OPERATIONS AND SUPPLY CHAIN MANAGEMENT

EIGHTH EDITION

International Student Version

Roberta S. Russell

Professor

Virginia Polytechnic Institute and State University

Bernard W. Taylor III

R. B. Pamplin Professor

Virginia Polytechnic Institute and State University

WILEY

Operations and Supply Chain Management, ISV
Eight Edition

Authorised reprint by Wiley India Pvt. Ltd., 4435-36/7, Ansari Road, Daryaganj, New Delhi-110002.

Cover Image: Vladimir Kolobov/iStockphoto

Reprint: 2017

Printed at: *Chaudhry Press, Delhi*

ISBN: 978-81-265-5682-3

>ABOUT THE AUTHORS

Bernard W. Taylor III and Roberta S. Russell

Bernard W. Taylor III is the Pamplin Professor of Management Science and Head of the Department of Business Information Technology in the Pamplin College of Business at Virginia Polytechnic Institute and State University. He received a Ph.D. and an M.B.A. from the University of Georgia and a B.I.E. from the Georgia Institute of Technology. He is the author of the book *Introduction to Management Science* (11th ed.) and co-author of *Management Science* (4th ed.), both published by Prentice Hall. Dr. Taylor has published over 80 articles in such journals as *Operations Research, Management Science, Decision Sciences, IIE Transactions, Journal of the Operational Research Society, Computers and Operations Research, Omega*, and the *International Journal of Production Research*, among others. His paper in *Decision Sciences* (with P. Y. Huang and L. P. Rees) on the Japanese kanban production system received the Stanley T. Hardy Award for its contribution to the field of production and operations management. He has served as President of the Decision Sciences Institute (DSI) as well as Program Chair, Council Member, Vice President, Treasurer, and as the Editor of *Decision Line*, the newsletter of DSI. He is a Fellow of DSI and a recipient of their Distinguished Service Award. He is a former President, Vice-President, and Program Chair of the Southeast Decision Sciences Institute and a recipient of their Distinguished Service Award. He teaches management science and production and operations management courses at both the undergraduate and graduate level. He has received the University Certificate of Teaching Excellence on four occasions, the Pamplin College of Business Certificate of Teaching Excellence Award, and the Pamplin College of Business Ph.D. Teaching Excellence Award at Virginia Tech.

Roberta S. Russell is a Professor of Business Information Technology in the Pamplin College of Business at Virginia Polytechnic Institute and State University. She received a Ph.D and a B.S. from Virginia Polytechnic Institute and State University and an M.B.A. from Old Dominion University. Dr. Russell's primary research and teaching interests are in the areas of operations and supply chain management, with special emphasis on humanitarian and healthcare operations. She has published in *Journal of Operations Management, Decision Sciences, IIE Transactions, International Journal of Production Research, IEEE Transactions, Annals of Operations Research, Computers and Operations Research*, and others. She is also co-author of the Prentice Hall book *Service Management and Operations*. Dr. Russell is a member of DSI, ASQ, POMS, and IIE. She is currently serving as President of the APICS Foundation and as Co-Chair of the Supply Chain Academic Talent Initiative (SCTAI). Dr. Russell is a Certified Fellow in Production and Inventory Management (CFPIM) and is recognized as a Certified Supply Chain Management Professional (CSCP). She is past Vice President of POMS, past President of the Southwest Virginia Chapter of APICS and has held numerous offices in Southeast DSI. Her consulting experience with IBM, AT&T, Dupont, Courtaulds, Xaloy, Newport News Shipbuilding and others brings a practical perspective into the classroom. She has received the Pamplin College of Business Certificate of Teaching Excellence on two occasions, the University Certificate of Teaching Excellence, and the MBA Association's Outstanding Professor Award. Dr. Russell teaches both undergraduate and graduate students in the classroom and online. She is frequently called upon to give workshops on teaching with technology, and has incorporated her experiences into the ancillary material that accompanies this text.

>CONTENTS

***Appendices A to D are available online at www.wiley.com/college/russell**

PREFACE

Changes in the Eighth Edition

This new eighth edition is organized around the important and prevalent topic of operations as the creation of value along the supply chain. We describe how every chapter topic fits within a supply chain framework in a company or organization in an increasingly global operating environment. To reflect this emphasis, the title of the text has been changed to *Operations and Supply Chain Management*. Two chapters deal directly with supply chain management: Chapter 10, Designing the Supply Chain, and Chapter 11, Global Procurement and Distribution. However, every chapter includes material relating the chapter topics to supply chain management in a global operating environment. In addition, Chapter 5, Designing Services, reflects the expanding presence and importance of the service sector in operations management. We have also added new material throughout the book on the increasingly important OM topics of sustainability, corporate social responsibility, and risk and resilience. To help us show how the OM topics in this new edition fit together within a supply chain framework, we open each chapter with a specific example about one product, *denim jeans*. Denim jeans are an ideal product to use as an example to introduce all the various operations and supply chain management topics in this text because it's a familiar and popular product to our readers, its supply chain is global, and its production process is straightforward and interesting.

In addition to opening each chapter with a denim jeans example, this new edition also includes "Along the Supply Chain" boxes that describe real-world business applications of OM topics at companies around the world. Many of these boxes focus on the increasingly important topics of sustainability and global supply chains. The boxes conclude with critical thinking questions that can be used for assignments and in-class or online discussion.

Chapter 1 focuses on examples of excellence in operations management, current issues in operations and supply chain management, and the strategic design of operations and supply chain management. Chapter 2, Ensuring Quality, emphasizes the necessity and use of quality management systems throughout the supply chain. Chapter 3 introduces statistical process control as essential to ensuring quality along the supply chain.

Chapter 4 has expanded sections on Design for the Environment and Collaborative Product Design Systems. Chapter 5 incorporates new statistics on the service economy, the blending of products and services, and expanded tools for service design. A streamlined waiting line analysis section is also included in the chapter. Chapter 6 emphasizes process analysis skills and includes revised material on making wise outsourcing decisions. Chapter 7 incorporates strategies for capacity management, facility selection and design, green facilities and examples of various service layouts.

Chapter 8, Human Resources, has an increased emphasis on sustainability in the workplace, especially among global suppliers of U.S. companies, as well as increased attention to employee cultural and diversity issues. Chapter 9, Managing Projects, has an increased focus on cultural and diversity issues in the management of global projects, plus a new section on project risk and how to manage it. Chapter 10, Designing the Supply Chain, has a new section on risk and resilience in global supply chains, and increased attention to global sustainability issues. Chapter 11, Global Procurement and Distribution, also addresses sustainability issues, and a new section has been added on spend analysis. Chapter 12, Forecasting Demand, includes a new section on the increasingly important IT topic of data mining, and Chapter 13, Inventory Management, emphasizes its important role in controlling costs along a global supply chain.

Chapter 14 emphasizes the need for effective Aggregate Planning for Sales and Operations, and includes a section on Revenue Management. Chapter 15, Enterprise Resource Planning, updates resource planning with discussions of cloud computing, in-memory computing, collaborative resource planning and product lifecycle management. Chapter 16 expands JIT and Lean Production to lean services, including lean supply chains, and lean and the environment. Chapter 17 incorporates employee scheduling, artificial intelligence, and theory of constraints, along with traditional scheduling methods.

In addition to this new topical coverage, this edition also includes new updated exhibits in every chapter reflecting the latest versions of *Excel*, *OM Tools,* and *Microsoft Project*. *Excel*, *OM Tools* or *MS Project* files of every exhibit in the text are available to instructors and students on request. For instructors, a printable *Solutions Manual* in Word is supplemented with *Excel* or *Microsoft Project* files for virtually every problem and case in the text.

Major Text Themes

OPERATIONS STRATEGY: CREATING VALUE ALONG THE SUPPLY CHAIN

A company's plan for being competitive is its strategy. The success of a strategic plan is largely determined by how well a company coordinates all of its internal processes, including operations, with its suppliers and customers to produce products and services that provide value. Throughout this book, we try to show how the functions and processes described in each chapter fit into a company's strategic design for the creation of value. In each chapter, we emphasize the need for considering the overall strategic implications of particular operating decisions.

One way in which companies can gain a competitive edge is by deploying the basic functions of operations management in a more effective manner than their rivals, e.g., build a better supply chain. Therefore, we give literally dozens of examples that explain how companies deploy specific operations functions along their supply chain to provide value and make them successful. Throughout the book, "Along the Supply Chain" boxes describe how successful companies have gained a competitive edge through operations.

GLOBAL OPERATIONS

Companies and organizations today must increasingly compete in a global marketplace. The establishment of new trade agreements between countries, innovations in information technology, and improvements in transport and shipping are just a few of the factors that have enabled companies to develop global supply chains. The opening of the global marketplace has only served to introduce more competitors and make competition tougher, thus making strategic supply chain design even more important for achieving success. In this edition, we introduce this global aspect of operations into every chapter. In each chapter, we include examples that touch on the impact of global operations relative to the topic under discussion, and we discuss how globalization affects supply chain management.

SUSTAINABILITY

Environmental concerns are changing every aspect of operations and supply chain management from product and service design, to supplier sourcing, to manufacture and delivery. In virtually every chapter of this text we address the impact of "sustainability" (i.e., meeting present needs without sacrificing future resources) and give examples of "green practices". For example, in Chapter 4 on product design, we discuss the design for environment lifecycle, eco-labeling, recycling and reuse, and sustainable operations. In Chapter 6 on processes we discuss green manufacturing; and in Chapter 7 on facilities we discuss LEED certified green buildings. In Chapter 8 we discuss how companies achieve a sustainable work place when they have suppliers around the world. In Chapter 10 on supply chain management we discuss sustainable sourcing in a global environment; and in Chapter 16 on lean systems we discuss lean and the environment.

SERVICES AND MANUFACTURING

We have attempted to strike a balance between manufacturing and service operations in this book. Traditionally, operations and supply chain management was thought of almost exclusively in a manufacturing context. However, in the United States and other industrialized nations, there has been a dramatic shift toward service industries. Thus, managing service operations is an important area of study. In many cases, operations and supply chain management processes and techniques are indistinguishable between service and manufacturing. However, in many other instances, service operations present unique situations and problems that require focused attention and unique solutions. We have tried to reflect the uniqueness of service operations by providing focused discussions on service operations throughout the text. For example, in Chapter 2 on quality management we specifically address the importance of quality management in service companies, in Chapter 5 on service design we emphasize the differences in design considerations between manufacturing and services, and in Chapter 14 we discuss aggregate planning in services. One type of service examined in virtually every chapter in the book is health care.

QUALITATIVE AND QUANTITATIVE PROCESSES

We have also attempted to strike a balance between the qualitative (or managerial) aspects of operations management and the quantitative aspects. In the contemporary world of operations management, the quantitative and technological aspects are probably more important than ever. The ability to manage people and resources effectively, to motivate, organize, control, evaluate, and adapt to change, have become critical to competing in today's global markets. Thus, throughout this book we seek to explain and clearly demonstrate how the successful operations manager manages, and how to use quantitative techniques and technology when they are applicable.

However, we attempt to present these quantitative topics in a way that's not overly complex or mathematically intimidating. Above all, we want to show how the quantitative topics fit in with, and complement, the qualitative aspects of operations management. We want you to be able to see both "the forest and the trees."

Teaching and Learning Support Features

This text is accompanied by many features and supplements both in the text and on request for students and instructors.

PEDAGOGY IN THE TEXTBOOK

"Along the Supply Chain" Boxes

These boxes are located in every chapter in the text. They describe the application of operations in a real-world company, organization or agency related to specific topics in each chapter. They emphasize how companies effectively compete with operations management in the global marketplace. The descriptions of operations at actual companies in these boxes help the student understand how specific OM techniques and concepts are used by companies, which also make the topics and concepts easier to understand. In addition, we have added discussion questions to these boxes to help students and teachers "connect" the example to the chapter topics.

Examples

The primary means of teaching the various quantitative topics in this text is through examples. These examples are liberally distributed throughout the text to demonstrate how problems are solved in a clear, straightforward approach to make them easier to understand.

Solved Problems

At the end of each chapter, just prior to the homework questions and problems, there is a section with solved examples to serve as a guide for working the homework problems. These examples are solved in a detailed, step-by-step manner.

Key Formulas

These summaries at the end of each chapter include all of the key quantitative formulas introduced in the chapter in one location for easy reference.

Homework Problems, Questions, and Cases

Our text contains a large number of end-of-chapter exercises for student assignments, including questions, problems, and advanced case problems. Answers to selected odd-numbered problems are included in the back of the book. As we mention in the following "Resources for Instructors" section, Excel spreadsheet solution files are available to the instructor for the majority of the end-of-chapter problems and cases.

Excel Files of Exhibits

Excel is used extensively throughout the text to solve various quantitative problems and many Excel illustrations are provided throughout the text.

Every Excel spreadsheet used to prepare the examples in the text is available on companion website for student and on request at acadmktg@wiley.com for instructors. They are organized by chapter and are listed by their exhibit number. Notice the file name is simply the exhibit number plus the topic (i.e, Exhibit 12.1. Forecasting). Please look in each file carefully. In many cases, several sheets in one file have been used to display different parts of a problem, such as a graphical solution as well as a numerical solution. Example files are also available for MS Project files in Chapter 9.

Online Resources For Students, www.wiley.com/college/russell

No other innovation has affected operations management in the past few years as much as computer technology and the Internet, and this is no less true in education. Therefore, we make full use of this technology as a learning and teaching medium in the courses we teach and in our text. Students can link to the text website where an exciting set of Internet resources have been compiled.

Here are some of the items found on the text website:

- ***Web links*** for companies and concepts discussed in each chapter can be accessed online. These provide enrichment for those students who want to learn more about a topic, and serve as a valuable resource for student assignments and papers.
- ***Internet Exercises*** provide up-to-date access to current issues in operations. These add immediacy to classroom discussions and ensure that operations management topics remain relevant to the student.
- ***Practice Quizzes*** are provided online where students can get immediate feedback on their progress.
- ***Appendices***

Resources for Instructors on Request

The following resources are available for instructors on request:

Instructor's Manual The Instructor's Manual, updated by the authors, features, chapter outlines, teaching notes, experiential exercises, alternate examples to those provided in the text, pause and reflect questions for classroom discussion, and suggested online videos to use in class or assign for homework.

Test Bank Fully revised from the previous edition by Scott Hedin of Gonzaga University this test bank consists of true/false, multiple-choice, short answer, and essay questions. All questions have been carefully accuracy-checked to ensure the highest quality of materials for our customers. The questions are also available electronically on the textbook support site. The Computerized Test Bank, for use on a

PC running Windows, is from a test-generating program that allows instructors to modify and add questions in order to customize their exams.

PowerPoint Presentation Slides The PowerPoint presentation slides, revised by Lance Matheson of Virginia Tech, include outlines for every chapter, exhibits from the text, and additional examples, providing instructors with a number of learning opportunities for students. Lecture notes accompany each slide.

Solutions Manual The Solutions Manual, updated by the authors, features detailed answers to end-of-chapter questions, homework problems, and case problems.

Excel Homework Solutions and Excel Exhibit Files Excel solution files for the instructor are provided for the majority of these problems. In addition, Microsoft Project solution files are provided for most of the homework problems in Chapter 9. Excel worksheets for class handouts or homework assignments are provided for QFD, process flow charts, MRP matrices, and others. Excel exhibit files for every example in the text solved with Excel are provided as templates for solving similar problems.

OM Tools or MS Project Files OM Tools is an Excel add-in designed to accompany the Russell/Taylor text. The software consists of 18 modules with over 60 problem types. OM Tools is easy to use and interpret, and is accompanied by a help file with text references.

Virtual Tours are online tours of service and production facilities. A Virtual Tours Master List, organized by industry, contains links to over 200 online tours that instructors may use for assignments or classroom presentation.

To request, please write a mail to acadmktg@wiley.com

// ACKNOWLEDGMENTS

The writing and revision of a textbook, like any large project, requires the help and creative energy of many people, and this is certainly not the exception. We especially appreciate the confidence, support, help, and friendship of our editor at Wiley. We also thank the Wiley staff members who helped with our book including:

Brian Kamins, Project Editor; Lise Johnson, Executive Editor; Alison Morris, Product Designer; Elena Santa-Maria, Media Specialist; Kelly Simmons, Sr. Marketing Manager; Valerie A. Vargas, Production Editor; and numerous other people who work behind the scenes to whom we never saw or talked. We are indebted to the reviewers of the text including: Robert Donnelly; Robert Aboolian, California State University San Marcos; Ajay Aggarwal, Millsaps College; Fred Anderson, Indiana University of Pennsylvania; Beni Asllani, University of Tennessee Chattanooga; Anteneh Ayanso, University of Connecticut, Storrs; Brent Bandy, University of Wisconsin, Oshkosh; Joe Biggs, California Polytechnic State University; Tom Bramorski, University of Wisconsin, Whitewater; Kimball Bullington, Middle Tennessee State University; Cem Canel, University of North Carolina, Wilmington; Janice Cerveny, Florida Atlantic University; Robert Clark, SUNY Stony Brook; Ajay Das, Baruch College CUNY; Kathy Dhanda, University of Portland; Susan Emens, Kent State University; Yee Fok, University of New Orleans; Phillip Fry, Boise State University; Mark Gershon, Temple University; Robert Greve, Oklahoma State University; Robert Frese, Maryville University; Jay Jayaram, University of South Carolina, Columbia; Vaidy Jayaraman, University of Miami; Serge Karalli, DePaul University; William Kime, University of New Mexico; Peter Klein, Ohio University; Howard Kraye, University of New Mexico, Albuquerque; John Kros, East Carolina University; Gopalan Kutty, Mansfield University; Bingguang Li, Albany State University; Royce Lorentz, Slippery Rock University; Sheldon Lou, California State University, San Marcos; Ken Mannino, Milwaukee School of Engineering; Lance Matheson, Virgina Tech; Duncan McDougall, Plymouth State University; Jaideep Motwani, Grand Valley State University; Hilary Moyes, University of Pittsburgh; Barin Nag, Towson University; Ozgur Ozluk, San Francisco State University; Amer Qureshi, University of Texas Arlington; Jim Robison, Sonoma State University; Raj Selladurai, Indiana University Northwest; Robert Setaputro, University of Wisconisin, Milwaukee; Jacob Simons, Georgia Southern University; Marilyn Smith, Winthrop University; Donna Stewart, University of Wisconsin, Stout; Donald Stout, St. Martin's College; Dothang Truong, Fayetteville State University; Elizabeth Trybus, California State University, Northridge; Ray Vankataraman, Pennsylvania State University, Erie; Timothy Vaughan, University of Wisconsin, Eau Claire; Mark Vrobelfski, University of Arizona; Gustavo Vulcano, New York University; Kevin Watson, University of New Orleans; Michel Whittenberg, University of Texas, Arlington; Hulya Yazici, University of Wisconsin, La Crosse; Jinfeng Yue, Middle Tennessee State University; and Xiaoqun Zhang, Pennsylvania State University, Harrisburg. We also thank the reviewers of the sixth edition including: Ajay Aggarwal, Millsaps College; Binguang Li, Albany State University; Christina McCart, Roanoke College; Cuneyt Altinoz, East Carolina University; Dana Johnson, Michigan Technical University; David Frantz, Indiana University; Donald Stout, St. Martin's University; Doug Hales, University of Rhode Island; Drew Stapleton, University of Wisconsin, LaCrosse; Fataneh Taghaboni-Dutta, University of Michigan, Flint; Ike Ehie, Kansas State University; John Hebert, University of Akron; John Kros, East Carolina University; Kaushik Sengupta, Hofstra University; Larry White, Eastern Illinois University; Lewis Coopersmith, Rider University; Mohammad Sedaghat, Fairleigh Dickinson University; Morgan Henrie, University of Alaska, Anchorage; Phil Fry, Boise State University; Robert Aboolian, California State University, San Marcos; Robert Clark, SUNY, Stony Brook; Scott Hedin, Gonzaga University; Susan Emens, Kent State University, Trumbull; Tom Wilder, California State University, Chico; Zhiwei Zhu, University of Louisiana, Lafayette.

They contributed numerous suggestions, comments, and ideas that dramatically improved and changed this edition. We offer our sincere thanks to these colleagues and hope that they can take some satisfaction in their contribution to our final product. We wish to thank our students who have class-tested, critiqued, and contributed to the first seven editions and this eighth edition from a consumer's point of view. We thank colleagues Kellie Keeling, University of Denver, for her extensive work on OM Tools; Laura Clark, Virginia Tech, for her help with WileyPLUS; Ronny Richardson, Southern Polytechnic, State University, who accuracy checked all of the supplements for this text; and graduate students Sai Panigrahi and Franklin Warren, for their assistance in numerous capacities. We are especially grateful to Tracy McCoy and Sylvia Seavey at Virginia Tech for their unstinting help, hard work, and patience.

R.S.R and B.W.T

CHAPTER 1

Operations and Supply Chain Strategy

LEARNING OBJECTIVES

AFTER READING THIS CHAPTER, YOU WILL BE ABLE TO:

- Describe what the operations function is and how it relates to other business functions.
- Discuss the key factors that have contributed to the evolution of operations and supply chain management.
- Discuss how and why businesses operate globally, and the importance of globalization in supply chain management.
- Calculate and interpret productivity measures used for measuring competitiveness.
- Discuss the importance of operations and supply chain management to a firm's strategy, and the process of developing, aligning and deploying strategy.

YOUR JEANS ARE YOU

There is no more popular garment worldwide than jeans. Jeans symbolize the American west, youth, and hard work and, because they shrink and fade with wear, YOU and the life you've lived in them.

Although jeans are most associated with the German immigrant to the United States, Levi Strauss, the name *jeans* comes from the "Genoese" sailors in Italy who wore trousers made of indigo fabric, called "serge de Nimes," made in Nimes, France. De Nimes fabric, or denim, is cross woven of white and indigo cotton yarn. Since the indigo dye does not penetrate both yarns, the cloth fades with time. The precise manner in which it fades and conforms to the body is related to how the consumer "wears" the jeans; thus, jeans take on a personal patina with time.

Jeans production ranges from mass produced to hand crafted. Jeans are produced in over 150 countries worldwide and worn in virtually every country on earth, by people of all ages, backgrounds, and social status. Cotton is grown in the United States, India, China, and Turkey. It is spun into yarn and dyed. For the most part, the spinning, dyeing, and weaving of cloth takes place in the factories of southeast Asia, and the cutting and sewing in Mexico, China, Bangladesh, Vietnam, and Pakistan.

We use jeans throughout this text to illustrate the principles of operations and supply chain management. Our journey will take us from quality and design, to processes, technologies, and logistics; from field to factory to distributor to consumer; from your corner store to around the world. We'll plan, source, make, deliver, and evaluate the most up-to-date material on supply chain management. Throughout this journey, we'll make the study of operations personal to you, as you navigate your own path through knowledge acquisition to your educational and career goals.

Operations management designs, operates, and improves productive systems—systems for getting work done. The food you eat, the movies you watch, the stores in which you shop, and the books you read are provided to you by the people in operations. Operations managers are found in banks, hospitals, factories, and government. They design systems, ensure quality, produce products, and deliver services. They work with customers and suppliers, the latest technology, and global partners. They solve problems, reengineer processes, innovate, and integrate. Operations is more than planning and controlling; it's doing. Whether it's superior quality, speed-to-market, customization, or low cost, excellence in operations is critical to a firm's success.

Operations is often defined as a transformation process. As shown in Figure 1.1, inputs (such as material, machines, labor, management, and capital) are transformed into outputs (goods and services). Requirements and feedback from customers are used to adjust factors in the transformation process, which may in turn alter inputs. In operations management, we try to ensure that the transformation process is performed efficiently and that the output is of greater *value* than the sum of the inputs. Thus, the role of operations is to create value. The transformation process itself can be viewed as a series of activities along a **value chain** extending from supplier to customer.

The input–transformation–output process is characteristic of a wide variety of operating systems. In an automobile factory, sheet steel is formed into different shapes, painted and finished, and then assembled with thousands of component parts to produce a working automobile. In an aluminum factory, various grades of bauxite are mixed, heated, and cast into ingots of different sizes. In a hospital, patients are helped to become healthier individuals through special care,

Figure 1.1
Operations as a Transformation Process

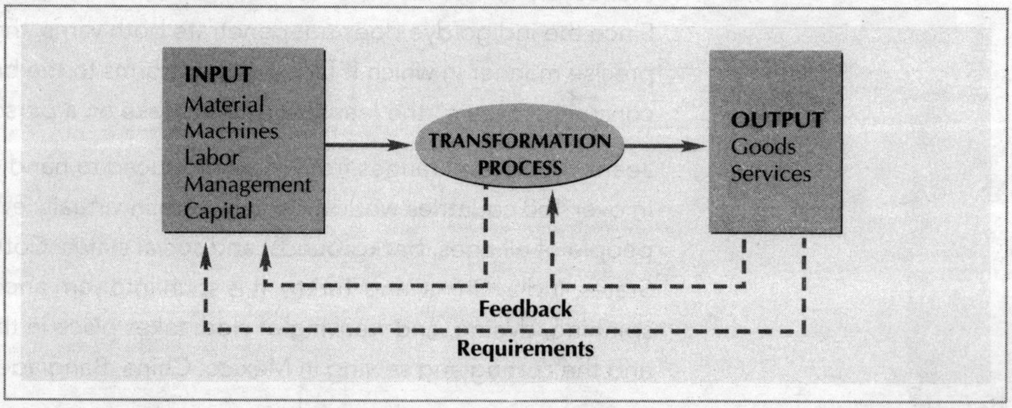

meals, medication, lab work, and surgical procedures. Obviously, "operations" can take many different forms. The transformation process can be

physical,	as in manufacturing operations;
locational,	as in transportation or warehouse operations;
exchange,	as in retail operations;
physiological,	as in healthcare;
psychological,	as in entertainment; or
informational,	as in communication.

The Operations Function

Activities in operations management (OM) include organizing work, selecting processes, arranging layouts, locating facilities, designing jobs, measuring performance, controlling quality, scheduling work, managing inventory, and planning production. Operations managers deal with people, technology, and deadlines. These managers need good technical, conceptual, and behavioral skills. Their activities are closely intertwined with other functional areas of a firm.

The four primary functional areas of a firm are marketing, finance, operations, and human resources. As shown in Figure 1.2, for most firms, operations is the technical core or "hub" of the organization, interacting with the other functional areas and suppliers to produce goods and provide services for customers. For example, to obtain monetary resources for production, operations provides finance and accounting with production and inventory data, capital budgeting requests, and capacity expansion and technology plans. Finance pays workers and suppliers, performs cost analyses, approves capital investments, and communicates requirements of shareholders and financial markets. Marketing provides operations with sales forecasts, customer orders, customer feedback, and information on promotions and product development. Operations, in turn, provides marketing with information on product or service availability, lead-time estimates, order status, and delivery schedules. For personnel needs, operations relies on human resources to recruit, train, evaluate, and

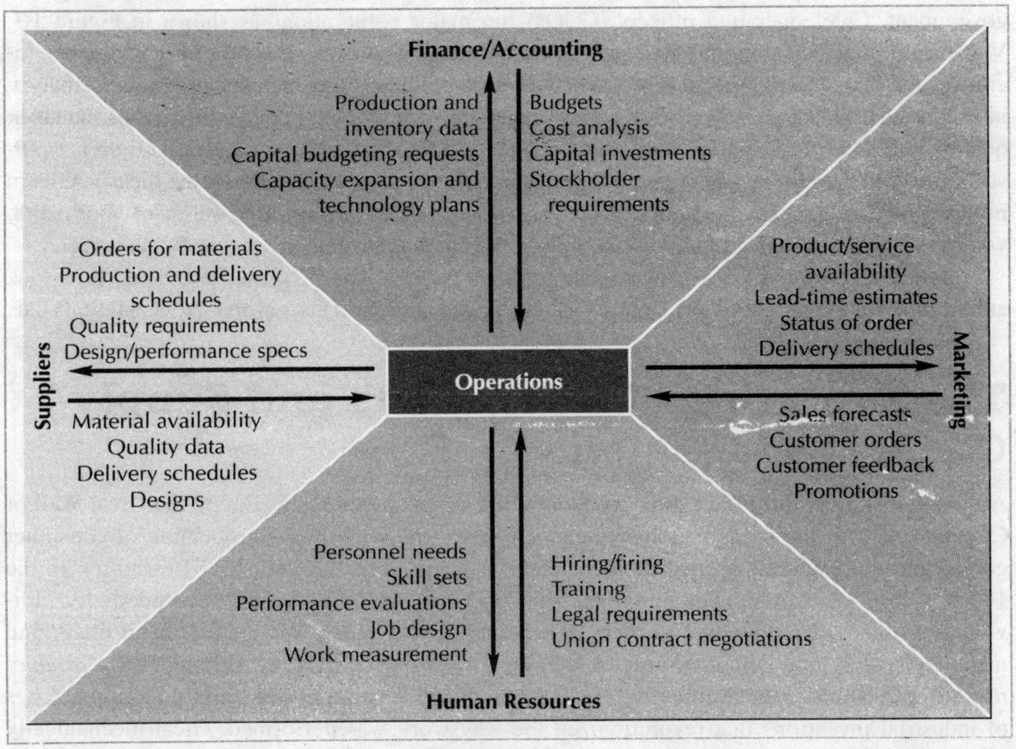

Figure 1.2
Operations as the Technical Core

Figure 1.3

Sample Organizational Structure

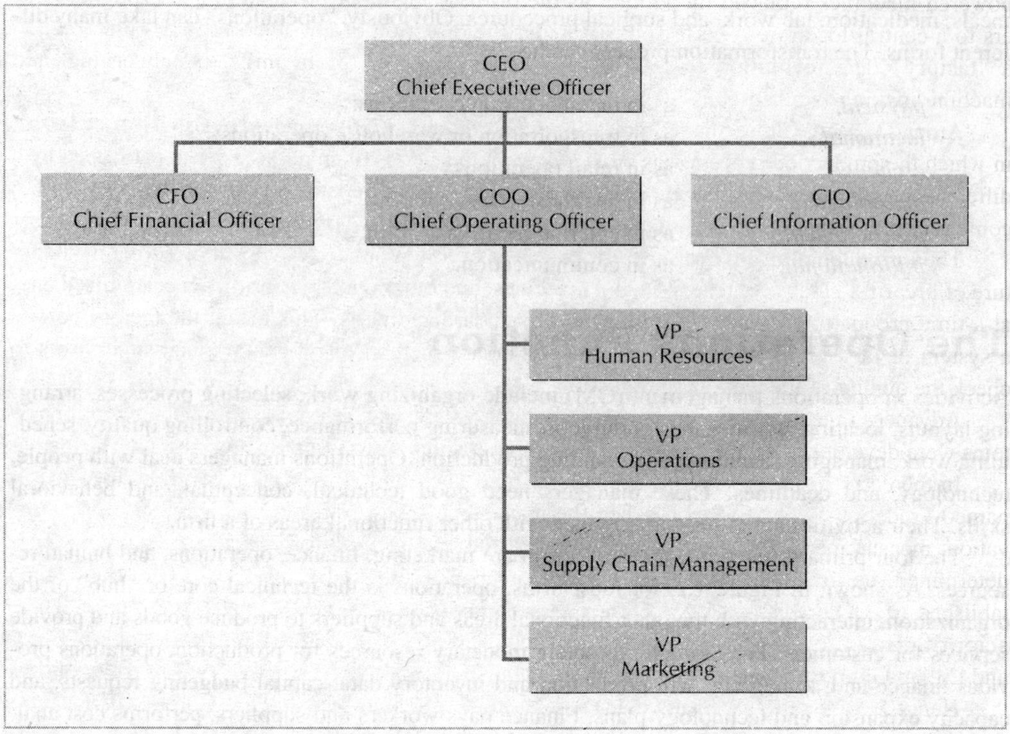

compensate workers and to assist with legal issues, job design, and union activities. Outside the organization, operations interacts with suppliers to order materials or services, communicate production and delivery requirements, certify quality, negotiate contracts, and finalize design specifications.

As a field of study, operations brings together many disciplines and provides an integrated view of business organizations. Operations managers are in demand in business, industry, and government. Chief operating officers (COOs) run major corporations as shown in Figure 1.3, Vice-presidents of Operations and Supply Chain Management oversee scores of departments, facilities, and employees. Typical jobs for new college graduates include business process analyst, inventory analyst, project coordinator, unit supervisor, supply chain analyst, materials manager, quality assurance specialist, production scheduler, and logistics planner. Even if you do not pursue a career in operations and supply chain management, you'll be able to use the ideas you learn in this course to organize work, ensure quality, and manage processes. Regardless of your major, you can apply some aspect of operations and supply chain management to your future career.

Now that you are aware of how operations might relate to your interests, let's take a brief look at how the field of operations and supply chain management (OSM) has evolved to its present state.

The Evolution of Operations and Supply Chain Management

Although history is full of amazing production feats—the pyramids of Egypt, the Great Wall of China, as well as the roads and aqueducts of Rome—the widespread production of consumer goods, and thus, operations management, did not begin until the Industrial Revolution in the 1700s. Prior to that time, skilled craftspersons and their apprentices fashioned goods for individual customers from studios in their own homes. Every piece was unique, hand-fitted, and made entirely by one person, a process known as **craft production**. Although *craft production* still exists today, the availability of coal, iron ore, and steam power set into motion a series of industrial inventions that revolutionized the way work was performed. Great mechanically powered machines replaced the laborer as the primary factor of production and brought workers to a central location to perform tasks under the direction of an "overseer" in a place called a "factory." The revolution first took hold in textile mills, grain mills, metalworking, and machine-making facilities.

Around the same time, Adam Smith's *Wealth of Nations* (1776) proposed the **division of labor**, in which the production process was broken down into a series of small tasks, each performed by a different worker. The specialization of the workers on limited, repetitive tasks allowed them to become very proficient at those tasks and further encouraged the development of specialized machinery.

The introduction of **interchangeable parts** by Eli Whitney (1790s) allowed the manufacture of firearms, clocks, watches, sewing machines, and other goods to shift from customized one-at-a-time production to volume production of standardized parts. This meant the factory needed a system of measurements and inspection, a standard method of production, and supervisors to check the quality of the worker's production.

Advances in technology continued through the 1800s. Cost accounting and other control systems were developed, but management theory and practice were virtually nonexistent.

In the early 1900s an enterprising laborer (and later chief engineer) at Midvale Steel Works named Frederick W. Taylor approached the management of work as a science. Based on observation, measurement, and analysis, he identified the best method for performing each job. Once determined, the methods were standardized for all workers, and economic incentives were established to encourage workers to follow the standards. Taylor's philosophy became known as **scientific management**. His ideas were embraced and extended by efficiency experts Frank and Lillian Gilbreth, Henry Gantt, and others. One of Taylor's biggest advocates was Henry Ford.

Henry Ford applied scientific management to the production of the Model T in 1913 and reduced the time required to assemble a car from a high of 728 hours to 1½ hours. A Model T chassis moved slowly down a conveyor belt with six workers walking alongside it, picking up parts from carefully spaced piles on the floor and fitting them to the chassis.[1] The short assembly time per car allowed the Model T to be produced in high volumes, or "en masse," yielding the name **mass production**.

American manufacturers became adept at mass production over the next 50 years and easily dominated manufacturing worldwide. The human relations movement of the 1930s, led by Elton Mayo and the Hawthorne studies, introduced the idea that worker motivation, as well as the technical aspects of work, affected productivity. Theories of motivation were developed by Frederick Herzberg, Abraham Maslow, Douglas McGregor, and others. Quantitative models and techniques spawned by the operations research groups of World War II continued to develop and were applied successfully to manufacturing and services. Computers and automation led still another upsurge in technological advancements applied to operations. These events are summarized in Table 1.1.

From the Industrial Revolution through the 1960s, the United States was the world's greatest producer of goods and services, as well as the major source of managerial and technical expertise. But in the 1970s and 1980s, industry by industry, U.S. manufacturing superiority was challenged by lower costs and higher quality from foreign manufacturers, led by Japan. Several studies published during those years confirmed what the consumer already knew—U.S.-made products of that era were inferior and could not compete on the world market. Early rationalizations that the Japanese success in manufacturing was a cultural phenomenon were disproved by the successes of Japanese-owned plants in the United States, such as the Matsushita purchase of a failing Quasar television plant in Chicago from Motorola. Part of the purchase contract specified that Matsushita had to retain the entire hourly workforce of 1000 persons. After only two years, with the identical workers, half the management staff, and little or no capital investment, Matsushita doubled production, cut assembly repairs from 130% to 6%, and reduced warranty costs from $16 million a year to $2 million a year. You can bet Motorola took notice, as did the rest of U.S. industry.

The **quality revolution** brought with it a realization that production should be tied to consumer demand. Product proliferation, shortened product lifecycles, shortened product development

[1]David Halberstam, *The Reckoning* (New York: William Morrow, 1986), pp. 79–81.

TABLE 1.1 Historical Events in Operations Management

Era	Events/Concepts	Dates	Originator
Industrial Revolution	Steam engine	1769	James Walt
	Division of labor	1776	Adam Smith
	Interchangeable parts	1790	Eli Whitney
Scientific Management	Principles of scientific management	1911	Frederick W. Taylor
	Time and motion studies	1911	Frank and Lillian Gilbreth
	Activity scheduling chart	1912	Henry Gantt
	Moving assembly line	1913	Henry Ford
Human Relations	Hawthorne studies	1930	Elton Mayo
	Motivation theories	1940s	Abraham Maslow
		1950s	Frederick Herzberg
		1960s	Douglas McGregor
Operations Research	Linear programming	1947	George Dantzig
	Digital computer	1951	Remington Rand
	Simulation, waiting line theory, decision theory, PERT/CPM	1950s	Operations research groups
	MRP	1960s	Joseph Orlicky, IBM, and others
	EDI, CIM	1970s	Auto industry, DARPA
Quality Revolution	JIT (just-in-time)	1970s	Taiichi Ohno (Toyota)
	TQM (total quality management)	1980s	W. Edwards Deming, Joseph Juran
	Strategy and operations		Wickham Skinner, Robert Hayes
	Reengineering	1990s	Michael Hammer, James Champy
	Six Sigma	1990s	GE, Motorola
Internet Revolution	Internet, WWW	1990s	ARPANET, Tim Berners-Lee
	ERP, supply chain management		SAP, Oracle, Dell
	E-commerce	2000s	Amazon, Yahoo, eBay, Google and others
Globalization	World Trade Organization	1990s	GATT
	European Union		Europe
	Global supply chains	2000s	China, India
	Outsourcing		Emerging economies
	Services Science		IBM
Sustainability	Global warming	Today	Numerous companies, scientists, statesmen and goverments
	Carbon footprint		
	Green products		
	Corporate social responsibility (CSR)		World Economic Forum
	UN Global Compact		United Nations

times, changes in technology, more customized products, and segmented markets did not fit mass production assumptions. Using a concept known as just-in-time, Toyota changed the rules of production from mass production to **lean production**, a system that prizes flexibility (rather than efficiency) and quality (rather than quantity).

The renewed emphasis on quality and the *strategic importance* of operations made some U.S. companies competitive again. Others continued to stagnate, buoyed temporarily by the expanding economies of the Internet era and globalization. Productivity soared as return on investment in information technology finally came to fruition. New types of businesses and business models emerged, such as Amazon, Google, and eBay, and companies used the Internet to connect with customers and suppliers around the world. The inflated expectations of the dot-com era came to an end and, coupled with the terrorist attacks of 9/11 and their aftermath, brought many companies back to reality, searching for ways to cut costs and survive in a global economy. They found relief in the emerging economies of China and India, and began accelerating the outsourcing of not only goods production, but services, such as information technology, call centers, and other business processes. The outsourcing of business processes brought with it a new awareness of business-to-business (B2B) services and the need for viewing services as a science.

With more and more activities taking place outside the enterprise in factories, distribution centers, offices and stores overseas, managers needed to develop skills in coordinating operations across a global supply chain. The field of **supply chain management** was born to manage the flow of information, products, and services across a network of customers, enterprises, and supply chain partners. In Figure 1.1, we depicted operations as a transformation process. Extending that analogy in Figure 1.4, supply chain management concentrates on the input and output sides of transformation processes. Increasingly, however, as the transformation process is performed by

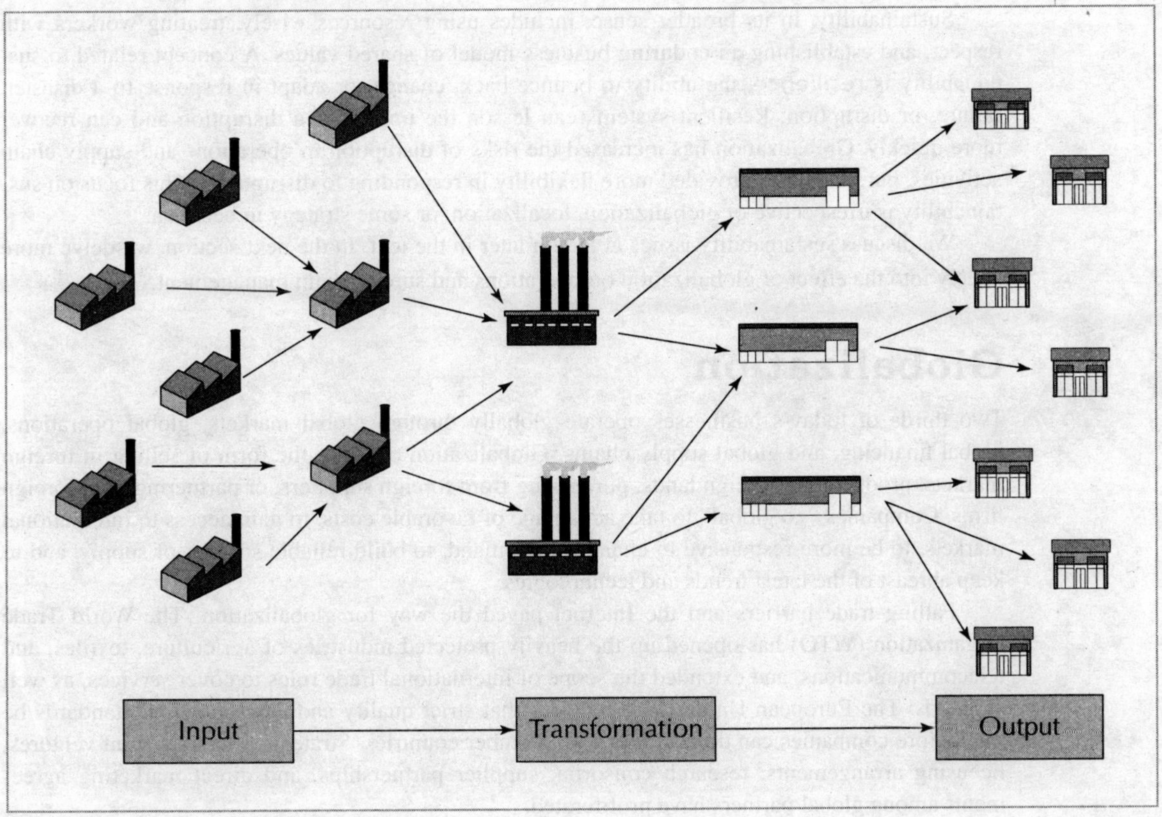

Figure 1.4
Supply Chain Management

suppliers who may be located around the world, the supply chain manager is also concerned with the timeliness, quality, and legalities of the supplier's operations.

The era of globalization was in full swing in 2008 when a financial crisis brought on by risky loans, inflated expectations, and unsavory financial practices brought the global economy to a standstill. Operations and supply chain management practices based on assumptions of growth had to be reevaluated for declining markets and resources. Companies began to reassess the value of their business, their customers, and their suppliers with an eye toward focusing on the most critical factors to sustain their business through the downturn.

The next phase in the evolution of OSM is the *Era of Sustainability*, in which countries, companies, and industries evaluate what it takes to sustain the health of their enterprise or people in the long term. This is especially important in light of changes in the environment, natural and man-made disasters, and the competitive landscape.

A recent UN Global Compact Survey reports that 93% of CEOs believe sustainability issues will be critical to the future success of their business. Companies that evaluate firm performance agree. Bloomberg Financials includes an ESG (environment, social, and governance) tool that, among other things, evaluates a company's environmental performance with an Environmental Disclosure Score and data on total energy consumption, energy efficient policies, and various sustainability practices. Bloomberg also reports on itself, and claims that every dollar spent on sustainability has saved the company two dollars in operating costs.

Similarly, Dow Jones Sustainability Indexes (DJSI) track the performance of leading sustainability-driven companies worldwide. Returns for companies listed in DJSI are typically higher than the regular Dow Jones Index (DJI). Investors believe that emphasizing sustainability is indicative of an "enlightened and disciplined management," and that an enhanced reputation and more loyal customers translate into higher returns.

Sustainability, in its broader sense, includes using resources wisely, treating workers with respect, and establishing an enduring business model of shared values. A concept related to sustainability is **resilience**, the ability to bounce back, change, or adapt in response to a disaster, failure, or disruption. Resilient systems can lesson the impact of a disruption and can recover more quickly. Globalization has increased the risks of disruption in operations and supply chain activities, but it has also provided more flexibility in responding to disruptions. This focus on sustainability is irrespective of globalization, localization, or some strategy in between.

We discuss sustainability issues at length later in the text. In the next section, we delve more deeply into the effect of globalization on operations and supply chain management.

Globalization

Two thirds of today's businesses operate globally through global markets, global operations, global financing, and global supply chains. Globalization can take the form of selling in foreign markets, producing in foreign lands, purchasing from foreign suppliers, or partnering with foreign firms. Companies "go global" to take advantage of favorable costs, to gain access to international markets, to be more responsive to changes in demand, to build reliable sources of supply, and to keep abreast of the latest trends and technologies.

Falling trade barriers and the Internet paved the way for globalization. The World Trade Organization (WTO) has opened up the heavily protected industries of agriculture, textiles, and telecommunications, and extended the scope of international trade rules to cover services, as well as goods. The European Union (EU) requires that strict quality and environmental standards be met before companies can do business with member countries. Strategic alliances, joint ventures, licensing arrangements, research consortia, supplier partnerships, and direct marketing agreements among global partners have proliferated.

Figure 1.5 shows the hourly wage rates (including benefits) in U.S. dollars for production workers in 15 selected countries. Wage rates in Norway are the highest at $64 an hour, with comparable rates in Switzerland. The United States and Japan pay wages of $35 an hour, while

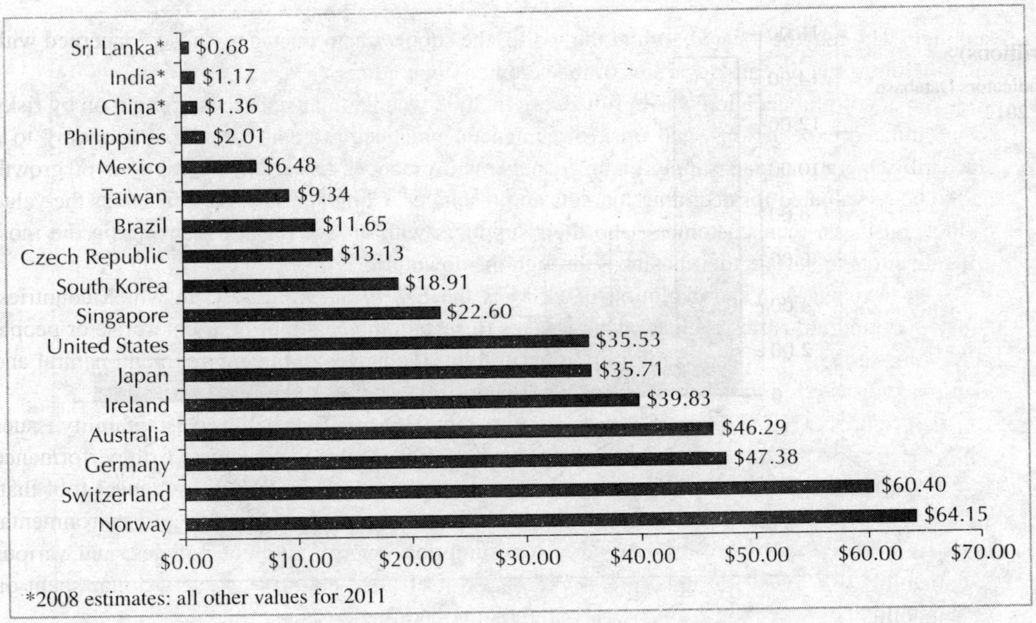

Figure 1.5

Hourly Compensation Costs for Production Workers (in U.S. Dollars)

SOURCE: Bureau of Labor Statistics, International Comparisons of Hourly Compensation Costs in Manufacturing, 2011, Washington, DC: December 19, 2012.

China, India, and Sri Lanka exhibit the lowest wage rates of $1.36, $1.17, and $0.68 an hour. To put the wage differentials in perspective, a U.S. worker receives roughly the equivalent sum of money for working 45 minutes as a Sri Lankan worker earns in a 40-hour week. This is a major factor in moving production to the low-cost countries of Asia.

China accounts for 20% of the world's population and is the world's largest manufacturer, employing more production workers than the United States, United Kingdom, Germany, Japan, Italy, Canada, and France combined. Its 1.3 billion people represent not only an immense labor market, but a huge consumer market as well. As China's industrial base multiplies, so does its need for machinery and basic materials, and as more companies move to China, so do their suppliers and their supplier's suppliers. Although initially the preferred location for the production of low-tech goods such as toys, textiles, and furniture, China has become a strategic manufacturing base for nearly every industry worldwide.

The scale of manufacturing in China is mind-boggling. For example, Foxconn (the trade name of Taiwan's Hon Hai Precision Industry Company) has two enormous industrial complexes in mainland China. The Guangdong Province site employs and houses approximately 270,000 workers, with its own dormitories, restaurants, hospital, police force, chicken farm, and soccer stadium. There are 40 separate production facilities "on campus," each dedicated to one of its major customers such as Apple, Dell, Motorola, Sony, Nintendo, and HP. Foxconn is the world's largest electronics manufacturer and China's largest exporter. It also represents a shorter supply chain because it *makes* components as well as *assembles* final products. Currently, Foxconn is expanding production into Mexico and Brazil to better serve the Americas. We will talk more about Foxconn later in the text.

Let's take a look at the health of the global economy in terms of GDP, trade in goods as a percent of GDP, and percentage manufacturing output by country. Figure 1.6 shows the gross domestic product (GDP) for the largest economies in 2011. Note that U.S. GDP is more than twice that of China, and China's is more than twice that of Germany. However, Germany and Mexico beat out both China and the United States in trade as a percentage of GDP, as shown in

Figure 1.6

GDP per Capita (in $US trillions)

SOURCE: World Development Indicators Database, The World Bank, December 21, 2012.

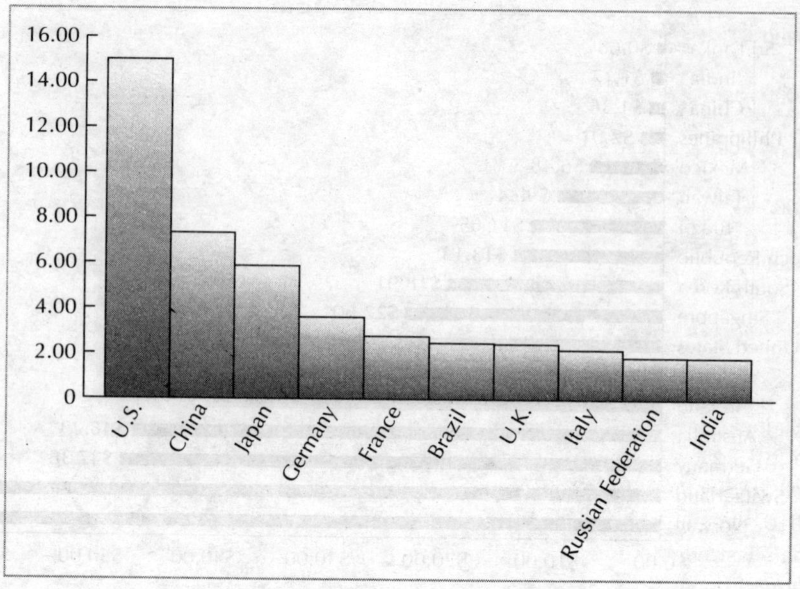

Figure 1.7

Trade in Goods as a Percent of GDP

SOURCE: The World Bank, Merchandise trade (% of GDP), http://data.worldbank.org/indicator/TG.VAL.TOTL.GD.ZS, accessed January 11, 2013.

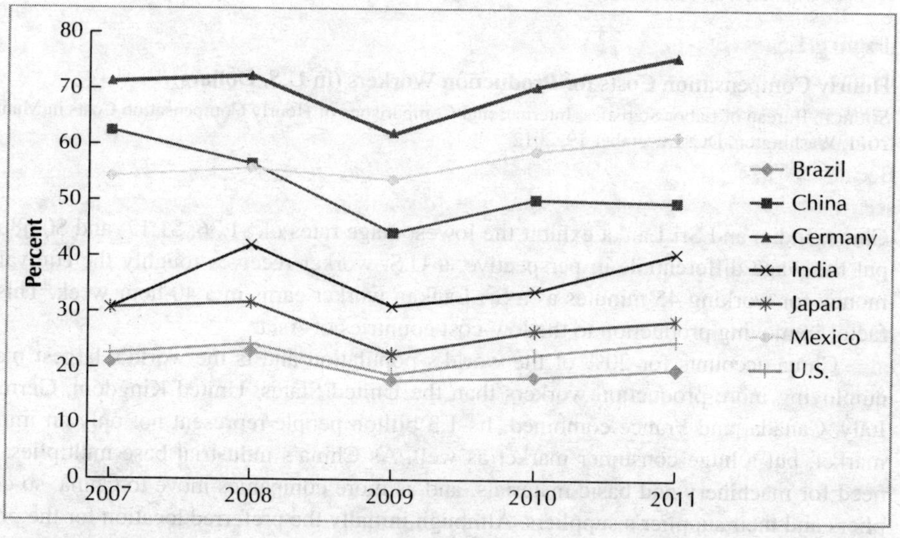

Figure 1.7. The United States, Brazil, and to some extent, Japan, are producing goods and services for their own markets, rather than exporting them.

Trade dropped in all of the economies in 2009 as the recession hit and stores were no longer placing orders for goods. Most countries have returned to their pre-recession trade, with Germany and Mexico gaining orders, most likely from an increase in near-shoring (i.e., companies outsourcing to companies nearby geographically) at the expense of China. India has also recovered well. China's slowdown in trade could be attributed to a higher percent of its factory output filling domestic demand for goods. The predominance of global supply chains means that intermediate goods cross borders many more times than they did when products and their components were manufactured in one country. That explains why the volume of trade declines more sharply than GDP during downturns and why trade accelerates faster than GDP when the global economy picks up.

Finally, let's examine production output from 2004 to 2011 for the world's largest manufacturing economies, as shown in Figure 1.8. In 2004, China held a slight edge over Germany as the world's third largest manufacturing economy. By 2006, China had surpassed Germany and was tied with Japan as the second largest manufacturer. Thus began a meteoric rise until 2010, where China edged ahead of the United States, producing 19.8% of the world's goods as compared to

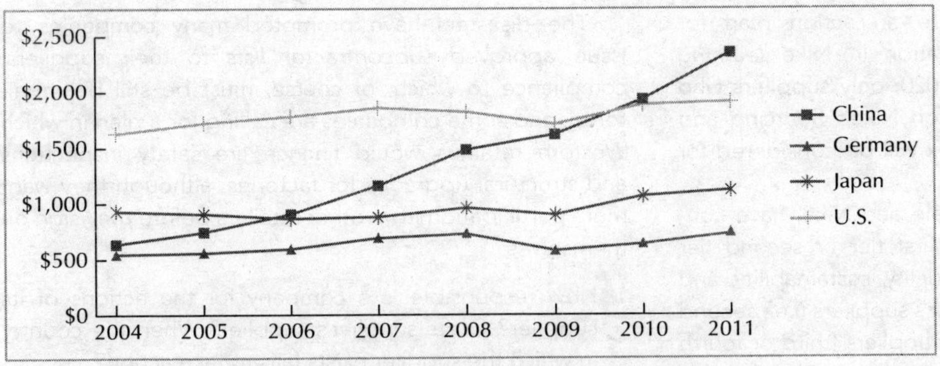

Figure 1.8

Manufacturing Output (in $US trillions)

SOURCE: United Nations, "GDP and its breakdown at current prices in US Dollars," National Accounts Aggregates Database, http://unstats.un.org/unsd/snaama/dnllist.asp, accessed January 14, 2013.

the United States' 19.4%. Then in 2011, China's manufacturing output soared. Preliminary data from 2013 show a slower rate of increase for Chinese manufacturing (single digits rather than double digits), but have China comfortably in the lead as the world's largest manufacturer. Prior to 2010, the United States had led world output in manufacturing since the 1930s. Prior to 2010, China's last number one ranking came in 1830, when it accounted for 30% of the world's production of goods.

Low labor costs, economies of scale, and a strong infrastructure (by Asian standards) have drawn goods production to China. But while China's manufacturing prowess may seem unbeatable, its one-child policy and aging workforce are causing labor costs to rise. Coupled with China's poor reputation for quality and uncertainty of consumer demand, companies are increasingly sourcing from other low-cost countries, particularly India, Bangladesh, Indonesia, Vietnam, and Eastern Europe. Because of its proximity to the United States, Mexico and several Central American countries are seeing a resurgence in orders, as well. Quality, reliability, and security problems also affect outsourcing decisions, as do questions of worker rights and environmental concerns.

Managing global operations and quality in a far-reaching supply chain is an added challenge for operations and supply chain managers. Physical distance, business decisions by suppliers, and different mores, laws, and legal systems in other countries can make it harder to maintain control over supplier activities. The following "Along the Supply Chain" box shows how companies such as Apple and Nike have handled such problems with their supply chain partners.

ALONG THE SUPPLY CHAIN

Human Rights and the Extended Supply Chain

One of the problems with outsourcing, particularly if suppliers are located far away, is monitoring their performance for quality, sustainability, and labor compliance. Apple came under fire after worker suicides and injuries revealed poor labor practices at its electronics contract manufacturer, Foxconn. In response, Apple published a complete list of its suppliers for the first time, opened up its supplier factories to outside inspectors (i.e., the Fair Labor Association), reinforced its supplier code of conduct, and prescribed a remediation program for Foxconn.

Simply monitoring supplier factories hasn't worked for Nike, the company most frequently associated with sweatshop labor in the 1990s. Nike saw factories improve during audits, only to return to their old ways soon afterward. Now, in addition to audits, Nike uses training, incentives, and lean manufacturing principles (discussed in Chapter 16) to work with its suppliers to improve conditions. Nike's *Sustainable Manufacturing Training* brings factory managers together with government officials, trade unions, International Labor Organization representatives, and other stakeholders to develop the systems and skills necessary for compliance. Following the training, suppliers participate in a six-month follow-up project with a lean production

(Continued)

facilitator (or *sensei*) to execute an action plan for improvement. Ongoing participation in Nike *learning communities* is required. As of 2020, only suppliers who have received an A or B rating on Nike's Sourcing and Manufacturing Sustainability Index will be considered for contract manufacturing.

Most companies, such as Apple and Nike, have contractual arrangements with their first tier or second tier suppliers only. That leaves the quality, sustainability, and working conditions of their supplier's suppliers (i.e., second or third tier) and those supplier's suppliers (third or fourth tier) unmonitored. The difficulty in regulating this *extended supply chain* was brought to light by recent industrial disasters in Bangladesh. On November 24, 2012, an apparel factory fire at Tazreen Fashions in Bangladesh killed 112 people. Evidence points to overcrowded conditions, lack of sprinkler systems, and locked doors. And then on April 24, 2013, at Rana Plaza in Bangledesh, an eight-story building housing several garment factories, collapsed, killing 1,127, making it one of the worst industrial disasters ever.

The fire at the Tazreen factory left behind charred clothing with Walmart, Disney, and Sears labels, among others. Although the factory was not an authorized manufacturer of those brands, it served as a supplier or subcontractor to manufacturers who *were* authorized. Likewise, even as labels and documents linked the Rana Plaza collapse to major brands like the Children's Place and Benetton, many companies were quick to distance themselves from the catastrophe or downplay their connection to the factory.

The disasters have prompted many companies to issue *approved subcontractor lists* to their suppliers, compliance to which, of course, must be still be monitored, and some companies are calling for a plan in which Western retailers would finance fire safety inspections and structural upgrades for factories, although they want more participation from other retailers before they sign on themselves.

1. How responsible is a company for the actions of its supplier? Of its supplier's supplier? When the country in which the supplier exists fails to take action?
2. What are the difficulties in relying on monitoring to enforce suitable working conditions in supplier factories? What other remedies would you recommend?
3. Compare Apple's supplier problems with Nike's and those of the apparel industry. Would the same remedies work in each case? Which case is more difficult? Why?

Sources: Based on Charles Duhigg and Steven Greenhouse, "Electronic Giant Vowing Reforms in China Plants," *The New York Times* (March 29, 2012); *Nike, Inc. Sustainable Business Performance Summary,* 2012. Available at http://www.nikeresponsibility.com/; Jim Yardley, "Horrific Fire Revealed a Gap in Safety for Global Brands," *The New York Times* (December 6, 2012); Julfikar Ali Manik, Steven Greenhouse, and Jim Yardley, "Western Firms Feel Pressure as Toll Rises in Bangladesh," *The New York Times* (April 26, 2013), available at http://www.nytimes.com/2013/04/26/world/asia/bangladeshi-collapse-kills-many-garment-workers.html?pagewanted=all; and Saeed Ahmed and Leone Lakhani, "Bangladesh Building Collapse: An End to Recovery Efforts, A Promise of a New Start," CNN (May 14, 2013), available at http://www.cnn.com/2013/05/14/world/asia/bangladesh-building-collapse-aftermath/?hpt=hp_t2.

Productivity and Competitiveness

A global marketplace for products and services means more customers and more intense competition. In the broadest terms, we speak of competitiveness in reference to other *countries* rather than to other companies. That's because how effectively a nation competes in the global marketplace affects the economic success of the nation and the quality of life for its citizens. The OECD (Organization for Economic Cooperation and Development) defines **competitiveness** as "the degree to which a nation can produce goods and services that meet the test of international markets while simultaneously maintaining or expanding the real incomes of its citizens." The most common measure of competitiveness is productivity. Increases in productivity allow wages to grow without producing inflation, thus raising the standard of living. Productivity growth also represents how quickly an economy can expand its capacity to supply goods and services.

Productivity is calculated by dividing units of output by units of input.

$$\text{Productivity} = \frac{\text{Output}}{\text{Input}}$$

Output can be expressed in units or dollars in a variety of scenarios, such as sales made, products produced, customers served, meals delivered, or calls answered. *Single-factor productivity* compares output to individual inputs, such as labor hours, investment in equipment, material

TABLE 1.2 Measures of Productivity

Single-Factor Productivity

$$\frac{\text{Output}}{\text{Labor}} \qquad \frac{\text{Output}}{\text{Materials}} \qquad \frac{\text{Output}}{\text{Capital}}$$

Multifactor Productivity

$$\frac{\text{Output}}{\text{Labor + Materials + Overhead}} \qquad \frac{\text{Output}}{\text{Labor + Energy + Capital}}$$

Total Factor Productivity

$$\frac{\text{Goods and services produced}}{\text{All inputs used to produce them}}$$

usage, or square footage. *Multifactor productivity* relates output to a combination of inputs, such as (labor + capital) or (labor + capital + energy + materials). Capital can include the value of equipment, facilities, inventory, and land. *Total factor productivity* compares the total quantity of goods and services produced with all the inputs used to produce them. These productivity formulas are summarized in Table 1.2. Note when several factors are included in a formula, they should be expressed in common terms, such as dollars.

EXAMPLE 1.1

CALCULATING PRODUCTIVITY

Osborne Industries is compiling the monthly productivity report for its board of directors. From the following data, calculate (a) labor productivity, (b) machine productivity, and (c) the multifactor productivity of output per dollars spent on labor, machine, materials, and energy. The average labor rate is $15 an hour, and the average machine usage rate is $10 an hour.

Units produced	100,000
Labor hours	10,000
Machine hours	5,000
Cost of materials	$35,000
Cost of energy	$15,000

SOLUTION

(a) $\text{Labor productivity} = \dfrac{\text{Output}}{\text{Labor hours}} = \dfrac{100{,}000}{10{,}000} = 10 \text{ units/hour}$

(b) $\text{Machine productivity} = \dfrac{\text{Output}}{\text{Machine hours}} = \dfrac{100{,}000}{5{,}000} = 20 \text{ units/hour}$

(c)
$$\text{Multifactor productivity} = \frac{\text{Output}}{\text{(Labor costs + Machine costs + Material costs + Energy costs)}}$$
$$= \frac{100{,}000}{(10{,}000 \times \$15) + (5{,}000 \times \$10) + \$35{,}000 + \$15{,}000}$$
$$= \frac{100{,}000}{\$250{,}000} = 0.4 \text{ units per dollar spent}$$

The Excel solution to this problem is shown in Exhibit 1.1.

EXHIBIT 1.1 Osborne Industries

EXCEL FILE

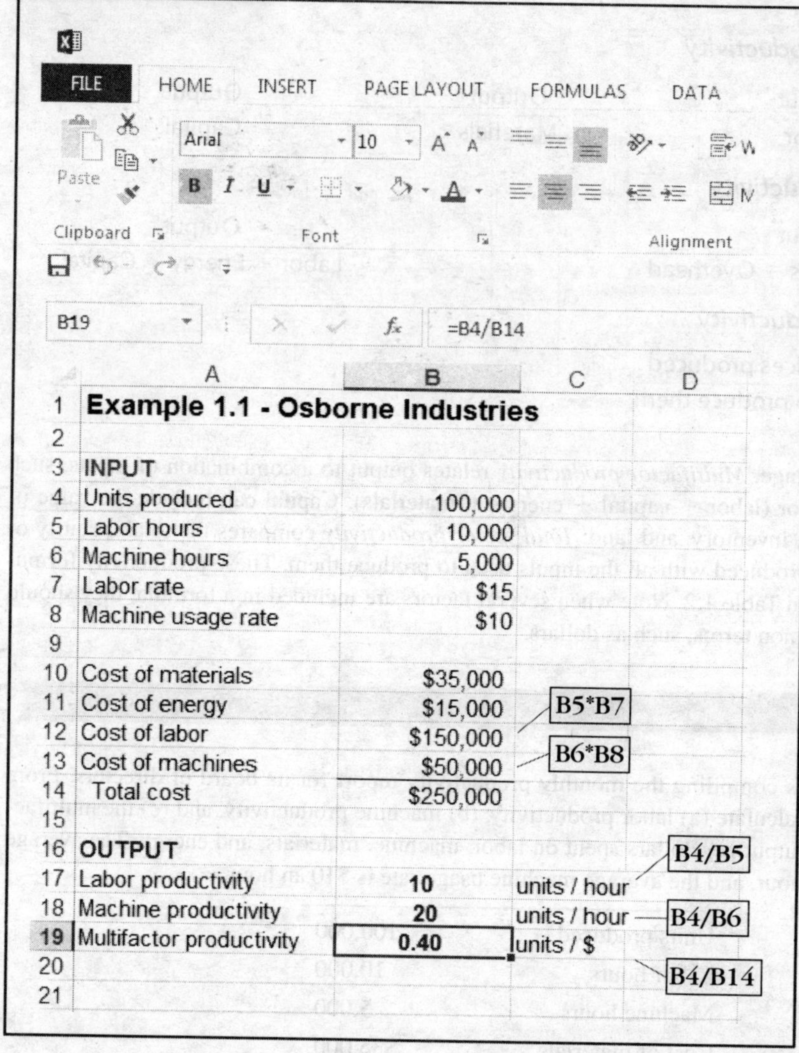

	A	B	C
1	**Example 1.1 - Osborne Industries**		
2			
3	**INPUT**		
4	Units produced	100,000	
5	Labor hours	10,000	
6	Machine hours	5,000	
7	Labor rate	$15	
8	Machine usage rate	$10	
9			
10	Cost of materials	$35,000	
11	Cost of energy	$15,000	
12	Cost of labor	$150,000	
13	Cost of machines	$50,000	
14	Total cost	$250,000	
15			
16	**OUTPUT**		
17	Labor productivity	**10**	units / hour
18	Machine productivity	**20**	units / hour
19	Multifactor productivity	**0.40**	units / $
20			
21			

The most common input in productivity calculations is labor hours. Labor is an easily identified input to virtually every production process. Productivity is a relative measure. Thus, productivity statistics provided in government reports typically measure percent changes in productivity from month to month, quarter to quarter, year to year, or over a number of years.

Productivity statistics can be misleading. Examining the formula for productivity, *output/input,* it becomes apparent that productivity can be increased in different ways. For example, a country or firm may increase productivity by decreasing input faster than output. Thus, although the company may be retrenching, its productivity is increasing. Seldom is this avenue for increasing productivity sustainable. Let's look at some recent productivity statistics.

Figure 1.9(a) shows the growth rate in productivity for select countries from 2010 to 2011. Continuing to recover from the global recession, labor productivity increased in 15 of the 19 countries shown, with an average increase of 2%. The Czech Republic, Singapore, and South Korea showed the greatest increases in productivity of 10%, 8%, and 6%, respectively. Examining the inputs and outputs more closely in Figure 1.9(b), we find that the Czech Republic, Singapore, United Kingdom, Spain, France, and Denmark increased their output while at the same time decreasing their input, a remarkable achievement. The United States, Belgium, Germany, Sweden, Taiwan, and South Korea expanded their input and saw an increase in output, some countries more successfully than others. Japan appears to be in retrenchment mode,

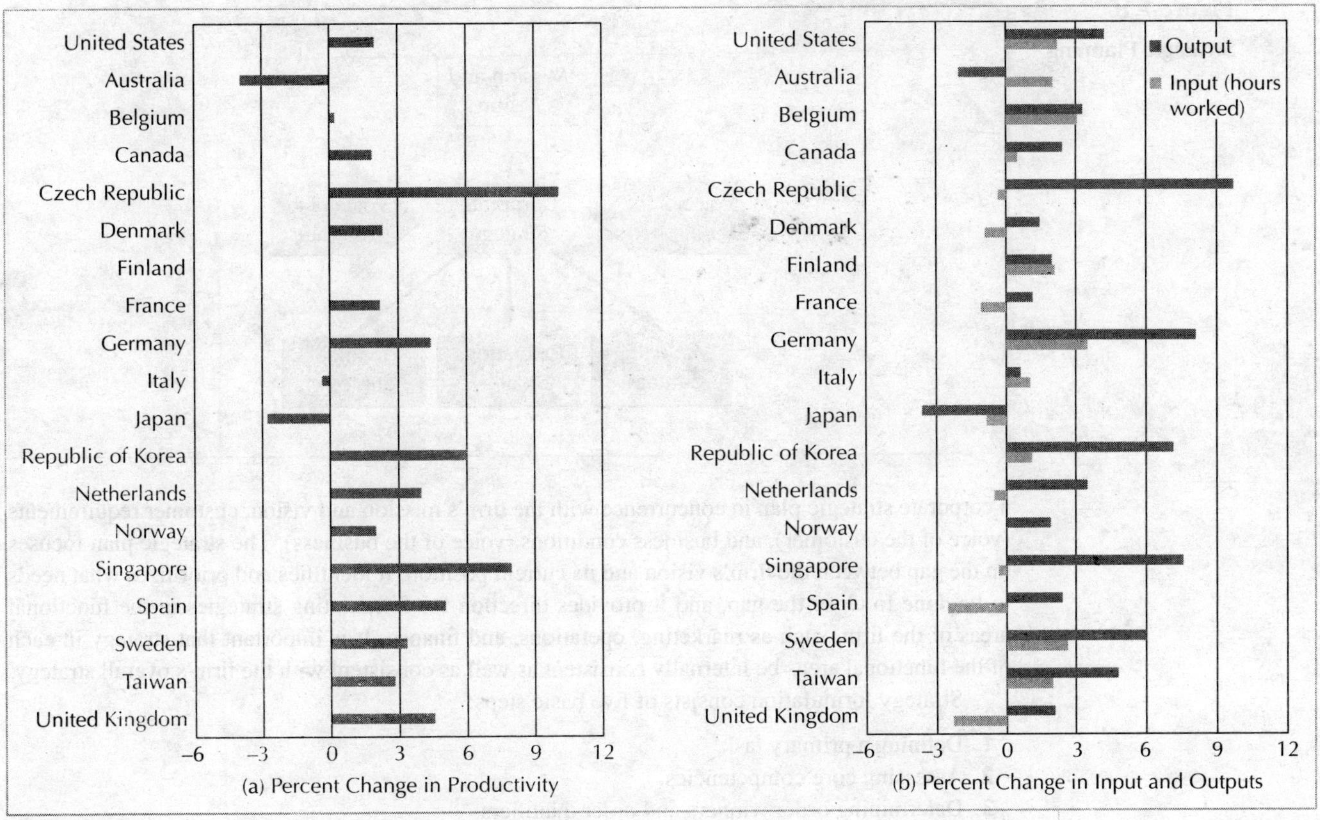

Figure 1.9

Changes in Productivity, Inputs, and Outputs in Select Countries

SOURCE: U.S. Bureau of Labor Statistics. *International Comparisons of Manufacturing Productivity and Unit Labor Costs Trends, 2011, http://www.bls.gov/news.release/prod4.t01.htm*, accessed January 14, 2013.

decreasing both its input and output, for a decrease in productivity of 2.8%. Australia added more hours but did not increase output; thus, its productivity dropped by 4%. Finland and Italy increased input but did not see a corresponding increase in output. Productivity is a relative measure, and exploring both the input and output side of the equation helps to explain how a country is trying to compete in the global economy.

Productivity statistics also assume that if more input were available, output would increase at the same rate. This may not be true, as there may be limits to output other than those on which the productivity calculations are based. Furthermore, productivity emphasizes *output produced,* not *output sold*. If products produced are not sold, inventories pile up and increases in output can actually accelerate a company's decline.

As the business world becomes more competitive, firms must find their own path to sustainable competitive advantage. Effectively managed operations are important to a firm's competitiveness. How a firm chooses to compete in the marketplace is the subject of the next section: *Strategy and Operations*.

Strategy and Operations

Strategy is how the mission of a company is accomplished. It unites an organization, provides consistency in decisions, and keeps the organization moving in the right direction. Operations and supply chain management play an important role in corporate strategy.

As shown in Figure 1.10, the strategic planning process involves a hierarchy of decisions. Senior management, with input and participation from different levels of the organization, develops

Figure 1.10
Strategic Planning

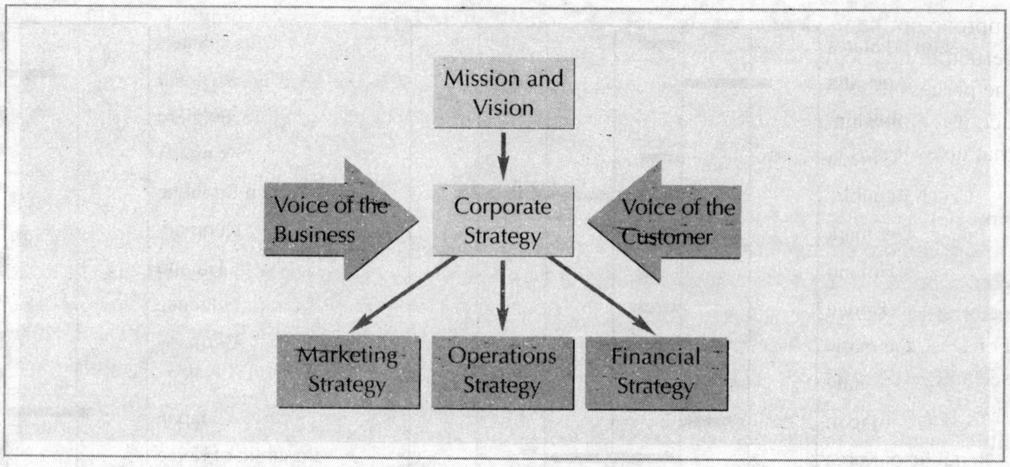

a corporate strategic plan in concurrence with the firm's mission and vision, customer requirements (voice of the customer), and business conditions (voice of the business). The strategic plan focuses on the gap between the firm's vision and its current position. It identifies and prioritizes what needs to be done to close the gap, and it provides direction for formulating strategies in the functional areas of the firm, such as marketing, operations, and finance. It is important that strategy in each of the functional areas be internally consistent as well as consistent with the firm's overall strategy.

Strategy formulation consists of five basic steps:

1. Defining a primary task.
2. Assessing core competencies.
3. Determining order winners and order qualifiers.
4. Positioning the firm.
5. Deploying the strategy.

PRIMARY TASK

The **primary task** represents the purpose of a firm—what the firm is in the business of doing. It also determines the competitive arena. As such, the primary task should not be defined too narrowly. For example, Norfolk Southern Railway is in the business of transportation, not railroads. Paramount is in the business of communication, not making movies. Amazon's business is providing the fastest, easiest, and most enjoyable shopping experience, while Disney's is making people happy! The primary task is usually expressed in a firm's *mission* statement.

Mission statements clarify what business a company is in—for Levi Strauss it's "branded casual apparel"; for Intel it's supplying "building blocks to the Internet economy"; for Binney & Smith (Crayola) it's "colorful visual expression"; for Currency Doubleday it's "ideas that link business with life's meaning"; for eBay it's "trading communities"; and for Merck it's "preserving and improving human life." Mission statements are the "constitution" for an organization, the corporate directive, but they are no good unless they are supported by strategy and converted into action. Thus, the next step in strategy formulation is assessing the core competencies of a firm.

CORE COMPETENCIES

Core competency is what a firm does better than anyone else, its *distinctive competence*. A firm's core competence can be exceptional service, higher quality, faster delivery, or lower cost. One company may strive to be first to the market with innovative designs, whereas another may look for success arriving later but with better quality.

Based on experience, knowledge, and know-how, core competencies represent *sustainable competitive advantages*. For this reason, products and technologies are seldom core competencies. The advantage they provide is short-lived, and other companies can readily purchase, emulate, or improve on them. Core competencies are more likely to be *processes*, a company's ability to *do* certain things better than a competitor. Thus, while a particular product is not a core competence, the process of developing new products is. For example, while the iPod was a breakthrough product, it is Apple's ability to turn out hit product after hit product (e.g., iPhone, iPad, MacBook, etc.) that gives it that competitive advantage.

Core competencies are not static. They should be nurtured, enhanced, and developed over time. Close contact with the customer is essential to ensuring that a competence does not become obsolete. Core competencies that do not evolve and are not aligned with customer needs can become *core rigidities* for a firm. Walmart and Dell, seemingly unstoppable companies in their field, went astray when they failed to update their competencies to match changes in customer desires. For Dell, the low cost and mail-order delivery of computers did not match the customer's desire to see and test computers before purchase, or to receive personalized after-purchase customer service. For Walmart, the obsession with lower costs led to image problems of a behemoth corporation with little regard for employees, suppliers, or local communities. Customers preferred to pay slightly more for the better designed products of more community-involved companies like Target. To avoid these problems, companies need to continually evaluate the characteristics of their products or services that prompt customer purchase; that is, the order qualifiers and order winners.

ORDER WINNERS AND ORDER QUALIFIERS

A firm is in trouble if the things it does best are not important to the customer. That's why it's essential to look toward customers to determine what influences their purchase decision.

Order qualifiers are the characteristics of a product or service that qualify it to be considered for purchase by a customer. An **order winner** is the characteristic of a product or service that wins orders in the marketplace—the final factor in the purchasing decision. For example, when purchasing a Blu-ray player, customers may determine a price range (order qualifier) and then choose the product with the most features (order winner) within that price range. Or they may have a set of features in mind (order qualifiers) and then select the least expensive player (order winner) that has all the required features.

Order winners and order qualifiers can evolve over time, just as competencies can be gained and lost. Japanese and Korean automakers initially competed on price but had to ensure certain levels of quality before the U.S. consumer would consider their product. Over time, the consumer was willing to pay a higher price (within reason) for the assurance of a superior-quality Japanese car. Price became a qualifier, but quality won the orders. Today, high quality, as a standard of the automotive industry, has become an order qualifier, and innovative design or superior gas mileage wins the orders.

As shown in Figure 1.11, order qualifiers will only take a firm so far. The customer expects the qualifiers, but is not "wowed" by them. For example, a low price might be a qualifier, but reducing the price further may not win orders if the features or design are not adequate. At a minimum, a firm

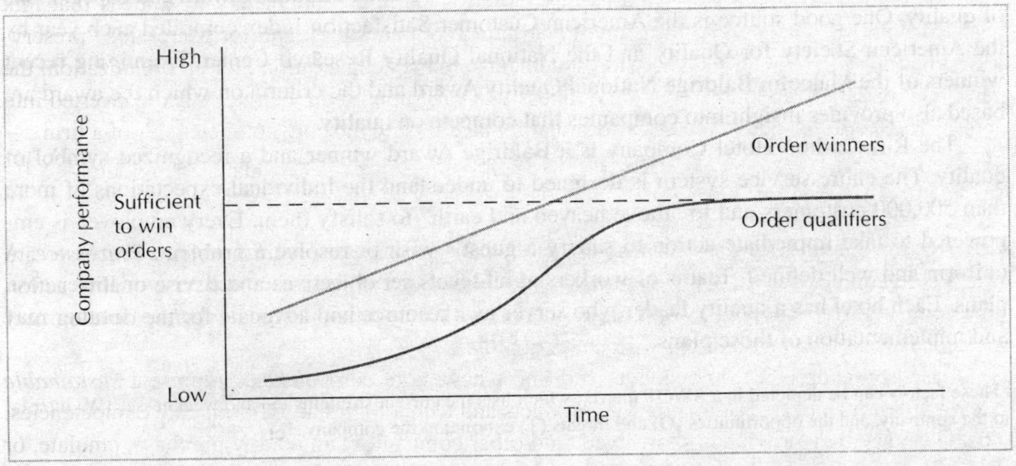

Figure 1.11

Order Winners and Order Qualifiers

SOURCE: Adapted from Nigel Slack, Stuart Chambers, Robert Johnston, and Alan Betts, *Operations and Process Management*, Prentice Hall, 2006, p. 47.

should meet the qualifiers. To excel, the firm needs to develop competencies that are in tune with the order winners. Marketing helps to identify these qualifiers and winners. Oftentimes, these characteristics are in the purview of operations and supply chain management, such as cost, speed to the market, speed of delivery, or customization. Other characteristics such as product or service design are supported by operations and supply chain management, but are not completely under their control.

POSITIONING THE FIRM

No firm can be all things to all people. Strategic **positioning** involves making choices—choosing one or two important things on which to concentrate and doing them extremely well. A firm's positioning strategy defines how it will compete in the marketplace—what unique value it will deliver to the customer. An effective positioning strategy considers the strengths and weaknesses of the organization, the needs of the marketplace, and the positions of competitors.[2]

Let's look at firms that have positioned themselves to compete on cost, speed, quality, and flexibility.

Competing on Cost

Companies that compete on cost relentlessly pursue the elimination of all waste. In the past, companies in this category produced standardized products for large markets. They improved yield by stabilizing the production process, tightening productivity standards, and investing in automation. Today, the entire cost structure is examined for reduction potential, not just direct labor costs. High-volume production and automation may or may not provide the most cost-effective alternative. A lean production system provides low costs through disciplined operations.

Competing on Speed

More than ever before, speed has become a source of competitive advantage. The Internet has conditioned customers to expect immediate response and rapid product shipment. Service organizations such as McDonald's, LensCrafters, and FedEx have always competed on speed. Now manufacturers are discovering the advantages of *time-based competition,* with build-to-order production and efficient supply chains. In the fashion industry where trends are temporary, Gap's six-month time-to-market can no longer compete with the nine-day design-to-rack lead time of Spanish retailer Zara. Read about Zara and its competitor Uniqlo in the "Along the Supply Chain" box on the next page.

Competing on Quality

Most companies approach quality in a defensive or reactive mode; quality is confined to minimizing defect rates or conforming to design specifications. To compete on quality, companies must view it as an opportunity to please the customer, not just a way to avoid problems or reduce rework costs.

To please the customer, one must first understand customer attitudes toward and expectations of quality. One good source is the American Customer Satisfaction Index compiled each year by the American Society for Quality and the National Quality Research Center. Examining recent winners of the Malcolm Baldrige National Quality Award and the criteria on which the award are based also provides insight into companies that compete on quality.

The Ritz-Carlton Hotel Company is a Baldrige Award winner and a recognized symbol of quality. The entire service system is designed to understand the individual expectations of more than 500,000 customers and to "move heaven and earth" to satisfy them. Every employee is empowered to take immediate action to satisfy a guest's wish or resolve a problem. Processes are uniform and well defined. Teams of workers at all levels set objectives and devise quality action plans. Each hotel has a quality leader who serves as a resource and advocate for the development and implementation of those plans.

[2]These factors can be depicted in a SWOT matrix, which lists the current strengths (S) and weaknesses (W) internal to the company, and the opportunities (O) and threats (T) external to the company.

ALONG THE SUPPLY CHAIN

Two Different Strategies—ZARA and Uniqlo

Zara is the world's largest fashion retailer and the lead brand in Inditex's wildly successful fashion empire. Zara, along with Sweden's H&M and Spain's Mango, are part of the fast fashion movement that has changed customer expectations of how retail stores should operate. These retailers are known for fresh design, rapid replenishment, and operational excellence. Zara, however, is the fastest and most profitable of the three.

For traditional retailers, garment production is outsourced to low-cost countries in Asia, and 80% of orders are placed six months to a year before they arrive in stores, leaving little room for new orders to be placed if fashion needs change. In contrast, Zara keeps more than half of its production in its own nearby factories, and leaves 85% of this in-house capacity open for in-season adjustments. The remainder of production, primarily standard offerings like t-shirts, is outsourced to China, Bangladesh, Vietnam, or Brazil. Although this production arrangement results in significantly higher labor costs than most garment manufacturers (including H&M and Mango), the fast turnaround time more than makes up for the difference, as described next.

At Zara's 14 highly automated factories, fabric is rolled out for cutting by computer-controlled equipment on 600-foot tables with patterns arranged to minimize waste. Cut fabric is sent to a network of 300 small sewing shops in nearby Galicia or Portugal, to be returned in a matter of days to the main factory for quality checks, pressing, tagging, and bagging. Finished garments are transported hung on overhead conveyors through an underground tunnel to the distribution center for automatic sorting (by country, then store) via bar codes. Orders to Europe are sent by truck, and to the United States and Asia by air, to arrive within 48 hours, twice weekly to every store. More than 2.6 million items move through the distribution center each week (that's 60,000 items per hour) to deliver 10,000 new designs to stores over the course of a year.

Since new merchandise is arriving at Zara stores twice a week and inventory of each item is kept low, customers are conditioned to visit the stores often and to purchase items right away. That means 80% to 90% of Zara's clothes are sold at full price and new fashions can be introduced as trends emerge (with an amazing design-to-hanger time as low as nine days). Zara also sports a 62% profit margin, unheard of in retail.

Uniqlo, a subsidiary of Japan's Fast Retailing, takes a different approach. It sells similarly priced products, but more basic items such as t-shirts, jeans, and sweaters that are not as easily susceptible to fashion whims. Seventy percent of Uniqlo's products are manufactured in China, the remainder in Japan. Uniqlo concentrates on classic "parts" of an outfit, and the quality of fit and fabric, rather than the latest style. It controls cost by limiting the number of items in the store, and by planning production a full year or more in advance of delivery. Relationships with suppliers are thus long-term (e.g., 10-year agreements) and production steady. Further, Uniqlo can spend time thoroughly testing materials and new designs, and work with suppliers to make sure the production of those items is exact. Its profit margin of 18% is countered by a high sales volume.

1. Zara has begun an online presence. What changes might be necessary to its business model to support online sales?
2. Zara currently has 45 stores in the United States and over 400 in China. Uniqlo aims for 1000 stores in the United States and 500 in China by 2015. Why the disparity?
3. Find information on the web about production strategies at GAP, Mango, and H&M. Compare these to Zara and Uniqlo. Which of the strategies most aligns with how you shop as a customer?
4. Zara's business model has been called unsustainable. Uniqlo's has been called boring. Do you agree? Explain.

Sources: Based on Suzy Hansen, "How Zara Grew Into the World's Largest Fashion Retailer," *The New York Times* (November 9, 2012); Seth Stevenson, "Polka Dots Are In? Polka Dots It Is! How Zara Gets Fresh Styles to Stores Insanely Fast," *Slate* (June 21, 2012); Christopher Bjork, "Inditex Goes from Strength to Strength," *The Wall Street Journal* (December 12, 2012); Ryan Tate, "Uniqlo's CEO on His Long, 'Crazy' Fight for the Future of Retail," *Wired* (October 10, 2012); Kerry Dolan, "Uniqlo: How Japanese Billionaire Tadashi Yanai Plans to Clothe America," *Forbes* (October 5, 2012); Greg Petro, "The Future of Retailing," *Forbes* (October 23, 2012).

Competing on Flexibility

Marketing always wants more variety to offer its customers. Manufacturing resists this trend because variety upsets the stability (and efficiency) of a production system and increases costs. The ability of manufacturing to respond to variation has opened up a new level of competition. **Flexibility** has become a competitive weapon. It includes the ability to produce a wide variety of products, to introduce new products and modify existing ones quickly, and to respond to customer needs.

National Bicycle Industrial Company fits bicycles to exact customer measurements. Bicycle manufacturers typically offer customers a choice among 20 or 30 different models. National offers 11,231,862 variations and delivers within two weeks at costs only 10% above standard models. Computerized design and computer-controlled machinery allow customized products to be essentially mass produced. The popular term for this phenomenon is **mass customization**.

Competing on Innovation

Companies that compete on innovation establish a corporate culture that encourages risk taking, challenges the status quo, accepts failure as part of the learning process, and celebrates successes. Three such companies are Apple, Google, and 3M. Apple *thinks different* to create incredibly fresh, beautiful game-changing designs. Google's open culture has produced such innovations as Google Street View, Google Fiber, Google People Finder (for disasters), Google Driverless Vehicles, and Google Glass. 3M defines itself as a global innovation company that never stops inventing. Ranging from Post-It notes to micro-needle skin patches designed to replace hypodermic needles, 3M produces hundreds of small innovations each year that improve how products or services operate. Like Google, 3M sets aside 20% of its engineers' time to be spent on projects of their own choosing. 3M also gives out $100,000 genius grants to its employees and has its own venture capitalist program that supports disruptive, early-stage innovations outside of the company's existing portfolio.

Innovation is exciting; however, it is not a competitive advantage if it cannot be transformed into marketable and profitable products or services. That's where operations and supply chain management come into play. We'll discuss their role more directly in Chapter 4 on Product Design.

STRATEGY DEPLOYMENT

Implementing strategy can be more difficult than formulating strategy. Strategies unveiled with much fanfare may never be followed because they are hard to understand, too general, or unrealistic. Strategies that aim for results five years or so down the road mean very little to the worker who is evaluated on his or her daily performance. Different departments or functional areas in a firm may interpret the same strategy in different ways. If their efforts are not coordinated, the results can be disastrous.

Consider Schlitz Brewing Company, whose strategy called for reduced costs and increased efficiency. Operations achieved its goals by dramatically shortening its brewing cycle—and, in the process, lost six of every 10 customers when the clarity and taste of the beer suffered. The efficiency move that was to make the company the most profitable in its industry instead caused its stock value to plummet from $69 per share to $5 per share. Schiltz has since been sold to Pabst Brewing Company, who combed through company documents and interviewed retired Schlitz brewmasters and taste-testers to derive and reintroduce the original 1960s "with gusto" formula.

Strategy deployment converts a firm's positioning strategy and resultant order winners and order qualifiers into specific performance requirements. Companies struggling to align day-to-day decisions with corporate strategy have found success with two types of planning systems—policy deployment and the balanced scorecard.

Policy Deployment

Policy deployment, also known as hoshin planning, is adapted from Japan's system of *hoshin kanri*, which is roughly translated from Japanese as "shining metal pointing direction"—a compass.

Policy deployment tries to focus everyone in an organization on common goals and priorities by translating corporate strategy into measurable objectives throughout the various functions and levels of the organization. As a result, everyone in the organization should understand the strategic plan, be able to derive several goals from the plan, and determine how each goal ties into their own daily activities.

Suppose the corporate strategic plan of competing on speed called for a reduction of 50% in the length of the supply chain cycle. Senior management from each functional area would assess how their activities contribute to the cycle, confer on the feasibility of reducing the cycle by 50%, and

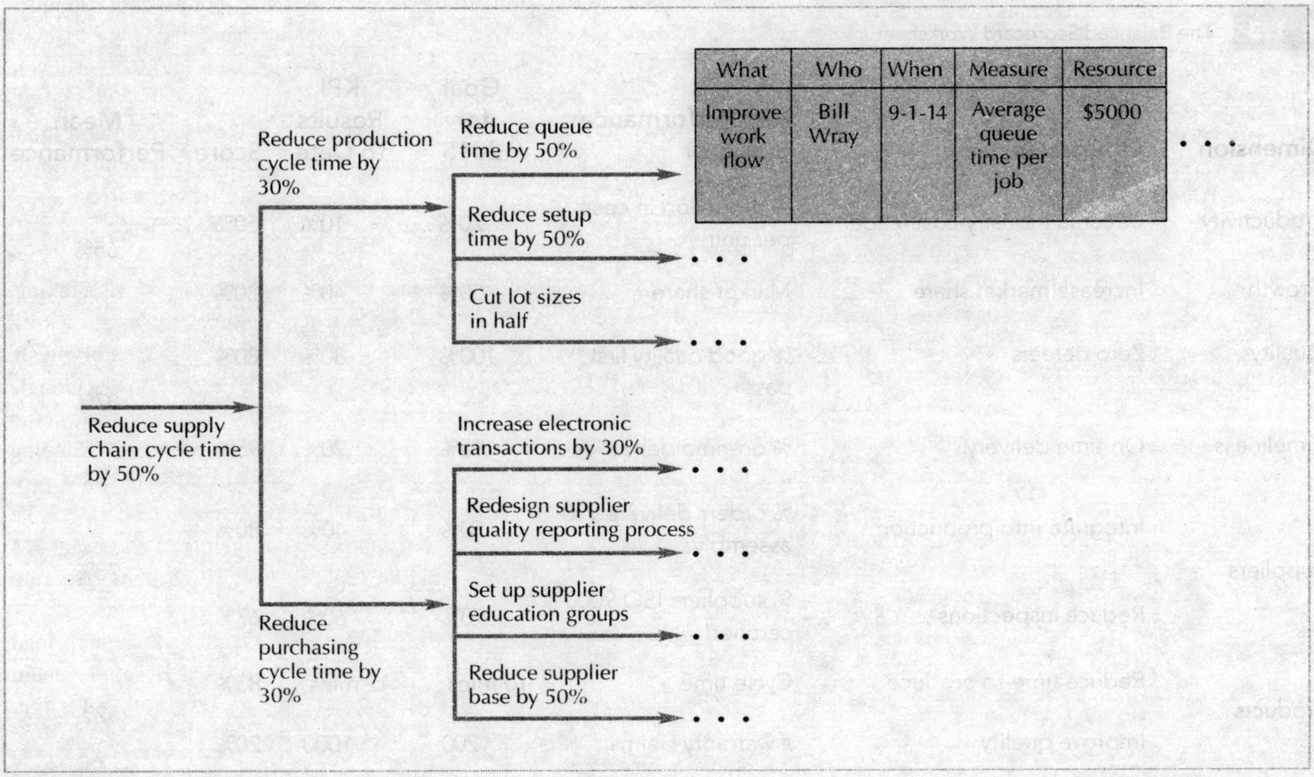

Figure 1.12

Derivation of an Action Plan Using Policy Deployment

agree on each person's particular role in achieving the reduction. Marketing might decide that creating strategic alliances with its distributors would shorten the average time to release a new product. Operations might try to reduce its purchasing and production cycles by reducing its supplier base, certifying suppliers, using e-procurement, and implementing a just-in-time (JIT) system. Finance might decide to eliminate unnecessary approval loops for expenditures, begin prequalifying sales prospects, and explore the use of electronic funds transfer (EFT) in conjunction with operations' lean strategy.

The process for forming objectives would continue in a similar manner down the organization with the *means* of achieving objectives for one level of management becoming the *target*, or objectives, for the next level. The outcome of the process is a cascade of action plans (or **hoshins**) aligned to complete each functional objective, which will, in turn, combine to achieve the strategic plan.

Figure 1.12 shows an abbreviated operations action plan for reducing supply chain cycle time. Policy deployment has become more popular as organizations become more geographically dispersed and culturally diverse.

Balanced Scorecard

The **balanced scorecard**, developed by Robert Kaplan and David Norton,[3] examines a firm's performance in four critical areas:

1. *Finances*—How should we look to our shareholders?
2. *Customers*—How should we look to our customers?
3. *Processes*—At which business processes must we excel?
4. *Learning and Growing*—How will we sustain our ability to change and improve?

[3] See Robert S. Kaplan and David P. Norton, "Transforming the Balanced Scorecard from Performance Measurement to Strategic Management," *Accounting Horizons* (March 2001), pp. 87–104; and Robert S. Kaplan and David P. Norton, "Having Trouble with Your Strategy? Then Map It," *Harvard Business Review* (September/October 2000), pp. 167–176.

TABLE 1.3 The Balanced Scorecard Worksheet

	Dimension	Objectives	Key Performance Indicator	Goal for 2015	KPI Results to Date	Score	Mean Performance
Finances	Productivity	Become industry cost leader	% reduction in cost per unit	20%	10%	50%	65%
	Growth	Increase market share	Market share	50%	40%	80%	
Customers	Quality	Zero defects	% good quality first pass	100%	80%	80%	87%
	Timeliness	On-time delivery	% on-time deliveries	95%	90%	95%	
Processes	Suppliers	Integrate into production	% orders delivered to assembly	50%	40%	80%	73%
		Reduce inspections	% suppliers ISO 9000 certified	90%	60%	67%	
	Products	Reduce time to produce	Cycle time	10 mins.	12 mins.	83%	52%
		Improve quality	# warranty claims	200	1000	20%	
	Distribution	Reduce transportation costs	% FTL shipments	75%	30%	40%	40%
	Service	Improve response to customer inquiries	% queries satisfied on first pass	90%	60%	67%	67%
	Risk	Reduce inventory obsolescence	Inventory turnover	12	6	50%	50%
		Reduce customer backlog	% orders backlogged	10%	20%	50%	
Learning & Growing	Human capital	Develop quality improvement skills	# of Six Sigma Black Belts	25	2	8%	35%
			% trained in SPC	80%	50%	63%	
	Information capital	Provide technology to improve processes	% customers who can track orders	100%	60%	60%	61%
			% suppliers who use EDI	80%	50%	63%	
	Organizational capital	Create innovative culture	# of employee suggestions	100	60	60%	55%
			% products new this year	20%	10%	50%	

It's called a *balanced* scorecard because more than financial measures are used to assess performance. Operational excellence is important in all four areas. How efficiently a firm's assets are managed, products produced, and services provided affect the financial health of the firm. Identifying and understanding targeted customers helps determine the processes and capabilities the organization must concentrate on to deliver value to the customer. The firm's ability to improve those processes and develop competencies in new areas is critical to sustaining competitive advantage.

Table 1.3 is a balanced scorecard worksheet. The worksheet selects areas of the strategy map to incorporate in annual objectives for the company. The objectives are then operationalized with **key performance indicators (KPI)**. The goals for the year are given, and the KPI results are recorded. The score converts the different performance measures into percentage completed. For example, if the goal is to achieve 12 inventory turns a year and the company manages only 6, then the goal is 50% achieved. The mean performance column averages the score for each dimension. The scorecard performance can be visualized in many ways, two of which are illustrated in Figures 1.13 and 1.14.

Figure 1.13 is a radar chart of the balanced scorecard. Goals 0% to 40% achieved appear in the red "danger" zone, 40% to 80% achieved are in the yellow "cautionary" zone, and 80% to 100%

Figure 1.13

A Radar Chart of the Balanced Scorecard

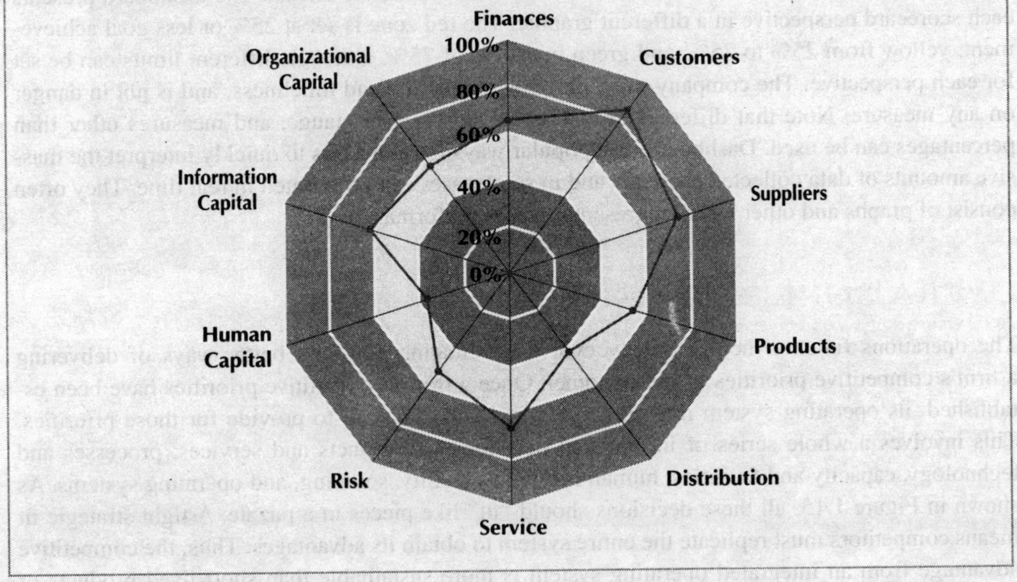

Figure 1.14

A Dashboard for the Balanced Scorecard

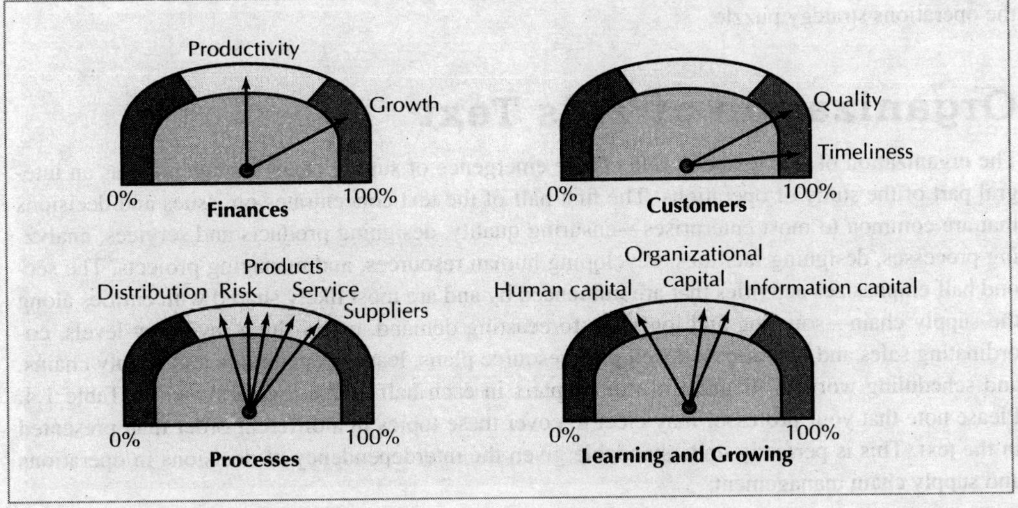

Figure 1.15

An Integrated Operations Strategy

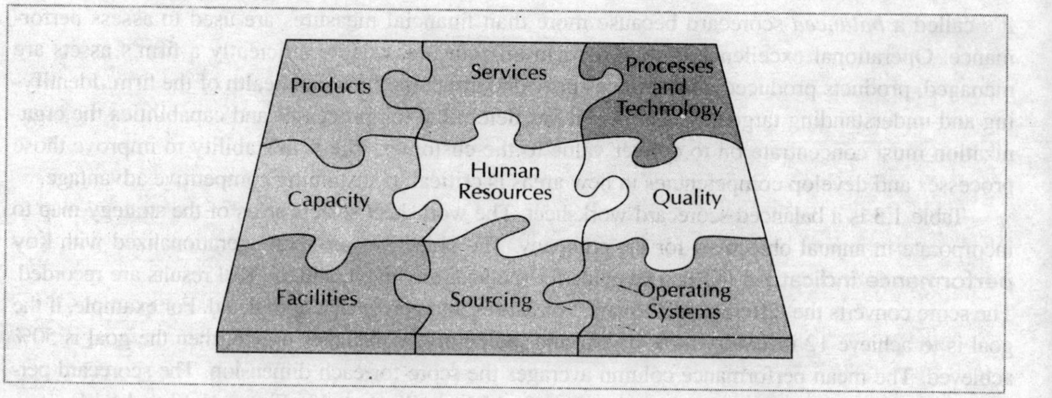

achieved are in the green "moving ahead" zone. In this example, the company is in the danger zone for human capital and distribution, but is doing well with growth, quality, timeliness, and service. Figure 1.14 shows the same information in an alternative format. The dashboard presents each scorecard perspective in a different graphic. The red zone is set at 25% or less goal achievement, yellow from 25% to 75%, and green in excess of 75%, although different limits can be set for each perspective. The company excels in growth, quality, and timeliness, and is not in danger on any measure. Note that different limits can be set for each gauge, and measures other than percentages can be used. Dashboards are popular ways for managers to quickly interpret the massive amounts of data collected each day and in some cases can be updated in real time. They often consist of graphs and other visual representations of performance.

OPERATIONS STRATEGY

The operations function helps strategy evolve by creating new and better ways of delivering a firm's competitive priorities to the customer. Once a firm's competitive priorities have been established, its operating system must be configured and managed to provide for those priorities. This involves a whole series of interrelated decisions on products and services, processes and technology, capacity and facilities, human resources, quality, sourcing, and operating systems. As shown in Figure 1.15, all these decisions should "fit" like pieces in a puzzle. A tight strategic fit means competitors must replicate the entire system to obtain its advantages. Thus, the competitive advantage from an integrated operating system is more sustainable than short-lived products or technologies. Beginning with quality, the remaining chapters in Part I put together the pieces of the operations strategy puzzle.

Organization of This Text

The organization of this textbook reflects the emergence of supply chain management as an integral part of the study of operations. The first half of the text concentrates on issues and decisions that are common to most enterprises—ensuring quality, designing products and services, analyzing processes, designing facilities, developing human resources, and managing projects. The second half emphasizes activities that are influenced by and are most likely shared with entities along the supply chain—sourcing and logistics, forecasting demand, establishing inventory levels, coordinating sales and operations, developing resource plans, leaning operations and supply chains, and scheduling work. A diagram of the chapters in each half of the text is shown in Table 1.4. Please note that your professor may elect to cover these topics in a different order than presented in the text. This is perfectly understandable given the interdependency of decisions in operations and supply chain management.

TABLE 1.4 Organization of the Text

Part I—Operations Management	
Chapter 1	Operations and Supply Chain Strategy
Chapter 2	Ensuring Quality
Chapter 3	Process Capability and Statistical Process Control
Chapter 4	Product Design
Chapter 5	Designing Services
Chapter 6	Designing Processes
Chapter 7	Planning Facilities and Capacity
Chapter 8	Human Resources
Chapter 9	Managing Projects
Part II—Supply Chain Management	
Chapter 10	Designing the Supply Chain
Chapter 11	Global Procurement and Distribution
Chapter 12	Forecasting Demand
Chapter 13	Inventory Management
Chapter 14	Aggregate Planning for Sales and Operations
Chapter 15	Enterprise Resource Planning
Chapter 16	JIT and Lean Production
Chapter 17	Scheduling

Learning Objectives of This Course

The learning objectives of this course are threefold:

1. ***To gain an appreciation of the strategic importance of operations and supply chain management in a global business environment and to understand how operations relates to other business functions.*** Regardless of your major, as you pursue a career in business, you will need to understand the basic issues, capabilities, and limitations of operations and supply chains. By the conclusion of this course, you will be able to describe the impact of operations and supply chain management on other functions within a firm, as well as on the competitive position of the firm. You will also be more aware of the global nature of operations and the complexity of supply chains.
2. ***To develop a working knowledge of the concepts and methods related to designing and managing operations and creating value along the supply chain.*** In this course, you will learn the basic steps involved in bringing a product to market from its design through production and delivery. You will also learn such skills as how to forecast demand, lay out a facility, manage a project, work with suppliers, and schedule work.
3. ***To develop a skill set for continuous improvement.*** From this course, you will gain the ability to conceptualize how systems are interrelated, to organize activities effectively, to analyze processes critically, to make decisions based on data, and to push for continual process improvement. These skills will serve you well in whatever career you choose.

SUMMARY

Operations can be viewed as a transformation process that converts inputs into outputs of greater value.

Operations management is the study of processes directly related to the creation and distribution of goods and services. Increasingly, these operations are taking place outside of the boundaries of a traditional enterprise. Thus, while today's managers need to understand how to manage operations efficiently within their own firm, they also need to develop skills in coordinating operations across a global supply chain. This text teaches students how to analyze processes, ensure quality, create value, and manage the flow of information, products and services across a network of customers, enterprises, and supply chain partners.

Firms choose to compete in different ways. A firm's *strategy* defines how it will compete in the marketplace—in its own best way. Strategy formulation involves defining the primary task, assessing core competencies, determining order winners and order qualifiers, and positioning the firm. An effective strategy meets the order qualifiers and excels on the order winners. A competitive position is not sustainable unless the operating system that supports it is configured and managed effectively.

Policy deployment is a planning system that helps align day-to-day operating decisions with the company's overall strategy. The *balanced scorecard* reinforces a firm's strategy by providing customer-oriented and process-oriented measures of performance, in addition to traditional financial measures.

Decision making for the future can be scary at best. Fortunately, there are quantitative tools available for making decisions under uncertain conditions. The supplement to this chapter reviews several of them for us.

QUESTIONS

1-1. What activities are involved in the operations function? How does operations interact with other functional areas?

1-2. What constitutes "operations" at (a) a bank, (b) a retail store, (c) a hospital, (d) a cable TV company?

1-3. Briefly describe how operations has evolved from the Industrial Revolution to Globalization.

1-4. What is competitiveness? How is it measured? How has the Internet affected competitiveness?

1-5. Investigate the role of government in improving industrial competitiveness. Begin with the U.S. Council on Competitiveness at www.compete.org. Find a similar site for at least one other country. Compare their priorities and initiatives.

1-6. Describe the global activities of a corporation of your choice. How many foreign plants or suppliers do they have? Where are they located? How much of their business is foreign? Are any global strategies evident?

1-7. Choose an industry on which you will be the class "expert" for the duration of this course. Write an initial profile of major players, customers, structure, and competitive issues.

1-8. Find an interesting website related to the operations function in a firm with which you are familiar. Write a summary of what you find.

1-9. Look for articles related to supply chain online or at *Fortune, Bloomberg Businessweek,* or CNN. How do they relate to the primary topics discussed in this chapter?

1-10. The World Bank ranks countries in terms of globalization. Go to the research section of *www.worldbank.com* and choose four countries to compare.

1-11. The World Trade Organization has its advocates and its adversaries. Find out more about the organization by visiting its website at *www.wto.org*. What kinds of activities does the organization support? What rules and regulations does it enforce? Who are its member states, and how is membership achieved?

1-12. Cultural differences can make it difficult to do business in other countries. Go to *www.worldbusinessculture.com* and choose a country to explore. Share your discoveries with your professor and classmates in a one- to two-page write-up.

1-13. Much of the negotiation in trade agreements centers on ethical/legal issues such as intellectual property protection, bribery and payoffs, and copyright and patent infringement. Transparency International at *www.transparency.org* publishes a bribery index by country. Report on which countries and industries are most susceptible to bribery.

1-14. Ethics is easier when there are laws to fall back on. Search the Internet for information on the Foreign Corrupt Practices Act. Briefly describe what it entails. Then find two companies that explicitly state a code of conduct on their website and, in particular, reference the Foreign Corrupt Practices Act. How does each company approach the issue?

1-15. Gather mission or vision statements from four different companies. What do they tell you about the organizations? Is their mission or vision reflected in the way they do business?

1-16. List and explain the five steps of strategy formulation. Follow the steps to outline a strategy for a company or organization with which you are familiar.

1-17. Explain the concept of core competencies in your own words. Provide examples of a core competency for a bank, a retail store, and an auto manufacturer.

1-18. What is your core competency? Make a list of the core competencies you will need to compete successfully in the job market. Design a strategy for developing the competencies that you do not have and capitalizing on the competencies that you do have.

1-19. What is the difference between an order winner and an order qualifier? Tell how you have used the two concepts in a purchasing decision.

1-20. Discuss the requirements from an operations perspective of competing on (a) quality, (b) cost, (c) flexibility, (d) speed, (e) innovation, and (f) service. Give examples of manufacturing or service firms that successfully compete on each of the criteria listed.

1-21. What role should operations play in corporate strategy?

1-22. Name several strategic decisions that involve operations and supply chain management.

1-23. Why do companies need policy deployment? What does it do?

1-24. What is the balanced scorecard? How does it relate to operations?

1-25. Examine the annual reports of a company of your choosing over three years. Use quotes from the reports to describe the company's overall strategy and its specific goals each year. Pay special attention to sustainability strategies. How well do you think the company deploys its strategy?

1-26. Use either policy deployment or a balanced scorecard to map out a personal strategy for your future.

PROBLEMS

1-1. It is time for the annual performance review of Go-Com's account executives. Account values and hours spent each week acquiring and servicing accounts are shown below. Each agent works approximately 45 weeks out of the year, but the time spent on accounts each week differs considerably. How would you rate the performance of each individual? Which agent is most productive? Which agents show the most potential?

Agents	Albert	Bates	Cressey	Duong
New accounts	$100,000	$40,000	$80,000	$200,000
Existing accounts	$40,000	$40,000	$150,000	$100,000
Labor hours	40	20	60	80

1-2. The Bureau of Labor Statistics collects input and output data from various countries for comparison purposes. Labor hours are the standard measure of input. Calculate the output per hour from the following data. Which country is most productive?

	Labor Hours	Units of Output
United States	89.5	136
Germany	83.6	100
Japan	72.7	102

1-3. Omar Industries maintains production facilities in several locations around the globe. Average monthly cost data and output levels are given in the following tables.

a. Calculate the labor productivity of each facility.
b. Calculate the multifactor productivity of each facility.
c. If Omar needed to close one of the plants, which one would you choose?

Units (in 000s)	Cincinnati	Frankfurt	Guadalajara	Beijing
Finished goods	10,000	12,000	5,000	8,000
Work-in-process	1,000	2,200	3,000	6,000

Costs (in 000s)	Cincinnati	Frankfurt	Guadalajara	Beijing
Labor costs	$3,500	$4,200	$2,500	$800
Material costs	$3,500	$3,000	$2,000	$2,500
Energy costs	$1,000	$1,500	$1,200	$800
Transportation costs	$250	$2,500	$2,000	$5,000
Overhead costs	$1,200	$3,000	$2,500	$500

1-4. Carpet City recorded the following data on carpet installations over the past week. Use the data to calculate the average rate (in yards per hour) at which carpet can be installed.

Installation	1	2	3
Square yards	1225	1435	2500
No. of workers	4	3	5
No. of hours per worker	3	5	6

1-5. Posey Ceramics makes ceramic vases for a chain of department stores. The output and cost figures over the past four weeks are shown here. Labor costs $10 an hour, and materials are $4 a pound. Calculate the (a) labor productivity (in hrs), (b) material productivity (in lbs), and (c) multifactor productivity for each week. Comment on the results.

Week	1	2	3	4
Units of output	2000	4000	5000	7000
No. of workers	4	4	5	6
Hours per week per worker	40	48	56	70
Material (lbs)	286	570	720	1000

1-6. True Value Jeans currently produces 60 pairs of jeans in an eight-hour day. The costs of production include:

Raw material	$10.00/pair
Labor	3 workers, $20/hour
Energy	$1/hour of machine time
Machines	3 machines, $10/hour

a. Calculate the labor productivity for True Value, i.e., how many jeans can be produced per hour of labor?
b. Calculate the multifactor productivity for True Value, i.e., how many pairs of jeans can be produced per dollar spent?

CASE STUDY

Evaluating the Need for Project Management Training at Polytechnical

Project Management Research Committee, China (PMRC) originated in 1991 with the commitment of developing China's project-management-specific discipline. The Polytechnical University has been in communications with PMRC about establishing a master of project management degree program. The Polytechnical School of Technology Management believes there is a real need for this program. Polytechnical's preliminary research has identified that project management is one of the fastest demand growing degrees in Asia. The literature shows that this discipline provides a real return to the organizations who use it and there appears to be an adequate supply of China-trained, qualified, and degreed project managers. Preliminary market research has identified an existing master's degree program at the neighboring Technical Management University.

You have been brought on as a project management training consultant. Your job is to work with Polytechnical's Technology Management team. The objective of this effort is to (a) determine if there is a need for the program and, if so, (b) develop a compelling business case to move forward.

1. Develop a high-level plan that will assist in determining if there is a need for this program.
2. Identify four or five key performance indicators that will help Polytechnical develop a balanced scorecard for this program.

REFERENCES

AT&T Quality Steering Committee. *Policy Deployment: Setting the Direction for Change.* Indianapolis: AT&T Technical Publications Center, 1992.

Christensen, Clayton. *The Innovator's Dilemma.* New York: Harper Business, 2003.

Engardio, Pete, and Dexter Roberts. "The China Price." *Business Week* (December 6, 2004).

Friedman, Thomas. *The World Is Flat.* New York: Farrar, Straus and Giroux, 2005.

Friedman, Thomas. *Hot, Flat, and Crowded*, New York: Farrar, Straus and Giroux, 2008.

Friedman, Thomas, and Michael Mandelbaum, *That Used to Be Us.* New York: Picador, 2012.

Hammer, Michael. *Beyond Reengineering.* New York: Harper-Collins, 1996.

Hayes, Robert, Gary Pisano, David Upton, and Steven Wheelwright. *Operations Strategy and Technology: Pursuing the Competitive Edge.* Hoboken, NJ: John Wiley, 2005.

Hill, Terry. *Manufacturing Strategy: Test and Cases*, 3rd ed. Homewood, IL: Irwin, 2000.

Jones, Patricia, and Larry Kahaner. *Say It and Live It: The 50 Corporate Mission Statements That Hit the Mark.* New York: Currency Doubleday, 1995.

Kaplan, Robert, and David Norton. *Strategy Maps: Converting Intangible Assets into Tangible Outcomes.* Boston: Harvard Business School Press, 2004.

King, Bob. *Hoshin Planning: The Developmental Approach.* Springfield, MA: GOAL/QPC, 1989.

Leonard-Barton, Dorothy. *Wellsprings of Knowledge: Building and Sustaining the Sources of Innovation.* Boston: Harvard Business School Press, 1995.

Manufacturing Studies Board. *Towards a New Era in Manufacturing: The Need for a National Vision.* Washington, DC: National Academy Press, 1986.

Peters, Tom. *Thriving on Chaos.* New York: Alfred A. Knopf, 1987.

Midler, Paul. *Poorly Made in China.* Hoboken, NJ: John Wiley and Sons, Inc., 2011.

Porter, Michael. *On Competition.* Boston: Harvard Business School Publishing, 2008.

Quade, Walter. "Beginner's Guide to the Asian Supply Chain." *Inside Supply Management* (March 2004), pp. 8–9.

Snyder, R. *Fugitive Denim: A Moving Story of People and Pants in the Borderless World of Global Trade* (New York: Norton, 2009).

Hegarty, S. "How Jeans Conquered the World," BBC World Service, January 28, 2012.

Skinner, Wickham. *Manufacturing: The Formidable Competitive Weapon.* New York: John Wiley, 1985.

Skinner, Wickham. "Three Yards and a Cloud of Dust: Industrial Management at Century End." *Production and Operations Management* 5, no. 1 (Spring 1996): 15–24.

Voss, Christopher. "Operations Management—from Taylor to Toyota—and Beyond." *British Journal of Management* 6 (December 1995), S17–S29.

Womack, James, Daniel Jones, and Daniel Roos. *The Machine that Changed the World.* New York: Macmillan, 1990.

CHAPTER 2

Ensuring Quality

LEARNING OBJECTIVES

AFTER READING THIS CHAPTER, YOU WILL BE ABLE TO:

- Discuss and define the dimensions of quality.
- Articulate the benefits and costs of good quality, and the costs of poor quality.
- Understand how quality management systems have evolved and be able to assess the stage of quality evolution a particular company exhibits.
- Utilize quality tools and the DMAIC methodology in problem solving.
- Explain the philosophy and magnitude of Six Sigma quality.
- Recognize quality awards and ISO certifications.

QUALITY AND VALUE IN DENIM JEANS

Denim jeans are a global wardrobe staple with about 2 billion pairs of jeans worth nearly $55 billion sold worldwide each year (70% in the United States, European Union, and China). About 780 million pairs of jeans are sold annually in the United States; virtually all U.S. consumers own at least one pair of denim jeans, and, on average, seven pairs. However, regardless of the price of their jeans, which generally average a little less than $40 but can approach $500, American consumers expect them to last longer and be more durable than any other piece of clothing in their closets. U.S. jeans retailers generally acknowledge that while price is the top factor for most consumer clothing decisions, it is less of a factor when buying denim jeans; consumers see the *value* in paying a little more for jeans that have "better" quality (i.e., a better fit and will last longer). Among women jeans buyers, price is the fourth most important factor behind other quality attributes, and among men less than half view price as important when buying jeans. As such, quality is perhaps the most important factor to the various companies up and down the denim jeans supply chain around the world that grow cotton, manufacture denim cloth, produce denim jeans, and sell jeans to consumers.

How the customer perceives "value" in denim jeans is a key factor that drives the quality management (QM) programs of most major denim jeans companies like Levi Strauss and VF Corporation (Lee and Wrangler jeans). There are a number of attributes that affect the feel, look, and fit of denim jeans, and thus distinguish their quality. For example, jeans buyers have historically been willing to pay more for jeans with a higher cotton content (resulting in a better "feel"), and apparel consumers, in general, believe better quality clothing is made from natural fibers (like cotton). Different fabric qualities are determined by not only the quality of the cotton used but also the manufacturing process used to make it; more expensive processes that spin the cotton into fabric unevenly give the fabric more character and depth. How the fabric is cut and sewn; how it is dyed; how it is ultimately washed in the finishing process (which can sometimes exceed all of the other production costs combined); the various trim items such as rivets, buttons, and zippers; and fit, are distinguishing quality attributes.

To be successful in the highly competitive global denim jeans market, companies must rely on well-conceived and managed quality management programs throughout their supply chains to ensure that they are able to provide the value their customers demand.

In this chapter we will discuss what quality is, and how companies develop effective quality management (QM) programs to satisfy their customers.

Sources: Based on Maggie Kalogeropoulos, "Understanding Denim," www.askmen.com; "Denim Jeans: State of the U.S. Market," *Cotton Incorporated Supply Chain Insights* (2011), www.lifestylemonitor.cottoninc.com; and, Summer R. Oakes, "Textile Talk: Denim Nation—Series 1.1," www.source4style.com/trends/the-academy/.

What is Quality?

Asked "What is quality?" one of our students replied, "Getting what you pay for." Another student added that to her, quality was "getting *more* than you paid for!" The *Oxford American Dictionary* defines quality as "a degree or level of excellence."

The American Society for Quality (ASQ) defines quality as "a subjective term for which each person has his or her own definition. In technical usage, quality can have two meanings: (1) The characteristics of a product or service that bear on its ability to satisfy stated or implied needs and (2) A product or service free of deficiencies." Obviously, quality can be defined in many ways, depending on who is defining it and the product or service it refers to. In this section we provide a perspective on what quality means to customers and companies.

QUALITY FROM THE CUSTOMER'S PERSPECTIVE

A business organization produces goods and services to meet its customers' needs. Customers want value and quality has become a major factor in the value of products and service. Customers know that certain companies produce better-quality products than others, and they buy accordingly. That means a firm must consider how the consumer defines quality. The customer can be a manufacturer purchasing raw materials or parts, a store owner or retailer purchasing products to sell, or someone who purchases retail products or services over the Internet. W. Edwards Deming, author and consultant on quality, says that "The consumer is the most important part of the production line. Quality should be aimed at the needs of the consumer, present and future." From this perspective, product and service quality is determined by what the customer wants and is willing to pay for. Since customers have different product needs, they will have different quality expectations. This results in a commonly used definition of quality as a service's or product's *fitness for its intended use*, or **fitness for use**: how well does it do what the customer or user thinks it is supposed to do and wants it to do?

Products and services are designed with intentional differences in quality to meet the different wants and needs of individual consumers. A Mercedes and a Ford truck are equally "fit for use," in the sense that they both provide automobile transportation for the consumer, and each may meet the quality standards of its individual purchaser. However, the two products have obviously been designed differently for different types of consumers. This is commonly referred to as the **quality of design**—the degree to which quality characteristics are designed into the product. Although designed for the same use, the Mercedes and Ford differ in their performance, features, size, and various other quality characteristics.

DIMENSIONS OF QUALITY FOR MANUFACTURED PRODUCTS

The *dimensions of quality* for manufactured products a consumer looks for include the following[1]:

1. Performance: The basic operating characteristics of a product; for example, how well a car handles or its gas mileage.
2. Features: The "extra" items added to the basic features, such as a stereo CD or a leather interior in a car.
3. Reliability: The probability that a product will operate properly within an expected time frame; that is, that a TV will work without repair for about seven years.
4. Conformance: The degree to which a product meets preestablished standards.
5. Durability: How long the product lasts; its life span before replacement. A pair of L.L. Bean boots, with care, might be expected to last a lifetime.
6. Serviceability: The ease of getting repairs, the speed of repairs, and the courtesy and competence of the repair person.
7. Aesthetics: How a product looks, feels, sounds, smells, or tastes.
8. Safety: Assurance that the customer will not suffer injury or harm from a product; an especially important consideration for automobiles.
9. Other perceptions: Subjective perceptions based on brand name, advertising, and the like.

These quality characteristics are weighed by the customer relative to the cost of the product. In general, customers will pay for the level of quality they can afford. If they feel they are getting what they paid for (or more), then they tend to be satisfied with the quality of the product.

DIMENSIONS OF QUALITY FOR SERVICES

The dimensions of quality for a service differ somewhat from those of a manufactured product. Service quality is more directly related to time and the interaction between employees and the customer. Evans and Lindsay[2] identify the following dimensions of service quality.

1. Time and timeliness: How long must a customer wait for service, and is it completed on time? For example, is an overnight package delivered overnight?
2. Completeness: Is everything the customer asked for provided? For example, is a mail order from a catalog company complete when delivered?

[1]Adapted from D. A. Garvin, "What Does Quality Really Mean?" *Sloan Management Review* 26, issue 1 (1984): 25–43.
[2]J. R. Evans and W. M. Lindsay, *The Management and Control of Quality*, 3rd ed. (St. Paul, MN: West, 1996).

3. Courtesy: How are customers treated by employees? For example, are catalog phone operators at L.L. Bean nice and are their voices pleasant?
4. Consistency: Is the same level of service provided to each customer each time? Is your newspaper delivered on time every morning?
5. Accessibility and convenience: How easy is it to obtain the service? For example, when you call L.L. Bean does the service representative answer quickly?
6. Accuracy: Is the service performed right every time? Is your bank or credit card statement correct every month?
7. Responsiveness: How well does the company react to unusual situations, which can happen frequently in a service company? For example, how well is a telephone operator at L.L. Bean able to respond to a customer's questions about a catalog item not fully described in the catalog?

QUALITY FROM THE PRODUCER'S PERSPECTIVE

Now we need to look at quality the way a producer or service provider sees it: how value is created. We already know that product development is a function of the quality characteristics (i.e., the product's fitness for use) the customer wants, needs, and can afford. Product or service design results in design specifications that should achieve the desired quality. However, once the product design has been determined, the producer perceives quality to be how effectively the production process is able to conform to the specifications required by the design, referred to as the **quality of conformance**. What this means is quality during production focuses on making sure that the product meets the specifications required by the design.

Examples of the quality of conformance: If new tires do not conform to specifications, they wobble. If a hotel room is not clean when a guest checks in, the hotel is not functioning according to the specifications of its design; it is a faulty service. From the producer's perspective, good-quality products conform to specifications—they are well made; poor-quality products are not made well—they do not conform to specifications.

Achieving quality of conformance depends on a number of factors, including the design of the production process (distinct from product design), the performance level of machinery, equipment and technology, the materials used, the training and supervision of employees, and the degree to which statistical quality-control techniques are used. When equipment fails or is maladjusted, when employees make mistakes, when material and parts are defective, and when supervision is lax, design specifications are generally not met. Key personnel in achieving conformance to specifications include the engineering staff, supervisors and managers, and, most important, employees.

An important consideration from the customer's perspective of product quality is product or service price. From the producer's perspective, an important consideration is achieving quality of conformance at an acceptable cost. Product cost is also an important design specification. If products or services cannot be produced at a cost that results in a competitive price, then the final product will not have acceptable value—the price is more than the consumer is willing to pay given the product's quality characteristics. Thus, the quality characteristics included in the product design must be balanced against production costs.

A FINAL PERSPECTIVE ON QUALITY

We approached quality from two perspectives, the customer's and the producer's. These two perspectives are dependent on each other, as shown in Figure 2.1. Although product design is customer-motivated, it cannot be achieved without the coordination and participation of the production process. When a product or service is designed without considering how it will be produced, it may be impossible for the production process to meet design specifications or it may be so costly to do so that the product or service must be priced prohibitively high.

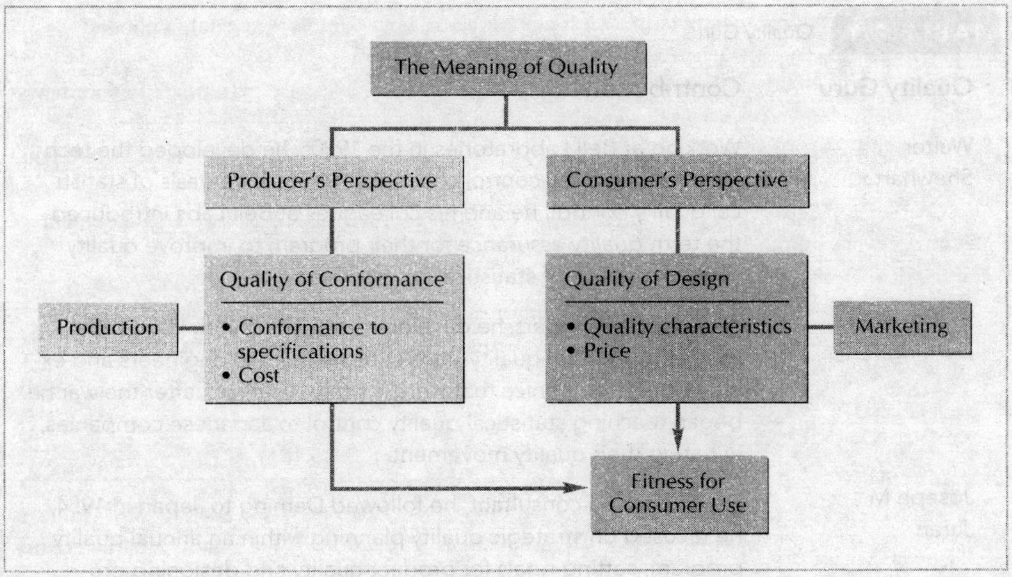

Figure 2.1
The Meaning of Quality

Figure 2.1 depicts the meaning of quality from the producer's and consumer's perspectives. The final determination of quality is fitness for use, which is the customer's view of quality. It is the consumer who makes the final judgment regarding quality, and so it is the customer's view that must dominate.

Quality Management System

To make sure that products and services have the quality they have been designed for, strategy to achieve quality throughout the organization is required. This approach to the management of quality throughout the entire organization and supply chain has evolved into what is generally referred to as a quality management system (QMS).

THE EVOLUTION OF QUALITY MANAGEMENT

A handful of prominent individuals summarized in Table 2.1 have had a profound impact on the importance of quality in the United States, Japan, and other countries. Of these "quality gurus," W. Edwards Deming has been the most prominent.

In the 1940s Deming worked at the Census Bureau, where he introduced the use of statistical process control to monitor the mammoth operation of key-punching data from census questionnaires onto millions of punch cards. During World War II, Deming developed a national program of 8- and 10-day courses to teach statistical quality-control techniques to over 10,000 engineers at companies that were suppliers to the military during the war. By the end of World War II he had an international reputation.

In 1950 Deming began teaching statistical quality control to Japanese companies. As a consultant to Japanese industries and as a teacher, he was able to convince them of the benefits of statistical quality control. He is a major figure in the Japanese quality movement, and in Japan he is frequently referred to as the father of quality control.

Deming's approach to quality management advocated continuous improvement of the production process to achieve conformance to specifications and reduce variability. He identified two primary sources of process improvement: eliminating common causes of quality problems, such

TABLE 2.1 Quality Gurus

Quality Guru	Contribution
Walter Shewhart	Working at Bell Laboratories in the 1920s, he developed the technical tools such as control charts that formed the basis of statistical quality control; he and his colleagues at Bell Labs introduced the term *quality assurance* for their program to improve quality through the use of statistical control methods.
W. Edwards Deming	A disciple of Shewart, he developed courses during World War II to teach statistical quality-control techniques to engineers and executives of companies that were military suppliers; after the war he began teaching statistical quality control to Japanese companies, initiating their quality movement.
Joseph M. Juran	An author and consultant, he followed Deming to Japan in 1954; he focused on strategic quality planning within an annual quality program, setting goals for product quality and designing processes to achieve those goals; quality improvement is achieved by focusing on projects to solve problems and securing breakthrough solutions.
Armand V. Feigenbaum	In his 1951 book, *Quality Control: Principles, Practices and Administration*, he introduced the concept of total quality control and continuous quality improvement as a companywide strategic commitment requiring the involvement of all functions in the quality process, not just manufacturing; discovered by the Japanese in the 1950s at about the same time as Juran's visit; from 1958 to 1968, he was director of manufacturing operations and quality control at GE.
Philip Crosby	In his 1979 book, *Quality Is Free*, he emphasized that the costs of poor quality (including lost labor and equipment time, scrap, downtime and lost sales) far outweigh the cost of preventing poor quality; in his 1984 book, *Quality Without Tears*, he defined absolutes of quality management—quality is defined as conformance to requirements, quality results from prevention, the performance standard is "zero defects."
Kaoru Ishikawa	This Tokyo University professor promoted the use of quality circles and developed the "fishbone" (cause and effect) diagram to diagnose quality problems; he emphasized the importance of the internal customer, that is, that a quality organization is first necessary in order to produce quality products or services.

as poor product design and insufficient employee training, and eliminating special causes, such as specific equipment or an operator. Deming emphasized the use of statistical quality-control techniques to reduce variability in the production process. He dismissed the then widely used approach of final product inspection as a means of ensuring good quality as coming too late to reduce product defects. Primary responsibility for quality improvement, he said, was employees' and management's. He promoted extensive employee involvement in a quality improvement program, and he recommended training for workers in quality-control techniques and methods.

TABLE 2.2 W. E. Deming's 14 Points

1.	Create a constancy of purpose toward product improvement to achieve long-term organizational goals.
2.	Adopt a philosophy of preventing poor-quality products instead of acceptable levels of poor quality as necessary to compete internationally.
3.	Eliminate the need for inspection to achieve quality by relying instead on statistical quality control to improve product and process design.
4.	Select a few suppliers or vendors based on quality commitment rather than competitive prices.
5.	Constantly improve the production process by focusing on the two primary sources of quality problems, the system and employees, thus increasing productivity and reducing costs.
6.	Institute worker training that focuses on the prevention of quality problems and the use of statistical quality-control techniques.
7.	Instill leadership among supervisors to help employees perform better.
8.	Encourage employee involvement by eliminating the fear of reprisal for asking questions or identifying quality problems.
9.	Eliminate barriers between departments, and promote cooperation and a team approach for working together.
10.	Eliminate slogans and numerical targets that urge employees to achieve higher performance levels without first showing them how to do it.
11.	Eliminate numerical quotas that employees attempt to meet at any cost without regard for quality.
12.	Enhance worker pride, artisanry, and self-esteem by improving supervision and the production process so that employees can perform to their capabilities.
13.	Institute vigorous education and training programs in methods of quality improvement throughout the organization, from top management down, so that continuous improvement can occur.
14.	Develop a commitment from top management to implement the previous 13 points.

Deming's overall philosophy for achieving improvement is embodied in his 14 points, summarized in Table 2.2.

Deming is also credited with the development of the *Deming Wheel*, although it was originally formulated by Walter Shewart, and later recast and renamed by the Japanese as the *plan-do-check-act (PDCA) cycle*. The PDCA cycle is a four-stage process for continuous quality improvement that complements Deming's 14 points, as shown in Figure 2.2. Years later, Deming once again modified the original Shewart cycle as a circle flow diagram for learning and improvement of a product and process that he called the *plan-do-study-act (PDSA) cycle* (also shown in Figure 2.2). The PDCA cycle later formed the basis for the Six Sigma five-step DMAIC breakthrough strategy (we'll talk about this in the "Six Sigma" section later in this chapter).

Deming's approach to quality embodied in his 14 points and PDCA cycle are the foundation for today's quality management systems employed by many successful companies.

Figure 2.2

The Deming Wheel (PDCA Cycle)

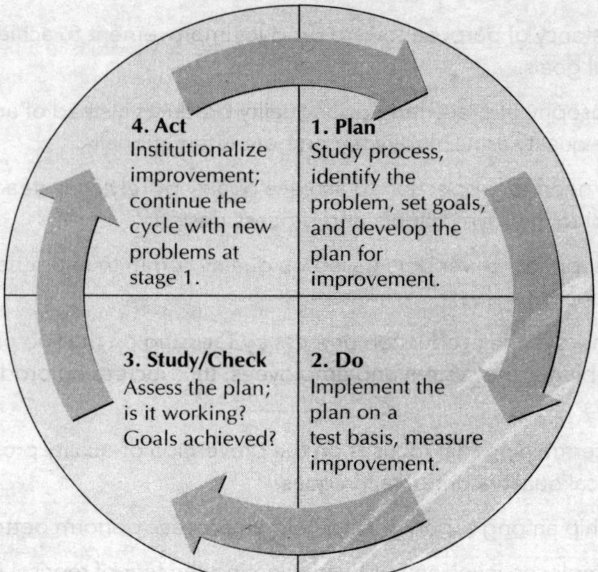

Quality Tools

A major cornerstone of the commitment to quality improvement prescribed by Deming and the other early quality gurus is the need to identify and prevent the causes of quality problems, or defects. These individuals prescribed a number of "tools" to identify the causes of quality problems that are still widely used today, including Pareto charts, process flowcharts, checksheets, histograms, scatter diagrams, statistical process control charts, and cause-and-effect diagrams. In fact, as noted previously, Deming traveled to Japan primarily to teach statistical process control techniques. These popular tools became the basis for the quality management programs developed by many companies. In this section we will briefly describe some of these tools, which are summarized in Figure 2.3.

PROCESS FLOWCHARTS

A **process flowchart** is a diagram of the steps in a job, operation, or process. It enables everyone involved in identifying and solving quality problems to have a clear picture of how a specific operation works and a common frame of reference. It also enables a process improvement team to understand the interrelationship of the departments and functions that constitute a process. This helps focus on where problems might occur and if the process itself needs fixing. Development of the flowchart can help identify quality problems by helping the problem solvers better understand the process. Flowcharts are described in greater detail in Chapters 6 and 8.

CAUSE-AND-EFFECT DIAGRAMS

A **cause-and-effect diagram**, also called a **fishbone** or Ishikawa diagram, is a graphical description of the elements of a specific quality problem and the relationship among those elements. It is used to identify the causes of a quality problem so it can be corrected. Cause-and-effect

Figure 2.3

Quality Tools

Process Flowchart

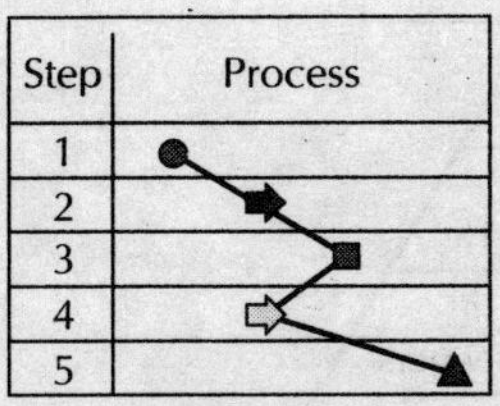

A diagram of the steps in a process; helps focus on where in a process a quality problem might exist.

Cause-and-Effect Diagram

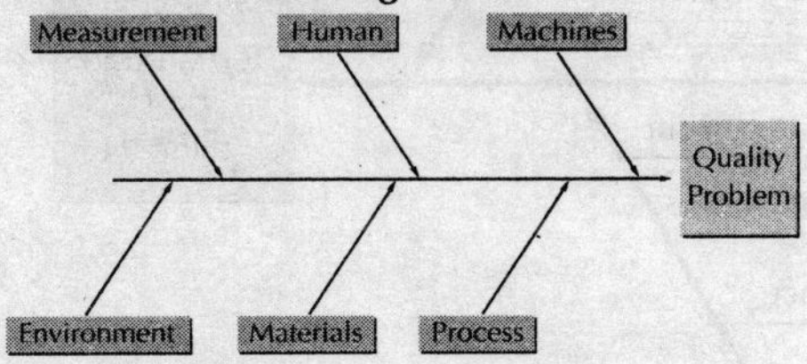

Also called a "fishbone" diagram; a graph of the causes of a quality problem divided into categories.

Check Sheet

Items	1	2	3	4
Dirt	✓✓			✓✓
Old		✓		✓
Temp.	✓	✓✓	✓✓	
Fault	✓✓✓		✓✓	

A fact-finding tool for tallying the number of defects for a list of previously identified problem causes.

Pareto Analysis

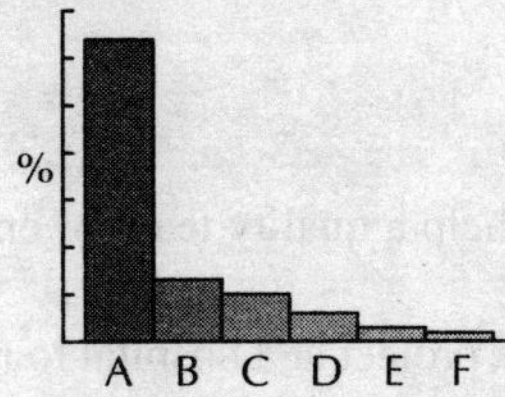

A diagram for tallying the percentage of defects resulting from different causes to identify major quality problems.

Histogram

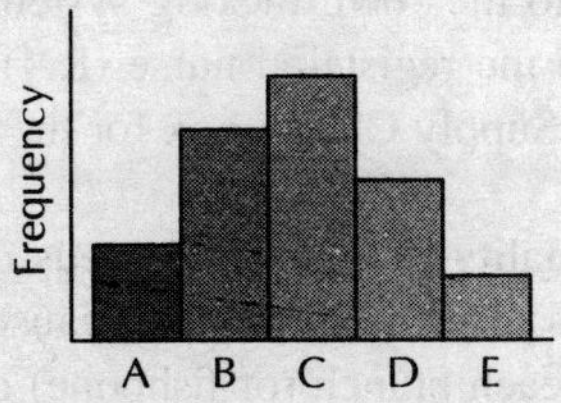

A diagram showing the frequency of data related to a quality problem.

Scatter Diagram

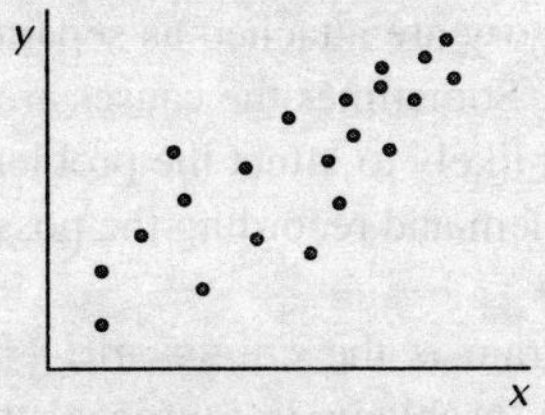

A graph showing the relationship between two variables in a process; identifies a pattern that may cause a quality problem.

Statistical Process Control Chart

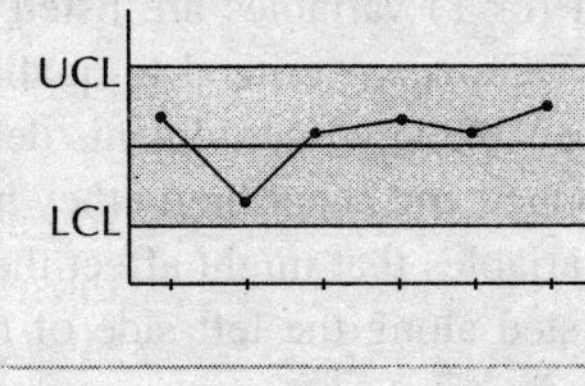

A chart with statistical upper and lower limits; if the process stays between these limits over time, it is in control and a problem does not exist.

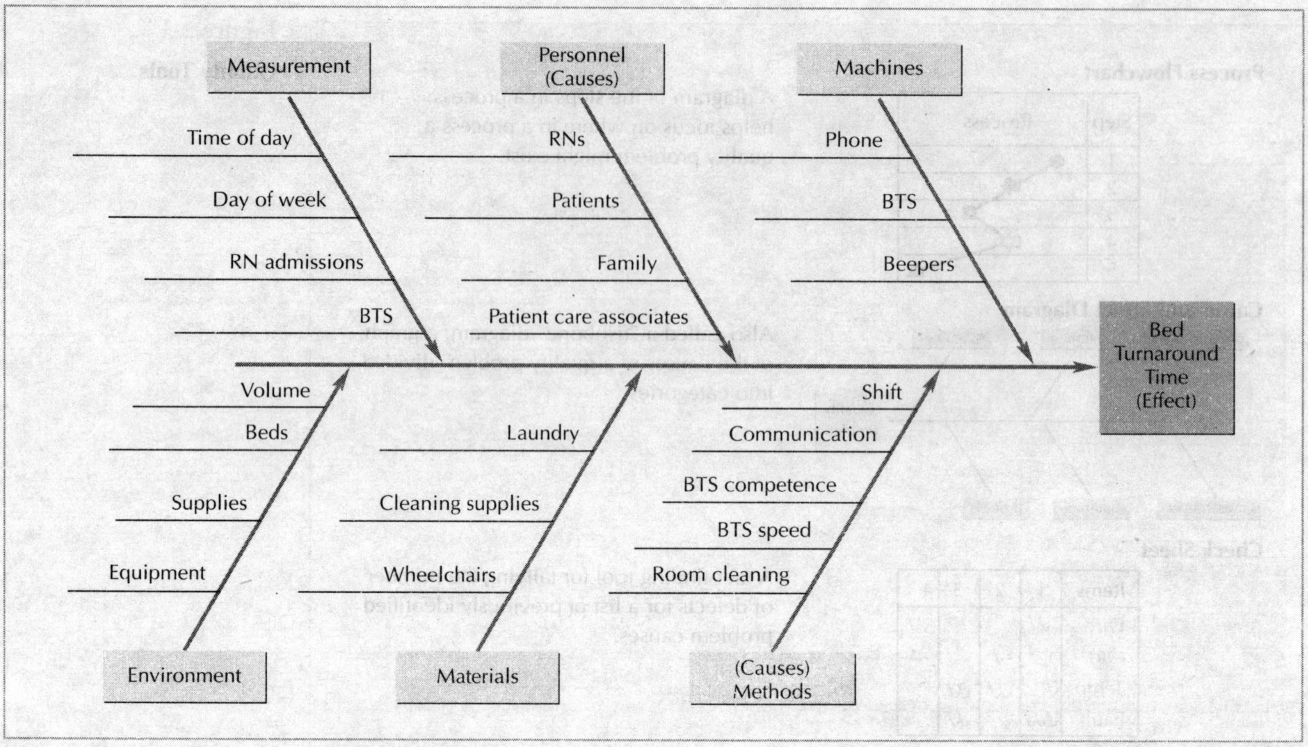

Figure 2.4
A Cause-and-Effect Diagram

diagrams are usually developed as part of *brainstorming* to help a quality team of employees and managers identify causes of quality problems.

Figure 2.4 is a cause-and-effect diagram for a Six Sigma project at a hospital to reduce delays in patient bed turnaround time, which creates a patient flow problem throughout the hospital. The primary cause of the problem is suspected to be related to the "bed tracking system" (BTS), an electronic system that indicates the status of each bed to the registered nurse (RN) who admits patients and assigns them to a room. (See the "Along the Supply Chain" box for the North Shore University Hospital on page 54.)

The "effect" box at the end of the diagram is the quality problem that needs correction. A center line connects the effect box to the major categories of possible problem causes, displayed as branches off of the center line. The box at the end of each branch (or fishbone) describes the cause category. The diagram starts out in this form with only the major categories at the end of each branch. Individual causes associated with each category are attached as separate lines along the length of the branch during the brainstorming process. Sometimes the causes are rank-ordered along the branches in order to identify those that are most likely to affect the problem. The cause-and-effect diagram is a means for thinking through a problem and recording the possible causes in an organized and easily interpretable manner.

A complementary tool related to the fishbone diagram is the **cause-and-effect matrix**, which is used to prioritize the potential causes of quality problems in a process that might first be identified using a cause-and-effect diagram. The output (or *Y*) variables are listed along the top of the matrix. These are also referred to as CTQs or CTQCs, (i.e., "critical-to-quality characteristics") and they are measurable characteristics that express the key requirements defined by a customer. CTQCs are what the customer expects from a product, and accordingly they have a significant impact on customer satisfaction. The input (or *X*) variables that might affect the outcome of process (i.e., the potential causes of an outcome) are listed along the left side of the matrix

			Key Output (Y) Variables (*CTQCs*)							
			1	2	3	4	5	6		
			Turnaround time	Patient flow	Physician time	Emergency dept.	Patient time	Operating room		Rank of X Variables/ Importance to Customer
	Key Input (X) Variables	Customer rank	1	3	2	5	6	4		
		Weight	*10*	*9*	*9*	*7*	*7*	*8*	Score	
1	BTS		9	8	10	8		5	348	3
2	Beepers		7	5	8		5		222	7
3	Volume		7	10	6	7	5	5	338	4
4	Beds		4		9				121	10
5	Time of day		3	4	5	4	10		209	8
6	Day of week		9	10	6			6	282	5
7	Communication		9	8	10	8	7	9	429	1
8	BTS competence		10	9	7		7	7	349	2
9	Room cleaning		7	5	3		8	4	230	6
10	Supplies		8	9					161	9

(8)(10) + (9)(9) = 161

Figure 2.5

A Cause-and-Effect Matrix

(or grid). The CTQCs are ranked or weighted in terms of importance to the customer; then, the relationship between causes and effects (CTQs) are weighted or ranked; and finally, an overall score is calculated for the causes (or *X* variables). The causes with the highest score should be addressed first in improvement efforts because they will have the largest impact on customer satisfaction. Figure 2.5 shows a cause-and-effect matrix for the hospital bed turnaround time example. Note that staff communication has the highest score, and thus, the greatest impact on how satisfied the customers are with the overall process.

CHECKSHEETS AND HISTOGRAMS

Checksheets are frequently used in conjunction with histograms, as well as with Pareto diagrams. A *checksheet* is a fact-finding tool used to collect data about quality problems. A typical check sheet for quality defects tallies the number of defects for a variety of previously identified problem causes. When the check sheet is completed, the total tally of defects for each cause can be used to create a *histogram* or a Pareto chart, as shown in Figure 2.6.

PARETO ANALYSIS

Pareto analysis is a method of identifying the causes of poor quality. It was devised in the early 1950s by the quality expert Joseph Juran. He named this method after a nineteenth-century Italian economist, Vilfredo Pareto, who determined that a small percentage of the people accounted for most of the wealth. Pareto analysis is based on Juran's finding that most quality problems and costs result from only a few causes. For example, he discovered in a textile mill that almost 75% of all defective cloth was caused by only a few weavers, and in a paper mill he studied, more than 60% of the cost of poor quality was attributable to a single category of defects. Correcting the few major causes of most of the quality problems will result in the greatest cost impact.

Pareto analysis can be applied by tallying the number of defects for each of the different possible causes of poor quality in a product or service and then developing a frequency distribution from the data. This frequency distribution, referred to as a *Pareto diagram*, is a useful visual aid for focusing on major quality problems.

The quality problem for hospital bed turnaround time is described in the previous section on cause-and-effect diagrams (Figure 2.4). In this case, a defect is anytime the turnaround time

Figure 2.6
Pareto Chart

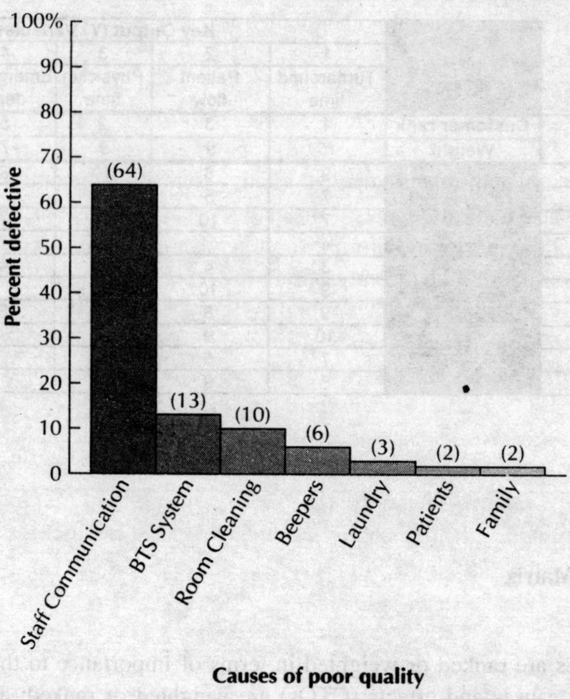

exceeds 150 minutes for a patient out of a sample of 195 patients. Some of the causes of this problem are as follows:

Cause	Number of Defects	Percentage
Staff communication	83	64%
BTS system	17	13
Room cleaning	13	10
Beepers	7	6
Laundry	4	3
Patients	3	2
Family	3	2
	130	100

For each cause of poor quality, the number of defects attributed to that cause has been tallied. This information is then converted into the Pareto chart shown in Figure 2.6.

This Pareto chart identifies the major cause of poor quality to be poor staff communication. Correcting the problem will result in the greatest quality improvement. However, the other problems should not be ignored. Continual quality improvement is the long-term goal. The Pareto diagram simply identifies the quality problems that will result in the greatest immediate impact on quality improvement.

SCATTER DIAGRAMS

Scatter diagrams graphically show the relationship between two variables, such as the brittleness of a piece of material and the temperature at which it is processed. One temperature reading should result in a specific degree of brittleness representing one point on the diagram. Many such points on the diagram visually show a pattern between the two variables and a relationship or lack of one. This diagram could be used to identify a particular quality problem associated with the baking process.

PROCESS CONTROL CHARTS AND STATISTICAL QUALITY CONTROL

We discuss control charts and other statistical quality-control methods in Chapter 3. For now, it is sufficient to say that a control chart is a means for measuring if a process is doing what it is supposed to do, like a thermostat monitoring room temperature. It is constructed with a horizontal line through the middle of a chart representing the process average or norm. It also has a line below this center line representing a lower control limit and a line above it for the upper control limit. Samples from the process are taken over time and measured according to some attribute. In its simplest form, if the measurement is within the upper and lower control limits, the process is said to be in control and there is no quality problem, but if the measurement is outside the limits, then a problem probably exists and should be investigated and corrected.

Statistical quality-control methods such as the process control chart are important tools for quality improvement. Employees who are provided with extensive training in statistical quality-control methods are able to identify quality problems and their causes and to make suggestions for improvement. (See the "Along the Supply Chain" box on page 54 to see how a control chart is used to monitor hospital bed turnaround times.)

TQM and QMS

Total quality management (TQM) has been the most prominent and visible approach to quality to evolve from the work of Deming and the early quality gurus. TQM originated in the 1980s as a Japanese-style management approach to quality improvement, and became very popular during the 1990s, being adopted by thousands of companies. Although it has taken on many meanings, it was (and still is) a philosophy for managing an organization centered on quality and customer satisfaction as "the" strategy for achieving long-term success. It requires the active involvement, participation and cooperation of everyone in the organization, and encompasses virtually all of its activities and processes. To achieve and sustain this pervasive focus on quality requires a significant long-term commitment on the part of the organization's leadership. Deming's 14 points and the philosophies and teachings of the early quality gurus are clearly embodied in the basic principles of TQM:

1. Quality can and must be *managed*.
2. The *customer* defines quality, and customer satisfaction is the top goal; it is a requirement and is not negotiable.
3. Management must be involved and provide *leadership*.
4. Continuous quality improvement is "the" *strategic* goal, which requires planning and organization.
5. Quality improvement is the responsibility of every *employee*; all employees must be trained and educated to achieve quality improvement.
6. Quality problems are found in *processes*, and problems must be prevented, not solved.
7. The quality *standard* is "no defects."
8. Quality must be *measured*; improvement requires the use of *quality tools*, and especially statistical process control.

TQM has been supplanted to a large extent by what is most commonly referred to as a **quality management system (QMS)**. This approach (or term) has evolved out of the ISO certification process that many companies around the world have gone through; essentially ISO certifies a company's "quality management system," and much of the ISO's written materials refer directly to "quality management systems." (ISO certification is discussed in greater detail in a separate section later in this chapter.) A QMS is not as much of a philosophy as TQM; rather, it is a system that complements a company's other systems and functions. It is a systematic approach to achieving quality and hence customer satisfaction, and while it suggests no less commitment to that goal than TQM, it maintains less of a core strategic focus that TQM. Further, since a QMS is not a "philosophy," it more naturally is designed to meet the individual needs and circumstances of a particular company. It outlines the policies and procedures necessary to improve and control specific (but not all) processes that will lead to improved business performance. A QMS tends to focus more on individual projects that have a quantifiable impact (i.e., increased profitability). Some companies have adopted the Malcolm Baldrige National Quality Award criteria as its QMS; another well-known QMS is Six Sigma (discussed in detail in a later section).

Regardless of the term a company uses to identify its approach to achieving quality improvement, and the possible differences between TQM and a QMS or other approaches, there are certain common characteristics of companywide approaches to quality improvement, such as customer satisfaction and employee involvement, topics we will talk about next.

The Focus of Quality Management—Customers

The main focus of Deming's 14 points, TQM, and all QMSs is to achieve customer satisfaction. The reason is simple: Customers who are very happy and delighted are less likely to switch to a competitor, which translates to profits. A high level of satisfaction creates an emotional bond instead of simply a rational preference. Research by companies has shown that there is a direct link between customer satisfaction and attrition rates, indicating that delighted customers are less likely to defect than dissatisfied customers. Figure 2.7 highlights some of the "facts" that are generally known to exist about customer satisfaction.

Figure 2.7

The Impact of Customer Satisfaction

- It costs 5 or 6 times more to attract a new customer than it does to keep an existing one.
- Between 94 and 96 percent of dissatisfied customers don't complain, they just walk away and about 91 percent of them don't come back.
- Between 54 and 70 percent of customers who complain will do business with the company again if their complaints are resolved satisfactorily; this number increases to around 95 percent if the complaint is resolved quickly.
- A typical dissatisfied customer will tell 8 to 10 people about their problem; one in five will tell 20 (and the Internet now makes it possible to tell thousands). A satisfied complainer will tell an average of five people about how a problem was resolved to their satisfaction.
- It takes about 12 positive service encounters to make up for a single negative one.
- Only about five percent of customers who cannot buy a product because it's out of stock return to make the originally planned purchase.
- Around 68 percent of customers stop doing business with suppliers because they perceive an attitude of indifference toward them; only 14 percent leave because they are dissatisfied with a product, and only 9 percent leave for competitive reasons.
- Between 80 and 90 percent of customers who defect say they are "satisfied;" but "very satisfied" customers are four to seven times more likely to repeat their purchase within the next 18 months than those who were merely "satisfied."
- An increase of as little as five percent in customer retention can result in an 80 to 100 percent increase in profits.
- Businesses with low quality service average only one percent return on sales and lose market share at a rate of two percent annually; businesses with high-quality service average a 12 percent return on sales and gain market share at the rate of 6 percent annually (and charge significantly higher prices).

Source: The British Quality Foundation, "Back to Basics," *Quality World* 32, issue 5 (May 2006): p. 37.

QUALITY MANAGEMENT IN THE SUPPLY CHAIN

Most companies not only have customers they want to satisfy, but they are also customers of other companies, their *suppliers*, within a company's supply chain. Companies know that to satisfy its customers requires not only their own commitment to quality, but also the support and resources of its suppliers. This is especially true of companies that outsource many of their activities to suppliers. Companies and their suppliers joined together in a supply chain must work together to meet the needs of the company's customers. A partnership exists between the supplier and its customer wherein the supplier is expected to manage its own quality effectively so that the company it supplies can count on the quality of the materials, parts, and services it receives.

Many companies reduce their number of suppliers in order to have more direct influence over their suppliers' quality and delivery performance, which was one of Deming's 14 points. It is based on the notion that if a company has a major portion of a supplier's business, then the supplier is more willing to meet the customer's quality standards. The company and supplier enter into a business relationship referred to as **partnering**, in which the supplier agrees to meet the company's quality standards, and in return the company enters into a long-term purchasing agreement with the supplier that includes a stable order and delivery schedule.

In order to ensure that its supplier meets its quality standards, a company will often insist that the supplier adopt a QMS similar to its own, or a company's QMS will include its suppliers. Still other companies require that their suppliers achieve ISO 9000 certification (see page 68), an international quality standard that ensures a high industry standard of quality as its QMS; some

ALONG THE SUPPLY CHAIN

Achieving Quality in Target's Supply Chain

Target, a *Fortune 500* company headquartered in Minneapolis, Minnesota, is one of the largest and best-known retail chains in the United States, with over 1,700 stores in 49 states, over 365,000 employees, and revenues over $70 billion. Target's supply chain includes 26 distribution centers across the United States and four warehouse centers near U.S. coastal ports that receive overseas shipments from suppliers around the world. For its hard good (nonfabric) products such as toys, furniture, electronics, sporting goods, and kitchen goods, Target works with over 3,000 factories around the world, and because of its large network of suppliers and factories, realizing its commitment to total quality requires constant diligence.

Quality is an essential component of Target's global sourcing process so that quality is achieved while products are moving through the supply chain before they reach store shelves. The ultimate goal is to drive variability out of the supply chain. However, with an enormous number of hard good products coming from those 3,000 factories, the opportunities for variability to enter the supply chain are substantial. Suppliers are required to sign a "standards of supplier engagement" agreement that clearly spells out Target's quality requirements. When a factory enters the Target supply chain, it is subjected to a thorough evaluation with a rating system that includes an assessment of product quality, which determines if a supplier can use the factory. Also, every factory must meet Target's global social compliance requirements regarding worker treatment, which are nonnegotiable and are the most important part of Target's partnering relationship with its suppliers.

Target works with existing factories and suppliers that experience failures to improve performance. However, repeated failures result in an end to the relationship. Target uses various statistical quality control tools in its evaluations, plus it also employs Six Sigma throughout its supply chain and business processes, in formal project management, problem solving, and process improvement.

Research how other large companies with a global supply chains might use formal rating systems to evaluate suppliers.

Sources: Based on William H. Murphy, "Bull's Eye: An Inside Look at How Target Ensures Quality in a Complex Supply Chain," *Quality Progress* (June 2010), pp. 22–29; and the Target website at www.target.com.

companies require their suppliers to follow Baldrige National Quality Award guidelines or even enter the Baldrige Award competition as their QMS.

At the other end of a company's spectrum from its suppliers is its direct relationship with its own customers. An important component of any QMS is the company's ability to measure customer satisfaction; to "hear" what the customer wants. The company needs to know if its QMS is effective. Is the company meeting customer expectations? Are its products or services meeting their fitness for use definition? Is it what the customer wants, does the customer like it, does the customer need it, would the customer like it changed? A QMS requires that some form of measurement system be in place to answer these questions and provide data about the customer's level of satisfaction. It is a well-established fact of consumer behavior that unhappy customers will tell almost twice as many others about their quality problems as they will about satisfactory products or services.

MEASURING CUSTOMER SATISFACTION

For most companies, figuring out what satisfies customers (i.e., what they want and need) is easier said than done. It requires that a company somehow gather information on what the customer wants and needs, disseminate that information throughout the company, use that information to improve its products and processes and develop new products, and then monitor customer satisfaction to ensure that the customer's needs are being met. The primary means for garnering information from customers, and measuring customer satisfaction is the customer survey. The customer survey is a means for companies to listen to what is often referred to as the "voice of the customer (VoC)." Applicants for the Malcolm Baldrige National Quality Award are expected to provide measures of customer satisfaction typically through customer surveys. Motorola, a two-time Baldrige Award winner, contracts with an independent survey firm to conduct regularly scheduled surveys with its customers around the world to help Motorola determine how well it's meeting its customers' needs.

J.D. Power and Associates is an independent, third-party company that provides companies in the automotive, energy/communications, travel, financial, and home-building industries with feedback from their customers based on surveys that they conduct. They also annually present awards to companies that have excelled in their industry based on independently financed consumer opinion studies. Award-winning companies are allowed to license the use of J.D. Power and Associates awards in advertising. For example, for 2012 Lexus was the highest-ranked automobile brand for quality (i.e., problem free), while the Toyota Corolla was the top-ranked compact car. For 2011, Holiday Inn had the highest "guest satisfaction" for mid-scale hotels (with full service), while Embassy Suites was the highest ranked in the "upper upscale" category; Apple ranked highest in customer satisfaction for smartphones, and Samsung ranked highest for traditional mobile phones.

The *American Customer Satisfaction Index (ACSI)* was established in 1994 through a partnership of the University of Michigan Business School, the American Society for Quality (ASQ), and the international consulting firm CFI Group. The ACSI is funded in part by corporate subscribers who receive industry benchmarking data and company-specific information about financial returns from improving customer satisfaction.

ACSI measures customer satisfaction with the goods and services of seven economic sectors, 39 industries (including e-commerce and e-business), and more than 200 companies and 70 federal and local government agencies. The ACSI reports scores on a 0 to 100 scale, which are based on econometric modeling of data obtained from telephone interviews with customers. From random-digit-dial (RDD) telephone samples (and Internet samples for e-commerce and e-business), more than 65,000 consumers are identified and interviewed annually.

ACSI scores are posted on their website at www.theacsi.org. For example, in 2011, Amazon was ranked highest in the "Internet retail" category with an ACSI score of 86, one of the highest scores ever recorded in any service industry. In the automobile category, Lexus, Cadillac, and

Toyota were tied for the highest ranked with a score of 87. Apple ranked first in computers with a score of 87, and in cell phones with a score of 83; while in apparel VF (e.g., Wrangler and Lee jeans) ranked first with a score of 83 (Levi Strauss ranked third with a score of 81).

The Role of Employees in Quality Improvement

Job training and employee development are major features of a successful quality management program. Increased training in job skills results in improved processes that improve product quality. Training in quality tools and skills such as statistical process control enable employees to diagnose and correct day-to-day problems related to their job. This provides employees with greater responsibility for product quality and greater satisfaction for doing their part to achieve quality. When achievement is reinforced through rewards and recognition, it further increases employee satisfaction. At Ritz-Carlton, first-year employees receive over 300 hours of training. Marriott employees are trained to view breakdowns in service as opportunities for satisfying customers; for example, they may send a gift and note of apology to customers who have experienced a problem in the hotel.

In our previous discussions, the importance of customer satisfaction as an overriding company objective was stressed. However, another important aspect of a successful QMS is internal customer (e.g., employee) satisfaction. It is unlikely that a company will be able to make its customers happy if its employees are not happy. For that reason, many successful companies conduct employee satisfaction surveys just as they conduct customer surveys.

When employees are directly involved in the quality management process, it is referred to as **participative problem solving**. Employee participation in identifying and solving quality problems has been shown to be effective in improving quality, increasing employee satisfaction and morale, improving job skills, reducing job turnover and absenteeism, and increasing productivity.

Participative problem solving is usually within an *employee-involvement (EI)* program, with a team approach. We will look at some of these programs for involving employees in quality management, including kaizen, quality circles, and process improvement teams.

KAIZEN AND CONTINUOUS IMPROVEMENT

Kaizen is the Japanese term for *continuous improvement*, not only in the workplace but also in one's personal life, home life, and social life. In the workplace, kaizen means involving everyone in a process of gradual, organized, and continuous improvement. Every employee within an organization should be involved in working together to make improvements. If an improvement is not part of a continuous, ongoing process, it is not considered kaizen. Kaizen is most closely associated with *lean systems,* an approach to continuous improvement throughout the organization that is the subject of Chapter 16.

Employees are most directly involved in kaizen when they are determining solutions to their own problems. Employees are the real experts in their immediate workspace. In its most basic form, kaizen is a system in which employees identify many small improvements on a continual basis and implement these improvements themselves. This is actually the application of the steps in the Deming Wheel (Figure 2.2) at its most basic, individual level. Employees identify a problem, come up with a solution, check with their supervisor, and then implement it. This works to involve all employees in the improvement process and gives them a feeling that they are really participating in quality improvement, which in turn keeps them excited about their jobs. Nothing motivates someone more than when they come up with a solution to their own problem. Small individual changes have a cumulative effect in improving entire processes, and with this level of participation improvement occurs across the entire organization. No companywide quality management program can succeed without this level of total employee involvement in continuous improvement.

Employees at Dana Corporation's Spicer Driveshaft Division, North America's largest independent manufacturer of driveshafts and a 2000 Malcolm Baldrige National Quality Award winner, participate in a kaizen-type program. On average, each employee submits three suggestions for improvements per month and almost 80% of these ideas are implemented. The company also makes use of kaizen "blitzes" in which teams brainstorm, identify, and implement ideas for improvement, sometimes as often as every three or four weeks. Companywide, Dana Corporation employees implemented almost 2 million ideas in one year alone.

QUALITY CIRCLES

One of the first team-based approaches to quality improvement was quality circles. Called quality-control circles in Japan when they originated during the 1960s, they were introduced in the United States in the 1970s, and they are still used today. A **quality circle** is a small, voluntary group of employees and their supervisor(s), comprising a team of about 8 to 10 members from the same work area or department. The supervisor is typically the circle moderator, promoting group discussion but not directing the group or making decisions; decisions result from group consensus. A circle meets about once a week during company time in a room designated especially for that purpose, where the team works on problems and projects of their own choice. These problems may not always relate to quality issues; instead, they focus on productivity, costs, safety, or other work-related issues in the circle's area. Quality circles follow an established procedure for identifying, analyzing, and solving quality-related (or other) problems. Figure 2.8 is a graphical representation of the quality circle process.

Figure 2.8
The Quality Circle Process

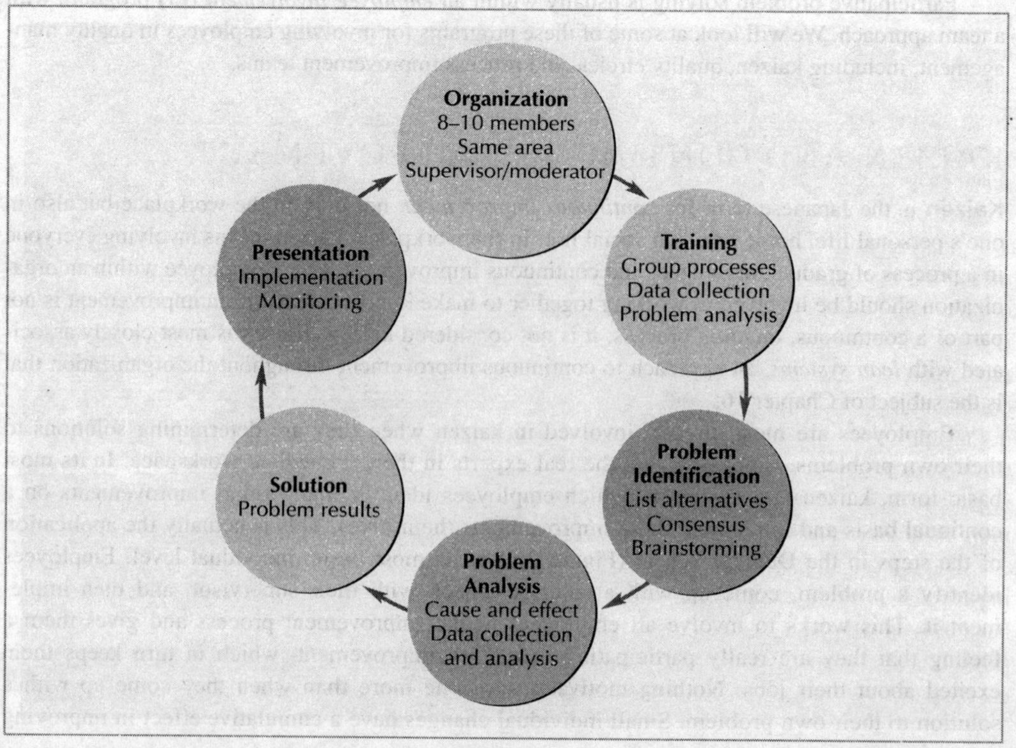

PROCESS IMPROVEMENT TEAMS

Process improvement teams, also called quality improvement teams (QIT), focus attention on business processes rather than separate company functions. It was noted previously that quality circles are generally composed of employees and supervisors from the same work area or department, whereas process improvement teams tend to be cross-functional or even cross-business between suppliers and their customers. A process improvement team would include members from the various interrelated functions or departments that constitute a process. For example, a process improvement team for customer service might include members from distribution, packaging, manufacturing, and human resources. A key objective of a process improvement team is to understand the process the team is addressing in terms of how all the parts (functions and departments) work together. The process is then measured and evaluated, with the goal of improving the process to make it more efficient and the product or service better. A key tool in helping the team understand how the process works is a *process flowchart*, a quality tool we discussed in greater detail in the section on "Quality Tools."

Quality in Services

From our discussion so far it is clear that most quality management approaches evolved in manufacturing companies like Toyota, GE, and Motorola. However, toward the end of the last century, service companies began to embrace quality management. This was important because the service sector is the largest segment of the U.S. economy, employing almost three times as many people as manufacturing industries.

Service organizations and manufacturing companies both convert inputs into outputs—products or services—through a productive process. Both manufacturing and services use the same kinds of inputs—resources such as physical facilities, capital, materials, equipment, and people. In some instances the processes and products are similar. For example, both Toyota and McDonald's produce a tangible, physical product (cars and hamburgers) assembled from component parts. However, in pure service industries such as law, hotels, entertainment, communication, engineering, education, clubs, real estate, banks, retail, healthcare, and airlines, the processes are less similar and the products are not as tangible. The "products" provided by these organizations are not typically a physical item that can be held or stored. The customer of a manufacturer tends to interact only at the output end of the production process. The customer of a service often interacts directly with the production process, consuming services like legal advice, a classroom lecture, or an airline flight as they are being produced. Services tend to be customized and provided at the convenience of the customer; for example, doctors prescribe individually to patients. In addition, services tend to be labor intensive, while manufacturing is more capital intensive. Thus, human contact and its ramifications are an important part of the process of producing services.

If a manufactured item is defective, the defect can usually be felt or seen, and counted or measured. The improvement (or deterioration) in a product's quality can likewise be measured. It's not the same for service. A service cannot be held, felt, stored, and used again. A service output is not always tangible; thus, it is not as easy to measure service defects. The dimensions of service quality include timeliness, courtesy, consistency, accuracy, convenience, responsiveness, and completeness—all hard to measure beyond a subjective assessment by the customer. This does not mean that the potential for quality improvement is any less in services. Each day thousands of travelers check into and out of Ritz-Carlton Hotels, UPS handles and delivers millions of packages, and Visa processes millions of credit transactions worldwide. However, it is sometimes more difficult to assess defects in service and thus more difficult to measure customer satisfaction.

Disney World, for example, has had to develop a "different" view of quality from a manufacturing company. In some ways, a theme park is similar to an assembly line except that Disney's rides have to work flawlessly all the time. However, the Disney experience is not just about defect-free rides. It is also about customer emotions and expectations, which are likely to vary widely. Customers have different tolerance levels for things that go wrong. When there is a long line at a ride, the

ALONG THE SUPPLY CHAIN

Two-Time Baldrige National Quality Award Winner, Ritz-Carlton Hotels

The Ritz-Carlton Hotel Company is one of only two two-time recipients of the Malcolm Baldrige National Quality Award, having won in 1992 and 1999, and the only hotel company ever to receive the award. An independently operated division of Marriott International, Inc., it manages 79 luxury hotels in 26 countries around the world. In 2010 alone, the hotel company received 121 quality awards from the travel industry.

The Ritz-Carlton's commitment to its total quality management program comes from the top down; approximately a quarter of each senior executive's time is devoted to quality-related matters, and top executives and the senior quality-management team meet weekly to review quality measures and guest satisfaction. The hotel motto, "We are ladies and gentlemen, serving ladies and gentlemen," and its three service steps—a warm and sincere greeting using the guest's name, anticipation of and fulfillment of each guest's needs, and a fond farewell and warm goodbye using the guest's name—reflect the company's commitment to guest satisfaction through its employees.

Ritz-Carlton is recognized as an industry and corporate leader in employee training. Employees are carefully selected; for every employee selected, 10 others applied. New employees attend a two-day corporate orientation that's followed by extensive training that results in job certification. In their first year employees receive an average of 300 hours of training, and 100 hours of training every year thereafter. The company spends around 10% of its total payroll expenses on training. Training is reinforced by routine skills testing for more than 75% of its employees, and each hotel has a daily lineup at which employees reaffirm their commitment to quality.

To help it meet its goal of total elimination of problems and defects, the Ritz-Carlton gathers and tracks data on a daily basis for quality-related parameters such as annual guest-room preventive maintenance cycles, percentage of check-ins with no wait lines, time spent to achieve industry best clean-room appearance, and time to service an occupied guest room. To cultivate customer loyalty Ritz-Carlton uses a companywide, cross-functional guest recognition database called "Mystique;" a tool created to meet and anticipate returning customers' preferences and requirements. Information gathered during various types of customer contacts, such as check-in requests, responses to service requests by overnight guests, or post-event reviews with meeting planners, are systematically entered into the database, which holds over a million files. A system called CARE (Clean and Repair Everything) that coordinates housekeeping with the preventive maintenance schedule ensures that all guestrooms are guaranteed to be defect-free every 90 days, the most defect-free guestrooms in the industry. Daily quality reports derived from data submitted from each of 720 hotel working areas help to identify problems before a guest does. Employees armed with quality processes and tools ranging from nine-step quality improvement teams to guest surveys examine every hotel process. To ensure that guests' problems are resolved quickly, employees are required to act immediately. Any employee can spend up to $2,000 and demand assistance from other employees to immediately correct a guest's problem or respond to a complaint.

The Ritz-Carlton Company has became known for its influence on service in a wide range of industries, through the creation of The Ritz-Carlton Learning Institute and The Ritz-Carlton Leadership Center, where nearly 50,000 executives from other companies worldwide have come to learn, and be trained in, the Ritz-Carlton principles of quality service.

In independent customer surveys, between 92% and 97% of guests leave the hotel with a positive impression, and 99% said they were satisfied with their overall Ritz-Carlton experience, compared with under 70% for their nearest luxury hotel competitor. As a result, hotel revenue per available room (the industry's measure of market share) has exceeded the industry average by more than 300%.

The Ritz-Carlton is an expensive luxury hotel chain. Do you think this enables it to have an approach to quality that less expensive, economy-class hotel chains cannot afford? Is revenue a factor in implementing a successful QMS, or is it a result?

Source: National Quality Program at the National Institute of Standards and Technology, http://www.quality.nist.gov.

issue is not just the length of the wait, but how a customer feels about waiting. Disney addresses this problem by being innovative; costumed characters entertain customers waiting in line.

QUALITY ATTRIBUTES IN SERVICES

Timeliness, or how quickly a service is provided, is an important dimension of service quality, and it is not difficult to measure. The difficulty is determining what is "quick" service and what is "slow" service. How long must a caller wait to place a phone catalogue order before it is considered poor service? The answer, to a large extent, depends on the caller's expectations: "too long" is not the same for everyone. Varying expectations make it difficult to determine an exact specification.

Quality management in services must focus also on employee performance related to intangible, difficult-to-measure quality dimensions. The most important quality dimensions may be how correctly and pleasantly employees are able to provide service. That is why service companies such as Federal Express, Starbucks, Avis, Disney, and Ritz-Carlton Hotels have well-developed quality management programs that focus on employee performance, behavior, and training, and serve as "**benchmarks**" for other companies. Service companies lose more customers because either their service is poor or their competitor's is better, than for any other reason, including price.

McDonald's has a reputation for high-quality service resulting from its application of established quality management principles. It provides fresh food promptly on demand. Restaurant managers meet with customer groups on a regular basis and use questionnaires to identify quality "defects" in its operation. It monitors all phases of its process continuously from purchasing to restrooms to restaurant decor and maintenance. It empowers all employees to make spot decisions to dispose of unfresh food or to speed service. The McDonald's workforce is flexible so that changes in customer traffic and demand can be met promptly by moving employees to different tasks. Food is sampled regularly for taste and freshness. Extensive use is made of information technology for scheduling, cash register operation, food inventory, cooking procedures, and food assembly processes—all with the objective of faster service. All of these quality improvement procedures are standard and similar to approaches to quality improvement that could be found in a manufacturing firm.

Six Sigma

Six Sigma was first developed at Motorola, and they and other companies have had a great deal of success with it as reported in the "Along the Supply Chain" box on page 51. A number of companies have credited Six Sigma with billions of dollars in cost savings and increased profits, and these reported successes have led many other large and small companies to adopt all or some of the Six Sigma methodology. As a result, Six Sigma is currently one of the most popular quality management systems in the world.

Basically, Six Sigma is a project-oriented methodology (or system) that provides businesses with the tools and expertise to improve their processes. This increase in performance through a decrease in process variation leads to defect reduction (to near zero) and an increase in product and service quality and increased profits. In its simplest form, Six Sigma is based on Deming's PDCA cycle and Joseph Juran's assertion that "all quality improvement occurs on a project-by-project" basis, with elements of kaizen-type employee involvement. In this section, we will provide a more detailed description of the elements and components of Six Sigma. Figure 2.9 illustrates the primary elements of a Six Sigma program.

THE SIX SIGMA GOAL—3.4 DPMO

Six Sigma is a process for developing and delivering virtually perfect products and services. The word "sigma" is a familiar statistical term for the standard deviation, a measure of variability around the mean of a normal distribution. In Six Sigma it is a measure of how much a given product or process deviates from perfection, or zero defects. The main idea behind Six Sigma is that

Figure 2.9
Six Sigma

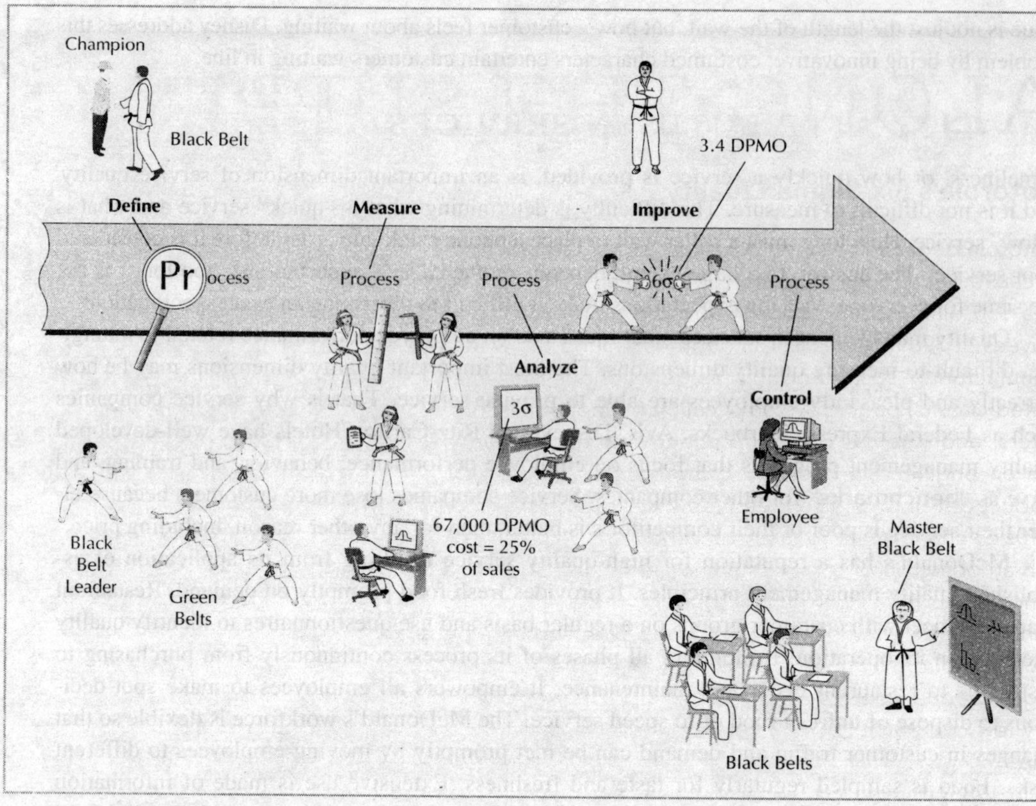

if the number of "defects" in a process can be measured, then it can be systematically determined how to eliminate them and get as close to zero defects as possible. In Six Sigma, "as close to zero defects as possible" translates into a statistically based numerical goal of *3.4 defects per million opportunities* (DPMO), which is the near elimination of defects from a process, product, or service. This is a goal far beyond the quality level at which most companies have traditionally operated. Through the reduction of variation in all processes (i.e., achieving the Six Sigma goal), the overall performance of the company will be improved and significant overall cost savings will be realized.

THE SIX SIGMA PROCESS

As implemented by Motorola, Six Sigma follows four basic steps—*align*, *mobilize*, *accelerate*, and *govern*. In the first step, "align," senior executives create a *balanced scorecard* (see Chapter 1) of strategic goals, metrics and initiatives to identify the areas of improvement that will have the greatest impact on the company's bottom line. Process owners (i.e, the senior executives who supervise the processes) "champion" the creation of high-impact improvement projects that will achieve the strategic goals.

In the second step, "mobilize," project teams are formed and empowered to act. The process owners select "Black Belts" to lead well-defined improvement projects. The teams follow a step-by-step, problem-solving approach referred to as *DMAIC*.

In the third step, "accelerate," improvement teams made up of Black Belt and Green Belt team members with appropriate expertise use an action-learning approach to build their capability and execute the project. This approach combines training and education with project work and coaching. Ongoing reviews with project champions ensure that projects progress according to an aggressive timeline.

ALONG THE SUPPLY CHAIN

Motorola's Six Sigma Quality

Motorola began in the late 1920s as a small manufacturer of car radios (hence the name *Motorola*). It has grown to a $30 billion corporation with more than 68,000 employees at 320 facilities in 73 countries around the world, manufacturing such products as semiconductors, integrated circuits, paging systems, cellular telephones, computers, and wireless communications systems. Motorola was an engineering-oriented company that focused on product development to create new markets. In the mid-1970s, it changed its focus from products to customers, with an objective of total customer satisfaction. Motorola is now recognized as having one of the best quality management systems in the world. In 1988, it was among the first group of winners of the prestigious Malcolm Baldrige National Quality Award and in 2002, it was one of very few companies to win the Baldrige Award a second time.

In 1986, it invented Six Sigma and in 1987, Motorola announced its goal of "Six Sigma" quality. This goal effectively changed the focus of quality in the United States, where quality levels had traditionally been measured in terms of percentages or parts per hundred. Motorola's Six Sigma has since become a benchmark standard that many other companies have adopted. Six Sigma has evolved from a metric (or standard) achieved through the application of various methodologies into a complete quality management system (QMS). GE, Ford, Coors, Boeing, Xerox, Bank of America, Honeywell, Kraft Foods, Intel, Microsoft, NASA, Dannon, UPS, Sony, and Texaco are just a few of the companies that have adopted Six Sigma as their quality management system. Motorola has reported over $17 billion in savings with Six Sigma. The companies that have adopted Six Sigma see it as the basis for a "best-in-class" philosophy and a long-term business strategy to achieve overall business improvement. The fundamental objective of Six Sigma is to focus on improvement in key processes and transactions within a company. In this way, waste and cost are driven out as quality and processes improve, and customer satisfaction and loyalty, and thus profits, are increased through continuous business improvement.

All of the companies cited above are large, well-known, national or international firms. What do you think some of the obstacles might be for a smaller company to implement a Six Sigma program? Are certain features and components of Six Sigma more applicable than others to a small company?

Source: Motorola Website, www.motorola.com.

In the final step, "govern," executive process owners monitor and review the status of improvement projects to make sure the system is functioning as expected. Leaders share the knowledge gained from the improvement projects with other parts of the organization to maximize benefit.

In the next few sections we describe some components of the Six Sigma process in greater detail.

IMPROVEMENT PROJECTS

The first step in the Six Sigma process is the identification of improvement projects. These projects are selected according to business objectives and the goals of the company. As such, they normally have a significant financial impact. These projects are not one-time, unique activities as projects are typically thought of, but team-based activities directed at the continuing improvement of a process.

Once projects are identified, they are assigned a **champion** from upper management who is responsible for project success, providing resources and overcoming organizational barriers. Champions are typically paid a bonus tied to the successful achievement of Six Sigma goals.

THE BREAKTHROUGH STRATEGY: DMAIC

At the heart of Six Sigma is the **breakthrough strategy**, a five-step process applied to improvement projects. The five steps in the breakthrough strategy are very similar to Deming's four-stage PDCA cycle (Figure 2.2), although more specific and detailed. The breakthrough strategy steps are *define, measure, analyze, improve*, and *control* (DMAIC), shown in Figure 2.9.

DEFINE: The problem is defined, including who the customers are and what they want, to determine what needs to improve. It is important to know which quality attributes are most important to the customer, what the defects are, and what the improved process can deliver.

MEASURE: The process is measured; data are collected and compared to the desired state.

ANALYZE: The data are analyzed in order to determine the cause of the problem.

IMPROVE: The team brainstorms to develop solutions to problems; changes are made to the process, and the results are measured to see if the problems have been eliminated. If not, more changes may be necessary.

CONTROL: If the process is operating at the desired level of performance, it is monitored to make sure the improvement is sustained and no unexpected and undesirable changes occur.

ALONG THE SUPPLY CHAIN

Six Sigma Highlights

- A Six Sigma team at North Carolina Baptist Hospital reduced the time for getting heart attack patients from the emergency room into the cardiac catheterization lab for treatment by an average of 41 minutes.
- A Bechtel project team working on the Channel Tunnel Rail Link in the United Kingdom used Six Sigma to save hundreds of hours on different tunneling jobs.
- A Six Sigma project for truck modification at Volvo's North American Truck Division resulted in cost savings of over $1 million; other projects improved forecasting processes and reduced fuel tank replacement down time.
- A Six Sigma team at Ford fixed a body-side molding problem and the resulting process improvements saved $100,000 annually in waste elimination and eliminated customer complaints about the body-side molding lifting off of the car.
- A Six Sigma project at HSBC Securities (USA) to improve the bottom line performance of its U.S. futures business increased net income from $1.9 million to $7.1 million, a 274% increase, with a 10% reduction in staff.
- Since implementing Six Sigma in 1999, Ford experienced a 27% decrease in warranty spending in a two-year period and credits Six Sigma with savings of over $2 billion.
- Royal Mail, one of the United Kingdom's largest employers with over 196,000 employees, used Six Sigma for one project to centralize a key process and halved the process workforce from 450 to 220.
- Since implementing Six Sigma on a corporatewide basis in 1997, Citibank has seen five- and ten-time defect reductions; examples include decreased response times for credit card applications and fewer errors in customer statements.
- Houston's Memorial Hermann Hospital used Six Sigma to increase its reimbursement percentage from Medicare services, resulting in savings of $62 million, an almost 50% improvement.
- Six Sigma projects at Bank of America saved the company in excess of $2 billion in 2005 and over $1 billion in 2009; the company completes thousands of Six Sigma projects each year.
- A Six Sigma project at Telefonica (Argentina) to eliminate broadband Internet outages saved the company $400,000 annually and won the Gold Award at ASQ International Team Excellence Award competition.
- A Six Sigma continuous improvement model at Honeywell Federal Manufacturing & Technologies resulted in annual savings from increased productivity and innovations of $27 million, a 20% improvement in energy conservation, and $65 million in supply chain savings, and won the company the 2009 Baldrige Award.

BLACK BELTS AND GREEN BELTS

The project leader who implements the DMAIC steps is called a **Black Belt**. Black Belts hold full-time positions and are extensively trained in the use of statistics and quality-control tools, as well as project and team management. A Black Belt assignment normally lasts two years during which the Black Belt will lead 8 to 12 projects from different areas in the company, each lasting about one quarter. A Black Belt is certified after two successful projects. Black Belts are typically very focused change agents who are on the fast track to company advancement. Figure 2.10 describes some of the most important tools used by Black Belts at Motorola.

Master Black Belts monitor, review, and mentor Black Belts across all projects. They are primarily teachers who are selected based on their quantitative skills, and on their teaching and

Quality Function Deployment (QFD)

Developed by the Japanese and first used in the United States by the auto industry in 1983, QFD is a system and set of procedures for understanding customer needs, what "value" means to a customer, and how customers are satisfied, and then translating that information into the design and development process for a product or service. Six Sigma teams use QFD to focus on what means most to the customer. (QFD is described in detail in Chapter 4, "Product Design.")

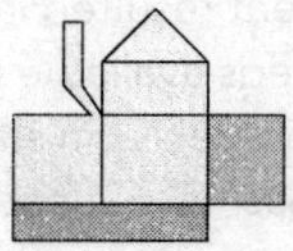

Cause and Effect (C&E) Matrix

The C&E Matrix is primarily used in the "measure" step of the five-step DMAIC process. It helps Six Sigma teams working on an improvement project to identify and prioritize causes of a problem found in a process. It is described in more detail earlier in this chapter on page 38.

Input (x)	Output (y)			Score
1	10	5		50
2	8		8	30
3		9	7	40

Failure Modes and Effects Analysis (FMEA)

FMEA is a tool for analyzing potential reliability problems and weaknesses in a product or process during the development stage, before they actually occur, when they are easier to fix. Six Sigma teams use FMEA to identify how new products, processes or services might fail and then identify actions to prevent the failures. There are different types of FMEAs for systems, design, process, service and software. FMEA is also discussed in Chapter 4, "Product Design."

Failure Mode	Cause	Effect	Action

t-Test

The t-test is a statistical measure used to determine if there is a statistical (and not a random) difference in the means between two groups of data. It is used in Six Sigma to validate test results from small sample sizes. It was first developed at the Guinness brewery to help select the best barley for Guinness beer.

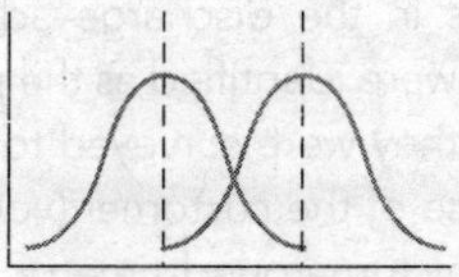

Statistical Process Control (SPC) Chart

SPC charts are used to monitor a process over time to determine if any variation in the process is the result of a cause or problem. They are constructed with a centerline representing an average, and lines above and below the centerline representing statistical upper and lower control limits. The SPC chart is one of the key tools for monitoring and improving quality specifically identified by Deming and the other quality gurus. A more detailed discussion of SPC charts is presented on page 41 in this chapter and it is the subject of Chapter 3.

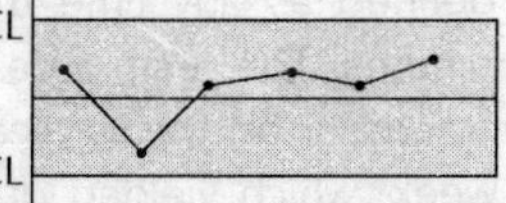

Design of Experiments (DOE)

A statistical technique that is used in Six Sigma to collect, analyze and interpret data. A DOE is a structured, organized method for determining the relationship between factors (Xs) affecting a process and the output of that process (Y). In this method, one or more input variables are controlled at two or more levels to determine if and how one or more output variables change.

Main Effects	Level 1	Level 2
A	10	20
B	30	50
C		
D		
E		

Source: Motorola University, "Six Tools Every Six Sigma Black Belt Loves," http://mu.motorola.com/six_sigma_lessons/(2004).

Figure 2.10

Six Sigma Tools

ALONG THE SUPPLY CHAIN

North Shore University Hospital: A Six Sigma Project Example

North Shore University Hospital in Manhasset, New York, is part of the North Shore-Long Island Jewish Health System, the third largest nonsectarian health system in the United States with 14 hospitals. The hospital used Six Sigma on a project to reduce delays in bed assignment turnaround time. The problem analysis showed that delays in the post-anesthesia care unit and the emergency department resulted in the hospital not always having the staff or beds available to accept additional patients, which resulted in delays in start times in the operating room and a decrease in patient and physician satisfaction. It was subsequently realized that staff were incorrectly using the bed tracking system (BTS), the electronic system that indicates the status of each bed. Delays in bed turnaround time resulted in delayed notification of a ready bed to the RN (registered nurse) responsible for the patient admission process. This led to delays in the operating room and emergency department and impacted the patient flow throughout the hospital. The bed turnaround time project focused on one surgical nursing unit that had 2,578 discharged patients in one year.

During the "define" stage of the Six Sigma DMAIC process, the project team developed a process map of the steps in the discharge–admission process. The admission RNs were identified as the primary customers of the process and they were surveyed to establish process targets. These "voice of the customer (VoC)" responses helped establish a target turnaround time of 120 minutes with an upper limit of 150 minutes. In the "measure" stage of DMAIC, a defect was defined as any time the turnaround time exceeded 150 minutes. The team measured the process by having a team member on the surgical unit monitor the process for one week, which yielded data on 195 patients. Based on the data (which showed 130 defects), the team calculated a DPMO of 672,725, which translated to a score of 1 sigma. The average turnaround time was 226 minutes. The team then developed a cause-and-effect diagram to help identify all the variables that affected the turnaround time.

During the "analyze" step of the DMAIC process, the variables that impacted the turnaround time process were discussed, targeted for statistical analysis, and prioritized. The team investigations at this stage showed that a communication failure and a technical failure at two key steps in the process caused significant delays. The team realized that the staff lacked proficiency in the use of the BTS. The lack of communication between the admission RNs and other patient care team members was identified as a priority, as was the lack of timely notification of a ready bed to the admission RN. Several solutions were developed to resolve these problems, including staff training and the use of improved documentation about discharge patients, laminated bedside cards, and reformatted beepers for RNs to accelerate the process. In the "improve" step, the turnaround time was reduced from a mean of 226 minutes to 90 minutes, which resulted in a metric of 2.3 sigma by the time the project ended. In the "control" step moving range and SPC charts were used to monitor turnaround times, and the turnaround time continued to improve to 69 minutes.

The results of this project were subsequently applied to all nursing units in the hospital. Patient satisfaction scores improved in two categories related to readiness for discharge and speed of the discharge process. Since initiating its Six Sigma program, the health system has completed over 60 Six Sigma projects and trained 24 Black Belts, 70 Green Belts, and two master Black Belts.

Identify a process in a hospital, restaurant, school, or other service that you think might be improved by the Six Sigma DMAIC process, and discuss how you would apply it, including the specific DMAIC stages.

Source: A. Pellicone and M. Martocci, "Faster Turnaround Time," *Quality Progress* 39, no. 3 (March 2006): pp. 31–36.

mentoring ability. As such, they are a resource for project teams and Black Belts. They also hold full-time positions and are usually certified after participating in about 20 successful projects, half while a Black Belt and half as a Master Black Belt.

Project team members are **Green Belts**, which is not a full-time position; they do not spend all of their time on projects. Green Belts receive similar training to Black Belts but somewhat less of it.

At General Electric, employees are not considered for promotion to any management position without Black Belt or Green Belt training. It is part of the Six Sigma overall strategy that as Black Belts and Green Belts move into management positions they will continue to promote and advance Six Sigma in the company. A generally held perception is that companies that have successfully implemented Six Sigma have one Black Belt for every 100 employees and one Master Black Belt for every 100 Black Belts. This will vary according to the size of the company and the number of projects regularly undertaken. At GE, Black Belt projects typically save $250,000 or more and Green Belt projects frequently yield savings in the $50,000 to $75,000 range.

In Six Sigma, all employees receive training in the Six Sigma breakthrough strategy, statistical tools, and quality-improvement techniques. Employees are trained to participate in Six Sigma project teams. Because quality is considered to be the responsibility of every employee, every employee must be involved in, motivated by, and knowledgeable about Six Sigma.

DESIGN FOR SIX SIGMA

An important element of the Six Sigma system is **Design for Six Sigma (DFSS)**, a systematic project methodology for designing products and processes that meet customer expectations and can be produced at Six Sigma quality levels. Also known as **DMADV**, it follows the same basic five-step approach as the DMAIC breakthrough strategy with Master Black Belts, Black Belts, and Green Belts, and makes extensive use of statistical tools and design techniques, training, and measurement. The five DMADV steps are *define* design goals consistent with customer demand; *measure* and identify characteristics that are "critical to quality" (CTQs), product capabilities, process capabilities, and risks: *analyze* design alternatives and select the best design; *design* details and optimize the design; and *verify* the design and implement the production process. However, it employs this strategy earlier, up front in the design phase and developmental stages. This is a more effective and less expensive way to achieve the Six Sigma goal than fixing problems after the product or process is already developed and in place.

LEAN SIX SIGMA

A recent trend in quality management is **Lean Six Sigma** (also known as Lean Sigma), which integrates Six Sigma and "lean systems." Lean systems is the subject of Chapter 16 so we do not offer a detailed presentation of it at this point; rather we will discuss lean systems in general terms and how they relate to Six Sigma.

Lean is a systematic method for reducing the complexity of a process and making it more efficient by identifying and eliminating sources of waste in a process (such as materials, labor, and time) that hinder flow. Lean basically seeks to optimize process flows through the organization in order to create more value for the customer with less work; i.e., get the product through the process faster. The lean process management philosophy was derived mainly from the Toyota Production System (including push and pull production, JIT, and kanbans; see Chapter 16) that has been very effective in manufacturing. As in the case of TPS, lean is basically a more sophisticated extension of earlier efforts to achieve efficiency (i.e., speed) in a manufacturing process by OM pioneers like Henry Ford and Frederick R Taylor.

The lean approach to process improvement includes five steps. First, it is determined what creates value for the customer, i.e., quality from the customer's perspective discussed earlier in this chapter. Second, the sequence of activities (in the process) that create value, called the "value stream," is identified, and those activities that do not add value are eliminated from the production process. Third, waste (such as inventory or long process times) along the value stream is removed through process improvements. Fourth, the process is made responsive to the customer's needs; i.e., making the product or service available when the customer needs it. Finally, lean continually repeats the attempt to remove waste (nonvalue activity) and improve flow; it seeks perfection. As such, lean is more of a philosophical approach to continuous improvement by eliminating waste throughout the organization everywhere along the value stream by involving everyone in the organization.

Lean Six Sigma attempts to combine the best features of lean and Six Sigma. As we have discussed, Six Sigma is a disciplined and very organized approach for improving processes and preventing defects. It employs a specific program (DMAIC) to identify and eliminate waste and achieve perfection (no defects). By focusing on reducing and controlling variation in targeted processes in an organization (via projects), Six Sigma improves the organization's performance. Through process improvement methods lean attempts to eliminate waste and accelerate process efficiency and flow times, thus increasing value to the customer. Lean improvements cause products to flow through processes faster while Six Sigma improves quality and prevents defects by reducing variation through individual projects. Six Sigma identifies the key factors in the performance of a process and sets them at their best level. Lean reduces the complexity of processes everywhere by eliminating waste that can slow down process flow. Lean focuses on what should not be done in a process and removes it; Six Sigma considers what should be done and how to get it right for all time.

The common link between the two is that they both seek to improve processes and provide value to the customer; however, they go about it in different ways. The proponents of Lean Six Sigma believe the two approaches complement each other, and that combining them can result in greater benefits than implementing them separately. However, others consider lean and Six Sigma to be mostly incompatible; Six Sigma is considered to be more of a management tool

ALONG THE SUPPLY CHAIN

Six Sigma Success at Telefonica Group

Telefonica Group, headquartered in Spain, is the world's third largest telecommunications company, providing cell phone and landline communications, broadband, and paid TV services in Europe, the United States, and Latin America. Worldwide it has over 265 million customers, three-quarters of whom are cell phone users. Telefonica's Argentine mobile cell phone communication subsidiary, Movistar, with 16 million customers and 4,000 employees, has been a company leader in quality deployment throughout Telefonica. Movistar first deployed Six Sigma and lean philosophy in 2002 and through 2011 had undertaken more than 200 improvement projects with goals of cost reduction, productivity improvement, service-level increases, process redesign, and quality assurance, resulting in cumulative savings of $245 million. In this same period over 165 champions, 200 Black Belts, and over 900 Green Belts have been trained. Projects are developed according to three key practices—an improvement community, workshops, and an inheritance stage.

The improvement community is made up of Master Black Belts and Black Belts that deliver training in quality improvement, act as facilitators in workshops, and mentor Champions, Blacks Belts, and Green Belts in the correct use of quality improvement tools, providing examples of best practices, helping with team formation, and problem solving. The improvement community facilitates workshops where projects are developed and where team members from similar process improvement projects share their experiences, analyses and conclusions. After a project team completes the DMAIC stages, quality leaders, together with the team's Champion and Black Belt, conduct a team performance evaluation, which is followed by a one-year inheritance period. The team's best-performing Green Belt is deemed the project heir whose responsibility it is to make sure the "improve" and "control" actions of the DMAIC are correctly implemented.

The success of the Movistar quality improvement program using Six Sigma has resulted in Telefonica replicating it throughout its organization, and joining with key suppliers in training and quality project ventures.

Search the Internet and identify another global company that has successfully implemented Six Sigma and discuss its experiences.

Source: Based on Matias G. Thompson and Veronica Rosano, "A Decade of Distinction," *Quality Progress* 44, no. 11 (November 2011): pp. 30–35.

(i.e., a program), whereas lean is a philosophical approach to process improvement that, like the Toyota Production System, is most effective in a mass manufacturing setting.

THE BOTTOM LINE—PROFITABILITY

The criterion for selecting Six Sigma projects by executives is typically based on the financial impact of the improvement expected from the project—how it will affect the bottom line. This focus on profitability for initiating quality improvement projects is one of the factors that distinguishes Six Sigma from TQM.

In *Quality Is Free*, Philip Crosby states that, "Quality is not only free, it is an honest-to-everything profit maker." Gary L. Tooker, former CEO and vice chairman of Motorola, in response to the question, "Is there a link between quality and profitability?" responded that "We've saved several billion dollars over the last year because of our focus on quality improvement and the Six Sigma initiative . . . . there is no doubt about the fact that it has enhanced our bottom line."

This is only the tip of a mountain of conclusive evidence that quality improvement and profitability are closely related. As quality improves, the costs associated with poor quality decline. Quality improvements result in increased productivity. As the quality of a company's products or services improves, it becomes more competitive and its market share increases. Customers' perception of a company's products as being of high quality and its competitive posture enable the company to charge higher prices. Taken together, these things result in higher profitability.

Example 2.1 describes a scenario illustrating the impact of profitability that can result from a Six Sigma project.

EXAMPLE 2.1

THE IMPACT OF SIX SIGMA ON PROFIT

The Medtek Company produces parts for an electronic bed tracking system (BTS) it sells to medical suppliers and hospitals. It contracted for and sold 1,000 units of one of its products during the past quarter for $1,000, each resulting in total sales of $1,000,000. During the quarter, the company incurred variable costs (e.g., direct labor, materials, and energy) of $600,000, so that the unit variable cost was $600. The company also incurred fixed costs of $350,000 (for items such as plant and equipment, and management salaries) during the quarter. This resulted in a (before-tax) profit of $50,000, as shown in the following income statement:

Sales	$1,000,000
Variable costs	600,000
Fixed costs	350,000
Profit	$50,000

However, now let's consider another factor—the company currently operates with a 10% defects rate and the defective products cannot be reworked. Since the company sold 1,000 products, it actually had to produce 1,111 units (i.e., 1,000/0.90 = 1,111), or 111 extra units to compensate for the scrapped units. The variable cost includes this cost of making scrap so the unit variable cost is really $540.05 (i.e., $600,000/1111 = $540.05). The company has paid a "quality tax" (sometimes called the "hidden factory") of $59,946 (i.e., 111 scrap units × $540.05 per unit = $59,946).

Now let's assume that the company implements a successful Six Sigma improvement project and it achieves a defect level of 3.4 DPMO, or virtually zero defects. The elimination

(*Continued*)

of defects will (at a minimum) erase the variable costs consumed by making those 111 scrap units. The effect of the elimination of this "quality tax" is shown in the following revised income statement:

Sales	$1,000,000
Variable costs	540,054
Fixed costs	350,000
Profit	$109,946

The company's profit has more than doubled! An approximate 10% reduction in variable costs because of Six Sigma has resulted in a 120% increase in profit. And, the company has actually increased its capacity to 1,111 units without spending more on plant and equipment.

Next assume that the company spent $120,000 on the Six Sigma project to eliminate defects. If the project was completed in one quarter and the company expects to benefit from the project for 3 years, or 12 quarters, the company should add $10,000 to fixed costs on its income statement:

Sales	$1,000,000
Variable costs	540,054
Fixed costs	360,000
Profit	$99,946

The increase in profit is $49,946 (i.e., $99,946 − 50,000 = $49,946), which is still almost double the profit before Six Sigma. Ignoring interest rates this represents about a 33% return on the company's investment in the Six Sigma project:

$$\text{Return} = \frac{100(49{,}946 - 10{,}000)}{120{,}000}$$

$$= 33.3\%$$

Source: S. Bisgaard and J. Freiesleben, "Six Sigma and the Bottom Line," *Quality Progress* 39, no. 9 (September 2004): pp. 57–62.

The Cost of Quality

According to legendary quality guru Armand Feigenbaum, "Quality costs are the foundation for quality systems economics." Quality costs have traditionally served as the basis for evaluating investments in quality programs. The costs of quality are those incurred to achieve good quality and to satisfy the customer, as well as costs incurred when quality fails to satisfy the customer. Thus, quality costs fall into two categories: the cost of achieving good quality, also known as the *cost of quality assurance*, and the cost associated with poor-quality products, also referred to as the *cost of not conforming* to specifications.

Two recent trends are driving a renewed interest within organizations for measuring quality costs. First, the most recent version of ISO 9000 emphasizes measurements and requires that quality improvement be quantifiably demonstrated. Maintaining quality cost data can provide ISO auditors with evidence of improvement in an organization applying for ISO certification. Second, the popularity and proliferation of Six Sigma, which emphasizes the financial impact of projects as a measure of improvement, has created a need in organizations for quality cost data in order to determine project success.

THE COST OF ACHIEVING GOOD QUALITY

The costs of a quality management program are *prevention costs* and *appraisal costs*. **Prevention costs** are the costs of trying to prevent poor-quality products from reaching the customer. Prevention reflects the quality philosophy of "do it right the first time," the goal of a quality management program. Examples of prevention costs include:

QUALITY PLANNING COSTS: The costs of developing and implementing the quality management program.

PRODUCT-DESIGN COSTS: The costs of designing products with quality characteristics.

PROCESS COSTS: The costs expended to make sure the productive process conforms to quality specifications.

TRAINING COSTS: The costs of developing and putting on quality training programs for employees and management.

INFORMATION COSTS: The costs of acquiring and maintaining (typically on computers) data related to quality, and the development and analysis of reports on quality performance.

Appraisal costs are the costs of measuring, testing, and analyzing materials, parts, products, and the productive process to ensure that product-quality specifications are being met. Examples of appraisal costs include:

INSPECTION AND TESTING: The costs of testing and inspecting materials, parts, and the product at various stages and at the end of the process.

TEST EQUIPMENT COSTS: The costs of maintaining equipment used in testing the quality characteristics of products.

OPERATOR COSTS: The costs of the time spent by operators to gather data for testing product quality, to make equipment adjustments to maintain quality, and to stop work to assess quality.

Appraisal costs tend to be higher in a service organization than in a manufacturing company and, therefore, are a greater proportion of total quality costs. Quality in services is related primarily to the interaction between an employee and a customer, which makes the cost of appraising quality more difficult. Quality appraisal in a manufacturing operation can take place almost exclusively in-house; appraisal of service quality usually requires customer interviews, surveys, questionnaires, and the like.

THE COST OF POOR QUALITY

The cost of poor quality (COPQ) is the difference between what it actually costs to produce a product or deliver a service and what it would cost if there were no defects. Most companies find that defects, rework, and other unnecessary activities related to quality problems significantly inflate costs; estimates range as high as 20% to 30% of total revenues. This is generally the largest quality cost category in a company, frequently accounting for 70% to 90% of total quality costs. This is also where the greatest cost improvement is possible.

The cost of poor quality can be categorized as *internal failure costs* or *external failure costs*. **Internal failure costs** are incurred when poor-quality products are discovered before they are delivered to the customer. Examples of internal failure costs include:

SCRAP COSTS: The costs of poor-quality products that must be discarded, including labor, material, and indirect costs.

REWORK COSTS: The costs of fixing defective products to conform to quality specifications.

PROCESS FAILURE COSTS: The costs of determining why the production process is producing poor-quality products.

PROCESS DOWNTIME COSTS: The costs of shutting down the productive process to fix the problem.

PRICE-DOWNGRADING COSTS: The costs of discounting poor-quality products—that is, selling products as "seconds."

External failure costs are incurred after the customer has received a poor-quality product and are primarily related to customer service. Examples of external failure costs include:

CUSTOMER COMPLAINT COSTS: The costs of investigating and satisfactorily responding to a customer complaint resulting from a poor-quality product.

PRODUCT RETURN COSTS: The costs of handling and replacing poor-quality products returned by the customer. In the United States, it is estimated that product returns reduce company profitability by an average of 4% annually.

WARRANTY CLAIMS COSTS: The costs of complying with product warranties.

PRODUCT LIABILITY COSTS: The litigation costs resulting from product liability and customer injury.

LOST SALES COSTS: The costs incurred because customers are dissatisfied with poor-quality products and do not make additional purchases.

Internal failure costs tend to be low for a service, whereas external failure costs can be quite high. A service organization has little opportunity to examine and correct a defective internal process, usually an employee–customer interaction, before it actually happens. At that point it becomes an external failure. External failures typically result in an increase in service time or inconvenience for the customer. Examples of external failures include a customer waiting too long to place a catalogue phone order; a catalogue order that arrives with the wrong item, requiring the customer to repackage and send it back; an error in a charge card billing statement, requiring the customer to make phone calls or write letters to correct it; sending a customer's orders or statements to the wrong address; or an overnight mail package that does not arrive overnight.

MEASURING AND REPORTING QUALITY COSTS

Collecting data on quality costs can be difficult. The costs of lost sales, of responding to customer complaints, of process downtime, of operator testing, of quality information, and of quality planning and product design are all costs that may be difficult to measure. These costs must be estimated by management. Training costs, inspection and testing costs, scrap costs, the cost of product downgrading, product return costs, warranty claims, and liability costs can usually be measured. Many of these costs are collected as part of normal accounting procedures.

Management wants quality costs reported in a manner that can be easily interpreted and is meaningful. One format for reporting quality costs is with **index numbers**, or indices. Index numbers are ratios that measure quality costs relative to some base value, such as the ratio of quality costs to total sales revenue or the ratio of quality costs to units of final product. These index numbers are used to compare quality management efforts between time periods or between departments or functions. Index numbers themselves do not provide very much information about the effectiveness of a quality management program. They usually will not show directly that a company is producing good- or poor-quality products. These measures are informative only when they are compared to some standard or other index. Some common index measures are:

LABOR INDEX: The ratio of quality cost to direct labor hours; it has the advantage of being easily computed (from accounting records) and easily understood, but it is not always effective for long-term comparative analysis when technological advances reduce labor usage.

COST INDEX: The ratio of quality cost to manufacturing cost (direct and indirect cost); it is easy to compute from accounting records and is not affected by technological change.

SALES INDEX: The ratio of quality cost to sales; it is easily computed, but it can be distorted by changes in selling price and costs.

Production index: The ratio of quality cost to units of final product; it is easy to compute from accounting records but is not effective if a number of different products exist.

Example 2.2 illustrates several of these index numbers.

EXAMPLE 2.2

AN EVALUATION OF QUALITY COSTS AND QUALITY INDEX NUMBERS

The H&S Motor Company produces small motors (e.g., 3 hp) for use in lawnmowers and garden equipment. The company instituted a quality management program in 2011 and has recorded the following quality cost data and accounting measures for four years.

	Year			
	2011	**2012**	**2013**	**2014**
Quality Costs				
Prevention	$27,000	41,500	74,600	112,300
Appraisal	155,000	122,500	113,400	107,000
Internal failure	386,400	469,200	347,800	219,100
External failure	242,000	196,000	103,500	106,000
Total	$810,400	829,200	639,300	544,400
Accounting Measures				
Sales	$4,360,000	4,450,000	5,050,000	5,190,000
Manufacturing costs	1,760,000	1,810,000	1,880,000	1,890,000

The company wants to assess its quality management program and develop quality index numbers using sales and manufacturing cost bases for the four-year period.

SOLUTION

The H&S Company experienced many of the typical outcomes when its quality management program was instituted. Approximately 78% of H&S's total quality costs are a result of internal and external failures, not unlike many companies. Failure costs frequently contribute 50 to 90% of overall quality costs. The typical reaction to high failure costs is to increase product monitoring and inspection to eliminate poor-quality products, resulting in high appraisal costs. This appeared to be the strategy employed by H&S when its quality management program was initiated in 2011. In 2012, H&S was able to identify more defective items, resulting in an apparent increase in internal failure costs and lower external failure costs (as fewer defective products reached the customer).

During 2011 and 2012, prevention costs were modest. However, prevention is critical in reducing both internal and external failures. By instituting quality training programs, redesigning the production process, and planning how to build in product quality, companies are able to reduce poor-quality products within the production process and prevent them from reaching the customer. This was the case at H&S, because prevention costs increased by more than 300% during the four-year period. Since fewer poor-quality products are being made, less monitoring and inspection is necessary, and appraisal costs thus decline. Internal and external failure costs are also reduced because of a reduction in defective products. In general, an increase in expenditures for prevention will result in a decrease in all other quality-cost categories. It is also not uncommon for a quality management program to isolate one or two specific quality problems that, when prevented, have a large impact on overall quality cost reduction. Quality problems are not usually evenly distributed throughout the product process; a few isolated problems tend to result in the majority of poor-quality products.

(Continued)

The H&S Company also desired to develop index numbers using quality costs as a proportion of sales and manufacturing costs, generally two of the more popular quality indexes. The general formula for these index numbers is

$$\text{Quality index} = \frac{\text{total quality costs}}{\text{base}}(100)$$

For example, the index number for 2006 sales is

$$\text{Quality cost per sale} = \frac{\$810{,}400(100)}{4{,}360{,}000}$$
$$= 18.58$$

The quality index numbers for sales and manufacturing costs for the four-year period are given in the following table.

Year	Quality Sales Index	Quality Manufacturing Cost Index
2011	18.58	46.04
2012	18.63	45.18
2013	12.66	34.00
2014	10.49	28.80

These index numbers alone provide little insight into the effectiveness of the quality management program; however, as a standard to make comparisons over time they can be useful. The H&S Company quality index numbers reflect dramatically improved quality during the four-year period. Quality costs as a proportion of both sales and manufacturing costs improved significantly. Quality index numbers do not provide information that will enable the company to diagnose and correct quality problems in the production process. They are useful in showing trends in product quality over time and reflecting the impact of product quality relative to accounting measures with which managers are usually familiar.

THE QUALITY–COST RELATIONSHIP

In Example 2.2 we showed that when the sum of prevention and appraisal costs increased, internal and external failure costs decreased. Recall that prevention and appraisal costs are the costs of achieving good quality, and internal and external failure costs are the costs of poor quality. In general, when the cost of achieving good quality increases, the cost of poor quality declines.

Philip Crosby's fourth absolute from his 1984 book *Quality Without Tears* explains that the dollar *cost of quality* is the difference between the price of nonconformance, the cost of doing things wrong (i.e., the cost of poor quality), and the price of conformance, the cost of doing things right (i.e., the cost of achieving good quality). He estimates that the cost of doing things wrong can account for 20 to 35% of revenues, while the cost of doing things right is typically 3 to 4%. As such, managers should determine where the cost of quality is occurring and find out what causes it.

Companies committed to quality improvement know that the increase in sales and market share resulting from increased customer satisfaction offsets the costs of achieving good quality.

Furthermore, as a company focuses on good quality, the cost of achieving good quality will be less because of the improvements in technologies and processes that will result from the quality improvement effort. These companies are frequently the ones that seek to achieve *zero defects*, the goal of Six Sigma.

The Japanese first recognized that the costs of poor quality had been traditionally underestimated. These costs did not take into account the customer losses that can be attributed to a reputation for poor quality. The Japanese viewed the cost associated with a reputation for poor quality to be quite high. A General Accounting Office report on companies that have been Baldrige Quality Award finalists has shown that corporate-wide quality improvement programs result in higher worker motivation, improved employee relations, increased productivity, higher customer satisfaction, and increased market share and profitability.

The Effect of Quality Management on Productivity

In the previous section we saw how an effective quality management program can help to reduce quality-related costs and improve market share and profitability. Quality management can also improve productivity—the number of units produced from available resources.

PRODUCTIVITY

Productivity is a measure of a company's effectiveness in converting inputs into outputs. It is broadly defined as

$$\text{Productivity} = \frac{\text{output}}{\text{input}}$$

An output is the final product from a service or production process, such as an automobile, a hamburger, a sale, or a catalogue order. Inputs are the parts, material, labor, capital, and so on that go into the productive process. Productivity measures, depending on the outputs and inputs used, are labor productivity (output per labor-hour) and machine productivity (output per machine-hour).

Improving quality by reducing defects will increase good output and reduce inputs. In fact, virtually all aspects of quality improvement have a favorable impact on different measures of productivity. Improving product design and production processes, improving the quality of materials and parts, and improving job designs and work activity will all increase productivity.

MEASURING PRODUCT YIELD AND PRODUCTIVITY

Product **yield** is a measure of output used as an indicator of productivity. It can be computed for the entire production process (or for one stage in the process) as follows:

$$\begin{aligned}\text{Yield} = {} & (\text{total input})(\%\text{ good units}) \\ & + (\text{total input})(1 - \%\text{ good units})(\%\text{ reworked})\end{aligned}$$

or

$$Y = (I)(\%G) + (I)(1 - \%G)(\%R)$$

where

I = planned number units of product started in the production process
$\%G$ = percentage of good units produced
$\%R$ = percentage of defective units that are successfully reworked

In this formula, yield is the sum of the percentage of products started in the process (or at a stage) that will turn out to be good quality plus the percentage of the defective (rejected) products that are reworked. Any increase in the percentage of good products through improved quality will increase product yield.

EXAMPLE 2.3

COMPUTING PRODUCT YIELD

The H&S Motor Company starts production for a particular type of motor with a steel motor housing. The production process begins with 100 motors each day. The percentage of good motors produced each day averages 80% and the percentage of poor-quality motors that can be reworked is 50%. The company wants to know the daily product yield and the effect on productivity if the daily percentage of good-quality motors is increased to 90%.

SOLUTION

$$\text{Yield} = (I)(\%G) + (I)(1 - \%G)(\%R)$$
$$Y = 100(0.80) + 100(1 - 0.80)(0.50)$$
$$= 90 \text{ motors}$$

If product quality is increased to 90% good motors, the yield will be

$$Y = 100(0.90) + 100(1 - 0.90)(0.50)$$
$$= 95 \text{ motors}$$

A 10 percentage-point increase in quality products results in a 5.5% increase in productivity output.

Now we will expand our discussion of productivity to include product manufacturing cost. The manufacturing cost per (good) product is computed by dividing the sum of total direct manufacturing cost and total cost for all reworked units by the yield, as follows:

$$\text{Product cost} = \frac{(\text{direct manufacturing cost per unit})(\text{input}) + (\text{rework cost per unit})(\text{reworked units})}{\text{yield}}$$

or

$$\text{Product cost} = \frac{(K_d)(I) + (K_r)(R)}{Y}$$

where

K_d = direct manufacturing cost per unit
I = input
K_r = rework cost per unit
R = reworked units
Y = yield

EXAMPLE 2.4

COMPUTING PRODUCT COST PER UNIT

The H&S Motor Company has a direct manufacturing cost per unit of \$30, and motors that are of inferior quality can be reworked for \$12 per unit. From Example 2.3, 100 motors are produced daily, 80% (on average) are of good quality and 20% are defective. Of the defective motors, half can be reworked to yield good-quality products. Through its quality management program, the company has discovered a problem in its production process that, when corrected (at a minimum cost), will increase the good-quality products to 90%. The company wants to assess the impact on the direct cost per unit of improvement in product quality.

SOLUTION

The original manufacturing cost per motor is

$$\text{Product cost} = \frac{(K_d)(I) + (K_r)(R)}{Y}$$

$$\text{Product cost} = \frac{(\$30)(100) + (\$12)(10)}{90 \text{ motors}}$$

$$= \$34.67 \text{ per motor}$$

The manufacturing cost per motor with the quality improvement is

$$\text{Product cost} = \frac{(\$30)(100) + (\$12)(10)}{95 \text{ motors}}$$

$$\text{Product cost} = \$32.21 \text{ per motor}$$

The improvement in the production process as a result of the quality management program will result in a decrease of \$2.46 per unit, or 7.1%, in direct manufacturing cost per unit as well as a 5.5% increase in product yield (computed in Example 2.3), with a minimal investment in labor, plant, or equipment.

In Examples 2.3 and 2.4, we determined productivity measures for a single production process. However, it is more likely that product quality would be monitored throughout the production process at various stages. Each stage would result in a portion of good-quality, "work-in-process" products. For a production process with *n* stages, the yield, *Y* (without reworking), is

$$Y = (I)(\%g_1)(\%g_2)\cdots(\%g_n)$$

where

I = input of items to the production process that will result in finished products

g_i = good-quality, work-in-process products at stage i

EXAMPLE 2.5

COMPUTING PRODUCT YIELD FOR A MULTISTAGE PROCESS

At the H&S Motor Company, motors are produced in a four-stage process. Motors are inspected following each stage, with percentage yields (on average) of good-quality, work-in-process units as follows.

Stage	Average Percentage Good Quality
1	0.93
2	0.95
3	0.97
4	0.92

(Continued)

The company wants to know the daily product yield for product input of 100 units per day. Furthermore, it would like to know how many input units it would have to start with each day to result in a final daily yield of 100 good-quality units.

SOLUTION

$$
\begin{aligned}
Y &= (I)(\%g_1)(\%g_2)(\%g_3)(\%g_4)\\
&= (100)(0.93)(0.95)(0.97)(0.92)\\
Y &= 78.8 \text{ motors}
\end{aligned}
$$

Thus, the production process has a daily good-quality product yield of 78.8 motors.

To determine the product input that would be required to achieve a product yield of 100 motors, I is treated as a decision variable when Y equals 100:

$$
\begin{aligned}
I &= \frac{Y}{(\%g_1)(\%g_2)(\%g_3)(\%g_4)}\\
I &= \frac{100}{(0.93)(0.95)(0.97)(0.92)}\\
&= 126.8 \text{ motors}
\end{aligned}
$$

To achieve output of 100 good-quality motors, the production process must start with approximately 127 motors.

THE QUALITY–PRODUCTIVITY RATIO

Another measure of the effect of quality on productivity combines the concepts of quality index numbers and product yield. Called the **quality–productivity ratio (QPR)**,[3] it is computed as follows:

$$
\text{QPR} = \frac{\text{good quality units}}{(\text{input units})(\text{unit processing cost}) + (\text{reworked units})(\text{rework cost})}(100)
$$

This is actually a quality index number that includes productivity and quality costs. The QPR increases if either processing cost or rework costs or both decrease. It increases if more good-quality units are produced relative to total product input (i.e., the number of units that begin the production process).

EXAMPLE 2.6

COMPUTING THE QUALITY PRODUCTIVITY RATIO (QPR)

The H&S Motor Company produces small motors at a processing cost of \$30 per unit. Defective motors can be reworked at a cost of \$12 each. The company produces 100 motors per day and averages 80% good-quality motors, resulting in 20% defects, 50% of which can be reworked prior to shipping to customers. The company wants to examine the effects of (1) increasing the production rate to 200 motors per day; (2) reducing the processing cost to \$26 and the rework cost to \$10; (3) increasing, through quality improvement, the product yield of good-quality products to 95%; and (4) the combination of 2 and 3.

[3]E. E. Adam, J. E. Hershauer, and W. A. Ruch, *Productivity and Quality: Measurement as a Basis of Improvement*, 2nd ed. (Columbia, MO: Research Center, College of Business and Public Administration, University of Missouri, 1986).

SOLUTION

The QPR for the base case is computed as follows.

$$QPR = \frac{80 + 10}{(100)(\$30) + (10)(\$12)}(100)$$

$$= 2.89$$

Case 1. Increase input to production capacity of 200 units.

$$QPR = \frac{160 + 20}{(200)(\$30) + (20)(\$12)}(100)$$

$$= 2.89$$

Increasing production capacity alone has no effect on the QPR; it remains the same as the base case.

Case 2. Reduce processing cost to \$26 and rework cost to \$10.

$$QPR = \frac{80 + 10}{(100)(\$26) + (10)(\$10)}(100)$$

$$= 3.33$$

These cost decreases cause the QPR to increase.

Case 3. Increase initial good-quality units to 95%.

$$QPR = \frac{95 + 2.5}{(100)(\$30) + (2.5)(\$12)}(100)$$

$$= 3.22$$

Again, the QPR increases as product quality improves.

Case 4. Decrease costs and increase initial good-quality units.

$$QPR = \frac{95 + 2.5}{(100)(\$26) + (2.5)(\$10)}(100)$$

$$= 3.71$$

The largest increase in the QPR results from decreasing costs and increasing initial good-quality product through improved quality.

Quality Awards

The Baldrige Award, Deming Prize, and other award competitions have become valuable and coveted prizes for U.S. companies eager to benefit from the aura and reputation for quality that await the winners, and the decreased costs and increased profits that award participants and winners have experienced. They have also provided widely used sets of guidelines to help companies implement an effective quality management system (QMS), and winners provide quality standards, or "benchmarks," for other companies to emulate.

THE MALCOLM BALDRIGE AWARD

The Malcolm Baldrige National Quality Award is given annually to up to 18 organizations in six categories: manufacturing, services, small businesses, nonprofits (with less than 500 full-time employees), healthcare, and education. It was created by law in 1987 (named after former Secretary of Commerce Malcolm Baldrige, who died in 1987) to (1) stimulate U.S. companies to improve quality, (2) establish criteria for businesses to use to evaluate their individual quality-improvement efforts, (3) set as examples those companies that were successful in improving quality, and (4) help other U.S. organizations learn how to manage quality by disseminating information about the award winners' programs.

The award criteria focus on the soundness of the approach to quality improvement, the overall quality management program as it is implemented throughout the organization, and customer satisfaction. The seven major categories of criteria by which companies are examined are leadership; strategic planning; customer focus; measurement, analysis, and knowledge management; workforce focus; operations focus; and results.

The Baldrige Award has had a major influence on U.S. companies, thousands of which request applications from the government each year to obtain a copy of the award guidelines and criteria for internal use in establishing a quality management system. Many companies have made the Baldrige criteria for quality their own, and have also demanded that their suppliers submit applications for the Malcolm Baldrige National Quality Award. Since its inception in 1987, it has been estimated that the economic benefits of the Baldrige Program as a ratio compared to its costs is 820 to 1. Companies that have won the Baldrige Quality Award and have become known as leaders in quality include Motorola, Xerox, Cadillac, Federal Express, Ritz Carlton, and IBM. These and other Baldrige Award winners have become models or benchmarks for other companies to emulate in establishing their own quality management systems.

OTHER AWARDS FOR QUALITY

The creation and subsequent success of the Baldrige Award has spawned a proliferation of national, international, government, industry, state, and individual quality awards. The American Society for Quality (ASQ) sponsors a number of national individual awards, including, among others, the Armand V. Feigenbaum Medal, the Deming Medal, the E. Jack Lancaster Medal, the Edwards Medal, the Shewart Medal, and the Ishikawa Medal.

The President's Quality Award was established in 1989 to recognize federal government organizations that improve their overall performance and capabilities, demonstrate mature approaches to quality throughout the organization, and demonstrate a sustained trend in high-quality products and services that result in effective use of taxpayer dollars.

Prominent international awards include the EFQM (formerly the European Foundation for Quality Management) Excellence Award that recognizes outstanding businesses in European countries, with similar scope and criteria to Baldrige Award, the UK Excellence Award, the German National Quality Award, the Canada Awards for Excellence, the Deming Prize (Japan), and the Japan Quality Award.

ISO 9000

The International Organization for Standardization (ISO), headquartered in Geneva, Switzerland, has as its members the national standards organizations for more than 157 countries. The ISO member for the United States is the American National Standards Institute (ANSI). The purpose of ISO is to facilitate global consensus agreements on international quality standards. It has resulted in a system for certifying suppliers to make sure they meet internationally accepted standards for quality management. It is a nongovernment organization and is not a part of the United Nations.

During the 1970s it was generally acknowledged that the word *quality* had different meanings within and among industries and countries and around the world. In 1979 the ISO member representing the United Kingdom, the British Standard Institute (BSI), recognizing the need for standardization for quality management and assurance, submitted a formal proposal to ISO to develop international standards for quality assurance techniques and practices. Using standards that already existed in the United Kingdom and Canada as a basis, ISO established generic quality standards, primarily for manufacturing firms, that could be used worldwide.

STANDARDS

Standards are documented agreements that include technical specifications or other precise criteria to be used consistently as rules, guidelines, or definitions to ensure that materials, products processes, and services are fit for their purpose. For example, the format for credit cards and phone cards was derived from ISO standards that specify such physical features as the cards' thickness so that they can be used worldwide. Standards, in general, increase the reliability and effectiveness of goods and services used around the world and as a result make life easier for everyone.

The ISO 9000 series of quality management standards, guidelines, and technical reports was first published in 1978, and it is reviewed at least every five years. It was most recently revised and updated in 2008. ISO 9000:2008, *Quality Management Systems—Fundamentals and Vocabulary*, is the starting point for understanding the standards. It defines the fundamental terms and definitions used in the ISO 9000 family of standards, guidelines, and technical reports. ISO 9001:2008, *Quality Management Systems—Requirements*, is the requirement standard a company uses to assess its ability to meet customer and applicable regulatory requirements in order to achieve customer satisfaction. ISO 9004:2008, *Quality Management Systems—Guidelines for Performance Improvements*, provides detailed guidance to a company for the continual improvement of its quality management system in order to achieve and sustain customer satisfaction. The ISO 9000 family includes 10 more published standards and guidelines; however, these three are the most widely used and applicable to the majority of companies.

CERTIFICATION

Many companies around the world require that companies they do business with (e.g., suppliers) have ISO 9001 certification. In that way, despite possible language, technology, and cultural differences, a company can be sure that the company it's doing business with meets uniform standards—that is, they are "on the same page." ISO 9001:2008 is the only standard in the ISO 9000 family that carries third-party *certification* (referred to as *registration* in the United States). A third-party company called a registrar is the only authorized entity that can award ISO 9001 certification. Registrars are accredited by an authoritative national body and are contracted by companies to evaluate their quality management system to see if it meets the ISO 9001 standards; if the company does, it is issued an ISO 9000 certification, which is recognized around the world. Over a million organizations around the world have been certified.

ISO 9001:2008 primarily serves as a basis for benchmarking a company's quality-management system. Quality management, in ISO terms, measures how effectively management determines the company's overall quality policy, its objectives, and its responsibilities, as well as its quality policy implementation. A company has to fulfill all of the requirements in ISO 9001:2008 to be certified (except for activities and functions it does not perform at all). Customer satisfaction is an explicit requirement. Thus, to be certified, a company must identify and review customer requirements, ensure that customer requirements are met, and be able to measure and monitor customer satisfaction. The company must also be able to show that measuring and monitoring customer satisfaction leads to corrective and preventive actions when nonconformance (to the standards) is found—that is, continual improvement. This type of analysis of customer satisfaction requires a large amount of data collection and processing.

IMPLICATIONS OF ISO 9000 FOR U.S. COMPANIES

Originally, ISO 9000 was adopted by the 12 countries of the European Community (EC)—Belgium, Denmark, France, Germany, Greece, Ireland, Italy, Luxembourg, the Netherlands, Portugal, Spain, and the United Kingdom. The governments of the EC countries adopted ISO 9000 as a uniform quality standard for cross-border transactions within the EC and for international transactions. The EC has since evolved into the European Union (EU) with 25 member countries.

These EU countries and many others are specifically acknowledging that they prefer suppliers with ISO 9000 certification. To remain competitive in international markets, U.S. companies must comply with the standards in the ISO 9000 series. Some products in the EU, for example, are "regulated" to the extent that the products must be certified to be in ISO 9000 compliance by an EU-recognized accreditation registrar. Most of these products have health and safety considerations. However, companies discovered that to remain competitive and satisfy customer preferences, their products had to be in compliance with ISO 9000 requirements even if these products were not specifically regulated.

The United States exports more than $250 billion annually to the EU market, much of it to France, Germany, Italy, Spain, and the United Kingdom. Most of these exports are affected in some way by ISO 9000 standards.

ALONG THE SUPPLY CHAIN

ISO 9001 Certification at Monarcas Morelia

Monarcas Morelia (named for the Monarch butterfly) is a professional soccer team in the Mexican Football Federation First Division league, which consists of 19 professional teams. It is the first international-level club soccer team to achieve ISO 9001 certification. The team is owned by TV Azteca, a Spanish-language television networks producer, which is owned by Grupo Salinas (GS), a $3.1 billion conglomerate created by Ricardo Salinas. Executives at TV Azteca and Grupo Salinas learned through the ISO certification process at TV Azteca and other GS subsidiaries that a quality management system (QMS) creates value and compels managers to seek continuous improvement and customer satisfaction. In 1998 Monarcas Morelia was at the bottom of the First Division and losing money. The philosophy of Ricardo Salinas was that every GS company must create value, and the football team was no exception. In 1999, eight months after it developed its QMS, Monarcas Morelia began earning a profit, in 2000 it won the Mexican Football Championship for the first time in team history, and in 2002 it finished in second place.

A necessary first step in developing a QMS was for Monarcas Morelia to define its customers, which was determined to be a large, diverse group including fans, investors, employees, visiting teams and their fans, the media, referees, sponsors, charities, and members of its youth development team, Basic Forces, and their families. The quality team led by team president, Alvaro Davila, focused on benchmarking to transform the team's management and seek continual improvement—just as any business would. He visited teams in Argentina, Spain and Germany, and adopted their successful strategies for winning, promoting goodwill and earning profits. He arranged exhibition games and player exchange programs, including a contract with the Chicago Fire of the U.S. MLS. In order to keep the 30,000-seat Morelia, Mexico stadium (including seats, bathrooms, vending outlets and lighting fixtures) in top condition, and continually improve it, the team relied on the steps of the Japanese *gemba kaizen* process (where *gemba* means "where the action is" and *kaizen* means "continuous improvement"). The team also established a customer-friendly security system with guards trained to prevent violence and promote a family-friendly atmosphere.

Pick an "entertainment" service like a college or professional athletic team, a theater, or an amusement park and discuss the ways it might benefit from a QMS.

Source: A. Tolumes, "Pitch Perfect," *Qualityworld* 32, issue 1 (January 2006): pp. 23–26.

Companies are also pressured within the United States to comply with ISO 9000 by more and more customers. For example, the U.S. Department of Defense, and specifically the Department of the Navy, as well as private companies like DuPont, 3M, and AT&T, have adopted ISO 9000. They recognize the value of these standards for helping to ensure top-quality products and services and required that their suppliers comply with ISO 9000.

In the EC registration system, the third-party assessors of quality are referred to as *notified bodies*; that is, the 12 EC governments *notify* one another as to which organization in their country is the officially designated government-approved quality assessor. The notified bodies ultimately certify a company with a European Conformity (CE) mark. The CE mark must be on any product exported from the United States that is ISO 9000-regulated. It is illegal to sell a regulated product in a store in the EC without the CE mark. For a supplier in the United States to export regulated products to an EC country, it must be accredited by European registrars—notified bodies within the EC. However, more and more EC companies are requiring ISO 9000 certification for suppliers of products that fall in the unregulated categories, and eventually all products exported to the EC will probably require certification. It is also important that U.S. companies obtain accreditation with a notified body that has widespread positive recognition in the EC so that they will have broad access to markets in the EC.

The U.S. member of the ISO, the American National Standards Institute (ANSI) designated the American Society for Quality (ASQ), as the sponsoring organization for ISO 9000 in the United States. ASQ and ANSI created the Registrar Accreditation Board (RAB) to act as an accrediter of third-party registrars in the United States.

ALONG THE SUPPLY CHAIN

Orkin Uses ISO Certification to Improve Service Quality

Orkin, Inc., headquartered in Atlanta, with 8,000 employees and more than 400 U.S. locations, is a leader in pest control services for residential and commercial customers. Approximately a third of Orkin's revenue is from its commercial business, which provides pest control for hospitals, hotels, food processing plants, and similar business facilities that have a very low tolerance for pests.

In the 1990s, as a number of Orkin's commercial customers achieved ISO certification, they wanted to partner with suppliers that subscribed to the same quality management standards, while at the same time Orkin wanted to achieve a higher level of consistency of quality service across its branches. Over time the company developed a quality assurance (QA) team that was responsible for developing a companywide quality management process that would eventually earn Orkin ISO 9001 certification in 2005.

Orkin's QA team is composed of experienced quality professionals who have worked at Orkin for an average of 30 years, and who have completed ISO technical courses and audit coursework. The team conducts approximately 200 commercial branch internal audits each year. A typical audit takes one QA member four days and consists of nine administrative reviews, four vehicle inspections, and 10 on-site customer inspections. Auditors document their findings in a two-page summary and each branch receives a score on administration, employee training, and on-site service evaluations. In accordance with ISO 9001:2008, if a branch fails any part of an audit, a formal corrective process is required and the QA team performs a follow-up audit within 90 to 120 days. However, even branches that receive very high scores are given areas of improvement to work on. Since achieving ISO certification, Orkin decreased its commercial business cancellation rate, saving approximately $600,000 per year, established companywide consistency in the quality of its service, and improved customer satisfaction from 95.8% to 97.7% for customers who rated Orkin's service as excellent or good.

Although Orkin franchises branches overseas, its ISO certification was directed at U.S. customers; why do you think it believed it had a need to meet international standards for quality?

Source: Based on Mark Udell and Mike Buffingtion, "Eradicating Inconsistency," *Quality Progress* 45, no. 3 (March 2012): pp. 38–44.

ISO REGISTRARS

A registrar is an organization that conducts audits by individual auditors. Auditors are skilled in quality systems and the manufacturing and service environments in which an audit will be performed. The registrar develops an audit team of one or more auditors to evaluate a company's quality program and then report back to the registrar. An organization that wants to become a registrar must be accredited by the Registrar Accreditation Board (RAB) founded by the American Society for Quality Control, which links the U.S. with ISO 9000 standards. Once RAB accredits a registrar, the registrar can then authorize its registered suppliers to use the RAB certificate in advertising, indicating compliance with ISO 9000.

ISO certification, or registration as it is called in the United States, is accomplished by a registrar through a series of document reviews and facility visits and audits. The registrar's auditors review a company's procedures, processes, and operations to see if the company conforms to the ISO quality management system standards. The registrar looks at a variety of things, including the company's administrative, design, and production processes; quality system documentation; personnel training records; management reviews; and internal audit processes. The registration process might typically include an initial document review that describes the company's quality management system, followed by the development of an audit plan and then the audit itself. This is usually followed by semiannual or annual surveillance audits to make sure the quality system is being maintained. The registration process can take from several weeks up to a year, depending on how ready the company is for registration. A RAB accredited registrar does not "help" the company attain certification either by giving advice or consulting.

SUMMARY

In our discussion of quality management in this chapter, certain consistencies or commonalities have surfaced. The most important perspective of quality is the customer's; products and services must be designed to meet customer expectations and needs for quality. A total commitment to quality is necessary throughout an organization for it to be successful in improving and managing product quality. This commitment must start at the top and filter down through all levels of the organization and across all areas and departments. Employees need to be active participants in the quality-improvement process and must feel a responsibility for quality. Employees must feel free to make suggestions to improve product quality, and a systematic procedure is necessary to involve workers and solicit their input. Improving product quality is cost-effective; the cost of poor quality greatly exceeds the cost of attaining good quality. Quality can be improved with the effective use of statistical quality-control methods. In fact, the use of statistical quality control has been a pervasive part of our discussions on quality management, and it has been identified as an important part of any quality-management program. In the following chapter we concentrate on statistical quality-control methods and principles.

KEY FORMULAS

Quality Index Numbers

$$\text{Quality index} = \frac{\text{total quality costs}}{\text{base}}(100)$$

Product Yield

$$Y = (I)(\%G) + (I)(1 - \%G)(\%R)$$

Manufacturing Cost per Product

$$\text{Product cost} = \frac{(K_d)(I) + (K_r)(R)}{Y}$$

Multistage Product Yield

$$Y = (I)(\%g_1)(\%g_2)\cdots(\%g_n)$$

Quality-Productivity Ratio

$$\text{QPR} = \frac{\text{good quality units}}{(\text{input units})(\text{processing cost}) + (\text{reworked units})(\text{rework cost})}(100)$$

SOLVED PROBLEMS

1. PRODUCT YIELD

A manufacturing company has a weekly product input of 1,700 units. The average percentage of good-quality products is 83%. Of the poor-quality products, 60% can be reworked and sold as good-quality products. Determine the weekly product yield and the product yield if the good-product quality is increased to 92%.

SOLUTION

Step 1. Compute yield according to the following formula:

$$Y = (I)(G\%) + (I)(1 - \%G)(\%R)$$

$$Y = (1{,}700)(0.83) + (1{,}700)(0.17)(0.60)$$
$$= 1{,}584.4 \text{ units}$$

Step 2. Increase %G to 92%:

$$Y = (1{,}700)(0.92) + (1{,}700)(0.08)(0.60)$$
$$= 1{,}645.6 \text{ units}$$

2. QUALITY–PRODUCTIVITY RATIO

A retail telephone catalogue company takes catalogue orders from customers and then sends the completed orders to the warehouses to be filled. An operator processes an average of 45 orders per day. The cost of processing an order is $1.15, and it costs $0.65 to correct an order that has been filled out incorrectly by the operator. An operator averages 7% bad orders per day, all of which are reworked prior to filling the customer order. Determine the quality–productivity ratio for an operator.

SOLUTION

Compute the quality–productivity ratio according to the following formulas:

$$QPR = \frac{\text{good quality units}}{(\text{input})(\text{processing cost}) + (\text{defective units})(\text{rework cost})}(100)$$

$$QPR = \frac{45}{(45)(\$1.15) + (3.15)(\$0.65)}(100)$$
$$= 83.65$$

QUESTIONS

2-1. A number of quality management philosophies hold that prevention costs are the most critical quality-related costs. Explain the logic behind this premise.

2-2. Describe the primary contribution to quality management of each of the following: W. E. Deming, Joseph Juran, Phillip Crosby, Armand Feigenbaum, and Kaoru Ishikawa.

2-3. Describe the impact that the creation of the Malcolm Baldrige Award has had on quality improvement in the United States.

2-4. More companies probably fail at implementing quality-management programs than succeed. Discuss the reasons why a quality-management program might fail.

2-5. Select a service provider and discuss the dimensions of quality on which a customer might evaluate it.

2-6. Select two competing service providers that you are familiar with or can visit, such as fast-food restaurants, banks, or retail stores, and compare how they interact with customers in terms of quality.

2-7. Develop a hypothetical quality-improvement program for the class in which you are using this textbook. Evaluate the class according to the dimensions of quality for a service. Include goals for quality improvement and ways to measure success.

2-8. Identify a company or organization from which you have received poor-quality products or services, describe the nature of the defects, and suggest ways in which you might improve quality.

2-9. Identify a company or organization from which you have received high-quality products and describe the characteristics that make them high-quality.

2-10. Why has ISO 9000 become so important to U.S. firms that do business overseas?

2-11. Go to the Baldrige Award website, http://www.quality. nist.gov, and research several companies that have won the Malcolm Baldrige Award. Describe any common characteristics that the quality-management programs in those companies have.

2-12. The discussion in this chapter has focused on the benefits of implementing a quality management program; however, many companies do not have such a program. Discuss the reasons why you think a company would not adopt a quality management program.

2-13. Access a website of a company that sells products to the general public on the Internet. Discuss the quality attributes of the site, and evaluate the quality of the website.

2-14. For an airline you have flown on list all of the quality "defects" you can recall. Discuss whether you think the airline exhibited overall good or poor quality. If it exhibited good quality, explain what made it so; if it exhibited poor quality, what actions do you think could be taken by the airline to improve quality?

2-15. Identify three websites that you think are poor quality and three that are good quality. What common characteristics are exhibited by the group of poor-quality sites? the group of good-quality sites? Compare the two groups.

2-16. Amazon operates what is considered to be an "open market" wherein it provides space and opportunity on its website for independent, competing companies to sell products. Discuss the type of quality problems that this arrangement might pose for Amazon, and how it might deal with quality problems in this kind of open marketplace environment.

2-17. Identify a service provider that you have experienced more than normal quality problems with, list the type of quality problems you have experienced, and suggest ways to correct these problems.

2-18. Discuss how you think sustainability issues are related to quality issues in a company.

2-19. Some companies, like Target and Amazon, are known for outstanding quality. Discuss why you think the processes and systems they use have not, or cannot, be applied to companies that are sometimes known for poor quality, like airlines.

2-20. Many companies have outsourced their customer service activity to overseas providers, most visibly computer, credit card, and airline companies. The quality issues this kind of outsourcing has created have become known to such a large extent that they are often parodied in the media. Discuss why you think companies persist in outsourcing such an important quality-related process as customer service, and what steps these companies might employ to improve the quality of their customer service if they continue to outsource it.

2-21. When Apple introduces new products, it is speculated that it markets first-generation versions of the product without first correcting all of the possible quality problems that might exist, preferring instead to let their customers do their product testing for them and discover any problems. This is a cost-effective process that doesn't seem to hurt Apple's reputation for high quality or sales. Why do you think this is?

2-22. One of the difficult aspects of global supply chain management is ensuring quality across a number of different suppliers. Discuss how a company can ensure quality along its supply chain.

2-23. Within a company's supply chain, identify and discuss some of the different supply chain processes where quality issues might arise.

2-24. Research the companies on the annual Gartner Supply Chain "Top 25" (at www.gartner.com) and identify some of the quality management characteristics they share.

2-25. Find an article from *Quality Progress* about a specific company's supply chain quality and write a brief report similar to the "Along the Supply Chain" about Target's supply chain in this chapter.

2-26. Research the website of a company that is known to be a leading user and proponent of Six Sigma (like some of those identified in this chapter), and discuss what they say about their use of Six Sigma.

2-27. Develop a fishbone diagram for the possible causes of flight delays.

2-28. Observe a business with which you are familiar and interact with frequently, such as a restaurant or food service, a laundry service, your bank, or the college bookstore. Develop a Pareto chart that encompasses the major service defects of the business, identify the most significant service problems and suggest how quality could be improved.

2-29. Joseph Juran created a "quality spiral" showing that each element of the business process, each function, not just the end product, is important. Describe how each of the following business process areas might impact quality: marketing, engineering, purchasing/sourcing, human resources, and distribution.

2-30. Using the Internet, research the winner of an international quality award at one of the award websites and write a brief report.

2-31. Go to the Malcolm Baldrige Award website, www.quality.nist.gov, and write a brief report on one of the most recent years' Baldrige Award winners similar to the "Along the Supply Chain" boxes in this chapter.

2-32. Write a brief summary on how a company relates quality management to sustainability by researching *Quality Progress* or the Internet.

2-33. Develop a fishbone diagram for the possible causes of your car not starting.

2-34. Describe the differences among Black Belts, Green Belts, and Master Black Belts in a Six Sigma program.

2-35. Describe the steps in the Six Sigma breakthrough strategy for quality improvement.

2-36. Develop a quality-improvement project in a situation you are familiar with such as a current or former job, a part-time job, a restaurant, your college bookstore, your dorm or apartment, a local business, and so on, and describe how you would apply the steps of the Six Sigma breakthrough strategy.

2-37. Develop a Six Sigma-type quality improvement project employing the DMAIC steps for your own personal health such as losing weight, improving your diet, exercise, etc.

2-38. Develop a Six Sigma-type project employing the DMAIC steps for improving any phase of your personal life that you feel may be "defective."

2-39. Visit your university infirmary and study the process in-patients follow to see a doctor and describe a quality improvement project to improve this process.

2-40. The Japanese are generally credited with starting the global quality revolution that in the 1970s became an integral part of corporate culture, and eventually led to the development of quality improvement programs systems like TQM and Six Sigma. Research and write a report about what Japan did to initiate the quality movement and why it differed from what was being done in the United States.

2-41. Describe the general steps a company must go through to obtain ISO 9001:2008 certification.

2-42. Select a retail store you are familiar with such as a grocery store, J. Crew, Macy's, Best Buy, Target, etc., and identify what might be considered as "defects" in their processes and how improvement might be measured.

2-43. ISO 9000 and the Malcolm Baldrige Award competition are both programs that seek to achieve recognition for outstanding quality, one in the form of a certificate and the other in the form of an award. Discuss how the two are similar and different, and how they might complement each other.

2-44. In the ongoing national debate about healthcare that is likely to continue for years, one view holds that quality improvement (and corresponding cost reduction) across the industry is fundamentally not possible because the direct consumer (i.e., the patient) is not who pays the bill; for most people the insurance company is. Since insurance companies do not directly receive the service provided, they cannot assess how well "value" is being delivered, and neither the customer nor the insurance company are motivated to reduce costs. Discuss this phenomenon of the healthcare industry and make a case for why you think it is accurate or inaccurate. Also address in your discussion how healthcare insurance differs from other forms of personal insurance.

PROBLEMS

2-1. Backwoods American, Inc., produces expensive water-repellent, down-lined parkas. The company implemented a total quality-management program in 2005. Following are quality-related accounting data that have been accumulated for the five-year period after the program's start.

	Year				
	2006	2007	2008	2009	2010
Quality Costs (000s)					
Prevention	$3.2	10.7	28.3	42.6	50.0
Appraisal	26.3	29.2	30.6	24.1	19.6
Internal failure	39.1	51.3	48.4	35.9	32.1
External failure	118.6	110.5	105.2	91.3	65.2
Accounting Measures (000s)					
Sales	$2,700.6	2,690.1	2,705.3	2,310.2	2,880.7
Manufacturing cost	420.9	423.4	424.7	436.1	435.5

a. Compute the company's total failure costs as a percentage of total quality costs for each of the five years. Does there appear to be a trend to this result? If so, speculate on what might have caused the trend.

b. Compute prevention costs and appraisal costs, each as a percentage of total costs, during each of the five years. Speculate on what the company's quality strategy appears to be.

c. Compute quality-sales indices and quality-cost indices for each of the five years. Is it possible to assess the effectiveness of the company's quality-management program from these index values?

d. List several examples of each quality-related cost—that is, prevention, appraisal, and internal and external failure—that might result from the production of parkas.

2-2. The Backwoods American company in Problem 2-1 produces approximately 20,000 parkas annually. The quality management program the company implemented was able to improve the average percentage of good parkas produced by 2% each year, beginning with 83% good-quality parkas in 2003. Only about 20% of poor-quality parkas can be reworked.

a. Compute the product yield for each of the five years.

b. Using a rework cost of $12 per parka, determine the manufacturing cost per good parka for each of the five years. What do these results imply about the company's quality management program?

2-3. The Omega Shoe Company manufactures a number of different styles of athletic shoes. Its biggest seller is the X-Pacer running shoe. In 2008 Omega implemented a quality-management program. The company's shoe production for the past three years and manufacturing costs are as follows:

	Year		
	2008	2009	2010
Units produced/input	32,000	34,600	35,500
Manufacturing cost	$278,000	291,000	305,000
Percent good quality	78%	83%	90%

Only one-quarter of the defective shoes can be reworked, at a cost of $2 apiece. Compute the manufacturing cost per good product for each of the three years and indicate the annual percentage increase or decrease resulting from the quality-management program.

2-4. The Colonial House Furniture Company manufactures four-drawer oak filing cabinets in six stages. In the first stage, the boards forming the walls of the cabinet are cut; in the second stage, the front drawer panels are woodworked; in the third stage, the boards are sanded and finished; in the fourth stage, the boards are cleaned, stained, and painted with a clear finish; in the fifth stage, the hardware for pulls, runners, and fittings is installed; and in the final stage, the cabinets are assembled. Inspection occurs at each stage of the process, and the average percentages of good-quality units are as follows:

Stage	Average Percentage Good Quality
1	87%
2	91%
3	94%
4	93%
5	93%
6	96%

The cabinets are produced in weekly production runs with a product input for 300 units.

a. Determine the weekly product yield of good-quality cabinets.

b. What would weekly product input have to be in order to achieve a final weekly product yield of 300 cabinets?

2-5. The Backwoods American company operates a telephone order system for a catalogue of its outdoor clothing products. The catalogue orders are processed in three stages. In the first stage, the telephone operator enters the order into the computer; in the second stage, the items are secured and batched in the warehouse; and in the final stage, the ordered products are packaged. Errors can be made in orders at any of these stages, and the average percentage of errors that occurs at each stage are as follows.

Stage	% Errors
1	12%
2	8%
3	4%

If an average of 320 telephone orders are processed each day, how many errorless orders will result?

2-6. The total processing cost for producing the X-Pacer running shoe in Problem 2-5 is $18. The Omega Shoe Company starts production of 650 pairs of the shoes weekly, and the average weekly yield is 90%, with 10% defective shoes. One quarter of the defective shoes can be reworked at a cost of $3.75.

a. Compute the quality-productivity ratio (QPR).

b. Compute the QPR if the production rate is increased to 800 pairs of shoes per week.

c. Compute the QPR if the processing cost is reduced to $16.50 and the rework cost to $3.20.

d. Compute the QPR if the product yield is increased to 93% good quality.

2-7. Airphone, Inc., manufactures cellular telephones at a processing cost of $47 per unit. The company produces an average of 250 phones per week and has a yield of 87% good-quality phones, resulting in 13% defective phones, all of which can be reworked. The cost of reworking a defective telephone is $16.

a. Compute the quality-productivity ratio (QPR).

b. Compute the QPR if the company increased the production rate to 320 phones per week while reducing the processing cost to $42, reducing the rework cost to $12, and increasing the product yield of good-quality telephones to 94%.

2-8. For the Medtek Company in Example 2.1, determine the break-even point (in sales) and draw the break-even diagram for both cases described in the example—with defects and without. (Refer to Chapter 6, for a description of break-even analysis.) Discuss the significance of the difference between the two break-even points.

2-9. The Blue Parrot is an expensive restaurant in midtown open only for dinner. Entrees are set at a fixed price of $42. In a typical month, the restaurant will serve 3,600 entrees. Monthly variable costs are $61,200, and fixed costs are $31,000 per month. Customers or waiters send back 8% of the entrees because of a defect, and they must be prepared again; they cannot be reworked. The restaurant owners hired a qualified Black Belt to undertake a Six Sigma project at the restaurant to eliminate all defects in the preparation of the entrees (i.e., 3.4 DPMO). Compare the profit in both situations, with and without defects, and indicate both the percentage decrease in variable costs and the percentage increase in profits following the Six Sigma project. Assuming that the restaurant paid the Black Belt $25,000 to achieve zero defects, and the restaurant owners plan to amortize this payment over a three-year period (as a fixed cost), what is the restaurant return on its investment (without applying an interest rate)? Discuss some other aspects of quality improvement at the restaurant that might result from the Six Sigma project.

2-10. A Black Belt has identified the following key input (X) and output (Y) variables for the process of laundering your clothes in your washing machine at home:

Input (X) Variables	Output (Y) Variables
Sort laundry	Clothes clean
Cycle	Clothes not damaged
Wash temperature	Colors okay
Rinse temperature	Lint free
Stain treatment	Stains removed
Load size	Smell fresh/no odors
Fabric softener	
Detergent	
Bleach	
Type of washer	

Develop a cause-and-effect diagram for this process of washing clothes. Next develop a cause-and-effect matrix and use your own insight and judgment about the process to rank and weight the output (*Y*) variables, assign a numerical score to each *X-Y* combination, develop overall scores for each *X* variable, and then rank the *X* variables in terms of importance.

2-11. A retail website sells a variety of products including clothes, electronics, furniture, sporting goods, books, video games, CDs and DVDs, among other items. An average customer order is $47. Weekly total variable costs are $365,000 and weekly fixed costs are $85,000. The company averages 18,400 orders per week and 12% of all orders are returned for a variety of reasons besides the customer not liking the product, including product misinformation on the website, errors in fulfilling the order, incomplete orders, defective product, breakage, etc. Thirty percent of all returned orders are turned around and refilled correctly per the customer's desire, but at a cost (for handling, packaging, and mailing) of $8 per order, while the remaining 70% of returned orders are lost. In addition, it is estimated that half of the customers associated with lost orders will not return to the website at a cost of $15 per order. Determine the weekly cost of poor quality for the website. The company can implement a quality improvement program for $800,000 a year that will reduce the percentage of returned orders to 2%; should the company invest in the program? How should the company address its quality problem, i.e., what processes does it likely need to improve? Why would zero defects not eliminate returned orders?

CASE STUDY

Quality Control and Yield at China Technology Ltd.

China Technology Ltd. Is a high-technology research and development firm which also manufactures and distributes its cell phones through various distribution outlets. The high technology industry is an extremely completive market, especially the cell phone industry which must compete with the global suppliers.

Cell phones have a very short life cycle as consumers continually require newer features and capabilities. Style, user friendliness, and high quality are minimum consumer bars which China Technology Ltd. must meet to remain competitive in the market place.

Recently China Technology Ltd. has seen an increasing rate of defects in their highly popular Dual SIM Mobile Phone, TV and JAVA product. An analysis of the returned products and consumer complaints indicates that the keyboard S and A keys are sticking so when one or the other key is pressed the other key is entered as well.

The keyboards are manufactured in a three-stage process. The following table identifies the individual stages and percent good and percent rework at each stage. China Technology Ltd. has identified that the keyboard defect occurs during stage 1. At this stage the individual key mounting location is determined. The keyboard printed circuit board machine is failing to maintain the correct distance between the S and A key locations.

Until a new key board manufacturing machine can be installed China Technology Ltd. must deliver 5,000 new units per month that will function correctly. Subsequent testing can ensure that no bad units are shipped. How many input units are required to achieve a monthly output yield of 5,000 units?

Assembly Stage	Average Percentage Good Quality	Average Percentage Reworked
1	97%	15%
2	98%	55%
3	96%	75%

REFERENCES

Crosby, P. B. *Quality is Free*. New York: McGraw-Hill, 1979.

Deming, W. E. *Out of the Crisis*. Cambridge, MA: MIT Center for Advanced Engineering Study, 1986.

Evans, J. R., and W. M. Lindsay. *The Management and Control of Quality*. 3rd ed. St. Paul, MN: West, 1996.

Feigenbaum, A. V. *Total Quality Control*. 3rd ed. New York: McGraw-Hill, 1983.

Garvin, D. A. *Managing Quality*. New York: Free Press/Macmillan, 1988.

Ishikawa, K. *Guide to Quality Control*. 2nd ed. White Plains, NY: Kraus International Publications, 1986.

Juran, J. M. *Juran on Planning for Quality*. New York: Free Press/Macmillan, 1988.

Juran, J. M., and F. M. Gryna, Jr. *Quality Planning and Analysis*. 2nd ed. New York: McGraw-Hill, 1980.

Montgomery, D. C. *Introduction to Statistical Quality Control*. 2nd ed. New York: John Wiley, 1991.

Taguchi, G. *Introduction to Quality Engineering*. Tokyo: Asian Productivity Organization, 1986.

CHAPTER 3

Process Capability and Statistical Process Control

LEARNING OBJECTIVES

AFTER READING THIS CHAPTER, YOU WILL BE ABLE TO:

- Explain when and how to use statistical process control to ensure the quality of products and services.
- Discuss the rationale and procedure for constructing control charts.
- Utilize attribute control charts to determine if a process is in control.
- Utilize variable control charts to determine if a process is in control.
- Identify control chart patterns and describe appropriate data collection.
- Develop control charts using Excel and OM Tools.
- Assess the process capability of a process.

QUALITY CONTROL IN DENIM FABRIC PRODUCTION

Because of the importance of quality to denim jeans purchasers, process control techniques are employed at every stage of the denim jeans supply chain. One hundred percent inspection and process control results in both the removal of defects and the control and adjustment of machinery and processes to eliminate future defects.

In the typical denim fabric production process, each bale of cotton is inspected for handling and shipping damage. In a series of processes, the cotton fibers are blended, cleaned, disentangled, and aligned, and then elongated and twisted into yarn that is spun onto tubes. In each of these processes, fibers are inspected for length and damage, and the weight per unit length is closely monitored by sophisticated electronic systems. The yarn is tested and monitored with sensors to ensure the quality of physical attributes such as surface structure, visual appearance, and durability. Some of the yarn is used as filler and sent directly to weaving while some of the yarn is sent to a process called *warping*, where it is pulled together and wrapped in sheets of parallel strands around beams called warps, or condensed into ropes of yarn and wrapped around a beam called a *log.* These beams of yarn then go through a dyeing process.

The Indigo dyeing process traditionally used for denim is unique among all commercial dyeing methods, and it's one thing that gives denim its special appeal. The properties of Indigo dye account for the wide variety of color designs that are available for denim jeans. However, it's also temperamental and difficult to work with because it is insoluble in water and will not dye cotton fiber. As a result, it is combined with several chemicals to make it water-soluble and allow the outer layers of the cotton yarn to absorb the dye.

In the dyeing process, the yarn is dipped through a series of dye vats containing the chemically altered Indigo (or in some cases, artificially created Indigo). The yarn goes down into vats and then up and over rollers, where it oxidizes, and then back down into the vats. The number of times it is dipped and the concentration of the Indigo determine the deepness and darkness of the blue color. The variables inherent in the dyeing process from the chemicals and the machinery make it subject to a high level of possible variation, hence the need for very stringent process control techniques in order to ensure quality. Electronic instruments linked to the dye vats continuously monitor yarn color so the process can be automatically adjusted if variation enters the dyeing process and it goes out of normal control.

Denim fabric is produced by weaving two sets of yarns. The dyed warp yarn on beams is fed into the front of a loom, that separates the dyed yarn threads into alternating top and bottom layers, while the undyed filler yarn passes through these layers from the side (using projectiles or air jets) at right angles. This gives denim its familiar look where the blue threads show on the outside of your jeans and the undyed threads make the inside of the jeans look white. As the yarn becomes fabric and is collected on rolls, it is subjected to visual and mechanical inspection to find defects. Modern looms employ online microprocessors that transmit data to computers for quality control.

During weaving, the yarns are stretched beyond their natural length and as a result, the fabric can shrink as much as 15%. However, jeans manufacturers will generally only accept shrinkage up to around 3%. To prevent shrinkage, the fabric is *sanforized,* a chemical and mechanical process that fixes the length and width of the fabric so that it doesn't shrink during the subsequent cutting and sewing processes, or later, during wearing and washing the finished jeans. During this process, temperature, moisture, and compression are critical quality variables that must be tested and controlled. Before the finished fabric is packaged and shipped up the supply chain to the jeans producers, it is subjected to extensive quality inspection to check properties such as length and width, weight, shrinkage, stiffness, tensile and tear strength, and the color shade. It is also checked for any defects that might have occurred (and been missed) during all production processes, sometimes using sophisticated camera systems that continually photograph the front and back of the fabric to identify defects.

In this chapter, we will learn about the fundamentals of statistical process control (SPC) that companies use to monitor and test production processes so that they won't produce defects.

After World War II, W. E. Deming, the quality expert and consultant, was invited to Japan by the Japanese government to give a series of lectures on improving product reliability. This was probably the single most important event that started the Japanese toward a global quality revolution. These lectures were based on statistical quality control, and they became a cornerstone of the Japanese commitment to quality management.

A major topic in statistical quality control is *statistical process control*. **Statistical process control (SPC)** is a statistical procedure using control charts to see if any part of a production process is not functioning properly and could cause poor quality. SPC is used to inspect and measure the production process to see if it is varying from what it is supposed to be doing. If there is unusual or undesirable variability, the process is corrected so that defects will not occur. In this way, statistical process control is used to prevent poor quality before it occurs. It is such an important part of quality management that nearly all workers at all levels in companies committed to quality management are given extensive and continual training in SPC. Conversely, in many companies the reason cited for failure to achieve high quality is the lack of comprehensive training for employees in SPC methods. U.S. companies successful in quality management train employees in SPC methods and make extensive use of SPC for continuous process improvement.

The Basics of Statistical Process Control

Process control is achieved by taking periodic **samples** from the process and plotting these sample points on a chart, to see if the process is within statistical control limits. A sample can be a single item or a group of items. If a sample point is outside the limits, the process may be out of control, and the cause is sought so that the problem can be corrected. If the sample is within the control limits, the process continues without interference but with continued monitoring. In this way, SPC prevents quality problems by correcting the process before it starts producing defects.

No production process produces exactly identical items, one after the other. All processes contain a certain amount of variability that makes some variation between units inevitable. There are two reasons why a process might vary. The first is the inherent random variability of the process, which depends on the equipment and machinery, engineering, the operator, and the system used for measurement. This kind of variability is a result of natural occurrences. The other reason for variability is unique or special causes that are identifiable and can be corrected. These causes tend to be nonrandom and, if left unattended, will cause poor quality. These might include equipment that is out of adjustment, defective materials, changes in parts or materials, broken machinery or equipment, operator fatigue or poor work methods, or errors due to lack of training.

SPC IN QUALITY MANAGEMENT

Companies use SPC to see if their processes are in control—working properly. This requires that companies provide SPC training on a continuing basis that stresses that SPC is a tool individuals can use to monitor production or service process *for the purpose of making improvements*. Through the use of statistical process control, employees can be made responsible for quality in their area: to identify problems and either correct them or seek help in correcting them. By continually monitoring the production process and making improvements, the employee contributes to the goal of continuous improvement and few or no defects.

The first step in correcting the problem is identifying the causes. In Chapter 2 we described several quality-control tools used for identifying causes of problems, including brainstorming, Pareto charts, histograms, checksheets, quality circles, and fishbone (cause-and-effect) diagrams.

When an employee is unable to correct a problem, management typically initiates problem solving. This problem-solving activity may be within a group like a quality circle, or it may be less formal, including other employees, engineers, quality experts, and management. This group will brainstorm the problem to seek out possible causes. Alternatively, quality problems can be corrected through Six Sigma projects.

ALONG THE SUPPLY CHAIN

Using Sampling and Statistics to Analyze MillerCoors Distribution Network Performance

MillerCoors is a U.S. manufacturer of beer brands including Miller, Coors, Molson, and Blue Moon, operating 10 breweries with a network of over 500 distributors servicing over 700,000 retail accounts, including supermarkets, bars, and restaurants. All U.S. breweries are required by law (emanating from the repeal of prohibition) to use a three-tier distribution system with a wholesaler/distributor layer between the brewery and the retail customer. An advantage of this system is that the distributor has direct local contact with retailers, which can help them develop a locally engaged market strategy. However, the distribution network must also be efficient and cost effective in order to deliver the brewer's products to retailers fresh, timely and damage free.

MillerCoors collects data from its distributors for seven attributes, weighted according to business considerations—expired products, processes, product damage, in-house audits, incorrect product staging, quality certifications, and consumer complaints. Data are collected using facility inspections and retail account audits; the latter collected by visiting a sample of 15, 20, or 25 random retailers based on the size of the distributor. This results in over 6,000 of the brewer's national retail accounts being audited each year. These data are used to develop a performance ranking of distributors based on a scaled score of each of the seven quality attributes (computed by using the *z* value for a normal distribution). The final rankings are developed by multiplying each distributor's score by the weighting factors, and adding the seven attribute scores for each distributor, and then "curving" (like grades are curved in a class) the summed distributor scores to develop a systemwide comparison based on performance. One direct outcome of the evaluation process was discovering (using a process flow diagram) that there was excessive and inefficient package handling in the distribution system.

Identify another company with a national distribution network and discuss how it might use a similar sampling process to evaluate distributor's performance.

Source: Based on Tony Gojanovic and Ernie Jiminez, "Brewed Awakening, Beer Maker Uses Statistical Methods to Improve How Its Products Are Distributed," *Quality Progress* 43, no. 4 (April 2010): pp 38–44.

QUALITY MEASURES: ATTRIBUTES AND VARIABLES

The quality of a product or service can be evaluated using either an *attribute* of the product or service or a *variable measure*. An **attribute** is a product characteristic such as color, surface texture, cleanliness, or perhaps smell or taste. Attributes can be evaluated quickly with a discrete response such as good or bad, acceptable or not, or yes or no. Even if quality specifications are complex and extensive, a simple attribute test might be used to determine whether or not a product or service is defective. For example, an operator might test a light bulb by simply turning it on and seeing if it lights. If it does not, it can be examined to find out the exact technical cause for failure, but for SPC purposes, the fact that it is defective has been determined.

A **variable measure** is a product characteristic that is measured on a continuous scale such as length, weight, temperature, or time. For example, the amount of liquid detergent in a plastic container can be measured to see if it conforms to the company's product specifications. Or the time it takes to serve a customer at McDonald's can be measured to see if it is quick enough. Since a variable evaluation is the result of some form of measurement, it is sometimes referred to as a *quantitative* classification method. An attribute evaluation is sometimes referred to as a *qualitative* classification, since the response is not measured. Because it is a measurement, a variable classification typically provides more information about the product—the weight of a product is more informative than simply saying the product is good or bad.

SPC APPLIED TO SERVICES

Control charts have historically been used to monitor the quality of manufacturing processes. However, SPC is just as useful for monitoring quality in services. The difference is the nature of the "defect" being measured and monitored. Using Motorola's definition—*a failure to meet customer requirements in any product or service*—a defect can be an empty soap dispenser in a restroom or an error with a phone catalog order, as well as a blemish on a piece of cloth or a faulty tray on a DVD player. Control charts for service processes tend to use quality characteristics and measurements such as time and customer satisfaction (determined by surveys, questionnaires, or inspections). Following is a list of several different services and the quality characteristics for each that can be measured and monitored with control charts:

HOSPITALS: Timeliness and quickness of care, staff responses to requests, accuracy of lab tests, cleanliness, courtesy, accuracy of paperwork, speed of admittance and checkouts.

GROCERY STORES: Waiting time to check out, frequency of out-of-stock items, quality of food items, cleanliness, customer complaints, checkout register errors.

AIRLINES: Flight delays, lost luggage and luggage handling, waiting time at ticket counters and check-in, agent and flight attendant courtesy, accurate flight information, passenger cabin cleanliness and maintenance.

FAST-FOOD RESTAURANTS: Waiting time for service, customer complaints, cleanliness, food quality, order accuracy, employee courtesy.

CATALOG-ORDER COMPANIES: Order accuracy, operator knowledge and courtesy, packaging, delivery time, phone order waiting time.

INSURANCE COMPANIES: Billing accuracy, timeliness of claims processing, agent availability and response time.

WHERE TO USE CONTROL CHARTS

Most companies do not use control charts for every step in a process. Although that might be the most effective way to ensure the highest quality, it is costly and time consuming. In most manufacturing and service processes, there are clearly identifiable points where control charts should be used. In general, control charts are used at critical points in the process where historically the process has shown a tendency to go out of control, and at points where if the process goes out of control, it is particularly harmful and costly. For example, control charts are frequently used at the beginning of a process to check the quality of raw materials and parts, or supplies and deliveries for a service operation. If material and parts are bad to begin with, it is a waste of time and money to begin the production process with them. Control charts are also used before a costly or irreversible point in the process, after which the product is difficult to rework or correct; before and after assembly or painting operations that might cover defects; and before the outgoing final product or service is shipped or delivered.

Control Charts

Control charts are graphs that visually show if a sample is within statistical **control limits**. They have two basic purposes: to establish the control limits for a process and then to monitor the process to indicate when it is out of control. Control charts exist for attributes and variables; within each category there are several different types of control charts. We will present four commonly used control charts, two in each category: *p*-charts and *c*-charts for attributes and *mean* ($\bar{x}$) and *range* (*R*) control charts for variables. Even though these control charts differ in how they measure process control, they all have certain similar characteristics. They all look alike, with a line through the center of a graph that indicates the process average and lines above and below the center line that represent the upper and lower limits of the process, as shown in Figure 3.1.

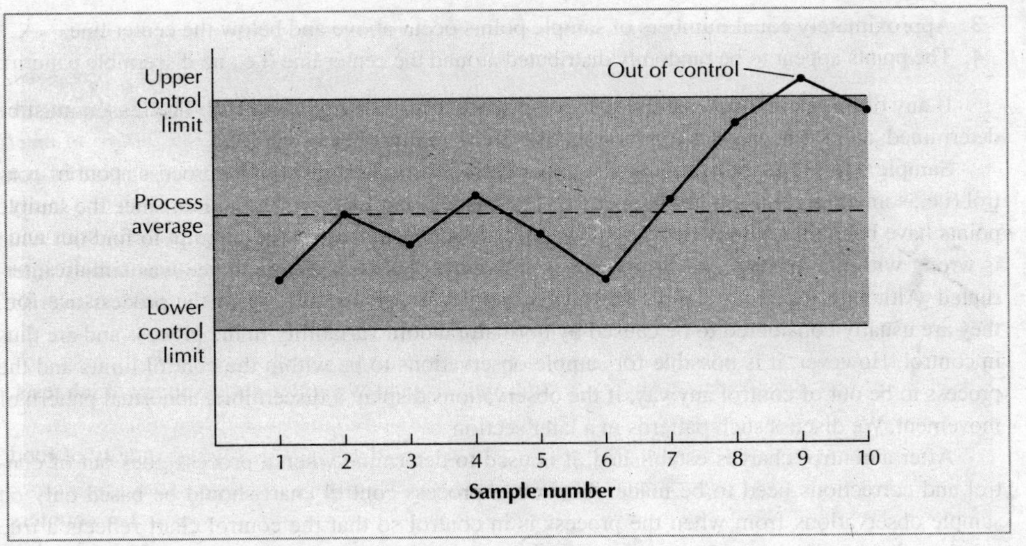

Figure 3.1
Process Control Chart

The formulas for conducting upper and lower limits in control charts are based on a number of standard deviations, z, from the process average (e.g., center line) according to a normal distribution. Occasionally, z is equal to 2.00 but most frequently is 3.00. A z value of 2.00 corresponds to an overall normal probability of 95%, and $z = 3.00$ corresponds to a normal probability of 99.73%.

The normal distribution in Figure 3.2 shows the probabilities corresponding to z values equal to 2.00 and 3.00 standard deviations (σ).

The smaller the value of z, the more narrow the control limits are and the more sensitive the chart is to changes in the production process. Control charts using $z = 2.00$ are often referred to as having 2-sigma (2σ) limits (referring to two standard deviations), whereas $z = 3.00$ means 3-sigma (3σ) limits.

Management usually selects $z = 3.00$ because if the process is in control, it wants a high probability that the sample values will fall within the control limits. In other words, with wider limits, management is less likely to (erroneously) conclude that the process is out of control when points outside the control limits are due to normal, random variations. Alternatively, wider limits make it harder to detect changes in the process that are not random and have an assignable cause. A process might change because of a nonrandom, assignable cause and be detectable with the narrower limits but not with the wider limits. However, companies traditionally use the wider control limits.

Each time a sample is taken, the mathematical average of the sample is plotted as a point on the control chart as shown in Figure 3.1. A process is generally considered to be in control if, for example,

1. There are no sample points outside the control limits.
2. Most points are near the process average (i.e., the center line), without too many close to the control limits.

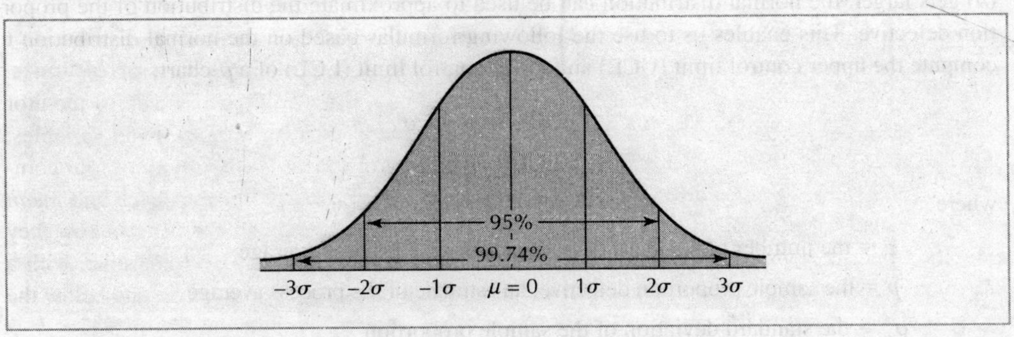

Figure 3.2
The Normal Distribution

3. Approximately equal numbers of sample points occur above and below the center line.
4. The points appear to be randomly distributed around the center line (i.e., no discernible pattern).

If any of these conditions are violated, the process may be *out of control*. The reason must be determined, and if the cause is not random, the problem must be corrected.

Sample 9 in Figure 3.1 is above the upper control limit, suggesting the process is out of control (i.e., something unusual has happened). The cause is not likely to be random since the sample points have been moving toward the upper limit, so management should attempt to find out what is wrong with the process and bring it back in control. Perhaps the employee was simply interrupted. Although the other samples display some degree of variation from the process average, they are usually considered to be caused by normal, random variability in the process and are thus in control. However, it is possible for sample observations to be within the control limits and the process to be out of control anyway, if the observations display a discernible, abnormal pattern of movement. We discuss such patterns in a later section.

After a control chart is established, it is used to determine when a process goes out of control and corrections need to be made. As such, a process control chart should be based only on sample observations from when the process is in control so that the control chart reflects a true benchmark for an in-control process. However, it is not known whether the process is in control until the control chart is first constructed. Therefore, when a control chart is first developed if the process is found to be out of control, the process should be examined and corrections made. A new center line and control limits should then be determined from a new set of sample observations. This "corrected" control chart is then used to monitor the process. It may not be possible to discover the cause(s) for the out-of-control sample observations. In this case, a new set of samples is taken, and a completely new control chart constructed. Or it may be decided simply to use the initial control chart, assuming that it accurately reflects the process variation.

Control Charts for Attributes

The quality measures used in *attribute control charts* are discrete values reflecting a simple decision criterion such as good or bad. A **p-chart** uses the proportion of defective items in a sample as the sample statistic; a **c-chart** uses the actual number of defects per item in a sample. A *p*-chart can be used when it is possible to distinguish between defective and nondefective items and to state the number of defectives as a percentage of the whole. In some processes, the proportion defective cannot be determined. For example, when counting the number of blemishes on a roll of upholstery material (at periodic intervals), it is not possible to compute a proportion. In this case a *c*-chart is required.

p-CHART

With a *p*-chart, a sample of *n* items is taken periodically from the production or service process, and the proportion of defective items in the sample is determined to see if the proportion falls within the control limits on the chart. Although a *p*-chart employs a discrete attribute measure (i.e., number of defective items) and thus is not continuous, it is assumed that as the sample size (n) gets larger, the normal distribution can be used to approximate the distribution of the proportion defective. This enables us to use the following formulas based on the normal distribution to compute the upper control limit (UCL) and lower control limit (LCL) of a *p*-chart:

$$\text{UCL} = \bar{p} + z\sigma_p$$
$$\text{LCL} = \bar{p} - z\sigma_p$$

where

z = the number of standard deviations from the process average

$\bar{p}$ = the sample proportion defective; an estimate of the process average

σ_p = the standard deviation of the sample proportion

The sample standard deviation is computed as

$$\sigma_p = \sqrt{\frac{\overline{p}(1 - \overline{p})}{n}}$$

where n is the sample size.

Example 3.1 demonstrates how a p-chart is constructed.

EXAMPLE 3.1

CONSTRUCTION OF A p-CHART

The Western Jeans Company produces denim jeans. The company wants to establish a p-chart to monitor the production process and maintain high quality. Western believes that approximately 99.74% of the variability in the production process (corresponding to 3-sigma limits, or $z = 3.00$) is random and thus should be within control limits, whereas 0.26% of the process variability is not random and suggests that the process is out of control.

The company has taken 20 samples (one per day for 20 days), each containing 100 pairs of jeans ($n = 100$), and inspected them for defects, the results of which are as follows.

Sample	Number of Defectives	Proportion Defectives
1	6	.06
2	0	.00
3	4	.04
4	10	.10
5	6	.06
6	4	.04
7	12	.12
8	10	.10
9	8	.08
10	10	.10
11	12	.12
12	10	.10
13	14	.14
14	8	.08
15	6	.06
16	16	.16
17	12	.12
18	14	.14
19	20	.20
20	18	.18
	200	

The proportion defective for the population is not known. The company wants to construct a p-chart to determine when the production process might be out of control.

(Continued)

SOLUTION

Since p is not known, it can be estimated from the total sample:

$$\bar{p} = \frac{\text{total defectives}}{\text{total sample observations}}$$

$$= \frac{200}{20(100)}$$

$$= 0.10$$

The control limits are computed as follows:

$$\text{UCL} = \bar{p} + z\sqrt{\frac{\bar{p}(1-\bar{p})}{n}}$$

$$= 0.10 + 3.00\sqrt{\frac{0.10(1-0.10)}{100}} = 0.190$$

$$\text{LCL} = \bar{p} - z\sqrt{\frac{\bar{p}(1-\bar{p})}{n}}$$

$$= 0.10 - 3.00\sqrt{\frac{0.10(1-0.10)}{100}} = 0.010$$

The p-chart, including sample points, is shown in the following figure:

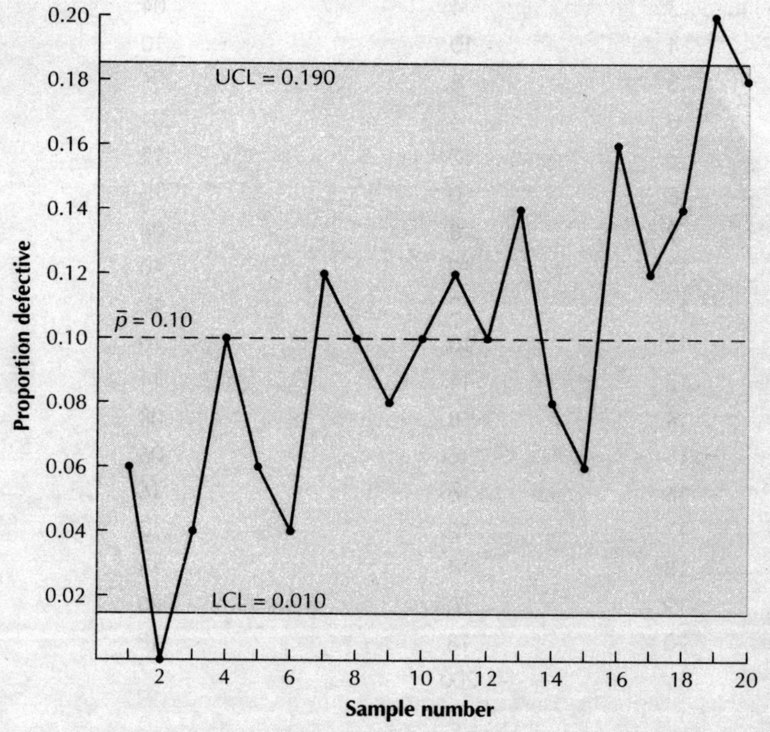

The process was below the lower control limits for sample 2 (i.e., during day 2). Although this could be perceived as a "good" result since it means there were very few defects, it might also suggest that something was wrong with the inspection process during that week that should be checked out. If there is no problem with the inspection process, then management would want to know what caused the quality of the process to improve. Perhaps "better" denim material came from a new supplier that week or a different operator was working.

The process was above the upper limit during day 19. This suggests that the process may not be in control and the cause should be investigated. The cause could be defective or maladjusted machinery, a problem with an operator, defective materials (i.e., denim cloth), or a number of other correctable problems. In fact, there is an upward trend in the number of defectives throughout the 20-day test period. The process was consistently moving toward an out-of-control situation. This trend represents a pattern in the observations, which suggests a nonrandom cause. If this was the actual control chart used to monitor the process (and not the initial chart), it is likely this pattern would have indicated an out-of-control situation before day 19, which would have alerted the operator to make corrections. Patterns are discussed in a separate section later in this chapter (page 96).

This initial control chart shows two out-of-control observations and a distinct pattern of increasing defects. Management would probably want to discard this set of samples and develop a new center line and control limits from a different set of sample values after the process has been corrected. If the pattern had not existed and only the two out-of-control observations were present, these two observations could be discarded, and a control chart could be developed from the remaining sample values.

Once a control chart is established based solely on natural, random variation in the process, it is used to monitor the process. Samples are taken periodically, and the observations are checked on the control chart to see if the process is in control.

c-CHART

A *c*-chart is used when it is not possible to compute a proportion defective and the actual number of defects must be used. For example, when automobiles are inspected, the number of blemishes (i.e., defects) in the paint job can be counted for each car, but a proportion cannot be computed, since the total number of possible blemishes is not known. In this case a single car is the sample. Since the number of defects per sample is assumed to derive from some extremely large population, the probability of a single defect is very small. As with the *p*-chart, the normal distribution can be used to approximate the distribution of defects. The process average for the *c*-chart is the mean number of defects per item, $\bar{c}$, computed by dividing the total number of defects by the number of samples. The sample standard deviation, σ_c, is $\sqrt{\bar{c}}$. The following formulas for the control limits are used:

$$\text{UCL} = \bar{c} + z\sigma_c$$

$$\text{LCL} = \bar{c} - z\sigma_c$$

EXAMPLE 3.2

CONSTRUCTION OF A C-CHART

The Ritz Hotel has 240 rooms. The hotel's housekeeping department is responsible for maintaining the quality of the rooms' appearance and cleanliness. Each individual housekeeper is responsible for an area encompassing 20 rooms. Every room in use is thoroughly cleaned and its supplies, toiletries, and so on are restocked each day. Any defects that the housekeeping staff notice that are not part of the normal housekeeping service are supposed to be reported to hotel maintenance. Every

(Continued)

room is briefly inspected each day by a housekeeping supervisor. However, hotel management also conducts inspection tours at random for a detailed, thorough inspection for quality-control purposes. The management inspectors not only check for normal housekeeping service defects like clean sheets, dust, room supplies, room literature, or towels, but also for defects like an inoperative or missing TV remote, poor TV picture quality or reception, defective lamps, a malfunctioning clock, tears or stains in the bedcovers or curtains, or a malfunctioning curtain pull. An inspection sample includes 12 rooms, that is, one room selected at random from each of the twelve 20-room blocks serviced by a housekeeper Following are the results from 15 inspection samples conducted at random during a one-month period:

Sample	Number of Defects
1	12
2	8
3	16
4	14
5	10
6	11
7	9
8	14
9	13
10	15
11	12
12	10
13	14
14	17
15	15
	190

The hotel believes that approximately 99% of the defects (corresponding to 3-sigma limits) are caused by natural, random variations in the housekeeping and room maintenance service, with 1% caused by nonrandom variability. It wants to construct a *c*-chart to monitor the housekeeping service.

SOLUTION

Because *c*, the population process average, is not known, the sample estimate, $\bar{c}$, can be used instead:

$$\bar{c} = \frac{190}{15} = 12.67$$

The control limits are computed using $z = 3.00$, as follows:

$$\text{UCL} = \bar{c} + z\sqrt{\bar{c}} = 12.67 + 3\sqrt{12.67} = 23.35$$

$$\text{LCL} = \bar{c} - z\sqrt{\bar{c}} = 12.67 - 3\sqrt{12.67} = 1.99$$

The resulting *c*-chart, with the sample points, is shown in the following figure:

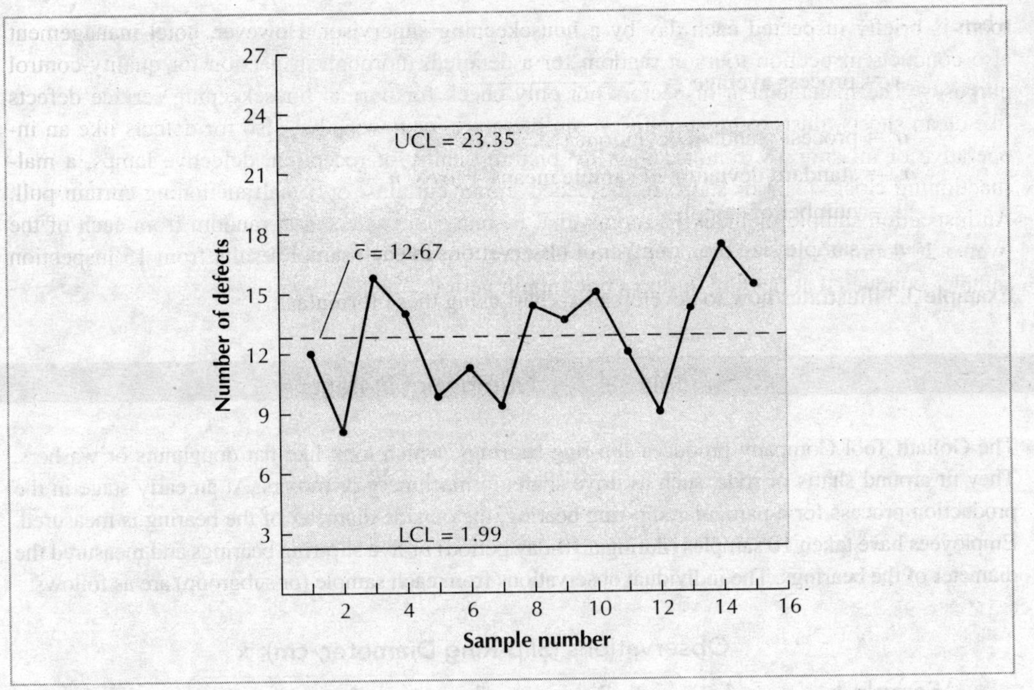

All the sample observations are within the control limits, suggesting that the room quality is in control. This chart would be considered reliable for monitoring the room quality in the future.

Control Charts for Variables

Variable control charts are used for continuous variables that can be measured, such as weight or volume. Two commonly used variable control charts are the range chart, or *R*-chart, and the mean chart, or $\bar{x}$-chart. A **range (*R*-) chart** reflects the amount of dispersion present in each sample; a **mean ($\bar{x}$-) chart** indicates how sample results relate to the process average or mean. These charts are normally used together to determine whether a process is in control.

MEAN ($\bar{x}$-) CHART

In a mean (or $\bar{x}$-) control chart, each time a sample of a group of items is taken from the process, the mean of the sample is computed and plotted on the chart. Each sample mean ($\bar{x}$) is a point on the control chart. The samples taken tend to be small, usually around 4 or 5. The center line of the control chart is the overall process average, that is, the mean of the sample means.

The $\bar{x}$-chart is based on the normal distribution. It can be constructed in two ways depending on the information that is available about the distribution. If the standard deviation of the distribution is known from past experience or historical data, then formulas using the standard deviation can be used to compute the upper and lower control limits. If the standard deviation is not known, then a table of values based on sample ranges is available to develop the upper and lower control limits. We will first look at how to construct an $\bar{x}$-chart when the standard deviation is known.

The formulas for computing the upper control limit (UCL) and lower control limit (LCL) are

$$\text{UCL} = \bar{\bar{x}} + z\sigma_{\bar{x}}$$

$$\text{LCL} = \bar{\bar{x}} - z\sigma_{\bar{x}}$$

where

$$\bar{\bar{x}} = \text{process average} = \frac{\bar{x}_1 + \bar{x}_2 + \cdots + \bar{x}_n}{k}$$

σ = process standard deviation

$\sigma_{\bar{x}}$ = standard deviation of sample means = $\sigma/\sqrt{n}$

k = number of samples

n = sample size (i.e., number of observations in each sample)

Example 3.3 illustrates how to develop an $\bar{x}$-chart using these formulas.

EXAMPLE 3.3

CONSTRUCTING AN $\bar{X}$-CHART

The Goliath Tool Company produces slip-ring bearings, which look like flat doughnuts or washers. They fit around shafts or rods, such as drive shafts in machinery or motors. At an early stage in the production process for a particular slip-ring bearing, the outside diameter of the bearing is measured. Employees have taken 10 samples (during a 10-day period) of five slip-ring bearings and measured the diameter of the bearings. The individual observations from each sample (or subgroup) are as follows:

	Observations (Slip-Ring Diameter, cm), x					
Sample k	1	2	3	4	5	$\bar{x}$
1	5.02	5.01	4.94	4.99	4.96	4.98
2	5.01	5.03	5.07	4.95	4.96	5.00
3	4.99	5.00	4.93	4.92	4.99	4.97
4	5.03	4.91	5.01	4.98	4.89	4.96
5	4.95	4.92	5.03	5.05	5.01	4.99
6	4.97	5.06	5.06	4.96	5.03	5.01
7	5.05	5.01	5.10	4.96	4.99	5.02
8	5.09	5.10	5.00	4.99	5.08	5.05
9	5.14	5.10	4.99	5.08	5.09	5.08
10	5.01	4.98	5.08	5.07	4.99	5.03
						50.09

From past historical data it is known that the process standard deviation is .08. The company wants to develop a control chart with 3-sigma limits to monitor this process in the future.

The process average is computed as

$$\bar{\bar{x}} = \frac{50.09}{10} = 5.01$$

The control limits are

$$\begin{aligned} \text{UCL} &= \bar{\bar{x}} + z\sigma_{\bar{x}} \\ &= 5.01 + 3(.08/\sqrt{5}) \\ &= 5.12 \end{aligned}$$

$$\begin{aligned} \text{LCL} &= \bar{\bar{x}} - z\sigma_{\bar{x}} \\ &= 5.01 - 3(.08/\sqrt{5}) \\ &= 4.90 \end{aligned}$$

None of the sample means ($\bar{x}$) falls outside these control limits, which indicates that the process is *in control* and this is an accurate control chart.

In the second approach to developing an $\bar{x}$-chart, the following formulas are used to compute the control limits:

$$UCL = \bar{\bar{x}} + A_2\bar{R}$$

$$LCL = \bar{\bar{x}} - A_2\bar{R}$$

where $\bar{\bar{x}}$ is the average of the sample means and $\bar{R}$ is the average range value. A_2 is a tabular value that is used to establish the control limits. Values of A_2 are included in Table 3.1. They were

TABLE 3.1 Factors for Determining Control Limits for $\bar{x}$- and *R*-Charts

Sample Size	Factor for $\bar{x}$ Chart	Factors for *R*-Chart	
n	A_2	D_3	D_4
2	1.88	0	3.27
3	1.02	0	2.57
4	0.73	0	2.28
5	0.58	0	2.11
6	0.48	0	2.00
7	0.42	0.08	1.92
8	0.37	0.14	1.86
9	0.34	0.18	1.82
10	0.31	0.22	1.78
11	0.29	0.26	1.74
12	0.27	0.28	1.72
13	0.25	0.31	1.69
14	0.24	0.33	1.67
15	0.22	0.35	1.65
16	0.21	0.36	1.64
17	0.20	0.38	1.62
18	0.19	0.39	1.61
19	0.19	0.40	1.60
20	0.18	0.41	1.59
21	0.17	0.43	1.58
22	0.17	0.43	1.57
23	0.16	0.44	1.56
24	0.16	0.45	1.55
25	0.15	0.46	1.54

developed specifically for determining the control limits for $\bar{x}$-charts and are comparable to three-standard deviation (3σ) limits. These table values are frequently used to develop control charts.

EXAMPLE 3.4

AN $\bar{X}$-CHART

The Goliath Tool Company desires to develop an $\bar{x}$-chart using table values. The sample data collected for this process with ranges is shown in the following table.

	Observations (Slip-Ring Diameter, cm), x						
Sample *k*	1	2	3	4	5	$\bar{x}$	R
1	5.02	5.01	4.94	4.99	4.96	4.98	0.08
2	5.01	5.03	5.07	4.95	4.96	5.00	0.12
3	4.99	5.00	4.93	4.92	4.99	4.97	0.08
4	5.03	4.91	5.01	4.98	4.89	4.96	0.14
5	4.95	4.92	5.03	5.05	5.01	4.99	0.13
6	4.97	5.06	5.06	4.96	5.03	5.01	0.10
7	5.05	5.01	5.10	4.96	4.99	5.02	0.14
8	5.09	5.10	5.00	4.99	5.08	5.05	0.11
9	5.14	5.10	4.99	5.08	5.09	5.08	0.15
10	5.01	4.98	5.08	5.07	4.99	5.03	0.10
						50.09	1.15

The company wants to develop an $\bar{x}$-chart to monitor the process.

SOLUTION

$\bar{R}$ is computed by first determining the range for each sample by computing the difference between the highest and lowest values as shown in the last column in our table of sample observations. These ranges are summed and then divided by the number of samples, ***k***, as follows:

$$\bar{R} = \frac{\sum R}{k} = \frac{1.15}{10} = 0.115$$

$\bar{\bar{x}}$ is computed as follows:

$$\bar{\bar{x}} = \frac{\sum \bar{x}}{k} = \frac{50.09}{10} = 5.01 \text{ cm}$$

Using the value of $A_2 = 0.58$ for $n = 5$ from Table 3.1 and $\bar{R} = 0.115$, we compute the control limits as

$$\text{UCL} = \bar{\bar{x}} + A_2\bar{R}$$
$$= 5.01 + (0.58)(0.115) = 5.08$$

$$\text{LCL} = \bar{\bar{x}} - A_2\bar{R}$$
$$= 5.01 - (0.58)(0.115) = 4.94$$

The $\bar{x}$-chart defined by these control limits is shown in the following figure. Notice that the process is on the UCL for sample 9; in fact, samples 4 to 9 show an upward trend. This would suggest that the process variability is subject to nonrandom causes and should be investigated.

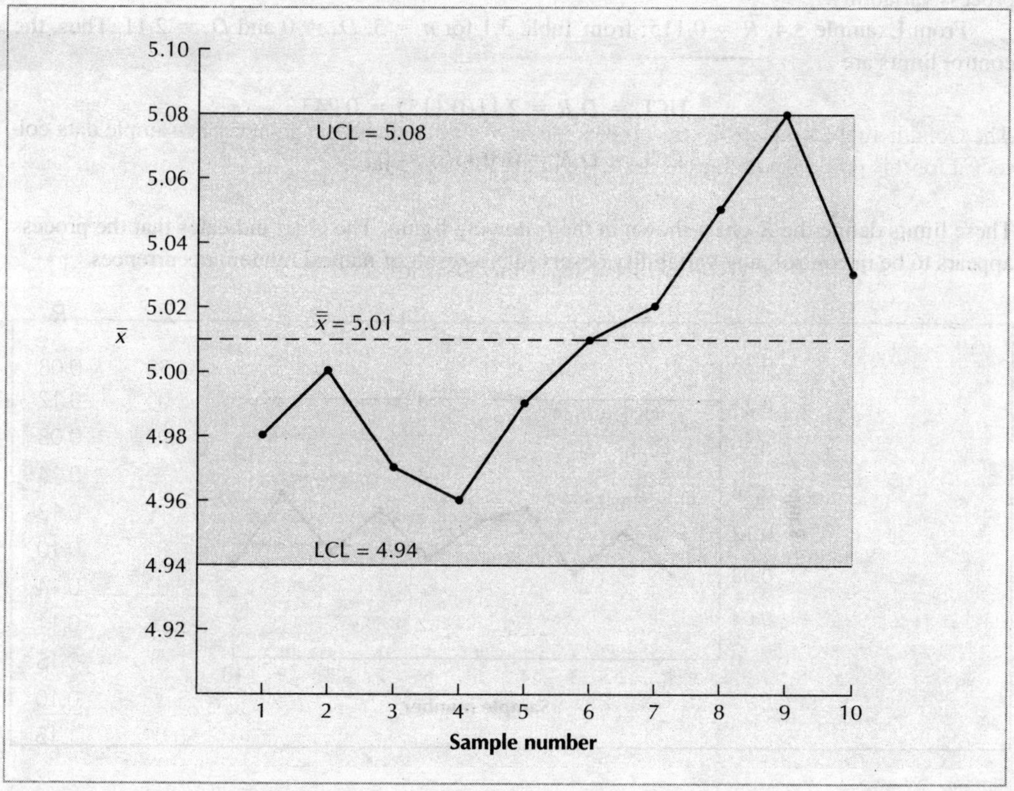

RANGE (R-) CHART

In an R-chart, the **range** is the difference between the smallest and largest values in a sample. This range reflects the process variability instead of the tendency toward a mean value. The formulas for determining control limits are

$$\text{UCL} = D_4\bar{R}$$

$$\text{LCL} = D_3\bar{R}$$

$\bar{R}$ is the average range (and center line) for the samples,

$$\bar{R} = \frac{\sum R}{k}$$

where

R = range of each sample

k = number of samples (subgroups)

D_3 and D_4 are table values like A_2 for determining control limits that have been developed based on range values rather than standard deviations. Table 3.1 also includes values for D_3 and D_4 for sample sizes up to 25.

EXAMPLE 3.5

CONSTRUCTING AN *R*-CHART

The Goliath Tool Company from Examples 3.3 and 3.4 wants to develop an *R*-chart to control process variability.

From Example 3.4, $\bar{R} = 0.115$; from Table 3.1 for $n = 5$, $D_3 = 0$ and $D_4 = 2.11$. Thus, the control limits are

$$\text{UCL} = D_4\bar{R} = 2.11(0.115) = 0.243$$

$$\text{LCL} = D_3\bar{R} = 0(0.115) = 0$$

These limits define the *R*-chart shown in the following figure. The chart indicates that the process appears to be in control; any variability observed is a result of natural random occurrences.

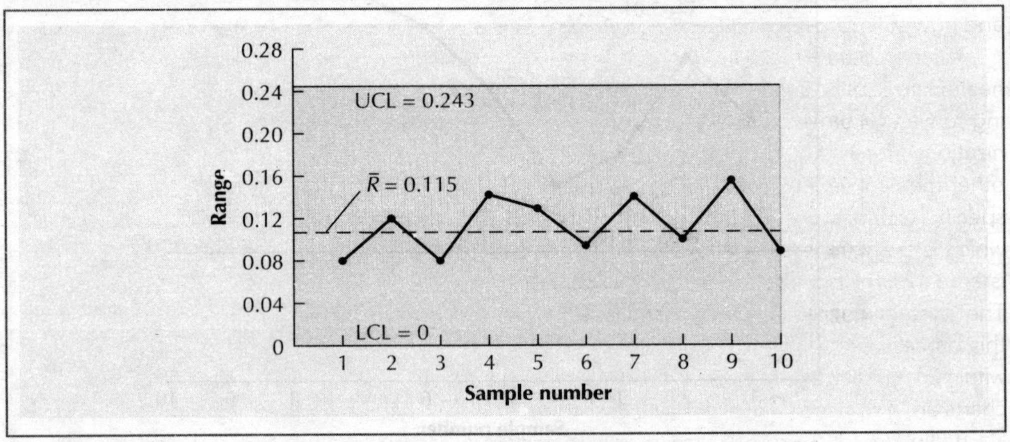

This example illustrates the need to employ the *R*-chart and the $\bar{x}$-chart together. The *R*-chart in this example suggests that the process is in control, since none of the ranges for the samples are close to the control limits. However, the $\bar{x}$-chart in Example 3.4 suggests that the process is not in control. In fact, the ranges for samples 8 and 10 were relatively narrow, whereas the means for these samples were relatively high. The use of both charts together provided a more complete picture of the overall process variability.

USING $\bar{X}$- AND *R*-CHARTS TOGETHER

The $\bar{x}$-chart is used with the *R*-chart under the premise that both the process average and variability must be in control for the process to be in control. This is logical. The two charts measure the process differently. It is possible for samples to have very narrow ranges, suggesting little process variability, but the sample averages might be beyond the control limits.

For example, consider two samples, the first having low and high values of 4.95 and 5.05 centimeters, and the second having low and high values of 5.10 and 5.20 centimeters. The range of both is 0.10 centimeters, but $\bar{x}$ for the first is 5.00 centimeters and $\bar{x}$ for the second is 5.15 centimeters. The two sample ranges might indicate the process is in control and $\bar{x} = 5.00$ might be okay, but $\bar{x} = 5.15$ could be outside the control limit.

Conversely, it is possible for the sample averages to be in control, but the ranges might be very large. For example, two samples could both have $\bar{x} = 5.00$ centimeters, but sample 1 could have a range between 4.95 and 5.05 ($R = 0.10$ centimeter) and sample 2 could have a range between 4.80 and 5.20 ($R = 0.40$ centimeter). Sample 2 suggests the process is out of control.

ALONG THE SUPPLY CHAIN

Using Control Charts for Improving Healthcare Quality

The National Health Service (NHS) in the United Kingdom makes extensive use of SPC charts to improve service delivery to patients. SPC charts are frequently developed using Excel spreadsheets. Employees throughout NHS attend a two-day training course where they learn about *X*- and *R*-charts and their application. They also learn about Deming's 14 points and principles of quality management and how to improve processes in their own operation.

The number of possible applications of SPC charts for a healthcare facility is very high, with many applications relating to waiting times (as is the case with many service organizations); for example, the time to see a doctor, nurse, or other medical staff member, or to get medical results. One specific example in the NHS is "door to needle" times, which is the time it takes after a heart attack patient is registered into the hospital to receive an appropriate injection. The systemwide goverment-mandated target value for this process is that 75% of heart patients receive treatment within 20 minutes of being received into the hospital. Control charts are also used to monitor administrative errors.

Bellin Health System is an integrated healthcare organization serving Green Bay, Wisconsin, and the surrounding region. It specializes in cardiac care and its 167-bed hospital is known as the region's heart center. In addition it operates a psychiatric center, 20 regional clinics, and a college of nursing. Bellin's quality management program is based on improving processes by identifying measures of success, setting goals for improvement that can be measured, applying Deming's PDCA cycle (see Chapter 2) for improving processes, and using statistical process control charts to monitor processes for stability and to see if improvement efforts are successful. Bellin has over 1,250 quality indicators reported monthly, quarterly, or annually, and over 90% are monitored with SPC charts. For example, one such quality indicator is for compliance with the Centers for Disease Control guidelines on healthcare hand hygiene, which Bellin measures across its entire system. The lack of hand hygiene is a leading cause of fatal hospital-borne infections, and thus a very important quality indicator. The quality resource department (QRD) at Bellin uses a *p*-chart to monitor hand hygiene for system nursing care, where the control measure is the portion of hand opportunities that meet the criteria divided by the total number of opportunities available to meet the criteria. Using SPC charts, Bellin was able to improve the hand hygiene process such that a 90% target level was acheived. Throughout the Bellin Health System, control charts are employed to identify special cause variations outside the norm in processes that require improvement. SPC has become an essential part of the continuous quality improvement program at Bellin used by all members of the organization to improve service and healthcare, and reduce costs.

Identify and discuss other applications of SPC charts in a healthcare facility that you think might improve processes.

Sources: Based on M. Owen, "From Sickness to Health," *Qualityworld* 29, issue 5 (August 2003): pp. 18–22; and C. O'Brien and S. Jennings, *Quality Progress* 41, no. 3 (March 2008): pp. 36–43.

It is also possible for an *R*-chart to exhibit a distinct downward trend in the range values, indicating that the ranges are getting narrower and there is less variation. This would be reflected on the $\bar{x}$-chart by mean values closer to the center line. Although this occurrence does not indicate that the process is out of control, it does suggest that some nonrandom cause is reducing process variation. This cause must be investigated to see if it is sustainable. If so, new control limits would need to be developed. Sometimes an $\bar{x}$-chart is used alone to see if a process is improving, perhaps toward a specific performance goal.

In other situations, a company might have studied and collected data for a process for a long time and already knows what the mean and standard deviation of the process are; all it wants to do is monitor the process average by taking periodic samples. In this case it would be appropriate to use the mean chart where the process standard deviation is already known, as shown in Example 3.3.

Control Chart Patterns

Even if a control chart indicates that a process is in control, it is possible that the sample variations within the control limits are not random. If the sample values display a consistent pattern, even within the control limits, it suggests that this pattern has a nonrandom cause that might warrant investigation. We expect the sample values to "bounce around" above and below the center line, reflecting the natural random variation in the process that will be present. However, if the sample values are consistently above (or below) the center line for an extended number of samples or if they move consistently up or down, there is probably a reason for this behavior; that is, it is not random. Examples of nonrandom patterns are shown in Figure 3.3.

A pattern in a control chart is characterized by a sequence of sample observations that display the same characteristics—also called a **run**. One type of pattern is a sequence of observations either above or below the center line. For example, three values above the center line followed by two values below the line represent two runs of a pattern. Another type of pattern is a sequence of sample values that consistently go up or go down within the control limits. Several tests are available to determine if a pattern is nonrandom or random.

One type of **pattern test** divides the control chart into three "zones" on each side of the center line, where each zone is one standard deviation wide. These are often referred to as 1-sigma, 2-sigma, and 3-sigma limits. The pattern of sample observations in these zones is then used to determine if any nonrandom patterns exist. Recall that the formula for computing an

Figure 3.3
Control Chart Patterns

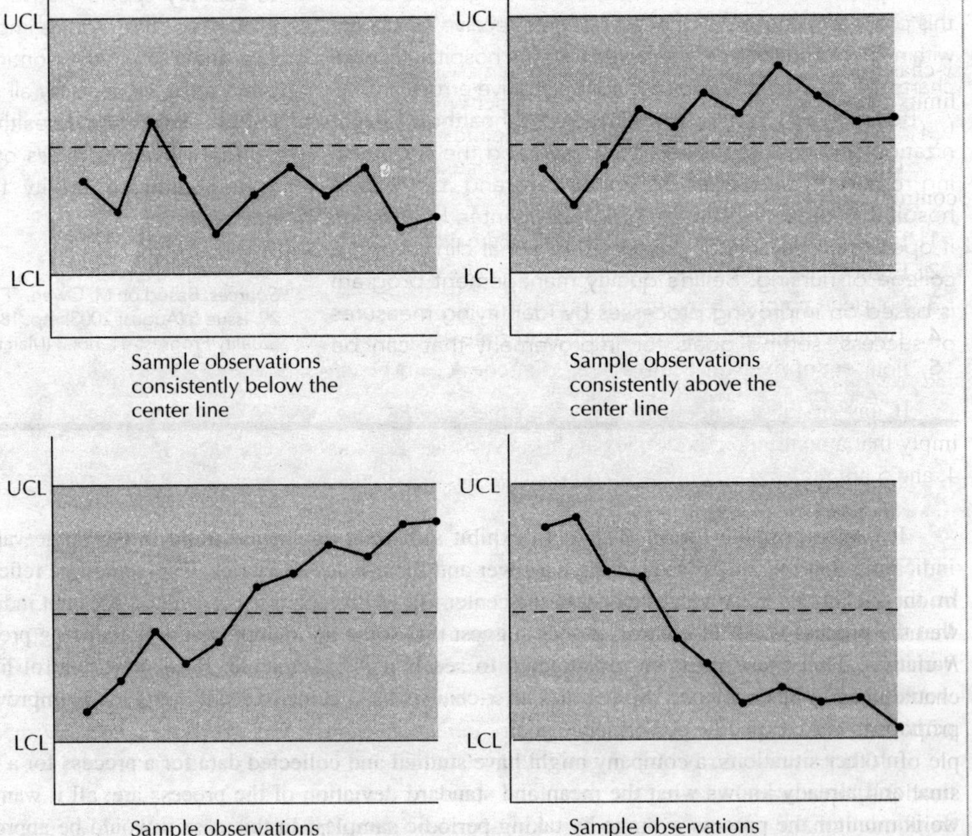

Sample observations consistently below the center line

Sample observations consistently above the center line

Sample observations consistently increasing

Sample observations consistently decreasing

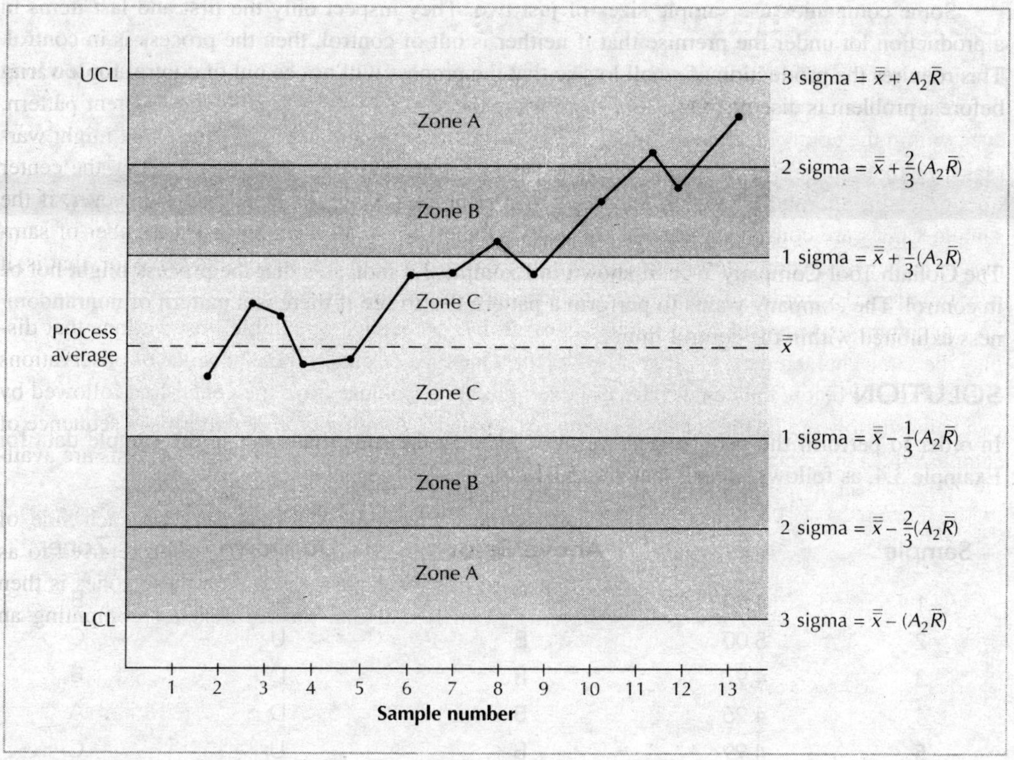

Figure 3.4

Zones for Pattern Tests

$\bar{x}$-chart uses A_2 from Table 3.1, which assumes 3 standard deviation control limits (or 3-sigma limits). Thus, to compute the dividing lines between each of the three zones for an $\bar{x}$-chart, we use $^1/_3A_2$. The formulas to compute these zone boundaries are shown in Figure 3.4.

There are five general guidelines associated with the zones for identifying patterns in a control chart where none of the observations are beyond the control limits:

1. Eight consecutive points on one side of the center line
2. Eight consecutive points up or down
3. Fourteen points alternating up or down
4. Two out of three consecutive points in zone A (on one side of the center line)
5. Four out of five consecutive points in zone A or B on one side of the center line

If any of these guidelines applied to the sample observations in a control chart, it would imply that a nonrandom pattern exists and the cause should be investigated. In Figure 3.4, rules 1, 4, and 5 are violated. Example 3.6 on the next page demonstrates how a pattern test is performed.

SAMPLE SIZE DETERMINATION

In our examples of control charts, sample sizes varied significantly. For p-charts and c-charts, we used sample sizes in the hundreds and as small as one item for a c-chart, whereas for $\bar{x}$- and R-charts we used samples of four or five. In general, larger sample sizes are needed for attribute charts because more observations are required to develop a usable quality measure. A population proportion defective of only 5% requires five defective items from a sample of 100. But, a sample of 10 does not even permit a result with 5% defective items. Variable control charts require smaller sample sizes because each sample observation provides usable information—for example, weight, length, or volume. After only a few sample observations (as few as two), it is possible to compute a range or a sample average that reflects the sample characteristics. It is desirable to take as few sample observations as possible, because they require the operator's time to take them.

Some companies use sample sizes of just two. They inspect only the first and last items in a production lot under the premise that if neither is out of control, then the process is in control. This requires the production of small lots so that the process will not be out of control for too long before a problem is discovered.

EXAMPLE 3.6

PERFORMING A PATTERN TEST

The Goliath Tool Company $\bar{x}$-chart shown in Example 3.4 indicates that the process might not be in control. The company wants to perform a pattern test to see if there is a pattern of nonrandomness exhibited within the control limits.

SOLUTION

In order to perform the pattern test, we must identify the runs that exist in the sample data for Example 3.4, as follows. Recall that $\bar{\bar{x}} = 5.01$ cm.

Sample	$\bar{x}$	Above/Below	Up/Down	Zone
1	4.98	B	—	B
2	5.00	B	U	C
3	4.97	B	D	B
4	4.96	B	D	A
5	4.99	B	U	C
6	5.01	—	U	C
7	5.02	A	U	C
8	5.05	A	U	B
9	5.08	A	U	A
10	5.03	A	D	B

No pattern rules appear to be violated.

Size may not be the only consideration in sampling. It may also be important that the samples come from a homogeneous source so that if the process is out of control, the cause can be accurately determined. If production takes place on either one of two machines (or two sets of machines), mixing the sample observations between them makes it difficult to ascertain which operator or machine caused the problem. If the production process encompasses more than one shift, mixing the sample observation between shifts may make it more difficult to discover which shift caused the process to move out of control.

SPC with Excel and OM Tools

Computer software and spreadsheet packages are available that perform statistical quality control analysis, including the development of process control charts. We will demonstrate how to develop a statistical process control chart on the computer using Excel and OM Tools. The Excel spreadsheet in Exhibit 3.1 shows the data for Example 3.1 in which we constructed a p-chart to monitor the production process for denim jeans at the Western Jeans Company. The values for $\bar{p}$, UCL, and LCL have been computed using formulas embedded in cells I4, I5, and I6. To construct our control chart, it is necessary to enter the values for the control chart mean ($\bar{p}$) and upper and

EXHIBIT 3.1

EXCEL FILE

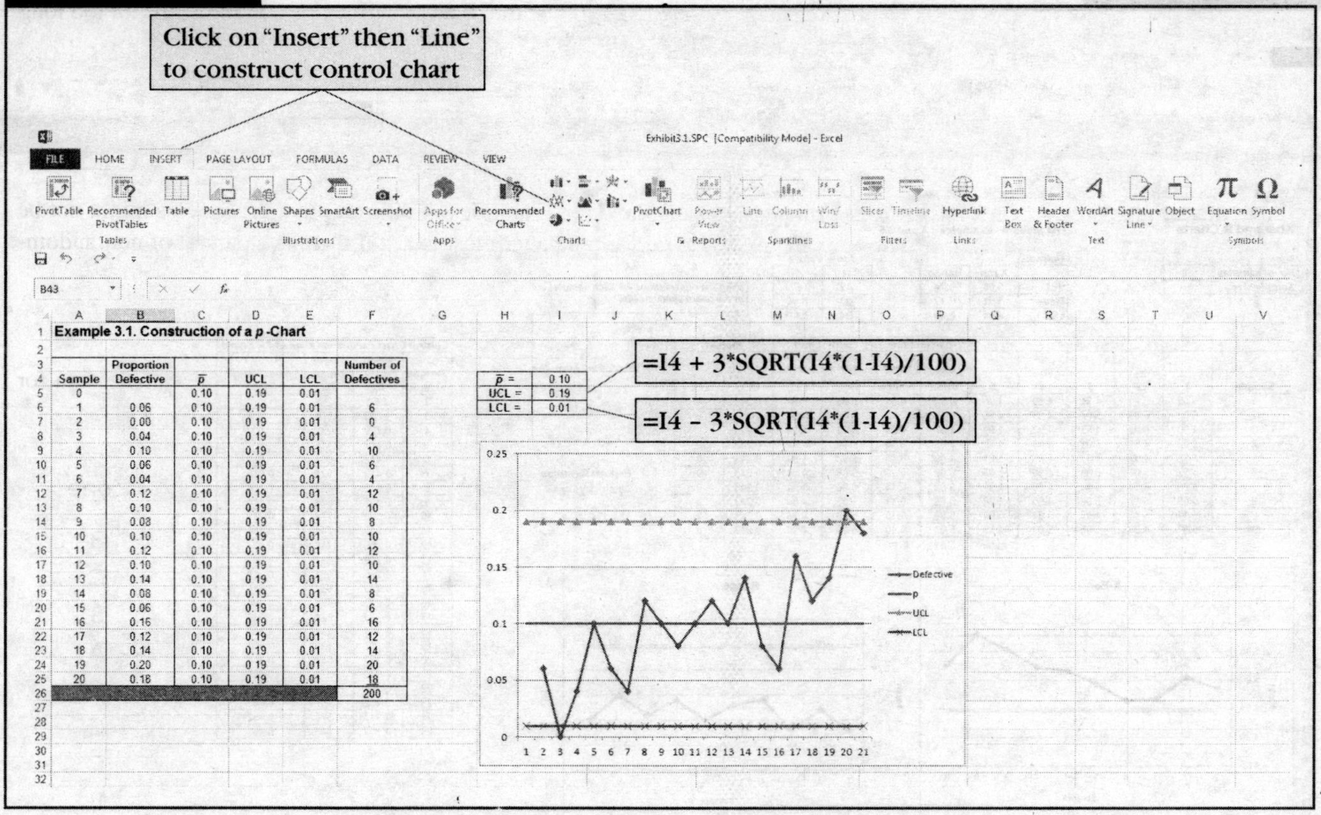

Sample	Proportion Defective	$\bar{p}$	UCL	LCL	Number of Defectives
0		0.10	0.19	0.01	
1	0.06	0.10	0.19	0.01	6
2	0.00	0.10	0.19	0.01	0
3	0.04	0.10	0.19	0.01	4
4	0.10	0.10	0.19	0.01	10
5	0.06	0.10	0.19	0.01	6
6	0.04	0.10	0.19	0.01	4
7	0.12	0.10	0.19	0.01	12
8	0.10	0.10	0.19	0.01	10
9	0.08	0.10	0.19	0.01	8
10	0.10	0.10	0.19	0.01	10
11	0.12	0.10	0.19	0.01	12
12	0.10	0.10	0.19	0.01	10
13	0.14	0.10	0.19	0.01	14
14	0.08	0.10	0.19	0.01	8
15	0.06	0.10	0.19	0.01	6
16	0.16	0.10	0.19	0.01	16
17	0.12	0.10	0.19	0.01	12
18	0.14	0.10	0.19	0.01	14
19	0.20	0.10	0.19	0.01	20
20	0.18	0.10	0.19	0.01	18
					200

lower control limits (UCL and LCL) in columns B, C, D, and E for all 20 sample points. This will provide the data points to construct UCL and LCL lines on the control chart.

The Excel file for the example problem spreadsheet shown in Exhibit 3.1 is provided on the text website, as are all Excel exhibits in the text. These files can be easily accessed and downloaded for use. The exhibit spreadsheets can often be used as templates for solving end-of-chapter homework problems.

The control chart shown in the lower-right-hand corner of Exhibit 3.1 was constructed by clicking on the "Insert" tab on the toolbar at the top of the spreadsheet, then covering the data points **B4:E25**. The next step was to click on the "Charts" tab and select a line chart, then after clicking "OK," the chart in Exhibit 3.1 appeared.

Exhibit 3.2 shows the $\bar{x}$-chart and *R*-chart developed in Examples 3.4 and 3.5 using the "quality control" module from the OM Tools software. Notice that it is only necessary to input the sample data from the $\bar{x}$-chart example in order to develop both control charts.

Process Capability

Control limits are occasionally mistaken for tolerances; however, they are quite different things. Control limits provide a means for determining natural variation in a production process. They are statistical results based on sampling. **Tolerances** are design specifications reflecting customer requirements for a product. They specify a range of values above and below a designed target value (also referred to as the *nominal value*) within which product units must fall to be acceptable. For example, a bag of potato chips might be designed to have a net weight of 9.0 oz of chips with a tolerance of ±0.5 oz. The design tolerances are thus between 9.5 oz (the *upper specification limit*) and 8.5 oz (the *lower specification limit*). The packaging process must be capable of performing

EXHIBIT 3.2 OM TOOLS

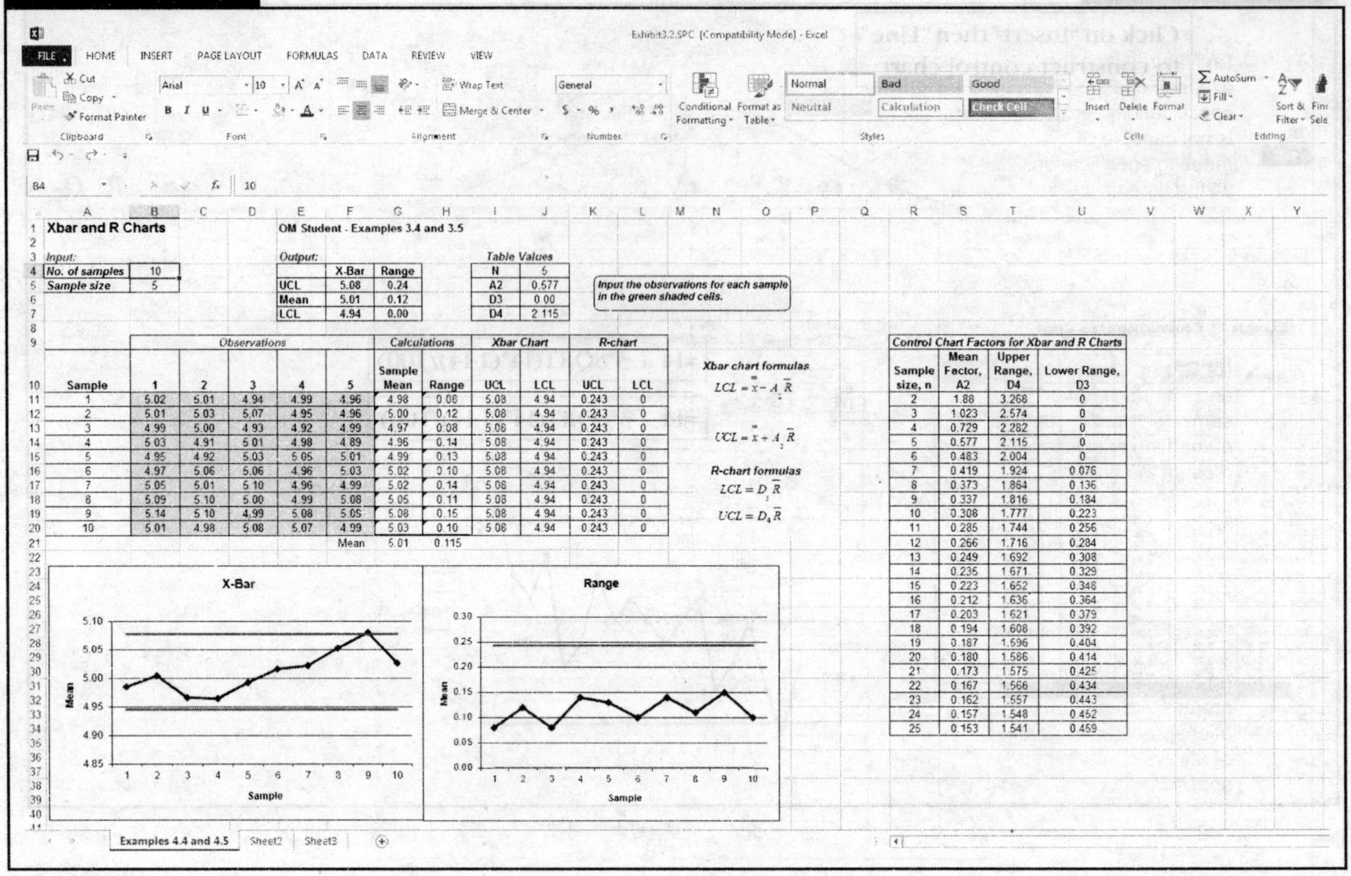

within these design tolerances or a certain portion of the bags will be defective, that is, underweight or overweight. Tolerances are not determined from the production process; they are externally imposed by the designers of the product or service. Control limits, on the other hand, are based on the production process, and they reflect process variability. They are a statistical measure determined from the process. It is possible for a process in an instance to be statistically "in control" according to control charts, yet the process may not conform to the design specifications. To avoid such a situation, the process must be evaluated to see if it can meet product specifications before the process is initiated, or the product or service must be redesigned.

Process capability refers to the natural variation of a process relative to the variation allowed by the design specifications. In other words, how capable is the process of producing acceptable units according to the design specifications? Process control charts are used for process capability to determine if an existing process is capable of meeting design specifications.

The three main elements associated with process capability are process variability (the natural range of variation of the process), the process center (mean), and the design specifications. Figure 3.5 shows four possible situations with different configurations of these elements that can occur when we consider process capability.

Figure 3.5*a* depicts the natural variation of a process, which is greater than the design specification limits. The process is not capable of meeting these specification limits. This situation will result in a large proportion of defective parts or products. If the limits of a control chart measuring natural variation exceed the specification limits or designed tolerances of a product, the process cannot produce the product according to specifications. The variation that will occur naturally, at random, is greater than the designed variation.

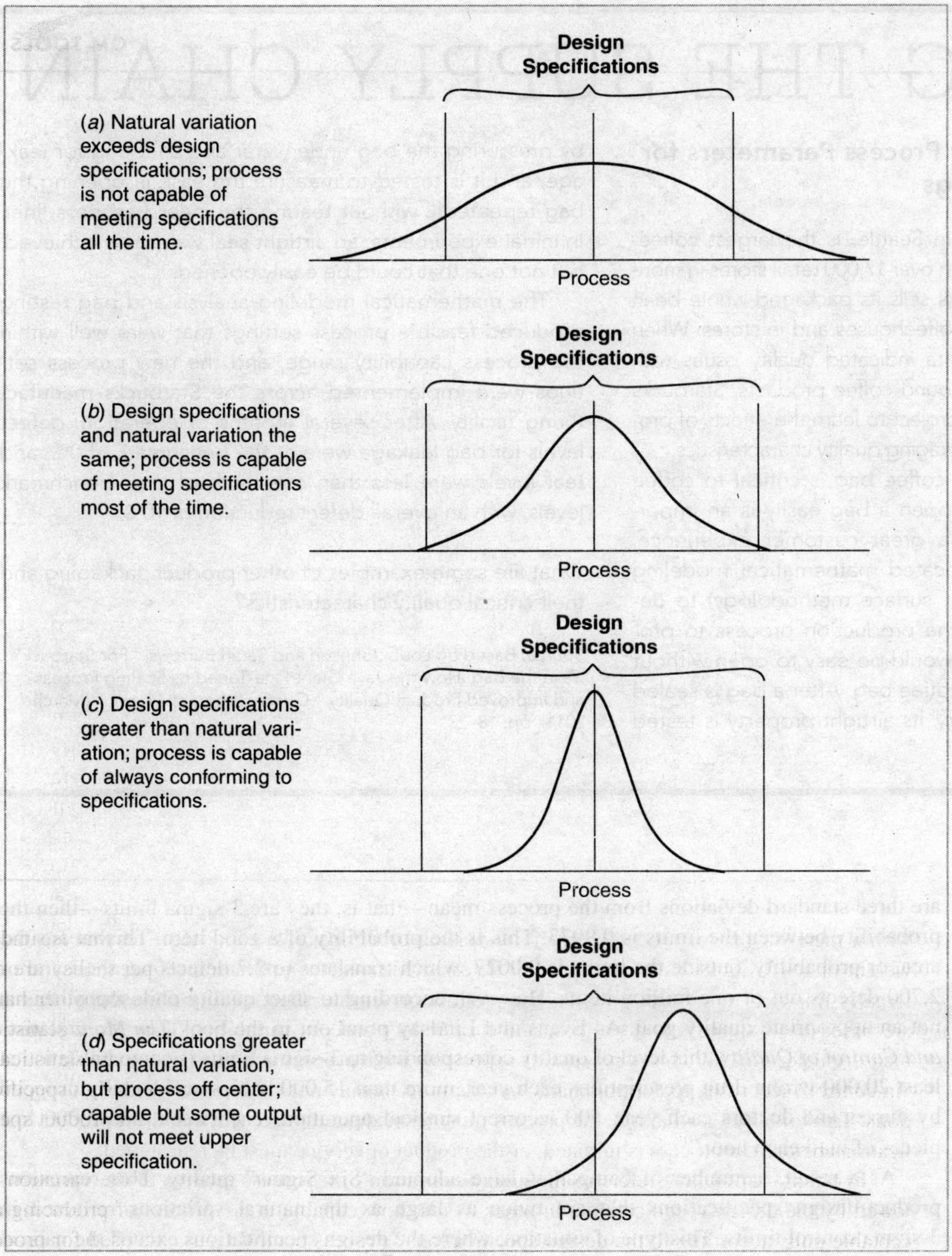

Figure 3.5

Process Capability

Parts that are within the control limits but outside the design specification must be scrapped or reworked. This can be very costly and wasteful. Alternatives include improving the process or redesigning the product. However, these solutions can also be costly. As such, it is important that process capability studies be done during product design, and before contracts for new parts or products are entered into.

Figure 3.5*b* shows the situation in which the natural control limits and specification limits are the same. This will result in a small number of defective items, the few that will fall outside the natural control limits due to random causes. For many companies, this is a reasonable quality goal. If the process distribution is normally distributed and the natural control limits

ALONG THE SUPPLY CHAIN

Determining Quality Process Parameters for Starbucks Coffee Bags

Starbucks, headquartered in Seattle, is the largest coffeehouse chain in the world with over 17,000 retail stores in more than 55 countries. Starbucks sells its packaged whole bean and ground coffees in its coffeehouses and in stores. When voice-of-customer (VoC) data indicated quality issues with the packaging of its one-pound coffee products, Starbucks engineers embarked on a project to learn the effects of process parameters on key packaging quality characteristics.

The airtight seal on a coffee bag is critical to coffee quality, but the ability to open a bag easily is an important factor in providing a great customer experience. Starbucks used a sophisticated mathematical modeling approach (called response surface methodology) to determine the settings for the production process to produce an airtight seal that would be easy to open without damaging the top of the coffee bag. After a bag is sealed with bag-sealing machinery, its airtight property is tested by pressuring the bag underwater and checking for leakage, and it is tested to measure the ease in opening the bag repeatedly without tearing the inner freshness liner. In initial experiments, an airtight seal was easily achieved, but not one that could be easily opened.

The mathematical modeling analysis and bag testing produced feasible process settings that were well within the process capability range, and the new process settings were implemented across the Starbucks manufacturing facility. After several months of operation, defect levels for bag leakage were at the benchmark of 0%, and tear levels were less than one-tenth of their benchmark levels, with an overall defect reduction of 90%.

What are some examples of other product packaging and their critical quality characteristics?

Source: Based on Louis Johnson and Sarah Burrows, "For Starbuck's It's in the Bag: How the Java Giant Fine-Tuned Its Sealing Process and Improved Product Quality," *Quality Progress* 44, no. 3 (March 2011): pp. 18–23.

are three standard deviations from the process mean—that is, they are 3-sigma limits—then the probability between the limits is 0.9973. This is the probability of a good item. This means the area, or probability, outside the limits is 0.0027, which translates to 2.7 defects per thousand or 2,700 defects out of one million items. However, according to strict quality philosophy, this is not an appropriate quality goal. As Evans and Lindsay point out in the book *The Management and Control of Quality*, this level of quality corresponding to 3-sigma limits is comparable to "at least 20,000 wrong drug prescriptions each year, more than 15,000 babies accidentally dropped by nurses and doctors each year, 500 incorrect surgical operations each week, and 2,000 lost pieces of mail each hour."[1]

As a result, a number of companies have adopted "Six Sigma" quality. This represents product-design specifications that are twice as large as the natural variations reflected in 3-sigma control limits. This type of situation, where the design specifications exceed the natural control limits, is shown graphically in Figure 3.5*c*. The company would expect that almost all products will conform to design specifications—as long as the process mean is centered on the design target. Statistically, Six Sigma corresponds to only 0.000 000 2% defects or 0.002 defective parts per million (PPM), which is only two defects per billion! However, when Motorola announced in 1989 that it would achieve Six Sigma quality in five years, they translated this to be 3.4 defects per million. How did they get 3.4 defects per million from 2 defects per billion? Motorola took into account that the process mean will not always exactly correspond to the design target; it might vary from the nominal design target by as much as 1.5 sigma (the scenario in Figure 3.5*d*), which translates to a Six Sigma defect rate of 3.4 defects per million.

[1]J. R. Evans and W. M. Lindsay, *The Management and Control of Quality*, 3rd ed. (Minneapolis: West, 1993), 602.

This value has since become the standard for Six Sigma quality in industry and business. Applying this same scenario of a 1.5-sigma deviation from the process mean to the more typical 3-sigma level used by most companies, the defect rate is not 2,700 defects per million, but 66,810 defects per million.

As indicated, Figure 3.5*d* shows the situation in which the design specifications are greater than the process range of variation; however, the process is off center. The process is capable of meeting specifications, but it is not because the process is not in control. In this case a percentage of the output that falls outside the upper design specification limit will be defective. If the process is adjusted so that the process center coincides with the design target (i.e., it is centered), then almost all of the output will meet design specifications.

Determining process capability is important because it helps a company understand process variation. If it can be determined how well a process is meeting design specifications, and thus what the actual level of quality is, then steps can be taken to improve quality. Two measures used to quantify the capability of a process, that is, how well the process is capable of producing according to design specifications, are the capability ratio (C_p) and the capability index (C_{pk}).

PROCESS CAPABILITY MEASURES

One measure of the capability of a process to meet design specifications is the *process capability ratio* (C_p). It is defined as the ratio of the range of the design specifications (the tolerance range) to the range of the process variation, which for most firms is typically $\pm 3\sigma$ or 6σ.

$$C_p = \frac{\text{tolerance range}}{\text{process range}}$$

$$= \frac{\text{upper specification limit} - \text{lower specification limit}}{6\sigma}$$

If C_p is less than 1.0, the process range is greater than the tolerance range, and the process is not capable of producing within the design specifications all the time. This is the situation depicted in Figure 3.5*a*. If C_p equals 1.0, the tolerance range and the process range are virtually the

EXAMPLE 3.7

COMPUTING C_p

The Munchies Snack Food Company packages potato chips in bags. The net weight of the chips in each bag is designed to be 9.0 oz, with a tolerance of ±0.5 oz. The packaging process results in bags with an average net weight of 8.80 oz and a standard deviation of 0.12 oz. The company wants to determine if the process is capable of meeting design specifications.

SOLUTION

$$C_p = \frac{\text{upper specification limit} - \text{lower specification limit}}{6\sigma}$$

$$= \frac{9.5 - 8.5}{6(0.12)}$$

$$= 1.39$$

Thus, according to this process capability ratio of 1.39, the process is capable of being within design specifications.

same—the situation shown in Figure 3.5*b*. If C_p is greater than 1.0, the tolerance range is greater than the process range—the situation depicted in Figure 3.5*c*. Thus, companies would logically desire a C_p equal to 1.0 or greater, since this would indicate that the process is capable of meeting specifications.

A second measure of process capability is the *process capability index* (C_{pk}). The C_{pk} differs from the C_p in that it indicates if the process mean has shifted away from the design target, and in which direction it has shifted—that is, if it is off center. This is the situation depicted in Figure 3.5*d*. The process capability index specifically measures the capability of the process relative to the upper and lower specifications.

$$C_{pk} = \text{minimum}\left[\frac{\bar{\bar{x}} - \text{lower specification}}{3\sigma}, \frac{\text{upper specification} - \bar{\bar{x}}}{3\sigma}\right]$$

If the C_{pk} index is greater than 1.00, then the process is capable of meeting design specifications. If C_{pk} is less than 1.00, then the process mean has moved closer to one of the upper or lower design specifications, and it will generate defects. When C_{pk} equals C_p, this indicates that the process mean is centered on the design (nominal) target.

EXAMPLE 3.8

COMPUTING C_{PK}

Recall that the Munchies Snack Food Company packaged potato chips in a process designed for 9.0 oz of chips with a tolerance of ±0.5 oz. The packaging process had a process mean ($\bar{\bar{x}}$) of 8.80 oz and a standard deviation of 0.12 oz. The company wants to determine if the process is capable, and if the process mean is on or off center.

$$C_{pk} = \text{minimum}\left[\frac{\bar{\bar{x}} - \text{lower specification}}{3\sigma}, \frac{\text{upper specification} - \bar{\bar{x}}}{3\sigma}\right]$$

$$= \text{minimum}\left[\frac{8.80 - 8.50}{3(0.12)}, \frac{9.5 - 8.80}{3(0.12)}\right]$$

$$= \text{minimum}\,[0.83, 1.94]$$

$$= 0.83$$

Although the C_p of 1.39 computed in Example 3.7 indicated that the process is capable (it is within the design specifications), the C_{pk} value of 0.83 indicates the process mean is off center. It has shifted toward the lower specifications limit; that means underweight packages of chips will be produced. Thus, the company needs to take action to correct the process and bring the process mean back toward the design target.

PROCESS CAPABILITY WITH EXCEL AND OM TOOLS

Exhibit 3.3 shows the Excel solution screen for the computation of the process capability ratio and the process capability index for Examples 3.7 and 3.8. The formula for the process capability index in cell D16 is shown on the formula bar at the top of the screen.

Exhibit 3.4 shows the computation of the process capability ratio and the process capability index for Example 3.7 and 3.8 using the "quality control" module from the OM Tools software.

EXHIBIT 3.3

EXCEL FILE

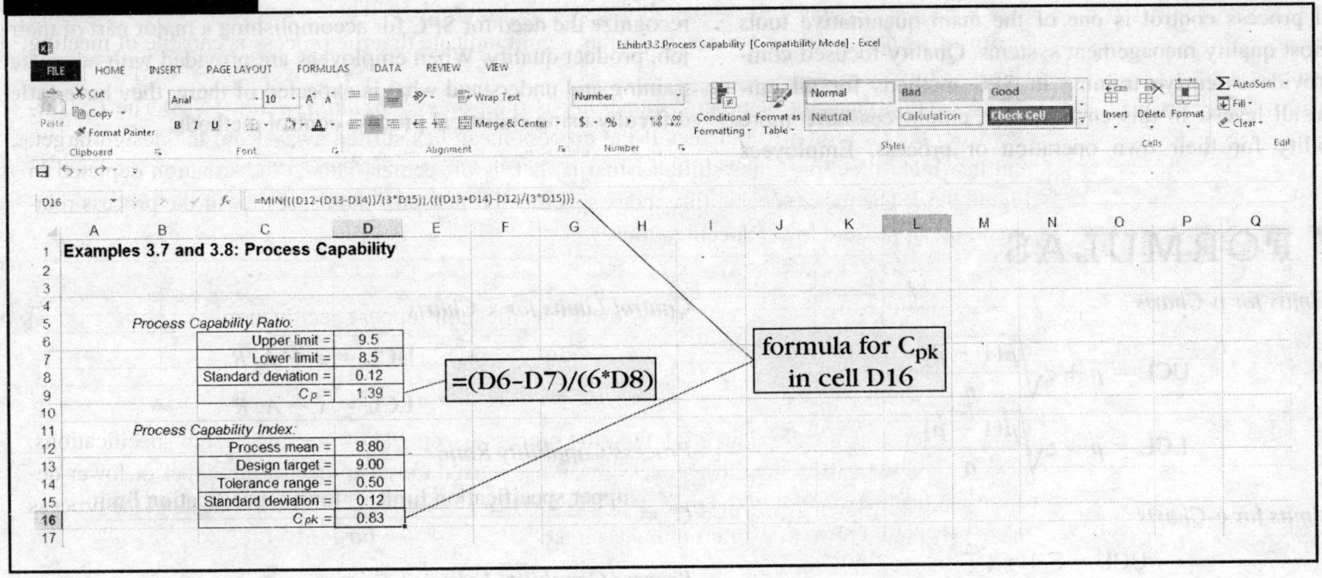

EXHIBIT 3.4

OM TOOLS

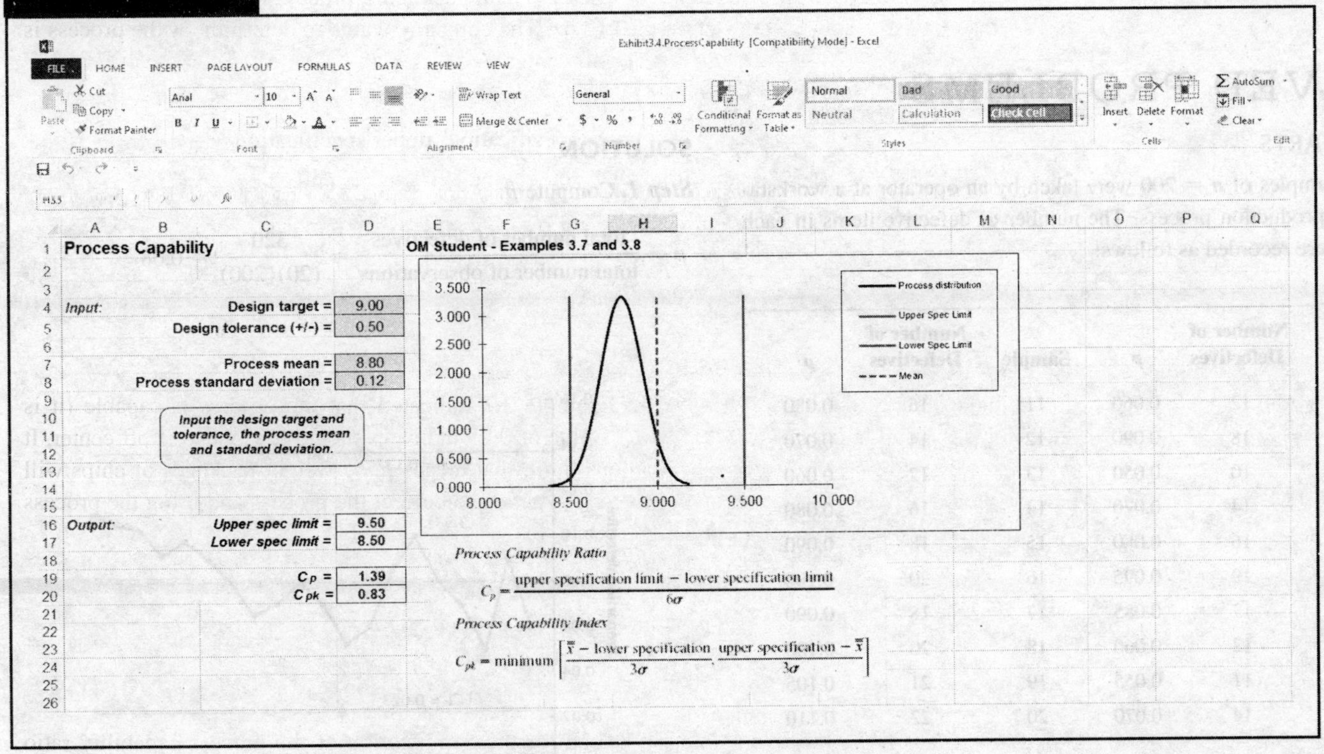

SUMMARY

Statistical process control is one of the main quantitative tools used in most quality management systems. Quality-focused companies provide extensive training in SPC methods for all employees at all levels. In this environment, employees have more responsibility for their own operation or process. Employees recognize the need for SPC for accomplishing a major part of their job, product quality. When employees are provided with adequate training and understand what is expected of them, they have little difficulty using statistical process control methods.

KEY FORMULAS

Control Limits for p*-Charts*

$$UCL = \bar{p} + z\sqrt{\frac{\bar{p}(1-\bar{p})}{n}}$$

$$LCL = \bar{p} - z\sqrt{\frac{\bar{p}(1-\bar{p})}{n}}$$

Control Limits for c*-Charts*

$$UCL = \bar{c} + z\sqrt{\bar{c}}$$

$$LCL = \bar{c} - z\sqrt{\bar{c}}$$

Control Limits for R*-Charts*

$$UCL = D_4\bar{R}$$

$$LCL = D_3\bar{R}$$

Control Limits for $\bar{x}$*-Charts*

$$UCL = \bar{\bar{x}} + A_2\bar{R}$$

$$LCL = \bar{\bar{x}} - A_2\bar{R}$$

Process Capability Ratio

$$C_p = \frac{\text{upper specification limit} - \text{lower specification limit}}{6\sigma}$$

Process Capability Index

$$C_{pk} = \text{minimum} \times \left[\frac{\bar{\bar{x}} - \text{lower specification}}{3\sigma}, \frac{\text{upper specification} - \bar{\bar{x}}}{3\sigma}\right]$$

SOLVED PROBLEMS

1. *p*-CHARTS

Twenty samples of $n = 200$ were taken by an operator at a workstation in a production process. The number of defective items in each sample were recorded as follows:

Sample	Number of Defectives	p	Sample	Number of Defectives	p
1	12	0.060	11	16	0.080
2	18	0.090	12	14	0.070
3	10	0.050	13	12	0.060
4	14	0.070	14	16	0.080
5	16	0.080	15	18	0.090
6	19	0.095	16	20	0.100
7	17	0.085	17	18	0.090
8	12	0.060	18	20	0.100
9	11	0.055	19	21	0.105
10	14	0.070	20	22	0.110

Management wants to develop a *p*-chart using 3-sigma limits. Set up the *p*-chart and plot the observations to determine if the process was out of control at any point.

SOLUTION

Step 1. Compute $\bar{p}$:

$$\bar{p} = \frac{\text{total number of defectives}}{\text{total number of observations}} = \frac{320}{(20)(200)} = 0.08$$

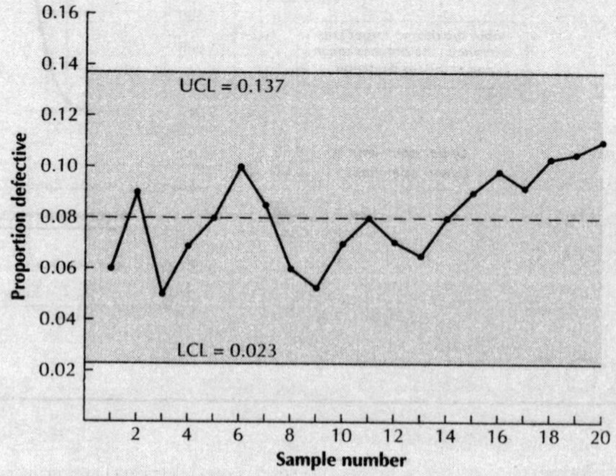

2. PATTERN TESTS

In the preceding problem, even though the control chart indicates that the process is in control, management wants to use pattern tests to further determine if the process is in control.

SOLUTION

Step 1. Determine the "up-and-down" and "above-and-below" runs and zone observations. Construct the zone boundaries on the control chart as follows.

Step 2. Determine the control limits:

$$\text{UCL} = \bar{p} + z\sqrt{\frac{\bar{p}(1-\bar{p})}{n}} = 0.08 + (3.00)(0.019) = 0.137$$

$$\text{LCL} = \bar{p} - z\sqrt{\frac{\bar{p}(1-\bar{p})}{n}} = 0.08 - (3.00)(0.019) = 0.023$$

Step 3. Construct the $\bar{p}$-chart with $\bar{p} = 0.08$, UCL = 0.137, and LCL = 0.023. The process does not appear to be out of control.

Sample	Above/Below $\bar{p} = 0.08$	Up/Down	Zone
1	B	—	B
2	A	U	C
3	B	D	B
4	B	U	C
5	A	U	C
6	A	U	B
7	A	D	C
8	B	D	B
9	B	D	B
10	B	U	C
11	A	U	C
12	B	D	C
13	B	D	C
14	A	U	C
15	A	U	C
16	A	U	B
17	A	D	C
18	A	U	B
19	A	U	B
20	A	U	B

(*Note*: Ties are broken in favor of A and U.)

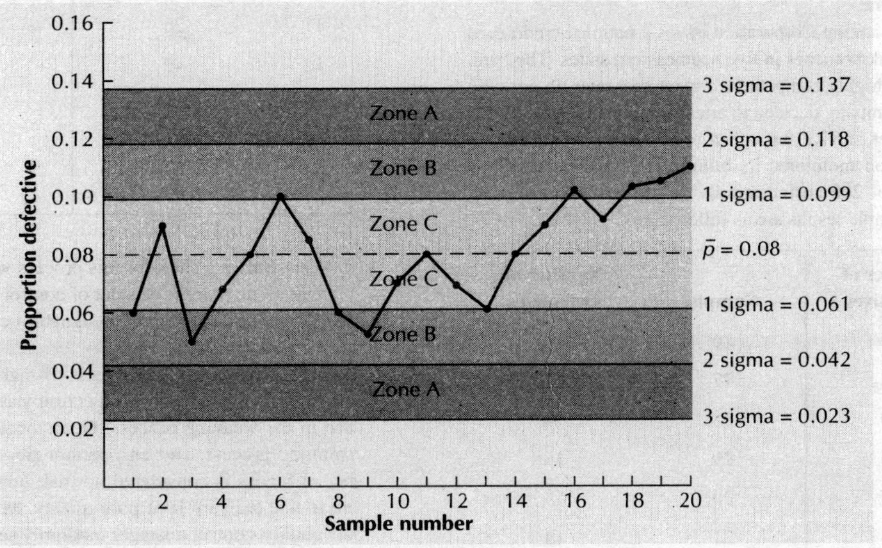

Because four of five consecutive points are in Zone B (i.e., points 16 to 20), it suggests that nonrandom patterns may exist and that the process may not be in control.

PROBLEMS

3-1. The Great North Woods Clothing Company sells specialty outdoor clothing through its catalog. A quality problem that generates customer complaints occurs when a warehouse employee fills an order with the wrong items. The company has decided to implement a process control plan by inspecting the ordered items after they have been obtained from the warehouse and before they have been packaged. The company has taken 30 samples (during a 30-day period), each for 100 orders, and recorded the number of defective orders in each sample, as follows:

Sample	Number of Defectives	Sample	Number of Defectives
1	12	16	6
2	14	17	3
3	10	18	7
4	16	19	10
5	18	20	14
6	19	21	18
7	14	22	22
8	20	23	26
9	18	24	20
10	17	25	24
11	9	26	18
12	11	27	19
13	14	28	20
14	12	29	17
15	7	30	18

Construct a *p*-chart for the company that describes 99.74% (3σ) of the random variation in the process, and indicate if the process seems to be out of control at any time.

3-2. The Commonwealth Banking Corporation issues a national credit card through its various bank branches in five southeastern states. The bank credit card business is highly competitive and interest rates do not vary substantially, so the company decided to attempt to retain its customers by improving customer service through a reduction in billing errors. The credit card division monitored its billing department process by taking daily samples of 200 customer bills for 30 days and checking their accuracy. The sample results are as follows:

Sample	Number of Defectives	Sample	Number of Defectives
1	7	16	10
2	12	17	12
3	9	18	14
4	6	19	16
5	5	20	15
6	8	21	13
7	10	22	9
8	11	23	10
9	14	24	12
10	10	25	15
11	9	26	14
12	6	27	16
13	3	28	12
14	2	29	15
15	8	30	14

Develop a *p*-chart for the billing process using 3σ control limits and indicate if the process is out of control.

3-3. The Great North Woods Clothing Company is a mail-order company that processes thousands of mail and telephone orders each week. It has a customer service number to handle customer order problems, inquiries, and complaints. The company wants to monitor the number of customer calls that can be classified as complaints. The total number of complaint calls the customer service department has received for each of the last 30 weekdays are shown as follows:

Day	Complaint Calls	Day	Complaint Calls
1	27	16	19
2	15	17	12
3	38	18	17
4	41	19	18
5	19	20	26
6	23	21	31
7	21	22	14
8	16	23	18
9	33	24	26
10	35	25	27
11	26	26	35
12	42	27	20
13	40	28	12
14	35	29	16
15	25	30	15

a. Construct a *c*-chart for this process with 3σ control limits and indicate if the process was out of control at any time.

b. What nonrandom (i.e., assignable) causes might result in the process being out of control?

3-4. One of the stages in the process of making denim cloth at the Southern Mills Company is to spin cotton yarn onto spindles for subsequent use in the weaving process. Occasionally the yarn breaks during the spinning process, and an operator ties it back together. Some number of breaks is considered normal; however, too many breaks might mean that the yarn is of poor quality. In order to monitor this process, the quality-control manager randomly selects a spinning machine each hour and checks the number of breaks during a 15-minute period. Following is a summary of the observations for the past 20 hours:

Sample	Number of Breaks	Sample	Number of Breaks
1	3	6	3
2	2	7	2
3	4	8	4
4	1	9	0
5	5	10	2

Sample	Number of Breaks	Sample	Number of Breaks
11	3	16	6
12	4	17	5
13	6	18	7
14	7	19	8
15	8	20	6

Construct a *c*-chart using 3σ limits for this process and indicate if the process was out of control at any time.

3-5. Telecom manufactures electronic components for computers. One measure it uses to monitor the quality of its distribution process is the number of customer invoice errors. The distribution center manager monitored the company's order processing and distribution by recording the number of invoice errors for 30 days. The sample results are as follows:

Day	Number of Errors	Day	Number of Errors
1	4	16	6
2	6	17	9
3	2	18	12
4	5	19	10
5	1	20	11
6	3	21	8
7	4	22	8
8	7	23	7
9	6	24	3
10	5	25	4
11	10	26	7
12	8	27	10
13	9	28	12
14	9	29	12
15	7	30	14

Construct a *c*-chart with 3σ limits for invoice errors and indicate if the process was out of control at any time.

3-6. BooksCDs.com sells books, videos, DVDs, and CDs through its website. The company ships thousands of orders each day from seven national distribution centers. BooksCDs.com wants to establish a *p*-chart to monitor the quality of its distribution process, specifically the number of "problem" orders. A problem order is one that is delivered to a customer late (i.e., after five days), incorrect or incomplete. The company sampled 500 orders every other day for 20 samples and tracked them to final customer delivery, the results of which are as follows:

Sample	Number of Problems Orders	Sample	Number of Problems Orders
1	14	11	38
2	22	12	24
3	36	13	15
4	17	14	12
5	25	15	10
6	41	16	16
7	18	17	9
8	19	18	21
9	26	19	18
10	28	20	12

Construct a *p*-chart for this process using 3σ limits and indicate if the process was out of control.

3-7. Valtec Electronics fills orders for its electronic components and parts by truck to customers through several distribution centers. A measure of its supply chain responsiveness is order fulfillment lead time, which is the number of days from when a company receives an order to when it is delivered to the customer. A distribution center manager has taken 20 samples of five orders each during the month and recorded the lead time for each as follows:

Samples	Load Time (Days)				
1	1.3	2.4	0.7	3.0	1.8
2	2.1	1.2	1.0	2.5	3.6
3	4.2	3.3	2.6	1.5	3.0
4	1.6	2.1	2.8	0.9	1.5
5	2.6	3.0	1.4	4.6	1.9
6	0.8	2.7	5.8	3.7	4.5
7	2.6	3.5	3.1	3.6	1.4
8	3.4	6.1	1.5	2.5	2.8
9	3.1	2.5	2.2	2.9	1.8
10	2.4	4.8	5.9	3.2	4.4
11	1.9	2.7	3.4	2.2	0.4
12	6.1	4.9	2.1	3.6	5.2
13	1.2	3.4	2.8	2.3	4.5
14	2.4	2.9	3.4	2.3	2.5
15	3.7	7.0	1.4	2.4	3.3
16	3.6	2.7	4.8	2.0	1.7
17	0.4	1.8	6.5	3.2	4.8
18	5.3	2.9	3.4	4.8	4.4
19	2.7	3.6	2.9	4.1	5.2
20	4.7	2.0	2.0	3.1	1.8

Construct an $\bar{x}$-chart to be used in conjunction with an R-chart using 3σ limits for these data and indicate if the process is in control.

3-8. The Startrac Coffee Company is an international coffeehouse chain. The company has a contract with a Mexican supplier for paper cups, lids, and insulated sleeves. Startrac management has found that the paper cups sometimes leak around the lid, dripping the contained beverage on their customers. The leaks can be caused by several factors, including defective manufacturing, damage during shipping and handling, and even how the lids are placed on the cups by employees. The company has sampled 1,000 filled cups each week for 20 weeks from a number of different randomly selected store locations around the country, with the following number of cups that leak.

Sample	Defective Cups	Sample	Defective Cups
1	78	11	123
2	116	12	71
3	49	13	87
4	51	14	43
5	37	15	91
6	63	16	63
7	77	17	107
8	106	18	54
9	31	19	73
10	28	20	65

Construct a p-chart for the cups using 3σ limits and indicate if the process was out of control, and if the control chart is reliable to monitor cup quality in the future. Visit your favorite coffee shop and see if your beverage cup leaks, and if so, try to determine what the cause might be.

3-9. The Southern Mills Company produces denim cloth. During the weaving process, dyed yarn on large, round beams is fed into looms where it is woven into cloth. During this weaving process, the yarns are stretched beyond their natural length. As a result, the woven fabric can shrink as much as 15%; however, shrinkage of only as much as 3% is the acceptable limit for Southern's customers. To prevent shrinkage, the fabric is put through a chemical process, but beams of fabric can still exceed the shrinkage limit. The Southern quality management team has taken a sample of 100 finished fabric beams each day for one month (i.e., 30 days) and tested them for shrinkage. The results of this inspection process showing the number of fabric beams that exceed the 3% shrinkage limit are as follows:

Sample	Defective Beams	Sample	Defective Beams
1	6	7	8
2	9	8	6
3	11	9	6
4	3	10	12
5	10	11	7
6	14	12	10

Sample	Defective Beams	Sample	Defective Beams
13	6	22	14
14	5	23	17
15	9	24	22
16	12	25	13
17	15	26	16
18	6	27	12
19	3	28	10
20	4	29	9
21	8	30	9

Develop a p-chart for fabric shrinkage using 3σ control limits and indicate if the process is out of control.

3-10. A machine at the Pacific Fruit Company fills boxes with raisins. The labeled weight of the boxes is 9 oz. The company wants to construct an R-chart to monitor the filling process and make sure the box weights are in control. The quality-control department for the company sampled five boxes every two hours for three consecutive working days. The sample observations are as follows:

Samples	Box Weights (oz)				
1	9.06	9.13	8.97	8.85	8.46
2	8.52	8.61	9.09	9.21	8.95
3	9.35	8.95	9.20	9.03	8.42
4	9.17	9.21	9.05	9.01	9.53
5	9.21	8.87	8.71	9.05	9.35
6	8.74	8.35	8.50	9.06	8.89
7	9.00	9.21	9.05	9.23	8.78
8	9.15	9.20	9.23	9.15	9.06
9	9.98	8.90	8.81	9.05	9.13
10	9.03	9.10	9.26	9.46	8.47
11	9.53	9.02	9.11	8.88	8.92
12	8.95	9.10	9.00	9.06	8.95

Construct an R-chart from these data with 3σ control limits, plot the sample range values, and comment on process control.

3-11. The City Square Grocery and Meat Market has a large meat locker in which a constant temperature of approximately 40 °F should be maintained. The market manager has decided to construct an R-chart to monitor the temperature inside the locker. The manager had one of the market employees take sample temperature readings randomly five times each day for 20 days in order to gather data for the control chart. Following are the temperature sample observations:

Samples	Temperature (°F)				
1	46.3	48.1	42.5	43.1	39.6
2	41.2	40.5	37.8	36.5	42.3

Samples	Temperature (°F)				
3	40.1	41.3	34.5	33.2	36.7
4	42.3	44.1	39.5	37.7	38.6
5	35.2	38.1	40.5	39.1	42.3
6	40.6	41.7	38.6	43.5	44.6
7	33.2	38.6	41.5	40.7	43.1
8	41.8	40.0	41.6	40.7	39.3
9	42.4	41.6	40.8	40.9	42.3
10	44.7	36.5	37.3	35.3	41.1
11	42.6	43.5	35.4	36.1	38.2
12	40.5	40.4	39.1	37.2	41.6
13	45.3	42.0	43.1	44.7	39.5
14	36.4	37.5	36.2	38.9	40.1
15	40.5	34.3	36.2	35.1	36.8
16	39.5	38.2	37.6	34.1	38.7
17	37.6	40.6	40.3	39.7	41.2
18	41.0	34.3	39.1	45.2	43.7
19	40.9	42.3	37.6	35.4	34.8
20	37.6	39.2	39.3	41.2	37.6

a. Construct an *R*-chart based on these data using 3σ limits, and plot the 20 sample range values.

b. Does it appear that the temperature is in control according to the criteria established by management?

3-12. The Oceanside Apparel Company manufactures expensive, polo-style men's and women's short-sleeve knit shirts at its plant in Jamaica. The production process requires that material be cut into large patterned squares by operators, which are then sewn together at another stage of the process. If the squares are not of a correct length, the final shirt will be either too large or too small. In order to monitor the cutting process, management takes a sample of four squares of cloth every other hour and measures the length. The length of a cloth square should be 36 inches, and historically, the company has found the length to vary across an acceptable average of 2 inches.

a. Construct an *R*-chart for the cutting process using 3σ limits.

b. The company has taken 10 additional samples with the following results:

Samples	Measurements (in.)			
1	37.3	36.5	38.2	36.1
2	33.4	35.8	37.9	36.2
3	32.1	34.8	39.1	35.3
4	36.1	37.2	36.7	34.2
5	35.1	38.6	37.2	33.6
6	33.4	34.5	36.7	32.4
7	38.1	39.2	35.3	32.7
8	35.4	36.2	36.3	34.3
9	37.1	39.4	38.1	36.2
10	32.1	34.0	35.6	36.1

Plot the new sample data on the control chart constructed in part (a) and comment on the process variability.

3-13. For the sample data provided in Problem 3-10, construct an $\bar{x}$-chart in conjunction with the *R*-chart, plot the sample observations, and, using both $\bar{x}$- and *R*-charts, comment on the process control.

3-14. For the sample data provided in Problem 3-11, construct an $\bar{x}$-chart in conjunction with the *R*-chart, plot the sample observations, and, using both $\bar{x}$- and *R*-charts, comment on the process control.

3-15. Using the process information provided in Problem 3-12, construct an $\bar{x}$-chart in conjunction with the *R*-chart, plot the sample observations provided in part (b), and, using both $\bar{x}$- and *R*-charts, comment on the process control.

3-16. Use pattern tests to determine if the sample observations used in the $\bar{x}$-chart in Problem 3-13 reflect any nonrandom patterns.

3-17. Use pattern tests to determine if the sample observations in Problem 3-3 reflect any nonrandom patterns.

3-18. Use pattern tests to determine if the sample observations in Problem 3-11 reflect any nonrandom patterns.

3-19. Use pattern tests to determine if the sample observations used in the $\bar{x}$-chart in Problem 3-14 reflect any nonrandom patterns.

3-20. The National Bank of Warwick is concerned with complaints from customers about its drive-through window operation. Customers complain that it sometimes takes too long to be served and since there are often cars in front of and behind a customer, they cannot leave if the service is taking a long time. To correct this problem, the bank installed an intercom system so the drive-through window teller can call for assistance if the line backs up or a customer has an unusually long transaction. The bank's objective is an average customer's waiting and service time of approximately 3 minutes. The bank's operations manager wants to monitor the new drive-through window system with SPC. The manager has timed five customers' waiting and service times at random for 12 days as follows:

	Observation Times (min)				
Sample	1	2	3	4	5
1	3.05	6.27	1.35	2.56	1.05
2	7.21	1.50	2.66	3.45	3.78
3	3.12	5.11	1.37	5.20	2.65
4	2.96	3.81	4.15	5.01	2.15
5	3.25	3.11	1.63	1.29	3.74
6	2.47	2.98	2.15	1.88	4.95
7	6.05	2.03	3.17	3.18	2.34
8	1.87	2.65	1.98	2.74	3.63
9	3.33	4.15	8.06	2.98	3.05
10	2.61	2.15	3.80	3.05	3.16
11	3.52	5.66	1.18	3.45	2.07
12	3.18	7.73	2.06	1.15	3.11

Develop an $\bar{x}$-chart to be used in conjunction with an *R*-chart to monitor this drive-through window process and indicate if the process is in control using these charts.

3-21. Metro Food Products is a food produce distributor that serves a number of restaurants, grocery stores and schools from a central distribution center and warehouse. Poor forecasting, late deliveries from its suppliers, food mishandling, and order cancellations can result in food spoilage in its warehouse. It has collected the following daily dollar value of spoiled food in its warehouse for four randomly selected days each month for a year.

	Waste Value ($)/Day			
Month	**1**	**2**	**3**	**4**
1	1,126	784	1,996	1,175
2	2,705	906	2,775	408
3	3,836	1,037	771	1,562
4	720	2,063	690	3,558
5	2,458	1,558	1,806	2,003
6	1,406	3,698	1,729	1,529
7	3,338	2,706	2,885	1,781
8	917	1,380	5,433	1,004
9	2,415	788	1,193	753
10	2,604	611	764	1,761
11	937	2,756	1,308	3,407
12	327	3,055	2,005	1,107

Construct a control chart for Metro using 3σ limits to monitor the dollar value food produce waste and indicate if the process is in control, and if the control chart would be reliable to monitor the process in the future.

3-22. Martha's Wonderful Cookie Company makes a special super-chocolate-chip peanut butter cookie. The company would like the cookies to average approximately eight chocolate chips apiece. Too few or too many chips distort the desired cookie taste. Twenty samples of five cookies each during a week have been taken and the chocolate chips counted. The sample observations are as follows:

Samples	**Chips per Cookie**				
1	7	6	9	8	5
2	7	7	8	8	10
3	5	5	7	6	8
4	4	5	9	9	7
5	8	8	5	10	8
6	7	6	9	8	4
7	9	8	10	8	8
8	7	6	5	4	5
9	9	10	8	9	7
10	11	9	9	10	6
11	5	5	9	8	8
12	6	8	8	5	9
13	7	3	7	8	8
14	6	9	9	8	8
15	10	8	7	8	6
16	5	6	9	9	7
17	6	10	10	7	3
18	11	4	6	8	8
19	9	5	5	7	7
20	8	8	6	7	3

Construct an $\bar{x}$-chart in conjunction with an *R*-chart using 3σ limits for these data and comment on the cookie-production process.

3-23. Thirty patients who check out of the Rock Creek County Regional Hospital each week are asked to complete a questionnaire about hospital service. Since patients do not feel well when they are in the hospital, they typically are very critical of the service. The number of patients who indicated dissatisfaction of any kind with the service for each 30-patient sample for a 16-week period is as follows:

Sample	**Number of Dissatisfied Patients**	**Sample**	**Number of Dissatisfied Patients**
1	6	9	6
2	3	10	6
3	10	11	5
4	7	12	3
5	2	13	2
6	9	14	8
7	11	15	12
8	7	16	8

Construct a control chart to monitor customer satisfaction at the hospital using 3σ limits and determine if the process is in control.

3-24. The Great Outdoors Clothing Company, a mail-order catalog operation, contracts with the Federal Parcel Service to deliver all of its orders to customers. As such, Great Outdoors considers Federal Parcel to be part of its QMS program. Great Outdoors processes orders rapidly and requires Federal Parcel to pick them up and deliver them rapidly. Great Outdoors has tracked the delivery time for five randomly selected orders for 12 samples during a two-week period as follows:

Sample	**Delivery Time (days)**				
1	2	3	3	4	3
2	3	3	6	2	1
3	4	3	3	2	2
4	6	1	5	3	3
5	2	4	1	4	4
6	5	1	3	3	3
7	2	3	3	2	1
8	1	1	3	1	2
9	6	3	3	3	3
10	6	7	5	5	6
11	6	1	1	3	2
12	5	5	3	1	3

Construct an $\bar{x}$-chart in conjunction with an R-chart using 3σ limits for the delivery process.

3-25. The Great Outdoors Clothing Company in Problem 3-24 has designed its packaging and delivery process to deliver orders to a customer within 3 business days ±1 day, which it tells customers. Using the process mean and control limits developed in Problem 3-24, compute the process capability ratio and index, and comment on the capability of the process to meet the company's delivery commitment.

3-26. Martha's Wonderful Cookie Company in Problem 3-22 has designed its special super-chocolate-chip peanut butter cookies to have 8 chocolate chips with tolerances of ±2 chips. Using the process mean and control limits developed in Problem 3-22, determine the process capability ratio and index, and comment on the capability of the cookie production process.

3-27. The Pacific Fruit Company in Problem 3-10 has designed its packaging process for boxes to hold a net weight (nominal value) of 9.0 oz. of raisins with tolerances of ±0.5 oz. Using the process mean and control limits developed in Problem 3-10, compute the process capability ratio and index, and comment on the capability of the process to meet the company's box weight specifications.

3-28. Elon Corporation manufactures parts for an aircraft company. It uses a computerized numerical controlled (CNC) machining center to produce a specific part that has a design (nominal) target of 1.275 inches with tolerances of ±0.024 inch. The CNC process that manufactures these parts has a mean of 1.281 inches and a standard deviation of 0.008 inch. Compute the process capability ratio and process capability index, and comment on the overall capability of the process to meet the design specifications.

3-29. The Elon Company manufactures parts for an aircraft company using three computerized numerical controlled (CNC) turning centers. The company wants to decide which machines are capable of producing a specific part with design specifications of 0.0970 inch ±0.015 inch. The machines have the following process parameters—machine 1 ($\bar{\bar{x}} = 0.0995$, $\sigma = 0.004$); machine 2 ($\bar{\bar{x}} = 0.1002$, $\sigma = 0.009$); and, machine 3 ($\bar{\bar{x}} = 0.095$, $\sigma = 0.005$). Determine which machines (if any) are capable of producing the products within the design specifications.

3-30. At Samantha's Super Store, the customer service area processes customer returns, answers customer questions and provides information, addresses customer complaints, and sells gift certificates. The manager believes that if customers must wait longer than 8 minutes to see a customer service representative they get very irritated. The customer service process has been designed to achieve a customer wait time of between 6 and 12 minutes. The store manager has conducted 10 samples of five observations each of customer waiting time over a two-week period as follows:

Sample	Wait Time (min)				
1	8.3	9.6	10.2	7.4	3.1
2	2.8	5.9	6.7	8.3	9.2
3	11.3	7.4	16.2	20.1	9.5
4	10.7	7.5	9.8	11.3	4.5
5	4.3	12.4	10.6	16.7	11.3
6	5.3	9.7	10.8	11.3	7.4
7	18.2	12.1	3.6	9.5	14.2
8	8.1	10.3	8.9	7.2	5.6
9	9.3	12.4	13.7	7.3	5.2
10	6.7	8.5	8.0	10.1	12.3

Construct an $\bar{x}$-chart in conjunction with an R-chart to monitor customer service wait time, and comment on the capability of the service area to meet its designated goal.

3-31. Metropolitan General Hospital is a city-owned and -operated public hospital. Its emergency room is the largest and most prominent in the city. Approximately 70% of emergency cases in the city come or are sent to Metro General's emergency room. As a result, the emergency room is often crowded and the staff is overworked, causing concern among hospital administrators and city officials about the quality of service and healthcare the emergency room is able to provide. One of the key quality attributes administrators focus on is patient waiting time—that is, the time between when a patient checks in and registers and when the patient first sees an appropriate medical staff member. Hospital administration wants to monitor patient waiting time using statistical process control charts. At different times of the day over a period of several days, patient waiting times were recorded at random with the following results:

	Waiting Times (min)				
Sample	1	2	3	4	5
1	27	18	20	23	19
2	22	25	31	40	17
3	16	15	22	19	23
4	35	27	16	20	24
5	21	33	45	12	22
6	17	15	22	20	30
7	25	21	26	33	19
8	15	38	23	25	31
9	31	26	24	35	32
10	28	23	29	20	27

a. Develop an $\bar{x}$-chart to be used in conjunction with an R-chart to monitor patient waiting time and indicate if the process appears to be in control.

b. The city has established a requirement that emergency room patients have a waiting time of 25 minutes ±5 minutes. Based on the results in part (a), is the emergency room capable of meeting this requirement with its current process?

3-32. The three most important quality attributes at Mike's Super Service fast-food restaurant are considered to be good food, fast service, and a clean environment. The restaurant manager uses a combination of customer surveys and statistical measurement tools to monitor these quality attributes. A national marketing and research firm has developed data showing that when customers are in line up to five minutes, their perception of that waiting time is only a few minutes; however, after five minutes customer perception of their waiting time increases exponentially. Furthermore, a five-minute average waiting time results in only 2% of customers leaving. The manager wants to monitor speed of service using a statistical process control chart. At six different times during the day over a period of 15 days, the manager had an employee time customers' waiting times (from the time they entered an order line to the time they received their order) at random, with the following results:

	Waiting Times (min)					
Sample	1	2	3	4	5	6
1	6.3	2.7	4.5	3.9	5.7	5.9
2	3.8	6.2	7.1	5.4	5.1	4.7
3	5.3	5.6	6.2	5.0	5.3	4.9
4	3.9	7.2	6.4	5.7	4.2	7.1
5	4.6	3.9	5.1	4.8	5.6	6.0
6	5.5	6.3	5.2	7.4	8.1	5.9
7	6.1	7.3	6.5	5.9	5.7	8.4
8	2.2	3.6	5.7	5.3	5.6	5.0
9	6.5	4.7	5.1	9.3	6.2	5.3
10	4.7	5.8	5.4	5.1	5.0	5.9
11	3.4	2.9	1.6	4.8	6.1	5.3
12	4.5	6.3	5.4	5.7	2.1	3.4
13	7.4	3.9	4.2	4.9	5.6	3.7
14	5.7	5.3	4.1	3.7	5.8	5.7
15	6.0	3.6	2.4	5.4	5.5	3.9

a. Develop an $\bar{x}$-chart to be used in conjunction with an *R*-chart to monitor speed of service and indicate if the process is in control using this chart.

b. Management at Mike's Super Service restaurant wants customers to receive their orders within 5 minutes ± 1 minute, and it has designed its ordering and food preparation process to meet that goal. Using the process mean and control limits developed in (a), compute the process capability ratio and index, and indicate if the process appears to be capable of meeting the restaurant's goal for speed of service.

3-33. The family of a patient at County General Hospital complained when the patient fell in the hospital and broke her hip. The family was threatening a lawsuit, and there had been some negative publicity about the hospital in the local media suggesting that patient falls might be common. The hospital administration decided to investigate this potential problem by developing a control chart based on two years of monthly data for the number of patient falls each month as follows:

Month	Falls	Month	Falls
1	3	13	1
2	2	14	1
3	4	15	4
4	3.5	16	3
5	0	17	6
6	2	18	3
7	2	19	5
8	4	20	2
9	4	21	1
10	2.5	22	2.5
11	1.5	23	2.5
12	3	24	1.5

Develop a control chart with 3σ limits to monitor patient falls, and discuss if you think there appears to be a quality problem at the hospital.

3-34. The time from when a patient is discharged from North Shore Hospital to the time the discharged patient's bed is ready to be assigned to a new patient is referred to as the bed assignment turnaround time. If the bed turnaround time is excessive, it can cause problems with patient flow and delay medical procedures throughout the hospital. This can cause long waiting times for physicians and patients, thus creating customer dissatisfaction. The admissions RN has assigned a patient care associate to measure the bed turnaround time for a randomly selected bed each morning, afternoon, and evening for 30 days. Following are the bed turnaround time sample observations:

Day	Bed Turnaround Times (min)		
1	127	135	167
2	140	155	122
3	112	128	97
4	223	135	154
5	181	155	160
6	103	158	145
7	146	135	167
8	104	122	115
9	136	158	137
10	145	163	106
11	84	146	125
12	169	152	208
13	216	124	163
14	190	178	103
15	148	205	144
16	157	151	126
17	142	102	95
18	166	178	159
19	177	211	204
20	98	91	158
21	133	160	152
22	212	131	138
23	180	165	134
24	88	126	108
25	95	156	138
26	156	202	177
27	144	157	165
28	184	171	106
29	138	142	155
30	150	99	148

a. Develop an x-chart to be used in conjunction with an R-chart using 3σ limits to monitor the bed turnaround times and indicate if the process is in control using these charts.

b. Is the hospital capable of consistently achieving bed turnaround times of 120 minutes ± 15 minutes without improving the process?

CASE STUDY

Quality Control at Korean Specialty Foods

Korean Specialty Foods Ltd. (KSF) has established a Tokyo-located restaurant as an initial step in adding more locations based on customer acceptance. Japanese consumers are concerned with affordability, public perception, health trends and the quality of the food. Therefore, foreign companies looking to break into the Japanese food service industry, either as an operator or as a supplier, must take these concerns into consideration.

While planning the new restaurant, KSF utilized Japan Statistical Resources Ltd. (JSR) to identify key characteristics that the Japanese consumer would be most influenced by. JSR identified that Japanese consumers are very selective clients: they expect their meals to be presented correctly the first time and are becoming increasingly concerned with the quality of the food that they are eating. They want assurances that the food is being produced with care and that all safety measures are being taken.

The selective nature of the clientele and highly competitive marketplace are correlated such that if the client's first meal is not judged as great, the probability of his or her return business is very low. Each meal needs to be perfect each and every time if KSF is to develop a faithful return business client list.

KSF management and quality consultants developed a customer satisfaction survey that they would like to use to develop a process control chart to monitor quality. The restaurant is open six hours a day. At random times, six customers are asked to rate their dining experience according to the survey.

This survey was conducted over a two-week period with the following results:

sample	Cust 1	Cust 2	Cust 3	Cust 4	Cust 5	Cust 6
1	7	9	1	12	5	5
2	11	1	7	12	8	3
3	7	5	3	7	2	5
4	12	7	11	5	1	11
5	4	3	5	8	4	2
6	5	11	9	7	8	7
7	7	4	6	6	3	7
8	3	12	7	8	8	9
9	1	6	6	3	8	4
10	9	10	5	2	4	7
11	1	11	3	4	11	1
12	7	12	6	2	4	12
13	2	12	11	4	12	1
14	4	8	6	9	3	5

Develop a process control chart for KSF to monitor the quality of its service using 2 standard deviations. Discuss how KSF can use this information to improve the quality.

REFERENCES

Charbonneau, H. C., and G. L. Webster. *Industrial Quality Control*. Englewood Cliffs, NJ: Prentice Hall, 1978.

Dodge, H. F., and H. G. Romig. *Sampling Inspection Tables—Single and Double Sampling*. 2nd ed. New York: Wiley.

Duncan, A. J. *Quality Control and Industrial Statistics*. 4th ed. Homewood, IL: Irwin, 1974.

Evans, James R., and William M. Lindsay. *The Management and Control of Quality*. 3rd ed. St. Paul, MN: West, 1993.

Fetter, R. B. *The Quality Control System*. Homewood, IL: Irwin, 1967.

Grant, E. L., and R. S. Leavenworth. *Statistical Quality Control*. 5th ed. New York: McGraw-Hill, 1980.

Montgomery, D. C. *Introduction to Statistical Quality Control*. 2nd ed. New York: Wiley, 1991.

CHAPTER 4

Product Design

LEARNING OBJECTIVES

AFTER READING THIS CHAPTER, YOU WILL BE ABLE TO:

- Explain the importance of the product design process and provide an overview of each step of the process.
- Calculate the reliability and availability of a product or service.
- Understand the technologies involved in designing new products and their related production processes.
- Utilize techniques for analyzing design failures and eliminating unnecessary design features.
- Explain why and how each step of the product lifecycle can be changed for improved environmental stewardship, and provide examples of programs that support green efforts.
- Use quality function deployment as a design tool.

DESIGNER JEANS

More important than price or durability is the cut, the fit or the "look" of a pair of jeans. This is especially true of designer jeans made from premium denim where cost is not a limiting factor. These jeans sell from $200 to $800 a pair and are made primarily in the United States and Japan.

One of the factors that makes these jeans so desirable is the quality of the denim fabric. Japan has numerous small fabric mills that produce only premium denim. Cole Mills in Greensboro, North Carolina, is the primary producer of premium denim in the United States. Both Cole and the Japanese mills use smaller vintage shuttle looms (rather than modern projectile looms) to produce premium denim fabric with selvage edges, a looser weave and more irregularities (called slubs) that bring character and uniqueness to the denim as it fades and wears.

The dyeing or "wash" of denim is another indication of a premium denim product. Most denim producers use synthetic dyes; however, many Japanese producers, including R By 45rpm, use natural indigo dye. Indigo adds considerable time and expense to production (three to six months more) but produces a deep blue color that resists fading (which may or may not be desirable).

Los Angeles is a hub for jean designers, where 7 For All Mankind, Citizens of Humanity, J Brand, True Religion, AG, Marc Nelson and others have set up design and production facilities. One of the reasons for this trend is the tight-knit community of fashion designers in LA; another is the skill of LA washhouses. Even Tears of Bleu designer, Caius Olowu, uses American washhouses; his jeans are cut and sewn in Okiyama, Japan, then sent to LA for their signature wash, before returning to Japan to be sold.

Producing and selling domestically reduces the time to fill orders from 12 weeks to 2 weeks for Hudson Jeans, and makes 7 For All Mankind much more responsive to changes in styles and finishing. Matching the product to the customer, and the process to the product, are keys to a sustainable company success, whether the product is 'premium' or just regular.

In this chapter, we'll learn about the product design process, the impact of good designs, and how to improve both the quality and speed of design.

Sources: Based on K. Tran, "L.A. Jeansmakers Put Premium on Local Production," *Women's Wear Daily* (November 11, 2011); C. Binkley, "How Can Jeans Cost $300?" *Wall Street Journal* (July 7, 2011).

New products and services are the lifeblood of an organization. Designs can provide a competitive edge by bringing new ideas to the market quickly, doing a better job of satisfying customer needs, or being easier to manufacture, use, and repair.

Design is a critical process for a firm. Strategically, it defines a firm's customers, as well as its competitors. It capitalizes on a firm's core competencies and determines what new competencies need to be developed. It is also the most obvious driver of change—new products and services can rejuvenate an organization, define new markets, and inspire new technologies.

The design process itself is beneficial because it encourages companies to look outside their boundaries, bring in new ideas, challenge conventional thinking, and experiment. Product and service design provide a natural venue for learning, breaking down barriers, working in teams, and integrating across functions.

The Design Process

Design has a tremendous impact on the quality of a product or service. Poor designs may not meet customer needs or may be so difficult to make that quality suffers. Costly designs can result in overpriced products that lose market share. If the design process is too lengthy, a competitor may capture the market by being the first to introduce new products, services, or features. However, rushing to be first to the market can result in design flaws and poor performance, which totally negate first-mover advantages. Design may be an art, but the design process must be managed effectively.

An effective design process:

- Matches product or service characteristics with customer requirements.
- Ensures that customer requirements are met in the simplest and least costly manner.

Figure 4.1
The Design Process

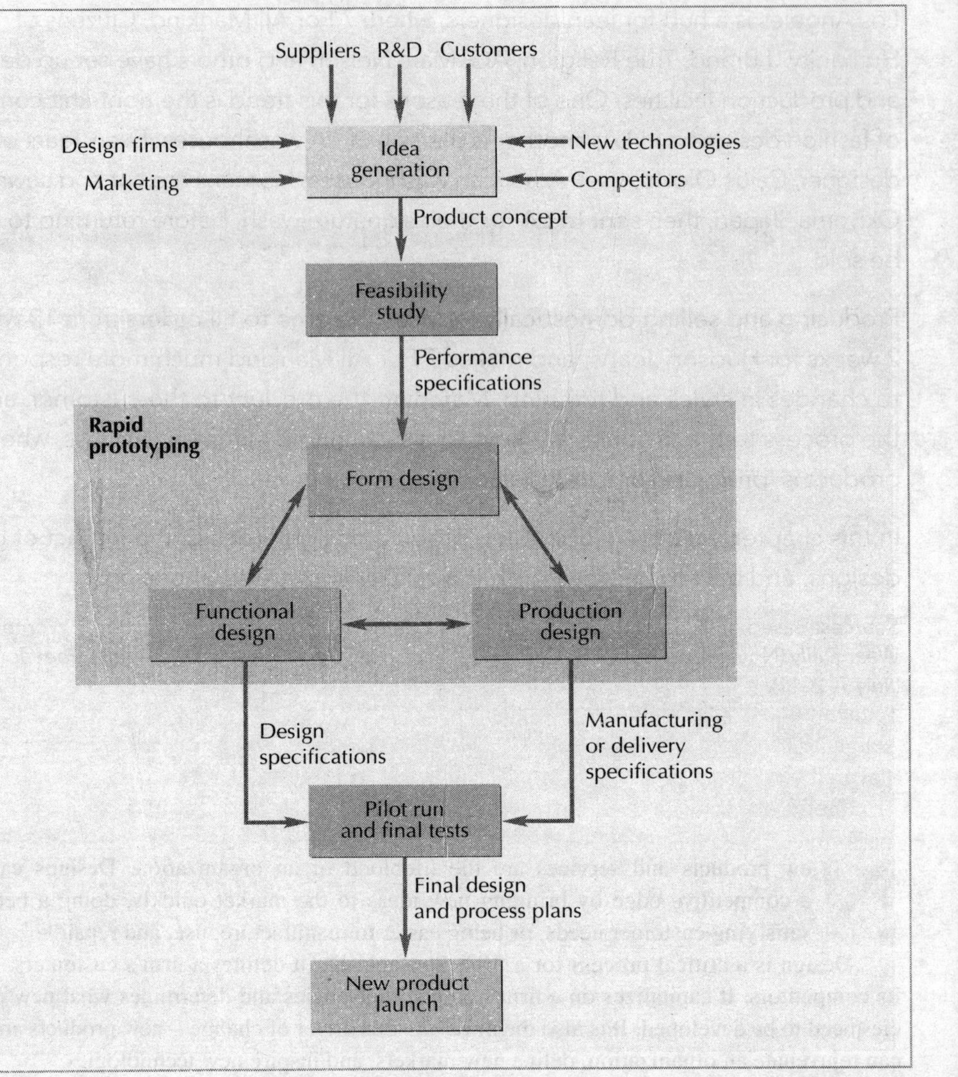

- Reduces the time required to design a new product or service.
- Minimizes the revisions necessary to make a design workable.

Product design defines the appearance of the product, sets standards for performance, specifies which materials are to be used, and determines dimensions and tolerances. Figure 4.1 outlines the design process from idea generation to product launch. Let's examine each step in detail.

IDEA GENERATION

The design process begins with understanding the customer and actively identifying customer needs. Ideas for new products or improvements to existing products can be generated from many sources, including a company's own R&D department, customer complaints or suggestions, marketing research, suppliers, salespersons in the field, factory workers, and new technological developments. Competitors are also a source of ideas for new products or services. Perceptual maps, benchmarking, and reverse engineering can help companies learn from their competitors.

Perceptual maps compare customer perceptions of a company's products with competitors' products. Consider the perceptual map of breakfast cereals in terms of taste and nutrition

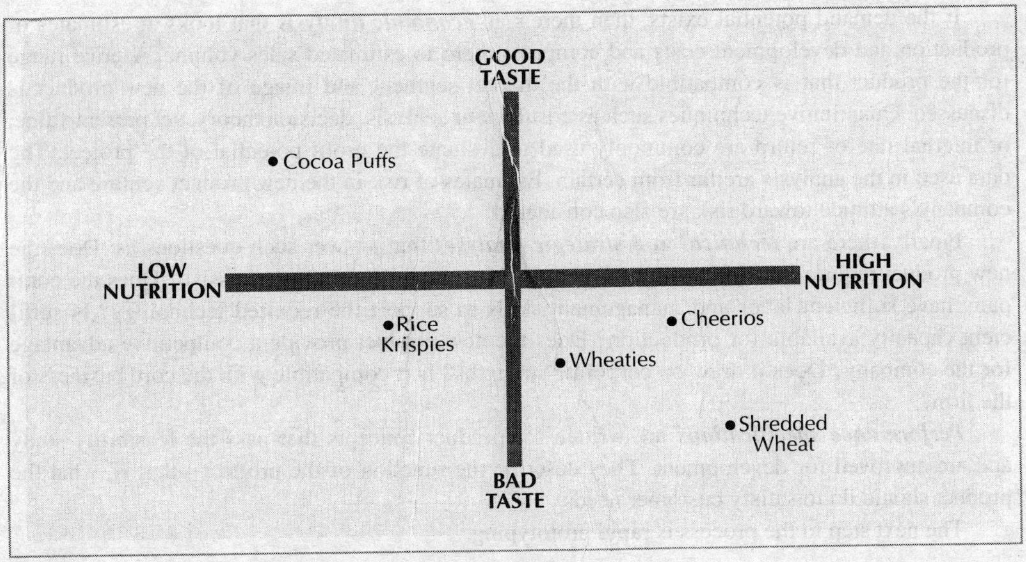

Figure 4.2
A Perceptual Map of Breakfast Cereals

shown in Figure 4.2. The lack of an entry in the good-taste, high-nutrition category suggests there are opportunities for this kind of cereal in the market. This is why Cheerios introduced honey-nut and apple-cinnamon versions while promoting its "oat" base. Fruit bits and nuts were added to wheat flakes to make them more tasty and nutritious. Shredded Wheat opted for more taste by reducing its size and adding a sugar frosting or berry filling. Rice Krispies, on the other hand, sought to challenge Cocoa Puffs in the "more tasty" market quadrant with marshmallow and fruit-flavored versions.

Benchmarking refers to finding the best-in-class product or process, measuring the performance of your product or process against it, and making recommendations for improvement based on the results. The benchmarked company may be in an entirely different line of business. For example, American Express is well known for its ability to get customers to pay up quickly; Disney World, for its employee commitment; FedEx, for its speed; McDonald's, for its consistency; and Xerox, for its benchmarking techniques.

Reverse engineering refers to carefully dismantling and inspecting a competitor's product to look for design features that can be incorporated into your own product. Ford used this approach successfully in its design of the Taurus automobile, assessing 400 features of competitors' products and copying, adapting, or enhancing more than 300 of them, including Audi's accelerator pedal, Toyota's fuel-gauge accuracy, and BMW's tire and jack storage.

For many products and services, following consumer or competitors' leads is not enough; customers are attracted by superior technology and creative ideas. In these industries, research and development is the primary source of new product ideas. Expenditures for R&D can be enormous ($27 million a day at Toyota) and investment risky (only 1 in 20 ideas ever becomes a product and only 1 in 10 new products is successful). In addition, ideas generated by R&D may follow a long path to commercialization.

FEASIBILITY STUDY

Marketing takes the ideas that are generated and the customer needs that are identified from the first stage of the design process and formulates alternative product and service concepts. The promising concepts undergo a feasibility study that includes several types of analyses, beginning with a ***market analysis***. Most companies have market researchers who can design and evaluate customer surveys, interviews, focus groups, or market tests. The market analysis assesses whether there's enough demand for the proposed product to invest in developing it further.

If the demand potential exists, then there's an ***economic analysis*** that looks at estimates of production and development costs and compares them to estimated sales volume. A price range for the product that is compatible with the market segment and image of the new product is discussed. Quantitative techniques such as cost/benefit analysis, decision theory, net present value, or internal rate of return are commonly used to evaluate the profit potential of the project. The data used in the analysis are far from certain. Estimates of risk in the new product venture and the company's attitude toward risk are also considered.

Finally, there are ***technical* and *strategic analyses*** that answer such questions as: Does the new product require new technology? Is the risk or capital investment excessive? Does the company have sufficient labor and management skills to support the required technology? Is sufficient capacity available for production? Does the new product provide a competitive advantage for the company? Does it draw on corporate strengths? Is it compatible with the core business of the firm?

Performance specifications are written for product concepts that pass the feasibility study and are approved for development. They describe the function of the product—that is, what the product should do to satisfy customer needs.

The next step in the process is rapid prototyping.

Rapid Prototyping and Concurrent Design

Designers take general performance specifications and transform them into a physical product or service with technical design specifications. The process involves building a prototype, testing the prototype, revising the design, retesting, and so on until a viable design is determined.

Rapid prototyping, as the name implies, creates preliminary design models that are quickly tested and either discarded (as fast failures) or further refined. The models can be physical or electronic, rough facsimiles or full-scale working models. The iterative process involves *form* and *functional design*, as well as *production design*.

It is important that these design decisions be performed *concurrently* at the rapid prototype stage. Design decisions affect sales strategies, efficiency of manufacture, assembly quality, speed of repair, and product cost. Design decisions overlap and early changes in the design are less disruptive than those made late in the process. Effective designs, as shown in Figure 4.3, break down the series of walls between functional areas and involve persons from different backgrounds and areas of expertise early in the design process. This process of jointly and iteratively developing a design is called **concurrent design**.

Concurrent design improves both the quality of the design and the time-to-market. This is especially true with the design of component parts to be completed by a supplier. Rather than designing the parts and giving the design specs to a supplier to complete, concurrent design involves the supplier in the design process. For example, a company may share with a potential supplier the performance specs and ask the supplier to complete the design so that the part performs properly and fits within space, weight, and cost parameters.

In the next sections, we discuss the three types of concurrent designs: form, functional, and production design.

FORM DESIGN

Form design refers to the physical appearance of a product—its shape, color, size, and style. Aesthetics such as image, market appeal, and personal identification are also part of form design. In many cases, functional design must be adjusted to make the product look or feel right. For example, the form design of Mazda's Miata sports car went further than looks—the exhaust had to have a certain "sound," the gearshift lever a certain "feel," and the seat and window arrangement the proper dimensions to encourage passengers to ride with their elbows out. Apple products have great form and functional design.

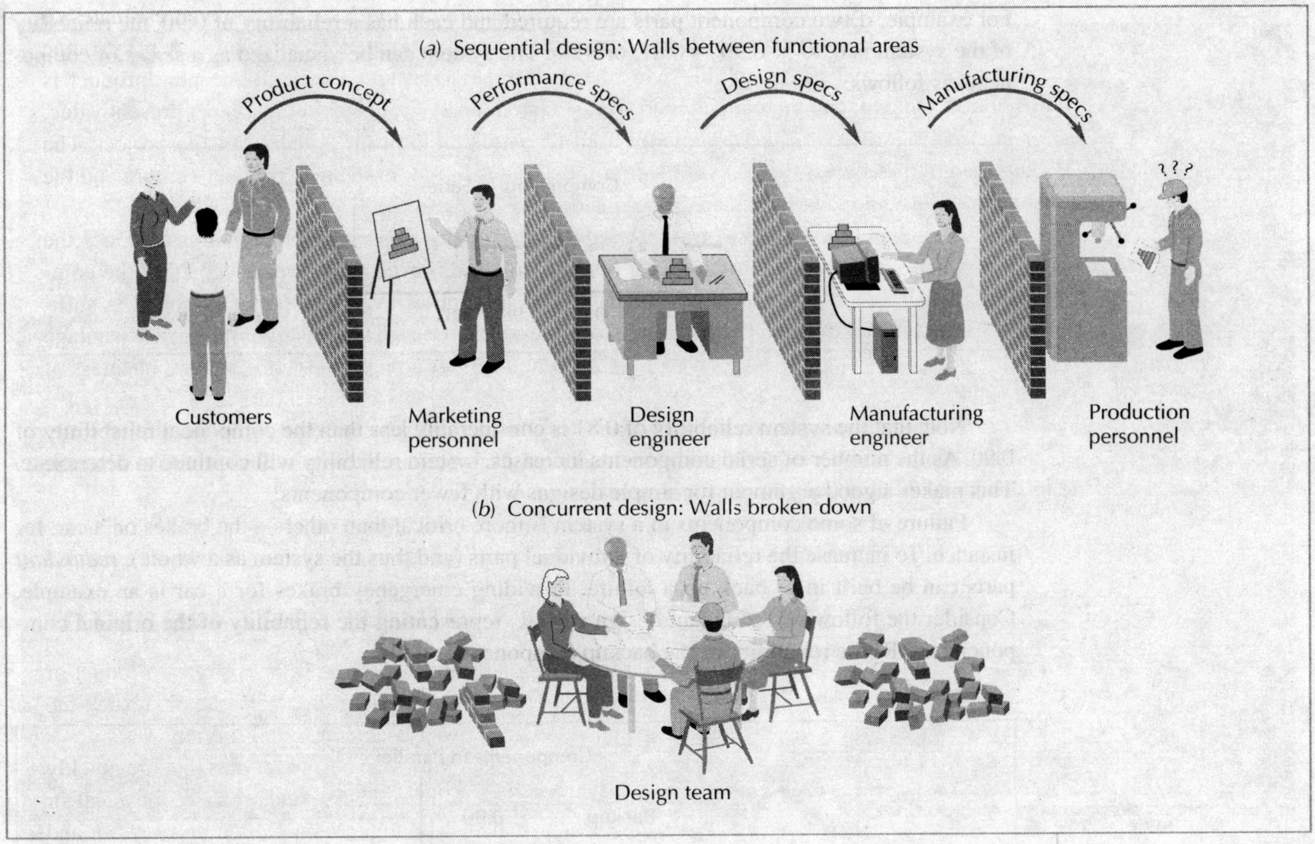

Figure 4.3

Concurrent Design, Breaking Down Barriers

FUNCTIONAL DESIGN

Functional design is concerned with how the product performs. It seeks to meet the performance specifications of fitness for use by the customer. Three performance characteristics considered during this phase of design are *reliability*, *maintainability*, and *usability*.

Reliability

Reliability is the probability that a given part or product will perform its intended function for a specified length of time under normal conditions of use. You may be familiar with reliability information from product warranties. A hair dryer might be guaranteed to function (i.e., blow air with a certain force at a certain temperature) for one year under normal conditions of use (defined to be 300 hours of operation). A car warranty might extend for three years or 50,000 miles. Normal conditions of use would include regularly scheduled oil changes and other minor maintenance activities. A missed oil change or mileage in excess of 50,000 miles in a three-year period would not be considered "normal" and would nullify the warranty.

A product or system's reliability is a function of the reliabilities of its component parts and how the parts are arranged. If all parts must function for the product or system to operate, then the system reliability is the *product* of the component part reliabilities.

$$R_s = (R_1)(R_2) \ldots (R_n), \text{ where } R_n \text{ is the reliablity of the } n\text{th component.}$$

For example, if two component parts are required and each has a reliability of 0.90, the reliability of the system is $0.90 \times 0.90 = 0.81$, or 81%. The system can be visualized as a *series* of components as follows:

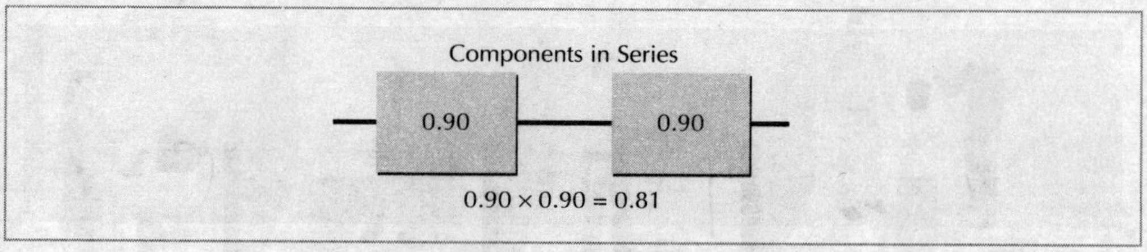

Note that the system reliability of 0.81 is considerably less than the component reliabilities of 0.90. As the number of serial components increases, system reliability will continue to deteriorate. This makes a good argument for simple designs with fewer components!

Failure of some components in a system is more critical than others—the brakes on a car, for instance. To increase the reliability of individual parts (and thus the system as a whole), *redundant* parts can be built in to back up a failure. Providing emergency brakes for a car is an example. Consider the following redundant design with R_1 representing the reliability of the original component and R_2 the reliability of the backup component.

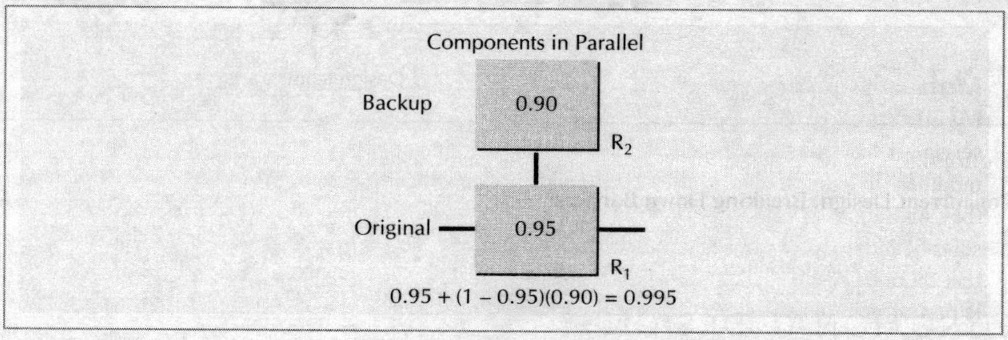

These components are said to operate in *parallel*. If the original component fails (a 5% chance), the backup component will automatically kick in to take its place—but only 90% of the time. Thus, the reliability of the system is[1]

$$\begin{aligned} R_s &= R_1 + (1 - R_1)(R_2) \\ &= 0.95 + (1 - 0.95)(0.90) = 0.995 \end{aligned}$$

Reliability can also be expressed as the length of time a product or service is in operation before it fails, called the *mean time between failures* (MTBF). In this case, we are concerned with the distribution of failures over time, or the *failure rate*. The MTBF is the reciprocal of the failure rate (MTBF = 1/failure rate). For example, if your laptop battery fails four times in 20 hours of operation, its failure rate would be $4/20 = 0.20$, and its MTBF $= 1/0.20 = 5$ hours.

Reliability can be improved by simplifying product design, improving the reliability of individual components, or adding redundant components. Products that are easier to manufacture or assemble, are well maintained, and have users who are trained in proper use have higher reliability.

[1]The reliability of parallel components can also be calculated as $R_s = 1 - [(1 - R_1)(1 - R_2)\ldots]$.

EXAMPLE 4.1

RELIABILITY

Determine the reliability of the system of components shown below.

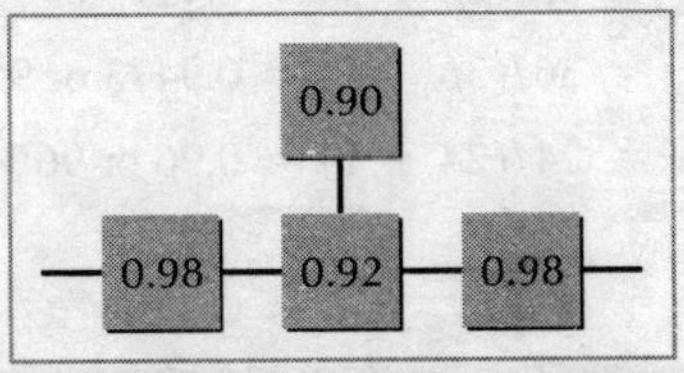

SOLUTION

First, reduce the system to a *series* of three components,

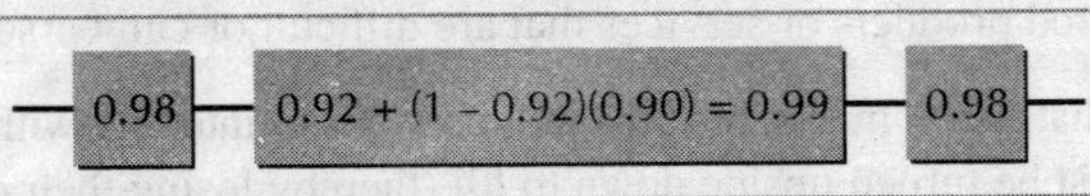

Then calculate the reliability of the series.

$$0.98 \times 0.99 \times 0.98 = 0.951$$

Maintainability

Maintainability (also called *serviceability*) refers to the ease and/or cost with which a product or service is maintained or repaired. Products can be made easier to maintain by assembling them in modules, like computers, so that entire control panels, cards, or disk drives can be replaced when they malfunction. The location of critical parts or parts subject to failure affects the ease of disassembly and, thus, repair. Instructions that teach consumers how to anticipate malfunctions and correct them themselves can be included with the product. Specifying regular maintenance schedules is part of maintainability, as is proper planning for the availability of critical replacement parts.

One quantitative measure of maintainability is mean time to repair (MTTR). Combined with the reliability measure of MTBF, we can calculate the average availability or "uptime" of a system as

$$\text{System Availability (SA)} = \frac{\text{MTBF}}{\text{MTBF} + \text{MTTR}}$$

EXAMPLE 4.2

SYSTEM AVAILABILITY

Amy Russell must choose a service provider for her company's e-commerce site. Other factors being equal, she will base her decision on server availability. Given the following server performance data, which provider should she choose?

Provider	MTBF (hr)	MTTR (hr)
A	60	4.0
B	36	2.0
C	24	1.0

(Continued)

SOLUTION

$$SA = \frac{MTBF}{MTBF + MTTR}$$

$$SA_A = 60/(60 + 4) = 0.9375 \text{ or } 94\%$$

$$SA_B = 36/(36 + 2) = 0.9473 \text{ or } 95\%$$

$$SA_C = 24/(24 + 1) = 0.96 \text{ or } 96\%$$

Amy should choose Provider C.

Usability

All of us have encountered products or services that are difficult or cumbersome to use. Consider:

- Cup holders in cars that, when in use, hide the radio buttons or interfere with the stick shift.
- Salt shakers that must be turned upside down to fill (thereby losing their contents).
- Speakers in laptop computers that are covered by your wrists as you type.
- Doors that you can't tell whether to pull or push.
- Remote controls with more and more buttons of smaller and smaller size for multiple products.
- Levers for popping the trunk of a car and unlocking the gas cap located too close together.

These are usability issues in design. **Usability** is what makes a product or service easy to use and a good fit for its targeted customer. It is a combination of factors that affect the user's experience with a product, including: ease of learning, ease of use and ease of remembering how to use, frequency and severity of errors, and user satisfaction with the experience.

Although usability engineers have long been a part of the design process, their use has skyrocketed with electronics, computer software, and website design. Forrester Research estimates that 50% of potential sales from websites are lost from customers who cannot locate what they need. Researchers have found that Internet users have a particularly low tolerance for poorly designed sites and cumbersome navigation.

Apple revolutionized the computer industry with its intuitive, easy-to-use designs and continues to do so with its sleek and functional iPods, iPads, and iPhones. Microsoft employs over 140 usability engineers. Before a design is deemed functional, it must go through usability testing. Simpler, more standardized designs are usually easier to use. They are also easier to produce, as we'll see in the next section.

PRODUCTION DESIGN

Production design is concerned with how the product will be made. Designs that are difficult to make often result in poor-quality products. Engineers tend to overdesign products, with too many features, options, and parts. Lack of knowledge of manufacturing capabilities can result in designs that are impossible to make or require skills and resources not currently available. Many times, production personnel find themselves redesigning products on the factory floor. Late changes in design are both costly and disruptive. An adjustment in one part may necessitate an adjustment in other parts, "unraveling" the entire product design. That's why production design is considered in the preliminary design phase. Recommended approaches to production design include *simplification, standardization, modularity, design for manufacture*, and *design for supply chain*.

Design **simplification** attempts to reduce the number of parts, subassemblies, and options in a product. It also means avoiding tools, separate fasteners, and adjustments. We'll illustrate simplification with an example. Consider the case of the toolbox shown in Figure 4.4. The company wants to increase productivity by using automated assembly. The initial design in

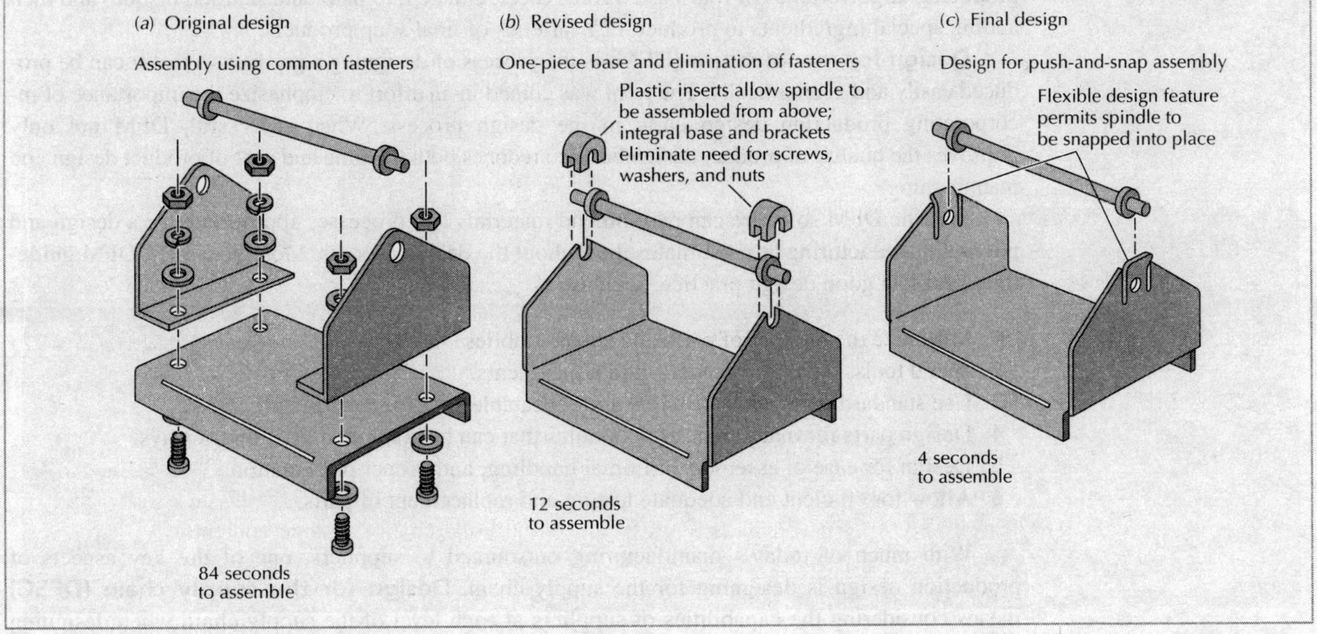

Figure 4.4
Design Simplification

SOURCE: Adapted from G. Boothroyd and P. Dewhurst, "Product Design. . . . Key to Successful Robotic Assembly," *Assembly Engineering* (September 1986), pp. 90–93.

Figure 4.4*a* contains 24 common parts (mostly nuts and bolts fasteners) and requires 84 seconds to assemble. The design does not appear to be complex for manual assembly but can be quite complicated for a robot to assemble.

As shown in Figure 4.4*b*, the team assigned to revise the design simplified the toolbox by molding the base as one piece and eliminating the fasteners. Plastic inserts snap over the spindle to hold it in place. The number of parts was reduced to four, and the assembly time cut to 12 seconds. This represents a significant gain in productivity, from 43 assemblies per hour to 300 assemblies per hour.

Figure 4.4*c* shows an even simpler design, consisting of only two parts, a base and spindle. The spindle is made of flexible material, allowing it to be snapped downward into place in a quick, one-motion assembly. Assembly time is reduced to 4 seconds, increasing production to 900 assemblies an hour. With this final design, the team agreed that the assembly task was too simple for a robot. Indeed, many manufacturers have followed this process in rediscovering the virtues of simplification—in redesigning a product for automation, they find that automation isn't necessary!

Using standard parts in a product or throughout many products saves design time, tooling costs, and production worries. **Standardization** makes possible the interchangeability of parts among products, resulting in higher-volume production and purchasing, lower investment in inventory, easier purchasing and material handling, fewer quality inspections, and fewer difficulties in production. Some products, such as light bulbs, batteries, and DVDs, benefit from being totally standardized. For others, being different is a competitive advantage. The question becomes how to gain the cost benefits of standardization without losing the market advantage of variety and uniqueness.

One solution is **modular design**. Modular design consists of combining standardized building blocks, or *modules*, in a variety of ways to create unique finished products. Modular design is common in the electronics industry and the automobile industry. Toyota's Camry, Corolla, and Lexus share the same body chassis. Even Campbell's Soup Company practices modular design by producing large volumes of four basic broths (beef, chicken, tomato, and seafood bisque) and then adding special ingredients to produce 125 varieties of final soup products.

Design for manufacture (DFM) is the process of designing a product so that it can be produced easily and economically. The term was coined in an effort to emphasize the importance of incorporating production design early in the design process. When successful, DFM not only improves the quality of product design but also reduces both the time and cost of product design and manufacture.

Specific DFM software can recommend materials and processes appropriate for a design and provide manufacturing cost estimates throughout the design process. More generally, DFM guidelines promote good design practice, such as:

1. Minimize the number of parts and subassemblies.
2. Avoid tools, separate fasteners, and adjustments.
3. Use standard parts when possible and repeatable, well-understood processes.
4. Design parts for many uses, and modules that can be combined in different ways.
5. Design for ease of assembly, minimal handling, and proper presentation.
6. Allow for efficient and adequate testing and replacement of parts.

With much of today's manufacturing outsourced to suppliers, one of the key aspects of production design is designing for the supply chain. **Design for the supply chain (DFSC)** means considering the capabilities of suppliers at each level of the supply chain when designing the product. It also involves controlling product variation, designing components that can be used in multiple products (called *component commonality*), and building universal designs (i.e., that can be used in different countries). Choosing supply chain partners early in the design stage, and working with them to finalize the design, enhance manufacturing capabilities, and reserve long-term capacity, are essential to meeting new product launch goals for both quality and time-to-market. That's why at Samsung, the supply chain part of the organization is physically located in R&D, and why at Apple, designers practically live at supplier factories during product launches to oversee quality and tweak design or manufacture as needed.

FINAL DESIGN AND PROCESS PLANS

In the preliminary design stage, prototypes are built and tested. After several iterations, a pilot run of the process is conducted. Adjustments are made as needed before the final design is agreed on. In this way, the *design specifications* for the new product have considered how the product is to be produced, and the *manufacturing* or *delivery specifications* more closely reflect the intent of the design. This should mean fewer revisions in the design as the product is manufactured and service provided. Design changes, known as engineering change orders (ECOs), are a major source of delay and cost overruns in the product development process.

The *final design* consists of detailed drawings and specifications for the new product or service. The accompanying *process plans* are workable instructions for manufacture, including necessary equipment and tooling, component sourcing recommendations, job descriptions and procedures for workers, and computer programs for automated machines. We discuss process planning in more detail in Chapter 6.

Good design is aided by the use of technology. The next section describes technology in design.

Technology in Design

New products for more segmented markets have proliferated over the past decade. Changes in product design are more frequent, and product lifecycles are shorter. IBM estimates the average life of its new product offerings is about six months. The ability to get new products to the market quickly has revolutionized the competitive environment and changed the nature of manufacturing.

Part of the impetus for the deluge of new products is the advancement of technology available for designing products. It begins with computer-aided design (CAD) and includes related technologies such as computer-aided engineering (CAE), computer-aided manufacturing (CAM), and collaborative product design (CPD).

Computer-aided design (CAD) is a software system that uses computer graphics to assist in the creation, modification, and analysis of a design. A geometric design is generated that includes not only the dimensions of the product but also tolerance information and material specifications. The ability to sort, classify, and retrieve similar designs from a CAD database facilitates standardization of parts, prompts ideas, and eliminates building a design from scratch.

CAD-generated products can also be tested more quickly. Engineering analysis, performed with a CAD system, is called **computer-aided engineering (CAE)**. CAE retrieves the description and geometry of a part from a CAD database and subjects it to testing and analysis on the computer screen without physically building a prototype. CAE can maximize the storage space in a car trunk, detect whether plastic parts are cooling evenly, and determine how much stress will cause a bridge to crack. With CAE, design teams can watch a car bump along a rough road, the pistons of an engine move up and down, a golf ball soar through the air, or the effect of new drugs on virtual DNA molecules. Advances in virtual reality and motion capturing technology allow designers and users to experience the design without building a physical prototype.

The ultimate design-to-manufacture connection is a **computer-aided design/computer-aided manufacturing (CAD/CAM)** system. CAM is the acronym for *computer-aided manufacturing*. CAD/CAM involves the automatic conversion of CAD design data into processing instructions for computer-controlled equipment and the subsequent manufacture of the part as it was designed. This integration of design and manufacture can save enormous amounts of time, ensure that parts and products are produced *precisely* as intended, and facilitate revisions in design or customized production.

Besides the time savings, CAD and its related technologies have also improved the *quality* of designs and the products manufactured from them. The communications capabilities of CAD may be more important than its processing capabilities in terms of design quality. CAD systems enhance communication and promote innovation in multifunctional design teams by providing a visual, interactive focus for discussion. Watching a vehicle strain its wheels over mud and ice prompts ideas on product design and customer use better than stacks of consumer surveys or engineering reports. New ideas can be suggested and tested immediately, allowing more alternatives to be evaluated. To facilitate discussion or clarify a design, CAD data can be sent electronically between designer and supplier or viewed simultaneously on computer screens by different designers in physically separate locations. Rapid prototypes can be tested more thoroughly with CAD/CAE. More prototypes can be tested as well. CAD improves every stage of product design and is especially useful as a means of integrating design and manufacture.

With so many new designs and changes in existing designs, a system is needed to keep track of design revisions. Such a system is called **product lifecycle management (PLM)**. PLM stores, retrieves, and updates design data from the product concept, through manufacturing, revision, service, and retirement of the product.

COLLABORATIVE PRODUCT DESIGN SYSTEMS

The benefits of CAD-designed products are magnified when combined with the ability to share product-design files and work on them in real time from physically separate locations. Collaborative design can take place between designers in the same company, between manufacturers and suppliers, or between manufacturers and customers. Manufacturers can send out product designs electronically with request for quotes (RFQ) from potential component suppliers. Or performance specs can be posted to a website from which suppliers can create and transmit their own designs. Designs can receive final approval from customers before expensive processing takes place. A complex design can involve hundreds of suppliers. The Web allows them to work together throughout the design and manufacturing processes, not just at the beginning and the end.

Software systems for collaborative design are loosely referred to as **collaborative product design (CPD)**. These systems provide the interconnectivity and translation capabilities necessary for collaborative work across platforms, departments, and companies. In conjunction with PLM systems, they also manage product data, set up project workspaces, and follow product development through the entire product lifecycle.

Collaborative design accelerates product development, helps to resolve product launch issues, and improves the quality of the design. Designers can conduct virtual review sessions, test "what if" scenarios, assign and track design issues, communicate with multiple tiers of suppliers, and create, store, and manage project documents.

These virtual review sessions often include the design review tools presented in the next section.

Design Quality Reviews

Before finalizing a design, formal procedures for analyzing possible failures and rigorously assessing the value of every part and component should be followed. Three such techniques are failure mode and effects analysis, fault tree analysis, and value analysis.

Failure mode and effects analysis (FMEA) is a systematic approach to analyzing the causes and effects of product failures. It begins with listing the functions of the product and each of its parts. Failure modes are then defined and ranked in order of their seriousness and likelihood of failure. Failures are addressed one by one (beginning with the most catastrophic), causes are hypothesized, and design changes are made to reduce the chance of failure. The objective of FMEA is to anticipate failures and prevent them from occurring. Table 4.1 shows a partial FMEA for potato chips.

Fault tree analysis (FTA) is a visual method of analyzing the *interrelationship* among failures. FTA lists failures and their causes in a tree format using two hatlike symbols, one with a straight line on the bottom representing *and*, and one with a curved line on the bottom for *or*. Figure 4.5 shows a partial FTA for a food manufacturer who has a problem with potato chip breakage. In this analysis, potato chips break because they are too thin *or* because they are too brittle. The options for fixing the problem of too-thin chips—increasing thickness or reducing size—are undesirable, as indicated by the Xs. The problem of too-brittle chips can be alleviated by adding more moisture *or* having fewer ridges *or* adjusting the frying procedure. We choose to adjust the frying procedure, which leads to the question of how hot the oil should be *and* how long to fry the chips. Once these values are determined, the issue of too-brittle chips (and thus chip breakage) is solved, as indicated.

TABLE 4.1 Failure Mode and Effects Analysis for Potato Chips

Failure Mode	Cause of Failure	Effect of Failure	Corrective Action
Stale	Low moisture content, expired shelf life, poor packaging	Tastes bad, won't crunch, thrown out, lost sales	Add moisture, cure longer, better package seal, shorter shelf life
Broken	Too thin, too brittle, rough handling, rough use, poor packaging	Can't dip, poor display, injures mouth, choking, perceived as old, lost sales	Change recipe, change process, change packaging
Too Salty	Outdated recipe, process not in control, uneven distribution of salt	Eat less, drink more, health hazard, lost sales	Experiment with recipe, experiment with process, introduce low-salt version

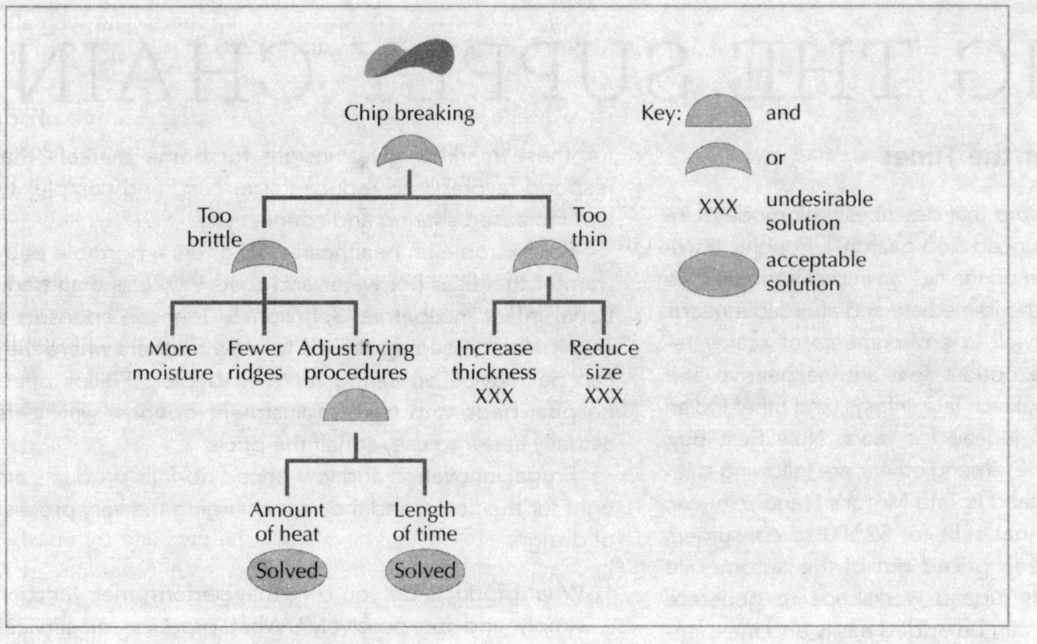

Figure 4.5

Fault Tree Analysis for Potato Chips

Value analysis (VA) (also known as value engineering) was developed by General Electric in 1947 to eliminate unnecessary features and functions in product designs. It has re-emerged as a technique for use by multifunctional design teams. The design team defines the essential functions of a component, assembly, or product using a verb and a noun. For example, the function of a container might be described as *holds fluid*. Then the team assigns a value to each function and determines the cost of providing the function. With that information, a ratio of value to cost can be calculated for each item. The team attempts to improve the ratio by either reducing the cost of the item or increasing its worth. Updated versions of value analysis also assess the environmental impact of materials, parts, and operations. This leads us to the next section on design for environment.

Design for Environment

Sustainability is the ability to meet present needs without compromising those of future generations. It is not only a lofty goal, but a practical one as companies worldwide are discovering the cost savings and consumer goodwill that green practices provide. For example, by eliminating excessive packaging on its private label toy line, Walmart saved $2.4 million a year in shipping costs, 3,800 trees, and 1 million barrels of oil. Installing auxiliary power sources in its fleet of trucks (instead of idling the engine while drivers sleep) saved $26 million in fuel costs. Baling plastic refuse for recycling and resale provided an additional $28 million in revenue. Buoyed by these successes, Walmart began mandating that its suppliers meet certain environmental (and cost-saving) standards such as reduced packaging, condensed liquids, green product formulations, and sustainable design. A sustainability scorecard for suppliers is now included in eco-labeling of Walmart products. For companies that supply Walmart and other large corporations, it became evident that the place to start meeting environmental requirements is with green product design, or what is more globally referred to as *design for environment* (DFE).

Design for environment (DFE) involves many aspects of design, such as designing products from recycled material, reducing hazardous chemicals, using materials or components that can be recycled after use, designing a product so that it is easier to repair than discard, and

ALONG THE SUPPLY CHAIN

Jugaad, Design for the Times

India has a Hindi slang word that describes their mode of innovation, *jugaad* (pronounced "joo-gaardh"). Roughly translated, it means "invention on the fly," an improvisational style of innovation based on the immediate and affordable needs of customers. It works well in environments of scarce resources where workable options that are inexpensive and quick to implement are valued. Tata, Infosys, and other Indian corporations have used jugaad for years. Now Best Buy, Cisco Systems, and Oracle, among others, are following suit.

One example of jugaad is Tata Motor's Nano mini-car, a bare-bones product that sells for $2,500 to consumers who had heretofore been priced out of the automobile market. Best Buy holds jugaad workshops to generate new product ideas that can be added easily and inexpensively to existing stores (e.g., home healthcare equipment). Cisco likes the Indian approach of affordability and scale. Repurposing existing ideas and technologies in simple ways helps to reduce R&D spending and adds to high-margin products.

This is similar to the micro-financing success in third-world countries, where small loans applied to basic needs can make a big difference. In fact, there is a reversal in the trend in design from multinationals who would typically "trickle down" ideas and products from affluent Western nations, to "trickling up" ideas and solutions from third-world countries. GE, Procter & Gamble, Nokia, and others are watching how Asian and African consumers handle medical equipment, foods, and cell phones. Designing for these markets gives insight for home markets that respond favorably to reduced size, cost, and complexity, and increased sharing and connectivity.

For example, in healthcare, GE offers a portable baby warmer that uses hot water and costs 99% less than traditional infant incubators. Johnson & Johnson sponsors a Text4baby messaging service for new mothers where they can get advice on caring for their babies. Philips offers hospital beds with fewer adjustment options, which are actually easier to use, at half the price.

Frugal innovation and low-priced no-frills products are right for the times, and they are changing the very process of design.

1. What products do you own that perform their function simply and inexpensively? What products or services would you like to see redesigned by a jugaad process?
2. Are there any products or services that you prefer to be designed more carefully and more futuristically and thus would not be good candidates for jugaad?
3. Get in the jugaad mindset by visiting www.frugalsolutions.org/ and discussing the best ideas.

Sources: Reena Jana, "India's Next Export—Innovation," *BusinessWeek* (December 2, 2009); Reena Jana, "Innovation Trickles Down," *BusinessWeek* (March 11, 2009); Navi Radjou, Jaideep Prabhu and Simone Ahuja, "Finding the Jugaad for U.S. Health Care," *CNN Global* (November 9, 2012); http://globalpublicsquare.blogs.cnn.com/2012/11/09/finding-the-jugaad-for-u-s-healthcare/; Philip McClellan, "Is Jugaad Going Global?" *The New York Times* (October 11, 2012); Peter Hesseldahl, "Jugaad Innovation," *Innovation Management* (December 12, 2012).

minimizing unnecessary packaging. As shown in Figure 4.6, it extends across the product lifecycle from raw material sourcing to manufacture to consumer use to end-of-life recycling, reuse, or disposal. We discuss each of these areas below.

GREEN SOURCING

Design for environment begins with using less material, and, where possible, using recycled material, organic material (e.g., that has not been treated with chemicals), nontoxic material and conflict-free material. The material should also be renewable, not endangered or scarce, and durable, so that the product will last. Suppliers should be vetted to ensure that their processes are environmentally sound, and should be located nearby so that greenhouse gases are minimized in transportation. Finally, the design should be rationalized so that only the needed features (and thus material) are included, and so that the product is saleable and will not end up, unused, in landfills. Standard procurement practices focus on meeting design specifications, without the customer comes to buy, but the service may persuade or dissuade a customer from making the purchase.

In this chapter, we'll learn about the principles of service design and the importance of a well-designed customer experience.

Source: Based on "Denim Jeans: State of the U.S. Market," *Cotton Incorporated Supply Chain Insights* (2011); www.levistrauss.com

The Service Economy

Services are the predominant force in our society. In the United States, services account for 80% of the labor force, 94% of job growth, and 81% of GDP. Globally, services account for over 50% of the economies of Brazil, Russia, Japan, Germany, India, and China. The impact of supporting services on product success has turned product-producing companies into service providers. Increased outsourcing of business services demands more in-depth understanding of the service product and standards for quality. Service computing has prompted a new level of understanding of customer requirements and design theory. Major societal problems, such as education, healthcare, disaster relief, and government services, depend on complex customer-focused processes and benefit significantly from an innovative and interdisciplinary approach to their study and analysis. This unprecedented shift in customer, corporate, and societal demand for services and the management of corresponding resources has created a critical need for the study, analysis, and design of service systems.

The rise of the service sector is not just a U.S. phenomenon. As shown in Figure 5.1, all of the countries listed, with the exception of Turkey, China, and India, employ more than 50%

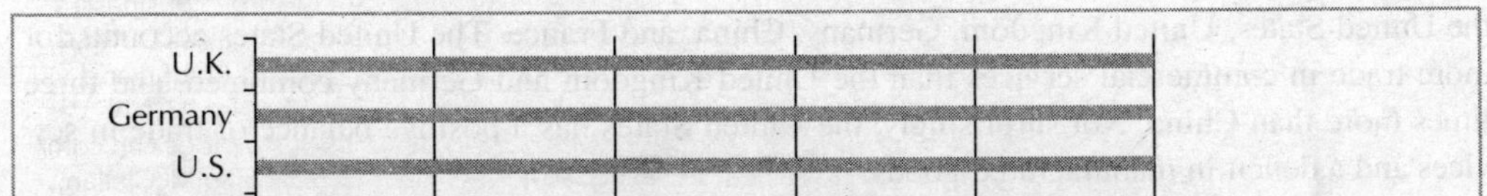

Figure 5.1

Percent of Employment by Industry Sector, Select Countries

SOURCE: The World Bank, 2012.

Figure 5.2

Percent of GDP by Industry Sector, U.S.

SOURCE: Economic Report of the President, Table B12, U.S. Government Printing Office (February 2012).

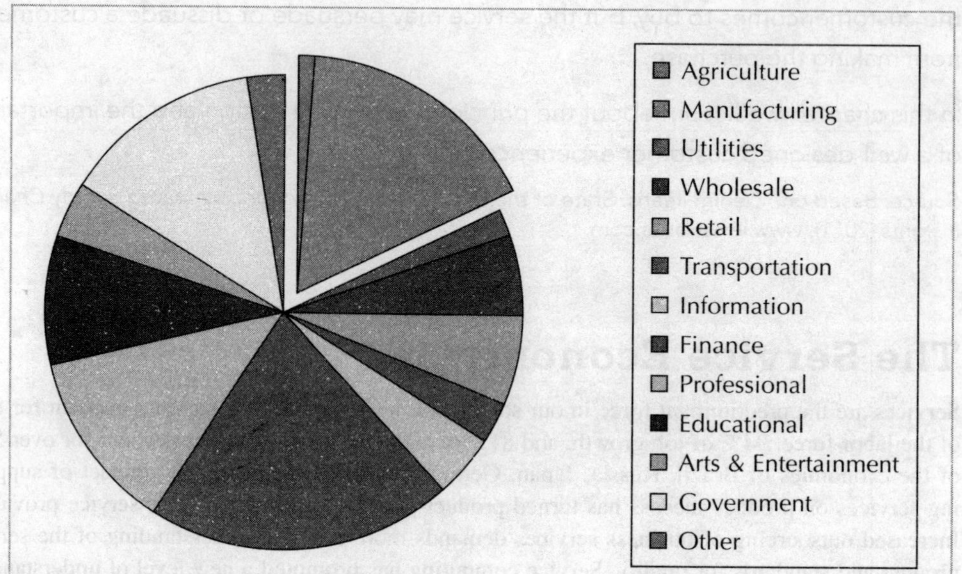

of their workforce in the service sector. Services represent the fastest-growing sector of the global economy, accounting for two-thirds of global output and nearly 20% of global trade. Services also account for a large percentage of GDP worldwide.

Figure 5.2 shows U.S. figures on percent of GDP by industry sector. The two slices pulled out from the pie are agriculture, which accounts for 1.1% of GDP, and manufacturing with 16.7%. The remainder of GDP, over 80%, is attributed to services. Financial services, alone, exceed manufacturing's contribution. Government services, professional services, and educational services contribute on average 13%, 12%, and 9% to GDP, respectively. The leading service exporters are the United States, United Kingdom, Germany, China, and France. The United States accounts for more trade in commercial services than the United Kingdom and Germany combined, and three times more than China. Not surprisingly, the United States has a positive balance of trade in services and a deficit in manufactured goods.

In this chapter, we discuss the characteristics of services, the service design process, tools for service design, and waiting line theory for service improvement.

Characteristics of Services

Services are acts, deeds, performances, or relationships that produce time, place, form, or psychological utilities for customers. A cleaning service saves the customer *time* from doing the chores himself. Department stores and grocery stores provide many commodities for sale in one convenient *place*. An online broker puts together information in a *form* more usable for the investor. A night out at a restaurant or movie provides *psychological* refreshment in the middle of a busy workweek.

Services can also be defined in contrast to goods. A **good** is a tangible object that can be created and sold or used later. A service is intangible and perishable. It is created and consumed simultaneously. Although these definitions may seem straightforward, the distinction between goods and services is not always clear-cut. For example, when we purchase a car, are we purchasing a good or the service of transportation? A flat-screen TV is a manufactured good, but what use is it without the service of television broadcasting? When we go to a fast-food restaurant, are we buying the service of having our food prepared for us, or are we buying goods that happen to be ready-to-eat food items?

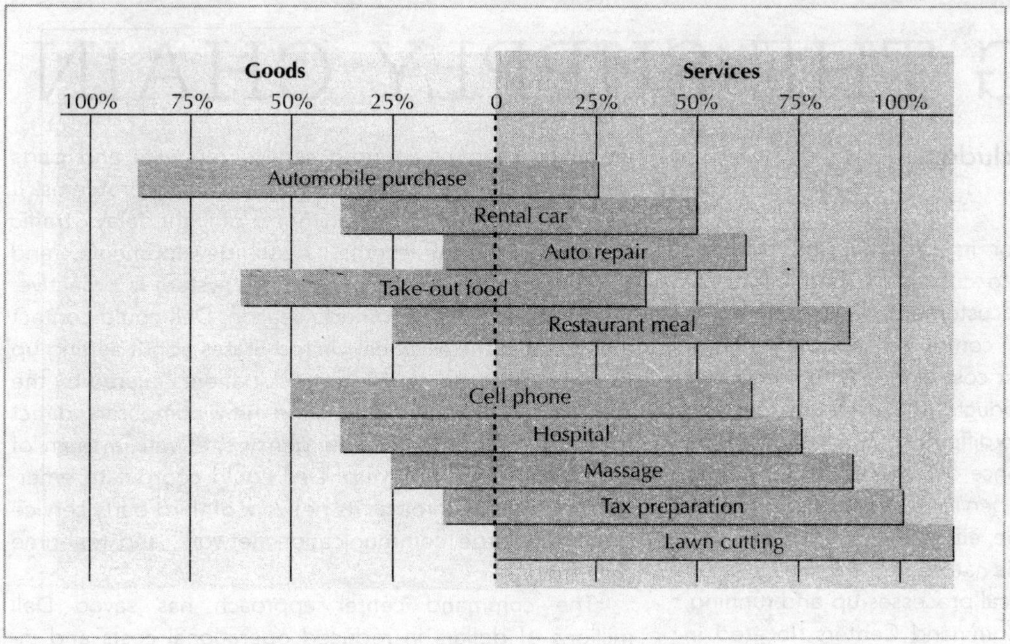

Figure 5.3

A Continuum from Goods to Services

SOURCE: Adapted from Earl W. Sasser, R. P. Olsen, and D. Daryl Wyckoff, *Management of Service Operations* (Boston: Allyn & Bacon, 1978), p. 11.

In reality, almost all purchases of goods are accompanied by *facilitating services*, and almost every service purchase is accompanied by *facilitating goods*. Thus, the key to understanding the difference between goods and services lies in the realization that these items are not completely distinct but rather are two poles on a continuum, as shown in Figure 5.3.

Understanding the different characteristics of services can help us better design service activities and the systems for their delivery.

Services can be distinguished from manufacturing by the following eight characteristics. Although not all services possess each of these characteristics, they do exhibit at least some of them to some degree.

1. ***Services are intangible***. It is difficult to design something you cannot see, touch, store on a shelf, or try on for size. Services are *experienced*, and that experience may be different for each individual customer. Designing a service involves describing what the customer is supposed to "experience," which can be a difficult task. Designers begin by compiling information on the way people think, feel, and behave (called *psychographics*).

   Because of its intangibility, consumers perceive a service to be more risky to purchase than a product. Cues (such as physical surroundings, server's demeanor, and service guarantees) need to be included in service design to help form or reinforce accurate perceptions of the service experience and reduce the consumer's risk.

   The quality of a service experience depends largely on the customer's service *expectations*. Expectations can differ according to a customer's knowledge, experience, and self-confidence.

   Customers also have different expectations of different types of service providers. You probably expect more from a department store than from a discount store, or from a car dealer's service center than from an independent repair shop. Understanding the customer and his or her expectations is essential in designing good service.

2. ***Service output is variable***. This is true because of the various service providers employed and the variety of customers they serve, each with his or her own special needs. Even though customer demands vary, the service experience is expected to remain consistent. According to a recent survey, the most important measures of service quality to the customer are reliability and consistency. Service design, then, must strive for predictability

ALONG THE SUPPLY CHAIN

Dell's Service Now Includes Disaster Recovery

Dell Computers, known for its breakthrough business model of direct shipping to customers, had been losing sales in recent years as customer buying preferences changed to "experiencing" computers in storefronts, or purchasing based on lowest cost alone. With computers considered commodity products, the profit margin was low and competition stiff. To differentiate its product from others, the company that once outsourced its call center to India, turned to superior service—and not your run-of-the-mill customer service line, either.

Recognizing the strategic nature of IT services and the importance of keeping critical processes up and running, Dell created five Global Command Centers, located in Austin, Texas; Limerick, Ireland; Kawasaki, Japan; Xiamen, China; and Penang, Malaysia. These customer-focused centers not only coordinate parts logistics worldwide and respond quickly to customer requests; they also monitor potential supply chain problems (such as natural disasters) and help their customers develop contingency plans to keep their own computer networks operational.

The command centers are NASA-like with computer consoles arranged in a tiered auditorium facing huge wall-mounted computer screens. The screens display live information feeds of service requests, maps, live video, news and weather via a custom-designed technology platform called Clear View monitoring. Supporting the center are 30,000 technical experts worldwide and thousands of local field engineers who can be dispatched to perform local repairs. Spare parts can also be routed from over 600 global parts depots.

Clear View is a combination of business activity-monitoring software, business process management, and expert system. It interacts with a geographic information system (GIS) that matches requests to parts locations, and identifies patterns in both service requests and parts delivery that might predict trends or future problems. It also evaluates the potential impact of flight delays, traffic congestion, local events, news developments, and weather on time-to-repair. And the system is proactive. For example, during tornado season, Dell could contact a hospital in the Midwest United States about setting up its own command center to track patients injured by the tornado. Further, it could send new computers direct from the factory to an emergency site, with a team of engineers to set them up. Dell could coordinate emergency response through its network of third-party service providers, large communication network, and real-time data feeds.

The command center approach has saved Dell millions of dollars in reduced operational costs and increased supply chain efficiency. The expertise learned from operating the centers has prepared the company for mobilizing IT resources for large-scale customer events, security breaches, or natural disasters of its own. More importantly, the centers have made it possible for Dell to reach out and help customers deal with disruptions and delays beyond either party's control—that is, to become a valued partner beyond the computers it sells.

1. Compare the customer base of Dell computers versus Apple computers. What is the source of competitive advantage for each company?
2. Discuss the capabilities that Dell command centers bring to the company and its customers. How can Dell afford to operate these command centers and aid its customers in times of disruption? What is the payback?
3. Think about how Dell has blurred the line between products and services. What other examples can you think of when this has occurred?

Source: Based on James Cooke, "Inside Dell's global command centers," *Supply Chain Quarterly*, no. 3 (2012).

or robustness. Examples of services known for their consistency include McDonald's, Marriott, and ServiceMaster. Extensive employee training, set operating procedures, and standardized materials, equipment, and physical environments are used by these companies to increase consistency.

3. ***Services have higher customer contact***. The service "encounter" between service provider and customer *is* the service in many cases. Making sure the encounter is a positive one is part of service design. This involves giving the service provider the skills and authority necessary

to complete a customer transaction successfully. Studies show a direct link between service provider motivation and customer satisfaction. Moreover, service providers are not motivated primarily by compensation but rather by concurrence with the firm's "service concept" and being able to perform their job competently.

High customer contact can interfere with the efficiency of a service and make it difficult to control its quality (i.e., there is no opportunity for testing and rework). However, direct contact with customers can also be an advantage for services. Observing customers experiencing a service generates new service ideas and facilitates feedback for improvements to existing services.

4. ***Services are perishable***. Because services can't be inventoried, the timing and location of delivery are important. Service design should define not only *what* is to be delivered but also *where* and *when*.
5. ***The service and the service delivery are inseparable***. That means service design and process design must occur concurrently. (This is one area in which services have an advantage over manufacturing—it has taken manufacturing a number of years to realize the benefits of concurrent design.) In addition to deciding what, where, and when, service design also specifies *how* the service should be provided. "How" decisions include the degree of customer participation in the service process, which tasks should be done in the presence of the customer (called front-room activities) and which should be done out of the customer's sight (back-room activities), the role and authority of the service provider in delivering the service, and the balance of "touch" versus "tech" (i.e., how automated the service should be).
6. ***Services tend to be decentralized and geographically dispersed***. Many service employees are on their own to make decisions. Although this can present problems, careful service design will help employees deal successfully with contingencies. Multiple service outlets can be a plus in terms of rapid prototyping. New ideas can be field-tested with a minimum disturbance to operations. McDonald's considers each of its outlets a "laboratory" for new ideas.
7. ***Services are consumed more often than products***, so there are more opportunities to succeed or fail with the customer. Jan Carlzon, former president of SAS Airlines, calls these opportunities "moments of truth." Services are confronted with thousands of moments of truth each day. Careful design and redesign of the service encounter can help make each moment of truth a positive experience. In a sense, the service environment lends itself more readily to continuous improvement than does the manufacturing environment.
8. ***Services can be easily emulated***. Competitors can copy new or improved services quickly. New ideas are constantly needed to stay ahead of the competition. As a result, new service introductions and service improvements occur even more rapidly than new product introductions.

The Service Design Process

Services that are allowed to just happen rarely meet customer needs. World-class services that come to mind—McDonald's, Nordstrom, FedEx, Disney World—are all characterized by impeccable design. McDonald's plans every action of its employees (including 49 steps to making perfect french fries); Nordstrom creates a pleasurable shopping environment with well-stocked shelves, live music, fresh flowers in the dressing rooms, and legendary salespersons; FedEx designs every stage of the delivery process for efficiency and speed; and Disney World in Japan was so well designed that it impressed even the zero-defect Japanese.

Service design is more comprehensive and occurs more often than product design. The inherent variability of service processes requires that the service system be carefully designed. Figure 5.4 shows the service design process beginning with a service concept and ending with service delivery.

Figure 5.4

The Service Design Process

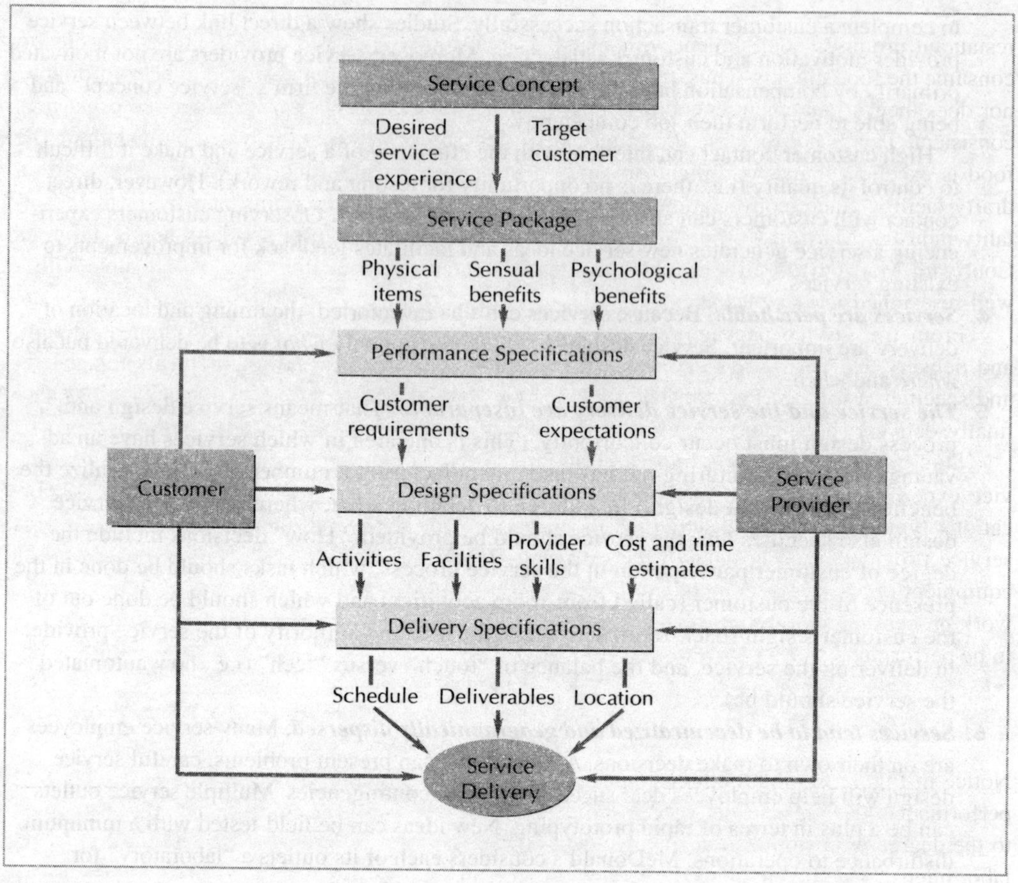

The **service concept** defines the target customer and the desired customer experience. It also defines how the service is different from others and how it will compete in the marketplace. Sometimes services are successful because their service concept fills a previously unoccupied niche or differs from the generally accepted mode of operation. For example, Citibank offers 15-minute mortgage approvals through online computer networks with real estate offices, credit bureaus, and builder's offices, and an expert system loan-application advisor. Amazon excels at customer service for online orders, and eBay's worldwide reach creates more lively auctions with a huge community of buyers and sellers. Shouldice Hospital performs only inguinal hernia operations, for which its doctors are very experienced and its facilities carefully designed. Local anesthesia is used; patients walk into and out of the operating room under their own power; and telephones, televisions, and dining facilities are located in a communal area some distance from patient rooms. As a result, patients quickly become ambulatory, are discharged within hours (compared to normal week-long stays), and pay one-third less for their operations.

From the service concept, a **service package** is created to meet customer needs. The package consists of a mixture of physical items, sensual benefits, and psychological benefits. For a restaurant the physical items consist of the facility, food, drinks, tableware, napkins, and other touchable commodities. The sensual benefits include the taste and aroma of the food and the sights and sounds of the people. Psychological benefits are rest and relaxation, comfort, status, and a sense of well-being.

Effective service design recognizes and defines *all* the components of a service package. Finding the appropriate mix of physical items and sensual and psychological benefits, and designing them to be consistent with each other and the service concept, are also important. A fast-food restaurant promises nourishment with speed. The customer is served quickly and is expected to consume the food quickly. Thus, the tables, chairs, and booths are not designed to be comfortable, nor does their arrangement encourage lengthy or personal conversations. The service package is consistent. This is not the case for an upscale restaurant located in a renovated train station. The food is excellent, but it is difficult to enjoy a full-course meal sitting on wooden benches in a drafty facility, where conversations echo and tables shake when the trains pass by. In the hospitality industry, Marriott Corporation is known for its careful design of specialty hotels. From its Courtyard Marriott to Fairfield Inn to residential centers, each facility "fits" its clientele with a well-researched service package.

From the service package, service specifications are developed for performance, design, and delivery. **Performance specifications** outline expectations and requirements for general and specific customers. Performance specifications are converted into design specifications and, finally, delivery specifications (in lieu of manufacturing specifications).

Design specifications must describe the service in sufficient detail for the desired service experience to be replicated for different individuals at numerous locations. The specifications typically consist of activities to be performed, skill requirements and guidelines for service providers, and cost and time estimates. Facility size, location, and layout, as well as equipment needs, are also included. **Delivery specifications** outline the steps required in the work process, including the work schedule, deliverables, and the locations at which the work is to be performed.

THE SERVICE-PROCESS MATRIX

Notice in Figure 5.4 that both customers and service providers may be involved in determining performance, design, and delivery specifications. Service processes can be classified according to the degree of customization (involvement of the customer in service design and delivery) and labor intensity (involvement of the service provider in service design and delivery).

Figure 5.5 shows a service-process matrix based on these two service characteristics. A *professional service*, such as accountant, lawyer, or doctor, is highly customized and very labor intensive. A *service shop*, such as schools and hospitals, is less customized and labor intensive

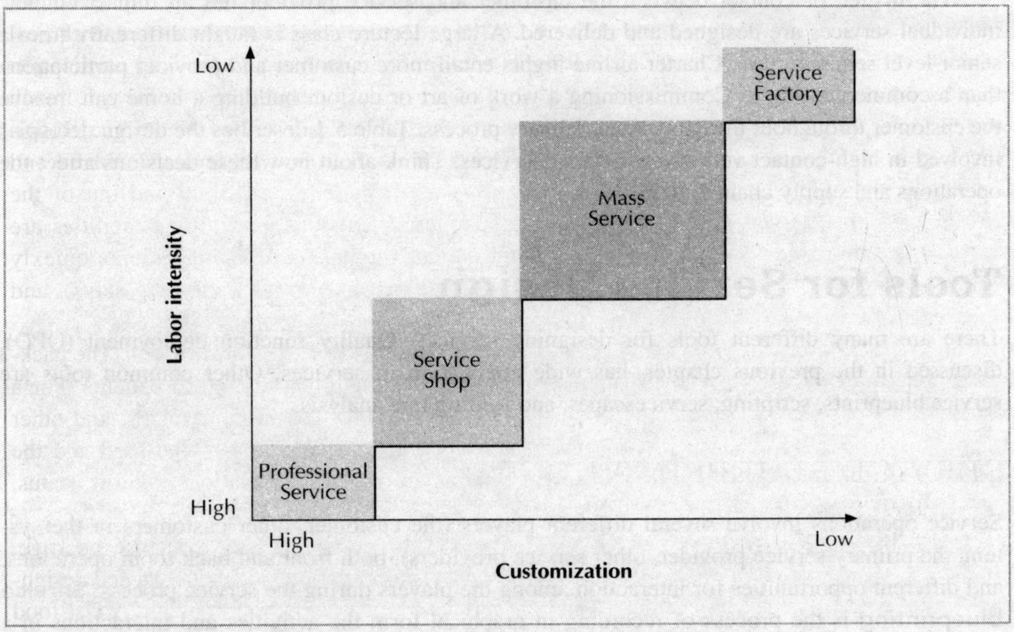

Figure 5.5
The Service-Process Matrix
SOURCE: Adapted from Roger Schmenner, "How Can Service Businesses Survive and Prosper?" *Sloan Management Review* 27, issue 3 (1986): 29.

TABLE 5.1 Differences in Design for High-Contact Services

Design Decision	High-Contact Service	Low-Contact Service
Facility location	Convenient to customer	Near labor or transportation source
Facility layout	Must look presentable, accommodate customer needs, and facilitate interaction with customer	Designed for efficiency
Quality control	More variable since customer is involved in process; customer expectations and perceptions of quality may differ; customer present when defects occur	Measured against established standards; testing and rework possible to correct defects
Capacity	Excess capacity required to handle peaks in demand	Planned for average demand
Worker skills	Must be able to interact well with customers and use judgment in decision making	Technical skills
Scheduling	Must accommodate customer schedule	Customer concerned only with completion date
Service process	Mostly front-room activities; service may change during delivery in response to customer	Mostly back-room activities; planned and executed with minimal interference
Service package	Varies with customer; includes environment as well as actual service	Fixed, less extensive

Source: Adapted from R. Chase, N. Aquilano, and R. Jacobs, *Operations Management for Compensative Advantage* (New York: McGraw-Hill, 2001), p. 210.

but still attentive to individual customers. A *mass service*, such as retailing and banking, offers the same basic services to all customers and allows less interaction with the service provider. Services with the least degree of customization and labor intensity, such as airlines and trucking, are most like manufactured products and are thus best processed by a *service factory*.

The degree of contact between the customer and service provider has an impact on how individual services are designed and delivered. A large lecture class is taught differently from a senior-level seminar class. Charter airline flights entail more customer and provider participation than a commercial flight. Commissioning a work of art or custom building a home can involve the customer throughout the design and delivery process. Table 5.1 describes the design decisions involved in high-contact versus low-contact services. Think about how these decisions affect the operations and supply chain system.

Tools for Service Design

There are many different tools for designing services. Quality function deployment (QFD), discussed in the previous chapter, has wide application in services. Other common tools are service blueprints, scripting, servicescapes, and waiting line analysis.

SERVICE BLUEPRINTING

Service operations involve several different players (the customer, other customers in the system, the primary service provider, other service providers), both front and back room operations, and different opportunities for interaction among the players during the service process. **Service blueprinting** is the process of recording in graphical form the activities and interactions in a

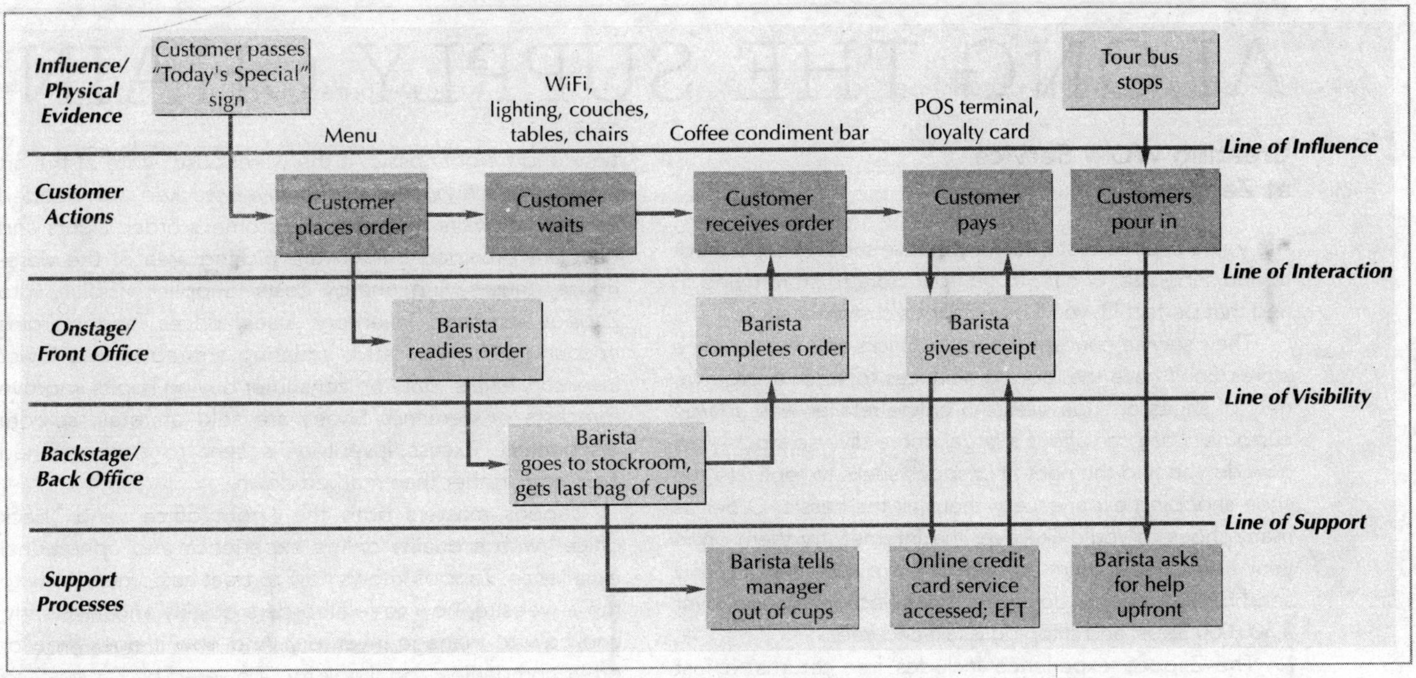

Figure 5.6

A Service Blueprint for a Coffee Shop

service process. The term *blueprinting* is used to reinforce the idea that services need to be as carefully designed as a physical product and documented with a blueprint of their own.

Figure 5.6 shows a sample service blueprint for a coffee shop operation. The blueprint consists of five components or lanes: (1) influence and physical evidence; (2) customer actions; (3) onstage provider actions (i.e., front office); (4) backstage provider actions (i.e., back office); and (5) support processes. Lines separate these components of the service encounter. The **line of influence** shows activities designed to influence the customer to enter the service facility, and the physical evidence to take action throughout the service process. The **line of interaction** is where the customer interacts with the service provider face-to-face. The **line of visibility** separates front-office (or onstage) activities from back-office (or backstage) activities. In this example, the barista prepares the coffee in front of the customer, but must go backstage to retrieve cups from the stockroom. The **line of support** is where the service provider interacts with backstage support personnel to complete their tasks. Moving these various lines on the service blueprint allows the designer to experiment with expanding or decreasing the activities in each area. For example, the barista could disappear behind a curtain to prepare the coffee, or the customer could serve the coffee herself and interact with the service provider only when paying.

In services there are constant tradeoffs between customer service and efficiency. Starbucks has redesigned the role of its barista several times, at one point reducing the number of baristas and thus requiring them to prepare several customer orders at a time, and more recently, increasing quality by asking baristas to prepare no more than two orders at a time, starting the second order while the first is being readied. A service blueprint can specify the exact process for serving a customer (including whether a barista rings up an order or simply prepares the order) and can codify rules (such as when to call in additional baristas). The consistency with which a service is provided is an important measure of service quality and customer satisfaction.

ALONG THE SUPPLY CHAIN

Creating WOW Service at Zappos

Are you a Zappos customer? If you love shoes, have a hard-to-find shoe size, or hate to go from store to store trying to find that perfect fit, you'll be a Zappos customer soon.

Their service concept is simple. Bricks-and-mortar shoe stores don't have the room or finances to stock a large variety of shoes or shoe sizes. An online retailer with a large customer base can afford a larger, more diverse stock—but how do you find the right fit? Zappos seeks to replicate the shoe shopping experience without all the hassle. Order as many shoes as you'd like over the Internet, try them on in your home, wear them around to make sure they fit, and send back those you don't like. The selection is huge (over 2,500,000 SKUs) and shipping is fast and free.

The Zappos experience includes free returns, a fast and responsive website, top-name brands, elaborate product descriptions, real customer reviews, and a 24-hour call center. Call center operators are knowledgeable and friendly, answer the phone within 20 seconds, have the authority to resolve disputes and spend as much time as necessary with each customer (longest recorded customer call—10 hours). Most orders are updated to next-day delivery, and customers have 365 days to return unwanted merchandise. Collectively, these deliver WOW service, one of Zappos' 10 core values.

So how does Zappos do it? To compensate for free shipping and call center expenses, the company has to be very cost conscious. There are no fancy headquarters or separate offices for executives. The West Coast and East Coast locations are smart and low-cost. Programming is coded in-house using open source software. Warehousing and distribution are handled at its own fulfillment center. The fulfillment center is located near UPS's worldwide air hub (Worldport) at the Louisville, Kentucky, airport where hourly pickups from UPS allow overnight delivery to more locations. Returns are sent by ground. Zappos trucks pick up merchandise from its suppliers at the docks to save time and freight costs. At the warehouse, state-of-the-art robots (from Kiva) transport shelves stocked with needed items to workers who *pick* a customer's order. Lights and heat are provided only in the picking area of the warehouse, thus saving energy costs. Supplier visibility into Zappos' on-hand inventory, sales, prices, and margins encourages collaborative ordering strategies and lower inventory levels. Data on consumer buying habits improve forecasts of demand. Shoes are sold at retail, seldom discounted. Excess inventory is sent to Zappo-owned 6pm.com, rather than marked down.

Zappos masters both the "front office" and "back office" with a quality online experience and operational excellence. Zappos knows how to treat customers, how to run a website, how to fulfill orders quickly and efficiently, and how to manage inventory. And now it does that for other companies, too. Look for "Powered by Zappos" on your favorite website. As CEO Tony Hsieh says, "Zappos is a service company that just happens to sell shoes," and now other merchandise, too.

1. Zappos has an interesting corporate culture. Go to the company website and read about the company and its management. What advantage does this culture provide?
2. Amazon now owns Zappos. What are the similarities and differences between the two companies? What changes would you anticipate at each company as a result of the merger?
3. Read about UPS Worldport on the web and watch a video about the facility on National Geographic's *Ultimate Factories*. How does the strategic partnership with UPS enhance Zappos' customer service model?

Sources: Based on Tony Hsieh, "Why I Sold Zappos," *Inc.* (June 6, 2010); "Zappos.com: Developing a Supply Chain to Deliver WOW," Stanford School of Business, Case GS-65, 2009; Jessie Scanlon, "How Kiva Robots Help Zappos and Walgreens," *Business Week* (April 15, 2009); Christopher Palmeri, "Zappos Retails Its Culture," *Business Week* (December 30, 2009); Martha White, "Zappos Service Call Lasts 10 Hours," NBC News.com, 10-31-12; *Ultimate Factories*, National Geographic Channel, http://channel.nationalgeographic.com/channel/ultimate-factories/videos/ups-worldport/.

FRONT-OFFICE AND BACK-OFFICE ACTIVITIES

In manufacturing firms, the focus of activities is on the back office (i.e., producing products efficiently), whereas in service firms, the focus is on the front office, interacting with the customer. Every firm needs both a front and back office, but firms may structure these in different ways.

In the front office, the customer interface can be an individual, the service provider, or a self-service kiosk or machine. The interactions in the front office influence the customer's perception of the service and thus are critical to a successful design. Typical front office goals are courtesy, transparency, responsiveness, usability, and fun.

The back-office processes material or information to support the front-office needs. Typical goals of the back office are efficiency, productivity, standardization, and scalability.

Obvious conflicts exist between front and back offices. Connecting the front and back offices in a meaningful way and encouraging the flow of information and support are two of the challenges of service design. Designing the service with an eye to the entire system will help alleviate some of the tensions. Mass customization is an example of a front/back compromise. Instead of giving customers the freedom to order anything they want, present a menu of options from which the customer may choose. This provides some stability to the back office, while also being responsive to the customer.

SERVICESCAPES

It is precisely because services are so intangible that physical cues to service quality are needed. **Servicescapes** design: (1) the space and function where the service takes places; (2) the ambient conditions, such as music, temperature, décor, and noise; and (3) signs, symbols, and artifacts. It is important that the servicescape be consistent with the service concept, and that all the elements be consistent with each other.

Servicescapes have proved to be extremely important to customer perceptions of service quality and to their satisfaction with the service.

QUANTITATIVE TECHNIQUES

There are many quantitative techniques for improving the service process. One of the most common and powerful is waiting line analysis, covered in the next several sections.

Waiting Line Analysis for Service Improvement

Anyone who goes shopping, to the post office, or to a movie experiences the inconvenience of waiting in line. Not only do people spend time waiting in lines, but machinery waits in line to be serviced or repaired, trucks line up to be loaded or unloaded at a shipping terminal, and planes wait to take off and land. Waiting takes place in virtually every productive process or service. Since the time spent by people and things waiting in line is a valuable resource, the reduction of waiting time is an important aspect of operations management.

Companies are able to reduce waiting time and provide faster service by increasing their service capacity, which usually means adding more servers—that is, more tellers, more mechanics, or more checkout clerks. However, increasing service capacity has a monetary cost, and therein lies the basis of waiting line analysis: the tradeoff between the cost of improved service and the cost of making customers wait.

Waiting lines are analyzed with a set of mathematical formulas that comprise a field of study called *queuing theory*. Different queuing models and mathematical formulas exist to deal with different types of waiting line systems. Although we discuss several of the most common types of queuing systems, we do not investigate the mathematical derivation of the queuing formulas. They are generally complex and not really pertinent to our understanding of the use of waiting line analysis to improve service.

ELEMENTS OF WAITING LINE ANALYSIS

Waiting lines form because people or things arrive at a server faster than they can be served. This does not mean that the service operation is understaffed or does not have the capacity to handle the influx of customers. Most businesses and organizations have sufficient serving capacity available to handle their customers *in the long run*. Waiting lines result because customers do not arrive at a constant, evenly paced rate, nor are they all served in an equal amount of time. Customers arrive at random times, and the time required to serve each individual is not the same. A waiting line is continually increasing and decreasing in length (and is sometimes empty) but in the long run approaches an average length and waiting time. For example, your local bank may have enough tellers to serve an average of 100 customers in an hour, and in a particular hour only 60 customers might arrive. However, at specific points in time during the hour, waiting lines may form because more than an average number of customers arrive and they have transactions that require more than the average amount of time.

Decisions about waiting lines and the management of waiting lines are based on these averages for customer arrivals and service times. They are used in queuing formulas or models to compute **operating characteristics** such as the average number of customers waiting in line and the average time a customer must wait in line. Different sets of formulas are used, depending on the type of waiting line system being investigated. A bank drive-up teller window at which one bank clerk serves a single line of customers in cars is different from a single line of passengers at an airline ticket counter that are served by three or four airline agents. In this section, we present the elements that make up waiting lines before looking at waiting line formulas.

The Waiting Line

The basic elements of a waiting line are the calling population, arrivals, servers, and the waiting line or **queue**. The relationship between these elements is shown in Figure 5.7 for the simplest type of *waiting line system*, a single server with a single queue. Following is a brief description of each of these waiting line elements.

The Calling Population

In our discussions of waiting lines, a customer is a person or thing that wants service from an operation. The **calling population** is the source of the customers to the waiting line system, and it can be either *infinite* or *finite*. An infinite calling population assumes such a large number of potential customers that it is always possible for one more customer to arrive to be served. For example, for the department store in Figure 5.7, we assume the calling population is infinite; to have, that is, the whole town or geographic area.

A finite calling population has a specific, countable number of potential customers. Examples of a finite calling population are a repair person in a shop who is responsible for a fixed number of machines to work on, a trucking terminal that services a fleet of 10 trucks, or a nurse assigned to attend to only 12 patients.

The Arrival Rate

The **arrival rate** is the rate at which customers arrive at the service facility during a specified period. This rate can be estimated from empirical data derived from studying the system or a similar system, or it can be an average of these empirical data. For example, if 100 customers arrive at a store checkout counter during a 10-hour day, we could say the arrival rate averages 10 customers per hour. However, it might be that no customers would arrive during one hour and 20 customers would arrive during another hour. Arrivals are assumed to be independent of each other and to vary randomly over time.

The variability of arrivals at a service facility often conform to a probability distribution. Arrivals could be described by many distributions, but it has been determined (through years of research and the practical experience of people in the field of queuing) that the number of

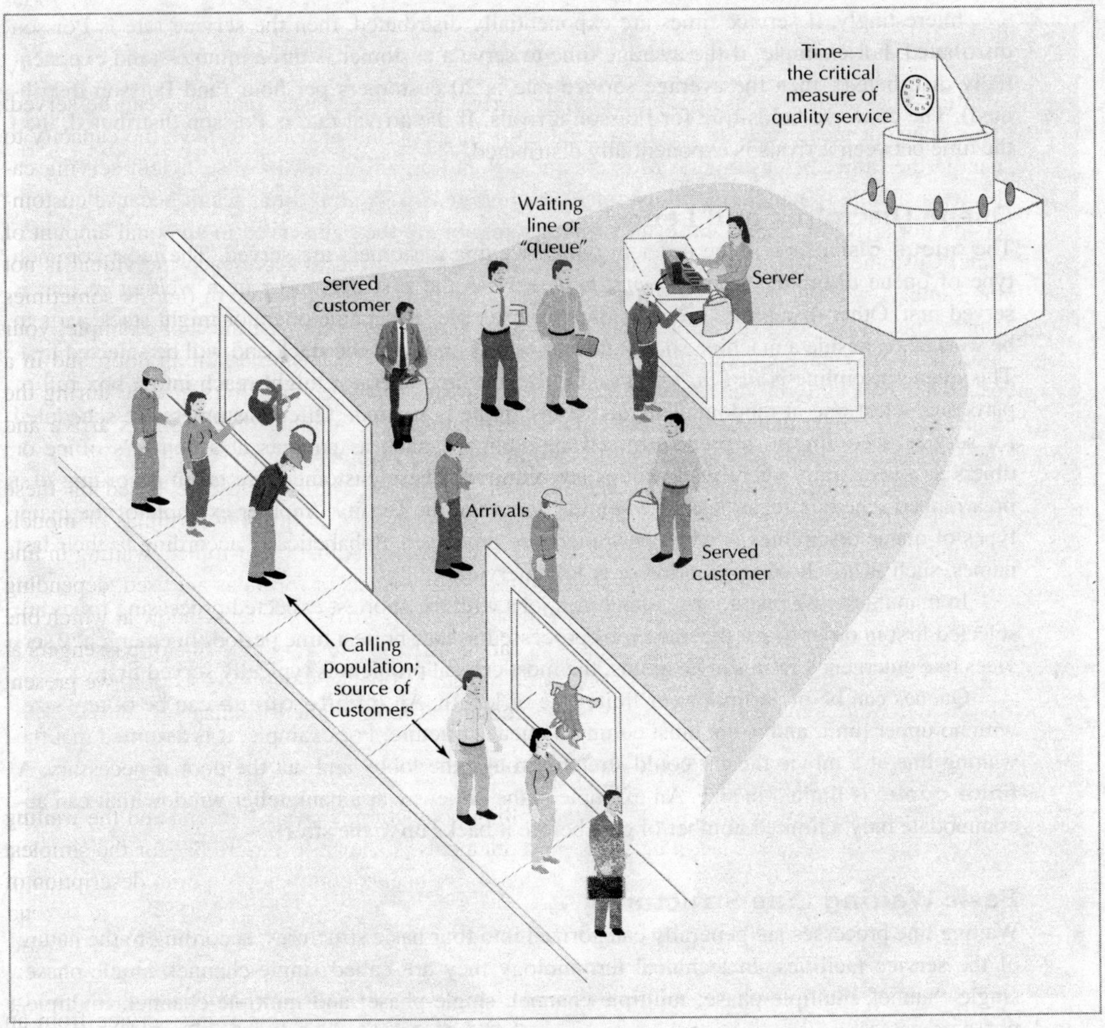

Figure 5.7

Elements of a Waiting Line System

arrivals per unit of time at a service facility can frequently be described by a *Poisson distribution*. In queuing, the average arrival rate, or how many customers arrive during a period of time, is signified by λ.

For the models presented in this chapter, we assume there is no *balking* (refusing to join a line), *reneging* (leaving a line), or *jockeying* (changing lines) by customers in the waiting line system. We also assume that the arrival rate is less than the service rate (or else the line would grow infinitely long).

Service Times

In waiting line analysis, arrivals are described in terms of a *rate*, and service in terms of *time*. **Service times** in a queuing process may also be any one of a large number of different probability distributions. The distribution most commonly assumed for service times is the negative *exponential distribution*. Although this probability distribution is for service *times*, service must be expressed as a *rate* to be compatible with the arrival rate. The average service rate, or how many customers can be served in a period of time, is expressed as μ.

Empirical research has shown that the assumption of negative exponentially distributed service times is not valid as often as is the assumption of Poisson-distributed arrivals. For actual applications of queuing analysis, the assumptions for both arrival rate and service time distribution would have to be verified.

Interestingly, if service times are exponentially distributed, then the service rate is Poisson distributed. For example, if the average time to serve a customer is three minutes (and exponentially distributed), then the average service rate is 20 customers per hour (and Poisson distributed). The converse holds true for Poisson arrivals. If the arrival rate is Poisson distributed, then the time between arrivals is exponentially distributed.

Queue Discipline and Length

The **queue discipline** is the order in which waiting customers are served. The most common type of queue discipline is *first come, first served*—the first person or item waiting in line is served first. Other disciplines are possible. For example, a machine operator might stack parts to be worked on beside a machine so that the last part is on top of the stack and will be selected first. This queue discipline is *last in, first out*. Or the machine operator might reach into a box full of parts and select one at random. This queue discipline is *random*. Often customers are scheduled for service according to a predetermined appointment, such as patients at a dentist's office or diners at a restaurant where reservations are required. These customers are taken according to a prearranged schedule regardless of when they arrive at the facility. Another example of the many types of queue disciplines is when customers are processed alphabetically according to their last names, such as at school registration or at job interviews.

In manufacturing operations, sometimes jobs with the shortest expected processing times are selected first in order to get the most jobs processed in the shortest time period. In emergency services like emergency rooms at hospitals, the most critical problem is typically served first.

Queues can be of an infinite or finite size or length. An **infinite queue** can be of any size, with no upper limit, and is the most common queue structure. For example, it is assumed that the waiting line at a movie theater could stretch through the lobby and out the door if necessary. A **finite queue** is limited in size. An example is the driveway at a bank teller window that can accommodate only a limited number of cars before it backs up to the street.

Basic Waiting Line Structures

Waiting line processes are generally categorized into four basic structures, according to the nature of the service facilities. In technical terminology they are called single-channel, single-phase; single-channel, multiple-phase; multiple-channel, single-phase; and multiple-channel, multiple-phase processes.

The number of **channels** in a queuing process is the number of parallel servers available. The number of **phases**, on the other hand, denotes the number of sequential servers each customer must go through to complete service. An example of a *single-channel, single-phase* queuing operation is a post office with only one postal clerk waiting on a single line of customers. This is more commonly called simply a *single-server* waiting line. A post office with several postal clerks waiting on a single line of customers is an example of a *multiple-channel, single-phase* process or simply a *multiple-server* waiting line. These are the two basic waiting line structures we will focus on in this chapter.

The other two waiting line structures we mentioned have multiple phases; that is, they have a sequence of servers, one following another. For example, when patients go to a clinic for treatment or check into a hospital, they first wait in a reception room, then they may go to an office to fill out some paperwork. When they get to the treatment room, the patients receive an initial checkup or treatment from a nurse, followed by treatment from a doctor. This arrangement constitutes a *single-channel, multiple-phase* queuing process. If there are several doctors and nurses, the process is a *multiple-channel, multiple-phase process*. Another example of a multiple-phase system is a manufacturing assembly line in which a product is worked on at several sequential machines or by several sequential operators at workstations. These are more complex structures and are beyond the scope of this text.

You may quickly visualize a familiar waiting situation that fits none of these categories of waiting line structures. The four waiting line structures we have described are simply the four

TABLE 5.2 Queuing System Operating Characteristics

Notation	Operating Characteristic
L	Average number of customers in the system (waiting and being served)
L_q	Average number of customers in the waiting line
W	Average time a customer spends in the system (waiting and being served)
W_q	Average time a customer spends waiting in line
P_0	Probability of no (i.e., zero) customers in the system
P_n	Probability of n customers in the system
ρ	Utilization rate; the proportion of the time the system is in use

basic general categories; but there are many variations, which often require very complex mathematical formulas to analyze. In some cases they can only be analyzed using simulation (the topic of Supplement 12). However, the basic fundamentals of waiting line analysis for the simpler queuing models that we will discuss in this chapter are relevant to the analysis of all queuing problems, regardless of their complexity.

OPERATING CHARACTERISTICS

The mathematics used in waiting line analysis do not provide an optimal, or "best," solution. Instead they generate measures referred to as *operating characteristics* that describe the performance of the waiting line system and that management uses to evaluate the system and make decisions. It is assumed these operating characteristics will approach constant, average values after the system has been in operation for a long time, which is referred to as a *steady state*. These basic operating characteristics used in a waiting line analysis are defined in Table 5.2.

TRADITIONAL COST RELATIONSHIPS IN WAITING LINE ANALYSIS

There is generally an inverse relationship between the cost of providing service and the cost of making customers wait, as reflected in the cost curves in Figure 5.8. As the level of service, reflected by the number of servers, goes up, the cost of service increases, whereas waiting cost decreases. In the traditional view of waiting line analysis, the level of service should coincide with the minimum point on the total cost curve.

The cost of providing the service is usually reflected in the cost of the servers, such as the cost of the tellers at a bank, postal workers at a post office counter, or the repair crew in a plant or shop. As the number of servers is increased to reduce waiting time, service cost goes up. Service cost is normally direct and easy to compute. The cost of waiting is not as easy to determine. The major determinant of waiting cost is the loss of business that might result because customers get tired of waiting or frustrated and leave. This business loss can be temporary (a single event) or permanent (the customer never comes back). The cost due to a loss of business is especially difficult to determine, since it is not part of normal accounting records, although some trade organizations for businesses and industries occasionally provide such data. Other types of waiting costs include the loss of production time and salary for employees waiting to use machinery or load and unload vehicles.

Figure 5.8

The Cost Relationship in Waiting Line Analysis

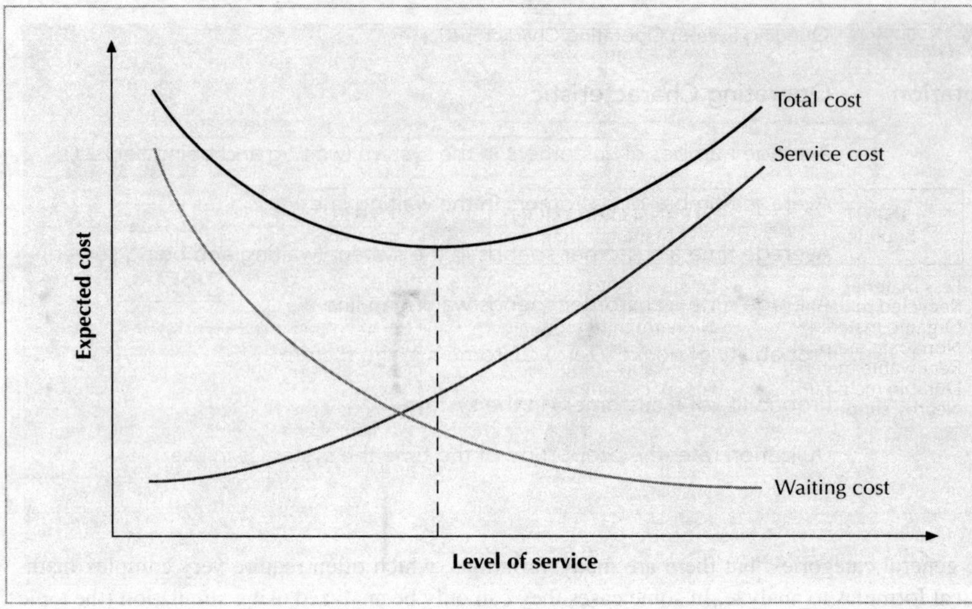

Most companies and organizations that have waiting as an integral part of their service process usually establish a goal for customer waiting time that corresponds to a level of service they want to achieve. For example, Taco Bell has determined that a three-minute average waiting time will result in only 2.5% of customers leaving, which they consider to be an acceptable service goal. Bank of America has a similar waiting time goal for serving its bank customers. The U.S. Postal Service has a goal of five minutes to serve its retail customers.

THE PSYCHOLOGY OF WAITING

In some instances, it is not possible to reduce waiting times, or other important issues besides cost may be involved. When these situations occur, the problem of providing quality service often depends more on psychological solutions. In other words, the organization will try to make waiting more palatable. For example, long lines are fairly common at Disney World, especially at certain peak times during the day. Although it is unlikely that any company has analyzed the technical aspects of waiting more than Disney, customers must still wait for long periods of time at certain shows, exhibits, and rides. Given the limited physical capacity of some attractions, the time required for a customer to complete them, and the large flow of customers, it is simply not possible to make the lines shorter or the service quicker without letting fewer people into the park. In these cases Disney management attempts to improve service in other ways to reduce customer dissatisfaction. For example, it makes use of costumed characters to entertain customers waiting in line and distract them from the long waits. Mobile vendors sell food, drinks, and souvenirs to people in line. Disney provides accurate wait times, which are more tolerable than vague ones, and provides frequent updates. For customers who are particularly annoyed by long waits, Disney sells special passes that allow customers to go to the front of the line for some attractions and to get into the park early before its normally scheduled opening.

Waiting rooms, such as at a doctor's office, provide magazines and newspapers for customers to read while waiting. Televisions are occasionally available in auto repair waiting areas, in airport terminals, or in bars and lounges of restaurants where customers wait. Mirrors are purposely located near elevators to distract people while they wait. Supermarkets locate magazines

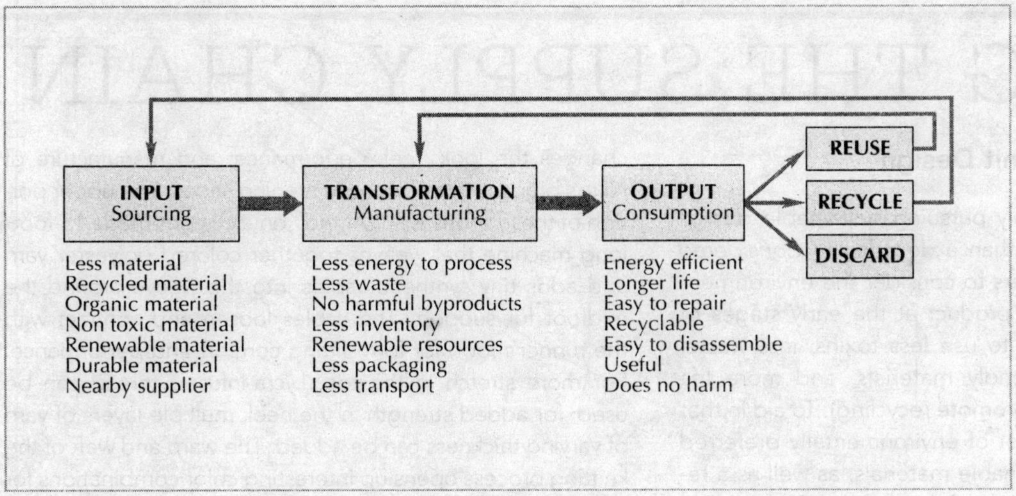

Figure 4.6
Design for Environment Lifecycle

considering how this occurs. Strictly written requests for quotes or proposals (RFQs or RFPs) make it difficult for potential suppliers to suggest alternate materials, methods, or technologies. In green sourcing, suppliers are encouraged to suggest more environmentally friendly materials, methods, and processes, especially if these also reduce cost. Suppliers and designers may brainstorm to develop new materials or methods. Sustainability becomes part of the strategic sourcing process. Greening the supply chain is discussed more thoroughly in Chapter 10 on Supply Chain Strategy and Design. Nike's CEO Mark Parker calls sustainability our generation's defining issue. Read about Nike's green sourcing and design in the "Along the Supply Chain" box that follows.

GREEN MANUFACTURE

In the manufacturing process, green design is concerned with the energy needed to produce the product, whether that energy is renewable, how much waste or harmful byproducts are generated from the process, and if that waste can be recycled or byproduct disposed of safely. Production should be carefully planned so that inventory is minimized, and the manufacturing plant should be located in close proximity to customers to minimize transportation and its affect on greenhouse gas emissions. The product should have minimal packaging and the boxes or bins used for transportation should be reusable.

Carbon footprints measure the amount of carbon dioxide (CO_2) and other greenhouse gases that contribute to global warming and climate change. A product's carbon footprint is calculated by estimating the greenhouse gas emissions from the energy used in manufacturing and transporting the product along its supply chain, the energy used in stocking and selling the product, the energy used by the consumer in using the product, and the energy used to recycle and dispose of the product at the end of its useful life. Carbon footprints are part of a more comprehensive lifecycle assessment initiative supported by IS0 14000 environmental standards. IS0 14000 standards provide guidelines and certifications for environmental requirements of doing business in certain countries, and are often used to qualify for foreign aid, business loans, and reduced insurance premiums.

A manufacturing plant's carbon footprint can be determined from the processing, waste, and transport that take place across the products it produces. Recycling, renewable resources, clean energy, efficient operations, and proper waste disposal can help mitigate the environmental impact of manufacturing.

ALONG THE SUPPLY CHAIN

Consider Nike's Flyknit Design

Nike has been aggressively pursuing sustainable design and production for more than a decade. Its *Considered Design* ethos asks designers to consider the environmental impact of a proposed product at the early stages of development; specifically, to use less toxins, less waste, more environmentally friendly materials, and more life cycle assessments (which promote recycling). To aid in that pursuit, Nike provides a list of environmentally preferred materials (EPM) and sustainable materials, as well as a restricted substances list (RSL) and restricted packaging list, to its suppliers and designers. A *Considered Index* is then calculated to evaluate the proposed design. Products or designs are scored on the use of solvents, waste, materials, treatments (such as fading or distressing), and innovation. Only those products with scores significantly higher than the Nike average are designated as "Considered."

The company has also developed a *Sourcing & Manufacturing Sustainability Index* (SMSI) that assesses contract factory performance on sustainability measures such as lean production, environmental performance (water, energy, carbon, waste), health and safety, and labor management factors. The company's recycling program, called *Reuse-A-Shoe*, has recycled more than 21 million pairs of athletic shoes to create public basketball courts, athletic tracks, and playground surfaces around the world. Sustainability is now one of Nike's core values, as noted in its recent annual report.

How appropriate, then, that one of Nike's biggest commercial successes is also an environmental success—a 5.6 ounce running shoe called the Flyknit. The Flyknit design changes the look, feel, performance, and manufacture of Nike's biggest sales category, running shoes. The upper portion of these shoes are "knitted" on a custom-made 15-foot-long machine that weaves together colored polyester yarn and adds tiny synthetic cables into the weave around the midfoot for support. The cables loosen and contract with the runner's foot, for form-fitting comfort and performance. For more stretch in the toe, Lycra-infused thread can be used; for added strength in the heel, multiple layers of yarn of varying thickness can be added. The warp and weft of the knitting process opens up interesting color combinations for the shoes as well. In the future, a shoe might be knitted to fit the particular needs of a customer's feet (even if that means a different knit pattern for the left foot than the right).

The Flyknit has 35 fewer pieces to assemble than a traditional shoe and produces very little waste. Since there is no cutting, sewing, stitching or gluing, the labor requirements and cost of manufacture are considerably less, too. This promises to be a game-changer for Nike, both in terms of profitability *and* the environment.

1. Why do you think Nike is so concerned about sustainability and the environment? Is that a trend among large corporations, or an anomaly?
2. It's not often that a design totally changes an industry. Can you think of any other designs that have played that role? Comment on the competitive landscape for both the Flyknit and the example you find.

Sources: Based on Nike corporate website, http://nikeinc.com/pages/responsibility, accessed January 5, 2013; Matt Townsend, "Is Nike's Flyknit the Swoosh of the Future?" *Business Week* (March 15, 2012).

GREEN CONSUMPTION

Images of overflowing landfills, toxic streams, and global warming have prompted governments worldwide to enact laws and regulations protecting the environment and rewarding environmental stewardship.

Extended producer responsibility (EPR) is a concept that holds companies responsible for their product even after its useful life. German law mandates the collection, recycling, and safe disposal of computers and household appliances, including stereos, televisions, washing machines, dishwashers, and refrigerators. Some manufacturers pay a tax for recycling; others include the cost of disposal in a product's price. Norwegian law requires producers and importers of electronic equipment to recycle or reuse 80% of the product. Twenty-five U.S. states now have ***takeback*** laws that require the return and recycling of batteries, appliances, and other electronics. Brazil considers all packaging that cannot be recycled hazardous waste. The European Union requires that 80% of the weight of discarded cars must be reused or recycled. Companies responsible for disposing of their own products are more conscious of the design decisions that generated the excess and the toxic waste that can be expensive to process.

Figure 4.7

International Eco-labels

These eco-labels are from the European Union, Germany, Korea, Japan, Norway, Taiwan, Canada, and the United States.

SOURCE: http://www.gdrc.org/sustbiz/green/doc-label_ programmes.html.

Once purchased, green design affects how efficiently the product uses energy, how long the product will last (i.e., reliability), if the product can be repaired instead of discarded (i.e., maintainability) and whether it can be recycled at the end of its useful life. If recyclable, the product should be easy to disassemble. Finally, the product should not cause harm to the customer or the environment (e.g., lead in toys or toxic fumes), and it should serve a useful purpose.

It's in the company mission statement, "Build the best product, cause no unnecessary harm, use business to inspire and implement solutions to the environmental crisis," but few would expect even outdoors retailer Patagonia to begin a "don't buy" campaign. "Don't buy this jacket, don't buy this shirt . . . unless you really need it," said the ad appearing on Black Friday in *The New York Times*. Limiting consumption is part of sustainability, even if it seems ill-fitted for an economy based on growth and consumer spending. Companies can also design a product that has a longer useful life, is easier to repair than discard, can be recycled into other products, or is more environmentally friendly to use.

Consumers can find help in identifying green products with **eco-labeling** and rating agencies. Eco-labeling, such as Germany's Blue Angel designation or the United States' Energy Star rating, gives the seal of approval to environmentally safe products and encourages informed consumer purchases. Mobile apps, like the Good Guide, let consumers evaluate the environmental rating of a product by scanning its bar code. Figure 4.7 shows several international eco-labels.

RECYCLING AND REUSE

When a product reaches the end of its useful life, it can be recycled, reused, or discarded (usually to a landfill). Recycling and reuse close the design loop, and are the ideal for sustainability. Unfortunately, that rarely happens for electronic products, less than 20% of which are recycled.

Increased consumption of electronic products has skyrocketed in recent years, producing 30 to 50 million metric tons of e-waste annually worldwide. In the United States alone, almost half a million mobile devices are discarded every day. To complicate matters, electronics contain lead, cadmium, mercury, and other hazardous wastes, which can leech into groundwater and create severe health and environmental problems.

Design factors such as product life, recoverable value, ease of repair, and disposal cost affect the consumer's decision to recycle, discard, or continue to use. Many products are discarded because they are difficult or expensive to repair. Materials from discarded products may not be recycled if the product is difficult to disassemble. That's why companies like Hewlett-Packard and Xerox design their products for disassembly. As a result, HP has been able to disassemble and refurbish 12,000 tons of equipment annually with less than 1% waste.

Xerox, a leader in **remanufacturing**, designs its copiers for multiple lifecycles. Old models can be refurbished or upgraded with new controls, software, and features because the basic form (i.e., rack or frame) and design layout of the machine remains the same. In a discarded copier with 8,000 parts, over 90% can typically be reused. Disassembly is easier because parts are labeled and those that are likely to default or become obsolete at the same time are clustered together. The remanufacturing process involves disassembling and sorting the parts, inspecting them, cleaning them, reprocessing them, then reassembly, final inspection, and testing.

One of the more amazing recycled products on the market is polar fleece, made from recycled soda bottles. But that is not where the journey ends. Patagonia, which makes garments from polar fleece, accepts worn-out fleece, wool, and other garments from its customers and completely recycles them. Discarded garments are cut into bits, pulverized into small pellets, purified, polymerized, melted, and spun into new fabric for new garments, thus completing the cycle in a cradle-to-cradle design. Through its Common Threads recycling program, Patagonia saves 38 million pounds of carbon dioxide emissions each year and creates 20% of its products from post-consumer waste.

Whether it's greening a design or making other design changes to please the customer, companies need a procedure for ensuring that the myriad of design decisions are consistent and reflective of customer needs. Such a technique, *quality function deployment*, is discussed in the next section.

Quality Function Deployment

Imagine that two engineers are working on two different components of a car sunroof simultaneously but separately.[2] The "insulation and sealing" engineer develops a new seal that will keep out rain, even during a blinding rainstorm. The "handles, knobs, and levers" engineer is working on a simpler lever that will make the roof easier to open. The new lever is tested and works well with the old seal. Neither engineer is aware of the activities of the other. As it turns out, the combination of heavier roof (due to the increased insulation) and lighter lever means that the driver can no longer open the sunroof with one hand! Hopefully, the problem will be detected in prototype testing before the car is put into production. At that point, one or both components will need to be redesigned. Otherwise, cars already produced will need to be reworked and cars already sold will have to be recalled. None of these alternatives is pleasant, and they all involve considerable cost.

Could such problems be avoided if engineers worked in teams and shared information? Not entirely. Even in design teams, there is no guarantee that all decisions will be coordinated. Ford and Firestone have worked together for over 75 years. But teamwork did not prevent Firestone tires designed to fit the Ford Explorer from failing when inflated to Ford specifications. A formal method is needed for making sure that everyone working on a design project knows the design objectives and is aware of the interrelationships of the various parts of the design. Similar communications are needed to translate the voice of the customer to technical design requirements. Such a process is called quality function deployment (QFD).

Quality functional deployment (QFD) uses a series of matrix diagrams that resemble connected houses. The first matrix, dubbed the *house of quality*, converts customer requirements

[2]Adapted from Bob King, *Better Designs in Half the Time* (Methuen, MA: GOAL/QPC, 1989), pp. 1.1–1.3.

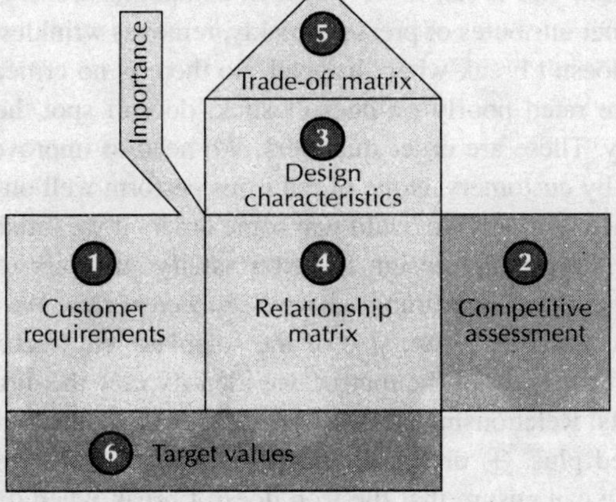

Figure 4.8

Outline of the House of Quality

into product design characteristics. As shown in Figure 4.8, the house of quality has six sections: a customer requirements section, a competitive assessment section, a design characteristics section, a relationship matrix, a tradeoff matrix, and a target values section. Let's see how these sections interrelate by building a house of quality for a steam iron.

Our customers tell us they want an iron that presses quickly, removes wrinkles, doesn't stick to fabric, provides enough steam, doesn't spot fabric, and doesn't scorch fabric (see Figure 4.9). We enter those attributes into the *customer requirements* section of the house. For easier reference, we can group them into a category called "Irons well." Next we ask our customers to rate the list of requirements on a scale of 1 to 10, with 10 being the most important. Our customers rate presses quickly and doesn't scorch fabric as the most important attributes, with a score of 9. A second group of attributes, called "Easy and safe to use" is constructed in a similar manner.

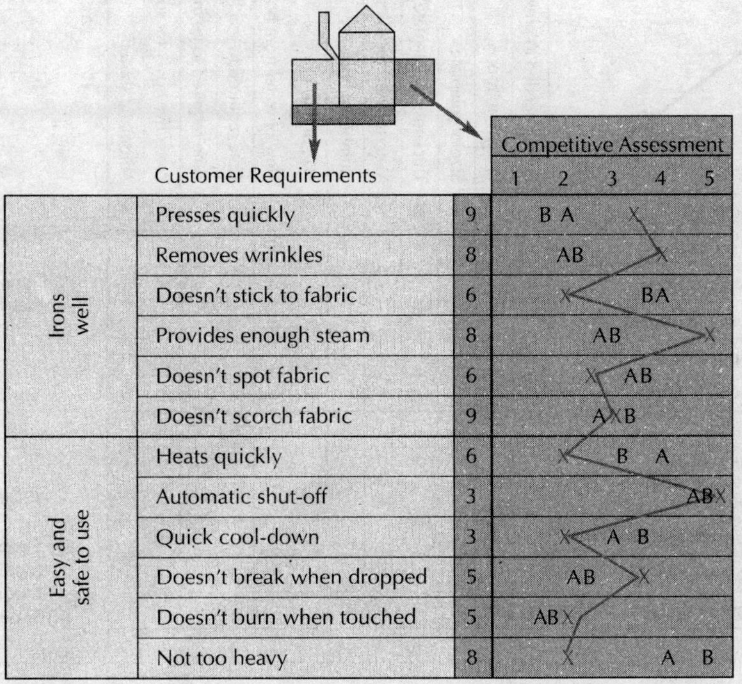

Figure 4.9

A Competitive Assessment of Customer Requirements

Next, we conduct a *competitive assessment*. On a scale of 1 to 5 (with 5 being the highest), customers evaluate our iron (we'll call it "X") against competitor irons, A and B. We see that our iron excels on the customer attributes of presses quickly, removes wrinkles, provides enough steam, automatic shutoff, and doesn't break when dropped. So there is no critical need to improve those factors. However, we are rated poorly on doesn't stick, doesn't spot, heats quickly, quick cool-down, and not too heavy. These are order qualifiers. We need to improve these factors just to be considered for purchase by customers. None of the irons perform well on doesn't scorch fabric, or doesn't burn when touched. Perhaps we could win some orders if we satisfied these requirements.

In order to change the product design to better satisfy customer requirements, we need to translate those requirements to measurable *design characteristics*. We list such characteristics (energy needed to press, weight of iron, size of the soleplate, etc.) across the top of the matrix shown in Figure 4.10. In the body of the matrix, we identify *how* the design characteristics relate to customer requirements. Relationships can be positive, + or minus, −. Strong relationships are designated with a circled plus, ⊕ or ⊖. Examine the plusses and minuses in the row *Doesn't break when dropped*. We can ensure that the iron doesn't break when dropped by increasing the weight of the iron, increasing the size of the soleplate, increasing the thickness of the soleplate, or adding a protective cover. Of those options, making the soleplate thicker has the strongest impact.

Product design characteristics are interrelated also, as shown in the roof of the house in Figure 4.11. For example, increasing the thickness of the soleplate would increase the weight of the iron but decrease the energy needed to press. Also, a thicker soleplate would decrease the flow of water through the holes, and increase the time it takes for the iron to heat up or cool down. Designers must take all these factors into account when determining a final design.

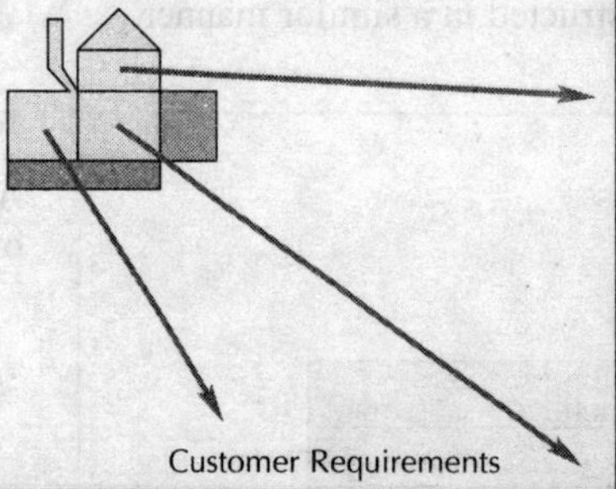

Design characteristics

	Customer Requirements	Energy needed to press	Weight of iron	Size of soleplate	Thickness of soleplate	Material used for soleplate	Number of holes	Size of holes	Flow of water from holes	Time required to reach 450° F	Time required to go from 450° to 100° F	Protective cover for soleplate	Automatic shutoff
Irons well	Presses quickly	−	⊖	+	+	+				−			
	Removes wrinkles		⊕		+		+	+	+				
	Doesn't stick to fabric		−			⊕			+	⊕		+	
	Provides enough steam			+			+	+	+				
	Doesn't spot fabric					+	−	−	⊖				
	Doesn't scorch fabric				+	⊕			+	−	⊖		
Easy and safe to use	Heats quickly			−	−					⊕		−	
	Automatic shut-off										+		⊕
	Quick cool-down			−	⊖	+					⊕		
	Doesn't break when dropped		+	+	⊕							+	
	Doesn't burn when touched				+						+	⊕	+
	Not too heavy	+	⊖	−	−	⊕						−	

Relationship matrix

Relationships

⊕ Strong positive
\+ Medium positive
− Medium negative
⊖ Strong negative

Figure 4.10

Converting Customer Requirements to Design Characteristics

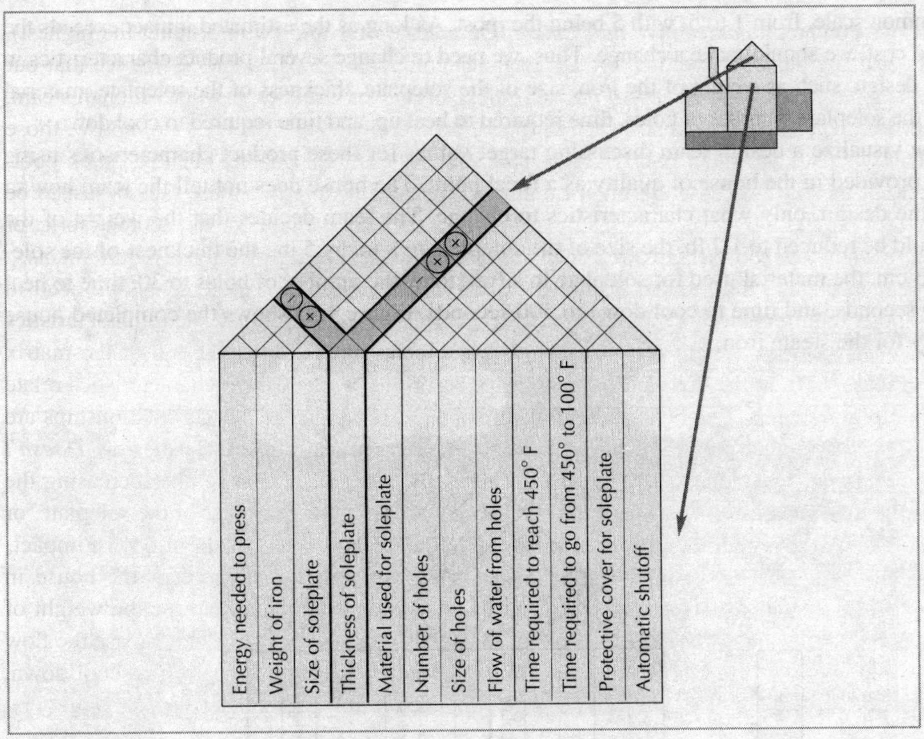

Figure 4.11

The Tradeoff Matrix: Effects of Increasing Soleplate Thickness

The last section of the house, shown in Figure 4.12, adds quantitative measures to our design characteristics. Measuring our iron X against competitors A and B, we find that our iron is heavier, larger, and has a thicker soleplate. Also, it takes longer to heat up and cool down, but requires less energy to press and provides more steam than other irons. To decide which design characteristics to change, we compare the estimated impact of the change with the estimated cost. We rate these factors

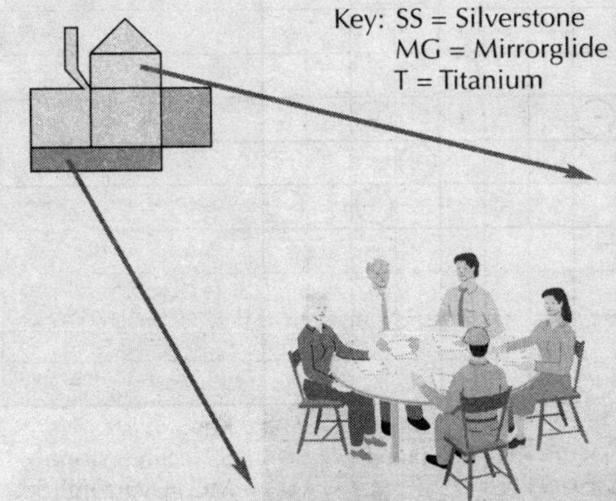

Key: SS = Silverstone
MG = Mirrorglide
T = Titanium

	Energy needed to press	Weight of iron	Size of soleplate	Thickness of soleplate	Material used for soleplate	Number of holes	Size of holes	Flow of water from holes	Time required to reach 450° F	Time required to go from 450° to 100° F	Protective cover for soleplate	Automatic shutoff
Objective measures: Units of measure	ft-lb	lbs	in.	cm	ty	ea	mm	oz/s	sec	sec	Y/N	Y/N
Objective measures: Iron A	3	1.4	8×4	2	SS	27	15	0.5	45	500	N	Y
Objective measures: Iron B	4	1.2	8×4	1	MG	27	15	0.3	35	350	N	Y
Objective measures: Our iron (X)	2	1.7	9×5	4	T	35	15	0.7	50	600	N	Y
Estimated impact	3	4	4	4	5	4	3	2	5	5	3	0
Estimated cost	3	3	3	3	4	3	3	3	4	4	5	2
Target values		1.2	8×5	3	SS	30			30	500		
Design changes		*	*	*	*	*			*	*		

Figure 4.12

Targeted Changes in Design

on a common scale, from 1 to 5, with 5 being the most. As long as the estimated impact exceeds the estimated cost, we should make a change. Thus, we need to change several product characteristics in our new design, such as weight of the iron, size of the soleplate, thickness of the soleplate, material used for the soleplate, number of holes, time required to heat up, and time required to cool down.

Now visualize a design team discussing target values for these product characteristics using the data provided in the house of quality as a focal point. The house does not tell the team how to change the design, only what characteristics to change. The team decides that the weight of the iron should be reduced to 1.2 lb, the size of the soleplate to 8 in. by 5 in., the thickness of the soleplate to 3 cm, the material used for soleplate to silverstone, the number of holes to 30, time to heat up to 30 seconds, and time to cool down to 500 seconds. Figure 4.13 shows the completed house of quality for the steam iron.

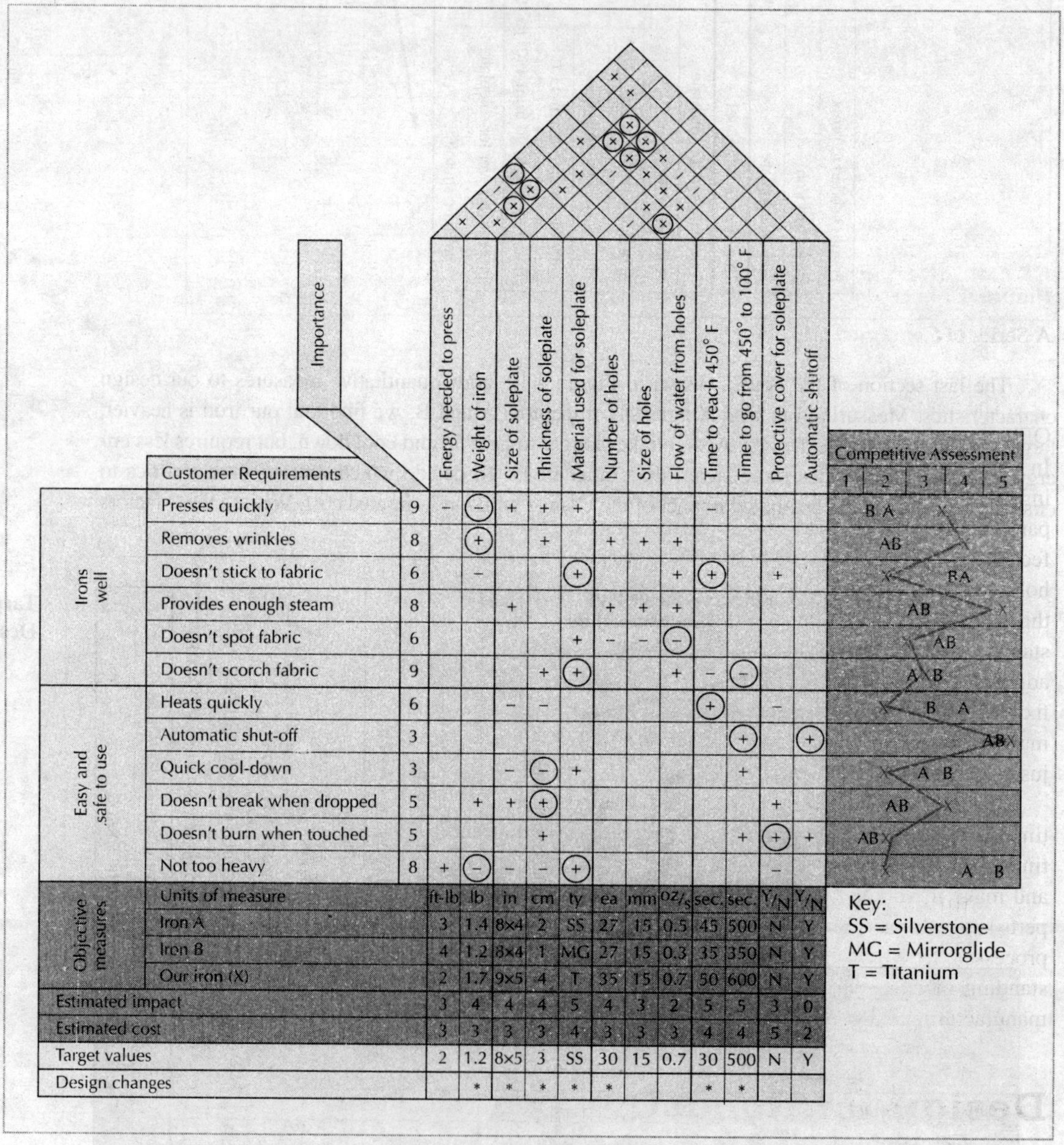

Figure 4.13

The Completed House of Quality for a Steam Iron

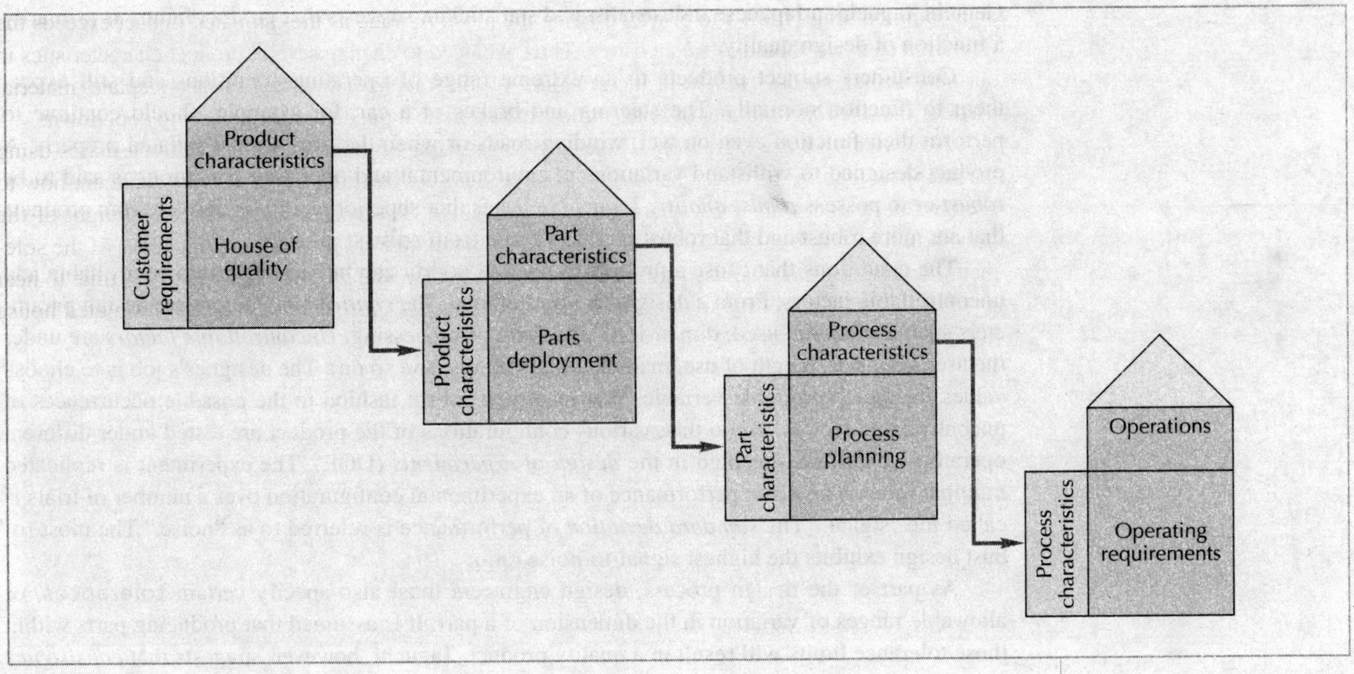

Figure 4.14

A Series of Connected QFD Houses

The house of quality is the most popular QFD matrix. However, to understand the full power of QFD, we need to consider three other houses that can be linked to the house of quality (Figure 4.14). In our example, suppose we decide to meet the customer requirement of "heats quickly" by reducing the thickness of the soleplate. The second house, *parts deployment*, examines which component parts are affected by reducing the thickness of the soleplate. Obviously, the soleplate itself is affected, but so are the fasteners used to attach the soleplate to the iron, as well as the depth of the holes and connectors that provide steam. These new part characteristics then become inputs to the third house, *process planning*. To change the thickness of the soleplate, the dyes used by the metal-stamping machine to produce the plates will have to change, and the stamping machine will require adjustments. Given these changes, a fourth house, *operating requirements*, prescribes how the fixtures and gauges for the stamping machine will be set, what additional training the operator of the machine needs, and how process control and preventive maintenance procedures need to be adjusted. Nothing is left to chance—all bases are covered from customer to design to manufacturing.

In comparison with traditional design approaches, QFD forces management to spend more time defining the new product changes and examining the ramifications of those changes. More time spent in the early stages of design means less time is required later to revise the design and make it work. This reallocation of time shortens the design process considerably. Some experts suggest that QFD can produce better product designs in *half* the time of conventional design processes. In summary, QFD is a communications and planning tool that promotes better understanding of customer demands, produces better understanding of design interactions, involves manufacturing in the design process, and provides documentation of the design process.

Design for Robustness

A product can fail because it was manufactured wrong in the factory—*quality of conformance*—or because it was designed incorrectly—*quality of design*. Quality-control techniques, such as statistical process control (SPC) discussed in Chapter 3, concentrate on quality of conformance.

Genichi Taguchi, a Japanese industrialist and statistician, suggests that product failure is primarily a function of design quality.

Consumers subject products to an extreme range of operating conditions and still expect them to function normally. The steering and brakes of a car, for example, should continue to perform their function even on wet, winding roads or when the tires are not inflated properly. A product designed to withstand variations in environmental and operating conditions is said to be *robust* or to possess *robust quality*. Taguchi believes that superior quality is derived from products that are more robust and that robust products come from **robust design**.

The conditions that cause a product to operate poorly can be separated into controllable and uncontrollable factors. From a designer's point of view, the *controllable factors* are design parameters such as material used, dimensions, and form of processing. *Uncontrollable factors* are under the user's control (length of use, maintenance, settings, and so on). The designer's job is to choose values for the controllable variables that react in a robust fashion to the possible occurrences of uncontrollable factors. To do this, various configurations of the product are tested under different operating conditions specified in the *design of experiments* (DOE). The experiment is replicated multiple times. The *mean* performance of an experimental configuration over a number of trials is called the "signal." The *standard deviation* of performance is referred to as "noise." The most robust design exhibits the highest signal-to-noise ratio.

As part of the design process, design engineers must also specify certain **tolerances**, or allowable ranges of variation in the dimension of a part. It is assumed that producing parts within those tolerance limits will result in a quality product. Taguchi, however, suggests that *consistency* is more important to quality than being within tolerances. He supports this view with the following observations:

- Consistent errors can be more easily corrected than random errors.
- *Parts* within tolerance limits may produce *assemblies* that are not within limits.
- Consumers have a strong preference for product characteristics near their ideal values.

Let's examine each of these observations.

Consistent mistakes are easier to correct. Consider the professor who always starts class 5 minutes late. Students can adjust their arrival patterns to coincide with the professor's, or the professor's clock can be set ahead by 5 minutes. But if the professor sometimes starts class a few minutes early, sometimes on time, and other times 10 minutes late, the students are more apt to be frustrated, and the professor's behavior will be more difficult to change.

Consistency is especially important for assembled products. The assembly of two parts that are near opposite tolerance limits may result in *tolerance stack-ups* and poor quality. For example, a button diameter that is small (near to the lower tolerance limit) combined with a buttonhole that is large (near to its upper tolerance limit) results in a button that won't stay fastened. Although it is beyond the scope of this book, Taguchi advises how to set tolerance limits so that tolerance stack-up can be avoided.

Manufacturing tolerances define what is acceptable or unacceptable quality. Parts or products measured outside tolerance limits are considered defective and are either reworked or discarded. Parts or products within the limits are considered "good." Taguchi asserts that although all the parts or products within tolerances may be acceptable, they are not all of the same quality. Consider a student who earns an average grade of 60 in a course. He or she will pass, whereas a student who earns an average grade of 59 will fail. A student with a 95 average will also pass the course. Taguchi would claim that there is negligible difference between the quality of the students with averages of 59 and 60, even though one was "rejected" and the other was not. There is, however, a great deal of difference in the quality of the student with an average of 60 and the student with an average of 95. Furthermore, a professor in a subsequent class or a prospective employer will be able to detect the difference in quality and will overwhelmingly prefer the student who passed the course with a 95 average. Quality near the target value is preferable to quality that simply conforms to specifications.

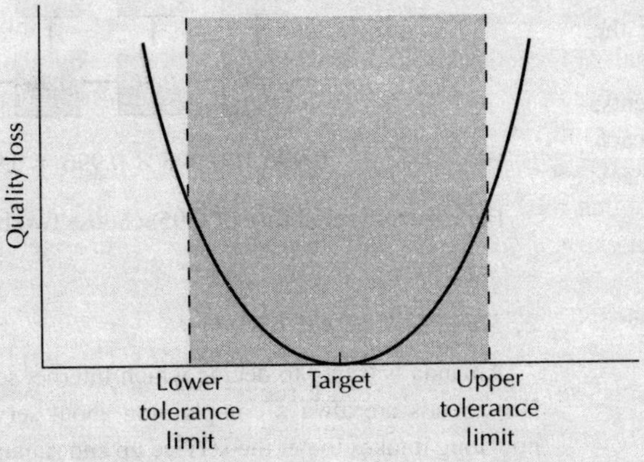

Figure 4.15
Taguchi's Quality Loss Function

Taguchi quantified customer preferences toward on-target quality in the *quality loss function* (QLF). The quadratic function, graphed in Figure 4.15, implies that a customer's dissatisfaction (or quality loss) increases geometrically as the actual value deviates from the target value. The quality loss function is used to emphasize that customer preferences are strongly oriented toward *consistently* meeting quality expectations. *Design for Six Sigma* (DFSS) uses the Taguchi method to reduce variability in design.

SUMMARY

New products and services enhance a company's image, invigorate employees, and help a firm to grow and prosper. The design process begins with ideas formulated into a product concept. Once a product concept passes a feasibility study, performance specs are given to designers who develop and test prototype designs. For selected prototypes, design and manufacturing specs are taken through a pilot run where the design is finalized and the planning for product launch begins.

Time-to-market can be accelerated by using design teams, concurrent design, design for manufacture concepts, and CAD/CAM systems. The quality of design can be improved through design reviews, design for environment, quality function deployment, and robust design.

KEY FORMULAS

Reliability in series

$$R_s = (R_1)(R_2)\ldots(R_n)$$

Reliability in parallel

$$R_s = R_1 + (1 - R_1)R_2$$

or

$$R_s = 1 - [(1 - R_1)(1 - R_2)\ldots(1 - R_n)]$$

Mean time between failures

$$\text{MTBF} = \frac{\text{time}}{\text{\# failures}}$$

System availability

$$\text{SA} = \frac{\text{MTBF}}{\text{MTBF} + \text{MTTR}}$$

SOLVED PROBLEMS

1. RELIABILITY

Jack McPhee, a production supervisor for McCormick, Inc., is committed to the company's new quality efforts. Part of the program encourages making product components in-house to ensure higher quality levels and instill worker pride. The system seems to be working well. One assembly, which requires a reliability of 0.95, is normally purchased from a local supplier. Now it is being assembled in-house from three components that each boast a reliability of 0.96.

a. Customer complaints have risen in the three months since McCormick started doing its own assembly work. Can you explain why?
b. What level of component reliability is necessary to restore the product to its former level of quality?
c. Jack can't increase the reliability of the individual components; however, he can add a backup with a reliability of 0.90 to each component. If the backups have a reliability of 0.90, how many will be needed to achieve a 0.95 reliability for the assembly?

SOLUTION

a.

$$0.96 \times 0.96 \times 0.96 = 0.885$$

Complaints are valid

b. $\sqrt[3]{0.95} = 0.983$

Each component would need a reliability of 0.983 to guarantee an assembly reliability of 0.95

c.

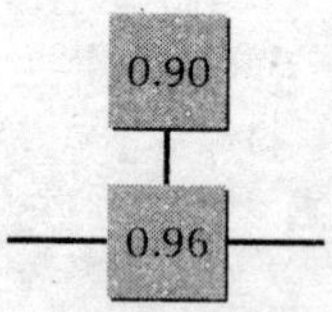

Components in parallel

$$0.96 + (1 - 0.96)(0.90) = 0.996$$

One backup

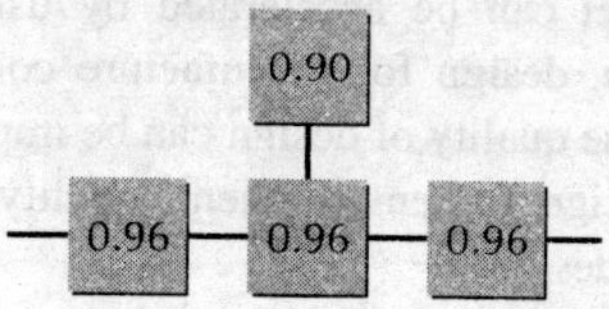

$$0.96 \times 0.996 \times 0.96 = 0.918$$

Two backups

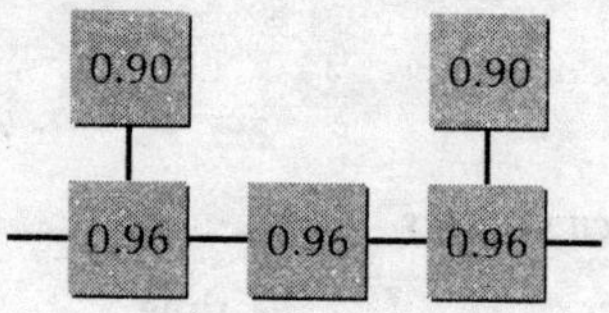

$$0.996 \times 0.96 \times 0.996 = 0.952$$

Three backups

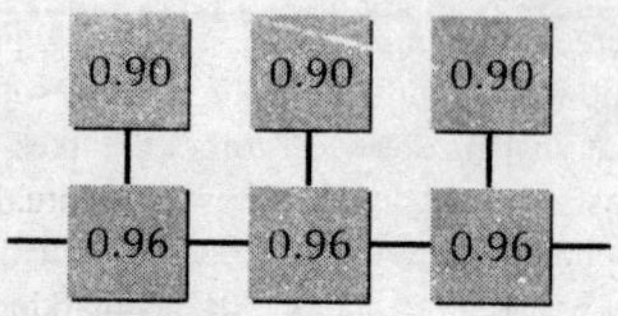

$$0.996 \times 0.996 \times 0.996 = 0.988$$

For a system reliability of 0.95, choose two backups.

2. SYSTEM AVAILABILITY

Amanda is trying to decide which Internet service provider to use. Her friends are always complaining about service interruptions and how long it takes to get the service up and running again. Amanda is a conscientious student and wants reliable access to the Internet. With that goal in mind, she has collected data on mean time between failures (MTBF) and mean time to repair (MTTR) for three Internet service providers. Given that cost and speed are comparable among the three options, which provider would you recommend?

PROVIDER	MTBF	MTTR
MostTel	20	1
Star	40	4
CableX	80	6

SOLUTION

PROVIDER	MTBF	MTTR	SYSTEM AVAILABILITY
MostTel	20	1	20/(20 + 1) = 0.952
Star	40	4	40/(40 + 1) = 0.909
CableX	80	6	80/(80 + 6) = 0.930

Choose MostTel

QUESTIONS

4-1. Describe the strategic significance of design. How can organizations gain a competitive edge with product or service design?

4-2. Look around your classroom and make a list of items that impede your ability to learn. Classify them as problems in *quality of design* or *quality of conformance*.

4-3. Give an example of a product or service you have encountered that was poorly designed. Read about more bad designs at the bad designs website, www.baddesigns.com. Make a list of the factors that make a design unworkable.

4-4. Sometimes failures provide the best opportunities for new products and services. Read the Post-It Note story at www.3m.com. Search the web for at least one other failure-to-success story.

4-5. *BusinessWeek* sponsors a best design competition each year. Read about this year's winners and write a brief summary about what makes these designs special.

4-6. Automakers often post concept cars on their websites. Find out how the design process for these cars differs. Which cars do you think will be commercially successful? Why?

4-7. Construct a perceptual map for the following products or services: (a) business schools in your state or region, (b) software packages, and (c) car rental/car sharing services. Label the axes with the dimensions you feel are most relevant. Explain how perceptual maps are used.

4-8. Read about benchmarking at the American Productivity and Quality Center website, www.apqc.org, and the Benchmarking Exchange website, www.benchnet.com. What is benchmarking? What types of things do these organizationsbenchmark? How are the studies conducted? If possible, access one of the free benchmarking reports and summarize its findings.

4-9. Find out if your university benchmarks itself against other universities. If so, write a summary of the characteristics that are considered, the measures that are used, and the results. Do the data support your views as a customer?

4-10. What kinds of analyses are conducted in a feasibility study for new products?

4-11. Differentiate between performance specifications, design specifications, and manufacturing specifications. Write sample specifications for a product or service of your choosing.

4-12. How are reliability and maintainability related? Give an example for a product or service you have experienced.

4-13. Explain how simplification and standardization can improve designs. How does modular design differ from standardization?

4-14. How can design teams improve the quality of design? Relate your experiences in working in teams. What were the advantages and disadvantages?

4-15. Discuss the concept of concurrent design. What are the advantages of this approach? How would you apply concurrent design to a group project?

4-16. What does design for manufacture entail? List several techniques that can facilitate the DFM process. How do DFM and DFSC differ?

4-17. Describe the objectives of failure mode and effect analysis, fault tree analysis, and value analysis. Apply one of the techniques to a project, computer assignment, or writing assignment you have recently completed.

4-18. Access the Environmental Protection Agency at www.epa.gov/ to read about the U.S. government's commitment to environmental product design. Compare the U.S. approach to those of other countries.

4-19. Search the Internet for two or more companies that publish sustainability reports. What are the main components of each company's green initiatives? How do their approaches differ?

4-20. Link to the International Standards Organization at www.iso.org, and explore ISO 14000. What do these standards entail? How werethey developed? How does a company attain ISO 14001 certification? Why would it want to?

4-21. What is the purpose of QFD? Find out if companies really use QFD by visiting the QFD Institute at www.qfdi.org, and summarizing one of their case studies.

4-22. Discuss the concept of robust design. Give an example of a robust product or service.

4-23. How does CAD relate to CAE and CAM? How do CAD and the Internet promote collaborative design?

PROBLEMS

4-1. Calculate the reliability of the following system.

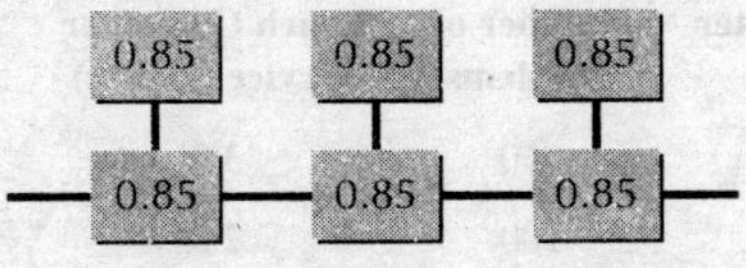

4-2. Competition for a new generation of computers is so intense that MicroTech has funded three separate design teams to create the new systems. Due to varying capabilities of the team members, it is estimated that team A has a 90% probability of coming up with an acceptable design before the competition, team B has an 80% chance, and team C has a 70% chance. What is the probability that MicroTech will beat the competition with its new computers?

4-3. MagTech assembles Blu-ray players from four major components arranged as follows:

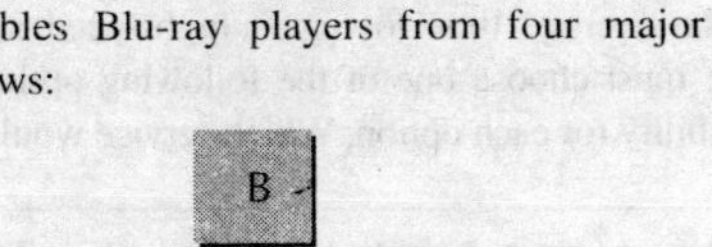

The components can be purchased from three different vendors, who have supplied the following reliability data:

	Vendor		
Component	**1**	**2**	**3**
A	0.94	0.85	0.92
B	0.86	0.88	0.90
C	0.90	0.93	0.95
D	0.93	0.95	0.90

a. If MagTech has decided to use only one vendor to supply all four components, which vendor should be selected?

b. Would your decision change if all the components were assembled in series?

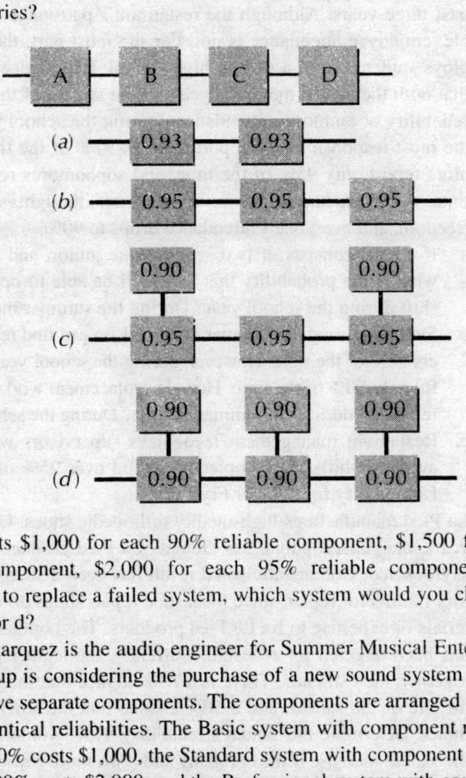

If it costs $1,000 for each 90% reliable component, $1,500 for each 93% component, $2,000 for each 95% reliable component, and $10,000 to replace a failed system, which system would you choose, a or b? c or d?

4-4. Omar Marquez is the audio engineer for Summer Musical Enterprises. The group is considering the purchase of a new sound system consisting of five separate components. The components are arranged in series with identical reliabilities. The Basic system with component reliabilities of 80% costs $1,000, the Standard system with component reliabilities of 90% costs $2,000, and the Professional system with component reliabilities of 99% costs $5,000. The cost of a failure during a performance is $50,000.

a. Calculate the reliability of each system. Which system would you recommend?
b. Omar has learned that each system described above can also be purchased in a Plus configuration, where each component has an identical backup, for double the original cost. Which system would you recommend now?

4-5. Dfinity promises its customers that network services are of 90% reliability. The network consists of three serial nodes, each of which must work for the network to be operational. Consistent with its customer guarantee, the reliability of each node is 90%; however, the company has been receiving complaints about its service.
a. Calculate the reliability of the network. Are customer complaints justified?
b. Dfinity is considering adding nodes to its network structure so that each of the current nodes is "backed up" by a lesser node with a reliability of 80%. What is the reliability of this revised network?

4-6. Identify, Inc. guarantees that it can correctly identify individuals from three pieces of information—date of birth, place of birth, and profession. In reality, whether Identify can keep that guarantee is dependent on the reliability of the information provided. Calculate the probability of correctly identifying an individual if:
a. The three pieces of information each has a 75% chance of being correct.
b. The date of birth is 99% correct, the profession is 50% correct, and the place of birth is 70% correct.
c. The date of birth is found in two publications, each with a 60% chance of being correct, the profession is from an association membership with an 80% accuracy, and the place of birth is self-reported on one site with a 50% chance of veracity and confirmed by a tabloid with a 40% reliability.
d. Which of the scenarios above has the highest reliability?

4-7. Lisa Garrett has been a shift scheduler at a local fast-food chain for the past three years. Although the restaurant's patronage is relatively stable, employee attendance is not. For the most part, the restaurant employs students from a nearby high school. Experience has taught Lisa that both the age of the employee and the season of the year affect the reliability of employee attendance. During the school year, seniors are the most responsible and report to work 97% of the time, whereas juniors report only 95% of the time, and sophomores report 90% of the time. After graduation, however, students' thoughts turn to fun and freedom, and everyone's attendance drops to 90%.
a. If a shift consists of two seniors, one junior, and one sophomore, what is the probability that Lisa will be able to operate with a full shift during the school year? During the summer months?
b. Suppose during the summer months, Lisa can find replacement workers 90% of the time. However, during the school year, she is successful only 80% of the time. How do replacement workers improve shift reliability during the summer months? During the school year?
c. Restaurant management recognizes supervisors with a Super Fry award if shifts are completely staffed over 95% of the time. Does Lisa qualify for a Super Fry?

4-8. La Pied manufactures high-quality orthopedic shoes. Over the past five years, the general public has "found" La Pied products, and sales have skyrocketed. One unanticipated result has been a sharp increase in factory returns for repair, since local shoe repair shops do not have the materials or expertise to fix La Pied products. The popular walking sandal has been targeted for redesign. Currently, the leather pieces are glued together, then stitched. There is a 70% chance that the glue will last for the life of the sandal, and a 50% chance that the stitching will remain intact. Determine the sandal's reliability. How would the reliability of the sandal increase if the company adds two more rows of stitching?

4-9. The Management Department recently purchased a small copier for faculty use. Although the workload of the office staff has improved somewhat, the secretaries are still making too many trips to the Dean's office when the departmental copier is out of service. Sylvia, the departmental secretary, has been keeping track of failure rates and service times. With a mean time between failures of 100 hours and a mean time to repair of 24 hours, how much of the time is the new copier available for faculty use?

4-10. As a regional sales manager, Nora Burke travels frequently and relies on her cell phone to keep up to date with clients. She has tried three different service providers, Airway, Bellular, and CyCom, with varying degrees of success. The number of failures in a typical eight-hour day and the average time to regain service are shown below. Nora's contract is up for renewal. Which cellular service should she use?

Cellular Co.	Number of Failures	Time to Regain Service
Airway	10	2 minutes
Bellular	8	4 minutes
CyCom	3	10 minutes

4-11. Nadia Algar is the overworked IT resource person for her department. In the next round of computer purchases, she is determined to recommend a vendor who does a better job of documenting possible errors in the system and whose customer service line is more responsive to the needs of her colleagues. Nadia compiled the following data over an eight-week observation period. Assuming 40 hours per week, which computer vendor should Nadia pursue?

Computer Vendor	Number of Problems	Mean Time to Reach Customer Service (Hours)	Mean Time to Fix Problem (Hours)
JCN	50	3.0	2.0
Bell	100	2.0	1.0
Comtron	250	1.0	0.5

4-12. Derek is disappointed in his high-speed Internet service. Although the Internet is seldom down, it kicks into slow mode quite often, which Derek considers to be a failure. He has tried three service providers with varying degrees of success. The number of failures in a typical eight-hour day and the average time to regain high-speed service are shown below. Derek must choose one of the following options. Calculate the system availability for each option. Which service would you recommend?

ISP	Number of Failures	Time to Regain Service
Xceptional	12	2 minutes
Yourizon	4	4 minutes
Zelltell	3	10 minutes

4-13. Students often complain that the requirements of assignments or projects are unclear. From the student's perspective, whoever can guess what the professor wants wins the highest grade. Thus, grades appear to be assigned somewhat arbitrarily. If you have ever felt that way, here is your chance to clarify that next project or assignment.

Construct a house of quality for a paper or project. View the professor as the customer. For the perceptual map, have your professor compare one of your papers with typical A, B, or C papers. When you have completed the exercise, give your opinion on the usefulness of QFD for this application.

4-14. Create a house of quality for a computer. Develop customer requirements related to ease of use, cost, capabilities, and connectivity. Make sure the customer requirements are a "wish list" stated in nontechnical terms.

4-15. Create a QFD example from your own experience. Describe the product or service to be designed and then complete a house of quality using representative data. Explain the entries in the house and how target values were reached. Also, describe how other houses might flow from the initial house you built. Finally, relate how QFD improves the design process for the example you chose.

CASE STUDY

China PC Customer Acceptance Elevation

China Business Bi-Weekly recently compiled a list of rapidly advancing Chinese engineered, manufactured and sold products. One of the leading products is the newly released PC. While the PC manufacturer is extremely happy with the national acceptance, its market share is just under 15%. The remaining 85% of the market is supplied by various international brands.

To advance its PC market share, it is planning a major redesign. The firm has contacted you to participate in a focus group. The focus group will compare a Japan competitor product (J) and a U.S. competitor product (U) against the China firm's product (C).

Using the following table, identify your top PC requirements that are deemed essential if you were to buy the product. The competitive assessment cells have been filled in. Write a short report on the resulting competitive assessment.

Competitive Assessment

Customer Requirements	1	2	3	4	5
		U & C	J	C	C
		C	J	U	
		J	U	C	
		U	J		
		U	J & C		
	J	C	U		

REFERENCES

Atasu, Atalay, and Luk Wassenhove. "Getting to Grips with Take-back Laws." *IESE Insight* (July/August 2011), pp. 29–35.

Baldwin, C., and K. Clark. *Design Rules: The Power of Modularity*. Boston: MIT Press, 2000.

Blackburn, J. (ed.). *Time-Based Competition: The Next Battleground*. Homewood, IL: Irwin, 1991.

Bowen, H. K., K. Clark, and C. Holloway. *The Perpetual Enterprise Machine*. New York: Oxford University Press, 1994.

Goleman, Daniel. *Ecological Intelligence*. New York: Broadway Books, 2009.

Hawkens, Paul. *The Ecology of Commerce*. New York: Harper Collins, 1994.

Hauser, J. R., and D. Clausing. "The House of Quality." *Harvard Business Review* (May–June 1988), pp. 63–73.

Hegarty, S. "How Jeans Conquered the World." BBC World Service (January 28, 2012).

Kelley, T., Jonathan Littman, and Tom Peters, *The Art of Innovation: Lessons in Creativity from IDEO*. New York: Currency/ Doubleday, 2001.

King, B. *Better Designs in Half the Time*. Methuen, MA: GOAL/QPC, 1989.

Leonard-Barton, D. *Wellsprings of Knowledge: Building and Sustaining the Sources of Innovation*. Boston: Harvard Business School Press, 1995.

McDonough, William, and Michael Braungart, *Cradle to Cradle*, New York: North Point Press. 2002.

Miller, Reed, Jeremy Gregory, Huabo Duan, and Randoph Kirchain. "Characterizing Transboundary Flows of Used Electronics: Summary Report." Materials System Laboratory, MIT (January 2012).

Nidumolu, Ram, C. K. Prahlad, and M. R. Rangaswami, "Why Sustainability Is Now the Key Driver for Innovation." *Harvard Business Review* (September 2009).

Snyder, R. *Fugitive Denim: A Moving Story of People and Pants in the Borderless World of Global Trade*. New York: Norton, 2009.

Stoll, H. "Design for Manufacture." *Manufacturing Engineering* (January 1988), pp. 67–73.

Sullivan, L. P. "Quality Function Deployment." *Quality Progress* 19, no. 6 (1986): p. 39.

Taguchi, G., and D. Clausing. "Robust Quality." *Harvard Business Review* (January–February 1990), pp. 65–75.

Unruh, Gregory. "The Biosphere Rules," *Harvard Business Review* (February 2008).

Whitney, D. "Manufacturing by Design." *Harvard Business Review* (July–August 1988), pp. 83–91.

Womack, J. P., D. T. Jones, and D. Roos. *The Machine that Changed the World*. New York: Macmillan, 1990.

CHAPTER 5

Designing Services

LEARNING OBJECTIVES

AFTER READING THIS CHAPTER, YOU WILL BE ABLE TO:

- Evaluate the impact of services on jobs and the economy.
- Appreciate and articulate the differences between products and services.
- Utilize tools for envisioning and designing quality services.
- Map out service processes and suggest process improvements.
- Model waiting lines and evaluate their performance for service improvement.

FINDING THAT PERFECT PAIR OF JEANS

In mid-level retail stores, more space is allocated to denim jeans than any other product category. Finding the perfect pair of jeans sends more consumers shopping than any other apparel product. Jeans come in a variety of sizes, lengths, and styles—bootcut, straight cut, skinny leg; relaxed fit, curvy fit, skinny fit, curvy-skinny fit; low rise, high rise, mid-rise; dark rinse, light rinse, distressed; and faded, honeycombed, or whiskered. The list goes on. Levi's, for example, has 49 different-numbered styles of jeans in its 500 series alone, from the classic button-front shrink-to-fit 501, to the bootcut-stretch 584. No wonder jeans shopping can be frustrating. That's where the retailer comes in.

While jeans can be purchased online, most customers prefer to purchase their jeans in retail stores where they can try on the jeans, get expert advice (from the store clerk or their friends) and purchase complementary products. The retail store provides a "service" to its customers by gathering many different products together in one place where a customer can conveniently sample the product (i.e., try it on), purchase it, and immediately carry it home. The store also displays styles and product combinations and provides product information and reassurance on purchases. If a customer is dissatisfied with a product, items can be returned—in most cases, without penalty or cost. How the jeans are displayed, how the store is laid out, the ambience of the store, and the look and feel of the products are all part of the service experience. The product is what and other "impulse-purchase" items at the checkout counter, not only as a diversion while waiting but as potential purchases. All these tactics are designed to improve the quality of service that requires waiting without actually incurring the cost of reducing waiting time.

Some service companies attempt to handle customer arrivals in a "smarter" way, by providing selective preferential treatment to certain types of customers in order to reduce their waiting time. For example, grocery stores have express lanes for customers with only a few purchases. Airlines and car rental agencies issue special cards to frequent-use customers or customers who pay an additional fee that allows them to join special waiting lines at their check-in counters. Telephone retailers check the phone numbers of incoming calls, and based on a customer's sales history, route the call to more experienced or specialized salespeople.

For some critical service providers, waiting times of any duration are simply not allowable. A police or fire department must provide sufficient service capacity so that calls for assistance can have quick response. This often results in long periods of underutilization where police officers, or firefighters are not doing anything. In these cases, cost takes a back seat to service.

WAITING LINE MODELS

The simplest, most basic waiting line structure is the *single-server* model. We run into this type of waiting line every day. When you buy a cup of coffee at your local Starbucks, when you go to a professor's office, when you use the copier in the library, and when you buy a ticket to see a movie, you wait in line to be served by one server.

The Basic Single-Server Model

There are several variations of the single-server waiting line system; however, in the basic single-server model we assume the following:

- Poisson arrival rate
- Exponential service times
- First-come, first-served queue discipline
- Infinite queue length
- Infinite calling population

The basic operating characteristics of this single-server model are computed using the following formulas, where λ = mean arrival rate, μ = mean service rate, and n = the number of customers in the waiting line system, including the customer being served (if any).

The probability that no customers are in the queuing system (either in the queue or being served) is

$$P_0 = \left(1 - \frac{\lambda}{\mu}\right)$$

The probability of exactly n customers in the queuing system is

$$P_n = \left(\frac{\lambda}{\mu}\right)^n \cdot P_0 = \left(\frac{\lambda}{\mu}\right)^n\left(1 - \frac{\lambda}{\mu}\right)$$

The average number of customers in the queuing system (i.e., the customers being serviced and in the waiting line) is

$$L = \frac{\lambda}{\mu - \lambda}$$

The average number of customers in the waiting line is

$$L_q = \frac{\lambda^2}{\mu(\mu - \lambda)}$$

The average time a customer spends in the queuing system (i.e., waiting and being served) is

$$W = \frac{1}{\mu - \lambda} = \frac{L}{\lambda}$$

The average time a customer spends waiting in line to be served is

$$W_q = \frac{\lambda}{\mu(\mu - \lambda)}$$

The probability that the server is busy and a customer has to wait, known as the **utilization factor**, is

$$\rho = \frac{\lambda}{\mu}$$

The probability that the server is idle and a customer can be served is

$$I = 1 - \rho = 1 - \frac{\lambda}{\mu} = P_0$$

Remember that these operating characteristics are averages that result over a period of time; they are not absolutes. In other words, customers who arrive at the bookstore checkout counter will not find 3.2 customers in line. There could be no customers or 1, 2, 3, or 4 customers. The value 3.2 is simply an average over time, as are the other operating characteristics. Notice that there are four customers in the system ($L = 4$) and 3.2 customers in line ($L_q = 3.2$). The difference is only 0.8 customer being served because 20% of the time, there is no customer being served ($I = .20$). Also note that the total time in the system of 10 minutes ($W = 10$) is exactly equal to the waiting time of 8 minutes ($W_q = 8$) plus the service time of 2 minutes (i.e., 60/30).

Service Improvement Analysis

The operating characteristics developed from the queuing formulas in Example 5.1 indicate the quality of service at the Tech auxiliary bookstore. The average waiting time of eight minutes is excessive and would likely cause customers to become frustrated and leave without making a purchase. Normally, a waiting time of two to three minutes is the most a customer will comfortably tolerate at a store like this. Thus, the bookstore management could use the operating characteristics to formulate new strategies to improve service and then test these strategies.

For example, the bookstore might consider adding another employee to assist the present operator. This would enable more customers to be served in less time, thus increasing the service rate. If the service rate were increased from 30 customers per hour to 40 customers per hour, the waiting time would be reduced to only 2.25 minutes. Management would then have to decide whether the cost of the new employee is worth the reduction in waiting time. Alternatively, the bookstore could be redesigned to add an additional cash register as well as another employee to operate it. This would have the effect of reducing the arrival rate. If exiting customers split evenly between the two cash registers, then the arrival rate at each register would decrease from 24 per hour to 12 per hour with a resulting customer waiting time of 1.33 minutes. Again, management would have to determine whether the reduction in waiting time is worth the cost of a new cash register and employee. This is the crux of waiting line analysis: determining whether the improvement in service is worth the cost to achieve it.

Solution of the Single-Server Model with Excel

Excel can be used to solve all of the queuing models in this chapter. The Excel solution screen for the single-server model for the auxiliary bookstore at Tech in Example 5.1 is shown in Exhibit 5.1. Excel files for this exhibit and all other exhibits in this chapter can be downloaded from the text website.

EXAMPLE 5.1

A SINGLE-SERVER MODEL

The auxiliary bookstore in the student center at Tech is a small facility that sells school supplies and snacks. It has one checkout counter where one employee operates the cash register. The cash register and operator represent the server in this waiting line system; the customers who line up at the counter to pay for their selections form the waiting line.

Customers arrive at a rate of 24 per hour according to a Poisson distribution ($\lambda = 24$), and service times are exponentially distributed, with a mean rate of 30 customers per hour ($\mu = 30$). The bookstore manager wants to determine the operating characteristics for this waiting line system.

SOLUTION

The operating characteristics are computed using the queuing formulas for the single-server model as follows:

$$P_0 = \left(1 - \frac{\lambda}{\mu}\right) = \left(1 - \frac{24}{30}\right)$$

$= 0.20$ probability of no customers in the system

$$L = \frac{\lambda}{\mu - \lambda} = \frac{24}{30 - 24}$$

$= 4$ customers on the average in the queuing system

$$L_q = \frac{\lambda^2}{\mu(\mu - \lambda)} = \frac{(24)^2}{30(30 - 24)}$$

$= 3.2$ customers on the average in the waiting line

$$W = \frac{1}{\mu - \lambda} = \frac{1}{30 - 24}$$

$= 0.167$ hour (10 minutes) average time in the system per customer

$$W_q = \frac{\lambda}{\mu(\mu - \lambda)} = \frac{24}{30(30 - 24)}$$

$= 0.133$ hour (8 minutes) average time in the waiting line per customer

$$\rho = \frac{\lambda}{\mu} = \frac{24}{30}$$

$= 0.80$ probability that the server will be busy and the customer must wait

$$I = 1 - \rho = 1 - 0.80$$

$= 0.20$ probability that the server will be idle and a customer can be served

Advanced Single-Server Models

There are many variations of the single-server model, as shown in Figure 5.9. The most common are: constant service times, finite queue length, and finite calling populations.

Constant service times occur most often when automated equipment or machinery performs the service. Examples are vending machines, car washes, and many manufacturing operations.

Finite queue lengths occur when there is a physical limitation to the length of the waiting line. For example, this can occur when cars waiting at a bank for an ATM machine are prohibited from extending into the street.

EXHIBIT 5.1 Single Server

EXCEL FILE

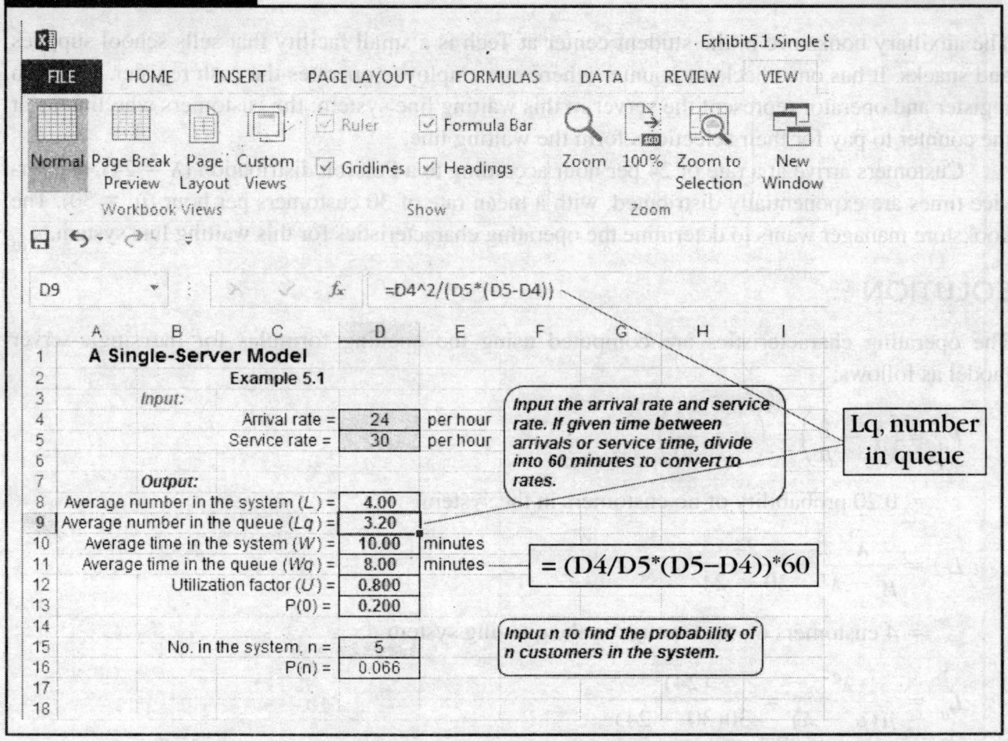

A *finite calling population refers* to a situation when the number of "customers" that can arrive to a system is limited, such as invitation-only events, student advisees, or maintenance for a fleet of rental cars.

The formulas for these models, included in the *Summary of Key Formulas* at the end of the chapter, can be quite involved. For that reason, all of these models, along with the single-server model and the multiple-server model discussed in the next section, can be solved with the Excel

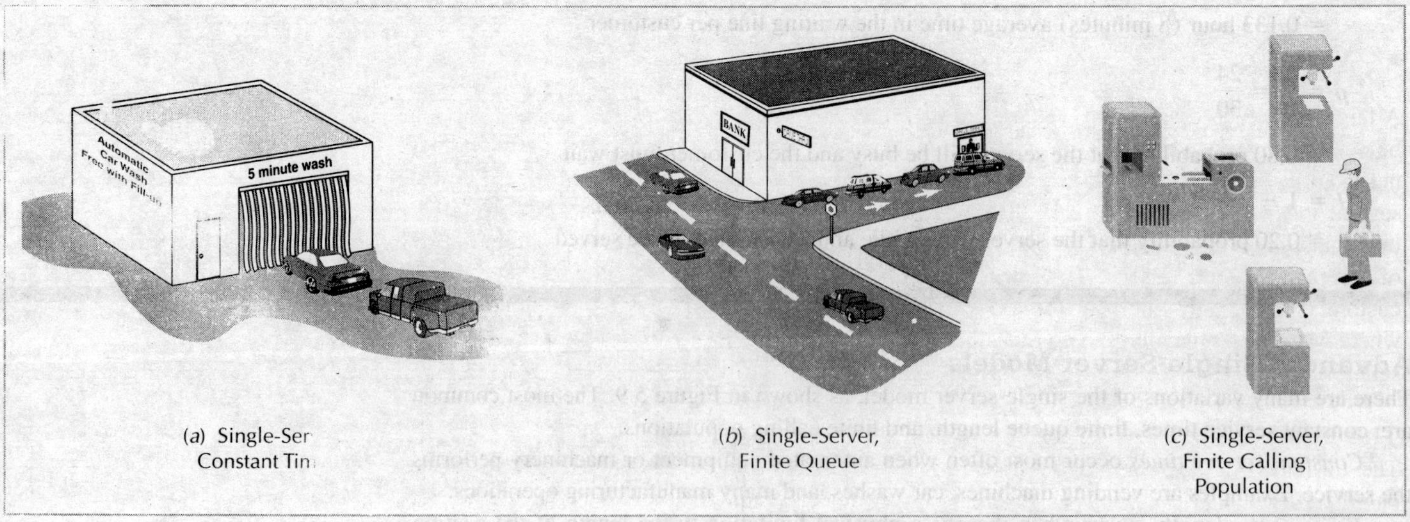

Figure 5.9

Advanced Single-Server Models

EXHIBIT 5.2 Advanced Single-Server Models

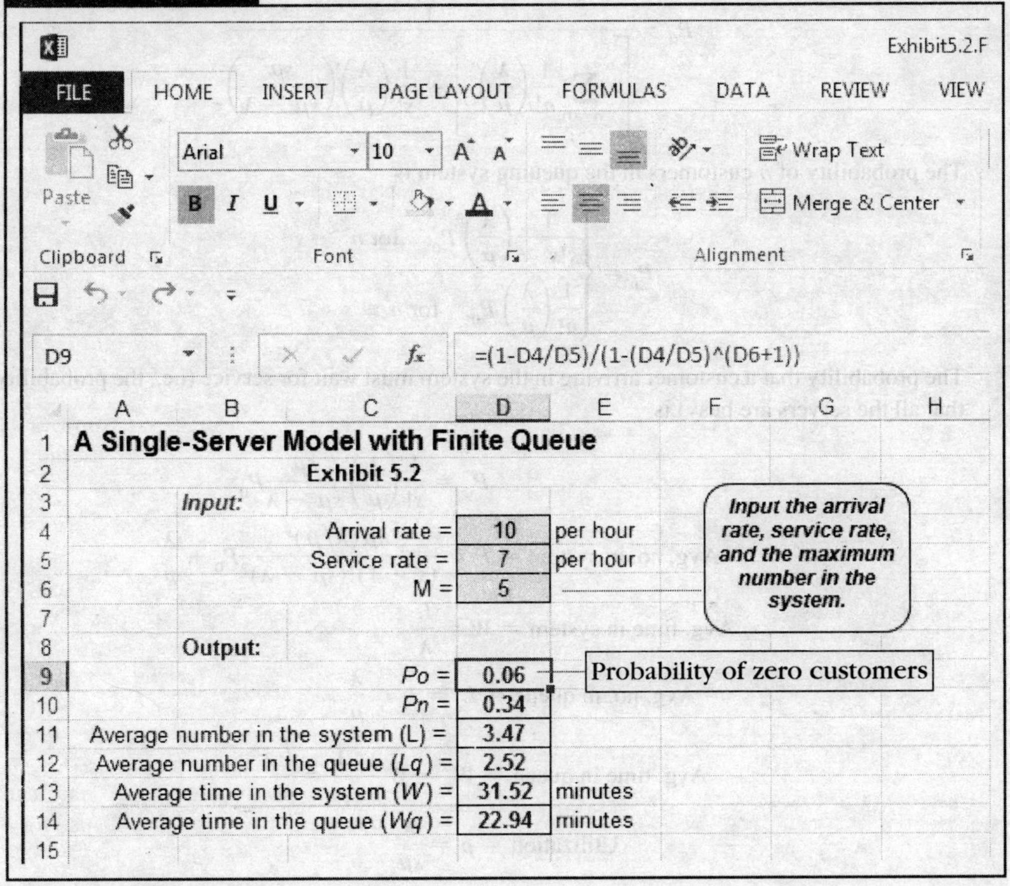

add-in that accompanies this book, *OM Tools*. Exhibit 5.2 shows the OM Tools solution to a single-server finite queue problem.

MULTIPLE-SERVER MODEL

A large number of operational waiting line systems include multiple servers. These models can be very complex, so in this section we present only the most basic multiple-server (or channel) waiting line structure. This system includes a single waiting line and a service facility with several independent servers in parallel. An example of a multiple-server system is an airline ticket and check-in counter, where passengers line up in a roped-off single line waiting for one of several agents for service. The same waiting line structure is found at the post office, where customers in a single line wait for service from several postal clerks, or at a multiplex theater where customers typically line up in a single line to buy movie tickets from one of several ticket sellers.

The Basic Multiple-Server Model

The formulas for determining the operating characteristics for the multiple-server model are based on the same assumptions as the single-server model—Poisson arrival rate, exponential service times, infinite calling population and queue length, and FIFO queue discipline. Also, recall that in the single-server model, $\mu > \lambda$; however, in the multiple-server model, $s\mu > \lambda$, where s is the number of servers. The operating characteristics formulas are as follows:

The probability that there are no customers in the system (all servers are idle) is

$$P_0 = \frac{1}{\left[\sum_{n=0}^{n=s-1} \frac{1}{n!}\left(\frac{\lambda}{\mu}\right)^n\right] + \frac{1}{s!}\left(\frac{\lambda}{\mu}\right)^s\left(\frac{s\mu}{s\mu - \lambda}\right)}$$

The probability of n customers in the queuing system is

$$P_n = \begin{cases} \dfrac{1}{s!s^{n-s}}\left(\dfrac{\lambda}{\mu}\right)^n P_0, & \text{for } n > s \\ \dfrac{1}{n!}\left(\dfrac{\lambda}{\mu}\right)^n P_0, & \text{for } n \leq s \end{cases}$$

The probability that a customer arriving in the system must wait for service (i.e., the probability that all the servers are busy) is

$$P_w = \frac{1}{s!}\left(\frac{\lambda}{\mu}\right)^s \frac{s\mu}{s\mu - \lambda} P_0$$

$$\text{Avg. no. in system} = L = \frac{\lambda\mu(\lambda/\mu)^s}{(s-1)!(s\mu - \lambda)^2} P_0 + \frac{\lambda}{\mu}$$

$$\text{Avg. time in system} = W = \frac{L}{\lambda}$$

$$\text{Avg. no. in queue} = L_q = L - \frac{\lambda}{\mu}$$

$$\text{Avg. time in queue} = W_q = W - \frac{1}{\mu} = \frac{L_q}{\lambda}$$

$$\text{Utilization} = \rho = \frac{\lambda}{s\mu}$$

EXAMPLE 5.2

A MULTIPLE-SERVER WAITING LINE SYSTEM

The student health service at Tech has a waiting room in which chairs are placed along a wall, forming a single waiting line. Some students have health problems that only require a nurse. The students are served by three nurses, each located in a separate room. Students are treated on a first-come, first-served basis.

The health service administrator wants to analyze this queuing system because excessive waiting times can make students angry and they complain. Students have a medical problem and thus are impatient anyway. Waiting increases their impatience.

A study of the health service for a six-month period shows that an average of 10 students arrive per hour (according to a Poisson distribution), and an average of four students can be served per hour by a nurse (Poisson distributed). Compare a three-server versus four-server system.

SOLUTION

$\lambda = 10$ students per hour

$\mu = 4$ students per hour per service representative

$s = 3$ service representatives

$s\mu = (3)(4) = 12\ (>\lambda = 10)$

Three-server system

$$P_0 = \frac{1}{\left[\sum_{n=0}^{n=s-1} \frac{1}{n!}\left(\frac{\lambda}{\mu}\right)^n\right] + \frac{1}{s!}\left(\frac{\lambda}{\mu}\right)^s\left(\frac{s\mu}{s\mu - \lambda}\right)}$$

$$= \frac{1}{\left[\frac{1}{0!}\left(\frac{10}{4}\right)^0 + \frac{1}{1!}\left(\frac{10}{4}\right)^1 + \frac{1}{2!}\left(\frac{10}{4}\right)^2\right] + \frac{1}{3!}\left(\frac{10}{4}\right)^3 \frac{3(4)}{3(4) - 10}}$$

$= 0.045$ probability that no customers are in the health service.

$$L = \frac{\lambda\mu(\lambda/\mu)^s}{(s-1)!(s\mu - \lambda)^2}P_0 + \frac{\lambda}{\mu}$$

$$= \frac{(10)(4)(10/4)^3}{(3-1)![3(4) - 10]^2}(0.045) + \frac{10}{4}$$

$= 6$ students in the health service

$$W = \frac{L}{\lambda} = \frac{6}{10}$$

$= 0.60$ hour or 36 minutes in the health service

$$L_q = L - \frac{\lambda}{\mu} = 6 - \frac{10}{4}$$

$= 3.5$ students waiting to be served

$$W_q = \frac{L_q}{\lambda} = \frac{3.5}{10}$$

$= 0.35$ hour, or 21 minutes waiting in line

$$P_w = \frac{1}{s!}\left(\frac{\lambda}{\mu}\right)^s \frac{s\mu}{s\mu - \lambda}P_0$$

$$= \frac{1}{3!}\left(\frac{10}{4}\right)^3 \frac{3(4)}{3(4) - (10)}(0.045)$$

$= 0.703$ probability that a student must wait for service (i.e., that there are three or more students in the system)

The health service administrator has observed that students are frustrated by the waiting time of 21 minutes and the 0.703 probability of waiting. To try to improve matters, the administrator is considering adding another nurse. The operating characteristics for this system must be recomputed with $s = 4$ nurses.

Four-server system

Substituting $s = 4$ along with λ and μ in the queuing formulas results in the following operating characteristics:

$P_0 = 0.073$ probability that no students are in the health service

$L = 3.0$ students in the health service

$W = 0.30$ hour, or 18 minutes, in the health service

$L_q = 0.5$ students waiting to be served

W_q = 0.05 hour, or 3 minutes, waiting in line

P_w = 0.31 probability that a student must wait for service

These results are significantly better: waiting time is reduced from 21 minutes to 3 minutes. This improvement in the quality of the service would have to be compared to the cost of adding an extra nurse.

EXHIBIT 5.3 Multiple-Server Waiting Line in Excel

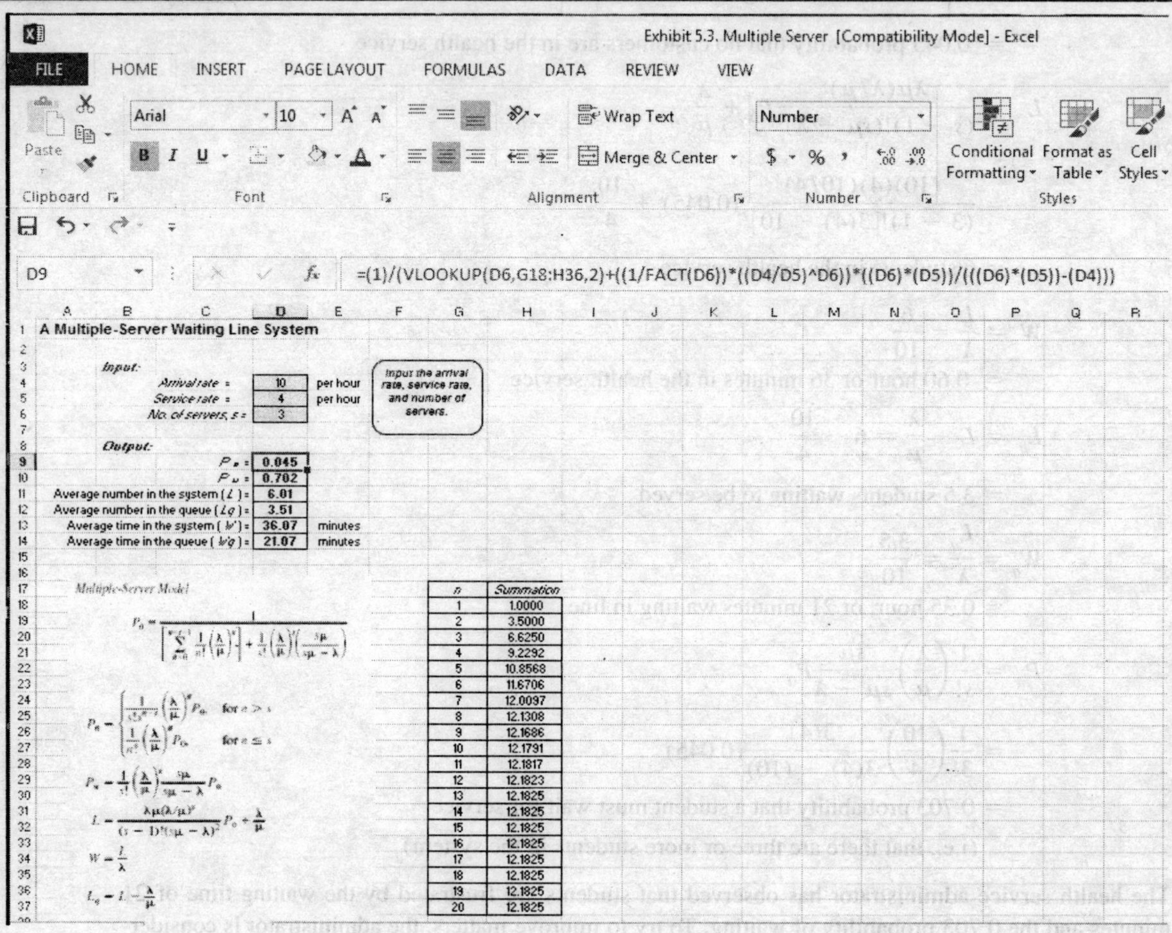

Explanation of Excel functions used in Exhibit 5.3

FACT (number)

A factorial is a count of the number of ways a group of items can be arranged (also called a permutation). The mathematical symbol for factorial is !. For example, 5! = 5 * 4 * 3 * 2 * 1 = 120. In Excel, FACT (5) = 120.

VLOOKUP (lookup value, table array, column number that contains the value to be returned).

VLOOKUP searches for a value in the first column of a table array and returns a value in the same row from another column in the table array. In this example, VLOOKUP(D6,G18:H36,2) looks up the number of servers, s, in the first column of the table and returns the value from the second column, which calculates the summation portion of the P_0 formula.

SUMMARY

Services represent the fastest-growing sector of the global economy and account for two thirds of global output, one third of global employment, and nearly 20% of global trade. The world's most industrialized nations are predominantly service economies.

Service design and operations present unique challenges due to the intangible nature of services, the inherent variability in service delivery, and the co-production of value by the customer and service provide. The design process involves developing a service concept, defining the service package, and determining performance, design, and delivery specifications. Design tools such as service blueprints, servicescapes, service scripts, and waiting line analysis facilitate the design process.

Since waiting is an integral part of many service-related operations, it is an important area of analysis. The mathematical formulas presented in this chapter for modeling various waiting line structures provide the basis for designing and improving service systems.

KEY FORMULAS

Single-Server Model

$$P_0 = 1 - \frac{\lambda}{\mu} \qquad W = \frac{1}{\mu - \lambda}$$

$$P_n = \left(\frac{\lambda}{\mu}\right)^n \left(1 - \frac{\lambda}{\mu}\right) \qquad W_q = \frac{\lambda}{\mu(\mu - \lambda)}$$

$$L = \frac{\lambda}{\mu - \lambda} \qquad \rho = \frac{\lambda}{\mu}$$

$$L_q = \frac{\lambda^2}{\mu(\mu - \lambda)} \qquad I = 1 - \frac{\lambda}{\mu}$$

where λ = arrival rate

μ = service rate

Single-Server Model with Finite Calling Population

$$P_0 = \frac{1}{\sum_{n=0}^{N} \frac{N!}{(N-n)!}\left(\frac{\lambda}{\mu}\right)^n} \qquad W_q = \frac{L_q}{(N - L)\lambda}$$

$$L_q = N - \left(\frac{\lambda + \mu}{\lambda}\right)(1 - P_0) \qquad W = W_q + \frac{1}{\mu}$$

$$L = L_q + (1 - P_0) \qquad P_n = \frac{N!}{(N-n)!}\left(\frac{\lambda}{\mu}\right)^n P_0$$

where N = population size

Single-Server Model with Finite Queue

$$P_0 = \frac{1 - \lambda/\mu}{1 - (\lambda/\mu)^{M+1}} \qquad W = \frac{L}{\lambda(1 - P_M)}$$

$$P_n = (P_0)(\lambda/\mu)^n, n \le M \qquad W_q = W - \frac{1}{\mu}$$

$$L = \frac{\lambda/\mu}{1 - \lambda/\mu} - \frac{(M+1)(\lambda/\mu)^{M+1}}{1 - (\lambda/\mu)^{M+1}}$$

$$L_q = L - \frac{\lambda(1 - P_M)}{\mu}$$

where M = maximum number allowed in the system

Single-Server Model with Constant Service Times

$$P_0 = 1 - \frac{\lambda}{\mu} \qquad W_q = \frac{L_q}{\lambda}$$

$$L_q = \frac{\lambda^2}{2\mu(\mu - \lambda)} \qquad W = W_q + \frac{1}{\mu}$$

$$L = L_q + \frac{\lambda}{\mu} \qquad \rho = \frac{\lambda}{\mu}$$

Multiple-Server Model

$$P_0 = \frac{1}{\left[\sum_{n=0}^{n=s-1} \frac{1}{n!}\left(\frac{\lambda}{\mu}\right)^n\right] + \frac{1}{s!}\left(\frac{\lambda}{\mu}\right)^s\left(\frac{s\mu}{s\mu - \lambda}\right)}$$

$$P_n = \begin{cases} \frac{1}{s!s^{n-s}}\left(\frac{\lambda}{\mu}\right)^n P_0, & \text{for } n > s \\ \frac{1}{n!}\left(\frac{\lambda}{\mu}\right)^n P_0, & \text{for } n \le s \end{cases}$$

$$P_w = \frac{1}{s!}\left(\frac{\lambda}{\mu}\right)^s \frac{s\mu}{s\mu - \lambda} P_0$$

$$L = \frac{\lambda\mu(\lambda/\mu)^s}{(s-1)!(s\mu - \lambda)^2} P_0 + \frac{\lambda}{\mu}$$

$$W = \frac{L}{\lambda}$$

$$L_q = L - \frac{\lambda}{\mu}$$

$$W_q = W - \frac{1}{\mu}$$

where s = number of servers

SOLVED PROBLEMS

1. SINGLE-SERVER MODEL

The new-accounts officer at the Citizens Northern Savings Bank enrolls all new customers in checking accounts. During the three-week period in August encompassing the beginning of the new school year at State University, the bank opens a lot of new accounts for students. The bank estimates that the arrival rate during this period will be Poisson distributed with an average of four customers per hour. The service time is exponentially distributed with an average of 12 minutes per customer to set up a new account. The bank wants to determine the operating characteristics for this system to determine if the current person is sufficient to handle the increased traffic.

SOLUTION

Determine operating characteristics for the single-server system:

$$\lambda = 4 \text{ customers per hour arrive}$$

$$\mu = 5 \text{ customers per hour are served}$$

$$P_0 = \left(1 - \frac{\lambda}{\mu}\right) = \left(1 - \frac{4}{5}\right)$$

$$= 0.20 \text{ probability of no customers in the system}$$

$$L = \frac{\lambda}{\mu - \lambda} = \frac{4}{5 - 4}$$

$$= 4 \text{ customers on average in the queuing system}$$

$$L_q = \frac{\lambda^2}{\mu(\mu - \lambda)} = \frac{4^2}{5(5 - 4)}$$

$$= 3.2 \text{ customers on average waiting}$$

$$W = \frac{1}{\mu - \lambda} = \frac{1}{5 - 4}$$

$$= 1 \text{ hour average time in the system}$$

$$W_q = \frac{\lambda}{\mu(\mu - \lambda)} = \frac{4}{5(5 - 4)}$$

$$= 0.80 \text{ hour (48 minutes) average time waiting}$$

$$P_w = \frac{\lambda}{\mu} = \frac{4}{5}$$

$$= 0.80 \text{ probability that the new-accounts officer will be busy and that a customer must wait}$$

The average waiting time of 48 minutes and the average time in the system are excessive, and the bank needs to add an extra employee during the busy period.

2. MULTIPLE-SERVER MODEL

The Citizens Northern Bank wants to compute the operating characteristics if an extra employee were added to assist with new-accounts enrollments.

SOLUTION

Determine the operating characteristics for the multiple-server system:

$$\lambda = 4 \text{ customers per hour arrive}$$

$$\mu = 5 \text{ customers per hour are served}$$

$$s = 2 \text{ servers}$$

$$P_0 = \frac{1}{\left[\sum_{n=0}^{n=s-1} \frac{1}{n!}\left(\frac{\lambda}{\mu}\right)^n\right] + \frac{1}{s!}\left(\frac{\lambda}{\mu}\right)^s\left(\frac{s\mu}{s\mu - \lambda}\right)}$$

$$= \frac{1}{\left[\frac{1}{0!}\left(\frac{4}{5}\right)^0 + \frac{1}{1!}\left(\frac{4}{5}\right)^1\right] + \frac{1}{2!}\left(\frac{4}{5}\right)^2\frac{(2)(5)}{(2)(5) - 4}}$$

$$= 0.429 \text{ probability that no customers are in the system}$$

$$L = \frac{\lambda\mu(\lambda/\mu)^s}{(s-1)!(s\mu - \lambda)^2}P_0 + \frac{\lambda}{\mu}$$

$$= \frac{(4)(5)(4/5)^2}{1![(2)(5) - 4]^2}(0.429) + \frac{4}{5}$$

$$= 0.952 \text{ customer on average in the system}$$

$$L_q = L - \frac{\lambda}{\mu} = 0.952 - \frac{4}{5}$$

$$= 0.152 \text{ customer on average waiting to be served}$$

$$W = \frac{L}{\lambda} = \frac{0.952}{4}$$

$$= 0.238 \text{ hour (14.3 minutes) average time in the system}$$

$$W_q = \frac{L_q}{\lambda} = \frac{0.152}{4}$$

$$= 0.038 \text{ hour (2.3 minutes) average time in line}$$

$$P_w = \frac{1}{s!}\left(\frac{\lambda}{\mu}\right)^s \frac{s\mu}{s\mu - l}P_0$$

$$= \frac{1}{2!}\left(\frac{4}{5}\right)^2 \frac{(2)(5)}{(2)(5) - 4}(0.429)$$

$$= 0.229 \text{ probability that a customer must wait}$$

The waiting time with the multiple-server model is 2.3 minutes, which is a significant improvement over the previous system; thus, the bank should add the second new-accounts officer.

QUESTIONS

5-1. How would you define a service?

5-2. List eight characteristics of services and explain what impact each characteristic has on the design process.

5-3. Describe the service package for (a) a bank, (b) an airline, and (c) a lawn service.

5-4. Generate as many ideas as you can for additional services or improvements in service delivery for (a) banking, (b) higher education, and (c) healthcare.

5-5. Explain the components of a service blueprint.

5-6. Identify 10 real-life examples of queuing systems with which you are familiar.

5-7. Why must the utilization factor in a single-server model be less than one?

5-8. Give five examples of real-world queuing systems with finite calling populations.

5-9. List the elements that define a queuing system.

5-10. How can the results of queuing analysis be used by a decision maker for making decisions?

5-11. What is the mean effective service rate in a multiple-server model, and what must be its relationship to the arrival rate?

5-12. For each of the following queuing systems, indicate if it is a single- or multiple-server model, the queue discipline, and if its calling population is infinite or finite:

a. Hair salon
b. Bank
c. Laundromat
d. Doctor's office
e. Adviser's office
f. Airport runway
g. Service station
h. Copy center
i. Team trainer
j. Mainframe computer

5-13. For Example 5.1 in this chapter, discuss why the multiple-server model would or would not be appropriate as an alternative to reduce waiting time.

5-14. Discuss briefly the relationship between waiting line analysis and quality improvement.

5-15. Define the four basic waiting line structures and give an example of each.

5-16. Describe the traditional cost relationship in waiting line analysis.

5-17. a. Is the following statement true or false? The single-phase, single-channel model with Poisson arrivals and undefined service times will always have larger (i.e., greater) operating characteristic values (i.e., W, W_q, L, L_q) than the same model with exponentially distributed service times. Explain your answer.

b. Is the following statement true or false? The single-phase, single-channel model with Poisson arrivals and constant service times will always have smaller (i.e., lower) operating characteristic values (i.e., W, W_q, L, L_q) than the same model with exponentially distributed service times. Explain your answer.

5-18. Under what conditions can the basic single-server and multiple-server models be used to analyze a multiple-phase waiting line system?

5-19. Why do waiting lines form at a service facility even though there may be more than enough service capacity to meet normal demand in the long run?

5-20. Provide an example of when a first-in, first-out (FIFO) rule for queue discipline would not be appropriate.

5-21. Under what conditions will the single-channel, single-phase queuing model with Poisson arrivals and undefined service times provide the same operating characteristics as the basic model with exponentially distributed service times?

5-22. What types of waiting line systems have constant service times?

5-23. Compare traditional car rental services with zipcar and car2go. Each of these has a different service concept. Explain.

PROBLEMS

5-1. McBurger's fast-food restaurant has a drive-through window with a single server who takes orders from an intercom and is also the cashier. The window operator is assisted by other employees who prepare the orders. Customers arrive at the ordering station prior to the drive-through window every 3.6 minutes (exponentially distributed) and the service time is 2.4 minutes (exponentially distributed). Determine the average length of the waiting line and the waiting time. Discuss the quality implications of your results. If you decide that the quality of the service could be improved, indicate what things you might do to improve quality.

5-2. The ticket booth on the Tech campus is operated by one person, who is selling tickets for the annual Tech versus State football game on Saturday. The ticket seller can serve an average of 12 customers per hour (Poisson distributed); on average, 8 customers arrive to purchase tickets each hour (Poisson distributed). Determine the average time a ticket buyer must wait and the portion of time the ticket seller is busy.

5-3. The Peachtree Airport in Atlanta serves light aircraft. It has a single runway and one air traffic controller to land planes. It takes an airplane 8 minutes to land and clear the runway (exponentially distributed). Planes arrive at the airport at the rate of 5 per hour (Poisson distributed).

a. Determine the average number of planes that will stack up waiting to land.

b. Find the average time a plane must wait in line before it can land.

c. Calculate the average time it takes a plane to clear the runway once it has notified the airport that it is in the vicinity and wants to land.

d. The FAA has a rule that an air traffic controller can, on the average, land planes a maximum of 45 minutes out of every hour. There must be 15 minutes of idle time available to relieve the tension. Will this airport have to hire an extra air traffic controller?

5-4. The National Bank of Union City currently has one outside drive-up teller. It takes the teller an average of three minutes (exponentially distributed) to serve a bank customer. Customers arrive at the drive-up window at the rate of 12 per hour (Poisson distributed). The bank operations officer is currently analyzing the possibility of adding a second drive-up window at an annual cost of $20,000. It is assumed that arriving cars would be equally divided between both windows. The operations officer estimates that each minute's reduction in customer waiting time would increase the bank's revenue by $2,000 annually. Should the second drive-up window be installed? What other factors should be considered in the decision besides cost?

5-5. The Escargot is a small French restaurant with 6 waiters and waitresses. The average service time at the restaurant for a table (of any size) is 80 minutes (exponentially distributed). The restaurant does not take reservations and parties arrive for dinner (and stay and wait) every 16 minutes (Poisson distributed). The restaurant is concerned that a lengthy waiting time might hurt its business in the long run. What is the current waiting time and queue length for the restaurant? Discuss the quality implications of the current waiting time and any actions the restaurant might take.

5-6. Cakes baked by the Freshfood Bakery are transported from the ovens to be packaged by one of three wrappers. Each wrapper can wrap an average of 120 cakes per hour (Poisson distributed). The cakes are brought to the wrappers at the rate of 300 per hour (Poisson distributed). If a cake sits longer than 5 minutes before being wrapped, it will not be fresh enough to meet the bakery's quality control standards. Does the bakery need to hire another wrapper?

5-7. The Draper Clinic has two general practitioners who see patients daily. An average of 6.5 patients arrive at the clinic per hour (Poisson distributed). Each doctor spends an average of 15 minutes (exponentially distributed) with a patient. The patients wait in a waiting area until one of the two doctors is able to see them. However, since patients typically do not feel well when they come to the clinic, the doctors do not believe it is good practice to have a patient wait longer than an average of 20 minutes. Should this clinic add a third doctor, and, if so, will this alleviate the waiting problem?

5-8. The Wearever Shoe Company is going to open a new branch at a mall, and company managers are attempting to determine how many salespeople to hire. Based on an analysis of mall traffic, the company estimates that customers will arrive at the store at the rate of 9 per hour (Poisson distributed), and from past experience at its other branches, the company knows that salespeople can serve an average of 6 customers per hour (Poisson distributed). How many salespeople should the company hire in order to maintain a company policy that on average a customer should have to wait for service no more than 30% of the time?

5-9. When customers arrive at Gilley's Ice Cream Shop, they take a number and wait to be called to purchase ice cream from one of the counter servers. From experience in past summers, the store's staff knows that customers arrive at the rate of 35 per hour (Poisson distributed) on summer days between 3:00 P.M. and 10:00 P.M. and a server can serve 15 customers per hour on average (Poisson distributed). Gilley's wants to make sure that customers wait no longer than 5 minutes for service. Gilley's is contemplating keeping three servers behind the ice cream counter during the peak summer hours. Will this number be adequate to meet the waiting time policy?

5-10. Huang's television-repair service receives an average of four TV sets per 8-hour day to be repaired. The service manager would like to be able to tell customers that they can expect their TV back in 3 days. What average repair time per set will the repair shop have to achieve to provide 3-day service on the average? (Assume that the arrival rate is Poisson distributed and repair times are exponentially distributed.)

5-11. The Seaboard Shipping Company has a warehouse terminal in Spartanburg, South Carolina. The capacity of each terminal dock is three trucks. As trucks enter the terminal, the drivers receive numbers, and when one of the three dock spaces becomes available, the truck with the lowest number enters the vacant dock. Truck arrivals are Poisson distributed, and the unloading and loading times (service times) are exponentially distributed. The average arrival rate at the terminal is five trucks per hour, and the average service rate per dock is two trucks per hour (30 minutes per truck).

a. Compute L, L_q, W, and W_q.

b. The management of the shipping company is considering adding extra employees and equipment to improve the average service time per terminal dock to 25 minutes per truck. It would cost the company $18,000 per year to achieve this improved service. Management estimates that it will increase its profit by $750 per year for each minute it is able to reduce a truck's waiting time. Determine whether management should make the investment.

c. Now suppose that the managers of the shipping company have decided that truck waiting time is excessive and they want to reduce it. They have determined that there are two alternatives available for reducing the waiting time. They can add a fourth dock, or they can add extra employees and equipment at the existing docks, which will reduce the average service time per location from the original 30 minutes per truck to 23 minutes per truck. The costs of these alternatives are approximately equal. Management desires to implement the alternative that reduces waiting time by the greatest amount. Which alternative should be selected?

5-12. Drivers who come to get their licenses at the department of motor vehicles have their photograph taken by an automated machine that develops the photograph onto the license card and laminates the complete license. The machine requires a constant time of 4.5 minutes to develop a completed license. If drivers arrive at the machine at the mean rate of 11 per hour (Poisson distributed), determine the average length of the waiting line and the average waiting time.

5-13. A vending machine at Municipal Airport dispenses hot coffee, hot chocolate, or hot tea in a constant service time of 30 seconds. Customers arrive at the vending machine at a mean rate of 50 per hour, Poisson distributed. Determine the average length of the waiting line and the average time a customer must wait.

5-14. Norfolk, Virginia, a major seaport on the East Coast, has a ship coal-loading facility. Currently, coal trucks filled with coal arrive at the port facility at the mean rate of 149 per day (Poisson distributed). The facility operates 24 hours a day. The coal trucks are unloaded one at a time on a first-come, first-served basis by automated mechanical equipment that empties the trucks in a constant time of eight minutes per truck, regardless of truck size. The port authority is negotiating with a coal company for an additional 30 trucks per day. However, the coal company will not use this port facility unless the port authority can assure them that their coal trucks will not have to wait to be unloaded at the port facility for more than 12 hours per truck on the average. Can the port authority provide this assurance?

5-15. The Riverton Police Department has eight patrol cars that are on constant call 24 hours per day. A patrol car requires repairs every 30 days, on average, according to an exponential distribution. When a patrol car is in need of repair it is driven into the motor pool, which has a repairperson on duty at all times. The average time required to repair a patrol car is 12 hours (exponentially distributed). Determine the average time a patrol car is not available for use and the average number of patrol cars out of service at any one time, and indicate if the repair service seems adequate.

5-16. The Crosstown Cab Company has four cabs on duty during normal business hours. The cab company dispatcher receives requests for service every seven minutes, on average, according to an exponential distribution. The average time to complete a trip is 20 minutes (exponentially distributed). Determine the average number of customers waiting for service and the average time a customer must wait for a cab.

5-17. A retail catalog operation employs a bank of six telephone operators who process orders using computer terminals. When a terminal breaks down, it must be disconnected and taken to a nearby electronics repair shop, where it is repaired. The mean time between terminal breakdowns is six working days, and the mean time required to repair a terminal is two working days (both exponentially distributed). As a result of lost sales, it costs the mail-order operation an estimated $50 per day in lost profits each day a terminal is out for repair. The company pays the electronics repair shop $3,000 per year on a service agreement to repair the terminals. The company is considering the possibility of signing a new service agreement with another electronics repair shop that will provide substitute terminals while the broken ones are at the repair shop. However, the new service agreement would cost the mail-order operation $15,000 per year. Assuming that there are 250 working days in a year, determine what the mail-order operation should do.

5-18. The Ritz Hotel has enough space for six taxicabs to load passengers, line up, and wait for guests at its entrance. Cabs arrive at the hotel every 10 minutes and if a taxi drives by the hotel and the line is full it must drive on. Hotel guests require taxis every five minutes on average and then it takes a cab driver an average of 3.5 minutes to load passengers and luggage and leave the hotel (exponentially distributed).

a. What is the average time a cab must wait for a fare?

b. What is the probability that the line will be full when a cab drives by and it must drive on?

5-19. The local Quick Burger fast food restaurant has a drive-through window. Customers in cars arrive at the window at the rate of 10 per hour (Poisson distributed). It requires an average of four minutes (exponentially distributed) to take and fill an order. The restaurant chain has a service goal of an average waiting time of three minutes.

a. Will the current system meet the restaurant's service goal?

b. If the restaurant is not meeting its service goal, it can add a second drive-in window that will reduce the service time per customer to 2.5 minutes. Will the additional window enable the restaurant to meet its service goal?

c. During the two-hour lunch period the arrival rate of drive-in customers increases to 20 per hour. Will the two-window system be able to achieve the restaurant's service goal during the rush period?

5-20. From 3:00 P.M. to 8:00 P.M. the local Big-W Supermarket has a steady arrival of customers. Customers finish shopping and arrive at the checkout area at the rate of 80 per hour (Poisson distributed). It is assumed that when customers arrive at the cash registers they will divide themselves relatively evenly so that all the checkout lines are even. The average checkout time at a register is seven minutes (exponentially distributed). The store manager's service goal is for customers to be out of the store within 12 minutes (on average) after they complete their shopping and arrive at the cash register. How many cash registers must the store have open in order to achieve the manager's service goal?

5-21. Customers arrive at the lobby of the exclusive and expensive Ritz Hotel at the rate of 40 per hour (Poisson distributed) to check in. The hotel normally has three clerks available at the desk to check guests in. The average time for a clerk to check in a guest is four minutes (exponentially distributed). Clerks at the Regency are paid $12 per hour and the hotel assigns a goodwill cost of $2 per minute for the time a guest must wait in line. Determine if the present check-in system is cost effective; if it is not, recommend what hotel management should do.

5-22. Jim Carter builds custom furniture, primarily cabinets, bookcases, small tables, and chairs. He only works on one piece of furniture for a customer at a time. It takes him an average of five weeks (exponentially distributed) to build a piece of furniture. An average of 14 customers approach Jim to order pieces of furniture each year (Poisson distributed); however, Jim will only take a maximum of eight advance orders. Determine the average time a customer must wait to receive a furniture order once it is placed and how busy Jim is. What is the probability that a customer will be able to place an order with Jim?

5-23. The Dominion Landing theme park has a new water ride, the Raging Rapids. The ride holds 36 people in boat-cars and it takes 4.1 minutes to complete the ride circuit. It also takes the ride attendants another 3.5 minutes (with virtually no variation) to load and unload passengers. Passengers arrive at the ride during peak park hours at the rate of 4.4 per minute (Poisson distributed). Determine the length of the waiting line for the ride.

5-24. The food court at Tech has a single checkout counter over the weekends staffed by one employee who takes an average of 2 minutes to checkout a customer. Students arrive to the food court at a rate of 25 per hour. The campus newspaper has recently published complaints from students about slow service in the food court on weekends. Use queuing theory to calculate the following:

a. The average number of students in the system

b. The average number of students in the waiting line

c. The average time a student spends in the line

d. The probability that the cashier would be busy and thus the student would have to wait

e. What assumptions about the distribution of arrival rates and service rates are you making in deriving the above values? Are the student complaints valid? Discuss.

5-25. After reviewing your report above, Tech has decided to improve the checkout process through training, clearer signage about prices, and bar code stickers on the most popular items purchased. With the improvements in place, it now takes an average of 1.5 minutes to check out a customer from the food court. As a result of the shorter checkout lines, more students are visiting the food court on weekends, arriving at an average rate of 30 customers per hour. Recalculate the measures above (a through d in Problem 5-24). Has customer service improved in the new system?

CASE STUDY

Improving the Pharmacy Experience

Yao Fun Small Town Pharmacy is the only location one can obtain prescription drugs from. With the limited options of where one can buy the prescribed drugs, the pharmacy is a very busy place. The local technical university sent its operations management class to observe the average customer experience and record it according to the specific steps an average customer experiences. The following was the final class listing:

1. Customer arrives.
2. Customer takes a ticket.
3. Customer waits at a comfortable chair location.
4. Customer is called to the pharmacy window.
5. Customer hands the pharmacist the prescription.
6. Customer returns to the waiting area until his/her prescription is called.
7. Customer's number is called.
8. Pharmacist hands the prescription over and provides guidance and advice on how to take the drugs.
9. Customer travels to the cashier line.
10. Customer waits in line to pay for the prescription.
11. Customer pays for the prescription.
12. Customer leaves.

a. Create a service blueprint of the procedure.

b. Identify opportunities for improving the overall process.

REFERENCES

Bitner, M. J., A. Ostrom, and F. Morgan, "Service Blueprinting: A Practical Technique for Service Innovation," California Management Review, Vol. 50, No. 3 (2008).

Cooper, R. B. *Introduction to Queuing Theory*, 2nd ed. New York: North Holland, 1981.

Davis, M., and J. Heineke. *Operations Management*. New York: McGraw-Hill/ Irwin, 2004.

Fitzsimmons, J., and M. Fitzsimmons. *Service Management*. New York: McGraw-Hill/Irwin, 2004.

Gross, D., and C. Harris. *Fundamentals of Queuing Theory*, 2nd ed. New York: Wiley, 1985.

Hillier, F. S., and O. S. Yu. *Queuing Tables and Graphics*. New York: North Holland, 1981.

Jacobs, R., and R. Chase. *Operations and Supply Chain Management*. New York: McGraw-Hill/ Irwin, 2014.

Jargon, J. "At Starbucks, Baristas Told No More Than Two Drinks," *The Wall Street Journal* (October 13, 2010).

Kleinrock, L. *Queuing Systems*, vols. 1 and 2. New York: Wiley, 1975.

Lee, A. *Applied Queuing Theory*. New York: St. Martin's Press, 1966.

Lovelock, C. H. and J. Wirtz. *Services Marketing*. Englewood Cliffs, NJ. Prentice Hall, 2011.

Morse, P. M. *Queues, Inventories, and Maintenance*. New York: Wiley, 1958.

Prahalad, C. K., and Venkat Ramaswamy. *The Future of Competition: Co-creating Unique Value with Customers*. Boston: Harvard Business School Press, 2004.

Saaty, T. L. *Elements of Queuing Theory with Applications*. New York: Dover, 1983.

Sampson, S. E. Understanding Service Businesses. Salt Lake City, UT: Brigham Young University, 1999.

Shostack, G. L. "Designing Services That Deliver." *Harvard Business Review* (January–February 1984), pp. 133–139.

Solomon, S. L. *Simulation of Waiting Line Systems*. Upper Saddle River, NJ: Prentice Hall, 1983.

White, J. A., J. W. Schmidt, and G. K. Bennett. *Analysis of Queuing Systems*. New York: Academic Press, 1975.

Zeithaml, V. *Service Quality*. Cambridge, MA: Marketing Science Institute, 2004

CHAPTER 6

Designing Processes

LEARNING OBJECTIVES

AFTER READING THIS CHAPTER, YOU WILL BE ABLE TO:

- Evaluate strategic options in process planning, including whether or not to outsource.
- Differentiate among different types of production processes.
- Understand the effect of volume and standardization on process selection.
- Appreciate the difficulties in translating a design to a process.
- Use simple flowcharting tools to improve everyday processes.
- Investigate the use of technology in manufacturing and service processes.

MAKING THE RIGHT OUTSOURCING DECISION

VF Corporation, formerly Vanity Fair Mills, is the world's largest apparel maker and the producer of Wrangler and Lee jeans, as well as many other apparel brands. VF employs over 29,000 supply chain associates who produce 1.25 million items each day. Currently, 70% of VF's apparel production is outsourced to 1,500 factories in more than 40 countries. The remaining 30% is produced in-house at 38 company-owned facilities.

VF uses three strategies for production: (1) vertical integration (i.e., in-house manufacturing), (2) transactional outsourcing, and (3) the third way. VF-owned factories use the latest processes, technology, and management. These in-house factories allow VF to keep its expertise in process and product innovation. Transactional outsourcing is used for low-cost or standard products and components. The third way is a strategic partnership between VF and its suppliers in which VF personnel and, sometimes, equipment and technology, are located in the supplier plant to monitor production and ensure product quality.

In Asia, where there are several third-way suppliers, VF has two innovation and development centers for jeanswear. These centers house sample "factories" where design and production work together to literally make new products before releasing them to the supplier factories. Jeans, in particular, need more than a sewing pattern or CAD design to communicate the look of the product. Getting the wash, the fading and the whiskering right requires more expertise, and practice. By using these "demo" factories, third way suppliers are able to ramp up production and accurately reproduce new designs within a two-week window.

VF's long-term strategy is to have 40% of its production in its own factories, 40% in third-way sourcing, and 20% in transactional sourcing.

In this chapter, we talk about planning, improving, and innovating processes, as well as how to make wise outsourcing and technology decisions.

Sources: Based on R. Lewis, "QA with Eric C. Wiseman, chairman, president, and CEO of VF Corporation," *The Robin Report* (September 10, 2012); Tom Glaser, *APAC & China 2017 Plan: Supply Chain*, www.vfinchina.com, September 19, 2012. For more information on the third way, see G. Pisano and P. Adams, "VF Brands: Global Supply Chain Strategy," Case 610022, Harvard Business School, 2009.

A **process** is a group of related tasks with specific inputs and outputs. Processes exist to create value for the customer, the shareholder, or society. *Process design* defines what tasks need to be done and how they are to be coordinated among functions, people, and organizations. Planning, analyzing, and improving processes is the essence of operations management. Processes are planned, analyzed, and redesigned as required by changes in strategy and emerging technology.

Process strategy is an organization's overall approach for physically producing goods and providing services. Process decisions should reflect how the firm has chosen to compete in the marketplace, reinforce product decisions, and facilitate the achievement of corporate goals. A firm's process strategy defines its:

- ***Vertical integration:*** The extent to which the firm will produce the inputs and control the outputs of each stage of the production process.
- ***Capital intensity:*** The mix of capital (i.e., equipment, automation) and labor resources used in the production process.
- ***Process flexibility:*** The ease with which resources can be adjusted in response to changes in demand, technology, products or services, and resource availability.
- ***Customer involvement:*** The role of the customer in the production process.

In this chapter we examine the planning, analysis, and innovation of processes, as well as technology decisions related to those processes.

Process Planning

Process planning determines *how* a product will be produced or a service provided. It decides which components will be made in-house and which will be purchased from a supplier, selects processes, and develops and documents the specifications for manufacture and delivery. In this section, we discuss outsourcing decisions, process selection, and process plans.

OUTSOURCING

A firm that sells the product, assembles the product, makes all the parts, and extracts the raw material is completely **vertically integrated**. But most companies cannot or will not make all of the parts that go into a product. A major strategic decision, then, is how much of the work should be done outside the firm. The decision involves questions of dependence, competency-building, and proprietary knowledge, as well as cost.

On what basis should particular items be made in-house? When should items be outsourced? How should suppliers be selected? What type of relationship should be maintained with suppliers—arm's length, controlling, partnership, alliance? What is expected from the suppliers? How many suppliers should be used? How can the quality and dependability of suppliers be ensured? How can suppliers be encouraged to collaborate?

For process planning, we need to decide which items will be purchased from an outside supplier and which items will be produced in our own factories. More advanced sourcing decisions and a discussion of the questions posed above are covered in Chapter 10.

The basic outsourcing decision rests on an evaluation of the following factors:

1. ***Cost.*** Would it be cheaper to make the item or buy it? to perform the service in-house or outsource it? The cost of *buying* the item from a supplier includes the purchase price, transportation costs, and various tariffs, taxes, and fees (referred to as landed cost in Chapter 10). The cost of coordinating production over long distances and increased inventory levels to cover demand during a lengthy lead time can also run high. The cost of *making* the item includes labor, material, and overhead. Existing overhead does not disappear when some products are outsourced. Spreading overhead over fewer products can actually increase unit costs.

   In some situations a company may decide to buy an item rather than make it (or vice versa) when, from a cost standpoint, it would be cheaper to do otherwise. The remaining factors in this list represent noneconomic factors that can influence or dominate the economic considerations.
2. ***Capacity.*** Companies that are operating at less than full capacity may elect to make components rather than buy them, especially if maintaining a level workforce or capability to produce is important. Sometimes the available capacity is not sufficient to make all the components, so choices have to be made. Typically, it is better to produce more customized or volatile products in-house, and to outsource steady products with high volume/high standardization.
3. ***Quality.*** The capability to provide quality parts consistently is an important consideration in the outsourcing decision. It is easier to control the quality of items produced in your own factory. However, standardization of parts, supplier certification, and supplier involvement in design can improve the quality of supplied parts. In the event that quality becomes a problem, increased monitoring of the supplier can significantly increase costs.
4. ***Speed.*** The savings from purchasing an item from a far-off vendor can be eaten up by the lengthy transit time of offshore shipments. At other times, a smaller supplier can be more flexible, and can adapt more quickly to design and technology changes. Of course, speed is useful only if it is reliable.
5. ***Reliability.*** Suppliers need to be reliable in both the quality and the timing of what they supply. Unexpected delays in shipments or partially filled orders because of quality rejects can wreak havoc with the manufacturing system. Many companies today are requiring that their suppliers meet certain quality and delivery standards to be certified as an approved supplier. As discussed in Chapter 2, the most common quality certification is ISO 9000. Other companies assess huge penalties for unreliable supply. Some automakers, for example, fine their suppliers $30,000 for each *hour* an order is late.
6. ***Expertise.*** Companies that are especially good at making or designing certain items may want to keep control over their production. Coca-Cola would not want to release its formula to a supplier, even if there were guarantees of secrecy. Although automakers might outsource many of their component parts, they need proprietary control over major components such as engines, transmissions, and electronic guidance systems. Japanese, Taiwanese, and Korean firms are currently learning U.S. expertise in aircraft design and manufacture by serving as suppliers of component parts. Chinese markets are often flooded with cheap knockoffs of goods manufactured by suppliers in that country. The protection of intellectual property is a major concern in extended supply chains.

Figure 6.1
The Sourcing Continuum

The outsourcing decision can be made along a continuum from a single purchasing decision to a joint venture, as shown in Figure 6.1.

Single contracts are used if the outsourcing decision is temporary, or the products are standardized (like commodities) and suppliers are chosen based on lowest cost. Strategic alliances signify that the supplier is an important long-term partner, and the cost or consequences of switching suppliers would be significant. Companies share more information with strategic suppliers and work with them to solve problems or improve processes. Joint ventures are used when entering a foreign country for the first time, or as a condition for operating in another country. Risks, resources, and rewards are shared among equity partners of a joint venture.

PROCESS SELECTION

The next step in process planning is to select a production process for those items we will produce in-house. Production processes can be classified into projects, batch production, mass production, and continuous production.

Projects take a long time to complete, involve a large investment of funds and resources, and produce one item at a time to consumer order. Examples include construction projects, shipbuilding, new-product development, and aircraft manufacturing.

Batch production processes many different jobs through the production system at the same time in groups or batches. Products are typically made to customer order, volume (in terms of customer order size) is low, and demand fluctuates. Examples of batch production include printers, bakeries, machine shops, education, and furniture making.

Mass production produces large volumes of a standard product for a mass market. Product demand is stable, and product volume is high. Goods that are mass produced include automobiles, televisions, personal computers, fast food, and most consumer goods.

Continuous production is used for *very* high-volume commodity products that are *very* standardized. The system is *highly* automated and is typically in operation continuously 24 hours a day. Refined oil, treated water, paints, chemicals, and foodstuffs are produced by continuous production.

The process chosen to create the product or service must be consistent with product and service characteristics. The most important product characteristics (in terms of process choice) are degree of *standardization* and *demand volume*. Figure 6.2 shows a product-process matrix that matches product characteristics with process choice.

The best process strategy is found on the diagonal of the matrix. Companies or products that are off the diagonal have either made poor process choices or have found a means to execute a competitive advantage. For example, technological advancements in flexible automation allow Motorola to mass produce customized pagers. Volvo and Rolls Royce occupy a special market niche by producing cars in a crafted, customized fashion. Examples of poor process choice include Texas Instruments' attempt to produce consumer products for mass markets by the same process that had been successful in the production of scientific products for specialized markets, and Corning's production of low-volume consumer items, such as range covers, with the same continuous process used for other items formed from glass.

Table 6.1 summarizes the characteristics of each type of process. As we move from projects to continuous production, demand volume increases; products become more standardized; systems become more capital-intensive, more automated, and less flexible; and customers become less involved.

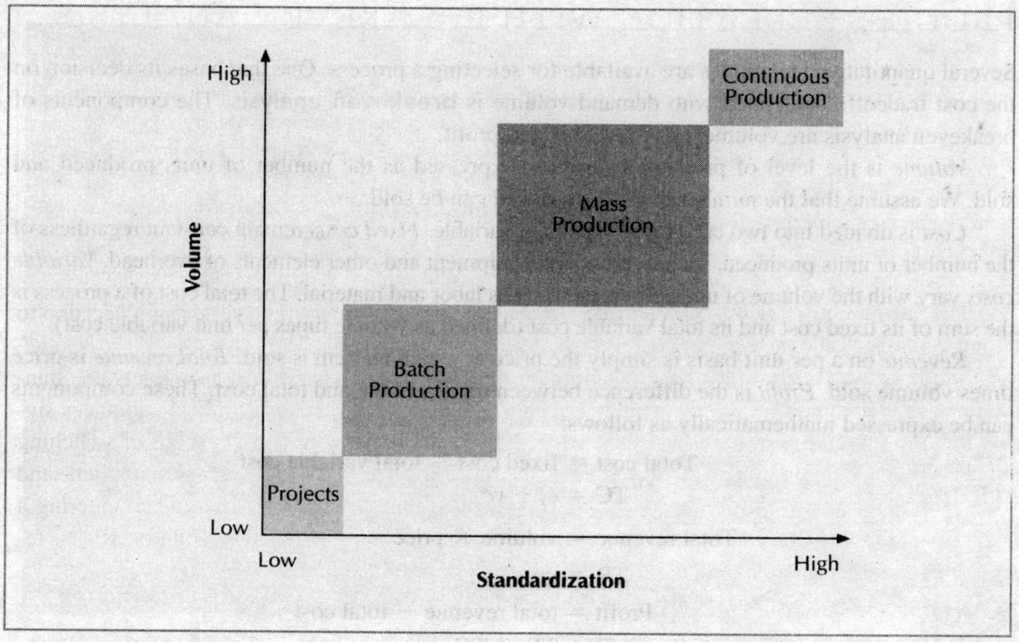

Figure 6.2

The Product-Process Matrix

SOURCE: Adapted from Robert Hayes and Steven Wheelwright, *Restoring the Competitive Edge: Competing Through Manufacturing* (New York, John Wiley & Sons, 1984), p. 209.

TABLE 6.1 Types of Processes

	Project	Batch Production	Mass Production	Continuous Production
Type of product	Unique	Made-to-order (customized)	Made-to-stock (standardized)	Commodity
Type of customer	One-at-a-time	Few individual customers	Mass market	Mass market
Product demand	Infrequent	Fluctuates	Stable	Very stable
Demand volume	Very low	Low to medium	High	Very high
No. of different products	Infinite variety	Many, varied	Few	Very few
Production system	Long-term project	Discrete, job shops	Repetitive, assembly lines	Continuous, process industries
Equipment	Varied	General-purpose	Special-purpose	Highly automated
Primary type of work	Specialized contracts	Fabrication	Assembly	Mixing, treating, refining
Worker skills	Experts, craftspersons	Wide range of skills	Limited range of skills	Equipment monitors
Advantages	Custom work, latest technology	Flexibility, quality	Efficiency, speed, low cost	Highly efficient, large capacity, ease of control
Disadvantages	Nonrepetitive, small customer base, expensive	Costly, slow, difficult to manage	Capital investment, lack of responsiveness	Difficult to change, far-reaching errors, limited variety
Examples	Construction, shipbuilding, spacecraft	Machine shops, print shops, bakeries, education	Automobiles, televisions, computers, fast food	Paint, chemicals, foodstuffs

PROCESS SELECTION WITH BREAKEVEN ANALYSIS

Several quantitative techniques are available for selecting a process. One that bases its decision on the cost tradeoffs associated with demand volume is **breakeven analysis**. The components of breakeven analysis are volume, cost, revenue, and profit.

Volume is the level of production, usually expressed as the number of units produced and sold. We assume that the number of units produced can be sold.

Cost is divided into two categories: fixed and variable. *Fixed costs* remain constant regardless of the number of units produced, such as plant and equipment and other elements of overhead. *Variable costs* vary with the volume of units produced, such as labor and material. The total cost of a process is the sum of its fixed cost and its total variable cost (defined as volume times per unit variable cost).

Revenue on a per-unit basis is simply the price at which an item is sold. *Total revenue* is price times volume sold. *Profit* is the difference between total revenue and total cost. These components can be expressed mathematically as follows:

$$\text{Total cost} = \text{fixed cost} + \text{total variable cost}$$
$$TC = c_f + vc_v$$
$$\text{Total revenue} = \text{volume} \times \text{price}$$
$$TR = vp$$
$$\text{Profit} = \text{total revenue} - \text{total cost}$$
$$Z = TR - TC$$
$$= vp - (c_f + vc_v)$$

where

c_f = fixed cost
v = volume (i.e., number of units produced and sold)
c_v = variable cost per unit
p = price per unit

In selecting a process, it is useful to know at what volume of sales and production we can expect to earn a profit. We want to make sure that the cost of producing a product does not exceed the revenue we will receive from the sale of the product. By equating total revenue with total cost and solving for v, we can find the volume at which profit is zero. This is called the **breakeven point**. At any volume above the breakeven point, we will make a profit. A mathematical formula for the breakeven point can be determined as follows:

$$TR = TC$$
$$vp = c_f + vc_v$$
$$vp - vc_v = c_f$$
$$v(p - c_v) = c_f$$
$$v = \frac{c_f}{p - c_v}$$

EXAMPLE 6.1

BREAKEVEN ANALYSIS

Travis and Jeff own Up Right Paddlers, a new startup company with the goal of designing, making, and marketing stand-up paddle boards for streams and rivers. A new fitness craze, stand-up paddle boards are similar to surfboards in appearance, but are used by individuals to navigate down rivers in an upright position with a single long pole (or paddle), instead of sitting in tubes or rafts and floating down. The boards are constructed from heavy-duty raft material that is inflatable, rather than the fiberglass material used in surfboards. Unlike surfboards that market for \$500 to \$1,000 each, paddle boards are typically sold for between \$100 and \$400. Since Travis and Jeff are just starting out and the demand for paddle boards on the East Coast has not been firmly established, they anticipate selling their product for \$100 each. Travis estimates the fixed cost for equipment and space will be \$20,000, and the material and labor costs will run \$50 per unit. What volume of demand will be necessary for Travis and Jeff to break even on their new venture?

SOLUTION

$$\text{Fixed cost} = c_f = \$2{,}000$$

$$\text{Variable cost} = c_v = \$50 \text{ per board}$$

$$\text{Price} = p = \$100 \text{ per board}$$

$$v = \frac{c_f}{p - c_v} = \frac{2000}{100 - 50} = 40 \text{ units}$$

The solution is shown graphically in the following figure. The x-axis represents production or demand volume, and the y-axis represents dollars of revenue, cost, or profit. The total revenue line extends from the origin, with a slope equal to the unit price of a board. The total cost line intersects the y-axis at a level corresponding to the fixed cost of the process and has a slope equal to the per-unit variable cost. The intersection of these two lines is the breakeven point. If demand is less than the breakeven point, the company will operate at a loss. But if demand exceeds the breakeven point, the company will be profitable. The company needs to sell more than 40 paddle boards to make a profit.

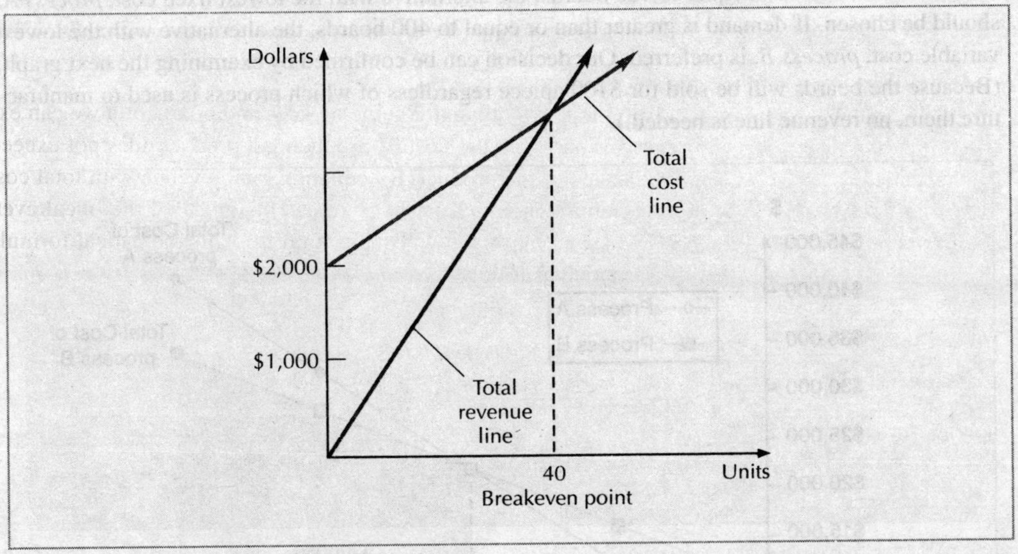

Breakeven analysis is especially useful when evaluating different degrees of automation. More automated processes have higher fixed costs but lower variable costs. The "best" process depends on the anticipated volume of demand for the product and the tradeoffs between fixed and variable costs. Example 6.2 shows how breakeven analysis can guide the selection of a process among several alternatives. The example uses this procedure:

1. Formulate a total cost equation for each process considered.
2. Calculate the ***point of indifference*** between two alternative processes (i.e., the volume at which the total cost of manufacturing is the same for the two processes) by setting their total cost equations equal to each other and solving for *v*, demand volume.
3. Above the point of indifference, choose the alternative with the lowest variable cost.
4. Below the point of indifference, choose the alternative with the lowest fixed cost.

EXAMPLE 6.2

PROCESS SELECTION

Jeff, the more optimistic of the two owners of UpRight Paddlers, believes that demand for paddle boards will exceed the breakeven point of 40 units calculated in Example 6.1. He proposes spending $10,000 in fixed costs to buy more automated equipment that would reduce the materials and labor cost to $30 per board. The boards would sell for $100, regardless of which manufacturing process is chosen. Compare the two processes and determine for what level of demand each process would be preferred. Label Travis's proposal as Process A and Jeff's proposal as Process B.

SOLUTION

$$\begin{aligned} \textit{Process A} \quad & \quad \textit{Process B} \\ \$2{,}000 + \$50v &= \$10{,}000 + \$30v \\ \$20v &= \$8{,}000 \\ v &= 400 \text{ units} \end{aligned}$$

If demand is less than or equal to 400 boards, the alternative with the lowest fixed cost, *process A*, should be chosen. If demand is greater than or equal to 400 boards, the alternative with the lowest variable cost, *process B*, is preferred. Our decision can be confirmed by examining the next graph. (Because the boards will be sold for $100 apiece regardless of which process is used to manufacture them, no revenue line is needed.)

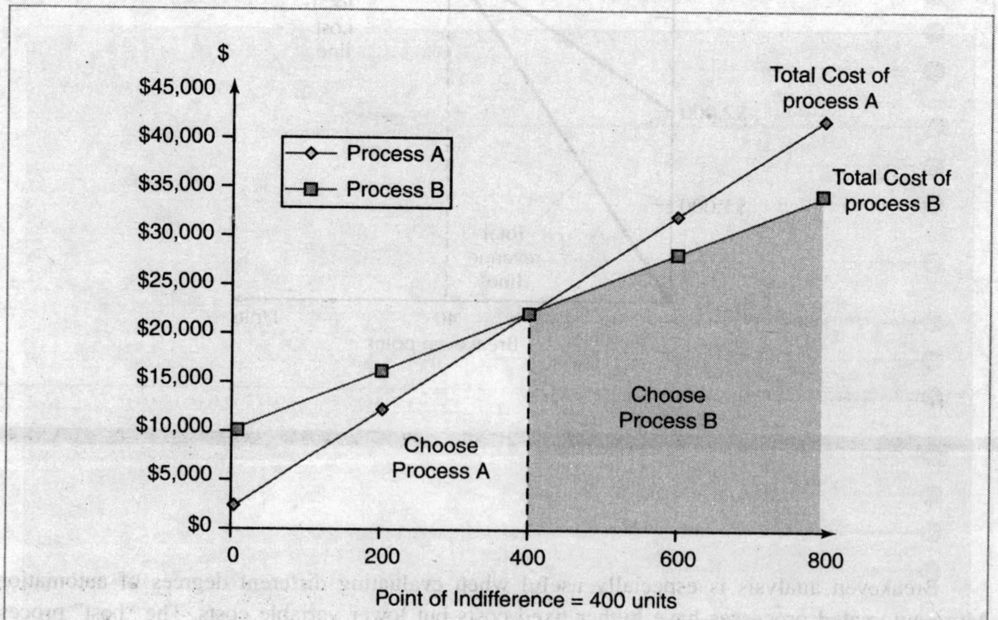

PROCESS PLANS

Process plans are a set of documents that detail manufacturing and service delivery specifications. They begin with detailed drawings of product design (usually from a CAD system) and include **assembly charts** or bills of material (showing the parts and materials needed and how they are to be assembled together), *operations sheets* or routing sheets (listing the operations to be performed with details on equipment, tools, skills, etc.), and *quality-control checksheets* (specifying quality standards and quality data to be recorded).

Process plans are used in both manufacturing and service settings. A hospital, for example, has a set of process plans (often called protocols) for different types of medical procedures and service plans for each particular patient. Similarly, in manufacturing, some process plans are standard, and others are created for each customer order. Figure 6.3 shows an assembly chart for a Big Mac. Figure 6.4 shows an operations sheet for a plastic molded vacuum cleaner attachment.

Process Analysis

Process analysis is the systematic examination of all aspects of a process to improve its operation—to make it faster, more efficient, less costly, or more responsive to the customer. The basic tools of process analysis are process flowcharts, diagrams, and maps. Exhibit 6.1 shows the various flowcharts available in Microsoft Visio to map out business processes.

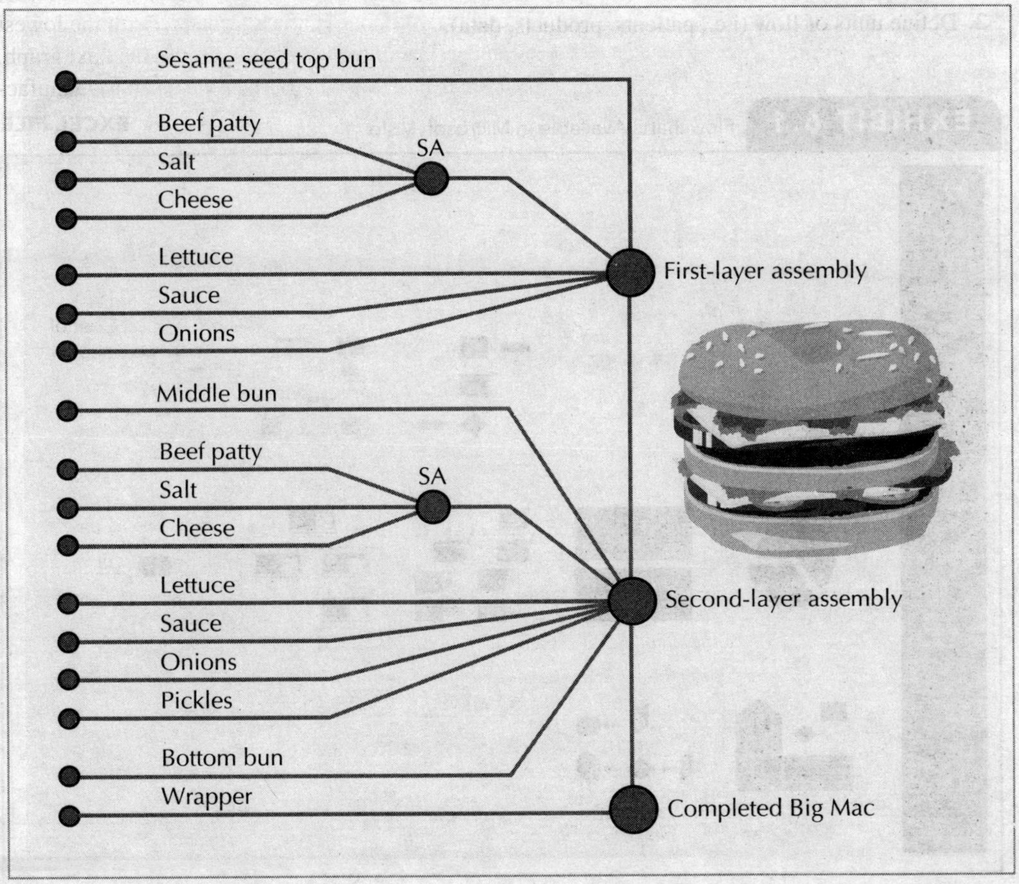

Figure 6.3
An Assembly Chart for a Big Mac

Figure 6.4

An Operations Sheet for a Plastic Part

Part name	Crevice Tool
Part No.	52074
Usage	Hand-Vac
Assembly No.	520

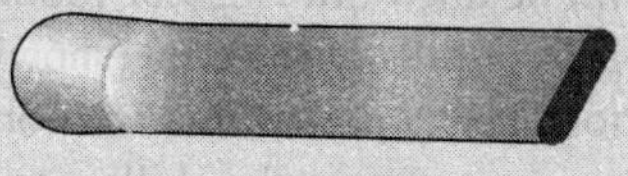

Oper. No.	*Description*	*Dept.*	*Machine/Tools*	*Time*
10	Pour in plastic bits	041	Injection molding	1 min
20	Insert mold	041	#076	2 min
30	Check settings and start machine	041	113, 67, 650	20 min
40	Collect parts and lay flat	051	Plastics finishing	10 min
50	Remove and clean mold	042	Parts washer	15 min
60	Break off rough edges	051	Plastics finishing	10 min

These flowcharts come in many different sizes, shapes, and forms; several are depicted in this chapter. While the format and symbols used may vary, the "process" of building a flowchart follows these steps:

1. Determine objectives.
2. Define process boundaries.
3. Define units of flow (i.e., patients, products, data).

EXHIBIT 6.1 Flowcharts Available in Microsoft Visio

EXCEL FILE

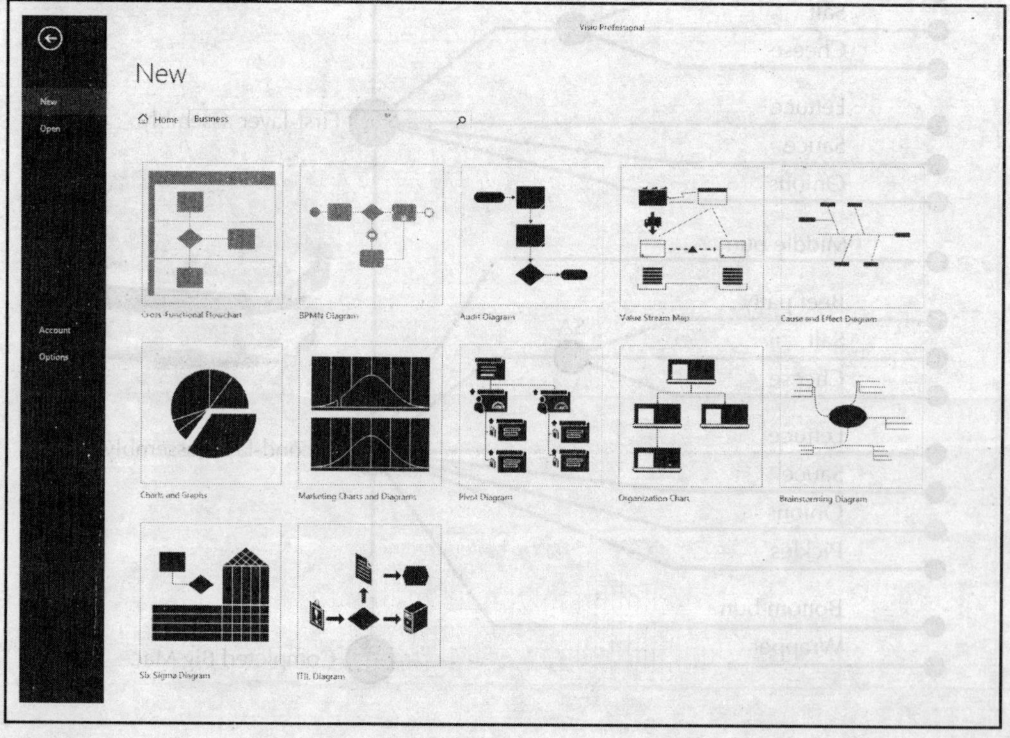

4. Choose type of chart.
5. Observe process and collect data.
6. Map out process.
7. Validate chart (with user, expert, or observation).

PROCESS FLOWCHARTS

The classic **process flowchart** looks at the manufacture of a product or delivery of a service from a broad perspective. The chart uses five standard symbols, shown in Figure 6.5, to describe a process: ○ for operations, □ for inspections, ⇒ for transportation, D for delay, and ▽ for storage. The details of each process are not necessary for this chart; however, the time required to perform each process and the distance between processes are often included. By incorporating nonproductive activities (*inspection, transportation, delay, storage*), as well as productive activities (*operations*), process flowcharts may be used to analyze the efficiency of a series of processes and to suggest improvements. They also provide a standardized method for documenting the steps in a process and can be used as a training tool. Automated versions of these charts are available that will superimpose the charts on floor plans of facilities. In this fashion, bottlenecks can be identified and layouts can be adjusted. Process flowcharts are used in both manufacturing and service operations. They are a basic tool for process innovation, as well as for job design.

Process improvement teams are likely to make a first pass at diagramming a process, with adhesive notes plastered on large sheets of paper connected with hand-drawn arrows. As documentation of the process becomes more complete, departments or companies may prefer particular symbols to represent inputs, outputs, decisions, activities, and resources.

Flowcharts can take many forms, from freehand drawings to animated simulations. Exhibit 6.2 shows a simple flowchart created in Excel. More sophisticated flowcharting tools are available from Microsoft Visio, SmartDraw (www.smartdraw.com), iGrafx (www.igrafx.com), and others. You may be able to download free trial copies of the software for limited periods of time.

Date: 9-30-15 Location: Graves Mountain
Analyst: TLR Process: Applesauce

Step	Operation	Transport	Inspect	Delay	Storage	Description of process	Time (min)	Distance (feet)
1	●	⇨	□	D	▽	Unload apples from truck	20	
2	○	➡	□	D	▽	Move to inspection station		100 ft
3	○	⇨	■	D	▽	Weigh, inspect, sort	30	
4	○	➡	□	D	▽	Move to storage		50 ft
5	○	⇨	□	D	▼	Wait until needed	360	
6	○	➡	□	D	▽	Move to peeler		20 ft
7	●	⇨	□	D	▽	Peel and core apples	15	
8	○	⇨	□	D	▼	Soak in water until needed	20	
9	●	⇨	□	D	▽	Place on conveyor	5	
10	○	➡	□	D	▽	Move to mixing area		20 ft
	Page 1 of 3					Total	450	190 ft

Figure 6.5
A Process Flowchart of Apple Processing

EXCEL FILE

EXHIBIT 6.2 Flowcharts in Excel

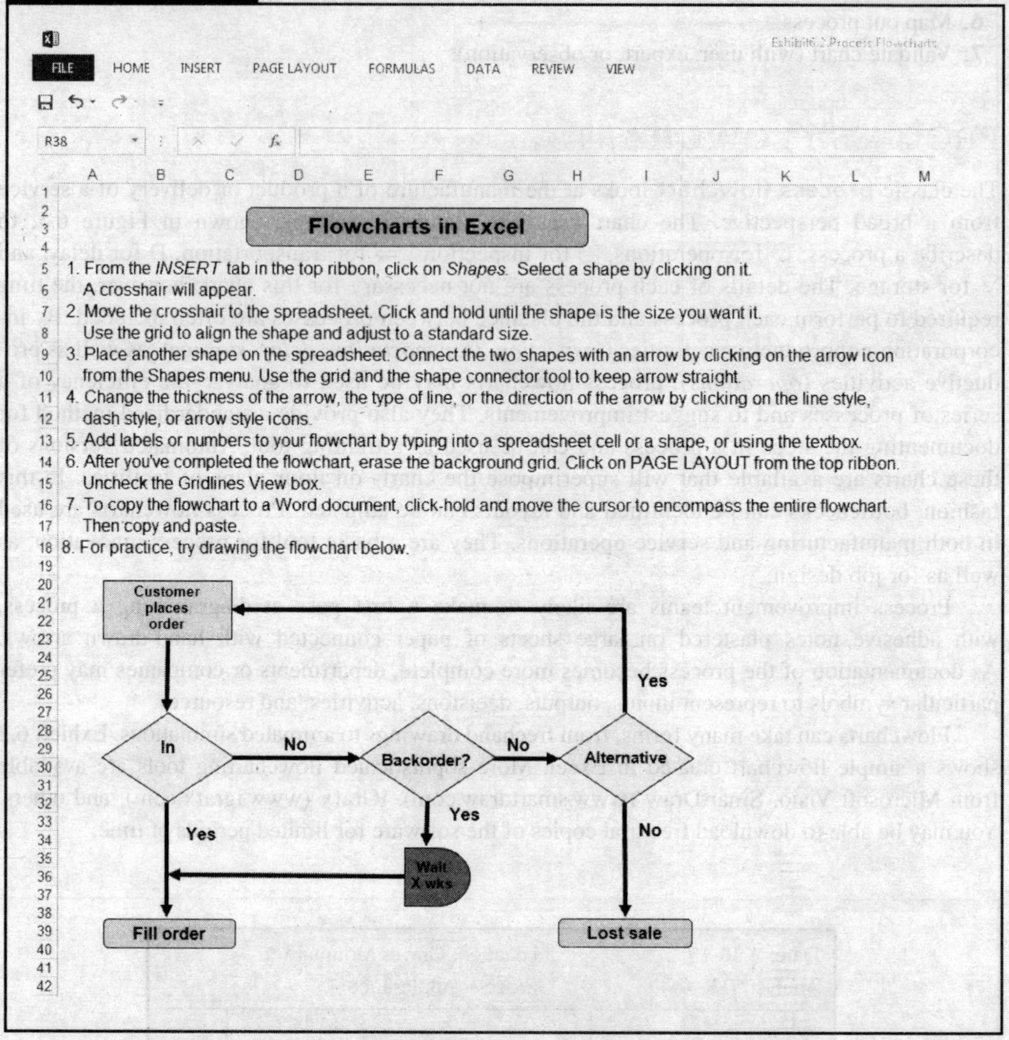

Figure 6.6 shows a *process map*, or swimlane chart, so called because it maps out the activities performed by various people in the process. Often process maps will include a time scale as well. Figure 6.7 shows a simple value chain flowchart from supplier to customer.

Processes are analyzed to reduce cost, speed time-to-completion, increase customer satisfaction, and, for environmental reasons, to reduce energy consumption or increase sustainability.

Process Innovation

Processes are *planned* in response to new facilities, new products, new technologies, new markets, or new customer expectations. Processes should be *analyzed* for improvement on a continuous basis. When continual improvement efforts have been exhausted and performance expectations still cannot be reached with an existing process, it is time to completely redesign or innovate the process.

Process innovation[1] projects are typically chartered in response to a *breakthrough* goal for rapid, dramatic improvement in process performance. Performance improvement of 50% to 100% within 12 months is common. In order to achieve such spectacular results, an innovation team is

[1]Process innovation is also known as business process reengineering (BPR), process redesign, restructuring, and many other company-specific terms.

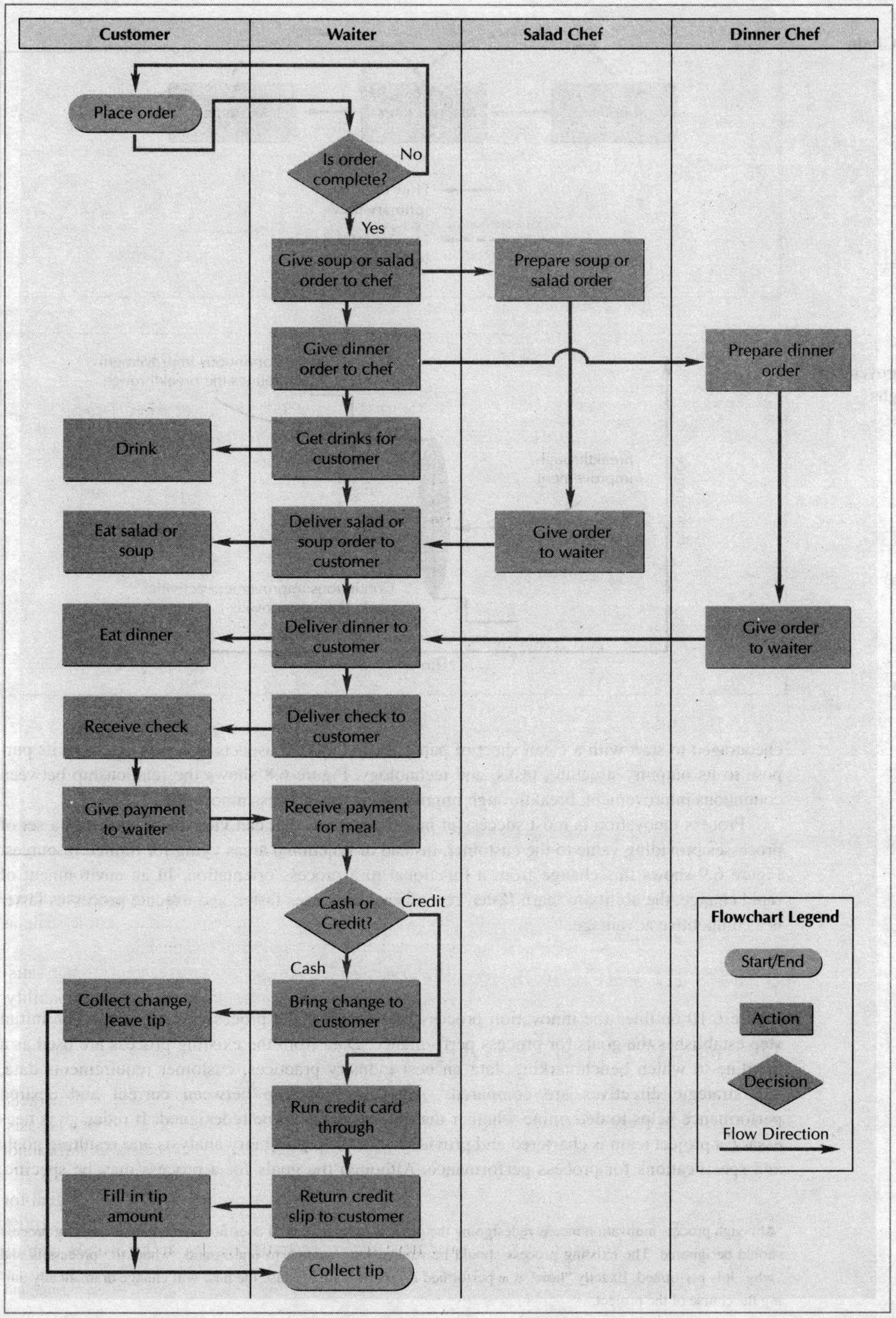

Figure 6.6

A Process Map or Swimlane Chart of Restaurant Service

SOURCE: www.SmartDraw.com

EXCEL FILE

Figure 6.7

A Simple Value Chain Flowchart

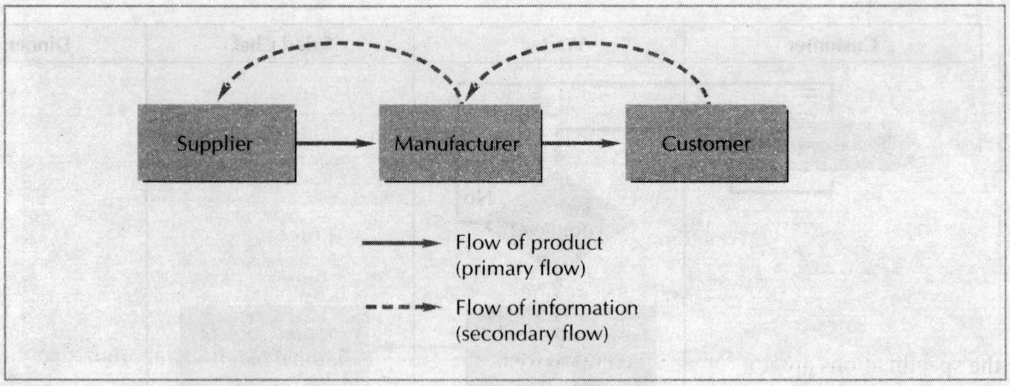

Figure 6.8

Continuous Improvements and Breakthroughs

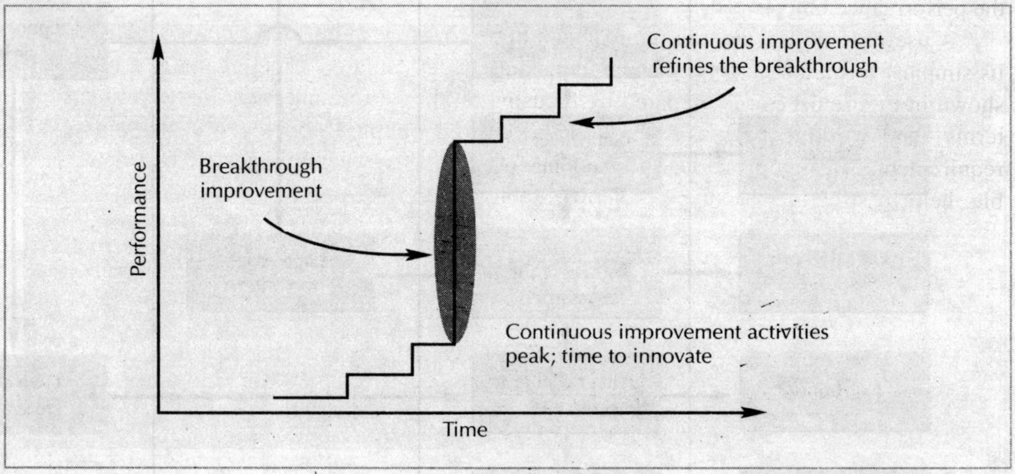

encouraged to start with a clean sheet of paper and rethink all aspects of a process, from its purpose to its outputs, structure, tasks, and technology. Figure 6.8 shows the relationship between continuous improvement, breakthrough improvement, and process innovation.

Process innovation is most successful in organizations that can view their system as a set of processes providing value to the customer, instead of functional areas vying for limited resources. Figure 6.9 shows this change from a functional to a process orientation. In an environment of rapid change, the ability to learn faster, reconfigure processes faster, and execute processes faster is a competitive advantage.

STEPS IN PROCESS INNOVATION

Figure 6.10 outlines the innovation process. Let's review the process step by step. The initial step establishes the goals for process performance. Data from the existing process are used as a baseline to which benchmarking data on best industry practices, customer requirements data, and strategic directives are compared.[2] Analyzing the gap between current and desired performance helps to determine whether the process needs to be redesigned. If redesign is necessary, a project team is chartered and provided with the preliminary analysis and resulting goals and specifications for process performance. Although the goals for a process may be specific,

[2]Although process innovation means redesigning the process from scratch, it does not mean that the existing process should be ignored. The existing process should be studied long enough to understand "what" the process is and "why" it is performed. Exactly "how" it is performed is less relevant because the how will change dramatically during the course of the project.

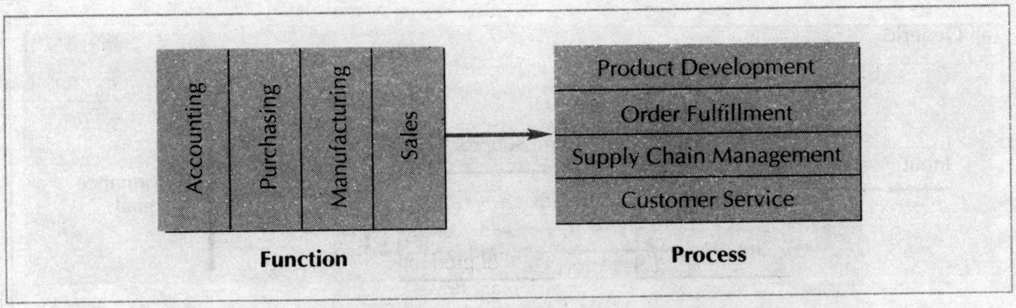

Figure 6.9

From Function to Process

the specifications are not (or else the creativity of the group is hampered). It is important that the project team be convinced that total redesign of the process is absolutely necessary to achieve the performance objectives.

A useful tool in beginning the redesign of a process is a *high-level process map*. Pared to its simplest form, a high-level map contains only the essential building blocks of a process. As shown in Figure 6.11, it is prepared by focusing on the performance goal—stated in customer terms—and working backward through the desired output, subprocesses, and initial input requirements. Design principles, such as performing subprocesses in parallel whenever possible, help to structure the map efficiently. Table 6.2 lists several additional design principles

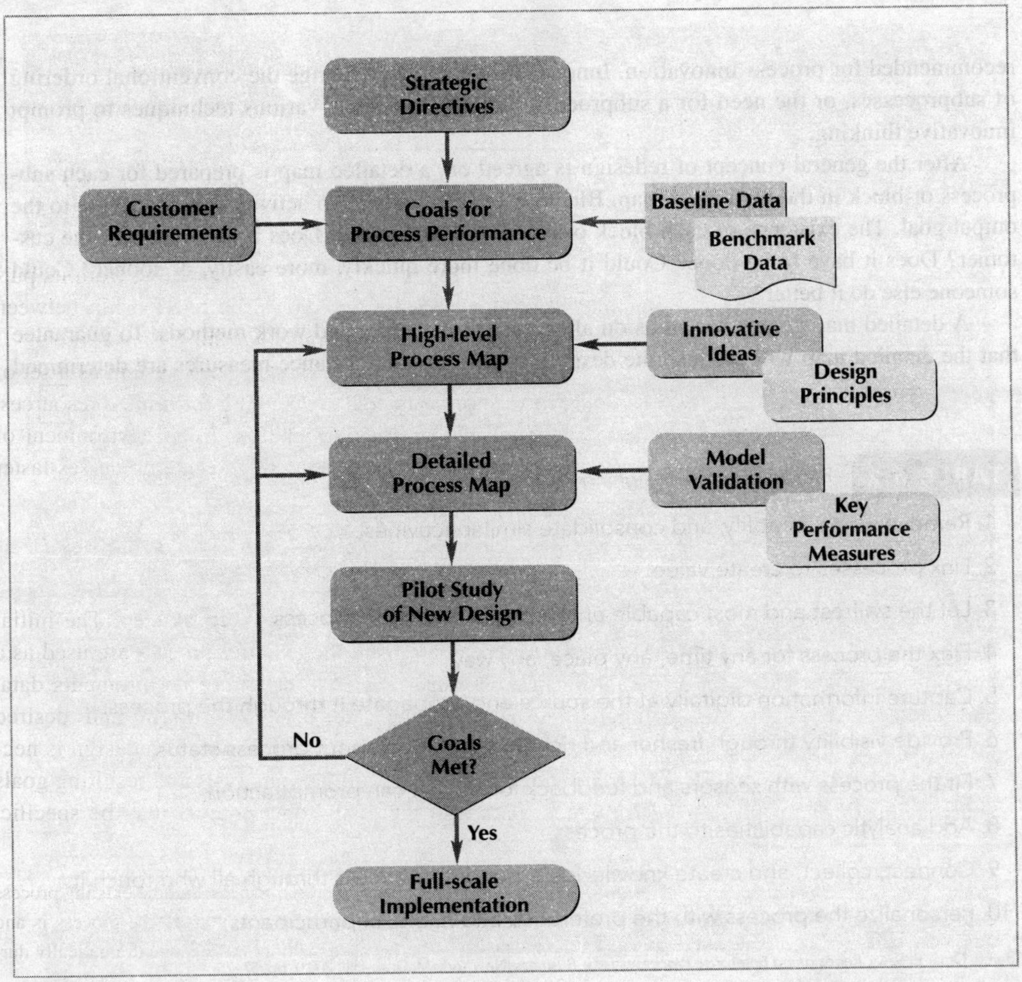

Figure 6.10

Process Innovation

Figure 6.11
A High-Level Process Map

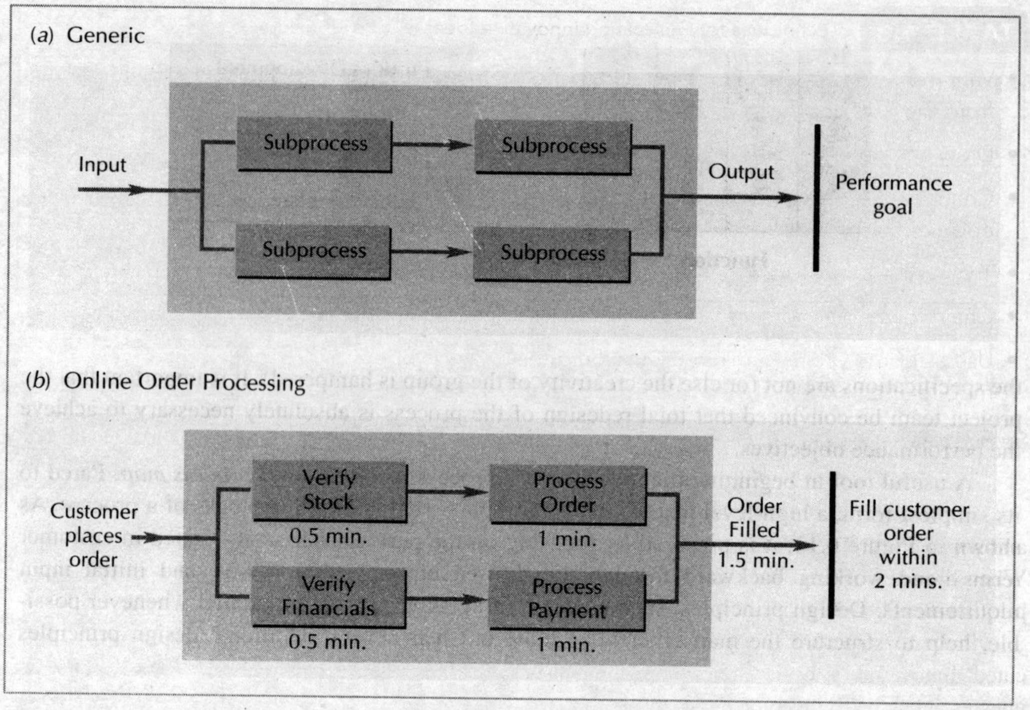

recommended for process innovation. Innovative ideas can challenge the conventional ordering of subprocesses, or the need for a subprocess. Table 6.3 presents various techniques to prompt innovative thinking.

After the general concept of redesign is agreed on, a detailed map is prepared for each subprocess or block in the high-level map. Blocks are added only if an activity can contribute to the output goal. The existence of each block or activity is challenged: Does it add value for the customer? Does it have to be done? Could it be done more quickly, more easily, or sooner? Could someone else do it better?

A detailed map guides decisions on allocation of resources and work methods. To guarantee that the detailed map will produce the desired results, key performance measures are determined

TABLE 6.2 Principles for Redesigning Processes

1. Remove waste, simplify, and consolidate similar activities.
2. Link processes to create value.
3. Let the swiftest and most capable enterprise execute the process.
4. Flex the process for any time, any place, any way.
5. Capture information digitally at the source and propagate it through the process.
6. Provide visibility through fresher and richer information about process status.
7. Fit the process with sensors and feedback loops that can prompt action.
8. Add analytic capabilities to the process.
9. Connect, collect, and create knowledge around the process through all who touch it.
10. Personalize the process with the preference and habits of participants.

Source: Omar El Sawy, *Redesigning Enterprise Processes for e-Business* (New York: McGraw-Hill, 2001), pp. 57–75.

TABLE 6.3 Techniques for Generating Innovative Ideas

• Vary the entry point to a problem. (In trying to untangle fishing lines, it's best to start from the fish, not the poles!)
• Draw analogies. (A previous solution to an old problem might work.)
• Change your perspective. (Think like a customer; bring in persons who have no knowledge of the process.)
• Try inverse brainstorming. (What would increase cost? displease the customer?)
• Chain forward as far as possible. (If I solve this problem, what is the next problem?)
• Use attribute brainstorming. (How would this process operate if . . . our workers were mobile and flexible? there were no monetary constraints? we had perfect knowledge?)

Source: Adapted from AT&T Quality Steering Committee, *Reengineering Handbook* (Indianapolis: AT&T Technical Publications Center, 1991).

and set in place. The model is also validated through simulation, interviewing, and partial testing. When the team is satisfied that the performance objective can be reached with the new design, a pilot study is conducted.

Process innovation is not like other projects, which can be carefully planned and flawlessly executed. Innovation is by definition something new and untested. Milestones, costs, and benefits are guesses at best. A pilot study allows the team to try something, see if it works, modify it, and try again.

After a successful pilot study, full-scale implementation can begin. Since process innovation involves radical change, the transition period between introducing the changed process and the incorporation of the new process into day-to-day operations can be difficult. The redesigned process may involve changing the way executives manage, the way employees think about their work, or how workers interact. The transition needs to be managed with a special concern for the "people" aspects of change. The innovation process is complete when the transition has been weathered and the new process consistently reaches its objective.

The concept of process innovation emerged in response to rapid changes in technology that rendered existing processes obsolete. In the next section, we discuss the impact of technology decisions and provide resources for a more in-depth study of technology.

Technology Decisions

Technology decisions involve large sums of money and can have a tremendous impact on the cost, speed, quality, and flexibility of operations. More importantly, they define the future capabilities of a firm and set the stage for competitive interactions. Thus, it is dangerous to delegate technology decisions to technical experts or financial analysts. A manager's ability to ask questions and understand the basic thrust of proposed technology is invaluable in making wise technology choices.

In this section we discuss the financial justification of new technology, followed by a brief technology primer.

FINANCIAL JUSTIFICATION OF TECHNOLOGY

After it is decided that a part will be produced or service provided in-house, specific technology decisions can be made. Alternatives include using, replacing, or upgrading existing equipment, adding additional capacity, or purchasing new equipment. Any alternative that involves an outlay of funds is considered a *capital investment*. Capital investments involve the commitment of funds in the present with an expectation of returns over some future time period. The expenditures are usually large and can have a significant effect on the future profitability of a firm. These decisions are analyzed carefully and typically require top management approval.

The most effective quantitative techniques for capital investment consider the time value of money as well as the risks associated with benefits that will not accrue until the future. These techniques, known collectively as *capital budgeting* techniques, include payback period, net present value, and internal rate of return. Detailed descriptions can be found in any basic finance text. Although capital budgeting techniques are beyond the scope of this text, we do need to comment on several factors that are often overlooked in the financial analysis of technology.

Purchase cost The initial investment in equipment consists of more than its basic purchase price. The cost of special tools and fixtures, installation, training, maintenance, and engineering or programming adjustments can represent a significant additional investment. Operating costs are often underestimated as well.

Operating costs To assess more accurately the requirements of the new technology, it is useful to consider, step by step, how the equipment will be operated, started, stopped, loaded, unloaded, changed over, upgraded, networked, maintained, repaired, cleaned up, speeded up, and slowed down.

Annual savings Most new technology is justified based on direct labor savings. However, other savings can actually be more important. For example, a more efficient process may be able to use less material and require less machine time or fewer repairs, so that downtime is reduced. A process that produces a better-quality product can result in fewer inspections and less scrap and rework. New processes (especially those that are automated) may significantly reduce safety costs, in terms of compliance with required regulations, as well as fines or compensation for safety violations.

Revenue enhancement Increases in revenue due to technology upgrades or new-equipment purchases are often ignored in financial analysis because they are difficult to predict. Improvements in product quality, price reductions due to decreased costs, and more rapid or dependable delivery can increase market share and, thus, revenue. Flexibility of equipment can also be important in adapting to the changing needs of the customer.

Replacement analysis As existing equipment ages, it may become slower, less reliable, and obsolete. The decision to replace old equipment with state-of-the-art equipment depends in large measure on the competitive environment. If a major competitor upgrades to a newer technology that improves quality, cost, or flexibility and you do not, your ability to compete will be severely damaged. In some industries, technology changes so rapidly that a replacement decision also involves determining whether this generation of equipment should be purchased or if it would be better to wait for the next generation. Replacement analysis maps out different schedules for equipment purchases over a two- to five-year period and selects a replacement cycle that will minimize cost.

Risk and uncertainty Investment in new technology can be risky. Estimates of equipment capabilities, length of life, and operating cost may be uncertain. Because of the risk involved, financial analysts tend to assign higher hurdle rates (i.e., required rates of return) to technology investments, making it difficult to gain approval for them.

Piecemeal analysis Investment in equipment and new technology is also expensive. Rarely can a company afford to automate an entire facility all at once. This has led to the proposal and evaluation of equipment purchases in a piecemeal fashion, resulting in pieces of technology that don't fit into the existing system and fail to deliver the expected returns.

A TECHNOLOGY PRIMER

Technology is important in both manufacturing and service operations. Cars now have hundreds of embedded systems performing thousands of computerized functions. Pacemakers, vending machines, Xerox copiers, and store shelves notify the manufacturer when repairs or restocking are needed. Coming soon are clothes that measure the wearer's vital statistics and notify a physician or change medication regimes when necessary, and refrigerators that pre-order ingredients to match weekly menus or order milk when the supply is low. We discuss many of the information technology advances that support these systems in more detail in Chapter 10. In this section, we present a brief overview of technology advances in manufacturing systems.

Technology in manufacturing includes computer-aided design, robots, automated guided vehicles, computer numerically controlled machines, automated storage and retrieval systems, and flexible manufacturing systems. Automated manufacturing systems integrated through computer technology are aptly called **computer-integrated manufacturing (CIM)**. With the advent of the Internet and the increased globalization of both markets and production, CIM has become more digital and collaborative.

CIM (also called e-manufacturing) involves sharing real-time data with trading partners and customers and making collaborative decisions about production based on that data. In order to collaborate, information must be converted into electronic form, protocols for communication must be established, and infrastructure must be in place for connectivity with customers, suppliers, and partners. Rather than making huge volumes of standard products in anticipation of demand, e-manufacturing uses real-time information on customer orders and productive capacity across the supply chain to speed customized products directly to the customer. Figure 6.12 shows the components of CIM categorized by product, process, manufacturing, and information technologies. Table 6.4 serves as a technology primer, briefly defining the terms listed in the figure. Additive manufacturing is discussed in the "Along the Supply Chain" box that follows.

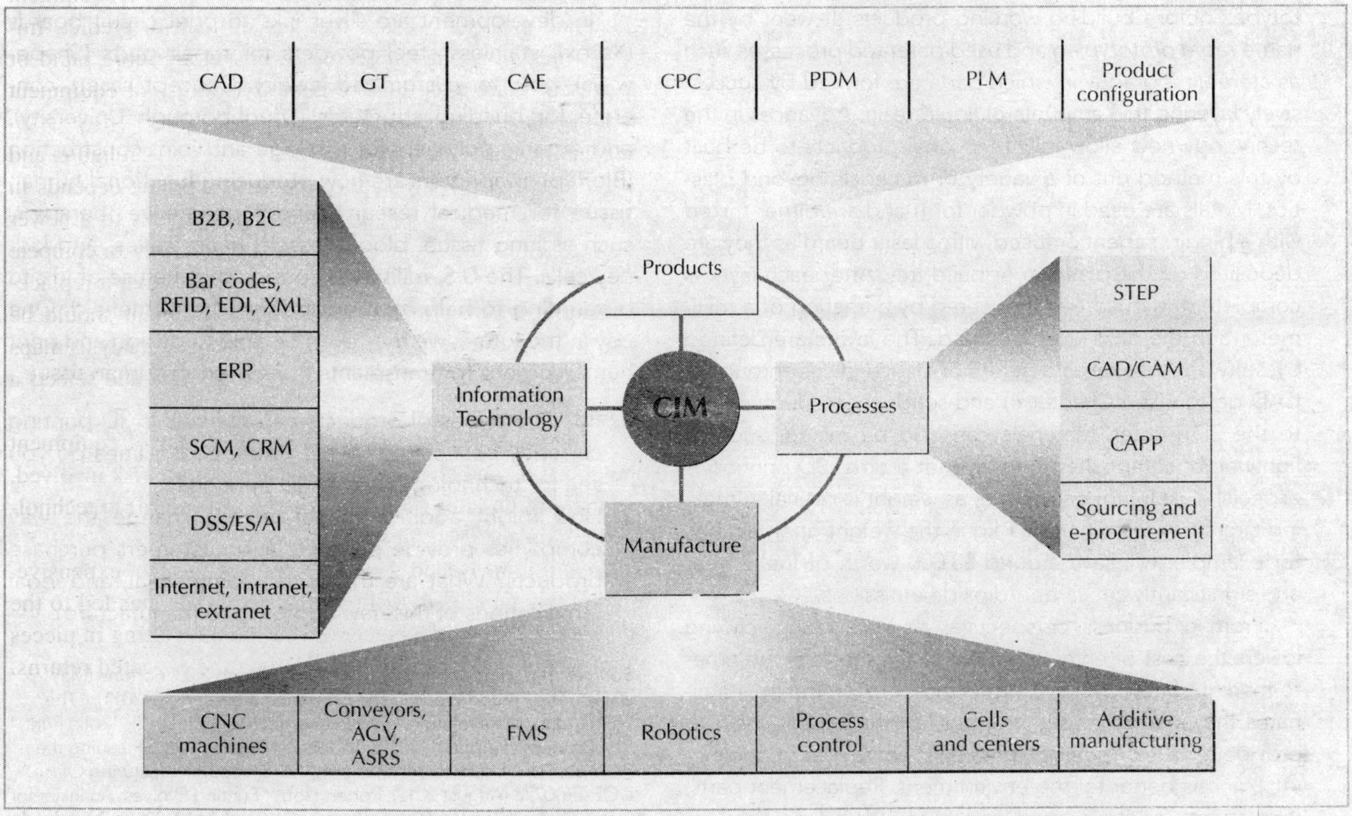

Figure 6.12

Components of Advanced Manufacturing

ALONG THE SUPPLY CHAIN

3D Printing and Other Advances in Additive Manufacturing

Traditional manufacturing works by subtraction—that is, carving out a part or product from a solid block of metal or wood, often resulting in 90% of the material being cut away. Additive manufacturing builds up a part or product by spraying layers of material back and forth across a build platform as directed by a special CAD model. It converts a digital model into a 3D product, and since the process resembles how a dot-matrix printer operates, it's called 3D printing. Similar to those desktop printers, a 3D printer can be purchased and operated on your desktop to produce a vast variety of shapes, parts, and products. Right now, the time required to "print" those parts can be lengthy—two to three hours, or overnight—and precision is limited, but there are some interesting possibilities that make this technology revolutionary.

Additive manufacturing technology has actually been available for some time and has been used to prepare prototypes before building working products. It went by the name *rapid prototyping* and used patented processes such as *stereolithography* in which parts are formed by successively layering thin amounts of liquid resin. Advances in the technology now allow fully functional products to be built by this method out of a variety of materials beyond plastics. Metals are used in powder form and are either mixed with a binding agent or fused with a laser beam as they are deposited on the platform or build tray. After each layer is complete, the build tray is lowered by a fraction of a millimeter and the next layer is added. The layers are defined by software that takes a series of digital slices through a CAD design (see Chapter 4) and sends those descriptions to the 3D printer. Materials can also be mixed, such as lightweight composites, one layer at a time. 3D printing is especially useful for aerospace, as weight is critical in making aircraft. A reduction of 1 kg in the weight of an airliner, for example, will save around $3,000 worth of fuel a year and significantly cut carbon-dioxide emissions.

From a business perspective, additive manufacturing lowers the cost of entry into an industry, shortens the time-to-market of new designs, allows mass customization, eliminates the need for costly inventory or the supply chain to provide it, saves resources (materials, energy, labor, tooling, etc.), and is better for the environment. Replacement parts, for example, can be printed instead of ordered; no need for stocking thousands of parts in inventory, or making them in advance of need. Think about how much weight could be jettisoned from aircraft carriers or spacecraft with no need for those extra parts; or how your local Advanced Auto store would house a printer or two, instead of shelves of inventory. Some stores or repair centers may cease to exist because individuals would have their own "printers."

3D printing can also create more intricate designs (and more rounded shapes) than is possible from conventional manufacturing, and it can make production profitable at lower volumes (nixing economies of scale). For example, since each item is created separately rather than from a mold, a build tray could hold 100 items that are different in design and produce them at the same cost as 100 items of the same design. Invisalign currently uses 3D printing in this way to produce customized retainers for its large suite of patients who need new ones every two weeks as part of the orthodontic procedure. It's also used to produce custom orthotics, hearing aids, and dental crowns faster and at a much reduced cost than traditional means.

In development are silver inks to print circuit boards (Xerox), stainless steel powders for repair parts (Shapeways), gold for customized jewelry (Concept Laser), concrete for building structures (Loughborough University), and organic polymers for cartilage and joint construction (BioRap). Bioprinters are now producing functional human tissue for medical research and regenerative therapies, such as lung tissue, blood vessels, heart valves, and kidney cells. The U.S. military is considering the use of in situ bioprinting to help treat wounds on the battlefield. One day in the future, we may even be able to design and print human organs for transplants from layering human tissue.

1. For what types of products and markets is 3D printing currently best suited? What future possibilities do you see for technology such as 3D printing?
2. How might additive manufacturing change the way companies provide products and customers purchase products? What are the social, commercial, and legal ramifications of this new approach to manufacture?

Sources: Based on Johnny Ryan, "Manufacturing 2.0," *Fortune* (May 23, 2011); "The Printed World," *The Economist* (February 10, 2011); "The Third Industrial Revolution," *The Economist* (April 21, 2012); "Solid Print," *The Economist* (April 21, 2012); "Additive Manufacturing: Pursuing the Promise," U.S. Department of Energy, Advanced Manufacturing Office, DOE/EE-0776 (August 2012); Robert Hotz, "Printing Evolves: An Inkjet for Living Tissue," *The Wall Street Journal* (September 18, 2012), D1.

TABLE 6.4 A Technology Primer

Product Technology		
CAD	Computer-aided design	Creates and communicates designs electronically
GT	Group technology	Classifies designs into families for easy retrieval and modification
CAE	Computer-aided engineering	Tests the functionality of CAD designs electronically
CPC	Collaborative product commerce	Facilitates electronic communication and exchange of information among designers and suppliers
PDM	Product data management	Keeps track of design specs and revisions for the life of the product
PLM	Product lifecycle management	Integrates the decisions of those involved in product development, manufacturing, sales, customer service, recycling, and disposal
Product configuration		Defines products "configured" by customers who have selected among various options, usually from a website
Process Technology		
STEP	Standard for exchange of product model data (ISO 10303)	Set standards for communication among different CAD vendors; translates CAD data into requirements for automated inspection and manufacture
CAD/CAM	Computer-aided design and manufacture	The electronic link between automated design (CAD) and automated manufacture (CAM)
CAPP	Computer-aided process planning	Generates process plans based on a database of similar requirements
E-procurement		Electronic purchasing of items from e-marketplaces, auctions, or company websites
Manufacturing Technology		
CNC	Computer numerically controlled	Machines controlled by software code to perform a variety of operations with the help of automated tool changers; also collects processing information and quality data
FMS	Flexible manufacturing system	A collection of CNC machines connected by an automated material handling system to produce a wide variety of parts
Robots		Manipulators that can be programmed to perform repetitive tasks; more consistent than workers but less flexible
Conveyors		Fixed-path material handling; moves items along a belt or overhead chain; "reads" packages and diverts them to different directions; can be very fast
AGV	Automatic guided vechicle	A driverless truck that moves material along a specified path; directed by wire or tape embedded in the floor or by radio frequencies; very flexible
ASRS	Automated storage and retrieval system	An automated warehouse—some 26 stories high—in which items are placed in a carousel-type storage system and retrieved by fast-moving stacker cranes; controlled by computer

Process Control		Continuous monitoring of automated equipment; makes real-time decisions on ongoing operation, maintenance, and quality
CIM	Computer-integrated manufacturing	Automated manufacturing systems integrated through computer technology; also called e-manufacturing
3D printing	Additive manufacturing	Building up a product layer by layer from digital instructions
Information Technology		
B2B	Business-to-business	Electronic transactions between businesses, usually over the Internet
B2C	Business-to-consumer	Electronic transactions between businesses and their customers, usually over the Internet
Internet		A global information system of computer networks that facilitates communication and data transfer
Intranet		Communication networks internal to an organization; can be password (i.e., firewall) protected sites on the Internet
Extranet		Intranets connected to the Internet for shared access with select suppliers, customers, and trading partners
Bar codes		A series of vertical lines printed on most packages that identifies the item and other information when read by a scanner
RFID	Radio frequency identification tags	An integrated circuit embedded in a tag that can send and receive information; a 21st-century bar code with read/write capabilities
EDI	Electronic data interchange	A computer-to-computer exchange of business documents over a proprietary network; very expensive and inflexible
XML	Extensible markup language	A programming language that enables computer-to-computer communication over the internet by tagging data before it is sent
ERP	Enterprise resource planning	Software for managing the basic requirements of an enterprise, including sales & marketing, finance & accounting, production & materials management, and human resources
SCM	Supply chain management	Software for managing the flow of goods and information among a network of suppliers, manufacturers, and distributors
CRM	Customer relationship management	Software for managing interactions with customers and compiling and analyzing customer data
DSS	Decision support systems	An information system that helps managers make decisions; includes a quantitative modeling component and an interactive component for what-if? analysis
ES	Expert systems	A computer system that uses an expert knowledge base to diagnose or solve a problem
AI	Artificial intelligence	A field of study that attempts to replicate elements of human thought in computer processes; includes expert systems, genetic algorithms, neural networks, and fuzzy logic (see Chapter 17)

SUMMARY

Important issues in process design are types of processes, process planning, analysis and innovation, and technology decisions. The type of production process selected depends primarily on demand volume and degree of product standardization. *Projects* are produced one at a time to customer order. *Batch production* is used to process a variety of low-volume jobs. *Mass production* produces large volumes of a standard product for a mass market. *Continuous production* is used for very-high-volume commodity products.

Process planning consists of converting product designs into workable instructions for manufacture. They often take the form of assembly charts, process flowcharts, operations sheets, and manufacturing or delivery specifications. On a broader scale, process planning involves process selection, technology decisions, and decisions on outsourcing. Process analysis drives the continuous improvement of operations; process innovation drives breakthrough improvements.

KEY FORMULAS

Breakeven point

$$v = \frac{c_f}{p - c_v}$$

Point of indifference

$$\left| \frac{c_{f2} - c_{f1}}{c_{v1} - c_{v2}} \right|$$

SOLVED PROBLEMS

Texloy Manufacturing Company must select a process for its new product, TX2, from among three different alternatives. The following cost data have been gathered:

	PROCESS A	PROCESS B	PROCESS C
Fixed cost	\$10,000	\$40,000	\$70,000
Variable cost	\$5/unit	\$2/unit	\$1/unit

For what volume of demand would each process be desirable?

SOLUTION

If v represents the number of TX2s demanded (and, we assume, produced), then

$$\begin{aligned}\text{Total cost for process A} &= \$10{,}000 + \$5v\\ \text{Total cost for process B} &= \$40{,}000 + \$2v\\ \text{Total cost for process C} &= \$70{,}000 + \$1v\end{aligned}$$

Next, we calculate the points of indifference between each pair of processes by equating their total costs and solving for demand volume, v. Always begin with the process that has the lowest fixed cost and compare it to the process with the next lowest fixed cost, and so on. For this example that means we'll compare process A to process B and process B to process C.

Comparison 1: Process A versus Process B

$$\begin{aligned}&\textit{Process A} \qquad\qquad \textit{Process B}\\ &\$10{,}000 + \$5v = \$40{,}000 + \$2v\\ &v = 10{,}000 \text{ units}\end{aligned}$$

If demand is less than or equal to 10,000, we should choose the alternative with the lowest fixed cost, process A. Conversely, if demand is greater than 10,000, we should choose the aternative with the lowest variable cost, process B. At 10,000 units we can actually choose either A or B.

Comparison 2: Process B versus Process C

$$\begin{aligned}&\textit{Process B} \qquad\qquad \textit{Process C}\\ &\$40{,}000 + \$2v = \$70{,}000 + \$1v\\ &v = 30{,}000 \text{ units}\end{aligned}$$

If demand is greater than 30,000 units, we should choose process C. If demand is less than 30,000 but greater than 10,000 (see comparison 1), we should choose process B. At 30,000, we can choose either B or C.

The Excel solution to this problem is shown in Exhibit 6.3.

To summarize, from the graph in Exhibit 6.3 and our decision rules, we can recommend the following process selection:

- Below 10,000 units, choose process A.
- Between 10,000 and 30,000 units, choose process B.
- Above 30,000 units, choose process C.

EXHIBIT 6.3 Using Excel for the Point of Indifference **EXCEL FILE**

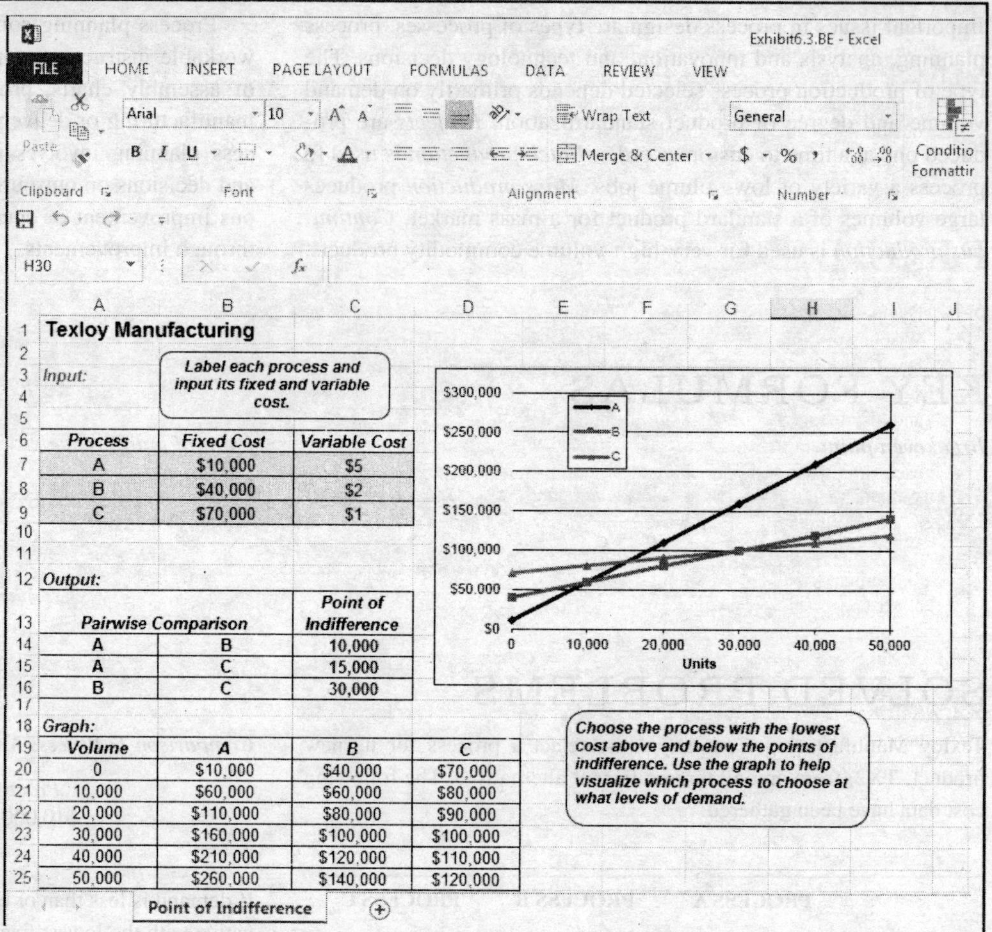

Texloy Manufacturing

Input:

Process	*Fixed Cost*	*Variable Cost*
A	$10,000	$5
B	$40,000	$2
C	$70,000	$1

Output:

Pairwise Comparison		*Point of Indifference*
A	B	10,000
A	C	15,000
B	C	30,000

Graph:

Volume	*A*	*B*	*C*
0	$10,000	$40,000	$70,000
10,000	$60,000	$60,000	$80,000
20,000	$110,000	$80,000	$90,000
30,000	$160,000	$100,000	$100,000
40,000	$210,000	$120,000	$110,000
50,000	$260,000	$140,000	$120,000

QUESTIONS

6-1. Discuss the types of decisions that are involved in creating a process strategy. Apply the four elements of process strategy to the process of completing a project or paper for one of your classes. Does the process differ from class to class?

6-2. List and explain six factors that affect the decision to outsource. Explain the sourcing continuum.

6-3. Describe the four basic types of production processes. What are the advantages and disadvantages of each? When should each be used?

6-4. What are the major cost factors considered in process selection? How is breakeven analysis used for process selection?

6-5. What kind of information do the following documents communicate?

a. Assembly chart
b. Operations sheet
c. Process flowchart

6-6. What does process planning entail? How would process planning differ for batch and continuous processes?

6-7. Explain the basic steps involved in process innovation.

6-8. Our thinking process, limited by the paradigms under which we operate, can become very rigid. Try these out-of-box thinking exercises:

a. Where does the letter *Z* belong in this pattern, above or below the line? Why?

```
BCD    G  J     OPQRS  U
A   EF  HI  KLMN      T  VWXY
```

b. What letter comes next in the following pattern? Why?

OTTFF-

c. Connect the nine dots below with four straight lines. Do not lift your pencil.

• • •
• • •
• • •

d. Circle the three errors in the following sentence: There is three mistakes in this sentence.

6-9. Describe the factors often overlooked in the financial justification of new technology.

6-10. Briefly discuss the components of CIM or e-manufacturing. In what ways can companies collaborate in producing goods and services? Report on at least one web source on collaborative manufacturing, e-manufacturing, or additive manufacturing.

6.11. Read about issues in outsourcing from a search on the web. Then, examine the website of a company with which you are familiar for its outsourcing strategy and supplier policies.

6.12. Create a flowchart for the process of building flowcharts described on pages 238 and 239.

6.13. Explore the sustainability requirements of production outsourced to different parts of the world.

PROBLEMS

6-1. David Austin recently purchased a chain of dry cleaners in northern Wisconsin. Although the business is making a modest profit now, David suspects that if he invests in a new press, he could recognize a substantial increase in profits. The new press costs $15,400 to purchase and install and can press 40 shirts an hour (or 320 per day). David estimates that with the new press, it will cost $0.25 to launder and press each shirt. Customers are charged $1.10 per shirt.

a. How many shirts will David have to press to break even?

b. So far, David's workload has varied from 50 to 200 shirts a day. How long would it take to break even on the new press at the low-demand estimate? At the high-demand estimate?

c. If David cuts his price to $0.99 a shirt, he expects to be able to stabilize his customer base at 250 shirts per day. How long would it take to break even at the reduced price of $0.99? Should David cut his price and buy the new press?

6-2. Soft Key is trying to determine how best to produce its newest product, DVORK keyboards. The keyboards could be produced in-house using either process A or process B, or purchased from a supplier. Cost data are given below. For what levels of demand should each process be chosen?

	Fixed Cost	Variable Cost
Process A	$ 8,000	$10
Process B	$20,000	$ 4
Supplier	$ 0	$20

6-3. NanoTech is ready to begin production of its exciting new technology. The company is evaluating three methods of production: (A) a small production facility with older equipment, (B) a larger production facility that is more automated, and (C) subcontracting to an electronics manufacturer in Singapore. The costs of each alternative are shown below. Determine for what level of demand each production process should be chosen.

Process	Fixed Cost	Variable Cost
A	$200,000	$40
B	$600,000	$20
C	$ 0	$60

6-4. Creative Designs makes intricate jewelry out of precious metal. The company is introducing a new line and needs to select a manufacturing process. Three options are available. The first involves using a mold to mass produce the design for pendants, earrings, and bracelets. The second option laser cuts the design from a block of metal using a pattern directed by the software. The third option builds the design out of metal powder (gold, silver, and bronze) via a 3D printer. The company is uncertain about demand for the new design.

Option	Fixed Cost	Variable Cost
1	$10,000	$10
2	$ 5,000	$30
3	$ 3,000	$50

a. If Creative Designs expects to sell 200 pieces of the new design, which process should it use?

b. If Creative Designs expects to sell 1,000 pieces of the new design, which process should it use?

c. Create a decision rule that specifies which process to select for different levels of demand.

6-5. Gemstone Quarry is trying to decide whether to invest in a new material-handling system. The current system (which is old and completely paid for) has an annual maintenance cost of $10,000 and costs approximately $25 to transport each load of material. The two new systems that are being considered vary both in sophistication and cost. System 1 has a fixed cost of $40,000 and a cost per load estimated at $10. System 2 has a fixed cost of $100,000 but a per-load cost of $5. At what volume of demand (i.e., number of loads) should Gemstone purchase System 1? System 2?

6-6. Tribal Systems, Inc., is opening a new plant and has yet to decide on the type of process to employ. A labor-intensive process would cost $10,000 for tools and equipment and $14 for labor and materials per item produced. A more automated process costs $50,000 in plant and equipment but has a labor/material cost of $8 per item produced. A fully automated process costs $300,000 for plant and equipment and $2 per item produced. If process selection were based solely on lowest cost, for what range of production would each process be chosen?

6-7. Sandra Saunders and her design team are analyzing the production costs for three alternative monitor designs. Given the cost information below, and assuming form and function are similar for each design, which monitor design would you recommend?

Monitor	Fixed Cost	Variable Cost
A	$ 700,000	$250
B	$1,000,000	$125
C	$1,500,000	$100

6-8. Keisha has been inundated with product-of-the-month offers from various marketing companies. She is considering joining a club that allows movies to be streamed from a members-only website, but can't decide which membership offers the best deal. Given the cost information below, which club would you recommend for Keisha?

Club	Membership fee	Cost per movie
Almost Free Flicks	$ 40	$5
Best Movies	$ 65	$4
Choice Cinema	$100	$3

6-9. Pete Patel is the sports liaison for the student government association. During the fall semester, the group promotes school spirit with "orange effect" t-shirts. The shirts feature a special screen-printed logo that can be expensive to make. Pete's supplier, Classic Tees, has quoted three prices for the shirts with differing logo packages.

a. If the t-shirts are sold for $6 each, how many shirts would have to be sold to break even with Package 1?

b. Pete is considering selling the shirts for $8 each. What is the break-even point for packages 1 and 2 with an $8 price?

c. Which logo package would you recommend if Pete expects to sell 75 shirts? 200 shirts?

d. Assuming the shirts would be sold at the same price regardless of the logo package, create a decision rule for Pete to use based on anticipated sales volume.

Package	Cost of Logo	Cost per Shirt
1	$300	$4
2	$100	$6
3	$ 0	$8

6-10. Sized Rite is trying to determine how best to produce its new line of shoes for expanded feet. Demand for its w-i-d-e products is uncertain. Given the alternative processes and costs below, determine at what level of demand you would choose each process.

	Fixed Cost	Variable Cost
Process A	$20,000	$ 5
Process B	$10,000	$10
Supplier C	$ 0	$20

CASE STUDY

Selecting Yokohama's New Control System

Yokohama Electric Utility Organization has a very good computer system controlling the electrical power supply system to the city. While the current computer network has received routine and frequent updates, the core system is 15 years old and annual operation and maintenance costs are increasing. At the present time, it is costing the electric company $500,000 to operate and maintain the current system. The utility has asked the current system vendor how much it would cost to update the full system to the current version, both hardware and software. The vendor has estimated it would cost $1,500,000 to upgrade and it would take about 24 months. There would be a complete power outage about every four months during the upgrade process.

The utility company has asked two world-recognized leaders in the electric utility computer systems business to provide quotes to replace the current system. Vendor 1 has offered to replace the system for $1,200,000. To accomplish this work, they will require the utility firm's engineers to assist at an estimated cost of $250,000. The new operation and maintenance cost, at the end of the 18-month project, is estimated at $200,000 per year. Vendor 2 has offered to install a new system for $1,800,000 and they will need the same utility resource support at an estimated cost of $275,000. They will take about 16 months to complete the project, at which time operation and maintenance cost should drop to $350,000 per year.

a. Which alternative would you recommend they go with if the operation and maintenance costs are estimated for a 10-year period (ignore net present value calculations)?

b. What other things should the utility company take into consideration in making this decision?

REFERENCES

"3D Printing: The printed world," *The Economist* (February 10, 2011), http://www.economist.com/node/18114221/print, accessed February 17, 2012.

"Print Me a Stradivarius," *The Economist* (February 10, 2011), http://www.economist.com/node/18114327/print, accessed February 17, 2012.

Bedworth, D., M. Henderson, and P. Wolfe. *Computer-Integrated Design and Manufacturing*. New York: McGraw-Hill, 1991.

Bylinsky, Gene. "Hot New Technologies for American Factories." *Fortune Now* (June 26, 2000).

El Sawy, Omar. *Redesigning Enterprise Processes for e-Business*. New York: McGraw-Hill, 2001.

Foston, L. *Fundamentals of Computer Integrated Manufacturing*. Upper Saddle River, NJ: Prentice Hall, 1991.

Hammer, Michael, and James Champy. *Reengineering the Corporation*. New York: HarperCollins, 1993.

Hammer, Michael, and Steven Stanton. *The Reengineering Revolution*. New York: HarperCollins, 1995.

Hayes, Robert, Gary Pisano, David Upton, and Steven Wheelwright. *Operations Strategy and Technology: Pursuing the Competitive Edge*. Hoboken, NJ: Wiley, 2005.

Hunt, V. Daniel. *Process Mapping*. New York: Wiley, 1996.

Keen, Peter. *The Process Edge*. Boston: Harvard Business School Press, 1997.

Nevens, J., D. Whitney, T. DeFazio, A. Edsall, R. Gustavson, R. Metzinger, and W. Dvorak. *Concurrent Design of Products and Process: A Strategy for the Next Generation in Manufacturing*. New York: McGraw-Hill, 1989.

Noori, H. *Managing the Dynamics of New Technology*. Upper Saddle River, NJ: Prentice Hall, 1990.

Richards, Bill. "Superplant." *eCompany Now* (November 2000).

Skinner, W. *Manufacturing: The Formidable Competitive Weapon*. New York: Wiley, 1985.

Teresko, John. "The Dawn of e-Manufacturing." *Industry Week* (October 2, 2000).

Valery, N. "Factory of the Future." *The Economist* (May 30, 1987), pp. 3–18.

Worldwide Robotics Survey and Directory. Pittsburgh: The Robotic Institute of America, 1999.

Zurawski, Laura, and Mark Hoske. "E-manufacturing: A Catchy Name for What You Should be Doing Anyway." *Control Engineering* (February 13, 2001).

CHAPTER 7

Planning Facilities and Capacity

LEARNING OBJECTIVES

AFTER READING THIS CHAPTER, YOU WILL BE ABLE TO:

- Evaluate different strategies for capacity expansion.
- Explain the concepts of economies of scale, best operating level, and capacity cushion.
- Describe the advantages and disadvantages of different types of layouts in both manufacturing and service settings.
- Visualize work flow and utilize algorithmic problem solving to lay out a facility.
- Create and evaluate hybrid layouts and hybrid solutions to problems.

CUT 'N SEW JEAN SHOPS

In cut and sew factories, the various components of a pair of jeans are cut from denim material in the cutting room and then "bundled" together to be distributed to individual sewers in the sewing room. The sewers untie the bundle, perform their task, then rebundle it to be passed on to the next process. This is called a progressive bundling system (PBS).

Since most sewers are paid on a piece-rate system (i.e., by how many pieces they can sew in a day) regardless of the production of subsequent sewers, considerable work-in-process (WIP) can build up, as shown in the photo above. It is also true that once the fabric is spread on the cutting table, as many pairs of jeans as possible are cut and bundled for distribution. Thus, on any given day, 60% to 70% more garments may be cut than can be assembled by the sewers. A typical garment factory would employ more than 2,000 workers, house 1,500 sewing machines, and produce over 350,000 garments per day in a one-shift operation.

An improvement to the PBS system is a type of modular or cellular production, where garment components are released to a team of sewers who work together to complete the garment. Production is paced by what the next sewer can handle. If one sewer in the team gets behind, another sewer can help out. The cells or modules operate as mini-factories with interchangeable tasks among the 5 to 15 workers, and group incentives are based on achieving quality goals, as well as output goals. Under the modular sewing system, WIP is cut considerably and quality increases. The space requirements are reduced, too, with less work-in-process, fewer supervisors, fewer quality inspectors, and fewer workers to move the bundles around. Output in both systems is similar, but modular production costs less (after the initial cross-training) due to the reduction in rework. In addition, cycle time is cut by one-third.

In this chapter, we'll learn about the importance of arranging work in a facility to meet both quality and productivity goals.

Sources: Based on F. Abernathy, J. Dunlop, J. Hammond, and D. Weil, *A Stitch in Time: Lean Retailing and the Transformation of Manufacturing—Lessons from the Apparel and Textile Industries* (New York: Oxford Press, 1999); E. Dirgar, and Z. Ondogan, "An Application for Modular Production Systems on Apparel," http://www.espire.com.pk/meeting/o7kwqx2amo.pdf; Brandix company website, http://www.brandix.com/brandix/casualwear.php.

Capacity Planning

Capacity is the maximum capability to produce. Capacity planning takes place at several levels of detail. We discuss long-term capacity planning in this chapter, intermediate-term capacity planning in Chapter 14, and short-term capacity planning in Chapters 15 and 16.

Long-term **capacity planning** is a strategic decision that establishes a firm's overall level of resources. It extends over a time horizon long enough to obtain those resources—usually a year or more for building or expanding facilities or acquiring new businesses. Capacity decisions affect product lead times, customer responsiveness, operating costs, and a firm's ability to compete. Inadequate capacity can lose customers and limit growth. Excess capacity can drain a company's resources and prevent investments in more lucrative ventures. *When* to increase capacity and *how much* to increase it are critical decisions.

Figure 7.1*a, b,* and *c* show three basic strategies for the timing of capacity expansion in relation to a steady growth in demand.

1. ***Capacity lead strategy***. Capacity is expanded in anticipation of demand growth. This aggressive strategy is used to lure customers from competitors who are capacity constrained or to gain a foothold in a rapidly expanding market. It also allows companies to respond to unexpected surges in demand and to provide superior levels of service during peak demand periods.
2. ***Average capacity strategy***. Capacity is expanded to coincide with average expected demand. This is a moderate strategy in which managers are certain they will be able to sell at least some portion of expanded output, and endure some periods of unmet demand. Approximately half of the time capacity leads demand, and half of the time capacity lags demand.
3. ***Capacity lag strategy***. Capacity is increased after an increase in demand has been documented. This conservative strategy produces a higher return on investment but may lose customers in the process. It is used in industries with standard products and cost-based or weak competition. The strategy assumes that lost customers will return from competitors after capacity has expanded.

Consider higher education's strategy in preparing for a tripling of the state's college-bound population in the next decade. An established university, guaranteed applicants even in lean years, may follow a capacity lag strategy. A young university might lead capacity expansion in hopes of capturing students not admitted to the more established universities. A community college may

Figure 7.1

Capacity Expansion Strategies

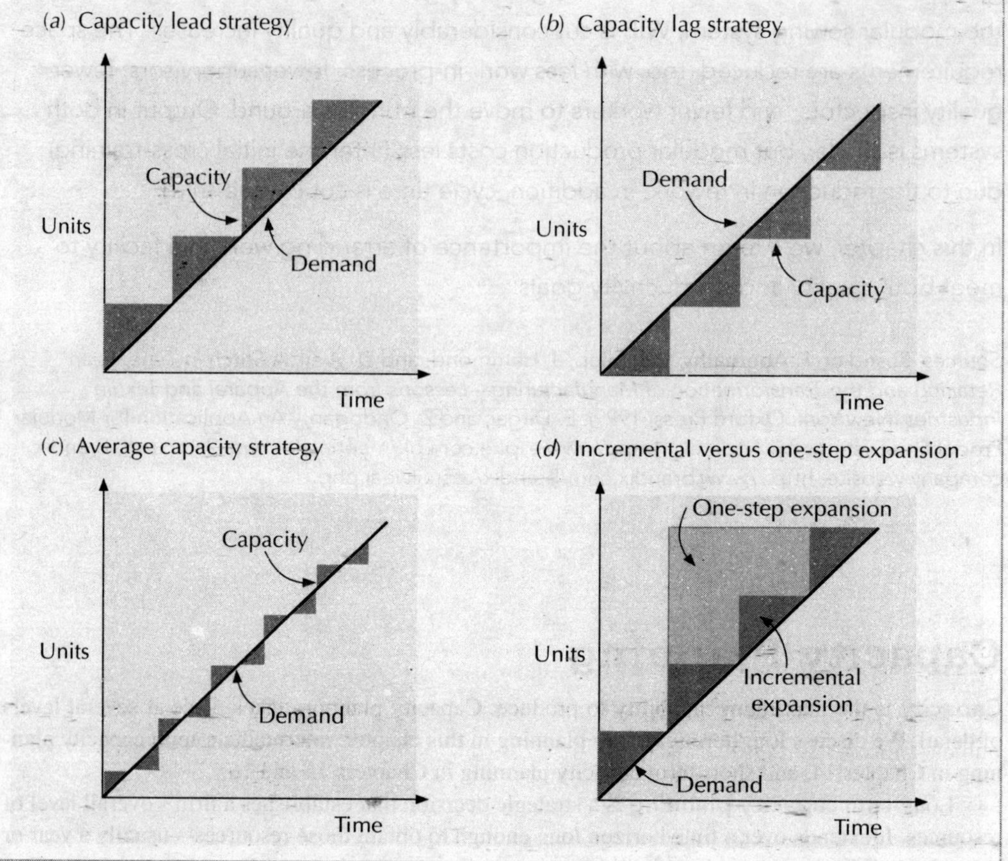

choose the average capacity strategy to fulfill its mission of educating the state's youth but with little risk.

How much to increase capacity depends on (1) the volume and certainty of anticipated *demand;* (2) *strategic objectives* in terms of growth, customer service, and competition; and (3) the *costs* of expansion and operation.

Capacity can be increased incrementally or in one large step, as shown in Figure 7.1*d*. Incremental expansion is less risky but more costly. An attractive alternative to expanding capacity is *outsourcing*, in which suppliers absorb the risk of demand uncertainty.

The **best operating level** for a facility is the percent of capacity utilization that minimizes average unit cost. Rarely is the best operating level at 100% of capacity—at higher levels of utilization, productivity slows and things start to go wrong. Average capacity utilization differs by industry. An industry with an 80% average utilization would have a 20% **capacity cushion** for unexpected surges in demand or temporary work stoppages. Large-capacity cushions are common in industries in which demand is highly variable, resource flexibility is low, and customer service is important. Utilities, for example, maintain a 20% capacity cushion. Capital-intensive industries with less flexibility and higher costs maintain cushions under 10%. Airlines maintain a negative cushion by overbooking flights. Best operating level can also refer to the most economic size of a facility.

Figure 7.2 shows the best operating level—in this case, the number of rooms for a hotel—as the point at which the *economies of scale* have reached their peak and the **diseconomies of scale** have not yet begun.

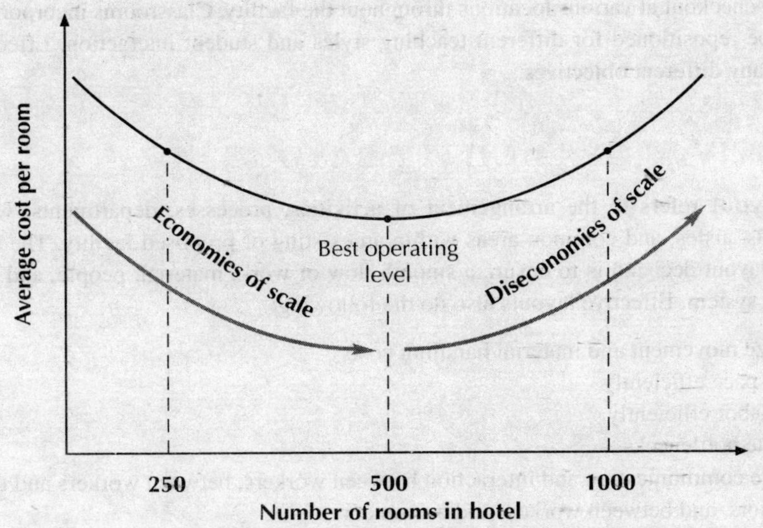

Figure 7.2

Best Operating Level for a Hotel

Economies of scale occur when it costs less per unit to produce or operate at high levels of output. This holds true when:

- Fixed costs can be spread over a larger number of units,
- Production or operating costs do not increase linearly with output levels,
- Quantity discounts are available for material purchases, and
- Operating efficiency increases as workers gain experience.

The electronics industry provides a good case example of economies of scale. The average cost per chip placement for printed circuit-board assembly is 32 cents in factories with a volume of 25 million placements, 15 cents in factories with 200 million placements, and only 10 cents in factories with 800 million placements.[1]

Capacity decisions provide a framework for further facility decisions, such as where to locate a new facility and how to arrange the flow of work in the facility. Facility location is discussed in the supplement to this chapter. The remainder of the chapter presents various alternatives for laying out a facility.

Facilities

Facilities make a difference. They can provide a competitive edge by enabling and leveraging the latest process concepts. For example, Bank of America has created an exemplary facility showcasing green design. Green buildings can save energy costs and increase worker productivity. Facility design has an impact on both quality and productivity. Facilities affect how efficiently workers can do their jobs, how much and how fast goods can be produced, how difficult it is to automate a system, and how responsive the system can be to changes in product or service design, product mix, or demand volume. Facilities must be planned, located, and laid out.

Facility layouts are more flexible than ever before. Factories that once positioned shipping and receiving departments at one end of the building now construct T-shaped buildings so that deliveries

[1]"High Volumes Yield Profits for High-Tech Factories." *HE Solutions* (April 1996), p. 8.

can be made directly to points of use within the factory. Stores sport portable kiosks for customer inquiry and checkout at various locations throughout the facility. Classrooms incorporate desks on wheels to be repositioned for different teaching styles and student interaction. Effective layouts can have many different objectives.

OBJECTIVES OF FACILITY LAYOUT

Facility layout refers to the arrangement of activities, processes, departments, workstations, storage areas, aisles, and common areas within an existing or proposed facility. The basic objective of the layout decision is to ensure a smooth flow of work, material, people, and information through the system. Effective layouts also do the following:

- Minimize movement and material handling costs
- Utilize space efficiently
- Utilize labor efficiently
- Eliminate bottlenecks
- Facilitate communication and interaction between workers, between workers and their supervisors, and between workers and customers
- Reduce manufacturing cycle time and customer service time
- Eliminate wasted or redundant movement
- Facilitate the entry, exit, and placement of material, products, and people
- Incorporate safety and security measures
- Promote product and service quality
- Encourage proper maintenance activities
- Provide a visual control of activities
- Provide flexibility to adapt to changing conditions
- Increase capacity.

Basic Layouts

Layouts can take many different forms. In the next section, we discuss three basic layout types: process, product, and fixed-position. Later in the chapter, we discuss three hybrid layouts: cellular layouts, flexible manufacturing systems, and mixed-model assembly lines.

PROCESS LAYOUTS

Process layouts, also known as *functional layouts*, group similar activities together in departments or work centers according to the process or function they perform. For example, in a machine shop, all drills would be located in one work center, lathes in another work center, and milling machines in still another work center. In a department store, women's clothes, men's clothes, children's clothes, cosmetics, and shoes are located in separate departments. A process layout is characteristic of service shops, job shops, or batch production, i.e., intermittent operations that serve different customers with different needs. The volume of each customer's order is low, and the sequence of operations required to complete a customer's order can vary considerably.

The equipment in a process layout is general purpose, and the workers are skilled at operating the equipment in their particular department. The advantage of this layout is flexibility. The disadvantage is inefficiency. Jobs or customers do not flow through the system in an orderly manner, backtracking is common, movement from department to department can take a considerable amount of time, and queues tend to develop. In addition, each new arrival may require that an operation be set up differently for its particular processing requirements. Although workers can operate a number of machines or perform a number of different tasks in a single department, their workload often fluctuates—from queues of jobs or customers waiting to be processed to idle time

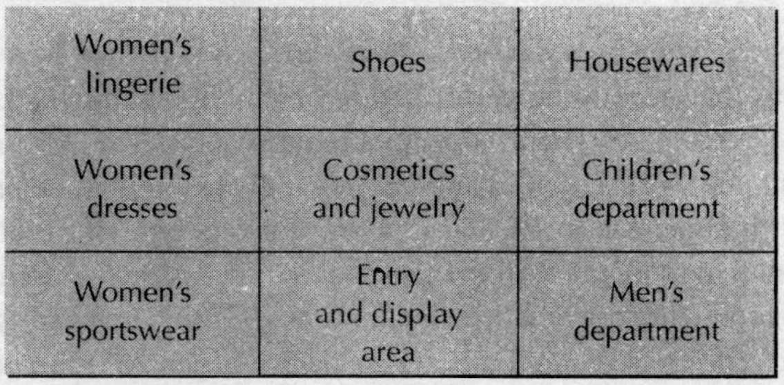

Figure 7.3

A Process Layout in Services

between jobs or customers. Figures 7.3 and 7.4 show schematic diagrams of process layouts in services and manufacturing.

Material storage and movement are directly affected by the type of layout. Storage space in a process layout is large to accommodate the large amount of in-process inventory. The factory may look like a warehouse, with work centers strewn between storage aisles. In-process inventory is high because material moves from work center to work center in batches waiting to be processed. Finished goods inventory, on the other hand, is low because the goods are being made for a particular customer and are shipped out to that customer on completion.

Process layouts in manufacturing firms require flexible material handling equipment (such as forklifts, carts or AGVs) that can follow multiple paths, move in any direction, and carry large loads of in-process goods. A *forklift* moving pallets of material from work center to work center needs wide aisles to accommodate heavy loads and two-way movement. Scheduling of forklifts is typically controlled by radio dispatch and varies from day to day and hour to hour. Routes have to be determined and priorities given to different loads competing for pickup.

Process layouts in service firms require large aisles for customers to move back and forth and ample display space to accommodate different customer preferences.

The major layout concern for a process layout is where to locate the departments or machine centers in relation to each other. Although each job or customer potentially has a different route through the facility, some paths will be more common than others. Past information on customer orders and projections of customer orders can be used to develop patterns of flow through the shop.

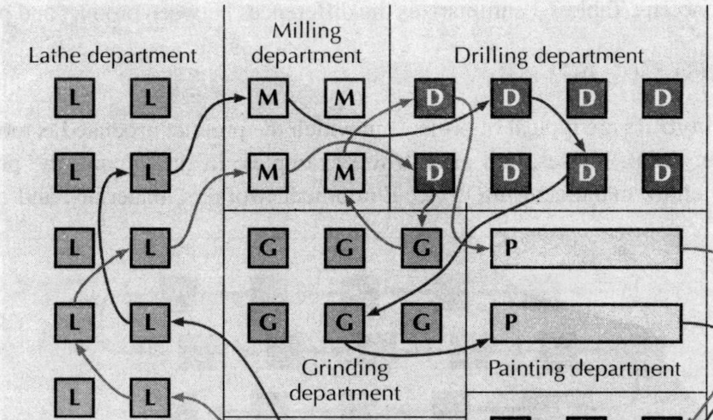

Figure 7.4

A Process Layout in Manufacturing

PRODUCT LAYOUTS

Product layouts, better known as *assembly lines*, arrange activities in a line according to the sequence of operations that need to be performed to assemble a particular product. Each product has its own "line" specifically designed to meet its requirements. The flow of work is orderly and efficient, moving from one workstation to another down the assembly line until a finished product comes off the end of the line. Since the line is set up for one type of product or service, special machines can be purchased to match a product's specific processing requirements. Product layouts are suitable for mass production or repetitive operations in which demand is stable and volume is high. The product or service is a standard one made for a general market, not for a particular customer. Because of the high level of demand, product layouts are more automated than process layouts, and the role of the worker is different. Workers perform narrowly defined assembly tasks that do not demand as high a wage rate as those of the more versatile workers in a process layout.

The advantage of the product layout is its efficiency and ease of use. The disadvantage is its inflexibility. Significant changes in product design may require that a new assembly line be built and new equipment be purchased. This is what happened to U.S. automakers when demand shifted to smaller cars. The factories that could efficiently produce six-cylinder engines could not be adapted to produce four-cylinder engines. A similar inflexibility occurs when demand volume slows. The fixed cost of a product layout (mostly for equipment) allocated over fewer units can send the price of a product soaring.

The major concern in a product layout is balancing the assembly line so that no one workstation becomes a bottleneck and holds up the flow of work through the line. Figure 7.5 shows the product flow in a product layout. Contrast this with the flow of products through the process layout shown in Figure 7.4.

A product layout needs material moved in one direction along the assembly line and always in the same pattern. Conveyors are the most common material handling equipment for product layouts. Conveyors can be *paced* (automatically set to control the speed of work) or *unpaced* (stopped and started by the workers according to their pace). Assembly work can be performed *online* (i.e., on the conveyor) or *offline* (at a workstation serviced by the conveyor).

Aisles are narrow because material is moved only one way, it is not moved very far, and the conveyor is an integral part of the assembly process, usually with workstations on either side. Scheduling of the conveyors, once they are installed, is simple—the only variable is how fast they should operate.

Storage space along an assembly line is quite small because in-process inventory is consumed in the assembly of the product as it moves down the assembly line. Finished goods, however, may require a separate warehouse for storage before they are shipped to dealers or stores to be sold.

Product and process layouts look different, use different material handling methods, and have different layout concerns. Table 7.1 summarizes the differences between product and process layouts.

FIXED-POSITION LAYOUTS

Fixed-position layouts are typical of projects in which the product produced is too fragile, bulky, or heavy to move. Ships, houses, and aircraft are examples. In this layout, the product remains stationary for the entire manufacturing cycle. Equipment, workers, materials, and other resources

Figure 7.5
A Product Layout

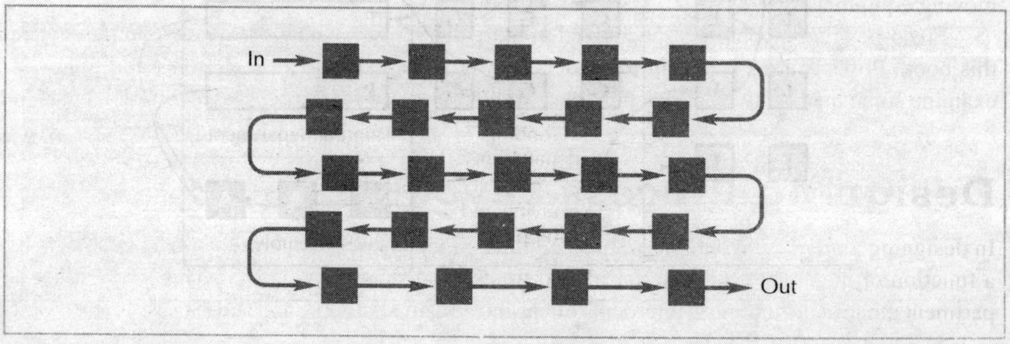

TABLE 7.1 A Comparison of Product and Process Layouts

	Product Layout	Process Layout
1. Description	Sequential arrangement of activities	Functional grouping of activities
2. Type of process	Continuous, mass production, mainly assembly	Intermittent, job shop, batch production, mainly fabrication
3. Product	Standardized, made to stock	Varied, made to order
4. Demand	Stable	Fluctuating
5. Volume	High	Low
6. Equipment	Special purpose	General purpose
7. Workers	Limited skills	Varied skills
8. Inventory	Low in-process, high finished goods	High in-process, low finished goods
9. Storage space	Small	Large
10. Material handling	Fixed path (conveyor)	Variable path (forklift)
11. Aisles	Narrow	Wide
12. Scheduling	Part of balancing	Dynamic
13. Layout decision	Line balancing	Machine location
14. Goal	Equalize work at each station	Minimize material handling cost
15. Advantage	Efficiency	Flexibility

are brought to the production site. Equipment utilization is low because it is often less costly to leave equipment idle at a location where it will be needed again in a few days, than to move it back and forth. Frequently, the equipment is leased or subcontracted because it is used for limited periods of time. The workers called to the work site are highly skilled at performing the special tasks they are requested to do. For instance, pipefitters may be needed at one stage of production, and electricians or plumbers at another. The wage rate for these workers is much higher than minimum wage. Thus, if we were to look at the cost breakdown for fixed-position layouts, the fixed cost would be relatively low (equipment may not be owned by the company), whereas the variable costs would be high (due to high labor rates and the cost of leasing and moving equipment).

Fixed-position layouts are specialized to individual projects and thus are beyond the scope of this book. Projects are covered in more detail in the next chapter. In the sections that follow, we examine some quantitative approaches for designing product and process layouts.

Designing Process Layouts

In designing a process layout, we want to minimize movement or material handling cost, which is a function of the amount of material moved times the distance it is moved. This implies that departments that incur the most interdepartment movement should be located closest to each other, and those that do not interact should be located further away. Two techniques used to design process layouts, block diagramming and relationship diagramming, are based on logic and the visual representation of data.

BLOCK DIAGRAMMING

We begin with data on historical or predicted movement of material between departments in the existing or proposed facility. This information is typically provided in the form of a from/to chart, or *load summary chart*. The chart gives the average number of **unit loads** transported between the departments over a given period of time. A unit load can be a single unit, a pallet of material, a bin of material, or a crate of material—however material is normally moved from location to location. In automobile manufacturing, a single car represents a unit load. For a ball-bearing producer, a unit load might consist of a bin of 100 or 1,000 ball bearings, depending on their size.

The next step in designing the layout is to calculate the *composite movements* between departments and rank them from most movement to least movement. Composite movement, represented by a two-headed arrow, refers to the back-and-forth movement between each pair of departments.

Finally, trial layouts are placed on a grid that graphically represents the relative distances between departments in the form of uniform blocks. The objective is to assign each department to a block on the grid so that *nonadjacent loads* are minimized. The term *nonadjacent* is defined as a distance farther than the next block, either horizontally, vertically, or diagonally. The trial layouts are scored on the basis of the number of nonadjacent loads. Ideally, the optimal layout would have zero nonadjacent loads. In practice, this is rarely possible, and the process of trying different layout configurations to reduce the number of nonadjacent loads continues until an acceptable layout is found.

EXAMPLE 7.1

PROCESS LAYOUT

Barko, Inc., makes *bark scalpers*, processing equipment that strips the bark off trees and turns it into nuggets or mulch for gardens. The facility that makes bark scalpers is a small-job shop that employs 50 workers and is arranged into five departments: (1) bar stock cutting, (2) sheet metal, (3) machining, (4) painting, and (5) assembly. The average number of loads transported between the five departments per month is given in the accompanying load summary chart. The current layout of the facility is shown schematically on the 2 × 3 grid. Notice that there is quite a bit of flexibility in the facility, as indicated by the six possible locations (i.e., intersections) available for five departments. In addition, the forklift used in the facility is very flexible, allowing horizontal, vertical, and diagonal movement of material.

Barko management anticipates that a new bark scalper plant will soon be necessary and would like to know if a similar layout should be used or if a better layout can be designed. You are

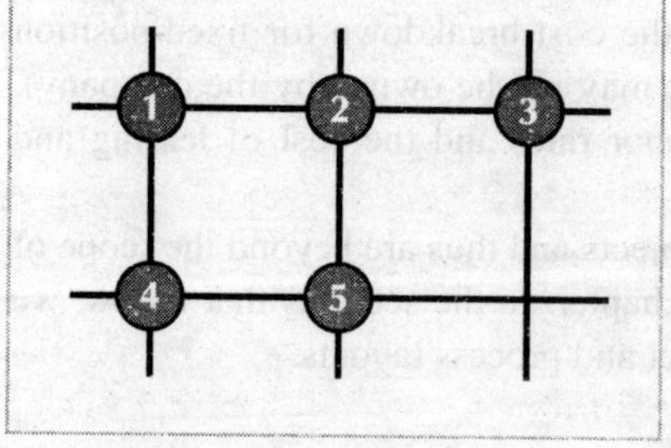

Load Summary Chart

from/to Department	Department 1	2	3	4	5
1	—	100	50		
2		—	200	50	
3	60		—	40	50
4		100		—	60
5		50			—

asked to evaluate the current layout in terms of nonadjacent loads, and if needed, propose a new layout on a 2 × 3 grid that will minimize the number of nonadjacent loads.

SOLUTION

In order to evaluate the current layout, we need to calculate the composite, or back-and-forth, movements between departments. For example, the composite movement between department 1 and department 3 is the sum of 50 loads moved from 1 to 3, plus 60 loads moved from 3 to 1, or 110 loads of material. If we continue to calculate composite movements and rank them from highest to lowest, the following list results:

Composite	*Movements*	*Composite*	*Movements*
2 ↔ 3	200 loads	3 ↔ 5	50 loads
2 ↔ 4	150 loads	2 ↔ 5	50 loads
1 ↔ 3	110 loads	3 ↔ 4	40 loads
1 ↔ 2	100 loads	1 ↔ 4	0 loads
4 ↔ 5	60 loads	1 ↔ 5	0 loads

Next, we evaluate the "goodness" of the layout by scoring it in terms of nonadjacent loads. The results are shown visually in Grid 1.

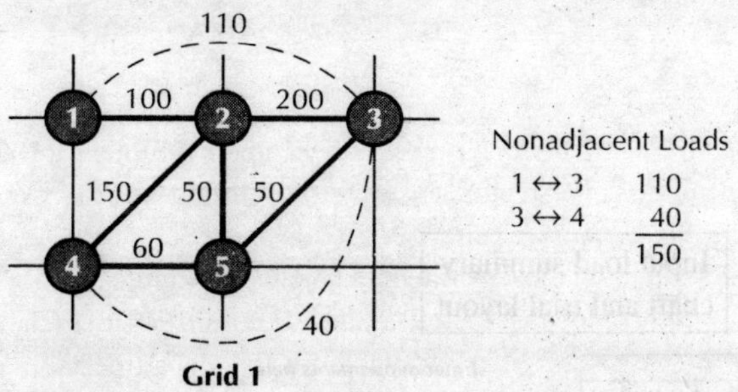

Grid 1

The adjacent moves are marked with a solid line and the nonadjacent moves are shown with a curved dashed line to highlight the fact that material is moved farther than we would like, that is, across more than one square. Following our composite movement list, 2 ↔ 3 and 2 ↔ 4 are adjacent moves, but 1 ↔ 3 is not. Our nonadjacent score starts with 110 loads of material from 1 ↔ 3. Continuing down our list, all moves are adjacent and are marked with solid lines until 3 ↔ 4. Movement 3 ↔ 4 is nonadjacent, so we designate it as such and add 40 loads to our nonadjacent score. The remaining movements have zero loads. Thus, our score for this layout is 110 + 40 = 150 nonadjacent loads.

To improve the layout, we note that departments 3 and 4 should be located adjacent to department 2, and that departments 4 and 5 may be located away from department 1 without adding to the score of nonadjacent loads. Let's put departments 4 and 5 on one end of the grid and department 1 on the other and then fill in departments 2 and 3 in the middle. The revised solution is shown in Grid 2. The only nonadjacent moves are between departments 1 and 4, and 1 and 5. Since no loads of material are moved along those paths, the score for this layout is zero.

(*Continued*)

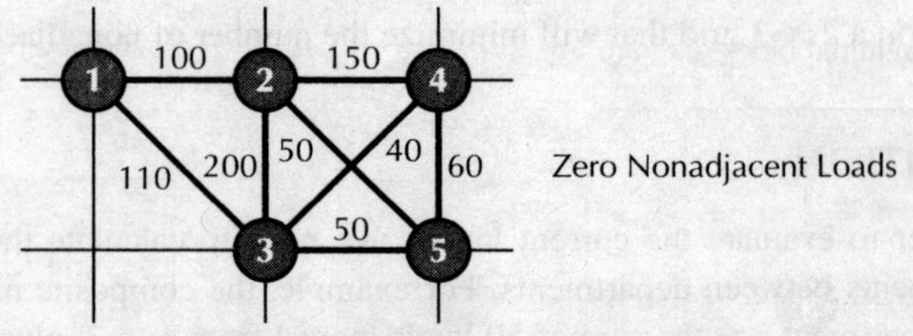

Grid 2

The Excel setup for this problem is shown in Exhibit 7.1.

The layout solution in Grid 2 represents the relative position of each department. The next step in the layout design is to add information about the space required for each department. Recommendations for workspace around machines can be requested from equipment vendors or found in safety regulations or operating manuals. In some cases, vendors provide templates

EXHIBIT 7.1 Using Excel for Process Layouts

EXCEL FILE

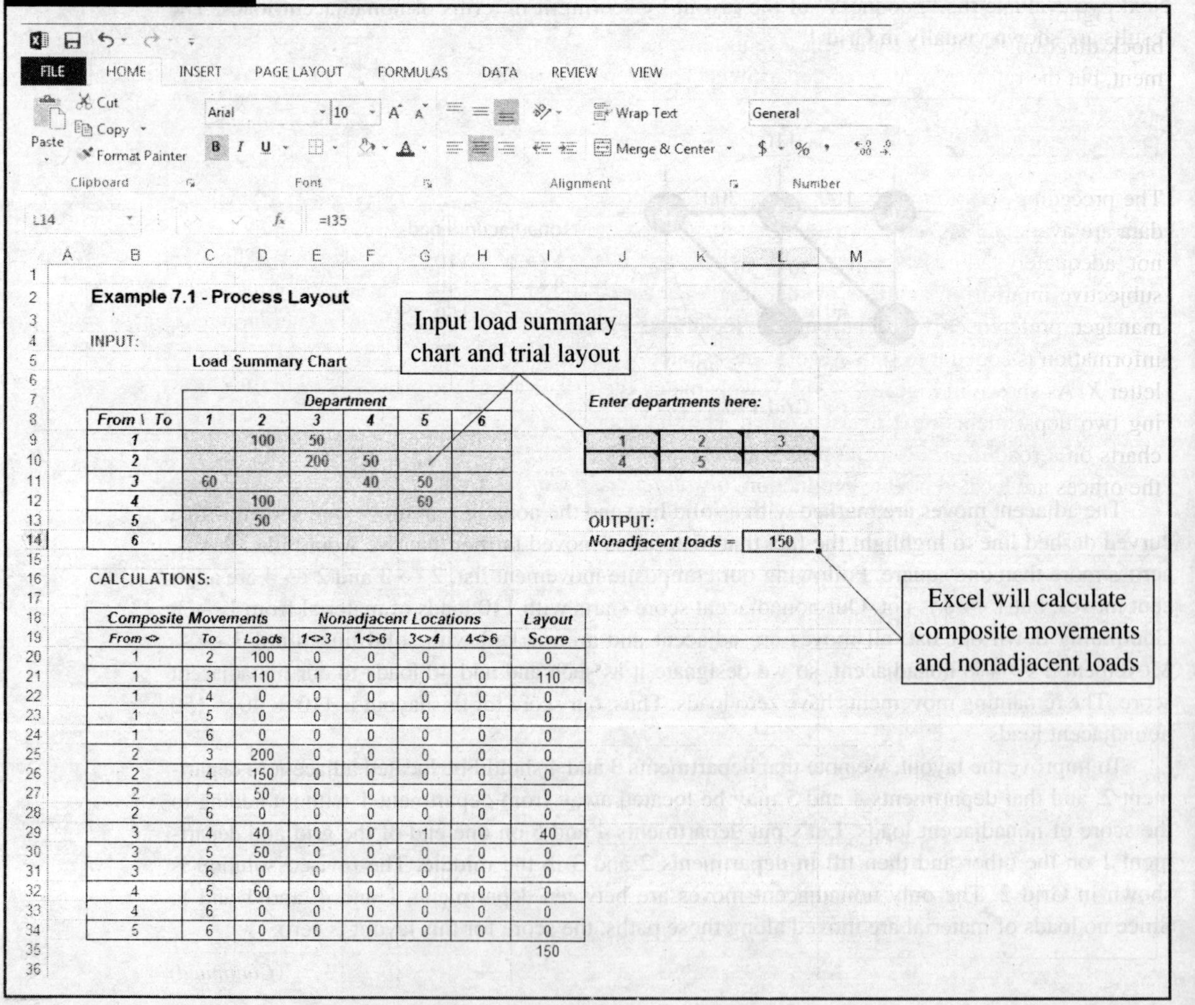

Load Summary Chart

From \ To	1	2	3	4	5	6
1		100	50			
2			200	50		
3	60			40	50	
4		100			60	
5		50				
6						

Enter departments here:

1	2	3
4	5	

OUTPUT: Nonadjacent loads = 150

Composite Movements			Nonadjacent Locations				Layout
From <>	To	Loads	1<>3	1<>6	3<>4	4<>6	Score
1	2	100	0	0	0	0	0
1	3	110	1	0	0	0	110
1	4	0	0	0	0	0	0
1	5	0	0	0	0	0	0
1	6	0	0	0	0	0	0
2	3	200	0	0	0	0	0
2	4	150	0	0	0	0	0
2	5	50	0	0	0	0	0
2	6	0	0	0	0	0	0
3	4	40	0	0	1	0	40
3	5	50	0	0	0	0	0
3	6	0	0	0	0	0	0
4	5	60	0	0	0	0	0
4	6	0	0	0	0	0	0
5	6	0	0	0	0	0	0
							150

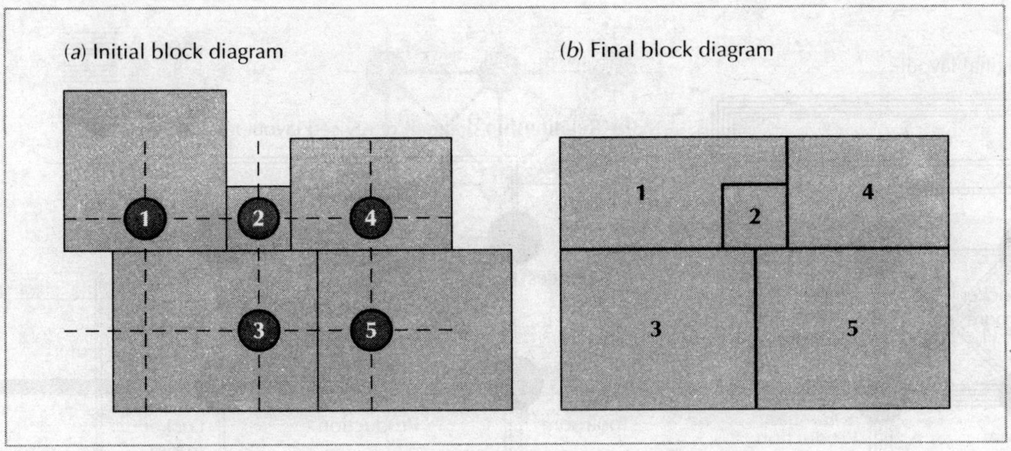

Figure 7.6
Block Diagrams

of equipment layouts, with work areas included. Workspace allocations for workers can be specified as part of job design, recommended by professional groups, or agreed on through union negotiations. A **block diagram** can be created by "blocking in" the work areas around the departments on the grid. The *final block diagram* adjusts the block diagram for the desired or proposed shape of the building. Standard building shapes include rectangles, L shapes, T shapes, and U shapes.

Figure 7.6*a* shows an initial block diagram for Example 7.1, and Figure 7.6*b* shows a final block diagram. Notice that the space requirements vary considerably from department to department, but the relative location of departments has been retained from the grid.

RELATIONSHIP DIAGRAMMING

The preceding solution procedure is appropriate for designing process layouts when quantitative data are available. However, in situations for which quantitative data are difficult to obtain or do not adequately address the layout problem, the load summary chart can be replaced with subjective input from analysts or managers. Richard Muther developed a format for displaying manager preferences for departmental locations, known as **Muther's grid.**[2] The preference information is coded into six categories associated with the five vowels, *A, E, I, O,* and *U,* plus the letter *X.* As shown in Figure 7.7, the vowels match the first letter of the closeness rating for locating two departments next to each other. The diamond-shaped grid is read similarly to mileage charts on a road map. For example, reading down the highlighted row in Figure 7.7, it is *okay* if the offices are located next to production, *absolutely necessary* that the stockroom be located next

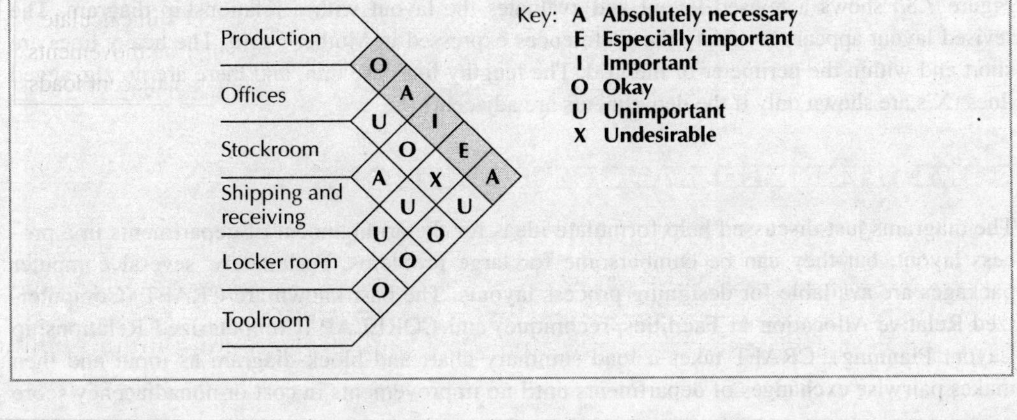

Figure 7.7
Muther's Grid

[2]R. Muther, *Systematic Layout Planning* (Boston: Industrial Education Institute, 1961).

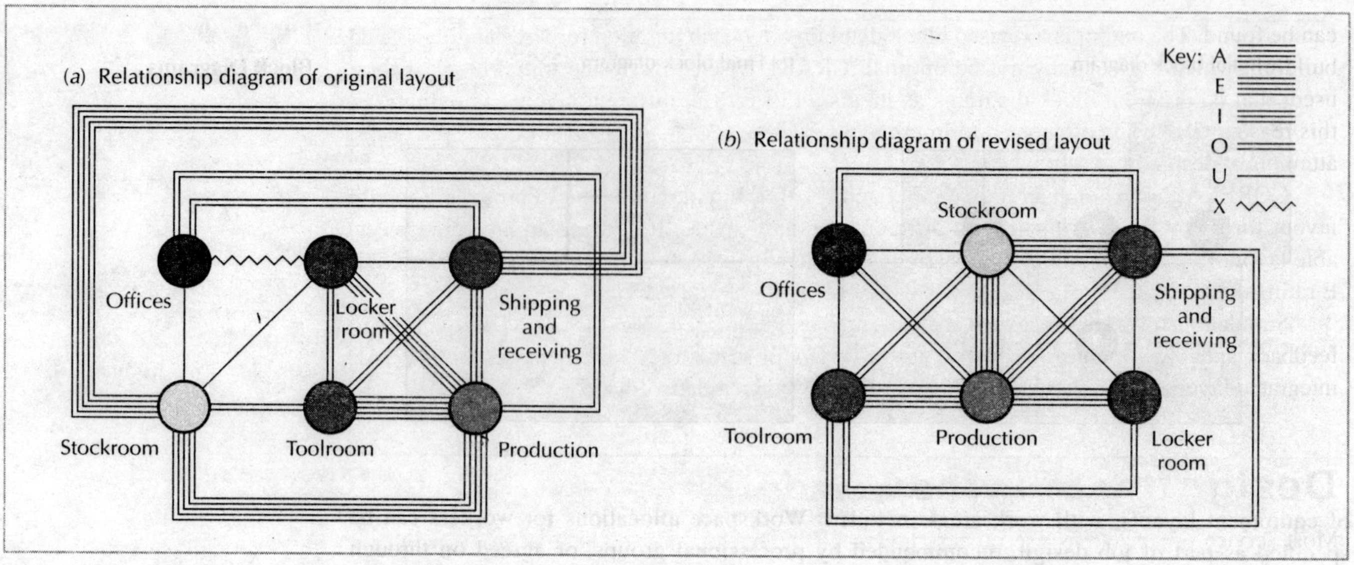

Figure 7.8

Relationship Diagrams

to production, *important* that shipping and receiving be located next to production, *especially important* that the locker room be located next to production, and *absolutely necessary* that the toolroom be located next to production.

The information from Muther's grid can be used to construct a **relationship diagram** that evaluates existing or proposed layouts. Consider the relationship diagram shown in Figure 7.8*a*. A schematic diagram of the six departments from Figure 7.7 is given in a 2 × 3 grid. Lines of different thicknesses are drawn from department to department. The thickest lines (three, four, or five strands) identify the closeness ratings with the highest priority—that is, for which departments it is *important, especially important*, or *absolutely necessary* that they be located next to each other. The priority diminishes with line thickness. *Undesirable* closeness ratings are marked with a zigzagged line. Visually, the best solution would show short heavy lines and no zigzagged lines (undesirable locations are noted only if they are adjacent). Thin lines (one or two strands, representing *unimportant* or *okay*) can be of any length and for that reason are sometimes eliminated from the analysis. An alternative form of relationship diagramming uses colors instead of line thickness to visualize closeness ratings.

From Figure 7.8*a*, it is obvious that production and shipping and receiving are located too far from the stockroom and that the offices and locker room are located too close to one another. Figure 7.8*b* shows a revised layout and evaluates the layout with a relationship diagram. The revised layout appears to satisfy the preferences expressed in Muther's grid. The heavy lines are short and within the perimeter of the grid. The lengthy lines are thin, and there are no zigzagged lines (X's are shown only if the departments are adjacent).

COMPUTERIZED LAYOUT SOLUTIONS

The diagrams just discussed help formulate ideas for the arrangement of departments in a process layout, but they can be cumbersome for large problems. Fortunately, several computer packages are available for designing process layouts. The best known are CRAFT (Computerized Relative Allocation of Facilities Technique) and CORELAP (Computerized Relationship Layout Planning). CRAFT takes a load summary chart and block diagram as input and then makes pairwise exchanges of departments until no improvements in cost or nonadjacency score can be found. The output is a revised block diagram after each iteration for a rectangular-shaped building, which may or may not be optimal. CRAFT is sensitive to the initial block diagram used; that is, different block diagrams as inputs will result in different layouts as outputs. For this reason, CRAFT is often used to improve on existing layouts or to enhance the best manual attempts at designing a layout.

CORELAP uses nonquantitative input and relationship diagramming to produce a feasible layout for up to 45 departments and different building shapes. It attempts to create an acceptable layout from the beginning by locating department pairs with A ratings first, then those with E ratings, and so on.

Simulation software for layout analysis such as PROMODEL and EXTEND provide visual feedback and allow the user to quickly test a variety of scenarios. Three-D modeling and CAD-integrated layout analysis are available in VisFactory and similar software.

Designing Service Layouts

Most service organizations use process layouts. This makes sense because of the variability in customer requests for service. Service layouts are designed in much the same way as process layouts in manufacturing firms, but the objectives may differ. For example, instead of minimizing the flow of materials through the system, services may seek to minimize the flow of paperwork or to maximize customer exposure to as many goods as possible. Grocery stores take this approach when they locate milk on one end of the store and bread on the other, forcing the customer to travel through aisles of merchandise that might prompt additional purchases.

In addition to the location of departments, service layouts are concerned with the circulation of customer traffic through the facility. There are a variety of ways to prompt the flow of customers through various processes or departments. You may have experienced a free-flow layout in The Disney Store, a grid layout in your grocery store, a spine layout in Barnes and Noble, or a circular layout in Kohl's department store. These layouts are shown in Figure 7.9. *Freeflow layouts* encourage browsing, increase impulse purchasing, and are flexible and visually appealing. *Grid layouts* encourage customer familiarity, are low cost, easy to clean and secure, and good for repeat customers. *Loop layouts* and *spine layouts* fall between the extremes of free flow and grids. They

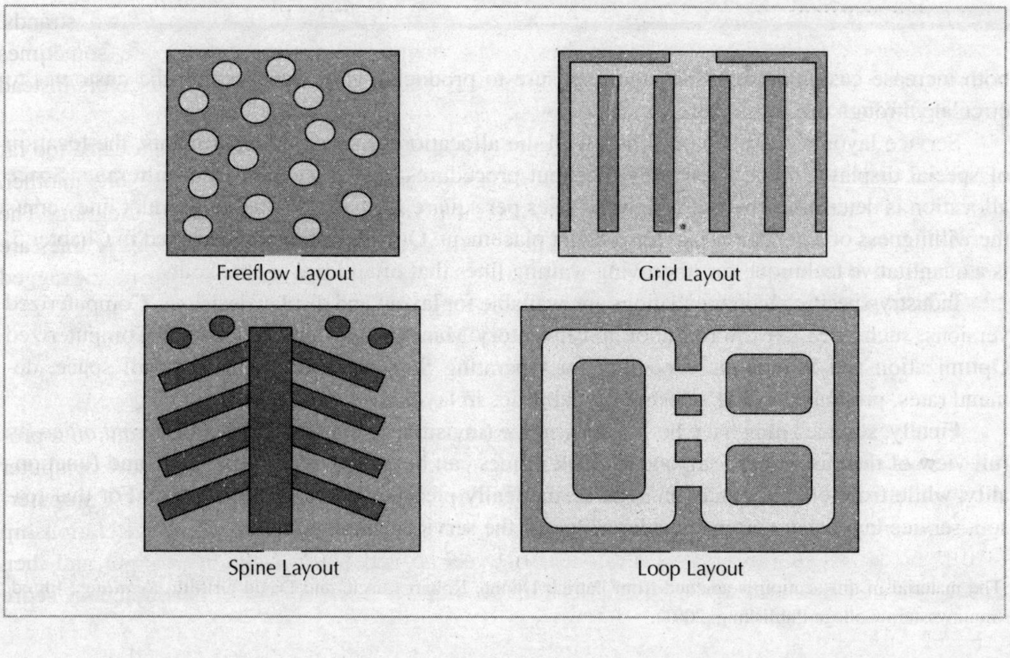

Figure 7.9
Types of Store Layouts

ALONG THE SUPPLY CHAIN

IKEA's Layout Design

IKEA, the world's largest furniture retailer, is known for its sleek, clean design of ready-to-assemble furniture and other household items. Based in Sweden but with retail outlets worldwide, the design of the store is a unifying brand feature. The stores are typically large blue and yellow big-box buildings that resemble a warehouse inside (think Home Depot), only with hundreds of showrooms that illustrate how to design living spaces with IKEA products. Navigation through the store, guided by one-way arrows on the floor and labels hanging from the ceiling, has been described as challenging, frustrating, and, often, infuriating. Customers follow one-way paths in a counter-clockwise direction that send them winding through the entire store and down two stories before checkout. Shortcuts are available but hard to find. You might wonder why a company known for its design has such a haphazard, inefficient facility layout.

British Professor Alan Penn says the layout is purposely long and confusing, encouraging shoppers to pick up items they may not have originally planned because, for one reason, they may not be able to find their way back to that part of the store again. That could be true, since over 60% of IKEA purchases are impulse buys. And for some customers, spending so much time in a store without buying something significant would seem wasteful.

IKEA's expansion into China has been well-received. Its stores are a cultural anomaly that draw thousands of curious newcomers and repeat customers daily. Chinese shoppers escape from crowded streets and small living spaces to lounge in IKEA showrooms, watch videos, work on their laptops, read, spread out a meal, take a nap, and literally spend the day. Many customers never purchase an item, but will continue to return to the store day after day. In Shanghai, a large group of seniors (500 to 700 people) gather weekly for free coffee and to meet potential suitors. A nearby McDonald's now offers space for nuptials.

1. Compare a grocery store layout with IKEA's. How are the goals of each store different? Similar?
2. IKEA has been successful in China, unlike Home Depot. Explain possible reasons.
3. Think about how layouts can affect human behavior. Give an example from your own experience.

Sources: Based on Alan Penn, University College London, online lecture, January 18, 2011, http://www.ucl.ac.uk/lhl/lhlpub_spring11/01-18012011; Rebecca Hill, "I Only Went in for Some Bedding . . ." *The Guardian* (January 31, 2011); Laurie Burkitt, "In China, IKEA Is a Swede Place for Senior Romance, Relaxation," *The Wall Street Journal* (December 1, 2011); Matthew Niederhauser, "Life in a Big Box," *Foreign Policy* (August 13, 2012).

both increase customer sightlines and exposure to products, while encouraging the customer to circulate through the entire store.[3]

Service layouts are also concerned with the allocation of space to departments, the location of special displays, the efficiency of checkout procedures, and protection from pilferage. Space allocation is determined by evaluating the sales per square foot of a product or product line versus the willingness of a vendor to pay for product placement. Queuing analysis, discussed in Chapter 5, is a quantitative technique for improving waiting lines that often form at checkouts.

Industry-specific recommendations are available for layout and display decisions. Computerized versions, such as SLIM (Store Labor and Inventory Management) and COSMOS (Computerized Optimization and Simulation Modeling for Operating Supermarkets), consider shelf space, demand rates, profitability, and stockout probabilities in layout design.

Finally, services may have both a *back office* (invisible to the customer) and a *front office* (in full view of the customer) component. Back offices can be organized for efficiency and functionality, while front office layouts must be aesthetically pleasing as well as functional. For that reason, service layouts are often considered part of the service design process.

[3]The material in this section is adapted from Patrick Dunne, Robert Lusch, and David Griffith, *Retailing*, 4th ed. (Southwestern College Publishing, 2001).

Designing Product Layouts

A product layout arranges machines or workers in a line according to the operations that need to be performed to assemble a particular product. From this description, it would seem the layout could be determined simply by following the order of assembly as contained in the bill of material for the product. To some extent, this is true. Precedence requirements, specifying which operations must precede others, which can be done concurrently and which must wait until later, are an important input to the product layout decision. But there are other factors that make the decision more complicated.

Product layouts or assembly lines are used for high-volume production. To attain the required output rate as efficiently as possible, jobs are broken down into their smallest indivisible portions, called *work elements*. Work elements are so small that they cannot be performed by more than one worker or at more than one workstation. But it is common for one worker to perform several work elements as the product passes through his or her workstation. Part of the layout decision is concerned with grouping these work elements into workstations so products flow through the assembly line smoothly. A *workstation* is any area along the assembly line that requires at least one worker or one machine. If each workstation on the assembly line takes the same amount of time to perform the work elements that have been assigned, then products will move successively from workstation to workstation with no need for a product to wait or a worker to be idle. The process of equalizing the amount of work at each workstation is called **line balancing.**

LINE BALANCING

Assembly-line balancing operates under two constraints: precedence requirements and cycle time restrictions.

Precedence requirements are physical restrictions on the *order* in which operations are performed on the assembly line. For example, we would not ask a worker to package a product before all the components were attached, even if he or she had the time to do so before passing the product to the next worker on the line. To facilitate line balancing, precedence requirements are often expressed in the form of a precedence diagram. The *precedence diagram* is a network, with work elements represented by circles or nodes and precedence relationships represented by directed line segments connecting the nodes. We will construct a precedence diagram later in Example 7.2.

Cycle time, the other restriction on line balancing, refers to the maximum amount of time the product is allowed to spend at each workstation if the targeted production rate is to be reached. *Desired cycle time* is calculated by dividing the time available for production by the number of units scheduled to be produced:

$$C_d = \frac{\text{production time available}}{\text{desired units of output}}$$

Suppose a company wanted to produce 120 units in an 8-hour day. The cycle time necessary to achieve the production quota is

$$C_d = \frac{(8 \text{ hours} \times 60 \text{ minutes/hour})}{(120 \text{ units})}$$

$$= \frac{480}{120} = 4 \text{ minutes}$$

Cycle time can also be viewed as the time between completed items rolling off the assembly line. Consider the three-station assembly line shown here.

4 minutes 4 minutes 4 minutes

Flow time = 4 + 4 + 4 = 12 minutes

Cycle time = max {4, 4, 4} = 4 minutes

It takes 12 minutes (i.e., 4 + 4 + 4) for each item to pass completely through all three stations of the assembly line. The time required to complete an item is referred to as its *flow time*. However, the assembly line does not work on only one item at a time. When fully operational, the line will be processing three items at a time, one at each workstation, in various stages of assembly. Every 4 minutes a new item enters the line at workstation 1, an item is passed from workstation 1 to workstation 2, another item is passed from workstation 2 to workstation 3, and a completed item leaves the assembly line. Thus, a completed item rolls off the assembly line every 4 minutes. This 4-minute interval is the actual cycle time of the line.

The *actual cycle time,* C_a, is the maximum workstation time on the line. It differs from the desired cycle time when the production quota does not match the maximum output attainable by the system. Sometimes the production quota cannot be achieved because the time required for one work element is too large. To correct the situation, the quota can be revised downward or parallel stations can be set up for the bottleneck element.

Line balancing is basically a trial-and-error process. We group elements into workstations recognizing time and precedence constraints. For simple problems, we can evaluate all feasible groupings of elements. For more complicated problems, we need to know when to stop trying different workstation configurations. The *efficiency* of the line can provide one type of guideline; the *theoretical minimum number of workstations* provides another. The formulas for efficiency, E, and minimum number of workstations, N, are

$$E = \frac{\sum_{i=1}^{j} t_i}{nC_a}; \qquad N = \frac{\sum_{i=1}^{j} t_i}{C_d}$$

where

t_i = completion time for element i
j = number of work elements
n = actual number of work stations
C_a = actual cycle time
C_d = desired cycle time

The total idle time of the line, called **balance delay**, is calculated as (1 − efficiency). Efficiency and balance delay are usually expressed as percentages. In practice, it may be difficult to attain the theoretical number of workstations or 100% efficiency.

The line balancing process can be summarized as follows:

1. Draw and label a precedence diagram.
2. Calculate the desired cycle time required for the line.
3. Calculate the theoretical minimum number of workstations.
4. Group elements into workstations, recognizing cycle time and precedence constraints.
5. Calculate the efficiency of the line.
6. Determine if the theoretical minimum number of workstations or an acceptable efficiency level has been reached. If not, go back to step 4.

EXAMPLE 7.2

LINE BALANCING

Real Fruit Snack Strips are made from a mixture of dried fruit, food coloring, preservatives, and glucose. The mixture is pressed out into a thin sheet, imprinted with various shapes, rolled, and packaged. The precedence and time requirements for each step in the assembly process are given below. To meet demand, Real Fruit needs to produce 6,000 fruit strips every 40-hour week. Design an assembly line with the fewest number of workstations that will achieve the production quota without violating precedence constraints.

	Work Element	Precedence	Time (min)
A	Press out sheet of fruit	—	0.1
B	Cut into strips	A	0.2
C	Outline fun shapes	A	0.4
D	Roll up and package	B, C	0.3

SOLUTION

First, we draw the precedence diagram as follows.

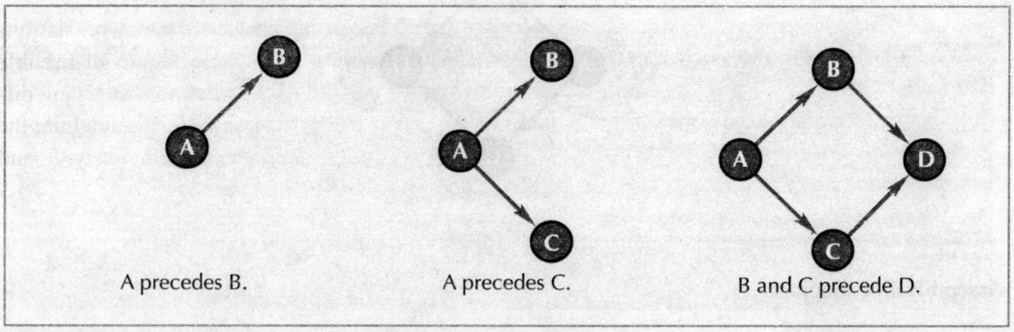

The precedence diagram is completed by adding the time requirements beside each node. Next, we calculate the desired cycle time and the theoretical minimum number of workstations:

$$C_d = \frac{40 \text{ hours} \times 60 \text{ minutes/hour}}{6000 \text{ units}} = \frac{2400}{6000} = 0.4 \text{ minutes}$$

$$N = \frac{0.1 + 0.2 + 0.3 + 0.4}{0.4} = \frac{1.0}{0.4} = 2.5 \approx 3 \text{ workstations (round up)}$$

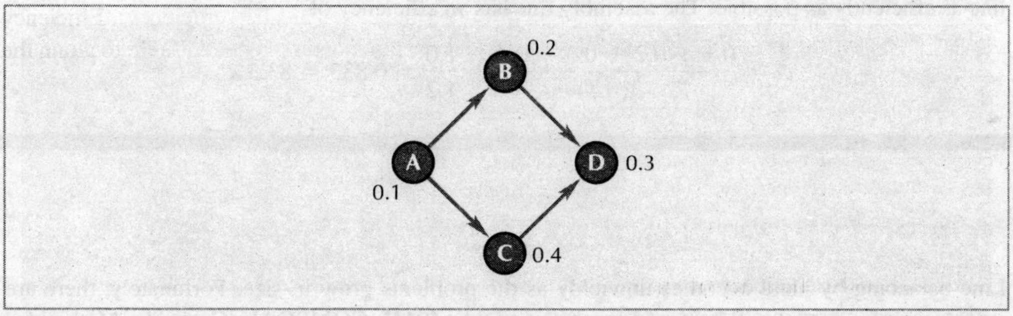

(Continued)

To balance the line, we must group elements into workstations so that the sum of the element times at each workstation is less than or equal to the desired cycle time of 0.4 minutes. Examining the precedence diagram, we begin with A since it is the only element that does not have a precedence. We assign A to workstation 1. B and C are now available for assignment. Cycle time is exceeded with A and C in the same workstation, so we assign B to workstation 1 and place C in a second workstation. No other element can be added to workstation 2, due to cycle time constraints. That leaves D for assignment to a third workstation. Elements grouped into workstations are circled on the precedence diagram and placed into workstations shown on the assembly line diagram.

Workstation	Element	Remaining Time	Remaining Elements
1	A	0.3	B, C
	B	0.1	C, D
2	C	0.0	D
3	D	0.1	none

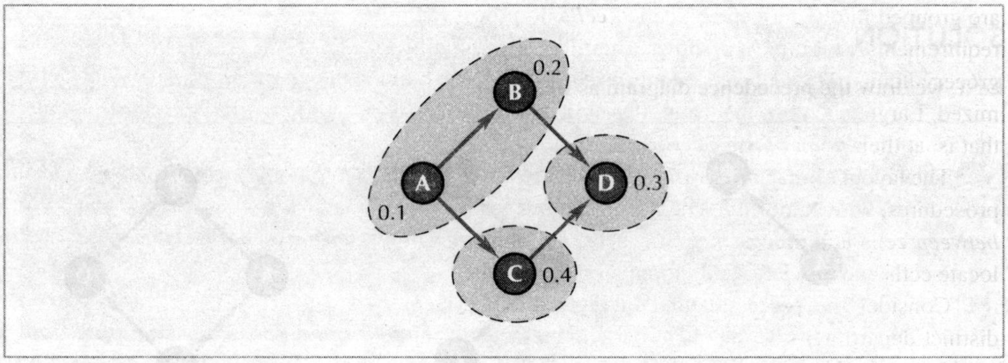

Assembly-line diagram:

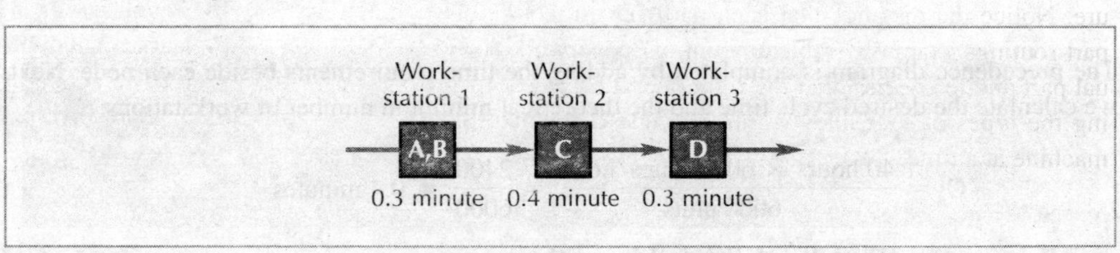

Since the theoretical minimum number of workstations was three, we know we have balanced the line as efficiently as possible. The assembly line has an efficiency of

$$E = \frac{0.1 + 0.2 + 0.3 + 0.4}{3(0.4)} = \frac{1.0}{1.2} = 0.833 = 83.3\%$$

COMPUTERIZED LINE BALANCING

Line balancing by hand becomes unwieldy as the problems grow in size. Fortunately, there are software packages that will balance large lines quickly. IBM's COMSOAL (Computer Method for Sequencing Operations for Assembly Lines) and GE's ASYBL (Assembly Line Configuration

Program) can assign hundreds of work elements to workstations on an assembly line. These programs, and most that are commercially available, do not guarantee optimal solutions. They use various *heuristics*, or rules, to balance the line at an acceptable level of efficiency. Five common heuristics are: longest operation time, shortest operation time, most number of following tasks, least number of following tasks, and ranked positional weight. Positional weights are calculated by summing the processing times of those tasks that follow an element. These heuristics specify the *order* in which work elements are considered for allocation to workstations. Elements are assigned to workstations in the order given until the cycle time is reached or until all tasks have been assigned. The most number of following tasks heuristic was used in Example 7.2.

Hybrid Layouts

Hybrid layouts modify and/or combine some aspects of product and process layouts. We discuss three hybrid layouts: cellular layouts, flexible manufacturing systems, and mixed-model assembly lines.

CELLULAR LAYOUTS

Cellular layouts attempt to combine the flexibility of a process layout with the efficiency of a product layout. Based on the concept of group technology (GT), dissimilar machines or activities are grouped into work centers, called *cells*, to process families of parts or customers with similar requirements. (Figure 7.10 shows a family of parts with similar shapes and a family of related grocery items.) The cells are arranged in relation to each other so that material movement is minimized. Large machines that cannot be split among cells are located near to the cells that use them, that is, at their *point of use*.

The layout of machines *within* each cell resembles a small assembly line. Thus, line-balancing procedures, with some adjustment, can be used to arrange the machines within the cell. The layout *between* cells is a process layout. Therefore, computer programs such as CRAFT can be used to locate cells and any leftover equipment in the facility.

Consider the process layout in Figure 7.11. Machines are grouped by function into four distinct departments. Component parts manufactured in the process layout section of the factory are later assembled into a finished product on the assembly line. The parts follow different flow paths through the shop. Three representative routings, for parts A, B, and C, are shown in the figure. Notice the distance that each part must travel before completion and the irregularity of the part routings. A considerable amount of "paperwork" is needed to direct the flow of each individual part and to confirm that the right operation has been performed. Workers are skilled at operating the types of machines within a single department and typically can operate more than one machine at a time.

Figure 7.10

Group Technology: (*a*) A family of similar parts; (*b*) A family of related grocery items.

SOURCE: Adapted from Mikell P. Groover, *Automation, Production Systems, and Computer Integrated Manufacturing* © 1987. Adapted by permission of Pearson Education, Inc., Upper Saddle River, NJ.

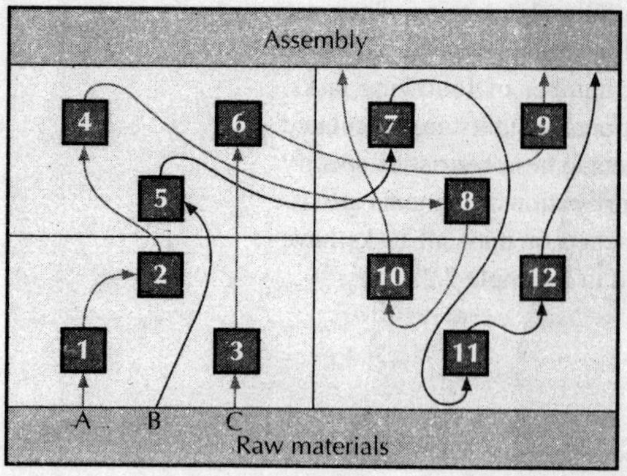

Parts	Machines 1	2	3	4	5	6	7	8	9	10	11	12
A	×	×		×				×		×		
B					×		×				×	×
C			×			×			×			
D	×	×		×				×		×		
E					×	×						×
F	×			×				×				
G			×			×			×			×
H							×				×	×

Figure 7.11

Original Process Layout with Routing Matrix

Figure 7.11 gives the complete part routing matrix for the eight parts processed through the facility. In its current form, there is no apparent pattern to the routings. **Production flow analysis (PFA)** is a group technology technique that reorders part routing matrices to identify families of parts with similar processing requirements. The reordering process can be as simple as using the "Data Sort" command in Excel for the most common machines, or as sophisticated as pattern-recognition algorithms from the field of artificial intelligence. Figure 7.12 shows the results of reordering. Now the part families and cell formations are clear. Cell 1, consisting of machines 1, 2, 4, 8, and 10, will process parts A, D, and F; Cell 2, consisting of machines 3, 6, and 9, will process products C and G; and Cell 3, consisting of machines 5, 7, 11, and 12, will process parts B, H, and E. A complete cellular layout showing the three cells feeding a final assembly line is also given in Figure 7.12. The representative part flows for parts A, B, and C are much more direct than those in the process layout. There is no backtracking or crisscrossing of routes, and the parts travel a

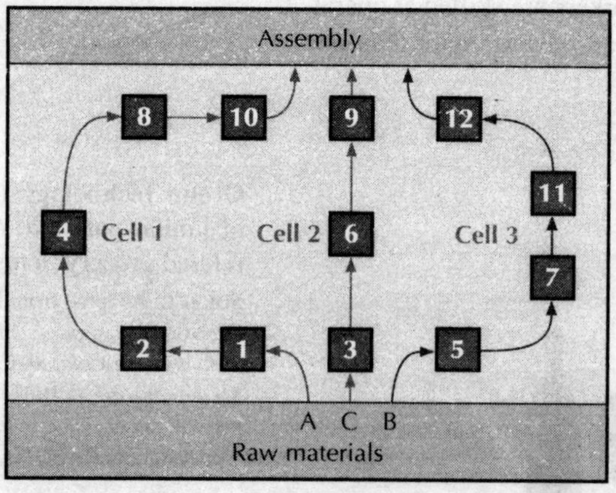

Parts	Machines 1	2	4	8	10	3	6	9	5	7	11	12
A	×	×	×	×	×							
D	×	×	×	×	×							
F	×		×	×								
C						×	×	×				
G						×	×	×				×
B									×	×	×	×
H										×	×	×
E							×		×			×

Cell 1: Parts A, D, F
Machines 1, 2, 4, 8, 10

Cell 2: Parts C, G
Machines 3, 6, 9

Cell 3: Parts B, H, E
Machines 5, 7, 11, 12

Figure 7.12

Revised Cellular Layout with Reordered Routing Matrix

shorter distance to be processed. Notice that parts G and E cannot be completely processed within cells 2 and 3, to which they have been assigned. However, the two cells are located in such a fashion that the transfer of parts between the cells does not involve much extra movement.

The U shape of cells 1 and 3 is a popular arrangement for manufacturing cells because it facilitates the rotation of workers among several machines. Workers in a cellular layout typically operate more than one machine, as was true in the process layout. However, workers who are assigned to each cell must now be multifunctional—that is, skilled at operating many different kinds of machines, not just one type, as in the process layout. In addition, workers are assigned a *path* to follow among the machines that they operate, which may or may not coincide with the path the product follows through the cell. Figure 7.13 shows a U-shaped manufacturing cell including worker paths.

Advantages of Cellular Layouts

Cellular layouts have become popular in the past decade as the backbone of modern factories. Cells can differ considerably in size, in automation, and in the variety of parts processed. As small interconnected layout units, cells are common in services, as well as manufacturing.

The advantages of cellular layouts are as follows:

- ***Reduced material handling and transit time***. Material movement is more direct. Less distance is traveled between operations. Material does not accumulate or wait long periods of time to be moved. Within a cell, the worker is more likely to carry a partially finished item from machine to machine than wait for material-handling equipment, as is characteristic of process layouts where larger loads must be moved farther distances.
- ***Reduced setup time***. Since similar parts are processed together, the adjustments required to set up a machine should not be that different from item to item. If it does not take that long to change over from one item to another, then the changeover can occur more frequently, and items can be produced and transferred in very small batches or lot sizes.

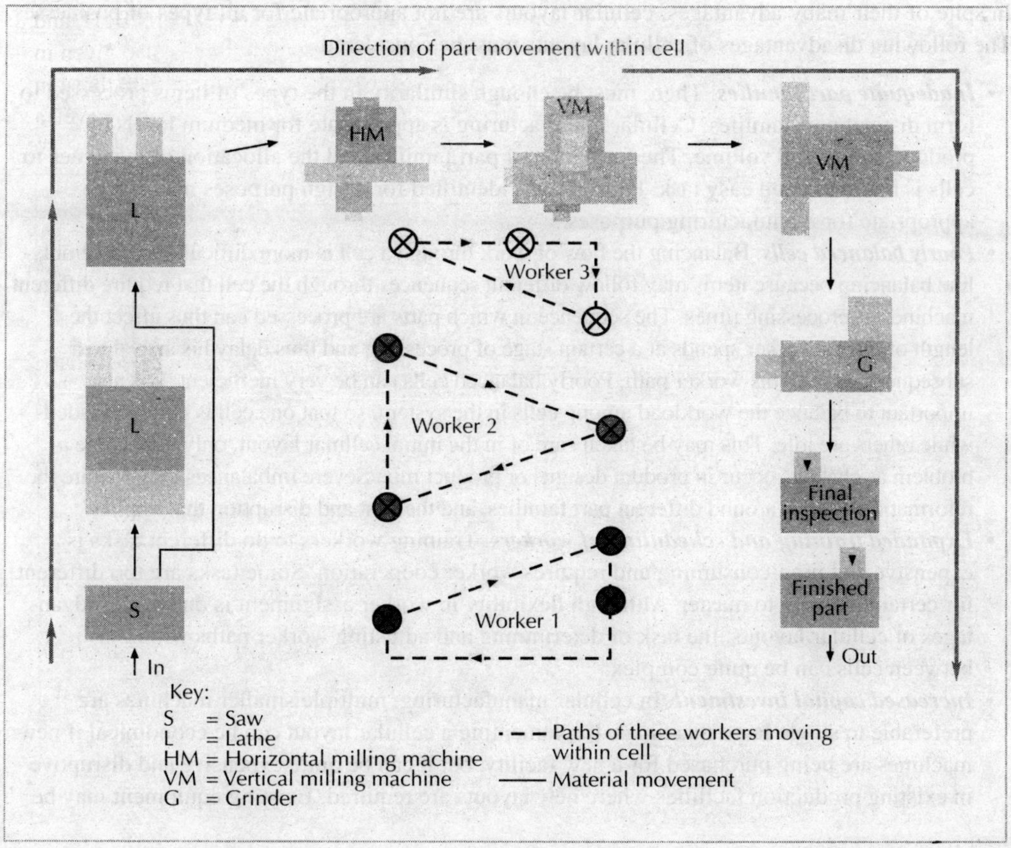

Figure 7.13

A Manufacturing Cell with Worker Paths

SOURCE: J.T. Black, "Cellular Manufacturing Systems Reduce Setup Time, Make Small Lot Production Economical." *Industrial Engineering* (November 1983). Reprinted with the permission of the Institute of Industrial Engineers, 3577 Parkway Lane, Suite 200, Norcross, GA 30092, 770-449-0461 © 1983.

- ***Reduced work-in-process inventory***. In a work cell, as with assembly lines, the flow of work is balanced so that no bottleneck or significant buildup of material occurs between stations or machines. Less space is required for storage of in-process inventory between machines, and machines can be moved closer together, thereby saving transit time and increasing communication.
- ***Better use of human resources***. Typically, a cell contains a small number of workers responsible for producing a completed part or product. The workers act as a self-managed team, in most cases more satisfied with the work that they do and more particular about the quality of their work. Labor in cellular manufacturing is a flexible resource. Workers in each cell are multifunctional and can be assigned to different routes within a cell or between cells as demand volume changes.
- ***Easier to control***. Items in the same part family are processed in a similar manner through the work cell. There is a significant reduction in the paperwork necessary to document material travel, such as where an item should be routed next, if the right operation has been performed, and the current status of a job. With fewer jobs processed through a cell, smaller batch sizes, and less distance to travel between operations, the progress of a job can be verified visually.
- ***Easier to automate***. Automation is expensive. Rarely can a company afford to automate an entire factory all at once. Cellular layouts can be automated one cell at a time. Figure 7.14 shows an automated cell with one robot in the center to load and unload material from several CNC machines and an incoming and outgoing conveyor. Automating a few workstations on an assembly line will make it difficult to balance the line and achieve the increases in productivity expected. Introducing automated equipment in a job shop has similar results, because the "islands of automation" speed up only certain processes and are not integrated into the complete processing of a part or product.

Disadvantages of Cellular Layouts

In spite of their many advantages, cellular layouts are not appropriate for all types of businesses. The following disadvantages of cellular layouts must be considered:

- ***Inadequate part families***. There must be enough similarity in the types of items processed to form distinct part families. Cellular manufacturing is appropriate for medium levels of product variety and volume. The formation of part families and the allocation of machines to cells is not always an easy task. Part families identified for design purposes may not be appropriate for manufacturing purposes.
- ***Poorly balanced cells***. Balancing the flow of work through a cell is more difficult than assembly-line balancing because items may follow different sequences through the cell that require different machines or processing times. The sequence in which parts are processed can thus affect the length of time a worker spends at a certain stage of processing and thus delay his arrival to a subsequent stage in his worker path. Poorly balanced cells can be very inefficient. It is also important to balance the workload among cells in the system, so that one cell is not overloaded while others are idle. This may be taken care of in the initial cellular layout, only to become a problem as changes occur in product designs or product mix. Severe imbalances may require the reformation of cells around different part families, and the cost and disruption that implies.
- ***Expanded training and scheduling of workers***. Training workers to do different tasks is expensive and time-consuming and requires worker cooperation. Some tasks are too different for certain workers to master. Although flexibility in worker assignment is one of the advantages of cellular layouts, the task of determining and adjusting worker paths within or between cells can be quite complex.
- ***Increased capital investment***. In cellular manufacturing, multiple smaller machines are preferable to single large machines. Implementing a cellular layout can be economical if new machines are being purchased for a new facility, but it can be quite expensive and disruptive in existing production facilities where new layouts are required. Existing equipment may be

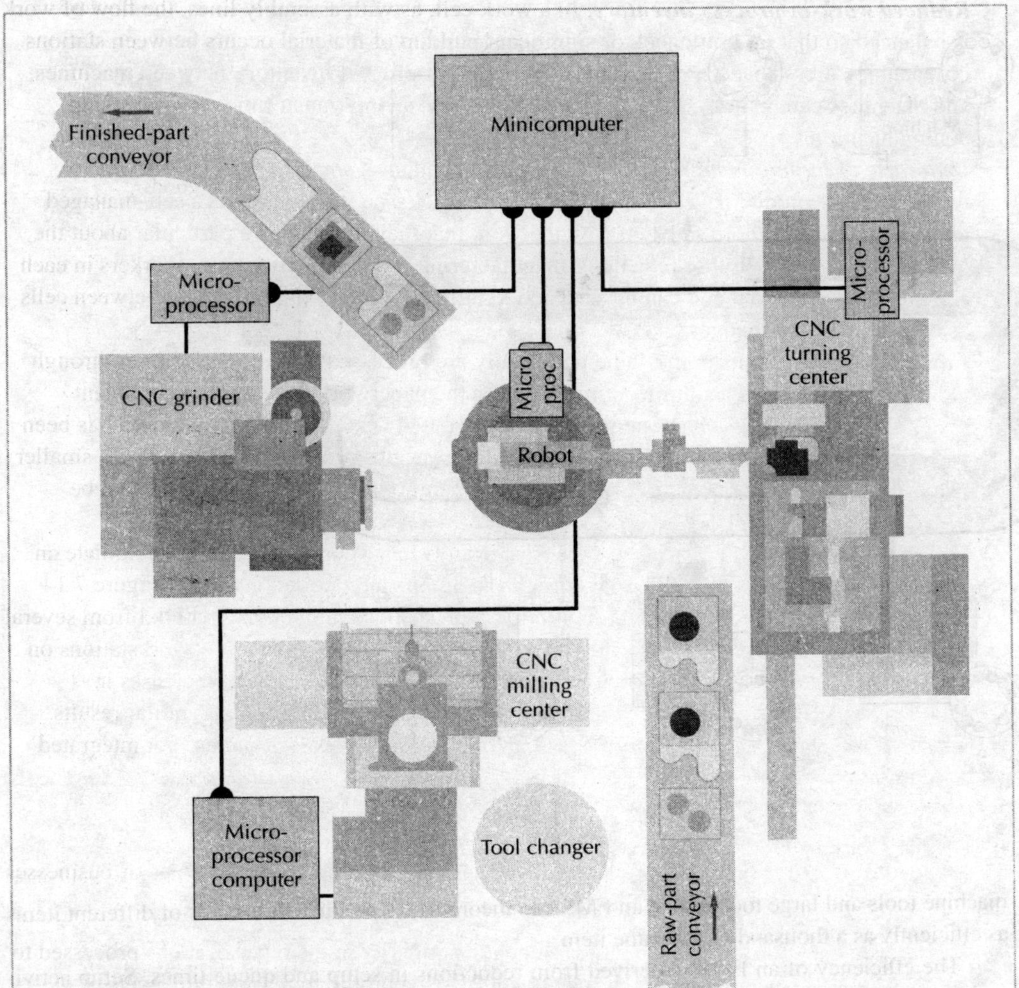

Figure 7.14

An Automated Manufacturing Cell

SOURCE: J. T. Black, "Cellular Manufacturing Systems Reduce Setup Time, Make Small Lot Production Economical." *Industrial Engineering* (November 1983). Reprinted with the permission of the Institute of Industrial Engineers, 3577 Parkway Lane, Suite 200, Norcross, GA 30092, 770-449-0461, © 1983.

too large to fit into cells or may be underutilized when placed in a single cell. Additional machines of the same type may have to be purchased for different cells. The cost and downtime required to move machines can also be high.

FLEXIBLE MANUFACTURING SYSTEMS

A **flexible manufacturing system (FMS)** consists of numerous programmable machine tools connected by an automated material handling system and controlled by a common computer network. It is different from traditional automation, which is fixed or "hard wired" for a specific task. *Fixed automation* is very efficient and can produce in very high volumes, but is not flexible. Only one type or model of product can be produced on most automated production lines, and a change in product design would require extensive changes in the line and its equipment.

An FMS combines flexibility with efficiency. Tools change automatically from large storage carousels at each machine, which hold hundreds of tools. The material-handling system (usually conveyors or automated guided vehicles) carries workpieces on pallets, which can be locked into a machine for processing. Pallets are transferred between the conveyor and machine automatically. Computer software keeps track of the routing and processing requirements for each pallet. Pallets communicate with the computer controller by way of bar codes or radio signals. Parts can be transferred between any two machines in any routing sequence. With a variety of programmable

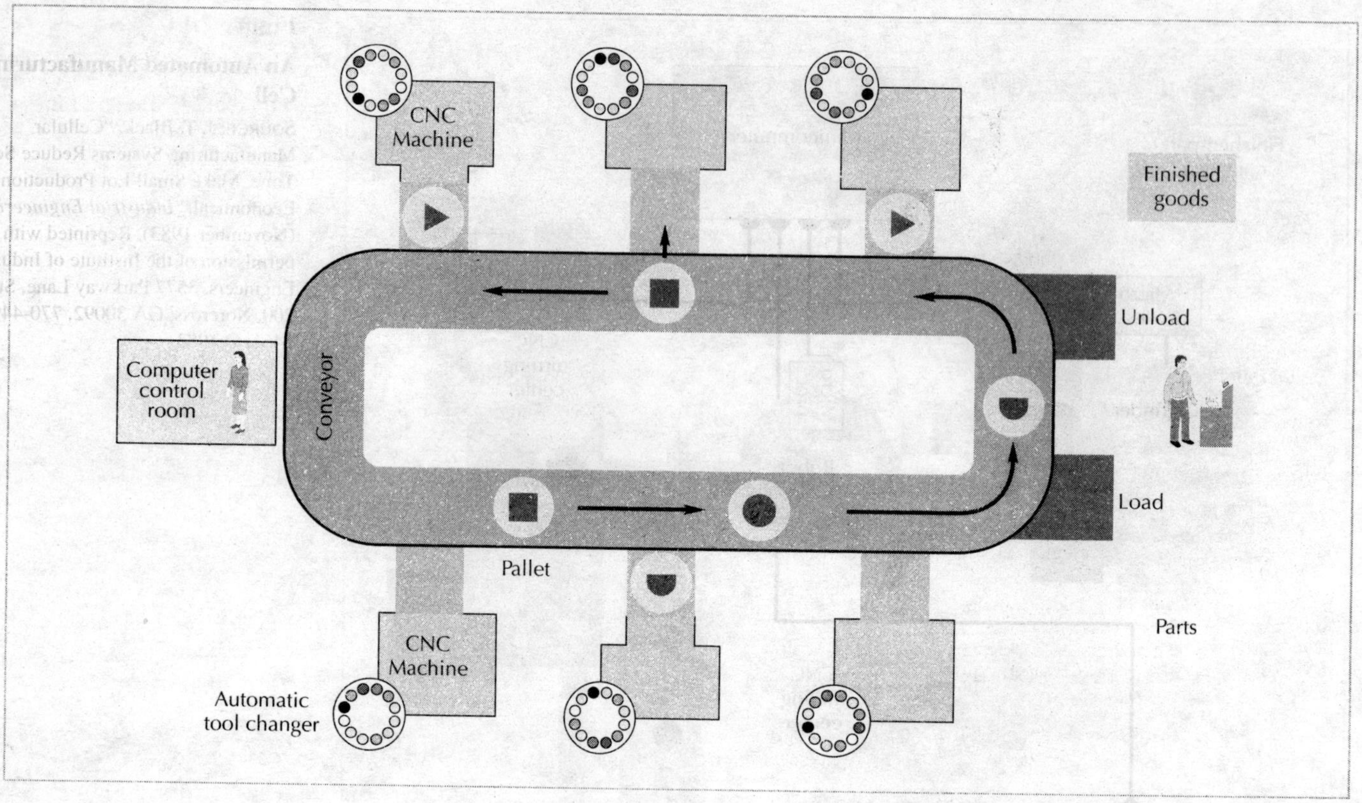

Figure 7.15

A Flexible Manufacturing System

machine tools and large tool banks, an FMS can theoretically produce thousands of different items as efficiently as a thousand of the same item.

The efficiency of an FMS is derived from reductions in setup and queue times. Setup activities take place *before* the part reaches the machine. A machine is presented only with parts and tools ready for immediate processing. Queuing areas at each machine hold pallets ready to move in the moment the machine finishes with the previous piece. The pallet also serves as a work platform, so no time is lost transferring the workpiece from pallet to machine or positioning and fixturing the part. The machines in an advanced FMS, such as five-axis CNC *machining centers*, simultaneously perform up to five operations on a workpiece that would normally require a series of operations on individual machines.

FMS layouts differ based on the variety of parts that the system can process, the size of the parts processed, and the average processing time required for part completion. Figure 7.15 shows a simple FMS where parts rotate on a conveyor until a machine is available for processing.

MIXED-MODEL ASSEMBLY LINES

Traditional assembly lines, designed to process a single model or type of product, can be used to process more than one type of product but not efficiently. Models of the same type are produced in long production runs, sometimes lasting for months, and then the line is shut down and changed over for the next model. The next model is also run for an extended time, producing perhaps half a year to a year's supply; then the line is shut down again and changed over for yet another model; and so on. The problem with this arrangement is the difficulty in responding to changes in customer demand. If a certain model is selling well and customers want more of it, they have to wait until the next batch of that model is scheduled to be produced. On the other hand, if demand is disappointing for models that have already been produced, the manufacturer is stuck with unwanted inventory.

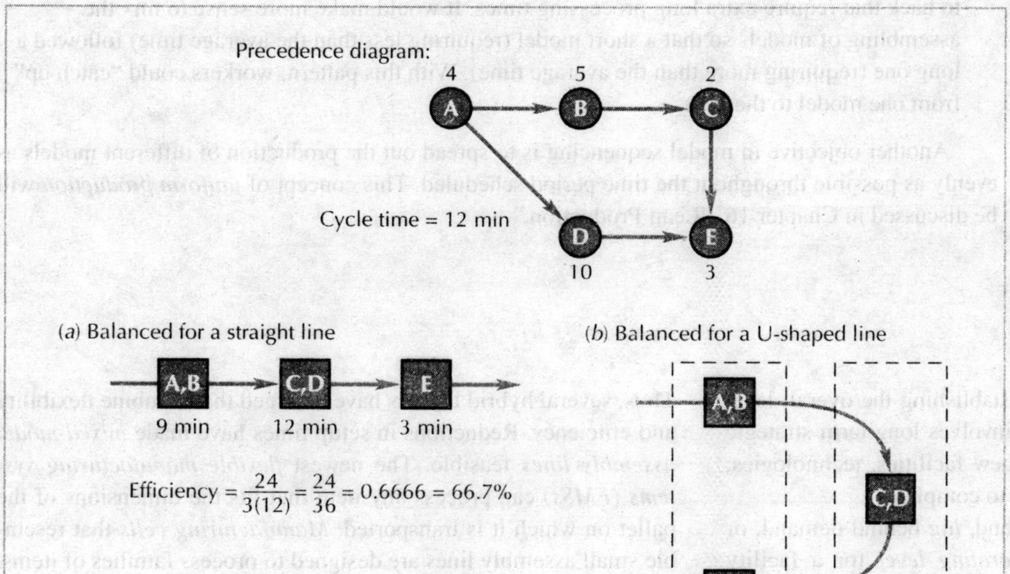

Figure 7.16

Balancing U-Shaped Lines

Recognizing that this mismatch of production and demand is a problem, some manufacturers concentrated on devising more sophisticated forecasting techniques. Others changed the manner in which the assembly line was laid out and operated so that it really became a **mixed-model assembly line**. First, they reduced the time needed to change over the line to produce different models. Then they trained their workers to perform a variety of tasks and allowed them to work at more than one workstation on the line, as needed. Finally, they changed the way in which the line was arranged and scheduled. The following factors are important in the design and operation of mixed-model assembly lines.

- ***Line balancing***. In a mixed-model line, the time to complete a task can vary from model to model. Instead of using the completion times from one model to balance the line, a distribution of possible completion times from the array of models must be considered. In most cases, the expected value, or average, times are used in the balancing procedure. Otherwise, mixed-model lines are balanced in much the same way as single-model lines.
- ***U-shaped lines***. To compensate for the different work requirements of assembling different models, it is necessary to have a flexible workforce and to arrange the line so that workers can assist one another as needed. Figure 7.16 shows how the efficiency of an assembly line can be improved when a U-shaped line is used.
- ***Flexible workforce***. Although worker paths are predetermined to fit within a set cycle time, the use of average time values in mixed-model lines will produce variations in worker performance. Hence, the flexibility of workers helping other workers makes a tremendous difference in the ability of the line to adapt to the varied length of tasks inherent in a mixed-model line.
- ***Model sequencing***. Since different models are produced on the same line, mixed-model scheduling involves an additional decision—the order, or sequence, of models to be run through the line. From a logical standpoint, it would be unwise to sequence two models back

to back that require extra long processing times. It would make more sense to mix the assembling of models so that a short model (requiring less than the average time) followed a long one (requiring more than the average time). With this pattern, workers could "catch up" from one model to the next.

Another objective in model sequencing is to spread out the production of different models as evenly as possible throughout the time period scheduled. This concept of *uniform production* will be discussed in Chapter 16, "Lean Production."

SUMMARY

Capacity planning is the process of establishing the overall level of productive resources for a firm. It involves long-term strategic activities, such as the acquisition of new facilities, technologies, or businesses, that take a year or more to complete.

Capacity expansion can *lead* demand, *lag* behind demand, or meet *average* demand. The *best operating level* for a facility often includes a *capacity cushion* for unexpected occurrences. The tendency of high levels of output to cost less per unit is known as *economies of scale*. This normally holds true up to a certain level of output, at which point *diseconomies of scale* can take over.

Facility decisions are an important part of operations strategy. An effective layout reflects a firm's competitive priorities and enables the firm to reach its strategic objectives. Batch production, which emphasizes flexibility, is most often organized into a *process layout*, whereas mass production uses a *product layout* for maximum efficiency. Because of their size and scope, projects tend to use *fixed-position layouts. Service layouts* may try to process customers through the system as quickly as possible or maximize customer exposure to products and services.

In the current manufacturing environment of new product introductions, rapidly changing technologies, and intense competition, the ability of a manufacturing system to adapt is essential. Thus, several hybrid layouts have emerged that combine flexibility and efficiency. Reductions in setup times have made *mixed-model assembly lines* feasible. The newest *flexible manufacturing systems (FMSs)* can process any item that fits the dimensions of the pallet on which it is transported. *Manufacturing cells* that resemble small assembly lines are designed to process families of items. Some companies are placing wheels and casters on their machines so that the cells can be adjusted as needed. Others are experimenting with modular conveyor systems that allow assembly lines to be rearranged while workers are on their lunch break.

As important as flexibility is, the cost of moving material is still a primary consideration in layout design. Today, as in the past, layout decisions are concerned with minimizing material flow. However, with reduced inventory levels, the emphasis has shifted from minimizing the *number* of loads moved to minimizing the *distance* they are moved. Instead of accumulating larger loads of material and moving them less often, machines are located closer together to allow the frequent movement of smaller loads. Planners who used to devote a considerable amount of time to designing the location of storage areas and the movement of material into and out of storage areas are now concerned with the rapid movement of material to and from the facility itself. The logistics of material transportation is discussed in Chapter 11.

KEY FORMULAS

Desired Cycle Time

$$C_d = \frac{\text{production time available}}{\text{desired units of output}}$$

Actual Cycle Time

$$C_a = \text{maximum workstation time}$$

Theoretical Minimum Number of Workstations

$$N = \frac{\sum_{i=1}^{j} t_i}{C_d}$$

Efficiency

$$E = \frac{\sum_{i=1}^{j} t_i}{nC_a}$$

Balance Delay

$$1 - \text{efficiency}$$

SOLVED PROBLEMS

1. PROCESS LAYOUT

Mohawk Valley Furniture Warehouse has purchased a retail outlet with six departments. The anticipated number of customers that move between the departments each week is given in the load summary chart.

a. Calculate the nonadjacent loads for the layout shown below.

b. Revise Mohawk's layout such that nonadjacent loads are minimized.

Initial Layout

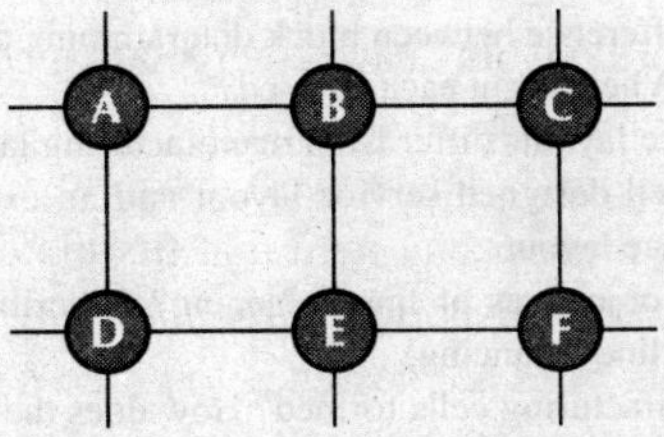

Load Summary Chart

Department	A	B	C	D	E	F
A	—	70				50
B		—			100	
C		70	—			
D			80			
E	40					30
F		60			100	—

SOLUTION

a.

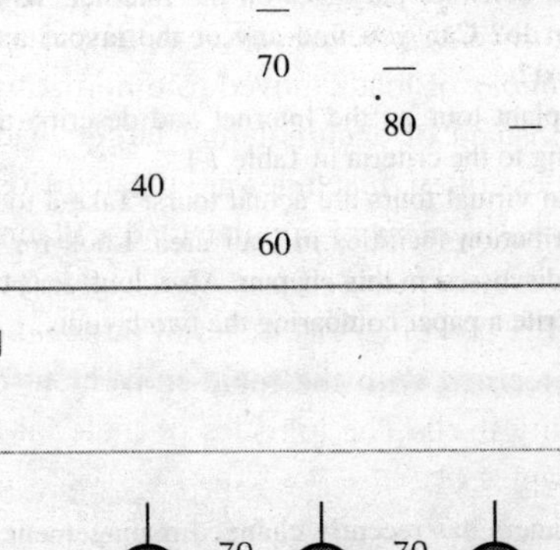

130 Nonadjacent loads

b.

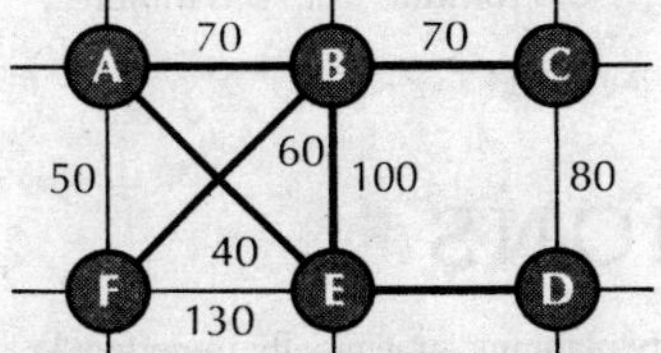

Zero nonadjacent loads

2. PRODUCT LAYOUT

The Basic Block Company needs to produce 4,000 boxes of blocks per 40-hour week to meet upcoming holiday demand. The process of making blocks can be broken down into six work elements. The precedence and time requirements for each element are as follows. Draw and label a precedence diagram for the production process. Set up a balanced assembly line and calculate the efficiency of the line.

Work Element	Precedence	Performance Time (Min)
A	—	0.10
B	A	0.40
C	A	0.50
D	—	0.20
E	C, D	0.60
F	B, E	0.40

SOLUTION

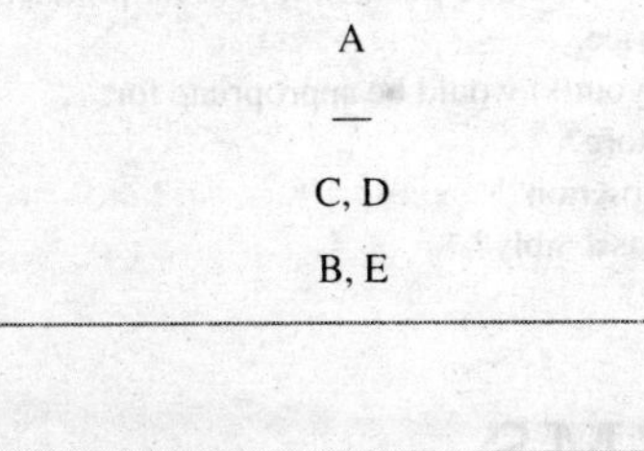

Start at the beginning of the network and group elements into workstations until cycle time has been reached. Do not violate precedence requirements.

$$C_d = \frac{\text{time}}{\text{units}} = \frac{40 \times 60}{4000} = \frac{2400}{4000} = 0.60$$

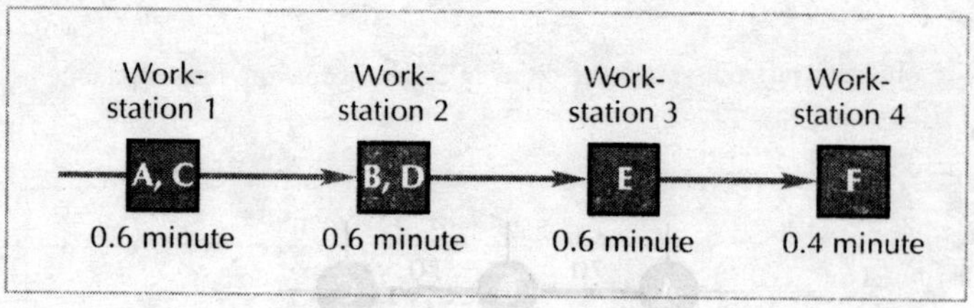

$$\text{Efficiency} = \frac{\sum t}{nC_a} = \frac{0.60 + 0.60 + 0.60 + 0.40}{4(0.60)}$$

$$= \frac{2.2}{2.4} = 91.67\%$$

QUESTIONS

7-1. Why is capacity planning strategically important?

7-2. Describe three strategies for expanding capacity. What are the advantages and disadvantages of incremental versus one-step expansion?

7-3. Explain economies and diseconomies of scale. Give an example of each.

7-4. Explore capacity planning at your university or place of business. How is capacity measured? What factors influence the acquisition and allocation of resources?

7-5. Look around your classroom. Which layout characteristics help the learning process, and which ones hinder it? How does layout affect the manner in which the class is taught?

7-6. Visit a local McDonald's, Burger King, and Taco Bell (or similar establishment). How do their layouts differ? Which appears to be most efficient? Why?

7-7. Does layout make a difference? Think of a time when the layout of a facility impeded a process with which you were involved. Think of a time when a layout made it easier for a process to be completed.

7-8. List five goals of facility layout. Give an example of a facility you know that emphasizes each goal.

7-9. Distinguish between a process and product layout. Give an example of each.

7-10. Give an example of a fixed-position layout for producing a product and providing a service.

7-11. What type of layout(s) would be appropriate for:

a. A grocery store?
b. Home construction?
c. Electronics assembly?
d. A university?

7-12. What are the fixed and variable cost tradeoffs among product, process, and fixed-position layouts? Draw a cost/volume graph to illustrate your answer.

7-13. What is the difference between block diagramming and relationship diagramming? When might each be used?

7-14. How do service layouts differ from manufacturing layouts? Give an example of a well-designed service layout and an example of a poorly designed service layout.

7-15. What are the objectives of line balancing? Describe several heuristic approaches to line balancing.

7-16. How are manufacturing cells formed? How does the role of the worker differ in cellular manufacturing?

7-17. Discuss the advantages and disadvantages of cellular layouts. How does a cellular layout combine a product and process layout?

7-18. Describe a flexible manufacturing system. How does it differ from a cellular layout?

7-19. How do mixed-model assembly lines differ from traditional assembly lines? What additional decisions are required?

7-20. Look for layout software packages on the Internet. What do systems like Proplanner do? Can you find any of the layout approaches discussed in the text?

7-21. Find a virtual plant tour on the Internet and describe the production system according to the criteria in Table 7.1.

7-22. Even better than virtual tours are actual tours. Take a tour of two production or distribution facilities in your area. Look for the basic and hybrid layouts discussed in this chapter. Also, look for bottlenecks and smooth flow. Write a paper comparing the two layouts.

PROBLEMS

7-1. Maureen Marcy is designing the layout for a new business in town, *The Collegiate Spa*. From visiting spas in neighboring towns, she has compiled the following data on movement between spa activities. Help Maureen determine where to locate each activity on a 2 × 3 grid so that nonadjacent moves are minimized.

From / To	1	2	3	4	5	6
1 Relaxation Lounge		50	25		75	
2 Facial	10					75
3 Massage	30			50		50
4 Power Shower						25
5 Mineral Bath		50				50
6 Sauna						

7-2. Spiffy Dry Cleaners has recently changed management, and the new owners want to revise the current layout. The store performs six main services: (1) laundry, (2) dry cleaning, (3) pressing, (4) alterations, (5) delivery, and (6) tuxedo rental. Each is located in a separate department, as shown here. The load summary chart gives the current level of interaction between the departments. Calculate the number of nonadjacent loads for the current layout. Design an alternative layout to minimize the number of nonadjacent loads.

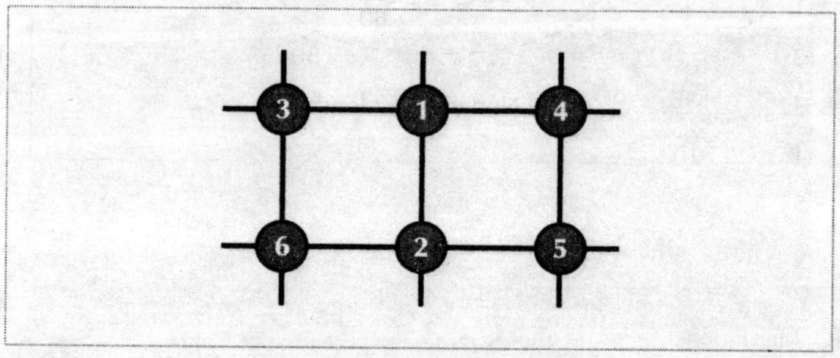

Load Summary Chart

From / To	1	2	3	4	5	6
1	—		125	40		
2		—	45	75		
3			—	20	235	200
4	60	30	10	—	85	50
5					—	10
6			40	30	150	—

7-3. Rent-With-Us Management Inc. has purchased a large housing complex and must decide where to locate its offices and service facilities. The company has learned that locating each service in a different apartment building helps control the behavior of tenants, but it would also like to keep unnecessary transit time to a minimum. Data collected on movements between facilities during a six-month period from a similar apartment complex are shown below. Construct a layout diagram on a 2 × 3 grid that minimizes nonadjacent movement.

Site to Site Travel

From / To	1	2	3	4	5
1 Management	—	20	35	25	20
2 Rent collection	50	—			35
3 Sales	40		—		10
4 Grounds	20			—	40
5 Maintenance	20	10		50	—

7-4. Avalanche, Inc. is a manufacturer of premium snow skis. The work is a combination of precision machining and skilled craftsmanship. Before completion, skis are processed back and forth between six different departments: (1) molding, (2) cutting, (3) fiberglass weaving, (4) gluing, (5) finishing, and (6) waxing. Avalanche is opening a new production facility and wants to lay it out as efficiently as possible. The number of loads of material moved from department to department at existing operations in other plants is shown below. Arrange the department for Avalanche's new plant in a 2 × 3 grid so that nonadjacent loads are minimized.

Load Summary Chart

From / To	1	2	3	4	5	6
1		100	75		100	60
2	10	—		45	60	
3	30		—		85	
4	100	50		—	70	
5	25	70	30	40	—	65
6	65				35	—

7-5. Marillion Hospital is building a satellite clinic in the Cold Harbor area of Richmond. The design committee has collected data on patient movement from similar facilities in hopes of making the new facility more efficient and customer-friendly.

Patient Movements

From / To	1	2	3	4	5	6
1 Intake	—	50	10	25	10	100
2 Exam room		—	30	40	20	20
3 Radiology		40	—	20	60	40
4 Laboratory		10	10	—	10	40
5 Orthopedics		30	20	10	—	30
6 Waiting room	40	60	50	20	50	—

Initial Layout

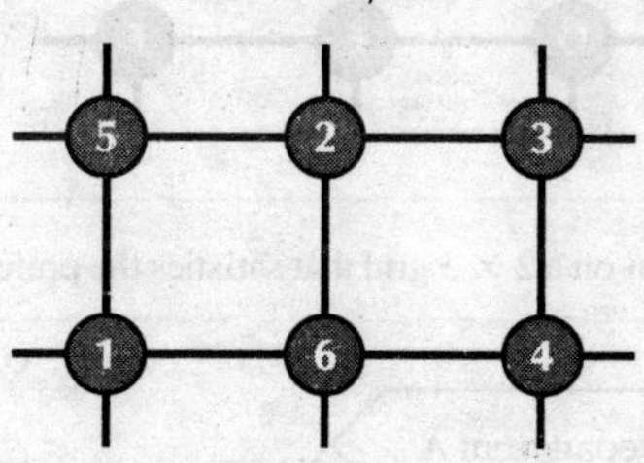

a. Calculate the nonadjacent loads for the initial layout.

b. Which pairwise exchange of departments would most improve the layout?

7-6. Tech Express provides technical assistance to customers through six separate departments. While much of the communication is electronic, it is helpful for departments working together on a customer's request to be physically located near to each other. Given the following data on customer "flow" between departments, design a layout on a 2 × 3 grid that will facilitate the maximum collaboration among departments. How much customer flow is nonadjacent?

Customer Flow

From / To	1	2	3	4	5	6
1	—	50	100	25	60	
2	40	—	80		150	
3	10	70	—	55		
4	10		80	—		
5	40			80	—	30
6		60	50			—

7-7. Flying Flags is opening a new theme park in southern Indiana. The park will have six main attractions: (a) animal kingdom, (b) Broadway shows, (c) carousel and other kiddie rides, (d) daredevil roller coasters, (e) eating places, and (f) flying machines. Data on customer flow patterns from similar parks is shown here, along with the layout for a similar park in

Virginia. Calculate the nonadjacent loads for the Virginia park; then improve the design for the new Indiana location.

From / To	1	2	3	4	5	6
1	—	20	100	10	10	20
2		—	30		50	
3		20	—			
4	50			—	50	300
5	30	50	60	40	—	50
6	10			200	60	—

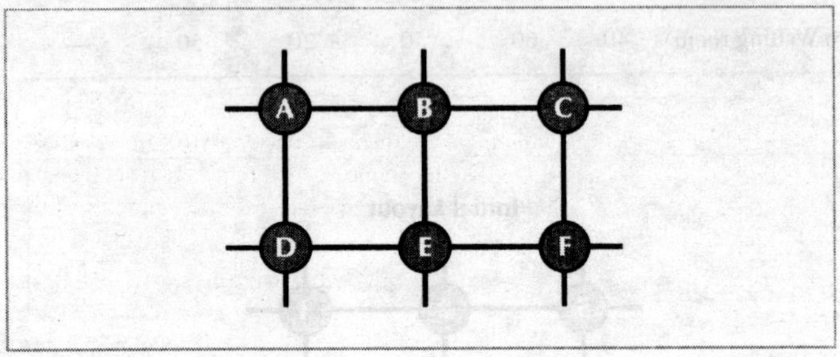

7-8. Design a layout on a 2 × 3 grid that satisfies the preferences listed here.

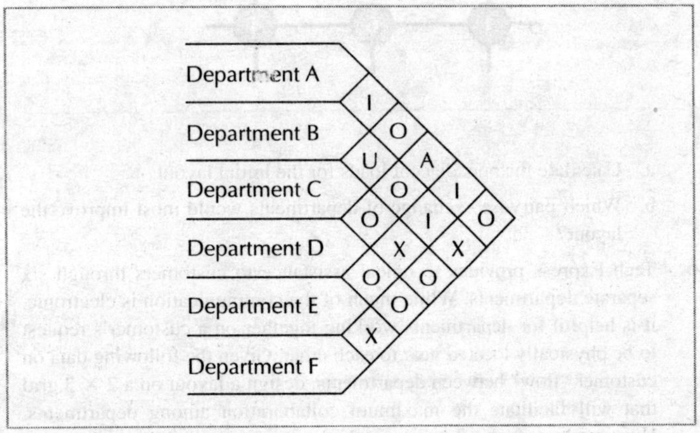

7-9. Design a layout on a 2 × 3 grid that satisfies these preferences.

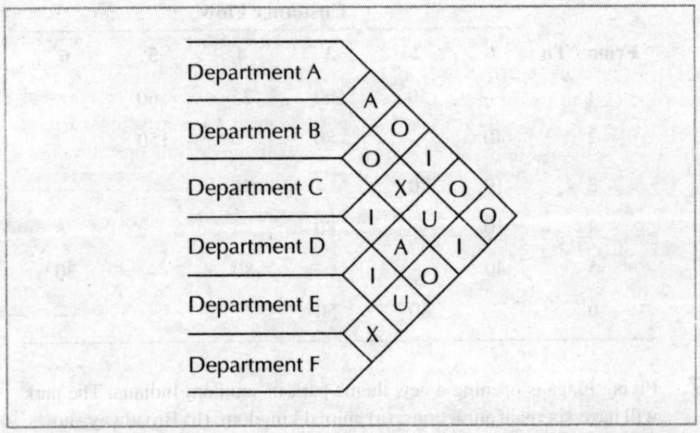

7-10. Best Vision is revamping its assembly lines to improve efficiency. As shown below, there are 10 steps to assembling a television set.

a If Best needs to produce 120 televisions in a 40-hour work week, how should the line be balanced? Given that one worker is assigned to each workstation, how many workers are required to operate the line? What is the efficiency of the line?

b If demand for televisions is reduced to 100 sets per 40-hour week, how many workers will be needed to man the line? Rebalance the line and recalculate its efficiency.

Task	Precedence	Time (min)
A	None	8
B	A	4
C	A	7
D	A	3
E	B	7
F	C, E	11
G	D	2
H	G	8
I	F, H	5
J	I	7

7-11. Professional Image Briefcases is an exclusive producer of handcrafted, stylish cases. The company assembles each case with care and attention to detail. This laborious process requires the completion of the six primary work elements listed here.

Work Element		Precedence	Time (min)
A	Tan leather	—	30
B	Dye leather	A	15
C	Shape case	B	10
D	Mold hinges and fixtures		5
E	Install hinges and fixtures	C, D	10
F	Assemble case	E	10

a. Construct a precedence diagram for the manufacturing of briefcases.
b. Compute the flow time required for assembling one briefcase and the cycle time necessary to assemble 50 cases in a 40-hour week.
c. Balance the line and compute its efficiency.
d. How would you change the line to produce 80 cases per week?

7-12. The TLB Yogurt Company must be able to make 600 party cakes in a 40-hour week. Use the following information to draw and label a precedence diagram, compute cycle time, compute the theoretical minimum number of workstations, balance the assembly line, and calculate its efficiency.

Work Element	Precedence	Performance Time (min)
A	—	1
B	A	2
C	B	2
D	A, E	4
E	—	3
F	C, D	4

7-13. Professor Garcia has assigned 15 cases in his OM Seminar class to be completed in a 15-week semester. The students, of course, are moaning and groaning that the caseload cannot possibly be completed in the time allotted. Professor Garcia sympathetically suggests that the students work in groups and learn to organize their work efficiently. Knowing when a situation is hopeless, the students make a list of the tasks that have to be completed in preparing a case. These tasks are listed here, along with precedence requirements and estimated time in days. Assuming students will work five days a week on this assignment, how many students should be assigned to each group, and what is the most efficient allocation of tasks? Can 15 cases be completed in a semester? Explain your answer.

Element	Description	Precedence	Time (days)
a	Read case	—	1
b	Gather data	a	4
c	Search literature	a	3
d	Load in data	b	1
e	Run computer analysis	d	4
f	Write/type case	c, e	4

7-14. The precedence diagram and task times (in minutes) for assembling McCauley's Mystifier are shown here. Set up an assembly line to produce 125 mystifiers in a 40-hour week. Balance the line and calculate its efficiency.

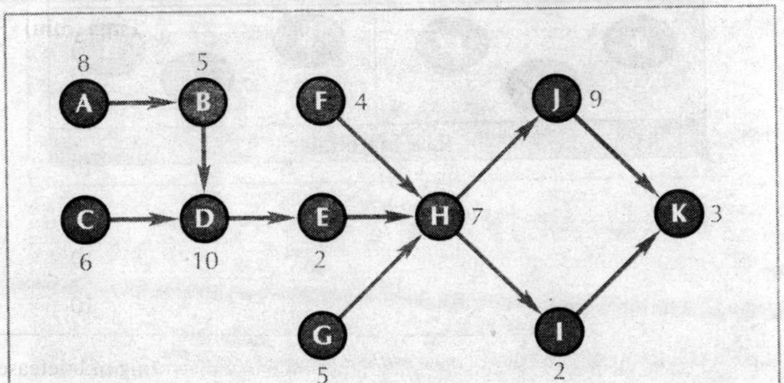

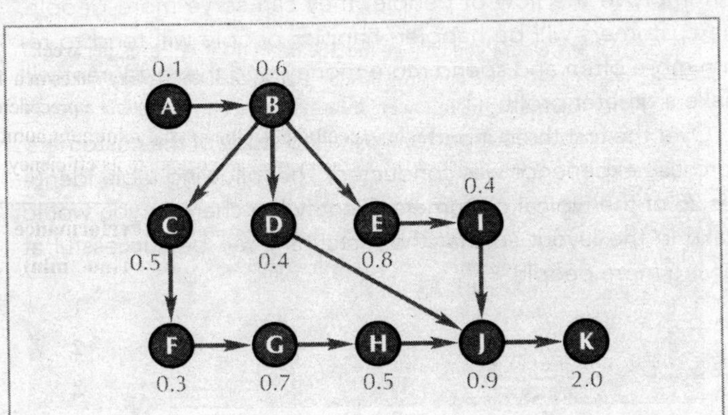

7-15. The Costplus Corporation has set a processing quota of 80 insurance claims per 8-hour day. The claims process consists of five elements, which are detailed in the following table. Costplus has decided to use an assembly-line arrangement to process the forms and would like to make sure they have set up the line in the most efficient fashion. Construct a precedence diagram for the claims process and calculate the cycle time required to meet the processing quota. Balance the assembly line and show your arrangement of workstations. Calculate the line's efficiency. How many claims can actually be processed on your line?

Element	Precedence	Time (min)
A	—	4
B	A	5
C	B	2
D	A	1
E	C, D	3

7-16. Given in the following table are the tasks necessary for the assembly of Fine Cedar Chests, the length of time needed to perform each task, and the operations that must be completed prior to subsequent operations.

Element	Precedence	Time (min)
A	None	2
B	A	4
C	B	5
D	None	5
E	D	3
F	None	1
G	F	2
H	C, E, G	4

a. Calculate the cycle time necessary to complete 300 cedar chests in a 35-hour week.

b. What is the minimum number of workstations that can be used on the assembly line and still reach the production quota? Balance the line and calculate the line's efficiency.

c. Rebalance the line with a cycle time of 9 minutes. How do the number of workstations, output, and line efficiency change?

7-17. Print-for-All is a family-owned print shop that has grown from a three-press two-color operation to a full-service facility capable of performing a range of jobs from simple copying to four-color printing, scanning, binding, and more. The company is moving into a new facility and would like some help arranging its 16 processes into an efficient, yet flexible, layout. A list of the most popular jobs and the processes associated with them is shown in the Print-for-All Process Manual below. Arrange the processes into cells to ensure an efficient *and* flexible operation.

Print-for-All Processes

Jobs	1	2	3	4	5	6	7	8	9	10	11	12	13	14	15	16
A	X	X										X				
B						X		X								
C	X						X							X		
D	X	X					X							X		
E				X		X										

Print-for-All Processes

Jobs	1	2	3	4	5	6	7	8	9	10	11	12	13	14	15	16
F						X		X			X					
G	X	X										X				
H					X					X					X	
I	X	X	X											X		
J						X					X					
K										X					X	X
L				X		X					X			X		
M		X							X			X				
N										X					X	X
O					X					X					X	X
P				X		X					X					
Q								X								

7-18. Jetaway, a small manufacturer of replacement parts for the aircraft industry, had always maintained a simple layout—all like machines were located together. That way the firm could be as flexible as possible in producing small amounts of the variety of parts its customers required. No one questioned the production arrangement until Chris Munnelly started to work for the company. Chris was actually hired to upgrade Jetaway's computer system. In the process of creating a database of part routings, Chris began to see similarities in the parts produced. A part routing matrix for nine of the most popular parts is shown below, along with a schematic of the factory layout.

Chris, who was already tired of being a programmer, decided to reorder the matrix and see what he could find. If he could identify distinct part families, he could reorganize the placement of machines into the cells he had been reading about in his business magazines. Maybe then someone would notice his management potential.

Help Chris gain status in Jetaway by creating a cellular layout for the company. Show your results in a schematic diagram. Be sure to include the reordered routing matrix.

Parts	Machines 1	2	3	4	5	6	7	8	9	10	11	12
A	×			×	×							
B		×	×			×						
C								×			×	
D	×			×	×		×					
E		×	×			×			×			×
F								×		×	×	
G	×				×		×					
H		×	×			×			×			
I								×		×		

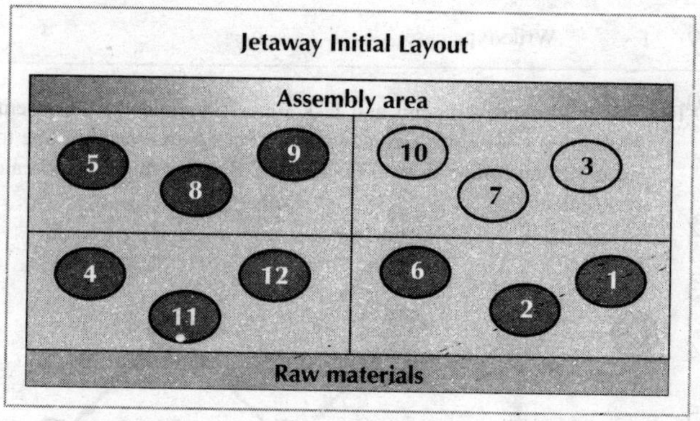

CASE STUDY

People Square Subway Restaurant Flow Optimization

A new fast-food restaurant has opened up in Shanghai's People Square subway station. The subway station is busy 24 hours a day, seven days a week so the fast-food restaurant is a welcome addition and a money-making proposition. The success of the restaurant has resulted in crowds of people trying to figure out what to buy, how to order it, where to pick things up, and where to pay for their purchase. The restaurant manager knows if they can improve the flow of people, they can serve more people, the customers will be happier; happier people will tend to return more often and spend more money, and the restaurant will make a greater profit.

Over the first three months, a detailed study of the customers' purchase experience was conducted. The following table identifies 25 of the typical customers. Identify the changes you would make in the layout so that the restaurant can be successful at serving more people.

Customer	Bakery	Fountain Drinks	Soups	Bottle Drinks	Fresh Fruit	Salads	Sandwiches	Tea or Cookies	Total Time (min)
1	X	X						X	4
2				X			X		1
3			X			X		X	3
4	X	X							3
5			X	X				X	6
6	X	X							9
7			X				X	X	5
8	X						X		5
9		X	X				X		5
10	X	X				X			10
11		X				X		X	7
12		X				X		X	3
13			X	X	X				4
14	X				X			X	5
15								X	9
16		X							3
17	X	X						X	8
18			X			X			7
19	X			X					7
20	X	X	X		X				6
21						X		X	1
22	X	X							1
23	X							X	9
24		X				X			7
25			X			X		X	1

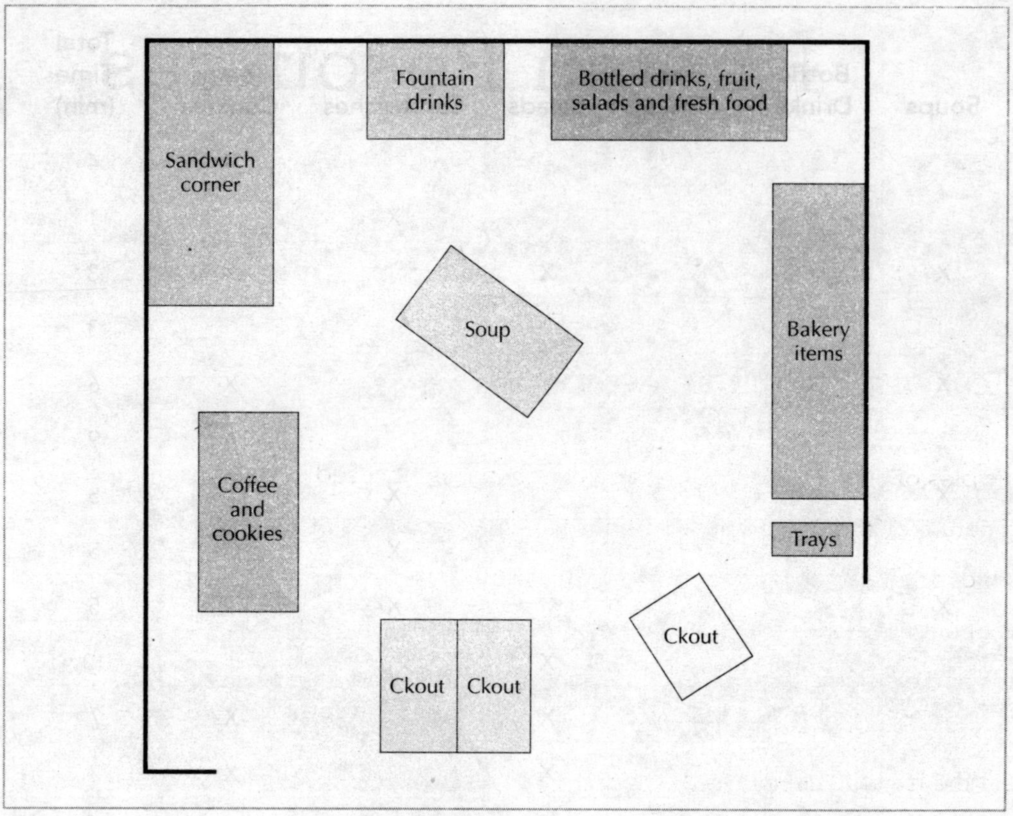

Figure 7.17

People Square Subway Restaurant Facility Layout

REFERENCES

Benjaafar, Saif, Sunderesh Heragu, and Shahrukh Irani. "Next Generation Factory Layouts: Research Challenges and Recent Progress." *Interfaces* (November/December 2002), pp. 58–78.

Black, J. T. *The Design of the Factory with a Future*. New York: McGraw-Hill, 1991.

Flanders, R. E. "Design, Manufacture and Production Control of a Standard Machine." *Transactions of ASME* 46 (1925).

Goetsch, D. *Advanced Manufacturing Technology*. Albany, NY: Delmar, 1990.

Hyer, Nancy, and Urban Wemmerlov. *Reorganizing the Factory: Competing Through Cellular Manufacturing*. Portland, OR: Productivity Press, 2002.

Jablonowski, J. "Reexamining FMSs." *American Machinist*, Special Report 774 (March 1985).

Luggen, W. *Flexible Manufacturing Cells and Systems*. Upper Saddle River, NJ: Prentice Hall, 1991.

Monden, Y. *Toyota Production System*, 3rd ed. Atlanta: IIE Press, 1993.

Muther, R. *Systematic Layout Planning*. Boston: Industrial Education Institute, 1961.

Russell, R. S., P. Y. Huang, and Y. Y. Leu. "A Study of Labor Allocation in Cellular Manufacturing." *Decision Sciences* 22 (3; 1991), pp. 594–611.

Sumichrast, R. T., R. S. Russell, and B. W. Taylor. "A Comparative Analysis of Sequencing Procedures for Mixed-Model Assembly Lines in a Just-In-Time Production System." *International Journal of Production Research* 30 (1; 1992), pp. 199–214.

Towards a New Era in Manufacturing Studies Board. Washington, DC: National Academy Press, 1986.

CHAPTER 8

Human Resources

LEARNING OBJECTIVES

AFTER READING THIS CHAPTER, YOU WILL BE ABLE TO:

- Discuss the basic principles of human resource management in quality-focused companies.
- Discuss the changing nature of and contemporary trends in human resources management.
- Explain different methods of employee compensation.
- Describe the benefits of employee diversity and give examples of diversity initiatives.
- Describe the attributes and elements of a good job design.
- Use various tools to conduct a job analysis.
- Determine and explain the learning curve effect for work improvement.

A GLOBAL COMMITMENT TO HUMAN RESOURCES AT LEVI STRAUSS & COMPANY

In 1991 Levi Strauss & Company was the first global apparel company to establish a workplace code of conduct, called "Terms of Engagement" (TOE), for its manufacturing suppliers. Based on United Nations human rights and labor documents, the TOE defines labor, health and safety, and environmental requirements for Levi Strauss's over 700 global suppliers in 42 countries. In 1999 and 2005, it strengthened protections of the rights of workers to form unions and participate in collective bargaining. In addition to interacting with its suppliers and local communities, Levi Strauss also engages governments at all levels in strengthening and enforcing labor laws. The company has established a strong program to monitor and assess its suppliers to determine how well they are meeting its TOE codes, using full-time factory assessors around the world who understand the company's standards, and who are experts in local languages, laws, cultures, and business environments. Every supplier factory has regular assessments that include on-site and off-site meetings with workers, management interviews, reviews of factory records, and health and safety and environmental inspections. Areas of improvement are identified and corrective action plans developed, and follow-up visits are conducted to ensure that suppliers complete the plans in a timely manner. In 2011, Levi Strauss developed plans to recommit itself to improving the quality of life for workers by going beyond monitoring supplier compliance according to various benchmarks, to directly engage suppliers to develop new factory-level programs that focus on worker and community well-being. This revised approach focuses on UN-inspired goals for economic empowerment, family well-being, equality, education and professional development, and a safe and healthy environment. Levi Strauss understands that in the long run, this commitment to workers around the world will strengthen factories, improve efficiency and productivity, and ultimately create an environment for business success that will increase its bottom line.

Source: The Levi Strauss & Company website at www.levistrauss.com/sustainability.

Employees—the people who work in an organization—are "resources," as important as other company resources, such as natural resources and technology. In fact, it is the one resource that all companies have available to them. A company in Taiwan, Japan, or Denmark may have different and few natural resources, certainly fewer than U.S. companies have, but they all have people. With the same or superior technologies as their competitors, and with good people, foreign companies can compete and thrive. Increasingly, *skilled* human resources are the difference between successfully competing or failing.

The traditional view of employees or labor was not so much as a valuable resource, but as a replaceable part of the productive process that must be closely directed and controlled. The trend toward quality management, more than anything else, changed this perspective. W. E. Deming, the international quality expert, emphasized that good employees who are always improving are the key to successful quality management and a company's ultimate survival. More than half of Deming's 14 points for quality improvement relate to employees. His point is that if a company is to attain its goals for quality improvement and customer service, its employees must be involved and committed. However, to get employees "with the program," the company must regard them and manage them as a valuable resource. Moreover, the company must have a commitment to its employees.

Another thing that has changed the way companies regard employees and work is the shift in the U.S. economy toward the service sector and away from manufacturing. Since services tend to be more people-intensive than capital-intensive, human resources are becoming a more important competitive factor for service companies. Advances in information technologies have also changed the working environment, especially in service companies. Because they rely heavily on information technology and communication, services need employees who are technically skilled and can communicate effectively with customers. They also need flexible employees who can apply these skills to a variety of tasks and who are continuously trained to keep up with rapid advances in information technology.

Increasing technological advances in equipment and machinery have also resulted in manufacturing work that is more technically sophisticated. Employees are required to be better educated, have greater skill levels and technical expertise, and are expected to take on greater responsibility. This work environment is a result of changing technologies and international market conditions, global competition that emphasizes diverse products, and an emphasis on product and service quality.

In this chapter we first discuss employees' role in achieving a company's goals for quality. Next we provide a perspective on how work has developed and changed in the United States and then look at some of the current trends in human resources. We will also discuss some of the traditional aspects of work and job design.

Human Resources and Quality Management

Most successful quality-oriented firms today recognize the importance of their employees when developing a competitive strategy. Quality management is an integral part of most companies' strategic design, and the role of employees is an important aspect of quality management. To change management's traditional control-oriented relationship with employees to one of cooperation, mutual trust, teamwork, and goal orientation necessary in a quality-focused company generally requires a long-term commitment as a key part of a company's strategic plan.

In the traditional management–employee relationship, employees are given precise directions to achieve narrowly defined individual objectives. They are rewarded with merit pay based on individual performance in competition with their coworkers. Often individual excellence is rewarded while other employees look on in envy. In a successful quality management program, employees are given broad latitude in their jobs, they are encouraged to improvise, and they have the power to use their own initiative to correct and prevent problems. Strategic goals are for quality and customer service instead of maximizing profit or minimizing cost, and rewards are based on group achievement. Instead of limited training for specific, narrowly defined jobs, employees are trained in a broad range of skills so they know more about the entire productive process, making them flexible in where they can work.

To manage human resources from this perspective, a company must focus on employees as a key, even central, component in their strategic design. All of the Malcolm Baldrige National Quality Award winners have a pervasive human resource focus. Companies that successfully integrate this kind of "employees first" philosophy into their strategic design share several common characteristics. Employee training and education are recognized as necessary long-term investments. Strategic planning for product and technological innovation is tied to the development of employees' skills, not only to help in the product development process but also to carry out innovations as they come to fruition. Motorola provides employees with 160 hours of training annually to keep up with technological changes and to learn how to understand and compete in newly emerging global markets.

To make sure their strategic design for human resources is working, companies regularly monitor employee satisfaction using surveys and make changes when problems are identified. All Baldrige Quality Award-winning companies conduct annual employee surveys, to assess employee satisfaction and make improvements.

A safe, healthy working environment is a basic necessity to keep employees satisfied. Successful companies provide special services like recreational activities, day care, flexible work hours, cultural events, picnics, and fitness centers. Notice that these are services that treat employees like customers, an acknowledgment that there is a direct and powerful link between employee satisfaction and customer satisfaction.

Strategic goals for quality and customer satisfaction require teamwork and group participation. Quality-oriented companies want all employees to be team members to identify and solve quality-related problems. Team members and individuals are encouraged to make suggestions to improve processes. The motivation for employee suggestions is viewed as that of a concerned family member, not as a complainant or as "sticking one's nose in."

It is important that employees understand what the strategic goals of the company are and that they feel like they can participate in achieving these goals. Employees need to believe they make a difference in order to be committed to goals and have pride in their work. Employee commitment and participation in the strategic plan can be enhanced if employees are involved in the planning process, especially at the local level. As the strategic plan passes down through the organization to the employee level, employees can participate in the development of local plans to achieve overall corporate goals.

The Changing Nature of Human Resource Management

The principles of *scientific management* developed by F. W. Taylor in the 1880s and 1890s dominated operations management during the first part of the twentieth century. Taylor's approach was to break jobs down into their most elemental activities and to simplify job designs so that only limited skills were required to learn a job, thus minimizing the time required for learning. This approach divided the jobs requiring less skill from the work required to set up machinery and maintain it, which required greater skill. In Taylor's system, a **job** is the set of all the tasks performed by a worker and **tasks** are individual activities consisting of *elements*, which encompass several **job motions**, or basic physical movements.

Scientific management broke down a job into its simplest elements and motions, eliminated unnecessary motions, and then divided the tasks among several workers so that each would require only minimal skill. This system enabled companies to hire large numbers of cheap, unskilled laborers, who were basically interchangeable and easily replaced. If a worker was fired or quit, another could easily be placed on the job with virtually no training expense. In this system, the timing of job elements (by stopwatch) enabled management to develop *standard times* for producing one unit of output. Workers were paid according to their total output in a *piece-rate system*. A worker was paid "extra" wages according to the amount he or she exceeded the "standard" daily output. Such a wage system is based on the premise that the single motivating factor for a worker to increase output is monetary reward.

F. W. Taylor's work was not immediately accepted or implemented. This system required high volumes of output to make the large number of workers needed for the expanded number of jobs cost effective. The principles of scientific management and mass production were brought together by Henry Ford and the assembly-line production of automobiles.

THE ASSEMBLY LINE

Between 1908 and 1929, Ford Motor Company created and maintained a mass market for the Model-T automobile, more than 15 million of which were eventually produced. During this period, Ford expanded production output by combining standardized parts and product design, continuous-flow production, and Taylor's scientific management. These elements were encompassed in the assembly-line production process.

On an assembly line, workers no longer moved from place to place to perform tasks, as they had in the factory/shop. Instead they remained at a single workplace, and the work was conveyed to them along the assembly line. Technology had advanced from the general-purpose machinery available at the turn of the century, which required the abilities of a skilled machinist, to highly specialized, semiautomatic machine tools, which required less skill to feed parts into or perform repetitive tasks. Fifteen thousand of these machines were installed at Ford's Highland Park plant. The pace of work was established mechanically by the line and not by the worker or management. The jobs along the line were broken down into highly repetitive, simple tasks.

The assembly line at Ford was enormously successful. The amount of labor time required to assemble a Model-T chassis was reduced from more than 12 hours in 1908 to a little less than 3 hours by 1913. By 1914 the average time for some tasks was as low as 1½ minutes. The basic assembly-line structure and many job designs that existed in 1914 remained virtually unchanged for the next 50 years.

LIMITATIONS OF SCIENTIFIC MANAGEMENT

Scientific management had obvious advantages. It resulted in increased output and lower labor costs. Workers could easily be replaced and trained at low cost, taking advantage of a large pool of cheap unskilled labor shifting from farms to industry. Because of low-cost mass production, the

U.S. standard of living was increased enormously and became the envy of the rest of the world. It also allowed unskilled, uneducated workers to gain employment based almost solely on their willingness to work hard physically at jobs that were mentally undemanding.

Scientific management also proved to have serious disadvantages. Workers frequently became bored and dissatisfied with the numbing repetition of simple job tasks that required little thought, ingenuity, or responsibility. The skill level required in repetitive, specialized tasks is so low that workers do not have the opportunity to prove their worth or abilities for advancement. Repetitive tasks requiring the same monotonous physical motions can result in unnatural physical and mental fatigue.

EMPLOYEE MOTIVATION

Modern psychologists and behaviorists in the 1950s and 1960s eschewed the principles of scientific management, and they developed theories (as summarized in Table 8.1) that proposed that in order to get employees to work productively and efficiently they must be motivated. **Motivation** is a willingness by an employee to work hard to achieve the company's goals because that effort satisfies some employee's need or objective. Thus, employee motivation is a key factor in achieving company goals such as product quality and creating a quality workplace. However, different things motivate employees. Obviously, financial compensation is a major motivating factor, but it is not the only one and may not be the most important. Other factors that motivate employees include self-actualization (such as integrity, responsibility, and naturalness), achievement and accomplishment, recognition, relationships with coworkers and supervisors, the type and degree of work supervision, job interest, trust and responsibility, and the opportunity for growth and advancement.

In general, job performance is a function of motivation combined with ability. Ability depends on education, experience, and training, and its improvement can follow a slow but clearly defined process. On the other hand, motivation can be improved more quickly, but there is no

TABLE 8.1 Evolution of Theories of Employee Motivation

Abraham Maslow's Pyramid of Human Needs ⇨ **Douglas McGregor's Theory X and Theory Y** ⇨ **Frederick Herzberg's Hygiene/Motivation Theories**

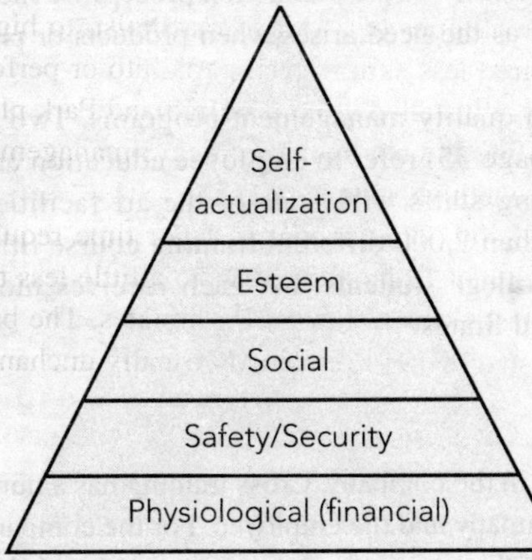

Theory X Employee
- Dislikes work
- Must be coerced
- Shirks responsibility
- Little ambition
- Security top motivator

Theory Y Employee
- Work is natural
- Self-directed
- Controlled
- Accepts responsibility
- Makes good decisions

Hygiene Factors
- Company policies
- Supervision
- Working conditions
- Interpersonal relations
- Salary, status, security

Motivation Factors
- Achievement
- Recognition
- Job interest
- Responsibility
- Growth
- Advancement

clear-cut process for motivating people. However, certain basic elements in job design and management have been shown to improve motivation, including

- positive reinforcement and feedback
- effective organization and discipline
- fair treatment of people
- satisfaction of employee needs
- setting of work-related goals
- design of jobs to fit the employee
- work responsibility
- empowerment
- restructuring of jobs when necessary
- rewards based on company as well as individual performance
- achievement of company goals

Contemporary Trends in Human Resource Management

During the last two decades of the twentieth century the competitive advantage gained by many Japanese companies in international markets, and especially in the automobile industry, caused U.S. firms to reevaluate their management practices vis-à-vis those of the Japanese. Human resource management is one area where there was a striking difference between Japanese and U.S. approaches and results. For example, in the 1980s one Japanese automobile company was able to assemble a car with half the blue-collar labor of a comparable U.S. auto company—about 14 hours in Japan, compared with 25 hours in the United States. Japan had not adopted the traditional Western approaches to work. Instead Japanese work allowed for more individual worker responsibility and less supervision, group work and interaction, higher worker skill levels, and training across a variety of tasks and jobs. There was initially a tendency among Americans to think that these characteristics were unique to the Japanese culture. However, the successes of U.S. companies such as Ford and Motorola in implementing quality-management programs, as well as successful Japanese companies operating in the United States, such as Nissan and Honda, showed that cultural factors were less important than management practices. As a result, certain contemporary trends in human resource management became the norm for successful companies in the United States and abroad.

JOB TRAINING

In companies with a commitment to quality, job training is extensive and varied. Expectations for performance and advancement from both the employee and management tend to be high. Typically, numerous courses are available for training in different jobs and functions. Job training is considered part of a structured career-development system that includes cross training and job rotation. This system of training and job rotation enhances the flexibility of the production process we mentioned earlier. It creates talent reserves that can be used as the need arises when products or processes change or the workforce is reduced.

Training is a major feature of all companies with quality management programs. Two of W. E. Deming's 14 points (See chapter 2, Table 2.2., page 35) refer to employee education and training. Most large companies have extensive training staffs with state-of-the-art facilities. FedEx has a television network that broadcasts more than 2,000 different training course titles to employees. Many UPS employees are part-time college students, but each receives more training than most skilled factory workers in the United States.

CROSS TRAINING

In **cross training** an employee learns more than one job in the company. Cross training has a number of attractive features that make it beneficial to the company and the employee. For the company it provides a safety measure with more job coverage in the event of employee resignations and absenteeism and sudden increases in a particular job activity. Employees are given more knowledge and variety so that they won't get as easily bored, they will find more value in what they do, and their interest level in the company will increase. Because of their increased knowledge, they will have the opportunity to move to other jobs within the company without leaving. Employees will respect each other because they will be more familiar with each other's jobs. However, cross training requires a significant investment in time and money, so the company should be committed to its implementation and sure of the benefits it hopes to realize from cross training.

Job rotation is not exactly the same as cross training. Cross training gives an employee the ability to move between jobs if needed. Job rotation requires cross training, but it also includes the horizontal movement between two or more jobs according to a plan or schedule. This not only creates a flexible employee, but it also reduces boredom and increases employee interest.

JOB ENRICHMENT

The objective of job enrichment is to create more opportunities for individual achievement and recognition by adding variety, responsibility, and accountability to the job. This can also lead to greater worker autonomy, increased task identity, and greater direct contact with other workers. Frederick Herzberg (Table 8.1) developed the following set of principles for job enrichment:

- Allow employees control over their own work and some of the supervisory responsibilities for the job, while retaining accountability, also called **vertical job enlargement**.
- Assign each worker a complete unit of work that includes all the tasks necessary to complete a process or product with clearly defined start and end points so that the employee feels a sense of closure and achievement. This is also called **horizontal job enlargement**.
- Provide additional authority and freedom for employees.
- Make periodic reports available to workers instead of just supervisors.
- Introduce new and more difficult tasks into the job.
- Encourage development of expertise by assigning individuals to specialized tasks.

EMPOWERMENT

Empowerment is giving employees responsibility and authority to make decisions. For quality management programs to work, it is generally conceded that employees must be empowered so that they are willing to innovate and act on their own in an atmosphere of trust and respect. Five of W. E. Deming's 14 points for quality improvement (see page 35) relate to employee empowerment. Empowerment requires employee education and training, and participation in goal setting. The advantages of empowerment include more attention to product quality and the ability to fix quality problems quickly, increased respect and trust among employees, lower absenteeism and higher productivity, more satisfying work, less conflict with management, and fewer middle managers. However, empowerment can also have some negative aspects. Employees may abuse the power given to them; empowerment may provide too much responsibility for some employees; it may create conflicts with middle management; it will require additional training for employees and managers that can be costly; group work, which often is an integral part of empowerment, can be time-consuming; and some employees may not make good decisions.

A Motorola sales representative is empowered to replace a customer's defective product up to six years after its purchase. GM plant employees can call in suppliers to help them solve problems. FedEx employees are empowered to do whatever it takes to ensure 100% customer satisfaction. The authority of employees to halt an entire production operation or line on their own initiative if they discover a quality problem is well documented at companies like AT&T. A Ritz-Carlton "lady or gentleman" can spend up to $2,000 without approval to immediately solve a guest's problem.

TEAMS

Empowerment and employee involvement are often realized through work groups or teams. Quality circles, discussed in Chapter 2, in which a group of 8 to 10 employees plus their supervisor work on problems in their immediate work area, is a well-known example of a team approach.

Teams can differ according to their purpose, level of responsibility, and longevity. Some teams are established to work on a specific problem and then disband; others are more long-term, formed to monitor a work area or process for continual improvement. Most teams are not totally democratic and have some supervisory oversight, although some have more authority than others. Quality circles typically have a supervisor in charge. In general, for teams to be effective, they must know what their purpose and roles are relative to the company's goals, as well as the extent of their empowerment, have the skills and training necessary to achieve their goals, and possess the ability to work together as a team.

Self-directed teams, though not totally independent, are usually empowered to make decisions and changes relative to the processes in their own work area. This degree of responsibility is based on trust and management's belief that the people who are closest to a work process know how to make it work best. Team members tend to feel more responsibility to make their solutions work, and companies typically reward teams for performance improvement.

Self-directed teams generally require more training to work together as a team; however, benefits include less managerial control (and fewer managers), quicker identification and solution of problems, more job satisfaction, positive peer pressure, and a feeling of "not wanting to let the team down" common to sports teams and military groups. On the other hand, such teams can have some negative aspects. Supervisors and managers may have difficulty adjusting to their changed role in which they monitor and oversee rather than direct work. Also, conflict among team members can hinder a team's effectiveness.

FLEXIBLE WORK SCHEDULES

Flexible work schedules or **flextime** are becoming an increasingly important workplace format. It refers to a variety of arrangements in which fixed times of arrival and departure are replaced by a combination of "core" or fixed time and flexible time. Core time is the designated period during which all employees are present, say 9:00 A.M. to 2:30 P.M. Flexible time is part of the daily work schedule where employees can choose their time of arrival and departure. In some cases, an employee may bank or credit hours—that is, work more hours one day and bank those hours in order to take a shorter work day in the future. In other cases, an employee may vary work days during the week, for example, work four 10-hour days followed by a three-day weekend. While flextime helps the company attract and retain employees and promotes job satisfaction, it can make it difficult to compensate for sudden changes in the workload or problems that can arise that require quick reactions.

ALTERNATIVE WORKPLACES AND TELECOMMUTING

An **alternative workplace** is a combination of nontraditional work locations, settings, and practices that supplements or replaces the traditional office. An alternative workplace can be a home office, a satellite office, a shared office, a shared desk or an open workspace where many employees work side by side. Another form of alternative workplace is telecommuting, performing work electronically wherever the worker chooses.

The motivation for companies to create alternative workplaces is primarily financial. Eliminating physical office space—that is, real estate—and reducing related overhead costs can result in significant cost reductions. In one five-year period, IBM realized $1 billion in real estate savings alone by equipping and training 17% of its worldwide workforce to work in alternative workplaces. Alternative workplaces can increase productivity by relieving employees of typical time-consuming office routines, allowing them more time to devote to customers. They can also help companies recruit and retain talented, motivated employees who find the flexibility of telecommuting or a home office very attractive. Eliminating commuting time to a remote office can save employees substantial work time. Customer satisfaction can also increase as customers find it easier to contact employees and receive more personalized attention.

In general, companies that use alternative workplaces employ a mix of different formats and tailor the workplace to fit specific company needs. There are also costs associated with establishing

ALONG THE SUPPLY CHAIN

Creating Sustainable Workplaces

Sustainability, the ability for a company to make a profit without sacrificing the resources of its people, the community, and the planet, is a movement that is gaining momentum throughout the workplace. Moreover, it is increasingly seen as having a positive impact on a business's bottom line, and as a factor in achieving its strategic goals. Widely adopted "green" practices include recycling of office products; energy-efficient equipment such as lighting systems that use occupancy sensors; laptops instead of desktops; automatic shutoffs for equipment; developing green "habits" of turning off lights when leaving a room, and not adjusting thermostats too high or too low; using recycled or refurbished supplies such as toner cartridges and printers; promoting alternative transportation like walking and biking, and public transportation; partnering with environmentally friendly suppliers; minimizing pollution during production processes; and participating in community "green" projects and events. Besides promoting sustainability, most of these activities also result in cost savings.

Telecommuting has become an effective "green" activity since it reduces employee travel, thereby reducing gasoline consumption and reducing carbon emissions. Studies show that the approximately 3 million U.S. employees who telecommute save almost 400 million gallons of gas and prevent the release of 3.6 million tons of greenhouse gases each year. If all 50 million U.S. employees who hold telework-compatible jobs and who want to work at home were allowed to, it would save $900 billion annually and reduce our Persian Gulf imports by over 45%. The energy saved annually would exceed the output of all renewable energy sources combined. Replacing employee travel with videoconferencing reduces airplane fuel consumption and carbon emissions, as well as saving airline travel costs. One telecommunications company, Vodafone, estimated that it eliminated 13,500 employee flights per year, which translates to a 5,500–ton reduction in carbon, by making extensive use of videoconferencing, and the reduction in travel costs paid for the videoconferencing equipment in one year.

Building energy-efficient buildings using solar paneling, radiant heat, and lots of windows saves energy while reducing costs. Going green is also an effective employee recruitment and retention tool for companies. According to various surveys, U.S. employees, especially younger workers, overwhelmingly (i.e., 80% to 90%) prefer to work in a "green" workplace with a company that is environmentally friendly. Companies have discovered that promoting "green" in the workplace creates a sense of achievement and pride among employees that translates to their jobs and operations. Extending quality improvement initiatives beyond just a company's functional processes to the workplace and environment is both good citizenship and good business.

Discuss some reasons a company might not want to participate in sustainable or green activities in the workplace.

Sources: Based on A. Fox, "Get in the Business of Being Green," *HR Magazine* 53, no. 6 (June 2008): pp. 45–50; K. Lister, and T. Harnish, "The State of Telework in the U.S.," *Telework Research Network* (June 2011), www.workshifting.com.

alternative workplace formats, including training, hardware and software, networks, phone charges, technical support, and equipment, although these costs are usually less than real estate costs, which are ever-increasing. Of course, alternative workplaces are not feasible for some companies, such as manufacturing companies, which require employees to be located at specific workstations, facilities, or stationary equipment or which require direct management supervision. Employees who work on an assembly line or in a hotel are not candidates for an alternative workplace. Alternative workplaces are more appropriate for companies that are informational—that is, they operate through voice and data communication between their employees and their customers.

One of the more increasingly common new alternative workplace formats is **telecommuting,** also referred to as "telework," and a "virtual workplace," in which employees work electronically from whatever location they choose, either exclusively or some of the time. It is estimated that about 40% of U.S. companies offer some form of telecommuting to employees. Companies that use telecommuting sites experience such benefits as lower real estate costs, reduced turnover, decreased

ALONG THE SUPPLY CHAIN

Telecommuting at Capital One, Bank of America, and Cisco

Credit card and banking company Capital One Financial Corporation, headquartered in McLean, Virginia, has 32,000 employees and worldwide revenues over $12 billion. It started its Future of Work (FOW) telecommuting program based on surveys that showed that employees who have the flexibility to telecommute are more satisfied in their jobs, are more committed to work, have less stress, work longer hours when they can do so according to their own schedule, and are more productive. In addition, it was discovered that at any one time 40% of employees' seats were vacant and desktops and land-line phones were being wasted. The company equipped its FOW employees with state-of-the-art mobile technology, including laptop computers, a voice-over Internet protocol connection that allowed them to work almost anywhere, and up to $1,000 from their managers to fix up their home offices. The company also reconfigured office space intu an open space design allowing mobile employees (who do not have assigned seats) to work side by side at large tables with hookups for their phones and laptops, but also include quiet zones and "huddle rooms" for small meetings. When employees need to be in "their office," they simply find a seat at a table, plug in, and start working. Virtually every employee said they were more satisfied with their ability to work uninterrupted than in their previous individual office environments, and reconfiguring office space allowed the company to house almost 2,000 employees in an area where 600 people were before; overall the company reduced its real estate costs by 20% Employees entering the FOW program do so voluntarily and receive extensive training to prepare them; employees who prefer a regular desk are referred to as "residents." Surveys of FOW employees show greater productivity, a more creative and stimulating work atmosphere, more workplace satisfaction, and happier, more satisfied employees.

Bank of America has a similar telecommuting program as Capital One, called "My Work." About 15% of its global workforce of over 280,000 people participate, working mostly from home 60% of the time, and using communal areas with mobile workstations when they come in to the company facilities. The company estimates it annually saves $5,500 per enrolled employee and overall $110 million, the largest part in real estate costs.

Cisco Systems, a global manufacturer of network equipment and systems, with over 63,000 employees in 165 countries around the world, estimates that its telecommuting programs have generated annual savings of over $275 million in productivity. On average, a Cisco employee telecommutes two days a week, and 60% of the time saved by an employee telecommuting is spent working. It found in a survey of a sample of employees working in their telecommuting programs around the world that almost 70% said they had higher productivity, 75% said the timeliness of their work improved, 67% said their overall work quality improved, 83% said that their ability to communicate with co-workers was the same, if not better, than working on-site, and 80% cited an improved quality of life with telecommuting.

Discuss some types of jobs that telecommuting and alternative workplaces would not be compatible with.

Sources: A. Pomeroy, "The Future is Now," *HR Magazine*, 52, no. 9 (September 2007): pp. 46–51; Shane Kite, "No Dress Code Required," *American Banker*, (January 1, 2011), at www.americanbanker.com/magazine/; Press Release, "Cisco Study Finds Telecommuting Significantly Increases Employee Productivity, Work-Life Flexibility and Job Satisfaction," *Cisco, The Network* (June 25, 2009), http://newsroom.cisco.com.

absenteeism and leave usage, increased productivity, and increased ability to comply with federal workplace laws such as the Americans with Disabilities Act. At PeopleSoft, telecommuting is the predominant form of work for the whole company. At IBM 40% of its employees telecommute, which has saved an estimated $2.9 billion in real estate costs since 1995. AT&T estimates it saves $550 million annually as a results of telecommunity.

It has been estimated that through telecommuting, absenteeism can be reduced by as much as 25%. For employees, telecommuting eliminates commuting time and travel costs, allows for a more flexible work schedule, and allows them to blend work with family and personal responsibilities.

Companies that offer telecommuting indicate productivity increases 10% to 20% and job satisfaction also increases, which can result in a higher employee retention rate.

Telecommuting also has negative aspects. It may negatively affect the relationship between employees and their immediate supervisors. Supervisors and middle managers may feel uncomfortable not having employees under direct visual surveillance. Furthermore, they may feel that they do not have control and authority over their employees if they are not physically present. In fact, some employees may not be well suited for telecommuting; they may not be self-motivated and may require more direct supervision and external motivation. The technology that allows employees to work anywhere, anytime, can also lead to employees who cannot "disconnect" from their jobs. Studies show that the biggest barrier to telecommuting is management fear and mistrust.

TEMPORARY AND PART-TIME EMPLOYEES

A trend among service companies in particular is the use of temporary, or *contingent*, employees. Part-time employees have accounted for over 40% of job growth in the retail industry during the last two decades. Fast-food and restaurant chains, retail companies, package delivery services, and financial firms tend to use a large number of temporary employees. Companies that have seasonal demand make extensive use of temporary employees. L.L. Bean needs a lot more telephone service operators, and UPS needs many more package sorters, in the weeks before Christmas. Sometimes a company will undertake a project requiring technical expertise its permanent employees do not have. Instead of reassigning or retraining its employees, the company will bring in temporary employees having the necessary expertise. Some firms *lease* people for jobs, especially for computer services. As companies downsize to cut costs, they turn to temporary employees to fill temporary needs without adding to their long-term cost base. People with computer skills able to work from home have also increased the pool of available temporary workers.

Unfortunately, temporary employees do not always have the commitment to goals for quality and service that a company might want. Companies dependent on temporary employees may not only suffer the inconsistent levels of their work ethic and skills, they may also sacrifice productivity for lower costs. To offset this possible inconsistency and to protect product and service quality, firms sometimes try to hire temporary employees only into isolated work areas away from their core businesses that most directly affect quality.

Part-time employment is a key aspect at some companies like UPS, which hires more than 95,000 part-time, seasonal employees; however part-time employment does not always have positive results. As part of a retooling plan at Home Depot, an attempt was made to change the sales floor staff mix from 30% part-time to 50% in order to cut costs and gain flexibility to cover busy times of the day. The plan was abandoned after customers complained about bad service and full-time employees complained about the part-timers' lack of commitment. It also violated the perception among employees that Home Depot was a place where someone could build a career.

Employee Compensation

Good human resource management practices or motivation factors cannot compensate for insufficient monetary rewards. If the reward is perceived as good, other things will motivate employees to give their best performance. Self-motivation can go only so far—it must be reinforced by financial rewards. Merit must be measured and rewarded regularly; otherwise performance levels will not be sustained.

TYPES OF PAY

The two traditional forms of employee payment are the hourly wage and the individual incentive, or piece-rate, wage, both of which are tied to time. The hourly wage is self-explanatory; the longer someone works, the more he or she is paid. In a piece-rate system, employees are paid for the number of units they produce during the workday. The faster the employee performs, the more output generated and the greater the pay. These two forms of payment are also frequently combined with a guaranteed base hourly wage and additional incentive piece-rate payments based on the number of units produced above a standard hourly rate of output. Other basic forms of compensation include straight salary, the most common form of payment for management, and commissions, a payment system usually applied to sales and salespeople.

An individual piece-rate system provides incentive to increase output, but it does not ensure high quality. It can do just the opposite! In an effort to produce as much as possible, the worker will become sloppy, take shortcuts, and pay less attention to detail. As a result, some quality-focused companies have tried to move away from individual wage incentive systems based on output and time. There has been a trend toward other measures of performance, such as quality, productivity, cost reduction, and the achievement of organizational goals. These systems usually combine an hourly base payment or even a salary with some form of incentive payment. However, incentives are not always individual but are tied to group, team, or company performance.

GAINSHARING AND PROFIT SHARING

Gainsharing is an incentive plan that includes employees in a common effort to achieve a company's objectives in which they share in the gains. Although gainsharing systems vary broadly, they all generally include some type of financial measurement and frequent feedback system to monitor company performance and distribute gains periodically in the form of bonuses. **Profit sharing** sets aside some portion of company profits and distributes it among employees, usually at the end of the fiscal year. The objective behind both incentive programs is to create a sense among employees that it is in their self-interest for the company to do well: the company wants employees to buy into the company's financial goals.

Both programs have been shown to result in an increase in employee productivity; however, gainsharing is different from profit sharing in several ways. Gainsharing programs provide frequent payouts or bonuses, sometimes weekly or monthly, while profit-sharing bonuses are awarded once a year. Thus, gainsharing provides a more frequent reinforcement of good performance for the average employee. It is also generally easier for average employees to see results of gainsharing than profit sharing. Gainsharing focuses more on performance measures that are directly linked to the performance of employees or groups of employees than does profit sharing. Gainsharing spells out clearly what employees need to do to achieve a short-term goal and what will happen when they do achieve it. Profit sharing does not have the same emphasis on specifically what needs to happen to achieve short-term (weekly or monthly) goals. For these reasons, profit sharing is typically an incentive program that is more applicable to higher level employees and executives.

Managing Diversity in the Workplace

Diversity in U.S. companies has been a critical management issue for several decades. However, as more and more companies move into the global marketplace, diversity has become an even more pervasive factor in human resource management around the world. The spread of global business combined with the geographic mobility of employees has resulted in companies with a more diverse workforce than ever before. U.S. companies outsource business activities and operate facilities and businesses overseas with a mix of foreign and U.S. management teams and employees, and foreign companies operate plants and businesses in the United States with similar mixes. According to the U.S. Bureau of Labor Statistics, 4 out of every 10 people entering the workforce during the decade from 1998 to 2008 were members of minority groups. In 2005, 14% of the working age population was Hispanic and by 2050 it is projected to be 31%.

In order to be successful with a diverse workforce, companies must provide a climate in which all employees feel comfortable, can do their job, feel like they are valued by the organization, and perceive that they are treated fairly. However, inequalities too often exist for employees

ALONG THE SUPPLY CHAIN

English in the Workplace

In the United States, foreign-born workers make up over 16% of the workforce, and this percentage is predicted to increase as U.S.-born workers decrease and immigration increases. Hispanics currently constitute about 15% of the population, and by 2050 this percentage is expected to double. As a result, there has been a growing diversity of languages in the workplace, and increasingly employers must rely on the non-English-speaking labor force to fill jobs. However, while foreign-born workers can get a job, they typically need English proficiency to advance, and low-wage companies like construction, hotels, and restaurants have discovered that non-English employees can hurt business. As a result, many companies have instituted their own in-house English language training programs as a competitive necessity.

English language programs can have many profitable benefits for employees and employers, including improving compliance with safety policies, boosting worker productivity (by improving comprehension), ensuring employees understand pay and benefits, improving customer service, preventing errors and waste, enhancing communication between workers and managers, and improving recruitment and retention. While some companies invest in their own English training programs, others work out arrangements with teaching institutions. For example, Hyatt Regency in Arlington, Virginia, receives vouchers from the county for employees to attend a 10-week series of evening classes. Marriott International has invested $500 million in portable, computerized recording devices to help Spanish-speaking workers learn English at home. McDonald's has initiated a program with a series of twenty-six 90-minute English classes for restaurant managers that it plans to expand in the future. However, despite the growing recognition of the need for English language training in the workplace, employer-provided training is still the exception, resulting in a number of legal issues for companies that seek to resolve the problem by only hiring workers who speak English. This would seem to be an untenable solution for the long run given the growing non-English-speaking workforce.

Source: Based on R. Zeidner, "One Workforce—Many Languages," *HR Magazine* 54, no. 1 (January 2009): p. 37.

because of race, gender, religion, cultural origin, age, and physical or mental limitations. The elimination of racism, sexism, cultural indifference, and religious intolerance cannot be mandated by higher management or managed by financial incentives. Companies as a whole, starting with top management, must develop a strategic approach to managing diversity in order to meet the challenges posed by a diverse workforce.

AFFIRMATIVE ACTION AND EQUAL OPPORTUNITY

In the United States, affirmative action and equal opportunity are sometimes confused with managing diversity, but they are not the same thing. Affirmative action is an outgrowth of laws and regulations and is government initiated and mandated. It contains goals and timetables designed to increase the level of participation by women and minorities to attain parity levels in a company's workforce. Affirmative action is not directly concerned with increasing company success or increasing profits. On the other hand, managing diversity is the process of creating a work environment in which all employees can contribute to their full potential in order to achieve a company's goals. It is voluntary in nature, not mandated. It seeks to improve internal communications and interpersonal relationships, resolve conflict, and in doing so increase product quality, productivity, and efficiency. Managing diversity is creating an environment where everyone works in concert to do the best job possible. Whereas affirmative action has a short-term result, managing diversity is a long-term process. The objective of managing diversity is to find a way to let everyone do their best so that the company can gain a competitive edge.

Although affirmative action and diversity management are not the same thing, they are not independent of each other. A company that successfully manages diversity and implements successful programs that eliminate diversity issues and discrimination will also eliminate costly affirmative action liability and government mandates.

DIVERSITY MANAGEMENT PROGRAMS

Although there is no magic formula for successfully **managing diversity**, education, awareness, communication, fairness, and commitment are critical elements in the process. We have explained on several occasions that employee training is an essential element in achieving product quality; the same holds true for creating a quality work environment for a diverse workforce. Prejudice feeds on ignorance. Employees must be educated about racial, gender, religious, and ethnic differences; they must be made aware of what it is like to be someone who is different from themselves. This also requires that lines of communication be open between different groups, and between employees and management. Most importantly, successful diversity management requires a commitment from top management. Although top management cannot mandate that the workplace be diversity friendly, strong leadership can successfully influence it.

A survey of *Fortune* 1000 companies conducted by the Society for Human Resource Management and *Fortune* magazine showed that diversity initiatives and programs can have a beneficial effect on company profits and success. Nearly all of the survey respondents (91%) indicated that their company's diversity initiatives helped them to maintain a competitive advantage by improving corporate culture (83%), improving employee morale (79%), decreasing interpersonal conflict among employees (58%), and increasing creativity (59%), and productivity (52%). Seventy-seven percent of the respondents indicated that their diversity initiatives improved employee recruitment, and 52% claimed they improved customer relations.

Many companies have discovered that a diverse workforce is no longer just a legally or culturally mandated requirement, but a beneficial aspect of their corporate culture that can have a bottom-line impact. At Frito-Lay, the snack food division of PepsiCo, the Latino Employee Network (called Adelante) played a major role in the development of Doritos Guacamole Flavored Tortilla Chips. Members of the network provided feedback on taste and packaging that ensured that the new product would be regarded as authentic. This helped make the new Doritos one of the most successful product launches in the company's history, with more than $100 million in sales in its first year. Aetna has discovered that it is critical for their employees to literally speak the language of their customers, making multilingual employees invaluable. Aetna often targets its recruiting efforts to identify individuals who can speak more than one language for specific functional segments in the company. Aetna, like many companies, has also found that diversity can impact community involvement and thus their marketplace. By supporting diversity-related community programs, Aetna enhances its presence and brand reputation in key markets, resulting in more business opportunities.

The most common diversity initiatives and programs are recruiting efforts designed to increase diversity; diversity training; education and awareness programs; and community outreach. However, these initiatives can be time consuming, costly, and sometimes generate false hopes.

One approach being used by a number of companies is to create groups or networks that enable employees with diverse backgrounds to interact with one another. Kodak has a number of diversity groups, including a Women's Forum and a gay-employees network, which collaborate on different workplace issues. Many employees belong to multiple groups and learn about each others' issues and concerns, which helps develop sensitivity and mutual respect. Unisys and AT&T have resource groups for disabled employees that allow them to provide suggestions for designing products to make them more accessible to people with disabilities. Other diversity initiatives that have shown success within companies include internships, mentoring programs, career management programs, and skill enhancement programs.

ALONG THE SUPPLY CHAIN

A Commitment to Diversity at UPS and Hershey's

Diversity affects business at UPS from many perspectives, including serving a diverse customer base of over 8 million customers in over 200 countries every day, working with a diverse supplier network, and maximizing the potential from the varied contributions of its diverse workforce. African-Americans, Hispanics, Asian-Pacific Americans, and other minorities make up 35% of the company's 350,000 employees in the United States. Minorities accounted for half of UPS's new employees in one recent year. Women represent 28% of the U.S. management team and 20% of the overall workforce. Minorities hold nearly 30% of the 63,000 U.S. management positions.

UPS expects every employee to maintain a daily commitment to diversity. UPS has a Diversity Steering Council, co-chaired by the company chairman and CEO and the senior vice president, Human Resources and Public Affairs, whose vision is to ensure that workforce, customer, and supplier diversity remain a visible core value within the company. The UPS Supplier Diversity Program is committed to providing opportunities to minority- and women-owned businesses and it encourages its majority suppliers to do so as well.

UPS has been consistently ranked by *Fortune* magazine each year as one of the "50 Best Companies for Minorities." It has been profiled as a leader in *Hispanic* magazine's annual corporate 100 list. UPS is annually named a "top corporation for Women's Business Enterprises" by the Women's Business Enterprise National Council. UPS received the coveted NAACP "Corporate Citizen of the Year Award." UPS placed third in DiversityInc.com's "Diversity Top 30" poll.

Hershey's is committed to a diverse and all-inclusive workforce. The company provides a variety of opportunities for its employees to learn and grow in the work environment and the community. Hershey's sponsors Diversity Councils and Affinity Groups that provide forums for employees to make and discuss recommendations on increasing productivity and improving the quality of the work environment. These include the Asian Affinity Group, the African American Affinity Group, and the Hispanic Affinity Group, which foster an environment of support, and cultural and personal growth and development, aimed at making Hershey's the employer of choice for these groups. Prism, a resource for gay, lesbian, bisexual, and transgender employees, seeks to improve the quality of the work environment for all of Hershey's employees. The Women's Council promotes and facilitates positive change related to women's issues through networking, work/life programs, and employee education, with a goal of making Hershey's one of the top 100 employers of choice for talented women. The Sales Diversity Council promotes advancements in diversity and inclusion across all levels of the sales organization. Hershey's also holds an annual companywide Inclusion Day celebrating the diversity of local communities.

"Lunch and Learn" speakers discuss such topics as new immigrant experiences to personal empowerment for women and minorities. An in-depth company website provides employees with information about an array of diversity subjects. Diversity email newsletters educate employees on specific aspects of diversity, and educate them about why these differences are important to Hershey's. All of these efforts at Hershey's are aimed at helping the company realize its vision of "Great People Building Great Brands."

Investigate and discuss how your college or university achieves and supports diversity among its employees, including faculty and staff, and whether or not you think it is effective and successful.

Sources: UPS website, http://www.ups.com, and The Hershey Company website at www.thehersheycompany.com.

GLOBAL WORKFORCE DIVERSITY AND SUSTAINABILITY ISSUES

Trends toward the globalization of companies, the use of global teams within and across companies, and global outsourcing have resulted in unique diversity issues. Cultural and language differences and geography are significant barriers to managing a globally diverse workforce. Emails, faxes, the Internet, phones, and air travel make managing a global workforce possible but not necessarily effective.

In the case of culturally diverse groups, differences may be more subtle, and defined diversity programs may be less effective in dealing with them. Some nationalities and cultures have a more relaxed view of time than, say, Americans or Europeans; deadlines are less important. In some cultures, religious and national holidays have more significance than in others. Americans will frequently work at home in the evening, stay late at work, or work over the weekend or on vacations, and on the average take less vacation time than employees in most European countries; in many foreign countries such behavior is unheard of. Some cultures seem to have their own rules of communication. An employee in a foreign country, for example, may politely nod yes in response to a question from a U.S. manager as a polite face-saving gesture, when in fact it's not an indication of agreement at all.

ALONG THE SUPPLY CHAIN

Target's Workplace Sustainability Standards for Its Global Suppliers' Employees

Target, a *Fortune 500* company headquartered in Minneapolis, Minnesota, is one of the largest and most well-known retail chains in the United States with over 1,700 stores in 49 states and over 365,000 employees. For its hard good (nonfabric) products, such as toys, furniture, electronics, sporting goods, and kitchen goods, Target works with over 3,000 factories around the world. When a factory joins the Target supply chain it is required to sign "a standards of supplier engagement" agreement that clearly spells out Target's requirements for employee treatment, which are nonnegotiable, and are the most important part of Target's partnering relationship with its suppliers. These requirements protect the Target brand by ensuring that its products are produced ethically and in accordance with its Standards of Vendor Engagement (SOVE), its Vendor Conduct Guide, and local laws. SOVE explicitly indicates that Target will not work with any company that does not comply with its ethical standards. Target's global business partners must provide safe and healthy workplaces that comply with local laws. If they provide residential facilities for their workers, they must be safe, healthy, and in compliance with local standards. There can be no forced or compulsory labor, no physical or mental punishment against employees, and no child (below age 14) labor.

While Target respects cultural differences, it believes workers should be employed based on their abilities, and suppliers are encouraged to eliminate workplace discrimination based on race, gender, personal characteristics, or beliefs. Suppliers should offer reasonable working hours and overtime, and workweeks should not exceed local laws or business customs. Target encourages its partners not to require more than a 60-hour workweek on a regularly scheduled basis (except for overtime compensated in compliance with local laws). Fair wages and benefits must be provided in compliance with local laws; in addition, partners are encouraged to improve wages and benefits to address the basic needs of workers and their families. Target requires its vendors to warrant that all goods are made in compliance with all applicable laws—both U.S. laws and the laws of the country in which the goods are produced, including the Fair Labor Standards Act of 1938, which governs how employers pay and treat their employees. Target has similar basic minimum requirements in countries where labor laws are not yet well developed. Target's vendor contracts authorize it to conduct unannounced social compliance audits at any time, which factories and suppliers must pass to continue as part of Target's supply chain. Each year Target's auditors conduct approximately 2,200 random, unannounced, mandatory audits at supplier factories in more than 40 countries.

Target has been a leader in creating a "sustainable" work environment for workers within its global supply chain. Identify other companies that have also been proactive in dealing with worker sustainability among their global suppliers.

Sources: Based on William H. Murphy, "Bull's Eye: An Inside Look at How Target Ensures Quality in a Complex Supply Chain," *Quality Progress* (June 2010), pp. 22–29; and the Target website at www.target.com.

Such cultural differences require unique forms of diversity management. Managers cannot interpret their employees' behavior through their own cultural background. It is important to identify critical cultural elements such as important holidays and a culturally acceptable work schedule, and to learn the informal rules of communication that may exist in a foreign culture among a diverse group of employees. It is often helpful to use a third party who is better able to bridge the cultural gap as a go-between. A manager who is culturally aware, and most importantly, speaks the language, is less likely to incorrectly interpret the behavior of diverse employees. Similarly, it is beneficial to teach employees the cultural norms for the organization so that they understand all the rules.

As a result of increased media attention, social networking, and Internet websites related to sustainability and social issues, there is an increased awareness of the plight of workers around the world, whose working conditions and treatment are generally perceived to be below acceptable norms. This has led to demands for major global companies (especially U.S. companies) to take responsibility for the condition of workers of the companies that they do business with in their extended supply chains. A number of high profile, socially conscious companies such as Walmart and Target have developed detailed employee standards with formal documentation, manuals, and audits that their suppliers are required to agree to, or not do business with these companies. These standards address working conditions related to areas such as compliance with local laws and regulations, voluntary labor, working hours, hiring practices, fair compensation, union organization and collective bargaining, health and safety, sanitation, living conditions, environmental laws, and corruption.

Job Design

In the preceding sections we have discussed how to motivate employees to perform well in their jobs. A key element in employee motivation and job performance is to make sure the employee is well suited for a job and vice versa. If a job is not designed properly and it is not a good fit for the employee, then it will not be performed well. Frederick Herzberg identified several attributes of good job design, as follows:

- An appropriate degree of repetitiveness
- An appropriate degree of attention and mental absorption
- Some employee responsibility for decisions and discretion
- Employee control over their own job
- Goals and achievement feedback
- A perceived contribution to a useful product or service
- Opportunities for personal relationships and friendships
- Some influence over the way work is carried out in groups
- Use of skills

In this section we will focus on the factors that must be considered in job design—the things that must be considered to create jobs with the attributes listed above.

THE ELEMENTS OF JOB DESIGN

The elements of job design fall into three categories: an analysis of the tasks included in the job, employee requirements, and the environment in which the job takes place. These categories address the questions of how the job is performed, who does it, and where it is done. Table 8.2 summarizes a selection of individual elements that would generally be considered in the job design process.

TASK ANALYSIS

Task analysis determines how to do each task and how all the tasks fit together to form a job. It includes defining the individual tasks and determining their most efficient sequence, their duration,

TABLE 8.2 Elements of Job Design

Task Analysis	Worker Analysis	Environmental Analysis
• Description of tasks to be performed	• Capability requirements	• Workplace location
• Task sequence	• Performance requirements	• Process location
• Function of tasks	• Evaluation	• Temperature and humidity
• Frequency of tasks	• Skill level	• Lighting
• Criticality of tasks	• Job training	• Ventilation
• Relationship with other jobs/tasks	• Physical requirements	• Safety
• Performance requirements	• Mental stress	• Logistics
• Information requirements	• Boredom	• Space requirements
• Control requirements	• Motivation	• Noise
• Error possibilities	• Number of workers	• Vibration
• Task duration(s)	• Level of responsibility	
• Equipment requirements	• Monitoring level	
	• Quality responsibility	
	• Empowerment level	

their relationship with other tasks, and their frequency. Task analysis should be sufficiently detailed so that it results in a step-by-step procedure for the job. The sequence of tasks in some jobs is a logical ordering; for example, the wedges of material used in making a baseball cap must be cut before they can be sewn together, and they must all be sewn together before the cap bill can be attached. The *performance requirements of a task* can be the time required to complete the task, the accuracy in performing the task to specifications, the output level or productivity yield, or quality performance. The performance of some tasks requires information such as a measurement (cutting furniture pieces), temperature (food processing), weight (filling bags of fertilizer), or a litmus test (for a chemical process).

WORKER ANALYSIS

Worker analysis determines the characteristics the worker must possess to meet the job requirements, the responsibilities the worker will have in the job, and how the worker will be rewarded. Some jobs require manual labor and physical strength, whereas others require none. Physical requirements are assessed not only to make sure the right worker is placed in a job but also to determine if the physical requirements are excessive, necessitating redesign. The same type of design questions must be addressed for mental stress.

ENVIRONMENTAL ANALYSIS

Environmental analysis refers to the physical location of the job in the production or service facility and the environmental conditions that must exist. These conditions include things such as proper temperature, lighting, ventilation, and noise. The production of microchips requires an extremely clean, climatically controlled, enclosed environment. Detail work, such as engraving or sewing, requires proper lighting; some jobs that create dust levels, such as lint in textile operations, require proper ventilation. Some jobs require a large amount of space around the immediate job area.

ERGONOMICS

Put simply, **ergonomics** as it is applied to work is fitting the task to the person. It deals with the interaction of work, technology, and humans. Ergonomics applies human sciences like anatomy, physiology, and psychology to the design of the work environment and jobs, and objects and equipment used in work. The objective of ergonomics is to make the best use of employees' capabilities while maintaining the employees' health and well-being. The job should never limit the employee or compromise an employee's capabilities or physical and mental health because of poor job design. Good ergonomics shortens learning times; makes the job easier with less fatigue; improves equipment maintenance; reduces absenteeism, labor turnover, and job stress and injury; and meets legislative requirements for health and safety. In order to achieve these objectives, the job activity must be carefully analyzed, and the demands placed on the employee must be understood.

The contribution of anatomy in ergonomics is the improvement of the physical aspect of the job: achieving a good physical fit between the employee and the things the employee uses on the job, whether it's a hand tool, a computer, a video camera, a forklift, or a lathe. Physiology is concerned with how the body functions. It addresses the energy required from the employee to do the job as well as the acceptable workload and work rate and the physical working conditions—heat, cold, light, noise, vibration, and space. Psychology is concerned with the human mind. Its objective is to create a good psychological fit between the employee and the job.

TECHNOLOGY AND AUTOMATION

The worker-machine interface is possibly the most crucial aspect of job design, both in manufacturing industries and in service companies where workers interface with computers. New technologies have increased the educational requirements and need for employee training. The development of computer technology and systems has heightened the need for workers with better skills and more job training.

During the 1990s, there was a substantial investment in new plants and equipment in the United States to compete globally. Companies developed and installed a new generation of automated equipment and robotics that enhanced their abilities to achieve higher output and lower costs. This new equipment also reduced the manual labor necessary to perform jobs and improved safety. Computer systems provided workers with an expanded array of information that increased their ability to identify and locate problems in the production process and monitor product quality. New job designs and redesigns of existing jobs were required that reflected these new technologies.

Job Analysis

Part of job design is to study the *methods* used in the work included in the job to see how it should be done. This has traditionally been referred to as *methods analysis*, or simply *work methods*.

Methods analysis is used to redesign or improve existing jobs. An analyst will study an existing job to determine if the work is being done in the most efficient manner possible; if all the present tasks are necessary; or if new tasks should be added. The analyst might also want to see how the job fits in with other jobs—that is, how well a job is integrated into the overall production process or a sequence of jobs. The development and installation of new machinery or equipment,

Figure 8.1

Symbols for a Process Flowchart

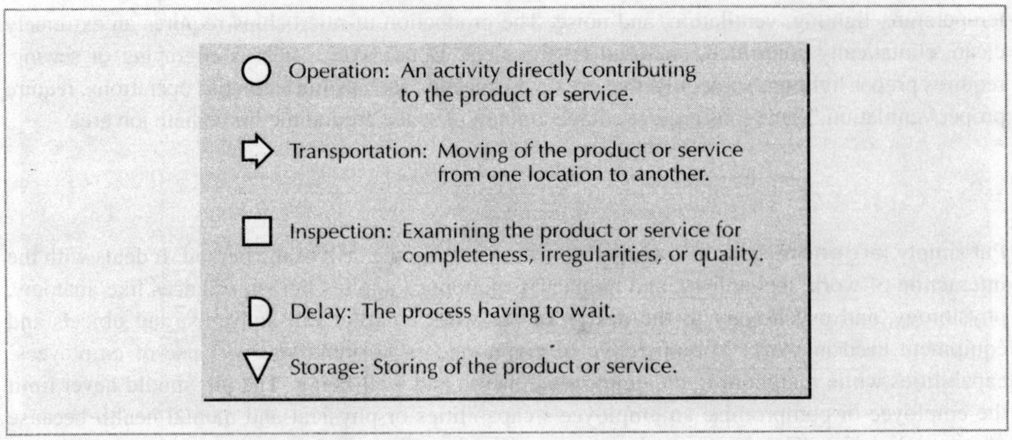

new products or product changes, and changes in quality standards can all require that a job be analyzed for redesign.

Methods analysis is also used to develop new jobs. In this case, the analyst must work with a description or outline of a proposed job and attempt to develop a mental picture of how the job will be performed.

The primary tools of methods analysis are a variety of charts that illustrate in different ways how a job or a work process is done. These charts allow supervisors, managers, and workers to see how a job is accomplished and to get their input and feedback on the design or redesign process. Two of the more popular charts are the *process flowchart* and the *worker-machine chart*.

PROCESS FLOWCHART

A **process flowchart** is used to analyze how the steps of a job or how a set of jobs fit together into the overall flow of the production process. Examples might include the flow of a product through a manufacturing assembly process, the making of a pizza, the activities of a surgical team in an operating room, or the processing of a catalogue mail or telephone order.

A process flowchart uses some basic symbols shown in Figure 8.1 to describe the tasks or steps in a job or a series of jobs. The symbols are connected by lines on the chart to show the flow of the process.

EXAMPLE 8.1

DEVELOPING A JOB PROCESS FLOWCHART

The QuikCopy Store does copying jobs for walk-in customers. When a customer comes in with a copy job, a desk operator fills out a work order (name, number of copies, quality of paper, and so on) and places it in a box. An operator subsequently picks up the job, makes the copies, and returns the completed job to the cashier, where the job transaction is completed. The store would like a job process flowchart that describes this sequence of tasks.

SOLUTION

The process flowchart for the steps in this copying job are shown in Figure 8.2. Although the process encompasses several operators and jobs, it focuses primarily on the tasks of the copy machine operator, who actually makes the copies.

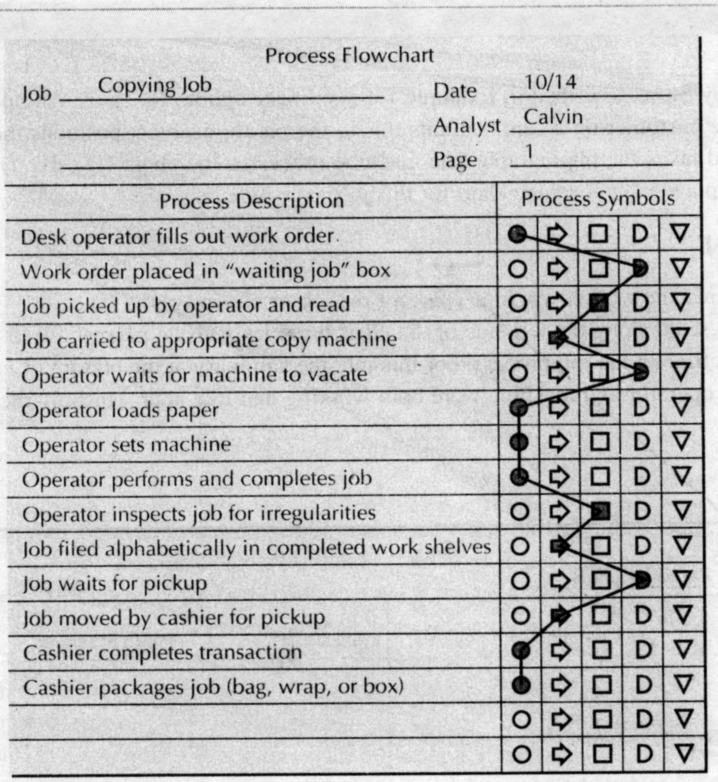

Figure 8.2

Process Flowchart of Copying Job

Often a process flowchart is used in combination with other types of methods analysis charts and a written job description to form a comprehensive and detailed picture of a job. Essentially, the methods analyst is a "job detective," who wants to get as much evidence as possible about a job from as many perspectives as possible in order to improve the job.

WORKER-MACHINE CHART

A **worker-machine chart** illustrates the amount of time a worker and a machine are working or idle in a job. This type of chart is occasionally used in conjunction with a process flowchart when the job process includes equipment or machinery. The worker-machine chart shows if the worker's time and the machine time are being used efficiently—that is, if the worker or machine is idle an excessive amount of time.

Another type of worker-machine chart is the *gang process chart*, which illustrates a job in which a team of workers are interacting with a piece of equipment or a machine. Examples include workers at a coal furnace in a steel mill or a military gunnery team on a battleship. A gang chart is constructed the same way as the chart in Figure 8.3, except there are columns for each of the different operators. The purpose of a gang process chart is to determine if the interaction between the workers is efficient and coordinated.

MOTION STUDY

The most detailed form of job analysis is **motion study**, the study of the individual human motions used in a task. The purpose of motion study is to make sure that a job task does not include

EXAMPLE 8.2

DEVELOPING A WORKER-MACHINE CHART

The QuikCopy Store described in Example 8.1 also makes photo ID cards. An operator types in data about the customer on a card, submits this to the photo machine, positions the customer for the photo, and takes the photograph. The machine processes the photo ID card. The store would like to develop a worker-machine chart for this job.

SOLUTION

Figure 8.3 shows the worker-machine chart for the job of making photo ID cards.

The time scale along the left side of the chart provides a visual perspective of the amount of work and idle time in the job process. For this job, the summary at the bottom of Figure 8.3 indicates that the operator and machine were both working and idle approximately the same amount of time.

Figure 8.3
Worker-Machine Chart

Worker–Machine Chart

Job Photo-ID Cards Date 10/14

Time (min)	Operator	Time (min)	Photo Machine
1–2	*Key in customer data on card*	*2.6*	*Idle*
3	*Feed data card in*	*0.4*	*Accept card*
	Position customer for photo	*1.0*	*Idle*
4	*Take picture*	*0.6*	*Begin photo process*
5–7	*Idle*	*3.4*	*Photo/card processed*
8–9	*Inspect card and trim edges*	*1.2*	*Idle*
10			

Summary

	Operator Time	%	Photo Machine Time	%
Work	*5.8*	*63*	*4.8*	*52*
Idle	*3.4*	*37*	*4.4*	*48*
Total	*9.2 min*	*100%*	*9.2 min*	*100%*

any unnecessary motion by the worker and to select the sequence of motions that ensure that the task is being performed in the most efficient way.

Motion study originated with Frank Gilbreth, a colleague of F. W. Taylor's at the beginning of the twentieth century. F.W. Taylor's approach to the study of work methods was to select the best worker among a group of workers and use that worker's methods as the standard by which other workers were trained. Alternatively, Gilbreth studied many workers and from among them picked the best way to perform each activity. Then he combined these elements to form the "one best way" to perform a task.

Gilbreth and his wife Lillian used movies to study individual work motions in slow motion and frame by frame, called *micromotion analysis*. Using motion pictures, the Gilbreths carefully categorized the basic physical elements of motion used in work.

The Gilbreths' research eventually evolved into a set of widely adopted *principles of motion study*, which companies have used as guidelines for the efficient design of work. These principles are categorized according to the efficient use of the *human body*, the efficient arrangement of the *workplace*, and the efficient use of *equipment and machinery*. The principles of motion study include about 25 rules for conserving motion. These rules can be grouped in the three categories shown in Table 8.3.

Motion study and scientific management complemented each other. Motion study was effective for designing the repetitive, simplified, assembly-line-type jobs characteristic of manufacturing operations. Frank Gilbreth's first subject was a bricklayer; through his study of this worker's motions, he was able to improve the bricklayer's productivity threefold. However, in Gilbreth's day, bricklayers were paid on the basis of how many bricks they could lay in an hour in a piece-rate wage system. Who would be able to find a bricklayer today paid according to such a system!

TABLE 8.3 Summary of General Guidelines for Motion Study

Efficient Use of the Human Body
• Work should be simplified, rhythmic, and symmetric.
• Hand/arm motions should be coordinated and simultaneous.
• The full extent of physical capabilities should be employed; all parts of the body should perform; the hand should never be idle.
• Energy should be conserved by letting machines perform tasks when possible, minimizing the distance of movements, and physical momentum should be in favor of the worker.
• Tasks should be simple, requiring minimal eye contact and minimal muscular effort, with no unnecessary motions, delays, or idleness.
Efficient Arrangement of the Workplace
• All tools, materials, and equipment should have a designated, easily accessible location that minimizes the motions required to get them.
• Seating and the general work environment should be comfortable and healthy.
Efficient Use of Equipment
• Equipment and mechanized tools enhance worker abilities.
• The use of foot-operated mechanized equipment that relieves the hand/arms of work should be maximized.
• Equipment should be constructed and arranged to fit worker use.

There has been a movement away from task specialization and simple, repetitive jobs in lieu of greater job responsibility and a broader range of tasks, which has reduced the use of motion study. Nevertheless, motion study is still employed for repetitive jobs, especially in service industries, such as postal workers in mailrooms, who process and route thousands of pieces of mail.

The Gilbreths, together with F. W. Taylor and Henry Gantt, are considered pioneers in operations management. The Gilbreths' use of motion pictures is still popular today. Computer-generated images are used to analyze an athlete's movements to enhance performance, and video cameras are widely used to study everything from surgical procedures in the operating room to telephone operators.

Learning Curves

A learning curve, or *improvement curve*, is a graph that reflects the fact that as workers repeat their tasks, they will improve performance. The learning curve effect was introduced in 1936 in an article in the *Journal of Aeronautical Sciences* by T. P. Wright, who described how the direct labor cost for producing airplanes decreased as the number of planes produced increased. This observation and the rate of improvement were found to be strikingly consistent across a number of airplane manufacturers. The premise of the learning curve is that improvement occurs because workers learn how to do a job better as they produce more and more units. However, it is generally recognized that other production-related factors also improve performance over time, such as methods analysis and improvement, job redesign, retooling, and worker motivation.

Figure 8.4 illustrates the general relationship defined by the learning curve; as the number of cumulative units produced increases, the labor time per unit decreases. Specifically, the learning curve reflects the fact that each time the number of units produced doubles, the processing time per unit decreases by a constant percentage.

The decrease in processing time per unit as production doubles will normally range from 10 to 20%. The convention is to describe a learning curve in terms of 1, or 100%, minus the percentage rate of improvement. For example, an 80% learning curve describes an improvement rate of 20% each time production doubles, a 90% learning curve indicates a 10% improvement rate, and so forth.

Figure 8.4
Learning Curve

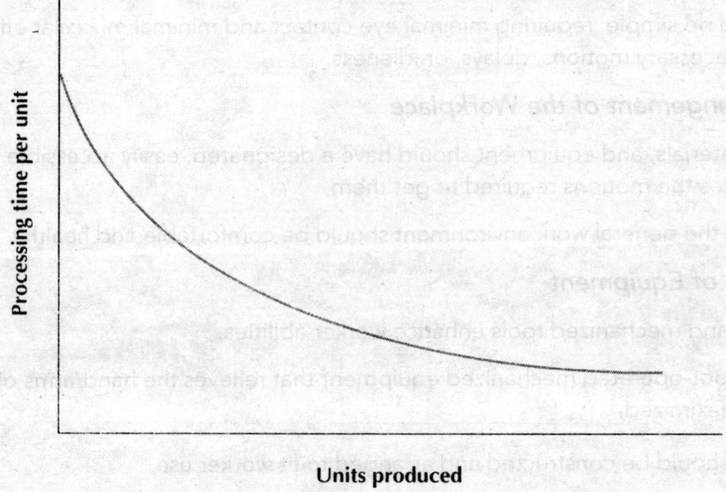

The learning curve in Figure 8.4 is similar to an exponential distribution. The corresponding learning curve formula for computing the time required for the nth unit produced is

$$t_n = t_1 n^b$$

where

t_n = the time required for the nth unit produced

t_1 = time required for the first unit produced

n = the cumulative number of units produced

b = ln r/ln 2, where r is the learning curve percentage (decimal coefficient)

Learning curves are useful for measuring work improvement for nonrepetitive, complex jobs requiring a long time to complete, such as building airplanes. For short, repetitive, and routine jobs, there may be little relative improvement, and it may occur in a brief time span during the first (of many) job repetitions. For that reason, learning curves can have limited use for mass production and assembly-line-type jobs. A learning curve for this type of operation sometimes achieves any improvement early in the process and then flattens out and shows virtually no improvement, as reflected in Figure 8.5.

Learning curves help managers project labor and budgeting requirements in order to develop production scheduling plans. Knowing how many production labor hours will be required over time can enable managers to determine the number of workers to hire. Also, knowing how many labor hours will eventually be required for a product can help managers make overall product cost estimates to use in bidding for jobs and later for determining the product selling price. However, product or other changes during the production process can negate the learning curve effect.

Although learning curves can be applied to many different businesses, its impact is most pronounced in businesses and industries that include complex, repetitive operations where the work pace is determined mostly by people, not machines. Examples of industries where the learning curve is used extensively include aerospace, electronics, shipbuilding, construction, and defense. The learning curve in the aerospace and shipbuilding industries is estimated to be 85%, while it is estimated to be 90% to 95% in the electronics industry. NASA, for example, uses the learning curve to estimate costs of space shuttle production and the times to complete tasks in space.

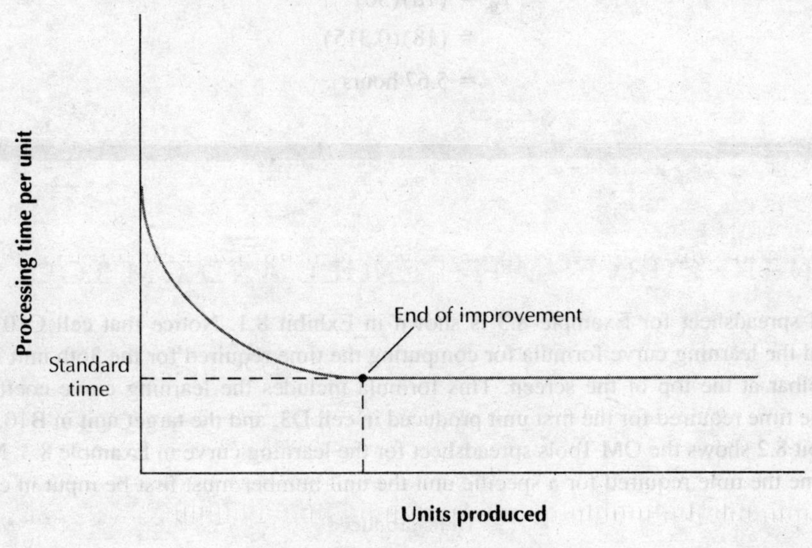

Figure 8.5

Learning Curve for Mass Production Job

EXAMPLE 8.3

DETERMINING THE LEARNING CURVE EFFECT

Paulette Taylor and Maureen Becker, two undergraduates at State University, produce customized personal computer systems at night in their apartment (hence the name of their enterprise, PM Computer Services). They shop around and purchase cheap components and then put together generic personal computers with customized features, for faculty, students, and local businesses. Each time they get an order, it takes them a while to assemble the first unit, but they learn as they go, and they reduce the assembly time as they produce more units. They have recently received their biggest order to date from the statistics department at State for 36 customized personal computers. It is near the end of the university's fiscal year, and the computers are needed quickly to charge them on this year's budget. Paulette and Maureen assembled the first unit as a trial and found that it took them 18 hours of direct labor. To determine if they can fill the order in the time allotted, they want to apply the learning curve effect to determine how much time the 9th, 18th, and 36th units will require to assemble. Based on past experience, they believe their learning curve is 80%.

SOLUTION

The time required for the 9th unit is computed using the learning curve formula:

$$t_n = t_1 n^b$$

$$t_9 = (18)(9)^{\ln(0.8)/\ln 2}$$

$$= (18)(9)^{-0.322} = 18/(9)^{0.322}$$

$$= (18)(0.493)$$

$$= 8.874 \text{ hours}$$

The times required for the 18th and 36th units are computed similarly:

$$t_{18} = (18)(18)^{\ln(0.8)/\ln 2}$$

$$= (18)(0.394)$$

$$= 7.092 \text{ hours}$$

and

$$t_{36} = (18)(36)^{\ln(0.8)/\ln 2}$$

$$= (18)(0.315)$$

$$= 5.67 \text{ hours}$$

LEARNING CURVES WITH EXCEL AND OM TOOLS

The Excel spreadsheet for Example 8.3 is shown in Exhibit 8.1. Notice that cell C10 is highlighted and the learning curve formula for computing the time required for the 36th unit is shown on the toolbar at the top of the screen. This formula includes the learning curve coefficient in cell D4, the time required for the first unit produced in cell D3, and the target unit in B10.

Exhibit 8.2 shows the OM Tools spreadsheet for the learning curve in Example 8.3. Note that to determine the time required for a specific unit the unit number must first be input in cells B11 to B13.

EXCEL FILE

EXHIBIT 8.1

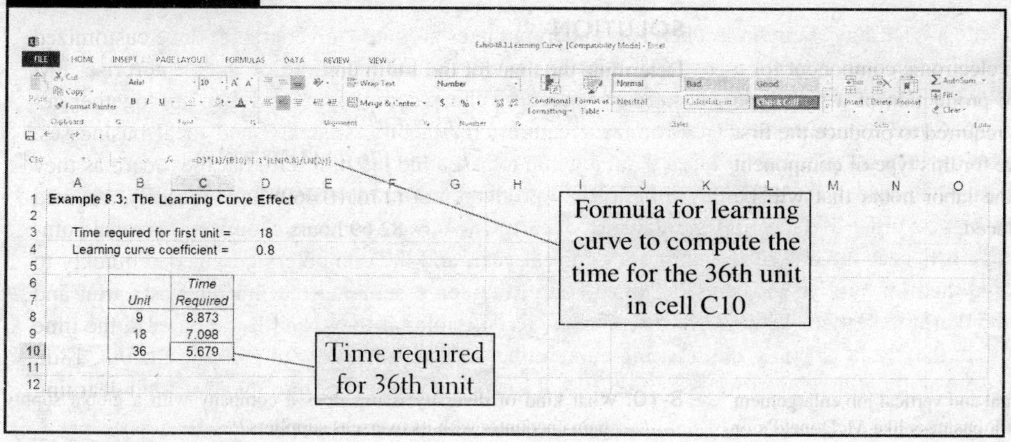

OM TOOLS

EXHIBIT 8.2

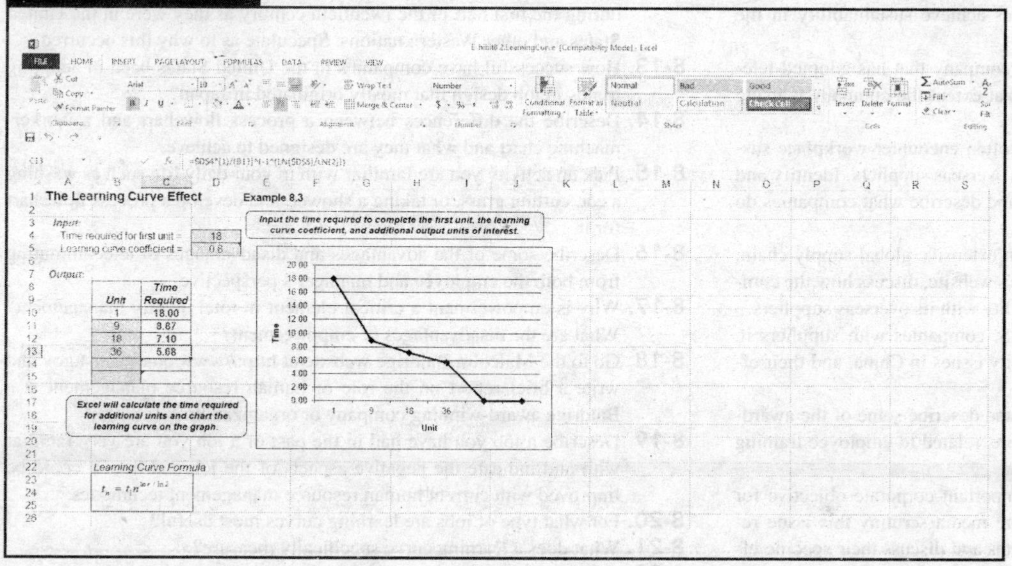

SUMMARY

As with many other areas in production and operations management, the quality movement and increased international competition have had a dramatic impact on human resources. Traditional approaches to work in the United States that once focused on task specialization, simplification, and repetition are being supplanted by approaches that promote higher job skill levels, broader task responsibility, more worker involvement, and, most importantly, worker responsibility for quality. A number of U.S. manufacturing and service firms have attempted to adopt new approaches to human resource management.

KEY FORMULAS

Learning Curve Formula

$$t_n = t_1 n^{\ln r/\ln 2}$$

SOLVED PROBLEMS

1. LEARNING CURVE

A military contractor is manufacturing an electronic component for a weapons system. It is estimated from the production of a prototype unit that 176 hours of direct labor will be required to produce the first unit. The industrial standard learning curve for this type of component is 90%. The contractor wants to know the labor hours that will be required for the 144th (and last) unit produced.

SOLUTION

Determine the time for the 144th unit.

$$t_n = t_1 n^b$$
$$t_{144} = (176)(144)^{\ln(0.9)/\ln 2}$$
$$= (176)(0.4698)$$
$$= 82.69 \text{ hours}$$

QUESTIONS

8-1. Explain the difference between horizontal and vertical job enlargement and how these concepts might work at a business like McDonald's or Starbucks.

8-2. How did the development of the assembly-line production process at Ford Motor Company popularize the scientific management approach to job design?

8-3. What are some of the ways companies achieve sustainability in the workplace?

8-4. Using the Internet, identify a specific company that has adopted telecommuting and discuss how and to what extent the company is using telecommuting and its impact.

8-5. Companies with global supply chains often encounter workplace sustainability issues and problems with its overseas suppliers. Identify and discuss some of these possible issues and describe what companies do to resolve them.

8-6. Identify a specific company that has an extensive global supply chain, and using the Internet and the company's website, discuss how the company is achieving workplace sustainability with its overseas suppliers.

8-7. Discuss the specific problems that U.S. companies with suppliers in China have with workplace sustainability issues in China, and their efforts to overcome these problems.

8-8. Research the Baldrige Award website and describe some of the award-winning companies initiatives and efforts related to employee training and education.

8-9. Workplace diversity has become an important corporate objective for many companies, partly because of the media scrutiny this issue receives. Research three company websites and discuss their specific efforts in achieving and sustaining diversity.

8-10. What kind of diversity issues does a company with a global supply chain encounter with its overseas suppliers?

8-11. What role do you think social media and the Internet have had in raising the public's consciousness about workplace issues both in the United States and abroad?

8-12. The principles of scientific management were not adopted in Japan during the first half of the twentieth century as they were in the United States and other Western nations. Speculate as to why this occurred.

8-13. How successful have companies in the United States been in adapting trends in job design that mostly originated in Japan?

8-14. Describe the differences between a process flowchart and a worker-machine chart and what they are designed to achieve.

8-15. Pick an activity you are familiar with in your daily life such as washing a car, cutting grass, or taking a shower, and develop a process flowchart for it.

8-16. Describe some of the advantages and disadvantages of telecommuting from both the employee and manager's perspective.

8-17. Why is empowerment a critical element in total quality management? What are the disadvantages of empowerment?

8-18. Go to the Malcolm Baldrige website at http://www.quality.nist.gov and write a brief report on the role of human resource management at a Baldrige award-winning company or organization.

8-19. Describe a job you have had in the past or a job you are very familiar with and indicate the negative aspects of the job and how it could be improved with current human resource management techniques.

8-20. For what type of jobs are learning curves most useful?

8-21. What does a learning curve specifically measure?

8-22. Discuss some of the uses and limitations of learning curves.

PROBLEMS

8-1. Nite-Site, Inc., manufactures image intensification devices used in products such as night-vision goggles and aviator's night-vision imaging systems. The primary customer for these products is the U.S. military. The military requires that learning curves be employed in the bid process for awarding military contracts. The company is planning to make a bid for 120 image intensifiers to be used in a military vehicle. The company estimates the first unit will require 80 hours of direct labor to produce. The industry learning curve for this particular type of product is 92%. Determine how many hours will be required to produce the 60th and 120th units.

8-2. Jericho Vehicles manufactures special-purpose all-terrain vehicles primarily for the military and government agencies in the United States and for foreign governments. The company is planning to bid on a new all-terrain vehicle specially equipped for desert military action. The company has experienced an 87% learning curve in the past for producing similar vehicles. Based on a prototype model, it estimates the first vehicle produced will require 1,600 hours of direct labor. The order is for 60 all-terrain vehicles. Determine the time that will be required for the 30th and 60th units.

8-3. PM Computer Services (described in Example 8.3) has received an order for 120 custom configured personal computers for a local business. Paulette and Maureen have so many orders that they can no longer perform the work themselves, and they must hire extra labor to assemble the units for this new order. They have hired eight students from the university to work part-time, 20 hours per week, to assemble the computers. Paulette and Maureen assembled a prototype unit and it required 26 hours of direct labor; from experience they know their computer assembly operation has an 84% learning curve. Approximately when will PM Computer Services be able to deliver the completed order?

8-4. The housekeeping staff at the five-star Ritz Hotel has a specific, detailed list of activities for cleaning an occupied room. Each activity is completed whether or not it looks like it is necessary. When the hotel hires a new housekeeper, it takes that employee about 55 minutes to clean a room the first time. The learning curve for this job is 92%, and the average minimum time for an experienced housekeeper to clean a room is 32 minutes. How many rooms will a newly hired housekeeper have to clean before it can be done in 32 minutes? If a housekeeper has an eight-hour work day with 1.5 hours off for lunch and breaks, how many work days will be required before the housekeeper is fully proficient and able to clean a room in the minimum average time?

8-5. Prior to the invention of the printing press in the mid-1400s, the process of producing fine books, called illuminated manuscripts, was strictly manual and performed by skilled craftsmen. A scribe would copy the manuscript in ornate handwriting (or calligraphy) from an original text called an exemplar, and artists decorated (or illuminated) the books with pictures. It is estimated that an apprentice scribe could initially copy approximately 50 lines per day. This roughly translates to about 15 minutes per line for a scribe just starting out. A scribe was generally thought to have completed his apprenticeship and was considered a craftsman after completing eight books where each book consisted of about 17,000 lines. (After eight books a scribe would show little additional improvement in accurate copying speed.) Assuming a learning curve of 91%, how long would it take for an experienced scribe to copy a line, and how many lines could he copy in a day?

8-6. Dale Computer Company accepts orders from customers for computers online through its website and configures and builds them to order at one of its distribution centers from components it orders from its various suppliers in the United States and overseas. It is continually retaining new suppliers as its computer models change and as new computing technologies are developed. It promises its customers that when an order is placed the customer will receive it quickly, typically within a week, which in turn requires that Dale's suppliers provide component parts as quickly as they are demanded. Normally Dale sets a target of three days for a supplier to deliver parts once they are ordered, and Dale uses SPC charts (see chapter 3) to monitor a supplier's delivery performance once this target value has been achieved. Dale has learned from past experiences working with many suppliers that it takes some time for new suppliers to improve their production and delivery processes to consistently meet Dale's target delivery time. It normally takes a supplier about 15 days to deliver Dale's first order. Determine approximately how many orders it will take a new supplier that has a 70% learning curve to be able to meet Dale's orders within the specified target time.

CASE STUDY

Entering the Global Market during a Recession

The world economic crash of 2008/9 created financial issues for many companies around the world. Japan, as the second largest world economy after the US, had its share of challenges and risks associated with the 1989 collapse of the Tokyo Stock Market Exchange and then the world recession of 2008/9.

Osaka Computer LLC is justifiably cautious about entering new markets but detailed global market analysis indicates that it has an opportunity to successfully expand its business by offering a new parallel-processing, technology-intensive, research-focused computer. Osaka Computer LLC has developed a prototype that preliminary market analysis indicates would be readily accepted in the research community.

The Osaka Computer LLC fabrication facility built two prototype units as a means to develop the costs of building this technologically advanced system. It understands that each computer must function 100% of the time when the equipment leaves the fabrication facility. The targeted research community is a close-knit organization that spreads informal information quickly through its ranks. Osaka Computer LLC cannot afford to have negative press within this close-knit group.

Based on historical records, the normal learning curve is 93%. Osaka Computer LLC also sees that once the fabricators have assembled 60 units, virtually all subsequent assemblies will require the same amount of time. The two prototype units required 89 minutes to assemble and complete the initial tests.

How long will it take to assemble a unit from the 60th unit on? What else should Osaka Computer LLC take into consideration, from a human resources perspective, for this potential opportunity?

REFERENCES

Barnes, R. M. *Motion and Time Study: Design and Measurement of Work*, 8th ed. New York: Wiley, 1980.

Belkaoui, A. *The Learning Curve*. Westport, CT: Quorum Books, 1986.

Emerson, H. P., and D. C. E. Maehring. *Origins of Industrial Engineering*. Atlanta: Institute of Industrial Engineers, 1988.

Evans, J. R., and W. M. Lindsay. *The Management and Control of Quality*, 3rd ed. St. Paul, MN: West, 1996.

Gilbreth, F. *Motion Study*. New York: Van Nostrand, 1911.

Herzberg, F. "One More Time: How Do You Motivate Employees?" *Harvard Business Review* 81 (1; January 2003), pp. 87–96.

Knights, D., H. Willmott, and D. Collinson, eds. *Job Redesign: Critical Perspectives on the Labor Process*. Hants, England: Gower, 1985.

Taylor, F. W. *The Principles of Scientific Management*. New York: Harper, 1911.

Wood, S., ed. *The Transformation of Work*. London: Unwin Hyman, 1989.

CHAPTER 9

Managing Projects

LEARNING OBJECTIVES

AFTER READING THIS CHAPTER, YOU WILL BE ABLE TO:

- Discuss the project planning process, including planning tools, evaluation methods, and key elements.
- Discuss the benefits of and strategies for dealing with diverse project groups.
- Explain the basics of project scheduling and the use of Gantt charts.
- Define enterprise project management and discuss the key elements in project control.
- Develop and analyze both deterministic probabilistic and project networks.
- Use Microsoft Project for network analysis.
- Determine and explain project crashing and time-cost tradeoffs.

PROJECTS TO ACHIEVE SUSTAINABILITY IN DENIM JEANS PRODUCTION

Sustainability is currently one of the most popular areas for project development and management among companies in the denim jeans industry. There are significant opportunities to engage in projects aimed at achieving sustainability goals throughout the denim jeans supply chain from cotton growers to denim jeans customers, and beyond. Cotton growers have undertaken projects to reduce water consumption for irrigation, use beneficial insects instead of chemical insecticides to control pests, improve farming practices to reduce the amount of chemicals used to grow cotton, and use farmland more productively to reduce the land area required to meet world cotton demand.

Textile production consumes over 2.5% of the world's total water use. Environmentally conscious denim companies have engaged in projects to conserve water and reduce water pollution among its global denim suppliers. Levi Strauss, the first denim jeans company to establish global water-quality guidelines for its suppliers, has undertaken a number of sustainability projects aimed at water conservation and reducing water pollution, including projects encouraging customers to reduce water usage in cleaning their jeans, which accounts for almost 50% of the water used during the life cycle of a pair of jeans. Gap, Inc., has embarked on projects to reduce energy consumption and greenhouse gas emissions in its U.S. operations. It has developed a program that requires companies in its global supply chain that launder its denim in the finishing process to properly treat wastewater before it's discharged into the environment. At the end of the denim jeans supply chain, one of the most unique sustainability projects has been the recycling of old jeans into a green, clean, and effective insulation product. Recycled denim insulation can be used anywhere fiberglass insulation is used, but unlike fiberglass, denim does not end up in landfills, and since it's free of irritants, it doesn't require handlers to wear protective clothing. "Green" building and construction projects increasingly include recycled denim insulation.

In this chapter we will learn how companies plan, manage, control, and schedule projects, including project management tools like CPM/PERT.

Sources: The Levi Strauss & Company website at www.levistrauss.com/sustainability; and, the Gap, Inc. website at www.gapinc.com.

In other chapters we discuss the scheduling of repetitive operations and **activities**, such as work scheduling and job scheduling, as an important aspect of managing an operation. Operational schedules are established to keep the flow of products or services through the supply chain on time. However, not all operational activities are repetitive; some are unique, occurring only once within a specified time frame. Such unique, one-time activities are referred to as **projects**.

Project management is the management of the work to develop and implement an innovation or change in an existing operation. It encompasses planning the project and controlling the project activities, subject to resource and budget constraints, to keep the project on schedule. Examples of projects include constructing facilities and buildings, such as houses, factories, a shopping mall, an athletic stadium, or an arena; developing a military weapons system, new aircraft, or new ship; launching a satellite system; constructing an oil pipeline, developing and implementing a new computer system; planning a rock concert, football bowl game, or basketball tournament; and introducing new products into the market.

Projects have become increasingly pervasive in companies in recent years. The nature of the global business environment is such that new machinery and equipment, as well as new production processes and computer support systems, are constantly evolving. This provides the capability of developing new products and services, which generates consumer demand for even greater product diversity. As a result, a larger proportion of total organizational effort now goes toward project-oriented activities than in the past. Thus, the planning and management of projects has taken on a more crucial role in operations management.

In this chapter we focus on project management using CPM and PERT network scheduling techniques that are popular because they provide a graph or visual representation of the interrelationship and sequence of individual project activities. However, before presenting the CPM/PERT technique, we will discuss the primary elements of the project management process—planning, scheduling, and control.

Project Planning

The general management process is concerned with the planning, organization, and control of an ongoing process or activity such as the production of a product or delivery of a service. Project management is different in that it requires a commitment of resources and people to an important undertaking that is not repetitive and involves a relatively short period of time, after which the management effort is dissolved. A project has a unique purpose, it is temporary, and it draws resources from various areas in the organization; as a result, it is subject to more uncertainty than the normal management process. Thus, the features and characteristics of the project management process tend to be unique.

Figure 9.1 provides an overview of the project management process, which encompasses three other major processes—planning, scheduling, and control. It also includes a number of the more prominent elements of these processes. In the remainder of this section, we will discuss some features of the project planning process, and in the following few sections we will discuss the scheduling and control processes.

ELEMENTS OF A PROJECT PLAN

Project plans generally include the following basic elements:

- *Objectives*—a detailed statement of what the project is to accomplish and how it will achieve the company's goals and meet the strategic plan; and an estimate of when it needs to be completed, the cost and the return.
- *Project scope*—a discussion of how to approach the project, the technological and resource feasibility, the major tasks involved, and a preliminary schedule; includes a justification of the project and what constitutes project success.
- *Contract requirements*—a general structure of managerial, reporting, and performance responsibilities, including a detailed list of staff, suppliers, subcontractors, managerial requirements and agreements, reporting requirements, and a projected organizational structure.
- *Schedules*—a list of all major events, tasks, and subschedules, from which a master schedule is developed.
- *Resources*—the overall project budget for all resource requirements and procedures for budgetry control.
- *Personnel*—identification and recruitment of personnel required for the project team, including special skills and training.
- *Control*—procedures for monitoring and evaluating progress and performance, including schedules and cost.
- *Risk and problem analysis*—anticipating and assessing uncertainties, problems and potential difficulties that might increase the risk of project delays and/or failure and threaten project success.

PROJECT RETURN

In order for a project to be selected to be undertaken it typically has to have some kind of positive gain or benefit for the organization that is considering it. In a business, one of the most popular measures of benefit is return on investment (ROI). ROI is a performance measure that is often used to evaluate the expected outcome of a project or to compare a number of different projects. To calculate ROI, the benefit (return) of a project is divided by the cost of the project; the result is expressed as a percentage or a ratio:

$$\text{ROI} = \frac{(\text{Gain from project} - \text{cost of project})}{\text{Cost of project}}$$

If a project does not have a positive ROI, or if there are other projects with a higher ROI, then the project might not be undertaken. ROI is a very popular metric for project planning because of its versatility and simplicity.

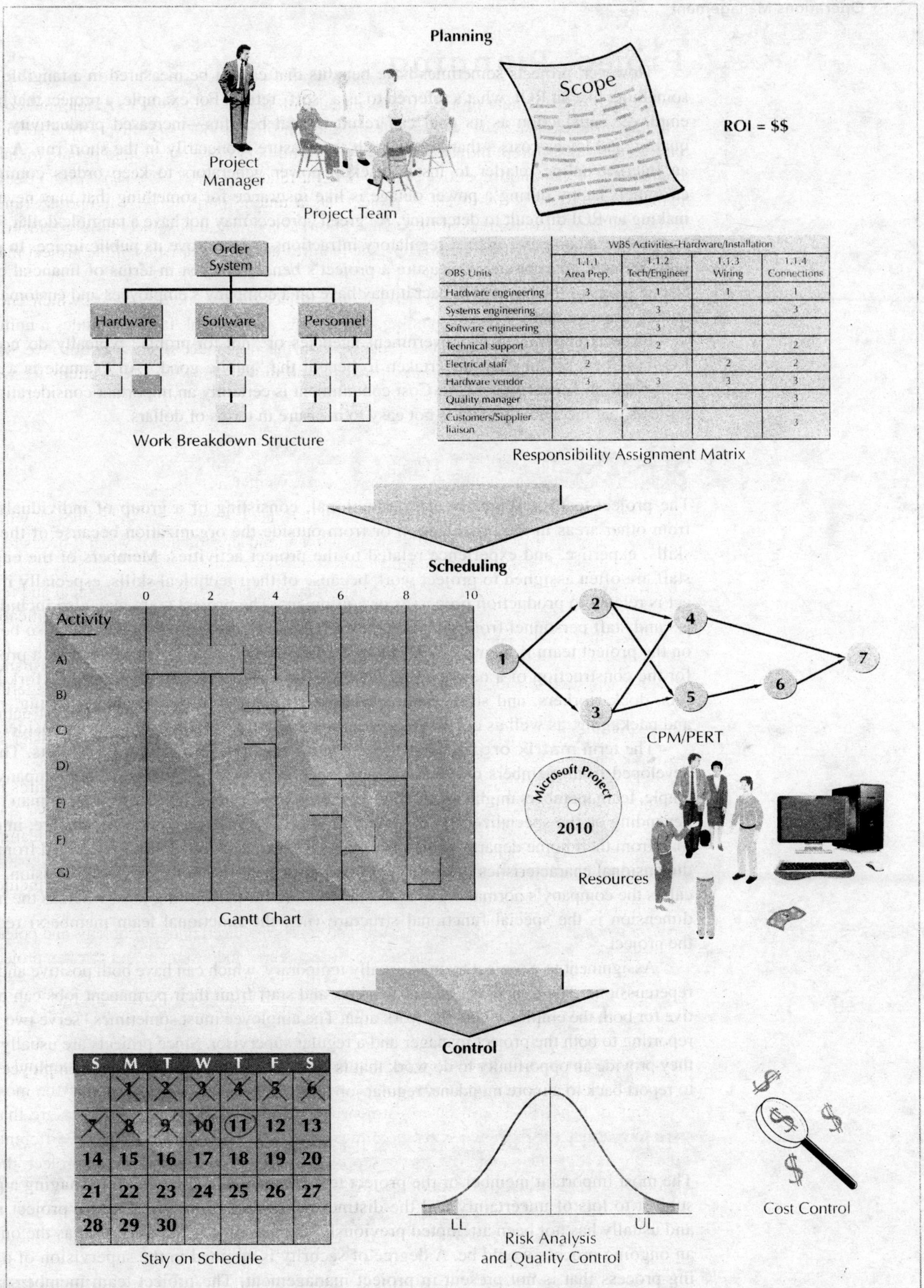

Figure 9.1

The Project Management Process

However, projects sometimes have benefits that cannot be measured in a tangible way with something like an ROI, what's referred to as a "soft" return. For example, a project that has raising employee satisfaction as its goal can result in real benefits—increased productivity, improved quality, and lower costs—that are difficult to measure monetarily in the short run. A project by an Internet online retailer to install backup power generators to keep orders coming in and customers happy during a power outage is like insurance for something that may never happen, making an ROI difficult to determine. A "green" project may not have a tangible dollar ROI, but it can protect a company against regulatory infractions and improve its public image. In general, it may be more appropriate to measure a project's benefit not just in terms of financial return, but also in terms of the positive impact it may have on a company's employees and customers, that is, quality improvement.

Projects undertaken by government agencies or "not-for-profits" typically do not have an ROI-type benefit; they are undertaken to benefit the "public good." An example is a project to fight AIDS in Africa (page 273). Cost containment is certainly an important consideration in such projects, but the actual benefit is not easy to measure in terms of dollars.

THE PROJECT TEAM

The project team is typically cross-functional, consisting of a group of individuals selected from other areas in the organization or from outside the organization because of their special skills, expertise, and experience related to the project activities. Members of the engineering staff are often assigned to project work because of their technical skills, especially if the project is related to production processes or equipment. The project team may also include managers and staff personnel from specific areas related to the project. Workers can also be involved on the project team if their job is a function of the project activity. For example, a project team for the construction of a new loading dock facility might include truck drivers, forklift operators, dock workers, and staff personnel and managers from purchasing, shipping, receiving, and packaging, as well as engineers to assess vehicle flow, routes, and space considerations.

The term **matrix organization** refers to a team approach to special projects. The team is developed from members of different functional areas or departments in the company. For example, team members might come from engineering, production, marketing, or human resources, depending on the specialized skills required by the project. The team members are, in effect, on loan from their home departments to work on a project. The term *matrix* is derived from the two-dimensional characteristics of this type of organizational structure. On one dimension, the vertical, is the company's normal organizational structure for performing jobs, whereas the horizontal dimension is the special functional structure (i.e., the functional team members) required by the project.

Assignment to a project team is usually temporary, which can have both positive and negative repercussions. The temporary loss of workers and staff from their permanent jobs can be disruptive for both the employee and the work area. The employee must sometimes "serve two masters," reporting to both the project manager and a regular supervisor. Since projects are usually exciting, they provide an opportunity to do work that is new and innovative, making the employee reluctant to report back to a more mundane, regular job after the project is completed.

THE PROJECT MANAGER

The most important member of the project team is the *project manager*. Managing a project is subject to lots of uncertainty and the distinct possibility of failure. Since a project is unique and usually has not been attempted previously, the outcome is not as certain as the outcome of an ongoing process would be. A degree of security is attained in the supervision of a continuing process that is not present in project management. The project team members are often from diverse areas of the organization and possess different skills, which must be coordinated into a single, focused effort to complete the project successfully. The project is subject to time

ALONG THE SUPPLY CHAIN

A Project to Fight AIDS in Swaziland

Swaziland in southern Africa has the highest rate of HIV infection in the world; the HIV rate is 42% among pregnant women, which passes the virus from mother to baby. In 2004, the Elizabeth Glaser Pediatric AIDS Foundation started an $8.5 million project, as part of a larger program in 19 African countries, to help prevent mother-to-baby transmission of the virus. Without intervention, approximately 40% of babies born to HIV-positive women can be infected during pregnancy, labor, and delivery or breastfeeding. A single dose of the drug nevirapine to mother and child can cut this rate in half, and a therapy program with a combination of drugs to stop HIV progression can reduce the rate to less than 2%. The project scope included expansion of the number of hospitals and clinics providing prevention services, and helping the government integrate comprehensive and sustainable HIV care and treatment into its health services. In addition to drug administration, the prevention program required a complex series of procedures including HIV testing and counseling, which required trained staff. The project team, working with the Swaziland Ministry of Health and with funding (and oversight) from the U.S. Agency for International Development, completed the project in 2010. The HIV mother-to-child prevention program was extended to 60 healthcare facilities, with the potential to reach over 85% of pregnant women in Swaziland, preventing more than 60% of infant HIV infections and benefiting 90,000 HIV-positive pregnant women.

Using the Internet, identify other disease-related projects.

Source: Based on Susie Ma, "Gift of Life," *PM Network* 25 (7); (July 2011), pp. 34–41.

and budgetary constraints that are not the same as normal work schedules and resource consumption in an ongoing process. There is usually more perceived and real pressure associated with project management than in a normal management position. However, there are potential opportunities, including demonstrating management abilities in a difficult situation, the challenge of working on a unique project, and the excitement of doing something new.

SCOPE STATEMENT

The **scope statement** is a document that provides a common understanding of a project. It includes a justification for the project that describes which factors created a need within the company for the project. It also includes an indication of what the expected results of the project will be and what will constitute project success. The scope statement might also include a list of the types of planning reports and documents that are part of the project management process.

A similar planning document is the **statement of work**. In a large project, the statement of work is often prepared for individual team members, groups, departments, subcontractors, and suppliers. This statement describes the work in sufficient detail so that the team members responsible for it know what is required and whether they have sufficient resources to accomplish the work successfully and on time. For suppliers and subcontractors it is often the basis for determining whether they can perform the work and for bidding on it. Some companies require that a statement of work be part of an official contract with a supplier or subcontractor.

WORK BREAKDOWN STRUCTURE

The **work breakdown structure (WBS)** is a tool used for project planning. The WBS organizes the work to be done on a project. In a WBS, a project is broken down into its major components, referred to as modules. These components are then subdivided into detailed subcomponents, which are further broken down into activities and, finally, individual tasks. The

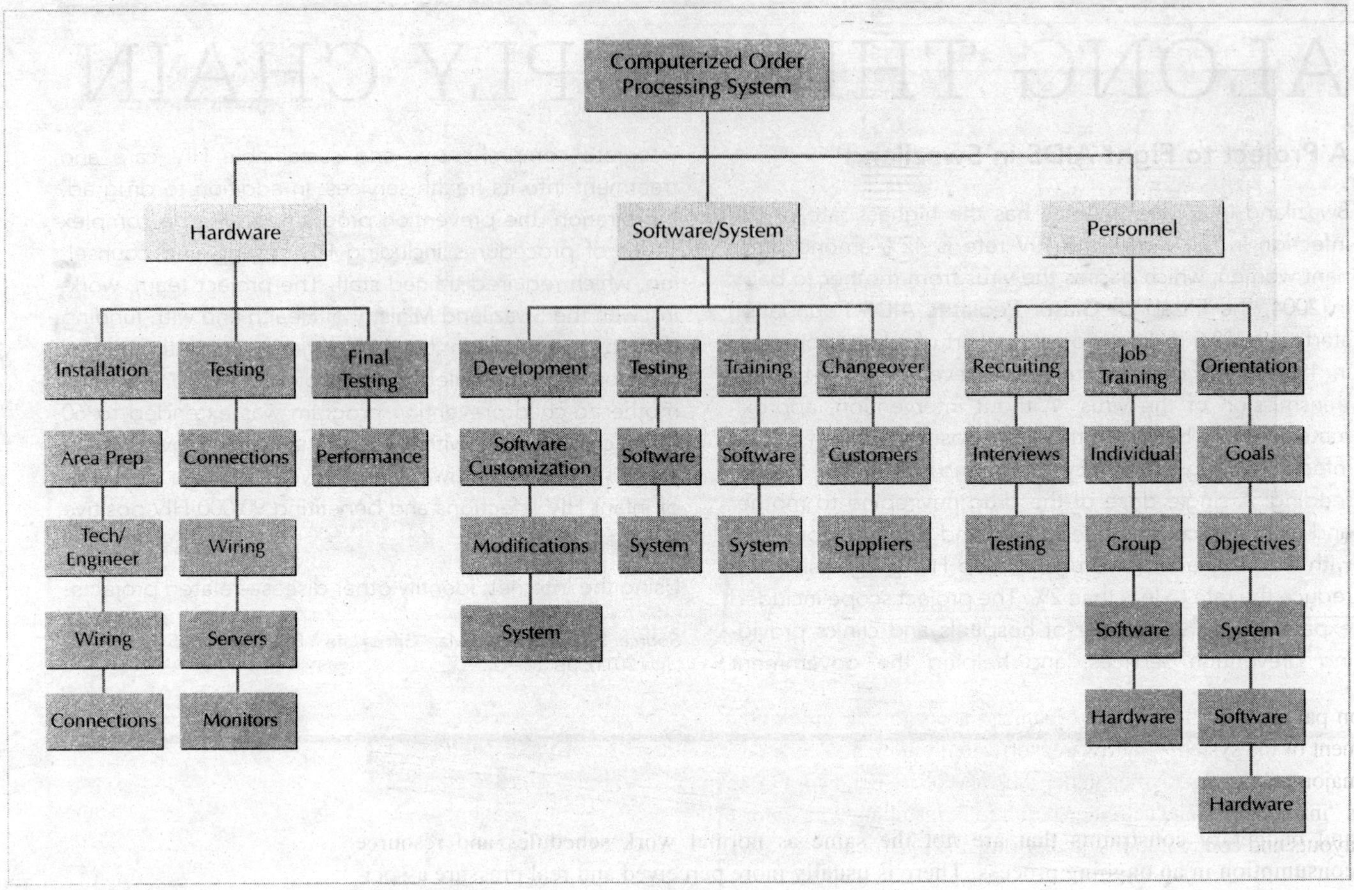

Figure 9.2

Work Breakdown Structure for a Computer Order Processing System Project

end result is a project hierarchical organizational structure made up of different levels, with the overall project at the top of the structure and the individual tasks for each activity at the bottom level. The WBS format is a good way to identify activities and to determine the individual task, module, and project workloads and resources required. It also helps to identify relationships between modules and activities as well as unnecessary duplication of activities. Finally, it provides the basis for developing and managing the project schedule, resources, and modifications.

There is no specific model to follow for the development of a WBS. It can be in the form of a chart or a table. It can be organized around project groups, project phases, or project tasks and events. However, experience has shown that there are two good ways for a project team to develop a WBS. One way is to start at the top and work one's way down, asking, "What components constitute this level?" until the WBS is developed in sufficient detail. The other way is simply to brainstorm the entire project, writing down each item on a sticky note and then organizing them together into the branches of a WBS. The upper levels of the WBS hierarchy tend to indicate the summary activities, major components, or functional areas involved in the project. They are typically described by nouns that indicate "what" is to be done. The lower levels of the WBS tend to describe the detailed work activities of the project required under the major components or areas. They are typically described by verbs that indicate "how" things are done.

Figure 9.2 shows a WBS for a project for installing a new computerized order processing system for a textile manufacturer that links customers, the manufacturer, and suppliers (see Example 9.1

OBS Units	WBS Activities–Hardware/Installation 1.1.1 Area Prep	1.1.2 Tech/Engineer	1.1.3 Wiring	1.1.4 Connections
Hardware engineering	3	1	1	1
Systems engineering		3		3
Software engineering		3		
Technical support	1	2		2
Electrical staff	2		2	2
Hardware vendor	3	3	3	3
Quality manager				3
Customer/supplier liaison				3

Level of responsibility: 1 = overall responsibility
2 = performance responsibility
3 = support

Figure 9.3
A Responsibility Assignment Matrix

on page 294). The WBS is organized according to the three major project categories for development of the system—hardware, software/system, and personnel. Within each of these categories the major tasks and activities under those tasks are detailed. For example, under hardware, a major task is "installation," and activities required in installation include area preparation, technical/engineering layouts and configurations, and wiring and electrical connections.

RESPONSIBILITY ASSIGNMENT MATRIX

After the work breakdown structure is developed, which organizes the project work into smaller, manageable elements, the project manager assigns the work elements to organizational units—departments, groups, individuals, or subcontractors—using an **organizational breakdown structure (OBS)**. The OBS is an organizational chart that shows which organizational units are responsible for work items. After the OBS is developed, the project manager can then develop a **responsibility assignment matrix (RAM)**. The RAM shows who in the organization is responsible for doing the work in the project. Figure 9.3 on the next page shows a RAM for the "Hardware/Installation" category from the work breakdown structure for the computerized order processing project shown in Figure 9.2. Notice that there are three levels of work assignment in the matrix, reflecting who is responsible for the work, who actually performs the work, and those who perform support activities. As with the WBS, both the OBS and RAM can take many different forms depending on the needs and preferences of the company, project team, and project manager.

PROJECT RISK

Every project has risks of varying size and degree. A risk is any uncertain factor, event, or occurrence that might potentially interfere with the progress and successful completion of a project. A risk is not a problem; it's the recognition that a problem might occur. By recognizing, understanding, and identifying potential problems in advance, and planning for them, the project team and manager can attempt to prevent them. It's the job of the project team and manager to manage and minimize the risk in their projects.

Managing project risks is best addressed in the planning stage. A risk management plan documents how risks will be managed throughout the project. In addition to identifying potential

ALONG THE SUPPLY CHAIN

Sustainability Projects Around the World

Sustainability or "green" projects are increasing around the world, not simply because they are a "good" thing for the world's environment but also because they can positively affect a company's bottom line. Studies estimate that the global market for environmental products and services will approach $3 trillion by 2020.

Most sustainability projects involve reducing energy consumption, resource use, and waste, and thus have cost-cutting implications. They uniquely mix cost cutting and savings with an inspiring sustainability message that appeals to both customers and stockholders; they provide an opportunity to achieve multiple benefits. They benefit the larger community, they benefit the environment, and they benefit the bottom line. The New York–based Environmental Defense Fund reaches out to firms to engage them in environmentally focused projects, but knows companies won't undertake such projects out of the goodness of their heart. It requires business-oriented incentives—bottom-line results and reduced regulatory risk.

British Petroleum (BP) has a portfolio of solar, wind, and hydrogen energy projects, and plans to spend $8 billion on alternative and renewable energy projects in the coming decade. GE Energy China has invested $15 billion in clean energy projects, including coal, wind, solar, and biofuel in China. Foster's, the Australian brewer, invested $14 million in a water management project at one of its breweries that allowed it to double its brewing capacity with only a 10% increase in water consumption, making it the most water-efficient brewery in the world. The Coca-Cola Foundation has provided $1 million to support four water infrastructure projects in developing countries. Finnish telecom company Nokia Siemens Networks plans to decrease the energy consumption of its building by 6% and increase the use of renewable energy in company operations by 50% in the next few years, initiatives that will reduce carbon dioxide emissions by about 2 million tons annually. Denmark's DONG Energy's Horns Rev 2 209-megawatt wind farm in the North Sea serves 200,000 households; 20% of the total power in Denmark is generated by wind energy. Morocco recently opened Africa's largest wind farm as part of a program to meet more than 40% of the country's power needs with renewable energy by 2020.

In the United States, over 3,000 schools and almost 6,000 universities have been certified by the Leadership in Energy and Environmental Design (LEED) program by undertaking sustainability projects such as solar panels or geothermal energy systems. Green schools save an average of $100,000 a year on operating costs by using 33% less energy and 32% less water. In Ohio, 250 LEED school projects are expected to save $1.4 billion over the next 40 years. (Plus, because schools are in use for many years, they have a much longer ROI payback period than private, commercial projects.) Hawaii's isolation in the Pacific makes it dependent on oil for 90% of its energy, and as a result makes it extremely vulnerable to price fluctuations and supply disruptions. To break itself of its oil dependency, it plans to launch sustainability projects requiring $20 billion in capital investment with a goal of using 70% clean energy for electricity and transportation by 2030.

Food distributor U.S. Foodservice undertook a project to reduce fuel throughout its vehicle fleet and achieved fuel cost savings of $8.2 million, and a corresponding reduction in carbon dioxide emissions of 22,000 tons in just three months. At mattress manufacturer Sealy, in just three months, sustainability projects in its manufacturing and delivery operations saved $1.2 million in fuel costs, reduced carbon dioxide emissions by 3000 tons, and saved $4 million in material costs while eliminating 650 tons of solid waste. A $450,000 project at the State University of New York at Buffalo to upgrade a quarter of its older computer servers with more energy-efficient models saved $150,000 in annual energy costs while increasing computing capacity by 50%.

Identify and discuss some potential "green" projects at your university.

Sources: Based on Shawn Henry, "Give and Take," *PM Network* 23 (8); (August 2009), pp. 28–33; Sarah Gale, "Survival of the Greenest," *PM Network* 23 (4); (April 2009), pp. 14–15; Tegan Jones and Sarah Gale, "Keeping the Faith," *PM Network* 23 (2); (February 2009), pp. 42–47; Sarah Gale, "Sink or Swim," *PM Network* 23 (3); (March 2009), pp. 16–17; Sarah Gale, "Measuring Up," *PM Network* 23 (7); (July 2009), pp. 14–15; Sarah Gale, "Aloha to Sustainability," *PM Network* 24 (6); (June 2010), pp. 14–15; Sarah Gale, "Little Green Schoolhouses," *PM Network* 26 (3); (March 2012), pp. 16–17; Sarah Gale, "A Closer Look, DONG Energy, North Sea," *PM Network* 24 (4); (April 2010), pp. 34–37.

risks, it specifies which team members are responsible for managing various areas of risk, how risks will be monitored throughout the project life cycle, how contingency plans for risks that materialize will be developed and implemented, and how project resources will be allocated to handle risk.

The approach to, managing project risk is proactive. The first step is to identify all of the possible risks that can be anticipated in the project. This might include such things as resource changes, wrong assumptions, a change in company objectives and needs, technology changes, changes in the company's competitive environment, and anything new in the project, like technology. After as many risks as possible are identified, they should each be evaluated in terms of their impact and possible eventuality (i.e., probability), and possibly quantified. Although any kind of risk evaluation and measurement is obviously an estimate, the objective is to have a process to compare the risks to one another in order to prioritize them in terms of which ones will most threaten project success. The most important risks that are controllable can be mitigated, and strategies should be developed to mitigate those that can't be controlled.

Successfully managing project risk can have a very positive impact; it can keep projects within budget and save money, maintain project schedules, and result in the project success and quality results hoped for.

Global Cultural and Diversity Issues in Project Management

In the existing global business environment, project teams form a mosaic of different genders, cultures, ethnicities, nationalities, religions, and races. Only by acknowledging and embracing this diversity will companies be able to attract the best people and achieve project success. Diversity offers a significant business advantage by providing a more well rounded perspective on a project from team members with different views, experiences, and values. The project leader must focus on creating common goals and objectives for the project by using good communication techniques and developing a cooperative environment that identifies common values and fosters mutual respect for differences. However, while a globally diverse project team can have advantages, project success typically requires respect for cultural differences and a management style that acknowledges these differences.

Global projects that involve companies and team members from different countries have expanded dramatically in recent years as a result of increased information and communication technology. Teamwork is a critical element in achieving project success, and in global projects, diversity among international team members can add an extra dimension to project planning. For projects to be successful, cultural differences, idiosyncrasies, and issues must be considered as important parts of the planning process. The basics of project management tend to be universal, but cultural differences in priorities, nuances, and terminology can result in communication failures. Since English is used widely around the world, language is not necessarily an overriding problem. However, often it is not what people say that matters but what they mean.

An example of one cultural difference that can play havoc with developing project schedules is the difference in work days and holidays in different countries. Southern Europeans take a lot of holidays, which can mess up a project schedule if they are not planned for. In the United States, you can ask people to move their vacations or work while on vacation (via phone or Internet), but in countries like France or Italy, don't ask. In India, the work ethic is closer to the European than the U.S. model: when the day ends it's over, and weekends are inviolate. In some cultures, certain days are auspicious for starting a new venture or ending a task.

Some cultures tend to be less aggressive than others, and team members will avoid confrontation so that when problems on a project occur (such as cost overruns or missed due dates) they will not be as aggressively addressed as they might be in the United States or in Germany, for

ALONG THE SUPPLY CHAIN

Cross-Cultural Project Teams

In today's global economy, cross-cultural project teams have become relatively common, but they still present unique situational problems that require an awareness of cultural differences on the part of U.S. team members and especially the project manager. In Saudi Arabia, Islam can play a significant role in a project; religious beliefs strongly influence how Saudis interact with foreigners in a business setting. For example, Saudi workers take time out several times a day for prayer, which will affect work schedules and productivity. Since Saudi women don't work alongside Saudi men, foreign women team members may create an uncomfortable situation. Being respectful of the culture is essential; thus, foreign women should always cover their heads. The Korean culture has a very strong work ethic, so foreign project team members should expect to work 16-hour days, seven days a week, whereas for the French, weekends and holidays are sacrosanct.

In projects in China, Chinese team members will sometimes show more deference and politeness than Americans are used to, thus avoiding useful criticisms that are expected by U.S. team members. While U.S. companies value individualism, Chinese companies, reflecting 2,000 years of traditional Confucian values, do not. Chinese project managers typically use a more collaborative leadership style than the more direct style of U.S. project managers. The Chinese word *guanxi* (gwan-shee) refers to the strong reliance of business on social connections. A Chinese business partner with strong, well-placed relationships can enhance project success. However, such relationships are developed slowly. The Chinese focus on the long term rather than the short-term view prevalent in many Western companies. Patience is a respected virtue in China, where time is used as a competitive tool. "Face" or *mianzi* (me-ahn-zee) is very important in China. Every conversation, meeting, meal, social, or business engagement is an opportunity for an individual to gain or lose stature. Rudeness, loudness, and anger have very negative consequences; raising your voice to a Chinese manager will cause shame and embarrassment, and brand the offending person as a barbarian. (While in the United States, the "squeaky wheel gets the grease," in China, the "loudest duck gets shot.") Rank is important in China; people of high rank are given an extraordinary degree of deference. As such, instructions from leaders are respected and followed, and advice from junior team members is not generally expected or valued. Humility helps; the U.S. way of doing business is not better than the Chinese way; it's just different. Gifts are important in China, not so much for their intrinsic value as for their symbolic value of respect. They should reflect a degree of thoughtfulness and effort—that is, not just a logo t-shirt.

U.S. project team members should research the culture of their team members; avoid stereotypes and not let them influence behavior; develop and show an interest in cultural differences and learn about local traditions; communicate effectively and not always assume you are being understood; and listen carefully and empathetically. Project managers should develop a skill known as *emotional intelligence*—the ability to read facial, verbal, and physical cues that reveal how a person from another culture is feeling. Team members and project managers need to develop a cultural sensitivity and understanding to see how cultural differences may impact the project environment in order to work together effectively to achieve project success, on time and within the budget.

Assume you are a project team member, and another team member is from a different country of your choice. Identify cultural differences between your two countries that you think might jeopardize project success.

Sources: Based on Bud Baker, "When in China …," *PM Network* 20 (6); (June 2006), pp. 24–25; Deborah Silver, "Abroad Spectrum," *PM Network* 23 (1); (January 2009), pp. 62–68; and Michelle Bowles, "Caution: Cultures Crossing," *PM Network* 25 (1); (January 2011), pp. 58–63.

example. Some team members in underdeveloped countries may bow to the perceived superiority of those from developed countries and not press their points aggressively even though they may be correct. Some people may simply have trouble working with others with cultural differences. Team members may think they do not understand team members from a foreign country, when it's actually their culture they don't understand.

In Asian countries, businesses typically employ a more methodical management style that values patience and building relationships. Project managers and team members in Japan consider establishing plans and providing direction to be more important managerial competencies than exist in the United States. What's considered to be micromanaging in the United States is the more common way of doing things in China. In Latin America, a formal management style with specific managerial direction is a cultural trait. Business relationships are built slowly over time and they are based on trust and a sense of personal integrity. In Latin countries, personal connections (that might include inquires into team members' personal lives) are often expected before business is transacted. In Malaysia, a "boss" has almost absolute power over subordinates, whereas in Austria, the perception is almost completely the opposite. The United States, Scandinavia, and many European countries fall somewhere in between. In countries like the United Kingdom, Sweden, and Denmark, people tend to cope with uncertainty and unexpected events much better than people in Italy and Portugal.

As a result, the project manager must address the issue of cultural diversity up front in the planning process. Project managers have to approach diversity differently from country to country. The project manager should never assume that something that works at home will work abroad or that what will work in country A will work in country B. This makes cultural research and communication important elements in the planning process. The manager must determine what cultural faux pas must be avoided—the things you don't do. It's important to discover at the start what holidays and cultural celebrations exist and the work ethic of team members.

The project manager must often find team members who are particularly adept at bridging cultural differences. It may be helpful to identify a team associate who can keep the project manager and other team members informed of important cultural differences. Although long-distance communication via phone or email is very easy, the face-to-face meeting is often better with someone with cultural differences, even with the added expense of travel.

Project Scheduling

The project schedule evolves from the planning documents we discussed in the previous section. It is typically the most critical element in the project management process, especially during the implementation phase (i.e., the actual project work), and it is the source of most conflict and problems. One reason is that frequently the single most important criterion for the success of a project is that it be finished on time. If a stadium is supposed to be finished in time for the first game of the season and it's not, there will be a lot of angry ticket holders; if a school building is not completed by the time the school year starts, there will be a lot of angry parents; if a shopping mall is not completed on time, there will be a lot of angry tenants; if a new product is not completed by the scheduled launch date, millions of dollars can be lost; and if a new military weapon is not completed on time, it could affect national security. Time is also a measure of progress that is very visible. It is an absolute with little flexibility; you can spend less money or use fewer people, but you cannot slow down or stop the passage of time.

Developing a schedule encompasses the following basic steps. First, *define the activities* that must be performed to complete the project; second, *sequence the activities* in the order in which they must be completed; next, *estimate the time* required to complete each activity; and finally, *develop the schedule* based on this sequencing and time estimates of the activities.

Because scheduling involves a quantifiable measure, time, several quantitative techniques, including the Gantt chart and CPM/PERT networks, are available that can be used to develop a project schedule. There are also various computer software packages that can be used to schedule projects, including the popular Microsoft Project. Later in this chapter we are going to discuss CPM/PERT and Microsoft Project in greater detail. For now, we are going to describe one of the oldest and most widely used scheduling techniques, the Gantt chart.

THE GANTT CHART

A **Gantt chart** (also called a *bar chart*) was developed by Henry Gantt, a pioneer in the field of industrial engineering, at the artillery ammunition shops of the Frankford Arsenal in 1914. The Gantt chart has been a popular project scheduling tool since its inception and is still widely used today. It is the direct precursor of the CPM/PERT technique, which we will discuss later.

The Gantt chart is a graph with a bar representing time for each activity in the project being analyzed. Figure 9.4 illustrates a Gantt chart of a simplified project description for building a house. The project contains only seven primary activities, such as designing the house, laying the foundation, ordering materials, and so forth. The first activity is "design house and obtain financing," and it requires three months to complete, shown by the bar from left to right across the chart. After the first activity is finished, the next two activities, "lay foundation" and "order and receive materials," can start simultaneously. This set of activities demonstrates how a **precedence relationship** works: the design of the house and the financing must precede the next two activities.

The activity "lay foundation" requires two months to complete, so it will be finished, at the earliest, at the end of month 5. "Order and receive materials" requires one month to complete, and it could be finished after month 4. However, observe that it is possible to delay the start of this activity one month until month 4. This delay would still enable the activity to be completed by the end of month 5, when the next activity, "build house," is scheduled to start. This extra time for the activity "order materials" is called slack. **Slack** is the amount by which an activity can be delayed without delaying any of the activities that follow it or the project as a whole. The remainder of the Gantt chart is constructed in a similar manner, and the project is scheduled to be completed at the end of month 9.

Figure 9.4
A Gantt Chart

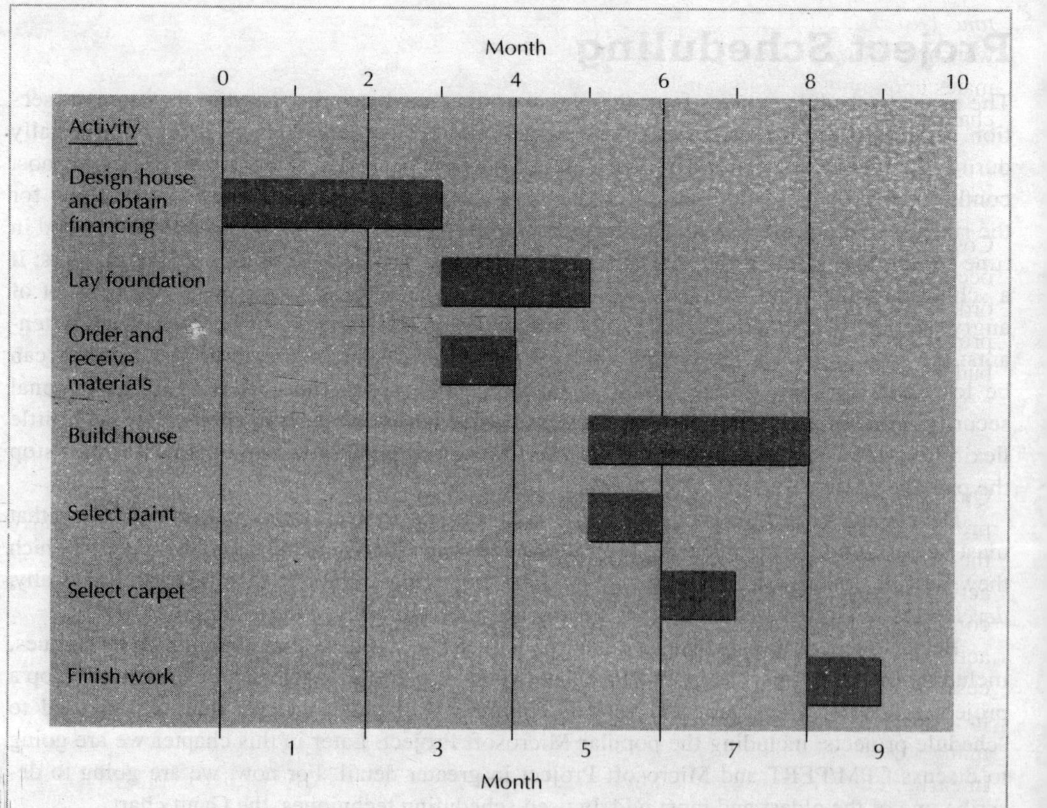

The Gantt chart provides a visual display of the project schedule, indicating when activities are scheduled to start, when they will be finished, and where extra time is available and activities can be delayed. The project manager can use the chart to monitor the progress of the activities and see which ones are ahead of schedule and which ones are behind schedule. The Gantt chart also indicates the precedence relationships between activities; however, these relationships are not always easily discernible. This problem is one of the disadvantages of the Gantt chart method, and it sometimes limits the chart's use to smaller projects with relatively few activities. The CPM/PERT network technique does not suffer this disadvantage.

Project Control

Project control is the process of making sure the project progresses toward a successful completion. It requires that the project be monitored and progress be measured so that any deviations from the project plan, and particularly the project schedule, are minimized. If the project is found to be deviating from the plan—that is, it is not on schedule, cost overruns are occurring, activity results are not as expected, and so on—then corrective action must be taken. In the rest of this section we will describe several key elements of project control, including time management, quality control, performance monitoring, and communication.

TIME MANAGEMENT

Time management is the process of making sure the project schedule does not slip and is on time. This requires the monitoring of individual activity schedules and frequent updates. If the schedule is being delayed to an extent that jeopardizes the project success, then the project manager may have to shift resources to accelerate critical activities. Some activities may have slack time, and resources can be shifted from them to activities that are not on schedule. This is referred to as *time–cost tradeoff*. However, this can also push the project cost above budget. In some cases, the work may need to be corrected or made more efficient. In other cases, original activity time estimates upon implementation may prove to be unrealistic, with the result that the schedule must be changed and the repercussions of such changes on project success evaluated.

COST MANAGEMENT

Cost management is often closely tied to time management because of the time–cost tradeoff occurrences that we mentioned previously. If the schedule is delayed, costs tend to increase in order to get the project back on schedule. Also, as the project progresses, some cost estimates may prove to be unrealistic or erroneous. Thus, it will be necessary to revise cost estimates and develop budget updates. If cost overruns are excessive, then corrective actions must be taken.

QUALITY MANAGEMENT

Quality management and control are an integral part of the project management process. The process requires that project work be monitored for quality and that improvements be made as the project progresses, just as in a normal production or manufacturing operation. Tasks and activities must be monitored to make sure that work is done correctly and that activities are completed correctly according to plan. If the work on an activity or task is flawed, subsequent activities may be affected, requiring rework, delaying the project, and threatening project success. Poor-quality work increases the risk of project failure, just as a defective part can result in a defective final product if not corrected. Thus, the principles of quality management and many of the same techniques for statistical analysis and statistical process control discussed in earlier chapters for traditional production processes can also be applied to the project management process.

PERFORMANCE MANAGEMENT

Performance management is the process of monitoring a project and developing timed (i.e., daily, weekly, monthly) status reports to make sure that goals are being met and the plan is being followed. It compares planned target dates for events, milestones, and work completion with dates actually achieved to determine whether the project is on schedule or behind schedule. Key measures of performance include deviation from the schedule, resource usage, and cost overruns. These reports are developed by the project manager and by individuals and organizational units with performance responsibility.

Earned value analysis (EVA) is a specific system for performance management. Activities "earn value" as they are completed. EVA is a recognized standard procedure for numerically measuring a project's progress, forecasting its completion date and final cost, and providing measures of schedule and budget variation as activities are completed. For example, an EVA metric such as "schedule variance" compares the work performed during a time period with the work that was scheduled to be performed. A negative variance means the project is behind schedule. "Cost variance" is the budgeted cost of work performed minus the actual cost of the work. A negative variance means the project is over budget. EVA works best when it is used in conjunction with a work breakdown structure (WBS) that compartmentalizes project work into small packages that are easy to measure. The drawbacks of EVA are that it's sometimes difficult to measure work progress and the time required for data measurement can be considerable.

COMMUNICATION

Communication needs for project and program management control in today's global business environment tend to be substantial and complex. The distribution of design documents, budget and cost documents, plans, status reports, schedules, and schedule changes in a timely manner is often critical to project success. As a result, more and more companies are using the Internet to communicate project information, and are using company intranet project websites to provide a single location for team members to access project information. Internet communication and software combined with faxing, videoconferencing systems, phones, handheld computers, and jet travel are enabling transnational companies to engage in global project management.

ENTERPRISE PROJECT MANAGEMENT

In many companies, project control takes place within the larger context of a multiple project environment. *Enterprise project management* refers to the management and control of a companywide portfolio of projects. In the enterprise approach to managing projects, a company's goals are achieved through the coordination of simultaneous projects. The company grows, changes, and adds value by systematically implementing projects of all types across the enterprise. The aggregate result of an organization's portfolio of projects becomes the company's bottom line. As such, program management is a managerial approach that sits above project management. Whereas project management concentrates on delivering a clearly defined, tangible outcome with its own scope and goals within a specified time frame, in a program management environment the company's goals and changes are achieved through a carefully planned and coordinated set of projects. Programs tend to cut across and affect all business areas and thus require a higher degree of cross-business functional coordination than individual projects.

AGILE PROJECT MANAGEMENT

Agile project management, a relatively recent addition to the project management lexicon, evolved out of the unique problems and challenges encountered in managing IT and software development projects. The agile approach to project management is very different from the formal, planned approach we have described so far. It focuses more on adaptability to rapid and unexpected change (i.e., uncertainty) in the project environment, which is especially prevalent in the IT and software development business.

Agile is a way to deal with change in project management by using an iterative and incremental approach. Unlike the traditional, straightforward and linear project management process with a predetermined and planned set of steps (i.e., a scope statement, project network, etc.), as, for example, would exist in a construction project, the agile method breaks down tasks into small increments with minimal planning. It promotes adaptive planning, evolutionary development, and an iterative approach, and encourages rapid and flexible response to changes. Its primary benefit is that it's adaptable to constant adjustments to change through a collaborative process. This type

ALONG THE SUPPLY CHAIN

Innovative "Cloud" Projects at Facebook, Google, and Apple

In recent years, Apple, Facebook, and Google have all opened new state-of-the-art data centers in North Carolina to support their cloud computing activates. Apple's new data center costing $1 billion encompasses a half million square-foot facility; Google's new building that supports over 55,200 servers cost $600 million; and Facebook's new 300,000 square-foot data center cost $400 million.

Facebook, the social networking service and website with almost a billion active users, undertook its project to move 1 terabyte (i.e., 1 trillion bytes) of data from the company's old data center that was approaching capacity to a new warehouse. The project had to occur seamlessly without disrupting the service for Facebook users and the revenue-generating internal work groups that rely on the network, and it had to be completed quickly, within a little over three months from conception. Moving a terabyte of data, which is the equivalent of 250 billion "likes" on Facebook, in a small amount of time without disrupting the website was a daunting task for the project team. The project was implemented in two stages. The first stage involved constructing and setting up the infrastructure. Team members had to choose and test the hardware, make selections, and have it all shipped, installed, and stacked with the necessary wiring, cooling and pipes, which involved coordination between the project team, the hardware team, and vendors. Vendors had to move quickly to deliver the hardware in a short time, and the project team had to test the equipment around the clock to make sure it was compatible with the company's systems.

In stage two the data had to be transferred safely and quickly. The project team made a calculated gamble by not loading the huge amount of data onto thousands of servers and physically moving them; instead they ramped up the company's own private network and flowed the data directly to the new site, risking that flowing so much information in a short amount of time would disrupt Facebook's entire website. The data transfer was successfully achieved in a three-week period (with a network flow rate of one gigabyte per second) by limiting and monitoring bandwidth throughout the transfer and constantly checking the flow to keep it in sync. The project was completed on time and with no delays or downtime. When the project was completed, the new center could hold eight times more data than the previous location, it managed the data more efficiently, and it cut millions of dollars from Facebook's energy bills while reducing the center's ecological footprint.

One of the problems of such large data centers is the energy they consume; it is estimated that data centers, in general, consume approximately 1.5% of the world's electricity. Google, in constructing its data center, pioneered unique technology to reduce energy consumption by keeping it hotter than what had been traditional in data centers. Typically, data centers are very chilly; however, Google keeps its data center warmer (around 77 degrees) by creating a "hot aisle," a space that takes hot air from the servers into water-filled coils, sending it outside the building to cool, then recirculating it back inside.

Can you think of any other, similar IT-related projects that a company like Amazon or Walmart might undertake?

Sources: Based on Sarah F. Gale, "A Closer Look, Facebook, Palo Alto, California," *PM Network* 24 (9); (September 2010), pp. 34–37; Patrick Thibodeau, "Apple, Google, Facebook Turn N.C. into Data Center Hub," *Computerworld* (June 3, 2011), www.computerworld.com; Jordan G. Teicher, "The Brain of the Beast: Google Reveals the Computers Behind the Cloud," www.npr.org (October 17, 2012).

of iterative process is more conducive to software projects, for example, that are subject to very rapid and unforeseen changes, which may be, in part, the result of customers not knowing entirely at the outset what they want the product to look like. Iterations are for short time frames (called time-boxes) that might last several weeks, at the end of which a working product (i.e., the software) is delivered and demonstrated to the customer. This reduces the overall risk and allows the project to adapt to changes quickly. For a software or IT development project, an iteration might not result in a market-ready product, with multiple iterations required for release of the full (software) product or new features.

Team composition in an agile project is usually cross-functional and typically includes a customer representative. Face-to-face communication among team members is emphasized, and is frequent, usually daily (in short meetings called *scrums*), which helps to reveal problems as they arise. Team size is typically small (5–9 people) to simplify team communication and collaboration. When a team works in different locations, they maintain daily contact through videoconferencing, voice, email, and so on. At the end of each iteration, stakeholders and the customer representative review progress and re-evaluate priorities with a view to optimizing the ROI and ensuring the project is aligned with customer needs and goals.

The agile approach differs from traditional project management by responding to change rather than following a plan; by relying on individuals who interact instead of formal processes and tools; and by frequently communicating and collaborating with the customer. As global business environments have become subject to more and more rapid and constant change, the agile approach to project management is spreading beyond IT and software development into other sectors, particularly business environments that are dynamic and turbulent, such as technology-based companies, financial services, insurance, telecommunications, pharmaceuticals, utilities, and manufacturing. While the agile approach has benefited some companies, it also has limitations and is not universally applicable to project management, even if the projects involve significant change. It requires small groups of experienced, talented, cross-functional team members that work well together, and some companies cannot (nor need to) adapt to the absence of a formal planning process.

CPM/PERT

In 1956, a research team at E. I. du Pont de Nemours & Company, Inc., led by a du Pont engineer, Morgan R. Walker, and a Remington-Rand computer specialist, James E. Kelley Jr., initiated a project to develop a computerized system to improve the planning, scheduling, and reporting of the company's engineering programs (including plant maintenance and construction projects). The resulting network approach is known as the *critical path method (CPM)*. At the same time, the U.S. Navy established a research team composed of members of the Navy Special Projects Office, Lockheed, and the consulting firm of Booz, Allen, and Hamilton, led by D. G. Malcolm. They developed a similar network approach for the design of a management control system for the development of the Polaris Missile Project (a ballistic missile-firing nuclear submarine). This network scheduling technique was named the *program evaluation and review technique*, or *PERT*. The Polaris project eventually included 23 PERT networks encompassing 3,000 activities.

Both CPM and PERT are derivatives of the Gantt chart and, as a result, are very similar. There were originally two primary differences between CPM and PERT. With CPM a single estimate for activity time was used that did not allow for any variation in activity times—activity times were treated as if they were known for certain, or "deterministic." With PERT, multiple time estimates were used for each activity that allowed for variation in activity times—activity times were treated as "probabilistic." The other difference was related to the mechanics of drawing the project network. In PERT, activities were represented as arcs, or arrowed lines, between two nodes, or circles, whereas in CPM activities were represented as the nodes or circles. However, over time CPM and PERT have been effectively merged into a single technique conventionally referred to as CPM/PERT.

The advantage of CPM/PERT over the Gantt chart is in the use of a network to depict the precedence relationships between activities. The Gantt chart does not clearly show precedence relationships, a disadvantage that limited its use to small projects. The CPM/PERT network is a more efficient and direct means of displaying precedence relationships. In other words, in a network it is visually easier to see the precedence relationships, which makes CPM/PERT popular with managers and other users, especially for large projects with many activities.

THE PROJECT NETWORK

A CPM/PERT network consists of *branches* and *nodes*, as shown in Figure 9.5. When CPM and PERT were first developed, they employed different conventions for constructing a network. With CPM the nodes, or circles in Figure 9.5, represented the project activities. The arrows in between the nodes indicated the precedence relationships between activities. For the network in Figure 9.5, activity 1, represented by node 1, precedes activity 2, and 2 precedes 3. This approach to network construction is called **activity-on-node (AON)**. With PERT the opposite convention was taken. The branches represented the activities, and the nodes in between them reflected **events**, or points in time such as the end of one activity and the beginning of another. In this approach, referred to as **activity-on-arrow (AOA)**, the activities are normally identified by the node numbers at the start and end of an activity. For example, activity 1–2 precedes activity 2–3 in Figure 9.5. In this book, we will focus on the AON convention, but we will also provide an overview of AOA networks.

AOA NETWORK

To demonstrate how these components are used to construct the two types of network, we will use our example project of building a house used in the Gantt chart in Figure 9.4. The comparable AOA CPM/PERT network for this project is shown in Figure 9.6. The precedence relationships are reflected in this network by the arrangement of the arrowed (or directed) branches in Figure 9.6. The first activity (1–2) in the project is to design the house and obtain financing. This activity must be completed before any subsequent activities can begin. Thus, activities 2–3, laying the foundation, and 2–4, ordering and receiving materials, can start only when node 2 is *realized*, indicating the event that activity 1–2 is finished. (Notice in Figure 9.6 that a time estimate of three months has been assigned for the completion of this activity.) Activity 2–3 and activity 2–4 can occur concurrently; neither depends on the other, and both depend only on the completion of activity 1–2.

When the activities of laying the foundation (2–3) and ordering and receiving materials (2–4) are completed, then activities 4–5 and 4–6 can begin simultaneously. However, before discussing these activities further, notice activity 3–4, referred to in the network as a dummy.

A **dummy** activity is inserted into the network to show a precedence relationship, but it does not represent any actual passage of time. Activities 2–3 and 2–4 have the precedence relationship shown in Figure 9.7*a*. However, in an AOA network, two or more activities are not allowed to share the same starting and ending nodes. Instead, activity 3–4 is inserted to give two activities separate end nodes and, thus, two separate identities as shown in Figure 9.7*b*. Notice, however, that a time of zero months has been assigned to activity 3–4. The dummy activity shows that

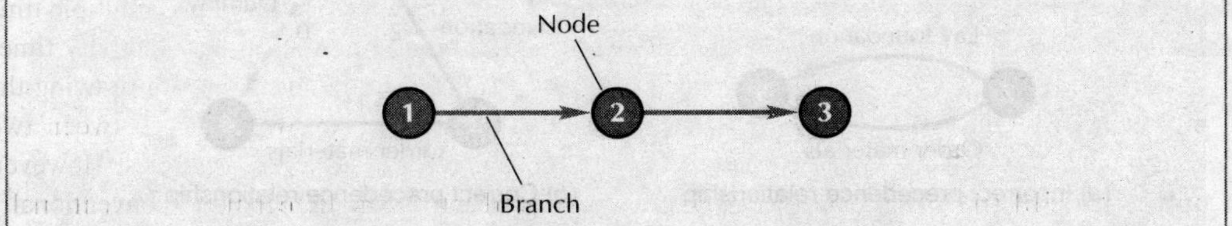

Figure 9.5
Network Components

Figure 9.6

The AOA Project Network for Building a House

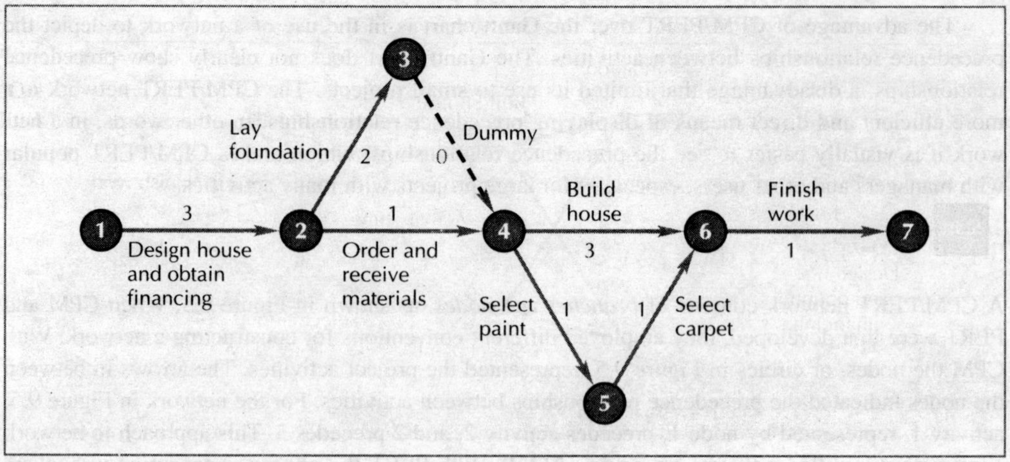

activity 2–3 must be completed prior to any activities beginning at node 4, but it does not represent the passage of time.

Returning to the network in Figure 9.6, we see that two activities start at node 4. Activity 4–6 is the actual building of the house, and activity 4–5 is the search for and selection of the paint for the exterior and interior of the house. Activity 4–6 and activity 4–5 can begin simultaneously and take place concurrently. Following the selection of the paint (activity 4–5) and the realization of node 5, the carpet can be selected (since the carpet color depends on the paint color). This activity can also occur concurrently with the building of the house (activity 4–6). When the building is completed and the paint and carpet are selected, the house can be finished (activity 6–7).

AON NETWORK

Figure 9.8 shows the comparable AON network to the AOA network in Figure 9.6 for our house building project. Notice that the activities and activity times are on the nodes and not on the activities as they were previously with the AOA network. The branches or arrows simply show the precedence relationships between the activities. Also, notice that there is no dummy activity; dummy activities are not required in an AON network since two activities will never be confused because they have the same start and end nodes. In general, both of the two methods accomplish the same thing, and the one that is used is usually a matter of individual preference. However, for our purposes the AON network has one distinct advantage—it is the convention used in the popular *Microsoft Project* software package, and because we want to demonstrate how to use this software, we will use the AON convention in this chapter.

Figure 9.7

Concurrent Activities

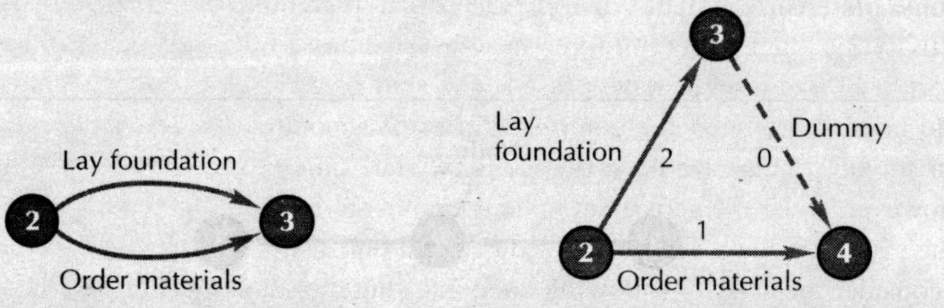

(*a*) Incorrect precedence relationship (*b*) Correct precedence relationship

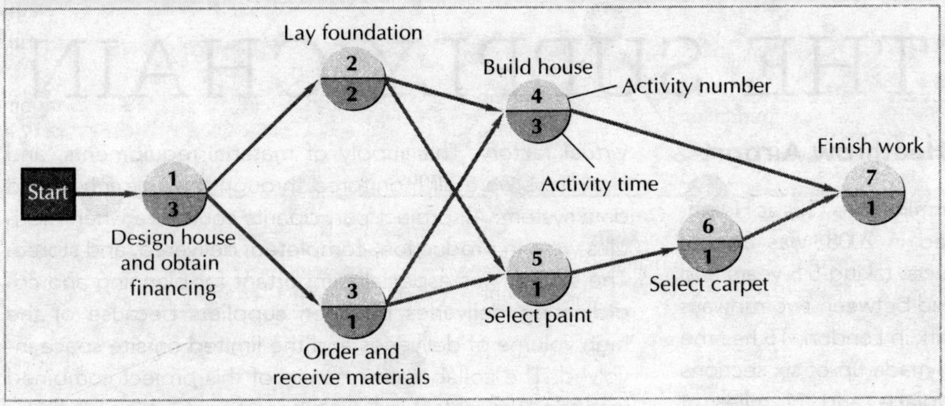

Figure 9.8
AON Network for House Building Project

THE CRITICAL PATH

A network path is a sequence of connected activities that runs from the start to the end of the network. The network in Figure 9.8 has several paths through it. In fact, close observations of this network show four paths, identified as A, B, C, and D:

A: 1 − 2 − 4 − 7
B: 1 − 2 − 5 − 6 − 7
C: 1 − 3 − 4 − 7
D: 1 − 3 − 5 − 6 − 7

The project cannot be completed (i.e., the house cannot be built) sooner than the time required by the longest path in the network, in terms of time. The path with the longest duration of time is referred to as the **critical path**.

By summing the activity times (shown in Figure 9.8) along each of the four paths, we can compute the length of each path, as follows:

Path A: 1 − 2 − 4 − 7
3 + 2 + 3 + 1 = 9 months
Path B: 1 − 2 − 5 − 6 − 7
3 + 2 + 1 + 1 + 1 = 8 months
Path C: 1 − 3 − 4 − 7
3 + 1 + 3 + 1 = 8 months
Path D: 1 − 3 − 5 − 6 − 7
3 + 1 + 1 + 1 + 1 = 7 months

Because path A is the longest, it is the critical path; thus, the minimum completion time for the project is nine months. Now let us analyze the critical path more closely. From Figure 9.9 we can see that activity 3 cannot start until three months have passed. It is also easy to see that activity 4 will not start until five months have passed. The start of activity 4 is dependent on two activities leading into node 4. Activity 2 is completed after five months, but activity 3 is completed at the end of four months. Thus, we have two possible start times for activity 4, five months and four months. However, since the activity at node 4 cannot start until all preceding activities have been finished, the soonest node 4 can be realized is five months.

Now consider the activity following node 4. Using the same logic as before, activity 7 cannot start until after eight months (five months at node 4 plus the three months required by activity 4) or after seven months. Because all activities preceding node 7 must be completed before activity 7 can start, the earliest this can occur is eight months. Adding one month for activity 7 to the start

ALONG THE SUPPLY CHAIN

The Terminal 5 Project at Heathrow Airport

British Airport Authority's (BAA) terminal five (T5) at Heathrow Airport in London, completed in 2008, was one of Europe's largest construction projects, taking 5.5 years and 60,000 people to complete. Located between two runways in a space equal in size to Hyde Park in London, T5 has the largest single-span roof in Europe, made up of six sections requiring 10 months to lift into place, and 11 miles of baggage conveyor belt. The facility, which cost £4.3 billion to build, increased Heathrow's capacity by 35 million annual passengers. For the first time in a project of this size and complexity, off-site prefabrication of over 2,800 component modules was used extensively. Assembled components were transported to the building site where they were bolted together, thereby reducing construction site time and disruption, and construction traffic at the airport. A web-based system enabled off-site project module manufacturers in Dover and Scotland to be coordinated though a *virtual factory*. The supply of material, equipments, and workflows were all monitored through this one integrated data system. All project participants could see when modules were in production, completed, delivered, and stored. The system was especially important for planning and coordinating deliveries between suppliers because of the high volume of deliveries and the limited on-site space involved. The collaborative nature of this project combined with the "virtual factory" web-based computer system, facilitated the performance of the integrated project teams, resulting in a reduction in construction times, a safer working environment, and better quality.

Discuss some of the unique problems that you think might exist for a project like this one that involves a facility with daily, heavy public usage.

Sources: John Summers, "The Virtual Factory," *Quality World* 31 (10); (October 2005), pp. 24–28; and Patricia Curmi, "Terminal Velocity," *Quality World* 33, (8); (August 2007), pp. 17–21.

time at node 7 gives a project duration of nine months. This is the time of the longest path in the network—the critical path.

This brief analysis demonstrates the concept of a critical path and the determination of the minimum completion time of a project. However, this was a cumbersome method for determining a critical path. Next, we discuss a mathematical approach to scheduling the project activities and determining the critical path.

ACTIVITY SCHEDULING

In our analysis of the critical path, we determined the earliest time that each activity could be finished. For example, we found that the earliest time activity 4 could start was five months. This time is referred to as the **earliest start time**, and it is expressed symbolically as **ES**.

Figure 9.9

Activity Start Times

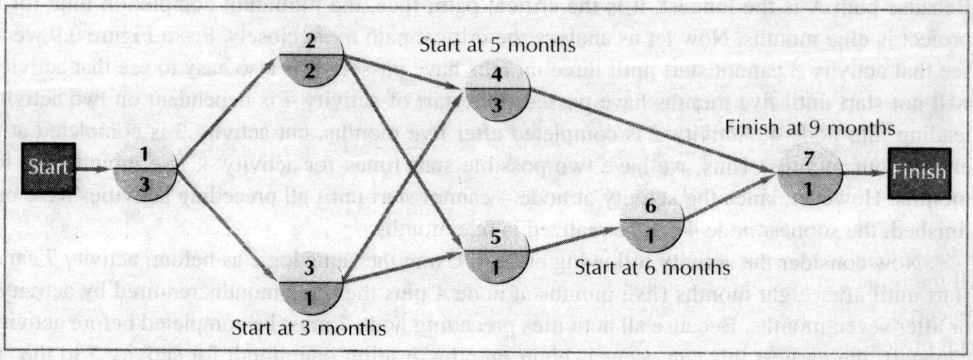

In order to show the earliest start time on the network as well as some other activity times, we will develop in the scheduling process, we will alter our node structure a little. Figure 9.10 shows the structure for node 1, the first activity in our example network for designing the house and obtaining financing.

To determine the earliest start time for every activity, we make a **forward pass** through the network. That is, we start at the first node and move forward through the network. The earliest start time for an activity is the maximum time in which all preceding activities have been completed—the time when the activity start node is realized.

The **earliest finish time (EF)**, for an activity is simply the earliest start time plus the activity time estimate. For example, if the earliest start time for activity 1 is at time 0, then the earliest finish time is three months. In general, the earliest start and finish times for an activity are computed according to the following mathematical relationship.

$$ES = \text{maximum (EF) of immediate predecessors}$$
$$EF = ES + t$$

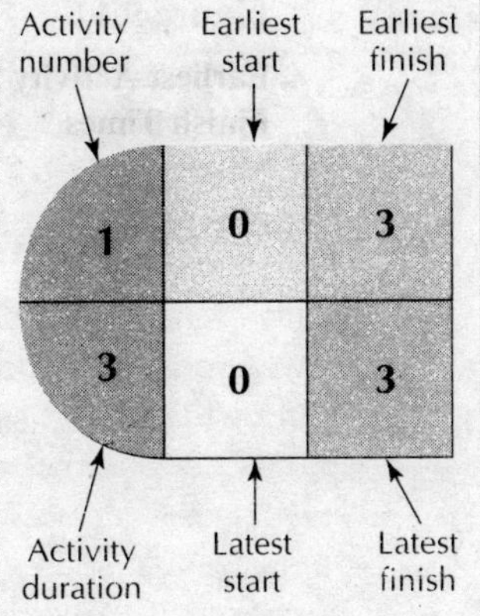

Figure 9.10

Node Configuration

The earliest start and earliest finish times for all the activities in our project network are shown in Figure 9.11.

The earliest start time for the first activity in the network (for which there are no predecessor activities) is always 0, or, ES = 0. This enables us to compute the earliest finish time for activity 1 as

$$\begin{aligned} EF &= ES + t \\ &= 0 + 3 \\ &= 3 \text{ months} \end{aligned}$$

The earliest start for activity 2 is

$$\begin{aligned} ES &= \text{max (EF immediate predecessors)} \\ &= 3 \text{ months} \end{aligned}$$

and the corresponding earliest finish time is

$$\begin{aligned} EF &= ES + t \\ &= 3 + 2 \\ &= 5 \text{ months} \end{aligned}$$

For activity 3 the earliest start time (ES) is three months, and the earliest finish time (EF) is four months.

Now consider activity 4, which has two predecessor activities. The earliest start time is

$$\begin{aligned} ES &= \text{max (EF immediate predecessors)} \\ &= \text{max } (5, 4) \\ &= 5 \text{ months} \end{aligned}$$

and the earliest finish time is

$$\begin{aligned} EF &= ES + t \\ &= 5 + 3 \\ &= 8 \text{ months} \end{aligned}$$

All the remaining earliest start and finish times are computed similarly. Notice in Figure 9.11 that the earliest finish time for activity 7, the last activity in the network, is nine months, which is the total project duration, or critical path time.

Figure 9.11
Earliest Activity Start and Finish Times

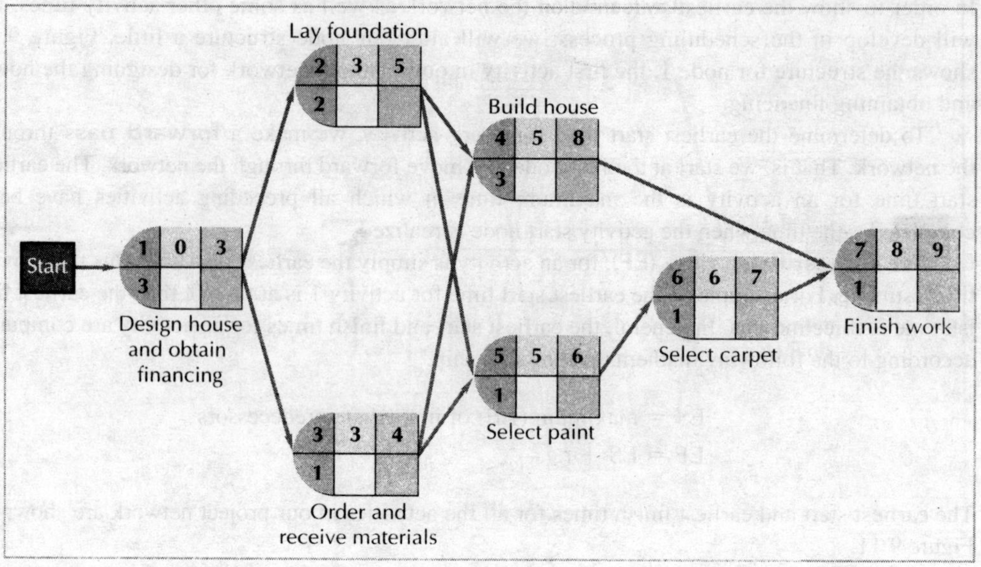

Companions to the earliest start and finish are the **latest start** and **latest finish times, LS** and **LF**. The latest start time is the latest time an activity can start without delaying the completion of the project beyond the project critical path time. For our example, the project completion time (and earliest finish time) at node 7 is nine months. Thus, the objective of determining latest times is to see how long each activity can be delayed without the project exceeding nine months.

In general, the latest start and finish times for an activity are computed according to the following formulas:

$$LS = LF - t$$
$$LF = \min \text{ (LS immediate following activities)}$$

Whereas a forward pass through the network is made to determine the earliest times, the latest times are computed using a **backward pass**. We start at the end of the network at node 7 and work backward, computing the latest times for each activity. Since we want to determine how long each activity in the network can be delayed without extending the project time, the latest finish time at node 7 cannot exceed the earliest finish time. Therefore, the latest finish time at node 7 is nine months. This and all other latest times are shown in Figure 9.12.

Starting at the end of the network, the critical path time, which is also equal to the earliest finish time of activity 7, is nine months. This automatically becomes the latest finish time for activity 7, or

$$LF = 9 \text{ months}$$

Using this value, the latest start time for activity 7 is

$$\begin{aligned} LS &= LF - t \\ &= 9 - 1 \\ &= 8 \text{ months} \end{aligned}$$

The latest finish time for activity 6 is the minimum of the latest start times for the activities following node 6. Since activity 7 follows node 6, the latest finish time is

$$\begin{aligned} LF_6 &= \min \text{ (LS following activities)} \\ &= 8 \text{ months} \end{aligned}$$

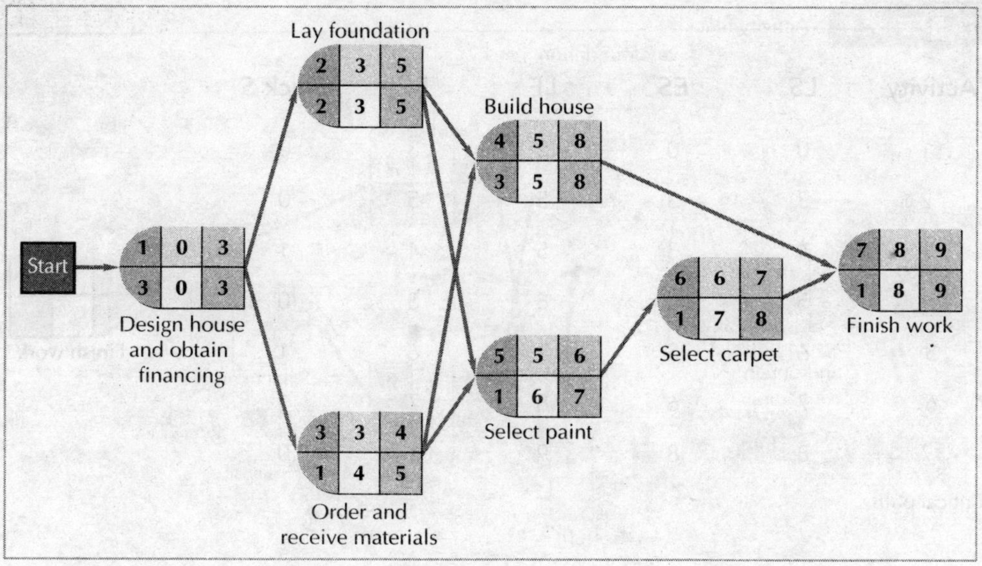

Figure 9.12

Latest Activity Start and Finish Times

The latest start time for activity 6 is

$$LS = LF - t$$
$$= 8 - 1$$
$$= 7 \text{ months}$$

For activity 4, the latest finish time (LF) is eight months, and the latest start time (LS) is five months; for activity 5, the latest finish time (LF) is seven months, and the latest start time (LS) is six months.

Now consider activity 3, which has two activities, 4 and 5, following it. The latest finish time is computed as

$$LF = \min(\text{LS following activities})$$
$$= \min(5, 6)$$
$$= 5 \text{ months}$$

The latest start time is

$$LS = LF - t$$
$$= 5 - 1$$
$$= 4 \text{ months}$$

All the remaining latest start and latest finish times are computed similarly. Figure 9.12 includes the earliest and latest start times and earliest and latest finish times for all activities.

ACTIVITY SLACK

The project network in Figure 9.12, with all activity start and finish times, highlights the critical path (1–2–4–7) we determined earlier by inspection. Notice that for the activities on the critical path, the earliest start times and latest start times are equal. This means that these activities on the critical path must start exactly on time and cannot be delayed at all. If the start of any activity on the critical path is delayed, then the overall project time will be increased. We now have an alternative way to determine the critical path besides simply inspecting the network. The activities on the critical path can be determined by seeing for which activities ES = LS or EF = LF. In Figure 9.12 the activities 1, 2, 4, and 7 all have earliest start times and latest start times that are equal (and EF = LF); thus, they are on the critical path.

TABLE 9.1 Activity Slack

Activity	LS	ES	LF	EF	Slack *S*
*1	0	0	3	3	0
*2	3	3	5	5	0
3	4	3	5	4	1
*4	5	5	8	8	0
5	6	5	7	6	1
6	7	6	8	7	1
*7	8	8	9	9	0

*Critical path.

For activities not on the critical path for which the earliest and latest start times (or earliest and latest finish times) are not equal, *slack* time exists. We introduced slack with our discussion of the Gantt chart in Figure 9.4. Slack is the amount of time an activity can be delayed without affecting the overall project duration. In effect, it is extra time available for completing an activity.

Slack, *S*, is computed using either of the following formulas:

$$S = \text{LS} - \text{ES}$$

or

$$S = \text{LF} - \text{EF}$$

For example, the slack for activity 3 is

$$\begin{aligned} S &= \text{LS} - \text{ES} \\ &= 4 - 3 \\ &= 1 \text{ month} \end{aligned}$$

If the start of activity 3 were delayed for one month, the activity could still be completed by month 5 without delaying the project completion time. The slack for each activity in our example project network is shown in Table 9.1. Table 9.1 shows there is no slack for the activities on the critical path (marked with an asterisk); activities not on the critical path have slack.

Notice in Figure 9.12 that activity 3 can be delayed one month and activity 5 that follows it can be delayed one more month, but then activity 6 cannot be delayed at all even though it has one month of slack. If activity 3 starts late at month 4 instead of month 3, then it will be completed at month 5, which will not allow activity 5 to start until month 5. If the start of activity 5 is delayed one month, then it will be completed at month 7, and activity 6 cannot be delayed at all without exceeding the critical path time. The slack on these three activities is called *shared slack*. This means that the sequence of activities 3–5–6 can be delayed two months jointly without delaying the project, but not three months.

Slack is beneficial to the project manager because it enables resources to be temporarily diverted from activities with slack and used for other activities that might be delayed for various reasons or for which the time estimate has proved to be inaccurate.

The times for the network activities are simply estimates, for which there is usually not a lot of historical basis (since projects tend to be unique undertakings). As such, activity time estimates are subject to quite a bit of uncertainty. However, the uncertainty inherent in activity time estimates can be reflected to a certain extent by using probabilistic time estimates instead of the single, deterministic estimates we have used so far.

Probabilistic Activity Times

In the project network for building a house in the previous section, all activity time estimates were single values. By using only a single activity time estimate, we are, in effect, assuming that activity times are known with certainty (i.e., they are deterministic). For example, in Figure 9.8, the time estimate for activity 2 (laying the foundation) is two months. Since only this one value is given, we must assume that the activity time does not vary (or varies very little) from two months. It is rare that activity time estimates can be made with certainty. Project activities are likely to be unique with little historical evidence that can be used as a basis to predict activity times. Recall that one of the primary differences between CPM and PERT is that PERT uses probabilistic activity times.

PROBABILISTIC TIME ESTIMATES

In the PERT-type approach to estimating activity times, three time estimates for each activity are determined, which enables us to estimate the mean and variance of a **beta distribution** of the activity times.

We assume that the activity times can be described by a beta distribution for several reasons. The beta distribution mean and variance can be approximated with three time estimates. Also, the beta distribution is continuous, but it has no predetermined shape (such as the bell shape of the normal curve). It will take on the shape indicated—that is, be skewed—by the time estimates given. This is beneficial, since typically we have no prior knowledge of the shapes of the distributions of activity times in a unique project network. Although other types of distributions have been shown to be no more or less accurate than the beta, it has become traditional to use the beta distribution to estimate probabilistic activity times.

The three time estimates for each activity are the **most likely time (m)**, the **optimistic time (a)**, and the **pessimistic time (b)**. The most likely time is a subjective estimate of the activity time that would most frequently occur if the activity were repeated many times. The optimistic time is the shortest possible time to complete the activity if everything went right. The pessimistic time is the longest possible time to complete the activity assuming everything went wrong. The person most familiar with an activity or the project manager makes these "subjective" estimates to the best of his or her knowledge and ability.

These three time estimates are used to estimate the mean and variance of a beta distribution, as follows:

$$\text{Mean (expected time): } t = \frac{a + 4m + b}{6}$$

$$\text{Variance: } \sigma^2 = \left(\frac{b - a}{6}\right)^2$$

where

a = optimistic time estimate

m = most likely time estimate

b = pessimistic time estimate

These formulas provide a reasonable estimate of the mean and variance of the beta distribution, a distribution that is continuous and can take on various shapes, or exhibit skewness.

Figure 9.13 illustrates the general form of beta distributions for different relative values of a, m, and b.

Figure 9.13

Examples of the Beta Distribution

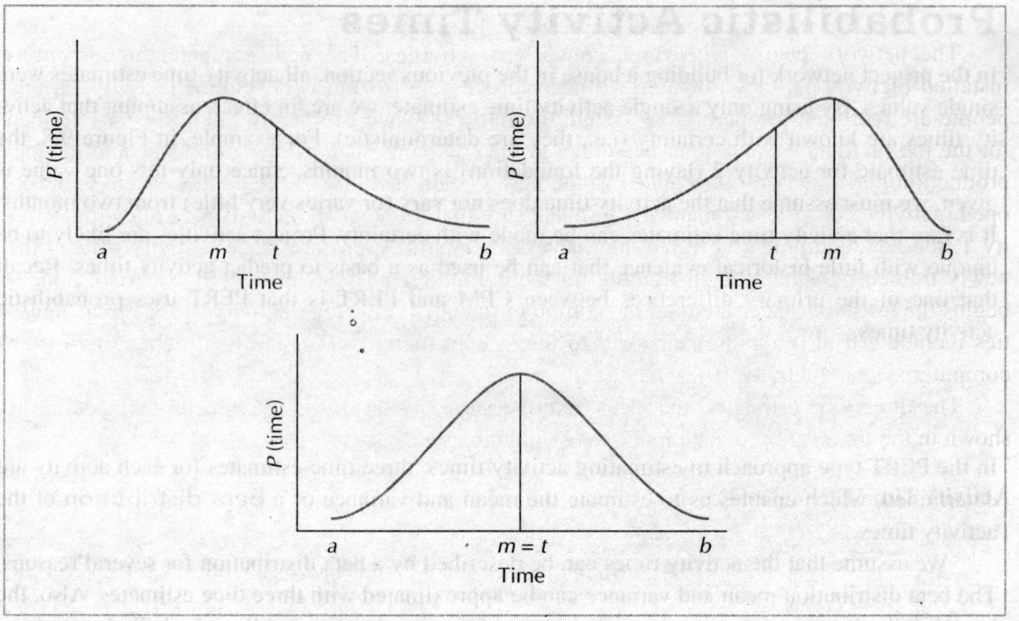

EXAMPLE 9.1

A PROJECT NETWORK WITH PROBABILISTIC TIME ESTIMATES

The Southern Textile Company has decided to install a new computerized order processing system that will link the company with customers and suppliers. In the past, orders were processed manually, which contributed to delays in delivery orders and resulted in lost sales. The new system will improve the quality of the service the company provides. The company wants to develop a project network for the installation of the new system. The network for the installation of the new order processing system is shown in the following figure.

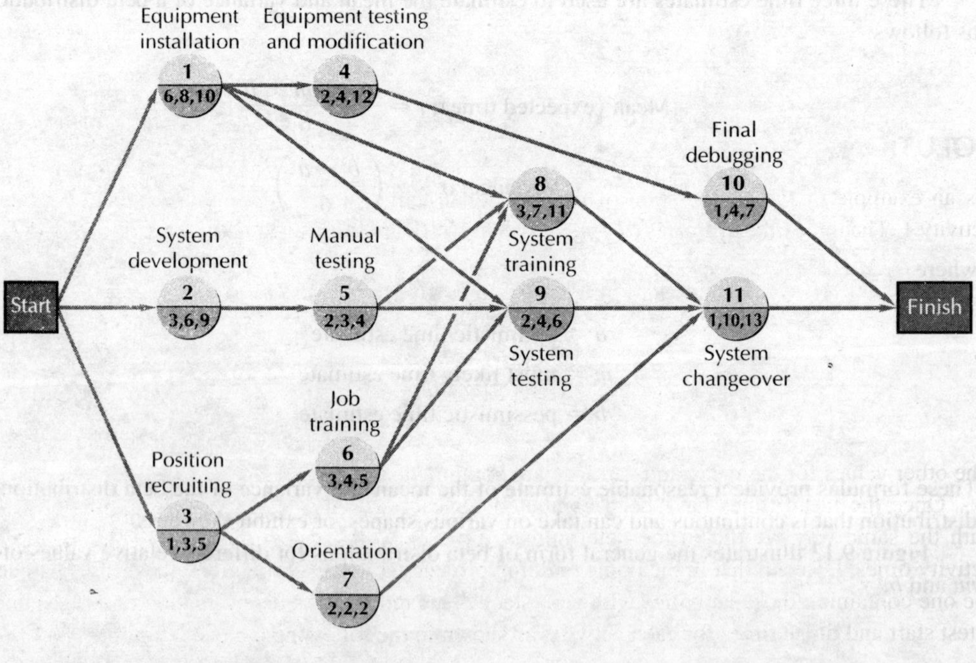

The network begins with three concurrent activities: The new computer equipment is installed (activity 1); the computerized order processing system is developed (activity 2); and people are recruited to operate the system (activity 3). Once people are hired, they are trained for the job (activity 6), and other personnel in the company, such as marketing, accounting, and production personnel, are introduced to the new system (activity 7). Once the system is developed (activity 2) it is tested manually to make sure that it is logical (activity 5). Following activity 1, the new equipment is tested, any necessary modifications are made (activity 4), and the newly trained personnel begin training on the computerized system (activity 8). Also, node 9 begins the testing of the system on the computer to check for errors (activity 9). The final activities include a trial run and changeover to the system (activity 11), and final debugging of the computer system (activity 10).

The three time estimates, the mean, and the variance for all the activities in the network as shown in the figure are provided in the following table:

Activity Time Estimates

	Time Estimates (weeks)			Mean Time	Variance
Activity	*a*	*m*	*b*	*t*	σ^2
1	6	8	10	8	0.44
2	3	6	9	6	1.00
3	1	3	5	3	0.44
4	2	4	12	5	2.78
5	2	3	4	3	0.11
6	3	4	5	4	0.11
7	2	2	2	2	0.00
8	3	7	11	7	1.78
9	2	4	6	4	0.44
10	1	4	7	4	1.00
11	1	10	13	9	4.00

SOLUTION

As an example of the computation of the individual activity mean times and variance, consider activity 1. The three time estimates ($a = 6, m = 8, b = 10$) are substituted in the formulas as follows:

$$t = \frac{a + 4m + b}{6} = \frac{6 + 4(8) + 10}{6} = 8 \text{ weeks}$$

$$\sigma^2 = \left(\frac{b - a}{6}\right)^2 = \left(\frac{10 - 6}{6}\right)^2 = \frac{4}{9} \text{ week}$$

The other values for the mean and variance are computed similarly.

Once the mean times have been computed for each activity, we can determine the critical path the same way we did in the deterministic time network, except that we use the expected activity times, *t*. Recall that in the home building project network, we identified the critical path as the one containing those activities with zero slack. This requires the determination of earliest and latest start and finish times for each activity, as shown in the following table and figure:

(*Continued*)

Activity Earliest and Latest Times and Slack

Activity	t	σ^2	ES	EF	LS	LF	S
1	8	0.44	0	8	1	9	1
2	6	1.00	0	6	0	6	0
3	3	0.44	0	3	2	5	2
4	5	2.78	8	13	16	21	8
5	3	0.11	6	9	6	9	0
6	4	0.11	3	7	5	9	2
7	2	0.00	3	5	14	16	11
8	7	1.78	9	16	9	16	0
9	4	0.44	9	13	12	16	3
10	4	1.00	13	17	21	25	8
11	9	4.00	16	25	16	25	0

From the table, we can see that the critical path encompasses activities 2–5–8–11, since these activities have no available slack. We can also see that the expected project completion time (t_p) is the same as the earliest or latest finish for activity 11, or $t_p = 25$ weeks. To determine the project variance, we *sum the variances for the activities on the critical path*. Using the variances shown in the table for the critical path activities, we can compute the total project variance as follows:

$$\sigma^2 = \sigma_2^2 + \sigma_5^2 + \sigma_8^2 + \sigma_{11}^2$$
$$= 1.00 + 0.11 + 1.78 + 4.00$$
$$= 6.89 \text{ weeks}$$

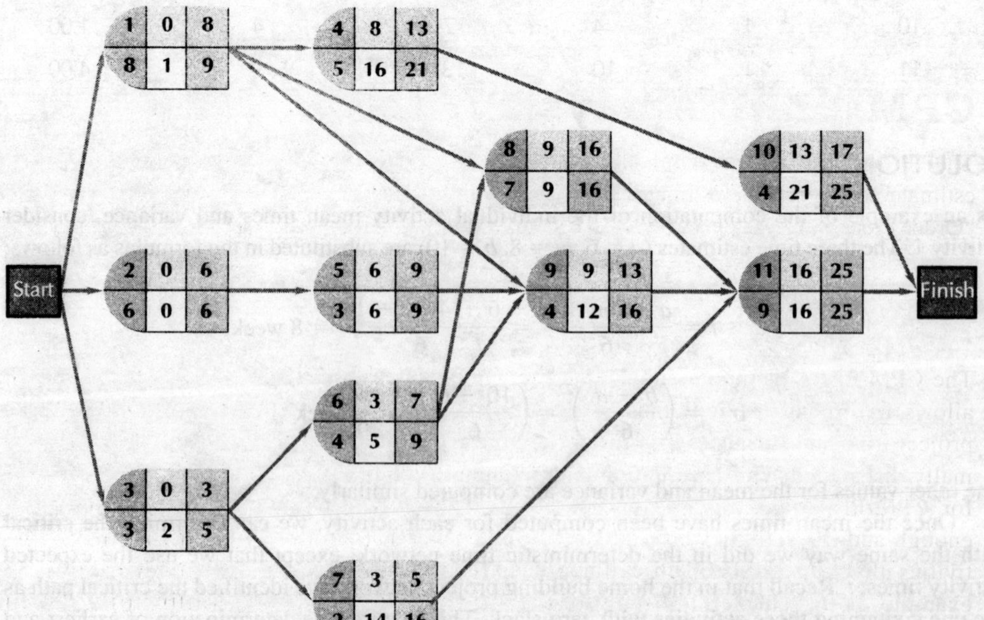

EXHIBIT 9.1

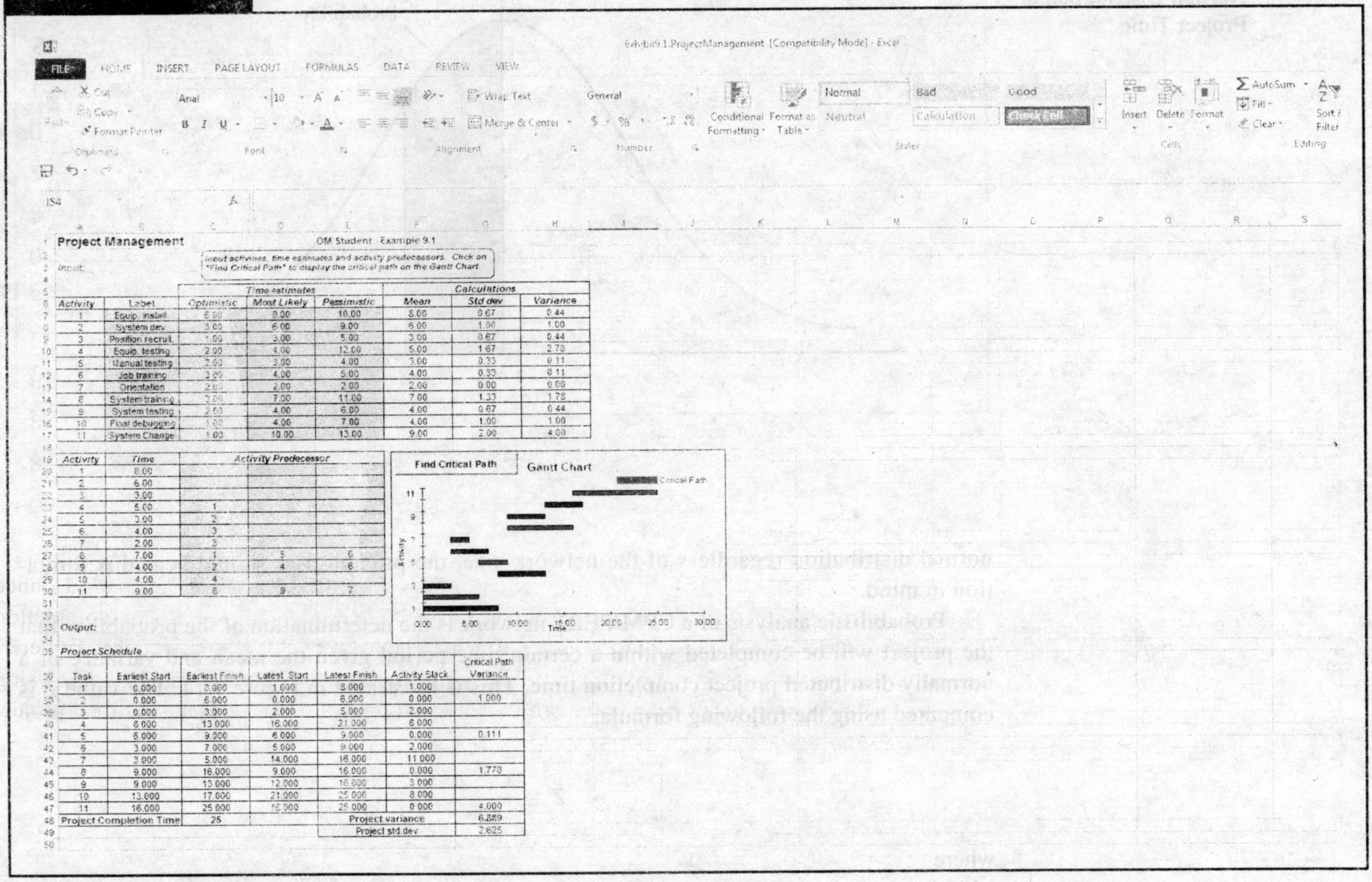

CPM/PERT Analysis with OM Tools

The "Project Management" module in OM Tools has the capability to develop both single-time estimate and three-time estimate networks. Exhibit 9.1 shows the OM Tools spreadsheet for the "Order Processing System" project in Example 9.1.

PROBABILISTIC NETWORK ANALYSIS

The CPM/PERT method assumes that the activity times are statistically independent, which allows us to sum the individual expected activity times and variances to get an expected project time and variance. It is further assumed that the network mean and variance are normally distributed. This assumption is based on the central limit theorem of probability, which for CPM/PERT analysis and our purposes states that if the number of activities is large enough and the activities are statistically independent, then the sum of the means of the activities along the critical path will approach the mean of a normal distribution. For the small examples in this chapter, it is questionable whether there are sufficient activities to guarantee that the mean project completion time and variance are normally distributed. Although it has become conventional in CPM/PERT analysis to employ probability analysis using the

Figure 9.14

Normal Distribution of Project Time

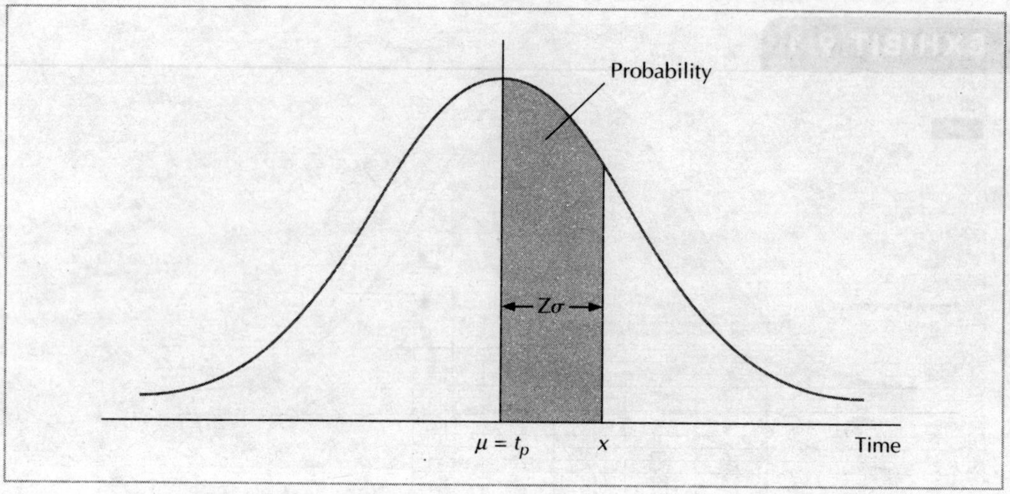

normal distribution regardless of the network size, the prudent user should bear this limitation in mind.

Probabilistic analysis of a CPM/PERT network is the determination of the probability that the project will be completed within a certain time period given the mean and variance of a normally distributed project completion time. This is illustrated in Figure 9.14. The value Z is computed using the following formula:

$$Z = \frac{x - \mu}{\sigma}$$

where

$\mu = t_p =$ project mean time

$x =$ the proposed project time

$Z =$ number of standard devisions x is from the mean

This value of Z is then used to find the corresponding probability in Table SC.1 (Supplement C).

EXAMPLE 9.2

PROBABILISTIC ANALYSIS OF THE PROJECT NETWORK

The Southern Textile Company in Example 9.1 has told its customers that the new order processing system will be operational in 30 weeks. What is the probability that the system will be ready by that time?

SOLUTION

The probability that the project will be completed within 30 weeks is shown as the shaded area in the accompanying figure. To compute the Z value for a time of 30 weeks, we must first compute the standard deviation (σ) from the variance (σ^2).

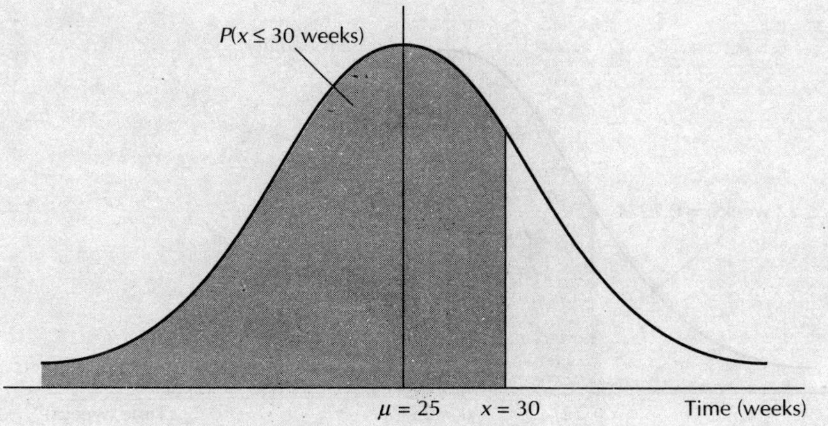

$$\sigma^2 = 6.89 \text{ weeks}$$
$$\sigma = \sqrt{6.89}$$
$$= 2.62 \text{ weeks}$$

Next we substitute this value for the standard deviation along with the value for the mean, 25 weeks, and our proposed project completion time, 30 weeks, into the following formula:

$$Z = \frac{x - \mu}{\sigma}$$
$$= \frac{30 - 25}{2.62}$$
$$= 1.91$$

A Z value of 1.91 corresponds to a probability of 0.4719 in Table SC.1 (Supplement C). This means that there is a 0.9719 probability of completing the project in 30 weeks or less (adding the probability of the area to the left of $\mu = 25$, or 0.5000, to 0.4719).

EXAMPLE 9.3

PROBABILISTIC ANALYSIS OF THE PROJECT NETWORK

A customer of the Southern Textile Company has become frustrated with delayed orders and told the company that if the new ordering system is not working within 22 weeks, it will not do any more business with the textile company. What is the probability the order processing system will be operational within 22 weeks?

SOLUTION

The probability that the project will be completed within 22 weeks is shown as the shaded area in the accompanying figure.

(Continued)

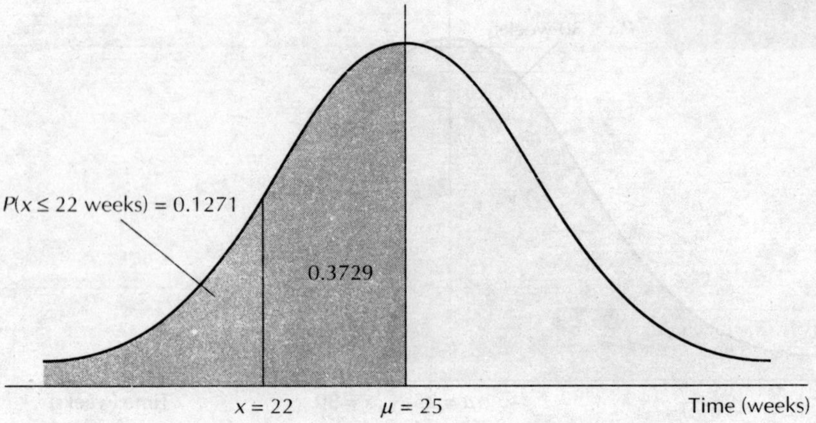

The probability of the project's being completed within 22 weeks is computed as follows:

$$Z = \frac{22 - 25}{2.62}$$
$$= \frac{-3}{2.62}$$
$$= -1.14$$

A Z value of -1.14 corresponds to a probability of 0.3729 in the normal table in Supplement C. Thus, there is only a 0.1271 (i.e., $0.5000 - 0.3729$) probability that the system will be operational in 22 weeks.

Microsoft Project

Microsoft Project is a popular and widely used software package for project management and CPM/PERT analysis. It is also relatively easy to use. We will demonstrate how to use Microsoft Project using the project network for building a house shown in Figure 9.8.

When you open *Microsoft Project,* a screen comes up for a new project, as shown in Exhibit 9.2. Notice that the "Gantt Chart Tools" tab on the toolbar ribbon at the top of the screen is highlighted. The initial step is to set the project up in this window. First type in the activity name, "Design and finance" under the "Task Name" column, and then type in the activity duration in the "Duration" column, which is three months for this activity. This only requires that you type "3 mo" and it will be recognized as 3 months. Next, type in a "Start" date, which we have selected to be "March 18, 2013." The start date can also be selected from the drop-down calendar. (Note that a start date must be designated for all starting activities that don't have predecessors, which for this example is only the first activity.) This first activity has no predecessor, so leave the "Predecessor" cell for this activity blank, and drop down to the next line to enter the next activity, "Lay foundation." Repeat the process followed for the first activity by typing in the duration, "2 mos," but do not type in the start and finish dates; the program will do this automatically once you start identifying activity predecessors. Toggle over to the "Predecessor" cell for this activity and type in "1" (indicating that activity 1 is the predecessor activity for this activity, 2. Next, drop down to the next line and type in the information for activity 3, "Order materials," the duration of "1 mo," and that its "Predecessor" is activity 1. Exhibit 9.3 shows our progress so far.

EXHIBIT 9.2

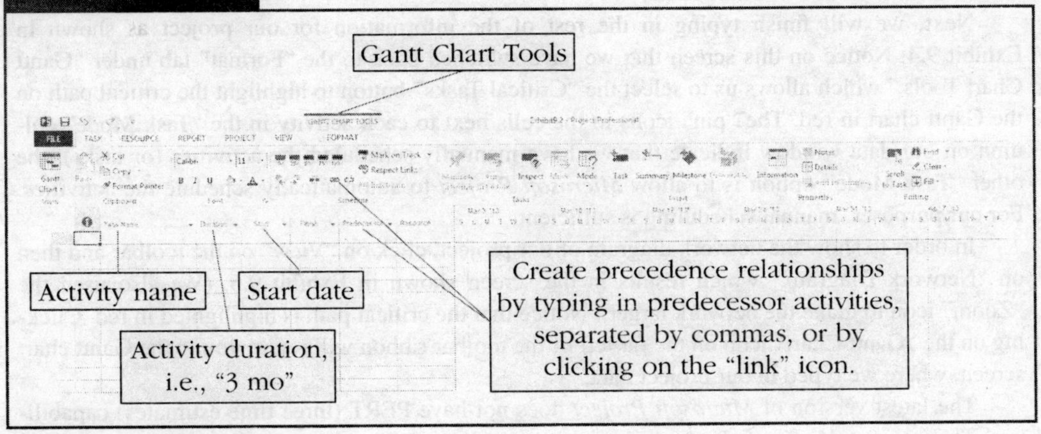

EXHIBIT 9.3

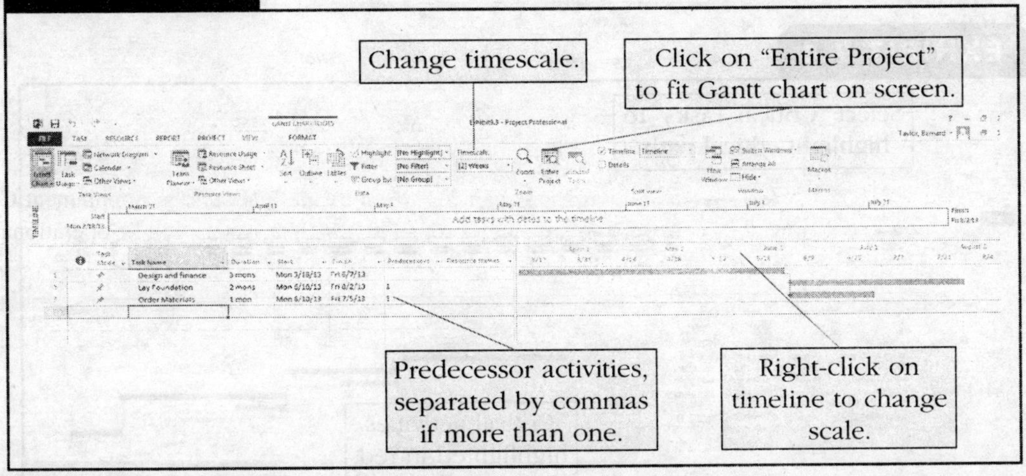

Before proceeding to finishing inputting the project data, we'll make a few comments. First, note the emerging Gantt chart forming on the calendar part of your window (on the right-hand part of the screen) for the activities we've entered. This chart might not be on your screen when you start because the timescale on the calendar does not conform to your start date. If the Gantt chart is not there, you can make it appear by moving the tab at the bottom of the calendar part of the screen ahead (i.e., to the right) until your start date appears, and this view should contain the beginning of your Gantt chart. Also, notice at the top of the window that we have switched to the "View" tab. On this toolbar ribbon, if you click on "Timescale," you can insert the time units of the project, which in this case is months, or you can accomplish the same thing by "right-clicking" on the timeline just above the Gantt chart and then clicking on "Timescale" from the drop-down menu. You can also condense the size of your Gantt chart to fit on the calendar part of your screen by clicking on the button on the "Entire Project" icon on the toolbar.

Microsoft Project uses a "standard" calendar for scheduling project activities; for example, it automatically removes weekend days as working days. Holidays and vacation days can also be designated by first clicking on the "Project" tab, then clicking on the "Change Working Time" icon. This will bring up a window with a calendar and menu for changing work times.

The activity predecessor relationships showing, for example, that activity 1 precedes activity 2, can also be established by placing the cursor on activity 1, then holding down the "Ctrl" key while clicking on activity 2 and then clicking on the "link" icon (i.e., the little chain link) from the "Task" tab under "Gantt Chart Tools."

Next, we will finish typing in the rest of the information for our project as shown in Exhibit 9.4. Notice on this screen that we have switched back to the "Format" tab under "Gantt Chart Tools," which allows us to select the "Critical Tasks" button to highlight the critical path on the Gantt chart in red. The "pin" icons in the cells next to each activity in the "Task Mode" column on our data window indicate that we have manually scheduled the activities (or tasks); the other "Task Mode" option is to allow *Microsoft Project* to automatically schedule the activities. For our purposes, manual scheduling is sufficient.

In order to show the network diagram of our project, click on "View" on the toolbar and then on "Network Diagram," which results in the screen shown in Exhibit 9.5. (We also used the "Zoom" icon to make the network larger.) Notice that the critical path is highlighted in red. Clicking on the "Gantt Chart" icon on the far left of the toolbar ribbon will return you to the Gantt chart screen, where we typed in our project data.

The latest version of *Microsoft Project* does not have PERT (three time estimates) capabilities. Thus, to use *Microsoft Project* when you have three time estimates you must first manually

EXHIBIT 9.4

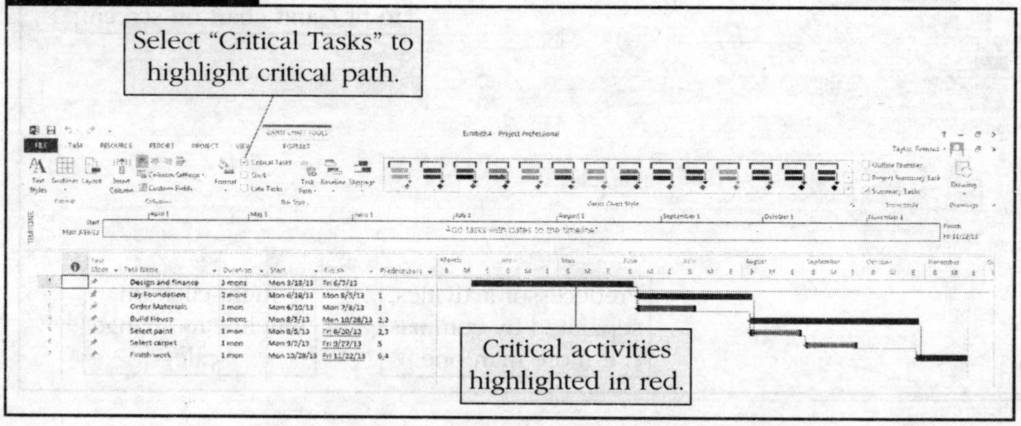

EXHIBIT 9.5

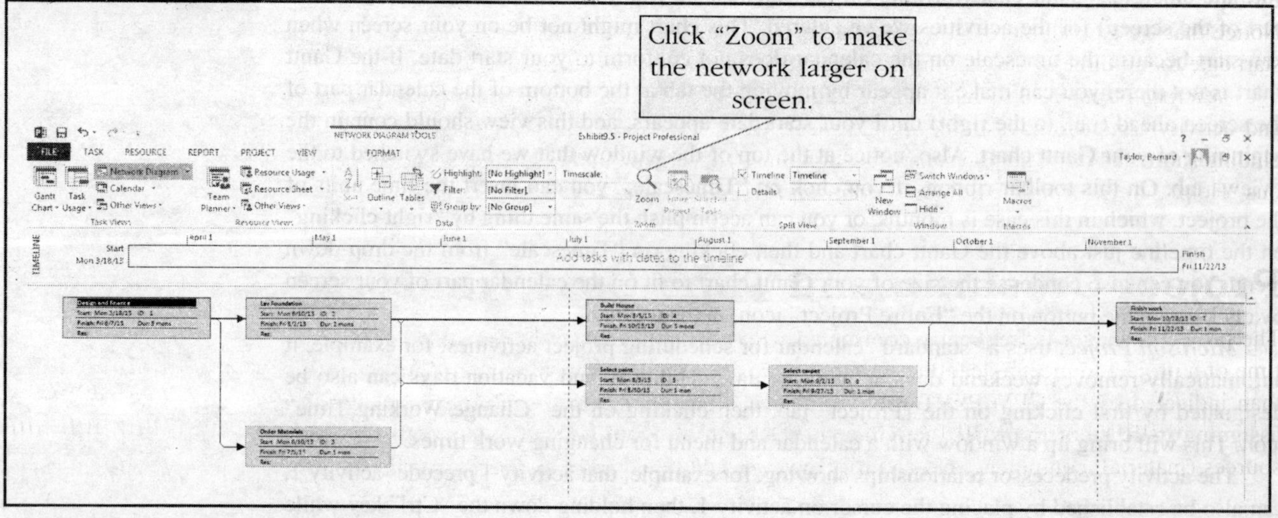

EXHIBIT 9.6

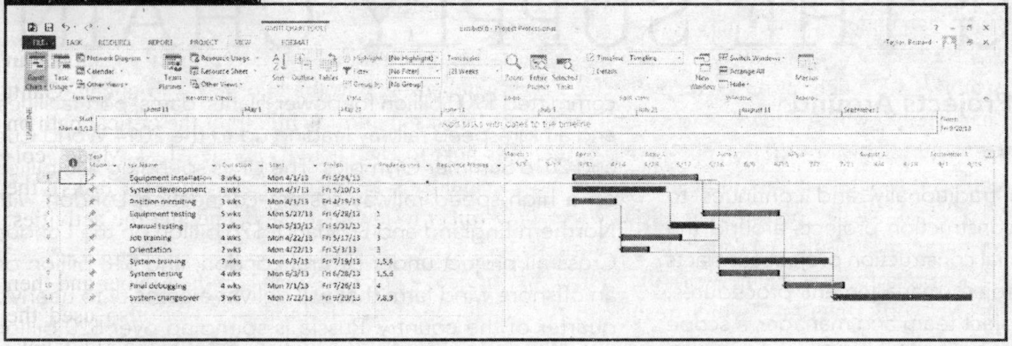

EXHIBIT 9.7

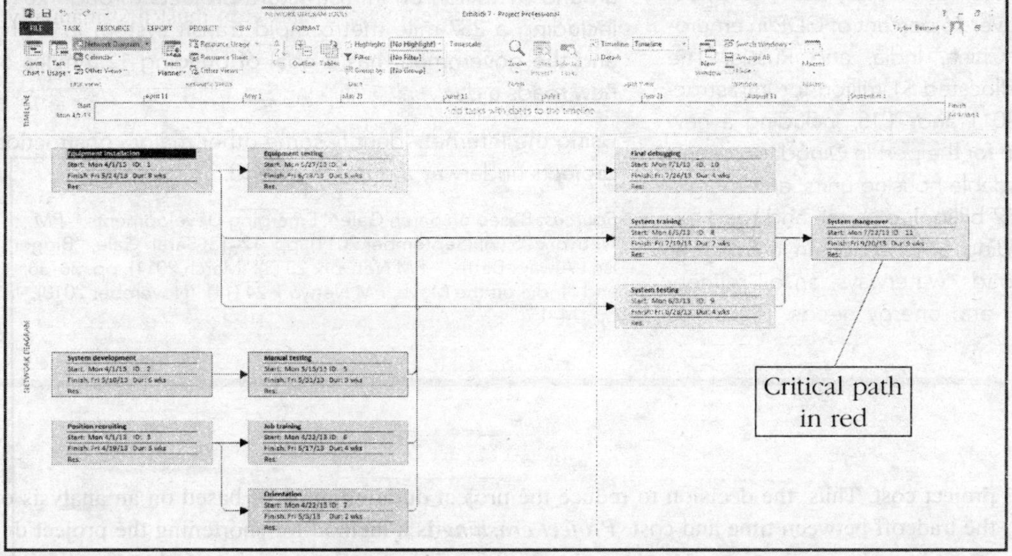

(or using Excel) compute the mean activity times and use these as single time estimates in *Microsoft Project*. Exhibit 9.6 shows the Gantt chart window for our "Order Processing System" project example where the mean activity time estimates are used. Exhibit 9.7 shows the network diagram. Notice that we gave this project a start date of April 1, 2013, which had to be designated as the start date for all three of our starting activities (that do not have predecessors): 1, 2, and 3.

Microsoft Project also has many additional tools and features, including project updating and activity completion, resource management, work stoppages, and changing work times, including shortened days, holidays, and vacation time. To learn about these features, access the various "Help" screens from the different *Microsoft Project* windows or press the F1 key.

Project Crashing and Time-Cost Tradeoff

The project manager is frequently confronted with having to reduce the scheduled completion time of a project to meet a deadline. In other words, the manager must finish the project sooner than indicated by the CPM/PERT network analysis. Project duration can often be reduced by assigning more labor to project activities, in the form of overtime, and by assigning more resources (material, equipment, and so on). However, additional labor and resources increase the

ALONG THE SUPPLY CHAIN

Construction Mega-Projects Around the World

Project management has traditionally, and continues to be, extensively used for construction projects around the world. Public and commercial construction project contracts typically require formal project management procedures, including a designated project team and manager, a scope statement, and project networks. The proliferation of construction projects has received an additional boost in recent years from economic stimulus monies by governments around the world. Studies estimate that by 2020, construction projects will make up over 16 percent of GDP in emerging global markets like China, India, and Russia. The Chinese government has allocated $1 trillion for infrastructure spending between 2011 and 2015, including a new airport in Beijing, expansion for the port in Qingdao (costing $15 billion), 36 million affordable housing units, and a high-speed railroad (costing $32 billion), plus rail and road extensions. Mexico is spending $141 billion in a five-year plan for ports, airports, roads, waterways, an oil refinery (for $7 billion), and water and energy needs. Brazil has committed $900 billion for power plants, dams, port facilities, and a high-speed railway leading up to the 2014 World Cup and 2016 Summer Olympics. The UK is spending $46 billion on a high-speed railway system connecting London with Northern England and Scotland; $26 billion on the London Crossrail project under central London; and $18 billion on an offshore wind farm that will deliver electricity to nearly a quarter of the country. Russia is spending over $20 billion for a natural gas pipeline stretching from Russia through the Black Sea to Bulgaria. India recently completed $514 billion in infrastructure projects, and expects to spend around $1 trillion on infrastructure projects through 2017, including a 257-mile metro rapid transit system in Delhi, and the government has a goal of building 12.5 miles of new roads a day.

Using the Internet, identify some other major construction projects underway around the world.

Sources: Based on Sarah Gale, "Emerging Developments," *PM Network* 25 (9); (September 2011), pp. 12–13; Sarah Gale, "Bigger Isn't Always Better," *PM Network* 25 (3); (March 2011), pp. 26–36; and "India on the Move, *PM Network* 24 (11); (November 2010), pp. 14–15.

project cost. Thus, the decision to reduce the project duration must be based on an analysis of the tradeoff between time and cost. *Project crashing* is a method for shortening the project duration by reducing the time of one (or more) of the critical project activities to less than its normal activity time. This reduction in the normal activity time is referred to as **crashing**. Crashing is achieved by devoting more resources, usually measured in terms of dollars, to the activities to be crashed.

PROJECT CRASHING

To demonstrate how project crashing works, we will employ the CPM/PERT network for constructing a house in Figure 9.8. This network is repeated in Figure 9.15, except that the activity times previously shown as months have been converted to weeks. Although this sample network encompasses only single-activity time estimates, the project crashing procedure can be applied in the same manner to PERT networks with probabilistic activity time estimates.

We will assume that the times (in weeks) shown on the network activities are the normal activity times. For example, 12 weeks are normally required to complete activity 1. Furthermore, we will assume that the cost required to complete this activity in the time indicated is $3,000. This cost is referred to as the *normal activity cost*. Next, we will assume that the building contractor has estimated that activity 1 can be completed in seven weeks, but it will cost $5,000 instead of $3,000 to complete the activity. This new estimated activity time is known as the **crash time**, and the cost to achieve the crash time is referred to as the **crash cost**.

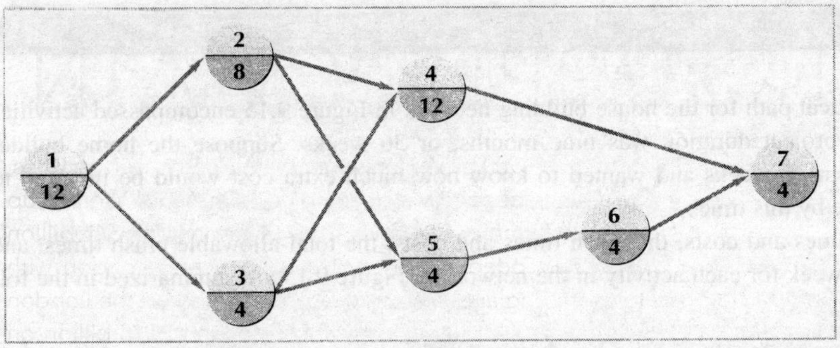

Figure 9.15

The Project Network for Building a House

Activity 1 can be crashed a total of five weeks (normal time − crash time = 12 − 7 = 5 weeks) at a total crash cost of \$2,000 (crash cost − normal cost = \$5,000 − 3,000 = \$2,000). Dividing the total crash cost by the total allowable crash time yields the crash cost per week:

$$\frac{\text{Total crash cost}}{\text{Total crash time}} = \frac{\$2000}{5} = \$400 \text{ per week}$$

If we assume that the relationship between crash cost and crash time is linear, then activity 1 can be crashed by any amount of time (not exceeding the maximum allowable crash time) at a rate of \$400 per week. For example, if the contractor decided to crash activity 1–2 by only two weeks (reducing activity time to 10 weeks), the crash cost would be \$800 (\$400 per week × 2 weeks). The linear relationships between crash cost and crash time and between normal cost and normal time are illustrated in Figure 9.16.

The objective of project crashing is to reduce project duration while minimizing the cost of crashing. Since the project completion time can be shortened only by crashing activities on the critical path, it may turn out that not all activities have to be crashed. However, as activities are crashed, the critical path may change, requiring crashing of previously noncritical activities to reduce the project completion time even further.

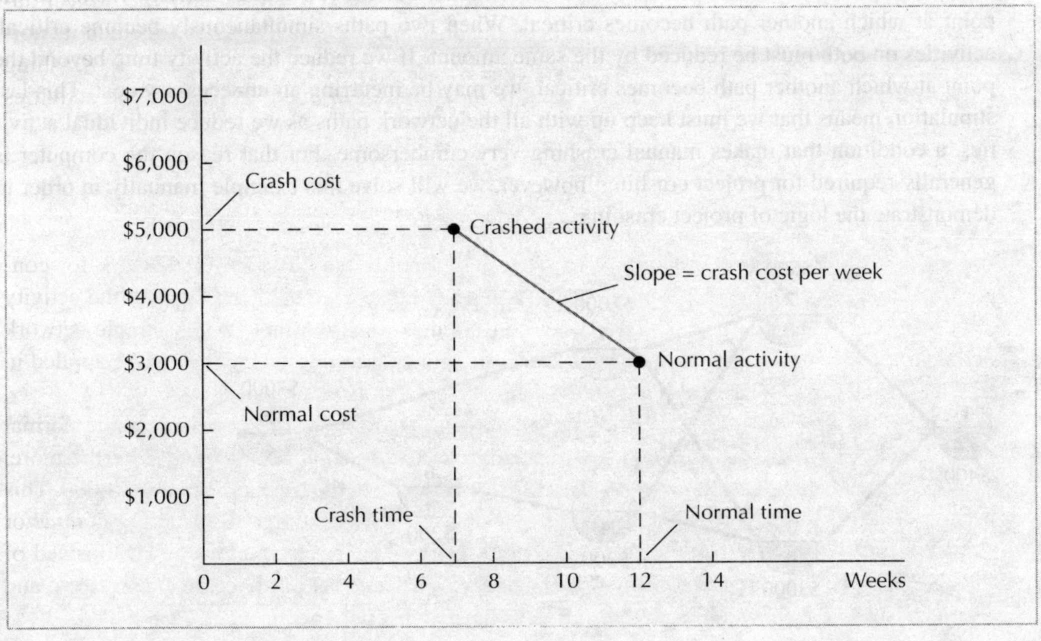

Figure 9.16

The Relationship Between Normal Time and Cost, and Crash Time and Cost

EXAMPLE 9.4

PROJECT CRASHING

Recall that the critical path for the house building network in Figure 9.15 encompassed activities 1–2–4–7 and the project duration was nine months, or 36 weeks. Suppose the home builder needed the house in 30 weeks and wanted to know how much extra cost would be incurred to complete the house by this time.

The normal times and costs, the crash times and costs, the total allowable crash times, and the crash cost per week for each activity in the network in Figure 9.15 are summarized in the following table:

Normal Activity and Crash Data

Activity	Normal Time (weeks)	Crash Time (weeks)	Normal Cost	Crash Cost	Total Allowable Crash Time (weeks)	Crash Cost per Week
1	12	7	$3,000	$5,000	5	$400
2	8	5	2,000	3,500	3	500
3	4	3	4,000	7,000	1	3,000
4	12	9	50,000	71,000	3	7,000
5	4	1	500	1,100	3	200
6	4	1	500	1,100	3	200
7	4	3	15,000	22,000	1	7,000
			$75,000	$110,700		

SOLUTION

We start by looking at the critical path and seeing which activity has the minimum crash cost per week. Observing the preceding table and the figure below, we see activity 1 has the minimum crash cost of $400. Activity 1 will be reduced as much as possible. The table shows that the maximum allowable reduction for activity 1 is five weeks, but we can reduce activity 1 only to the point at which another path becomes critical. When two paths simultaneously become critical, activities on both must be reduced by the same amount. If we reduce the activity time beyond the point at which another path becomes critical, we may be incurring an unnecessary cost. This last stipulation means that we must keep up with all the network paths as we reduce individual activities, a condition that makes manual crashing very cumbersome. For that reason the computer is generally required for project crashing; however, we will solve this example manually in order to demonstrate the logic of project crashing.

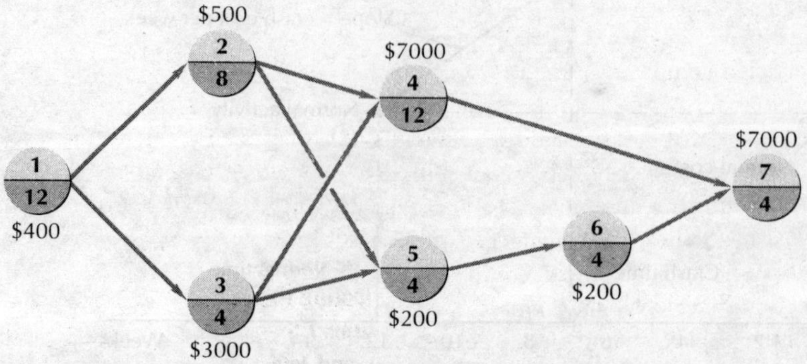

It turns out that activity 1 can be crashed by the total amount of five weeks without another path becoming critical, since activity 1 is included in all four paths in the network. Crashing this activity results in a revised project duration of 31 weeks at a crashing cost of $2,000. The revised network is shown in the following figure:

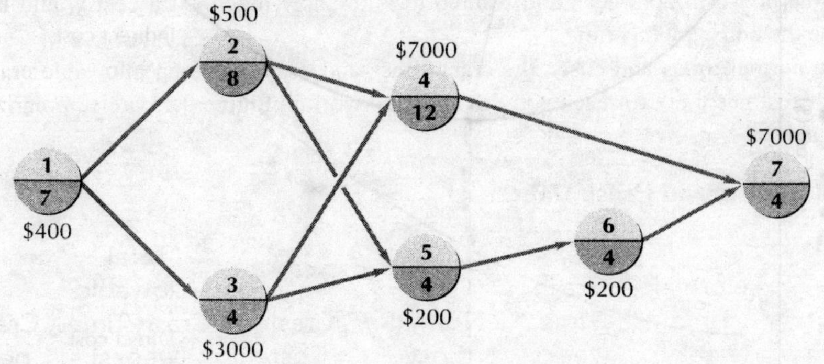

Since we have not reached our crashing goal of 30 weeks, we must continue, and the process is repeated. The critical path in the preceding figure remains the same, and the minimum activity crash cost on the critical path is $500 for activity 2. Activity 2 can be crashed a total of three weeks, but since the contractor desires to crash the network only to 30 weeks, we need to crash activity 2 by only one week. Crashing activity 2 by one week does not result in any other path becoming critical, so we can safely make this reduction. Crashing activity 2 to seven weeks (i.e., a one-week reduction) costs $500 and reduces the project duration to 30 weeks.

The total cost of crashing the project to 30 weeks is $2,500. The contractor could inform the customer that an additional cost of only $2,500 would be incurred to finish the house in 30 weeks.

Suppose we wanted to continue to crash this network, reducing the project duration down to the minimum time possible—that is, crashing the network the maximum amount possible. We can determine how much the network can be crashed by crashing each activity the maximum amount possible and then determining the critical path of this completely crashed network. For example, activity 1 is seven weeks, activity 2 is five weeks, 3 is three weeks, and so on. The critical path of this totally crashed network is 1–2–4–7, with a project duration of 24 weeks. This is the smallest amount of time in which the project can be completed. If we crashed all the activities by their maximum amount, the total crashing cost would be $35,700, computed by subtracting the total normal cost of $75,000 from the total crash cost of $110,700 in the preceding table. However, if we followed the crashing procedure outlined in this example, the network could be crashed to 24 weeks at a cost of $31,500, a savings of $4,000.

THE GENERAL RELATIONSHIP OF TIME AND COST

In our discussion of project crashing, we demonstrated how the project critical path time could be reduced by increasing expenditures for labor and other direct resources. The objective of crashing was to reduce the scheduled completion time to reap the results of the project sooner. However, there may be other reasons for reducing project time. As projects continue over time, they consume *indirect costs*, including the cost of facilities, equipment, and machinery, interest on investment, utilities, labor, personnel costs, and the loss of skills and labor from members of the project team who are not working at their regular jobs. There also may be direct financial penalties for not completing a project on time. For example, many construction contracts and government contracts have penalty clauses for exceeding the project completion date.

In general, project crashing costs and indirect costs have an inverse relationship: crashing costs are highest when the project is shortened, whereas indirect costs increase as the project duration increases. This time–cost relationship is illustrated in Figure 9.17. The best, or optimal, project time is at the minimum point on the total cost curve.

Figure 9.17

The Time–Cost Tradeoff

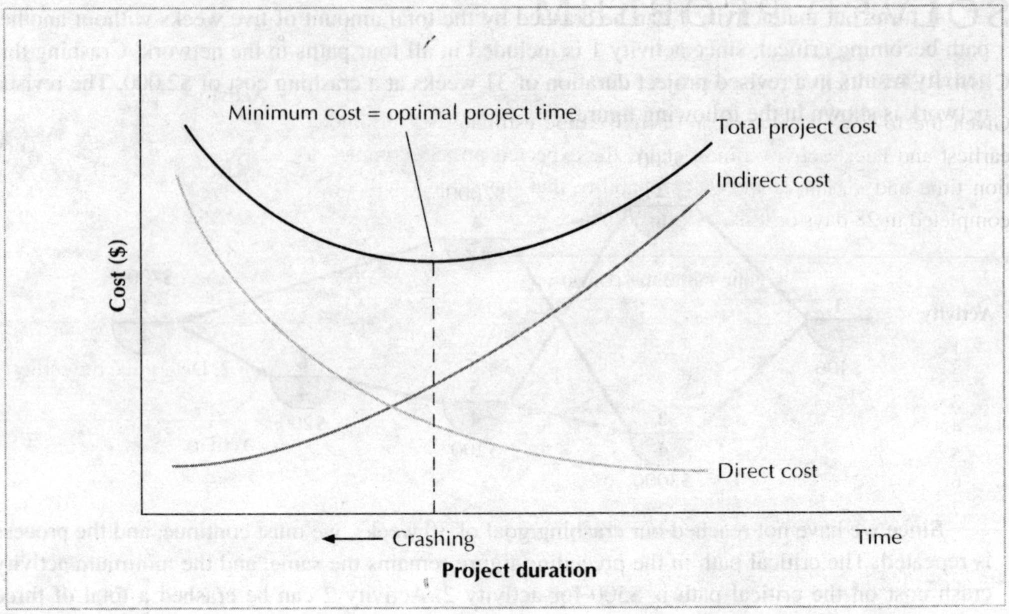

SUMMARY

Since the development of CPM/PERT in the 1950s, it has been applied in a variety of government agencies concerned with project control, including military agencies, NASA, the Federal Aviation Agency (FAA), and the General Services Administration (GSA). These agencies are frequently involved in large-scale projects involving millions of dollars and many subcontractors. CPM/PERT has also been widely applied in the private sector. Two of the areas of application of CPM/PERT in the private sector have been research and development (R&D) and construction.

One reason for this popularity is that a network analysis provides a visual display of the project that is easy for managers and staff to understand and interpret. It is a powerful tool for identifying and organizing the activities in a project and controlling the project schedule. However, beyond that it provides an effective focal point for organizing the efforts of management and the project team. Currently, hundreds of project management software packages are commercially available for personal computers, ranging in cost from several hundred dollars to thousands of dollars.

CPM/PERT also has certain limitations. The project manager tends to rely so heavily on the project network that errors in the precedence relationship or missing activities can be overlooked, until a point in time where these omissions become a problem. Attention to critical path activities can become excessive to the extent that other project activities may be neglected, or they may be delayed to the point that other paths become critical. Obtaining accurate single-time estimates and even three probabilistic time estimates is difficult and subject to a great deal of uncertainty. Since persons directly associated with the project activity within the organization are typically the primary source for time estimates, they may be overly pessimistic if they have a vested interest in the scheduling process or overly optimistic if they do not. Personal interests aside, it is frequently difficult to define, within the context of an activity, what an optimistic or pessimistic time means. Nevertheless, such reservations have not diminished the popularity of CPM/PERT because most people feel its usefulness far outweighs any speculative or theoretical drawbacks.

KEY FORMULAS

Earliest Start and Finish Times

$$\text{ES} = \max\ (\text{EF of immediately preceding activities})$$

$$\text{EF} = \text{ES} + t$$

Latest Start and Finish Times

$$\text{LS} = \text{LF} - t$$

$$\text{LF} = \min\ (\text{LS of immediately following activities})$$

Activity Slack

$$S = \text{LS} - \text{ES} = \text{LF} - \text{EF}$$

Mean Activity Time and Variance

$$t = \frac{a + 4m + b}{6}$$

$$\sigma^2 = \left(\frac{b - a}{6}\right)^2$$

SOLVED PROBLEM

CPM/PERT NETWORK ANALYSIS

Given the following network and activity time estimates, determine earliest and latest activity times, slack, the expected project completion time and variance, and the probability that the project will be completed in 28 days or less.

	Time Estimates (Days)		
Activity	***a***	***m***	***b***
1	5	8	17
2	7	10	13
3	3	5	7
4	1	3	5
5	4	6	8
6	3	3	3
7	3	4	5

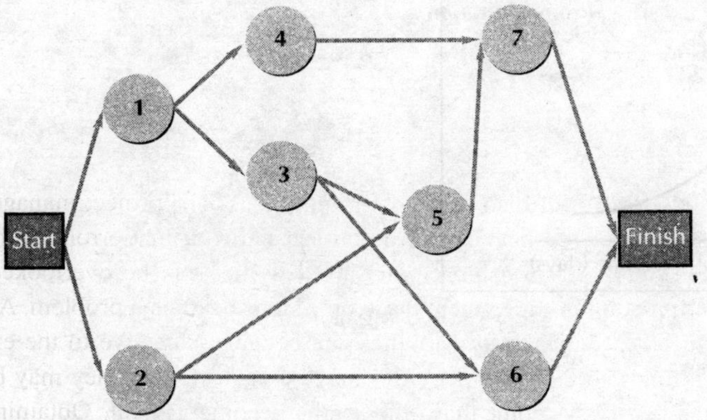

SOLUTION

Step 1. Compute the expected activity times and variances:

$$t = \frac{a + 4m + b}{6}$$

$$\sigma^2 = \left(\frac{b - a}{6}\right)^2$$

For example, the expected time and variance for activity 1 are

$$t = \frac{5 + 4(8) + 17}{6} = 9 \text{ days}$$

$$\sigma^2 = \left(\frac{17 - 5}{6}\right)^2 = 4 \text{ days}$$

These values and the remaining expected times and variances for each activity are shown in the following table:

Activity	*t*	σ^2
1	9	4
2	10	1
3	5	4/9
4	3	4/9
5	6	4/9
6	3	0
7	4	1/9

Step 2. Determine the earliest and latest activity times and activity slack:

Activity	*t*	ES	EF	LS	LF	*S*
1	9	0	9	0	9	0
2	10	0	10	4	14	4
3	5	9	14	9	14	0
4	3	9	12	17	20	8
5	6	14	20	14	20	0
6	3	14	17	21	24	7
7	4	20	24	20	24	0

As an example, the earliest start and finish times for activity 1 are

$$\begin{aligned} \text{ES} &= \max \text{ (EF immediate predecessors)} \\ &= 0 \\ \text{EF} &= \text{ES} + t \\ &= 0 + 9 \\ &= 9 \end{aligned}$$

The latest start and finish times for activity 7 are

$$\begin{aligned} \text{LF} &= \min \text{ (LS following activities)} \\ &= 24 \\ \text{LS} &= \text{LF} - t \\ &= 24 - 4 \\ &= 20 \end{aligned}$$

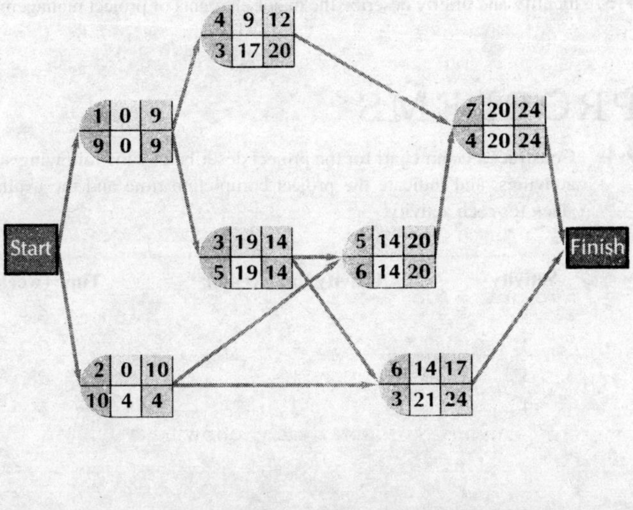

Step 3. Identify the critical path and compute expected project completion time and variance. Observing the preceding table and those activities with no slack (i.e., $s = 0$), we can identify the critical path as 1–3–5–7. The expected project completion time (t_p) is 24 days. The variance is computed by summing the variances for the activities in the critical path:

$$\sigma^2 = 4 + \frac{4}{9} + \frac{4}{9} + \frac{1}{9}$$
$$= 5 \text{ days}$$

Step 4. Determine the probability that the project will be completed in 28 days or less. The following normal probability distribution describes the probability analysis.

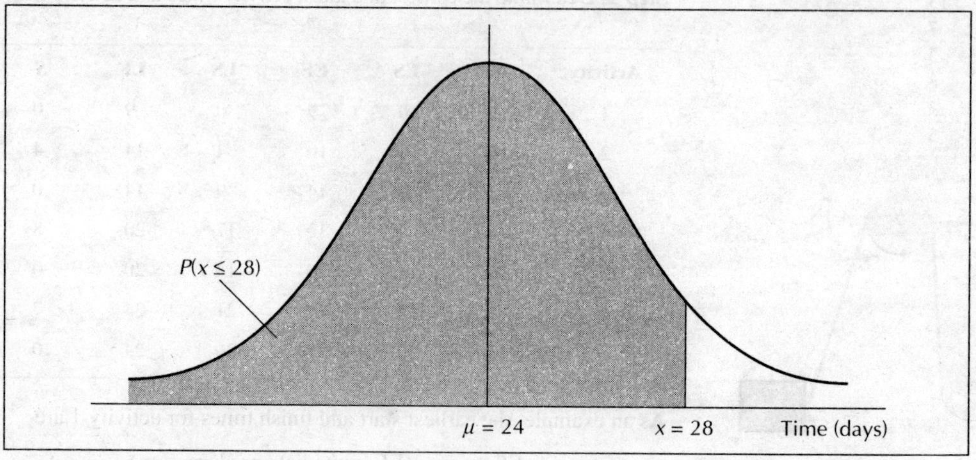

Compute Z using the following formula:

$$Z = \frac{x - \mu}{\sigma}$$
$$= \frac{28 - 24}{\sqrt{5}}$$
$$= 1.79$$

The corresponding probability from the normal table in Supplement C is 0.4633; thus,

$$P(x \leq 28) = 0.9633$$

QUESTIONS

9-1. What is the purpose of project crashing analysis?

9-2. Describe the process of manually crashing a project network.

9-3. Which method for determining activity time estimates, deterministic or probabilistic, do you perceive to be preferable? Explain.

9-4. Explain how a Gantt chart differs from a CPM/PERT network, and indicate the advantage of the latter.

9-5. Discuss the relationship of direct and indirect costs in project management.

9-6. Describe the limitations and disadvantages of CPM/PERT.

9-7. Describe the difference between activity-on-node and activity-on-arrow project networks.

9-8. Identify and briefly describe the major elements of project management.

9-9. Select an everyday "project" you are familiar with such as a class project, preparing a meal, making a pizza, or repairing your car. Develop a list of the activities, a CPM/PERT network (with time estimates), and a work breakdown schedule for the project.

9-10. Prepare a WBS for a spaghetti with meatballs dinner that includes a Caesar salad, a loaf of Italian bread, and wine. (Include the different components of the dinner at the upper level and the various detailed work activities required by each component at the lower level.)

9-11. Describe and discuss the cultural differences between the United States and a country of your choice that might affect the management of a project in this foreign country.

PROBLEMS

9-1. Construct a Gantt chart for the project described by the following set of activities, and indicate the project completion time and the available slack for each activity:

Activity	Activity Predecessor	Time (weeks)
1	—	3
2	—	7
3	1	2
4	2	5
5	2	6
6	4	1
7	5	4

9-2. Use the project activities that follow to determine the following:

a. Construct a Gantt chart; indicate the project completion time and slack for each activity.

b. Construct the CPM/PERT network, compute the length of each path in the network, and indicate the critical path.

Activity	Activity Predecessor	Time (weeks)
1	—	4
2	—	7
3	1	8
4	1	3
5	2	9
6	3	5
7	3	2
8	4, 5, 6	6
9	2	5

9-3. Construct a network from the information in the following table and identify all the paths in the network, compute the length of each, and indicate the critical path.

Activity	Activity Predecessor	Time (weeks)
1	—	7
2	—	10
3	1	6
4	2	5
5	2	4
6	3, 4	3
7	5, 6	2

9-4. For the network in Problem 9-3, determine the earliest start and finish times, latest start and finish times, and slack for each activity. Indicate how the critical path would be determined from this information.

9-5. Given the following network with activity times in months, determine the earliest start and finish times, latest start and finish times, and slack for each activity. Indicate the critical path and the project duration.

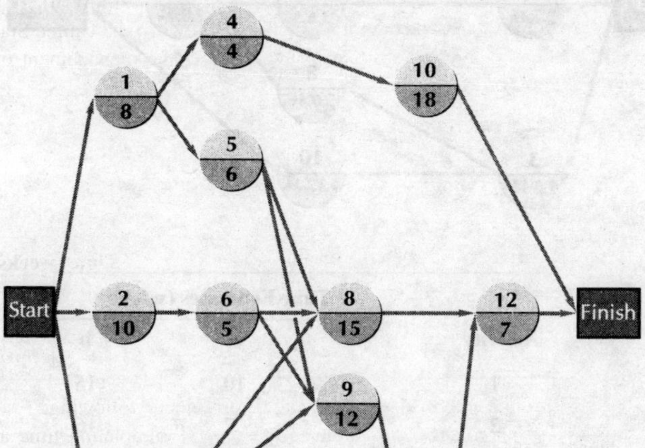

9-6. Given the following network with activity times in weeks, determine the earliest start and finish times, latest start and finish times, and slack for each activity. Indicate the critical path and the project duration.

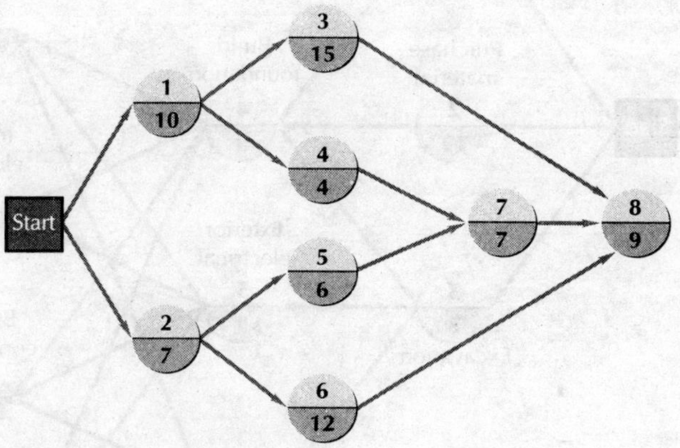

9-7. A marketing firm is planning to conduct a survey of a segment of the potential product audience for one of its customers. The planning process for preparing to conduct the survey consists of six activities with procedure relationships and activity time estimates as follows:

Activity	Description	Activity Predecessor	Time Estimates (days)
a	Determine survey objectives	—	3
b	Select and hire personnel	a	3
c	Design questionnaire	a	5
d	Train personnel	b, c	4
e	Select target audience	c	3
f	Make personnel assignments	d, e	2

a. Determine all paths through the network from node a to node f and the duration of each, and indicate the critical path.
b. Determine the earliest and latest activity start and finish times.
c. Determine the slack for each activity.

9-8. A group of developers is building a new shopping center. A consultant for the developers has constructed the CPM/PERT network on the following page and assigned activity times in weeks. Determine the earliest start and finish times, latest start and finish times, activity slack, critical path, and duration for the project.

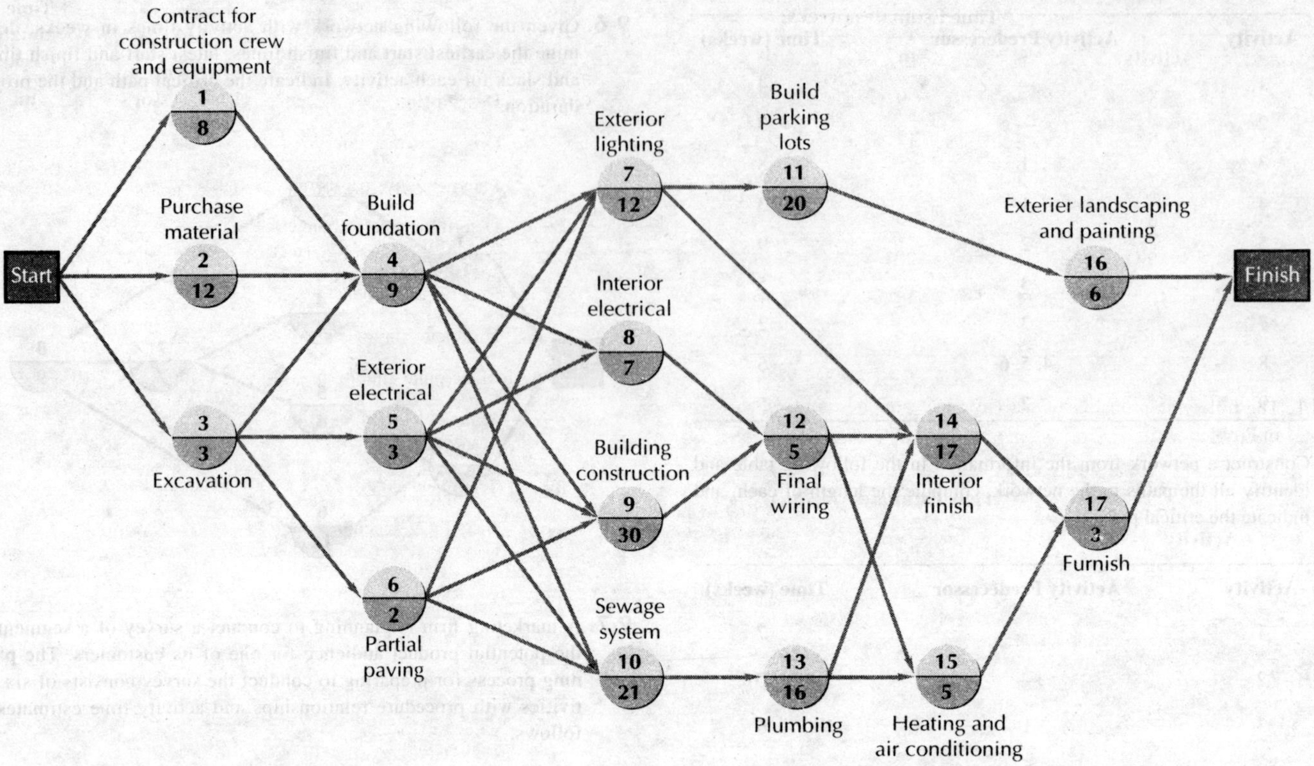

9-9. The management of a factory is going to erect a maintenance building with a connecting electrical generator and water tank. The activities, activity descriptions, and estimated durations are given in the following table:

Activity	Description	Activity Predecessor	Activity Duration (weeks)
a	Excavate	—	2
b	Erect building	a	6
c	Install generator	a	4
d	Install tank	a	2
e	Install maintenance equipment	b	4
f	Connect generator and tank to building	b, c, d	5
g	Paint on a finish	b	3
h	Check out facility	e, f	2

Construct the network for this project, identify the critical path, and determine the project duration time.

9-10. Given the following network (in the opposite column) and probabilistic activity time estimates, determine the expected time and variance for each activity and indicate the critical path.

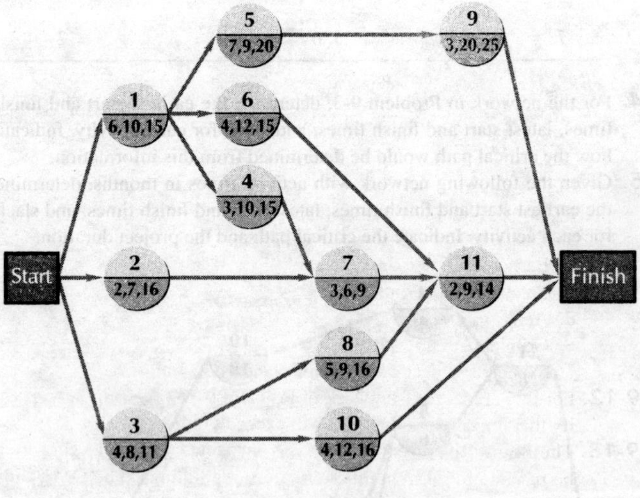

Activity	Time Estimates (weeks) a	m	b
1	6	10	15
2	2	7	16
3	4	8	11
4	3	10	15

	Time Estimates (weeks)		
Activity	a	m	b
5	7	9	20
6	4	12	15
7	3	6	9
8	5	9	16
9	3	20	35
10	4	12	16
11	2	9	14

9-11. The following probabilistic activity time estimates are for the network in Problem 9-5:

	Time Estimates (months)		
Activity	a	m	b
1	4	8	12
2	6	10	15
3	2	10	14
4	1	4	13
5	3	6	9
6	3	6	18
7	2	8	12
8	9	15	22
9	5	12	21
10	7	20	25
11	5	6	12
12	3	8	20

Determine the following:

a. Expected activity times
b. Earliest start and finish times
c. Latest start and finish times
d. Activity slack
e. Critical path
f. Expected project duration and standard deviation

9-12. For the CPM/PERT network in Problem 9-11, determine the probability that the network duration will exceed 50 months.

9-13. The Stone River Textile Mill was inspected by OSHA and found to be in violation of a number of safety regulations. The OSHA inspectors ordered the mill to alter some existing machinery to make it safer (e.g., add safety guards); purchase some new machinery to replace older, dangerous machinery; and relocate some machinery to make safer passages and unobstructed entrances and exits. OSHA gave the mill only 35 weeks to make the changes; if the changes were not made by then, the mill would be fined $300,000. The mill determined the activities in a PERT network that would have to be completed and then estimated the indicated activity times, as shown in the table below. Construct the PERT network for this project and determine the following:

			Time Estimates (Weeks)		
Activity	Description	Activity Predecessor	a	m	b
a	Order new machinery	—	1	2	3
b	Plan new physical layout	—	2	5	8
c	Determine safety changes in existing machinery	—	1	3	5
d	Receive equipment	a	4	10	25
e	Hire new employees	a	3	7	12
f	Make plant alterations	b	10	15	25
g	Make changes in existing machinery	c	5	9	14
h	Train new employees	d, e	2	3	7
i	Install new machinery	d, e, f	1	4	6
j	Relocate old machinery	d, e, f, g	2	5	10
k	Conduct employee safety orientation	h, i, j	2	2	2

a. Expected activity times
b. Earliest and latest activity times and activity slack
c. Critical path
d. Expected project duration and variance
e. The probability that the mill will be fined $300,000

9-14. On May 21, 1927, Charles Lindbergh landed at Le Bourget Field in Paris, completing his famous transatlantic solo flight. The preparation period prior to his flight was quite hectic and time was critical, since several other famous pilots of the day were also planning transatlantic flights. Once Ryan Aircraft was contracted to build the *Spirit of St. Louis*, it took only a little over 2½ months to construct the plane and fly it to New York for the takeoff. If CPM/PERT had been available to Charles Lindbergh, it no doubt would have been useful in helping him plan this project. Use your imagination and assume that a CPM/PERT network, shown in the figure on the next page, with the following estimated activity times, was developed for the flight.

	Time Estimates (days)		
Activity	a	m	b
1	1	3	5
2	4	6	10
3	20	35	50
4	4	7	12
5	2	3	5
6	8	12	25
7	10	16	21
8	5	9	15
9	1	2	2

(Continued)

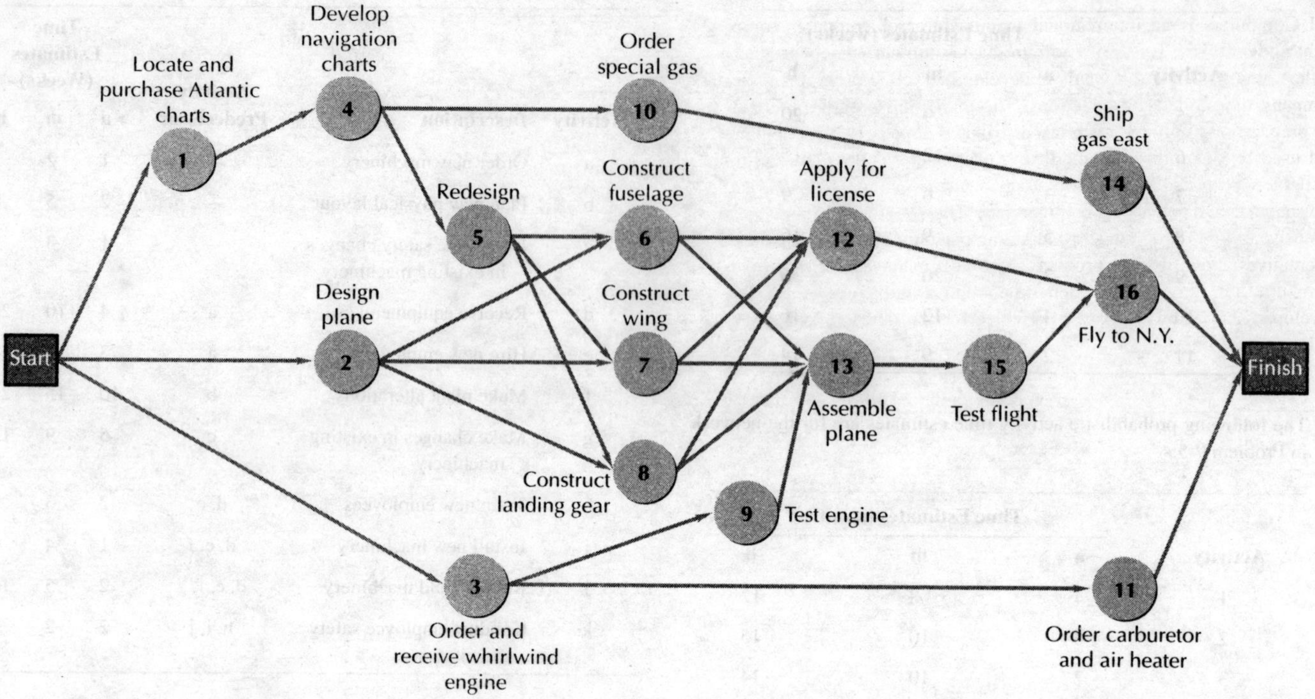

	Time Estimates (days)		
Activity	**a**	**m**	**b**
10	6	8	14
11	5	8	12
12	5	10	15
13	4	7	10
14	5	7	12
15	5	9	20
16	1	3	7

Determine the expected project duration and variance and the probability of completing the project in 67 days.

9-15. RusTech Tooling, Inc., is a large job shop operation that builds machine tools and dies to manufacture parts for specialized items. The company bids primarily on contracts for government-related activities to produce parts for things such as military aircraft, weapons systems, and the space program. The company is bidding on a contract to produce a component part for the fuselage assembly in a new space shuttle. A major criterion for selecting the winning bid besides low cost is the time required to produce the part. However, if the company is awarded the contract it will be held strictly to the completion date specified in the bid, and any delays will result in severe financial penalties. In order to determine the project completion time to put in its bid, the company has identified the project activities, precedence relationships, and activity times shown in the following table:

		Time Estimates (Weeks)		
Activity	**Activity Predecessor**	**a**	**m**	**b**
a	—	3	5	9
b	a	2	5	8
c	a	1	4	6
d	a	4	6	10
e	b	2	8	11
f	b	5	9	16
g	c	4	12	20
h	c	6	9	13
i	d	3	7	14
j	d	8	14	22
k	f, g	9	12	20
l	h, i	6	11	15
m	e	4	7	12
n	j	3	8	16
o	n	5	8	10

If RusTech, Inc., wants to be 90% certain that it can deliver the part without incurring a penalty, what time frame should it specify in the bid?

9-16. PM Computers is an international manufacturer of computer equipment and software. It is going to introduce a number of new products in the coming year, and it wants to develop marketing programs to accompany the product introductions. The marketing program includes the preparation of printed materials distributed directly by the company and used by the company's marketing personnel, vendors, and representatives; print advertising in regular magazines, trade journals, and newspapers; and television commercials. The program also includes extensive training programs for marketing personnel, vendors, and representatives about the new products. A project management team with members from the marketing department and manufacturing areas has developed the following list of activities for the development of the marketing program:

Activity	Description	Activity Predecessor	Time Estimates (days) a	m	b
a	Preliminary budget and plan approval	—	10	15	20
b	Select marketing personnel for training	—	5	9	12
c	Develop overall media plan	a	15	25	30
d	Prepare separate media plans	c	12	20	25
e	Develop training plan	c	5	8	12
f	Design training course	e	6	14	20
g	Train marketing personnel	b, f	16	20	25
h	Plan TV commercial with agency	d	15	25	35
i	Draft in-house print materials	d	8	15	20
j	Develop print advertising layouts with agency	d	16	23	30
k	Review print advertising layouts	j	4	9	12
l	Review TV commercial	h	3	7	12
m	Review and print in-house materials	i	3	5	7
n	Release advertising to print media	g, i, k,	2	4	8
o	Release TV commercials to networks	l	4	7	10
p	Final marketing personnel review	g, i, k	4	5	9
q	Run media advertising, mailings	m, n, o	15	20	30

Construct the network for this project and determine the activity schedule. Identify the critical path and determine the expected project duration time and variance. What is the probability the program can be completed within four months?

9-17. The following table provides the information necessary to construct a project network and project crash data:

Activity	Activity Predecessor	Activity Time (weeks) Normal	Crash	Activity Cost ($) Normal	Crash
1	—	20	8	1,000	1,480
2	—	24	20	1,200	1,400
3	—	14	7	700	1,190
4	1	10	6	500	820
5	3	11	5	550	730

a. Construct the project network.
b. Determine the maximum possible crash time for the network, and crash the network the maximum amount possible.
c. Compute the normal project cost and the cost of the crashed project.

9-18. The Eastern Shore Hospital has encountered a problem in bed turnaround time (i.e., the time taken to discharge a patient from a bed and admit a new patient). This, in turn, has caused delays in the hospital operating room, resulting in physician and patient dissatisfaction. The hospital initiated a Six Sigma project to resolve the problem, initially focusing on one surgical nursing unit, which had almost 3,000 patients in one year. The Six Sigma DMAIC process employed by the project team included the following project activities, activity times, and precedence relationships.

Activity	Description	Activity Predecessor	Time Estimates (days) a	m	b
a	Develop process map	—	4	7	10
b	VoC survey of RNs	a	6	12	15
c	Establish turnaround target time	b	2	5	8
d	Measure process, define defects	a, c	5	7	11
e	Cause & effect diagram (identify variables that effect turnaround time)	b	3	9	14
f	Statistical analysis of variables	e	4	6	10
g	Analyze possible solutions	c, d, f	5	9	14
h	Identify solution approach	g	3	7	9
i	Improve process	h	10	14	20
j	Monitor and control process with SPC	i	15	23	30
k	Apply improved process across hospital	j	12	18	25

Construct the network for this project. Determine the earliest and latest activity times and the critical path.

9-19. The Valley United Soccer Club is planning a soccer tournament for the weekend of April 29–30. The club's officers know that by March 30 they must send out acceptances to teams that have applied to enter, and by April 15 they must send out the tournament game schedule to teams that have been selected to play. Their tentative plan is to begin the initial activities for tournament preparation including sending out the application forms to prospective teams, on January 20. Following is a list of tournament activities, their precedence relationships, and estimates of their duration in days. Develop a project network for the club's tournament preparation process and determine the likelihood that they will meet their schedule milestones and complete the process according to the scheduled tournament start date of April 29.

Activity	Activity Description	Activity Predecessor	Time Estimates (days) a	m	b
a	Send application forms	—	5	7	10
b	Get volunteer workers	—	10	18	26
c	Line up referees	—	7	10	14
d	Reserve fields	—	14	21	35
e	Receive and process forms	a	30	30	30
f	Determine age divisions	b, c, d, e	4	9	12
g	Assign fields to divisions	f	4	7	10
h	Sell program ads	b	14	21	30
i	Acquire donated items for team gift bags	b	15	20	26
j	Schedule games	g	6	14	18
k	Design ads	h	5	8	10
l	Fill gift bags	i	9	12	17
m	Process team t-shirt orders	e	7	10	14
n	Send acceptance letters	f	4	7	12
o	Design and print programs	j, k, l, n	14	18	24
p	Put together registration boxes (programs, gifts, etc.)	o	5	7	10
q	Send out game schedules	j, k, l, n	5	8	12
r	Assign referees to games	j, k, l, n	4	7	10
s	Get trophies	f	20	28	35
t	Silk-screen t-shirts	m	12	17	25
u	Package team t-shirt orders	t	5	8	12

9-20. The Horizon Aircraft Company is preparing a contract proposal to submit to the Global Airlines Company for a new commercial aircraft, the JK60. Part of the proposal is a development and productions schedule for completion of the first aircraft. The project consists of three primary categories: (1) engine design and development; (2) development and production of the airframe (e.g., the aircraft body); and (3) the design and development of the aircraft avionics (e.g., the electronic systems, equipment, and other devices used to operate and control the aircraft). Following is a table listing the project activities with time estimates (in months).

Activity	Description	Activity Predecessor	Time Estimates (months) a	m	b
1	General design	—	6	10	24
2	Design engines	—	20	35	60
3	Airframe design	1	5	17	33
4	Avionics design	1	2	8	21
5	Develop test engine	2	6	9	15
6	Develop test airframe	3	7	12	17
7	Develop interim avionics	4	6	16	27
8	Engine development	2	18	25	42
9	Assemble test aircraft	5, 6, 7	5	8	11
10	Test avionics	4	4	11	16
11	Engine/airframe flight trials	9	5	10	13
12	Avionics flight trials	10	5	9	26
13	Engine production	8	10	15	18
14	Airframe production	11	11	14	21
15	Avionics production	11, 12	12	16	26
16	Final assembly/Finish	13, 14, 15	3	5	6

Develop the project network, and determine the critical path, the expected project duration, and variance. What is the probability the project will be completed within 8 years?

9-21. The Carriage Auto Parts Company near Nashville, Tennessee, is a direct supplier for the nearby Sigma auto manufacturing plant. In order to gain a competitive advantage and meet quality requirements by its customer, Carriage has undertaken a project to achieve ISO/TS 16949 registration. TS 16949 provides the requirements for the application of ISO 9001:2009 standards for automotive production and relevant service parts organizations. The goal of ISO/TS 16949 is the development of a quality management system that provides for continual improvement emphasizing defect prevention and the reduction of process variation and waste. (See Chapter 2 for a discussion of ISO certification.) The project management team has developed the following list of required activities necessary to achieve ISO certification:

Activity	Description	Activity Predecessor	Time Estimates (weeks) a	m	b
a	Appointment of company taskforce	—	1	2	3
b	Development of feasibility plan	a	2	3	4
c	Selection of third party registrar and auditor	b	1	2	3

Activity	Description	Activity Predecessor	Time Estimates (weeks) a	m	b
d	Development of quality manual, procedure, and instruction documents	b	10	14	20
e	Quality system training for all employees	b	4	7	10
f	Outside training for company quality managers and internal plant auditors	b	4	7	10
g	Plant preparation and organization to meet ISO 9001 standards including use of SPC charts to identify non-conforming processes	e	18	24	32
h	Preparation of ISO application documents with outside auditor; set schedule for submissions to registrar	c	4	6	10
i	Internal audit of plant	d, f, h, g	10	12	16
j	Corrective action plans for necessary process improvements	i	8	12	20
k	Outside auditor visit and audit	j	1	2	3
l	Corrective action plans developed based on auditor report and implemented	k	2	4	5
m	Follow-up visit and re-audit by auditor	l	1	2	4
n	Auditor recommendation to registrar for ISO certification	m	1	2	2

Construct the network for this project and determine the project schedule. Identify the critical path and determine the expected project duration time and variance. Determine the probabilities that the certification project can be completed within one year and within 18 months.

CASE STUDY

Music in the Quick Time

Aki had just called a meeting of the Technical Institute Programs and Music Committee to order.

"Okay, okay, everybody, quiet down. I have an important announcement to make," he shouted above the noise. The room got quiet and Aki started again, "Well, everyone wanted a big J-rock band for the concert. We have scored on Despairs showing up."

Everyone in the room cheered and started talking excitedly. Aki stood up, waved his arms, and shouted again, "Hey, calm down, everybody, and listen up." The room quietened again and everyone focused on Aki. "That is the good news. The bad news is they will be here in 21 days."

The committee groaned and seemed to share Dai's feeling when he shouted, "No way, man. It can't be done. Why can't they put it off for a couple of weeks so we can prepare better?"

Aki answered, "They're just starting their new tour and are looking for some warm-up concerts. They will be traveling near here for their first concert date in Tokyo and saw they had an email from us, so they said they could come now, but that's it—it's now or never."

He looked around the room at the solemn faces. "Look, you guys, we can handle this. Let's think of what we have to do. Come on, perk up. Let's make a list of everything we have to do to get ready and figure out how long it will take. So somebody tell me what we have to do first!"

Hisao shouted from the back of the room, "We have to find a place; you know, get an auditorium somewhere. I've done that before and it could take anywhere from 3 to 9 days but it should probably take 4."

Aki yelled, "Okay, that's great, go for it. What's next?"

Ichiro added in, "We need to print tickets and quick. It could take only a day if the printer isn't busy but it could take up to 5 days if it is. I would say it will take 3 days to obtain the tickets. But we don't want to print the tickets until we know where the auditorium will be." Aki and Hisao agreed, "Right, get the auditorium first, and then print the tickets."

Kenta identified that they would need to make hotel and transportation arrangements for the band and their entourage while they were here. "But we'd better not do that until we get the auditorium. That way if we can't find a place for the show, everything else falls through." He continued, "Depending on where we are looking, it could take as few as 5 days or as many as 12 days to book the room. I would say plan for 8 days."

Kin jumped in, "We also need to hire a company to set up the stage, take it down, run the lights and microphones, etc. Finding the right company may take 4 to 13 days but I think I can get it done in 5. But first, I need to know the location, in case the auditorium has prior agreements in place."

"How about advertising?" Juor asked. Kazuo seconded the need, saying, "Yes, advertising is going to be critical. We need pre-show advertising, and a press conference for the band when they are here. That means we need to contract a PR firm—that will take anywhere from 2 to 4 days, so let's plan on it taking 3." Juor added, "We can start that now as the location should be identified before we have them ready to go to work."

"What else?" asked Aki.

Hisao identified that the stage must be set up, someone has to check the lighting, etc., before the show, and estimated this would take at least 3 days, but depending on location, it could take 6 days, adding, "I think we can really finish in 4 days."

"We also need to start selling the tickets," Kin pointed out. "If we do a good job of advertising, they could go in a day, but sometimes it takes up to 8 days to sell out. I think the ticket office always plans on it taking 4 days to sell out for this type of concert."

Aki added, "Yes, but we need to know where the show will be, the tickets must be printed, and the PR firm must be working."

Kenta joined back in, "We then hold a press conference prior to the concert. We need to book the press room, notify the press, and tell them when we are going to hold the press conference. We want it in the same hotel where band is staying, so we need to have the rooms booked."

Aki agreed, but added, "We also want it close to the concert date, so let's say we must have the stage set up, as well as all tickets sold out. I think putting together the press conference will take 2 days at least, but it could take up to 5 days if unexpected things happen; I think we can pull it off in 3 days, assuming that the other three things are done and we can focus on this."

Everyone thought this was a workable plan.

Based on the input provided, develop a PERT schedule, and determine the expected duration, activity variance, early start, early finish, late start, late finish, slack, project variance, and probability that everything will be ready for the concert date.

REFERENCES

Burman, P. J. *Precedence Networks for Project Planning and Control*. New York: McGraw-Hill, 1972.

Cleland, D. I., and W. R. King. *Project Management Handbook*. New York: Van Nostrand Reinhold, 1983.

Levy, F., G. Thompson, and J. Wiest. "The ABC's of the Critical Path Method." *Harvard Business Review* 41(5; October 1963).

Moder, J., C. R. Phillips, and E. W. Davis. *Project Management with CPM and PERT and Precedence Diagramming*, 3rd ed. New York: Van Nostrand Reinhold, 1983.

O'Brian, J. *CPM in Construction Management*. New York: McGraw-Hill, 1965.

Wiest, J. D., and F. K. Levy. *A Management Guide to PERT/CPM*, 2nd ed. Upper Saddle River, NJ: Prentice Hall, 1977.

Designing the Supply Chain

LEARNING OBJECTIVES

AFTER READING THIS CHAPTER, YOU WILL BE ABLE TO:

- Describe the key characteristics and management strategies of the modern supply chain.
- Discuss sustainable supply chain practices and the impact of the environment on supply chain decisions.
- Describe the role of information technology in supply chains, and the need for supply chain integration.
- Present the SCOR model and calculate key performance indicators for monitoring supply chain performance.

THE DENIM JEANS SUPPLY CHAIN

The United States is the world's largest market for denim jeans. Out of the 2 billion pairs of jeans sold each year worldwide about 40% are sold in the United States. The favorite jeans of consumers are U.S. brands such as Levi's, Lee, Wrangler, Gap, Old Navy, and American Eagle. However, about 98% of all denim jeans sold in U.S. stores are imported from suppliers in countries around the world—even though the United States is the world's third largest cotton producer and the largest cotton exporter. This means that the denim jeans industry encompasses a supply chain that is geographically and financially one of the largest in the world, with the United States as a major (cotton) supplier on one end of the supply chain, and the predominant jeans consumer on the other end, but with virtually none of the production process in between. China, India, the United States, and Pakistan produce almost 80% of the world's cotton. Much of the cotton grown in China, India, and Pakistan supplies manufacturing facilities within these countries that produce denim cloth and then jeans, while cotton from the United States (as well as other major exporters like India, Brazil, and Australia) is exported to these countries, as well as to other major denim fabric and jeans producing countries like Mexico and Bangladesh. China, Mexico, and Bangladesh are the top jeans suppliers to the United States, accounting for almost 70% of U.S.

imports. Mexico is the largest supplier of men's and boy's jeans (approximately 40%), while China is the primary supplier for women's and girl's jeans (about 44%). The jeans manufacturing process can occur at facilities entirely within a country or between countries. For example, cotton grown in the United States can be shipped to China, where it is stored in warehouses, then transported by truck or rail to a Chinese facility where it is spun into yarn, which is then shipped to another city in China where denim cloth is produced, which is then shipped to Bangladesh where jeans are sewn, and buttons, rivets and zippers are added from other plants, before the finished denim jeans are shipped back to the United States to complete the supply chain.

In this chapter we will learn about supply chains and the key role supply chain management plays in successfully integrating all the operations and processes involved in producing a product like denim jeans.

Sources: Based on "Denim Jeans: State of the U.S. Market," 2011, http://www.lifestylemonitor.cottoninc.com; and, Summer R. Oakes, "Textile Talk: DenimNation-Series 1.1," 2011, http://www.source4style.com.

Supply Chains

Globalization and the evolution of information technology have provided the catalysts for supply chain management to become the strategic means for companies to manage quality, satisfy customers, and remain competitive. A **supply chain** encompasses all activities associated with the flow and transformation of goods and services from the raw materials stage to the end user (customer), as well as the associated information flows. In essence, it is all the assets, information, and processes that provide "supply." It is made up of many interrelated members, starting with raw material suppliers, and including parts and components suppliers, subassembly suppliers, the product or service producer, and distributors, and ending with the end-use customer.

Figure 10.1 illustrates the stages, facilities, and physical movement of products and services in a supply chain. The supply chain begins with suppliers, which can be as basic as raw material providers. These suppliers are referred to as *upstream* supply chain members, while the distributors, warehouses, and eventual end-use customers are referred to as *downstream* supply chain members. The stream at the bottom of the figure denotes the flow of goods and services (i.e., demand) as the supply chain moves downstream. Notice that the stream is very rough at the upstream end and gets smoother as it moves downstream, a characteristic we will discuss in greater detail later. Also note that "information" is at the center of Figure 10.1; it is the "heart and brains" of the supply chain, another characteristic we will talk more about later.

The supply chain in Figure 10.1 can represent a single producer directly linked to one level of suppliers and one set of end-use customers. A grocery store that gets food products like milk, eggs, or vegetables directly from a farmer (and not through a distributor) and sells them directly to the customer who consumes them reflects this basic level of supply chain. However, supply chains are more typically a series of linked suppliers and customers; every customer is in turn a supplier to the next, up to the final end user of the product or service. For example, Figure 10.2 (see pages 322 and 323) shows the supply chain for denim jeans, a straightforward manufacturing process with a distinct set of suppliers. Notice that the jeans manufacturer has suppliers that produce denim who in turn have suppliers who produce cotton and dye.

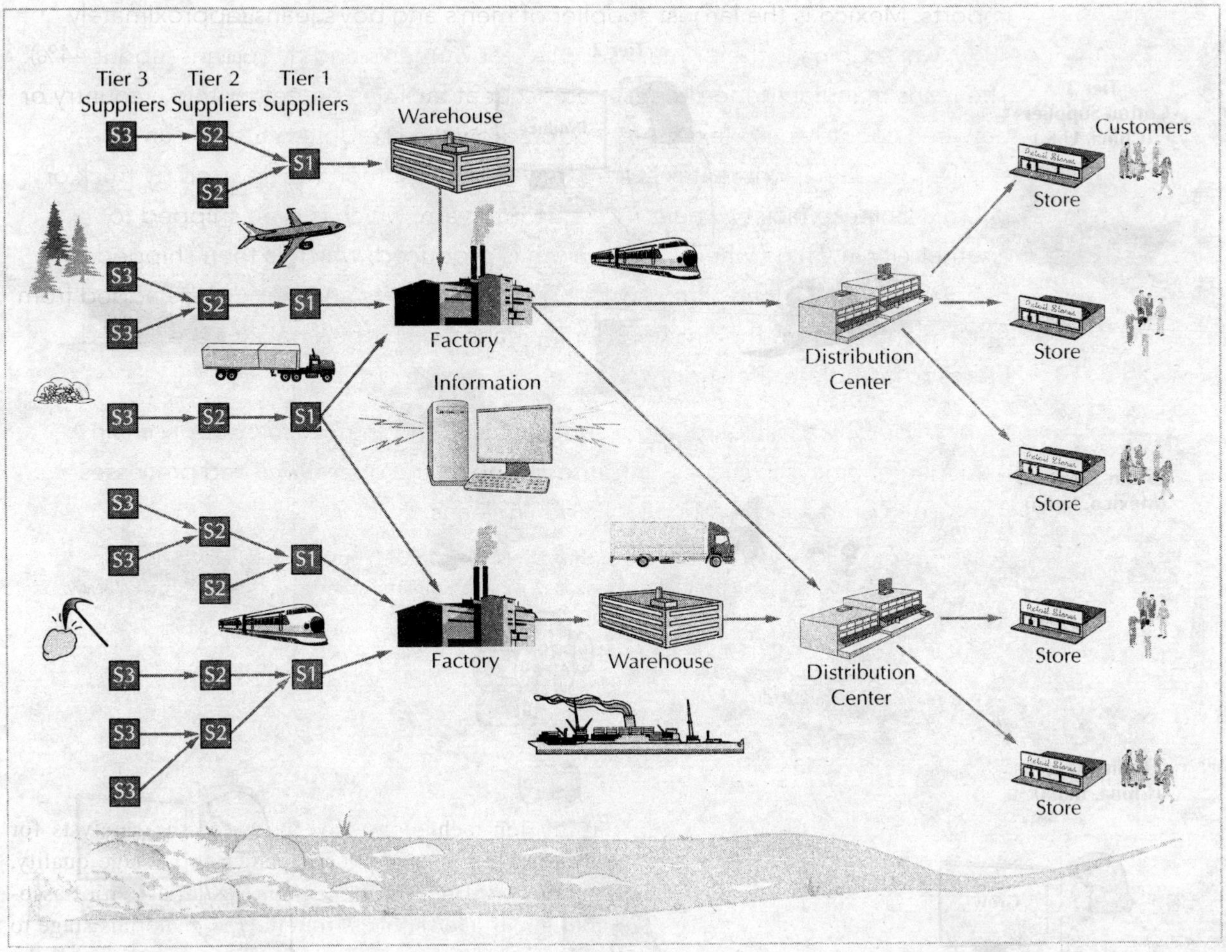

Figure 10.1

The Supply Chain

As Figures 10.1 and 10.2 show, the delivery of a product or service to a customer is a complex process, encompassing many different interrelated processes and activities. First, demand for a product or service is forecast, and plans and schedules are made to meet demand within a time frame. The product or service can require multiple suppliers (who have their own suppliers) who prepare and then ship parts and materials to manufacturing or service sites. A large manufacturer like General Electric or Procter & Gamble has thousands of suppliers including first-tier suppliers that supply it directly, second-tier suppliers that supply those suppliers, third-tier suppliers that supply second-tier suppliers, and so on. Parts and materials are transformed into final products or services. These products may then be stored at a distribution center or warehouse. Finally, these products are transported by carriers to external or internal customers. However, this may not be the final step at all, as these customers may transform the product or service further and ship it on to their customers. All of this is part of the supply chain—that is, the flow of goods and services from the materials stage to the end user.

The supply chain is also an integrated group of business processes and activities with the same goal—providing customer satisfaction. As shown in Figure 10.3, these processes include the **procurement** of services, materials, and components from suppliers; *production* of the products and services; and *distribution* of products to the customer including taking and filling orders. Information and information technology tie these processes together; it is what "integrates" them into a supply chain.

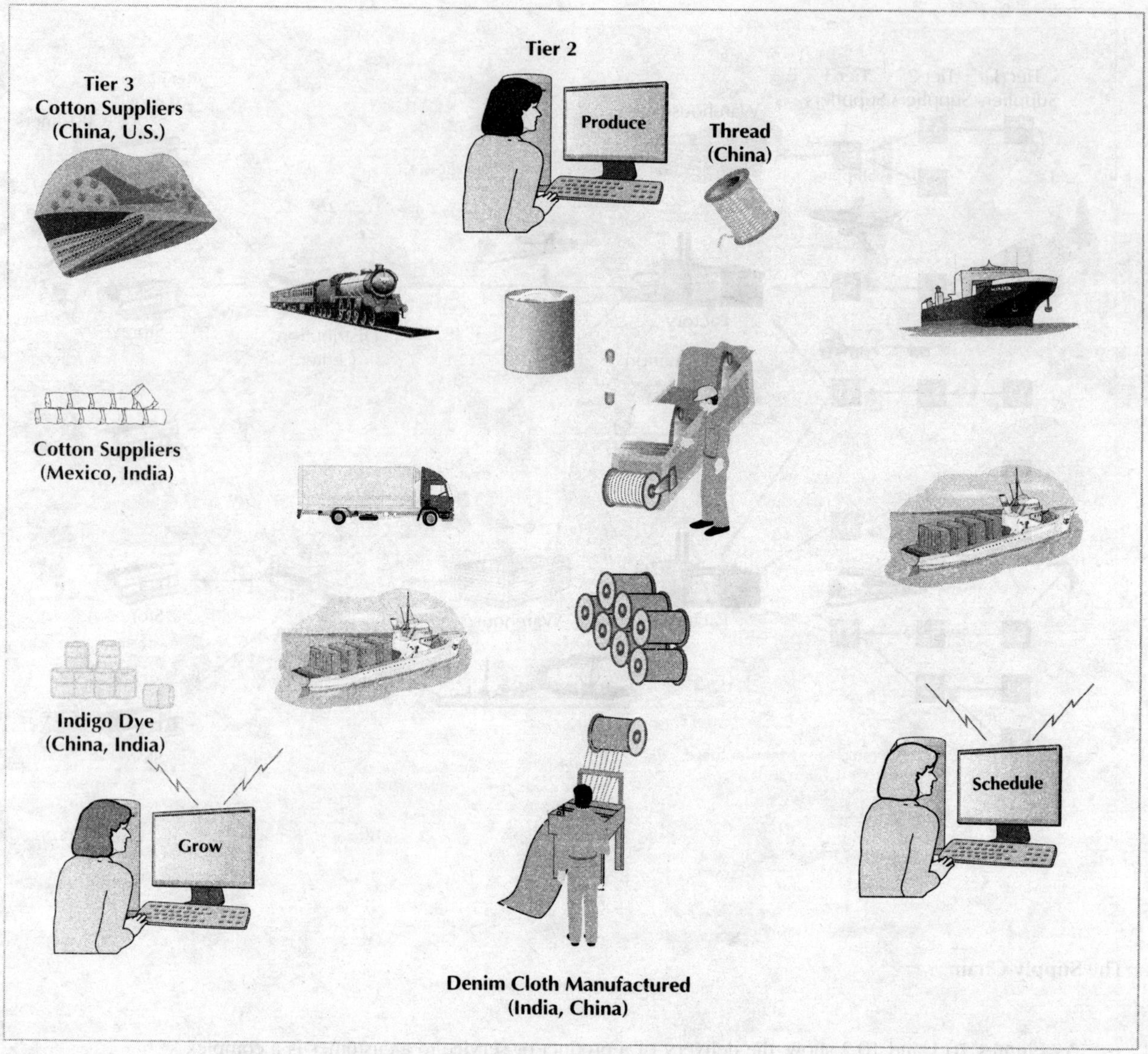

Figure 10.2

The Supply Chain for Denim Jeans

SUPPLY CHAINS FOR SERVICE PROVIDERS

Supply chains for services are sometimes not as easily defined as supply chains for manufacturing operations. Since the supply chain of a service provider does not always provide the customer with a physical good, its supply chain does not focus as much on the flow of physical items (material, parts, and subassemblies) through the supply chain. It instead may focus more on the human resources and support services necessary to provide its own service. The supply chain of a service provider also tends to be more compact and less extended than a manufacturing supply chain. It generally does not have as many tiers of suppliers, and its distribution network is smaller or nonexistent. However, supply chains of service companies are definable and can be effectively managed using many of the same principles. Service companies and organizations have suppliers (who have suppliers), and they distribute their products to customers (who may have their own customers). Although a hospital and HMO do not provide actual goods to its customers, they nevertheless purchase equipment, computers,

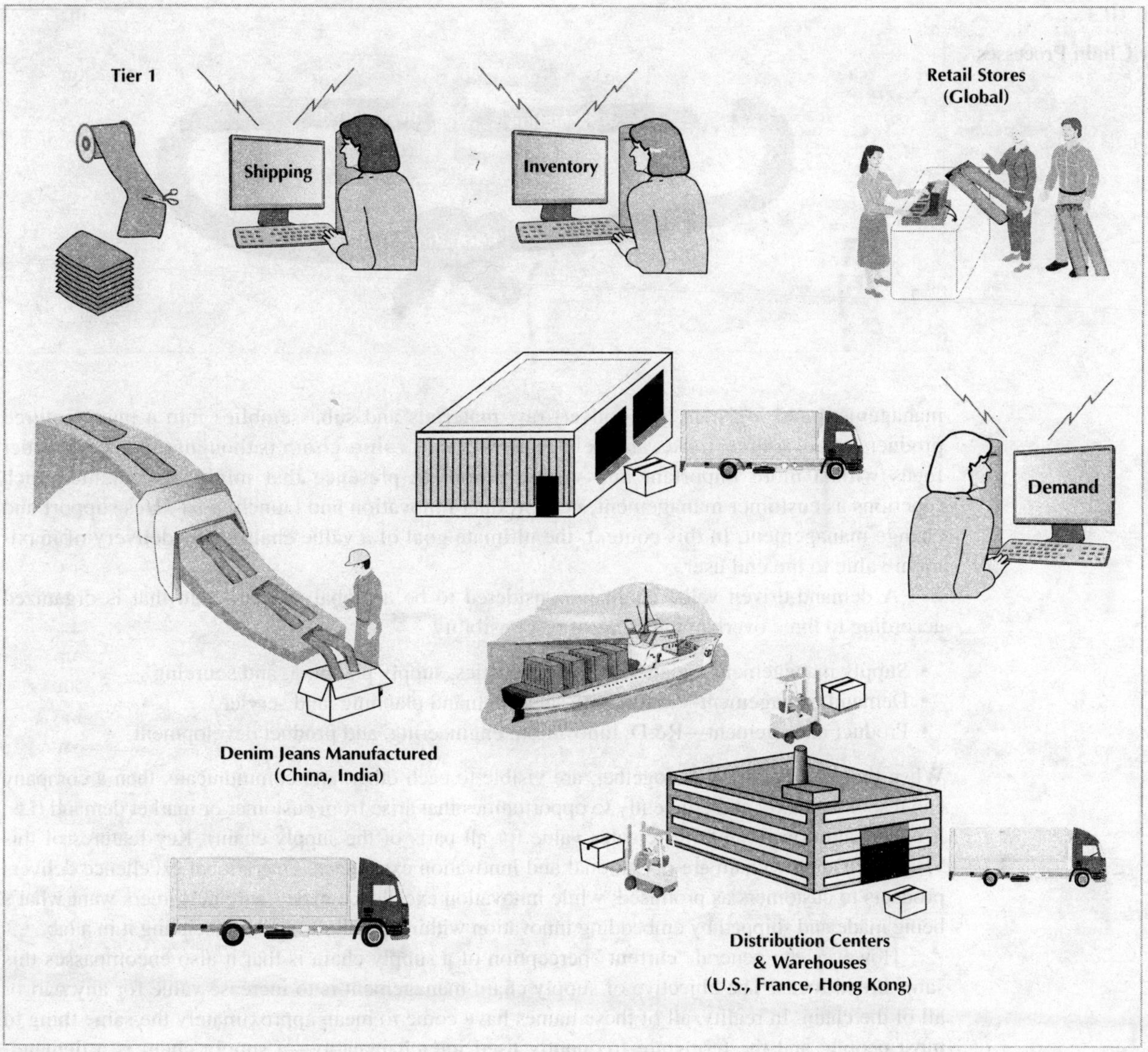

Figure 10.2
(continued)

drugs, and medical supplies from suppliers (who have suppliers). They also contract for services (such as food preparation or laundry); hire doctors, nurses, accountants, administrators, and staff; and provide healthcare. They have quality-management issues throughout their supply chain. They also encounter the same problems and inefficiencies as a manufacturing-based supply chain. Other service-oriented companies, like McDonald's, do, in fact, provide a physical product, and thus have a more discernible supply chain with distribution, transportation and inventory like a manufacturing company.

VALUE CHAINS

In recent years, terms such as *value chain* and *demand-driven value chain* have entered the supply chain lexicon and are sometimes used instead of, or interchangeably with, supply chain. Are there any differences among the various terms? The traditional view of a supply chain was that it focused somewhat narrowly on the activities and processes associated with material

Figure 10.3
Supply Chain Processes

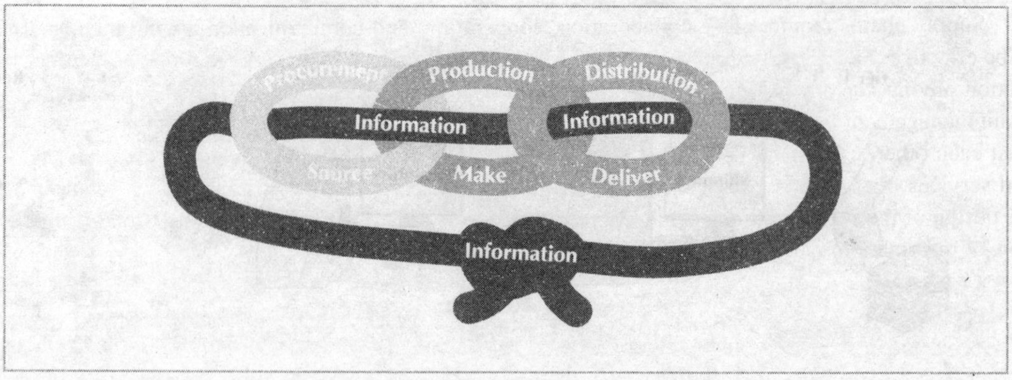

management and logistics that convert raw materials and subassemblies into a manufactured product—plan, source, make, and deliver. However, a **value chain** is thought to have a broader focus with a more important and visible corporate presence that might also include such functions as customer management, new product innovation and launch, post-sales support and change management. In this context, the ultimate goal of a value chain is the delivery of maximum value to the end user.

A demand-driven value chain is considered to be a global supply chain that is organized according to three overlapping areas of responsibility:

- Supply management—manufacturing, logistics, supply planning, and sourcing
- Demand management—marketing, sales, demand planning, and service
- Product management—R&D, innovation, engineering, and product development

When these processes work together, are visible to each other, and communicate, then a company can respond quickly and efficiently to opportunities that arise from customer or market demand (i.e., it is demand-driven, and thus creates value for all parts of the supply chain). Key features of this vision of a supply chain are operational and innovation excellence. Operational excellence delivers products to customers as promised; while innovation excellence makes sure customers want what's being made and shipped by embedding innovation within operations and not isolating it in a lab.

However, the general "current" perception of a supply chain is that it also encompasses this same broad focus. The objective of supply chain management is to increase value for any part or all of the chain. In reality, all of these names have come to mean approximately the same thing to most people, and the terms are frequently used interchangeably—a supply chain is a demand-driven value chain, and vice versa.

A common thread among these perceptions of supply, value, and demand chains is that of **value**. Value to the customer is good quality, a fair price, and fast and accurate delivery. To achieve value for the customer, the members of the supply chain must act as partners to systematically create value at every stage of the supply chain. Thus, companies not only look for ways to create value internally in their own production processes, but they also look to their supply chain partners to create value by improving product design and quality, enhancing supply chain performance and speed, and lowering costs. To accomplish these value enhancers, supply chain members must collaborate with each other and integrate their processes, topics that we will continually return to in this chapter.

The Management of Supply Chains

Supply chain management (SCM) focuses on integrating and managing the flow of goods and services and information through the supply chain in order to make it responsive to customer needs while lowering total costs. Traditionally, each segment of the supply chain was managed as a separate (stand-alone) entity focused on its own goals. However, to compete in today's global marketplace a company has to count on the combined and coordinated effort of all members of the supply chain.

Supply chains require close collaboration, cooperation, and communication among members to be effective. Suppliers, and their customers must share information. It is the rapid flow of information among customers, suppliers, distributors, and producers that characterizes today's supply chain management. Suppliers and customers must also have the same goals. They need to be able to trust each other. Customers need to be able to count on the quality and timeliness of the products and services of their suppliers. Furthermore, suppliers and customers must participate together in the design of the supply chain to achieve their shared goals and to facilitate communication and the flow of information.

SUPPLY CHAIN UNCERTAINTY AND INVENTORY

One of a company's main objectives in managing its supply chain is to synchronize the upstream flow of incoming materials, parts, subassemblies, and services with production and distribution downstream so that it can respond to uncertainty in customer demand without creating costly excess inventory. Examples of factors that contribute to uncertainty, and hence variability, in the supply chain are inaccurate demand forecasting, long variable lead times for orders, late deliveries, incomplete shipments, product changes, batch ordering, price fluctuations and discounts, and inflated orders. The primary negative effects of supply chain uncertainty and variability are lateness and incomplete orders. If deliveries from suppliers are late or incomplete, they slow down the flow of goods and services through the supply chain, ultimately resulting in poor-quality customer service. Companies cope with this uncertainty and try to avoid delays with their own form of "insurance," **inventory**.

Supply chain members carry buffer (or extra) inventory at various stages of the supply chain to minimize the negative effects of uncertainty and to keep goods and services flowing smoothly from suppliers to customers. For example, if a parts order arrives late (or does not arrive at all) from a supplier, the producer is able to continue production and maintain its delivery schedule to its customers by using parts it has stored in inventory for just such an occurrence.

Companies also accumulate inventory because they may order in large batches in order to keep down order and transportation costs or to receive a discount or special price from a supplier. However, inventory is very costly. Products sitting on a shelf or in a warehouse are just like money sitting there not being used when it could be used for something else. It is estimated that the cost of carrying a retail product in inventory for one year is over 25% of what the item cost. Inventory-carrying costs are over $300 billion per year in the United States. As such, suppliers and customers would like to minimize or eliminate it.

THE BULLWHIP EFFECT

Distorted information or the lack of information, such as inaccurate demand data or forecasts, from the customer end can ripple back upstream through the supply chain and magnify demand variability at each stage. This can result in high buffer inventories, poor customer service, missed production schedules, wrong capacity plans, inefficient shipping, and high costs. This phenomenon, which has been observed across different industries, is known as the **bullwhip effect**. It occurs when slight to moderate demand variability becomes magnified as demand information is transmitted back upstream in the supply chain. In Figure 10.1 the stream at the bottom of the figure reflects this occurrence; the flow is greater (and the waters more turbulent) further upstream. Figure 10.4 presents a detailed perspective of the bullwhip effect.

The bullwhip effect is created when supply chain members make ordering decisions with an eye to their own self-interest and/or they do not have accurate demand information from the adjacent supply chain members. If each supply chain member is uncertain and not confident about what the actual demand is for the succeeding member it supplies and is making its own demand forecast, then it will stockpile extra inventory to compensate for the uncertainty. In other words, they create a security blanket of inventory. As shown in Figure 10.4, demand for the end user is relatively stable and the inventory is small. However, if slight changes in demand occur, and the

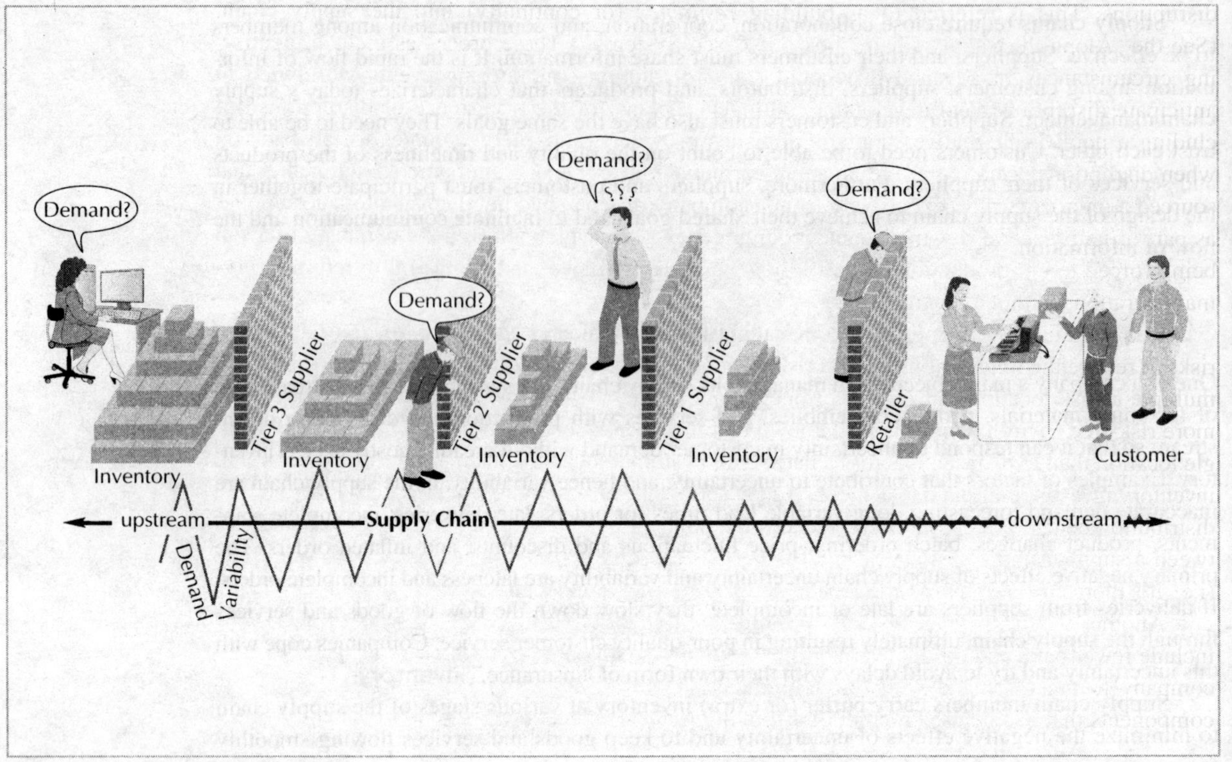

Figure 10.4
The Bullwhip Effect

distributor does not know why this change occurred, then the distributor will tend to overreact and increase its own demand, or conversely reduce its own demand too much if demand from its customer unexpectedly drops. This creates an even greater overreaction by the manufacturer who supplies the distributor and the suppliers who supply the manufacturer. One way to cope with the bullwhip effect is for supply chain members to share information, especially demand forecasts. If the supply chain exhibits *transparency*, then members can have access to each other's information, which reduces or eliminates uncertainty.

RISK MANAGEMENT

When supply chains stretch over long distances and multiple locations around the world, uncertainty, and therefore risk, increase. In "lean" supply chains, there is little redundancy and slack (i.e., inventory), so when disruptions occur—natural or otherwise—the effects can cascade through the supply chain, slowing or stopping normal operations and eventual customer order fulfillment. As suggested previously, one way to offset uncertainty is by carrying extra inventory at various points along the supply chain; however, as we have also noted, this is an expensive solution for handling uncertainty and risk; Instead, a number of innovative companies with top supply chains have begun to engage in formal "risk management" to cope with supply chain uncertainty.

Risk management requires due diligence to evaluate and anticipate the likelihood and possible impact of unexpected supply chain disruptions, which can be economic, marketplace, or natural, and plan ahead for them. In recent years, as a result of a global economic downturn and several natural disasters, including an earthquake in Japan, floods in Thailand, and a volcanic eruption in Iceland, companies have altered their approach to supply chain management to incorporate formal ongoing risk management processes to identify and plan for possible disruptions. This is referred to as building *resiliency* (or continuity) into the supply chain. (See the "Along the Supply Chain" box on "Cisco Systems.") These processes include identifying circumstances in advance that could cause disruptions, monitoring events worldwide to anticipate disruptions, and developing contingency plans for the occurrence of disruptions, including a pool of alternative suppliers, logistics providers, and energy sources to fall back on when disruptions occur. After the Japanese earthquake in 2011, one international automaker that sourced a microcontroller exclusively from a company in Japan had lined up an alternate supplier as part of its proactive risk management contingency plan, which allowed the company to avoid being forced to cut production by half following the earthquake, and enabled it to return to normal operations within a few months.

Risk pooling is an approach to managing risks in which an attempt is made to aggregate risks to reduce the impact of individual risks. One way to pool risks is to combine inventories from multiple at-risk locations into a few, or one, location, like a warehouse or distribution center, in a more risk-free environment. It is well known that it is more economical to hold inventory at a single location than to disperse it across a number of customer locations. Doing so reduces the overall inventory investment needed to achieve a target service level across all the customers supplied by a distribution center, which, in effect, reduces demand variability. Adding a distribution center between a supplier and a customer can also shorten lead times, which is another way to pool risks (i.e., it's more costly to meet variations in demand from several locations than from one).

Another way to manage risks is to build risk tradeoffs into product and service designs to include fewer parts and product variability. Reducing the number of product components allows a company to meet demand with fewer products and fewer suppliers. Having common product components that can be used in a lot of different products enables a company to pool its forecasts

ALONG THE SUPPLY CHAIN

Supply Chain Resiliency at Cisco Systems

Cisco Systems, the San Jose–based designer and manufacturer of networking equipment with annual revenues over $40 billion, has a global supply chain of more than 700 direct suppliers and five manufacturing partners in more than 30 countries. Its supply chain was ranked eighth best in *Gartner's* 2012 annual Top-25 ranking of supply chains. Cisco has a centralized risk management team within its supply chain operations organization that works with other organizational functions (like engineering and customer operations) to ensure supply chain resiliency in the face of possible disruptions. Cisco achieves resiliency through four processes. Product resiliency identifies risk tradeoffs early in the development and sourcing of new products. Supply chain resiliency identifies and mitigates circumstances that could limit recovery from a major disruption within a certain time frame. Business continuity planning compiles resiliency data points for critical suppliers including such things as emergency contacts, alternate power providers and estimated recovery time. The supply chain incident management process monitors events worldwide on a 24/7 basis for any potential disruption that could impact suppliers, transportation or manufacturing. These processes helped Cisco weather the Japanese earthquake in 2011 that impacted over a thousand unique component parts involving 65 suppliers in Japan. Cisco was able to execute 900 new supply sources three times faster than the average time and incurred only minimal customer order fulfillment disruption and virtually no loss of revenue. Cisco was able to react to similar natural disruptions, including floods in Thailand and an Iceland volcano eruption, due to its supply chain resiliency processes.

Do you think Cisco's centralized approach to risk management would be appropriate and useful for retail companies like P&G and Walmart?

Source: Based on Mary Siegfried, "Building a Resilient Supply Chain," *Inside Supply Management*, 23, no. 3 (April 2012): 24, http://www.ism.ws.

for component demand, resulting in fewer demand forecasts. (The more forecasts, the more chances for errors.) Reducing product offerings can have the same effect—it's easier to forecast demand for a smaller number of product configurations than a larger number. That is why automobile companies like Honda started offering packages of options on a few common vehicle bases rather than just providing the customer with a list of add-ons.

Supply Chain Sustainability

Achieving **sustainability**, also referred to as "going green," has become one of the most visible recent trends in operations and supply chain management. Sustainability, according to the United Nations, is "meeting present needs without compromising the ability of future generations to meet

ALONG THE SUPPLY CHAIN

Walmart's Commitment to Sustainability

Walmart, the world's third largest public corporation and largest retailer, with over 8,500 retail locations and more than 2 million employees around the world, has a global supply chain encompassing over 100,000 suppliers. The company has made a major commitment to have an environmentally sustainable supply chain in order to make a difference in the environment and communities around the world. In 2005, it established corporate sustainability goals "to be supplied 100 percent by renewable energy, create zero waste, and sell products that sustain our resources and the environment." To achieve these goals Walmart must closely monitor and scrutinize the environmental performance of its extended supply chain, suggest improvements to its suppliers, and help its suppliers implement sustainable solutions. Walmart has all of its U.S. suppliers complete a supplier sustainability assessment that measures supplier performance related to energy and climate, material efficiency, natural resources, and ethical production; this helps Walmart direct its suppliers on what they need to be doing to meet the company's sustainability goals.

Walmart has developed a number of sustainability initiatives, including a goal to eliminate 20 million metric tons of greenhouse gas (GHG) emissions (the amount of its direct emissions in 2010) from the company's global supply chain by 2016. The Energy Defense Fund (EDF) is collaborating with Walmart's top 200 suppliers in China to improve the energy efficiency of their factories. One energy initiative is to make Walmart's distribution fleet more efficient by working with suppliers to use fuel-saving technologies, load trucks more efficiently and improve routing, and use alternatively fueled trucks. The company has more than 180 renewable energy projects that provide 1.1 billion kilowatt hours annually, which is about 4% of the electricity Walmart buildings consume globally. The U.S. Environmental Protection Agency (EPA) ranks Walmart as the second-largest onsite green power generator in the United States. It has committed to sending zero waste to U.S. landfills by 2025.

In 2011, the company kept almost 81% of all waste from its U.S. operations out of landfills, which had the potential to reduce CO_2 emissions by 11.8 million tons annually. Its stores in China and Brazil divert over 50% of their operational waste from landfills, and its U.K. operator sends zero waste to landfills. It had a goal of reducing plastic shopping bag waste at its stores around the world by 33% by 2013, which translated to as much as 135 million pounds, and would potentially eliminate 290,000 metric tons of greenhouse gases and the use of 678,000 barrels of oil annually.

Walmart has increased the amount of locally grown produce (i.e., grown and sold in the same state) by 97%, which is 10% of all produce sold in its U.S. stores, with a goal of doubling the amount of locally grown produce it sells in the United States by 2015.

Not only does Walmart's commitment to sustainability make it a good global corporate citizen, but it is also good business.

Identify the company that is the EPA's top onsite green power generator and discuss its sustainability initiatives.

Sources: Based on the Walmart website at www.walmartstores.com/Sustainability/; and Erica Plambeck, and Lyn Denend, "The Greening of Walmart's Supply Chain . . . Revisited," *Supply Chain Management Review* 15, no. 5 (September/October 2011): 16–23.

their needs." Implicit in this definition is not depleting or abusing our natural resources like air, water, land, and energy in a way that's going to harm current or future generations. For businesses it also means sustaining human and social resources. However, to many companies, sustainability means becoming environmentally friendly and socially conscious (i.e., "green") at *the expense of competitiveness and higher costs.* A common perception among many U.S. and European corporations is that requiring suppliers, especially in developing countries, to use green practices is not feasible because they do not face the same governmental, cultural, and social pressures; that green manufacturing will require costly new equipment and processes; and that the customer market for products designed with green attributes is "soft." As a result, companies often view social and environmental responsibility separately from business objectives.

However, there is a growing realization among many companies that the social and environmental benefits of developing sustainable products do not have to come at the expense of reduced profits and competiveness. In an IBM survey of 320 global companies in 31 countries, almost 37% indicated that they were utilizing sustainability as part of their company's innovation and growth strategy. As these companies have learned, sustainability can, in fact, be cost-effective and profitable and provide the impetus for product and process innovations. Green initiatives can lower costs because fewer resources are used, and additional revenues can result from better products or new businesses. Although Toyota realized huge costs in developing its hybrid Prius, it created a whole new successful and potentially profitable product and market just as gasoline prices were rising. Further, by designing products that can be recycled or reused, companies can reduce waste, thereby lowering costs. Thus, while a commitment to green practices can create a better image for companies among consumers (and the government), they can also reduce costs and increase revenues.

The impetus for, and commitment to, sustainability generally comes from downstream in the supply chain and moves back upstream to include suppliers. Companies have found that suppliers can account for as much as 80% of the resources consumed in a product's supply chain. Companies must work with and guide suppliers to reduce the inefficient use of resources, reduce the use of raw materials, reduce waste, and recycle. Suppliers can be coerced into using green practices by threats, demands, or incentives, or a combination.

SUSTAINABILITY AND QUALITY MANAGEMENT

Many companies already have quality improvement programs in place that require suppliers to adhere to continuous improvement goals of eliminating returned products, thus reducing waste; poor quality translates to wasted resources. The same quality management focus on reducing waste can work to achieve sustainability goals. As we discussed in Chapter 2, the cost of poor quality can have a significant impact on a company's profitability and competitiveness, and quality costs may often come from suppliers along the supply chain, including the cost of materials, labor, and resources for reworking defective products; the cost of shipping delays and customer service errors; and the cost of product replacement and waste.

Improving fuel efficiency in a distribution fleet, having employees telecommute, using eco-friendly packaging materials, building energy efficient facilities, reducing the use of wooden pallets, and even turning the thermostat up in summer and down in winter are initiatives that improve processes and reduce costs, and also achieve sustainability goals. As part of the U.S. General Services Administration's smart building strategy, IBM is installing smart building technology in 50 of the federal government's highest-energy-consuming buildings, saving taxpayers $15 million annually. By consolidating distribution centers, COSCO, China's largest shipping and logistics services supplier, reduced its overall fuel costs by 25%. Dow Chemical estimates that its sustainability initiatives have saved more than $8 billion in fuel costs.

ALONG THE SUPPLY CHAIN

Achieving Sustainability While Reducing Costs and Increasing Profits

Walmart's globally recognized commitment to creating a sustainable supply chain has resulted in significant financial benefits for the company. As one example, the company used to spend $16 million annually to send plastic waste to landfills, which it now converts into plastic pellets that it sells back to its packaging suppliers, generating $28 million annually in income. Its sustainability initiatives starting in 2005 moved it from the lowest-ranked global retailer in terms of ethical reputation to third-ranked in just five years, which has helped Walmart secure permission to open new stores and increase sales in existing stores.

FedEx has a fleet of over 700 aircraft and 44,000 vehicles that consume an estimated 4 million gallons of fuel per day. As part of its sustainability efforts it is replacing old aircraft with new larger, more fuel-efficient Boeing aircraft that will reduce its fuel consumption by over 50% and increase shipping capacity by 20%, with a goal of reducing CO_2 emissions by 20% by 2020. FedEx has increased its use of hybrid and electric vans that are over 40% more fuel efficient, with a goal of improving its overall fleet fuel efficiency by 20% by 2020. It has developed software that will optimize aircraft routes and schedules; and four of its U.S. hub facilities and one in Germany utilize solar energy, reducing CO_2 emissions by almost 4,000 metric tons per year (which is equivalent to 440,000 gallons of gasoline). FedEx has also started a consulting firm to sell the energy expertise it has gained through its own sustainability initiatives.

At IBM, employee telecommuting saves the company more than $700 million in real estate costs each year. IBM estimates that its energy conservation projects in one year alone saved it $43 million in energy expenses. AT&T annually saves $550 million with telecommuting. Johnson Controls, a global *Fortune 500* company offering products and services to optimize energy and operational efficiencies of buildings, automotive batteries and interior systems for automobiles, became so adept at reducing its own greenhouse gas (GHG) emissions that it made sustainability a central part of its own product line and offers its "Internal Energy and Emissions Management System" to customers to help them reduce energy use and costs.

Cisco Systems established a business unit for recycling that increased the reuse of equipment from 5% to 45% and reduced recycling costs by 40% in four years; overall, the unit became a profit center that earned Cisco over $100 million in one year.

Procter & Gamble estimated that if U.S. households switched to cold-water clothes washing instead of heating water, we would save 80 billion kWh of electricity and reduce carbon dioxide emissions by 34 million tons. As a result, P&G developed new cold-water detergents, Tide Coldwater in the United States and Ariel Cool Clean in Europe. More popular in Europe than in the United States, cold-water washing rose from 2% to 21% in the United Kingdom, and in Holland it rose from 5% to 52%.

Clorox—upon discovering that household cleaning products are the second-biggest environmental concern in the United States next to cars, and that up to 35% of consumers consider environmental benefits when making purchases—spent three years and $20 million to develop its nonsynthetic Green Works line of cleaning products. Endorsed by the Sierra Club, in one year Green Works grew the natural cleaner market in the United States by 100 percent, and Clorox garnered a 40% share of the $200 million market. It then introduced biodegradable cleaning wipes and nonsynthetic detergents that compete directly with P&G products.

Waste Management, a $14 billion garbage disposal company, estimated that it was hauling $9 billion worth of reusable waste to landfills. It set up a new business unit, "Green Squad," to partner with companies in the United States to turn waste into profits—for example, it worked with Sony to collect electronic waste for recycling.

Look on the Internet and identify other "green" initiatives that companies have taken that reduce costs or increase profits.

Sources: Ram Nidumolu, C.K. Prahalad, and M.R. Rangaswami, "Why Sustainability Is Now the Key Driver of Innovation," *Harvard Business Review* 87, no. 9 (September 2009): pp. 57–64; Walmart website at www.walmart.com; and IBM website at www.ibm.com.

Information Technology: A Supply Chain Enabler

Information is the essential link between all supply chain processes and members. Computer and information technology allows real-time, online communications throughout the supply chain. Technologies that enable the efficient flow of products and services through the supply chain are referred to as "enablers," and information technology has become the most important enabler of effective supply chain management.

Supply chain managers like to use the phrase "in modern supply chain management, information replaces inventory." Although this statement is not literally true—companies need inventory at some point, not just information—information does change the way supply chains are managed, and these changes can lead to lower inventories. Without information technology, supply chain management would not be possible at the level it is currently being accomplished on a global basis. Some of the more important IT supply chain enablers are shown in Figure 10.5.

ELECTRONIC BUSINESS

E-business replaces physical processes with electronic ones. In e-business, supply chain transactions are conducted via a variety of electronic media, including electronic data interchange (EDI), email, electronic funds transfer (EFT), electronic publishing, image processing, electronic bulletin boards, shared databases, bar coding, fax, automated voice mail, CD-ROM catalogs, the Internet, websites, and so on. Companies are able to automate the process of moving information electronically between suppliers and customers. This saves both labor costs and time.

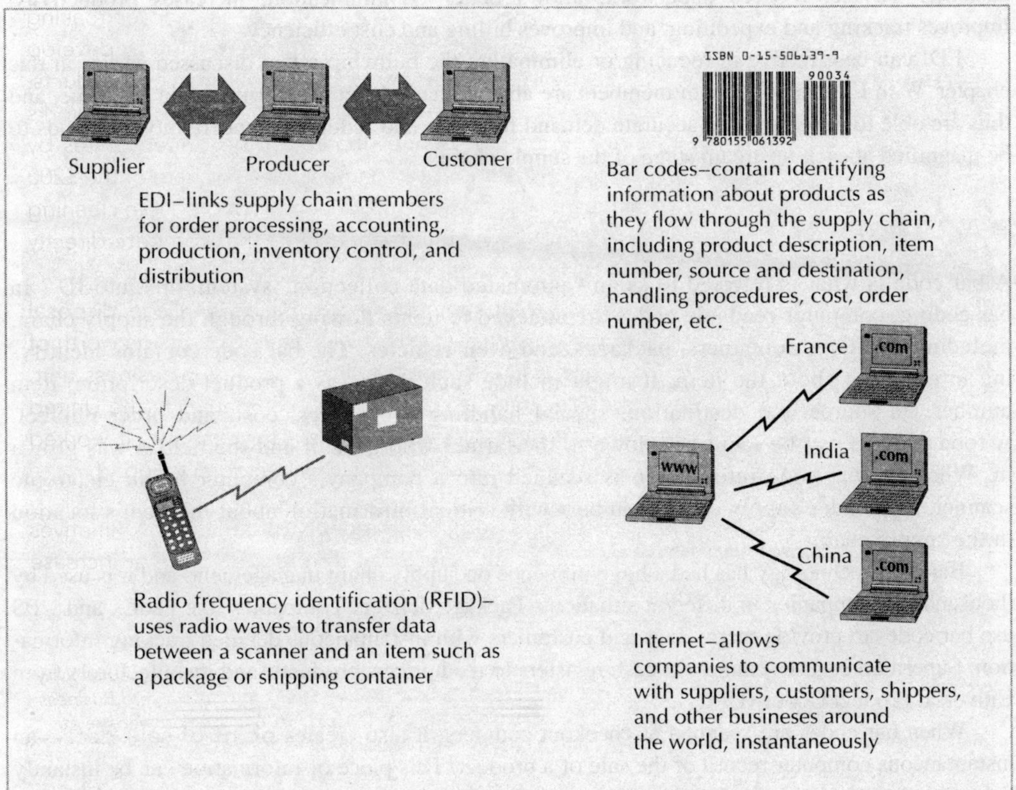

Figure 10.5
Supply Chain Enablers

Some of the features that e-business brings to supply chain management include:

- Cost savings and price reductions derived from lower transaction costs (including labor and document savings)
- Reduction or elimination of the role of intermediaries and even retailers and service providers, thus reducing costs
- Shortening supply chain response and transaction times for ordering and delivery
- Gaining a wider presence and increased visibility for companies
- Greater choices and more information for customers
- Improved service as a result of instant accessibility to services
- Collection and analysis of voluminous amounts of customer data and preferences
- The creation of virtual companies like Amazon.com that distribute only through the Web, which can afford to sell at lower prices because they do not need to maintain retail space
- Leveling the playing field for small companies, which lack resources to invest in infrastructure (plant and facilities) and marketing
- Gaining global access to markets, suppliers, and distribution channels

ELECTRONIC DATA INTERCHANGE

Electronic data interchange (EDI) is a computer-to-computer exchange of business documents in a standard format, which has been established by the American National Standards Institute (ANSI) and the International Standards Organization (ISO). It creates a data exchange that allows trading partners to use Internet transactions instead of paper when performing purchasing, shipping, and other business. EDI links supply chain members together for order processing, accounting, production, and distribution. It provides quick access to information, allows better customer service, reduces paperwork, allows better communication, increases productivity, improves tracking and expediting, and improves billing and cost efficiency.

EDI can be effective in reducing or eliminating the bullwhip effect discussed earlier in this chapter. With EDI, supply chain members are able to share demand information in real time, and thus are able to develop more accurate demand forecasts and reduce the uncertainty that tends to be magnified at each upstream stage of the supply chain.

BAR CODES

A bar code is what is referred to as an "automated data collection" system, or "auto-ID." In bar coding, computer-readable codes are attached to items flowing through the supply chain, including products, containers, packages, and even vehicles. The bar code contains identifying information about the item. It might include such things as a product description, item number, its source and destination, special handling procedures, cost, and order number. A food product can be identified down to the farmer who grew it and the field it was grown in. When the bar code information is scanned into a company's computer by an electronic scanner, it provides supply chain members with critical information about the item's location in the supply chain.

Bar code technology has had a huge influence on supply chain management, and it is used by thousands of companies in different situations. Package delivery companies like FedEx and UPS use bar codes to provide themselves and customers with instantaneous detailed tracking information. Supermarkets use scanners at cash registers to read prices, products, and manufacturers from Universal Product Codes (UPCs).

When bar codes are scanned at checkout counters, it also creates **point-of-sale data**—an instantaneous computer record of the sale of a product. This piece of information can be instantly transmitted throughout the supply chain to update inventory records. Point-of-sale data enable supply chain members—suppliers, producers, and distributors—to quickly identify trends, order parts and materials, schedule orders and production, and plan for deliveries.

RADIO FREQUENCY IDENTIFICATION

While a barcode is the most commonly used auto-ID system, a more technologically advanced system is **radio frequency identification (RFID)**. RFID technology uses radio waves to transfer data between a reader (that is, a scanner) and an item such as a shipping container or a carton. RFID consists of a tiny microchip and computer, often a small, thin ribbon, which can be put in almost any form—for example between layers of cardboard in a box, or on a piece of tape or a label. An RFID "tag" stores a unique identification number. RFID scanners transmit a radio signal via an antenna to "access" the tag, which then responds with its number. The tag could be an Electronic Product Code (EPC), which could be linked to databases with detailed information about a product item.

RFID has several advantages over barcodes. RFID tags do not need a direct "line of sight" to read, and many tags can be read simultaneously over a long distance. When products arrive at a location, such as a retail store, shipping dock, or warehouse, each barcode has to be scanned individually, whereas RFID readers placed at an entry site (like a door) can scan a whole pallet of different products automatically and instantaneously. As such, RFID provides complete visibility of product location, is faster, reduces labor usage, and is more accurate than barcodes. With barcodes it is difficult to know how much product is in a store; however, RFID readers inside a store (or warehouse) can continuously monitor what is available, and when the inventory reaches a certain level it can be reordered. When items are stored in a warehouse, the barcode on the item to be stored has to be scanned as well as the barcode fixed to the location; RFID eliminates these steps.

In a global supply chain, RFID tags make it possible for suppliers or retailers to know automatically what goods they have and where they are around the world. For example, a retailer could distinguish between three cartons of the same product and know that one was in the warehouse in

ALONG THE SUPPLY CHAIN

Managing Ford's Supply Chain Risks and Helping the Automaker's Recovery

In 2006, Ford mortgaged virtually the entire company against private bank loans of almost $27 billion (while rivals GM and Chrysler accepted $25 billion of government bail-out money). A condition of the loans was that its debt would have to be rated investment grade by two major rating agencies before Ford could get back its brand, buildings, and factories. By mid-2012, following three years of solid revenue growth, Ford received investment grade ratings from Fitch Ratings and Moody's Investor Services. In 2010, it surpassed Toyota as the second-largest auto seller in the United States.

A significant factor in Ford's recovery has been attributed to tight management of its large and complex supply chain. Ford builds around 6 million cars a year with a supply chain that includes 70 plants around the world drawing 34 billion parts from 1,400 tier 1 suppliers at 4,400 manufacturing sites, with as many as 10 tiers of suppliers between the automaker and its raw material sources. A key to Ford's supply chain management strategy was simplification, by building cars on a smaller number of base vehicles. This is one of the primary trends of the top company supply chains identified by *Gartner's* in its annual report (see the "Along the Supply Chain" box on page 327).

Ford also mirrored top supply chain performers by introducing *resiliency* in its supply chain through good risk planning. Ford was able to weather several major disruptions during its recovery, including a fire at the trim factory of a Michigan supplier and severe floods in Thailand that affected a tooling plant. The company worked to proactively identify the areas of greatest risk, especially among its tier 1 suppliers where disruptions could halt production, by keeping approved, qualified alternative suppliers available to minimize risk and prevent supply disruptions.

Using the Internet, identify some of the major natural, economic, or political global disruptions in the past five years that would have posed a risk situation to U.S. companies with a global supply chain.

Source: Based on Robert J. Bowman, "How Ford's Supply Chain Put the Company Back in the Driver's Seat," *SupplyChainBrain* (June 18, 2012), www.supplychainbrain.com.

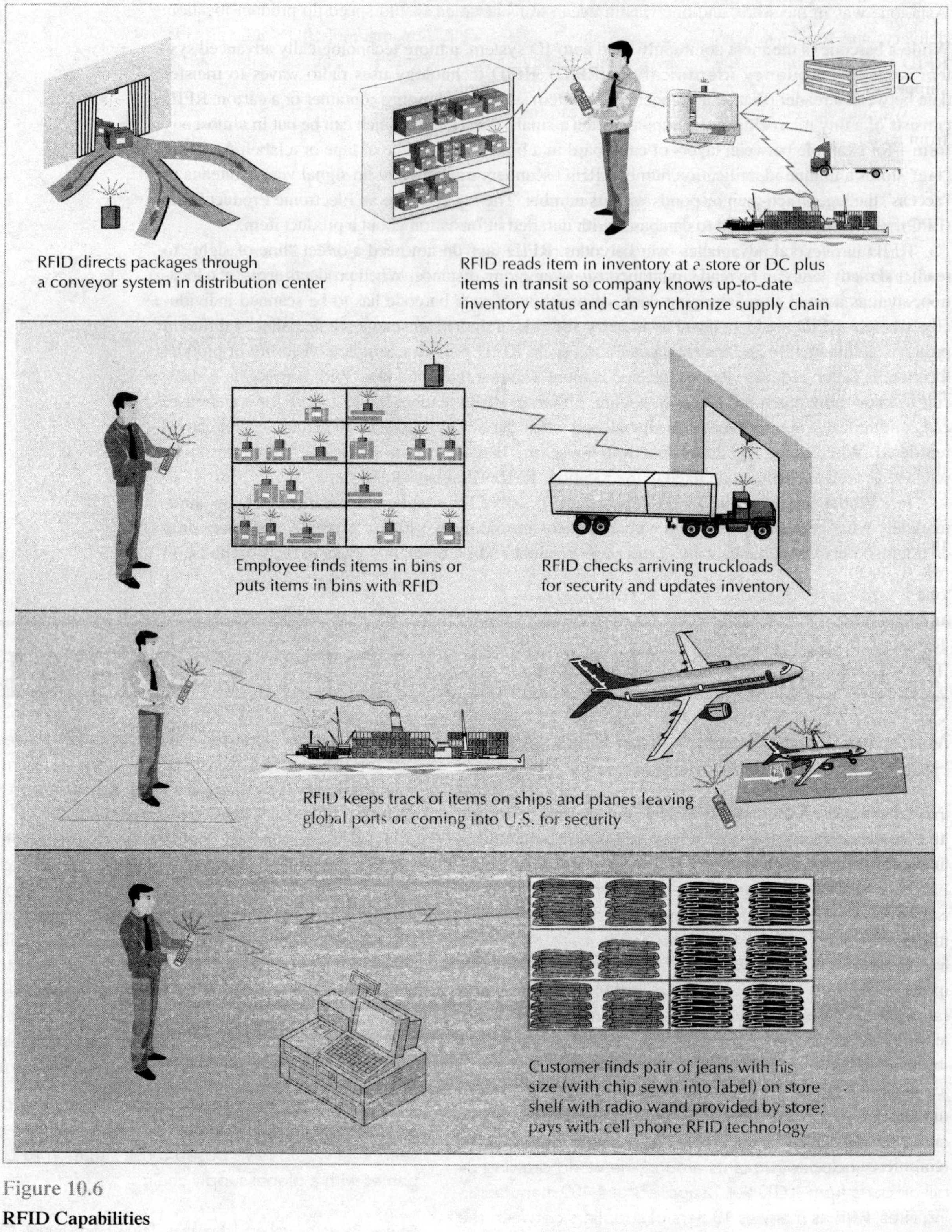

Figure 10.6

RFID Capabilities

Asia, one was in the store, and one was in ocean transit, which would speed up product location, delivery, and replenishment. Figure 10.6 shows some of the advantages RFID could provide. RFID technology also has obvious security benefits by being able to identify all items being shipped into the United States on an airplane or a ship.

Walmart, an early proponent of RFID, estimated that the following benefits would result from RFID:

- Labor to scan barcodes on cases and pallets will be eliminated.
- On-shelf monitoring will decrease stock-outs in stores.
- Product shrinkage, vendor fraud, and theft will be prevented.
- Tracking over 1 billion pallets annually will reduce distribution center costs.
- RFID will provide inventory visibility, enabling a 20% reduction in inventory levels.
- Savings of over $8 billion per year are projected.

However, RFID technology does have disadvantages. RFID technology is not yet standardized, which makes it difficult to track items that move from one system to another. Using RFID is more costly than using barcodes: individual RFID tags are expensive relative to barcodes, and the readers are costly. Radio waves don't go through metal and are diffused by water.

Walmart originally mandated that its top suppliers put RFID tags carrying EPC codes on their pallets and cases. However, a number of its suppliers balked due to technical problems and costs. Many consumer products such as toilet paper and detergent have very thin profit margins, so requiring tags on every pallet and case could turn profit into loss very quickly. Walmart also thought other retailers would follow their lead and also implement RFID on a wide scale, and when this didn't happen, suppliers were left with the cost of maintaining two inventory systems—one for Walmart and one for everyone else. As a result, Walmart scaled back its expectations for implementing RFID throughout its supply chain to a smaller number of top suppliers. Where RFID has found a niche is inside retail stores. Walmart, Macy's, Bloomingdale's, and Lord & Taylor are examples of retailers that are using RFID to track shelf inventory and maintain the right mix of sizes and styles for customers. It's much less costly and time-consuming to scan a store shelf with RFID tags than to use hand sorting or barcode scanning.

THE INTERNET

No technology has a bigger impact on supply chain management, and business in general, than the Internet. Through the Internet a business can communicate with customers and other businesses within its supply chain anywhere in the world in real time.

The Internet has eliminated geographic barriers, enabling companies to access markets and suppliers around the world that were previously inaccessible. By doing so, the Internet has shifted the advantage in the transaction process from the seller to the buyer, because the Internet makes it easier for companies to deal with many more suppliers around the world in order to get lower prices and better service.

The Internet adds speed and accessibility to the supply chain. Companies are able to reduce or eliminate traditional time-consuming activities associated with ordering and purchasing transactions by using the Internet to link directly to suppliers, factories, distributors, and customers. It enables companies to speed up ordering and delivery, track orders and delivery in real time, instantaneously update inventory information, and get instantaneous feedback from customers. This combination of accurate information and speed allows companies to reduce uncertainty and inventory. Internet commerce is expected to exceed $6 trillion in this decade.

BUILD-TO-ORDER (BTO)

Dell was the first computer company to move to a direct-sell-to-customers model over the Internet. Its popular build-to-order (BTO) models were initially based on telephone orders by customers. Dell created an efficient supply chain using a huge number of weekly purchase orders faxed to suppliers. However, Dell now sends out orders to suppliers over the Internet every few hours or less. Dell's suppliers are able to access the company's inventories and production plans, and they receive constant feedback on how well they are meeting shipping schedules.

Dell's website allows the customer to configure a PC with the desired features; to order and track the order status, allowing the customer to follow their purchase in real time from order to delivery; and to be notified by email as soon as the order is shipped. Also, Dell created secure private sites for corporate and public sector customers to provide access to service and support information customized to the customer's products. In addition, Dell provides online access to technical reference materials and self-diagnostic tools that include symptom-specific troubleshooting modules that walk customers interactively through common systems problems.

Supply Chain Integration

One of the keys to having a successful, efficient supply chain is to get the various supply chain members to collaborate and work together, that is, to get "in sync." This level of coordination is referred to as *supply chain integration*. Information technology is the key element in achieving supply chain integration through four areas—information sharing, collaborative planning, workflow coordination, and the adoption of new models and technologies. Table 10.1 describes the positive effect each of these elements can have on supply chain performance.

Information sharing includes any data that are useful to other members of the supply chain such as demand data, inventory stocks, and production and shipping schedules—anything that can help the supply chain members improve performance. Information needs to be transparent (i.e., not hidden) and easily accessible online. Collaborative planning defines *what* is done

TABLE 10.1 Supply Chain Integration

Information sharing among supply chain members • Reduced bullwhip effect • Early problem detection • Faster response • Builds trust and confidence
Collaborative planning, forecasting, replenishment, and design • Reduced bullwhip effect • Lower costs (material, logistics, operating, etc.) • Higher capacity utilization • Improved customer service levels
Coordinated workflow, production and operations, procurement • Production efficiencies • Fast response • Improved service • Quicker to market
Adopt new business models and technologies • Penetration of new markets • Creation of new products • Improved efficiency • Mass customization

with the information that is shared. Workflow coordination defines *how* supply chain partners work together to coordinate their activities. Finally, adopting new business models and technologies is how supply chain members redesign and improve their supply chain performance.

Collaborative planning, forecasting, and replenishment (CPFR) is a process for two or more companies in a supply chain to synchronize their individual demand forecasts in order to develop a single plan for meeting customer demand. With CPFR, parties electronically exchange a series of written comments and supporting data, which includes past sales trends, point-of-sale data, on-hand inventory, scheduled promotions, and forecasts. This allows participants to coordinate joint forecasts by concentrating on differences in forecast numbers. They review the data together, compare calculations, and collaborate on what is causing discrepancies. If there are no exceptions, they can develop a purchase order and ship. CPFR does not require EDI; data can be sent via spreadsheets or over the Internet. CPFR is actual collaboration because both parties do the work and both parties share in fixing the problems. Sharing forecasts in this type of collaborative system can result in a significant decrease in inventory levels for both the manufacturer and distributor since it tends to reduce the "bullwhip effect" and thus lower costs. Many companies, including General Mills, Procter & Gamble, Hershey's and Cisco Systems, participate in some form of CPFR with their suppliers.

Supply Chain Management (SCM) Software

Enterprise resource planning (ERP) is software that helps integrate the components of a company, including most of the supply chain processes, by sharing and organizing information and data among supply chain members. It transforms transactional data like sales into useful information that supports business decisions in other parts of the company. For example, when data such as a sale becomes available in one part of the business, it is transmitted through ERP software, which automatically determines the effects of the transaction on other areas, such as manufacturing, inventory, procurement, invoicing, distribution, and accounting, and on suppliers. Through these information flows, ERP organizes and manages a company's supply chain. Most ERP vendors systems handle external, Web-based interactions, and have software specifically for supply chain management called "SCM."

SAP was the first ERP software provider and is the largest, which has made it almost synonymous with ERP applications software. mySAP.com is the umbrella brand name for the SAP software. mySAP.com is a suite of Web-enabled SAP modules that allow a company to collaborate with its customers and business partners along its supply chain. When a customer submits an order, that transaction ripples throughout the company's supply chain, adjusting inventory, part supplies, accounting entries, production schedules and shipping schedules, and balance sheets. Different nations' laws, currencies, and business practices are embedded in the software, which enables it to translate sales transactions smoothly between business partners in different countries—for example, a company in Taiwan and its customer in Brazil.

ERP is discussed in greater detail in Chapter 15, "Resource Planning."

Measuring Supply Chain Performance

As we indicated in previous sections, inventory is a key element in supply chain management. On one hand, it enables a company to cope with uncertainty by serving as a buffer between stages in the supply chain. Inventory allows items to flow smoothly through the system to meet customer demand when stages are not in sync. On the other hand, inventory can be very costly. Thus, it is important for a company to maintain an efficient supply chain by lowering inventory levels (and costs) as much as possible. In order to accomplish this objective, several numerical measures, also called **key performance indicators (KPIs)** or metrics, are often used to measure supply chain performance. Three of the more widely used key performance indicators are *inventory turnover*, *inventory days of supply*, and *fill rate*.

KEY PERFORMANCE INDICATORS

Inventory turnover (or turns) is computed by dividing the cost of goods sold (i.e., the cost of annual sales) by the average aggregate inventory value:

$$\text{Inventory turns} = \frac{\text{Cost of goods sold}}{\text{Average aggregate value of inventory}}$$

The average aggregate value of inventory is the total value (at cost) of all items being held in inventory, including such things as raw materials, work-in-process (WIP), and finished goods. It is computed by summing for all individual inventory items, the product of the average number of units on hand in inventory at any one time multiplied by the unit value:

$$\text{Average aggregate value of inventory} = \sum (\text{average inventory for item } i) \times (\text{unit value item } i)$$

The cost of goods sold is only for finished goods, valued at cost, not the final sale price (which might include discounts or markups).

Every time product items are sold that are equal to the average amount of money that was invested in those items, then the inventory has been turned. An item whose inventory is sold (i.e., turns over) once a year has higher holding costs (for rent, utilities, insurance, theft, etc.) than one that turns over twice, three times, or more in that same time period. For example, if a firm that sells products that cost $10,000 in a year has a total revenue from the sale of these products of $15,000, the gross profit is $5,000. However, suppose instead the company only purchased $5,000 worth of products at the first of the year, and then just before running out of stock, it bought an additional $5,000 of products with part of the revenues from selling the first batch. The company still invested $10,000 in products and made revenues of $15,000, but only on an investment of $5,000. Which strategy is better—making $5,000 gross profit on an investment of $10,000 or $5,000? It is better to invest the smaller amount; with a $5,000 investment, the company has freed up $5,000 for part of the year to invest in other things it could make a profit on, and it has reduced its holding costs. However, the trick is to invest the minimum amount possible in products and reorder at just the right time to avoid stockouts. This is why a company with good supply chain management has more inventory turns than a company that does not.

A poor, or comparatively low, inventory turnover indicates that a large amount of inventory is required to satisfy demand. In general, a good (or poor) number of inventory turns is relative to what is being achieved at various stages across a company and what the industry norm is. Only comparisons of inventory turns for companies within the same industry are meaningful. Comparing a supermarket to a car dealer is not meaningful; a supermarket sells fast-moving products so its inventory turns will be higher than a car dealer that sells slow-moving items. In the 1980s, inventory turns for many manufacturing companies were less than five; however, the advent of lean production (see Chapter 16) and the increased focus on quality management and supply chain management have increased inventory turns in much of the manufacturing sector to about six turns per year for a typical company. Although this seems like a small change, it still represents a significant decrease in costs and increase in profits. On the other hand, a typical computer company or grocery store will have 12 turns or more per year.

Toyota had inventory turns in the 60s in the 1980s when its supply chain was mostly in Japan, but this has fallen to between 10 and 12 in recent years as it has expanded globally and the complexities of its supply chain have increased accordingly. High-tech companies typically have around six turns per year, but Dell has achieved inventory turns greater than 50, belying its supply chain success. On the other hand, pharmaceutical giant Pfizer has had recent inventory turns as low as 1.5. However, this does not mean that Pfizer is doing poorly financially—it has been very profitable. It does mean that perhaps it could manage its supply chain more efficiently.

Another commonly used KPI is days (or weeks) of supply. This is a measure of how many days (or weeks) of inventory is available at any point in time. It is computed by dividing the aggregate average value of inventory by the daily (or weekly) cost of goods sold,

$$\text{Days of supply} = \frac{\text{Average aggregate value of inventory}}{(\text{Cost of goods sold})/(365 \text{ days})}$$

Automotive companies typically carry about 60 days of finished goods supply.

Another frequently used KPI is **fill rate**. Fill rates are the fraction of orders placed by a customer with a supplier distribution center or warehouse that are filled within a specific period of time, typically one day. High fill rates indicate that inventory is moving from the supplier to the customer at a faster rate, which thereby reduces inventory at the distribution center. For example, Nabisco's fill rate for its Planter's peanuts at Wegman's grocery store chain is 97%, meaning that when the store places an order with the Nabisco distribution center, 97% of the time it is filled within one day.

PROCESS CONTROL

In Chapter 2, "Quality Management," we talked about various techniques that could be employed to monitor product and service quality. One of the more powerful techniques we presented was statistical process control, the subject of Chapter 3. Although we tend to think that process control is used to

EXAMPLE 10.1

COMPUTING KEY PERFORMANCE INDICATORS

The Tomahawk Motorcycle Company manufactures motorcycles. Last year the cost of goods sold was $425 million. The company had the following average value of production materials and parts, work-in-process, and finished goods inventory:

Production materials and parts	$ 4,629,000
Work-in-process	17,465,000
Finished goods	12,322,000
Total average aggregate value of inventory	$34,416,000

The company wants to know the number of inventory turns and days of supply being held in inventory.

SOLUTION

$$\text{Inventory turns} = \frac{\text{Cost of goods sold}}{\text{Average aggregate value of inventory}}$$

$$= \frac{\$425{,}000{,}000}{34{,}416{,}000}$$

$$\text{Inventory turns} = 12.3$$

$$\text{Days of supply} = \frac{\text{Average aggregate value of inventory}}{(\text{Cost of goods sold})/(365 \text{ days})}$$

$$= \frac{\$34{,}416{,}000}{(425{,}000{,}000)/(365)}$$

$$\text{Days of supply} = 29.6$$

monitor and control quality for manufacturing operations, it can also be used to monitor and control any of the processes in the supply chain. If products are defective, then the effects are obvious. However, other problems along the supply chain that create uncertainty and variability are most often caused by errors. If deliveries are missed or are late, if orders are lost, if errors are made in filling out forms, if items with high obsolescence rates (like PCs) or perishable items are allowed to stay too long in inventory, if demand forecast errors are made, if plant and equipment are not properly maintained, then the supply chain can be disrupted, thereby reducing supply chain performance. Thus, at any stage in the process, statistical process control charts can be used to monitor process performance.

SCOR

The **supply chain operations reference (SCOR)** model is a supply chain diagnostic tool that provides a cross-industry standard for supply chain management. It was developed and is maintained by the Supply Chain Council, a global not-for-profit trade association organized in 1996 with membership open to companies interested in improving supply chain efficiency primarily through the use of SCOR. The Supply Chain Council (SCC) has almost 1,000 corporate members around the world, including many Fortune 500 companies.

The purpose of the SCOR model is to define a company's current supply chain processes, quantify the performance of similar companies to establish targets to achieve "best-in-class" performance, and identify the practices and software solutions that will yield "best in class" performance. It is organized around a set of five primary management processes—plan, source, make, deliver, and return, as shown in Figure 10.7. These processes provide a common set of definitions, or building blocks, that SCOR uses to describe any supply chain, from simple to complex. This allows supply chains for different companies to be linked and compared.

A primary feature of the SCOR model is the use of a set of performance indicators or "metrics" to measure supply chain performance. These metrics are categorized as "customer focused" or "internally focused" as shown in Table 10.2. Customer focused metrics measure supply chain delivery reliability, responsiveness, and agility with respect to customers and suppliers. Internally focused metrics measure supply chain cost and asset management efficiency. The metrics may be used for multiple supply chain processes.

These metrics are used to develop a "SCORcard" that measures both a company's current supply chain performance for different processes and its competitor's metrics. The company then projects

Figure 10.7
Supply Chain Enablers

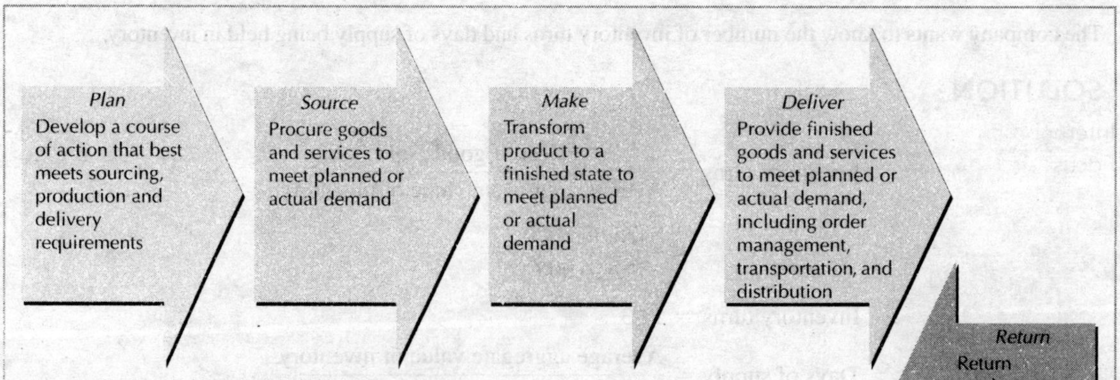

the level of metrics it needs to be on a par with its competitors, to have an advantage over its competitors, or to be superior. The value associated with these measured improvements in performance is then projected for the different performance attributes. For example, a company may know that the industry "median fill rate" is 90% and the industry best-in-class performance is 99%. The company has determined that its current fill rate is 65%, and that a fill rate of 90% will give it parity with its competitors, a 95% fill rate will give it an advantage, and a 99% fill rate will make it superior to most of its competitors. The company may then project that the improvement in its fill rate plus improvements in the other supply chain reliability attributes (i.e., delivery performance and perfect order fulfillment) will increase supply chain value by $10 million in revenue. This process wherein a company measures its current supply chain performance, compares it to its competition, and then projects the performance levels it needs to compete is referred to as "gap analysis." SCOR then provides a framework not only for measuring performance but for diagnosing problems and identifying practices and solutions that will enable a company to achieve its competitive performance objectives.

TABLE 10.2 SCOR Performance Metrics

	Performance Attribute	Performance Metric	Definition
Customer Focus	Supply chain delivery reliability	Delivery performance	Percentage of orders delivered on time and in full to the customer
		Fill rate	Percentage of orders shipped within 24 hours of order receipt
		Perfect order fulfillment	Percentage of orders delivered on time and in full, perfectly matched with order with no errors
	Supply chain responsiveness	Order fulfillment lead time	Time from order receipt to customer delivery; sourcing time; make time; delivery time
	Supply chain agility	Supply chain response time and risk	Time for the supply chain to respond to an unplanned significant change in demand without a cost penalty
		Production flexibility	Number of days to achieve an unplanned 20% change in orders without a cost penalty
Internal Focus	Supply chain cost	Supply chain management costs	The direct and indirect cost to plan, source, make, and deliver products and services
		Cost of goods sold	The direct and indirect cost of material and labor to produce a product or service
Internal Focus	Supply chain cost	Risk mitigation cost	Cost of identifying, evaluating, planning for and monitoring risks
		Warranty/return processing cost	Direct and indirect costs associated with returns including defective, planned maintenance, and excess inventory
	Supply chain asset management	Cash-to-cash cycle time	The number of days that cash is tied up as working capital
		Inventory days of supply	The number of days that cash is tied up as inventory
		Return on fixed assets	Fixed asset value for SCM processes
		Return on working capital	Accounts payable, receivable and inventory

SUMMARY

Supply chain management is one of the most important strategic aspects of operations management because it encompasses so many related functions. Who to buy materials from, how to transport goods and services, and how to distribute them in the most cost-effective, timely manner constitutes much of an organization's strategic planning. Contracting with the wrong supplier can result in poor-quality materials and late deliveries. Selecting the wrong mode of transportation or carrier can mean late deliveries to customers that will require high, costly inventories to offset. All of these critical functional supply chain decisions are complicated by the fact that they often occur in a global environment within cultures and markets at a distance and much different from those in the United States.

KEY FORMULAS

$$\text{Inventory turns} = \frac{\text{Cost of goods sold}}{\text{Average aggregate value of inventory}}$$

$$\text{Days of supply} = \frac{\text{Average aggregate value of inventory}}{(\text{Cost of goods sold})/(365 \text{ days})}$$

SOLVED PROBLEM

INVENTORY TURNS AND DAYS OF SUPPLY

A manufacturing company had the following average raw materials, work-in-process, and finished goods inventory on hand at any one time during the past year.

Raw Materials	Average Inventory	Unit Cost
1	135	$26.50
2	67	18.20
3	210	9.75
4	97	31.25
Work-in-Process		
5	40	$165.00
6	65	230.00
Finished Goods	**Average Inventory**	**Unit Cost**
7	25	$ 670.00
8	18	1,050.00
9	35	520.00

The company's cost of goods sold last year was $2.73 million, and it operates 365 days per year.

Determine the company's inventory turns and days of supply.

SOLUTION

Step 1. Compute the average aggregate value of inventory.

$$
\begin{aligned}
\text{Raw materials: } (135)(\$26.50) &= \$3{,}577.50 \\
(67)(18.20) &= 1{,}219.40 \\
(210)(9.75) &= 2{,}047.50 \\
(97)(31.25) &= 3{,}031.25 \\
\text{Work-in-process: } (40)(165) &= 6{,}600.00 \\
(65)(230) &= 14{,}950.00 \\
\text{Finished goods: } (25)(670) &= 16{,}750.00 \\
(18)(1050) &= 18{,}900.00 \\
(35)(520) &= 18{,}200.00 \\
\text{Total} & \ \ \$85{,}275.65
\end{aligned}
$$

Step 2. Compute inventory turns.

$$
\begin{aligned}
\text{Inventory turns} &= \frac{\text{Cost of good sold}}{\text{Average aggregate value of inventory}} \\
&= \frac{2{,}730{,}000}{85{,}275.65} \\
&= 32
\end{aligned}
$$

Step 3. Compute days of supply.

$$
\begin{aligned}
\text{Days of supply} &= \frac{\text{Average aggregate value of inventory}}{(\text{cost of goods sold})/(365)} \\
&= \frac{85{,}275.65}{(2{,}730{,}000)/(365)} \\
&= 11.4 \text{ days}
\end{aligned}
$$

QUESTIONS

10-1. Compare the supply chains, in general terms, for McDonald's and for Toyota.

10-2. Identify three service businesses in your community and describe their supply chains.

10-3. Discuss, in general, the differences in the supply chains of service providers and manufacturing companies.

10-4. Select a company and determine the type of suppliers it has, then indicate the criteria that you think the company might use to evaluate and select suppliers.

10-5. Locate an e-marketplace site on the Internet and describe it and the type of producers and suppliers it connects.

10-6. Explore the website of an ERP provider and describe the services that it indicates it provides.

10-7. Explain why radio frequency identification (RFID) offers enhanced opportunities for security in global transportation and distribution, and how this, in turn, could improve supply chain efficiency.

10-8. Walmart is one of the leaders in promoting the development and use of RFID and electronic product codes. Explain how Walmart uses RFID, why Walmart wants its suppliers to adopt RFID, and what obstacles have been shown to exist for this new technology.

10-9. It has been suggested that SCOR might serve as an international supply chain certification tool much like ISO certification for quality. Explain how you think SCOR might be used as a certification tool.

10-10. Identify and discuss the types of risk a company with a global supply chain might encounter with its overseas suppliers.

10-11. What are some of the ways companies manage risks in a global supply chain?

10-12. Identify the quality problems that a company might encounter with the following global supply chain components:

a. Oversesas suppliers
b. Container ships
c. Transportation
d. Packaging
e. Distribution
f. Warehousing

10-13. Identify a business that employs EDI in its supply chain management and describe how it is used.

10-14. Surf the Internet and identify a company with a strong commitment to sustainability and discuss its green initiatives.

10-15. What are some of the unique sustainability challenges that a company might face in a global supply chain?

10-16. What type of sustainability issues might a U.S. company face with a supplier in China? Mexico?

10-17. How are companies able to save money through their sustainability efforts?

10-18. How do sustainability initiatives differ between a service provider and a manufacturing firm?

PROBLEMS

10-1. The Fizer Drug Company manufactures over-the-counter and prescription drugs. Last year the company's cost of goods sold was $470 million. It carried average raw material inventory of $17.5 million, average work-in-process of $9.3 million, and average finished goods inventory of $6.4 million. The company operates 365 days per year. Compute the company's inventory turns and days of supply for last year.

10-2. The Ashton Furniture Company manufactures coffee tables and chests of drawers. Last year the company's cost of goods sold was $3,700,000, and it carried inventory of raw materials, work-in-process, and finished goods. Its average inventory levels for a 52-week business year were as follows:

Raw Materials	Average Inventory	Unit Cost
Oak	8,000	$6.00
Pine	4,500	4.00
Brass fixtures	1,200	8.00
Stains	3,000	2.00
Joiners	900	1.00
Work-in-Process		
Frames	200	$30
Drawers	400	10
Panels	600	50
Chests	120	110
Tables	90	90
Finished Goods		
Chests	300	$500
Coffee tables	200	350

Determine the number of inventory turns and the days of supply for the furniture company.

10-3. Barington Mills manufactures denim cloth from two primary raw materials: cotton and dye. Work-in-process includes lapped cotton, spun yarn, and undyed cloth, while finished goods includes three grades of dyed cloth. The average inventory amounts on hand at any one time last year and the unit costs are as follows:

Raw Materials	Average Inventory	Unit Cost
Cotton	70,000 lb.	$2.75
Dye	125,000 gal.	5.00
Work-in-Process		
Lapped cotton	2,000 rolls	$10.50
Spun yarn	5,000 spools	6.75
Undyed cloth	500 rolls	26.10
Finished Goods		
Grade 1 cloth	250 rolls	$65.00
Grade 2 cloth	190 rolls	80.00
Grade 3 cloth	310 rolls	105.00

The company operates 50 weeks per year, and its cost of goods sold for the past year was $17.5 million.

Determine the company's inventory turns and weeks of supply.

10-4. The PM Computer Company makes build-to-order (BTO) computers at its distribution center year round. The following table shows the average value (in $ millions) of component parts, work-in-process, and finished computers at the DC for the past four years.

	Year			
	1	2	3	4
Component parts	$20.5	27.8	30.8	37.3
Work-in-process	4.2	6.7	7.1	9.5
Finished computers	3.6	7.2	8.6	10.1
Cost of goods sold	226.0	345.0	517.0	680.0

a. Determine the number of inventory turns and the days of supply for each year.

b. As the company has grown, does it appear that the company's supply chain performance has improved? Explain your answer.

c. If the company wants to improve its supply chain performance, what items should it focus on? Why?

10-5. Solve Problem 3-5 in Chapter 3 to construct a *c*-chart for monitoring invoice errors at Telecom Manufacturing Company.

10-6. Solve Problem 3-6 in Chapter 3 to construct a *p*-chart to monitor order problems at BooksCDs.com

10-7. Solve Problem 3-7 in Chapter 3 to construct an *x*-chart in conjunction with an *R*-chart for order fulfillment lead time at Valtec Electronics.

CASE STUDY

Beating the Bad Weather

ABC Ulsan Oil Field Equipment Manufacturers is competing with Daejeon Suppliers to provide process control computers to the Sino-Russian gas pipeline under construction. Due to the remoteness of the pipeline construction, severe weather conditions, and short construction season, the construction firm must have the highest level of assurance that their suppliers can meet delivery dates.

The firm is looking at the options of buying larger quantities of materials and storing them on-site, or obtaining smaller shipments on a more frequent basis. If the construction firm were to buy in larger quantities, it would incur increased inventory costs due to the cost of storing the inventory and shrinkage. It would also have lost the use of capital funds (opportunity cost) as significant project funds would have been tied up in inventory.

The firm has been trying to determine the best quantitative method of comparing either purchasing larger or smaller material lots. The purchasing agent has suggested that they compare each option's inventory turns and days of supply as part of the decision-making process. The construction firm's management has tentatively agreed to use this input as it makes its final decision.

With the general agreement, the management of the construction firm has directed the purchasing agent to develop a spreadsheet showing the results and to provide a recommended way forward.

To this end, the purchasing agent began to derive the raw data that would be used for this analysis. A major difficulty was encountered in that the first request for data resulted in the external firms providing their total cost of goods sold and total aggregate inventory costs. The problem with this approach is the two firms provide a much wider set of materials to many other industries than just the material needed for this pipeline project.

The purchasing agent did not think it was appropriate to compare the full company data when just a minor portion was required for this job. As such, the purchasing agent requested that each firm provide the cost of goods sold and various inventories associated with just the material that would be provided. The following table contains the results of this second data set:

	Supplier 1	Supplier 2	Construction Firm
Cost of goods sold	$4,500,000	$3,500,000	$7,500,000
Raw materials	375,000	295,000	0
Work-in-process	25,000	30,000	150,000
Finished goods	750,000	700,000	145,000
Weeks work =	52	52	52
Days per week =	5	6	7

Based on the number of days worked, develop the days of supply and inventory turns values.

Do you think this is a fair comparison of the alternatives? Justify your answer.

REFERENCES

Chopra, S., and P. Meindl. *Supply Chain Management*, 2nd ed. Upper Saddle River, NJ: Prentice Hall, 2004.

Christopher, M. *Logistics and Supply Chain Management*. 2nd ed. Upper Saddle River, NJ: Prentice Hall, 1998.

Dornier, P., R. Ernst, M. Fender and P. Kouvelis. *Global Operations and Logistics*. New York: John Wiley & Sons, 1998.

Schechter, D., and G. Sander. *Delivering the Goods: The Art of Managing Your Supply Chain*. New York: John Wiley & Sons, 2002.

CHAPTER 11

Global Procurement and Distribution

LEARNING OBJECTIVES

AFTER READING THIS CHAPTER, YOU WILL BE ABLE TO:

- Discuss outsourcing as a strategic decision.
- Explain the basic elements of procurement, e-procurement and spend analysis.
- Describe distribution strategies, systems and processes.
- Assess the advantages and disadvantages of different modes of transportation.
- Discuss issues and trends in the global supply chain.

GLOBAL SUPPLY CHAIN MANAGEMENT AT LI & FUNG

Li & Fung Limited, headquartered in Hong Kong, is the world's leading consumer goods sourcing company supplying high volume, time-sensitive products like denim jeans to over 2,000 customers worldwide. It is the recognized world leader in supply chain management, providing a spectrum of services that covers the entire supply chain. It has over 240 offices and distribution centers with 37,000 employees in over 40 countries. Garments, including denim jeans, make up about two-thirds of Li & Fung's business; it is involved in the production of 40% to 50% of the clothes you'll find in any U.S. shopping mall.

Li & Fung's extensive global network of over 15,000 suppliers includes product design and development, raw material and factory sourcing, production planning and management, quality assurance, shipping and distribution, warehousing, customs brokerage, and export documentation. It manages the supply chain of large retailers such as Walmart, Kohl's, Target, Abercrombie & Fitch, Marks and Spencer, and Talbots, helping them (and all their customers) optimize the flow of inventory and information to reduce cost and improve service level. For products like denim jeans, Li & Fung finds raw materials and factories and takes on manufacturing responsibilities to make sure factories meet labor standards and deliver jeans at set prices and quickly (although Li & Fung generally owns few factories itself).

Several years ago, Li & Fung took over Liz Claiborne Inc.'s sourcing operations, which encompasses all aspects of its production, from acquiring materials to manufacturing and delivery. Liz Claiborne, which includes Juicy Couture and Lucky Brand jeans, retained its design and marketing functions—for example, it gives Li & Fung jeans designs, who bid them out worldwide to the manufacturer with the best combination of quality, speed-to-market, and price. Liz Claiborne recognized that Li & Fung, with its vast sourcing network and supply chain expertise, could manage its supply chain better than it could itself.

In this chapter we will learn how global supply chain companies like Li & Fung manage supply chains that stretch around the world.

Sources: Based on Li & Fung's website at www.lifunggroup.com; Bruce Einhorn, "Li & Fung: A Factory Sourcer Shines," May 14, 2009, http://www.businessweek.com/magazine; and Sandeep Agarwal, "Li & Fung—Operations, Emerging Supply Chain Changes & More…," October 8, 2011, http://www.denimandjeans.com.

In Chapter 10 we introduced the topic of supply chain management and focused on the strategy and design of supply chains. We discussed the various aspects, components and implications of supply chain management in a broad context, giving more of a *macro*-view of supply chains. Early in Chapter 10 in Figure 10.3, we identified the primary processes related to supply chain management—the procurement of supply, production, and the distribution of products and services. In this chapter we are going to focus more closely on two of these processes—procurement and distribution, which also includes transportation; this entails a more *micro*-view of supply chains. We will begin with a discussion of procurement, which is the process of obtaining *supply*: the goods and services that are used in the production process (whether it be goods or services).

Supply chains begin with supply at the farthest upstream point in the supply chain, inevitably from raw materials, as was shown in Figure 10.1. Purchased materials have historically accounted for about half of U.S. manufacturing costs, and many manufacturers purchase over half of their parts. Companies want the materials, parts, and services necessary to produce their products to be delivered on time, to be of high quality, and to be low cost, which are the responsibility of their suppliers. If deliveries are late from suppliers, a company will be forced to keep large, costly inventories to keep their own products from being late to their customers. Thus, purchasing goods and services from suppliers, or **procurement**, plays a crucial role in supply chain management.

Procurement

A key element in the development of a successful partnership between a company and a supplier is the establishment of linkages. The most important linkage is information flow; companies and suppliers must communicate—about product demand, about costs, about quality, and so on—in order to coordinate their activities. To facilitate communication and the sharing of information, many companies use teams. *Cross-enterprise teams* coordinate processes between a company and its supplier. For example, suppliers may join a company in its product-design process. Instead of a company designing a product and then asking a supplier if it can provide the required part or a company trying to design a product around an existing part, the supplier works with the company in the design process to ensure the most effective design possible. This form of cooperation makes use of the expertise and talents of both parties. It also ensures that quality features will be designed into the product.

In an attempt to minimize inventory levels, companies frequently require that their suppliers provide **on-demand**, also referred to as **direct-response**, delivery to support a just-in-time (JIT) or comparable inventory system. In **continuous replenishment**, a company shares real-time demand and inventory data with its suppliers, and goods and services are provided as they are needed. For the supplier, these forms of delivery often mean making more frequent, partial deliveries, instead of the large-batch orders suppliers have traditionally been used to filling. While large-batch orders are easier for the supplier to manage, and less costly, they increase the customer's inventory. They also reduce the customer's flexibility to deal with sudden market changes because of their large investment in inventory. Every part used at Honda's Marysville, Ohio, plant is delivered on a daily basis. Sometimes parts deliveries are required several times a day. This often requires that suppliers move their location to be close to their customer. For example, most of the U.S. suppliers for Honda are within a 150-mile radius of their Marysville, Ohio, assembly plant.

In addition to meeting their customers' demands for quality, lower inventory, and prompt delivery, suppliers are also expected to help their customers lower product cost by lowering the price of its goods and services. These customer demands on its suppliers—high quality, prompt delivery, and lower prices—are potentially very costly to suppliers. Prompt delivery of products and services as they are demanded from its customers may require the supplier to maintain excessive inventories itself. These demands require the supplier to improve its own processes and make its own supply chain more efficient. Suppliers require of their own suppliers what has been required of them—high quality, lower prices, process improvement, and better delivery performance.

OUTSOURCING

The selection of suppliers is called **sourcing**: suppliers are literally the "source" of supply. **Outsourcing** is the act of purchasing goods and services that were originally produced in-house from an outside supplier. Outsourcing is nothing new; for decades companies have outsourced as a short-term solution to problems such as an unexpected increase in demand, breakdowns in plants and equipment, testing products, or a temporary lack of plant capacity. However, outsourcing has become a long-term strategic decision instead of simply a short-term tactical one. Companies, especially large multinational companies, are moving more production, service, and inventory functions into the hands of suppliers. Figure 11.1 shows the three major categories of goods and services that companies tend to outsource.

Many companies are outsourcing as a strategic move so that they can focus more on their **core competencies**, that is, what they do best. They let a supplier do what the company is not very good at or doesn't have much experience with, what the supplier is most competent to do. Traditionally, many companies, especially large ones, attempted to own and operate all of their sources of supply and distribution along the supply chain so that they would have direct managerial control and reduce their dependence on potentially unreliable suppliers. They also thought it was more cost effective. However, this stretched these companies' resources thin, and they discovered they did not have the expertise to do everything well. In addition, management of unwieldy, complex supply chains was often difficult. Large inventories were kept throughout the supply chain to buffer against uncertainties and poor management practices. The recent trend toward outsourcing provides companies with greater flexibility and resources to focus on their own core competencies, and partnering relationships with suppliers give them with control. In addition, many companies are outsourcing in countries where prices for supply are lower, such as China.

By limiting the numbers of its suppliers, a company has more direct influence and control over the quality, cost, and delivery performance of a supplier if the company has a major portion of that supplier's volume of business. The company and supplier enter into a partnership in which the supplier agrees to meet the customer's quality standards for products and services and helps lower the customer's costs. The company can also stipulate delivery schedules from the supplier that enable it to reduce inventory. In return, the company enters into a long-term relationship with the supplier, providing the supplier with security and stability. It may seem that all the benefits of such

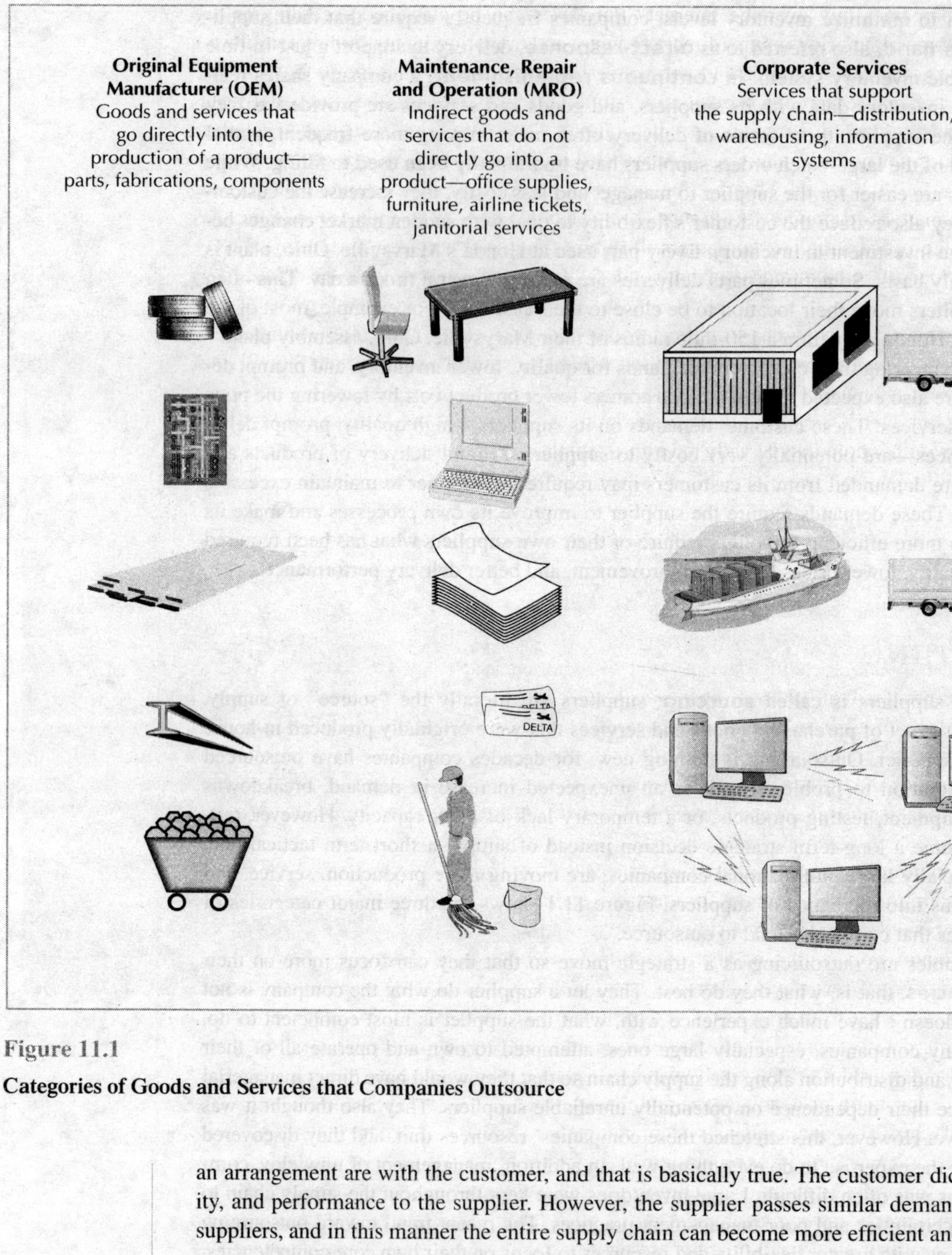

Figure 11.1

Categories of Goods and Services that Companies Outsource

an arrangement are with the customer, and that is basically true. The customer dictates cost, quality, and performance to the supplier. However, the supplier passes similar demands on to its own suppliers, and in this manner the entire supply chain can become more efficient and cost-effective.

E-Procurement

E-procurement is part of the business-to-business (B2B) commerce being conducted on the Internet, in which buyers make purchases directly from suppliers through their websites, by using software packages or through e-marketplaces, e-hubs, and trading exchanges. The Internet can streamline and speed up the purchase order and transaction process from companies. Benefits include lower transaction costs associated with purchasing, lower prices for goods and services, reduced labor (clerical) costs, and faster ordering and delivery times.

What do companies buy over the Internet? Purchases can be classified according to two broad categories: manufacturing inputs (direct products) and operating inputs (indirect products). Direct products are the raw materials and components that go directly into the production process of a product. Because they tend to be unique to a particular industry, they are usually purchased from industry-specific suppliers and distributors. They also tend to require specialized delivery; UPS does not typically deliver engine blocks. Indirect products do not go directly into the production of finished goods. They are the maintenance, repair, and operation (MRO) goods and services we mentioned previously (Figure 11.1). They tend not to be industry specific; they include things like office supplies, computers, furniture, janitorial services, and airline tickets. As a result, they can often be purchased from vendors like Staples, and they can be delivered by services like UPS.

More companies tend to purchase indirect goods and services over the Internet than direct goods. One reason is that a company does not have to be as careful about indirect goods since they typically cost less than direct products and they do not directly affect the quality of the company's own final product. Companies that purchase direct goods over the Internet tend to do so through suppliers with whom they already have an established relationship.

SPEND ANALYSIS

Spend analysis is a relatively recent addition to the supply chain management lexicon that has evolved out of the challenges encountered in managing procurement activities, especially in far-reaching, complex global business environments. It is a formal process of collecting, cleansing, classifying, and analyzing spending data in order to reduce procurement costs and improve the efficiency of the procurement process. Spend analysis attempts to assess the who, what, when, where, why, and how of a company's expenditure process and thereby answer the questions: How much is being spent? With which suppliers? Is the promised value being realized?

Spend data can come from many different sources including supplier data and contracts, purchasing transactions, financial data, and risk data. Figure 11.1 shows three basic categories of spend data—original equipment manufacturer (OEM); maintenance, repair, and operation (MRO); and corporate services. Within all of these categories, spend data can come from different suppliers, where there are too many suppliers for the same commodity. For example, in the OEM category a company could purchase office supplies and furniture from several different office supply companies and could work with a number of printing services, copier companies, and couriers; employees could use different travel agents, etc. Within the OEM and corporate services categories, spend data can come from an ERP system and accounts payable. Many companies attempt to consolidate this data on spreadsheets; however, even if all the data from multiple sources is accurately collected, in order to effectively manage spending and realize maximum cost savings, a formal process must be in place to analyze and manage spending, which is the basic premise of spend analysis. A formal spend analysis system can be automated with spend analysis software products, of which there are many, or by outsourcing spend analysis with an outside vendor.

Whatever automated system is used, companies that have a spend analysis process in place tend to have significantly lower procurement costs, have fewer suppliers, have a more efficient supply chain in terms of speed and quality, and tend to use more advanced e-procurement systems, such as vendor-managed inventory (see page 355). Spend analysis helps companies find opportunities to save money. This can be as simple as determining who is buying what within a company so that purchases can be consolidated and volume discounts can be achieved. This might also include the use of Pareto analysis to see which few items make up the largest spending categories. It can identify suppliers in different business units or in different geographic locations that are providing better buying terms than suppliers in other parts of the business; or it can indicate if contract prices are not being adhered to. One important potential benefit is the analysis of total supply chain cost for a product that integrates spend data not only for supply purchase cost but also for transportation, tariffs and duties, inventory carrying cost, insurance, and so on.

E-MARKETPLACES

E-marketplaces or e-hubs consolidate suppliers' goods and services at one Internet site like a catalogue. For example, e-hubs for MROs include consolidated catalogues from a wide array of suppliers that enable buyers to purchase low-value goods and services with relatively high transaction costs more cheaply and efficiently over the Internet. E-hubs for direct goods and services are similar in that they bring together groups of suppliers at a few easy-to-use websites.

E-marketplaces like Ariba provide a neutral ground on the Internet where companies can streamline supply chains and find new business partners. An e-marketplace also offers services such as online auctions where suppliers bid on order contracts, online product catalogs with multiple supplier listings that generate online purchase orders, and request-for-quote (RFQ) service through which buyers can submit an RFQ for their needs and users can respond.

REVERSE AUCTIONS

A process used by e-marketplaces for buyers to purchase items is the **reverse auction**. In a reverse auction, a company posts contracts for items it wants to purchase that suppliers can bid on. The auction is usually open for a specified time frame, and vendors can bid as often as they want in order to provide the lowest purchase price. When the auction is closed, the company can compare bids on the basis of purchase price, delivery time, and supplier reputation for quality. Some e-marketplaces restrict participation to vendors who have been previously screened or certified for reliability and product quality. Reverse auctions are not only used to purchase manufacturing items but are also being used to purchase services. For example, transportation exchanges hold reverse auctions for carriers to bid on shipping contracts and for air travel.

Sometimes companies use reverse auctions to create price competition among the suppliers it does business with; at other times, companies simply go through a reverse auction only to determine the lowest price without any intention of awarding a contract. It only wants to determine a baseline price to use in negotiations with its regular supplier. Companies that award contracts to low bidders in auctions can later discover their purchases are delivered late or not at all, and are of poor quality. Suppliers are often able to see online their rank in the bidding process relative to other bidders (who are anonymous), which provides pricing information to them for the future.

Distribution

Distribution encompasses all of the channels, processes, and functions, including warehousing and transportation, that a product passes through on its way to the final customer (end user). It is the actual movement of products and materials between locations. Distribution management involves managing the handling of materials and products at receiving docks, storing products and materials, packaging, and the shipment of orders. The focus of distribution, what it accomplishes, is referred to as **order fulfillment**. It is the process of ensuring on-time delivery of the customer's order.

Distribution and transportation are also often referred to as **logistics**. Logistics management in its broadest interpretation is similar to supply chain management. However, it is frequently more narrowly defined as being concerned with just transportation and distribution, in which case logistics is a subset of supply chain management. In this decade, total annual U.S. business logistics is over $1.3 trillion.

SPEED AND QUALITY

Distribution is not simply a matter of moving products from point A to point B. The driving force behind distribution and transportation in today's highly competitive business environment is *speed*. One of the primary quality attributes on which companies compete is speed of service. Customers have gotten used to instant access to information, rapid Internet-based order transactions, and quick delivery of goods and services. As a result, walking next door to check on what's in the warehouse is not nearly fast enough when customers want to buy a product now and a company has to let them know if it's in stock. That demands real-time inventory information. Calling a trucking firm and asking it when it will have a truck in the vicinity to pick up a delivery is not nearly fast enough when a customer has come to expect delivery in a few days or overnight. That also requires real-time information about carrier location, schedules, and capacity. Thus, the key to distribution speed is information, as it has been in our discussion of other parts of the supply chain.

INTERNET COMPANIES: AMAZON.COM

Distribution is a particularly important supply chain component for Internet companies like Amazon.com, whose supply chains consist almost entirely of supply and distribution. These companies have no production process; they simply sell and distribute products that they acquire from suppliers. They are not driven from the front end of the supply chain—the website—but by distribution at the back end. Their success ultimately depends on the capability to ship each order when the customer needs or wants it.

Figure 11.2 illustrates the order fulfillment process at Amazon.com when one of its millions of customers places an order via the Internet (or by phone). The order is transmitted to the closest distribution center (DC) where items are stored in a warehouse in shelved bins. Computers send workers to retrieve items from the shelves, and they place each item in a crate with other orders. When the crate is full it moves by conveyor through the plant to a central point. At this central sorting area, bar codes are matched with order numbers to determine which items go with which order, and the items that fulfill an order are sorted into chutes. The items that make up an order are placed in a box as they come off the chute with a new bar code that identifies the order. The boxes are then packed, taped, weighed, and shipped by a carrier, for example, the U.S. Postal Service or UPS.

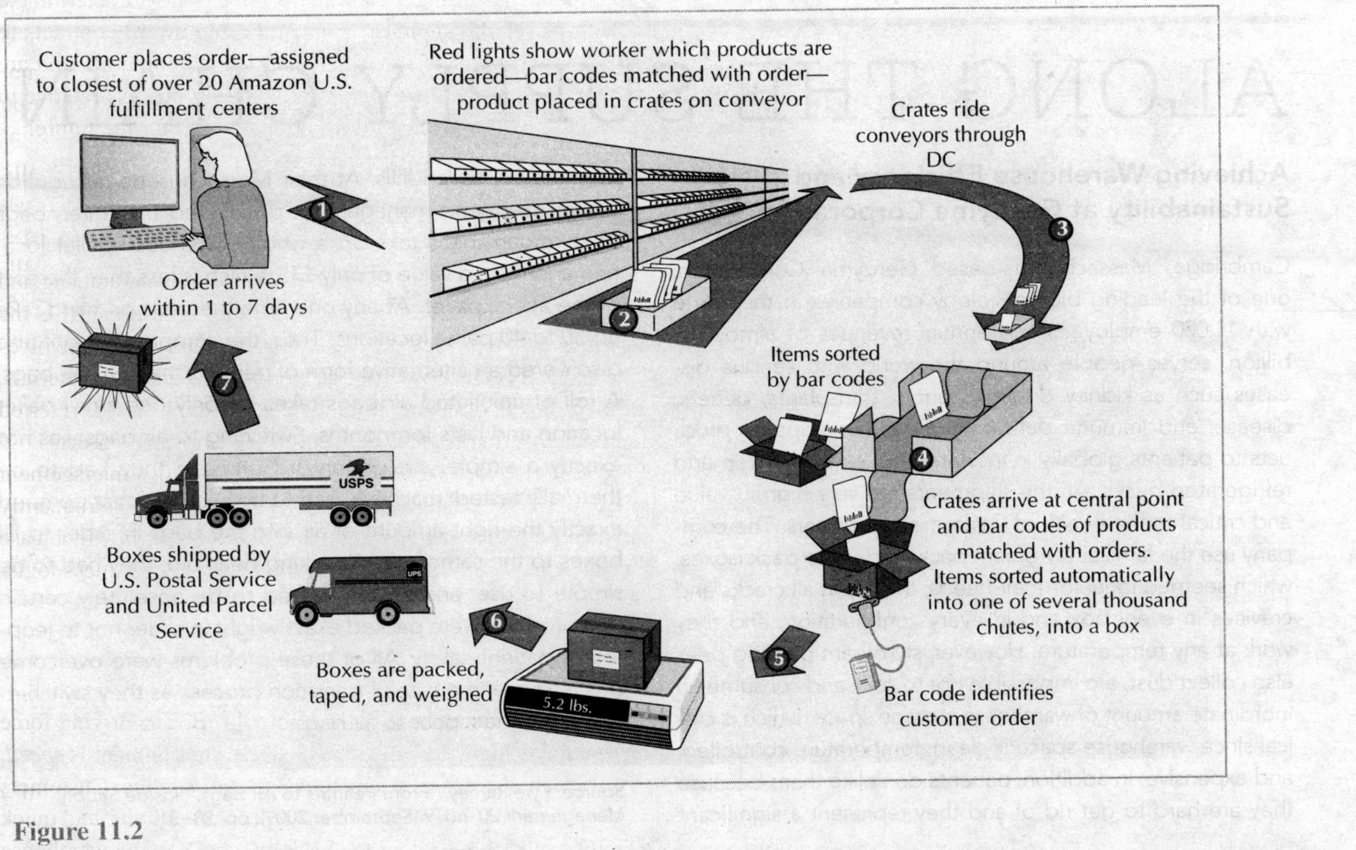

Figure 11.2
Order Fulfillment at Amazon.com

DISTRIBUTION CENTERS AND WAREHOUSING

Distribution centers, which typically incorporate warehousing and storage, are buildings that are used to receive, handle, store, package, and then ship products. Some of the largest business facilities in the United States are distribution centers. The Target Import DC in Lacey, Washington, has 2 million square feet of floor space—over 37 times bigger than the area of a football field and almost the same floor space as the Empire State Building.

As in other areas of supply chain management, information technology has a significant impact on distribution management. The Internet has altered how companies distribute goods by adding more frequent orders in smaller amounts and higher customer service expectations to the already difficult task of rapid response fulfillment. To fill Internet orders successfully, warehouses and distribution centers must be set up as "flow-through" facilities, using automated material-handling equipment to speed up the processing and delivery of orders.

Retailers have shifted from buying goods in bulk and storing them to pushing inventory and storage and final configuration back up the supply chain (upstream). They expect suppliers (and/or distributors) to make frequent deliveries of merchandise that includes a mix of different product items in small quantities (referred to as "mixed-pallet"), properly labeled, packed, and shipped in store-ready configurations. For example, some clothing retailers may want sweaters delivered already folded, ready for the store shelf, while others may want them to be on their own hangers. To handle retailer requirements adequately, distribution centers must be able to handle a variety of automated tasks.

POSTPONEMENT

Postponement moves some final manufacturing steps like assembly or individual product customization into the warehouse or distribution center. Generic products or component parts (like computer components) are stored at the warehouse, and then final products are built-to-order

ALONG THE SUPPLY CHAIN

Achieving Warehouse Efficiency and Sustainability at Genzyme Corporation

Cambridge, Massachusetts-based Genzyme Corporation, one of the leading biotechnology companies in the world with 11,000 employees and annual revenues of almost $5 billion, serves people around the world with serious diseases such as kidney disease, cancer, transplants, genetic disease, and immune deficiency. Genzyme ships its products to patients globally in insulated boxes with frozen and refrigerated bricks. All the shipments are very high in value and critical to the health of Genzyme's customers. The company use the familiar styrofoam packing peas to pack boxes, which seemed ideal for their needs; they fit in all cracks and crevices in every box and in every configuration, and they work at any temperature. However, styrofoam packing peas also collect dust, are impossible not to spill, and consume an inordinate amount of warehouse storage space, which is critical since warehouse space is clean, temperature controlled, and expensive. In addition, patients don't like them because they are hard to get rid of and they represent a significant contribution to landfills. At their Massachusetts distribution center, Genzyme management discovered that three bags of styrofoam peas take up a whole warehouse pallet location and have a value of only $75, which is less than the cost of the actual pallet. At any one time the peas on hand take up 30 to 40 pallet locations. Thus, the company sought and discovered an alternative form of packing material, air bags. A roll of uninflated air bags takes up only one small pallet location and lasts for months. Switching to air bags was not exactly a simple, straightforward process; they had to be thermally tested; machines had to be acquired that pumped exactly the right amount of air into the bags in order to fill boxes to the same extent packing peas did; they had to be simple to use; and Genzyme had to be absolutely certain that products were packed exactly right in order not to jeopardize patient safety. All of these problems were overcome by Genzyme in a careful transition process as they switched from Styrofoam peas to air bags.

Source: Kyle Ramey, "From Peanuts to Air Bags," *Inside Supply Management* 20, no. 9 (September 2009): pp. 30–31.

(BTO), or personalized, to meet individual customer demand. It is a response to the adage that whoever can get the desired product to the customer first gets the sale. Postponement actually pulls distribution into the manufacturing process, allowing lead times to be reduced so that demand can be met more quickly. However, postponement also usually means that a distributor must stock a large number of inventory items at the warehouse to meet the final assembly or customization requirements; this can create higher inventory-carrying costs. The manufacturing and distribution supply chain members must therefore work together to synchronize their demand forecasts and carefully manage inventory.

WAREHOUSE MANAGEMENT SYSTEMS

In order to handle the new trends and demands of distribution management, companies employ sophisticated, highly automated **warehouse management systems (WMS)** to run day-to-day operations of a distribution center and keep track of inventories. The WMS places an item

ALONG THE SUPPLY CHAIN

Adding a New Distribution Center to the Sephora Supply Chain

Sephora, the beauty products brand and chain of cosmetics stores, was founded in Paris and is owned by French conglomerate LVMH (Louis Vuitton Moet Hennessy). The Sephora supply chain includes more than 750 stores in 24 countries, carrying over 250 brands, along with its own private label. Sephora has over 280 stores in the United States and Canada, which until 2008 were served by a single 316,000 squarefoot distribution center in Belcamp, Maryland. Precipitated by its rapid growth and becoming the exclusive provider of beauty products for over 300 J.C. Penney stores across the United States in 2006, Sephora began investigating alternatives for its distribution network, including replacing the Belcamp facility with a larger, more optimally located distribution center, opening a second distribution center, or simply keeping the Belcamp facility. The company engaged an outside supply chain consulting firm to undertake a project to investigate these alternatives.

The project team, consisting primarily of Sephora's internal logistics team and members from the consulting firm, first developed a model of the existing Sephora distribution network to better understand how store replenishment worked and what level of service they needed. The network model included transactional data for its stores and Internet site, plus logistics data for freight costs, warehouse operating costs, shipment volumes, and store locations. Next, the objectives for the future distribution network were established, which required an understanding of future store growth patterns including possible locations.

After growth projections were included in the model, the team addressed two possible scenarios—what was the best East Coast site if Belcamp was closed, and if Belcamp stayed open, what was the best site for a second facility. For each scenario the model was evaluated with data for different possible locations, including the average cost per square foot and freight rates, and based on these model results the sites were rated and then ranked according to service cost. The model results showed first that the absolute optimal site was near Philadelphia, only 80 miles from Belcamp, such that the minimal savings in transportation costs would not offset the relocation costs, and thus Belcamp was fixed as one site. Next, the model was reevaluated for second-site candidates that would optimize transportation costs, lead times and expenses. Salt Lake City was selected as the site for the second distribution center because of not only optimal transportation costs, but also the support of local and state governments. The Salt Lake City distribution center opened in 2008 and relieved the capacity at Belcamp, increased Sephora's customer service capabilities, and reduced its shipping costs. In 2013, Sephora began considering a third North American distribution center as it expanded into Brazil and Mexico.

Do you think the process Sephora used to determine the site of its new distribution center could be universally applied to other retail companies?

Source: Based on Maida Napolitano, "Sephora's Gorgeous Network Reorganization," *Supply Chain Management Review* 15, no. 11 (November 2011): S40–S50.

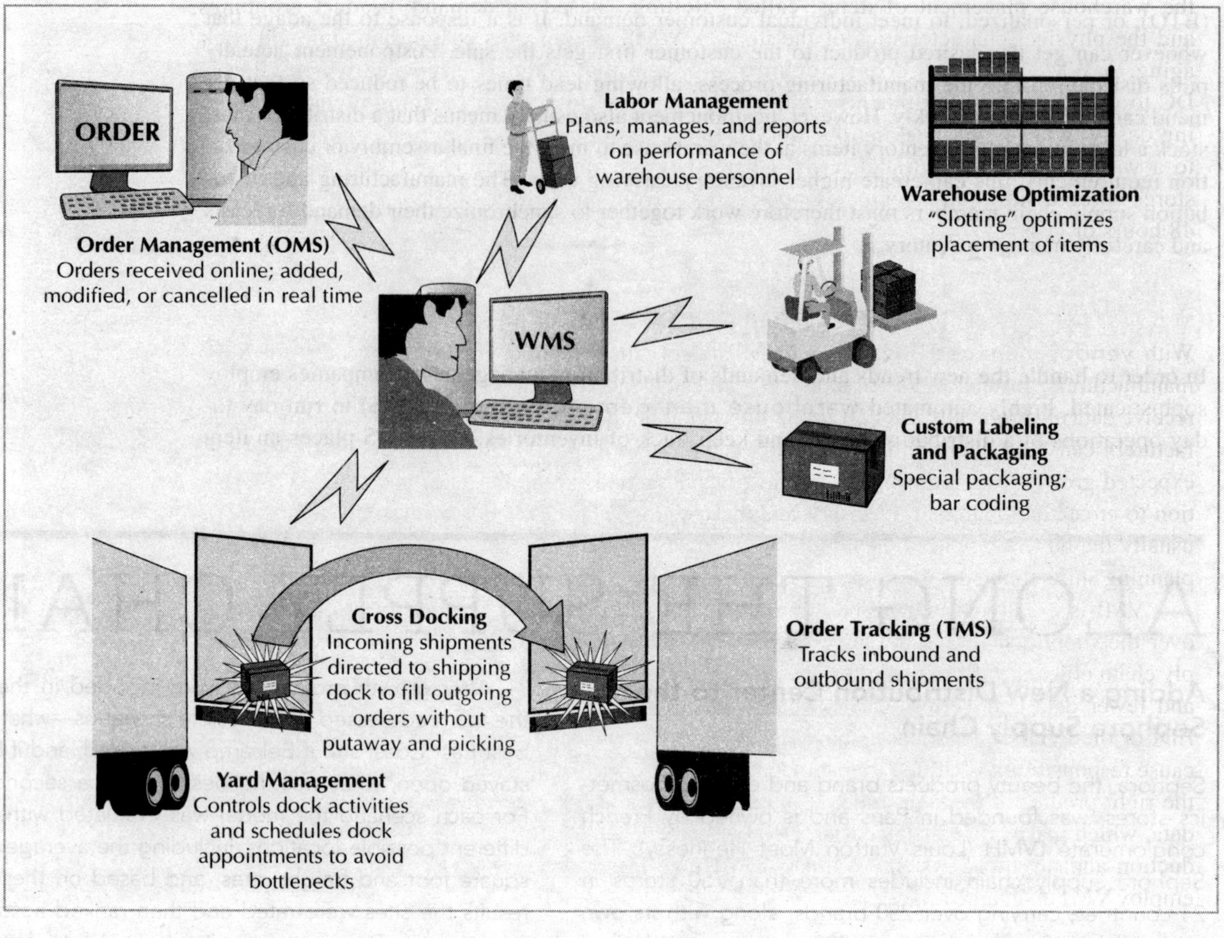

Figure 11.3
A Warehouse Management System (WMS)

in storage at a specific location (a *putaway*), locates and takes an item out of storage (a *pick*), packs the item, and ships it via a *carrier*. The WMS acknowledges that a product is available to ship, and, if it is not available, the system will determine from suppliers in real time when it will be available.

Figure 11.3 illustrates the features of a WMS. Orders flow into a WMS through an *order management system* (OMS). The OMS enables the distribution center to add, modify, or cancel orders in real time. When the OMS receives customer order information online, it provides a snapshot of product availability from the WMS and from suppliers via EDI. If an item is not in stock, the OMS looks into the supplier's production schedule to see when it will be available. The OMS then allocates inventory from the warehouse site to fill an order, establishes a delivery date, and passes these orders onto the transportation management system for delivery.

The *transportation management system (TMS)* allows the DC to track inbound and outbound shipments, to consolidate and build economical loads, and to select the best carrier based on cost and service. *Yard management* controls activities at the facility's dock and schedules dock appointments to reduce bottlenecks. *Labor management* plans, manages, and reports the performance level of warehouse personnel. *Warehouse optimization* optimizes the warehouse placement of items, called "slotting," based on demand, product groupings, and the physical characteristics of the item. A WMS also creates custom labeling and packaging. A WMS facilitates **cross-docking**, a system that Walmart originated which allows a DC to direct incoming shipments straight to a shipping dock to fill outgoing orders, eliminating costly putaway and picking operations. In a cross-docking system, products are delivered to a warehouse on a continual basis, where they are stored, repackaged, and distributed to stores without sitting in inventory. Goods "cross" from one loading dock to another, usually in 48 hours or less.

VENDOR-MANAGED INVENTORY

With **vendor-managed inventory (VMI)** (also called supplier managed inventory or SMI), manufacturers, instead of distributors or retailers, generate orders. Under VMI, manufacturers receive data electronically via EDI or the Internet about distributors' sales and stock levels. Manufacturers can see which items distributors carry, as well as several years of point-of-sale data, expected growth, promotions, new and lost business, and inventory goals, and use this information to create and maintain a forecast and an inventory plan. VMI is a form of "role reversal"—usually the buyer completes the administrative tasks of ordering; with VMI the responsibility for planning shifts to the manufacturer.

VMI is usually an integral part of supply chain collaboration. The vendor has more control over the supply chain and the buyer is relieved of administrative tasks, thereby increasing supply chain efficiency. Both manufacturers and distributors benefit from increased processing speed, and fewer data entry errors occur because communications are through computer-to-computer EDI or the Internet. Distributors have fewer stockouts; planning and ordering costs go down because responsibility is shifted to manufacturers; and service is improved because distributors have the right product at the right time. Manufacturers benefit by receiving distributors' point-of-sale data, which makes forecasting easier. Dell perfected VMI as part of its build-to-order (BTO) production and inventory system; Walmart and Home Depot are examples of companies that also employ VMI on a large scale.

COLLABORATIVE LOGISTICS

Rival companies are also finding ways to collaborate in distribution. They have found that by pooling their distribution resources, which can create greater economies of scale, they can reduce their costs.

For example, a company may find it is paying for too many half-empty trucks so they might move to collaborative logistics. Using the Internet as a central coordination tool among producers, carriers, and retailers, companies can share trucks and warehouse space with other companies, even competitors that are shipping to the same retail locations. At third-party logistics (3PL) providers, companies use a website to post the warehouse space they need or have available and share space, trucks, and expenses. The goal is that everyone, from suppliers to truckers to retailers, shares in the savings.

DISTRIBUTION OUTSOURCING

Another distribution alternative is outsourcing. Just as companies outsource production to suppliers that they once performed themselves, manufacturers are increasingly outsourcing distribution activities. The reason is basically the same for producers as it is for suppliers: outsourcing allows the company to focus on its core competencies. It also takes advantage of the expertise that distribution companies have developed. Outsourcing distribution activities to third-party logistics (3PL) providers tends to lower inventory levels and reduce costs for the outsourcing company, plus it allows companies to focus on its core competencies.

Transportation

In a supply chain, *transportation* is the movement of a product from one location to another as it makes its way to the end-use customer. Although supply chain experts agree that transportation sometimes falls through the supply chain management cracks, receiving less attention than it should, it can be a significant supply chain cost. For some manufacturing companies, transportation costs can be as much as 20% of total production costs and run as high as 6% of revenue. For some retail companies primarily involved in the distribution of goods, such as L.L. Bean and Amazon.com, transportation is not only a major cost of doing business, it is also a major determinant of quick delivery service. L.L. Bean ships over 15 million packages in a year—over one million in its busiest week—mostly by UPS.

The principal modes of transportation within the United States are railroads, air, truck, intermodal, water, package carriers, and pipeline. In the United States, the greatest amount of freight is shipped by trucking, followed by railroad, pipeline, and inland waterways. The different transport modes and some of their advantages and disadvantages are shown in Figure 11.4.

Railroads, with more than 160,000 miles of track in the United States, are cost-effective for transporting products such as raw materials, coal, minerals, ores, and especially containers over long distances. However, railroads operate on less flexible and slower schedules than trucks, and they usually cannot go directly from one business location to another as trucks can. Railroad freight service also has the worst record of quality performance of all modes of freight transport, with a higher incidence of product damage and almost 10 times more late deliveries than trucking.

Trucking is the main mode of freight transportation in the United States, annually carrying over 60% of U.S. freight tonnage, and generating almost 70% of the nation's total freight cost each year. Trucks provide flexible point-to-point service, delivering small loads over short and long distances over widely dispersed geographic areas.

Air freight is the most expensive and fastest mode of freight transportation. For companies that use air freight, service is more important than price. For some companies,

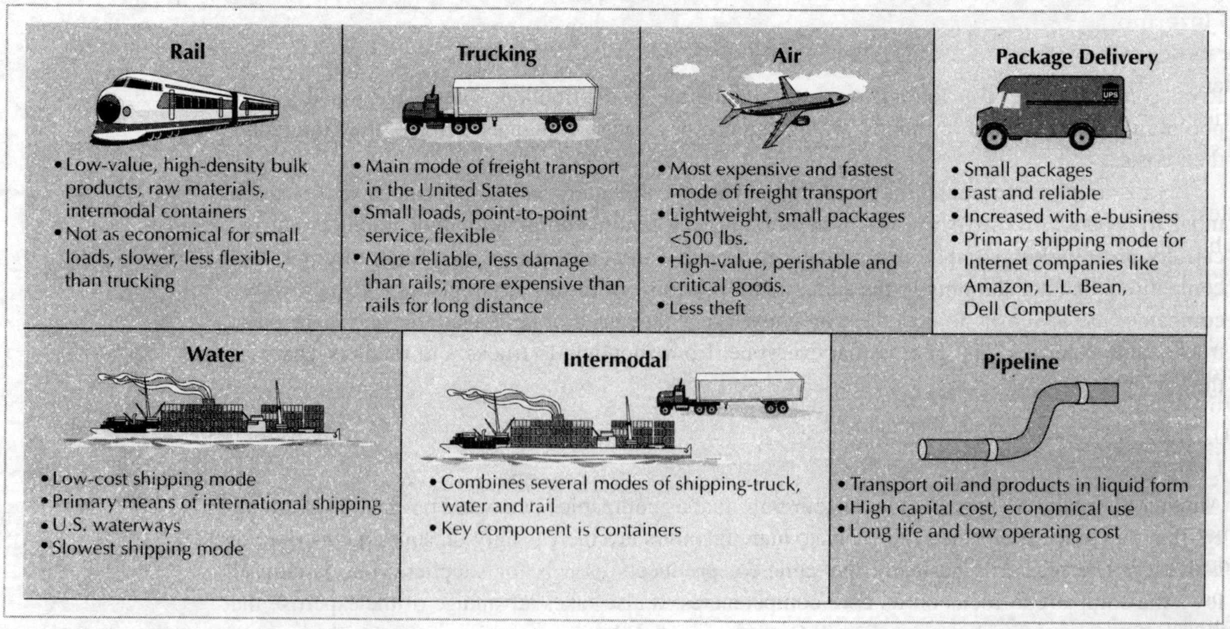

Figure 11.4

Transportation Modes

production stoppages because of missing parts or components can be much more expensive than the increased cost of air freight. For high-value goods such as pharmaceuticals, high technology, and consumer electronics, speed to market is important. In addition, shorter shipping times reduce the chances for theft and other losses. The general rule for international air freight is that anything that is physically or economically perishable has to move by air instead of by ship. The major product groups that are shipped by international air freight, from largest to smallest, are perishables, construction and engineering equipment, textiles and wearing apparel, documents and small package shipments, and computers, peripherals, and spare parts.

Air freight is growing particularly fast in Asia and specifically China. The lack of adequate ground infrastructure makes rail and trucking transport difficult between countries in Asia and regions in China. Companies with manufacturing plants in one place in Asia and suppliers in another often use air freight to connect the two.

Package carriers such as UPS, FedEx, and the U.S. Postal Service transport small packages, up to about 150 pounds. The growth of e-business has significantly increased the use of package carriers. Package carriers combine various modes of transportation, mostly air and truck, to ship small packages rapidly. They are not economical for large-volume shipments; however, they are fast and reliable, and they provide unique services that some companies must have. Package carriers have been innovative in the use of bar codes and the Internet to arrange and track shipments. The FedEx website attracts more than 1 million hits per day, and it receives 70% of its customer orders electronically. FedEx delivers around 7.5 million packages daily in over 220 countries.

Waterways in the United States include 26,000 navigable miles over inland waterways, canals, the Great Lakes, and along coastlines. Water transport is a slow but very low-cost form of shipping. It is limited to heavy, bulk items such as raw materials, minerals, ores, grains, chemicals, and petroleum products. If delivery speed is not a factor, water transport is cost competitive with railroads for shipping these kinds of bulk products. Water transport is the primary means of international shipping between countries separated by oceans for most products. Over 80% of freight imports into the U.S. arrive via ocean shipping.

Intermodal transportation combines several modes of transportation to move shipments. The most common intermodal combination in the United States is truck–rail–truck, and the truck–water–rail/truck combination is the primary means of global transport. Intermodal transportation carries over 35% of all freight shipments over 500 miles in the United States. Intermodal truck–rail shipping can be as much as 40% cheaper than long-haul trucking.

The key component in intermodal transportation is the *container*. Within the United States, containers are hauled as trailers attached to trucks to rail terminals, where they are double- or triple-stacked on railroad flatcars or specially designed "well cars," which feature a well-like lower section in which the trailer or container rides (70% of U.S. intermodal shipping over a million containers annually) is double-stacked. The containers are then transported to another rail terminal, where they are reattached to trucks for direct delivery to the customer. For overseas shipments, container ships transport containers to ports where they are off-loaded to trucks or rail for transport. Container traffic worldwide is over 430 million TEUs (i.e., 20-foot equivalent units, a standard size container) annually, with almost 10% in the United States.

There are over 2 million miles of *pipelines* in the United States, 75% of which are used primarily for transporting oil and petroleum products. Pipelines called slurry lines carry other products such as coal and kaolin that have been pulverized and transformed into liquid form. Once the product arrives at its destination, the water is removed, leaving the solid material. Although pipelines require a high initial capital investment to construct, they are economical because they can carry materials over terrain that would be difficult for trucks or trains to travel across, for example, the Trans-Alaska pipeline. Once in place, pipelines have a long life and are low cost in terms of operation, maintenance, and labor.

INTERNET TRANSPORTATION EXCHANGES

Internet transportation exchanges bring together shippers who post loads and carriers who post their available capacity in order to arrange shipments. In some exchanges, once the parties have matched up at a website, all the negotiation is done offline. In others, the online service manages the load matches automatically; the services match up shipments and carriers based on shipment characteristics, trailer availability, and the like. For example, shippers tender load characteristics, and the online service returns with recommendations on carrier price and service levels. Some services also provide an online international exchange structured as a reverse auction. The shippers will tender their loads, and carriers will bid on the shipment. Shipments remain up for bid until a shipper-specified auction closing time (like auctions on eBay). However, the lowest price, or lowest bid, is not always conducive to quality service. At some sites the low bid does not necessarily win; the service takes into account quality issues such as transit time, the carrier, and availability in addition to price.

Two of the more well-known Internet exchange services are www.nte.com (National Transportation Exchange) and www.freightquote.com. At these sites (and others like it) shippers and carriers identify their available shipment or capacity needs and their business requirements. The exchanges automatically match compatible shippers with carriers based on price and service. Automated processes make the trade within a few hours with no phone calls, invoices, and so on.

The Global Supply Chain

A number of factors have combined to create a global marketplace. International trade barriers have fallen, and new trade agreements between countries and nations have been established. The dissolution of communism opened up new markets in Russia and Middle and Eastern Europe, and the creation of the European Union resulted in the world's largest economic market—500 million people. Europe, with a total population of 730 million, is the largest, best-educated economic group in the world. Emerging markets in China, growing Asian export-driven economies, burgeoning global trading centers in Hong Kong and Singapore, and an increasingly robust economy in India, have linked with the rest of the world to form a vigorous global economic community. Global trade now exceeds $27 trillion per year.

Globalization is no longer restricted to giant companies. Technology advances have made it possible for middle-tier companies to establish a global presence. Companies previously regional in scope are using the Internet to become global overnight. Information technology is the "enabler" that lets companies gain global visibility and link disparate locations, suppliers, and customers. However, many companies are learning that it takes more than a glitzy website to be a global player. As with the domestic U.S. market, it takes a well-planned and coordinated supply chain to be competitive and successful.

OBSTACLES TO GLOBAL SUPPLY CHAIN MANAGEMENT

Moving products across international borders is like negotiating an intricate maze, riddled with potential pitfalls. For U.S. companies eager to enter new and growing markets, trading in foreign countries is not "business as usual." Global supply chain management, though global in nature, must still take into account national and regional differences. Customs, business practices, and regulations can vary widely from country to country and even within a country. Foreign markets are not homogeneous and often require customized service in terms of packaging and labeling. Quality can be a major challenge when dealing with emerging markets in countries with different languages and customers.

Some of the other major differences between domestic and global supply chain transactions include:

- Increased documentation for invoices, cargo insurance, letters of credit, ocean bills of lading or air waybills, and inspections

- Ever-changing regulations that vary from country to country, and govern the import and export of goods
- Trade groups, tariffs, duties, and landing costs
- Limited shipping modes and infrastructure
- Differences in communication technology and availability
- Different business practices as well as language barriers
- Government codes and reporting requirements that vary from country to country
- Numerous players, including forwarding agents, custom house brokers, financial institutions, insurance providers, multiple transportation carriers, and government agencies
- Numerous security regulations and requirements

DUTIES, TARIFFS, AND GLOBAL TRADING GROUPS

The proliferation of trade agreements has changed global markets and has accelerated global trade activity. Nations have joined together to form trading groups, also called **nation groups**, and customs unions, and within these groups, products move freely with no import tax, called **tariffs** or **duties**, charged on member products. The members of a group charge uniform import duties to nations outside their group, thus removing tariff trade barriers within the group and raising barriers for outsiders. The group adopts rules and regulations for freely transporting goods across borders that, combined with reduced tariffs, give member nations a competitive advantage over nonmembers. These trade advantages among member nations lower supply chain costs and reduce cycle time—that is, the time required for products to move through the supply chain.

Two of the most prominent international groups that trade with the United States are NAFTA, the North American Free Trade Agreement, and EU, the European Union trade group.

The World Trade Organization (WTO) is an international organization dealing with the global rules of trade. It ensures that trade flows as smoothly and freely as possible among its 155 members. The trade agreements and rules are negotiated and signed by governments, and their purpose is to help exporters and importers conduct business. Most-favored-nation trade (MFN) status is an arrangement in which WTO member countries must extend to other members the most favorable treatment given to any trading partner. For example, MFN status for China translates into lower duties on goods entering the United States, and fewer trade regulations for companies.

To overcome the obstacles and problems of global supply chain management, many companies hire one or more international **trade specialists**. Figure 11.5 summarizes the activities of different types of trade specialists.

LANDED COST

In global trade **landed cost** is the total cost of producing, storing, and transporting a product to the site of consumption or another port. It can include such costs as brokerage and logistics fees, port fees, custom duties, tariffs, taxes, insurance, currency conversion, and handling fees; as many as 80 components can be included in landed cost. However, 85% of these components fall into two broad categories: (1) transportation cost and duty, and (2) governmental charges such as **value added tax (VAT)** and excise tax. Landed costs are important because the duty assessed by different governments incorporates varying portions of landed costs. For example, for U.S. imports, duty is charged free on board (FOB) the factory. This means that transportation costs from the point of entry into the United States to the factory destination are not calculated as part of the import duty charge. However, in other countries the duty assessed can include the cost of transportation from beginning to end.

By knowing the landed cost of a product before it is purchased, a company can make more informed decisions, while poorly projected landed costs can balloon the price of a product move. Accurately estimating true landed costs helps avoid "clicker shock." Clicker shock occurs when an overseas customer places an order with a company that does not have the capability of calculating landed cost. Then the order gets shipped, and along the way tariffs get added on top—in some cases this can double the original purchase price.

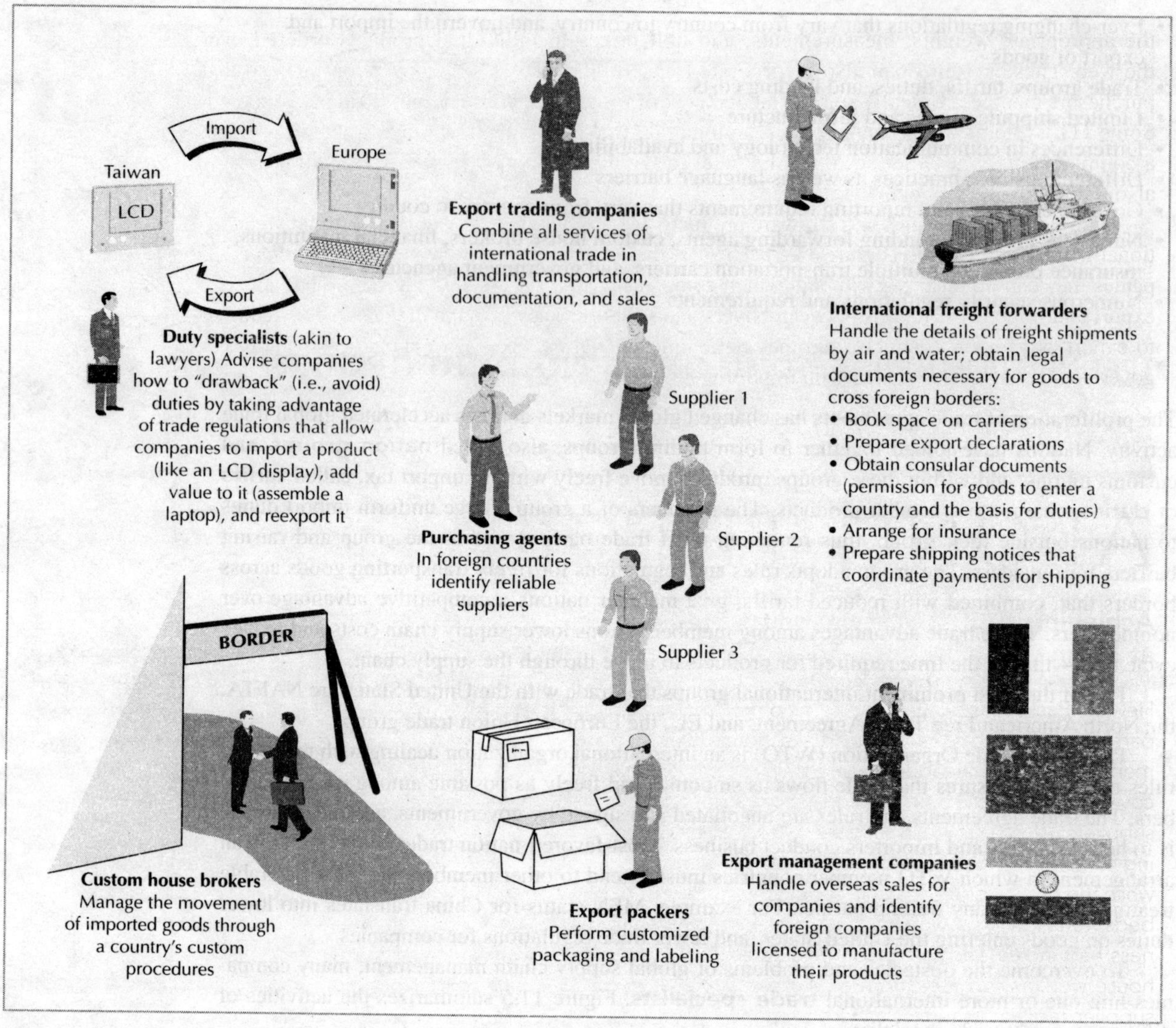

Figure 11.5

International Trade Specialists

WEB-BASED INTERNATIONAL TRADE LOGISTICS SYSTEMS

As we have indicated, global supply chain management involves a stunningly complex matrix of language barriers, currency conversions, international trade agreements, taxes, tariffs, embargoes, duties, quotas, document requirements, local rules, and new trading partners. These factors require an automated information technology solution for any company with any real volume of international shipments. International trade logistics (ITL) companies use web-based software products that link directly to customers' websites to eliminate or reduce the obstacles to global trade. They convert language and currency from the U.S. system into those used by many of the United States' trading partners, giving potential buyers in other nations easy access to product and price information. ITL systems also provide information on tariffs, duties, and customs processes and some link with financial institutions to facilitate letters of credit and payment. Through the use of extensive databases, these systems can attach the appropriate weights, measurements, and unit prices to individual products ordered over the web. These systems can also incorporate transportation costs and conversion rates so that purchasers can electronically see the landed cost of ordering a product and having it delivered. Some ITL systems use a landed cost search engine that calculates shipping costs online while a company enters an order so it will know exactly what the costs will be in U.S. funds. They also track global shipments.

Through their websites and software products, ITL companies do many of the things international trade specialists do (Figure 11.5). They let their customers know which international companies they can do business with and which companies can do business with them. They identify export and import restrictions between buyers and vendors. They provide the documents required to export and import products, and they determine the duties, taxes, and landed costs and other government charges associated with importing a product.

ALONG THE SUPPLY CHAIN

Achieving Global Sustainability at HP in China

Hewlett-Packard is committed to helping its global supply partners, specifically in China, make continuous improvements in their sustainable processes. In recent years HP discovered some disturbing labor practices among its Chinese suppliers. At one Chinese supplier, factory workers were taking turns using the same dormitory bed; one worker slept while the other worked. At another factory, hundreds of bunk beds were set up for workers in a big hall; the supplier's business had increased but it had not built additional space to house workers recruited from rural areas. At other overseas supplier facilities, chemicals were brought in without being properly evaluated, resulting in skin rashes among workers; in another factory, pallets of materials were stacked in front of stairwells, making the exits inaccessible in the event of fires; elsewhere workers were accumulating hours beyond allowable levels and workers' pay was docked as a disciplinary action, plus other unacceptable labor practices. Central European suppliers find it difficult to meet occupational safety and emergency preparedness practices while in Latin America, working hours and emergency preparedness are a challenge. However, in today's publicly transparent business climate, how a company like HP conducts itself in terms of its social and environmental responsibility is central to its reputation. HP is constantly under scrutiny from a variety of stakeholders including customers, stockholders, government and non-government agencies, media, and investors. In one recent global survey across a number of countries, 87% of consumer respondents expressed concern about the environmental and social impact of the products they buy.

The challenge for HP is how to make sure its suppliers in a long and diverse global supply chain meet HP's standards of sustainable conduct that ultimately reflect its own reputation. Most of its electronics suppliers are located in China so its sustainability efforts have been focused there. In dealing with suppliers in China, HP prefers to work with a supplier that is not meeting standards rather than dropping them. HP has implemented an Electronic Industry Code of Conduct and is using audits and supplier business reviews to monitor conformance and it is increasing sustainability weights on supplier scorecards. Some suppliers think sustainability only comes at a financial cost, so when possible, HP is trying to link it with quality initiatives that reduce costs. In its most recent round of supplier audits, 70% of the major nonconformances identified in its initial audits had been resolved, while the average number of major nonconformances per supplier facility decreased by 35% since the first audits were done. In addition, HP is making a concerted effort to push its commitment to sustainability further upstream in the supply chain, often partnering with its first-tier suppliers to audit sub-tier suppliers; by 2012, HP expected that suppliers representing 75% of its total purchases would have developed sustainability programs with their own suppliers.

Discuss some of the factors that you think might make it difficult for a large multinational company like HP to get its overseas suppliers to make a commitment to sustainability.

Source: Sonali Rammohan, "Toward a More Responsible Supply Chain: The HP Story," *Supply Chain Management Review* 13, no. 5 (July 2009): pp. 34–40.

Livingston International (www.livingstonintl.com) is an example of a global trade management company that enables customers through its web-based software products to calculate landed costs, screen for restricted parties, generate shipment documentation, and manage duties, and it also handles repairs and returns. It has an online library of trade regulations for different countries.

TRENDS IN GLOBALIZATION FOR U.S. COMPANIES

Two significant changes that prompted many U.S. companies to expand globally were the passage of NAFTA, which opened up business opportunities with Mexico, and the admission of China into the World Trade Organization. Approximately 700 of the Fortune 1000 companies have a portion of their operations, production components, or affiliates in Mexico. Besides cheap labor, Mexico is also close to the United States, and thus Mexican companies can meet the just-in-time requirements of many U.S. companies. However, Mexico's economic gains also lead to more jobs and increased worker skills, and as a result, higher wages, which, in turn, has led U.S. and foreign companies away from Mexico to China with its even lower wage rates. The hourly manufacturing wage rate in China is around $1.50 to $2.00, compared to approximately $4 in Mexico, $5 in Singapore, $9 in Taiwan, $28 in Japan, and $19 in the United States. As companies have moved their manufacturing into China because of lower labor costs, new low-cost Chinese suppliers have also emerged, and United States, Japanese, Taiwanese, and Korean suppliers (among others) have set up operations in China as well. This is basically the same pattern followed previously in Japan in the 1960s and 1970s and later in Korea, Taiwan, and Singapore before Mexico became a global hot spot.

Both Mexico and China have positive and negative aspects in terms of supply chain development for U.S. companies. You can ship from Mexico to the United States in about eight hours; however, it takes 21 to 23 days to ship from China. Many people speak English in Mexico, and many Americans speak Spanish; the same situation does not exist in China (although English is becoming more prevalent). Government regulations, especially in terms of business ownership, are sometimes restrictive in China, but in China a company can work 24 hours a day, 7 days a week, compared to an average workweek in Mexico of approximately 44 hours. Trade regulations and tariffs are increasingly being lowered in Mexico and China. Quality is a problem in both Mexico and China, where it can vary dramatically between companies. Chinese and Mexican suppliers generally lack quality-management systems, and do not often use statistical process control or have ISO certification, unless they are imposed by their global customers.

CHINA'S ROLE IN THE GLOBAL SUPPLY CHAIN

It has become commonplace for companies in the United States and abroad to develop a global supply chain by sourcing in low-cost countries, and no country has received more attention as a supplier than China. China has become one of the world's premier sources of supply. Walmart, for example, has more than 50,000 suppliers in China. Not only are companies looking to China as a low-cost supplier of goods and services, but some companies are relocating their procurement operations to China. IBM moved its global purchasing headquarters from Westchester County, New York, to Shenzhen, China—the first time IBM located the headquarters of one of its global corporate functions outside the United States. It relocated, in part, to help the company develop stronger relationships with its suppliers in China, and to have more control over quality and logistics.

Companies are looking to China (as well as other emerging low-cost sources of supply such as Central/Eastern Europe, India, Bangladesh, the Philippines, and Pacific Rim countries) for several reasons. There is an abundance of low-wage labor; China has a labor market of 750 million people, and the country's average hourly wage, although increasing, is still lower than in most other emerging markets. The average worker earns about $1.70 an hour, and migrant workers (who account for one-fifth of the labor market) typically earn less than $150 per month. Almost half of China's population has a middle-school or greater education. Most companies that are global sourcing also want to position their source countries as future markets, and China is one of the world's fastest-growing markets, and the world's second largest economy. China's exports increased by 500% and were almost $9 trillion in the first decade of this century. China's retail spending has been increasing by as much 12% to 16% annually in recent years. China has introduced a number of regulatory changes that has liberalized its market.

Traditionally, China exported consumer goods, clothing, and textiles; however, it is now increasingly exporting products with a higher technology content as its manufacturing sector matures. This is what most low-cost emerging countries do: ramp up with labor-intensive manufacturing and then migrate slowly toward more skilled, higher-value products and services. In particular, high-tech industries are looking to China as a low-cost supplier. Because high-tech companies operate on razor-thin margins, with intense competition and very fast product lifecycles, they have no choice but to look to countries like China as a source of low-cost supply. The Microsoft Xbox game system was first built in Mexico and Hungary, but production was shifted to China. Laptop computer manufacturing in Taiwan is moving to China.

United States companies generally follow one of several models in doing business in China. One option is to employ local third-party trading agents such as Chinese import and export companies (like Li & Fung) to help identify local suppliers, negotiate prices, and arrange logistics. Companies can develop their own international procurement offices (as IBM did) that have specialized teams performing different sourcing functions like logistics. This has proven to be the most successful, especially for large manufacturing firms.

Sourcing from China is not without challenges. Dramatic differences in organization, cultural relationships, and technology can result in significant problems to overcome. Many U.S. companies have spent years and resources building a network of reliable, high-quality suppliers, and disrupting that system in order to global outsource (often to remain competitive) can be a daunting task. Simply getting reliable information about Chinese suppliers in order to compare companies is much more difficult than in the United States. Information technology is less advanced and sophisticated in China than in the United States. Cultural relationships are more difficult to establish in China than in the United States. *Guanxi* (or personal relationships) will frequently trump commercial considerations in the negotiation process and in doing business. Worker turnover rates among low-skilled workers are extremely high, averaging 30–40% annually, and the turnover rate among new university graduates is also extremely high compared to industrialized nations.

Although China has become a burgeoning global supplier market, the country's underdeveloped transportation infrastructure, fragmented distribution systems, lack of sophisticated technology, limited logistics skills, regulatory restrictions, and local protectionism hinder efficient logistics and make supply chain management a challenge. Companies entering the Chinese market often find they cannot manage transportation and distribution as they might in their home country. The government-controlled rail service is China's cheapest distribution mode; however, capacity shortages often occur, although there has been significant investment in the railway infrastructure with over $350 billion spent between 2009 and 2012. Roads are the preferred mode of distribution for packaged finished goods; however, demand exceeds capacities, and China's road transport industry is fragmented although improving. Airfreight is subject to high prices, inadequate capacity, fragmented routes, and limited information exchange between airlines and freight forwarders. Ocean and inland water transport is the most developed distribution mode in China, and China's shipping companies rank among the world's largest. However, inland water distribution is sometimes underutilized because ports often cannot process and manage cargo efficiently, bureaucratic delays and theft are common, and some ports cannot accommodate larger vessels. Distribution is also hampered by poor warehousing, which is predominantly government controlled. Warehouse designs are inefficient with low ceilings and poor lighting, and goods are usually handled manually without warehouse automation.

Logistics oversight in China is shared by different government entities such as various planning and trade commissions, and this shared responsibility creates problems with things like customs clearance including excessive paperwork, inefficient procedures, and short business hours. Complicated and excessive regulatory controls are also common. Foreign trade companies must sell goods through distributors and cannot sell directly to stores, and they are forbidden to own distribution channels. A foreign company can sell goods manufactured in China, but it cannot sell or distribute goods imported into the country, including those produced by a company's plants outside of China. Thus, foreign companies must rely on small local distribution companies to move goods. Regulations also have created a shortage of third-party logistics providers.

However, despite these problems China's distribution and logistics sector is growing and improving rapidly. Trillions of dollars are being spent annually on new highways, airport construction and expansion, inland water transportation, and the construction of distribution and logistics centers. China's emergence as an economic power has forced the country to progressively remove regulations and restrictions that prevent foreign companies from participating in transportation and distribution functions, which has made it possible for foreign companies to establish subsidiaries and offices that manage a variety of supply chain functions. The demand for third-party logistics service providers has also expanded the outsourcing of logistics and transportation.

REVERSE GLOBALIZATION

U.S. and European companies expanded their supply chains and shifting operations into Asia, and specifically China, because of cheaper labor and raw materials. However, the trend toward partnering with Asian and Far Eastern suppliers shows signs of reversing itself as the gloss of global sourcing has begun to tarnish for some companies. With an improved infrastructure and a higher standard of living, China is rapidly approaching a level of parity with other developed nations, mirroring a transition experienced in the past by other foreign countries like Japan, Taiwan, and India. Wage rates in Asia are steadily rising, thus negating one of the primary reasons for global sourcing. While Far Eastern and Asian countries are instituting new laws and port and trade regulations, countries in Latin America, South America, and Canada are investing more in education and infrastructure and developing larger and more modern port facilities, making it more appealing to source in this hemisphere. Volatile oil prices have made it more costly to ship items long distances and more difficult to predict costs; oil prices now account for nearly half of total freight costs. Shipping products over long distances while companies are demanding faster delivery times in a JIT-type competitive environment have contributed to an increase in containerization and faster ship speeds, which have increased fuel consumption. Increases in global transport costs have now effectively offset many of the trade liberalization agreements of the last 30 years.

Combined with these factors are the continuing unreliability of delivery times in longer global supply chains and quality failures, in China in particular. (See the "Along the Supply Chain" box on "Reverse Globalization at K'NEX.") Surveys show that companies are increasingly concerned about the risk of poor product and supply chain quality (for example, the problem of lead paint in toys produced in China), and the infringement on intellectual property and security breaches in China. Long lead times resulting from distance and uncertainties in the shipping processes for global sourcing mean ordering far in advance, which can backfire if the product market changes or the economy sours. It is often difficult for U.S. companies to gain visibility into the financial health of foreign suppliers; during the recent global recession, many overseas suppliers went bankrupt, creating supply chain delays for U.S. buyers. All of these factors—increasing oil prices, higher foreign wage rates, increasing raw material costs, poor quality and long delivery times—have made what's referred to as *near-shore* sourcing, and redesigning supply chains with multilocal operations, in this hemisphere more attractive.

Gartner's 2012 annual survey of Top 25 supply chains, which included companies like Apple, Dell, Amazon, Cisco, Walmart, and Procter & Gamble, indicated that an emerging trend among companies with top-ranked supply chains was a reassessment of the tradeoff between global economies of scale and the demand for local responsiveness, and as a result, they were redesigning

ALONG THE SUPPLY CHAIN

Brazil as a Potential Near-Shore Supplier for the United States

U.S. companies increasingly concerned about problems with extended Asian supply chains, and Chinese suppliers in particular, are looking more closely at reverse globalization and near-shore suppliers. Brazil offers a number of advantages to U.S. companies as a near-shore supplier and as a consumer market. Since 2000, Brazilian exports have grown at an annual rate of 17%, positioning it, along with Russia, India, and China, as one of the world's foremost emerging economies and global trading partners. It ranks sixth in the world in GDP. With exports over $250 billion, it is the 24th leading exporter in the world, and enjoys a trade balance of over $30 billion. Seventeen percent of Brazil's exports flow to China, and 10% to the United States. Brazil has become a potential supply chain source for U.S. companies because of several factors. The country's electrical system is based mainly on hydroelectric power, which is inexpensive and sustainable. It has a favorable climate for agro-commodities, which has increased productivity compared to other Northern Hemisphere countries for almost all crops including soy, sugarcane, and wood. It has a wealth of natural resource reserves including iron ore, bauxite, and petroleum, making it relatively independent of resource shortages that have plagued other countries. It has become a major U.S. supplier of iron ore (with 8% of U.S. imports), pulp mill products (19%), and fruit and vegetable derivatives (3%). Brazil has an established sustainable ethanol production and distribution network that provides more than 80% of the energy for passenger vehicles produced and sold in the country, making it probably the first country that will be independent of fossil fuels for its light vehicle fleet. Import restrictions in the 1970s forced the country to develop a well-established local supply base of small industrial companies that support a variety of industry sectors. It has substantially lower labor costs compared to developed countries. The cost of trained automotive production and assembly labor is five times lower in Brazil than the United States, and nine times lower than Western Europe. Although China is a major sourcing and consumer market for many U.S. and European companies, Brazil's closeness to the United States in geography, distance, and time zone results in comparatively less risky, less expensive, more sustainable supply chains. Shipping routes do not pass through global hot spots in the Middle East freight rates are 30% lower than rates from Asia; and there are lower carbon emissions. In addition, the Western culture of Brazilian businessmen is more closely related to that of North Americans and Western Europeans. Brazil does have some drawbacks: the industrial capacity in some sectors is not of a sufficient scale to supply some U.S. mass production industries; advanced technology skills are insufficient in some high-tech industry sectors; and the country's infrastructure is lacking, and any exporter will likely be required to make a significant investment in order to achieve adequate shipping capacity and reliability. Still, Brazil offers enough positive benefits for many U.S. companies to start looking south for a new supply chain member.

Investigate and discuss some of the other countries that might be possible near-shore supply sources for the United States in the future.

Source: Ricardo Ruiz-Huidobro and Markus Stricker, "Brazil, A Country of Regeneration," *Inside Supply Management* 20, no. 9 (September, 2009): pp. 26–28.

their supply chains to support a more regionalized approach. Although these companies' supply chains may be designed to address a global marketplace, manufacturing and supply capabilities are being situated at numerous regional localities, rather than in a central location like China. This change is being driven by several factors including local government incentives, organized labor concessions, high annual wage increases and rising logistics expenses in China, combined with the demand to be more responsive to local markets.

Although wage rates are higher, many U.S. companies are moving operations and facilities back to the states, are partnering with U.S. suppliers or suppliers in this hemisphere, including South America, Mexico and the Caribbean, and some are insourcing. Near-shoring allows companies to reduce or avoid many of the risks associated with global sourcing, and shorter supply chains enable companies to gain more control and flexibility. Some companies, embracing customer concerns about service quality, are moving customer service and ordering processes from India back to the United States; even though it's more costly, maintaining customers and customer satisfaction is being recognized as the more important consideration.

SECURITY WITHIN GLOBAL SUPPLY CHAINS

The events of 9/11 affected global supply chains as they did much else in our lives. The two primary modes of transport in global supply chains are airfreight and ocean carriers, both of which enter the United States through portals from the outside world and thus are obvious security risks. The U.S. government, in concert with countries around the world, has adopted security measures that, besides increasing security, have added time to supply chain schedules and increased supply chain costs. Air and ocean carriers must file an advance manifest with the U.S. government 24 hours before loading the containers on a U.S.-bound ship or airplane so the government can conduct "risk screening." This 24-hour rule requires extensive documentation at the airport or seaport of origin, which can extend supply chain time by three to four days. Even if shipments

ALONG THE SUPPLY CHAIN

Reverse Globalization at K'NEX

In 2007 the Consumer Product Safety Commission issued 81 toy recalls, its most ever, to companies parents trusted like Fisher-Price, Mattel, and J.C. Penney. However, the Hatfield, Pennsylvania, construction toy maker K'NEX avoided these recalls because, unlike these other toy companies who experienced quality problems with Chinese suppliers, its products are "Made in the U.S.A." Although K'NEX has several Chinese suppliers, it closely monitors its manufacturing processes and quality practices to ensure they perform the same as their domestic U.S. suppliers. It has established long-term relationships with only two Chinese suppliers that have met its very stringent quality requirements. Companies have found that Chinese suppliers cannot be trusted to voluntarily adhere to quality standards and product specifications. Various surveys of U.S. companies have shown that China is "riskier" than any other global region for supplier and internal product quality failure. K'NEX uses safeguards with its Chinese suppliers, including a partnership with Hasbro, which has a quality control team in Chinese factories every week, quarterly inspections by K'NEX personnel, inspections performed by the Chinese government, and ISO 9001 certification. K'NEX also has devices that check for lead in its plants. All of these practices add to costs, but the avoidance of recent recalls made them worthwhile and cost-effective. While overall toy sales declined by 2% in 2007, in large part because of highly publicized recalls due to lead, K'NEX sales increased by 12%. Much of K'NEX's success was due to its ability to tout the fact that it is a U.S.-based manufacturer with almost 30% of its product volume made entirely in the United States. Since the toy industry recall in 2007, K'NEX has shifted as much as 50% of it production to the United States, partly because of concerns about quality and partly because of increasing labor cost in China. An added benefit to shifting more of its production back to the states is that it has a shorter supply chain and can delay product decisions longer. The toy market is very seasonal, with most sales occurring during the Christmas season; thus, if K'NEX is being supplied from China, to get products in stores by October, it must make product decisions in June. However, with a shorter domestic supply chain, these decisions can be delayed until mid-September.

Discuss some of the other reasons that you think might make companies decide to change to *near-shore* sourcing, and make their supply chains less global.

Source: Brett Krzykowski, "K'NEX Success," *Quality Progress* 41, no. 5 (May 2008): pp. 36–42.

reach the U.S. port on time, stricter customs inspections can leave the shipment tied up for hours or days. For example, food imports can be diverted for inspections for possible bioterrorism alterations. For airfreight, a delay of three or four days would negate the benefit of shipping by air at all. As a result of new security measures after 9/11, inventory levels increased almost 5%, requiring more than $75 billion in extra working capital, as companies coped with delays with buffer inventory. The cost of insuring U.S. imports increased from $36 billion in 2001 to over $40 billion to 2002. The Brookings Institute has estimated that the cost of slowing the delivery of imported goods by one day because of additional security checks is approximately $7 billion per year. These costs do not even include the costs of new people, technologies, equipment, surveillance, communication, and security systems, and training necessary for screening at airports and seaports around the world.

In 2003 the U.S. Customs and Border Protection (CPB) agency was established as part of the Department of Homeland Security to ensure that all imports and exports are legal and comply with U.S. laws and regulations. The CPB has implemented a comprehensive cargo security system designed to protect national security that includes the 24-hour manifest rule, a container security initiative, a customs-trade partnership against terrorism (C-PAT), nonintrusion inspection techniques, automated targeting systems, the national targeting center, and recently, the secure freight initiative. The secure freight initiative, announced in 2008, went into effect in January 2010. Also known as the "10+2" initiative, is intended to reduce the rise of terrorism by using the latest tracking and tracing, and communication and reporting, technologies. It provides for a detailed security account of goods and materials shipped into the United States, called the Importer Security Filing (ISF), that distinguishes between potentially risky cargo and lower risk cargo, and more efficiently allocates agency resources to focus on true security threats. ISF 10+2 is mandatory for all importers; it includes 10 specific data elements related to container manufacturer, seller, buyer, content, importer, schedule, origin, and destination, that must be electronically filed 24 hours before loading any container on a ship bound for the United States. The "+2" are data files which the carrier must file within 48 hours of the departure time, and include the location of all containers on the ship and information on the movement of containers and any status changes as they move through the supply chain. 10+2 was expected to increase annual supply chain shipping costs from $400 million to $700 million as a result of government filing fees and the additional reporting information required.

QUESTIONS

11-1. Pick a business you are familiar with and describe its primary transportation model and its transport routes.

11-2. Select a company that has a global supply chain and describe it, including purchasing, production, distribution, and transportation.

11-3. Locate an e-marketplace on the Internet and describe it and the type of suppliers, and producers it connects.

11-4. Locate a transportation exchange on the Internet, describe the services it provides to its users, and indicate some of the customers that use it.

11-5. Locate an international logistics provider on the Internet; describe the services it provides and identify some of its customers.

11-6. Walmart is one of the leaders in promoting the development and use of radio frequency identification (RFID) and electronic product codes. Explain how Walmart uses RFID in its procurement and distribution and why Walmart wants its suppliers to adopt RFID.

11-7. Explain how Walmart has used cross-docking to improve its supply chain efficiency.

11-8. Identify three countries (other than Canada and Mexico) that you think would be possible near-shore suppliers for U.S. companies and discuss their advantages and disadvantages.

11-9. Using the Internet, find an article and write a report about how an actual company is achieving sustainability though improved processes in its transportation and distribution functions.

11-10. Discuss some of the disadvantages of U.S. companies using Chinese suppliers that might drive them to near-shore their supply chains.

11-11. Describe what *spend analysis* is and how it can improve procurement activities for a company with a global supply chain.

11-12. Compare the positive and negative aspects of a U.S. company outsourcing in China, Mexico, and Brazil.

11-13. Apple, Amazon, and Procter & Gamble are recognized year after year as companies with top-rated global supply chains. Describe the supply chains of each company and discuss their similarities and differences.

11-14. Walmart employs numerous suppliers in China; describe some of the difficulties that it experiences in its sustainability efforts.

11-15. Using the Internet, identify a third-party logistics (3PL) provider and describe the type of services it offers and the advantages it might provide the outsourcing company.

11-16. Study the website of the World Trade Organization (WTO) and describe the type of services it provides its members—that is, what it is and what it does.

11-17. Describe the "10 benefits of the WTO trading system" outlined on the World Trade organization website.

11-18. Describe the differences among tariffs, duties, landed costs, and value-added taxes.

11-19. The World Trade Organization (WTO) maintains large databases about the trade statistics of its member countries on its website. Access a "trade profile" for a country of your choosing and the United States for the most recent available year, and write a summary report describing and comparing the trade profiles of the two countries.

11-20. Describe the European Union—what it is, its history, and how it promotes and advances international trade.

11-21. Using the Internet, identify an "international trade specialist" and describe the services it provides companies with a global supply chain.

11-22. Using the Internet, identify the five busiest global ports according to whatever measure of port traffic or volume you choose.

11-23. Write a report describing the North American Free Trade Agreement (NAFTA), including its history, what it is, what it does, and its effectiveness in promoting trade between its member companies.

CHAPTER 12

Forecasting Demand

LEARNING OBJECTIVES

AFTER READING THIS CHAPTER, YOU WILL BE ABLE TO:

- Discuss the strategic role of forecasting in supply chain management.
- Describe the forecasting process and identify the components of forecasting demand.
- Forecast demand using various time series models, including exponential smoothing, and trend and seasonal adjustments.
- Discuss and calculate various methods for evaluating forecast accuracy.
- Use Excel to create various forecast models.
- Develop forecasting models with linear and multiple regression analysis.

FORECASTING DENIM JEANS TRENDS

Denim jeans consumers may think that new apparel trends just happen out of the "blue," but that's rarely the case. Jeans looks, styles, and colors in most cases can be traced back months and often years, and are the result of vast amounts of data and information, sophisticated forecasting methodologies, and expert professional analysis. In the denim jeans industry, trends evolve over time, as distinct from fads, which are short term and are driven by extraneous factors like instant celebrity or a music video.

Most large-volume denim jeans brands such as Levi's, Gap, Lee, and Wrangler, and more fashionable brands like H&M, Calvin Klein, Tommy Hilfiger, and Zara, follow a similar methodology for trend forecasting. They first identify basic fundamental facts about past trends and forecasts such as the colors and styles that have had the greatest demand, then they determine what factors caused changes in the past and compare differences between past forecasts and what actually occurred. Next they determine what factors are most likely to affect future trends, which can be economic and technological changes as well as fashion changes.

Factors that go into denim jeans trend forecasting could include new cotton fiber innovations, the price and availability of cotton, advances in manufacturing processes and machinery, shifts in global manufacturing locations, shipping changes, shifting global markets (for example, into less economically developed countries), and sustainability issues, in addition to fashion factors like designs, styles, colors, media, blogs, celebrity, and apparel trade shows. The resulting information and data are used in forecasting tools and techniques to develop trend forecasts, with particular attention paid to accuracy and reliability.

Once the trend forecast is developed, it is closely monitored to determine reasons for significant deviations from what is actually happening, and the forecast is revised as needed. Ultimately it is this trend forecast, combined with shorter-term and seasonal forecasts, that drives a jeans company's global supply chain; and it is sudden changes in fashion trends and customer tastes that alter the forecast and make the denim jeans supply chain so complex and difficult to manage.

Source: Based on Randi Gollin, "Trend Forecasters Talk Fall/Winter 2012/2013," *Apparel Insiders*, www.apparelinsiders.com.

A forecast is a prediction of what will occur in the future. Meteorologists forecast the weather, sportscasters and gamblers predict the winners of football games, and companies attempt to predict how much of their product will be sold in the future. A forecast of product demand is the basis for most important planning decisions. Planning decisions regarding scheduling, inventory, production, facility layout and design, workforce, distribution, purchasing, and so on, are functions of customer demand. Long-range strategic plans by top management are based on forecasts of the type of products consumers will demand in the future and the size and location of product markets.

Forecasting is an uncertain process. It is not possible to predict consistently what the future will be, even with the help of a crystal ball or a deck of tarot cards. Management generally hopes to forecast demand with as much accuracy as possible, which is becoming increasingly difficult to do. In the current international business environment, consumers have more product choices and more information on which to base choices. They also demand and receive greater product diversity, made possible by rapid technological advances. This makes forecasting products and product demand more difficult. Consumers and markets have never been stationary targets, but they are moving more rapidly now than they ever have before.

Companies sometimes use **qualitative forecast methods** based on judgment, opinion, past experience, or best guesses, to make forecasts. A number of **quantitative forecasting methods** are also available to aid management in making planning decisions. In this chapter, we discuss two of the traditional types of mathematical forecasting methods, time series analysis and regression, as well as several nonmathematical, qualitative approaches to forecasting. Although no technique will result in a totally accurate forecast, these methods can provide reliable guidelines in making decisions.

The Strategic Role of Forecasting in Supply Chain Management

In today's global business environment, strategic planning and design tend to focus on supply chain management and quality management.

SUPPLY CHAIN MANAGEMENT

A company's supply chain encompasses all of the facilities, functions, and activities involved in producing a product or service from suppliers (and their suppliers) to customers (and their customers).

Supply chain functions include purchasing, inventory, production, scheduling, facility location, transportation, and distribution. All these functions are affected in the short run by product demand and in the long run by new products and processes, technology advances, and changing markets.

Forecasts of product demand determine how much inventory is needed, how much product to make, and how much material to purchase from suppliers to meet forecasted customer needs. This in turn determines the kind of transportation that will be needed and where plants, warehouses, and distribution centers should be located so that products and services can be delivered on time. Without accurate forecasts, large stocks of costly inventory must be kept at each stage of the supply chain to compensate for the uncertainties of customer demand. If there are insufficient inventories, customer service suffers because of late deliveries and stockouts. This is especially hurtful in today's competitive global business environment, where customer service and on-time delivery are critical factors. Figure 12.1 illustrates the effects of bad forecasting on the supply chain.

While accurate forecasts are necessary, completely accurate forecasts are never possible. Hopefully, the forecast will reduce uncertainty about the future as much as possible, but it will never eliminate uncertainty. Thus, all of the supply chain processes need to be flexible to respond to some degree of uncertainty.

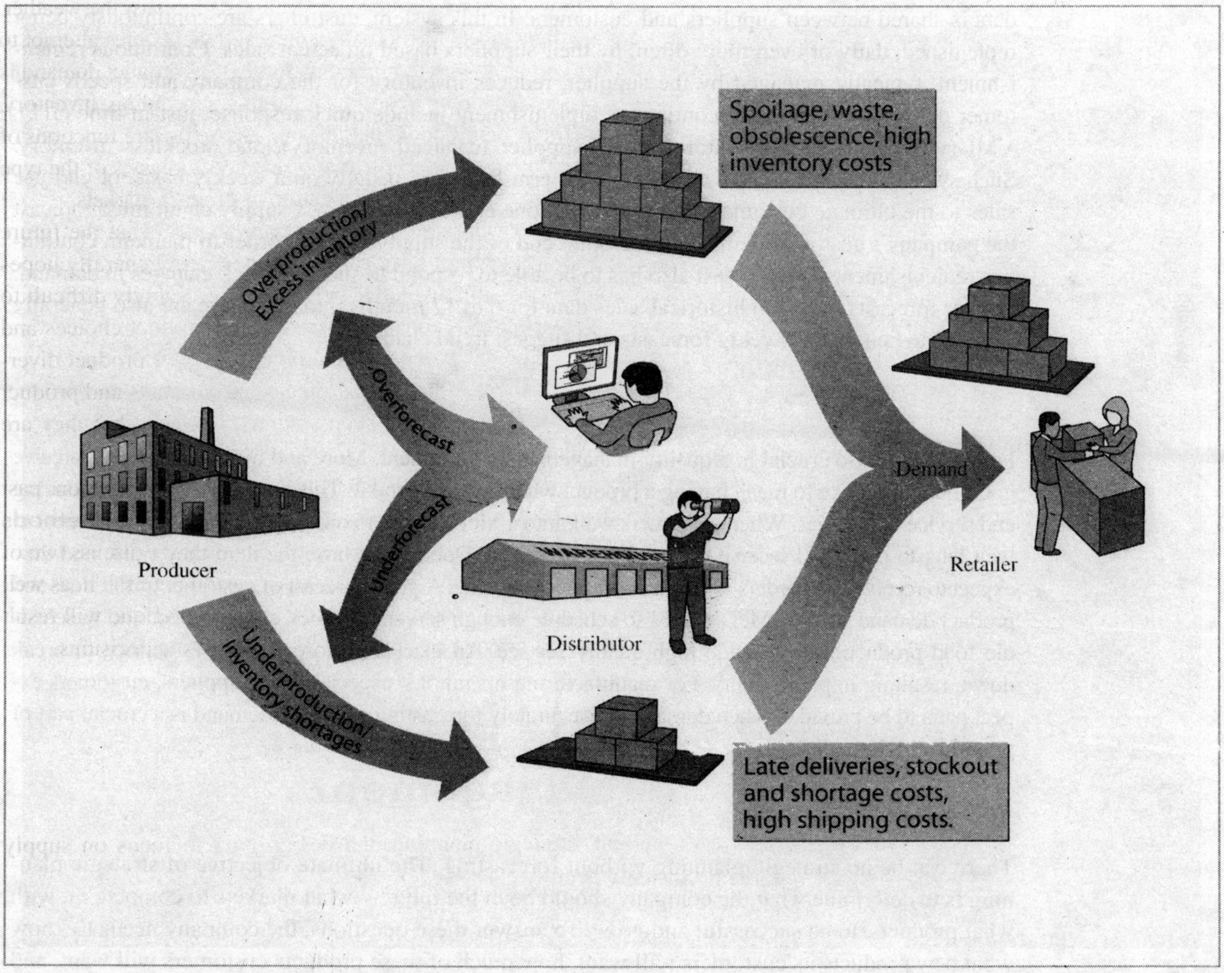

Figure 12.1
The Effect of Inaccurate Forecasting on the Supply Chain

In Chapter 10 on supply chain management, we talked about the "bullwhip effect" and its negative impact on the supply chain. The bullwhip effect is the distortion of information about product demand (including forecasts) as it is transmitted back through the supply chain toward suppliers. As demand moves further away from the ultimate end-use consumer, the variation in demand becomes greater and demand forecasts become less reliable. This increased variation can result in excessive, costly safety stock inventories at each stage in the supply chain and poorer customer service.

The bullwhip effect is caused when slight demand variability is magnified as information moves back upstream in the supply chain (see Figure 10.4). It is created when supply chain members make ordering decisions with an eye to their own self-interest and/or they do not have accurate demand forecasts from adjacent supply chain members. If each supply chain member is uncertain and not confident about what the actual demand is for the succeeding member it supplies, and it's making its own demand forecast, then it will stockpile extra inventory to compensate for the uncertainty; that is, the member creates a security blanket of inventory. One way to cope with the bullwhip effect is to develop demand forecasts that will reduce uncertainty and for supply chain members to share these forecasts with one another. Ideally, a single forecast of demand for the final customer in the supply chain would drive the development of subsequent forecasts for each supply chain member back up through the supply chain.

One trend in supply chain design is *continuous replenishment,* wherein continuous updating of data is shared between suppliers and customers. In this system, customers are continuously being replenished, daily or even more often, by their suppliers based on actual sales. Continuous replenishment, typically managed by the supplier, reduces inventory for the company and speeds customer delivery. Variations of continuous replenishment include quick response, just-in-time (JIT), VMI (vendor-managed inventory), SMI (supplier managed inventory), and stockless inventory. Such systems rely heavily on accurate short-term forecasts, usually on a weekly basis, of end-use sales to the ultimate customer. The supplier at one end of a company's supply chain must forecast the company's customer demand at the other end of the supply chain in order to maintain continuous replenishment. The forecast also has to be able to respond to sudden, quick changes in demand. Longer forecasts based on historical sales data for 6 to 12 months into the future are also generally required to help make weekly forecasts and suggest trend changes.

QUALITY MANAGEMENT

Forecasting is also crucial in a quality management environment. More and more, customers perceive good-quality service to mean having a product when they demand it. This holds true for manufacturing and service companies. When customers walk into a McDonald's to order a meal, they do not expect to wait long to place and receive orders. They expect McDonald's to have the item they want, and they expect to receive their orders within a short period of time. A good forecast of customer traffic flow and product demand enables McDonald's to schedule enough servers, to stock enough food, and to schedule food production to provide high-quality service. An inaccurate forecast causes service to break down, resulting in poor quality. For manufacturing operations, especially for suppliers, customers expect parts to be provided when demanded. Accurately forecasting customer demand is a crucial part of providing high-quality service.

STRATEGIC PLANNING

There can be no strategic planning without forecasting. The ultimate objective of strategic planning is to determine what the company should be in the future—what markets to compete in, with what products, to be successful and grow. To answer these questions, the company needs to know what new products its customers will want, how much of these products customers will want, and the level of quality and other features that will be expected in these products. Forecasting answers these questions and is a key to a company's long-term competitiveness and success. The determination of future new products and their design subsequently determines process design, the kinds

ALONG THE SUPPLY CHAIN

Supply Chain Forecasting at Heineken USA

Heineken is an international brewer based in Amsterdam with over 200 brands of beer sold in over 100 countries and with annual revenues over €14,000 million. Heineken brews, packages, and ships its Dutch brands, including Heineken, Heineken Premium Light, and Amstel Light, to Heineken USA on ocean carriers to seven U.S. ports in Miami, Charleston, Norfolk, New York, Houston, Long Beach, and Oakland, where it maintains warehouses and demand centers. Heineken thus operates a three-tier supply chain with a brewer, distributors, and retailers. Heineken ships full container loads directly from the ports to the warehouses of its largest distributors; for smaller distributors, loads are shipped from Heineken demand centers near the ports. A "depletion" forecast showing how much beer distributors are currently and historically selling to retailers is converted to a sales demand forecast, which indicates the amount of inventory the distributors will be buying from Heineken. Promotions and seasonal sales are factored into this demand forecast. The sales demand forecast is then used in Holland to create a production/replenishment plan for product supply. Distributors order beer over the Internet on a weekly basis at which time they also provide their three-month depletion forecast, which is a major input to the demand forecast that drives production in Holland. One week later they receive delivery from a port or demand center. Retailers order directly from the distributors. Since lead times are long (four to six weeks) and many consumers will switch beers if it is out of stock, forecasting at Heineken is critical. Underforecasting results in lost sales; overforecasting results in costly excess inventory, which becomes obsolete and is destroyed if it sits in inventory too long and is not absolutely fresh. However, there are no negative effects for the distributor if it provides a bad forecast; if it overforecasts, Heineken absorbs the excess inventory; if it underforecasts, Heineken transfers products from other demand centers to avoid stockouts. In the mid-2000s, because distributors suffered no ill effects from a bad forecast, the forecasting process had deteriorated badly in the Southeastern region. An incentive plan was developed to award American Express gift cards to individual distributor forecasters who have the best monthly, quarterly, and yearly forecast accuracy. The incentive program was a success; average monthly forecasts improved 10% in one year, which resulted in dependable forecasts to drive Heineken's supply chain.

Why do you think Heineken does not penalize its distributors for bad forecasts, but instead uses an incentive plan to entice them to provide better forecasts?

Source: Based on Brian Dershem, "Financial Incentives Improve the Supply Chain: Heineken's Journey," *The Journal of Business Forecasting* 26, issue 1 (Spring 2007): pp. 32–37.

of new equipment and technologies that will be needed, and the design of the supply chain, including the facilities, transportation, and distribution systems that will be required. These elements are ultimately based on the company's forecast of the long-run future.

Components of Forecasting Demand

The type of forecasting method to use depends on several factors, including the **time frame** of the forecast (i.e., how far in the future is being forecasted), the *behavior* of demand, and the possible existence of patterns (trends, seasonality, and so on), and the *causes* of demand behavior.

TIME FRAME

Forecasts are either short- to mid-range, or long-range. **Short-range (to mid-range) forecasts** are typically for daily, weekly, or monthly sales demand for up to approximately two years into the future, depending on the company and the type of industry. They are primarily used to determine production and delivery schedules and to establish inventory levels. At Hewlett-Packard, monthly forecasts for printers are constructed from 12 to 18 months into the future, while at Levi Strauss, weekly forecasts for jeans are prepared for five years into the future.

A **long-range forecast** is usually for a period longer than two years into the future. A long-range forecast is normally used for strategic planning—to establish long-term goals, plan new products for changing markets, enter new markets, develop new facilities, develop technology, design the supply chain, and implement strategic programs. At Unisys, long-range strategic forecasts project three years into the future; Hewlett-Packard's long-term forecasts are developed for years 2 through 6; and at Fiat, the Italian automaker, strategic plans for new and continuing products go 10 years into the future.

These classifications are generalizations. The line between short- and long-range forecasts is not always distinct. For some companies a short-range forecast can be several years, and for other firms a long-range forecast can be in terms of months. The length of a forecast depends a lot on how rapidly the product market changes and how susceptible the market is to technological changes.

DEMAND BEHAVIOR

Demand sometimes behaves in a random, irregular way. At other times it exhibits predictable behavior, with trends or repetitive patterns, which the forecast may reflect. The three types of demand behavior are *trends, cycles*, and *seasonal patterns.*

A **trend** is a gradual, long-term up or down movement of demand. For example, the demand for houses has followed an upward trend during the past few decades, without any sustained downward movement in the market. Trends are often the starting points for developing forecasts. Figure 12.2(*a*) illustrates a demand trend in which there is a general upward movement, or increase. Notice that Figure 12.2(*a*) also includes several random movements up and down. **Random variations** are movements that are not predictable and follow no pattern (and thus are virtually unpredictable). They are routine variations that have no "assignable" cause.

Figure 12.2

Forms of Forecast Movement

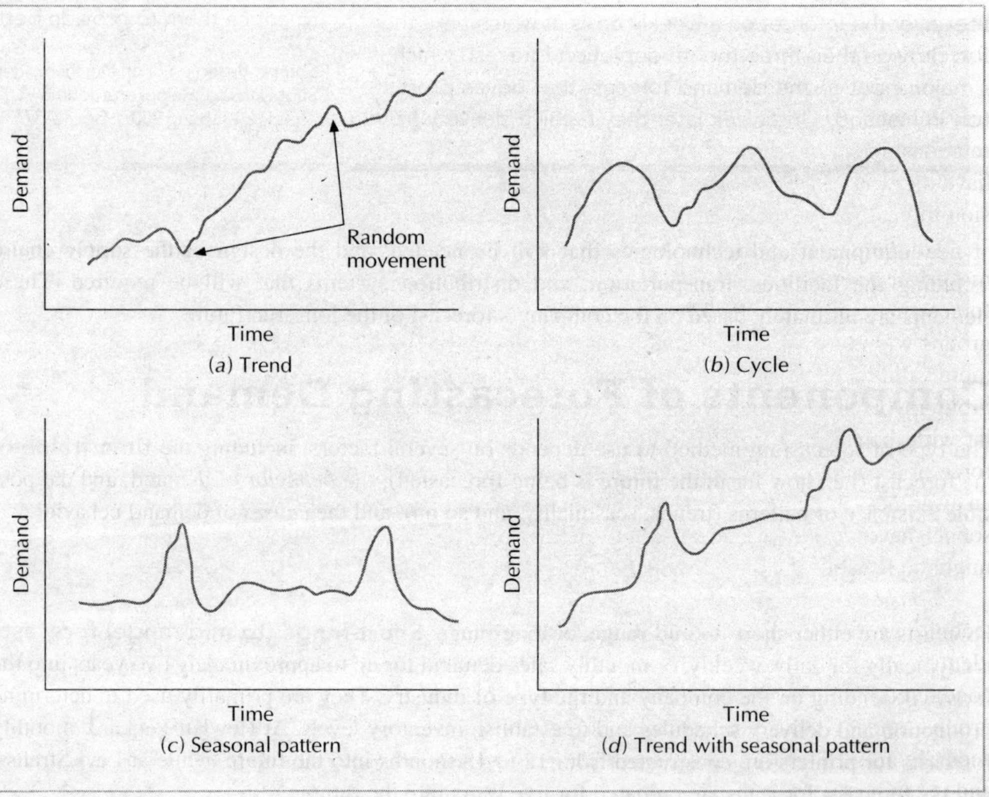

A **cycle** is an up-and-down movement in demand that repeats itself over a lengthy time span (i.e., more than a year). For example, new housing starts and, thus, construction-related products tend to follow cycles in the economy. Automobile sales also tend to follow cycles. The demand for winter sports equipment increases every four years before and after the Winter Olympics. Figure 12.2(*b*) shows the behavior of a demand cycle.

A **seasonal pattern** is an oscillating movement in demand that occurs periodically (in the short run) and is repetitive. Seasonality is often weather-related. For example, every winter the demand for snowblowers and skis increases, and retail sales in general increase during the holiday season. However, a seasonal pattern can occur on a daily or weekly basis. For example, some restaurants are busier at lunch than at dinner, and shopping mall stores and theaters tend to have higher demand on weekends. At FedEx, seasonalities include the month of the year, day of the week, and day of the month, as well as various holidays. Figure 12.2(*c*) illustrates a seasonal pattern in which the same demand behavior is repeated each year at the same time.

Demand behavior frequently displays several of these characteristics simultaneously. Although housing starts display cyclical behavior, there has been an upward trend in new house construction over the years. Demand for skis is seasonal; however, there has been an upward trend in the demand for winter sports equipment during the past two decades. Figure 12.2(*d*) displays the combination of two demand patterns, a trend with a seasonal pattern.

Instances when demand behavior exhibits no pattern are referred to as *irregular movements,* or variations. For example, a local flood might cause a momentary increase in carpet demand, or a competitor's promotional campaign might cause a company's product demand to drop for a time. Although this behavior has a cause and, thus, is not totally random, it still does not follow a pattern that can be reflected in a forecast.

FORECASTING METHODS

The factors discussed previously in this section determine to a certain extent the type of forecasting method that can or should be used. In this chapter we are going to discuss three basic types of forecasting: *time series methods, regression methods,* and *qualitative methods.*

Time series methods are statistical techniques that use historical demand data to predict future demand. **Regression** (or causal) **forecasting methods** attempt to develop a mathematical relationship (in the form of a regression model) between demand and factors that cause it to behave the way it does. Most of the remainder of this chapter will be about time series and regression forecasting methods. In this section we will focus our discussion on qualitative forecasting.

Qualitative (or judgmental) methods use management judgment, expertise, and opinion to make forecasts. Often called "the jury of executive opinion," they are the most common type of forecasting method for the long-term strategic planning process. There are normally individuals or groups within an organization whose judgments and opinions regarding the future are as valid or more valid than those of outside experts or other structured approaches. Top managers are the key group involved in the development of forecasts for strategic plans. They are generally most familiar with their firms' own capabilities and resources and the markets for their products. The sales force of a company represents a direct point of contact with the consumer. This contact provides an awareness of consumer expectations in the future that others may not possess. Engineering personnel have an innate understanding of the technological aspects of the type of products that might be feasible and likely in the future.

Consumer (or market) *research* is an organized approach using surveys and other research techniques to determine what products and services customers want and will purchase, and to identify new markets and sources of customers. Consumer and market research is normally conducted by the marketing department within an organization, by industry organizations and groups, and by private marketing or consulting firms. Although market research can provide accurate and useful forecasts of product demand, it must be skillfully and correctly conducted, and it can be expensive.

The **Delphi method** is a procedure for acquiring informed judgments and opinions from knowledgeable individuals using a series of questionnaires to develop a consensus forecast about what will occur in the future. It was developed at the Rand Corporation shortly after World War II to forecast the impact of a hypothetical nuclear attack on the United States. Although the Delphi method has been used for a variety of applications, forecasting has been one of its primary uses. It has been especially useful for forecasting technological change and advances.

Technological forecasting has become increasingly crucial to compete in the modern international business environment. New enhanced computer technology, new production methods, and advanced machinery and equipment are constantly being made available to companies. These advances enable them to introduce more new products into the marketplace faster than ever before. The companies that succeed manage to get a "technological" jump on their competitors by accurately predicting what technology will be available in the future and how it can be exploited. What new products and services will be technologically feasible, when they can be introduced, and what their demand will be are questions about the future for which answers cannot be predicted from historical data. Instead, the informed opinion and judgment of experts are necessary to make these types of single, long-term forecasts.

Data mining is a recent addition to the library of methods and techniques companies have available for forecasting, brought about by the evolution in information technology. It is a process and set of tools for analyzing large amounts of data in order to identify patterns, trends, and relationships among and between groups of customers, markets, and products. Data mining is made possible by the vast amounts of data that companies now have available to them from various electronic transactions throughout their supply chains, and the ability to store this amount of data inexpensively.

ALONG THE SUPPLY CHAIN

Global Supply Chain Forecasting at Hershey's

Global companies such as Hershey's have numerous opportunities to use forecasting along various points in its supply chain. Downstream in its supply chain, Hershey's attempts to forecast product demand, which is subject to uncertainties resulting from new and current products from competitors, competitors' promotional events and price changes, and changing consumer tastes for its own current and new products. Issues related to product quality and safety, ingredients, or packaging could adversely affect demand. Negative publicity related to product recalls due to contamination or product tampering, whether valid or not, might also negatively impact product demand. All of these factors affect the forecasting process. Upstream in its supply chain, Hershey's sources many different commodities including cocoa products, sugar, dairy products, peanuts, almonds, corn sweeteners, natural gas, and fuel oil. Commodities are subject to price volatility and changes in supply caused by numerous factors, including commodity market fluctuations and speculative influences; currency exchange rates; the effect of weather on crop yield and distribution channels; trade agreements among producing and consuming nations; political unrest in producing countries; and changes in governmental agricultural programs and energy policies. Other factors that can create uncertainties in its global supply chain and operations that make forecasting difficult include global economic and environmental changes that can result in interruptions in supply and decreased demand for its products overseas; changes in tariff and trade agreements; political instability; nationalization of Hershey's properties; and disruptions in shipping or reduced availability of freight transportation.

Given the various uncertainties inherent in the forecasting process at Hershey's, what kind of forecasting models might you suggest for the company?

Source: Hershey's website at www.thehersheycompany.com.

FORECASTING PROCESS

Forecasting is not simply identifying and using a method to compute a numerical estimate of what demand will be in the future. It is a continuing process that requires constant monitoring and adjustment illustrated by the steps in Figure 12.3.

In the next few sections, we present several different forecasting methods applicable for different patterns of demand behavior. Thus, one of the first steps in the forecasting process is

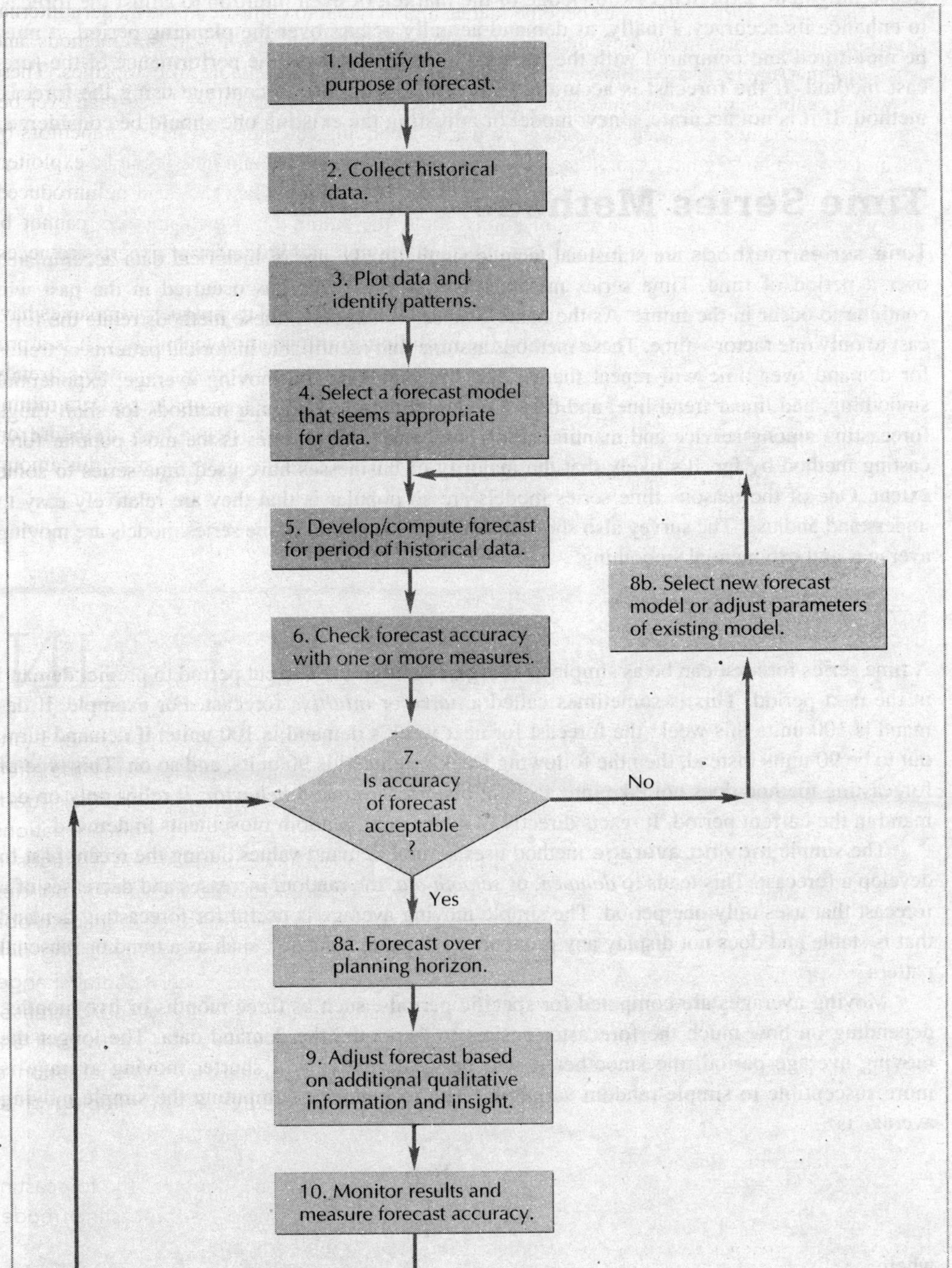

Figure 12.3

Steps of the Forecasting Process

to plot the available historical demand data and, by looking at them, to attempt to determine the forecasting method that best seems to fit the patterns the data exhibit. Historical demand is usually past sales or orders data. There are several measures for comparing historical demand with the forecast to see how accurate the forecast is. Following our discussion of the forecasting methods, we present several measures of forecast accuracy. If the forecast does not seem to be accurate, another method can be tried until an accurate forecast method is identified. After the forecast is made over the desired planning horizon, it may be possible to use judgment, experience, knowledge of the market, or even intuition to adjust the forecast to enhance its accuracy. Finally, as demand actually occurs over the planning period, it must be monitored and compared with the forecast in order to assess the performance of the forecast method. If the forecast is accurate, then it is appropriate to continue using the forecast method. If it is not accurate, a new model or adjusting the existing one should be considered.

Time Series Methods

Time series methods are statistical techniques that make use of historical data accumulated over a period of time. Time series methods assume that what has occurred in the past will continue to occur in the future. As the name *time series* suggests, these methods relate the forecast to only one factor—time. These methods assume that identifiable historical patterns or trends for demand over time will repeat themselves. They include the moving average, exponential smoothing, and linear trend line, and they are among the most popular methods for short-range forecasting among service and manufacturing companies. Time series is the most popular forecasting method by far. It's likely that the majority of businesses have used time series to some extent. One of the reasons time series models are so popular is that they are relatively easy to understand and use. The survey also showed that the most popular time series models are moving averages and exponential smoothing.

MOVING AVERAGE

A time series forecast can be as simple as using demand in the current period to predict demand in the next period. This is sometimes called a *naive* or *intuitive* forecast. For example, if demand is 100 units this week, the forecast for next week's demand is 100 units; if demand turns out to be 90 units instead, then the following week's demand is 90 units, and so on. This type of forecasting method does not take into account historical demand *behavior*; it relies only on demand in the current period. It reacts directly to the normal, random movements in demand.

The simple **moving average** method uses several demand values during the recent past to develop a forecast. This tends to *dampen*, or *smooth out,* the random increases and decreases of a forecast that uses only one period. The simple moving average is useful for forecasting demand that is stable and does not display any pronounced demand behavior, such as a trend or seasonal pattern.

Moving averages are computed for specific periods, such as three months or five months, depending on how much the forecaster desires to "smooth" the demand data. The longer the moving average period, the smoother it will be. (Alternatively, a shorter moving average is more susceptible to simple random variation.) The formula for computing the simple moving average is

$$MA_n = \frac{\sum_{i=1}^{n} D_i}{n}$$

where

n = number of periods in the moving average

D_i = demand in period i

EXAMPLE 12.1

COMPUTING A SIMPLE MOVING AVERAGE

The Heartland Produce Company sells and delivers food produce to restaurants and catering services within a 100-mile radius of its warehouse. The food supply business is competitive, and the ability to deliver orders promptly is a factor in getting new customers and keeping old ones. The manager of the company wants to be certain enough drivers and vehicles are available to deliver orders promptly and they have adequate inventory in stock. Therefore, the manager wants to be able to forecast the number of orders that will occur during the next month (i.e., to forecast the demand for deliveries).

From records of delivery orders, management has accumulated the following data for the past 10 months, from which it wants to compute three- and five-month moving averages.

Month	Orders	Month	Orders
January	120	June	50
February	90	July	75
March	100	August	130
April	75	September	110
May	110	October	90

SOLUTION

Let us assume that it is the end of October. The forecast resulting from either the three- or five-month moving average is typically for the next month in the sequence, which in this case is November. The moving average is computed from the demand for orders for the prior three months in the sequence according to the following formula:

$$MA_3 = \frac{\sum_{i=1}^{3} D_i}{3}$$

$$= \frac{90 + 110 + 130}{3}$$

$$= 110 \text{ orders for November}$$

The five-month moving average is computed from the prior five months of demand data as follows:

$$MA_5 = \frac{\sum_{i=1}^{5} D_i}{5}$$

$$= \frac{90 + 110 + 130 + 75 + 50}{5}$$

$$= 91 \text{ orders for November}$$

The three- and five-month moving average forecasts for all the months of demand data are shown in the following table. Actually, the manager would use only the forecast for November based on the most recent monthly demand. However, the earlier forecasts for prior months allow us to compare the forecast with actual demand to see how accurate the forecasting method is—that is, how well it does.

(Continued)

Three- and Five-Month Averages

Month	Orders per Month	Three-Month Moving Average	Five-Month Moving Average
January	120	—	—
February	90	—	—
March	100	—	—
April	75	103.3	—
May	110	88.3	—
June	50	95.0	99.0
July	75	78.3	85.0
August	130	78.3	82.0
September	110	85.0	88.0
October	90	105.0	95.0
November	—	110.0	91.0

Both moving average forecasts in the preceding table tend to smooth out the variability occurring in the actual data. This smoothing effect can be observed in the following figure in which the three-month and five-month averages have been superimposed on a graph of the original data.

The five-month moving average in the previous figure smooths out fluctuations to a greater extent than the three-month moving average. However, the three-month average more closely reflects the most recent data available to the produce company manager. In general, forecasts using the longer-period moving average are slower to react to recent changes in demand than those made using shorter-period moving averages. The extra periods of data dampen the speed with which the forecast responds. Establishing the appropriate number of periods to use in a moving average forecast often requires some amount of trial-and-error experimentation.

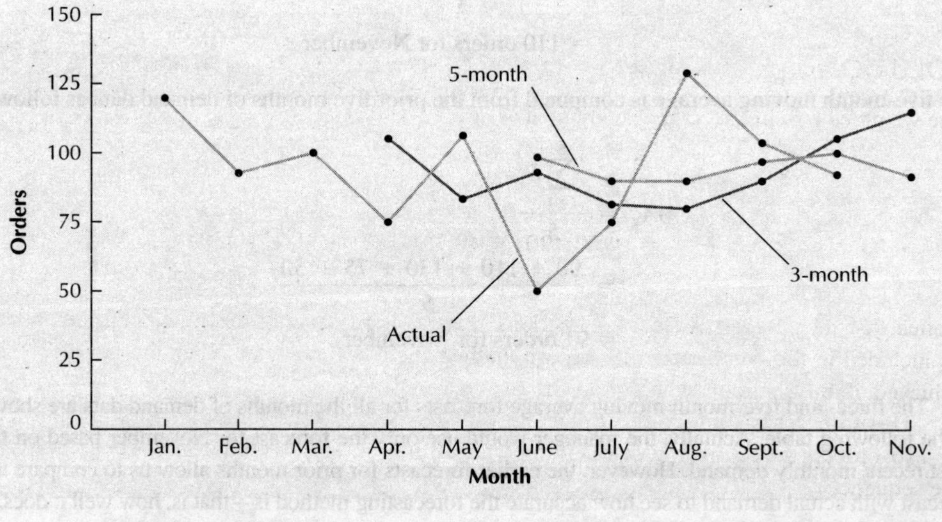

The disadvantage of the moving average method is that it does not react to variations that occur for a reason, such as cycles and seasonal effects. Factors that cause changes are generally ignored. It is basically a "mechanical" method that reflects historical data in a consistent way. However, the moving average method does have the advantage of being easy to use, quick, and relatively inexpensive. In general, this method can provide a good forecast for the short run, but it should not be pushed too far into the future.

WEIGHTED MOVING AVERAGE

The moving average method can be adjusted to more closely reflect fluctuations in the data. In the **weighted moving average** method, weights are assigned to the most recent data according to the following formula:

$$WMA_n = \sum_{i=1}^{n} W_i D_i$$

where

W_i = the weight for period i, between 0 and 100 percent

$\Sigma w_i = 1.00$

Determining the precise weights to use for each period of data usually requires some trial-and-error experimentation, as does determining the number of periods to include in the moving average. If the most recent periods are weighted too heavily, the forecast might overreact to a random fluctuation in demand. If they are weighted too lightly, the forecast might underreact to actual changes in demand behavior.

EXAMPLE 12.2

COMPUTING A WEIGHTED MOVING AVERAGE

The Heartland Produce Company in Example 12.1 wants to compute a three-month weighted moving average with a weight of 50% for the October data, a weight of 33% for the September data, and a weight of 17% for the August data. These weights reflect the company's desire to have the most recent data influence the forecast most strongly.

SOLUTION

The weighted moving average is computed as

$$\begin{aligned} WMA_3 &= \sum_{i=1}^{3} W_i D_i \\ &= (0.50)(90) + (0.33)(110) + (0.17)(130) \\ &= 103.4 \text{ orders} \end{aligned}$$

Notice that the forecast includes a fractional part, 0.4. In general, the fractional parts need to be included in the computation to achieve mathematical accuracy, but when the final forecast is achieved, it must be rounded up or down.

This forecast is slightly lower than our previously computed three-month average forecast of 110 orders, reflecting the lower number of orders in October (the most recent month in the sequence).

EXPONENTIAL SMOOTHING

Exponential smoothing is also an averaging method that weights the most recent data more strongly. As such, the forecast will react more to recent changes in demand. This is useful if the recent changes in the data are significant and unpredictable instead of just random fluctuations (for which a simple moving average forecast would suffice).

Exponential smoothing is one of the more popular and frequently used forecasting techniques, for a variety of reasons. Exponential smoothing requires minimal data. Only the forecast for the current period, the actual demand for the current period, and a weighting factor called a smoothing constant are necessary. The mathematics of the technique are easy for management to understand. Virtually all forecasting computer software packages include modules for exponential smoothing. Most importantly, exponential smoothing has a good track record of success. It has been employed over the years by many companies that have found it to be an accurate method of forecasting.

The exponential smoothing forecast is computed using the formula

$$F_{t+1} = \alpha D_t + (1 - \alpha)F_t$$

where

F_{t+1} = the forecast for the next period

D_t = actual demand in the present period

F_t = the previously determined forecast for the present period

α = a weighting factor referred to as the **smoothing constant**

The smoothing constant, α, is between 0.0 and 1.0. It reflects the weight given to the most recent demand data. For example, if $\alpha = 0.20$,

$$F_{t+1} = 0.20D_t + 0.80F_t$$

which means that our forecast for the next period is based on 20% of recent demand (D_t) and 80% of past demand (in the form of forecast F_t, since F_t is derived from previous demands and forecasts). If we go to one extreme and let $\alpha = 0.0$, then

$$\begin{aligned} F_{t+1} &= 0D_t + 1F_t \\ &= F_t \end{aligned}$$

and the forecast for the next period is the same as the forecast for this period. In other words, *the forecast does not reflect the most recent demand at all.*

On the other hand, if $\alpha = 1.0$, then

$$\begin{aligned} F_{t+1} &= 1D_t + 0F_t \\ &= 1D_t \end{aligned}$$

and we have considered only the most recent data (demand in the present period) and nothing else. Thus, the higher α is, the more sensitive the forecast will be to changes in recent demand, and the smoothing will be less. The closer α is to zero, the greater will be the dampening, or smoothing, effect. As α approaches zero, the forecast will react and adjust more slowly to differences between the actual demand and the forecasted demand. The most commonly used values of α are in the range of 0.01 to 0.50. However, the determination of α is usually judgmental and subjective and is often based on trial-and-error experimentation. An inaccurate estimate of α can limit the usefulness of this forecasting technique. (As α approaches 1.0, the forecast is the same as the naive result.)

EXAMPLE 12.3

COMPUTING AN EXPONENTIALLY SMOOTHED FORECAST

HiTek Computer Services repairs and services personal computers at its store, and it makes local service calls. It primarily uses part-time State University students as technicians. The company has had steady growth since it started. It purchases generic computer parts in volume at a discount from a variety of sources whenever it sees a good deal. Thus, they need a good forecast of demand for repairs so that they will know how many computer component parts to purchase and stock, and how many technicians to hire.

The company has accumulated the demand data shown in the accompanying table for repair and service calls for the past 12 months, from which it wants to consider exponential smoothing forecasts using smoothing constants (α) equal to 0.30 and 0.50.

Demand for Repair and Service Calls

Period	Month	Demand	Period	Month	Demand
1	January	37	7	July	43
2	February	40	8	August	47
3	March	41	9	September	56
4	April	37	10	October	52
5	May	45	11	November	55
6	June	50	12	December	54

SOLUTION

To develop the series of forecasts for the data in this table, we will start with period 1 (January) and compute the forecast for period 2 (February) using $\alpha = 0.30$. The formula for exponential smoothing also requires a forecast for period 1, which we do not have, so we will use the demand for period 1 as both *demand* and *forecast* for period 1. (Other ways to determine a starting forecast include averaging the first three or four periods or making a subjective estimate.) Thus, the forecast for February is

$$\begin{aligned} F_2 &= \alpha D_1 + (1 - \alpha)F_1 \\ &= (0.30)(37) + (0.70)(37) \\ &= 37 \text{ service calls} \end{aligned}$$

The forecast for period 3 is computed similarly:

$$\begin{aligned} F_3 &= \alpha D_2 + (1 - \alpha)F_2 \\ &= (0.30)(40) + (0.70)(37) \\ &= 37.9 \text{ service calls} \end{aligned}$$

The remainder of the monthly forecasts are shown in the following table. The final forecast is for period 13, January, and is the forecast of interest to HiTek:

$$\begin{aligned} F_{13} &= \alpha D_{12} + (1 - \alpha)F_{12} \\ &= (0.30)(54) + (0.70)(50.84) \\ &= 51.79 \text{ service calls} \end{aligned}$$

(Continued)

Exponential Smoothing Forecasts, $\alpha = 0.30$ and $\alpha = 0.50$

			Forecast, F_{t+1}	
Period	Month	Demand	$\alpha = 0.30$	$\alpha = 0.50$
1	January	37	—	—
2	February	40	37.00	37.00
3	March	41	37.90	38.50
4	April	37	38.83	39.75
5	May	45	38.28	38.37
6	June	50	40.29	41.68
7	July	43	43.20	45.84
8	August	47	43.14	44.42
9	September	56	44.30	45.71
10	October	52	47.81	50.85
11	November	55	49.06	51.42
12	December	54	50.84	53.21
13	January	—	51.79	53.61

This table also includes the forecast values using $\alpha = 0.50$. Both exponential smoothing forecasts are shown in the following figure together with the actual data.

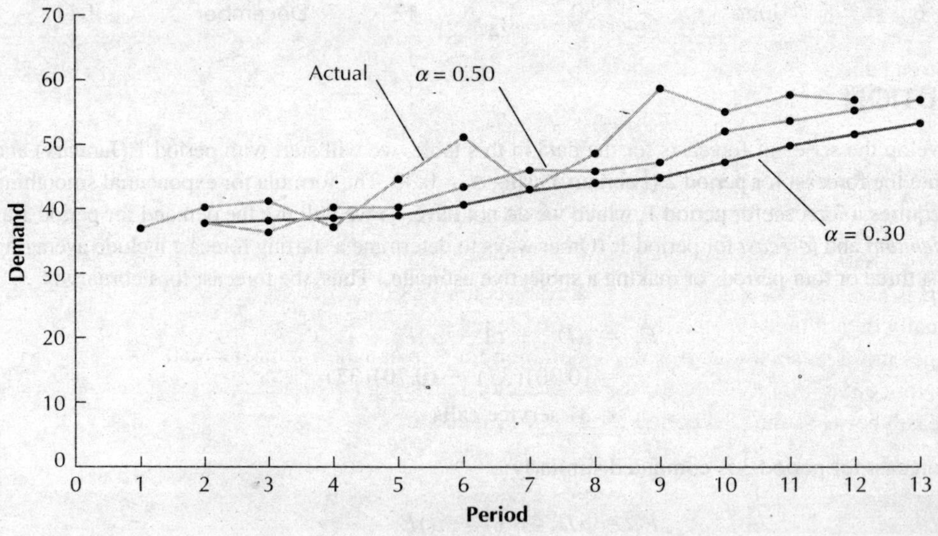

In Example 12.3, the forecast using the higher smoothing constant, $\alpha = 0.50$, seems to react more strongly to changes in demand than does the forecast with $\alpha = 0.30$, although both smooth out the random fluctuations in the forecast. Notice that both forecasts lag behind the actual demand. For example, a pronounced downward change in demand in July is not reflected in the forecast until August. If these changes mark a change in trend (i.e., a long-term upward or downward movement) rather than just a random fluctuation, then the forecast will always lag behind this trend. We can see a general upward trend in service calls throughout the year. Both forecasts tend to be consistently lower than the actual demand; that is, the forecasts lag the trend.

Based on simple observation of the two forecasts in Example 12.3, $\alpha = 0.50$ seems to be the more accurate of the two in the sense that it seems to follow the actual data more closely. (Later in this chapter we discuss several quantitative methods for determining forecast accuracy.) When demand is relatively stable without any trend, a small value for α is more appropriate to simply smooth out the forecast. When actual demand displays an increasing (or decreasing) trend, as is the case in the figure, a larger value of α is better. It will react more quickly to more recent upward or downward movements in the actual data. In some approaches to exponential smoothing, the accuracy of the forecast is monitored in terms of the difference between the actual values and the forecasted values. If these differences become larger, then α is changed (higher or lower) in an attempt to adapt the forecast to the actual data. However, the exponential smoothing forecast can also be adjusted for the effects of a trend.

In Example 12.3, the final forecast computed was for one month, January. A forecast for two or three months could have been computed by grouping the demand data into the required number of periods and then using these values in the exponential smoothing computations. For example, if a three-month forecast were needed, demand for January, February, and March could be summed and used to compute the average forecast for the next three-month period, and so on, until a final three-month forecast results. Alternatively, if a trend is present, the final period forecast can be used for an extended forecast by adjusting it by a trend factor.

ADJUSTED EXPONENTIAL SMOOTHING

The **adjusted exponential smoothing forecast** consists of the exponential smoothing forecast with a trend adjustment factor added to it:

$$AF_{t+1} = F_{t+1} + T_{t+1}$$

where

T = an exponentially smoothed trend factor

The trend factor is computed much the same as the exponentially smoothed forecast. It is, in effect, a forecast model for trend:

$$T_{t+1} = \beta(F_{t+1} - F_t) + (1 - \beta)T_t$$

where

T_t = the last period's trend factor

β = a smoothing constant for trend

β is a value between 0.0 and 1.0. It reflects the weight given to the most recent trend data. β is usually determined subjectively based on the judgment of the forecaster. A high β reflects trend changes more than a low β. It is not uncommon for β to equal α in this method.

Notice that this formula for the trend factor reflects a weighted measure of the increase (or decrease) between the next period forecast, F_{t+1}, and the current forecast, F_t.

EXAMPLE 12.4

COMPUTING AN ADJUSTED EXPONENTIALLY SMOOTHED FORECAST

HiTek Computer Services now wants to develop an adjusted exponentially smoothed forecast using the same 12 months of demand shown in the table for Example 12.3. It will use the exponentially smoothed forecast with $\alpha = 0.5$ computed in Example 12.3 with a smoothing constant for trend, β, of 0.30.

SOLUTION

The formula for the adjusted exponential smoothing forecast requires an initial value for T_t to start the computational process. This initial trend factor is often an estimate determined subjectively or based on past data by the forecaster. In this case, since we have a long sequence of demand data

(Continued)

(i.e., 12 months), we will start with the trend T_t equal to zero. By the time the forecast value of interest F_{13} is computed, we should have a relatively good value for the trend factor.

The adjusted forecast for February, AF_2, is the same as the exponentially smoothed forecast, since the trend computing factor will be zero (i.e., F_1 and F_2 are the same and $T_2 = 0$). Thus, we compute the adjusted forecast for March, AF_3, as follows, starting with the determination of the trend factor, T_3:

$$\begin{aligned} T_3 &= \beta(F_3 - F_2) + (1 - \beta)T_2 \\ &= (0.30)(38.5 - 37.0) + (0.70)(0) \\ &= 0.45 \end{aligned}$$

and

$$\begin{aligned} AF_3 &= F_3 + T_3 \\ &= 38.5 + 0.45 \\ &= 38.95 \text{ service cells} \end{aligned}$$

This adjusted forecast value for period 3 is shown in the accompanying table, with all other adjusted forecast values for the 12-month period plus the forecast for period 13, computed as follows:

$$\begin{aligned} T_{13} &= \beta(F_{13} - F_{12}) + (1 - \beta)T_{12} \\ &= (0.30)(53.61 - 53.21) + (0.70)(1.77) \\ &= 1.36 \end{aligned}$$

and

$$\begin{aligned} AF_{13} &= F_{13} + T_{13} \\ &= 53.61 + 1.36 \\ &= 54.97 \text{ service calls} \end{aligned}$$

Adjusted Exponential Smoothing Forecast Values

Period	Month	Demand	Forecast F_{t+1}	Trend T_{t+1}	Adjusted Forecast AF_{t+1}
1	January	37	37.00	—	—
2	February	40	37.00	0.00	37.00
3	March	41	38.50	0.45	38.95
4	April	37	39.75	0.69	40.44
5	May	45	38.37	0.07	38.44
6	June	50	41.68	1.04	42.73
7	July	43	45.84	1.97	47.82
8	August	47	44.42	0.95	45.37
9	September	56	45.71	1.05	46.76
10	October	52	50.85	2.28	53.13
11	November	55	51.42	1.76	53.19
12	December	54	53.21	1.77	54.98
13	January	—	53.61	1.36	54.96

The adjusted exponentially smoothed forecast values shown in the above table are compared with the exponentially smoothed forecast values and the actual data in the figure on the following page. Notice that the adjusted forecast is consistently higher than the exponentially smoothed forecast and is thus more reflective of the generally increasing trend of the actual data. However, in general, the pattern, or degree of smoothing, is very similar for both forecasts.

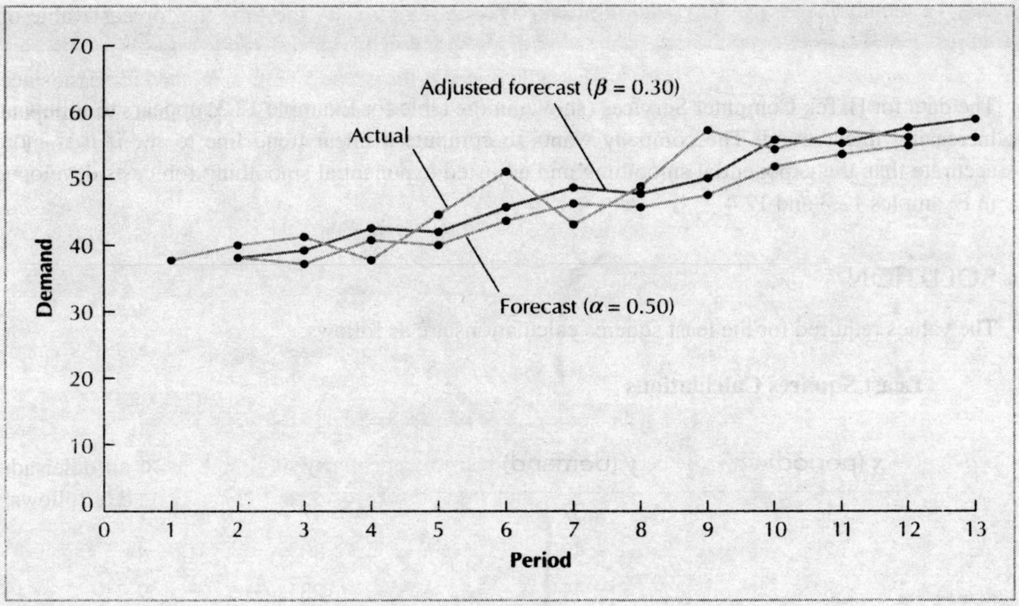

LINEAR TREND LINE

Linear regression is a method of forecasting in which a mathematical relationship is developed between demand and some other factor that causes demand behavior. However, when demand displays an obvious trend over time, a least squares regression line, or **linear trend line**, that relates demand to time can be used to forecast demand.

A linear trend line relates a dependent variable, which for our purposes is demand, to one independent variable, time, in the form of a linear equation:

$$y = a + bx$$

where

a = intercept (at period 0)

b = slope of the line

x = the time period

y = forecast for demand for period x

These parameters of the linear trend line can be calculated using the least squares formulas for linear regression:

$$b = \frac{\Sigma xy - n\bar{x}\bar{y}}{\Sigma x^2 - n\bar{x}^2}$$

$$a = \bar{y} - b\bar{x}$$

where

n = number of periods

$\bar{x} = \dfrac{\Sigma x}{n}$ = the mean of the x values

$\bar{y} = \dfrac{\Sigma y}{n}$ = the mean of the y values

EXAMPLE 12.5

COMPUTING A LINEAR TREND LINE

The data for HiTek Computer Services (shown in the table for Example 12.3) appears to follow an increasing linear trend. The company wants to compute a linear trend line to see if it is more accurate than the exponential smoothing and adjusted exponential smoothing forecasts developed in Examples 12.3 and 12.4.

SOLUTION

The values required for the least squares calculations are as follows:

Least Squares Calculations

x (period)	y (demand)	xy	x^2
1	37	37	1
2	40	80	4
3	41	123	9
4	37	148	16
5	45	225	25
6	50	300	36
7	43	301	49
8	47	376	64
9	56	504	81
10	52	520	100
11	55	605	121
12	54	648	144
78	557	3,867	650

Using these values, we can compute the parameters for the linear trend line as follows:

$$\bar{x} = \frac{78}{12} = 6.5$$

$$\bar{y} = \frac{557}{12} = 46.42$$

$$b = \frac{\Sigma xy - n\bar{x}\bar{y}}{\Sigma x^2 - n\bar{x}^2}$$

$$= \frac{3867 - (12)(6.5)(46.42)}{650 - 12(6.5)^2}$$

$$= 1.72$$

$$a = \bar{y} - b\bar{x}$$

$$= 46.42 - (1.72)(6.5)$$

$$= 35.2$$

Therefore, the linear trend line equation is

$$y = 35.2 + 1.72x$$

To calculate a forecast for period 13, let $x = 13$ in the linear trend line:

$$y = 35.2 + 1.72(13)$$
$$= 57.56 \text{ service calls}$$

The graph on the following page shows the linear trend line compared with the actual data. The trend line appears to reflect closely the actual data—that is, to be a good fit—and would thus be a good forecast model for this problem. However, a disadvantage of the linear trend line is that it will not adjust to a change in the trend, as the exponential smoothing forecast methods will; that is, it is assumed that all future forecasts will follow a straight line. This limits the use of this method to a shorter time frame in which you can be relatively certain that the trend will not change.

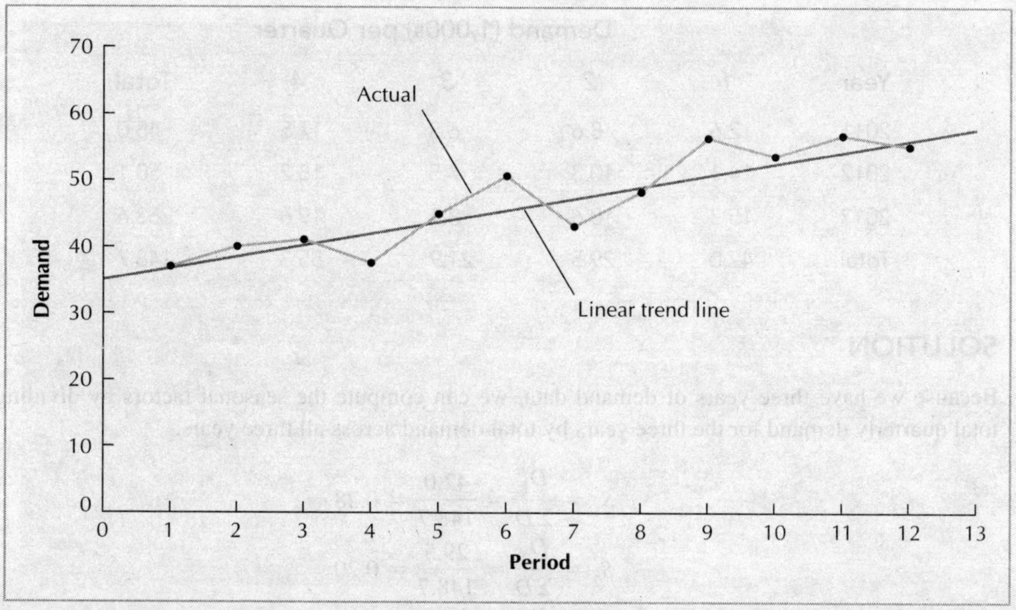

SEASONAL ADJUSTMENTS

A seasonal pattern is a repetitive increase and decrease in demand. Many demand items exhibit seasonal behavior. Clothing sales follow annual seasonal patterns, with demand for warm clothes increasing in the fall and winter and declining in the spring and summer as the demand for cooler clothing increases. Demand for many retail items, including toys, sports equipment, clothing, electronic appliances, hams, turkeys, wine, and fruit, increases during the holiday season. Greeting card demand increases in conjunction with special days such as Valentine's Day and Mother's Day. Seasonal patterns can also occur on a monthly, weekly, or even daily basis. Some restaurants have higher demand in the evening than at lunch or on weekends as opposed to weekdays. Traffic—hence sales—at shopping malls picks up on Friday and Saturday.

There are several methods for reflecting seasonal patterns in a time series forecast. We will describe one of the simpler methods using a *seasonal factor*. A **seasonal factor** is a numerical value that is multiplied by the normal forecast to get a seasonally adjusted forecast.

One method for developing a demand for seasonal factors is to divide the demand for each seasonal period by total annual demand, according to the following formula:

$$S_i = \frac{D_i}{\Sigma D}$$

The resulting seasonal factors between 0 and 1.0 are, in effect, the portion of total annual demand assigned to each season. These seasonal factors are multiplied by the annual forecasted demand to yield adjusted forecasts for each season.

EXAMPLE 12.6

COMPUTING A FORECAST WITH SEASONAL ADJUSTMENTS

Wishbone Farms raises turkeys to sell to a meat-processing company throughout the year. However, its peak season is obviously during the fourth quarter of the year, from October to December. Wishbone Farms has experienced the demand for turkeys for the past three years shown in the following table:

Demand for Turkeys at Wishbone Farms

	Demand (1,000s) per Quarter				
Year	1	2	3	4	Total
2011	12.6	8.6	6.3	17.5	45.0
2012	14.1	10.3	7.5	18.2	50.1
2013	15.3	10.6	8.1	19.6	53.6
Total	42.0	29.5	21.9	55.3	148.7

SOLUTION

Because we have three years of demand data, we can compute the seasonal factors by dividing total quarterly demand for the three years by total demand across all three years:

$$S_1 = \frac{D_1}{\Sigma D} = \frac{42.0}{148.7} = 0.28$$

$$S_2 = \frac{D_2}{\Sigma D} = \frac{29.5}{148.7} = 0.20$$

$$S_3 = \frac{D_3}{\Sigma D} = \frac{21.9}{148.7} = 0.15$$

$$S_4 = \frac{D_4}{\Sigma D} = \frac{55.3}{148.7} = 0.37$$

Next, we want to multiply the forecasted demand for the next year, 2011, by each of the seasonal factors to get the forecasted demand for each quarter. To accomplish this, we need a demand forecast for 2014. In this case, since the demand data in the table seem to exhibit a generally increasing trend, we compute a linear trend line for the three years of data in the table to get a rough forecast estimate:

$$\begin{aligned} y &= 40.97 + 4.30x \\ &= 40.97 + 4.30(4) \\ &= 58.17 \end{aligned}$$

Thus, the forecast for 2014 is 58.17, or 58,170 turkeys.

Using this annual forecast of demand, we find that the seasonally adjusted forecasts, SF_i, for 2014 are

$$\begin{aligned} SF_1 &= (S_1)(F_5) = (0.28)(58.17) = 16.28 \\ SF_2 &= (S_2)(F_5) = (0.20)(58.17) = 11.63 \\ SF_3 &= (S_3)(F_5) = (0.15)(58.17) = 8.73 \\ SF_4 &= (S_4)(F_5) = (0.37)(58.17) = 21.53 \end{aligned}$$

Comparing these quarterly forecasts with the actual demand values in the table, we see that they would seem to be relatively good forecast estimates, reflecting both the seasonal variations in the data and the general upward trend.

ALONG THE SUPPLY CHAIN

Demand Forecasting for Global Distribution at Zara

Zara is a subsidiary of the Inditex Group, one of the world's largest clothing retailers, that includes over 100 companies involved in textile design, manufacturing, and distribution. Zara is one of the world's most recognized and successful apparel retailers with more than 1,600 stores in 84 countries and annual revenues of over 6 billion euros. Its supply chain model involves frequent and rapid store changes with trendy fashion items provided at competitive prices. Within Zara's supply chain a continual flow of information from stores to designers conveys customer's changing tastes and instigates rapid orders for new designs from manufacturing suppliers.

Zara's supply chain includes four primary logistics platforms (warehouses and distribution centers) in Spain that receive finished clothing shipments from suppliers around the world and then ship items directly to stores around the world twice a week. The time between when orders are received at distribution centers to store delivery averages 24 hours in Europe and is less than 48 hours to U.S. and Asian stores. Individual store managers differentiate between major (S, M, and L) sizes and minor sizes (XXS, XXL, etc.), and when a store runs out of a major size for a clothing article it pulls all the item's inventory from the shelves and replaces it with a new article, so that customers won't be frustrated by wanting to buy an item that's not available in their size. The removed article may be returned to the store shelves if missing sizes can be shipped from warehouses, or the removed inventory may be transferred to another store where it is consolidated.

The challenge for Zara is to determine the exact number of units of each of eight sizes, of each of up to 3,000 items, to include in a shipment to each of its 1,500 stores. These order decisions, which across Zara's supply chain can reach several million each week, must be determined in a few hours after the store manager receives the relevant information including store inventory and the previous day's sales history. Any further delays can delay store replenishment by a day because of warehouse processing times and transportation schedules. Zara uses previous store shipment orders and past sales data to develop demand forecasts, which are combined with the current store and warehouse inventory to determine optimal shipment quantities that will maximize global sales. The demand forecasting model uses standard regression analysis to predict the upcoming weekly demand for each size of each article in each of Zara's stores.

As an apparel retailer, what are some of the unique supply chain forecasting factors that might affect Zara?

Sources: Based on Felipe Caro, Jeremie Gallien, Miguel Diaz, Javier Garcia, Jose Corredoira, Marcos Montes, Jose A. Ramos, and Juan Correa, "Zara Uses Operations Research to Reengineer Its Global Distribution Process," *Interfaces* 40, issue 1 (January–February 2010): pp. 71–84; and Zara website at www.zara.com.

Forecast Accuracy

A forecast is never completely accurate; forecasts will always deviate from the actual demand. This difference between the forecast and the actual is the **forecast error**. Although forecast error is inevitable, the objective of forecasting is that it be as slight as possible. A large degree of error may indicate that either the forecasting technique is the wrong one or it needs to be adjusted by changing its parameters (for example, α in the exponential smoothing forecast).

There are different measures of forecast error. We will discuss several of the more popular ones: mean absolute deviation (MAD), mean absolute percent deviation (MAPD), cumulative error, and average error or bias ($\overline{E}$).

MEAN ABSOLUTE DEVIATION

The **mean absolute deviation**, or **MAD**, is one of the most popular and simplest to use measures of forecast error. MAD is an average of the difference between the forecast and actual demand, as computed by the following formula:

$$\text{MAD} = \frac{\Sigma|D_t - F_t|}{n}$$

where

t = the period number

D_t = demand in period t

F_t = the forecast for period t

n = the total number of periods

$||$ = absolute value

EXAMPLE 12.7

MEASURING FORECASTING ACCURACY WITH MAD

In Examples 12.3, 12.4, and 12.5, forecasts were developed using exponential smoothing ($\alpha = 0.30$ and $\alpha = 0.50$), adjusted exponential smoothing ($\alpha = 0.50$, $\beta = 0.30$), and a linear trend line, respectively, for the demand data for HiTek Computer Services. The company wants to compare the accuracy of these different forecasts using MAD.

SOLUTION

We will compute MAD for all four forecasts; however, we will present the computational detail for the exponential smoothing forecast with $\alpha = 0.30$ only. The following table shows the values necessary to compute MAD for the exponential smoothing forecast:

Computational Values for MAD

Period	Demand, D_t	Forecast F_t ($\alpha_t = 0.30$)	Error (e_t) ($D_t - F_t$)	$\|D_t - F_t\|$
1	37	37.00	—	—
2	40	37.00	3.00	3.00
3	41	37.90	3.10	3.10
4	37	38.83	−1.83	1.83
5	45	38.28	6.72	6.72
6	50	40.29	9.69	9.69
7	43	43.20	−0.20	0.20
8	47	43.14	3.86	3.86
9	56	44.30	11.70	11.70
10	52	47.81	4.19	4.19
11	55	49.06	5.94	5.94
12	54	50.84	3.15	3.15
	557		49.32	53.38

[a]The computation of MAD will be based on 11 periods, periods 2 through 12, excluding the initial demand and forecast values for period 1 since they both equal 37.

Using the data in the table, MAD is computed as

$$\text{MAD} = \frac{\Sigma|D_t - F_t|}{n} = \frac{53.39}{11} = 4.85$$

The smaller the value of MAD, the more accurate the forecast, although viewed alone, MAD is difficult to assess. In this example, the data values were relatively small, and the MAD value of 4.85 should be judged accordingly. Overall, it would seem to be a "low" value; that is, the forecast appears to be relatively accurate. However, if the magnitude of the data values were in the thousands or millions, then a MAD value of a similar magnitude might not be bad, either. The point is, you cannot compare a MAD value of 4.85 with a MAD value of 485 and say the former is good and the latter is bad; they depend to a certain extent on the relative magnitude of the data.

One benefit of MAD is to compare the accuracy of several different forecasting techniques, as we are doing in this example. The MAD values for the remaining forecasts are as follows:

$$\text{Exponential smoothing}(\alpha = 0.50)\text{: MAD} = 4.04$$
$$\text{Adjusted exponential smoothing}(\alpha = 0.50, \beta = 0.30)\text{: MAD} = 3.81$$
$$\text{Linear trend line: MAD} = 2.29$$

Since the linear trend line has the lowest MAD value of 2.29, it would seem to be the most accurate, although it does not appear to be significantly better than the adjusted exponential smoothing forecast. Furthermore, we can deduce from these MAD values that increasing α from 0.30 to 0.50 enhanced the accuracy of the exponentially smoothed forecast. The adjusted forecast is even more accurate.

The **mean absolute percent deviation (MAPD)** measures the absolute error as a percentage of demand rather than per period. As a result, it eliminates the problem of interpreting the measure of accuracy relative to the magnitude of the demand and forecast values, as MAD does. The mean absolute percent deviation is computed according to the following formula:

$$\text{MAPD} = \frac{\Sigma|D_t - F_t|}{\Sigma D_t}$$

Using the data from the table in Example 12.7 for the exponential smoothing forecast ($\alpha = 0.30$) for HiTek Computer Services, we find

$$\text{MAPD} = \frac{53.39}{557} = 0.096 \text{ or } 9.6\%$$

A lower percent deviation implies a more accurate forecast. The MAPD values for our other three forecasts are

$$\text{Exponential smoothing}(\alpha = 0.50)\text{: MAPD} = 7.9\%$$
$$\text{Adjusted exponential smoothing}(\alpha = 0.50, \beta = 0.30)\text{: MAPD} = 7.5\%$$
$$\text{Linear trend line: MAPD} = 4.9\%$$

CUMULATIVE ERROR

Cumulative error is computed simply by summing the forecast errors, as shown in the following formula.

$$E = \Sigma e_t$$

A large positive value indicates that the forecast is probably consistently lower than the actual demand, or is biased low. A large negative value implies that the forecast is consistently higher than actual demand, or is biased high. Also, when the errors for each period are scrutinized, a preponderance of positive values shows the forecast is consistently less than the actual value and vice versa.

The cumulative error for the exponential smoothing forecast ($\alpha = 0.30$) for HiTek Computer Services can be read directly from the table in Example 12.7; it is simply the sum of the values in the "Error" column:

$$E = \Sigma e_t$$
$$= 49.31$$

This large positive error for cumulative error, plus the fact that the individual errors for all but two of the periods in the table are positive, indicates that this forecast is consistently below the actual demand. A quick glance back at the plot of the exponential smoothing ($\alpha = 0.30$) forecast in Example 12.3 visually verifies this result.

The cumulative error for the other forecasts are

$$\text{Exponential smoothing } (\alpha = 0.50){:}\ E = 33.21$$

$$\text{Adjusted exponential smoothing } (\alpha = 0.50, \beta = 0.30){:}\ E = 21.14$$

We did not show the cumulative error for the linear trend line. E will always be near zero for the linear trend line.

A measure closely related to cumulative error is the **average error**, or *bias*. It is computed by averaging the cumulative error over the number of time periods:

$$\bar{E} = \frac{\Sigma e_t}{n}$$

For example, the average error for the exponential smoothing forecast ($\alpha = 0.30$) is computed as follows. (Notice a value of 11 was used for n, since we used actual demand for the first-period forecast, resulting in no error, that is, $D_1 = F_1 = 37$.)

$$\bar{E} = \frac{49.32}{11} = 4.48$$

The average error is interpreted similarly to the cumulative error. A positive value indicates low bias, and a negative value indicates high bias. A value close to zero implies a lack of bias.

Table 12.1 summarizes the measures of forecast accuracy we have discussed in this section for the four example forecasts we developed in Examples 12.3, 12.4, and 12.5 for HiTek Computer Services. The results are consistent for all four forecasts, indicating that for the HiTek Computer Services example data, a larger value of α is preferable for the exponential smoothing forecast. The adjusted forecast is

TABLE 12.1 Comparison of Forecasts for HiTek Computer Services

Forecast	MAD	MAPD	E	$\bar{E}$
Exponential smoothing ($\alpha = 0.30$)	4.85	9.6%	49.31	4.48
Exponential smoothing ($\alpha = 0.50$)	4.04	8.5%	33.21	3.02
Adjusted exponential smoothing ($\alpha = 0.50, \beta = 0.30$)	3.81	7.5%	21.14	1.92
Linear trend line	2.29	4.9%	—	—

more accurate than the exponential smoothing forecasts, and the linear trend is more accurate than all the others. Although these results are for specific examples, they indicate how the different forecast measures for accuracy can be used to adjust a forecasting method or select the best method.

FORECAST CONTROL

There are several ways to monitor forecast error over time to make sure that the forecast is performing correctly—that is, the forecast is in control. Forecasts can go "out of control" and start providing inaccurate forecasts for several reasons, including a change in trend, the unanticipated appearance of a cycle, or an irregular variation such as unseasonable weather, a promotional campaign, new competition, or a political event that distracts consumers.

A **tracking signal** indicates if the forecast is consistently biased high or low. It is computed by dividing the cumulative error by MAD, according to the formula

$$\text{Tracking signal} = \frac{\Sigma(D_t - F_t)}{\text{MAD}} = \frac{E}{\text{MAD}}$$

The tracking signal is recomputed each period, with updated, "running" values of cumulative error and MAD. The movement of the tracking signal is compared to *control limits*: as long as the tracking signal is within these limits, the forecast is in control.

Typically, forecast errors are normally distributed, which results in the following relationship between MAD and the standard deviation of the distribution of error, σ:

$$1 \text{ MAD} \cong 0.8\sigma$$

This enables us to establish statistical control limits for the tracking signal that correspond to the more familiar normal distribution. For example, statistical control limits of ± 3 standard deviations, corresponding to 99.7% of the errors, would translate to ± 3.75 MADs; that is, $3\sigma \div 0.8 = 3.75$ MADs. Control limits of ± 2 to ± 5 MADs are used most frequently.

EXAMPLE 12.8

DEVELOPING A TRACKING SIGNAL

In Example 12.7, the mean absolute deviation was computed for the exponential smoothing forecast ($\alpha = 0.30$) for HiTek Computer Services. Using a tracking signal, monitor the forecast accuracy using control limits of ± 3 MADs.

SOLUTION

To use the tracking signal, we must recompute MAD each period as the cumulative error is computed.

Using MAD = 3.00, we find that the tracking signal for period 2 is

$$TS_2 = \frac{E}{\text{MAD}} = \frac{3.00}{3.00} = 1.00$$

The tracking signal for period 3 is

$$TS_3 = \frac{6.10}{3.05} = 2.00$$

(*Continued*)

The remaining tracking signal values are shown in the following table:

Tracking Signal Values

Period	Demand, D_t	Forecast, F_t	Error, $D_t - F_i$	$E = \Sigma(D_t - F_i)$	MAD	Tracking Signal
1	37	37.00	—	—	—	—
2	40	37.00	3.00	3.00	3.00	1.00
3	41	37.90	3.10	6.10	3.05	2.00
4	37	38.83	−1.83	4.27	2.64	1.62
5	45	38.28	6.72	10.99	3.66	3.00
6	50	40.29	9.69	20.68	4.87	4.25
7	43	43.20	−0.20	20.48	4.09	5.01
8	47	43.14	3.86	24.34	4.06	6.00
9	56	44.30	11.70	36.04	5.01	7.19
10	52	47.81	4.19	40.23	4.92	8.18
11	55	49.06	5.94	46.17	5.02	9.20
12	54	50.84	3.15	49.32	4.85	10.17

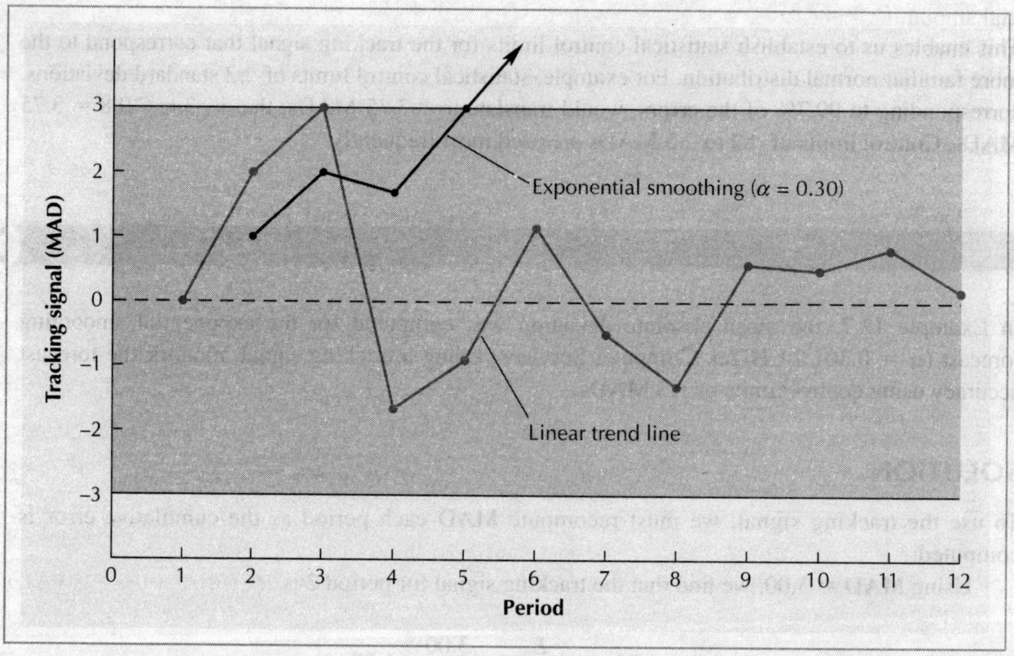

The tracking signal values in the table above move outside ±3 MAD control limits (i.e., ±3.00) in period 5 *and* continue increasing. This suggests that the forecast is not performing accurately or, more precisely, is consistently biased low (i.e., actual demand consistently exceeds the forecast). This is illustrated in the graph. Notice that the tracking signal moves beyond the upper limit of 3 following period 5 and continues to rise. For the sake of comparison, the tracking signal for the linear trend line forecast computed in Example 12.5 is also plotted on this graph.

Notice that it remains within the limits (touching the upper limit in period 3), indicating a lack of consistent bias.

Another method for monitoring forecast error is statistical control charts. For example, $\pm 3\sigma$ control limits would reflect 99.7% of the forecast errors (assuming they are normally distributed). The sample standard deviation, σ, is computed as

$$\sigma = \sqrt{\frac{\Sigma(D_t - F_t)^2}{n-1}}$$

This formula without the square root is known as the **mean squared error (MSE)**, and it is sometimes used as a measure of forecast error. It reacts to forecast error much as MAD does. (For our Example 12.8, MSE = 37.57.)

EXAMPLE 12.9

FORECAST ERROR WITH STATISTICAL CONTROL CHARTS

Using the same example for the exponential smoothing forecast ($\alpha = 0.30$) for HiTek Computer Services as in Example 12.8, we compute the standard deviation as

$$\sigma = \sqrt{\frac{375.61}{10}} = 6.13$$

Using this value of σ we can compute statistical control limits for forecast errors for our exponential smoothing forecast ($\alpha = 0.30$) example for HiTek Computer Services. Plus or minus 3σ control limits, reflecting 99.7% of the forecast errors, gives $\pm 3(6.13)$, or ± 18.39. Although it can be observed from the table in Example 12.8 that all the error values are within the control limits, we can still detect that most of the errors are positive, indicating a low bias in the forecast estimates. This is illustrated in the following graph of the control chart with the errors plotted on it.

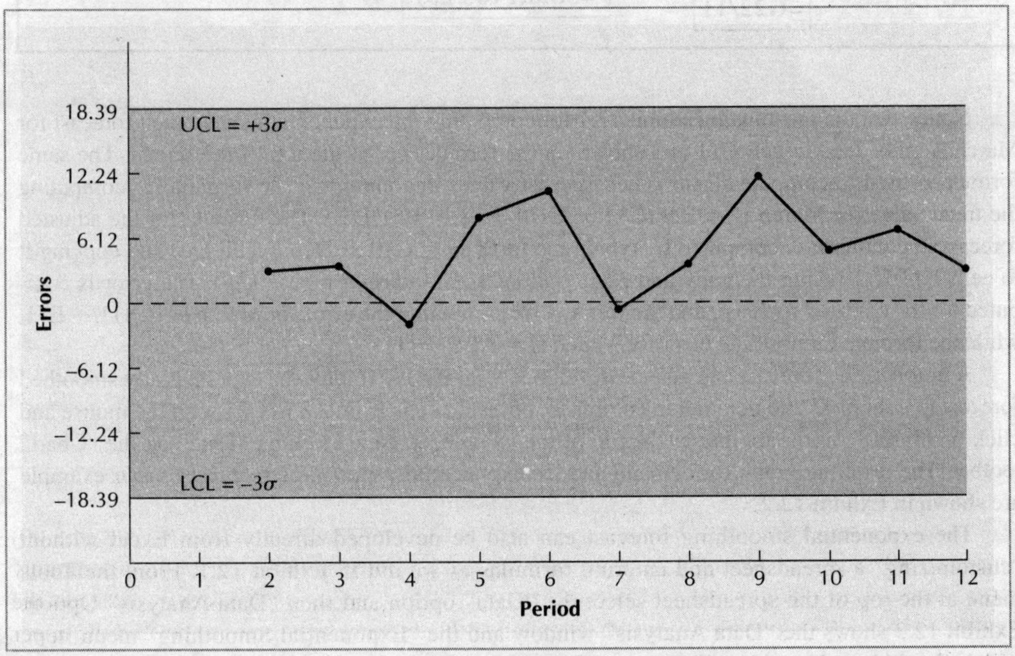

Time Series Forecasting Using Excel

Excel can be used to develop forecasts using the moving average, exponential smoothing, adjusted exponential smoothing, and linear trend line techniques. Various surveys of companies across different industries that use forecasting, show that over half use Excel spreadsheets for forecasting, and most use a variety of different forecasting software packages.

First we will demonstrate how to determine exponentially smoothed and adjusted exponentially smoothed forecasts using Excel, as shown in Exhibit 12.1. We will demonstrate Excel using Examples 12.3 and 12.4 for forecasting demand at HiTek Computer Services, including the Excel spreadsheets showing the exponentially smoothed forecast with $\alpha = 0.5$ and the adjusted exponentially smoothed forecast with $\beta = 0.3$. We have also computed the values for MAD, MAPD, and E.

EXHIBIT 12.1 **EXCEL FILE**

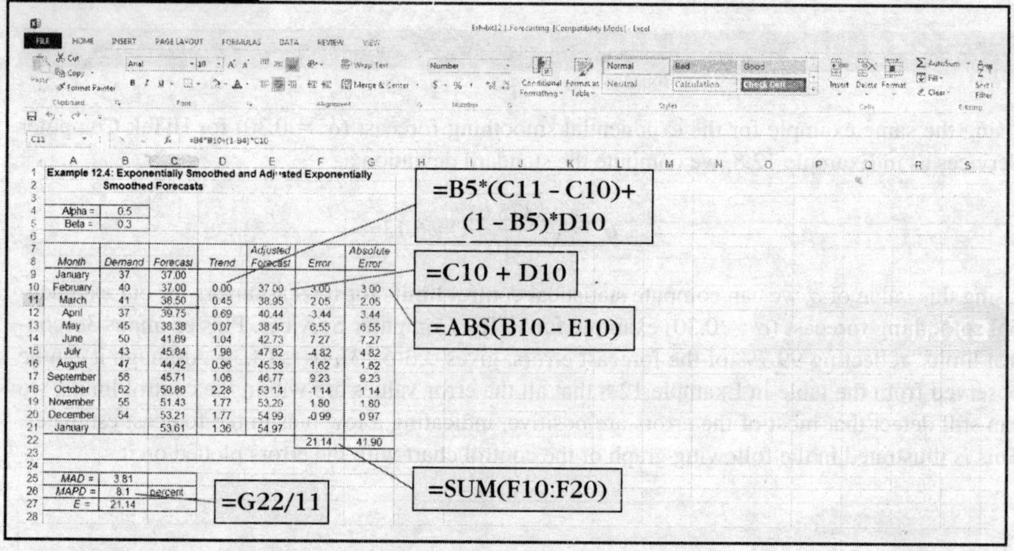

Notice that the formula in Exhibit 12.1 for computing the exponentially smoothed forecast for March is embedded in cell C11 and shown on the formula bar at the top of the screen. The same formula is used to compute all the other forecast values in column C. The formula for computing the trend value for March is = B5*(C11 − C10) + (1 − B5)*D10. The formula for the adjusted forecast in column E is computed by typing the formula = C10 + D10 in cell E10 and copying it to cells E11:E21 (using the copy and paste options from the right mouse key). The error is computed for the adjusted forecast, and the formula for computing the error for March is = B11 − E11, while the formula for absolute error for March is = ABS (F11).

A graph of the forecast can also be developed with Excel. To plot the exponentially smoothed forecast in column C and demand in column B, cover all cells from A8 to C21 with the mouse and click on "Insert" on the toolbar at the top of the worksheet. Next click on "Line" on the "Chart" toolbar. The resulting graph for demand and the exponentially smoothed forecast for our example are shown in Exhibit 12.2.

The exponential smoothing forecast can also be developed directly from Excel without "customizing" a spreadsheet and entering formulas as we did in Exhibit 12.1. From the Tools menu at the top of the spreadsheet select the "Data" option and then "Data Analysis" Option. Exhibit 12.3 shows the "Data Analysis" window and the "Exponential Smoothing" menu item, which should be selected by clicking on "OK." The resulting "Exponential Smoothing" window is shown in Exhibit 12.4. The "input range" includes the demand values in column B in Exhibit

EXCEL FILE

EXHIBIT 12.2

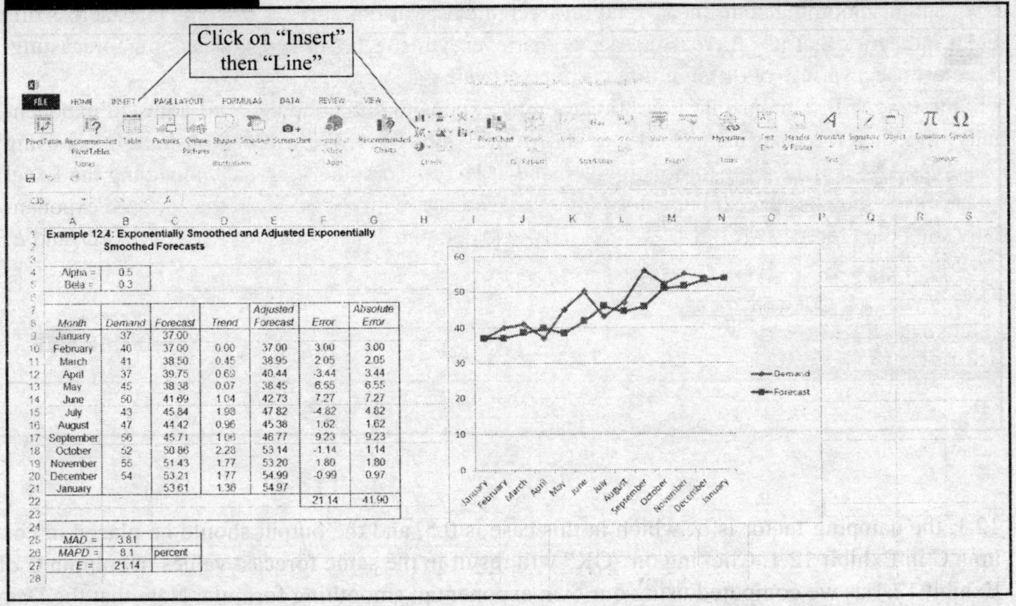

EXHIBIT 12.3

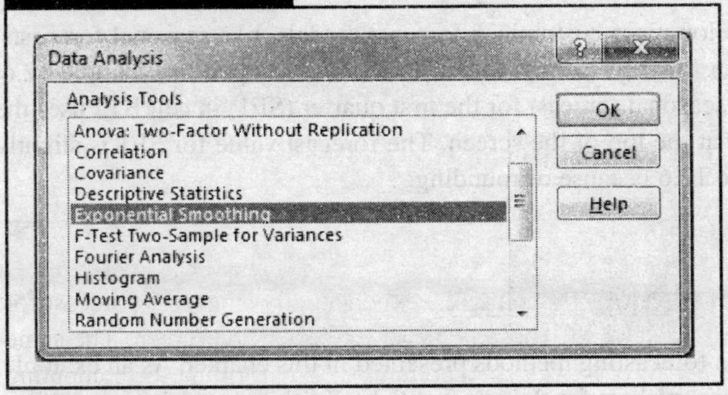

EXHIBIT 12.4

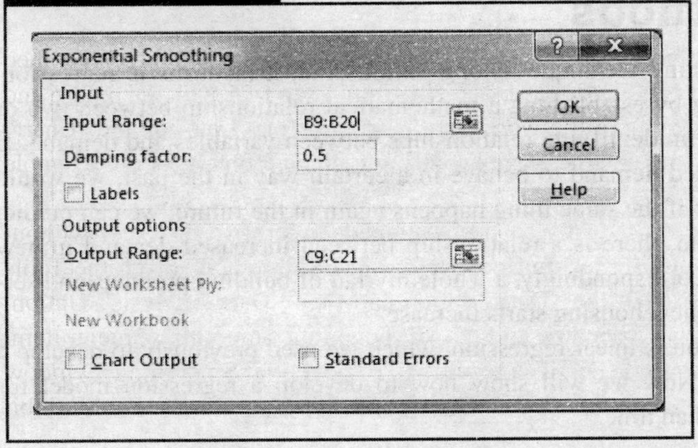

EXHIBIT 12.5 **EXCEL FILE**

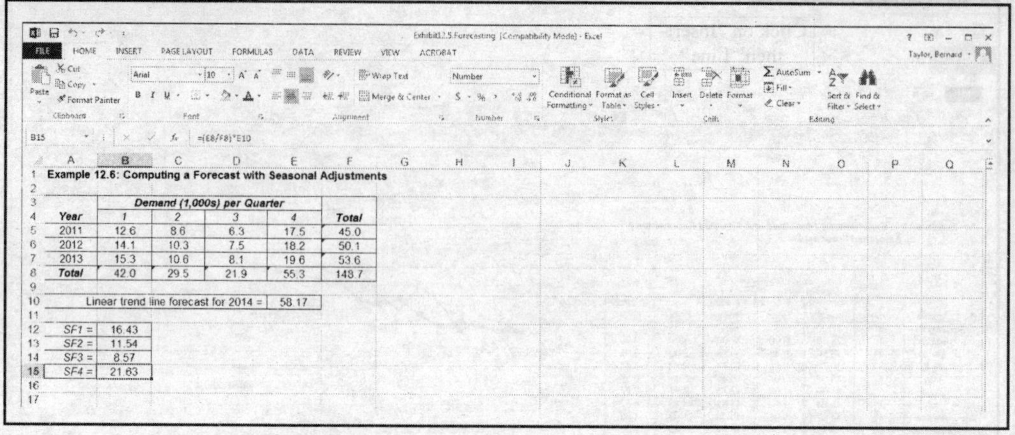

12.1, the damping factor is α, which in this case is 0.5, and the output should be placed in column C in Exhibit 12.1. Clicking on "OK" will result in the same forecast values in column C of Exhibit 12.1 as we computed using our own exponential smoothing formula. Note that the Data Analysis group of analysis tools does not have an adjusted exponential smoothing selection; that is one reason we developed our own customized spreadsheet in Exhibit 12.1. The "Data Analysis" tools also have a moving average menu item that you can use to compute a moving average forecast.

Excel can also be used to develop more customized forecast models, like seasonal forecasts. Exhibit 12.5 shows an Excel screen for the seasonal forecast model developed in Example 12.6. Notice that the computation of the seasonal forecast for the first quarter (SF1) in cell B12 uses the formula shown on the formula bar at the top of the screen. The forecast value for SF1 is slightly different from the value in Example 12.6 because of rounding.

FORECASTING WITH OM TOOLS

OM Tools has modules for all of the forecasting methods presented in this chapter. As an example, Exhibit 12.6 shows the OM Tools spreadsheet for the exponential smoothing model (α = 0.30) in Example 12.3.

Regression Methods

The second most popular forecasting technique among various industrial firms is regression. Regression is used for forecasting by establishing a mathematical relationship between two or more variables. We are interested in identifying relationships between variables and demand. If we know that something has caused demand to behave in a certain way in the past, we would like to identify that relationship so if the same thing happens again in the future, we can predict what demand will be. For example, there is a relationship between increased demand in new housing and lower interest rates. Correspondingly, a whole myriad of building products and services display increased demand if new housing starts increase.

The simplest form of regression is linear regression, which we used previously to develop a linear trend line for forecasting. Now we will show how to develop a regression model for variables related to demand other than time.

EXHIBIT 12.6 OM TOOLS

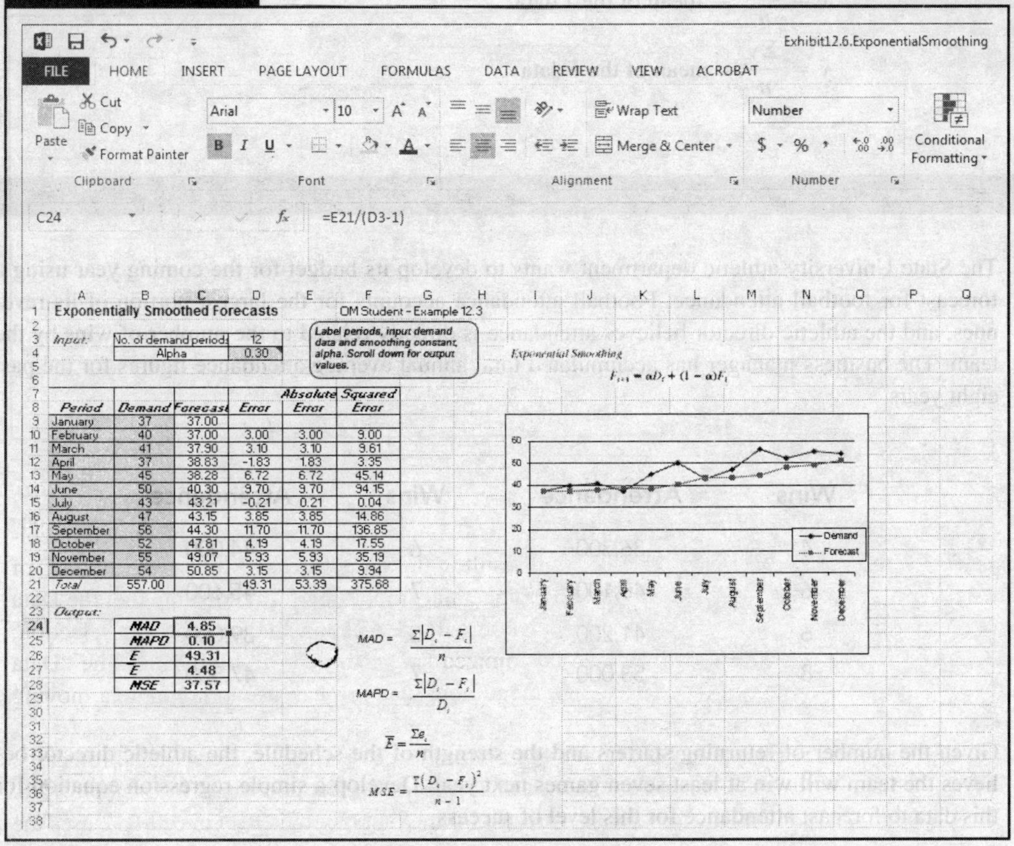

Period	Demand	Forecast	Error	Absolute Error	Squared Error
January	37	37.00			
February	40	37.00	3.00	3.00	9.00
March	41	37.90	3.10	3.10	9.61
April	37	38.83	-1.83	1.83	3.35
May	45	38.28	6.72	6.72	45.14
June	50	40.30	9.70	9.70	94.15
July	43	43.21	-0.21	0.21	0.04
August	47	43.15	3.85	3.85	14.86
September	56	44.30	11.70	11.70	136.85
October	52	47.81	4.19	4.19	17.55
November	55	49.07	5.93	5.93	35.19
December	54	50.85	3.15	3.15	9.94
Total	557.00		49.31	53.39	375.68

$$F_{t+1} = \alpha D_t + (1-\alpha)F_t$$

$$MAD = \frac{\Sigma|D_t - F_t|}{n} \qquad MAPD = \frac{\Sigma|D_t - F_t|}{D_t} \qquad \bar{E} = \frac{\Sigma e_t}{n} \qquad MSE = \frac{\Sigma(D_t - F_t)^2}{n-1}$$

LINEAR REGRESSION

Linear regression is a mathematical technique that relates one variable, called an *independent variable*, to another, the *dependent variable*, in the form of an equation for a straight line. A linear equation has the following general form:

$$y = a + bx$$

where

- y = the dependent variable
- a = the intercept
- b = the slope of the line
- x = the independent variable

Because we want to use linear regression as a forecasting model for demand, the dependent variable, y, represents demand, and x is an independent variable that causes demand to behave in a linear manner.

To develop the linear equation, the slope, b, and the intercept, a, must first be computed using the following least squares formulas:

$$a = \bar{y} - b\bar{x}$$

$$b = \frac{\Sigma xy - n\bar{x}\bar{y}}{\Sigma x^2 - n\bar{x}^2}$$

where

$$\bar{x} = \frac{\Sigma x}{n} = \text{mean of the } x \text{ data}$$

$$\bar{y} = \frac{\Sigma y}{n} = \text{mean of the } y \text{ data}$$

EXAMPLE 12.10

DEVELOPING A LINEAR REGRESSION FORECAST

The State University athletic department wants to develop its budget for the coming year using a forecast for football attendance. Football attendance accounts for the largest portion of its revenues, and the athletic director believes attendance is directly related to the number of wins by the team. The business manager has accumulated total annual average attendance figures for the past eight years.

Wins	Attendance	Wins	Attendance
4	36,300	6	44,000
6	40,100	7	45,600
6	41,200	5	39,000
8	53,000	7	47,500

Given the number of returning starters and the strength of the schedule, the athletic director believes the team will win at least seven games next year. Develop a simple regression equation for this data to forecast attendance for this level of success.

SOLUTION

The computations necessary to compute a and b using the least squares formulas are summarized in the accompanying table. (Note that y is given in 1,000s to make manual computation easier.)

Least Squares Computations

x (Wins)	y (Attendance, 1,000s)	xy	x^2
4	36.3	145.2	16
6	40.1	240.6	36
6	41.2	247.2	36
8	53.0	424.0	64
6	44.0	264.0	36
7	45.6	319.2	49
5	39.0	195.0	25
7	47.5	332.5	49
49	346.9	2,167.7	311

$$\bar{x} = \frac{49}{8} = 6.125$$

$$\bar{y} = \frac{346.9}{8} = 43.36$$

$$b = \frac{\Sigma xy - n\bar{x}\bar{y}}{\Sigma x^2 - n\bar{x}^2}$$

$$= \frac{(2167.7) - (8)(6.125)(43.36)}{(311) - (8)(6.125)^2}$$

$$= 4.06$$

$$a = \bar{y} - b\bar{x}$$

$$= 43.36 - (4.06)(6.125)$$

$$= 18.46$$

Substituting these values for a and b into the linear equation line, we have

$$y = 18.46 + 4.06x$$

Thus, for $x = 7$ (wins), the forecast for attendance is

$$y = 18.46 + 4.06(7)$$

$$= 46.88, \text{ or } 46{,}880$$

The data points with the regression line are shown in the following figure. Observing the regression line relative to the data points, it would appear that the data follow a distinct upward linear trend, which would indicate that the forecast should be relatively accurate. In fact, the MAD value for this forecasting model is 1.41, which suggests an accurate forecast.

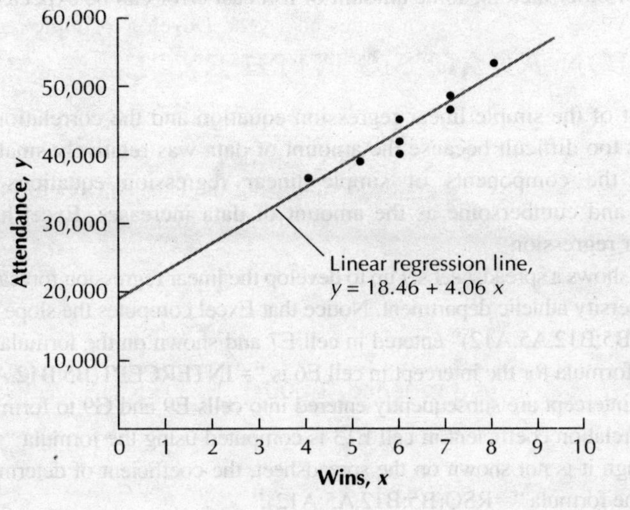

CORRELATION

Correlation in a linear regression equation is a measure of the strength of the relationship between the independent and dependent variables. The formula for the correlation coefficient is

$$r = \frac{n\Sigma xy - \Sigma x \Sigma y}{\sqrt{[n\Sigma x^2 - (\Sigma x)^2][n\Sigma y^2 - (\Sigma y)^2]}}$$

The value of r varies between -1.00 and $+1.00$, with a value of $+1.00$ indicating a strong linear relationship between the variables. If $r = 1.00$, then an increase in the independent variable will result in a corresponding linear increase in the dependent variable. If $r = -1.00$, an increase in the dependent variable will result in a linear decrease in the dependent variable. A value of r near zero implies that there is little or no linear relationship between variables.

We can determine the correlation coefficient for the linear regression equation determined in Example 12.9 by substituting most of the terms calculated for the least squares formula (except for Σy^2) into the formula for r:

$$r = \frac{(8)(2167.7) - (49)(346.9)}{\sqrt{[(8)(311) - (49)^2][(8)(15{,}224.7) - (346.9)^2]}}$$

$$= 0.947$$

This value for the correlation coefficient is very close to 1.00, indicating a strong linear relationship between the number of wins and home attendance.

Another measure of the strength of the relationship between the variables in a linear regression equation is the **coefficient of determination**. It is computed by squaring the value of r. It indicates the percentage of the variation in the dependent variable that is a result of the behavior of the independent variable. For our example, $r = 0.947$; thus, the coefficient of determination is

$$r^2 = (0.947)^2$$

$$= 0.897$$

This value for the coefficient of determination means that 89.7% of the amount of variation in attendance can be attributed to the number of wins by the team (with the remaining 10.3% due to other unexplained factors, such as weather, a good or poor start, or publicity). A value of 1.00 (or 100%) would indicate that attendance depends totally on wins. However, since 10.3% of the variation is a result of other factors, some amount of forecast error can be expected.

REGRESSION ANALYSIS WITH EXCEL

The development of the simple linear regression equation and the correlation coefficient for our example was not too difficult because the amount of data was relatively small. However, manual computation of the components of simple linear regression equations can become very time-consuming and cumbersome as the amount of data increases. Excel has the capability of performing linear regression.

Exhibit 12.7 shows a spreadsheet set up to develop the linear regression forecast for Example 12.10 for the State University athletic department. Notice that Excel computes the slope directly with the formula "=SLOPE(B5:B12,A5:A12)" entered in cell E7 and shown on the formula bar at the top of the spreadsheet. The formula for the intercept in cell E6 is "=INTERCEPT(B5:B12,A5:A12)." The values for the slope and intercept are subsequently entered into cells E9 and G9 to form the linear regression equation. The correlation coefficient in cell E13 is computed using the formula "=CORREL(B5:B12, A5:A12)." Although it is not shown on the spreadsheet, the coefficient of determination (r^2) could be computed using the formula "=RSQ(B5:B12,A5:A12)."

A linear regression forecast can also be developed directly with Excel using the "Data Analysis" option from the Tools menu we accessed previously to develop an exponentially smoothed forecast. Exhibit 12.8 shows the selection of "Regression" from the Data Analysis menu, and Exhibit 12.9 shows the Regression window. We first enter the cells from Exhibit 12.7 that include the y values (for attendance), B5:B12. Next enter the x value cells, A5:A12. The output range is the location on the spreadsheet where you want to put the output results. This range needs to be large (18 cells by 9 cells) and not overlap with anything else on the spreadsheet. Clicking on "OK" will result in the spreadsheet shown in Exhibit 12.10. (Note that the "Summary Output" has been slightly moved around so that all the results could be included on the screen in Exhibit 12.9.)

EXCEL FILE

EXHIBIT 12.7

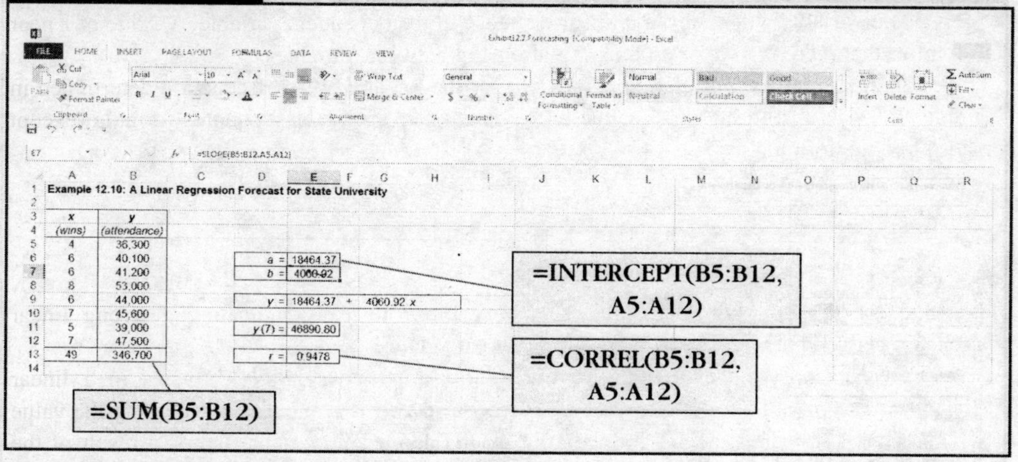

EXHIBIT 12.8

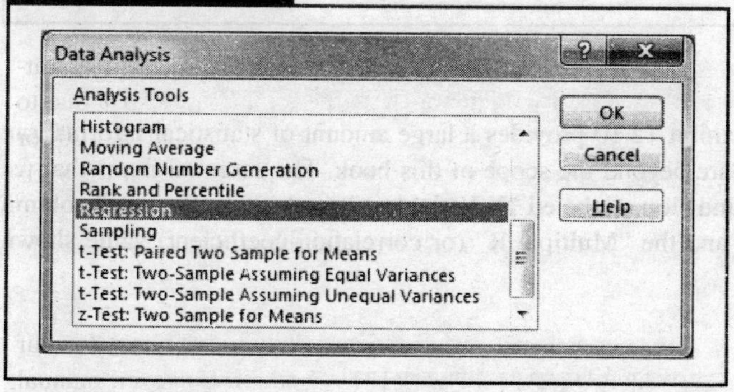

EXHIBIT 12.9

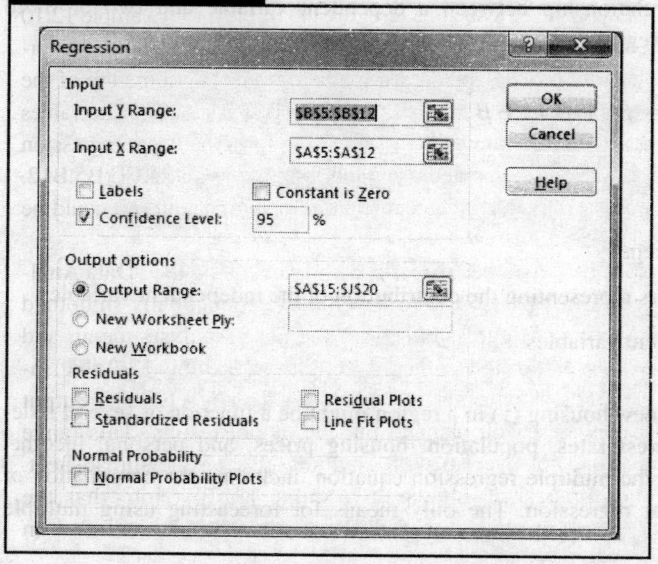

EXHIBIT 12.10

EXCEL FILE

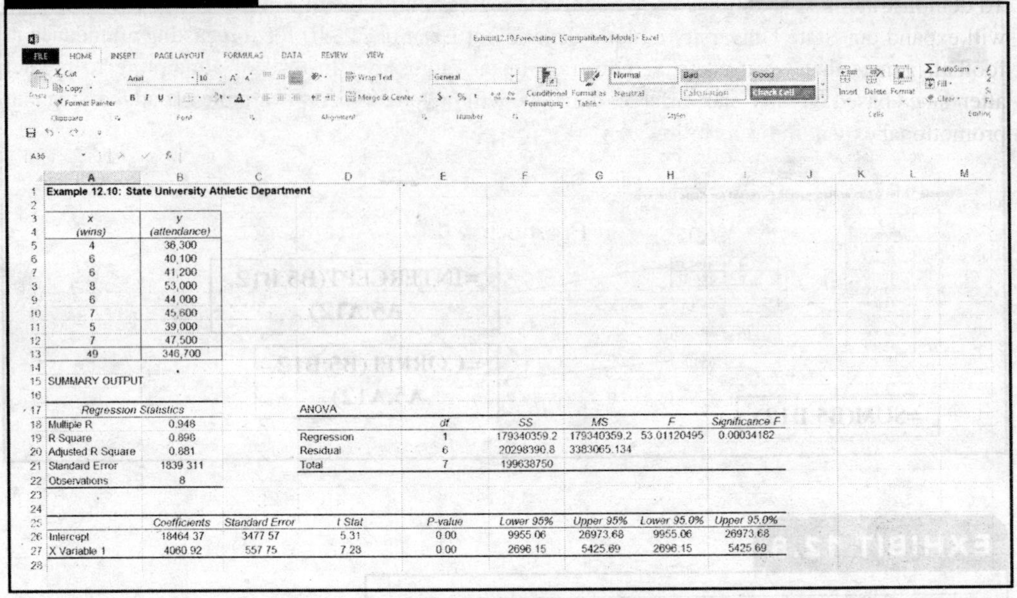

Example 12.10: State University Athletic Department

x (wins)	y (attendance)
4	36,300
6	40,100
6	41,200
8	53,000
6	44,000
7	45,600
5	39,000
7	47,500
49	346,700

SUMMARY OUTPUT

Regression Statistics	
Multiple R	0.948
R Square	0.898
Adjusted R Square	0.881
Standard Error	1839.311
Observations	8

ANOVA

	df	*SS*	*MS*	*F*	*Significance F*
Regression	1	179340359.2	179340359.2	53.01120495	0.00034182
Residual	6	20298390.8	3383065.134		
Total	7	199638750			

	Coefficients	*Standard Error*	*t Stat*	*P-value*	*Lower 95%*	*Upper 95%*	*Lower 95.0%*	*Upper 95.0%*
Intercept	18464.37	3477.57	5.31	0.00	9955.06	26973.68	9955.06	26973.68
X Variable 1	4060.92	557.75	7.28	0.00	2696.15	5425.69	2696.15	5425.69

The "Summary Output" in Exhibit 12.10 provides a large amount of statistical information, the explanation and use of which are beyond the scope of this book. The essential items that we are interested in are the intercept and slope (labeled "X Variable 1") in the "Coefficients" column at the bottom of the spreadsheet, and the "Multiple R" (or correlation coefficient) value shown under "Regression Statistics."

MULTIPLE REGRESSION WITH EXCEL

Another causal method of forecasting is **multiple regression**, a more powerful extension of linear regression. Linear regression relates demand to one other independent variable, whereas multiple regression reflects the relationship between a dependent variable and two or more independent variables. A multiple regression model has the following general form:

$$y = \beta_0 + \beta_1 x_1 + \beta_2 x_2 + \dots + \beta_k x_k$$

where

β_0 = the intercept

$\beta_1, \dots, \beta_k$ = parameters representing the contribution of the independent variables

$x_1, \dots, x_k$ = independent variables

For example, the demand for new housing (y) in a region might be a function of several independent variables, including interest rates, population, housing prices, and personal income. Development and computation of the multiple regression equation, including the compilation of data, is more complex than linear regression. The only means for forecasting using multiple regression is with a computer.

EXAMPLE 12.11

DEVELOPING A MULTIPLE REGRESSION FORECAST WITH EXCEL

To demonstrate the capability to solve multiple regression problems with Excel spreadsheets, we will expand our State University athletic department Example 12.10 for forecasting attendance at football games that we used to demonstrate linear regression. Instead of attempting to predict attendance based on only one variable, wins, we will include a second variable for advertising and promotional expenditures as follows:

Wins	Promotion ($)	Attendance
4	29,500	36,300
6	55,700	40,100
6	71,300	41,200
8	87,000	53,000
6	75,000	44,000
7	72,000	45,600
5	55,300	39,000
7	81,600	47,500

We will use the "Data Analysis" option (add-in) from the Tools menu at the top of the spreadsheet that we used in the previous section to develop our linear regression equation, and then the "Regression" option from the "Data Analysis" menu. The resulting spreadsheet with the multiple regression statistics is shown in Exhibit 12.11.

SOLUTION

Note that the data must be set up on the spreadsheet so that the two x variables are in adjacent columns (in this case A and B). Then we enter the "Input X Range" as **A4:B12** as shown in Exhibit 12.12.

The regression coefficients for our x variables, wins and promotion, are shown in cells B27 and B28. Thus, the multiple regression equation is formulated as

$$y = 19{,}094.42 + 3{,}560.99x_1 + 0.0368x_2$$

This equation can now be used to forecast attendance based on both projected football wins and promotional expenditure. For example, if the athletic department expects the team to win seven games and plans to spend $60,000 on promotion and advertising, the forecasted attendance is

$$\begin{aligned} y &= 19{,}094.42 + 3{,}560.99(7) + 0.0368(60{,}000) \\ &= 46{,}229.35 \end{aligned}$$

If the promotional expenditure is held constant, every win will increase attendance by 3,560.99, whereas if the wins are held constant, every $1,000 of advertising spent will increase attendance by 36.8 fans. This would seem to suggest that the number of wins has a more significant impact on attendance than promotional expenditures.

r^2, the coefficient of determination shown in cell B19, is 0.900, which suggests that 90% of the amount of variation in attendance can be attributed to the number of wins and the promotional expenditures. However, as we have already noted, the number of wins would probably appear to account for a larger part of the variation in attendance.

EXHIBIT 12.11

EXCEL FILE

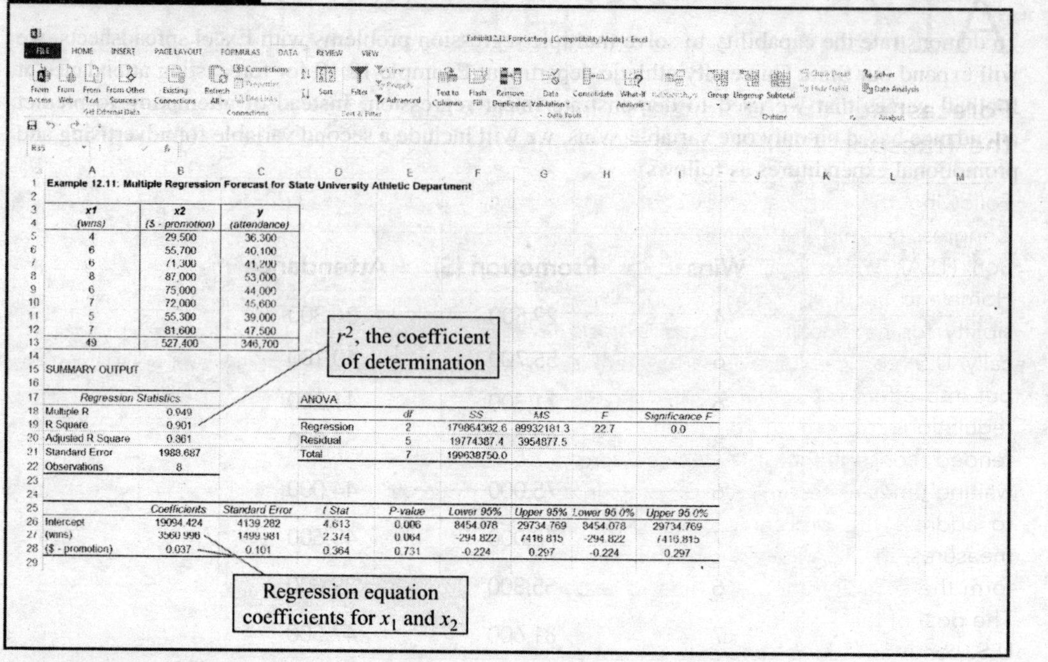

EXHIBIT 12.12

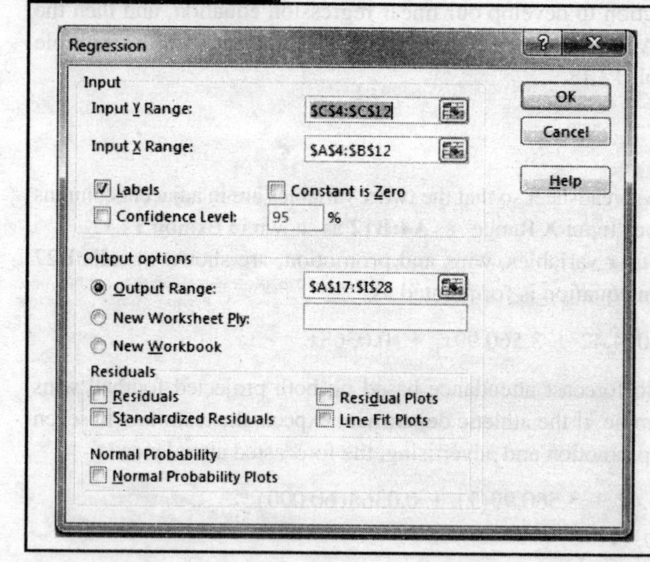

A problem often encountered in multiple regression is *multicollinearity,* or the amount of "overlapping" information about the dependent variable that is provided by several independent variables. This problem usually occurs when the independent variables are highly correlated, as in this example, in which wins and promotional expenditures are both positively correlated (i.e., more wins coincide with higher promotional expenditures and vice versa). (Possibly the athletic department increased promotional expenditures when it thought it would have a better team that would achieve more wins.) The topic of multicollinearity and how to cope with it is beyond the scope of this book and this brief section on multiple regression; however, most statistics textbooks discuss this topic in detail.

ALONG THE SUPPLY CHAIN

Forecasting Airport Security Gate Arrivals at the Transportation Security Administration

Following the terrorist attacks of September 11, 2001, Congress created the Transportation Security Administration (TSA), which became part of the Department of Homeland Security in March, 2003. The TSA has responsibility for national transportation security and, specifically, U.S. commercial aviation system security. The TSA put into effect a number of procedures, processes, and regulations to safeguard against terrorism, the unintended consequences of which were long lines and waiting times at security checkpoints in airports. In order to address the problems created by the new security measures, the TSA joined with the commercial airlines to form the U.S. Commercial Aviation Partnership (USCAP). The goal of this partnership was to maintain the health of U.S. commercial aviation while ensuring that security requirements were implemented efficiently and effectively. To achieve this goal, USCAP used their technical professionals to develop mathematical models to analyze, define, and predict the operational and economic effects of air travel security measures. The key component of this modeling effort was a model to forecast air travel passenger demand.

Previously most air travel forecasting models focused on long-term trends with time horizons of 5 to 20 years, which weren't effective for making near-term tactical decisions and reflecting the immediate impact of security policies. The model developed by USCAP used multiple regression to forecast passenger demand based on six causal factors: the economy (reflected by U.S. gross domestic product); ticket prices (represented by the average fare for a 1,000-mile trip); travel time (from door-to-door); fear (represented by the reduction in plane boardings due to an event causing fear); a hassle factor (created by the reduction in plane boardings due to an event causing hassle); and an operations factor (resulting from a reduction in plane boardings due to a reduction in operations caused by an event). A detailed regression analysis solver tool with special capabilities was developed for this model. The forecasting model was subsequently used as the basis for other analytical models to explore numerous questions concerning airport security procedures such as staffing for security screening, the number of screening lanes at airports, security processing times, security credentials for employees, and what-if? analyses of proposed security measures such as passenger security fees. The immediate financial savings of the models developed by USCAP, in addition to improved security procedures, were in the tens of billions of dollars with an estimated 20-year impact of over $100 billion.

Explain how you think the multiple regression forecasting results might be used to determine answers to the "what-if" questions; for example, how many screening lanes to open?

Source: Based on: R. Peterson, R. Bittel, C. Forgie, W. Lee and J. Nestor, "Using USCAP's Analytical Models, the Transportation Security Administration Balances the Impacts of Aviation Security Policies on Passengers and Airlines," *Interfaces* 37, issue 1 (January–February 2007): pp. 52–67.

Data Mining

At one time, business forecasters typically did not have enough data to develop accurate forecasts; however, that's no longer a problem. In fact, the situation is just the opposite—businesses are overwhelmed with data. Data are collected wherever and whenever a customer swipes a credit card or accesses a website, or a company employee scans a box or a pallet in a warehouse or goods on a store shelf. It is estimated that all the data in databases in the world double in less than every two years. In addition, large, inexpensive storage devises make it possible for companies to store this explosion of data. Thus, the problem for forecasters is no longer having enough data, it's how to use the huge amount of data they now have for forecasting purposes. Data mining helps forecasters use this wealth of data to develop useful forecasts.

USES FOR DATA MINING

Data mining is a process of exploring, categorizing, and modeling large amounts of data in order to identify meaningful, logical patterns and relationships among key variables. It is used to discover trends, predict future events, and assess possible courses of action. For example, police can use data mining to predict when and where crimes might occur; weather analysts use data mining to discover weather patterns and make forecasts; utility companies use data mining to forecast energy consumption under different weather conditions in different geographic regions; hotels can use data mining to determine returning customers' preferences. Data mining allows companies to search for useful information such as patterns or trends that might be useful for forecasting—for example, to determine if certain products are sold together, if events trigger the sale of certain products, or, if more of a product is sold in a certain geographic region. Data mining can help companies like Amazon or Barnes & Noble determine what types of books or music various groups of customers categorized by such things as age, gender, income, or location might prefer; or help denim jeans companies identify fashion trends as described in the introduction to this chapter.

Data mining for business forecasting purposes is different from time series and regression methods. In these traditional forecasting methods forecasters first attempt to determine if there is a pattern in the demand data such as a trend or seasonality, and then find the forecasting model (i.e., exponential smoothing, weighted average, regression, etc.) that best fits the data pattern. When they find a model that reflects the data, they use it to forecast future demand. The opposite happens with data mining; forecasters don't attempt to know what patterns may fit the data; many times, forecasters don't even know what kind of pattern they're looking for and or that may be found. Instead, data mining is a way of letting the data identify patterns and then using that information for forecasting.

TOOLS OF DATA MINING

Data mining uses and analyzes data that are stored in *databases*, *data warehouses*, and *data marts*. A database is a collection of related data organized to help a company analyze some relevant activity—for example, historical sales data for a specific product. A data warehouse is typically a company's repository for its own current and historical data, including information from its own operations (i.e., marketing, sales, ERP systems, and supply chain, and external data) for such things as markets, demographics, customers, materials, competitors, suppliers, and financial data. Data warehouses can be subdivided into data marts, which store subsets of data that hold special information, and data that is grouped to help the company make decisions. Data mining employs several tools or tasks that are used to extract patterns and relationships from databases, data warehouses, and data marts. All of these categories of tools employ various software packages, such as SAS, SPSS, and Excel products, to mine data—to import, process, and analyze data, and help identify patterns and relationships.

Association rule learning is a data mining tool that searches for relationships between variables, such as a retail store determining which apparel products are frequently purchased together by certain categories of customers, such as a shirt with denim jeans; or common features across a variety of product variations that a group of customers prefer. *Clustering analysis* is a tool that uses software packages to identify groups in the data that naturally fall together, such as suppliers who use a type of packaging or method of transportation, or an age or income group that purchases a type of jeans. *Classificatio*n tools attempt to distinguish different classes of objects or actions. For example, an email may be classified as "legitimate" or "spam," or a company or product (like jeans) may be considered "green" or not. *Prediction* tools are adopted from traditional forecasting methods, such as regression, for predicting a variable's value, like monthly demand. *Summarization* provides a compact representation of the data, including a report.

SUMMARY

Forecasts of product demand are a necessity for almost all aspects of operational planning. Short-range demand forecasts determine the daily resource requirements needed for production, including labor and material, as well as for developing work schedules and shipping dates and controlling inventory levels. Long-range forecasts are needed to plan new products for development and changes in existing products and to acquire the plant, equipment, personnel, resources, and supply chain necessary for future operations.

We have presented several methods of forecasting useful for different time frames. These quantitative forecasting techniques are easy to understand, simple to use, and not especially costly unless the data requirements are substantial. They also have exhibited a good track record of performance for many companies that have used them. For these reasons, regression methods, and especially time series, are popular.

When managers and students are first introduced to forecasting methods, they are sometimes surprised and disappointed at the lack of exactness of the forecasts. However, they soon learn that forecasting is not easy, and exactness is not possible. Nonetheless, companies that have the skill and experience to obtain more accurate forecasts than their competitors' will gain a competitive edge.

KEY FORMULAS

Moving Average

$$\text{MA}_n = \frac{\sum_{i=1}^{n} D_i}{n}$$

Weighted Moving Average

$$\text{WMA}_n = \sum_{i=1}^{n} W_i D_i$$

Exponential Smoothing

$$F_{t+1} = \alpha D_t + (1 - \alpha) F_t$$

Adjusted Exponential Smoothing

$$AF_{t+1} = F_{t+1} + T_{t+1}$$

Trend Factor

$$T_{t+1} = \beta(F_{t+1} - F_t) + (1 - \beta) T_t$$

Linear Trend Line

$$y = a + bx$$

Least Squares

$$b = \frac{\Sigma xy - n\overline{x}\overline{y}}{\Sigma x^2 - n\overline{x}^2}$$

$$a = \overline{y} - b\overline{x}$$

Seasonal Factor

$$S_i = \frac{D_i}{\Sigma D}$$

Seasonally Adjusted Forecast

$$\text{SF}_i = (S_i)(F_t)$$

Mean Absolute Deviation

$$\text{MAD} = \frac{\Sigma |D_t - F_t|}{n}$$

Mean Absolute Percent Deviation

$$\text{MAPD} = \frac{\Sigma |D_t - F_t|}{\Sigma D_t}$$

Cumulative Error

$$E = \Sigma e_t$$

Average Error (Bias)

$$\overline{E} = \frac{\Sigma e_t}{n}$$

Tracking Signal

$$\text{TS} = \frac{\Sigma (D_t - F_t)}{\text{MAD}} = \frac{E}{\text{MAD}}$$

Mean Squared Error

$$\text{MSE} = \frac{\Sigma (D_t - F_t)^2}{n - 1}$$

Linear Regression Equation

$$y = a + bx$$

Correlation Coefficient

$$r = \frac{n\Sigma xy - \Sigma x \Sigma y}{\sqrt{[n\Sigma x^2 - (\Sigma x)^2][n\Sigma y^2 - (\Sigma y)^2]}}$$

Coefficient of Determination

$$\text{Coefficient of determination} = r^2$$

SOLVED PROBLEMS

WileyPLUS

1. MOVING AVERAGE

A manufacturing company has monthly demand for one of its products as follows:

MONTH	DEMAND
February	520
March	490
April	550
May	580
June	600
July	420
August	510
September	610

Develop a three-period moving average forecast and a three-period weighted moving average forecast with weights of 0.50, 0.30, and 0.20 for the most recent demand values, in that order. Calculate MAD for each forecast, and indicate which would seem to be most accurate.

SOLUTION

Step 1. Compute the three-month moving average using the formula

$$MA_3 = \sum_{i=1}^{3} \frac{D_i}{3}$$

For May, the moving average forecast is

$$MA_3 = \frac{520 + 490 + 550}{3} = 520$$

Step 2. Compute the three-month weighted moving average using the formula

$$WMA_3 = \Sigma W_i D_i$$

For May, the weighted average forecast is

$$\begin{aligned} WMA_3 &= (0.50)(550) + (0.30)(490) + (0.20)(520) \\ &= 526.00 \end{aligned}$$

The values for both moving average forecasts are shown in the following table:

MONTH	DEMAND	MA_3	WMA_3
February	520		
March	490	—	—
April	550	—	—
May	580	520.00	526.00
June	600	540.00	553.00
July	420	576.67	584.00
August	510	533.33	506.00
September	610	510.00	501.00
October	—	513.33	542.00

Step 3. Compute the MAD value for both forecasts:

$$MAD = \frac{\Sigma|D_t - F_t|}{n}$$

The MAD value for the three-month moving average is 80.0, and the MAD value for the three-month weighted moving average is 75.6, indicating there is not much difference in accuracy between the two forecasts, although the weighted moving average is slightly better.

2. EXPONENTIAL SMOOTHING

A computer software firm has experienced the following demand for its "Personal Finance" software package:

PERIOD	UNITS
1	56
2	61
3	55
4	70
5	66
6	65
7	72
8	75

Develop an exponential smoothing forecast using $\alpha = 0.40$ and an adjusted exponential smoothing forecast using $\alpha = 0.40$ and $\beta = 0.20$. Compare the accuracy of the two forecasts using MAD and cumulative error.

SOLUTION

Step 1. Compute the exponential smoothing forecast with $\alpha = 0.40$ using the following formula:

$$F_{t+1} = \alpha D_t + (1 - \alpha)F_t$$

For period 2, the forecast (assuming $F_1 = 56$) is

$$\begin{aligned} F_2 &= \alpha D_t + (1 - \alpha)F_1 \\ &= (0.40)(56) + (0.60)(56) \\ &= 56 \end{aligned}$$

For period 3, the forecast is

$$\begin{aligned} F_3 &= (0.40)(61) + (0.60)(56) \\ &= 58 \end{aligned}$$

The remaining forecasts are computed similarly and are shown in the accompanying table.

Step 2. Compute the adjusted exponential smoothing forecast with $\alpha = 0.40$ and $\beta = 0.20$ using the formula

$$\begin{aligned} AF_{t+1} &= F_{t+1} + T_{t+1} \\ T_{t+1} &= \beta(F_{t+1} - F_t) + (1 - \beta)T_t \end{aligned}$$

Starting with the forecast for period 3 (since $F_1 = F_2$, and we will assume $T_2 = 0$),

$$T_3 = \beta(F_3 - F_2) + (1 - \beta)T_2$$
$$= (0.20)(58 - 56) + (0.80)(0)$$
$$= 0.40$$
$$AF_3 = F_3 + T_3$$
$$= 58 + 0.40$$
$$= 58.40$$

The remaining adjusted forecasts are computed similarly and are shown in the following table:

PERIOD	D_t	F_t	AF_t	$D_t - F_i$	$D_i - AF_t$
1	56	—		—	—
2	61	56.00	56.00	5.00	5.00
3	55	58.00	58.40	−3.00	−3.40
4	70	56.80	56.88	13.20	13.12
5	66	62.08	63.20	3.92	2.80
6	65	63.65	64.86	1.35	0.14
7	72	64.18	65.26	7.81	6.73
8	75	67.31	68.80	7.68	6.20
9	—	70.39	72.19	—	—
				35.97	30.60

Step 3. Compute the MAD value for each forecast:

$$MAD(F_t) = \frac{\Sigma|D_t - F_t|}{n}$$
$$= \frac{41.97}{7}$$
$$= 5.99$$
$$MAD(AF_t) = \frac{37.39}{7}$$
$$= 5.34$$

Step 4. Compute the cumulative error for each forecast:

$$E(F_t) = 35.97$$
$$E(AF_t) = 30.60$$

Because both MAD and the cumulative error are less for the adjusted forecast, it would appear to be the most accurate.

3. LINEAR REGRESSION

A local building products store has accumulated sales data for 2 × 4 lumber (in board feet) and the number of building permits in its area for the past 10 quarters:

QUARTER	BUILDING PERMITS x	LUMBER SALES (1,000S OF BOARD FEET), y
1	8	12.6
2	12	16.3
3	7	9.3
4	9	11.5
5	15	18.1
6	6	7.6
7	5	6.2
8	8	14.2
9	101	15.0
10	12	17.8

Develop a linear regression model for these data and determine the strength of the linear relationship using correlation. If the model appears to be relatively strong, determine the forecast for lumber given ten building permits in the next quarter.

SOLUTION

Step 1. Compute the components of the linear regression equation, $y = a + bx$, using the least squares formulas

$$\bar{x} = \frac{92}{10} = 9.2$$
$$\bar{y} = \frac{128.6}{10} = 12.86$$
$$b = \frac{\Sigma xy - n\bar{x}\bar{y}}{\Sigma x^2 - n\bar{x}^2}$$
$$= \frac{(1{,}290.3) - (10)(9.2)(12.86)}{(932) - (10)(9.2)^2}$$
$$b = 1.25$$
$$a = \bar{y} - b\bar{x}$$
$$= 12.86 - (1.25)(9.2)$$
$$a = 1.36$$

Step 2. Develop the linear regression equations:

$$y = a + bx$$
$$y = 1.36 + 1.25x$$

Step 3. Compute the correlation coefficient:

$$r = \frac{n\Sigma xy - \Sigma x \Sigma y}{\sqrt{[n\Sigma x^2 - (\Sigma x)^2][n\Sigma y^2 - (\Sigma y)^2]}}$$
$$= \frac{(10)(1290.3) - (92)(128.6)}{\sqrt{[(10)(932) - (92)^2][(10)(1{,}810.48) - (128.6)^2]}}$$
$$= 0.925$$

Thus, there appears to be a strong linear relationship.

Step 4. Calculate the forecast for $x = 10$ permits.

$$y = a + bx$$
$$= 1.36 + 1.25(10)$$
$$= 13.86 \text{ or } 13{,}860 \text{ board feet}$$

PROBLEMS

12-1. The manager of the Excom Service Station wants to forecast the demand for unleaded gasoline next month so that the proper number of gallons can be ordered from the distributor. The owner has accumulated the following data on demand for unleaded gasoline from sales during the past 10 months:

Month	Gasoline Demanded (gal)
October	800
November	725
December	630
January	500
February	645
March	690
April	730
May	810
June	1200
July	980

a. Compute an exponentially smoothed forecast using an α value of 0.30.

b. Compute an adjusted exponentially smoothed forecast ($\alpha = 0.30$ and $\beta = 0.20$).

c. Compare the two forecasts using MAPD and indicate which seems to be the most accurate.

12-2. The Intrepid mutual fund of growth stocks has had the following average monthly price for the past 10 months.

Month	Fund Price
1	62.7
2	63.9
3	68.0
4	66.4
5	67.2
6	65.8
7	68.2
8	69.3
9	67.2
10	70.1

Compute the exponentially smoothed forecast with $\alpha = 0.40$, the adjusted exponentially smoothed forecast with $\alpha = 0.40$ and $\beta = 0.30$, and the linear trend line forecast. Compare the accuracy of the three forecasts using cumulative error and MAD, and indicate which forecast appears to be most accurate.

12-3. The Oceanside Hotel is adjacent to City Coliseum, a 24,000-seat arena that is home to the city's professional basketball and ice hockey teams and that hosts a variety of concerts, trade shows, and conventions throughout the year. The hotel has experienced the following occupancy rates for the nine years since the coliseum opened:

Year	Occupancy Rate
1	75%
2	70
3	72
4	77
5	83
6	81
7	86
8	91
9	87

Compute an exponential smoothing forecast with $\alpha = 0.20$, an adjusted exponential smoothing forecast with $\alpha = 0.20$ and $\beta = 0.20$, and a linear trend line forecast. Compare the three forecasts using MAD and average error ($\overline{E}$), and indicate which forecast seems to be most accurate.

12-4. Globetron manufactures components for use in small electronic products such as computers, CD players, and radios at plants in Belgium, Germany, and France. The parts are transported by truck to Hamburg, where they are shipped overseas to customers in Mexico, South America, the United States, and the Pacific Rim. The company has to reserve space on ships months and sometimes years in advance, and thus needs an accurate forecasting model. Following are the number of cubic feet of container space the company has used in each of the past 18 months.

Month	Space (1,000s ft^3)	Month	Space (1,000s ft^3)
1	10.6	3	9.8
2	12.7	4	11.3

Month	Space (1,000s ft³)	Month	Space (1,000s ft³)
5	13.6	12	14.7
6	14.4	13	18.2
7	12.2	14	19.6
8	16.7	15	21.4
9	18.1	16	22.8
10	19.2	17	20.6
11	16.3	18	18.7

Develop a forecasting model that you believe would provide the company with relatively accurate forecasts for the next year and indicate the forecasted shipping space required for the next three months.

12-5. Backstreet's Pizza delivery service has randomly selected eight weekdays during the past month and recorded orders for pizza at four different time periods per day, as follows:

	Days							
Time Period	**1**	**2**	**3**	**4**	**5**	**6**	**7**	**8**
10:00 A.M.–3:00 P.M.	62	49	53	35	43	48	56	43
3:00 P.M.–7:00 P.M.	73	55	81	77	60	66	85	70
7:00 P.M.–11:00 P.M.	42	38	45	50	29	37	35	44
11:00 P.M.–2:00 P.M.	35	40	36	39	26	25	36	31

Develop a seasonally adjusted forecasting model for daily pizza demand and forecast demand for each of the time periods for a single upcoming day.

12-6. The Willow River Mining Company mines and ships coal. It has experienced the following demand for coal during the past eight years:

Year	Coal Sales (tons)
1	4,260
2	4,510
3	4,050
4	3,720
5	3,900
6	3,470
7	2,890
8	3,100

Develop an adjusted exponential smoothing model ($\alpha = 0.30$, $\beta = 0.20$) and a linear trend line model, and compare the forecast accuracy of the two using MAD. Indicate which forecast seems to be most accurate.

12-7. The Great Northwest Outdoor Company is a catalog sales operation that specializes in outdoor recreational clothing. Demand for its items is very seasonal, peaking during the holiday season and during the spring. It has accumulated the following data for order per "season" (quarter) during the past five years:

	Orders (1,000s)				
Quarter/Year	**1**	**2**	**3**	**4**	**5**
January–March	18.6	18.1	22.4	23.2	24.5
April–June	23.5	24.7	28.8	27.6	31.0
July–September	20.4	19.5	21.0	24.4	23.7
October–December	41.9	46.3	45.5	47.1	52.8

a. Develop a seasonally adjusted forecast model for these order data. Forecast demand for each quarter for year 6 (using a linear trend line forecast estimate for orders in 2011).

b. Develop a separate linear trend line forecast for each of the four seasons and forecast each season for year 6.

c. Which of the two approaches used in parts (a) and (b) appear to be the most accurate? Use MAD to verify your selection.

12-8. Townside Food Vending operates vending machines in office buildings, the airport, bus stations, colleges, and other businesses and agencies around town and operates vending trucks for building and construction sites. The company believes its sandwich sales follow a seasonal pattern. It has accumulated the following data for sandwich sales per season during the past four years.

	Sandwich Sales (1,000s)			
Season/Year	**1**	**2**	**3**	**4**
Fall	42.7	44.3	45.7	40.6
Winter	36.9	42.7	34.8	41.5
Spring	51.3	55.6	49.3	47.3
Summer	62.9	64.8	71.2	74.5

Develop a seasonally adjusted forecast model for these sandwich sales data. Forecast demand for each season for 2011 using a linear trend line estimate for sales in year 5. Do the data appear to have a seasonal pattern?

12-9. During the past five months, the emergency room at the new County Hospital has observed the number of patients during two parts of every other week—the weekend (Friday through Sunday) and weekdays (Monday through Thursday). They typically experience greater patient traffic on weekends than during the week:

	Number of Patients	
Week	**Weekend**	**Weekdays**
1	105	73
2	119	85
3	122	89
4	128	83
5	117	96
6	136	78
7	141	91
8	126	100
9	143	83
10	140	101

Develop a seasonally adjusted forecasting model for the number of patients during each part of the week for week 11.

12-10. The Highlands Craft Store makes and sells bowls and mugs that are hand-made by local artisans, at their craft store and through their website. Since making these items requires a special type of clay and a large amount of individual man-hours, for planning purposes, the company would like to forecast future demand, specifically through their website, which has increasingly become the primary source of their sales. Following is the company's website demand (in items sold) for the past 36 months.

Month	Sales	Month	Sales	Month	Sales
1	345	13	415	25	344
2	411	14	395	26	286
3	266	15	298	27	455
4	347	16	377	28	634
5	506	17	418	29	502
6	278	18	522	30	388
7	411	19	421	31	427
8	510	20	384	32	561
9	198	21	455	33	447
10	387	22	506	34	395
11	344	23	478	35	414
12	412	24	613	36	522

Develop a linear trend forecast model, an exponentially smoothed model ($\alpha = 0.20$) and a 5-month moving average forecast model and indicate which one seems best to forecast website demand.

12-11. Temco Industries has developed a forecasting model that was used to forecast during a 10-month period. The forecasts and actual demand are shown as follows:

Month	Actual Demand	Forecast Demand
1	160	170
2	150	165
3	175	157
4	200	166
5	190	183
6	220	186
7	205	203
8	210	204
9	200	207
10	220	203

Measure the accuracy of the forecast using MAD, MAPD, and cumulative error. Does the forecast method appear to be accurate?

12-12. Monitor the forecast in Problem 12-11 for bias using a tracking signal and a control chart with ±3 MAD. Does there appear to be any bias in the forecast?

12-13. Monitor the adjusted exponential smoothing forecast in Problem 12-6 for bias using a tracking signal and a control chart with ±3 MAD.

12-14. RAP Computers assembles computers from generic parts it purchases at discount and sells the units via phone orders it receives from customers responding to their ads in trade journals. The business has developed an exponential smoothing forecast model to forecast future computer demand. Actual demand for their computers for the past eight months is as follows:

Month	Demand	Forecast
March	120	—
April	110	120.0
May	150	116.0
June	130	129.6
July	160	129.7
August	165	141.8
September	140	151.1
October	155	146.7
November	—	150.0

a. Using the measure of forecast accuracy of your choice, ascertain if the forecast appears to be accurate.

b. Determine if a three-month moving average would provide a better forecast.

c. Use a tracking signal to monitor the forecast in part (a) for bias.

12-15. The Fieldale Dairy produces cheese, which it sells to supermarkets and food processing companies. Because of concerns about cholesterol and fat in cheese, the company has seen demand for its products decline during the past decade. It is now considering introducing some alternative low-fat dairy products and wants to determine how much available plant capacity it will have next year. The company has developed an exponential smoothing forecast with $\alpha = 0.40$ to forecast cheese. The actual demand and the forecasts from its model are shown as follows:

Year	Demand (1,000s lb)	Forecast
1	16.8	—
2	14.1	16.8
3	15.3	15.7
4	12.7	15.5
5	11.9	14.4
6	12.3	13.4
7	11.5	12.9
8	10.8	12.4

Assess the accuracy of the forecast model using MAD and cumulative error, and determine if the forecast error reflects bias using a tracking signal and ±3 MAD control limits. If the exponential smoothing forecast model is biased, determine if a linear trend model would provide a more accurate forecast.

12-16. The manager of the Commander Hotel near City Stadium believes that how well the local Blue Sox professional baseball team is playing has an impact on the occupancy rate at the hotel during the summer months. Following are the number of victories for the Blue Sox (in a 162-game schedule) for the past eight years and the hotel occupancy rates:

Year	Number of Blue Sox Wins	Occupancy Rate
1	70	81%
2	65	74
3	81	83
4	88	84
5	80	85
6	92	91
7	83	88
8	64	80

Develop a linear regression model for these data, and forecast the occupancy rate for next year if the Blue Sox wins 85 games. Does there appear to be a strong relationship between wins and occupancy rate?

12-17. Employees at Hubbell Engine Parts Company produce parts using precision machine tools according to exact design specifications. The employees are paid partially according to a piece rate system wherein if they work faster and produce more parts, they are eligible for monthly bonuses. Management suspects that this method of pay may contribute to a high number of defective parts. A specific part requires a normal, standard time of 23 minutes to produce. The quality control manager has checked the actual average times to produce this part for 10 different employees during 20 days selected at random during the past month, and determined the corresponding percentage of defective parts, as follows.

Average Time (min)	% Defective	Average Time (min)	% Defective
21.6	4.1	20.8	3.1
22.5	4.6	18.9	6.1
23.1	1.2	21.4	3.8
24.6	1.5	23.7	1.9
22.8	2.6	23.8	1.7
23.7	1.9	24.9	0.8
20.9	3.7	19.8	4.3
19.7	5.3	19.7	5.1
24.5	1.8	21.2	3.9
26.7	2.3	20.8	1.7

Develop a linear regression model relating average production time to percentage defects to determine if a relationship exists, and the percentage of defective items that would be expected with the normal production time of 23 minutes.

12-18. Apperson and Fitz is a chain of clothing stores that caters to high school and college students. It publishes a quarterly catalog and operates a website that features provocatively attired males and females. The website is very expensive to maintain, and company executives are not sure if the number of hits at the site relate to sales; that is, people may be looking at the site for the pictures rather than as potential customers. The webmaster has accumulated the following data for hits per month and orders placed at the website for the past 20 months.

Hits (1,000s)	Orders (1,000s)	Hits (1,000s)	Orders (1,000s)
34.2	8.2	46.7	9.1
28.5	5.7	43.5	7.2
36.7	9.1	52.6	10.7
42.3	7.5	61.8	9.3
25.8	6.3	37.3	3.1
52.3	10.4	28.9	4.4
35.2	7.5	26.4	5.2
27.9	6.2	39.4	6.8
31.4	4.8	44.7	8.4
29.4	5.3	46.3	7.9

Develop a linear regression model for these data and indicate if there appears to be a strong relationship between website hits and orders. What would be the forecast for orders with 60,000 hits per month?

12-19. ITown is a large computer discount store that sells computers and ancillary equipment and software in the town where State University is located. It has collected historical data on computer sales and printer sales for the past 10 years as follows:

Year	Personal Computer Sales	Printers Sold
1	1,045	381
2	1,610	579
3	860	312
4	1,211	501
5	975	296
6	1,117	415
7	1,066	535
8	1,310	592
9	1,517	607
10	1,246	473

a. Develop a linear trend line forecast to forecast printer demand in year 11.

b. Develop a linear regression model relating printer sales to computer sales to forecast printer demand in year 11 if 1500 computers are sold.

c. Compare the forecasts developed in parts (a) and (b) and indicate which one appears to be the best.

12-20. Develop an exponential smoothing model with $\alpha = 0.30$ for the data in Problem 12-19 to forecast printer demand in year 11, and compare its accuracy to the linear regression forecast developed in Problem 12-19(a).

12-21. Arrow Air is a regional East Coast airline. It has collected data for the percentage of available seats occupied on its flights for four quarters—(1) January–March, (2) April–June, (3) July–September, and (4) October–December—for the past five years. The company also has collected data for the average percentage fare discount for each of these quarters as follows:

Year	Quarter	% Seat Occupancy	% Average Fare Discount
1	1	63	21
	2	75	34
	3	76	18
	4	58	26
2	1	59	18
	2	62	40
	3	81	25
	4	76	30
3	1	65	23
	2	70	28
	3	78	30
	4	69	35
4	1	59	20
	2	61	35
	3	83	26
	4	71	30
5	1	60	25
	2	66	37
	3	86	25
	4	74	30

a. Develop a seasonally adjusted forecast model for seat occupancy. Forecast seat occupancy for year 6 (using a linear trend line forecast estimate for seat occupancy in year 6).

b. Develop linear regression models relating seat occupancy to discount fares to forecast seat occupancy for each quarter in year 6. Assume a fare discount of 20% for quarter 1, 36% for quarter 2, 25% for quarter 3, and 30% for quarter 4.

c. Compare the forecasts developed in parts (a) and (b) and indicate which one appears to be the best.

12-22. Develop an adjusted exponential smoothing forecast model ($\alpha = 0.40$ and $\beta = 0.40$) for the data in Problem 12-21 to forecast seat occupancy, and compare its accuracy with the seasonally adjusted model developed in Problem 12.21(a).

12-23. The consumer loan department at National Bank wants to develop a forecasting model to help determine its potential loan application volume for the coming year. Since adjustable-rate home mortgages are based on government long-term Treasury note rates, the bank has collected the following data for three- to five-year Treasury note interest rates for the past 24 years:

Year	Rate	Year	Rate	Year	Rate
1	5.77	9	9.71	17	7.68
2	5.85	10	11.55	18	8.26
3	6.92	11	14.44	19	8.55
4	7.82	12	12.92	20	8.26
5	7.49	13	10.45	21	6.80
6	6.67	14	11.89	22	6.12
7	6.69	15	9.64	23	5.48
8	8.29	16	7.06	24	6.09

Develop an appropriate forecast model for the bank to use to forecast Treasury note rates in the future, and indicate how accurate it appears to be compared to historical data.

12-24. The Vantage Fund is a balanced mutual fund that includes a mix of stocks and bonds. Following are the year-end share prices of the fund and Dow Jones Industrial Average for a 20-year period.

Year	Share Price	DJIA	Year	Share Price	DJIA
1	14.75	1,046	11	19.08	3,301
2	15.06	1,258	12	20.40	3,754
3	14.98	1,211	13	19.39	3,834
4	15.73	1,546	14	24.43	5,117
5	16.11	1,895	15	26.46	6,448
6	16.07	1,938	16	29.45	7,908
7	16.78	2,168	17	29.35	9,181
8	17.69	2,753	18	27.96	11,497
9	16.90	2,633	19	28.21	10,786
10	17.81	3,168	20	27.26	10,150

Develop a linear regression model for these data and forecast the fund share price for a DJIA of 12,000. Does there appear to be a strong relationship between the fund's share price and the DJIA?

12-25. Delaplane Computers gets most of its component parts from suppliers in Pacific Rim countries, who ship to the company's main distribution center near Long Beach, California, where computers are built to order for customers. This type of assembly operation at the company's distribution center allows it to carry little of its own inventory by pushing inventory down to its suppliers, who provide components as demanded. However, the suppliers also want to minimize their own inventory, and one way to do that is to develop an accurate demand forecast. Following is the demand data (units) from Delaplane for the past 24 months for one specific supplier who provides the screens for laptops:

Month	Year 1 Demand	Year 2 Demand
January	2,447	2,561
February	1,826	1,733
March	1,755	1,693
April	1,456	1,484
May	1,529	1,501
June	1,633	1,655

Month	Year 1 Demand	Year 2 Demand
July	2,346	2,412
August	3,784	4,017
September	4,106	3,886
October	3,006	2,844
November	2,257	2,107
December	3,212	3,415

Closely observe the demand data and develop a forecast model for year 3 that would be the most accurate for the supplier.

12-26. Chlorex, a household products company, has developed a natural, cold-water detergent called "Nature Clean." The company's marketing department thinks that sales jump when there are several major environmental (i.e., sustainability) episodes in the national media, such as an oil spill or the government issuing a major pollution report. Thus, the marketing department wants to develop a linear regression forecasting model that relates the number of "green" episodes reported monthly in the national media to monthly sales of the detergent. The marketing department had several staff members go through various media sources for the last two years and count the number of major national green episodes reported on, which, with monthly sales, is shown in the following table:

Month	Sales	Green Episodes	Month	Sales	Green Episodes
1	34,175	3	13	55,732	7
2	28,366	2	14	26,004	4
3	41,819	4	15	49,188	5
4	27,666	1	16	40,005	2
5	31,299	1	17	38,912	2
6	37,456	4	18	31,777	1
7	52,444	5	19	30,367	0
8	46,712	3	20	34,566	1
9	37,222	2	21	29,078	1
10	44,981	2	22	45,876	3
11	40,006	2	23	48,556	4
12	47,321	4	24	51,022	6

Develop a linear regression model and determine the sales forecast if three green episodes are reported in the media. Discuss the value and usefulness of this type of relational forecast for Chlorex's detergent sales.

12-27. Chlorex in Problem 12-26 is planning to introduce another "sustainable product," an all-purpose cleaner. The company is attempting to forecast what demand might be like five years into the future. However, it has no historical demand data to use to develop a forecast model. The marketing department has made its own estimate of first-year sales and acquired estimates for the new cleaner from four other sources—top management, the sales force, a household products trade association, and an independent marketing firm. Top management estimates first-year sales to be 34,000 units; the marketing department's estimate is 47,000 units; the sales force suggests 41,000 units; the trade association estimates first-year sales will be 28,000 units; and the independent marketing firm estimates sales will be 51,000 units. Using these estimates and the demand data and forecast model for the detergent in Problem 12-26, develop a forecast for planning purposes for year 5 for the new cleaner.

12-28. The Port of Charleston is considering an expansion of their container terminal. The port has experienced the following container throughput during the past 12 years, expressed as TEUs (i.e., 20 feet equivalent units, a standard unit of measure for containers).

Year	TEUs (1,000s)
1	526.1
2	549.4
3	606.0
4	627.0
5	695.7
6	734.9
7	761.1
8	845.4
9	1,021.1
10	1,137.1
11	1,173.6
12	1,233.4

a. Develop a linear trend line forecast for these data and forecast the number of TEUs for the next year.

b. How strong is the linear relationship for these data?

12-29. The County Arsenal Travel Soccer Club has boys and girls travel soccer teams at all age levels up to 18 years old. The club has been successful and grown in popularity over the years; however, an obstacle to its continued growth is a shortage of practice and game soccer fields in the area. The club has tried to make a case to the County Board of Supervisors for more soccer fields to accommodate the increasing number of kids who want to play on a club travel team. The number of kids who have played soccer on a club team, and the county's population for the last 10 years are as follows:

Year	Club Soccer Players	Town Population
1	246	38,060
2	235	38,021
3	259	38,110
4	261	38,125
5	276	38,240
6	290	38,231
7	327	38,306
8	318	38,477
9	335	38,506
10	331	38,583
11	339	38,609
12	351	38,745
13	366	39,003
14	401	39,062
15	427	39,114

The soccer club wants to develop a forecasting model to demonstrate to the board of supervisors its expected growth in the future.

a. Develop a linear trend line forecast to predict the number of soccer players the club can expect next year.
b. The county planning department has told the soccer club that the county expects to grow to a population of 39,300 by next year and to 40,000 in five years. Develop a linear regression model using the county's population as a predictor of the number of club soccer players and compare this forecasting model to the one developed in part (a). Which forecasting model should the club use to support its request for new fields?

12-30. Some members of management of the Fairface Cosmetics Firm believe that demand for its products is related to the promotional activities of local department stores where its cosmetics are sold. However, others in management believe that other factors, such as local demographics, are stronger determinants of demand behavior. The following data for local annual promotional expenditures for all Fairface products and local annual unit sales for Fairface lip gloss have been collected from 20 stores selected at random from different localities:

Store	Annual Unit Sales ($1,000s)	Annual Promotional Expenditures ($1,000s)
1	5.3	12.6
2	4.2	15.5
3	3.1	10.8
4	2.7	8.7
5	5.9	20.3
6	5.6	21.9
7	10.3	25.6
8	4.1	14.3
9	9.9	15.1
10	5.7	18.7
11	3.5	9.6
12	3.2	12.7
13	8.1	16.3
14	3.6	8.1
15	5.3	7.5
16	5.8	12.4
17	8.1	17.3
18	6.1	11.2
19	3.1	18.5
20	9.5	16.7

Based on these data, does it appear that the strength of the relationship between lip gloss sales and promotional expenditures is sufficient to warrant using a linear regression forecasting model? Explain your response.

12-31. The Pro Apparel company manufactures baseball-style caps with various team logos. The caps come in an assortment of designs and colors. The company has had monthly sales for the past 24 months as follows:

Month	Demand (1,000s)	Month	Demand (1,000s)
1	8.2	3	8.1
2	7.5	4	9.3
5	9.1	15	11.7
6	9.5	16	9.8
7	10.4	17	10.8
8	9.7	18	11.3
9	10.2	19	12.6
10	10.6	20	11.5
11	8.2	21	10.8
12	9.9	22	11.7
13	10.3	23	12.5
14	10.5	24	12.8

Develop a forecast model using the method you believe best, and justify your selection using a measure (or measures) of forecast accuracy.

12-32. In Problem 12-19, ITown believes its printer sales are also related to the average price of its printers. It has collected historical data on average printer prices for the past 10 years as follows:

Year	Average Printer Prices ($)
1	475
2	490
3	520
4	420
5	410
6	370
7	350
8	300
9	280
10	250

a. Using Excel, develop the multiple regression equation for these data.
b. What is the coefficient of determination for this regression equation?
c. Determine a forecast for printer sales based on personal computer sales of 1,500 units and an average printer price of $300.

12-33. The manager of the Salem police department motor pool wants to develop a forecast model for annual maintenance on police cars based on mileage in the past year and age of the cars. The following data have been collected for eight different cars:

Miles Driven	Car Age (years)	Maintenance Cost ($)
14,320	6	$1,120
15,100	7	1,610
17,415	8	1,545
9,370	3	900
7,230	3	650
12,045	5	1,500
8,100	2	550
6,300	3	730

a. Using Excel, develop a multiple regression equation for these data.
b. What is the coefficient of determination for this regression equation?
c. Forecast the annual maintenance cost for a police car that is four years old and will be driven 10,000 miles in one year.

12-34. The busiest time of the day at the Taco Town fast-food restaurant is between 11:00 A.M. and 2:00 P.M. Taco Town's service is very labor-dependent, and a critical factor for providing quick service is the number of employees on hand during this three-hour period. In order to determine the number of employees it needs during each hour of the three-hour lunch period, Taco Town requires an accurate forecasting model. Following are the number of customers served at Taco Town during each hour of the lunch period for the past 20 weekdays:

	Hour				Hour		
Day	**11–12**	**12–1**	**1–2**	**Day**	**11–12**	**12–1**	**1–2**
1	90	125	87	8	63	91	66
2	76	131	93	9	73	146	119
3	87	112	99	10	101	104	96
4	83	149	78	11	57	114	106
5	71	156	83	12	68	125	95
6	94	178	89	13	75	206	102
7	56	101	124	14	94	117	118
15	103	145	122	18	83	166	94
16	67	121	93	19	79	124	87
17	94	113	76	20	81	118	115

Develop a forecast model that you believe will best forecast Taco Town's customer demand for the next day and explain why you selected this model.

CASE STUDY

Beijing Specialty Noodle Export Business

The global economic crisis started in 2008 and has had a dramatic impact on Beijing Specialty Noodle Export Business. The world's leading economists are not in alignment on what the coming year will look like. Some economists are predicting a "double dip" scenario where the economy takes another major drop. Other economists are predicting a very small global economy growth of about 1%. A very small set of experts are predicting that the economy is at its turning point and that the global economy will expand by at least 3% next year.

Beijing Specialty Noodle's export experience shows that their export business is tied very closely to what is happening in the global economy. When the economy is growing, their exports grow as well.

The firm's leadership wants to forecast what their export business will be next year. Unfortunately the leading economic experts are not presenting a universal agreement on what to expect. The company's forecasting ability is also complicated as they have never lived through a global economic meltdown before and the duration of this experience is just three years. Thus, while they have a large data set of past performance, the timeframe for the economic meltdown is very small.

Beijing Specialty Noodle has contracted with you to build them a forecast for next year's exports. It is their view that the likelihood of a "double-dip" situation is very small. While some economists are stating this could happen, the majority of economists are predicting a global growth of 1% to 3%. They have provided you the following 15 years of data. Years 12–15 are those where the global economic meltdown occurred. They would like to have a year 16 forecast.

Assuming that the data for years 1–12 provide the best forecast model, they want you to compare exponential, adjusted exponential, and linear forecast models and provide a year 16 forecast for each model, based on year 15 sales. In other words, they want you to exclude years 13 and 14 from the forecast model and assume that year 15 is year 13. Identify at least one item that supports the use of any model over the others. What is the risk of ignoring years 13 and 14?

Year	Sales (1,000,000s)	Year	Sales (1,000,000s)
1	5	9	12.1
2	7	10	11.2
3	8	11	11.9
4	6	12	12
5	9	13	6.8
6	11	14	6.5
7	10	15	6.8
8	11.8		

REFERENCES

Box, G. E. P., and G. M. Jenkins. *Time Series Analysis: Forecasting and Control*, 2nd ed. Oakland, CA: Holden-Day, 1976.

Brown, R. G. *Statistical Forecasting for Inventory Control*. New York: McGraw-Hill, 1959.

Chambers, J. C., K. M. Satinder, and D. D. Smith. "How to Choose the Right Forecasting Technique." *Harvard Business Review* (July–August 1971), pp. 45–74.

Gardner, E. S. "Exponential Smoothing: The State of the Art." *Journal of Forecasting* 4(1; 1985).

Gardner, E. S., and D. G. Dannenbring. "Forecasting with Exponential Smoothing: Some Guidelines for Model Selection." *Decision Sciences* 11(2; 1980), pp. 370–383.

Makridakis, S., S. C. Wheelwright, and V. E. McGee. *Forecasting: Methods and Applications*, 2nd ed. New York: John Wiley, 1983.

Tersine, R. J., and W. Riggs. "The Delphi Technique: A Long-Range Planning Tool." *Business Horizons* 19(2; 1976).

CHAPTER 13

Inventory Management

LEARNING OBJECTIVES

AFTER READING THIS CHAPTER, YOU WILL BE ABLE TO:

- Explain why companies keep inventory and how advances in IT have impacted inventory decisions.
- Discuss the key elements and costs of inventory, and the relationship between inventory costs and customer service.
- Contrast continuous and periodic inventory systems, and classify inventory according to the ABC system.
- Utilize basic inventory models to calculate order quantity and related measures, as well as the annual cost of inventory.
- Determine the appropriate reorder point in a continuous inventory system based on a target service level.
- Calculate the order quantity for a periodic inventory system.

USING RFID TECHNOLOGY FOR DENIM JEANS INVENTORY MANAGEMENT

Radio-frequency identification (RFID) tags attached to consumer goods like denim jeans that can be scanned from a distance have been used to track inventory (specifically shipping pallets) moving through a company's supply chain. Walmart has been a leading proponent of the use of RFID technology to track inventory, and thus improve and enhance the efficiency of its global supply chain. More recently, RFID technology is moving into retail stores to improve inventory control at the store level. Walmart is using RFID tags in stores specifically to monitor and control its denim jeans inventory. Using a hand-held scanner, a Walmart employee can quickly learn which size of Wrangler jeans, for example, is not on the store shelf with an objective of making sure shelves are optimally stocked and thereby increasing sales and reducing inventory costs.

A common inventory problem at many retailers is inaccurate inventory levels created by manual counting mistakes that result in overstocks (having more inventory than it should have) and understocks (missing inventory that it should have). A study conducted by researchers at the University of Arkansas of men's and women's denim jeans departments at Bloomingdale's stores found an RFID system could improve inventory accuracy (decreasing overstocks and understocks) by more than 27%. The study also showed that by using RFID tags, the time required for biannual or end-of-year inventory counts of jeans (i.e., the familiar end-of-year "taking inventory") could be reduced by 96%; an average of over 4,700 items could be counted in an hour with RFID, compared to about 200 items per hour with a manual system using barcodes. With RFID technology, it would be possible to make storewide inventory counts much more often than once or twice a year—possibly every few weeks—or not have annual storewide counts at all because of the increased accuracy of RFID.

Another benefit of RFID technology identified by these studies is in the possible reduction of theft. Every year, denim jeans are consistently the most shoplifted clothing item in the country, and one of the most shoplifted consumer items overall. RFID would make it easier to see if jeans are stolen by employees from a store's inventory, and to identify shoplifters with stolen jeans by reading RFID tags as they leave stores.

In this chapter, we will learn about the different inventory models, techniques, and technologies that companies use to determine the lowest-cost amount of inventory to order and keep on hand, which is one of the primary objectives of supply chain management.

Sources: Based on Mary C. O'Connor, "Bloomingdale's Tests Item-Level RFID," *RFID Journal*, August 26, 2009, http://www.rfidjournal.com; and Michael Bustillo, "Walmart Radio Tags to Track Clothing," *Wall Street Journal*, July 23, 2010, http://www.wsj.com.

The objective of inventory management has been to keep enough inventory to meet customer demand and also be cost effective. However, inventory has not always been perceived as an area to control cost. Traditionally, companies maintained "generous" inventory levels to meet long-term customer demand because there were fewer competitors and products in a generally sheltered market environment. In the current global business environment, with more competitors and highly diverse markets in which new products and new product features are rapidly and continually introduced, the cost of inventory has increased due in part to quicker product obsolescence. At the same time, companies are continuously seeking to lower costs so they can provide a better product at a "lower" price.

Inventory is an obvious candidate for cost reduction. It is estimated that U.S. companies carry several trillion in inventory spread out along the supply chains. It is also estimated that the average holding cost of manufacturing goods inventory in the United States is approximately 30% of the total value of the inventory. That means if a company has $10 million worth of products in inventory, the cost of holding the inventory (including insurance, obsolescence, depreciation, interest, opportunity costs, storage costs, and so on) is approximately $3 million. If inventory could be reduced by half, to $5 million, then $1.5 million would be saved, a significant cost reduction.

The high cost of inventory has motivated companies to focus on efficient supply chain management and quality management. They believe that inventory can be significantly reduced by reducing uncertainty at various points along the supply chain. In many cases, uncertainty is created by poor quality on the part of the company or its suppliers or both. This can be in the form of variations in delivery times, uncertain production schedules caused by late deliveries, or large numbers of defects that require higher levels of production or service than what should be necessary, large fluctuations in customer demand, or poor forecasts of customer demand.

With efficient supply chain management, products or services are moved from one stage in the supply chain to the next according to a system of constant communication between customers and suppliers. Items are replaced as they are diminished without maintaining larger buffer stocks of inventory at each stage to compensate for late deliveries, inefficient service, poor quality, or uncertain demand. An efficient, well-coordinated supply chain reduces or eliminates these types of uncertainty so that this type of system will work.

Some companies maintain in-process, buffer inventories between production stages to offset irregularities and problems and keep the supply chain flowing smoothly. Quality-oriented companies consider large buffer inventories to be a costly crutch that masks problems and inefficiency primarily caused by poor quality. Adherents of quality management believe that inventory should be minimized. However, this works primarily for a production or manufacturing process. For the retailer who sells finished goods directly to the consumer or the supplier who sells parts or materials to the manufacturer, inventory is a necessity. Few shoe stores, discount stores, or department stores can stay in business with only one or two items on their shelves or racks. For these supply chains, the traditional inventory decisions of how much to order and when to order continue to be important. In addition, the traditional approaches to inventory management are still widely used by most companies.

In this chapter we review the basic elements of traditional inventory management and discuss several of the more popular models and techniques for making cost-effective inventory decisions. These decisions are basically *how much to order* and *when to order* to replenish inventory to an optimal level.

The Role of Inventory in Supply Chain Management

A company employs an inventory strategy for many reasons. The main reason is holding inventories of finished goods to meet customer demand for a product, especially in a retail operation. However, customer demand can also be a secretary going to a storage closet to get a printer cartridge or paper, or a carpenter getting a board or nails from a storage shed.

Since demand is usually not known with certainty, it is not possible to produce exactly the amount demanded. An additional amount of inventory, called safety, or buffer, stocks, is kept on hand to meet variations in product demand. In the *bullwhip effect* (which we have discussed previously in our chapters on supply chain and forecasting), demand information is distorted as it moves away from the end-use customer. This uncertainty about demand back upstream in the supply chain causes distributors, manufacturers, and suppliers to stock increasingly higher safety stock inventories to compensate.

Additional stocks of inventories are sometimes built up to meet demand that is seasonal or cyclical. Companies will continue to produce items when demand is low to meet high seasonal demand for which their production capacity is insufficient. For example, toy manufacturers produce large inventories during the summer and fall to meet anticipated demand during the holiday season. Doing so enables them to maintain a relatively smooth supply chain flow throughout the year. They would not normally have the production capacity or logistical support to produce enough to meet all of the holiday demand during that season. In the same way, retailers might find it necessary to keep large stocks of inventory on their shelves to meet peak seasonal demand, or for display purposes to attract buyers.

At the other end of the supply chain from finished goods inventory, a company might keep large stocks of parts and material inventory to meet variations in supplier deliveries. Inventory provides independence from vendors that a company does not have direct control over. Inventories of raw materials and purchased parts are kept on hand so that the production process will not be delayed as a result of missed or late deliveries or shortages from a supplier.

A company will purchase large amounts of inventory to take advantage of price discounts, as a hedge against anticipated price increases in the future, or because it can get a lower price by purchasing in volume. Walmart stores have been known to purchase a manufacturer's entire stock of soap powder or other retail item because they can get a very low price, which they subsequently pass on to their customers. Companies purchase large stocks of low-priced items when a supplier liquidates. In some cases, large orders will be made simply because the cost of ordering may be very high, and it is more cost-effective to have higher inventories than to order frequently.

Many companies find it necessary to maintain buffer inventories at different stages of their production process to provide independence between stages and to avoid work stoppages or delays. Inventories are kept between stages in the manufacturing process so that production can continue smoothly if there are temporary machine breakdowns or other work stoppages. Similarly, a stock of finished parts or products allows customer demand to be met in the event of a work stoppage or problem with transportation or distribution.

The Effects of Information Technology on Inventory Management

As we pointed out in previous chapters, information technology (IT) has become an enabler for effective supply chain management. Traditionally, inventory was owned by the buyer (as opposed to the supplier), it was kept at the buyer's location, and the buyer controlled how and when its inventory was replenished. However, in recent years these traditional aspects of inventory management have changed, due in large part to advances in IT. Because of technology and software—including such IT tools as enterprises resource planning (ERP) systems (including forecasting software), barcodes, radio frequency identification (RFID), EDI, and point-of-sales data—companies can track and locate inventory throughout their supply chain, which enables them to locate inventory somewhere other than their own facility, and control it remotely or have someone else control it. These technologies have enabled modern supply chain management practices such as vendor managed inventory (VMI), continuous replenishment programs (CRP), supplier hubs, and outsourcing operations to third-party service providers (3PL). In these practices, inventory can be located at the supplier's facility, at the buyer's, or somewhere in between. Unlike traditional practices, the supplier owns inventory until the buyer needs it and it is delivered, thus relieving the buyer of inventory costs; order sizes are reduced, deliveries (which the supplier pays for) are increased, and the buyer avoids maintaining storage facilities. However, for this to be effective, the supplier must be able to minimize its own inventory costs and optimize its own supply chain, which can be achieved if the buyer shares end-use demand and sales data with its suppliers through IT. This enables suppliers to make replenishment decisions and provide inventory to the buyer, as it's needed. A recent supply chain management practice is for inventory to be located at "supplier hubs" that are usually at, or in very close proximity to, the buyer, and are often owned and operated by a 3PL provider, which shifts all responsibility and liability for inventory to the suppliers that share the hub. For a supplier hub to work, the supply chain members—buyers, suppliers, and 3PL providers—must share information through information technology. The 3PL provider uses information provided by the buyer and suppliers (including forecasts and sales data) to consolidate shipping among suppliers, plan and execute all logistics, connect and coordinate all supply chain members through an IT system, and operate the hub facility. Supplier hubs are being used successfully by such companies as Dell, Apple, Fiat, Hewlett-Packard, Nokia, Cisco, Sam's Club, Samsung, and Volkswagen.

Inventory and Quality Management in the Supply Chain

A company maintains inventory to meet its own demand and its customers' demand for items in the supply chain. The ability to meet effectively internal organizational demand or external customer demand in a timely, efficient manner is referred to as the *level of customer service*. A primary objective of supply chain management is to provide as high a level of customer service in terms of on-time delivery as possible. This is especially important in today's highly competitive business environment, where quality is such an important product characteristic. Customers for finished goods usually perceive quality service as availability of goods they want when they want them. (This is equally true of internal customers, such as company departments or employees.) To provide this level of quality customer service, the tendency is to maintain large stocks of all types of items. However, there is a cost associated with carrying items in inventory, which creates a cost tradeoff between the quality level of customer service and the cost of that service.

As the level of inventory increases to provide better customer service, inventory costs increase, whereas quality-related customer service costs, such as lost sales and loss of customers, decrease. The conventional approach to inventory management is to maintain a level of inventory that reflects a compromise between inventory costs and customer service. However, according to the contemporary "zero defects" philosophy of quality management, the long-term benefits of quality in terms of larger market share outweigh lower short-term production-related costs, such as inventory costs. Attempting to apply this philosophy to inventory management is not simple because one way of competing in today's diverse business environment is to reduce prices through reduced inventory costs.

The Elements of Inventory Management

Inventory is a stock of items kept by an organization to meet internal or external customer demand. Virtually every type of organization maintains some form of inventory. Department stores and grocery stores carry inventories of all the retail products they sell; a nursery has inventories of different plants, trees, and flowers; a rental-car agency has inventories of cars; and a major league baseball team maintains an inventory of players on its minor league teams. Even a family household maintains inventories of items such as food, clothing, medical supplies, and personal hygiene products.

Most people think of inventory as a final product—a new car or a can of tomatoes—waiting to be sold to a retail customer. This is certainly one of its most important uses. However, especially in a manufacturing firm, inventory can take on forms besides finished goods, including:

- Raw materials
- Purchased parts and supplies
- Partially complete work in process (WIP)
- Items being transported
- Tools, and equipment

The purpose of *inventory management* is to determine the amount of inventory to keep in stock—how much to order and when to replenish, or order. In this chapter we describe several different inventory systems and techniques for making these determinations.

DEMAND

The starting point for the management of inventory is customer demand. Inventory exists to meet customer demand. Customers can be inside the organization, such as a machine operator waiting for a part or partially completed product to work on. Customers can also be outside the organization—for example, an individual purchasing groceries or a new DVD player. In either case, an essential determinant of effective inventory management is an accurate forecast of demand. For this reason, the topics of forecasting (Chapter 12) and inventory management are directly interrelated.

In general, the demand for items in inventory is either dependent or independent. **Dependent demand** items are typically component parts or materials used in the process of producing a final product. If an automobile company plans to produce 1,000 new cars, then it will need 5,000 wheels and tires (including spares). The demand for wheels is dependent on the production of cars—the demand for one item depends on demand for another item.

Cars, retail items, grocery products, and office supplies are examples of independent demand items. **Independent demand** items are final or finished products that are not a function of, or dependent on, internal production activity. Independent demand is usually determined by external market conditions and, thus, is beyond the direct control of the organization. In this chapter we focus on the management of inventory for independent demand items.

INVENTORY COSTS

Three basic costs are associated with inventory: carrying, or holding, costs; ordering costs; and shortage costs.

Carrying (or holding) costs are the costs of holding items in inventory. Annual inventory carrying costs in the United States are estimated to be over $400 billion. These costs vary with the level of inventory in stock and occasionally with the length of time an item is held. That is, the greater the level of inventory over a period of time, the higher the carrying costs. In general, any cost that grows linearly with the number of units in stock is a carrying cost. Carrying costs can include the following items:

- Facility storage (rent, depreciation, power, heat, cooling, lighting, security, refrigeration, taxes, insurance, etc.)
- Material handling (equipment)
- Labor
- Record keeping
- Borrowing to purchase inventory (interest on loans, taxes, insurance)
- Product deterioration, spoilage, breakage, obsolescence, pilferage

Carrying costs are normally specified in one of two ways. The usual way is to assign total carrying costs, determined by summing all the individual costs just mentioned, on a per-unit basis per time period, such as a month or year. In this form, carrying costs are commonly expressed as a per-unit dollar amount on an annual basis; for example, $10 per unit per year. Alternatively, carrying costs are sometimes expressed as a percentage of the value of an item or as a percentage of average inventory value. It is generally estimated that carrying costs range from 10% to 40% of the value of a manufactured item.

Ordering costs are the costs associated with replenishing the stock of inventory being held. These are normally expressed as a dollar amount per order and are independent of the order size. Annual ordering costs vary with the number of orders made—as the number of orders increases, the ordering cost increases. In general, any cost that increases linearly with the number of orders is an ordering cost. Costs incurred each time an order is made can include requisition and purchase orders, transportation and shipping, receiving, inspection, handling, and accounting and auditing costs.

Ordering costs react inversely to carrying costs. As the size of orders increases, fewer orders are required, reducing ordering costs. However, ordering larger amounts results in higher inventory levels and higher carrying costs. In general, as the order size increases, ordering costs decrease and carrying costs increase.

Shortage costs, also referred to as *stockout costs*, occur when customer demand cannot be met because of insufficient inventory. If these shortages result in a permanent loss of sales, shortage costs include the loss of profits. Shortages can also cause customer dissatisfaction and a loss of goodwill that can result in a permanent loss of customers and future sales. Some studies have shown that approximately 8% of shoppers will not find the product they want to purchase in stock, which will ultimately result in total lost sales of about 3%.

In some instances, the inability to meet customer demand or lateness in meeting demand results in penalties in the form of price discounts or rebates. When demand is internal, a shortage can cause work stoppages in the production process and create delays, resulting in downtime costs and the cost of lost production (including indirect and direct production costs).

Costs resulting from lost sales because demand cannot be met are more difficult to determine than carrying or ordering costs. Therefore, shortage costs are frequently subjective estimates and sometimes an educated guess.

Shortages occur because carrying inventory is costly. As a result, shortage costs have an inverse relationship to carrying costs—as the amount of inventory on hand increases, the carrying cost increases, whereas shortage costs decrease.

The objective of inventory management is to employ an inventory control system that will indicate how much should be ordered and when orders should take place so that the sum of the three inventory costs just described will be minimized.

Inventory Control Systems

An inventory system controls the level of inventory by determining how much to order (the level of replenishment) and when to order. There are two basic types of inventory systems: a *continuous* (or *fixed-order-quantity*) *system* and a *periodic* (or *fixed-time-period*) *system*. In a continuous system, an order is placed for the same constant amount whenever the inventory on hand decreases to a certain level, whereas in a periodic system, an order is placed for a variable amount after specific regular intervals.

CONTINUOUS INVENTORY SYSTEMS

In a **continuous inventory system** (also referred to as a *perpetual system* and a *fixed-order-quantity system*), a continual record of the inventory level for every item is maintained. Whenever the inventory on hand decreases to a predetermined level, referred to as the *reorder point*, a new order is placed to replenish the stock of inventory. The order that is placed is for a fixed amount that minimizes the total inventory costs. This amount, called the *economic order quantity*, is discussed in greater detail later.

A positive feature of a continuous system is that the inventory level is continuously monitored, so management always knows the inventory status. This is advantageous for critical items such as replacement parts or raw materials and supplies. However, maintaining a continual record of the amount of inventory on hand can also be costly.

A simple example of a continuous inventory system is a ledger-style checkbook that many of us use on a daily basis. Our checkbook comes with 300 checks; after the 200th check has been used (and there are 100 left), there is an order form for a new batch of checks. This form, when turned in at the bank, initiates an order for a new batch of 300 checks. Many office inventory systems use *reorder cards* that are placed within stacks of stationery or at the bottom of a case of pens or paper clips to signal when a new order should be placed. If you look behind the items on a hanging rack in a Kmart store, there will be a card indicating it is time to place an order for the item for an amount indicated on the card.

Continuous inventory systems often incorporate information technology tools to improve the speed and accuracy of data entry. A familiar example is the computerized checkout system with a laser scanner used by many supermarkets and retail stores. The laser scanner reads the universal product code (UPC), or bar code, from the product package; the transaction is instantly recorded and the inventory level updated. Such a system is not only quick and accurate, it also provides management with continuously updated information on the status of inventory levels. Many manufacturing companies' suppliers and distributors also use bar code systems and handheld laser scanners to inventory materials, supplies, equipment, in-process parts, and finished goods.

PERIODIC INVENTORY SYSTEMS

In a **periodic inventory system** (also referred to as a *fixed-time-period system* or a *periodic review system*), the inventory on hand is counted at specific time intervals—for example, every week or at the end of each month. After the inventory in stock is determined, an order is placed for an amount that will bring inventory back up to a desired level. In this system, the inventory level is not monitored at all during the time interval between orders, so it has the advantage of little or no required record keeping. The disadvantage is less direct control. This typically results in larger inventory levels for a periodic inventory system than in a continuous system to guard against unexpected stockouts early in the fixed period. Such a system also requires that a new order quantity be determined each time a periodic order is made.

An example of a periodic inventory system is a college or university bookstore. Textbooks are normally ordered according to a periodic system, wherein a count of textbooks in stock (for every course) is made after the first few weeks of a semester or quarter. An order for new textbooks for the next semester is then made according to estimated course enrollments for the next term (i.e., demand) and the amount remaining in stock. Smaller retail stores, drugstores, grocery stores, and offices sometimes use periodic systems—the stock level is checked every week or month, often by a vendor, to see how much should be ordered.

THE ABC CLASSIFICATION SYSTEM

The **ABC system** is a method for classifying inventory according to several criteria, including its dollar value to the firm. Typically, thousands of independent demand items are held in inventory by a company, especially in manufacturing, but a small percentage is of such a high dollar value to warrant close inventory control. In general, about 5% to 15% of all inventory items account for 70% to 80% of the total dollar value of inventory. These are classified as *A*, or *Class A*, items. *B* items represent approximately 30% of total inventory units but only about 15% of total inventory dollar value. *C* items generally account for 50% to 60% of all inventory units but represent only 5% to 10% of total dollar value. For example, a discount store such as Walmart normally stocks a relatively small number of televisions, a somewhat larger number of bicycles or sets of sheets, and hundreds of boxes of soap powder, bottles of shampoo, and AA batteries. Figure 13.1 shows the approximate ABC classes.

Figure 13.1
ABC Classifications

In ABC analysis, each class of inventory requires different levels of inventory monitoring and control—the higher the value of the inventory, the tighter the control. Class A items should experience tight inventory control; B and C require more relaxed (perhaps minimal) attention. However, the original rationale for ABC analysis was that continuous inventory monitoring was expensive and not justified for many items. The wide use of bar code scanners may have eroded that reasoning. At least for larger companies, bar codes have made continuous monitoring cheap enough to use for all item classes.

The first step in ABC analysis is to classify all inventory items as A, B, or C. Each item is assigned a dollar value, which is computed by multiplying the dollar cost of one unit by the annual demand for that item. All items are then ranked according to their annual dollar value, with, for example, the top 10% classified as A items, the next 30% as B items, and the last 60% as C items. These classifications will not be exact, but they have been found to be close to the actual occurrence in firms with remarkable frequency.

The next step is to determine the level of inventory control for each classification. Class A items require tight inventory control because they represent such a large percentage of the total dollar value of inventory. These inventory levels should be as low as possible, and safety stocks minimized. This requires accurate demand forecasts and detailed record keeping. The appropriate inventory control system and inventory modeling procedure to determine order quantity should be applied. In addition, close attention should be given to purchasing policies and procedures if the inventory items are acquired from outside the firm. B and C items require less stringent inventory control. Since carrying costs are usually lower for C items, higher inventory levels can sometimes be maintained with larger safety stocks. It may not be necessary to control C items beyond simple observation. In general, A items frequently require a continuous control system, where the inventory level is continuously monitored; a periodic review system with less monitoring will suffice for C items.

Although cost is the predominant reason for inventory classification, other factors such as scarcity of parts or difficulty of supply may also be reasons for giving items a higher priority. For example, long lead times for some parts might be a problem for a company in Australia ordering from Europe, thus requiring a higher-priority classification for those parts.

EXAMPLE 13.1

ABC SYSTEM CLASSIFICATION

The maintenance department for a small manufacturing firm has responsibility for maintaining an inventory of spare parts for the machinery it services. The parts inventory, unit cost, and annual usage are as follows:

Part	Unit Cost	Annual Usage
1	$ 60	90
2	350	40
3	30	130
4	80	60
5	30	100
6	20	180
7	10	170
8	320	50
9	510	60
10	20	120

(Continued)

The department manager wants to classify the inventory parts according to the ABC system to determine which stocks of parts should most closely be monitored.

SOLUTION

First rank the items according to their total value and also compute each item's percentage of total value and quantity.

Part	Total Value	% of Total Value	% of Total Quantity	% Cumulative
9	$30,600	35.9	6.0	6.0
8	16,000	18.7	5.0	11.0
2	14,000	16.4	4.0	15.0
1	5,400	6.3	9.0	24.0
4	4,800	5.6	6.0	30.0
3	3,900	4.6	13.0	43.0
6	3,600	4.2	18.0	61.0
5	3,000	3.5	10.0	71.0
10	2,400	2.8	12.0	83.0
7	1,700	2.0	17.0	100.0
	$85,400			

Based on simple observation, it appears that the first three items form a group with the highest value, the next three items form a second group, and the last four items constitute a group. Thus, the ABC classification for these items is as follows:

Class	Items	% of Total Value	% of Total Quantity
A	9, 8, 2	71.0	15.0
B	1, 4, 3	16.5	28.0
C	6, 5, 10, 7	12.5	57.0

Economic Order Quantity Models

In a continuous, or fixed-order-quantity, system when inventory reaches a specific level, referred to as the *reorder point*, a fixed amount is ordered. The most widely used and traditional means for determining how much to order in a continuous system is the **economic order quantity (EOQ)** model, also referred to as the economic lot-size model. The earliest published derivation of the basic EOQ model formula in 1915 is credited to Ford Harris, an employee at Westinghouse.

The function of the EOQ model is to determine the optimal order size that minimizes total inventory costs. There are several variations of the EOQ model, depending on the assumptions made about the inventory system. We will describe two model versions: the basic EOQ model and the production quantity model.

ALONG THE SUPPLY CHAIN

Determining Supply Chain Strategy by Evaluating Inventory Costs at Hewlett-Packard

Hewlett-Packard, with annual revenues exceeding $90 billion and 150,000 employees worldwide, is the *Fortune 500* 11th-ranked company. Although demand for PCs increased fivefold in the 1990s, becoming a veritable household product, many PC companies struggled to remain profitable. By the end of the 1990s, HP was struggling to make a profit in the increasingly competitive global PC market because of price cuts throughout the 1990s. Since prices were not really controllable, inventory costs became especially critical in the PC profit equation. Rapid technological advancements render new PC products obsolete in a few months, and, in general, it's believed that the value of a PC decreases at the rate of 1% per week. As such, holding any excess inventory was very costly.

In the late 1990s, in order to return its PC business to more sustainable profitability, HP undertook an extensive evaluation of its supply chain costs. It discovered that inventory-related costs were the main determinants of overall PC cost, and, in fact, in one year alone, inventory-related costs equaled the PC business's total operating margin. Further, HP determined that the traditional inventory carrying (or holding) costs (which encompass capital costs plus storage, taxes, insurance, breakage, etc.) accounted for less than 10% of the total inventory-related costs. HP identified four additional inventory costs in its PC business that were a major factor in overall supply chain costs. The single biggest inventory cost was determined to be the "component devaluation cost." This is the penalty cost HP incurred when the price dropped for excess components and parts (e.g., CPUs, memory, and chips) being held in inventory. HP held inventories of parts and components in factories, in distribution centers, and in transit, and would incur a devaluation cost at all of these points in its supply chain whenever a price reduction occurred. Another inventory cost is the "price protection cost," which occurs when the retail price of a product drops after it has already been shipped to the sales outlet. HP has to reimburse its sales partners for the difference in price for any unsold units, so its partners won't incur a loss. Given how fast PC products lose their value, excess inventory can result in large protection costs. A third inventory-related cost in the PC business is the "product return cost." This is the cost of a full refund HP pays its distributors when unsold products are returned; essentially it is a 100% price protection cost. In some cases, sales partners and distributors returned excess unsold inventory valued at more than 10% of a product's revenue. The fourth inventory cost is "obsolescence cost," which is the cost of writing off unsold products in inventory after the life of the product ends. Since PC products lifecycles are so short, there is the potential for large costs if excessive inventories are held. Related costs include price discounts for products that are about to be discontinued and the marketing costs to reduce inventory quickly. The Mobile Computing Division (which manufactures notebooks) was the first HP PC business unit to focus on all of these inventory-related costs in redesigning its supply chain. The original supply chain consisted of a central manufacturing facility with local product configuration occurring at regional sites. (In this configuration, about 40% of the total supply chain cost was related to inventory.) In the redesigned supply chain, there is a central manufacturing facility and products are air freighted directly to customers around the world. Positive results were immediate: in a two-year period, inventory-related costs dropped from almost 19% of total revenue to less than 4%, and the notebook division became profitable. As a result, all other HP PC operations began using these inventory costs to evaluate and redesign their supply chains.

Using the Internet as a research tool, compare Hewlett-Packard's inventory system and its methods for controlling inventory costs with a vendor-managed inventory (VMI) system (page 355).

Source: Based on G. Callioni, X. de Montgros, R. Slagmulder, L. N. Van Wassenhove, and L. Wright, "Inventory-Driven Costs," *The Harvard Business Review* 83, no. 3 (March 2005): pp. 135–141.

THE BASIC EOQ MODEL

The *basic EOQ model* is a formula for determining the optimal order size that minimizes the sum of carrying costs and ordering costs. The model formula is derived under a set of simplifying and restrictive assumptions, as follows:

- Demand is known with certainty and is constant over time.
- No shortages are allowed.
- Lead time for the receipt of orders is constant.
- The order quantity is received all at once.

These basic model assumptions are reflected in Figure 13.2, which describes the continuous-inventory **order cycle** system inherent in the EOQ model. An order quantity, Q, is received and is used up over time at a constant rate. When the inventory level decreases to the reorder point, R, a new order is placed; a period of time, referred to as the *lead time*, is required for delivery. The order is received all at once just at the moment when demand depletes the entire stock of inventory—the inventory level reaches 0—so there will be no shortages. This cycle is repeated continuously for the same order quantity, reorder point, and lead time.

As we mentioned, the economic order quantity is the order size that minimizes the sum of carrying costs and ordering costs. These two costs react inversely to each other. As the order size increases, fewer orders are required, causing the ordering cost to decline, whereas the average amount of inventory on hand will increase, resulting in an increase in carrying costs. Thus, in effect, the optimal order quantity represents a compromise between these two inversely related costs.

The total annual ordering cost is computed by multiplying the cost per order, designated as C_o, times the number of orders per year. Since annual demand, D, is assumed to be known and to be constant, the number of orders will be D/Q, where Q is the order size and

$$\text{Annual ordering cost} = \frac{C_o D}{Q}$$

The only variable in this equation is Q; both C_o and D are constant parameters. Thus, the relative magnitude of the ordering cost is dependent on the order size.

Total annual carrying cost is computed by multiplying the annual per-unit carrying cost, designated as C_c, by the average inventory level. The average inventory level is one-half of Q or $Q/2$, as shown in Figure 13.2.

$$\text{Annual carrying cost} = \frac{C_c Q}{2}$$

The total annual inventory cost is the sum of the ordering and carrying costs:

$$\text{TC} = \frac{C_o D}{Q} + \frac{C_c Q}{2}$$

Figure 13.2
The Inventory Order Cycle

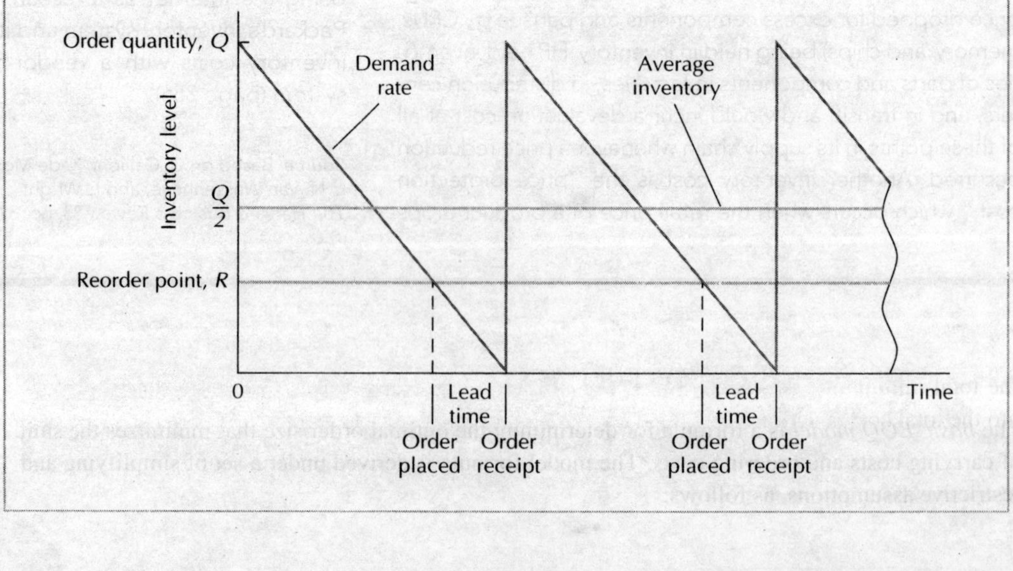

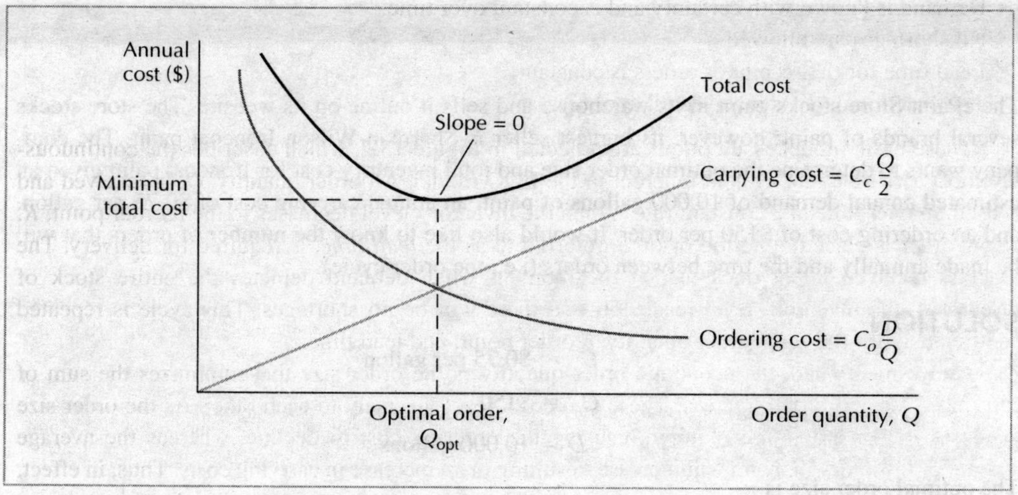

Figure 13.3
The EOQ Cost Model

The graph in Figure 13.3 shows the inverse relationship between ordering cost and carrying cost, resulting in a convex total cost curve.

The optimal order quantity occurs at the point in Figure 13.3 where the total cost curve is at a minimum, which coincides exactly with the point where the carrying cost curve intersects the ordering cost curve. This enables us to determine the optimal value of Q by equating the two cost functions and solving for Q:

$$\frac{C_o D}{Q} = \frac{C_c Q}{2}$$

$$Q^2 = \frac{2C_o D}{C_c}$$

$$Q_{\text{opt}} = \sqrt{\frac{2C_o D}{C_c}}$$

Alternatively, the optimal value of Q can be determined by differentiating the total cost curve with respect to Q, setting the resulting function equal to zero (the slope at the minimum point on the total cost curve), and solving for Q:

$$\text{TC} = \frac{C_o D}{Q} + \frac{C_c Q}{2}$$

$$\frac{\partial \text{TC}}{\partial Q} = -\frac{C_o D}{Q^2} + \frac{C_c}{2}$$

$$0 = -\frac{C_o D}{Q^2} + \frac{C_c}{2}$$

$$Q_{\text{opt}} = \sqrt{\frac{2C_o D}{C_c}}$$

The total minimum cost is determined by substituting the value for the optimal order size, Q_{opt}, into the total cost equation:

$$\text{TC}_{\min} = \frac{C_o D}{Q_{\text{opt}}} + \frac{C_c Q_{\text{opt}}}{2}$$

EXAMPLE 13.2

THE ECONOMIC ORDER QUANTITY

The ePaint Store stocks paint in its warehouse and sells it online on its website. The store stocks several brands of paint; however, its biggest seller is Sharman-Wilson Ironcoat paint. The company wants to determine the optimal order size and total inventory cost for Ironcoat paint given an estimated annual demand of 10,000 gallons of paint, an annual carrying cost of \$0.75 per gallon, and an ordering cost of \$150 per order. It would also like to know the number of orders that will be made annually and the time between orders (i.e., the order cycle).

SOLUTION

$$C_c = \$0.75 \text{ per gallon}$$
$$C_o = \$150$$
$$D = 10{,}000 \text{ gallons}$$

The optimal order size is

$$Q_{\text{opt}} = \sqrt{\frac{2C_oD}{C_c}}$$
$$= \sqrt{\frac{2(150)(10{,}000)}{(0.75)}}$$
$$= 2{,}000 \text{ gallons}$$

The total annual inventory cost is determined by substituting Q_{opt} into the total cost formula:

$$\text{TC}_{\min} = \frac{C_oD}{Q_{\text{opt}}} + \frac{C_cQ_{\text{opt}}}{2}$$
$$= \frac{(150)(10{,}000)}{2{,}000} + \frac{(0.75)(2{,}000)}{2}$$
$$= \$750 + 750$$
$$= \$1{,}500$$

The number of orders per year is computed as follows:

$$\text{Number of orders per year} = \frac{D}{Q_{\text{opt}}}$$
$$= \frac{10{,}000}{2{,}000}$$
$$= 5 \text{ orders per year}$$

Given that the company processes orders 311 days annually (365 days minus 52 Sundays, Thanksgiving, and Christmas), the order cycle is

$$\text{Order cycle time} = \frac{311 \text{ days}}{D/Q_{\text{opt}}}$$
$$= \frac{311}{5}$$
$$= 62.2 \text{ days}$$

The optimal order quantity, determined in this example and in general, is an approximate value, since it is based on estimates of carrying and ordering costs as well as uncertain demand (although all of these parameters are treated as known, certain values in the EOQ model). In practice it is desirable to round the Q values off to some nearby pragmatic value. The precision of a decimal place is generally not necessary. In addition, because the optimal order quantity is computed from a square root, errors or variations in the cost parameters and demand tend to be dampened. For instance, in Example 13.2, if the order cost had actually been 30% higher, or \$200, the resulting optimal order size would have varied only by a little under 10% (i.e., 2,190 gallons instead of 2,000 gallons). Variations in both inventory costs will tend to offset each other, since they have an inverse relationship. As a result, the EOQ model is relatively resilient to errors in the cost estimates and demand, or is *robust*, which has tended to enhance its popularity.

THE PRODUCTION QUANTITY MODEL

A variation of the basic EOQ model is the **production quantity model**, also referred to as the *gradual usage* and *non-instantaneous receipt model*. In this EOQ model the assumption that orders are received all at once is relaxed. The order quantity is received gradually over time, and the inventory level is depleted at the same time it is being replenished. This situation is commonly found when the inventory user is also the producer, as in a manufacturing operation where a part is produced to use in a larger assembly. This situation also can occur when orders are delivered continuously over time or when a retailer is also the producer.

The noninstantaneous receipt model is shown graphically in Figure 13.4. The inventory level is gradually replenished as an order is received. In the basic EOQ model, average inventory was half the maximum inventory level, or $Q/2$, but in this model variation, the maximum inventory level is not simply Q; it is an amount somewhat lower than Q, adjusted for the fact the order quantity is depleted during the order receipt period.

In order to determine the average inventory level, we define the following parameters unique to this model:

p = daily rate at which the order is received over time, also known as the *production rate*
d = daily rate at which inventory is demanded

The demand rate cannot exceed the production rate, since we are still assuming that no shortages are possible, and, if $d = p$, there is no order size, since items are used as fast as they are produced. For this model the production rate must exceed the demand rate, or $p \geq d$.

Observing Figure 13.4, we see that the time required to finish receiving an order is the order quantity divided by the rate at which the order is received, or Q/p. For example, if the order size is 100 units and the production rate, p, is 20 units per day, the order will be received over five days. The amount of inventory that will be depleted or used up during this time period is determined by

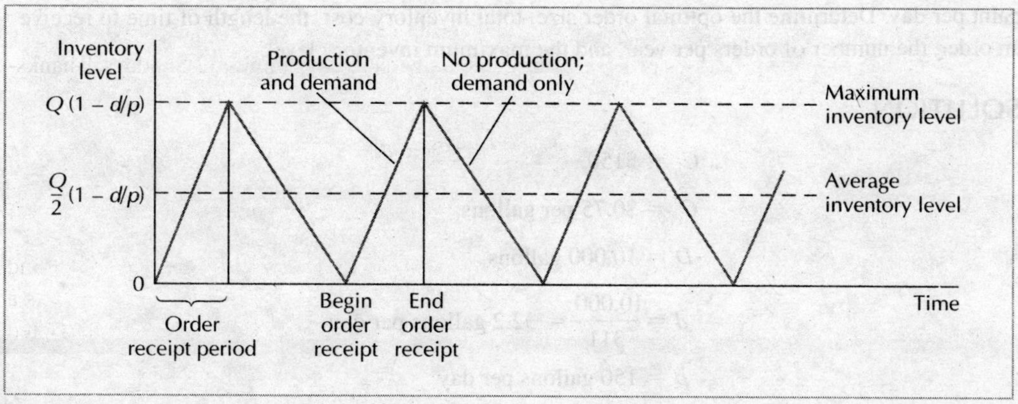

Figure 13.4
The Production Quantity Model

multiplying by the demand rate: $(Q/p)d$. For example, if it takes five days to receive the order and during this time inventory is depleted at the rate of two units per day, then 10 units are used. As a result, the maximum amount of inventory on hand is the order size minus the amount depleted during the receipt period, computed as

$$\text{Maximum inventory level} = Q - \frac{Q}{p}d$$

$$= Q\left(1 - \frac{d}{p}\right)$$

Since this is the maximum inventory level, the average inventory level is determined by dividing this amount by 2:

$$\text{Average inventory level} = \frac{1}{2}\left[Q\left(1 - \frac{d}{p}\right)\right]$$

$$= \frac{Q}{2}\left(1 - \frac{d}{p}\right)$$

The total carrying cost using this function for average inventory is

$$\text{Total carrying cost} = \frac{C_c Q}{2}\left(1 - \frac{d}{p}\right)$$

In this case the ordering cost, C_o, is often the setup cost for production.

Thus, the total annual inventory cost is determined according to the following formula:

$$\text{TC} = \frac{C_o D}{Q} + \frac{C_c Q}{2}\left(1 - \frac{d}{p}\right)$$

Solving this function for the optimal value Q,

$$Q_{\text{opt}} = \sqrt{\frac{2C_o D}{C_c\left(1 - \dfrac{d}{p}\right)}}$$

EXAMPLE 13.3

THE PRODUCTION QUANTITY MODEL

Assume that the ePaint Store has its own manufacturing facility in which it produces Ironcoat paint. The ordering cost, C_o, is the cost of setting up the production process to make paint. C_o = \$150. Recall that C_c = \$0.75 per gallon and D = 10,000 gallons per year. The manufacturing facility operates the same days the store is open (i.e., 311 days) and produces 150 gallons of paint per day. Determine the optimal order size, total inventory cost, the length of time to receive an order, the number of orders per year, and the maximum inventory level.

SOLUTION

$$C_o = \$150$$

$$C_c = \$0.75 \text{ per gallons}$$

$$D = 10{,}000 \text{ gallons}$$

$$d = \frac{10{,}000}{311} = 32.2 \text{ gallons per day}$$

$$p = 150 \text{ gallons per day}$$

The optimal order size is determined as follows:

$$Q_{\text{opt}} = \sqrt{\frac{2C_oD}{C_c\left(1 - \dfrac{d}{p}\right)}}$$

$$= \sqrt{\frac{2(150)(10{,}000)}{0.75\left(1 - \dfrac{32.2}{150}\right)}}$$

$$= 2{,}256.8 \text{ gallons}$$

Although an order of 2,256.8 gallons should be rounded to 2,257, we will use the 2,256.8 to compute total cost.

This value is substituted into the following formula to determine total minimum annual inventory cost:

$$\text{TC}_{\min} = \frac{C_oD}{Q} + \frac{C_cQ}{2}\left(1 - \frac{d}{p}\right)$$

$$= \frac{(150)(10{,}000)}{2{,}256.8} + \frac{(0.75)(2{,}256.8)}{2}\left(1 - \frac{32.2}{150}\right)$$

$$= \$1329$$

The length of time to receive an order for this type of manufacturing operation is commonly called the length of the *production run*.

$$\text{Production run} = \frac{Q}{p}$$

$$= \frac{2{,}256.8}{150}$$

$$= 15.05 \text{ days per order}$$

The number of orders per year is actually the number of production runs that will be made:

$$\text{Number of production runs (from orders)} = \frac{D}{Q}$$

$$= \frac{10{,}000}{2{,}256.8}$$

$$= 4.43 \text{ runs per year}$$

Finally, the maximum inventory level is

$$\text{Maximum inventory level} = Q\left(1 - \frac{d}{p}\right)$$

$$= 2{,}256.8\left(1 - \frac{32.2}{150}\right)$$

$$= 1{,}772 \text{ gallons}$$

Thus, ePaint will need to set aside storage space sufficient to accommodate these 1,772 gallons of paint.

SOLUTION OF EOQ MODELS WITH EXCEL

EOQ analysis can be done with Excel. The Excel solution screen for Example 13.2 is shown in Exhibit 13.1. The Excel screen for the production quantity model in Example 13.3 is shown in Exhibit 13.2.

EXHIBIT 13.1

EXCEL FILE

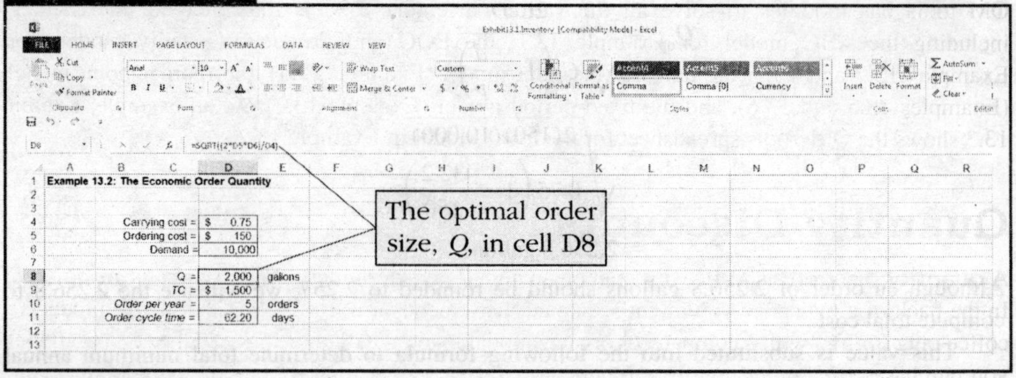

EXHIBIT 13.2

EXCEL FILE

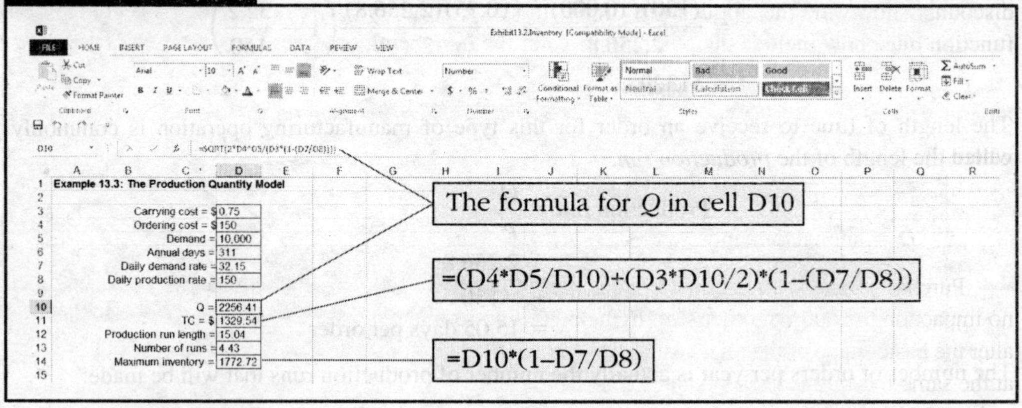

EXHIBIT 13.3

OM TOOLS

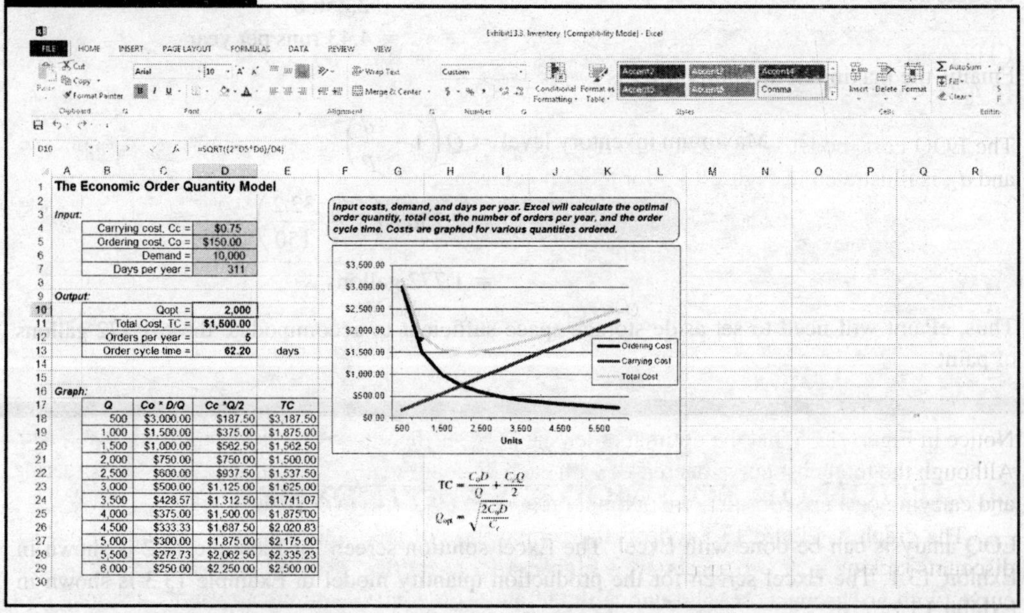

SOLUTION OF EOQ MODELS WITH OM TOOLS

OM tools has modules to solve all the various inventory models illustrated in this chapter, including the ABC model for Example 13.1, the EOQ and production quality models for Examples 13.2 and 13.3, the quantity discount model (Example 13.4), the reorder point model (Examples 13.5 and 13.6), and the fixed-period model (Example 13.7). As an example, Exhibit 13.3 shows the OM Tools spreadsheet for the EOQ Model in Example 13.2.

Quantity Discounts

A **quantity discount** is a price discount on an item if predetermined numbers of units are ordered. In the back of a magazine you might see an advertisement for a firm stating that it will produce a coffee mug (or hat) with a company or organizational logo on it, and the price will be $5 per mug if you purchase 100, $4 per mug if you purchase 200, or $3 per mug if you purchase 500 or more. Many manufacturing companies receive price discounts for ordering materials and supplies in high volume, and retail stores receive price discounts for ordering merchandise in large quantities.

The basic EOQ model can be used to determine the optimal order size with quantity discounts; however, the application of the model is slightly altered. The total inventory cost function must now include the purchase price of the item being ordered:

$$\text{TC} = \frac{C_oD}{Q} + \frac{C_cQ}{2} + PD$$

where

P = per-unit price of the item

D = annual demand

Purchase price was not considered as part of our basic EOQ formulation earlier because it had no impact on the optimal order size. In the preceding formula, PD is a constant value that would not alter the basic shape of the total cost curve; that is, the minimum point on the cost curve would still be at the same location, corresponding to the same value of Q. Thus, the optimal order size is the same no matter what the purchase price is. However, when a discount price is available, it is associated with a specific order size, which may be different from the optimal order size, and the customer must evaluate the tradeoff between possibly higher carrying costs with the discount quantity versus EOQ cost. As a result, the purchase price does affect the order-size decision when a discount is available.

QUANTITY DISCOUNTS WITH CONSTANT CARRYING COST

The EOQ cost model with constant carrying costs for a pricing schedule with two discounts, d_1 and d_2, is illustrated in Figure 13.5 for the following discounts:

Order Size	Price
0–99	$10
100–99	8(d_1)
200+	6(d_2)

Notice in Figure 13.5 that the optimal order size, Q_{opt}, is the same regardless of the discount price. Although the total cost curve decreases with each discount in price (i.e., d_1 and d_2), since ordering and carrying cost are constant, the optimal order size, Q_{opt}, does not change.

The graph in Figure 13.5 reflects the composition of the total cost curve resulting from the discounts kicking in at two successively higher order quantities. The first segment of the total cost curve (with no discount) is valid only up to 99 units ordered. Beyond that quantity, the total cost

Figure 13.5

Quantity Discounts with Constant Carrying Cost

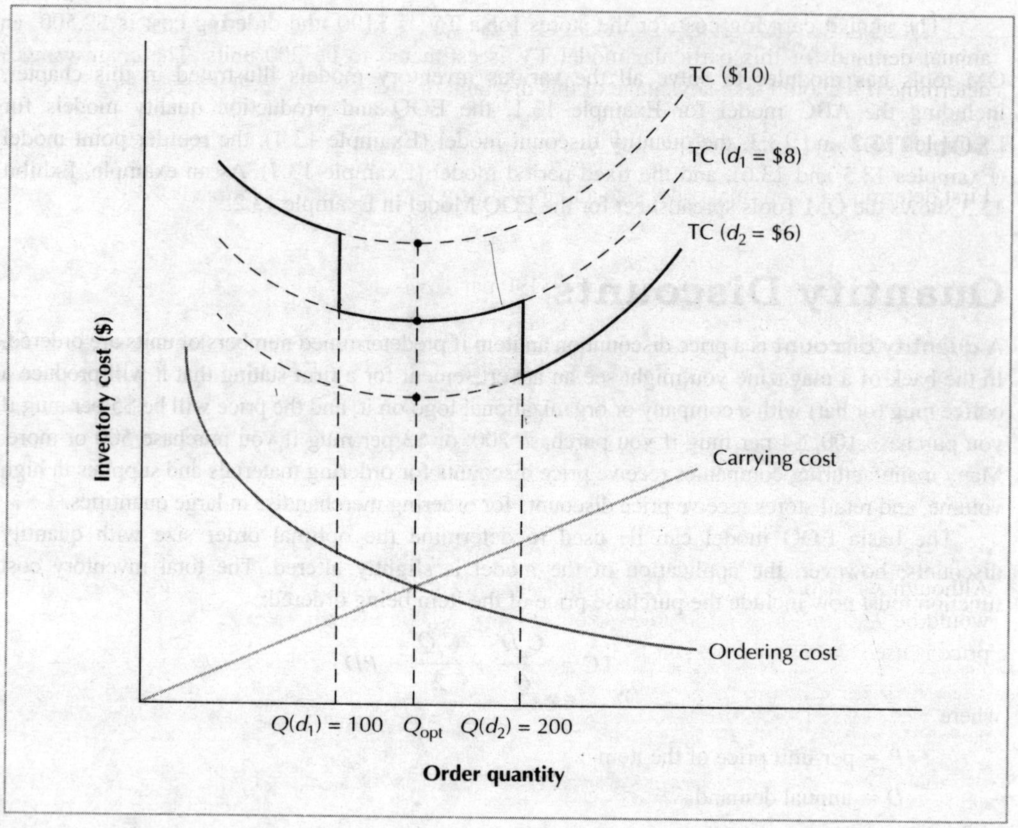

curve (represented by the topmost dashed line) is meaningless because above 100 units, there is a discount (d_1). Between 100 and 199 units, the total cost drops down to the middle curve. This middle-level cost curve is valid only up to 199 units because at 200 units, there is another, lower discount (d_2). So the total cost curve has two discrete steps, starting with the original total cost curve, dropping down to the next level cost curve for the first discount, and finally dropping to the third-level cost curve for the final discount.

Notice that the optimal order size, Q_{opt}, is feasible only for the middle level of the total cost curve, TC(d_1)—it does not coincide with the top level of the cost curve, TC, or the lowest level, TC(d_2). If the optimal EOQ order size had coincided with the lowest level of the total cost curve, TC(d_2), it would have been optimal order size for the entire discount price schedule. Since it does not coincide with the lowest level of the total cost curve, the total cost with Q_{opt} must be compared to the lower-level total cost using $Q(d_2)$ to see which results in the minimum total cost. In this case the optimal order size is 200.

EXAMPLE 13.4

A QUANTITY DISCOUNT WITH CONSTANT CARRYING COST

Avtek, a distributor of audio and video equipment, wants to reduce a large stock of televisions. It has offered a local chain of stores a quantity discount pricing schedule, as follows:

Quantity	Price
1–49	$1,400
50–89	1,100
90+	900

The annual carrying cost for the stores for a TV is \$190, the ordering cost is \$2,500, and annual demand for this particular model TV is estimated to be 200 units. The chain wants to determine if it should take advantage of this discount or order the basic EOQ order size.

SOLUTION

First determine the optimal order size and total cost with the basic EOQ model.

$$C_o = \$2{,}500$$
$$C_c = \$190 \text{ per TV}$$
$$D = 200 \text{ TVs per year}$$

$$Q_{\text{opt}} = \sqrt{\frac{2C_oD}{C_c}}$$
$$= \sqrt{\frac{2(2500)(200)}{190}}$$
$$= 72.5 \text{ TVs}$$

Although we will use $Q_{\text{opt}} = 72.5$ in the subsequent computations, realistically, the order size would be 73 televisions. This order size is eligible for the first discount of \$1,100; therefore, this price is used to compute total cost:

$$\text{TC}_{\min} = \frac{C_0D}{Q_{\text{opt}}} + \frac{C_cQ_{\text{opt}}}{2} + PD$$
$$= \frac{(2{,}500)(200)}{72.5} + \frac{(190)(72.5)}{2} + (1{,}100)(200)$$
$$\text{TC}_{\min} = \$233{,}784$$

Since there is a discount for a larger order size than 50 units (i.e., there is a lower cost curve), this total cost of \$233,784 must be compared with total cost with an order size of 90 and a discounted price of \$900:

$$\text{TC} = \frac{C_oD}{Q} + \frac{C_cQ}{2} + PD$$
$$= \frac{(2{,}500)(200)}{90} + \frac{(190)(90)}{2} + (900)(200)$$
$$= \$194{,}105$$

Since this total cost is lower (\$194,105 < \$233,784), the maximum discount price should be taken, and 90 units should be ordered. We know that there is no order size larger than 90 that would result in a lower cost, since the minimum point on this total cost curve has already been determined to be 73.

QUANTITY DISCOUNT MODEL SOLUTION WITH EXCEL

It is also possible to use Excel to solve the quantity-discount model with constant carrying cost. Exhibit 13.4 shows the Excel solution screen for Example 13.4. Notice that the selection of the appropriate order size, Q, that results in the minimum total cost for each discount range is determined by the formulas embedded in cells E8, E9, and E10. For example, the formula for the first quantity-discount range, "1–49," is embedded in cell E8 and shown on the formula bar at the top of the screen,

"=IF(D8≥B8,D8,B8)." This means that if the discount order size in cell D8 (i.e., $Q = 72.55$) is greater than or equal to the quantity in cell B8 (i.e., 1), then the quantity in cell D8 (72.55) is selected; otherwise the amount in cell B8 is selected. The formulas in cells E9 and E10 are constructed similarly. The result is that the order quantity for the final discount range, $Q = 90$, is selected.

Reorder Point

In our description of the EOQ models in the previous sections, we addressed how much should be ordered. Now we will discuss the other aspect of inventory management, when to order. The determinant of when to order in a continuous inventory system is the **reorder point**, the inventory level at which a new order is placed.

The reorder point for our basic EOQ model with constant demand and a constant lead time to receive an order is equal to the amount demanded during the lead time,

$$R = dL$$

where

d = demand rate per period (e.g., daily)

L = lead time

EXHIBIT 13.4 EXCEL FILE

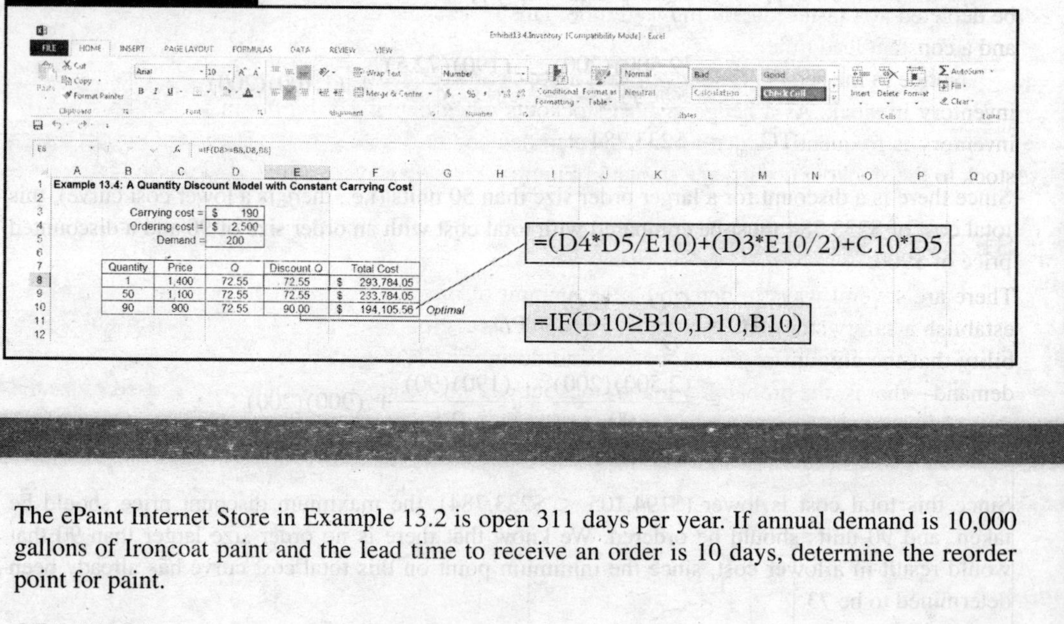

EXAMPLE 13.5

REORDER POINT FOR THE BASIC EOQ MODEL

The ePaint Internet Store in Example 13.2 is open 311 days per year. If annual demand is 10,000 gallons of Ironcoat paint and the lead time to receive an order is 10 days, determine the reorder point for paint.

SOLUTION

$$R = dL$$

$$= \left(\frac{10{,}000}{311}\right)(10)$$

$$= 321.54 \text{ gallons}$$

When the inventory level falls to approximately 321 gallons of paint, a new order is placed. Notice that the reorder point is not related to the optimal order quantity or any of the inventory costs.

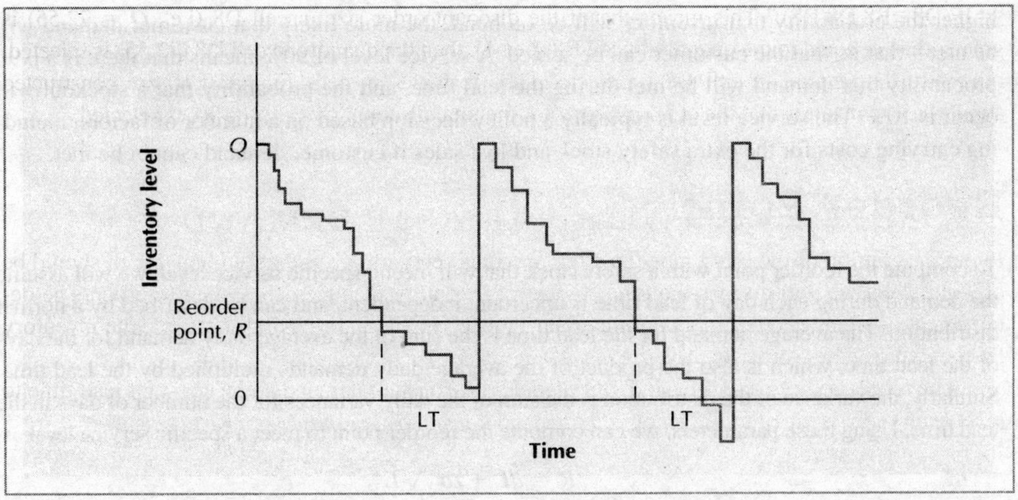

Figure 13.6

Variable Demand with a Reorder Point

SAFETY STOCKS

In Example 13.5, an order is made when the inventory level reaches the reorder point. During the lead time, the remaining inventory in stock will be depleted at a constant demand rate, such that the new order quantity will arrive at exactly the same moment as the inventory level reaches zero. Realistically, demand—and, to a lesser extent lead time—are uncertain. The inventory level might be depleted at a faster rate during lead time. This is depicted in Figure 13.6 for uncertain demand and a constant lead time.

Notice in the second order cycle that a **stockout** occurs when demand exceeds the available inventory in stock. As a hedge against stockouts when demand is uncertain, a **safety stock** of inventory is frequently added to the expected demand during lead time. The addition of a safety stock to the stockout occurrence shown in Figure 13.6 is displayed in Figure 13.7.

SERVICE LEVEL

There are several ways to determine the amount of the safety stock. One popular method is to establish a safety stock that will meet a specified **service level**. The service level is the probability that the amount of inventory on hand during the lead time is sufficient to meet expected demand—that is, the probability that a stockout will not occur. The term *service* is used, since the

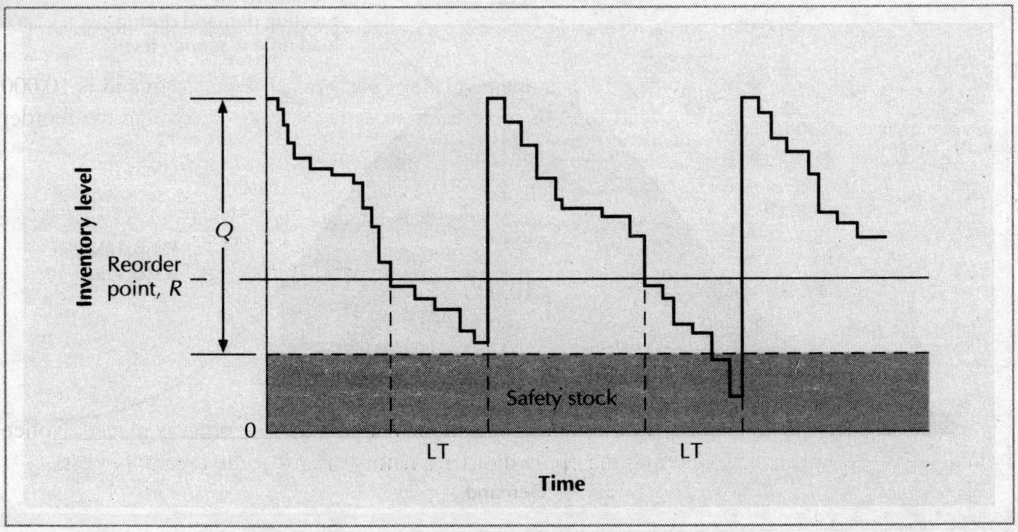

Figure 13.7

Reorder Point with a Safety Stock

higher the probability that inventory will be on hand, the more likely that customer demand will be met—that is, that the customer can be served. A service level of 90% means that there is a 0.90 probability that demand will be met during the lead time, and the probability that a stockout will occur is 10%. The service level is typically a policy decision based on a number of factors, including carrying costs for the extra safety stock and lost sales if customer demand cannot be met.

REORDER POINT WITH VARIABLE DEMAND

To compute the reorder point with a safety stock that will meet a specific service level, we will assume the demand during each day of lead time is uncertain, independent, and can be described by a normal distribution. The average demand for the lead time is the sum of the average daily demand for the days of the lead time, which is also the product of the average daily demands multiplied by the lead time. Similarly, the variance of the distribution is the sum of the daily variances for the number of days in the lead time. Using these parameters, we can compute the reorder point to meet a specific service level as

$$R = \bar{d}L + z\sigma_d\sqrt{L}$$

where

$\bar{d}$ = average daily demand

L = lead time

σ_d = the standard deviation of daily deman

z = number of standard deviations corresponding to the service level probability

$z\sigma_d\sqrt{L}$ = safety stock

The term $\sigma_d\sqrt{L}$ in this formula for the reorder point is the square root of the sum of the daily variances during lead time:

$$\text{Variance} = (\text{daily variance}) \times (\text{number of days of lead time})$$
$$= \sigma_d^2 L$$
$$\text{Standard deviation} = \sqrt{\sigma_d^2 L}$$
$$= \sigma_d\sqrt{L}$$

The reorder point relative to the service level is shown in Figure 13.8. The service level is the shaded area, or probability, to the left of the reorder point, R.

Figure 13.8

Reorder Point for a Service Level

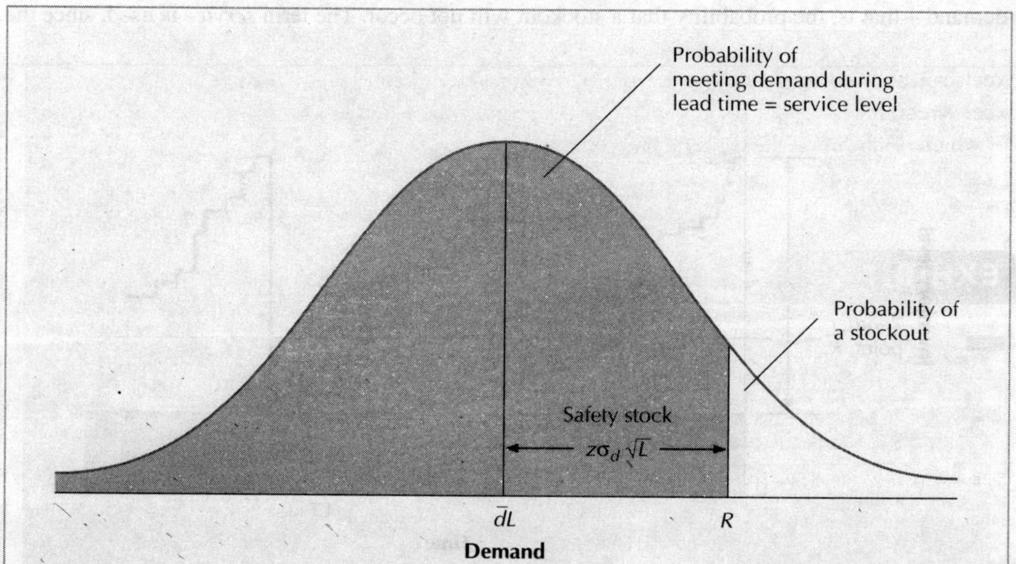

EXAMPLE 13.6

REORDER POINT FOR VARIABLE DEMAND

For the ePaint Internet Store in Example 13.2, we will assume that daily demand for Ironcoat paint is normally distributed with an average daily demand of 30 gallons and a standard deviation of 5 gallons of paint per day. The lead time for receiving a new order of paint is 10 days. Determine the reorder point and safety stock if the store wants a service level of 95%—that is, the probability of a stockout is 5%.

SOLUTION

$$\bar{d} = 30 \text{ gallons per day}$$
$$L = 10 \text{ days}$$
$$\sigma_d = 5 \text{ gallons per day}$$

For a 95% service level, the value of z (from the normal table in Supplement C) is 1.65. The safety stock is:

$$\begin{aligned}\text{Safety stock} &= z\sigma_d\sqrt{L}\\ &= (1.65)(5)(\sqrt{10})\\ &= 26.1 \text{ gallons}\end{aligned}$$

The reorder point is computed as follows:

$$\begin{aligned}R &= \bar{d}L + z\sigma_d\sqrt{L}\\ &= 30(10) + (1.65)(5)(\sqrt{10})\\ &= 300 + 26.1\\ &= 326.1 \text{ gallons}\end{aligned}$$

DETERMINING THE REORDER POINT WITH EXCEL

Excel can be used to determine the reorder point for variable demand. Exhibit 13.5 shows the Excel screen for Example 13.6. Notice that the reorder point is computed using the formula in cell E7, which is shown on the formula bar at the top of the screen.

EXHIBIT 13.5

EXCEL FILE

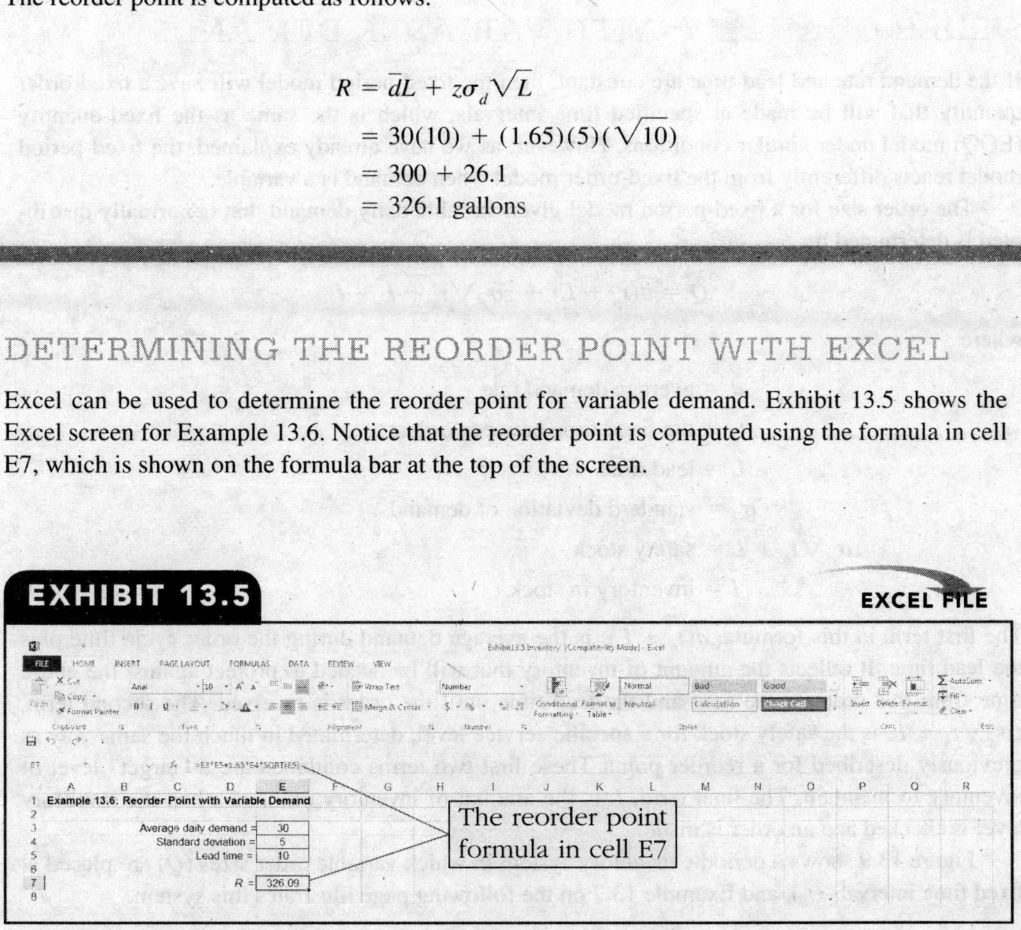

Order Quantity for a Periodic Inventory System

We defined a continuous, or fixed-order-quantity, inventory system as one in which the order quantity was constant and the time between orders varied. So far this type of inventory system has been the focus of our discussion. The less common *periodic*, or *fixed-time-period, inventory system* is one in which the time between orders is constant and the order size varies. Small retailers often use this sytem. Drugstores are one example of a business that sometimes uses a fixed-period inventory system. Drugstores stock a number of personal hygiene- and health-related products such as shampoo, toothpaste, soap, bandages, cough medicine, and aspirin.

Normally, the vendors who provide these items to the store will make periodic visits—every few weeks or every month—and count the stock of inventory on hand for their product. If the inventory is exhausted or at some predetermined reorder point, a new order will be placed for an amount that will bring the inventory level back up to the desired level. The drugstore managers will generally not monitor the inventory level between vendor visits but instead will rely on the vendor to take inventory.

Under this system, the vendor would bundle many small, low-cost items into a single order and delivery, thereby saving costs. Since the items are generally of low value, larger safety stocks will not pose a significant cost. Also, if the items are noncritical, even if there is a stockout, it is not a big deal. However, inventory might be exhausted early in the time period between visits, resulting in a stockout that will not be remedied until the next scheduled order. As a result, a larger safety stock for more critical items is sometimes required for the fixed-interval system.

ORDER QUANTITY WITH VARIABLE DEMAND

If the demand rate and lead time are constant, then the fixed-period model will have a fixed-order quantity that will be made at specified time intervals, which is the same as the fixed-quantity (EOQ) model under similar conditions. However, as we have already explained, the fixed-period model reacts differently from the fixed-order model when demand is a variable.

The order size for a fixed-period model given variable daily demand that is normally distributed is determined by

$$Q = \bar{d}(t_b + L) + z\sigma_d\sqrt{t_b + L} - I$$

where

$$\begin{aligned} \bar{d} &= \text{average demand rate} \\ t_b &= \text{the fixed time between orders} \\ L &= \text{lead time} \\ \sigma_d &= \text{standard deviation of demand} \\ z\sigma_d\sqrt{t_b + L} &= \text{safety stock} \\ I &= \text{inventory in stock} \end{aligned}$$

The first term in this formula, $\bar{d}(t_b + L)$, is the average demand during the order cycle time plus the lead time. It reflects the amount of inventory that will be needed to protect against the entire time from this order to the next and the lead time until the order is received. The second term, $z\sigma_d\sqrt{t_b + L}$, is the safety stock for a specific service level, determined in much the same way as previously described for a reorder point. These first two terms combined are a "target" level of inventory to maintain. The final term, I, is the amount of inventory on hand when the inventory level is checked and an order is made.

Figure 13.9 shows a periodic inventory system in which variable order sizes (Q) are placed at fixed time intervals (t_b), and Example 13.7 on the following page illustrates this system.

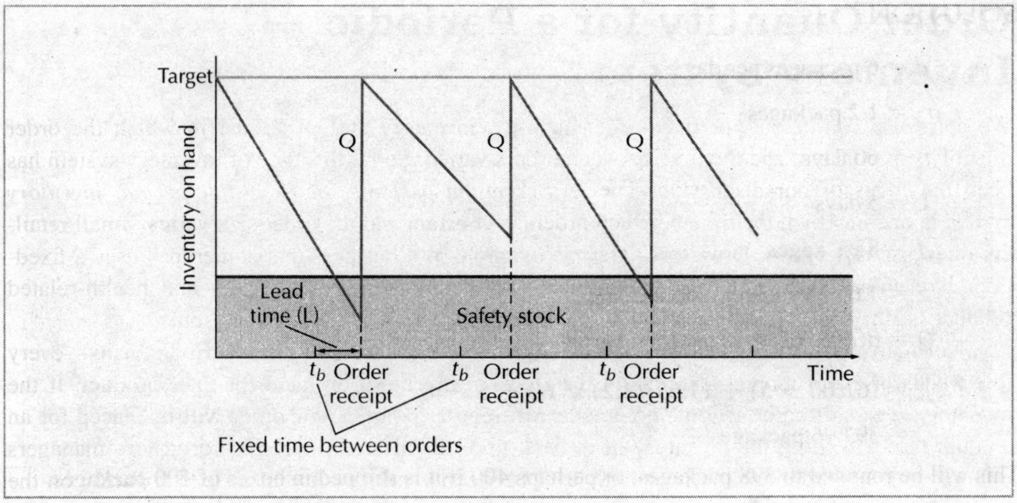

Figure 13.9

Periodic Inventory System

DETERMINING THE ORDER QUANTITY FOR THE FIXED-PERIOD MODEL WITH EXCEL

The order quantity for the fixed-period model with variable demand can be determined using Excel. The Excel screen for Example 13.7 is shown in Exhibit 13.6. Notice that the order quantity in cell D10 is computed with the formula shown on the formula bar at the top of the screen.

EXHIBIT 13.6

EXCEL FILE

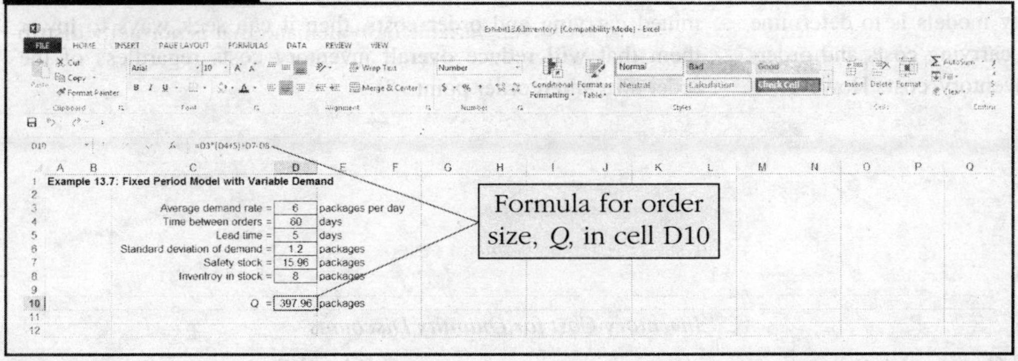

EXAMPLE 13.7

ORDER SIZE FOR FIXED-PERIOD MODEL WITH VARIABLE DEMAND

The KVS Pharmacy stocks a popular brand of over-the-counter flu and cold medicine. The average demand for the medicine is six packages per day, with a standard deviation of 1.2 packages. A vendor for the pharmaceutical company checks KVS's stock every 60 days. During one visit, the store had eight packages in stock. The lead time to receive an order is five days. Determine the order size for this order period that will enable KVS to maintain a 95% service level.

(Continued)

SOLUTION

$\bar{d} = 6$ packages per day

$\sigma_d = 1.2$ packages

$t_b = 60$ days

$L = 5$ days

$I = 8$ packages

$z = 1.65$ (for a 95% service level)

$$Q = \bar{d}(t_b + L) + z\sigma_d\sqrt{t_b + L} - I$$
$$= (6)(60 + 5) + (1.65)(1.2)\sqrt{60 + 5} - 8$$
$$= 397.96 \text{ packages}$$

This will be rounded to 398 packages, or perhaps 400 if it is shipped in boxes of 100 packages.

SUMMARY

The two types of systems for managing inventory are continuous and periodic, and we presented several models for determining how much to order and when to order for each system. However, we focused our attention primarily on the more commonly used continuous, fixed-order-quantity systems with EOQ models for determining order size and reorder points for determining when to order.

The objective of these order quantity models is to determine the optimal tradeoff between inventory carrying costs and ordering costs that would minimize total inventory cost. However, a drawback of approaching inventory management in this manner is that it can delude management into thinking that if it determines the minimum cost order quantity, it has achieved all it can in reducing inventory costs, which is not the case. Management should continually strive both to accurately assess and to reduce individual inventory costs. If management has accurately determined carrying and order costs, then it can seek ways to lower them that will reduce overall inventory costs regardless of the order size and reorder point.

KEY FORMULAS

Basic EOQ Model

$$TC = \frac{C_oD}{Q} + \frac{C_cQ}{2}$$

$$Q_{opt} = \sqrt{\frac{2C_oD}{C_c}}$$

EOQ Model with Noninstantaneous Receipt

$$TC = \frac{C_oD}{Q} + \frac{C_cQ}{2}\left(1 - \frac{d}{p}\right)$$

$$Q_{opt} = \sqrt{\frac{2C_oD}{C_c\left(1 - \frac{d}{p}\right)}}$$

Inventory Cost for Quantity Discounts

$$TC = \frac{C_oD}{Q} + \frac{C_cQ}{2} + PD$$

Reorder Point with Constant Demand and Lead Time

$$R = dL$$

Reorder Point with Variable Demand

$$R = \bar{d}L + z\sigma_d\sqrt{L}$$

Fixed-Time-Period Order Quantity with Variable Demand

$$Q = \bar{d}(t_b + L) + z\sigma_d\sqrt{t_b + L} - I$$

SOLVED PROBLEMS

1. BASIC EOQ MODEL

Electronic Village stocks and sells a particular brand of personal computer. It costs the store $450 each time it places an order with the manufacturer for the personal computers. The annual cost of carrying the PCs in inventory is $170. The store manager estimates that annual demand for the PCs will be 1,200 units. Determine the optimal order quantity and the total minimum inventory cost.

SOLUTION

$$D = 1{,}200 \text{ personal computers}$$

$$C_c = \$170$$

$$C_o = \$450$$

$$Q_{\text{opt}} = \sqrt{\frac{2C_oD}{C_c}}$$

$$= \sqrt{\frac{2(450)(1200)}{170}}$$

$$= 79.7 \text{ personal computers}$$

$$\text{TC} = \frac{C_oD}{Q_{\text{opt}}} + \frac{C_cQ_{\text{opt}}}{2}$$

$$= 450\left(\frac{1{,}200}{79.7}\right) + 170\left(\frac{79.7}{2}\right)$$

$$= \$13{,}549.91$$

2. PRODUCTION QUANTITY MODEL

I-75 Discount Carpets manufactures Cascade carpet, which it sells in its adjoining showroom store near the interstate. Estimated annual demand is 20,000 yards of carpet with an annual carrying cost of $2.75 per yard. The manufacturing facility operates the same 360 days the store is open and produces 400 yards of carpet per day. The cost of setting up the manufacturing process for a production run is $720. Determine the optimal order size, total inventory cost, length of time to receive an order, and maximum inventory level.

SOLUTION

$$C_o = \$720$$

$$C_c = \$2.75 \text{ per yard}$$

$$D = 20{,}000 \text{ yards}$$

$$d = \frac{20{,}000}{360} = 55.56 \text{ yards per day}$$

$$p = 400 \text{ yards per day}$$

$$Q_{\text{opt}} = \sqrt{\frac{2C_oD}{C_c\left(1 - \frac{d}{p}\right)}}$$

$$= \sqrt{\frac{2(720)(20{,}000)}{2.75\left(1 - \frac{55.56}{400}\right)}}$$

$$= 3{,}487.4 \text{ yards}$$

$$\text{TC}_{\text{min}} = \frac{C_oD}{Q} + \frac{C_cQ}{2}\left(1 - \frac{d}{p}\right)$$

$$= \frac{(720)(20{,}000)}{3{,}487.4} + \frac{(2.75)(3{,}487.4)}{2}\left(1 - \frac{55.6}{400}\right)$$

$$= \$8{,}258.33$$

$$\text{Production run} = \frac{Q}{p}$$

$$= \frac{3{,}487.4}{400}$$

$$= 8.72 \text{ days per order}$$

$$\text{Maximum inventory level} = Q\left(1 - \frac{d}{p}\right)$$

$$= 3{,}487.4\left(1 - \frac{55.6}{400}\right)$$

$$= 3{,}003 \text{ yards}$$

3. QUANTITY DISCOUNT

A manufacturing firm has been offered a particular component part it uses according to the following discount pricing schedule provided by the supplier.

Quantity	Unit cost
1–199	$65
200–599	59
600+	56

The manufacturing company uses 700 of the components annually, the annual carrying cost is $14 per unit, and the ordering cost is $275. Determine the amount the firm should order.

SOLUTION

First, determine the optimal order size and total cost with the basic EOQ model.

$$C_o = \$275$$

$$C_c = \$14$$

$$D = 700$$

$$Q_{\text{opt}} = \sqrt{\frac{2C_oD}{C_c}}$$

$$= \sqrt{\frac{2(275)(700)}{14}}$$

$$Q_{opt} = 165.83$$

$$TC = \frac{C_o D}{Q_{opt}} + \frac{C_c Q_{opt}}{2} + PD$$

$$= \frac{(275)(700)}{165.83} + \frac{(14)(165.83)}{2} + (\$65)(700)$$

$$= \$47,821$$

Next, compare the order size with the second-level quantity discount with an order size of 200 and a discount price of \$59.

$$TC = \frac{(275)(700)}{200} + \frac{(14)(200)}{2} + (59)(700)$$

$$= \$43,662.50$$

This discount results in a lower cost.

Finally, compare the current discounted order size with the fixed-price discount for $Q = 600$.

$$TC = \frac{(275)(700)}{600} + \frac{(14)(600)}{2} + (56)(700)$$

$$= \$43,720.83$$

Since this total cost is higher, the optimal order size is 200 with a total cost of \$43,662.50.

4. REORDER POINT WITH VARIABLE DEMAND

A computer products store stocks color graphics monitors, and the daily demand is normally distributed with a mean of 1.6 monitors and a standard deviation of 0.4 monitor. The lead time to receive an order from the manufacturer is 15 days. Determine the reorder point that will achieve a 98% service level.

SOLUTION

$$\bar{d} = 1.6 \text{ monitors per day}$$

$$L = 15 \text{ days}$$

$$\sigma_d = 0.4 \text{ monitor per day}$$

$$z = 2.05 (\text{for a } 98\% \text{ service level})$$

$$R = \bar{d}L + z\sigma_d\sqrt{L}$$

$$= (1.6)(15) + (2.05)(0.4)\sqrt{15}$$

$$= 24 + 3.18$$

$$= 27.18 = 28 \text{ monitors}$$

PROBLEMS

13-1. AV City stocks and sells a particular brand of laptop. It costs the firm \$625 each time it places an order with the manufacturer for the laptops. The cost of carrying one laptop in inventory for a year is \$130. The store manager estimates that total annual demand for the laptops will be 1,500 units, with a constant demand rate throughout the year. Orders are received within minutes after placement from a local warehouse maintained by the manufacturer. The store policy is never to have stockouts of the laptops. The store is open for business every day of the year except Christmas Day. Determine the following:

a. Optimal order quantity per order
b. Minimum total annual inventory costs
c. The number of orders per year
d. The time between orders (in working days)

13-2. AV City (Problem 13-1) assumed with certainty that the ordering cost is \$625/order and the inventory carrying cost is \$130/unit/year. However, the inventory model parameters are frequently only estimates that are subject to some degree of uncertainty. Consider four cases of variation in the model parameters as follows: (a) Both ordering cost and carrying cost are 10% less than originally estimated; (b) both ordering cost and carrying cost are 10% higher than originally estimated; (c) ordering cost is 10% higher and carrying cost is 10% lower than originally estimated; and (d) ordering cost is 10% lower and carrying cost is 10% higher than originally estimated. Determine the optimal order quantity and total inventory cost for each of the four cases. Prepare a table with values from all four cases and compare the sensitivity of the model solution to changes in parameter values.

13-3. A firm is faced with the attractive situation in which it can obtain immediate delivery of an item it stocks for retail sale. The firm has therefore not bothered to order the item in any systematic way. However, recently profits have been squeezed due to increasing competitive pressures, and the firm has retained a management consultant to study its inventory management. The consultant has determined that the various costs associated with making an order for the item stocked are approximately \$70 per order. She has also determined that the costs of carrying the item in inventory amount to approximately \$27 per unit per year (primarily direct storage costs and forgone profit on investment in inventory). Demand for the item is reasonably constant over time, and the forecast is for 16,500 units per year. When an order is placed for the item, the entire order is immediately delivered to the firm by the supplier. The firm operates six days a week plus a few Sundays, or approximately 320 days per year. Determine the following:

a. Optimal order quantity per order
b. Total annual inventory costs
c. Optimal number of orders to place per year
d. Number of operating days between orders, based on the optimal ordering

13-4. The Chemco Company uses a highly toxic chemical in one of its manufacturing processes. It must have the product delivered by special cargo trucks designed for safe shipment of chemicals. As such, ordering (and delivery) costs are relatively high, at \$3,600 per order. The chemical product is packaged in one-gallon plastic containers. The cost of holding the chemical in storage is \$50 per gallon per year. The annual demand for the chemical, which is constant over time, is 7,000 gallons per year. The lead time from time of order placement until receipt is 10 days. The company operates 310 working days per year. Compute the optimal order quantity, total minimum inventory cost, and the reorder point.

13-5. The Food Place Supermarket stocks Munchkin Cookies. Demand for Munchkins is 5,000 boxes per year (365 days). It costs the store $80 per order of Munchkins, and it costs $0.50 per box per year to keep the cookies in stock. Once an order for Munchkins is placed, it takes four days to receive the order from a food distributor. Determine the following:

a. Optimal order size
b. Minimum total annual inventory cost
c. Reorder point

13-6. Kroft Foods makes cheese to supply to stores in its area. The dairy can make 350 pounds of cheese per day, and the demand at area stores is 205 pounds per day. Each time the dairy makes cheese, it costs $175 to set up the production process. The annual cost of carrying a pound of cheese in a refrigerated storage area is $12. Determine the optimal order size and the minimum total annual inventory cost.

13-7. The Shotz Brewery produces an ale, which it stores in barrels in its warehouse and supplies to its distributors on demand. The demand for ale is 1,800 barrels per day. The brewery can produce 3,000 barrels per day. It costs $7,500 to set up a production run for ale. Once it is brewed, the ale is stored in a refrigerated warehouse at an annual cost of $60 per barrel. Determine the economic order quantity and the minimum total annual inventory cost.

13-8. The purchasing manager for the Pacific Steel Company must determine a policy for ordering coal to operate 12 converters. Each converter requires exactly 5 tons of coal per day to operate, and the firm operates 360 days per year. The purchasing manager has determined that the ordering cost is $80 per order, and the cost of holding coal is 20% of the average dollar value of inventory held. The purchasing manager has negotiated a contract to obtain the coal for $12 per ton for the coming year.

a. Determine the optimal quantity of coal to receive in each order.
b. Determine the total inventory-related costs associated with the optimal ordering policy (do not include the cost of the coal).
c. If five days' lead time is required to receive an order of coal, how much coal should be on hand when an order is placed?

13-9. The TransCanada Lumber Company and Mill processes 10,000 logs annually, operating 250 days per year. Immediately upon receiving an order, the logging company's supplier begins delivery to the lumber mill at the rate of 60 logs per day. The lumber mill has determined that the ordering cost is $1,600 per order, and the cost of carrying logs in inventory before they are processed is $15 per log on an annual basis. Determine the following:

a. The optimal order size
b. The total inventory cost associated with the optimal order quantity
c. The number of operating days between orders
d. The number of operating days required to receive an order

13-10. The Goodstone Tire Company produces a brand of tire called the Rainpath. The annual demand at its distribution center is 12,400 tires per year. The transport and handling costs are $2,600 each time a shipment of tires is ordered at the distribution center. The annual carrying cost is $3.75 per tire.

a. Determine the optimal order quantity and the minimum total annual cost.
b. The company is thinking about relocating its distribution center, which would reduce transport and handling costs to $1900 per order but increase carrying costs to $4.50 per tire per year. Should the company relocate based on inventory costs?

13-11. The Deer Valley Farm produces a natural organic fertilizer, which it sells mostly to gardeners and homeowners. The annual demand for fertilizer is 220,000 pounds. The farm is able to produce 305,000 pounds annually. The cost to transport the fertilizer from the plant to the farm is $620 per load. The annual carrying cost is $0.12 per pound.

a. Compute the optimal order size, the maximum inventory level, and the total minimum cost.
b. If the farm can increase production capacity to 360,000 pounds per year, will it reduce total inventory cost?

13-12. Tradewinds Imports is an importer of ceramics from overseas. It has arranged to purchase a particular type of ceramic pottery from a Korean artisan. The artisan makes the pottery in 120-unit batches and will ship only that exact amount. The transportation and handling cost of a shipment is $7,600 (not including the unit cost). The importer estimates its annual demand to be 1,400 units. What storage and handling cost per unit does it need to achieve in order to minimize its inventory cost?

13-13. JAL Trading is a Hong Kong manufacturer of electronic components. During the course of a year it requires container cargo space on ships leaving Hong Kong bound for the United States, Mexico, South America, and Canada. The company needs 280,000 cubic feet of cargo space annually. The cost of reserving cargo space is $7,000 and the cost of holding cargo space is $0.80/ft^3. Determine how much storage space the company should optimally order, the total cost, and how many times per year it should place an order to reserve space.

13-14. Southwood Furniture Company is a U.S.-based furniture manufacturer that offshored all of its actual manufacturing operations to China about a decade ago. It set up a distribution center in Hong Kong from which the company ships its items to the United States on container ships. The company learned early on that it could not rely on local Chinese freight forwarders to arrange for sufficient containers for the company's shipments, so it contracted to purchase containers from a Taiwanese manufacturer and then sell them to shipping companies at the U.S. ports the containers are shipped to. Southwood needs 715 containers each year. It costs $1,200 to hold a container at its distribution center, and it costs $6,000 to receive an order for the containers. Determine the optimal order size, minimum total annual inventory cost, number of annual orders, and time between orders.

13-15. In Problem 12-25 in Chapter 12, Delaplane Computers' supplier receives shipments of laptop screens from its manufacturing facility in the Philippines, which has, a maximum production rate of 200 units per day. Using the forecast of demand developed in 12-25, an annual carrying cost of $115.75 (which includes an average obsolescence cost), a shipping cost from Asia of $6,500 per shipment, and a lead time to receive an order of 25 days, determine the optimal order size, the minimum total annual inventory cost, the maximum inventory level, and the reorder point (given that the Delaplane assembly operation operates 365 days per year).

13-16. County Hospital orders syringes from a hospital supply firm. The hospital expects to use 40,000 per year. The cost to order and have the syringes delivered is $800. The annual carrying cost is $1.90 per syringe because of security and theft. The hospital supply firm offers the following quantity discount pricing schedule.

Quantity	Price
0–999	$3.40
10,000–19,999	3.20
20,000–29,999	3.00
30,000–39,999	2.80
40,000–49,999	2.60
50,000+	2.40

Determine the order size for the hospital.

13-17. The office manager for the Metro Life Insurance Company orders letterhead stationery from an office products firm in boxes of 500 sheets. The company uses 6,500 boxes per year. Annual carrying costs are $3 per box, and ordering costs are $28. The following discount price schedule is provided by the office supply company:

Order Quantity (boxes)	Price per Box
200–999	$16
1000–2999	14
3000–5999	13
6000+	12

Determine the optimal order quantity and the total annual inventory cost.

13-18. Determine the optimal order quantity and total annual inventory cost for boxes of stationery in Problem 13-17 if the carrying cost is 20% of the price of a box of stationery.

13-19. The 21,000-seat Air East Arena houses the local professional ice hockey, basketball, indoor soccer, and arena football teams as well as various trade shows, wrestling and boxing matches, tractor pulls, and circuses. Arena vending annually sells large quantities of soft drinks and beer in plastic cups with the name of the arena and the various team logos on them. The local container cup manufacturer that supplies the cups in boxes of 100 has offered arena management the following discount price schedule for cups:

Order Quantity (boxes)	Price per Box
2000–6999	$47
7000–11,999	43
12,000–19,999	41
20,000+	38

The annual demand for cups is 2.3 million, the annual carrying cost per box of cups is $1.90, and ordering cost is $320. Determine the optimal order quantity and total annual inventory cost.

13-20. Determine the optimal order quantity and total annual inventory cost for cups in Problem 13-19 if the carrying cost is 5% of the price of a box of cups.

13-21. The amount of denim used daily by the Southwest Apparel Company in its manufacturing process to make jeans is normally distributed with an average of 4,000 yards of denim and a standard deviation of 600 yards. The lead time required to receive an order of denim from the textile mill is a constant 7 days. Determine the safety stock and reorder point if the company wants to limit the probability of a stock-out and work stoppage to 5%.

13-22. In Problem 13-21, what level of service would a safety stock of 2,000 yards provide?

13-23. The Paramount Paper company produces paper from wood pulp ordered from a lumber products firm. The paper company's daily demand for wood pulp is normally distributed, with a mean of 9,000 pounds and a standard deviation of 1,900 pounds. Lead time is eight days. Determine the reorder point if the paper company wants to limit the probability of a stockout and work stoppage to 2%.

13-24. IM Systems assembles microcomputers from generic components. It purchases its color monitors from a manufacturer in Taiwan; thus, there is a long lead time of 25 days. Daily demand is normally distributed with a mean of 3.5 monitors and a standard deviation of 1.2 monitors. Determine the safety stock and reorder point corresponding to a 90% service level.

13-25. IM Systems (Problem 13-24) is considering purchasing monitors from a U.S. manufacturer that would guarantee a lead time of eight days, instead of from the Taiwanese company. Determine the new reorder point given this lead time and identify the factors that would enter into the decision to change manufacturers.

13-26. KVS Pharmacy fills prescriptions for a popular children's antibiotic, amoxicillin. The daily demand for amoxicillin is normally distributed with a mean of 200 ounces and a standard deviation of 80 ounces. The vendor for the pharmaceutical firm that supplies the drug calls the drugstore's pharmacist every 30 days and checks the inventory of amoxicillin. During a call, the druggist indicated the store had 60 ounces of the antibiotic in stock. The lead time to receive an order is four days. Determine the order size that will enable the drugstore to maintain a 99% service level.

13-27. Food Place Market stocks frozen pizzas in a refrigerated display case. The average daily demand for the pizzas is normally distributed, with a mean of 8 pizzas and a standard deviation of 2.5 pizzas. A vendor for a packaged food distributor checks the market's inventory of frozen foods every 10 days; during a particular visit there were no pizzas in stock. The lead time to receive an order is three days. Determine the order size for this order period that will result in a 98% service level. During the vendor's following visit there were 5 frozen pizzas in stock. What is the order size for the next order period?

13-28. The Mediterranean Restaurant stocks a red Chilean table wine it purchases from a wine merchant in a nearby city. The daily demand for the wine at the restaurant is normally distributed, with a mean of 18 bottles and a standard deviation of 4 bottles. The wine merchant sends a representative to check the restaurant's wine cellar every 30 days, and during a recent visit there were 25 bottles in stock. The lead time to receive an order is two days. The restaurant manager has requested an order size that will enable him to limit the probability of a stockout to 5%.

13-29. The Aztec Company stocks a variety of parts and materials it uses in its manufacturing processes. Recently, as demand for its finished goods has increased, management has had difficulty managing parts inventory; they frequently run out of some crucial parts and seem to have an endless supply of others. In an effort to control inventory more effectively, they would like to classify their inventory of parts according to the ABC approach. Following is a list of selected parts and the annual usage and unit value for each:

Item Number	Annual Usage	Unit Cost	Item Number	Annual Usage	Unit Cost
1	36	$350	16	60	$610
2	510	30	17	120	20
3	50	23	18	270	15
4	300	45	19	45	50
5	18	1,900	20	19	3,200
6	500	8	21	910	3
7	710	4	22	12	4,750
8	80	26	23	30	2,710
9	344	28	24	24	1,800
10	67	440	25	870	105
11	510	2	26	244	30
12	682	35	27	750	15
13	95	50	28	45	110

Item Number	Annual Usage	Unit Cost	Item Number	Annual Usage	Unit Cost
14	10	3	29	46	160
15	820	1	30	165	25

Classify the inventory items according to the ABC approach using dollar value of annual demand.

13-30. The EastCoasters Bicycle Shop stocks bikes; helmets; clothing; a variety of bike parts including chains, gears, tires, wheels; and biking accessories. The shop is in a storefront location on a busy street and it has very limited storage space for inventory. It often runs out of items and is unable to serve customers. To help manage its inventory, the shop would like to classify the stock using the ABC system. Following is a list of items the shop stocks and the annual demand and unit value for each:

Item Number	Annual Demand	Unit Cost	Item Number	Annual Demand	Unit Cost
1	10	$8	17	110	$23
2	18	16	18	74	18
3	36	30	19	8	610
4	9	1,230	20	10	935
5	4	760	21	7	270
6	3	810	22	5	1,400
7	19	420	23	5	900
8	56	35	24	46	67
9	105	17	25	32	160
10	27	350	26	101	45
11	19	36	27	83	12
12	12	115	28	54	16
13	7	2,300	29	14	42
14	10	245	30	9	705
15	6	665	31	7	37
16	18	28	32	16	26

Classify the inventory items according to the ABC approach using dollar value of annual demand.

CASE STUDY

Managing Supplies for Free Shoes for Kids

Free Shoes for Kids is a shoe manufacturing company with a heart. The firm originated five years ago when its founder saw that many children around the world had to go barefoot as shoes were either not available or cost-prohibitive to obtain. As such, the founder decided to establish a shoe manufacturing, distribution and retail sales firm. The commercial side of this business supports the real desire to help the needy children have a pair of shoes to wear. The firm's position is that for every pair of shoes they sell, it will give one pair to a needy child. To achieve this objective, the company must contain its costs and achieve the highest level of efficiencies.

Since the firm started, its offices, manufacturing facilities, and retail outlets have been concentrated in the United States. As the needy children are global in nature, the firm's founder is trying to decide if it could establish a second manufacturing and distribution center in the Pacific Rim. The Pacific Rim distribution center would focus its attention on needs within this geographic region while the US location would focus its attention on the rest of the global need.

The firm has acknowledged that the true demand is beyond its ability to meet in any single year. Thus, they must limit the number of shoes that go to the needy children to the number of shoes that are sold. The following table identifies the number of shoes that have been sold since the firm was formed.

Year	Shoes Sold
2005	43,280
2006	68,750
2007	155,200
2008	189,750
2009	256,080
2010	369,500

To establish the Pacific Rim location, the founder needs to identify the optimal order quantity for the 2011 forecasted demand. They believe a linear regression forecast will provide an adequate prediction.

The major product that they must order is the material for the rubberized shoe sole. This material comes in 9 m^2 sheets, each sheet can be used to produce 35 shoes. Each sheet costs $15.00 and each order costs the firm $25.00. Inventory costs are held to the lowest possible with an estimated annual cost of $0.35 per sheet.

The firm only works five days a week for all 52 weeks of the year. The material supplier says they can deliver the material to any major Pacific Rim city in 25 days.

a. What is the 2011 forecast?
b. What accuracy does this forecast have?
c. What is the optimal order quantity for the sheet of shoe material?
d. What is the total inventory cost for this item?
e. What is the reorder point?
f. How often are the orders placed?
g. How many orders should be placed a year?

REFERENCES

Brown, R. G. *Decision Rules for Inventory Management*. New York: Holt, Rinehart and Winston, 1967.

Buchan, J., and E. Koenigsberg. *Scientific Inventory Management*. Upper Saddle River, N.J.: Prentice Hall, 1963.

Buffa, E. S., and Jefferey Miller. *Production-Inventory Systems: Planning and Control*, rev. ed. Homewood, IL: Irwin, 1979.

Churchman, C. W., R. L. Ackoff, and E. L. Arnoff. *Introduction to Operations Research*. New York: Wiley, 1957.

Fetter, R. B., and W. C. Dalleck. *Decision Models for Inventory Management*. Homewood, IL: Irwin, 1961.

Greene, J. H. *Production and Inventory Control*. Homewood, IL: Irwin, 1974.

Hadley, G., and T. M. Whitin. *Analysis of Inventory Systems*. Upper Saddle River, N.J.: Prentice Hall, 1963.

McGee, J. F., and D. M. Boodman. *Production Planning and Inventory Control*, 2nd ed. New York: McGraw-Hill, 1967.

Starr, M. K., and D. W. Miller. *Inventory Control: Theory and Practice*. Upper Saddle River, N.J.: Prentice Hall, 1962.

Wagner, H. M. *Statistical Management of Inventory Systems*. New York: Wiley, 1962.

Whitin, T. M. *The Theory of Inventory Management*. Princeton, N.J.: Princeton University Press, 1957.

CHAPTER 14

Aggregate Planning for Sales and Operations

LEARNING OBJECTIVES

AFTER READING THIS CHAPTER, YOU WILL BE ABLE TO:

- Appreciate the interface of marketing, finance, and operations in S&OP planning.
- Describe the monthly S&OP process and the importance of reconciling differences.
- Utilize various tools and techniques to adjust capacity and manage demand.
- Evaluate a demand scenario and select an appropriate S&OP strategy.
- Describe hierarchical planning and the process of determining available-to-promise.
- Determine overbooking, single orders, and fare class strategies for revenue management in services.

SALES AND OPERATIONS PLANNING AT VF CORPORATION

The hierarchical planning process at VF Corporation (producer of Lee and Wrangler jeans, and a variety of outdoor and sports-related apparel) begins with a 3- to 5-year long-range plan for building the capacity needed to support strategic growth objectives, followed by a 1- to 3-year mid-range plan for ensuring the availability of materials to meet demand, and a 12- to 18-month sales and operations plan (S&OP) for optimizing inventory and customer service levels. VF must balance the ongoing and seasonal needs of its customers for product availability (such as colorful jeans in the spring) with the costs of production and inventory.

The sales and operations planning process is the mechanism achieving that balance. It involves monthly cross-functional S&OP review meetings to reach demand consensus, review inventory levels and forecasting accuracy, perform root cause analysis for underperforming KPIs, and solidify capacity plans. With S&OP, the Vans division of VF was able to increase customer service levels by 27%, reduce inventory by 53%, and increase profitability by 30%. With these kinds of results, it's no wonder S&OP is being implemented across VF's divisions.

In this chapter, we'll learn how companies such as VF plan their resource levels to balance supply and demand. We begin with a discussion of the nature of S&OP

and then continue with strategies for managing demand and adjusting capacity. We conclude with a discussion of hierarchical planning decisions, collaborative planning with trading partners, and aggregate planning for services.

Source: Based on Kerry Middlemas, "Using S&OP to Enable Future Growth," *2012 Best of the Best S&OP Conference*, APICS & IBF, Chicago, June 5, 2012.

The Sales and Operations Planning Process

Sales and operations planning (S&OP) is an aggregate planning process that determines the resource capacity a firm will need to meet its demand over an intermediate time horizon—6 to 12 months in the future. Within this time frame, it is usually not feasible to increase capacity by building new facilities or purchasing new equipment; however, it *is* feasible to hire or lay off workers, increase or reduce the workweek, add an extra shift, subcontract out work, use overtime, or build up and deplete inventory levels.

We use the term *aggregate* because the plans are developed for product lines or product families, rather than individual products. An aggregate operations plan might specify how many bicycles are to be produced but would not identify them by color, size, tires, or type of brakes. Resource capacity is also expressed in aggregate terms, typically as labor or machine hours. Labor hours would not be specified by type of labor, nor machine hours by type of machine. And they may be given only for critical processes.

For services, capacity is often limited by *space*—number of airline seats, number of hotel rooms, number of hospital beds. *Time* can also affect capacity. The number of customers who can be served lunch in a restaurant is limited by the number of seats, as well as the number of hours lunch is served. In some overcrowded schools, lunch begins at 10:00 A.M. so that all students can be served by 2:00 P.M.!

There are two objectives to sales and operations planning:

1. To establish a companywide game plan for allocating resources, and
2. To develop an economic strategy for meeting demand.

The first objective refers to the long-standing battle between the sales and operations functions within a firm. Personnel who are evaluated solely on sales volume have the tendency to make unrealistic sales commitments (either in terms of quantity or timing) that operations is expected to meet, sometimes at an exorbitant price. Operations personnel who are evaluated on keeping manufacturing costs down may refuse to accept orders that require additional financial resources (such as overtime wage rates) or hard-to-meet completion dates. The job of operations planning is to match forecasted demand with available capacity. If capacity is inadequate, it can usually be expanded, but at a cost. The company needs to determine if the extra cost is worth the increased revenue from the sale, and if the sale is consistent with the strategy of the firm. Thus, the aggregate plan should not be determined by manufacturing personnel alone; rather, it should be agreed on by top management from all the functional areas of the firm—operations, marketing, and finance. Because this is such an important decision, companies engage in a structured, collaborative decision-making process called *sales and operations planning (S&OP)*. Figure 14.1 outlines the S&OP process.

As shown in Figure 14.1, the sales and operations plan should reflect company policy (such as avoiding layoffs, limiting inventory levels, and maintaining a specified customer service level) and strategic objectives (such as capturing a certain share of the market or achieving targeted

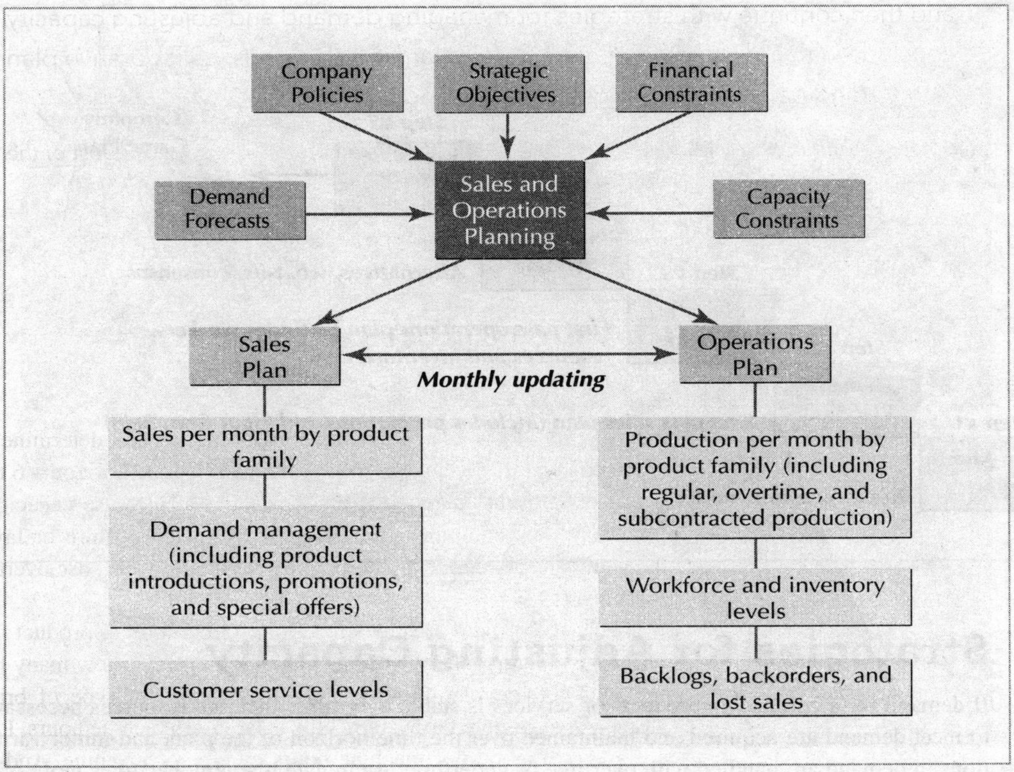

Figure 14.1
Sales and Operations Planning

levels of quality or profit). Other inputs include financial constraints, demand forecasts (from sales), and capacity constraints (from operations).

Given these inputs, the sales function develops a monthly sales plan. A forecasting model is run to create preliminary demand figures, then adjusted based on input from key customers and sales personnel in the field. The forecast is further adjusted for planned promotions, product introductions, and special offers. Finally, a customer service level is set that specifies the percent of customer demand that should be satisfied.

The sales plan is then shared with the operations function that must convert sales to production requirements as economically as possible. Operations develops a schedule of production per month by product family that includes the number of workers and other resources needed, and whether the production plan requires overtime or subcontracting. The production plan also shows anticipated inventory levels, backlog (work not yet completed), backorders (work performed later for customers willing to wait for their order), and lost sales (customers whose orders could not be completed or were not accepted).

The sales and operations planning process does not stop here. The two plans must be reconciled. Typically this involves creating an annual plan and updating it with monthly meetings that culminate in executive approval of the final plan. The process is diagrammed in Figure 14.2.

Because of the various factors and viewpoints considered, the sales and operations plan is often referred to as the company's *game plan* for the coming year, and deviations from the plan are carefully monitored. Monthly S&OP meeting reconcile differences in supply, demand, and new product plans.

An economic strategy for meeting demand can be attained by either *adjusting capacity* or *managing demand*. We discuss both approaches in the following sections. Please note that the terms *operations plan, production plan,* and *aggregate plan* are used interchangeably in this textbook.

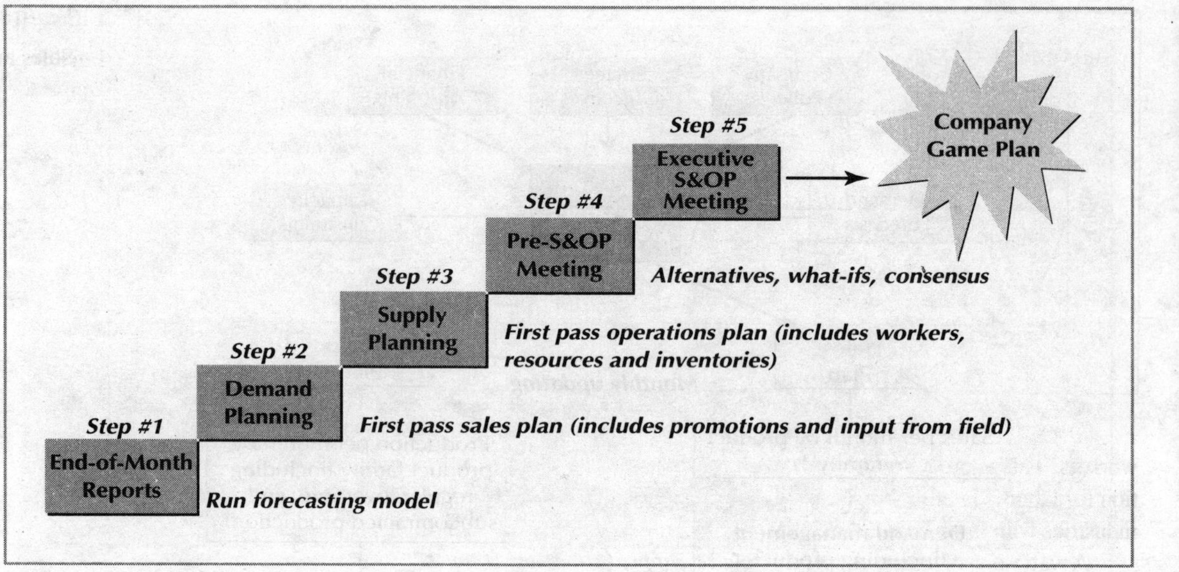

Figure 14.2
The Monthly S&OP Planning Process

Strategies for Adjusting Capacity

If demand for a company's products or services is stable over time, then the resources necessary to meet demand are acquired and maintained over the time horizon of the plan, and minor variations in demand are handled with overtime or undertime. Aggregate planning becomes more of a challenge when demand fluctuates over the planning horizon. For example, seasonal demand patterns can be met by:

1. Producing at a constant rate and using inventory to absorb fluctuations in demand (*level production*)
2. Hiring and firing workers to match demand (*chase demand*)
3. Maintaining resources for high-demand levels
4. Increasing or decreasing working hours (*overtime* and *undertime*)
5. Subcontracting work to other firms
6. Using part-time workers
7. Providing the service or product at a later time period (*backordering*)

When one of these alternatives is selected, a company is said to have a **pure strategy** for meeting demand. When two or more are selected, a company has a mixed strategy.

LEVEL PRODUCTION

The **level production** strategy, shown in Figure 14.3*a*, sets production at a fixed rate (usually to meet average demand) and uses inventory to absorb variations in demand. During periods of low demand, overproduction is stored as inventory, to be depleted in periods of high demand. The cost of this strategy is the cost of holding inventory, including the cost of obsolete or perishable items that may have to be discarded.

CHASE DEMAND

The **chase demand** strategy, shown in Figure 14.3*b*, matches the production plan to the demand pattern and absorbs variations in demand by hiring and firing workers. During periods of low demand, production is cut back and workers are laid off. During periods of high demand, production is increased and additional workers are hired. The cost of this strategy is the cost of hiring and firing

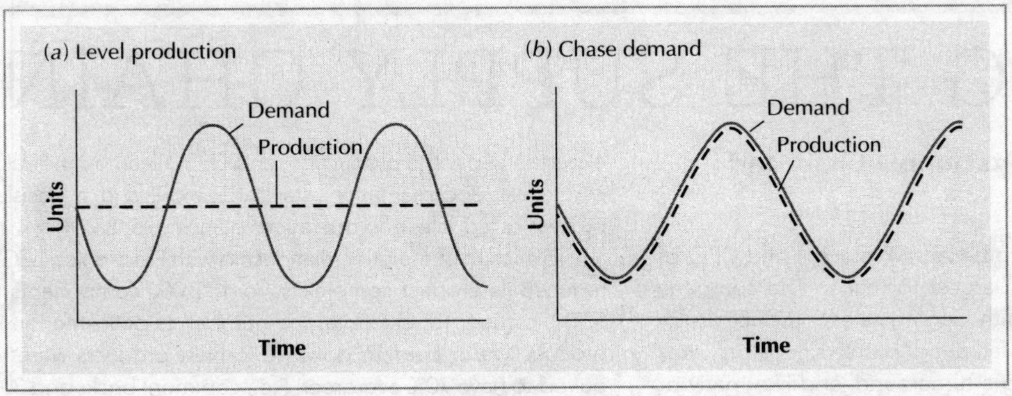

Figure 14.3
Pure Strategies for Meeting Demand

workers. This approach would not work for industries in which worker skills are scarce or competition for labor is intense, but it can be quite cost-effective during periods of high unemployment or for industries with low-skilled workers.

A variation of chase demand is *chase supply*. For some industries, the production planning task revolves around the supply of raw materials, not the demand pattern. Consider Motts, the applesauce manufacturer, whose raw material is available only 40 days during a year. The workforce size at its peak is 1,500 workers, but it normally consists of around 350 workers. Almost 10% of the company's payroll is made up of unemployment benefits—the price of doing business in that particular industry.

PEAK DEMAND

Maintaining resources for **peak demand** levels ensures high levels of customer service but can be very costly in terms of the investment in extra workers and machines that remain idle during low-demand periods. This strategy is used when superior customer service is important (as for Nordstrom's department store) or when customers are willing to pay extra for the availability of critical staff or equipment. Professional services trying to generate more demand may keep staff levels high, defense contractors may be paid to keep extra capacity "available," child-care facilities may elect to maintain staff levels for continuity when attendance is low, and full-service hospitals may invest in specialized equipment that is rarely used but is critical for the care of a small number of patients.

OVERTIME AND UNDERTIME

Overtime and *undertime* are common strategies when demand fluctuations are not extreme. A competent staff is maintained, hiring and firing costs are avoided, and demand is met temporarily without investing in permanent resources. Disadvantages include the premium paid for overtime work, a tired and potentially less efficient workforce, and the possibility that overtime alone may be insufficient to meet peak demand periods.

Undertime can be achieved by working fewer hours during the day or fewer days per week. In addition, vacation time can be scheduled during months of slow demand. For example, furniture manufacturers typically shut down the entire month of July, while shipbuilding goes dormant in December. During the recent recession, 35% of U.S. employers surveyed used unpaid furloughs in lieu of more layoffs to adjust to decreased demand. Europe routinely uses shorter workweeks and mandatory vacations in economic downturns.

SUBCONTRACTING

Subcontracting or outsourcing is a feasible alternative if a supplier can reliably meet quality and time requirements. This is a common solution for component parts when demand exceeds expectations for the final product. The outsourcing decision requires maintaining strong ties with

ALONG THE SUPPLY CHAIN

How LEGO Rebuilt Its Supply Chain and Found S&OP

In 2004, Jorgen Knudstorp became President and CEO of LEGO, the world's fourth largest toymaker. The company was in financial trouble with lagging sales, product proliferation, and high manufacturing costs. Knudstorp was charged with engineering a turnaround, and like many of his contemporaries, pursued a strategy of aggressive outsourcing to low-cost countries.

To tighten up finances and prepare for the new outsourcing strategy, LEGO divested itself of theme parks and other peripheral ventures, simplified its LEGO product sets, reeled in its distributors to focus on large retail outlets, and consolidated five European warehouses into one (to be managed by DHL). As an outsourcing partner, LEGO chose Flextronics, a reliable electronics manufacturing services (EMS) company headquartered in Singapore with factories around the world. U.S. production moved to Flextronics factories in Mexico, and production in Danish and Swiss factories moved to Flextronics-run factories in Hungary and the Czech Republic. Prior to the supply chain reorganization, LEGO had produced 90% of its items in-house; after the reorganization, LEGO was responsible for only 20% of production (the molding process and final packaging). Both companies were optimistic about a long-term mutually beneficial relationship, but it didn't take long for the relationship to sour, and in less than three years, the outsourcing contract was canceled.

What happened? Consider that the lifespan of LEGO products averages 16 to 18 months, more than 60% of production takes place in the second half of the year, and demand uncertainty means forecasts are only ±30% accurate. These types of operating conditions do not mesh with Flextronics' high-volume mass production forte, and in the outsourcing scenario, significantly lower costs of production did not materialize. All was not lost, however, since Flextronics acquired expertise in plastics production, and LEGO learned the value of process documentation, standardization, and a decision process called sales and operations planning, or S&OP.

As a result of the brief relationship with Flextronics, LEGO reduced its product complexity from 12,000 components to 5,500, cutting, for example, the number of policemen in its product lineup from 16 down to 2. New products were required to have 70% evergreen (i.e., common) bricks and 30% new (i.e., unique) bricks. Flextronics-run factories in Mexico and Eastern Europe reverted to LEGO management to produce products by region instead of by brand. S&OP brought sales, operations, and product development together to discuss and make changes in demand and production plans on a monthly basis, so that errant forecasts were corrected and over- or underproduction of product was avoided. Each monthly cycle began with data collection at the local level and ended with global S&OP meetings at the executive level. S&OP became "the glue" that held all workflows together, both inside and outside of the company.

By 2008, LEGO was receiving awards for outstanding supply chain management, and by 2011 the company was expanding its existing plants and building new ones.

1. With 90% of the world's toys produced in China, why do you think LEGO did not follow that route?
2. Knowing what you do about LEGO products, why do you think the company thought it important to retain the molding and final packaging processes?
3. How likely do you think LEGO would have learned the lessons it did without trying its hand at outsourcing?
4. Why is S&OP a valuable process for LEGO?

Sources: Based on Marcus Larsen, Torben Pedersen, and Dmitrij Slepniov, "The Lego Group: An Offshore Outsourcing Journey Toward a New Future," *Global Sourcing*, Gothenburg, 2010; Keith Oliver, Edouard Samkh, and Peter Heckmann, "Rebuilding Lego, Brick by Brick," *Strategy + Business*, 48 (Autumn 2007); The LEGO Group Annual Report 2004, 2008, and 2011, http://aboutus.lego.com/en-us/lego-group/annual-report/.

possible subcontractors and first-hand knowledge of their work. Disadvantages include reduced profits, loss of control over production, long lead times, and the potential that the subcontractor may become a future competitor.

PART-TIME WORKERS

Using *part-time workers* is feasible for unskilled jobs or in areas with large temporary labor pools (such as students, homemakers, or retirees). Part-time workers are less costly than full-time workers—they receive no healthcare or retirement benefits—and are more flexible—their hours usually vary considerably. Part-time workers have been the mainstay of retail, fast-food, and other services for some time and are becoming more accepted in manufacturing and government jobs. Japanese manufacturers traditionally use a large percentage of part-time or temporary workers. Part-time and temporary workers now account for one-third of the U.S. workforce, and are expected to increase as companies gingerly enter recovery from the recession.

BACKLOGS, BACKORDERING, AND LOST SALES

Companies that offer customized products and services accept customer orders and fill them at a later date. The accumulation of these orders creates a **backlog** that grows during periods of high demand and is depleted during periods of low demand. The planned backlog is an important part of the aggregate plan. For make-to-stock companies, customers who request an item that is temporarily out of stock may have the option of **backordering** the item. If the customer is unwilling to wait for the backordered item, the sale will be lost. Although in general both backorders and **lost sales** should be avoided, the aggregate plan may include an estimate of both. Backorders are added to the next period's requirements; lost sales are not.

Strategies for Managing Demand

Aggregate planning can also involve proactive demand management. Strategies for managing demand include:

- Shifting demand into other time periods with incentives, sales promotions, and advertising campaigns;
- Offering products or services with countercyclical demand patterns; and
- Partnering with suppliers to reduce information distortion along the supply chain.

Winter coat specials in July, bathing-suit sales in January, early-bird discounts on dinner, lower health club rates mid-mornings, and getaway weekends at hotels during the off-season are all attempts to shift demand into different time periods. Electric utilities are especially skilled at off-peak pricing. Promotions can also be used to extend high demand into low-demand seasons. Holiday gift buying is encouraged earlier each year, and beach resorts plan festivals in September and October to extend the season. Successful demand management depends on accurate forecasts of demand and accurate forecasts of the changes in demand brought about by sales, promotions, and special offers.

For industries with extreme variations in demand, offering products or services with countercyclical demand patterns helps smooth out resource requirements. This approach involves examining the idleness of resources and creating a demand for those resources. McDonald's offers breakfast to keep its kitchens busy during the prelunch hours, pancake restaurants serve lunch and dinner, and heating firms also sell air conditioners.

Amadas Industries, a small U.S. manufacturer of peanut harvesting equipment, does an especially good job of finding countercyclical products to smooth the load on its manufacturing facilities. The company operates a job shop production system with general-purpose equipment, 50 highly skilled workers, and a talented engineering staff. With these flexible resources, the company can make virtually anything its engineers can design. Inventories of finished goods are limited because of the significant investment in funds and the size of the finished product. Demand for the product is highly seasonal. Peanut-harvesting equipment is generally purchased on an as-needed basis from August to October, so during the spring and early summer, the company makes bark-scalping equipment for processing mulch and pine nuggets used by landscaping services. Demand for peanut-harvesting equipment is also affected by the weather each growing season, so during years of extensive drought, the company produces and sells irrigation equipment. The company also decided to market its products internationally with a special eye toward countries whose growing seasons are opposite to that of the United States. Thus, many of its sales are made in China and India during the very months when demand in the United States is low.

Another approach to managing demand recognizes the information distortion caused by ordering goods in batches along a supply chain. Even though a customer may require daily usage of an item, he or she probably does not purchase that item daily. Neither do retail stores restock their shelves continuously. By the time a replenishment order reaches distributors, wholesalers, manufacturers, and their suppliers, the demand pattern for a product can appear extremely erratic. This *bullwhip effect* was discussed in Chapter 10. To control the situation, manufacturers, their suppliers, and customers form partnerships in which demand information is shared and orders are placed in a more continuous fashion.

Quantitative Techniques for Aggregate Planning

One **aggregate planning** strategy is not always preferable to another. The most effective strategy depends on the demand distribution, competitive position, and cost structure of a firm or product line. Several quantitative techniques are available to help with the aggregate planning decision. In the sections that follow, we discuss pure and mixed strategies, linear programming, the *transportation method*, and other quantitative techniques.

PURE STRATEGIES

Solving aggregate planning problems involves formulating strategies for meeting demand, constructing production plans from those strategies, determining the cost and feasibility of each plan, and selecting the lowest cost plan from among the feasible alternatives. The effectiveness of the aggregate planning process is directly related to management's understanding of the cost variables involved and the reasonableness of the scenarios tested. Example 14.1 compares the cost of two pure strategies: *level production* and *chase demand*.

EXAMPLE 14.1

AGGREGATE PLANNING USING PURE STRATEGIES

The Good and Rich Candy Company makes a variety of candies in three factories worldwide. Its line of chocolate candies exhibits a highly seasonal demand pattern, with peaks during the winter months (for the holiday season and Valentine's Day) and valleys during the summer months (when chocolate tends to melt and customers are watching their weight). Given the following costs and quarterly sales forecasts, determine whether (a) level production or (b) chase demand would more economically meet the demand for chocolate candies:

Quarter	Sales Forecast (lbs)
Spring	80,000
Summer	50,000
Fall	120,000
Winter	150,000

Hiring cost = \$100 per worker
Firing cost = \$500 per worker
Inventory carrying cost = \$0.50 per pound per quarter
Regular production cost per pound = \$2.00
Production per employee = 1,000 pounds per quarter
Beginning workforce = 100 workers

SOLUTION

a. For the level production strategy, we first need to calculate average quarterly demand.

$$\frac{(80{,}000 + 50{,}000 + 120{,}000 + 150{,}000)}{4} = \frac{400{,}000}{4} = 100{,}000 \text{ pounds}$$

This becomes our planned production for each quarter. Since each worker can produce 1,000 pounds a quarter, 100 workers will be needed each quarter to meet the production requirements of 100,000 pounds. Production in excess of demand is stored in inventory, where it remains until it is used to meet demand in a later period. Demand in excess of production is met by using inventory from the previous quarter. The production plan and resulting inventory costs are as follows:

Quarter	Demand	Regular Production	Inventory
Spring	80,000	100,000	(100,000 − 80,000) = 20,000
Summer	50,000	100,000	(20,000 + 100,000 − 50,000) = 70,000
Fall	120,000	100,000	(70,000 + 100,000 − 120,000) = 50,000
Winter	150,000	100,000	(50,000 + 100,000 − 150,000) = 0
Total	*400,000*	*400,000*	*140,000*

Cost of Level Production Strategy = (400,000 × \$2.00) + (140,000 × \$.50) = \$870,000

b. For the chase demand strategy, production each quarter matches demand. To accomplish this, workers are hired at a cost of \$100 each and fired at a cost of \$500 each. Since each worker can produce 1,000 pounds per quarter, we divide the quarterly sales forecast by 1,000 to determine the required workforce size each quarter. We begin with 100 workers and hire and fire as needed. The production plan and resulting hiring and firing costs are given here.

Quarter	Demand	Regular Production	Workers Needed	Workers Hired	Workers Fired
Spring	80,000	80,000	80,000/1000 = 80		(100 − 80) = 20
Summer	50,000	50,000	50,000/1000 = 50		(80 − 50) = 30
Fall	120,000	120,000	120,000/1000 = 120	(120 − 50) = 70	
Winter	150,000	150,000	150,000/1000 = 150	(150 − 120) = 30	
Total	*400,000*	*400,000*		*100*	*50*

Cost of Chase Demand Strategy = (400,000 × \$2.00) + (100 × \$100) + (50 × \$500) = \$835,000

Comparing the cost of level production with chase demand, we find that chase demand is the best strategy for the Good and Rich line of candies.

The problem can also be solved using Excel. Exhibit 14.1 shows two worksheets from the Excel file, Exhibit 14.1.xls, available on the text website.

EXHIBIT 14.1a Level Production for Good and Rich **EXCEL FILE**

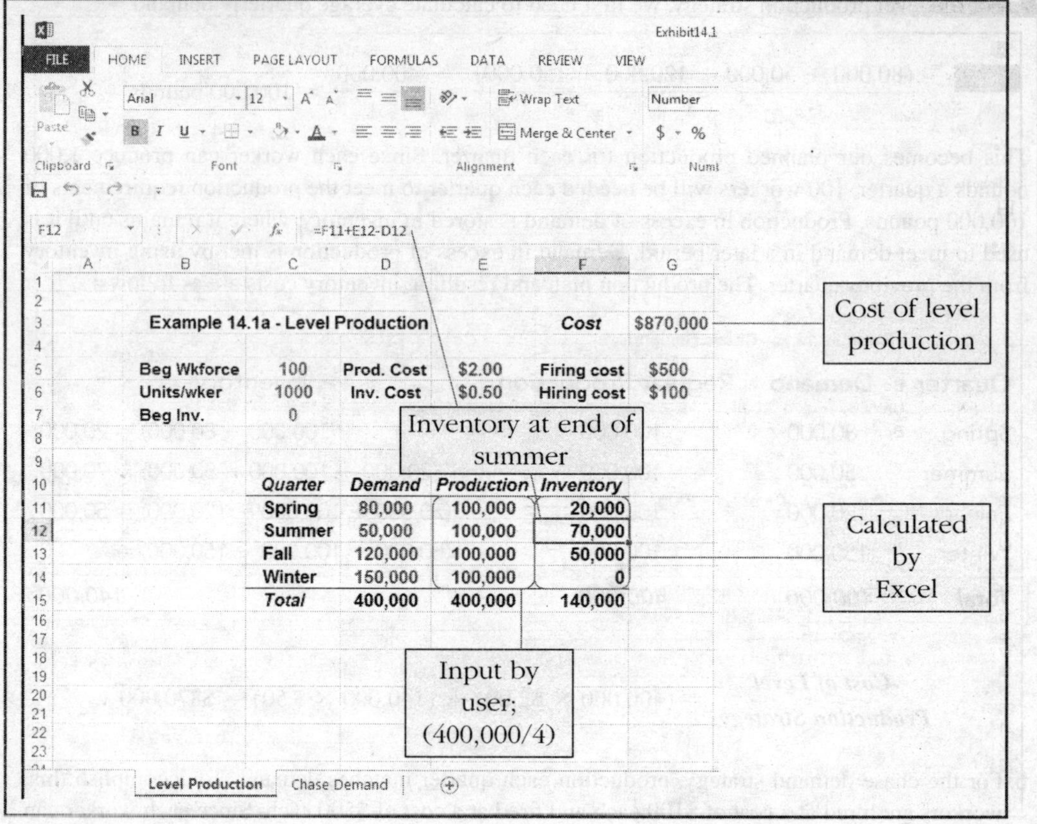

Although chase demand is the better strategy for Good and Rich from an economic point of view, it may seem unduly harsh on the company's workforce. An example of a good "fit" between a company's chase demand strategy and the needs of the workforce is Hershey's, located in rural Pennsylvania, with a demand and cost structure much like that of Good and Rich. The location of the manufacturing facility is essential to the effectiveness of the company's production plan. During the winter, when demand for chocolate is high, the company hires farmers from surrounding areas, who are idle at that time of year. The farmers are let go during the spring and summer, when they are anxious to return to their fields and the demand for chocolate falls. The plan is cost-effective, and the extra help is content with the sporadic hiring and firing practices of the company.

GENERAL LINEAR PROGRAMMING MODEL

Strategies for production planning may be easy to evaluate, but they do not necessarily provide an optimal solution. Consider the Good and Rich Company of Example 14.1. The *optimal* production plan is probably some combination of inventory and workforce adjustment. We could simply try different combinations and compare the costs (i.e., the trial-and-error approach), or we could find the optimal solution by using *linear programming*. If you are unfamiliar with linear programming, please review the supplement to this chapter. Example 14.2 develops an optimal production plan for Good and Rich chocolate candies using linear programming.

EXHIBIT 14.1b Chase Demand for Good and Rich

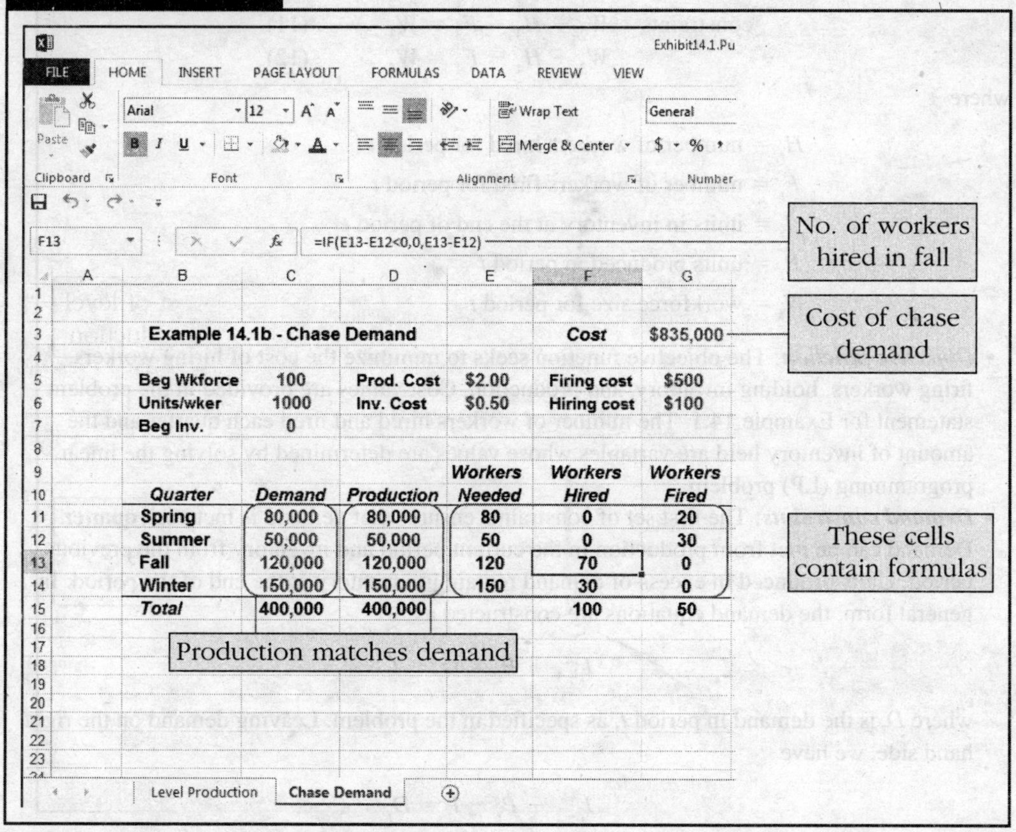

Example 14.1b - Chase Demand				Cost	$835,000
Beg Wkforce	100	Prod. Cost	$2.00	Firing cost	$500
Units/wker	1000	Inv. Cost	$0.50	Hiring cost	$100
Beg Inv.	0				
Quarter	Demand	Production	Workers Needed	Workers Hired	Workers Fired
Spring	80,000	80,000	80	0	20
Summer	50,000	50,000	50	0	30
Fall	120,000	120,000	120	70	0
Winter	150,000	150,000	150	30	0
Total	400,000	400,000		100	50

EXAMPLE 14.2

PRODUCTION PLANNING USING LINEAR PROGRAMMING

Formulate a linear programming model for Example 14.1 that will satisfy demand for Good and Rich chocolate candies at minimum cost. Solve the model with Excel Solver.

SOLUTION

Model Formulation:

$$\begin{aligned}\text{Minimize } Z = {} & \$100\,(H_1 + H_2 + H_3 + H_4) \\ & + \$500\,(F_1 + F_2 + F_3 + F_4) \\ & + \$0.50\,(I_1 + I_2 + I_3 + I_4) \\ & + \$2\,(P_1 + P_2 + P_3 + P_4)\end{aligned}$$

subject to

Demand constraints

$$\begin{aligned} P_1 - I_1 &= 80{,}000 \quad (1)\\ I_1 + P_2 - I_2 &= 50{,}000 \quad (2)\\ I_2 + P_3 - I_3 &= 120{,}000 \quad (3)\\ I_3 + P_4 - I_4 &= 150{,}000 \quad (4)\end{aligned}$$

Production constraints

$$\begin{aligned} 1{,}000W_1 &= P_1 \quad (5)\\ 1{,}000W_2 &= P_2 \quad (6)\\ 1{,}000W_3 &= P_3 \quad (7)\\ 1{,}000W_4 &= P_4 \quad (8)\end{aligned}$$

(Continued)

V

$$
\begin{array}{lrr}
 & 100 + H_1 - F_1 = W_1 & (9) \\
\text{Workforce} & W_1 + H_2 - F_2 = W_2 & (10) \\
\text{constraints} & W_2 + H_3 - F_3 = W_3 & (11) \\
 & W_3 + H_4 - F_4 = W_4 & (12)
\end{array}
$$

where

H_t = number of workers hired for period t

F_t = number of workers fired for period t

I_t = units in inventory at the end of period t

P_t = units produced in period t

W_t = workforce size for period t

- ***Objective function***: The objective function seeks to minimize the cost of hiring workers, firing workers, holding inventory, and production. Cost values are provided in the problem statement for Example 14.1. The number of workers hired and fired each quarter and the amount of inventory held are variables whose values are determined by solving the linear programming (LP) problem.
- ***Demand constraints***: The first set of constraints ensures that demand is met each quarter. Demand can be met from production in the current period and inventory from the previous period. Units produced in excess of demand remain in inventory at the end of the period. In general form, the demand equations are constructed as

$$I_{t-1} + P_t = D_t + I_t$$

where D_t is the demand in period t, as specified in the problem. Leaving demand on the right-hand side, we have

$$I_{t-1} + P_t - I_t = D_t$$

There are four demand constraints, one for each quarter. Since there is no beginning inventory, $I_0 = 0$, and it can be dropped from the first demand constraint.

- ***Production constraints***: The four production constraints convert the workforce size to the number of units that can be produced. Each worker can produce 1,000 units a quarter, so the production each quarter is 1,000 times the number of workers employed, or

$$1{,}000W_t = P_t$$

- ***Workforce constraints***: The workforce constraints limit the workforce size in each period to the previous period's workforce plus the number of workers hired in the current period minus the number of workers fired.

$$W_{t-1} + H_t - F_t = W_t$$

Notice the first workforce constraint shows a beginning workforce size of 100.

- ***Additional variables and constraints***: Additional variables, such as overtime and subcontracting, can be added to the LP formulation as needed. The cost of those variables is then added to the objective function. Additional constraints such as limiting the amount of overtime or subcontracting can also be added in the Solver model.

The LP formulation is solved using Excel Solver as shown in Exhibit 14.2b. The Excel file, Exhibit 14.2.xls, is available on the text website. The cost of the optimum solution is $832,000, an improvement of $3,000 over the chase demand strategy and $38,000 over the level production strategy.

EXHIBIT 14.2a Setting up the Spreadsheet

EXCEL FILE

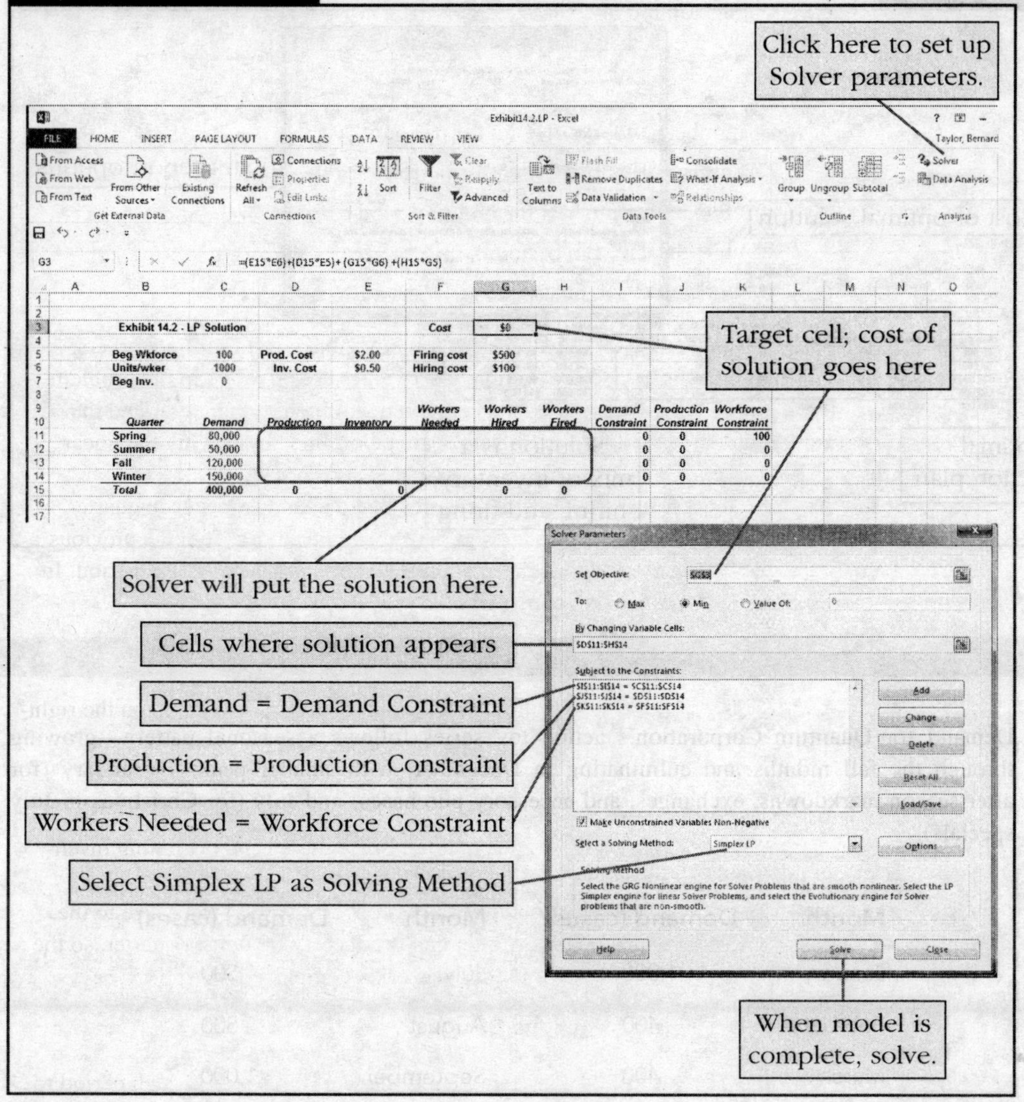

MIXED STRATEGIES

Most companies use **mixed strategies** for production planning. Mixed strategies can incorporate management policies, such as "no more than x% of the workforce can be laid off in one quarter" or "inventory levels cannot exceed x dollars." They can also be adapted to the quirks of a company or industry. For example, many industries that experience a slowdown during part of the year may simply shut down manufacturing during the low-demand season and schedule employee vacations during that time.

Example 14.3 compares pure and mixed strategies in a more extensive aggregate planning problem. Excel spreadsheets are used to make the calculations. The user inputs demand and cost data, as well as values for regular, overtime, and subcontracted production. The spreadsheet calculates resulting inventory levels, workforce levels, hiring/firing and total cost. The Excel file for this example, Exhibit 14.3.xls, is available on the textbook website. Although this problem can be solved by hand, you may wish to use the spreadsheet as a template for solving other aggregate planning problems.

EXHIBIT 14.2b Solver Solution **EXCEL FILE**

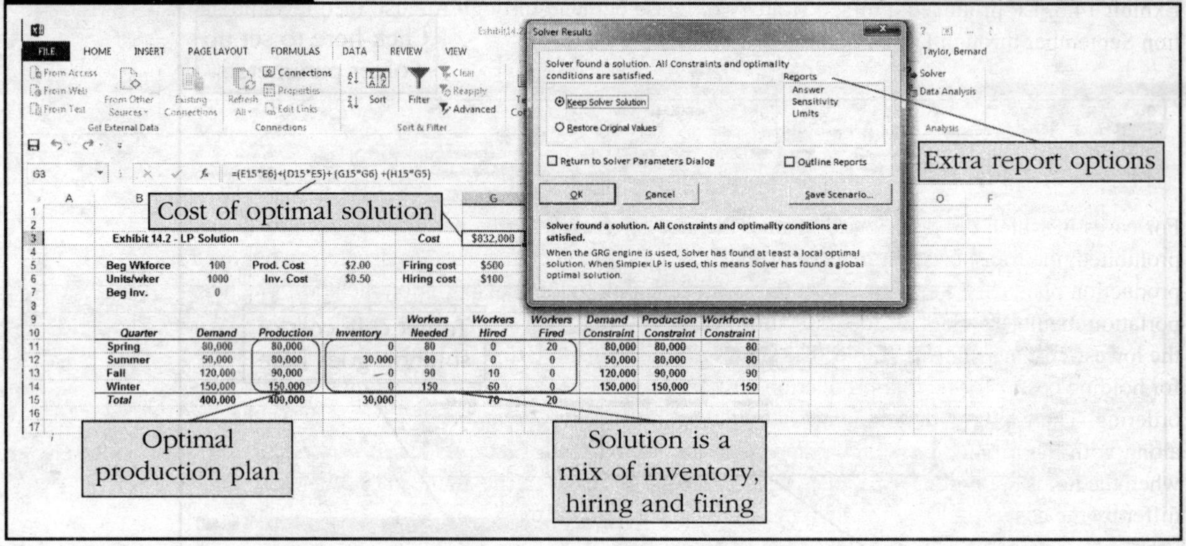

EXAMPLE 14.3

AGGREGATE PLANNING USING PURE AND MIXED STRATEGIES

Demand for Quantum Corporation's action toy series follows a seasonal pattern—growing through the fall months and culminating in December, with smaller peaks in January (for after-season markdowns, exchanges, and accessory purchases) and July (for Christmas-in-July specials).

Month	Demand (cases)	Month	Demand (cases)
January	1,000	July	500
February	400	August	500
March	400	September	1,000
April	400	October	1,500
May	400	November	2,500
June	400	December	3,000

Each worker can produce on average 100 cases of action toys each month. Overtime is limited to 300 cases, and subcontracting is unlimited. No action toys are currently in inventory. The wage rate is $10 per case for regular production, $15 for overtime production, and $25 for subcontracting. No stockouts are allowed. Holding cost is $1 per case per month. Increasing the workforce costs approximately $1,000 per worker; decreasing the workforce costs $500 per worker.

Management wishes to test the following scenarios for planning production:

a. Level production over the 12 months.
b. Produce to meet demand each month.
c. Solve the problem with linear programming (LP) using Excel Solver.

SOLUTION

Excel was used to evaluate the three planning scenarios. The solution printouts are shown in Exhibit 14.3. LP produced a mixed strategy of chase demand through August, then level production September through December.

THE TRANSPORTATION METHOD

For cases in which the decision to change the size of the workforce has already been made or is prohibited, the transportation method of linear programming can be used to develop an aggregate production plan. (See Supplement 10 for an introduction to the transportation method.) The transportation method gathers all the cost information into one matrix and plans production based on the lowest-cost alternatives. Table 14.1 shows a blank transportation tableau with *i* for inventory, *h* for holding cost, *r* for regular production cost, *o* for overtime, *s* for subcontracting, and *b* for backordering. The capital letters indicate individual capacities or demand. The periods of production, along with the production options, appear in the first column. The periods of use (regardless of when the items are produced) appear across the top row. Cost entries in the period-of-use columns differ by the cost of holding the item in inventory before its use.

EXHIBIT 14.3a Level Production for Quantum **EXCEL FILE**

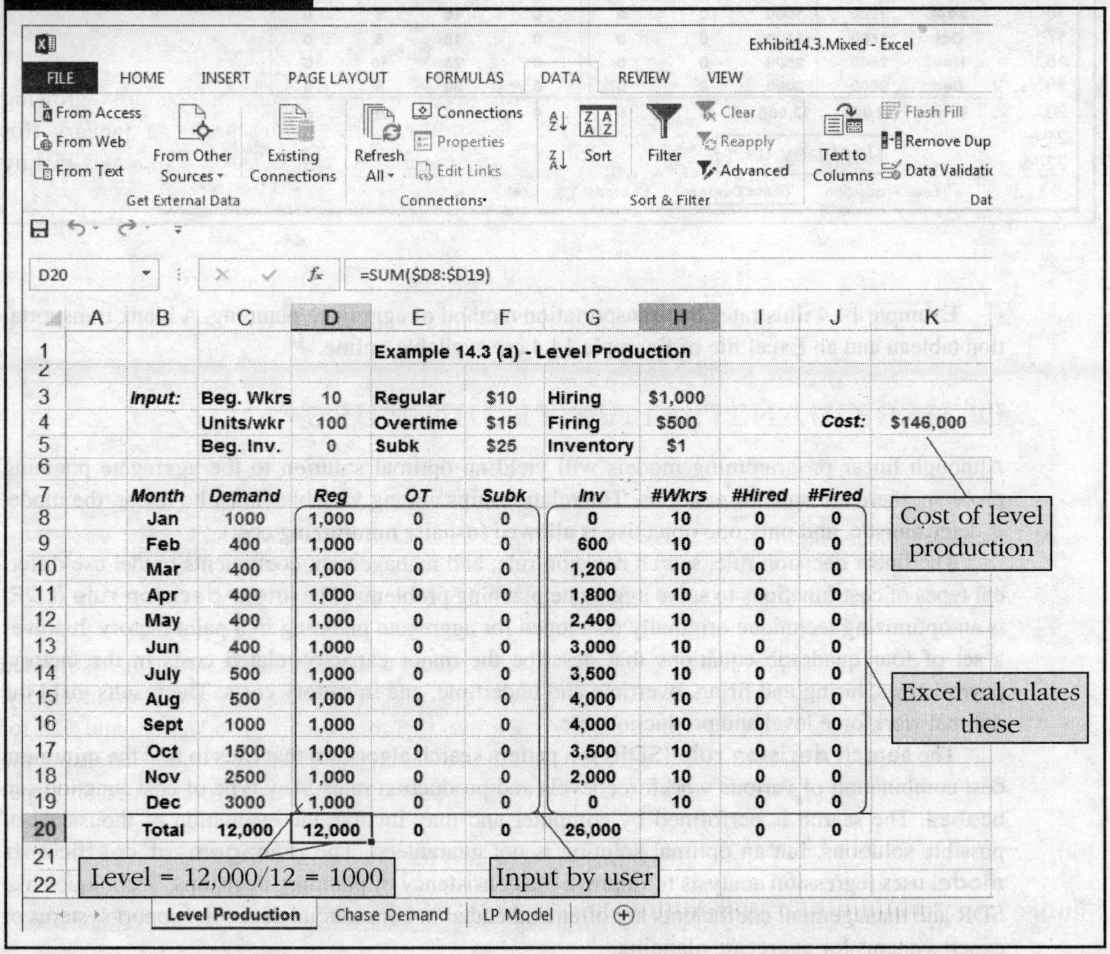

	A	B	C	D	E	F	G	H	I	J	K
1					Example 14.3 (a) - Level Production						
2											
3		*Input:*	Beg. Wkrs	10	Regular	$10	Hiring	$1,000			
4			Units/wkr	100	Overtime	$15	Firing	$500		*Cost:*	$146,000
5			Beg. Inv.	0	Subk	$25	Inventory	$1			
6											
7		*Month*	*Demand*	*Reg*	*OT*	*Subk*	*Inv*	*#Wkrs*	*#Hired*	*#Fired*	
8		Jan	1000	1,000	0	0	0	10	0	0	
9		Feb	400	1,000	0	0	600	10	0	0	
10		Mar	400	1,000	0	0	1,200	10	0	0	
11		Apr	400	1,000	0	0	1,800	10	0	0	
12		May	400	1,000	0	0	2,400	10	0	0	
13		Jun	400	1,000	0	0	3,000	10	0	0	
14		July	500	1,000	0	0	3,500	10	0	0	
15		Aug	500	1,000	0	0	4,000	10	0	0	
16		Sept	1000	1,000	0	0	4,000	10	0	0	
17		Oct	1500	1,000	0	0	3,500	10	0	0	
18		Nov	2500	1,000	0	0	2,000	10	0	0	
19		Dec	3000	1,000	0	0	0	10	0	0	
20		Total	12,000	12,000	0	0	26,000		0	0	
21											
22											

EXHIBIT 14.3b Chase Demand for Quantum

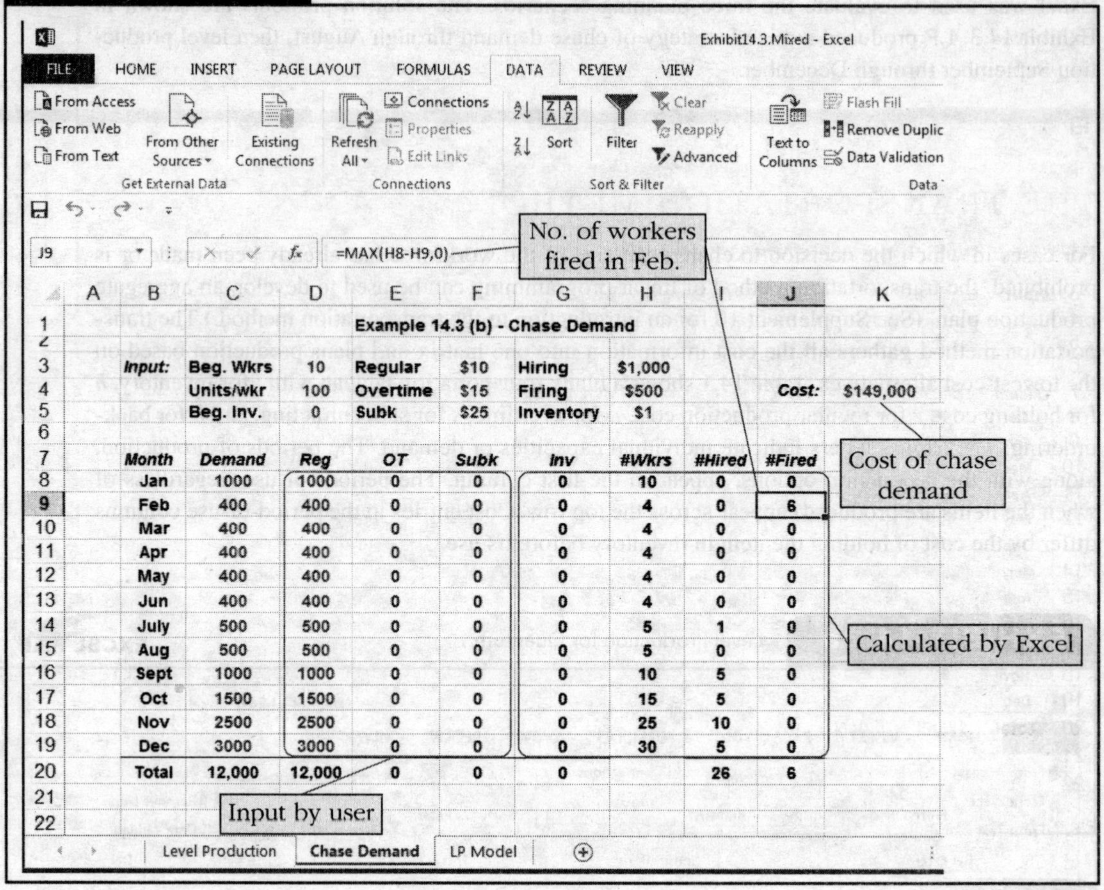

Example 14.3 (b) - Chase Demand

Input:	Beg. Wkrs	10	Regular	$10	Hiring	$1,000		
	Units/wkr	100	Overtime	$15	Firing	$500	*Cost:*	$149,000
	Beg. Inv.	0	Subk	$25	Inventory	$1		

Month	*Demand*	*Reg*	*OT*	*Subk*	*Inv*	*#Wkrs*	*#Hired*	*#Fired*
Jan	1000	1000	0	0	0	10	0	0
Feb	400	400	0	0	0	4	0	6
Mar	400	400	0	0	0	4	0	0
Apr	400	400	0	0	0	4	0	0
May	400	400	0	0	0	4	0	0
Jun	400	400	0	0	0	4	0	0
July	500	500	0	0	0	5	1	0
Aug	500	500	0	0	0	5	0	0
Sept	1000	1000	0	0	0	10	5	0
Oct	1500	1500	0	0	0	15	5	0
Nov	2500	2500	0	0	0	25	10	0
Dec	3000	3000	0	0	0	30	5	0
Total	12,000	12,000	0	0	0		26	6

Example 14.4 illustrates the transportation method of aggregate planning. A blank transportation tableau and an Excel file of Example 14.4 are available online.

OTHER QUANTITATIVE TECHNIQUES

Although linear programming models will yield an optimal solution to the aggregate planning problem, there are some limitations. The relationships among variables must be linear, the model is deterministic, and only one objective is allowed (usually minimizing cost).

The linear decision rule, search decision rule, and management coefficients model use different types of cost functions to solve aggregate planning problems. The **linear decision rule (LDR)** is an optimizing technique originally developed for aggregate planning in a paint factory. It solves a set of four quadratic equations that describe the major capacity-related costs in the factory: payroll costs, hiring and firing, overtime and undertime, and inventory costs. The results yield the optimal workforce level and production rate.

The **search decision rule (SDR)** is a pattern search algorithm that tries to find the minimum cost combination of various workforce levels and production rates. Any type of cost function can be used. The search is performed by computer and may involve the evaluation of thousands of possible solutions, but an optimal solution is not guaranteed. The **management coefficients model** uses regression analysis to improve the consistency of planning decisions. Techniques like SDR and management coefficients are often embedded in commercial decision support systems or expert systems for aggregate planning.

EXHIBIT 14.3c Linear Programming Solution for Quantum

EXCEL FILE

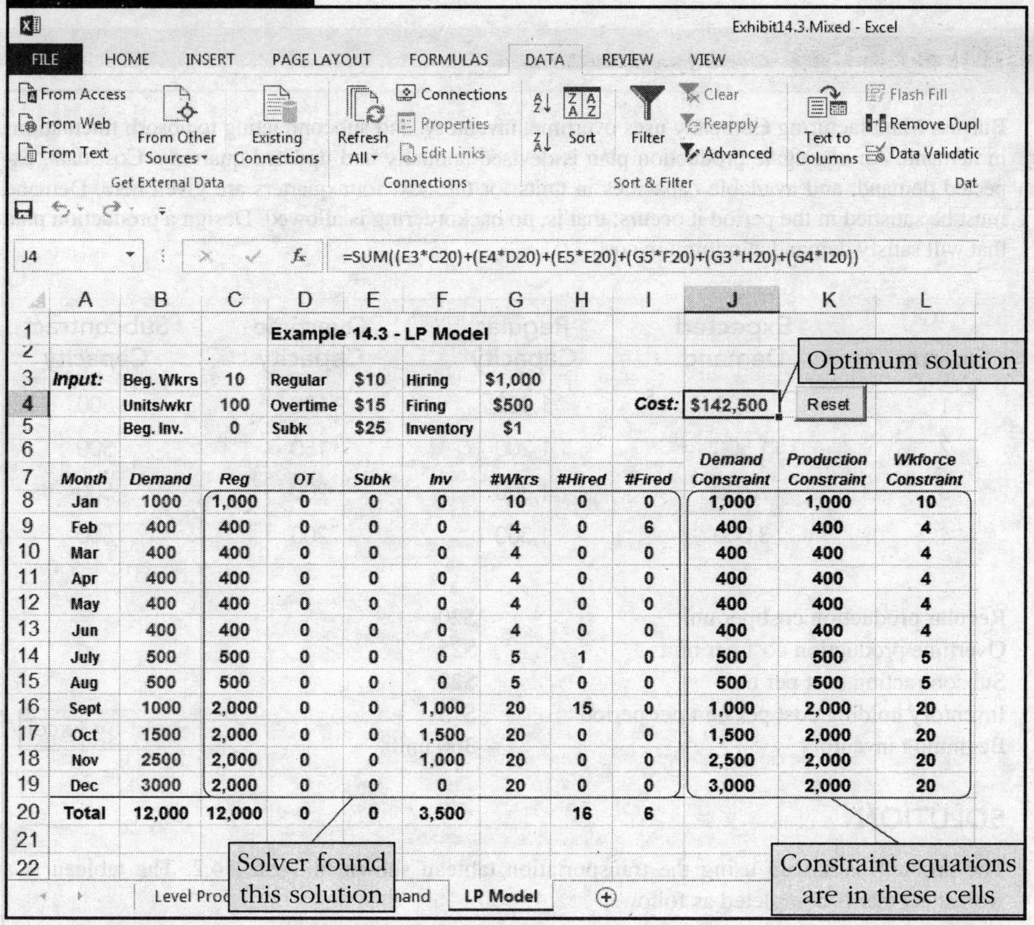

	A	B	C	D	E	F	G	H	I	J	K	L
1				Example 14.3 - LP Model								
2												
3	*Input:*	Beg. Wkrs	10	Regular	$10	Hiring	$1,000					
4		Units/wkr	100	Overtime	$15	Firing	$500		*Cost:*	$142,500		
5		Beg. Inv.	0	Subk	$25	Inventory	$1					
6												
7	*Month*	*Demand*	*Reg*	*OT*	*Subk*	*Inv*	*#Wkrs*	*#Hired*	*#Fired*	*Demand Constraint*	*Production Constraint*	*Wkforce Constraint*
8	Jan	1000	1,000	0	0	0	10	0	0	1,000	1,000	10
9	Feb	400	400	0	0	0	4	0	6	400	400	4
10	Mar	400	400	0	0	0	4	0	0	400	400	4
11	Apr	400	400	0	0	0	4	0	0	400	400	4
12	May	400	400	0	0	0	4	0	0	400	400	4
13	Jun	400	400	0	0	0	4	0	0	400	400	4
14	July	500	500	0	0	0	5	1	0	500	500	5
15	Aug	500	500	0	0	0	5	0	0	500	500	5
16	Sept	1000	2,000	0	0	1,000	20	15	0	1,000	2,000	20
17	Oct	1500	2,000	0	0	1,500	20	0	0	1,500	2,000	20
18	Nov	2500	2,000	0	0	1,000	20	0	0	2,500	2,000	20
19	Dec	3000	2,000	0	0	0	20	0	0	3,000	2,000	20
20	Total	12,000	12,000	0	0	3,500		16	6			
21												
22												

TABLE 14.1 Transportation Tableau

		Period of Use					
Period of Production		**1**	**2**	**3**	**4**	**Unused Capacity**	**Capacity**
	Beginning Inventory	0	h	$2h$	$3h$		I
1	Regular	r	$r + h$	$r + 2h$	$r + 3h$		R_1
	Overtime	o	$o + h$	$o + 2h$	$o + 3h$		O_1
	Subcontract	s	$s + h$	$s + 2h$	$s + 3h$		S_1
2	Regular	$r + b$	r	$r + h$	$r + 2h$		R_2
	Overtime	$o + b$	o	$o + h$	$o + 2h$		O_2
	Subcontract	$s + b$	s	$s + h$	$s + 2h$		S_2
3	Regular	$r + 2b$	$r + b$	r	$r + h$		R_3
	Overtime	$o + 2b$	$o + b$	o	$o + h$		O_3
	Subcontract	$s + 2b$	$s + b$	s	$s + h$		S_3
4	Regular	$r + 3b$	$r + 2b$	$r + b$	r		R_4
	Overtime	$o + 3b$	$o + 2b$	$o + b$	o		O_4
	Subcontract	$s + 3b$	$s + 2b$	$s + b$	s		S_4
	Demand	D_1	D_2	D_3	D_4		

h = holding cost per unit
r = regular production cost per unit
o = overtime cost per unit
s = subcontracting cost per unit
b = backordering cost per unit
D = demand
I = beginning inventory
R = regular capacity
O = overtime capacity
S = subcontracting capacity

EXAMPLE 14.4

THE TRANSPORTATION METHOD OF AGGREGATE PLANNING

Burruss Manufacturing Company uses overtime, inventory, and subcontracting to absorb fluctuations in demand. An aggregate production plan is devised annually and updated quarterly. Cost data, expected demand, and available capacities in units for the next four quarters are given here. Demand must be satisfied in the period it occurs; that is, no backordering is allowed. Design a production plan that will satisfy demand at minimum cost.

Quarter	Expected Demand	Regular Capacity	Overtime Capacity	Subcontract Capacity
1	900	1,000	100	500
2	1,500	1,200	150	500
3	1,600	1,300	200	500
4	3,000	1,300	200	500

Regular production cost per unit	\$20
Overtime production cost per unit	\$25
Subcontracting cost per unit	\$28
Inventory holding cost per unit per period	\$ 3
Beginning inventory	300 units

SOLUTION

The problem is solved using the transportation tableau shown in Table 14.2. The tableau is a worksheet that is completed as follows:

- To set up the tableau, demand requirements for each quarter are listed on the bottom row, and capacity constraints for each type of production (i.e., regular, overtime, or subcontracting) are placed in the far right column, around the rim of the table.
- Next, cost figures are entered into the small square at the corner of each cell. Starting with the beginning inventory row, inventory on hand in period 1 that is used in period 1 incurs zero cost. Inventory on hand in period 1 that is not used until period 2 incurs a \$3 holding cost. Inventory held until period 3, costs \$3 more, or \$6. Similarly, inventory held until period 4 costs an additional \$3, or \$9.
- For regular production, a unit produced in period 1 and used in period 1 costs \$20. A unit produced under regular production in period 1 but not used until period 2 incurs a production cost of \$20 plus an inventory cost of \$3, or \$23. If the unit is held until period 3, it costs \$3 more, or \$26. If held until period 4, it costs \$29. The cost calculations continue for overtime and subcontracting, beginning with production costs of \$25 and \$28, respectively.
- The costs for production in periods 2, 3, and 4 are determined in a similar fashion, with one exception. Half of the remaining transportation tableau is blocked out as infeasible. This occurs because no backordering is allowed for this problem, and production cannot take place in one period to satisfy demand for a period that has already passed.
- Now that the tableau is set up, we can begin to allocate units to the cells and develop our production plan. The procedure is to assign units to the lowest-cost cells in a column so that demand requirements for the column are met, yet capacity constraints of each row are not exceeded. Beginning with the first demand column for period 1, we have 300 units of

TABLE 14.2

EXCEL FILE

Period of Production		Period of Use 1	2	3	4	Unused Capacity	Capacity
	Beginning Inventory	300 (0)	— (3)	— (6)	— (9)		300
1	Regular	600 (20)	300 (23)	100 (26)	— (29)		1000
	Overtime	(25)	(28)	(31)	100 (34)		100
	Subcontract	(28)	(31)	(34)	(37)	500	500
2	Regular		1200 (20)	— (23)	— (26)		1200
	Overtime		(25)	(28)	150 (31)		150
	Subcontract		(28)	(31)	250 (34)	250	500
3	Regular			1300 (20)	— (23)		1300
	Overtime			200 (25)	— (28)		200
	Subcontract			(28)	500 (31)		500
4	Regular				1300 (20)		1300
	Overtime				200 (25)		200
	Subcontract				500 (28)		500
	Demand	900	1500	1600	3000	250	

beginning inventory available to us at no cost. If we use all 300 units in period 1, there is no inventory left for use in later periods. We indicate this fact by putting a dash in the remaining cells of the beginning inventory row. We can satisfy the remaining 600 units of demand for period 1 with regular production at a cost of $20 per unit.

- In period 2, the lowest-cost alternative is regular production in period 2. We assign 1,200 units to that cell and, in the process, use up all the capacity for that row. Dashes are placed in the remaining cells of the row to indicate that they are no longer feasible choices. The remaining units needed to meet demand in period 2 are taken from regular production in period 1 that is inventoried until period 2, at a cost of $23 per unit. We assign 300 units to that cell.
- Continuing to the third period's demand of 1,600 units, we fully utilize the 1,300 units available from regular production in the same period and 200 units of overtime production. The remaining 100 units are produced with regular production in period 1 and held until period 3, at a cost of $26 per unit. As noted by the dashed line, period 1's regular production has reached its capacity and is no longer an alternative source of production.
- Of the fourth period's demand of 3,000 units, 1,300 units come from regular production, 200 from overtime, and 500 from subcontracting in the same period. One hundred fifty more units can be provided at a cost of $31 per unit from overtime production in period 2 and 500 from subcontracting in period 3. The next-lowest alternative is $34 from overtime in period 1 or subcontracting in period 2. At this point, we can make a judgment call as to whether our workers want overtime or whether it would be easier to subcontract out the entire amount. As shown in Table 14.2, we decide to use overtime to its full capacity of 100 units and fill the remaining demand of 250 from subcontracting.
- The unused capacity column is filled in last. In period 2, 250 units of subcontracting capacity are available but unused. This information is valuable because it tells us the flexibility the company has to accept additional orders.

TABLE 14.3 The Production Plan

		Production Plan			
Period	Demand	Regular Production	Overtime	Subcontract	Ending Inventory
1	900	1,000	100	0	500
2	1,500	1,200	150	250	600
3	1,600	1,300	200	500	1,000
4	3,000	1,300	200	500	0
Total	7,000	4,800	650	1,250	2,100

The optimal production plan, derived from the transportation tableau, is given in Table 14.3.[2] The values in the production plan are taken from the transportation tableau one row at a time.

EXHIBIT 14.4 Using Excel for the Transportation Method of Aggregate Planning

EXCEL FILE

Exhibit14.4.Transpor

FILE HOME INSERT PAGE LAYOUT FORMULAS DATA REVIEW VIEW

O31

Exhibit 14.4 - The Transportation Method of Aggregate Planning

(Unit cost of each cell shown in brackets.)

Period of Production		Period of Use 1	2	3	4	Units Produced	Capacity	Unused Capacity
	Beg. Inventory	300 [0]	0 [3]	0 [6]	· [9]	300	300	0
1	Regular	600 [20]	300 [23]	100 [26]	[29]	1,000	1,000	0
	Overtime	[25]	0 [28]	0 [31]	100 [34]	100	100	0
	Subk	0 [28]	0 [31]	0 [34]	0 [37]	0	500	500
2	Regular	0	1,200 [20]	[23]	0 [26]	1,200	1,200	0
	Overtime	0	[25]	0 [28]	150 [31]	150	150	0
	Subk	0	[28]	0 [31]	250 [34]	250	500	250
3	Regular	0	0	1,300 [20]	0 [23]	1,300	1,300	0
	Overtime	0	0	200 [25]	0 [28]	200	200	0
	Subk	0	0	0 [28]	500 [31]	500	500	0
4	Regular	0	0	0	1,300 [20]	1,300	1,300	0
	Overtime	0	0	0	200 [25]	200	200	0
	Subk	0	0	0	500 [28]	500	500	0
	Units Produced	900	1,500	1,600	3,000	7,000	7,000	750
	Demand	900	1,500	1,600	3,000	7,000		
	Unmet Demand	0	0	0	0		Total Cost =	$153,550

There are multiple optimum solutions to this problem.

Production Plan

Period	Demand	Reg. Prod.	Overtime	Subk	Ending Inventory
1	900	1,000	100	0	500
2	1,500	1,200	150	250	600
3	1,600	1,300	200	500	1,000
4	3,000	1,300	200	500	0
Total	7,000	4,800	650	1,250	2,100

Total Cost = $153,550

Regular production for period 1

Cost of solution

[2] For this example, our initial solution to the production problem happens to be optimal. In other cases, it may be necessary to iterate to additional transportation tableaux before an optimal solution is reached. Students unfamiliar with the transportation method should review the topic in the Supplement to Chapter 11.

For example, the 1,000 units of a regular production for period 1 is the sum of 600 + 300 + 100 from the second row of the transportation tableau. Ending inventory is calculated by summing beginning inventory and all forms of production for that period, and then subtracting demand. For example, the ending inventory for period 1 is

$$\begin{aligned}&(\text{Beginning inventory} + \text{Regular production}\\&+ \text{Overtime production} + \text{Subcontracting}) - \text{Demand}\\&= (300 + 1000 + 100 + 0) - 900 = 500\end{aligned}$$

The cost of the production plan can be determined directly from the transportation tableau by multiplying the units in each cell times the cost in the corner of the cell and summing them. Alternatively, the cost can be determined from the production plan by multiplying the total units produced in each production category, or held in inventory, by their respective costs and summing them, as follows:

$$(4800 \times \$20) + (650 \times \$25) + (1250 \times \$28) + (2100 \times \$3) = \$153{,}550$$

An Excel solution to this problem is shown in Exhibit 14.4.

The Hierarchical Nature of Planning

Planning involves a hierarchy of decisions. By determining a strategy for meeting and managing demand, aggregate planning provides a framework within which shorter term production and capacity decisions can be made. The levels of production and capacity planning are shown in Figure 14.4. In production planning, the next level of detail is a *master production schedule*, in which weekly (not monthly or quarterly) production plans are specified by individual final product (not product line). At another level of detail, *material requirements planning* plans the production of the components that go into the final products. *Shop floor scheduling* schedules the manufacturing operations required to make each component.

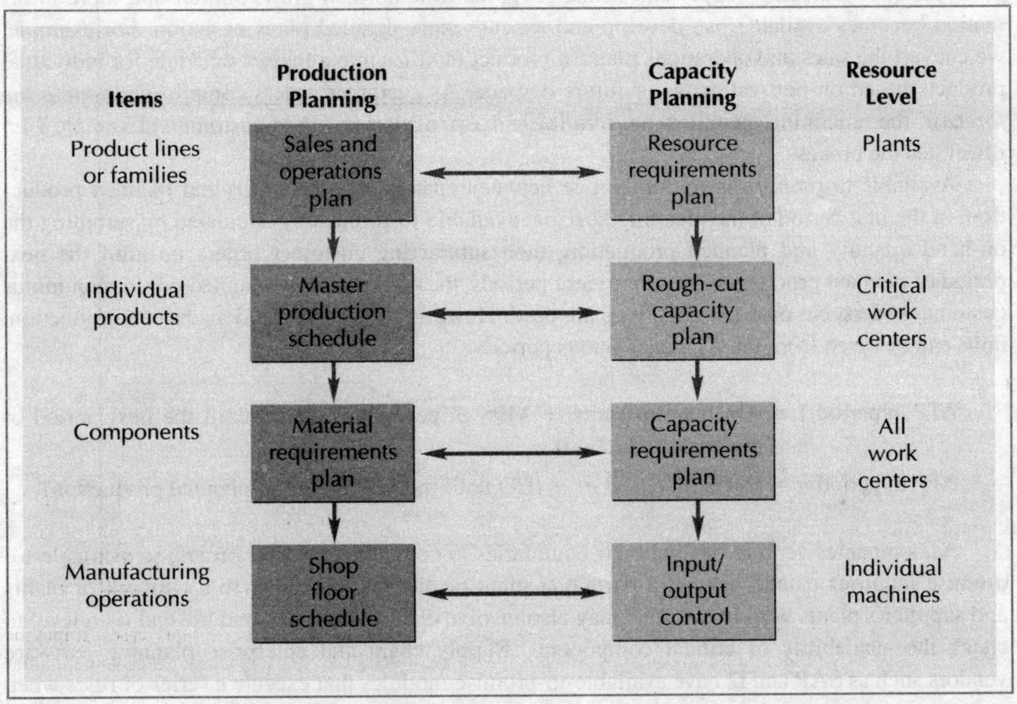

Figure 14.4
Hierarchical Planning

In capacity planning, we might develop a *resource requirements plan*, to verify that a sales and operations plan is doable, and a *rough-cut capacity plan* as a quick check to see if the master production schedule is feasible. One level down, we would develop a much more detailed *capacity requirements plan* that matches the factory's machine and labor resources to the material requirements plan. Finally, we would use *input/output control* to monitor the production that takes place at individual machines or work centers.

At each level, decisions are made within the parameters set by the higher-level decisions. The process of moving from the aggregate plan to the next level down is called **disaggregation**. We examine this process more thoroughly in Chapter 15. In the next section, we discuss two important tools for planning in an e-business environment: collaborative planning and available-to-promise.

COLLABORATIVE PLANNING

Collaborative planning is part of the supply chain process of collaborative planning, forecasting, and replenishment (CPFR) presented in Chapter 10. In terms of production, CPFR involves selecting the products to be jointly managed, creating a single forecast of customer demand, and synchronizing production across the supply chain. Consensus among partners is reached first on the sales forecast, then on the production plan. Although the process differs by software vendor, basically each partner has access to an Internet-enabled planning book in which forecasts, customer orders, and production plans are visible for specific items. Partners agree on the level of aggregation to be used. Events trigger responses by partners. Alerts warn partners of conditions that require special action or changes to the plan.

One example of an event that requires collaboration among trading partners is quoting available-to-promise dates for customers.

AVAILABLE-TO-PROMISE

In the current business environment of outsourcing and build-to-order products, companies must be able to provide the customer with accurate promise dates. Recall that S&OP is the company's *game plan* for matching supply and demand. As the time horizon grows shorter and more information becomes available, we develop and execute more detailed plans of action. For example, we convert the sales and operations plan for product families into a master schedule for individual products based on best estimates of future demand. As customer orders come in *consuming the forecast*, the remaining quantities are **available-to-promise** to future customers. Example 14.5 illustrates the process.

Available-to-promise is the difference between customer orders (CO) and planned production. In the first period of the planning horizon, available-to-promise is calculated by summing the on-hand quantity and planned production, then subtracting customer orders up until the next period of planned production. In subsequent periods, the ATP is simply planned production minus customer orders. No on-hand quantities are used. However, if customer orders exceed production, units can be taken from the ATP of previous periods.

ATP in period 1 = (On-hand quantity + MPS in period 1) − (CO until the next period of planned production)

ATP in period n = (MPS in period n) − (CO until the next period of planned production)

As companies venture beyond their boundaries to complete customer orders, so available-to-promise inquiries extend beyond a particular plant or distribution center to a network of plants and supplier's plants worldwide. ATP may also involve drilling down beyond the end item level to check the availability of critical components. Supply chain and enterprise planning software vendors such as SAP and i2 have available-to-promise modules that execute a series of rules when

EXAMPLE 14.5

AVAILABLE-TO-PROMISE

East Coast Bicycle Company has recently begun to accept customer orders over the Internet. The company uses both an aggregate production plan for families and a master production schedule for individual products. Now East Coast wants to add available-to-promise functionality to the planning process. Using the information given below, determine how many girls' 26" bikes are available-to-promise in April, May, and June.

Sales and Operations Plan

	Quarter			
Product Family	*1*	*2*	*3*	*4*
Juvenile Bikes	800	1,000	1,500	4,000

Master Production Schedule for Qtr 2

	April	May	June	Total
Boys' 26" Bike	150	100	150	400
Girls' 26" Bike	**100**	**100**	**100**	**300**
Boys' 20" Bike	30	20	50	100
Girls' 20" Bike	40	20	140	200
Total	320	240	440	1,000

Available-to Promise for Girls' 26" Bike

On Hand = 10	April	May	June	Total
Forecast	50	100	150	300
Customer Orders	70	110	50	230
Master Production Schedule	**100**	**100**	**100**	**300**
Available-to-Promise				

SOLUTION

The available-to-promise (ATP) row is calculated by summing the on-hand quantity with the scheduled production units and subtracting the customer orders up until the next period of planned production. The negative ATP in May is offset by using 10 units of ATP from April.

On Hand = 10	April	May	June
Forecast	50	100	150
Customer Orders	70	110	150
Master Production Schedule	100	100	100
Available-to-Promise	30	0	50

ATP in April = (10 + 100) − 70 = ~~40~~ 30
ATP in May = 100 − 110 = −10 Take excess units from April
ATP in June = 100 − 50 = 50

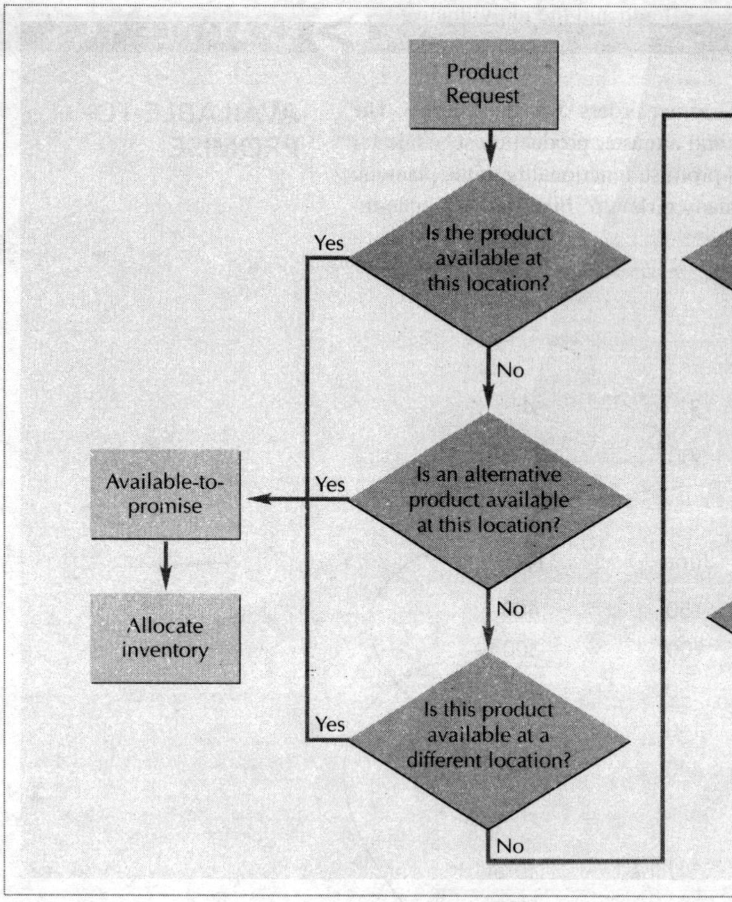

Figure 14.5

Rules-Based ATP

SOURCE: Adapted from SAP AG, "Global Available-to-Promise," http://www.sap.com/solutions/scm/apo/pdf/atp.pdf.

assessing product availability, and alert the planner when customer orders exceed or fall short of forecasts. The rules prescribe product substitutions, alternative sources, and allocation procedures as shown in Figure 14.5. When the product is not available, the system proposes a **capable-to-promise** date that is subject to customer approval.

Aggregate Planning for Services

The aggregate planning process is different for services in the following ways:

1. ***Most services cannot be inventoried***. It is impossible to store an airline seat, hotel room, or hair appointment for use later when demand may be higher. When the goods that accompany a service can be inventoried, they typically have a very short life. Newspapers are good for only a day; flowers, at most a week; and cooked hamburgers, only 10 minutes.
2. ***Demand for services is difficult to predict***. Demand variations occur frequently and are often severe. The exponential distribution is commonly used to simulate the erratic demand for services—high-demand peaks over short periods of time with long periods of low demand in between. *Customer service levels* established by management express the percentage of demand that must be met and, sometimes, how quickly demand must be met. This is an important input to aggregate planning for services.

3. ***Capacity is also difficult to predict***. The variety of services offered and the individualized nature of services make capacity difficult to predict. The "capacity" of a bank teller depends on the number and type of transactions requested by the customer. Units of capacity can also vary. Should a hospital define capacity in terms of number of beds, number of patients, size of the nursing or medical staff, or number of patient hours?
4. ***Service capacity must be provided at the appropriate place and time***. Many services have branches or outlets widely dispersed over a geographic region. Determining the range of services and staff levels at each location is part of aggregate planning.
5. ***Labor is usually the most constraining resource for services***. This is an advantage in aggregate planning because labor is very flexible. Variations in demand can be handled by hiring temporary workers, using part-time workers, or using overtime. Summer recreation programs and theme parks hire teenagers out of school for the summer. FedEx staffs its peak hours of midnight to 2 A.M. with area college students. McDonald's, Walmart, and other retail establishments woo senior citizens as reliable part-time workers. Workers can also be cross-trained to perform a variety of jobs and can be called upon as needed. A common example is the sales clerk who also stocks inventory. Less common are police officers who are cross-trained as firefighters and paramedics.

There are several services that have unique aggregate planning problems. Doctors, lawyers, and other professionals have emergency or priority calls for their service that must be meshed with regular appointments. Hotels and airlines routinely *overbook* their capacity in anticipation of customers who do not show up. Airlines design complex pricing structures for different routes and classes of customers. Planners incorporate these decisions in a process called revenue management.

REVENUE MANAGEMENT

Revenue management (also called *yield management*) seeks to maximize profit or yield from time-sensitive products and services. It is used in industries with inflexible and expensive capacity, perishable products or services, segmented markets, advanced sales, and uncertain demand. The types of problems addressed by revenue management include overbooking, partitioning demand into fare classes, and single order quantities.

Overbooking

Services with reservation systems can lose money when customers fail to show up, or cancel reservations at the last minute. It is not unusual for no-shows to account for 10% to 30% of an aircraft's available seats. Thus, hotels, airlines, and restaurants routinely overbook their capacity. Managers who underestimate the number of no-shows must then compensate a customer who has been "bumped" by providing the service free of charge at another time or place.

Fare Classes

Hotels, airlines, stadiums, and theaters typically offer different ticket prices for certain classes of seats or customers. Planners must determine the number of seats or rooms to allocate to these different fare classes. Too many high-priced seats can lose customers, while too few high-priced seats can lower profits. Sabre estimates that airlines make more profits from the 3% of customers who are "business travelers" than the rest of customers who have discounted fares.

With the volume of data now available from digital "footprints," companies can now offer one-to-one marketing deals to online customers, changing prices for each customer based on previous buying habits, or to close a sale for an item left in the shopping cart unpurchased. *Congestion prices* vary on the newest toll road for the D.C. metro region, where drivers may choose to pay a toll for access to less congested roadways. The price of the toll changes as traffic on the main road increases. Smart vending machines can change prices, too, depending on inventory levels or outside temperature.

Single Order Quantities

The useful life for products such as newspapers, flowers, baked goods, and seasonal items is so short that in many instances, only one order for production can take place. Determining the size of that single order can be difficult.

Table 14.4 shows the various types of revenue management problems with cost descriptions. In each of these problems, the cost of overestimating demand (times the probability that it will occur) must be balanced with the cost of underestimating demand and its probability of occurrence.

The optimum probability is where the cost of underestimating demand is equal to or just greater than the cost of overestimating demand. The derivation of the formula is shown below, followed by an example.

$$\text{Cost of underestimating demand} \geq \text{Cost of overestimating demand}$$

$$P(N \geq X)C_u \geq P(N < X)C_o$$

$$[1 - P(N < X)]C_u \geq P(N < X)C_o$$

$$P(N < X) \leq \frac{C_u}{C_u + C_o}$$

where

C_o = cost of overestimating demand or no-shows
C_u = cost of underestimating demand or no-shows
$P(N < X)$ = probability of overestimating demand or no-shows
$P(N \geq X)$ = probability of underestimating demand or no-shows
N = number of units demanded or no-shows
X = units ordered or overbooked

Given cost information and a distribution of demand or no-shows from past data, we can now match our planning policy with the optimum probability of overestimating demand. Example 14.6 illustrates the procedure for overbooking. A single order quantity problem is included in the solved problems at the end of this chapter.

TABLE 14.4 Types of Revenue Management Problems

Type of Problem	Type of Business	Probability of Overestimating Demand or No-Shows, $P(N < X)$	Optimal Probability of Demand or No-Show $\frac{C_u}{(C_u + C_o)}$	Cost Description
Overbooking	Hotel, airlines, restaurants	N = number of no-shows X = number of overbooked rooms or seats	C_o = cost of overbooking C_u = cost of underbooking	Replacement cost Lost profit
Fare Classes	Airlines, cruise ships, passenger trains, extended stay hotel	N = number of full-fare tickets that can be sold X = seats reserved for full-fare passengers	C_o = cost of overestimating full-fare passengers C_u = cost of underestimating full-fare passengers	Lost full-fare (Full-fare−discounted fare)
Premium Seats	Stadiums, theaters	N = number of premium tickets that can be sold X = seats reserved for premium ticket holders	C_o = cost of overestimating premium ticket sales C_u = cost of underestimating premium ticket sales	Lost regular revenue (Premium ticket−regular ticket revenue)
Single Order Quantities	Newspapers, magazines, florists, nurseries, bakeries, sale items	N = number of items that can be sold X = number of items ordered	C_o = cost of overestimating demand C_u = cost of underestimating demand	(Cost−salvage value) Lost profit

EXAMPLE 14.6

TYPES OF REVENUE MANAGEMENT PROBLEMS

Lauren Lacy, manager of the Lucky Traveler Inn in Las Vegas, is tired of customers who make reservations and then don't show up. Rooms rent for $100 a night and cost $25 to maintain per day. Overflow customers can be sent to the Motel 7 for $70 a night. Lauren's records of no-shows over the past six months are given below. Should the Lucky Traveler start overbooking? If so, how many rooms should be overbooked?

No-Shows	Probability
0	0.15
1	0.25
2	0.30
3	0.30

SOLUTION

$$C_o = \$70$$

$$C_u = \$100 - \$25 = \$75$$

$$P(N < X) \leq \frac{C_u}{C_u + C_o} = \frac{75}{75 + 70} = 0.517$$

Adding a cumulative probability column of no-shows being less than expected gives us:

No-Shows	Probability	$P(N < X)$	
0	0.15	0.00	
1	0.25	0.15	
2	0.30	0.40	←0.517
3	0.30	0.70	

The optimal probability of no-shows falls between 0.40 and 0.70. Since we are concerned with no-shows *less than or equal to* 0.517, we choose the next lowest value, or 0.40. Following across the table, the Lucky Traveler should overbook by two rooms.

SUMMARY

Sales and Operations Planning (S&OP) is a structured collaborative process for matching supply and demand. The sales plan and operations plan are expressed in aggregate terms, hence the name *aggregate planning*.

Aggregate planning is critical for companies with seasonal demand patterns and for services. Variations in demand can be met by *adjusting capacity* or *managing demand*. There are several mathematical techniques for aggregate planning, including linear programming, linear decision rule, search decision rule, and management coefficient model.

Production and capacity plans are developed at several levels of detail. The process of deriving more detailed production and capacity plans from the aggregate plan is called *disaggregation*. Collaborative planning sets production plans in concert with suppliers and trading partners. *Available-to-promise* often involves collaboration along a supply chain.

Aggregate planning for services is somewhat different from that for manufacturing because the variation in demand is usually more severe and occurs over shorter time frames. Fortunately, the constraining resource in most services is labor, which is quite flexible. Services use part-time workers, overtime, and undertime. *Revenue management* is a special aggregate planning tool for industries with time-sensitive products and segmented customer classes.

SOLVED PROBLEMS

1. Fabulous Fit Fibers produces a line of sweatclothes that exhibits a varying demand pattern. Given the following demand forecasts, production costs, and constraints, design a production plan for Fabulous Fit using the transportation method of LP. Also, calculate the cost of the production plan.

PERIOD	DEMAND
September	100
October	130
November	200
December	300

Maximum regular production	100 units/month
Maximum overtime production	50 units/month
Maximum subcontracting	50 units/month
Regular production costs	$10/unit
Overtime production costs	$25/unit
Subcontracting costs	$35/unit
Inventory holding costs	$5/unit/month
Beginning inventory	0

SOLUTION

Period of Used

Period of Production		*1*	*2*	*3*	*4*	*Unused Capacity*	*Capacity*
	Beginning inventory	[0]	[5]	— [10]	— [15]		0
1	Regular	100 [10]	— [15]	[20]	[25]		100
	Overtime	[25]	[30]	[35]	50 [40]		50
	Subcontract	[35]	[40]	[45]	[50]	50	50
2	Regular		100 [10]	— [15]	— [20]		100
	Overtime		30 [25]	20 [30]	— [35]		50
	Subcontract		[35]	[40]	30 [45]	20	50
3	Regular			100 [10]	— [15]		100
	Overtime			50 [25]	— [30]		50
	Subcontract			30 [35]	20 [40]		50
4	Regular				100 [10]		100
	Overtime				50 [25]		50
	Subcontract				50 [35]		50
	Demand	100	130	200	300		

PRODUCTION PLAN

PERIOD	DEMAND	*REGULAR PRODUCTION*	*OVER-TIME*	*SUBCONTRACT*	ENDING INVENTORY
Sept	100	100	50	0	50
Oct	130	100	50	30	100
Nov	200	100	50	50	100
Dec	300	100	50	50	0
Total	730	400	200	130	250

$$\text{Cost} = (400 \times \$10) + (200 \times \$25) + (130 \times \$35) + (250 \times \$5)$$
$$= 4{,}000 + 5{,}000 + 4{,}550 + 1{,}250$$
$$= \$14{,}800$$

2. Calculate the available-to-promise for periods 1, 3, and 5.

	PERIOD					
ON HAND = 50	*1*	*2*	*3*	*4*	*5*	*6*
Forecast	100	100	100	100	100	100
Customer orders	90	120	130	70	20	10
Master production schedule	200			200	200	
Available-to-promise						

SOLUTION

	PERIOD					
ON HAND = 50	*1*	*2*	*3*	*4*	*5*	*6*
Forecast	100	100	100	100	100	100
Customer orders	90	120	130	70	20	10
Master production schedule	200		200		200	
Available-to-promise	40		0		170	

ATP in period 1 = (50 + 200) − (90 + 120) = 40
ATP in period 3 = 200 − (130 + 70) = 0
ATP in period 5 = 200 − (20 + 10) = 170

3. Doughman Bakery bakes a variety of pastries, but none is more popular than its jumbo doughnuts. Doughnuts are made fresh every morning at 4:00 A.M. and sold throughout the day. Leftover doughnuts are put in a grab bag and sold at 75% discount the next day. Fresh doughnuts are sold for $1.20 each. The cost to make each doughnut is $0.45. The bakery has recorded first-day sales data for the last 200 days. Determine how many doughnuts Doughman Bakery should bake in the morning.

DOZENS OF DOUGHNUTS	FREQUENCY
2	14
3	18
4	26
5	32
6	30
7	26
8	20
9	18
10	12
11	2
12	2

SOLUTION

DOZENS OF DOUGHNUTS	FREQUENCY	PROBABILITY	P(N < X)
2	14	0.07	0.00
3	18	0.09	0.07
4	26	0.13	0.16
5	32	0.16	0.29
6	30	0.15	0.45
7	26	0.13	0.60
8	20	0.10	0.73
9	18	0.09	0.83 ← 0.833
10	12	0.06	0.92
11	2	0.01	0.98
12	2	0.01	0.99
Total	200	1.00	

$$C_u = \$1.20 - \$0.45 = \$0.75$$

$$C_o = \$0.45 - \$0.30 = \$0.15$$

$$P(N < X) \le \frac{C_u}{C_u + C_o} = \frac{0.75}{0.75 + 0.15} = 0.833$$

Doughman should make 9 dozen doughnuts.

QUESTIONS

14-1. What is the purpose of sales and operations planning? Describe the S&OP process.

14-2. List several alternatives for adjusting capacity. List several alternatives for managing demand.

14-3. Describe the output of aggregate planning. When is aggregate planning most useful?

14-4. How do linear programming, the linear decision rule, the search decision rule, and the management coefficients model differ in terms of cost functions and output?

14-5. Identify several industries that have highly variable demand patterns. Explore how they adjust capacity.

14-6. What options are available for altering the capacity of (a) an elementary school, (b) a prison, and (c) an airline?

14-7. Discuss the advantages and disadvantages of using part-time workers, subcontracting work, and building up inventory as strategies for meeting demand.

14-8. Describe the levels of production and capacity planning in the hierarchical planning process.

14-9. Explain the process of collaborative planning. How is available-to-promise involved?

14-10. Access a major vendor of business software, such as SAP or Oracle. Read about their demand management, available-to-promise, and production planning products. What kinds of capabilities do these systems have?

14-11. How is the aggregate planning process different when used for services rather than for manufacturing?

14-12. What does revenue management entail? What types of businesses, besides hotels and airlines, would benefit from revenue management? As a consumer, how do you view the practice?

PROBLEMS

14-1. Bioway, Inc., a manufacturer of medical supplies, uses aggregate planning to set labor and inventory levels for the year. While a variety of items are produced, a standard kit composed of basic supplies is used for planning purposes. Demand varies with seasonal illnesses and the quarterly ordering policies of hospitals. The average worker at Bioway can produce 1,000 kits a month at a cost of $9 per kit during regular production hours and $10 a kit during overtime production. Completed kits can also be purchased from outside suppliers at $12 each. Inventory carrying costs are $2 per kit per month. Overtime is limited to regular production, but subcontracting is unlimited. Due to high quality standards and extensive training, hiring and firing costs are $1,500 per worker. Bioway currently employs 25 workers. Given the demand forecast below, develop a six-month aggregate production plan for Bioway using (a) chase demand and (b) a mixed strategy where the current workforce is kept for April through August, and supplemented with overtime and subcontracting as needed.

Month	Demand
April	60,000
May	22,000
June	15,000
July	46,000
August	80,000
September	15,000

14-2. Rowley Apparel, manufacturer of the famous "Race-A-Rama" swimwear line, needs help planning production for next year. Demand for swimwear follows a seasonal pattern, as shown here. Given the following costs and demand forecasts, test these four strategies for meeting demand: (a) level production with overtime and subcontracting, as needed, (b) level production with backorders as needed, (c) chase demand, and (d) 3000 units regular production from April through September and as much regular, overtime, and subcontracting production in the other months as needed to meet annual demand. Determine the cost of each strategy. Which strategy would you recommend?

Month	Demand Forecast
January	1,000
February	500
March	500
April	2,000
May	3,000
June	4,000
July	5,000
August	3,000
September	1,000
October	500
November	500
December	3,000

Beginning workforce	8 workers
Subcontracting capacity	unlimited
Overtime capacity	2,000 units/month
Production rate per worker	250 units/month
Regular wage rate	$15 per unit
Overtime wage rate	$25 per unit
Subcontracting cost	$30 per unit
Hiring cost	$100 per worker
Firing cost	$200 per worker
Holding cost	$0.50 per unit/month
Backordering cost	$10 per unit/month

14-3. FansForYou is a small, privately owned company that manufactures fans. Large variations in demand due to seasonality have contributed to high costs for the company. FansForYou currently uses a level production strategy because it prefers not to hire and fire employees. However, if there is enough cost justification, the company will consider alternative production plans.

a. What is the cost of the current production plan?
b. How much would FansForYou save by using a chase demand strategy?
c. How much would FansForYou save by keeping a steady workforce of 20 workers and supplementing with overtime and subcontracting as needed?

Month	Demand
September	1,500
October	1,000
November	600
December	600
January	600
February	800
March	1,000
April	1,000
May	4,000
June	6,500
July	6,000
August	4,000

Beginning inventory	0
Beginning workforce	25 workers
Production rate	100 fans per worker per month
Regular production cost	$40 per fan
Overtime production cost	$60 per fan
Subcontracting cost	$70 per fan
Overtime capacity	Not to exceed regular production
Subcontracting capacity	Unlimited
Holding cost	$8 per fan
Hiring cost	$2,000
Firing cost	$3,000

14-4. Slopes & Sleds (S&S) makes skis, snowboards, and high-end sledding equipment. As shown below, the demand for its products is highly seasonal. The company employs 10 workers who can each produce 200 units of various equipment per month. The cost of regular production is

$8 per unit, overtime $12, and subcontracting $16. Overtime is limited to regular production each period. Subcontracting is unlimited. Hiring and firing costs are $500 per worker. Inventory holding costs are $2 per unit per month. Given the estimates of demand below, create an aggregate production plan for Slopes & Sleds using:

a. the current workforce level (supplemented with overtime and subcontracting as needed),
b. chase demand.

Month	Demand
January	6,400
February	7,000
March	1,500
April	500
May	600
June	1,400
July	1,600
August	2,000
September	1,400
October	1,500
November	5,200
December	6,900

14-5. Design a production plan for Rowley Apparel in Problem 14-2 using linear programming and Excel Solver.

14-6. Design a production plan for Slopes & Sleds in Problem 14-4 using linear programming and Excel Solver.

14-7. The global sourcing department of Slopes & Sleds (see Problems 14-4 and 14-6) has located a company in China that can make S&S products for $9 a unit. Revise the production plan using Solver. How much money can be saved by outsourcing to China? What other factors should be considered in the outsourcing decision?

14-8. The Wetski Water Ski Company is the world's largest producer of water skis. As you might suspect, water skis exhibit a highly seasonal demand pattern, with peaks during the summer months and valleys during the winter months. Given the following costs and quarterly sales forecasts, use the transportation method to design a production plan that will economically meet demand. What is the cost of the plan?

Quarter	Sales Forecast
1	50,000
2	150,000
3	200,000
4	52,000

Inventory carrying cost	$3.00 per pair of skis per quarter
Production per employee	1,000 pairs of skis per quarter
Regular workforce	50 workers
Regular capacity	50,000 pairs of skis
Overtime capacity	50,000 pairs of skis
Subcontracting capacity	40,000 pairs of skis
Cost of regular production	$50 per pair of skis
Cost of overtime production	$75 per pair of skis
Cost of subcontracting	$85 per pair of skis

14-9. Bits and Pieces uses overtime, inventory, and subcontracting to absorb fluctuations in demand. An annual production plan is devised and updated quarterly. Expected demand over the next four quarters is 600, 800, 1,600, and 1,900 units, respectively. The capacity for regular production is 1,000 units per quarter with an overtime capacity of 100 units a quarter. Subcontracting is limited to 500 units a quarter. Regular production costs $20 per unit, overtime $25 per unit, and subcontracting $30 per unit. Inventory holding costs are assessed at $3 per unit per period. There is no beginning inventory. Design a production plan that will satisfy demand at minimum cost.

14-10. Caltex uses overtime, inventory, and subcontracting to absorb fluctuations in demand. An annual production plan is devised and updated quarterly. Expected demand, available capacities, and costs for the next four quarters are given below. Design a production plan that will satisfy demand at minimum cost.

Period	Demand	Regular Capacity	Overtime Capacity	Subcontracting Capacity
1	1,500	1,000	200	500
2	1,900	1,000	200	500
3	500	1,000	200	500
4	2,000	1,000	200	500

Regular production cost per unit	$10
Overtime production cost per unit	$15
Subcontracting cost per unit	$20
Inventory holding cost per unit per period	$ 2

14-11. Robotic Pet Products uses overtime, inventory, and subcontracting to absorb fluctuations in demand. As expected, demand in the fourth quarter during the holiday season is particularly high, followed by first quarter demand for customers purchasing accessories for their R-pets. Given the demand and available capacities shown below, design a production plan that will satisfy demand at minimum cost.

Quarter	Demand	Regular Capacity	Overtime Capacity	Subcontracting Capacity
1	1,000	1,000	100	500
2	800	1,000	100	500
3	600	1,000	100	500
4	2,600	1,000	100	500

Regular production cost per unit	$10
Overtime production cost per unit	$15
Subcontracting cost per unit	$20
Inventory holding cost per unit per period	$ 3
Beginning inventory	100

14-12. Complete the available-to-promise table below.

	Period					
On hand = 10	*1*	*2*	*3*	*4*	*5*	*6*
Forecast	50	50	50	50	50	50
Customer Orders	56	17	75	50	16	14
Master Production Schedule	100		100		100	
Available-to-Promise						

14-13. Complete the following table. How many Bs are available-to-promise in week 2? How soon could you fill an order for 250 Bs?

	Period					
Bs on hand = 10	*1*	*2*	*3*	*4*	*5*	*6*
Forecast	100	100	100	100	100	100
Customer Orders	25	50	137	72	23	5
Master Production Schedule	100	100	100	100	100	100
Available-to-Promise						

14-14. The Blue Roof Inn overbooks two rooms a night. Room rates run $100 a night but cost only $30 to maintain. Bumped customers are sent to a nearby hotel for $80 a night. What is the cost of overbooking? What is the cost of underbooking? Given the following distribution of no-shows, should Blue Roof continue its current policy?

No-Shows	Probability
0	0.30
1	0.20
2	0.10
3	0.30
4	0.10

14-15. NorthStar Airlines runs daily commuter flights from Washington, D.C., to Chicago. The planes hold 60 passengers and cater to the business traveler with comparable business rates. The recent economic downturn has reduced the occupancy rate of flights to such an extent that NorthStar would like to offer a set number of seats at discount rates to gain more passengers. The board of directors is worried that discounted seats will cut into profit margins and will upset the regular business traveler. The ticket price for a business traveler is $350. Discounted tickets would sell for $120. Assuming that empty seats can be sold if discounted, use the following data gathered from 100 flights to determine how many seats should be discounted.

No. of Full-Fare Passengers	Frequency
10	15
20	25
30	25
40	20
50	10
60	5

14-16. Tariott Hotel rents rooms for $125 a night that cost approximately $50 per day to maintain. Overbooking is a common practice in the industry. Customers whose rooms have been leased to someone else are put up in a nearby hotel for $100 a night. Records show that during the past month, there were 10 days with zero no-shows, 5 days with 1 no-show, 6 days with 2 no-shows, and 9 days with 3 no-shows.

a. What is the cost of overbooking?
b. What is the cost of underbooking?
c. What is the optimum probability of no-shows for Tariott?
d. How many rooms should Tariott overbook?

CASE STUDY

Erin's Energy Plan

The discussion was getting heated. A brightly colored chart at the front of the room told the story all too well. At Waylan Industries, sales were up, profits down.

"Larry, there's no way we can hit our profit objective with your high cost of production. You've got to cut back."

"Why pick on me? We're running bare bones as it is. Last winter's energy prices really killed us. How can you cut costs with a 250% increase in energy prices?"

Everyone stared at Erin. Erin swallowed hard and spoke up. "You know, we've never had to stockpile fuel before and I'm not sure how far we can go in managing demand, but I've been collecting data on purchase options. . . ."

"Well, let's see it then."

"Although it's not how we purchase energy, I've converted the prices to millions of BTUs for comparison. Coal costs $8 per million BTUs, but we can only burn 500 million per quarter to stay within our environmental air standards. Natural gas costs $32 per million BTUs, and petroleum $46. We can burn 1,000 million BTUs of each per quarter. Coal and natural gas can be stored for later use at a holding cost of 30% of purchase price per quarter. The holding cost for petroleum is 20%. Electricity cannot be stored, but it can be reserved in advance. The cost of electricity also varies considerably by season of the year, as do our energy needs. The cost of electricity from the local utility is $20 per million BTUs in the spring, $40 in the summer, $24 in the fall, and $70 in the winter.

These are averages from last year. A nearby utility quotes slightly higher prices at $22, $44, $26, and $75 for spring, summer, fall, and winter. As far as availability is concerned, 4,000 million BTUs of electricity are available in the spring and fall, 5,000 in the summer and winter. We can save some money by contracting with the utilities in advance of the season. I've summarized the options in the table here, along with our energy needs. What I need now is some help analyzing the data. Larry, could you . . ."

Before Erin could finish, Tom spoke up. "Yes, Larry—you and Erin work up an energy plan—like those aggregate production plans you're always bringing in. And have it ready by Thursday."

Source: This case was developed with the help of Richard Hirsh, Professor of Science and Technology at Virginia Tech.

	USED IN							
	Spring		Summer		Fall		Winter	
PURCHASED IN	Utility A	Utility B	Utility A	Utility B	Utility A	Utility B	Utility A	Utility B
Spring	$20	$22	$40	$44	$20	$22	$45	$50
Summer			$40	$44	$22	$24	$50	$60
Fall					$24	$26	$60	$65
Winter							$70	$75
Demand	1,500		5,000		5,000		10,000	

Use Erin's data to develop an aggregate energy plan for Waylan Industries.

REFERENCES

Bowman, E. H. "Production Planning by the Transportation Method of Linear Programming." *Journal of Operations Research Society* (February 1956), pp. 100–103.

Bowman, E. H. "Consistency and Optimality in Managerial Decision Making." *Management Science* (January 1963), pp. 310– 321.

Buffa, E. S., and J. G. Miller. *Production-Inventory Systems: Planning and Control,* 3rd ed. Homewood, IL: Irwin, 1979.

Correll, J., and N. Edson. *Gaining Control*. New York: Wiley, 1998.

Haksever, C., B. Render, R. Russell and R. Murdick. *Service Operations and Management*. Upper Saddle River, NJ: Prentice Hall, 2000.

Holt, C., F. Modigliani, J. Muth, and H. Simon. *Planning Production, Inventories and Work Force*. Englewood Cliffs, NJ: Prentice Hall, 1960.

Palmatier, G. E., and C. Crum. *Enterprise Sales and Operations Planning*. Boca Raton: J. Ross Publishers, 2003.

SAP AG. "Global Available to Promise." December 1999. SAP AG 2000, APO ATP 3.0. http://www.sap.com/solutions/scm/apo/pdf/atp.pdf.

Taubert, W. "A Search Decision Rule for the Aggregate Scheduling Problem." *Management Science* (February 1968), pp. B343– 359.

Tersine, R. *Production/Operations Management: Concepts, Structure, and Analysis*. New York: Elsevier-North Holland, 1985.

Vollmann, T., W. Berry, and D. C. Whybark. *Manufacturing Planning and Control Systems,* 4th ed. Homewood, IL: Irwin, 1997.

Wallace, T. *Sales and Operations Planning—The How-to Handbook.* Columbus, OH: T. F. Wallace & Co., 2000.

CHAPTER 15

Enterprise Resource Planning

LEARNING OBJECTIVES

AFTER READING THIS CHAPTER, YOU WILL BE ABLE TO:

- Discuss the differences between independent and dependent demand systems.
- Describe the inputs and outputs to an MRP system, and execute the MRP process.
- Determine resource capacity and load percent, and perform load leveling on capacitated resources.
- Explain the hierarchical planning process for resources as a closed loop system, and discuss the assumptions on which this process is based.
- Describe basic ERP systems and the scope of their implementations, including the connection to SCM, CRM and PLM.
- Discuss the issues, advantages and drawbacks of the enterprise IT software systems that run today's global businesses.

SOFTWARE THAT RUNS THE COMPANY

VF Corporation is the world's largest apparel company, known for its Wrangler and Lee brand jeans, as well as Nautica, JanSport, Eastpak, Eagle Creek, Vans, Timberland, and North Face outdoor apparel. Although its corporate headquarters is located in Greensboro, North Carolina, VF brands are sold in more than 150 countries through 47,000 retailers in all channels of distribution, from mass merchandisers to department stores to specialty retailers. Sourcing and manufacturing are managed through VF's Global Supply Chain organization, which oversees the production of 500 million items annually at more than 1,400 owned or sourced facilities in locations around the world. VF needs a strong IT strategy to manage the flow of information across this large network of suppliers, manufacturers, distributors, and retailers.

Most large companies run their operations with an enterprise resource planning (ERP) system. The challenge for VF was to find a common ERP system that could be implemented across a geographically dispersed company that was growing rapidly through acquisitions.

VF chose market leader SAP for its ERP system, becoming the first major company to implement SAP's Apparel and Footwear (AFS) industry solution. The original plan was to use SAP's AFS off-the-shelf for its software needs, but VF found that SAP's software needed to be customized more than originally thought, due, in part, to additional measures such as inseam and waist size that were not normally included in sizing for other apparel garments. The implementation team worked with SAP to adapt planning software used in the cable industry that sizes products by length, gauge, and width, but that solution proved to be cumbersome. The order management system would need to work across multiple divisions and products, too, and that was causing difficulties. So, the original plan was scrapped in favor of using SAP along with "best-of-breed" solutions from other software vendors.

Thus, in addition to SAP, VF chose i2's Supply Chain Planner software to manage its global supply network; DeSL's product lifecyle management (PLM) software for product design; Infor PM for performance management; Manhattan Associates for warehouse and labor management; HSBC's Connect software for international electronic payments; Logility for demand planning and forecasting; and Alteryx for retail floor space management (RFSM). Clearly, building the decision support necessary for managing today's global supply chains is a monumental task.

In this chapter we learn about ERP systems and other software systems that run modern organizations, standardize decision making, and make operations and supply chains more efficient.

Sources: Based on Edward Cone, "Case 003: VF Corp.—Inching Along," *Baseline*, October 29, 2001; "VF Sportswear Goes Live with DeSL PLM in 60 days," company website, http://www.bluewatersoft-ware. com; "Saving Millions at VF Corporation Through Tighter Supply Chain Planning," i2 Customer Success Story, www.i2.com; "Fit for Growth at VF Corporation," Corporate Connectivity 2012, www. hbsc.com; "VF Corporation Launches First Large Scale Apparel Industry-Specific SAP Solution," company press release, June 2000, www.vfc.com; "VF Corporation Leverages IBM/i2 Alliance to Take Retail Supply Chain to Next Level," Hurwitz Group (July 2001); "Retail Leader VF Corporation Vaults Ahead with Spatial Analytics," *Directions Magazine*, July 19, 2012, http://vimeo.com/52714305.

Enterprise resource planning (ERP) systems provide the information infrastructure for today's corporations. They bring functions, processes, and resources together to meet customer needs and provide value to shareholders. ERP evolved from more modest versions of manufacturing resource planning aimed at providing material resources and machine/labor resources to support production plans. We begin this chapter by describing the resource planning systems of material requirements planning (MRP) and capacity requirements planning (CRP), and we end with a discussion of the scope and impact of more elaborate ERP systems, with extensions to customers and suppliers.

As a framework for discussion, Figure 15.1 shows the resource planning process from the sales and operations plan to manufacture. Recall that the *sales and operations plan* is for families of items and the *master production schedule* is for individual products. The *material requirements plan* translates the master production schedule into requirements for components, subassemblies, and raw materials. The *capacity requirements plan* converts the material plan into labor and machine requirements. Once the plans have been approved, purchase orders are released to suppliers and work orders are released to the shop. Purchased parts and manufactured parts are assembled in manufacture.

Figure 15.1

Resource Planning for Manufacturing

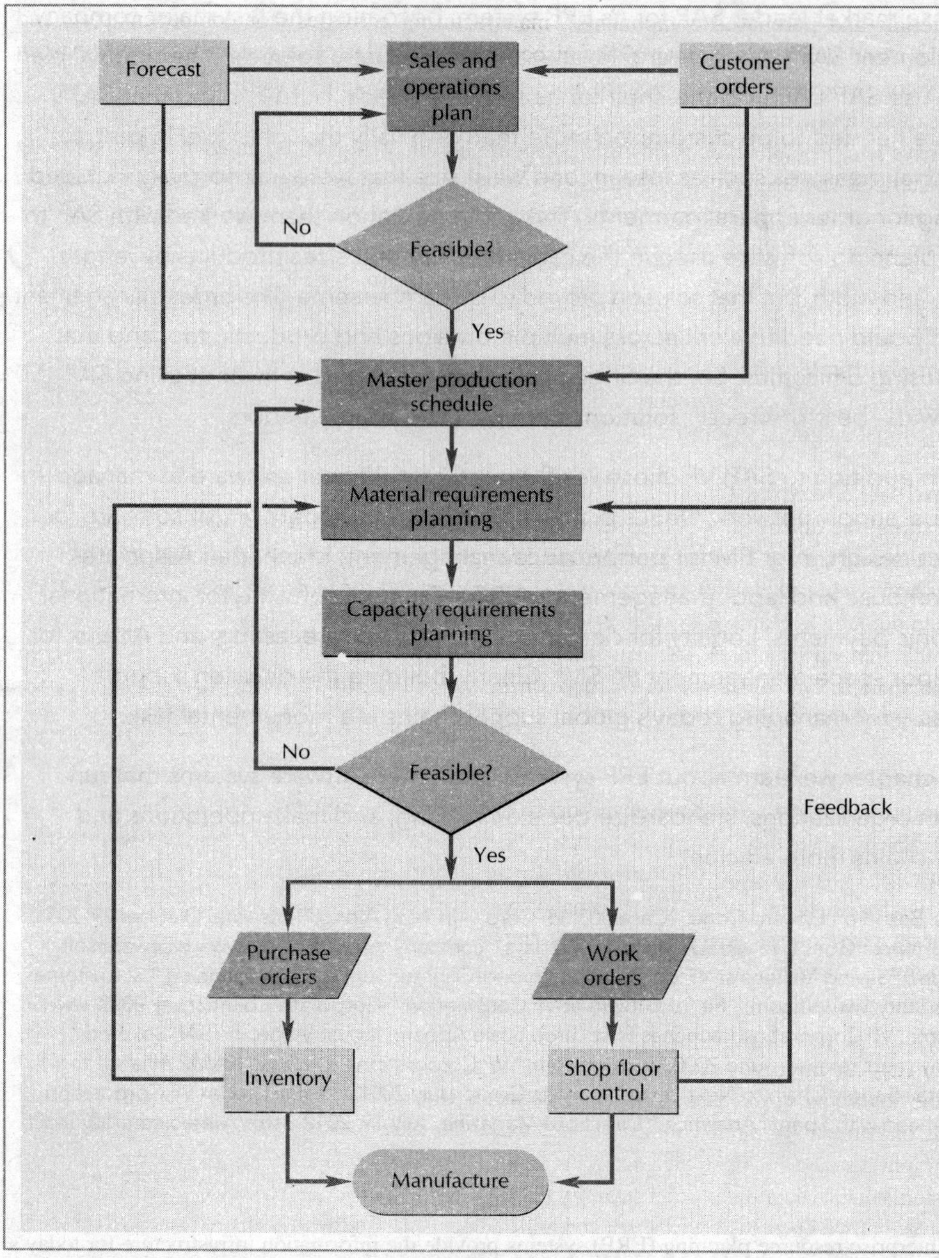

Material Requirements Planning (MRP)

Material requirements planning (MRP) is a computerized inventory control and production planning system. The main objective of any inventory system is to ensure that material is available when needed—which can easily lead to a tremendous investment of funds in unnecessary inventory. One objective of MRP is to maintain the lowest possible level of inventory. MRP does this by determining *when* component items are needed and scheduling them to be ready at that time, no earlier and no later.

MRP was the first inventory system to recognize that inventories of raw materials, components, and finished goods may need to be handled differently. In the process of planning inventory levels for these various types of goods, the system also planned purchasing activities (for raw materials and purchased components), manufacturing activities (for component parts and assemblies), and delivery schedules (for finished products). Thus, the system was more than an inventory control system; it became a production scheduling system as well.

One of the few certainties in a manufacturing environment is that things rarely go as planned—orders arrive late, machines break down, workers are absent, designs are changed, and so on. With its computerized database, MRP is able to keep track of the relationship of job orders so that if a delay in one aspect of production is unavoidable, other related activities can be rescheduled, too. MRP systems have the ability to keep schedules valid and up to date.

WHEN TO USE MRP

MRP is useful for dependent and discrete demand items, complex products, job shop production, and assemble-to-order environments. Managing component demand inventory is different from managing finished goods inventory.

Dependent Demand

For one thing, the demand for component parts does not have to be forecasted; it can be derived from the demand for the finished product. For example, suppose demand for a table, consisting of four legs and a tabletop, is 100 units per week. Then, demand for tabletops would also be 100 per week, and demand for table legs would be 400 per week. Demand for table legs is totally *dependent* on the demand for tables. The demand for tables may be forecasted, but the demand for table legs is calculated. The tables are an example of *independent demand*. The tabletop and table legs exhibit *dependent demand.*

Discrete Demand

Another difference between finished products and component parts is the continuity of their demand. For the inventory control systems in Chapter 13, we assumed that demand occurred at a constant rate. The inventory systems were designed to keep some inventory on hand at all times, enough, we hoped, to meet each day's demand. With component items, demand does not necessarily occur on a continuous basis. Let us assume in our table example that table legs are the last items to be assembled onto the tables before shipping. Also assume that it takes one week to make a batch of tables and that table legs are assembled onto the tabletops every Friday. If we were to graph the demand for table legs, as shown in Figure 15.2, it would be zero for Monday, Tuesday, Wednesday, and Thursday, but on Friday the demand for table legs would jump to 400. The same pattern would repeat the following week. With this scenario, we do not need to keep an inventory of table legs available on Monday through Thursday of any week. We need table legs only on Fridays. Looking at our graph, demand for table legs occurs in *lumps;* it is *discrete*, not continuous. Using an inventory system such as economic order quantity (EOQ) for component items would result in inventory being held that we know will not be needed until a later date. The excess inventory takes up space, soaks up funds, and requires additional resources for counting, sorting, storing, and moving.

Complex Products

Industries that manufacture complex products, requiring the coordination of component production, find MRP especially useful. A complex product may have hundreds of component parts, dozens of assemblies, and several levels of assembly. MRP tries to ensure that multiple components of an assembly are ready at the same time so that they can be assembled together. Products with simple structures do not need MRP to plan production or monitor inventory levels.

Erratic Orders

The advantages of MRP are more evident when the manufacturing environment is complex and uncertain. Manufacturing environments in which customer orders are erratic, each job takes a different path through the system, lead time is uncertain, and due dates vary, need an information system such as MRP to keep track of the different jobs and coordinate their schedules. The type of

Figure 15.2

Demand Characteristics for Finished Products and Their Components

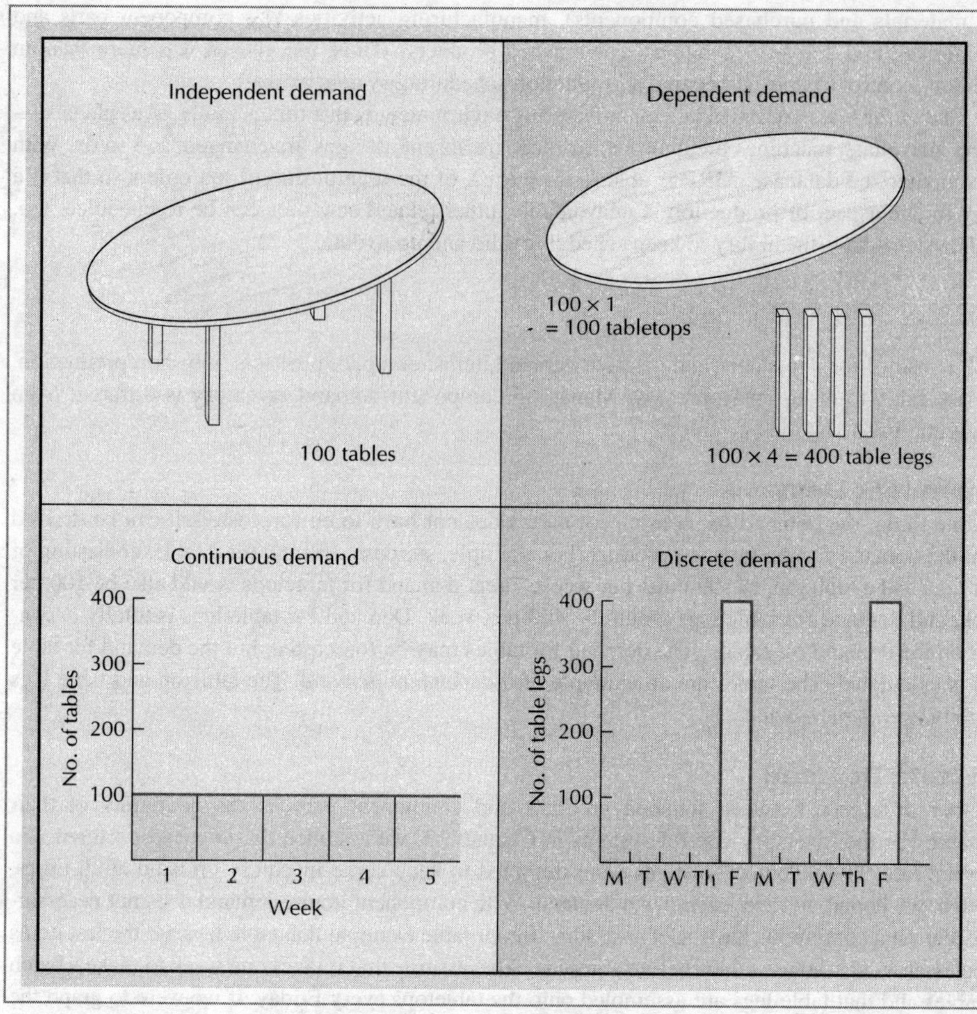

environment we are describing is characteristic of *batch*, or *job shop*, processes.[1] Although MRP is currently available for continuous and repetitive manufacturing, it was designed primarily for systems that produce goods in batches.

Assemble-to-Order

Finally, MRP systems are very useful in industries in which the customer is allowed to choose among different options. These products have many common components that are inventoried in some form before the customer order is received. For example, customers of a well-known electronics firm routinely expect delivery in six weeks on goods that take 28 weeks to manufacture. The manufacturer copes with this seemingly unrealistic demand by producing major assemblies and subassemblies in advance of the customer order and then completing the product on receipt of the order. This type of operation is called **assemble-to-order** or *build-to-order*.

Figure 15.3 shows the inputs to and outputs from the MRP process. There are three major inputs:

- Master production schedule
- Product structure file
- Item master file

[1]For a more thorough discussion of types of processes, see Chapter 6.

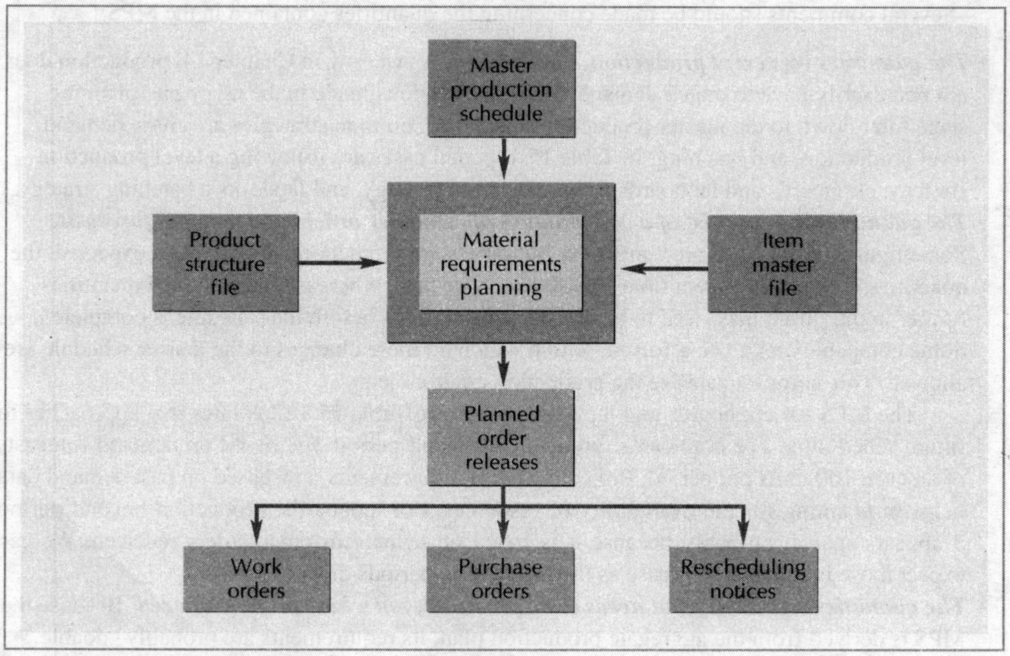

Figure 15.3

Material Requirements Planning

MASTER PRODUCTION SCHEDULE

The **master production schedule (MPS)**, also called the *master schedule*, specifies which end items or finished products a firm is to produce, how many are needed, and when they are needed. Recall that the sales and operations plan is a similar schedule for product lines or families, given by months or quarters of a year. The master production schedule works within the constraints of the aggregate production plan but produces a more specific schedule by individual products. The time frame is more specific, too. An MPS is usually expressed in days or weeks and may extend over several months to cover the complete manufacture of the items contained in the MPS. The total length of time required to manufacture a product is called its **cumulative lead time.**

The master production schedule drives the MRP process. The schedule of finished products provided by the master schedule is needed before the MRP system can do its job of generating production schedules for component items. Table 15.1 shows a sample master production schedule consisting of four end items produced by a manufacturer of specialty writing accessories.

TABLE 15.1 Master Production Schedule (MPS)

	Period				
MPS Item	**1**	**2**	**3**	**4**	**5**
Pencil case	125	125	125	125	125
Clipboard	85	95	120	100	100
Lapboard	75	120	47	20	17
Lapdesk	0	60	0	60	0

Several comments should be made concerning the quantities contained in the MPS:

- ***The quantities represent production, not demand.*** As we saw in Chapter 14, production does not necessarily have to match demand. Strategy decisions made in the aggregate planning stage filter down to the master production schedule. Common strategies are chase demand, level production, and batching. In Table 15.1, pencil cases are following a level production strategy, clipboards and lapboards a chase demand strategy, and lapdesks a batching strategy.
- ***The quantities may consist of a combination of customer orders and demand forecasts.*** Some figures in the MPS are confirmed, but others are predictions. As might be expected, the quantities in the more recent time periods are more firm, whereas the forecasted quantities further in the future may need to be revised several times before the schedule is completed. Some companies set a **time fence**, within which no more changes to the master schedule are allowed. This helps to stabilize the production environment.

  The MPS for clipboards and lapboards shown in Table 15.1 illustrates two approaches to future scheduling. For clipboards, production beyond period 3 is based on demand forecasts of an even 100 units per period. Projecting these requirements now based on past demand data helps in planning for the availability of resources. For lapboards, production beyond period 3 appears sparse, probably because it is based on actual customer orders received. We can expect those numbers to increase as the future time periods draw nearer.
- ***The quantities represent what needs to be produced, not what can be produced.*** Because the MPS is derived from the aggregate production plan, its requirements are probably "doable," but until the MRP system considers the specific resource needs and the timing of those needs, the feasibility of the MPS cannot be guaranteed. Thus, the MRP system is often used to *simulate* production to verify that the MPS is feasible or to confirm that a particular order can be completed by a certain date before the quote is given to the customer.
- ***The quantities represent end items that may or may not be finished products.*** The level of master scheduling can differ by type of production system. In make-to-stock companies, the MPS consists of finished products. In assemble-to-order companies, the MPS usually represents major subassemblies or modules. In make-to-order companies, the master schedule can consist of critical components, hard-to-get materials, and service parts. Separate final assembly schedules are then used for the finished product or customer order. As Figure 15.4 shows, companies usually master schedule at the smallest part of the product structure. To simplify discussions, we assume in this chapter that an end item is, in fact, the finished product.

PRODUCT STRUCTURE FILE

Once the MPS is set, the MRP system accesses the **product structure file** to determine which component items need to be scheduled. The product structure file contains a **bill of material (BOM)** for every item produced. The bill of material for a product lists the items that go into the product, includes a brief description of each item, and specifies when and in what quantity each item is needed in the assembly process.

Figure 15.4

Master Schedule at the Smallest Part of the Product Structure

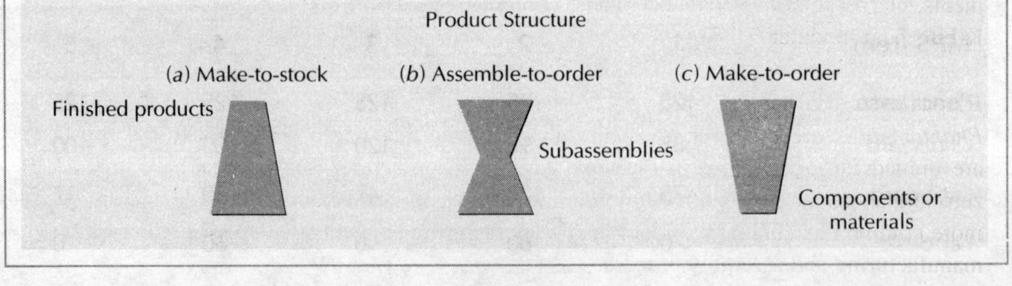

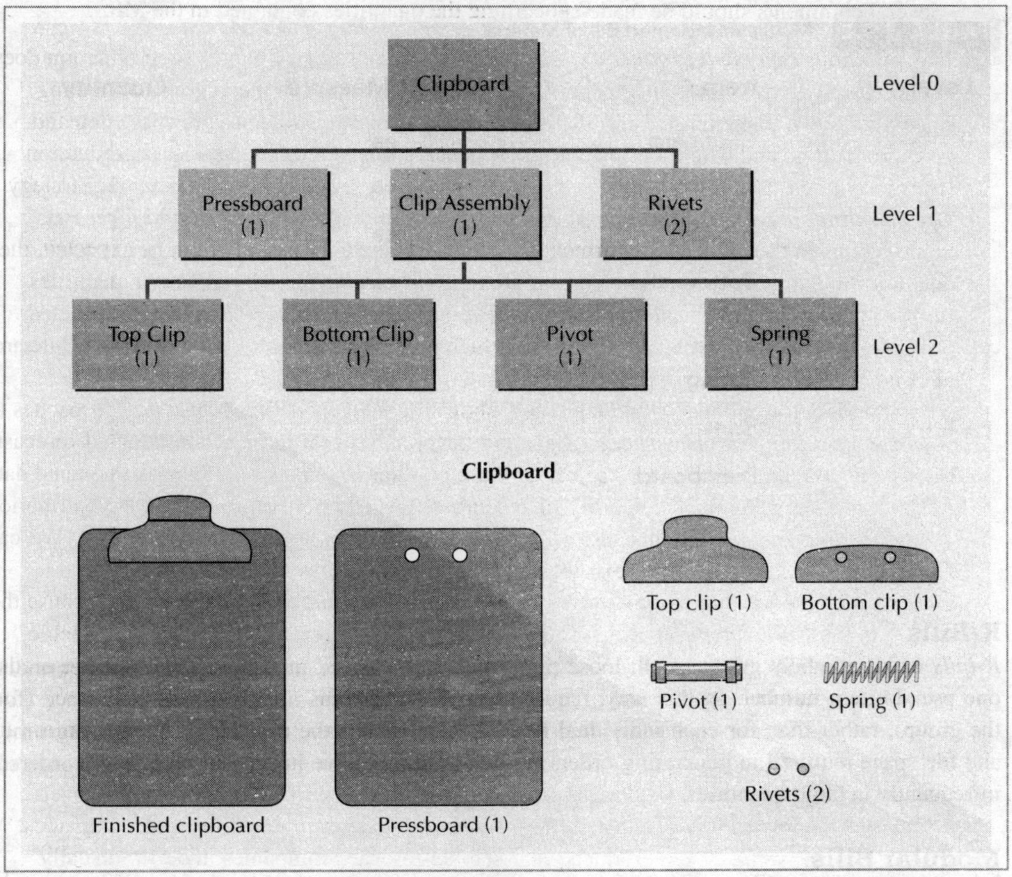

Figure 15.5

Product Structure Diagram for a Clipboard

When each item is needed can best be described in the form of a product structure diagram, shown in Figure 15.5 for a clipboard. An assembled item is sometimes referred to as a *parent*, and a component as a *child*. The number in parentheses with each item is the quantity of a given component needed to make *one* parent. Thus, one clip assembly, two rivets, and one pressboard are needed to make each clipboard. The clip assembly, rivets, and board appear at the same level of the product structure because they are to be assembled together.

A diagram can be converted to a computerized bill of material by labeling the levels in the product structure. The final product or end item at the top of the structure—in this case, the clipboard—is labeled level 0. The level number increases as we move down the product structure. The clipboard has three levels of assembly. The bill of material for the clipboard, listed in Table 15.2, shows some levels indented underneath others. This specifies which components belong to which parents and can easily be matched to the product structure diagram.

Several specialized bills of material have been designed to simplify information requirements, clarify relationships, and reduce computer processing time. They include phantom bills, K-bills, and modular bills.

Phantom Bills

Phantom bills are used for transient subassemblies that never see a stockroom because they are immediately consumed in the next stage of manufacture. These items have a lead time of zero and a special code so that no orders for them will be released. Phantom bills are becoming more common as companies adopt lean manufacturing concepts that speed products through the manufacturing and assembly process.

TABLE 15.2 Multilevel Indented Bill of Material

Level	Item	Unit of Measure	Quantity
0- - - -	Clipboard	ea	1
- 1- - -	Clip assembly	ea	1
- - 2- -	Top clip	ea	1
- - 2- -	Bottom clip	ea	1
- - 2- -	Pivot	ea	1
- - 2- -	Spring	ea	1
- 1- - -	Rivet	ea	2
- 1- - -	Pressboard	ea	1

K-Bills

K-bills or kit numbers group small, loose parts such as fasteners, nuts, and bolts together under one pseudo-item number. In this way, requirements for the items are processed only once (for the group), rather than for each individual item. K-bills reduce the paperwork, processing time, and file space required in generating orders for small, inexpensive items that are usually ordered infrequently in large quantities.

Modular Bills

Modular bills of material are appropriate when the product is manufactured in major subassemblies or modules that are later assembled into the final product with customer-designated options. With this approach, the end item in the master production schedule is not a finished product, but a major option or module. This reduces the number of bills of material that need to be input, maintained, and processed by the MRP system.

Consider the options available on the X10 automobile, partially diagrammed in Figure 15.6. Customers can choose among three engine types, eight exterior colors, three interiors, eight interior colors, and four car bodies. Thus, there are $3 \times 8 \times 3 \times 8 \times 4 = 2{,}304$ possible model configurations—and the same number of bills of material—unless modular bills are used. By establishing a bill of material for each option rather than each combination of options, the entire range of options can be accounted for by $3 + 8 + 3 + 8 + 4 = 26$ modular bills of material.

Modular bills of material also simplify forecasting and planning. The quantity per assembly for an option is given as a decimal figure, interpreted as a percentage of the requirements for the parent item. For example, from Figure 15.6, in preparation for an anticipated demand of 1,000 X10 automobiles, 1,000 engines are needed. Of those 1,000 engines, the master production schedule would generate requirements for 400 four-cylinder engines, 500 six-cylinder engines, and 100 eight-cylinder engines.

The creation of a product structure file can take a considerable amount of time. Accurate bills of material are essential to an effective MRP system. The bill of material must specify how a product is actually manufactured rather than how it was *designed* to be manufactured. Redundant or obsolete part numbers must be purged from the system. This may not seem like a big task, but in some companies every time a part is purchased from a different supplier, it is assigned a different part number. One firm in the process of implementing MRP was able to eliminate 6,000 extra part numbers from its database and dispose of thousands of dollars of obsolete inventory that had not previously been identified as such.

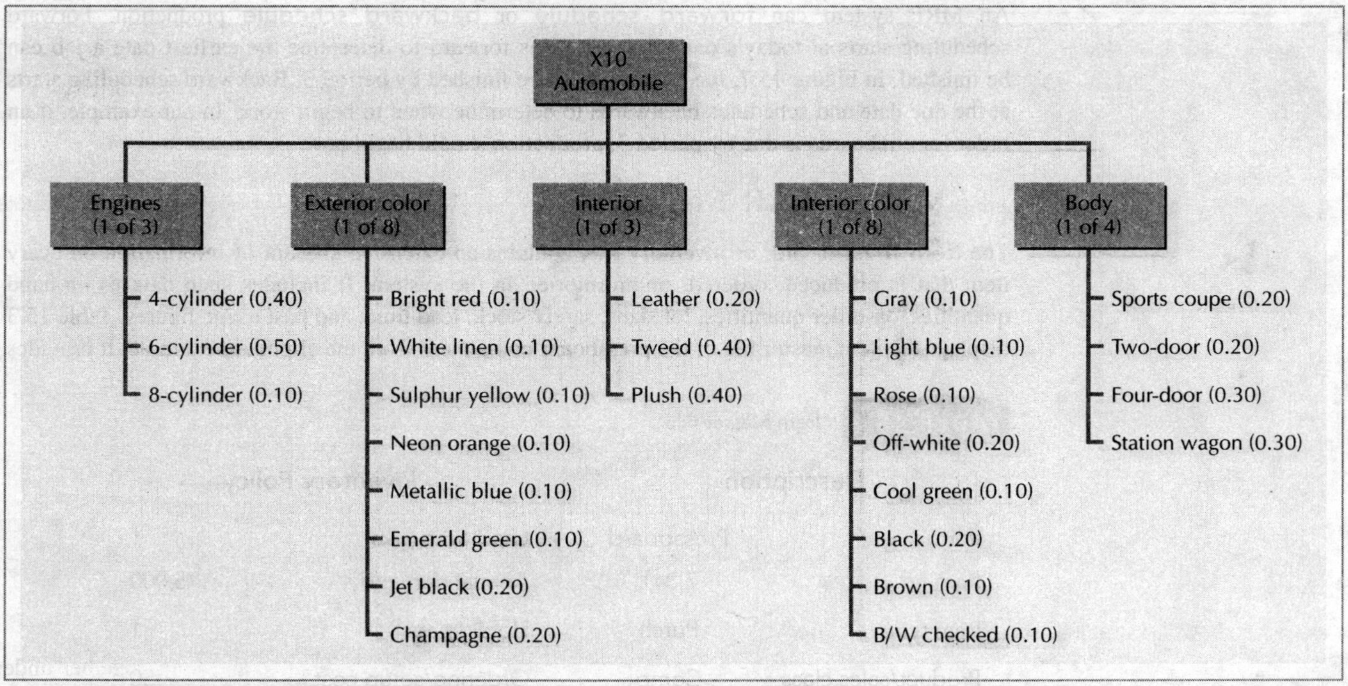

Figure 15.6

Modular Bills of Material

Time-Phased Bills

A **time-phased bill of material**, also known as a *time-phased assembly chart*, is basically a horizontal product structure diagram that graphically shows the lead time required to purchase or manufacture an item. Assuming the lead time for each item in the bill of material for a clipboard is one week, Figure 15.7 shows how long it will take to assemble a clipboard from scratch.

Figure 15.7

Time-Phased Assembly Chart

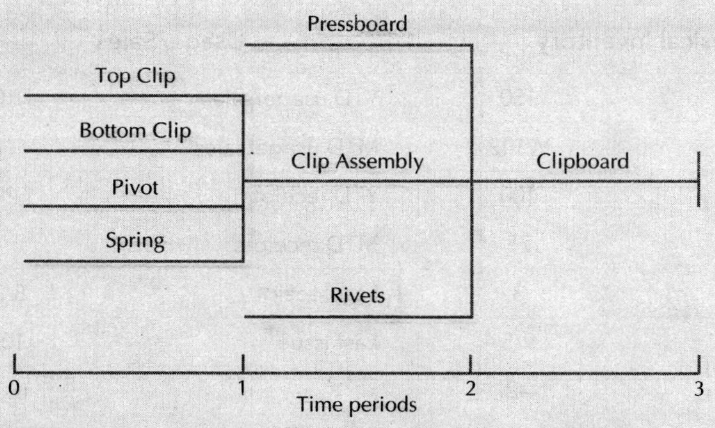

Forward scheduling: start at today's date and schedule forward to determine the earliest date the job can be finished. If each item takes one period to complete, the clipboards can be finished in three periods.

Backward scheduling: start at the due date and schedule backward to determine when to begin work. If an order for clipboards is due by period three, we should start production now.

An MRP system can **forward schedule** or **backward schedule** production. Forward scheduling starts at today's date and schedules forward to determine the earliest date a job can be finished. In Figure 15.7, the clipboard can be finished by period 3. Backward scheduling starts at the due date and schedules backwards to determine when to begin work. In our example, if an order for clipboards is due by period 3, production should begin now.

ITEM MASTER FILE

The **item master file**, or inventory file, contains an extensive amount of information on every item that is produced, ordered, or inventoried in the system. It includes such data as on-hand quantities, on-order quantities, lot sizes, safety stock, lead time, and past usage figures. Table 15.3 displays the item master file of the pressboard component from the clipboard example. It provides

TABLE 15.3 Item Master File

Description		Inventory Policy	
Item	Pressboard	Lead time (wks)	1
Item no.	7,341	Annual demand	5,000
Item type	Purch	Holding cost	1
Product/sales class	Comp	Ordering/setup cost	50
Value class	B	Safety stock	0
Buyer/planner	RSR	Reorder point	96
Vendor/drawing	07142	EOQ	707
Phantom code	N	Minimum order qty.	100
Unit price/cost	1.25	Maximum order qty.	500
Pegging	Y	Multiple order qty.	1
LLC	1	Policy code	3
Physical Inventory		**Usage/Sales**	
On hand	150	YTD usage/sales	1,100
Location	W142	MTD usage/sales	75
On order	100	YTD receipts	1,200
Allocated	75	MTD receipts	0
Cycle	3	Last receipt	8/25
Last count	9/5	Last issue	10/5
Difference	–2		
		Codes	
		Cost acct.	00754
		Routing	00326
		Engr.	07142

a detailed description of the item, specifies the inventory policy, updates the physical inventory count, summarizes the item's year-to-date or month-to-date usage, and provides internal codes to link this file with other related information in the MRP database.

The item master file is updated whenever items are withdrawn from or added to inventory or whenever an order is released, revised, or completed. Accuracy of inventory transactions is essential to MRP's ability to keep inventory levels at a minimum. It is estimated that 95% inventory accuracy is a prerequisite for an effective MRP system. Although technologies such as bar codes, voice-activated systems, and automated "picking" equipment can improve inventory accuracy considerably, a general overhaul of inventory procedures is often needed. This involves (1) maintaining orderly stockrooms; (2) establishing and enforcing procedures for inventory withdrawal; (3) ensuring prompt and accurate entry of inventory transactions; (4) taking physical inventory count on a regular basis; and (5) reconciling inventory discrepancies in a timely manner.

If you have ever taken part in an end-of-year inventory count, you can verify the wide discrepancies that are commonly found between what the records say is in inventory and what is physically there. Unfortunately, by the time the errors are discovered, it is too late to correct them or find out why they occurred. The slate is merely cleaned for next year's record, with the hope or promise that next time will be better.

Cycle counting involves taking physical count of at least some inventory items daily and reconciling differences as they occur. The system specifies which items are to be counted each day and may tie the frequency of the count to the frequency of orders for the item within the MRP system. Thus, items that are used more often are counted more often. The cycle counting system may also be related to the *ABC classification system* discussed in Chapter 13. *A* items would be counted more often than *B* items, perhaps weekly. *B* items would be counted monthly, and *C* items may still be counted only once a year. Approved cycle counting systems are accepted by the accounting standards boards as valid replacements for end-of-year physical inventories.

THE MRP PROCESS

The MRP system is responsible for scheduling the production of all items beneath the end item level. It recommends the release of work orders and purchase orders, and issues rescheduling notices when necessary.

The MRP process consists of four basic steps: (1) exploding the bill of material, (2) **netting** out inventory, (3) lot sizing, and (4) time-phasing requirements. The process is performed again and again, moving down the product structure until all items have been scheduled. An MRP matrix, as shown in Table 15.4, is completed for each item starting with level zero items. Identifying information at the top of the matrix includes the item name or number, the lowest level at

TABLE 15.4 The MRP Matrix

		Period				
Item Lot Size	LLC LT	1	2	3	4	5
Gross Requirements		*Derived from MPS or planned order releases of the parent*				
Scheduled Receipts		*On order and scheduled to be received*				
Projected on Hand	Beg. Inv	*Anticipated quantity on hand at the end of the period*				
Net Requirements		*Gross requirements net of inventory and scheduled receipts*				
Planned Order Receipts		*When orders need to be received*				
Planned Order Releases		*When orders need to be placed to be received on time*				

which the item appears in the product structure (called *low level code* or LLC), the time required to make or purchase an item (called *lead time* or LT), and the quantities in which an item is usually made or purchased (called *lot size*).

Entries in the matrix include gross requirements, scheduled receipts, projected on hand, net requirements, planned order receipts, and planned order releases. *Gross requirements* begin the MRP process. They are given in the master production schedule (MPS) for end items and derived from the parent for component items. *Scheduled receipts* are items on order that are scheduled to arrive in future time periods. *Projected on hand* is inventory currently on hand or projected to be on hand at the end of each time period as a result of the MRP schedule. *Net requirements* are what actually needs to be produced after on-hand and on-order quantities have been taken into account. *Planned order receipts* represent the quantities that will be ordered and when they must be received. These quantities differ from net requirements by **lot sizing** rules when production or purchasing is made in predetermined batches or lots. Common lot sizing rules include ordering in minimum or multiple quantities, using an EOQ or periodic order quantity, or ordering the exact quantities needed (called **lot-for-lot** or L4L). We discuss these techniques later in the chapter.

The last row of the matrix, *planned order releases*, determines when orders should be placed (i.e., released) so that they are received when needed. This involves offsetting or **time phasing** the planned order receipts by the item's lead time. Planned order releases at one level of a product structure generate gross requirements at the next lower level. When the MRP process is complete, the planned order releases are compiled in a planned order report.

LOT SIZING IN MRP SYSTEMS

Example 15.1 illustrates the use of minimum order quantities, multiple order quantities, and lot-for-lot sizing rules. Although the L4L approach is most consistent with the objectives of MRP, in some circumstances it is useful to order an amount different from what is needed. For example, *minimum order quantities* are typically used to take advantage of quantity discounts or to conform to vendor requirements, *maximum order quantities* are used for large or expensive items when space or funds are limited, and *multiple order quantities* accommodate packaging restrictions (such as a set number in a box, gallon containers, bundles, or pallet loads). Several additional lot sizing techniques are available with most MRP systems. These include economic order quantity (EOQ) and **periodic order quantity (POQ)**.

EXAMPLE 15.1

SCHOOL MATE PRODUCTS

School Mate offers a number of standard products to encourage writing outside of the classroom, including clipboards, lapdesks, lapboards, and pencil boxes. Rising costs and inventory levels have prompted the company to install a computerized planning and control system called MRP. The MPS and bill-of-material modules are up and running. Sample output follows. Before going live with the MRP module, School Mate has asked for a manual demonstration. Since manual calculations can be quite tedious, you have decided to prepare MRP matrices for only three items—the clipboard and lapdesk products, and a common component, pressboard. The master production schedule, abbreviated product structure diagrams, and inventory information are given below.

Master Production Schedule

	1	2	3	4	5
Clipboard	85	95	120	100	100
Lapdesk	0	60	0	60	0

Item Master File

	Clipboard	Lapdesk	Pressboard
On hand	25	20	150
On order (sch receipt)	175 (period 1)	0	0
LLC	0	0	1
Lot size	L4L	Mult 50	Min 100
Lead time	1	1	1

Product Structure Diagrams

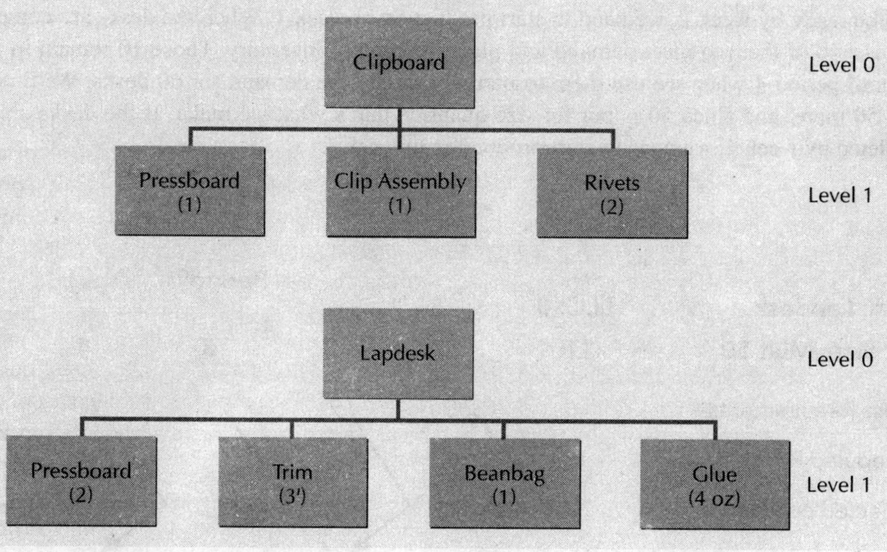

SOLUTION

We begin with the level 0 items, the clipboard and lapdesk. Since these are finished products, the *gross requirements* row is simply copied from the master production schedule for those items. We'll begin with the clipboard.

Item: Clipboard	LLC: 0	Period				
Lot Size: L4L	LT: 1	1	2	3	4	5
Gross Requirements		85	95	120	100	100
Scheduled Receipts		175				
Projected on Hand	25	115	20	0	0	0
Net Requirements		0	0	100	100	100
Planned Order Receipts				100	100	100
Planned Order Releases			100	100	100	

(*Continued*)

In period 1, we have 25 units on hand and 175 scheduled to be received. That gives us (25 + 175) = 200 units available. We use 85 of them to satisfy demand, leaving (200 − 85) = 115 units in inventory at the end of period 1. In period 2, we can meet demand from stock, leaving (115 − 95) = 20 units in inventory at the end of the period. In period 3, the 20 units on hand is not enough to cover our demand of 120 units. We need to make 100 more. Thus, our *net requirements* are 100 units. Since our lot sizing rule is lot-for-lot, we order exactly what we need, 100 units. Recall that our lead time is one week. If we wish to *receive* our order for 100 units in period 3, we must *place* the order one week in advance, in period 2. To meet demand in periods 4 and 5, we order 100 units in weeks 3 and 4, one week in advance of when we need them.

The MRP matrix for lapdesks appears below. To meet our demand for 60 units in period 2, we'll use the 20 units in stock and make 40 more. Before we release our work order for production, we check our lot sizing rule. It says we should make 50 lapdesks at a time. If the 50 desks are to be ready by week 2, we need to start production in week 1. When the desks are completed, we'll use 40 of them to meet demand and place 10 back in inventory. Those 10 remain in inventory until period 4 when we use them to partially satisfy the demand for 60 desks. We'll need to make 50 more, and since 50 is our lot size quantity, that's what we make. If the desks are to be completed by week 4, we need to start production in week 3.

Item: Lapdesk	LLC: 0	Period				
Lot Size: Mult 50	**LT: 1**	**1**	**2**	**3**	**4**	**5**
Gross Requirements		0	60	0	60	0
Scheduled Receipts						
Projected on Hand	20	20	10	10	0	0
Net Requirements			40		50	
Planned Order Receipts			50		50	
Planned Order Releases		50		50		

Pressboard is a purchased component cut to size and used in both the clipboard and the lapdesk. As shown below, its gross requirements are calculated by multiplying the planned order releases of each parent times the quantity per assembly contained in the bill of material. This process is called **explosion**. Since one pressboard is needed for every clipboard and two for every lapdesk, gross requirements for period 1 are (50 × 2) = 100; period 2, (100 × 1 = 100); period 3, (100 × 1) + (50 × 2) = 200; and period 4, (100 × 1) = 100.

With 150 units on hand, we can satisfy the demand in period 1 with 50 units left over. For period 2, we use the 50 in inventory and need 50 more. Because our lot sizing rule says we must order *at least* 100 units and it takes 1 week to process an order, we place an order for 100 pressboards in week 1. When the 100 boards come in, we use 50 of them and put 50 back in stock. To meet our demand in period 3, we use the 50 boards in stock and order 150 more. The order is placed in week 2 to arrive in week 3. To meet period 4's demand, we order 100 boards in week 3, one week in advance of delivery.

Item: Clipboard Lot Size: L4L	LLC: 0 LT: 1	Period 1	2	3	4	5
Planned Order Releases			100	100	100	

100 × 1   100 × 1   100 × 1

Item: Lapdesk Lot Size: Mult 50	LLC: 0 LT: 1	Period 1	2	3	4	5
Planned Order Releases		50		50		

50 × 2   50 × 2

Item: Pressboard Lot Size: Min 100	LLC: 1 LT: 1	Period 1	2	3	4	5
Gross Requirement		100	100	200	100	0
Scheduled Receipts						
Projected on Hand	150	50	50	0	0	0
Net Requirements			50	150	100	
Planned Order Receipts			100	150	100	
Planned Order Releases		100	150	100		

We have now completed the MRP calculations. To summarize the results, we construct a *planned order report* from the planned order release row of each matrix, as follows:

Planned Order Report

Item	Period 1	2	3	4	5
Clipboard		100	100	100	
Lapdesk	50		50		
Pressboard	100	150	100		

Economic Order Quantity

We discussed the economic order quantity for independent demand items in Chapter 13. The EOQ can be adapted for use with MRP if it is treated as a minimum order quantity. In addition, annual demand, D, is replaced with average demand per period, d, and carrying cost, C_c, is converted to a per-period amount. The EOQ is used only sparingly, usually at the finished product or raw material level, and does not perform well when demand is highly variable.

Periodic Order Quantity

The periodic order quantity (POQ) was created as a variation of the EOQ more suited to variable demand. POQ is calculated by dividing the EOQ by average demand. It represents the number of demand periods covered by each order. Thus, if the POQ were three, an order would be placed for three weeks worth of demand.

Example 15.2 compares the L4L, EOQ, and POQ lot sizing techniques.

EXAMPLE 15.2

ADVANCED LOT SIZING RULES

The Lifetime Sports Company has been using MRP to manufacture sports equipment for a number of years. Recently, Bob Sage, the operations manager, decided to investigate the use of lot sizing for MRP-generated orders. As a test case, Bob selected a typical product in their line of fishing rods and gathered weekly data over a month's time. Ordering costs are $60 per order, and carrying costs are $1 per unit per week. The beginning inventory is 30 units, and lead time is one week. Help Bob determine whether the L4L, EOQ, or POQ lot sizing technique is more appropriate.

Period	1	2	3	4	5
Gross Requirements	30	50	20	10	40

a.

$$C_o = \$60$$
$$C_c = \$1$$
$$d = (30 + 50 + 20 + 10 + 40)/5 = 30$$

With L4L, orders are placed for the exact amount needed. Total cost is calculated as (number of orders × ordering cost) + (total projected on hand × carrying cost). Beginning inventory that is used right away incurs no cost.

Item: Rod Lot Size: L4L	LLC: 0 LT: 1	Period 1	2	3	4	5
Gross Requirements		30	50	20	10	40
Scheduled Receipts						
Projected on Hand	30	0	0	0	0	0
Net Requirements			50	20	10	40
Planned Order Receipts			50	20	10	40
Planned Order Releases		50	20	10	40	

$$\text{Total cost of L4L} = (4 \times \$60) + (0 \times \$1) = \$240$$

b. $$\text{EOQ} = \sqrt{\frac{2(30)(60)}{1}} = 60 \quad \text{Use as a minimum order quantity.}$$

Item: Rod Lot Size: EOQ 60	LLC: 0 LT: 1	Period 1	 2	 3	 4	 5
Gross Requirements		30	50	20	10	40
Scheduled Receipts						
Projected on Hand	30	0	10	50	40	0
Net Requirements			50	10		
Planned Order Receipts			60	60		
Planned Order Releases		60	60			

$$\text{Total cost of EOQ} = (2 \times \$60) + [(10 + 50 + 40) \times \$1] = \$220$$

c. $POQ = Q/\bar{d} = 60/30 = 2$ period's worth of requirements

Item: Rod Lot Size: POQ 2	LLC: 0 LT: 1	Period 1	 2	 3	 4	 5
Gross Requirements		30	50	20	10	40
Scheduled Receipts						
Projected on Hand	30	0	20	0	40	0
Net Requirements			50		10	
Planned Order Receipts			70		50	
Planned Order Releases		70		50		

$$\text{Total cost of POQ} = (2 \times \$60) + [(20 + 40) \times \$1] = \$180$$

POQ is the lowest cost lot sizing technique for this example.

MRP OUTPUTS

The outputs of the MRP process are planned orders from the planned order release row of the MRP matrix. As shown in Figure 15.4, these can represent *work orders* to be released to the shop floor for in-house production or *purchase orders* to be sent to outside suppliers. MRP output can also recommend changes in previous plans or existing schedules. These *action notices,* or *rescheduling notices,* are issued for items that are no longer needed as soon as planned or for quantities that may have changed. One of the advantages of the MRP system is its ability to show the effect of change in one part of the production process on the rest of the system. It simulates the ordering, receiving, and use of raw materials, components, and assemblies into future time periods and issues warnings to the MRP planner of impending stockouts or missed due dates.

Table 15.5 shows a monthly *planned order report* for an individual item, in this case, item #2740. The report maps out the material orders planned and released orders scheduled to be completed in

TABLE 15.5 Planned Order Report

Item	#2740	Date	9-25-15
On hand	100	Lead time	2 weeks
On order	200	Lot size	200
Allocated	50	Safety stock	50

Date	Order No.	Gross Reqs.	Scheduled Receipts	Projected On Hand	Action	
				50		
9–26	AL 4416	25		25		
9–30	AL 4174	25		0		
10–01	GR 6470	50		−50		
10–08	SR 7542		200	150	Expedite SR	10–01
10–10	CO 4471	75		75		
10–15	GR 6471	50		25		
10–23	GR 6471	25		0		
10–27	GR 6473	50		−50	Release PO	10–13

Key: AL = allocated WO = work order
CO = customer order SR = scheduled receipt
PO = purchase order GR = gross requirement

anticipation of demand. Notice that safety stock is treated as a quantity not to be used and that a problem exists on 10-01, when projected on hand first goes negative. To correct this, the system suggests that the scheduled receipt of 200 units due on 10-08 be moved forward to 10-01. The MRP system will not generate a new order if a deficit can be solved by expediting existing orders. It is up to the MRP planner to assess the feasibility of expediting the scheduled receipt and to take appropriate action.

Table 15.6 shows an *MRP action report* for a family of items for which a particular MRP planner is responsible. It summarizes the action messages that have been compiled for individual

TABLE 15.6 MRP Action Report

Current date: 9-25-15

Item	Date	Order No.	Qty.	Action		
#2740	10-08	7542	200	Expedite	SR	10-01
#3616	10-09			Move forward	PO	10-07
#2412	10-10			Move forward	PO	10-05
#3427	10-15			Move backward	PO	10-25
#2516	10-20	7648	100	De-expedite	SR	10-30
#2740	10-27		200	Release	PO	10-30
#3666	10-31		50	Release	WO	10-24

items. On 10-08, we see the action message for item #2740 that appeared on the previous report. Notice the variety of action messages listed. Some suggest that planned orders be moved forward or backward. Others suggest that scheduled receipts be expedited or de-expedited.

It is the planner's job to respond to the actions contained in the action report. If a planner decides to **expedite** an order—that is, have it completed in less than its normal lead time—he or she might call up a supplier or a shop supervisor and ask for priority treatment. Giving one job higher priority may involve reducing the priority of other jobs. This is possible if the MRP action report indicates that some jobs are not needed as early as anticipated. The process of moving some jobs *forward* in the schedule (expediting) and moving other jobs *backward* (de-expediting) allows the material planner, with the aid of the MRP system, to fine-tune the material plan. Temporary lead time adjustments through overtime or outside purchases of material can also fix a timing problem in the MRP plan, but at a cost. An MRP action report that is exceedingly long or does not strike a balance between speeding up some orders and slowing down others can signify trouble. Action messages that recommend only the expediting of orders indicate an overloaded master schedule and an ineffective MRP system.

The MRP system, as the name implies, ensures that *material* requirements are met. However, material is not the only resource necessary to produce goods—a certain amount of labor and machine hours are also required. Thus, the next step in the planning process is to verify that the MRP plan is "feasible" by checking for the availability of labor and/or machine hours. This process is called *capacity requirements planning* and is similar to MRP.

Capacity Requirements Planning (CRP)

Capacity requirements planning (CRP) is a computerized system that projects the load from a given material plan onto the capacity of a system and identifies underloads and overloads. It is then up to the MRP planner to *level the load*—smooth out the resource requirements so that capacity constraints are not violated. This can be accomplished by shifting requirements, reducing requirements, or temporarily expanding capacity.

There are three major inputs to CRP, as shown in Figure 15.8:

- The *planned order* releases from the MRP process
- A *routing file,* which specifies which machines or workers are required to complete an order from the MRP plan, in what order the operations are to be conducted, and the length of time each operation should take
- An *open orders file,* which contains information on the status of jobs that have already been released but have not yet been completed

With this information, CRP can produce a load profile for each process or work center in the shop. The load profile compares released orders and planned orders with work center capacity.

CALCULATING CAPACITY

Capacity is the maximum capability to produce. It can be measured as units of output, dollars of output, hours of work, or number of customers processed over a specified period of time. Capacity is affected by the mix of products and services, the choice of technology, the size of a facility, and the resources allocated.

Rated capacity is the theoretical output that could be attained if a process were operating at full speed without interruption, exceptions, or downtime. Effective capacity takes into account the efficiency with which a particular product or customer can be processed, and the utilization of the scheduled hours or work. Effective capacity expressed in hours per day is calculated as:

$$\text{Effective daily capacity} = (\text{no. of machines or workers}) \times (\text{hours per shift}) \\ \times (\text{no. of shifts}) \times (\text{utilization}) \times (\text{efficiency})$$

Figure 15.8
Capacity Requirements Planning

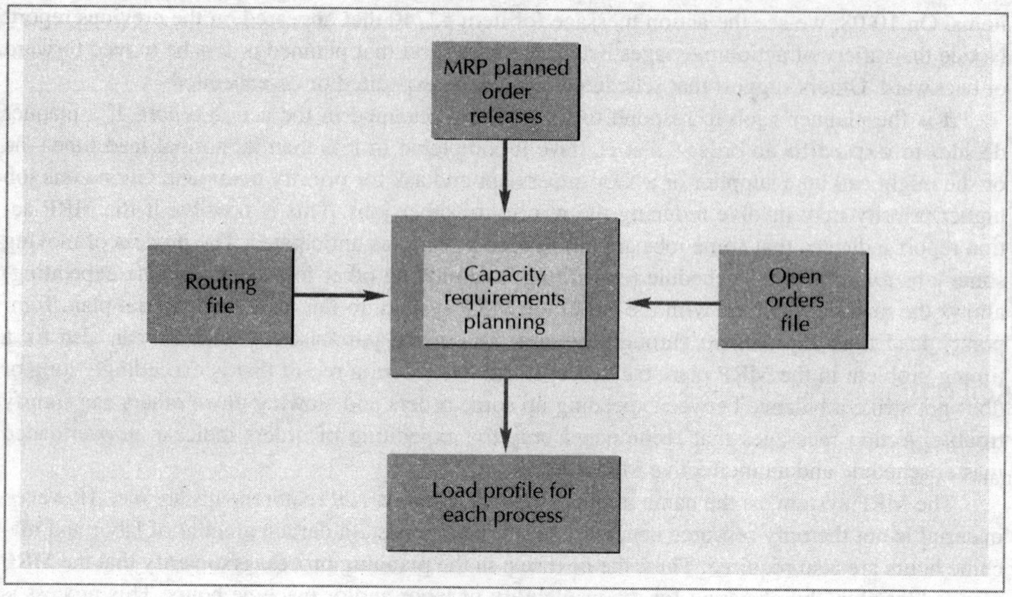

Utilization refers to the percentage of available working time that a worker actually works or a machine actually runs. Scheduled maintenance, lunch breaks, and setup time are examples of activities that reduce actual working time. **Efficiency** refers to how well a machine or worker performs compared to a standard output level. Standards can be based on past records of performance or can be developed from the work-measurement techniques discussed in Chapter 8. An efficiency of 100% is considered normal or standard performance, 125% is above normal, and 90% is below normal. Efficiency is also dependent on product mix. Some orders obviously will take longer than others to process, and some machines or workers may be better at processing certain types of orders.

Load is the standard hours of work (or equivalent units of production) assigned to a production facility. After load and capacity have been determined, a **load percent** can be calculated as

$$\text{Load percent} = \frac{\text{load}}{\text{capacity}} \times 100\%$$

Centers loaded above 100% will not be able to complete the scheduled work without some adjustment in capacity or reduction in load.

EXAMPLE 15.3

DETERMINING LOADS AND CAPACITIES

Copy Courier (CC) is a fledgling copy center in downtown Richmond run by two college students. Currently, the equipment consists of two high-speed copiers that can be operated by one operator. If the students work alone, it is conceivable that two shifts per day can be staffed. The students each work 8 hours a day, 5 days a week. They do not take breaks during the day, but they do allow themselves 30 minutes for lunch or dinner. In addition, they service the machines for about 30 minutes at the beginning of each shift. The time required to set up for each order varies by the type of paper, use of color, number of copies, and so on. Estimates of setup time are kept with each order. Since the machines are new, their efficiency is estimated at 90%.

Due to extensive advertising and new customer incentives, orders have been pouring in. The students need help determining the capacity of their operation and the current load on their facility. Use the following information to calculate the normal daily capacity of Copy Courier and to project next Monday's load and load percent.

Job No.	No. of Copies	Setup Time (min)	Run Time (min/unit)
10	500	5.2	0.08
20	1,000	10.6	0.10
30	5,000	3.4	0.12
40	4,500	11.2	0.14
50	2,000	15.3	0.10

SOLUTION

The machines and operators at Copy Courier are out of service for 1 hour each shift for maintenance and lunch. Utilization is thus 7/8, or 87.5%. Daily copy shop capacity is:

$$2 \text{ machines} \times 2 \text{ shifts} \times 8 \text{ hours/shift} \times 90\% \text{ efficiency}$$
$$\times\ 87.5\% \text{ utilization} = 25.2 \text{ hours or } 1{,}512 \text{ minutes}$$

The projected load for Monday of next week is as follows:

Job No.	Total × Time
z10	5.2 + (500 × 0.08) = 45.20
20	10.6 + (1,000 × 0.10) = 110.60
30	3.4 + (5,000 × 0.12) = 603.40
40	11.2 + (4,500 × 0.14) = 641.20
50	15.3 + (2,000 × 0.10) = 215.30
	1,615.70 minutes

$$\text{Load percent} = \frac{1{,}615.70}{1512} = 1.068 \times 100\% = 106.8\%$$

Copy Courier is overloaded 6.8%. Several options are available to alleviate the overload. If each worker extends his or her working day by approximately 36 minutes, the load percent will reduce to 99%. The same effect can be achieved by increasing efficiency to 97%. This may involve limiting the orders accepted to those that can be processed more efficiently, or grouping jobs by similar processing requirements so that setup time is reduced.

LOAD PROFILES

Load profiles are a graphical comparison of load versus capacity. As shown in Figure 15.9, the normal capacity of Department A is 40 hours per week. We can see that the machine is *underloaded* in periods 1, 5, and 6, and *overloaded* in periods 2, 3, and 4. Underloaded conditions can be leveled by:

1. Acquiring more work;
2. *Pulling work ahead* that is scheduled for later periods; or
3. Reducing normal capacity.

Figure 15.9

Initial Load Profile for Department A

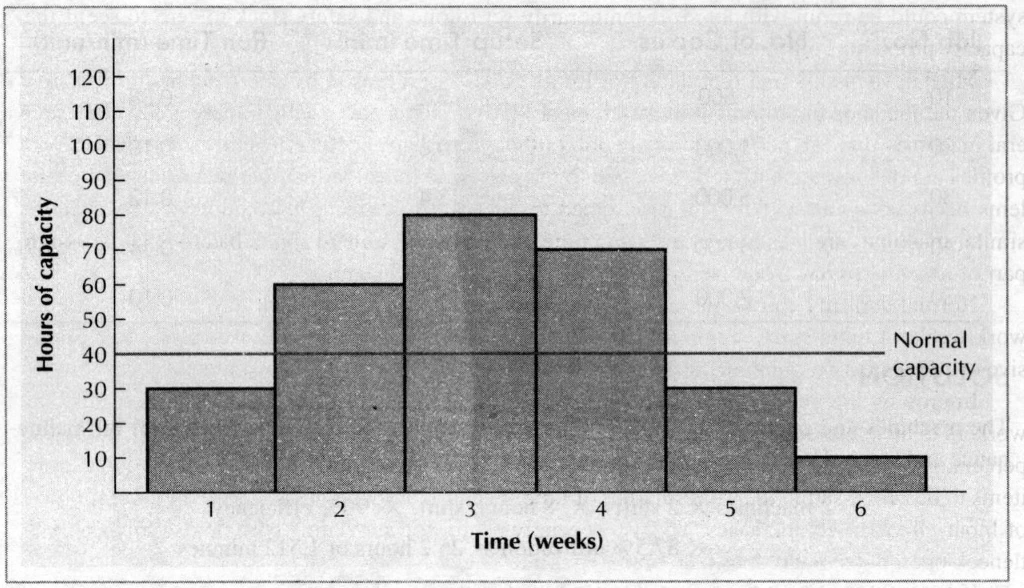

Additional work can be acquired by transferring similar work from other machines in the same shop that are near or over capacity, by making components in-house that are normally purchased from outside suppliers, or by seeking work from outside sources. Pulling work ahead seems like a quick and easy alternative to alleviate both underloads and overloads. However, we must remember that the MRP plan was devised based on an interrelated product structure, so the feasibility of scheduling work in an earlier time period is contingent on the availability of required materials or components. In addition, work completed prior to its due date must be stored in inventory and thus incurs a holding cost. When work is shifted to other time periods, the MRP plan should be rerun to check the feasibility of the proposed schedule.

If an underloaded condition continues for some time, reducing the size of the workforce may be necessary. Smaller underloads can be handled by reducing the length of the working day or workweek, by scheduling idled workers for training sessions or vacations, or by transferring workers to other positions at machine centers or processes where overloads are occurring.

OVERLOADS

Overloaded conditions are the primary concern of the MRP planner because an overloaded schedule left unchecked cannot possibly be completed as planned. Overloads can be reduced by:

1. Eliminating unnecessary requirements;
2. Rerouting jobs to alternative machines, workers, or work centers;
3. Splitting lots between two or more machines;
4. Increasing normal capacity;
5. Subcontracting;
6. Increasing the efficiency of the operation;
7. Pushing work back to later time periods; or
8. Revising the master schedule.

Some capacity problems are generated from an MRP plan that includes lot sizes, safety stock and unsubstantiated requirements for service parts or forecasted demand. To verify that a capacity overload is caused by "real" need, the planner might examine the MRP matrices of the items assigned to a machine center during an overloaded period as well as the matrices of the parents of those items processed, all the way up the product structure to the master schedule. Or, the MRP system could be rerun with lot sizes temporarily set to one and safety stock to zero to see if the capacity problem is eliminated.

MRP systems assume that an entire lot of goods is processed by one machine or operator. Given the job shop environment in which most MRP systems are installed, there are usually several machines that can perform the same job (although perhaps not as efficiently). With CRP, load profiles are determined with jobs assigned to the preferred machine first, but when capacity problems occur, jobs can certainly be reassigned to alternate machines. In addition, if two or more similar machines are available at the same time, it may be possible to *split* a batch—that is, assign part of an order to one machine and the remainder to another machine.

Normal capacity can be increased by adding extra hours to the work day, extra days to the work week, or extra shifts. Temporary overloads are usually handled with overtime. More extensive overloads may require hiring additional workers. Work can also be outsourced.

Improving the efficiency of an operation increases its capacity. Assigning the most efficient workers to an overloaded machine, improving the operating procedures or tools, or decreasing the percentage of items that need to be reworked or scrapped increases efficiency and allows more items to be processed in the same amount of time. Because output increases with the same amount of input, *productivity* increases. This is especially useful for alleviating chronic overloads at bottleneck operations, but it does take time to put into effect.

If later time periods are underloaded, it may be possible to push work back to those periods so that the work is completed but later than originally scheduled. There are two problems with this approach. First, postponing some jobs could throw the entire schedule off, meaning customers will not receive the goods when promised. This could involve a penalty for late delivery, loss of an order, or loss of a customer. Second, filling up the later time periods may preclude accepting new orders during those periods. It is normal for time periods further in the future to be underloaded. As these periods draw nearer, customer orders accelerate and begin taking up more of the system's capacity.

If all the preceding approaches to remedying overloads have been tried, but an overload still exists, the only option is to revise the master schedule. That means some customers will not receive goods as previously promised. The planner, in conjunction with the sales manager and master scheduler, determines which customers have the lowest priority and whether their orders should be postponed or canceled.

There are cost consequences associated with each of these alternatives, but there is usually no attempt to derive an optimal solution. More than likely, the MRP planner will use the options that produce a feasible solution quickly. In many manufacturing environments, new customer orders arrive daily, and feasible MRP plans can become infeasible overnight.

LOAD LEVELING

Figure 15.10 shows one possible remedy for the overloads shown in Figure 15.9. Ten hours of work are pulled ahead from period 2 to period 1. Ten hours of overtime are assigned in period 2. An entire 40-hour shift is added in period 3. Ten hours of work from period 4 are pushed back to period 5, and 20 hours are pushed back to period 6. This process of balancing underloads and overloads is called **load leveling.**

CRP *identifies* capacity problems, but the planner *solves* the problems. With experience, the task of shifting work and leveling loads is not as formidable as it appears. However, it is helpful if the initial load profile is as accurate as possible and if previous planning stages (i.e., sales and operations planning and master production scheduling) have considered capacity constraints. Some companies formalize capacity planning at each stage of production planning. *Resource requirements planning* is associated with the sales and operations plan, and *rough-cut capacity planning* is performed prior to the approval of a master schedule. Capacity requirements planning may still be performed on the material requirements plan, but its role is to fine-tune existing resources rather than to find or develop new resources.

Once the feasibility of an MRP plan has been verified by CRP, the plan can be executed by releasing orders in the time periods indicated. Normally, the ERP system automatically releases

Figure 15.10

Adjusted Load Profile for Department A

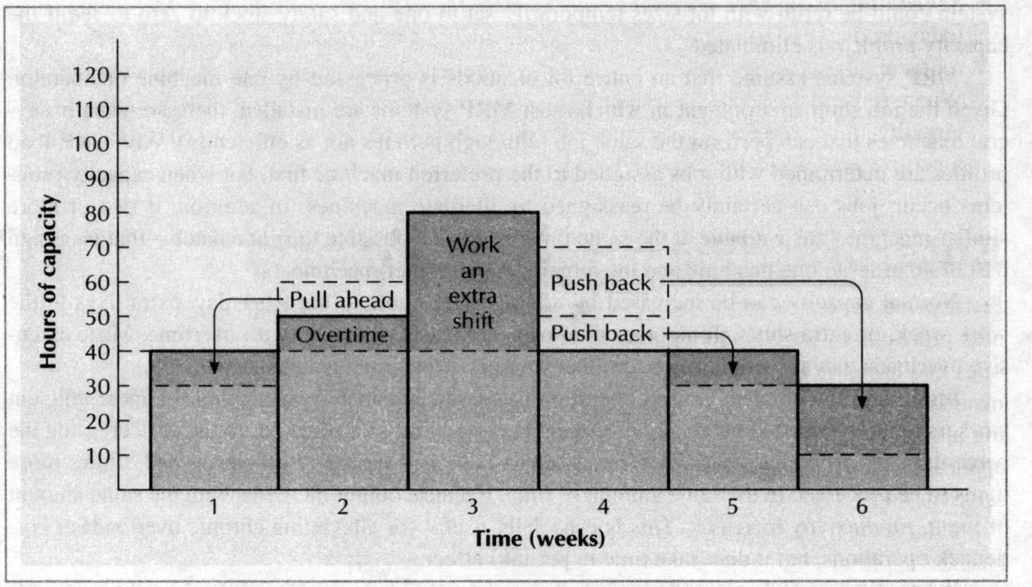

the orders. Work orders sent to the shop enter a shop floor control system, where daily scheduling and monitoring take place. When received, purchase orders are logged through the inventory system electronically before moving to manufacturing. Refer back to Figure 15.1. The figure shows the entire MRP process from the sales and operations plan to manufacture as a *closed-loop* system. The term is used to describe the numerous feedback loops between plans for production and available capacity.

RELAXING MRP ASSUMPTIONS

The MRP process described in the previous sections and depicted in Figure 15.1 makes certain assumptions about production resources and how they should be allocated. Today's ERP technology allows us to relax some of the more restrictive assumptions of MRP. For example, we have learned the following:

- ***Material is not always the most constraining resource.*** The iterative procedure described in the previous section for determining material availability first, then verifying capacity may not be relevant to some industries. If there are particular processes that constrain the system or other capacity constraints that are difficult to relax, then they should drive the schedule rather than the availability of materials. Similarly, a bill of material may not be as important as a *bill of labor, a bill of resources, a bill of distribution,* or *a bill of information.*
- ***Lead times can vary.*** Fixed lead times assume that either lot sizes will continue unchanged or that they have no bearing on lead time. Under this assumption, the lead time necessary to process an order would remain the same whether that order consists of 1 unit or 100 units, and whether the shop is operating empty or at capacity. ERP processors today are able to handle variable lead times, but users must determine how sensitive the system should be to parameters that change.
- ***Not every transaction needs to be recorded.*** MRP tries to keep track of the status of all jobs in the system and reschedules jobs as problems occur. In a manufacturing environment of speed and small lot sizes, this is cumbersome. It might take as long to *record* the processing of an item at a workstation as it does to process the item. Managers must assess how much processing detail is really needed in the common database and how much control is enough.
- ***The shop floor may require a more sophisticated scheduling system.*** Dynamic scheduling environments require a level of sophistication not present in most MRP systems. Chapter 17 introduces more advanced planning and control techniques for detailed scheduling.

- ***Scheduling in advance may not be appropriate for on-demand production***. Many companies today produce products on-demand from customers. The just-in-time or lean production environment, discussed in the next chapter, may produce better results under those circumstances. Whereas the master scheduling and bill-of-material explosion aspects of MRP are used in virtually all manufacturing environments, the MRP/CRP process may not be necessary in repetitive manufacturing driven by customer orders.

Enterprise Resource Planning (ERP)

Enterprise resource planning (ERP) is software that organizes and manages a company's business processes by sharing information across functional areas. It transforms transactional data like sales into useful information that supports business decisions in other parts of the company, such as manufacturing, inventory, procurement, invoicing, distribution, and accounting. In addition to managing all sorts of back-office functions, ERP connects with supply chain and customer management applications, helping businesses share information both inside and outside the company. Thus, ERP serves as the backbone for an organization's information needs, as well as its e-business initiatives.

Prior to ERP, most companies supported a full staff of program developers, who wrote their business applications from scratch or developed complicated interfaces to allow prepackaged applications from several vendors to pass data back and forth as necessary to complete business transactions throughout the enterprise. This process was costly, time-consuming, and error-prone. Communication among various areas of the business was difficult, and managers could not get a comprehensive view of how the business was doing at any point in time.

SAP, a German software company, created a generic ERP software package to integrate all business processes together for use by any business in the world. Established first in a mainframe version, the software was updated to client-server architecture just as companies began replacing their old legacy systems in preparation for the Y2K problem. Sales were robust, and with essentially one product, SAP became the third largest software company in the world.

With ERP, companies can integrate their accounting, sales, distribution, manufacturing, planning, purchasing, human resources, and other transactions into one application software. This enables transactions to be synchronized throughout the entire system. For example, a customer order entered into an ERP system automatically updates inventory levels, parts supplies, accounting entries, production schedules, shipping schedules, and balance sheets.

ERP systems help companies manage their resources efficiently and, at the same time, better serve their customers. Owens Corning replaced over 200 legacy systems with one ERP system. By coordinating customer orders, financial reporting, and global procurement, the company was able to save over $65 million. IBM Storage Systems reduced the time required to reprice its line of products from 5 days to 5 minutes, the time to ship a replacement part from 22 days to 3 days, and the time to complete a credit check from 20 minutes to 3 seconds. Microsoft saved $12 million annually just in early-payment discounts from vendors when its ERP system went live. Monsanto cut its production planning from 6 weeks to 3, reduced working capital, and enhanced its bargaining position with suppliers, saving the company an estimated $200 million a year.

Global companies and those that share data regularly benefit the most from ERP. Nation-specific laws, currencies, and business practices embedded in the system enable it to translate sales transactions smoothly between business units in different countries—for example, a company in Taiwan and its customer in Brazil.

ERP simplifies customer interaction and speeds production with its configure-to-order capabilities. Customers ordering online or through a sales rep can quickly choose from a variety of options, for which a bill of material is automatically generated and sent to production. National Park Service employees log on to a special segment of VF Corporation's website to purchase their uniforms. VF's ERP system makes sure the items selected are approved and automatically debits their clothing allowance. Walmart's 5,000 suppliers can link directly to a data warehouse to see how their products are selling and decide when to replenish the stock.

Data entered once into an ERP system, say from manufacturing, need not be reconciled with accounting or warehouse records because the records are all the same. With broader, more timely access to operating and financial data, ERP systems encourage flatter organizational structures and more decentralized decision making. At the same time, they centralize control over information and standardize processes. Standardized transactions make businesses more efficient; shared data helps solve problems.

ERP MODULES

ERP systems consist of a series of application modules that can be used alone or in concert. The modules are fully integrated, use a common database, and support processes that extend across functional areas. Transactions in one module are immediately available to all other modules at all relevant sites—corporate headquarters, manufacturing plants, suppliers, sales offices, and subsidiaries.

Although ERP modules differ by vendor, they are typically grouped into four main categories: (1) finance and accounting, (2) sales and marketing, (3) production and materials management, and (4) human resources. Figure 15.11 shows the type of information that flows between customers, suppliers, and these various functional areas.

Finance/Accounting

The *finance and accounting module* encompasses financial accounting, investment management, cost control, treasury management, asset management, and enterprise controlling. Included are cost centers, profit centers, activity-based costing, capital budgeting, and profitability analysis, as well as enterprise measures of performance. The finance module provides consistent financial data that is updated in real time and that links operational results with the financial effects of those results. For every physical transaction, the financial result is shown.

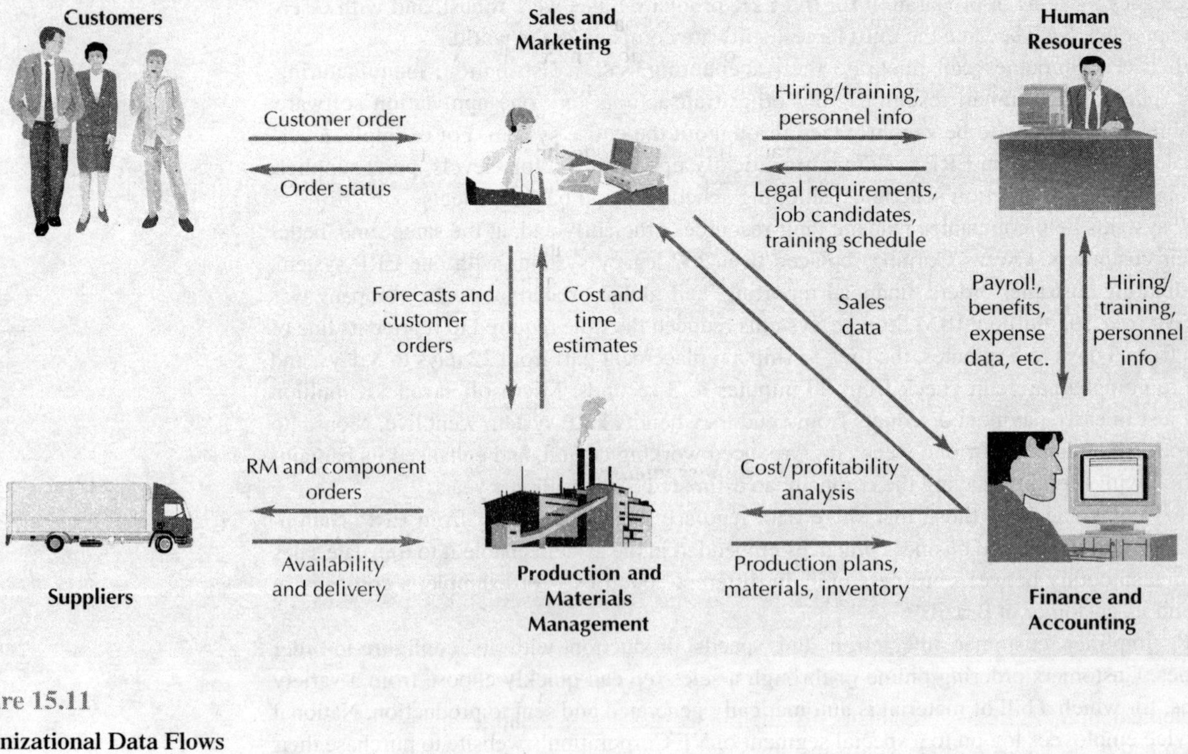

Figure 15.11

Organizational Data Flows

SOURCE: Adapted from Joseph Brady, Ellen Monk, and Bret Wagner, *Concepts in Enterprise Resource Planning* (Boston: Course Technology, 2001), pp. 7–12. NOTE: The flow between HR and Production is similar to that between HR and Sales. It was eliminated from the figure to simplify the diagram.

Sales/Marketing

The *sales and marketing module* supports customer-related activities such as order processing, product configuration, and delivery quotations. Pricing, promotions, availability, and shipping options are determined as sales orders are entered. The sales module allows for profitability analyses based on different pricing strategies with discounts and rebates, and the projection of accurate delivery dates. It can also look into the company's finished goods and work-in-process inventories as well as material availability to determine how quickly an order can be filled. Managers can reserve inventory for specific customers, request certain supplier options, and customize orders. Distribution requirements, transportation management, shipping schedules, and export controls are included in the module, as are billing, invoicing, rebate processing, product registrations, and customer complaints. Distribution is coordinated more closely with manufacturing and sales in order to maintain customer delivery schedules.

Production/Materials Management

The *production and materials management module* is set up to handle all types of manufacturing processes—make-to-order, assemble-to-order, repetitive, and continuous. The module interfaces with CAD programs; performs process planning, bill-of-material processing, and product costing; processes engineering change orders; plans material requirements (MRP); allocates resources; and schedules and monitors production. Kanbans, Gantt charts, master schedules, and available-to-promise are all supported. It links sales and distribution to materials management, production planning, and financial effects in real time. Inventory is adjusted instantly and resource planning is done on a daily basis. Materials management refers to supply-chain-related activities such as purchasing, inventory and warehouse functions, supplier evaluations, just-in-time (JIT) deliveries, and invoice verification.

Human Resources

The *human resources* module covers all personnel management tasks, including workforce planning, employee scheduling, training and development, payroll and benefits, travel expense reimbursement, applicant data, job descriptions, organization charts, and workflow analysis. It provides a database of personnel, maintains salary and benefits structures, and does payroll accounting as well.

Together, these modules form an integrated information technology strategy for effectively managing the entire enterprise. ERP connects processes that belong together, giving every employee fast, convenient access to the information required for their jobs. As shown in Figure 15.12, ERP creates a central repository for the company's data, enabling the company to perform various business analyses. A company can quickly access data in real time related to forecasting and planning, purchasing and materials management, product distribution, and accounting and financial management, so that it can deploy its resources quickly and efficiently. It can help schedule its production capacity to meet demand and reduce inventory levels. By consolidating information from sales, the company can better negotiate contracts and product prices, and determine their effect on the company's financial position. These types of decisions often require advanced analytic capabilities collectively called *business intelligence* or *business analytics*.

Both the scope and detail of ERP systems are impressive. In addition to the four major modules in an ERP system, there are hundreds of functional support modules. Many of the systems are table-driven, with over 8,000 tables to configure. As might be expected, these systems require considerable time and skill to implement. In the next section, we discuss issues in implementation.

ERP IMPLEMENTATION

ERP implementation has a checkered history of mammoth projects over budget and out of control. Dow Chemical spent half a billion dollars and seven years implementing an ERP system that has since been overhauled. FoxMeyer Drug claims that ERP implementation sent it into bankruptcy. ERP vendors and their customers have learned from these debacles, and the second-generation ERP systems are substantially different from the first generation, although they are still complex.

Figure 15.12
ERP's Central Database

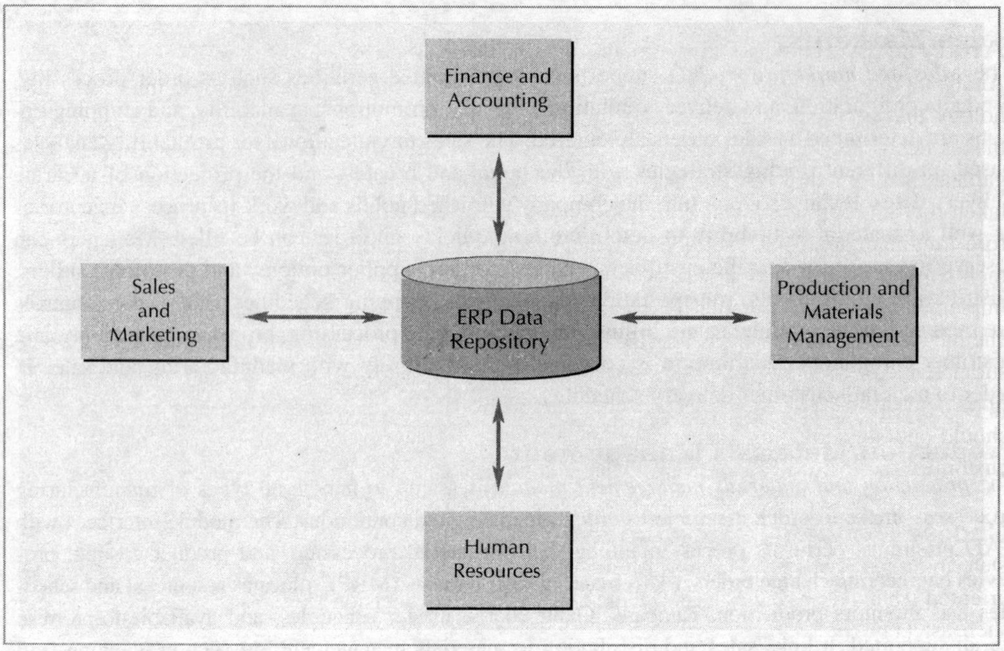

New ERP offerings sport stand-alone modules and open architecture. Companies can pick and choose the modules they want to install and can even choose a collection of modules from different vendors—the **best-of-breed** approach. While single-source ERP systems are easier to integrate, best-of-breed systems may provide a better match with organizational needs. Table 15.7 lists several enterprise software vendors and their area of expertise.

ERP implementation involves: (1) analyzing business processes, (2) choosing the modules to implement, (3) aligning the level of sophistication, (4) finalizing delivery and access, and (5) linking with external partners.

TABLE 15.7 Selected Enterprise Software Vendors and Their Area of Expertise

Vendor	Specialty
1. SAP	Large enterprise discrete manufacturing ERP, SCM
2. Oracle Corp.	Large enterprise discrete manufacturing and services
3. Oracle's PeopleSoft	Human resources and employee relationship management
4. Oracle's Siebel Systems	Customer relationship management (CRM)
5. Infor; JDA	Supply chain management (SCM)
6. PTC, EDS, Dassault Systems	Product lifecycle management (PLM)
7. Siemens Energy & Automation	Manufacturing execution systems (MES); energy
8. SunGard SCT	Public sector; education; financial services
9. QAD	Multinational midmarket manufacturing
10. Microsoft Dynamics	Small to midmarket ERP, CRM

Analyze Business Processes

Analyzing business processes is the first step in implementation. Since ERP is an integrated technology that pervades and connects all parts of a company, it usually alters the way a company makes decisions; thus, its implementation typically requires major changes in a company's organizational structure and business processes. Companies that have had success with ERP have taken the time to think about how their processes work and how they can best be integrated before "automating" them. To guide companies in this massive project, ERP vendors have designed their software around best practices for specific industries. Solution maps and stories of successful implementations are available for such industries as aerospace and defense, apparel, automotive, chemicals, consumer products, engineering and construction, healthcare, high-tech industries, insurance, media, oil and gas, pharmaceuticals, the public sector, real estate, retail, telecommunications, and utilities. Companies can either use the software as a blueprint for how their processes should operate and adjust their processes, or they can map out their own business processes and customize the software accordingly. Most companies try a combination of these approaches.

Choose Modules to Implement

Determining which ERP modules to implement and how they should be configured is a process-oriented (rather than technology-oriented) decision. The decision should be guided by questions such as: (1) Which processes have the biggest impact on customer relations? (2) Which processes would benefit the most from cross-functional or interorganizational integration? (3) Which processes should be standardized throughout the organization and which should be allowed to vary?

Small-market and midsize-market companies with time and budget constraints have an especially hard time implementing ERP. In response, software vendors like SAP have created a fast-track approach to ERP implementation. Based on the processes and applications that have proved most successful in the past, SAP has created 11 industry-specific best-practices templates designed to maximize efficiency and minimize customization. Plain vanilla, template-based modules chosen by the client are provided at a fixed price and implemented over a fixed timetable. The results are impressive. eCompany installed fully functional ERP modules for materials management, function planning, finance, and online retailing in three weeks for less than $200,000. Interactive Apparel implemented SAP's materials management, sales and distribution, warehouse management, and financial modules in nine weeks for less than $150,000.

Align Level of Sophistication

Knowing the level of sophistication needed for your business is also key to effective ERP implementation. QAD, a midmarket ERP vendor, offers industry-specific software to manufacturing companies and international clients. QAD software can be directed with instructions much simpler than those of larger ERP vendors. Instead of deploying a single system to manage all of a company's plants, QAD tailors its software to individual plants, then links them with corporate financial, distribution, and support functions. Since 65% of QAD's customers are international, its software incorporates country-specific methods for invoicing, accounting, and amortization. For example, QAD uses a model to decide how an incoming order from a trading partner should be handled, automatically processing transactions across enterprises, languages, and customs. QAD is known for both its ease of implementation and ease of use.

Finalize Delivery and Access

The Internet provides another aid to implementation. ERP vendors, including Oracle, and SAP, now offer their products through portals. The vendor hosts the application, which the customer accesses over the Internet with their browser. Portals are less expensive, so they give midsize market and smaller clients access to the same services as larger corporations. ERP services can also be accessed through third-party application service providers (ASPs). Redback Networks, for example, uses Qwest CyberSolutions to access Oracle's suite of enterprise solutions, including finance, order management, human resources, manufacturing, shipping, and inventory systems.

ALONG THE SUPPLY CHAIN

Under Armour at the Top of Its Game with ERP

Under Armour (UA) is a sports apparel company launched by a University of Maryland football player to market a new type of athletic shirt that fits tightly and wicks away moisture. The innovative new product was a hit with teammates and other athletes, and quickly found its way onto the shelves of Dick's Sporting Goods, creating an entirely new market for what has come to be known as "performance sports apparel." Today, Under Armour sells its products via the Internet, catalogs, and 17,000 sporting goods stores worldwide. In direct competition with giants Nike, Adidas, and Columbia Sportswear, it holds a 74% market share and boasts an average annual growth rate of 40% over the past 12 years.

Having a great product is only one avenue to success. Keeping costs down, suppliers reliable, and customers satisfied is equally important. For Under Armour, that means investing in IT for its business. CEO and founder Kevin Plank says, "We run this company much like a team. Sales and marketing is like offense. Manufacturing and distribution is like defense. Finance and IT are like our special teams." (*The Today Show*, NBC, April 15, 2009)

For its ERP system, Under Armour chose an out-of-the-box product with SAP'S Apparel and Footwear Solution for Consumer Products. Because the software had widespread use in the apparel industry (including Nike, Adidas, and Columbia Sportswear), UA proceeded with confidence to implement the system without modification. Eight months later, with the help of a 20-person implementation team and implementation partner, Metamor, Under Armour had finished the implementation process. The company was careful to schedule three mock "go-lives" to test the software in a safe environment without affecting ongoing operations.

The apparel industry is marked by rapid product introductions, seasonal demand, and lengthy supply chains. To meet customer due dates, increase inventory turns, and minimize markdowns, the supply chain must be both fluid and tightly controlled. SAP brought ATP (available-to-promise) functionality to Under Armour's supply chain that enabled the company to allocate inventory across customers and suppliers worldwide. UA can now close its books faster, bring new operations or countries online more readily, and make faster, more knowledgeable decisions with real-time data.

For those activities not covered in SAP'S basic software, UA chose outside vendors Dassault Systemes for PLM (product lifecycle management) software and Oracle for EDI (electronic data interchange) to electronically exchange key documents with suppliers. Both systems were implemented quickly and efficiently. More recently, UA implemented SAP's Advanced Planning & Optimization (APO) software to help develop sales projections, plan inventory, and synchronize strategic financial plans with new product launches. The software saved the company $1.2 million in purchases in only 30 days. APO was also essential in coordinating the activities of the three planning departments, demand planning, merchandise planning, and sales planning.

1. Think about the types of products offered and customers served by UA. What information and functionality would be needed for different market segments and customers?
2. What different activities would a demand planning, merchandise planning, and sales planning department have? Why might APO be helpful in coordinating these activities?

Sources: Based on Trey Palmisano, "From Rags to Microfiber: Inside the Rapid Rise of Under Armour," *Sports Illustrated* (April 2009); Merrill Douglas, "Jim Calo: Under Armour's Over Achiever," *Inbound Logistics* (September 2007); Beth Stackpole, "PLM's Vertical Challenge," *Managing Automation* (February 2008); and Maroushka Kanywani, "Why Under Armour Selected SAP," *Dashboard Insight* (January 2009); B. Booen, "The Under Armour Success Story: How SAP Improved the UA Supply Chain," *Supply Chain Digital* (March 10, 2011).

Link with External Partners

The value of e-business relies on a company's ability to integrate its internal processes with external suppliers, customers, and companies. First-generation ERP systems lacked the ability to interact outside the organization with other ERP systems, with e-businesses, or directly with customers. By the second generation of ERP, vendors had learned to create web-centric systems by consolidating data and allowing dynamic access from various clients. Software vendors have developed powerful new analytic tools and applications that capitalize on ERP's infrastructure. Examples of such software systems are customer relationship management, supply chain management, and product lifecycle management.

Customer Relationship Management (CRM)

Perhaps no new application reinforces the changing focus of ERP better than customer relationship management. **Customer relationship management (CRM)** software plans and executes business processes that involve customer interaction, such as marketing, sales, fulfillment, and service. CRM changes the focus from managing products to managing customers. With the advent of e-commerce, companies have the opportunity to sell directly to the customer. Marketing can be personalized to individual preferences and behaviors. A wealth of data on customer buying behavior is available from records of purchases and analysis of clickstreams. Special events, such as holidays or product promotions, can trigger customer purchases. Point-of-sale data from physical stores, mail-order purchases, and online purchases are monitored. All of these data go into a data warehouse, where they are analyzed for patterns (called *data mining*) from which predictions of future behavior are made.

Prospect information, customer profiles, sales-force automation, and campaign modules for direct mail and special sales promotions are managed with CRM. In addition to collecting and analyzing customer data, CRM provides decision support for forecasting demand, demand management, pricing products and services, quoting order delivery dates, and planning for customer service needs. Customer service includes tracking and tracing orders, returns, repairs, service, and warranty management. CRM interacts with supply chain management (SCM) software and ERP to ensure prompt and accurate order fulfillment, and to plan for future requirements.

Supply Chain Management (SCM)

As discussed in Chapter 10, **supply chain management (SCM)** software includes supply chain planning, supply chain execution, and supplier relationship management. *Planning* involves designing the supply chain network, demand planning, and collaborative supply planning. *Execution* involves fulfillment, manufacturing, and delivery. *Relationship management* handles all the interactions with suppliers from supplier certification to quality assurance, contracts, and agreements.

From the above list, you can see that the distinction between business software applications has become increasingly blurred as ERP vendors are adding more SCM functions, and SCM vendors are encroaching on ERP. SAP, whose ERP application runs most Fortune 500 companies, is now concentrating on a suite of new offerings in supply chain management, customer relationship management, and product lifecycle management. i2 technologies, now owned by JDA, has incorporated ERP functions into its TradeMatrix software. Oracle, known for its database management systems, emphasizes CRM, B2B, and business intelligence.

Product Lifecycle Management (PLM)

A new entry into business application software is **product lifecycle management (PLM)**. PLM manages product data through the life of the product, coordinates product and processes redesign, and collaborates with suppliers and customers in the design process.

PLM, CRM, ERP, and SCM make a powerful combination. Figure 15.13 shows how these types of software systems can work together. Customer and supplier collaboration on design with PLM can reduce time to market for new products and services. Similarly, customer and supplier collaboration in manufacturing via ERP helps speed the product to the customer. Design and manufacture collaborate in the DFMA (design for manufacture and assembly) process discussed in Chapter 4.

Connectivity, Integration, Big Data, and the Cloud

Getting ERP, PLM, CRM, and SCM systems talking to each other within a company is difficult. Getting them to communicate across hundreds of different companies and vendors is a daunting task. Using the same suite of products from one vendor facilitates integration, but most companies

Figure 15.13

ERP and Related Software Systems

SOURCE: Adapted from George Shaw, "Building the Lean Enterprise: Reducing Time to Market," *Industry Week*, webcast, June 14, 2001, www.industryweek.com/Events/TimeToMarket/pent0614.html.

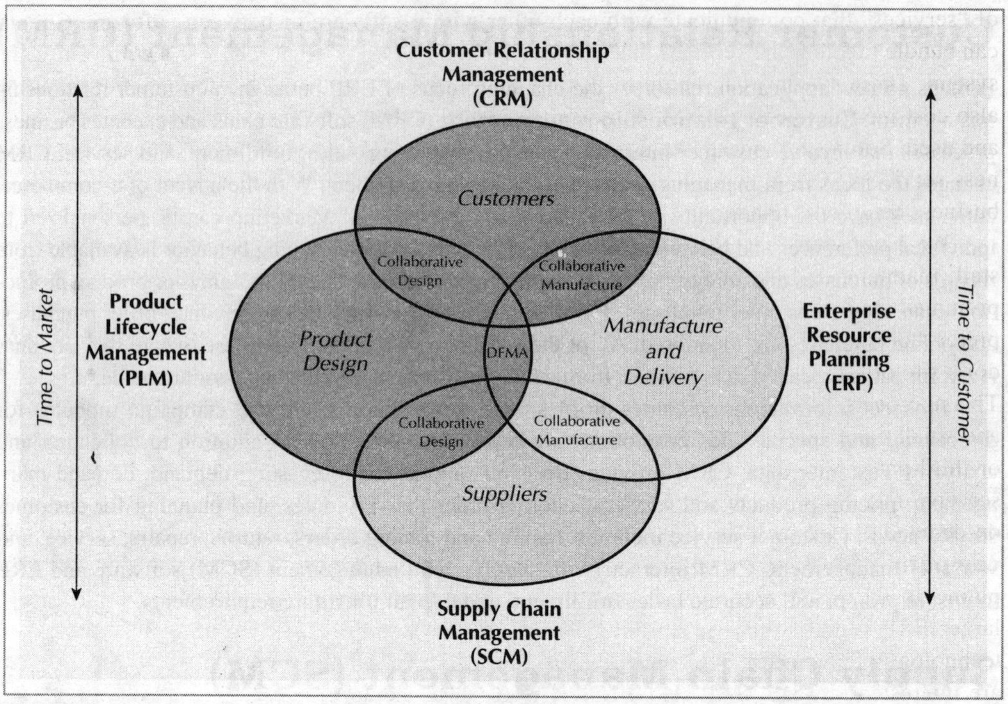

prefer a best-of-breed approach, buying the products or modules that best fit their business from a variety of vendors. It is common for e-business applications to come with application programming interfaces (APIs) that give other programs well-defined ways of speaking to them. But APIs that allow communication between application A and application B are overwhelmed when applications C, D, and E are added to the exchange. Enter third-party vendors that offer enterprise application integration (EAI). This software breaks down a complex business process into a series of transactions between applications. It then brokers those transactions in language each application can understand. That language is most likely **XML** (for extensible markup language); newer software uses XML extensively.

Electronic data interchange (EDI) used to be the language of business-to-business communication. While EDI is good at transmitting orders and invoices, it cannot change product descriptions, transmit product drawings, update in real time, or easily communicate with ERP systems. XML, on the other hand, was built for the Internet. Instead of downloading data from one system and reentering it into another, XML tags each chunk of data—such as part number, price, and delivery date—before sending it to a trading partner. The receiving XML-run system picks out the data by its tag and inserts it into the proper place in its ERP system. Thus, websites can communicate with websites, computers with computers.

IBM estimates that 70% of all code written today consists of interfaces, protocols, and other procedures to establish linkages among various systems. Connectivity and integration will continue to be an issue as new technologies emerge and the volume of data grows. There is no question that the amount of data in the world is increasing at an unparalleled rate; 90% in the past two years alone. These massive data streams containing both structured and unstructured data are known collectively as **big data**. Companies are challenged with where to store this amount of data, how to analyze it, and how to act on it. ERP systems and related CRM, SCM and PLM systems both feed and receive big data. *Business analytics* software connected to these systems hold great promise for helping decision makers make effective use of big data.

For many companies, purchasing an ERP software package means paying too much money for features and functionality they will never use. Recent trends in software engineering, such as SOA, can provide relief. **Service-oriented architecture (SOA)** is a collection of "services" that communicate with each other within software or between software. Clients can bundle together the services that they need and do not need to purchase the entire software system. These systems can be more flexible and efficient than current offerings, but they can also cost more to customize. SOA radically changes how software is designed, offered, sold, and used. Software vendors like the ability to reuse and share services across clients and business services. SOA also provides a means to deploy and quickly reconfigure applications as business conditions change.

We have seen that ERP software can be quite expensive and time consuming to install, maintain, and operate. The decomposition of large software systems into services has prompted another revolution in the way software is delivered to customers. Many companies prefer storing their data or accessing business software, such as ERP or CRM, from the vendor's site or a third-party host site, instead of installing, running and maintaining it in-house. This approach, known as **software as a service (SaaS)**, is gaining popularity in both large and small companies. In addition to providing the software on-demand to its clients, vendors or third-party providers also maintain and run the IT infrastructure, including the networks, servers, operating systems, and storage necessary to run the software. This broader view of on-demand IT services, usually delivered by a provider over the Internet, is known as **cloud computing**. Salesforce was the first business software vendor to successfully use cloud computing in the CRM market, followed by NetSuite for e-commerce and financials. Today's larger ERP vendors are also entering the cloud. For example, SAP offers *NetWeaver* as its technology platform for SOA and *Business ByDesign* for small to mid-sized businesses who are interested in SaaS. SAP also offers HANA, an in-memory database large enough to perform business analytics in real time on big data streams provided by multiple ERP systems and supply chain partners.

SUMMARY

Material requirements planning (MRP) is a computerized inventory control and production planning system. It has enjoyed widespread use in industry, primarily for batch manufacturing, as an information system that improves manufacturing decision making. MRP began as a system for ensuring that sufficient *material* was available when needed. However, in application, it became clear that material was not the only resource in short supply. Planning capabilities for machine and labor resources were added to the system in the form of *capacity requirements planning* (CRP).

MRP requires input from other functional areas of a firm, such as marketing and finance. As these areas began to see the power of a common database system, they encouraged the expansion of MRP into areas such as demand forecasting, demand management, customer order entry, accounts payable, accounts receivable, budgets, and cash flow analysis. Clearly, this enhanced version was more powerful than the original MRP system that ordered material and scheduled production. It provided a common database that the entire company could use. Its what if? capability proved invaluable in evaluating tradeoffs, and the easy access to information encouraged more sophisticated planning. Thus, MRP evolved into a more comprehensive *enterprise resource planning system,* or ERP.

ERP is a powerful software system that organizes and manages business processes across functional areas. In addition to managing all sorts of back-office functions, ERP connects with supply chain and customer management applications, helping businesses share information both inside and outside the company. ERP is essential to related software systems, such as customer relationship management (CRM), supply chain management (SCM), and product lifecycle management (PLM). Connectivity, integration, big data and the cloud are emerging issues in ERP implementation and success.

QUESTIONS

15-1. Describe a production environment in which MRP would be useful. Describe a production environment in which MRP would *not* be useful.

15-2. Explain with an example the difference between dependent and independent demand.

15-3. What are the objectives, inputs, and outputs of an MRP system?

15-4. How is a master production schedule created, and how is it used?

15-5. What is the purpose of phantom bills, K-bills, and modular bills of material?

15-6. What type of information is included in the item master file?

15-7. Describe cycle counting. How does it improve inventory performance?

15-8. Describe the MRP process, including netting, explosion, lot sizing, and time phasing.

15-9. What are the inputs to capacity requirements planning? Discuss several alternatives for leveling the load on a facility.

15-10. Discuss several assumptions of MRP and how they are being relaxed with new technology.

15-11. Explain how MRP could be applied to (a) the surgery suite of a hospital, (b) scheduling university classes, (c) a chain of restaurants, and (d) hotel renovations.

15-12. How does MRP differ from ERP? Find a description of an MRP module from a software vendor.

15-13. Access the website of an ERP vendor such as Oracle, SAP, Infor, JDA, or QAD. Make a list of the modules available. Choose one module to describe in detail.

15-14. What are the capabilities of customer relationship management (CRM) software? How do ERP and CRM relate?

15-15. What are the capabilities of supply chain management software? How do ERP and SCM relate?

15-16. Compare the ERP/CRM/SCM offerings of two different software vendors.

15-17. What is PLM? How does it relate to other business software?

15-18. Describe how the ERP systems from two different companies can converse.

15-19. While there are numerous ERP software vendors, the two largest are SAP and Oracle. Find out how these two companies compete, and compare their customers and product offerings.

15-20. Discuss the scope of ERP and difficulties in implementation.

15-21. Interview managers at three companies in your area about their use of ERP. How have their experiences been similar? What accounts for the similarities and differences?

15-22. APICS is a professional organization for operations and supply chain management. Find out if there is a local APICS chapter in your area. Attend a meeting and write a summary of the speaker's comments, or access *www.APICS.org* and read one of its online articles.

15-23. From articles in recent business magazines, describe the newest trends in big data, business analytics software, cloud computing, and in-memory computing.

SOLVED PROBLEMS

Complete the following MRP matrix for item X.

ITEM: X	LLC: 0	PERIOD							
LOT SIZE: MIN 50	**LT: 2**	*1*	*2*	*3*	*4*	*5*	*6*	*7*	*8*
Gross Requirements		20	30	50	50	60	90	40	60
Scheduled Receipts			50						
Projected on Hand	40								
Net Requirements									
Planned Order Receipts									
Planned Order Releases									

a. In what periods should orders be released, and what should be the size of those orders?

b. How would your answer change if the cost of ordering item X were $100, the cost of carrying were $2 a week, and the POQ lot sizing technique were used?

c. Which lot sizing technique yields the lowest total cost?

SOLUTION

a.

ITEM: X	LLC: 0	PERIOD							
LOT SIZE: MIN 50	**LT: 2**	*1*	*2*	*3*	*4*	*5*	*6*	*7*	*8*
Gross Requirements		20	30	50	50	60	90	40	60
Scheduled Receipts			50						
Projected on Hand	40	20	40	40	40	30	0	10	0
Net Requirements				10	10	20	60	40	50
Planned Order Receipts				50	50	50	60	50	50
Planned Order Releases		50	50	50	60	50	50		

b. $\bar{d} = 50 \qquad Q = \sqrt{\dfrac{2(50)(100)}{2}} = 70.711$

$C_o = \$100$

$C_c = \$2$

$$POQ = Q/\bar{d} = 1.41 \text{ or } 2 \text{ periods}$$

Item: X	LLC: 0	PERIOD							
LOT SIZE: POQ 2	**LT: 2**	*1*	*2*	*3*	*4*	*5*	*6*	*7*	*8*
Gross Requirements		20	30	50	50	60	90	40	60
Scheduled Receipts			50						
Projected on Hand	40	20	40	50	0	90	0	60	0
Net Requirements				10		60		40	
Planned Order Receipts				60		150		100	
Planned Order Releases		60		150		100			

c. $TC_{MIN50} = (6 \times \$100) + (180 \times \$2) = \$960$

$TC_{POQ2} = (3 \times \$100) + (260 \times \$2) = \$820$

Choose the POQ lot-sizing technique.

PROBLEMS

15-1. Referring to the product structure diagram for product A, determine:

a. how many Ks are needed for each A.
b. how many Es are needed for each A.
c. the low-level code for item E.

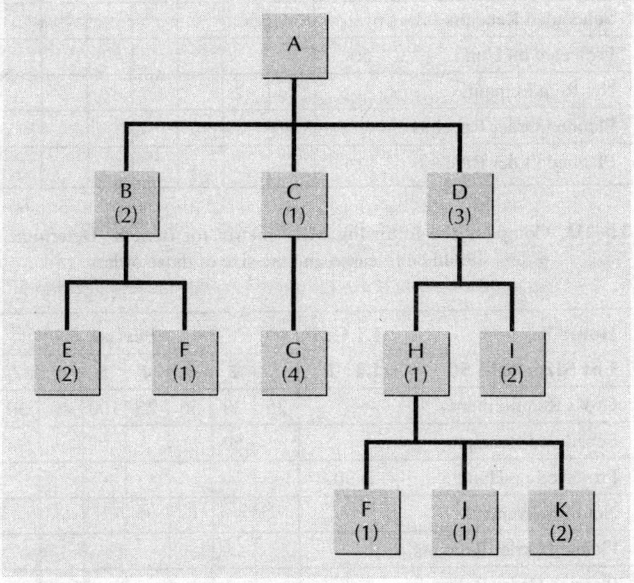

15-2. Construct a multilevel bill of material for product Z. How many Us are needed to make each Z? How many Ws are needed to make each Z?

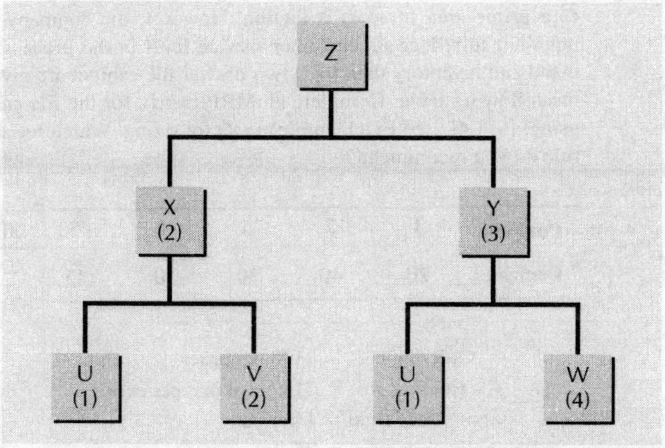

15-3. Draw a product structure diagram from the following bill of materials and calculate how many Ds are needed for each A.

Level	Item	Quantity
0- - -	A	1
- 1- - -	B	2
- - 2- -	D	3
- - 2- -	E	2
- 1- - -	C	4
- - 2- -	D	3
- - 2- -	F	1

15-4. Product A is assembled from two units of S1 and three units of S2. S1 is made of one unit of C1, four units of C2, and one unit of C3. S2 is made of three units of C2 and two units of C3.

a. Draw a product structure diagram for product A.
b. How many C3s are needed to fill an order for 100 As?
c. Assuming no inventory on hand, products take one day to assemble, subassemblies take two days and components take three days. When should an order be released for C3 if the 100 As are needed by day 7?

15-5. The Best Wheels Bicycle Company produces bicycles in different styles for boys and girls, in heights of 26 inches or 20 inches, and with 10 speeds, 3 speeds, or 1 speed.

a. How many different kinds of bicycles does Best Wheels make?
b. Construct a modular bill of material for Best Wheels (one level). Assume that bike sales are equally split between boys and girls, 26-inch bikes are preferred two-to-one to 20-inch bikes, and 3-speed bikes account for only 20% of sales. The remaining sales are divided equally between 10-speed and 1-speed bikes.
c. If bicycle sales are expected to reach 10,000 over the holiday shopping season, how many 26-inch bikes should Best Wheels plan to produce? How many 10-speed bikes?

15-6. From the product structure diagram for item X shown below, determine how many of each lower-level items (B through I) are needed to fill an order for 50 Xs.

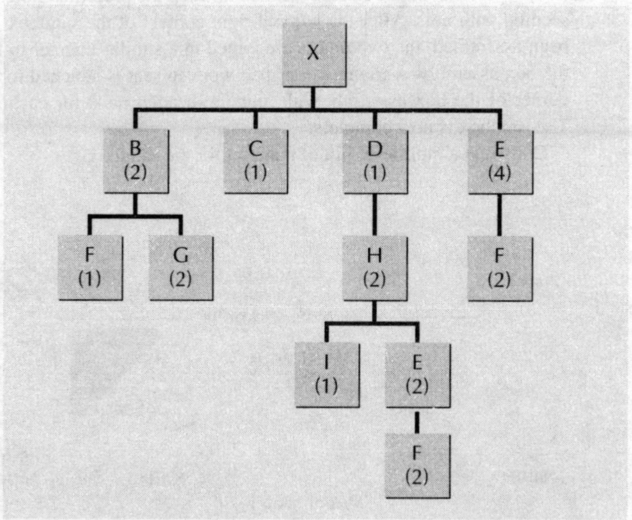

15-7. The Alpha Beta Company produces two products, A and B, that are made from components C and D. Given the following product structures, master scheduling requirements, and inventory information, determine when orders should be released for A, B, C, and D and the size of those orders.

	On Hand	Scheduled Receipts	Lot Size	MPS
A	10	0	L4L	100, period 8
B	5	0	L4L	200, period 6
C	140	0	Min 50	—
D	200	250, period 2	Mult 250	—

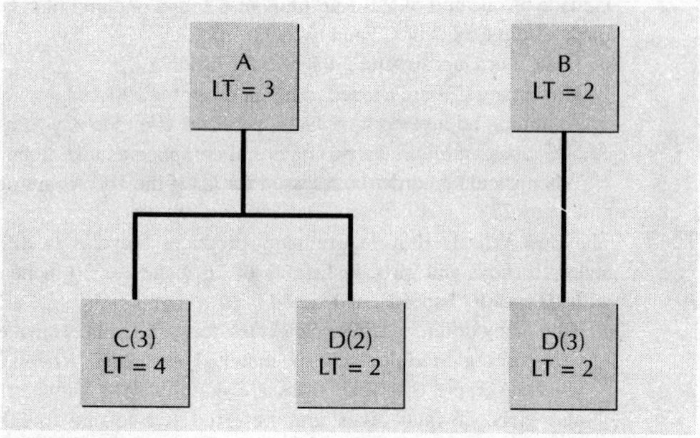

15-8. Kid's World sells outdoor play equipment for children. One of its most popular items is a 5-foot by 7-foot wooden sandbox shown below. General assembly instructions follow.

Assembly Instructions: The wood pieces for the sandbox are ordered precut and treated. Kid's World sands the wood, drills several holes in each piece as required for assembly, and coats each piece with 2 ounces of water sealer. The sides are then assembled one corner at a time by attaching a 1-foot wood strip cater-corner between a 5-foot and 7-foot side. Four bolts are inserted through the predrilled holes and secured with nuts. After the left and right corners of the sandbox have been assembled, the two pieces are joined in a similar manner to form the box assembly. A triangular-shaped wooden seat is attached to each corner of the box assembly with four flat-headed nails for each seat. The sandbox is now complete.

Construct a multilevel bill of material for the sandbox.

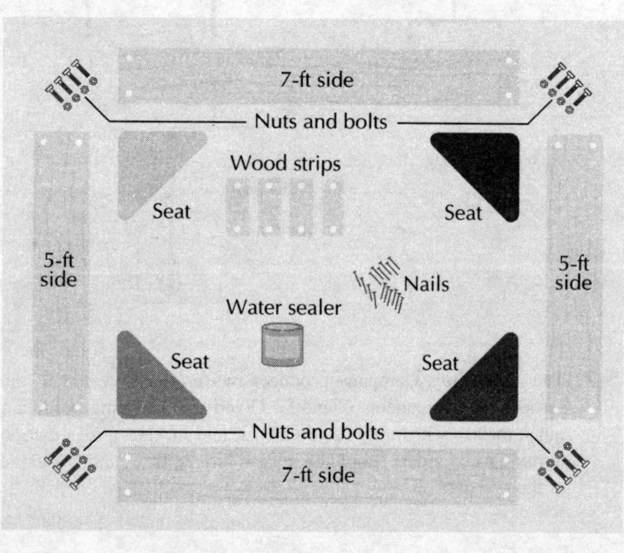

15-9. Complete the following MRP matrix for item A:

Item: A	LLC: 1	Period							
Lot Size: Mult 50	**LT: 2**	*1*	*2*	*3*	*4*	*5*	*6*	*7*	*8*
Gross Requirements		10	15	25	75	60	85	45	60
Scheduled Receipts									
Projected on Hand	50								
Net Requirements									
Planned Order Receipts									
Planned Order Releases									

15-10. Complete the following MRP matrix for Item X. Determine when orders should be released and the size of those orders.

Item: X	LLC: 0	Period							
Lot Size: Min 50	**LT: 2**	*1*	*2*	*3*	*4*	*5*	*6*	*7*	*8*
Gross Requirements		25	30	56	25	100	40	30	20
Scheduled Receipts			50						
Projected on Hand	30								
Net Requirements									
Planned Order Receipts									
Planned Order Releases									

15-11. Files and More, Inc. (F&M), a manufacturer of office equipment, uses MRP to schedule its production. Because of the current recession and the need to cut costs, F&M has targeted inventory as a prime area for cost reduction. However, the company does not want to reduce its customer service level in the process. Demand and inventory data for a two-drawer file cabinet are given in the following table. Complete an MRP matrix for the file cabinet using: (a) L4L, (b) EOQ, and (c) POQ lot sizing. Which lot-sizing rule do you recommend?

Period	1	2	3	4	5
Demand	20	40	30	10	45

Ordering cost = $100 per order
Holding cost = $1 per cabinet per period
Lead time = 1 period
Beginning inventory = 25

15-12. F&M's best-selling item is a standard office desk. The desk consists of four legs, one top, one drawer, two side panels, one back panel, and two drawer guides, as shown in the next column. Each side is assembled from a side panel, two legs, and a drawer guide. The base is formed from the back panel and two sides. In final assembly, the top is attached to the base and the drawer is slid into place. Lead times are two days for purchased items and one day for assembled items.

a. Construct a time-phased assembly chart for the desk.
b. With no inventory on hand, how long would it take to complete a customer order?

c. The desk sides, back, and drawer are metal. The top is woodgrain. F&M is considering making the desk top in its own factory. The top would take four days to manufacture. Would making the desk top in-house affect the time required to fill a customer order?

d. F&M's customers like the desk and its price, but would like to be able to get desks in three days. Which items should F&M keep in inventory to fill an order in three days?

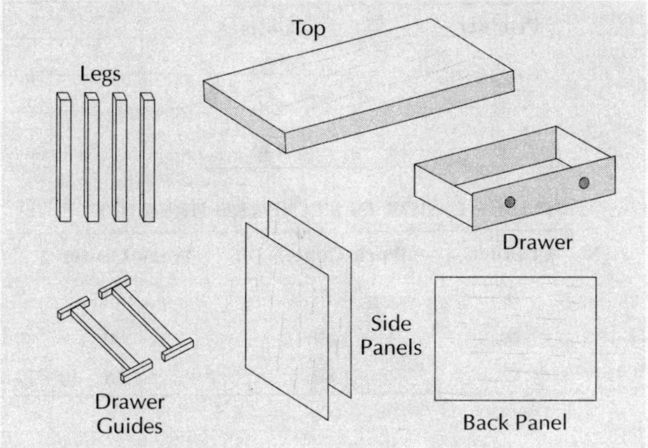

15-13. Daily demand for an item is shown here. Assume a holding cost of \$0.50 per unit per day, a setup cost of \$100 per setup, a lead time of one day and 70 units on hand. Determine when a work order should be released for the item and the size of the order using the L4L, EOQ, and POQ lot sizing techniques. Which technique produces the lowest total cost?

Period	1	2	3	4	5	6	7	8	9	10
Gross Requirements	50	30	25	35	40	50	35	45	70	75

15-14. Product A is assembled from one B and two Cs. Each item requires one or more operations, as indicated by the circles in the product structure diagram. Assume lead time is negligible. From the information given:

a. Develop a load profile chart for each of the three work centers.

b. Level the loads. Discuss possible consequences of shifting work to other periods.

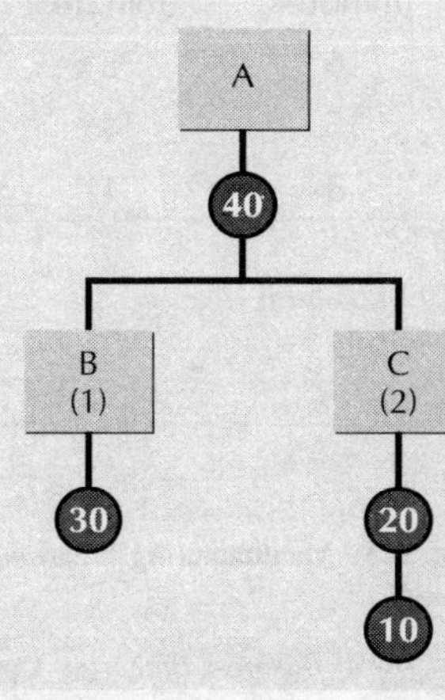

MASTER PRODUCTION SCHEDULE

Period	1	2	3	4	5	6
Product A	100	150	100	200	100	100

ROUTING AND WORK STANDARDS FILE

Operation	Item	Work Center	Standard Time per Unit (hr)
10	C	Machining	0.50
20	C	Heat treat	2.00
30	B	Machining	1.00
40	A	Assembly	0.40

15-15. Sitting on Maggie Brumfield's desk is the latest planned order report (shown below) from the company's MRP system. Maggie's job is to determine if there is enough capacity to handle the workload and to level the load if it's uneven. She gathers the latest cost figures and gets to work. Subcontracting and hiring extra workers are not options at this point, but overtime, pulling work ahead, and postponing work are. Regular production costs \$10 an hour and is limited to 40 hours a week. Overtime costs \$15 an hour and cannot exceed 40 extra hours (i.e., a double shift). An inventory cost of \$3 per period is assessed for each hour's worth of work performed in advance. Postponing work costs \$20 per period for each hour of work postponed.

a. Completely level the load by working the same number of hours each period (fractions of an hour are acceptable).

b. Economically level the load by assigning work that meets demand at the lowest possible cost. How much money is saved by economically leveling the load?

PLANNED ORDER REPORT

	Week			
Item	1	2	3	4
A	90			
B	100		250	
C		600		160
D	60			

PROCESSING TIMES

Item	Setup Time (min)	Run Time (min per unit)
A	15	3
B	30	15
C	50	10
D	45	4

15-16. The Best Wheels Bicycle Company has scheduled the production of the following bicycles this month.

		Week			
	Model	1	2	3	4
[B2610]	26-inch 10-speed	50	100	195	150
[B2003]	20-inch 3-speed	15	30	65	45
[B2001]	20-inch 1-speed	20	40	80	60

The two critical work centers for producing these bikes are welding and assembly. Welding has an efficiency of 95% and a utilization of 90%. Assembly has an efficiency of 90% and a utilization of 92%. The time required (in hours) by each bike in the two work centers is as follows:

	Welding	Assembly
B2610	0.20	0.18
B2003	0.15	0.15
B2001	0.07	0.10

Assume 40 hours is available per week for each work center. Calculate the capacity and load percent per work center per week.

15-17. Given the following information for products A, B, and C, determine the work load in work centers 1 and 2 for January, and the number of workers to assign to each work center. Assume full-time workers work a 40-hour week, 4 weeks per month, and part-time workers are available.

MASTER PRODUCTION SCHEDULE FOR JANUARY

Product	Units
A	60
B	220
C	140

BILL OF LABOR IN STANDARD HRS/UNIT

Product	Work Center 1	Work Center 2
A	1.70	.50
B	1.30	.90
C	1.80	.66

CASE STUDY

Does the New Business Make Sense?

A popular Hong Kong taxicab company does business in three service areas. It wants to expand its business to include dedicating a higher quality car for its elite customers. The cabs are identified as red with silver top (RS), green with white top (GW) and blue with white top (BW).

To appeal to this elite customer base, the cabs must be detailed between each customer and restocked with a range of beverages. Depending on the specific cab, this setup time varies.

As each cab is assigned to a specific service area, the number of clients serviced during the day varies and the duration of taxicab ride time varies as well.

To test the viability of this new venture, the firm will begin operation with 20 RS cabs, 25 GW cabs and 35 BW cabs. Each cab will be operated 16 hours a day. During these 16 hours, the cab drivers are allowed to take two 30-minute meal breaks; one 10-minute break about every 2.5 hours not exceeding 60 minutes in total over the 16 hours; and 15 minutes at the start and about mid-way through the day to refuel the cars.

In general, the firm believes that the assigned drivers are some of its most experienced and qualified personnel. Based on time studies, the firm is assigning them an efficiency rating of 96%.

Using the data in the table below, determine:

a. Utilization
b. Capacity
c. Projected load for each taxi sector
d. Overall load
e. Load percent

What would you recommend to the taxi company based on your findings?

Taxi	Number of Cabs	Setup Time (minutes)	Fare Time (minutes)	Number of Fares/Cab
RS	20	6	31	4
GW	25	15	46	3
BW	35	8	41	8

REFERENCES

Bancroft, N., H. Seip, and A. Spungel. *Implementing SAP R/3*. Greenwich, CT: Manning, 1998.

Bond, B., Y. Genovese, et al. "ERP Is Dead—Long Live ERP II." *Gartner Advisory Research Note* (October 4, 2000) http://www. gartner.com.

Bylinsky, G. "Heroes of U.S. Manufacturing." *Fortune* (March 19, 2001). http://www.fortune.com.

Curran, T., and G. Keller. *SAP/3 Business Blueprint*. Upper Saddle River, NJ: Prentice Hall, 1998.

Davenport, T. "Putting the Enterprise into the Enterprise System." *Harvard Business Review* (July/August 1998), pp. 121–131.

Davenport, T. *Mission Critical: Realizing the Promise of Enterprise Systems*. Boston: Harvard Business School Press, 2000.

ERP software vendors: www.sap.com, www.i2.com, www.oracle.com, www.QAD.com.

Jacobs, F.R., W.L. Berry, D.C. Whybark, and T.E. Vollman, *Manufacturing Planning and Control for Supply Chain Management*. New York: McGraw-Hill, 2010.

Kerstetter, J. "When Machines Chat." *BusinessWeek* (July 23, 2001), pp. 76–77.

Michel, R. "ERP Gets Redefined." *MSI Magazine* (February 1, 2001). http://www.manufacturingsystems.com.

Miller, D. "Tying It All Together." *The Industry Standard Magazine* (July 2, 2001). http://www.thestandard.net.

Monk, E. and B. Wagner. *Concepts in Enterprise Resource Planning*. Boston: Course Technology, 2013.

Pender, L. "Faster, Cheaper ERP." *CIO Magazine* (May 15, 2001). http://www.cio.com.

Peterson, K., K. Brant, et al. "Manufacturing Imperatives in Collaborative Commerce." *Gartner Advisory Research Note* (July 31, 2000). http://www.gartner.com.

Phillips, S. *Control Your ERP Destiny*. Street Smarts ERP. 2012.

Ptak, Carol, and Chad Smith, *Orlicky's Material Requirements Planning*. New York: McGraw Hill, 2011.

Savitz, E. "The End of ERP," *Forbes* (February 9, 2012).

Wight, O. *Production Planning and Inverntory Control in the Computer Age*. Boston: Cahners Books International., 1974.

Word, J. *SAP Hana Essentials*. Epistemy Press. 2012.

CHAPTER 16

JIT and Lean Production

LEARNING OBJECTIVES

AFTER READING THIS CHAPTER, YOU WILL BE ABLE TO:

- Explain how the basic elements of lean eliminate waste, create flow, and continuously improve operations.
- Assess the benefits of lean, as well as the difficulties in implementing lean systems.
- Explain how the complementary concepts of lean and six sigma work together for process improvement.
- Construct and interpret a value stream map.
- Use lean concepts and techniques to enhance environmental initiatives.
- Create strategies for implementing lean in service industries.

LEAN RETAILING AND THE JEANS SUPPLY CHAIN

While consumers may like sales, too much merchandise with sales tags attached indicates waste, poor planning, and lost revenue. Let's see what lean retailing would look like.

It is Sunday evening and a retailer places an order with a manufacturer for men's jeans in an assortment of styles, colors, fabric weight and finish, waist size, and inseam length. The order is electronic and includes specific instructions for pricing and tagging the jeans with barcodes and sorting them into cartons so that when they are unpacked they are "floor-ready." Delivery to the retailer is scheduled for Wednesday afternoon.

When retailers "go lean," they reduce their order sizes and order more frequently in response to customer demand for products. That causes a domino effect back through the apparel supply chain. Instead of producing large quantities of product months in advance of need, manufacturing is tightly coupled with retail demand and delivered with a shortened lead time. In order to respond to the retail order, manufacturers must get a quick response from their suppliers of fabric, rivets, zippers, thread, labels, and so on. This "pull" of the product from consumer to retailer to manufacturer to supplier is one of the basic elements of a lean system.

The apparel supply chain has seen many changes in recent years, with industry leaders emphasizing quick response, fast fashion, and lean production. This conflicts, however, with the pursuit of low labor costs in countries that are geographically distant. We will see how companies like Zara handle that contradiction.

In this chapter, we explore the origin of lean production, its elements and evolution, and how lean systems can be applied to global manufacturing and services.

Source: Based on D. Weil, "*Lean Retailing and Supply Chain Restructuring: Implications for Private and Public Governance,*" Princeton Institute for International and Regional Studies (March 2006); and S. Stevenson, "Polka Dots Are In? Polka Dots It Is!" *Slate Magazine* (June 2012).

Shortened product lifecycles, demanding customers, globalization, and e-commerce have placed intense pressure on companies for quicker response and shorter cycle times. One way to ensure a quick turnaround is by holding inventory. But inventory costs can easily become prohibitive, especially when product obsolescence is considered. A wiser approach is to make your operating system lean and agile, able to adapt to changing customer demands. We have talked extensively in this book about supply chains. Collaboration along a supply chain can work only if the participants coordinate their production and operate under the same rhythm. Companies have found this rhythm in a well-respected but difficult to implement philosophy called lean production.

Lean production means doing more with less—less inventory, fewer workers, less space. The term was coined by James Womack and Daniel Jones[1] to describe the Toyota Production System, widely recognized as the most efficient manufacturing system in the world.

The Toyota Production System evolved slowly over a span of 20 years. Initially known as **just-in-time (JIT)**, it emphasized minimizing inventory and smoothing the flow of materials so that material arrived just as it was needed or "just-in-time." As the concept widened in scope, the term *lean production* became more prevalent. Now the terms are often used interchangeably.

Taiichi Ohno, a former shop manager and later vice president of Toyota Motor Company, is the individual generally credited with the development of lean production. The idea of producing only what you need when you need it hardly seems the basis of a revolution in manufacturing, but the concept is deceptively simple. If you produce only what you need when you need it, there is no room for error. For lean production to work well, many fundamental elements must be in place—steady production, flexible resources, extremely high quality, reliable equipment, reliable suppliers, quick setups, and the discipline to maintain these elements.

In this chapter, we explore the elements of lean production and try to discover how they became part of Ohno's integrated management system, known as the *Toyota Production System*. We also explore the benefits and drawbacks of lean production and its implementation. We conclude with a discussion of lean services.

The Basic Elements of Lean Production

In the 1950s, the entire Japanese automobile industry produced 30,000 vehicles, fewer than a half day's production for U.S. automakers. With such low levels of demand, the principles of mass production that worked so well for U.S. manufacturers could not be applied in Japan. Furthermore, the Japanese were short on capital and storage space. So it seems natural that efforts to improve performance (and stay solvent) would center on reducing the asset that soaks up both funds and

[1] J. Womack and D. Jones, *The Machine that Changed the World* (New York: Macmillan, 1990).

space—inventory. What is significant is that a system originally designed to reduce inventory levels eventually became a system for continually improving all aspects of operations. The stage was set for this evolution by the president of Toyota, Eiji Toyoda, who gave a mandate to his people to "eliminate waste." Waste, or **muda**, was defined as "anything other than the minimum amount of equipment, materials, parts, space, and time which are absolutely essential to add value to the product."[2] Examples of the seven wastes in operations are shown in Figure 16.1.

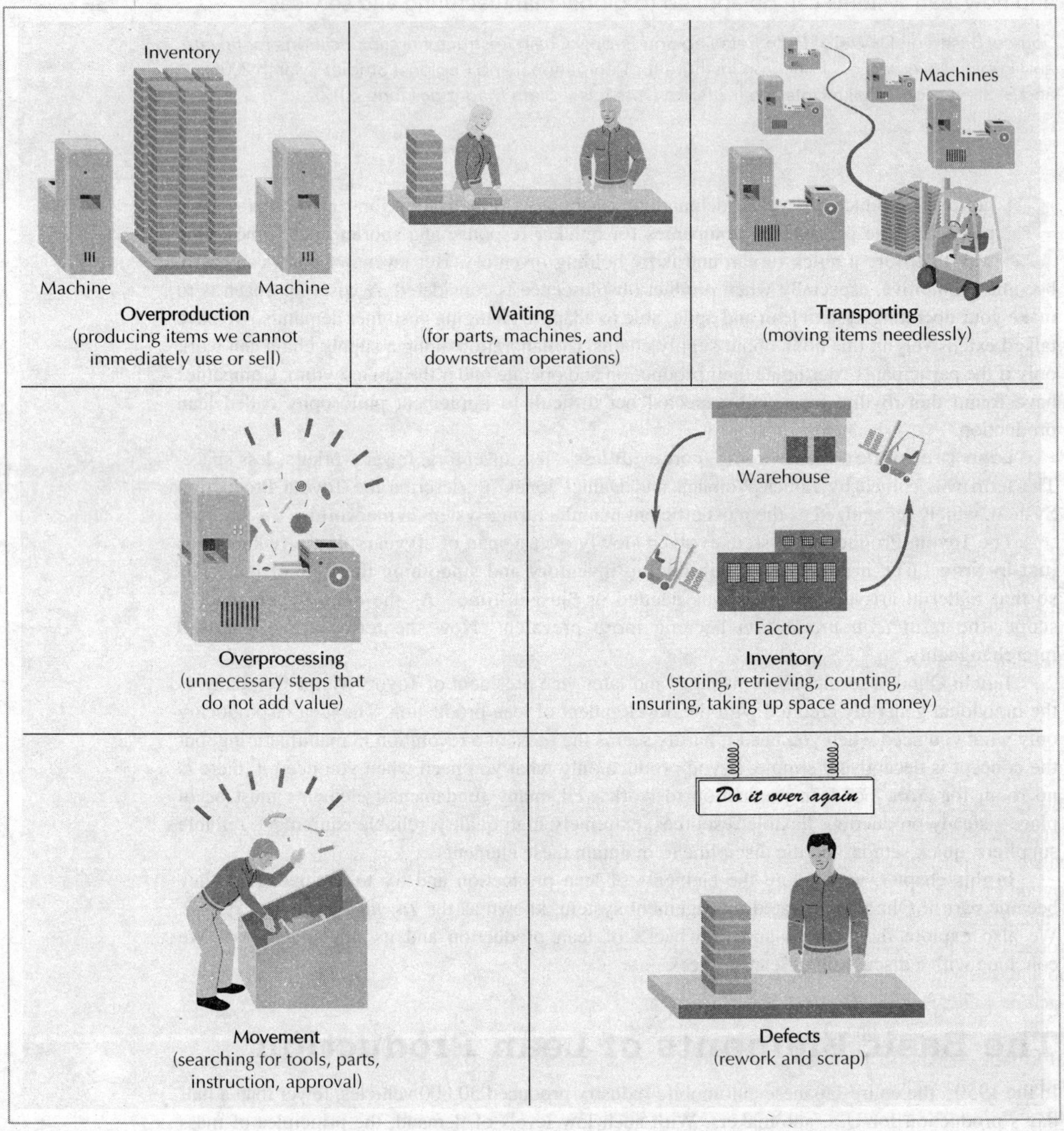

Figure 16.1
The Seven Wastes

[2]Ibid., pp. 8–9.

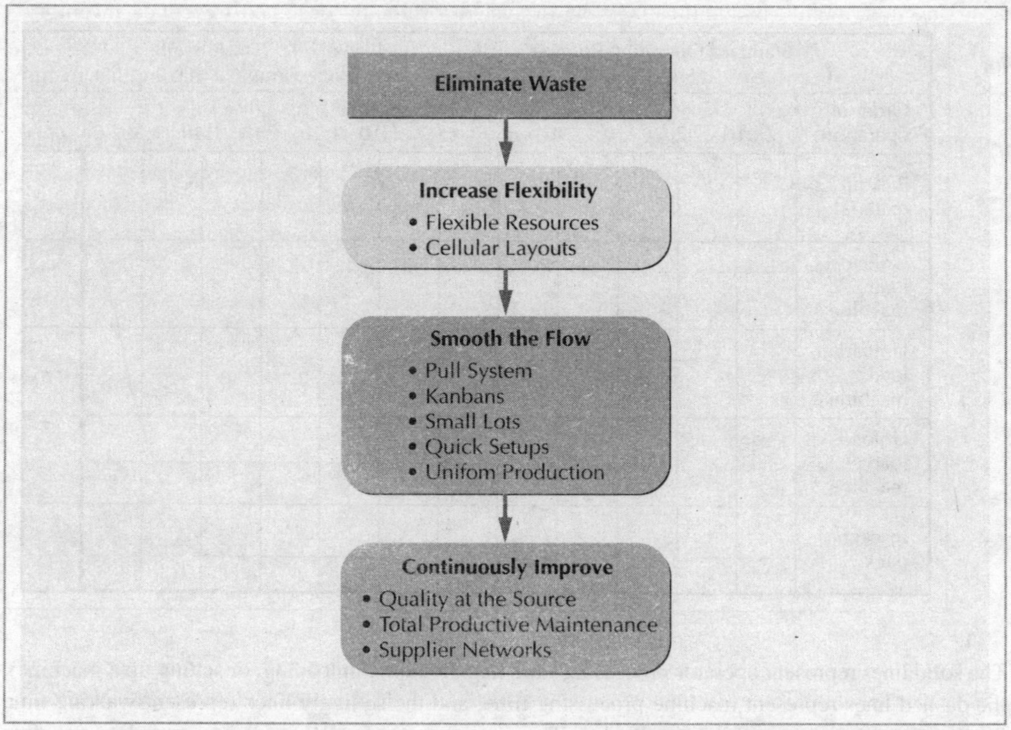

Figure 16.2

Elements of Lean Production

Lean production is the result of the mandate to eliminate waste. It is composed of ten elements:

1. Flexible resources
2. Cellular layouts
3. Pull system
4. Kanbans
5. Small lots
6. Quick setups
7. Uniform production levels
8. Quality at the source
9. Total productive maintenance
10. Supplier networks

These elements can be loosely organized into three phases, as shown in Figure 16.2. Let's explore each of these elements and determine how they work in concert.[3]

FLEXIBLE RESOURCES

The concept of flexible resources, in the form of **multifunctional workers** and **general-purpose machines**, is recognized as a key element of lean production, but most people do not realize that it was the first element to fall into place. Taiichi Ohno had transferred to Toyota from Toyoda textile mills with no knowledge of (or preconceived notions about) automobile manufacturing. His first attempt to eliminate waste (not unlike U.S. managers) concentrated on worker productivity. Borrowing heavily from U.S. time and motion studies, he set out to analyze every job and every machine in his shop. He quickly noted a distinction between the operating time of a machine and the operating time of the worker. Initially, he asked each worker to operate two machines rather than one. To make this possible, he located the machines in parallel lines or in L-formations. After a time, he asked workers to operate three or four machines arranged in a U-shape. The machines were no longer of the same type (as in a process layout) but represented a series of different processes common to a group of parts (i.e., a cellular layout).

The operation of different, multiple machines required additional training for workers and specific rotation schedules. Figure 16.3 shows a standard operating routine for an individual worker.

[3]Much of the material in these sections is adapted from Chapter 5 in Michael Cusomano's book, *The Japanese Automobile Industry* (Cambridge, MA: Harvard University Press), 1985.

Figure 16.3

Standard Operating Routine for a Worker

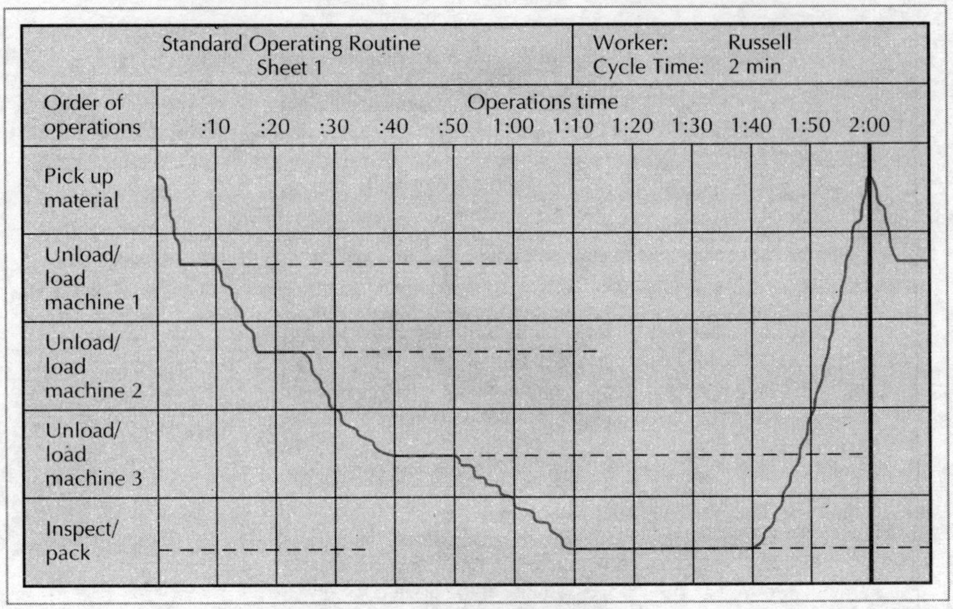

The solid lines represent operator processing time (e.g., loading, unloading, or setting up a machine), the dashed lines represent machine processing time, and the squiggly lines represent walking time for the operator from machine to machine. The time required for the worker to complete one pass through the operations assigned is called the operator *cycle time*.

Closely related to the concept of cycle time is *takt time*. "Takt" is the German word for baton, such as an orchestra leader would use to signal the timing at which musicians play. **Takt time**, then, is the pace at which production should take place to match the rate of customer demand. An operator's cycle time is coordinated with the takt time of the product or service being produced.

With single workers operating multiple machines, the machines themselves also required some adjustments. Limit switches were installed to turn off machines automatically after each operation was completed. Changes in jigs and fixtures allowed machines to hold a workpiece in place, rather than rely on the presence of an operator. Extra tools and fixtures were purchased and placed at their point of use so that operators did not have to leave their stations to retrieve them when needed. By the time Ohno was finished with this phase of his improvement efforts, it was possible for one worker to operate as many as 17 machines (the average was 5 to 10).

The flexibility of labor brought about by Ohno's changes prompted a switch to more flexible machines. Thus, although other manufacturers were interested in purchasing more specialized automated equipment, Toyota preferred small, general-purpose machines. A general-purpose lathe, for example, might be used to bore holes in an engine block and then do other drilling, milling, and threading operations at the same station. The waste of movement to other machines, setting up other machines, and waiting at other machines was eliminated.

CELLULAR LAYOUTS

While it is true that Ohno first reorganized his shop into **manufacturing cells** to use labor more efficiently, the flexibility of the new layout proved to be fundamental to the effectiveness of the system as a whole. The concept of cellular layouts did not originate with Ohno. It was first described by a U.S. engineer in the 1920s, but it was Ohno's inspired application of the idea that brought it to the attention of the world. We discussed cellular layouts (and the concept of group technology on which it is based) in Chapter 7. Let us review some of that material here.

Cells group dissimilar machines together to process a family of parts with similar shapes or processing requirements. The layout of machines within the cell resembles a small assembly line

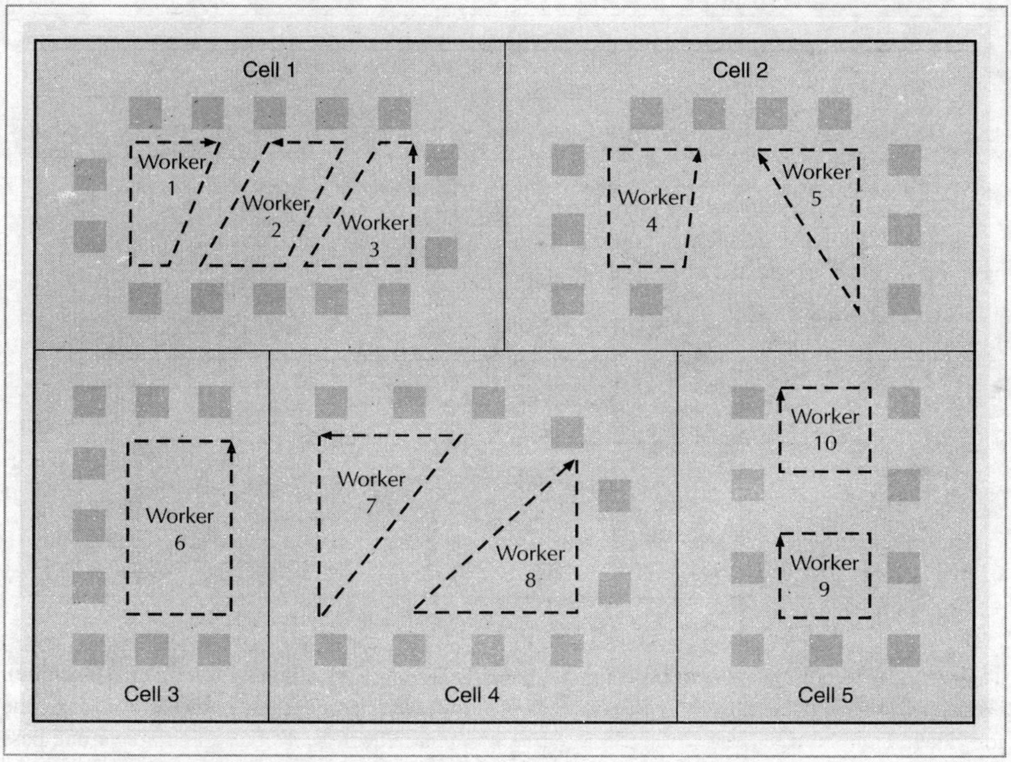

Figure 16.4

Cells with Worker Routes

and is usually U-shaped. Work is moved within the cell, ideally one unit at a time, from one process to the next by a worker as he or she walks around the cell in a prescribed path. Figure 16.4 shows a typical manufacturing cell with worker routes.

Work normally flows through the cell in one direction and experiences little waiting. In a one-person cell, the cycle time of the cell is determined by the time it takes for the worker to complete his or her path through the cell. This means that, although different items produced in the cell may take different amounts of time to complete, the time between successive items leaving the cell remains virtually the same because the worker's path remains the same. Thus, changes of product mix within the cell are easy to accommodate. Changes in volume or takt time can be handled by adding workers to or subtracting workers from the cell and adjusting their walking routes accordingly as shown in Figure 16.5.

Because cells produce similar items, setup time requirements are low and lot sizes can be reduced. Movement of output from the cells to subassembly or assembly lines occurs in small lots and is controlled by kanbans (which we discuss later). Cellular layouts, because of their manageable size, workflow, and flexibility, facilitate another element of lean production, the *pull system*.

THE PULL SYSTEM

A major problem in automobile manufacturing is coordinating the production and delivery of materials and parts with the production of subassemblies and the requirements of the final assembly line. It is a complicated process, not because of the technology, but because of the thousands of large and small components produced by thousands of workers for a single automobile. Traditionally, inventory has been used to cushion against lapses in coordination, and these inventories can be quite large. Ohno struggled for five years trying to come up with a system to improve the coordination between processes and thereby eliminate the need for large amounts of inventory. He finally got the idea for his *pull* system from another American classic, the supermarket. Ohno read (and later observed) that Americans do not keep large stocks of food at home. Instead, they make

Figure 16.5
Worker Routes Lengthen as Volume Decreases

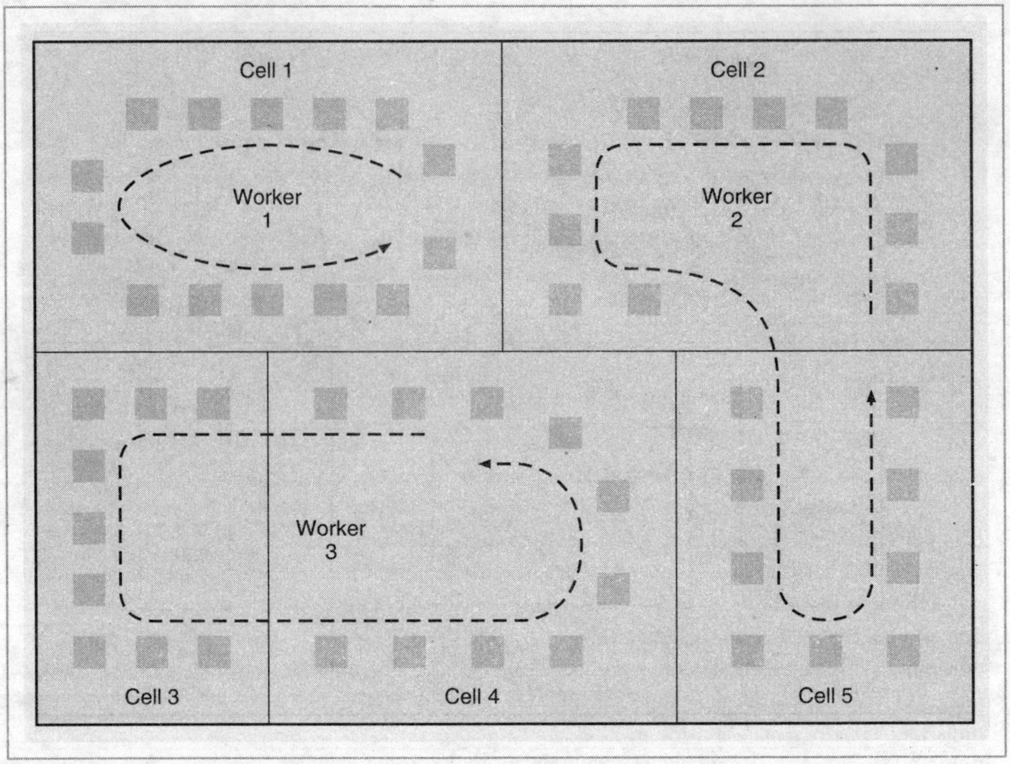

frequent visits to nearby supermarkets to purchase items as they need them. The supermarkets, in turn, carefully control their inventory by replenishing items on their shelves only as they are removed. Customers actually "pull through" the system the items they need, and supermarkets do not order more items than can be sold.

Applying this concept to manufacturing requires a reversal of the normal process/information flow, called a *push* system. In a **push system**, a schedule is prepared in advance for a series of workstations, and each workstation pushes its completed work to the next station. With the **pull system**, workers go back to previous stations and take only the parts or materials they need and can process immediately. When their output has been taken, workers at the previous station know it is time to start producing more, and they replenish the exact quantity that the subsequent station just took away. If their output is not taken, workers at the previous station simply stop production; no excess is produced. This system forces operations to work in coordination with one another. It prevents overproduction and underproduction; only necessary quantities are produced. "Necessary" is not defined by a schedule that specifies what ought to be needed; rather, it is defined by the operation of the shop floor, complete with unanticipated occurrences and variations in performance.

Although the concept of pull production seems simple, it can be difficult to implement because it is so different from normal scheduling procedures. After several years of experimenting with the pull system, Ohno found it necessary to introduce *kanbans* to exercise more control over the pull process on the shop floor.

KANBANS

Kanban is the Japanese word for card. In the pull system, each kanban corresponds to a standard quantity of production or size of container. A kanban contains basic information such as part number, brief description, type of container, unit load (i.e., quantity per container), preceding station (where it came from), and subsequent station (where it goes to). Sometimes the kanban is color-coded to indicate raw

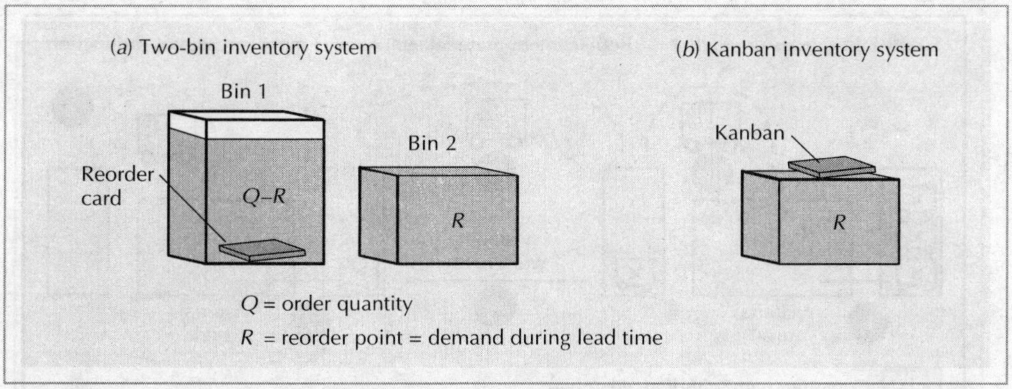

Figure 16.6
The Origin of Kanban

materials or other stages of manufacturing. The information on the kanban does not change during production. The same kanban can rotate back and forth between preceding and subsequent workstations.

Kanbans are closely associated with the fixed-quantity inventory system we discussed in Chapter 13. Recall that in the fixed-quantity system, a certain quantity, Q, is ordered whenever the stock on hand falls below a reorder point. The reorder point is determined so that demand can be met while an order for new material is being processed. Thus, the reorder point corresponds to demand during lead time. A visual fixed-quantity system, called the *two-bin system*, illustrates the concept nicely. Referring to Figure 16.6*a*, two bins are maintained for each item. The first (and usually larger) bin contains the order quantity minus the reorder point, and the second bin contains the reorder point quantity. At the bottom of the first bin is an order card that describes the item and specifies the supplier and the quantity that is to be ordered. When the first bin is empty, the card is removed and sent to the supplier as a new order. While the order is being filled, the quantity in the second bin is used. If everything goes as planned, when the second bin is empty, the new order will arrive and both bins will be filled again.

Ohno looked at this system and liked its simplicity, but he could not understand the purpose of the first bin. As shown in Figure 16.6*b*, by eliminating the first bin and placing the order card (which he called a *kanban*) at the top of the second bin, $(Q - R)$ inventory could be eliminated. In this system, an order is continually in transit. When the new order arrives, the supplier is reissued the same kanban to fill the order again. The only inventory that is maintained is the amount needed to cover usage until the next order can be processed. This concept is the basis for the kanban system.

Kanbans do not make the schedule of production; they maintain the discipline of pull production by authorizing the production and movement of materials. If there is no kanban, there is no production. If there is no kanban, there is no movement of material. There are many different types and variations of kanbans. The most sophisticated is probably the dual kanban system used by Toyota, which uses two types of kanbans: *production kanbans* and *withdrawal kanbans*. As their names imply, a **production kanban** is a card authorizing production of goods, and a **withdrawal kanban** is a card authorizing the movement of goods. Each kanban is physically attached to a container or cart. As shown in Figure 16.7, an empty cart signals production or withdrawal of goods. Kanbans are exchanged between containers as needed to support the pull process.

The dual kanban approach is used when material is not necessarily moving between two consecutive processes, or when there is more than one input to a process and the inputs are dispersed throughout the facility (as for an assembly process). If the processes are tightly linked, other types of kanbans can be used.

Figure 16.8*a* shows the use of kanban squares placed between successive workstations. A **kanban square** is a marked area that will hold a certain number of output items (usually one or two). If the kanban square following his or her process is empty, the worker knows it is time to begin production again. *Kanban racks*, also known as *supermarkets*, are illustrated in Figure 16.8*b*. When the allocated slots on a rack or shelf are empty, workers know it is time to begin a new round of production to fill up

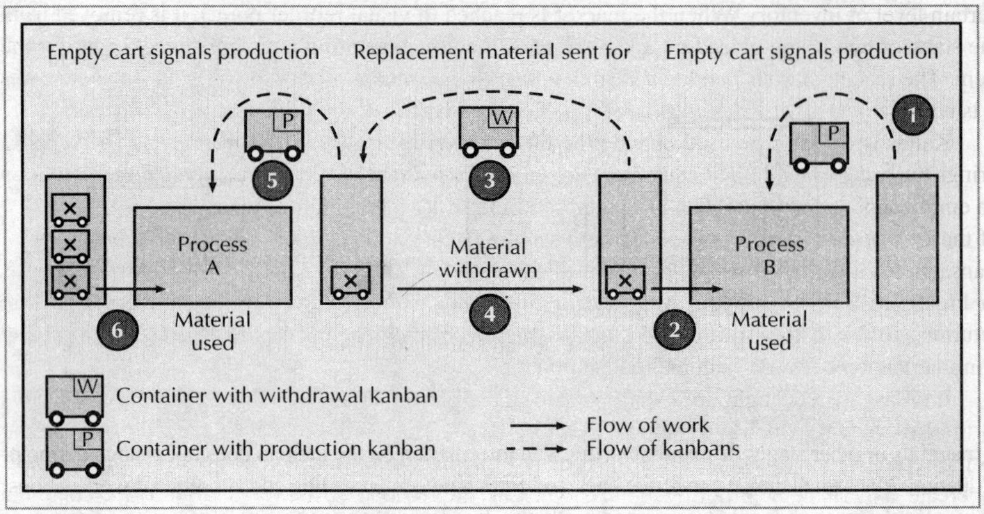

Figure 16.7
Dual Kanbans

the slots. Often, these racks or shelves will be open-backed and placed between two operations with the operator on one side using the material on the racks and the operator on the other side replenishing the material. If the distance between stations prohibits the use of kanban squares or racks, the signal for production can be a colored golf ball rolled down a tube, a flag on a post, a light flashing on a board, or an electronic or verbal message requesting more.

Signal kanbans are used when inventory between processes is still necessary. It closely resembles the reorder point system. As shown in Figure 16.8*c*, a triangular marker is placed at a

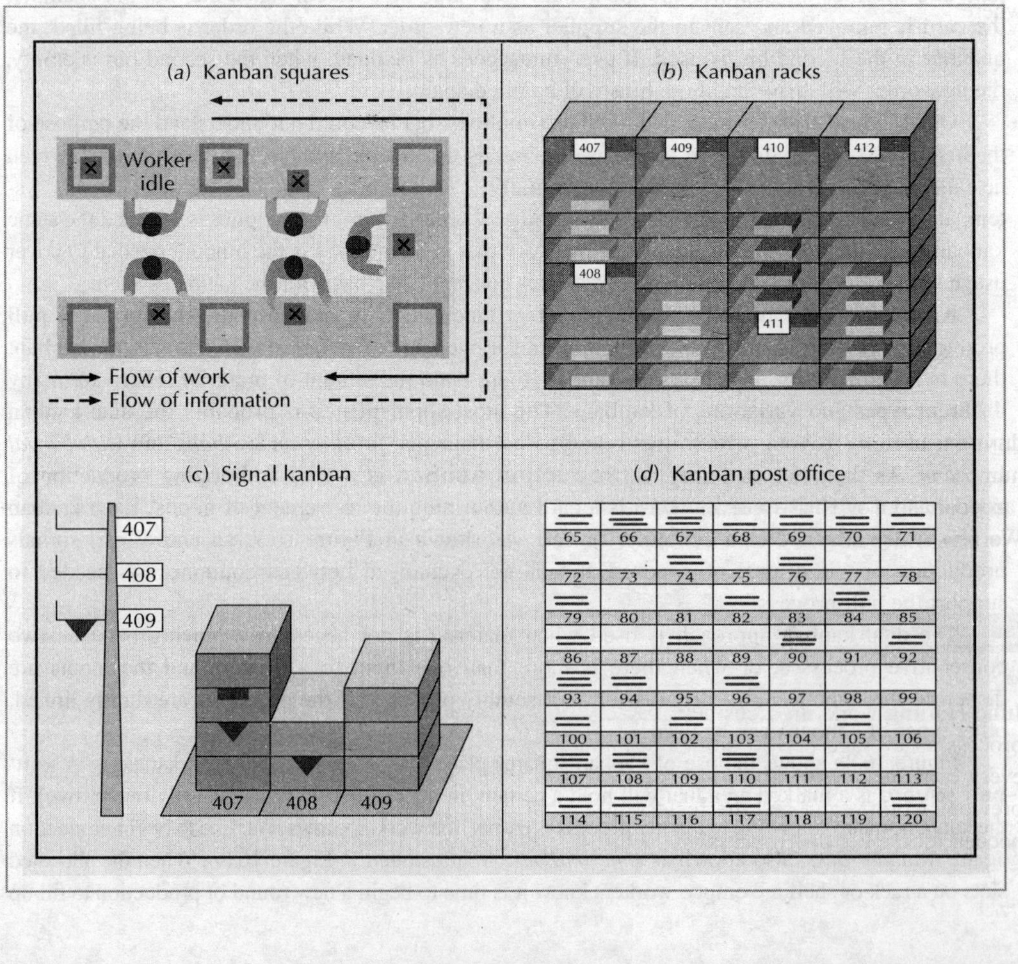

Figure 16.8
Other Types of Kanbans

certain level of inventory. When the marker is reached (a visual reorder point), it is removed from the stack of goods and placed on a kanban post, thereby generating a replenishment order for the item. The rectangular-shaped kanban in the diagram is called a **material kanban**. In some cases it is necessary to order the *material* for a process in advance of the initiation of the process.

Kanbans can also be used outside the factory to order material from suppliers. The supplier brings the order (e.g., a filled container) directly to its point of use in the factory and then picks up an empty container with kanban to fill and return later. It would not be unusual for 5,000 to 10,000 of these **supplier kanbans** to rotate between the factory and suppliers. To handle this volume of transactions, a kind of kanban "post office" can be set up, with the kanbans sorted by supplier, as in Figure 16.8*d*. The supplier then checks his or her "mailbox" to pick up new orders before returning to the factory. Bar-coded kanbans and electronic kanbans can also be used to facilitate communication between customer and supplier.

It is easy to get caught up with the technical aspects of kanbans and lose sight of the objective of the pull system, which is to reduce inventory levels. The kanban system is actually very similar to the reorder point system. The difference is in application. The reorder point system attempts to create a permanent ordering policy, whereas the kanban system encourages the continual reduction of inventory. We can see how that occurs by examining the formula for determining the number of kanbans needed to control the production of a particular item.

$$\text{No. of kanbans} = \frac{\text{average demand during lead time} + \text{safety stock}}{\text{container size}}$$

$$N = \frac{\bar{d}L + S}{C}$$

where

N = number of kanbans or containers

$\bar{d}$ = average number of units demanded over some time period

L = lead time; the time it takes to replenish an order (expressed in the same terms as demand)

S = safety stock; usually given as a percentage of demand during lead time but can be based on service level, lead time and the standard deviation of demand during lead time (as in Chapter 13)

C = container size

To force the improvement process, the container size is usually much smaller than the demand during lead time. At Toyota, containers can hold at most 10% of a day's demand. This allows the number of kanbans (i.e., containers) to be reduced one at a time. The smaller number of kanbans (and corresponding lower level of inventory) causes problems in the system to become visible. Workers and managers then attempt to solve the problems that have been identified.

EXAMPLE 16.1

DETERMINING THE NUMBER OF KANBANS

Julie Hurling works in a cosmetic factory filling, capping, and labeling bottles. She is asked to process an average of 150 bottles per hour through her work cell. If one kanban is attached to every container, a container holds 25 bottles, it takes 30 minutes to receive new bottles from the previous workstation, and the factory uses a safety stock factor of 10%, how many kanbans are needed for the bottling process?

(*Continued*)

SOLUTION

Given:

$$d = 150 \text{ bottles per hour}$$
$$L = 30 \text{ minutes} = 0.5 \text{ hour}$$
$$S = 0.10\,(150 \times 0.5) = 7.5$$
$$C = 25 \text{ bottles}$$

Then,

$$N = \frac{dL + S}{C} = \frac{(150 \times 0.5) + 7.5}{25}$$

$$= \frac{75 + 7.5}{25} = 3.3 \text{ kanbans or containers}$$

Round either up or down (three containers would force the factory to improve operations, and four would allow some slack).

SMALL LOTS

Small-lot production requires less space and capital investment than systems that incur large inventories. By producing small amounts at a time, processes can be physically moved closer together and transportation between stations can be simplified. In small-lot production, quality problems are easier to detect and workers show less tendency to let poor quality pass (as they might in a system that is producing huge amounts of an item anyway). Lower inventory levels make processes more dependent on each other. This is beneficial because it reveals errors and bottlenecks more quickly and gives workers an opportunity to solve them.

The analogy of water flowing over a bed of rocks is useful here. As shown in Figure 16.9, the inventory level is like the level of water. It hides problems but allows for smooth sailing. When the inventory level is reduced, the problems (or rocks) are exposed. After the exposed rocks are removed from the river, the boat can again progress, this time more quickly than before.

Although it is true that a company can produce in small lot sizes without using the pull system or kanbans, from experience we know that small-lot production in a push system is difficult to coordinate. Similarly, using large lot sizes with a pull system and kanbans would not be advisable. Let's look more closely at the relationship between small lot sizes, the pull system, and kanbans.

From the kanban formula, it becomes clear that a reduction in the number of kanbans (given a constant container size) requires a corresponding reduction in safety stock or in lead time itself. The need for safety stock can be reduced by making demand and supply more certain. Flexible resources allow the system to adapt more readily to unanticipated changes in demand. Demand fluctuations can also be controlled through closer contact with customers and better forecasting systems. Deficiencies in supply can be controlled through eliminating mistakes, producing only good units, and reducing or eliminating machine breakdowns.

Lead time is typically made up of four components:

- Processing time
- Move time
- Waiting time
- Setup time

Processing time can be reduced by reducing the number of items processed and the efficiency or speed of the machine or worker. *Move time* can be decreased if machines are moved closer

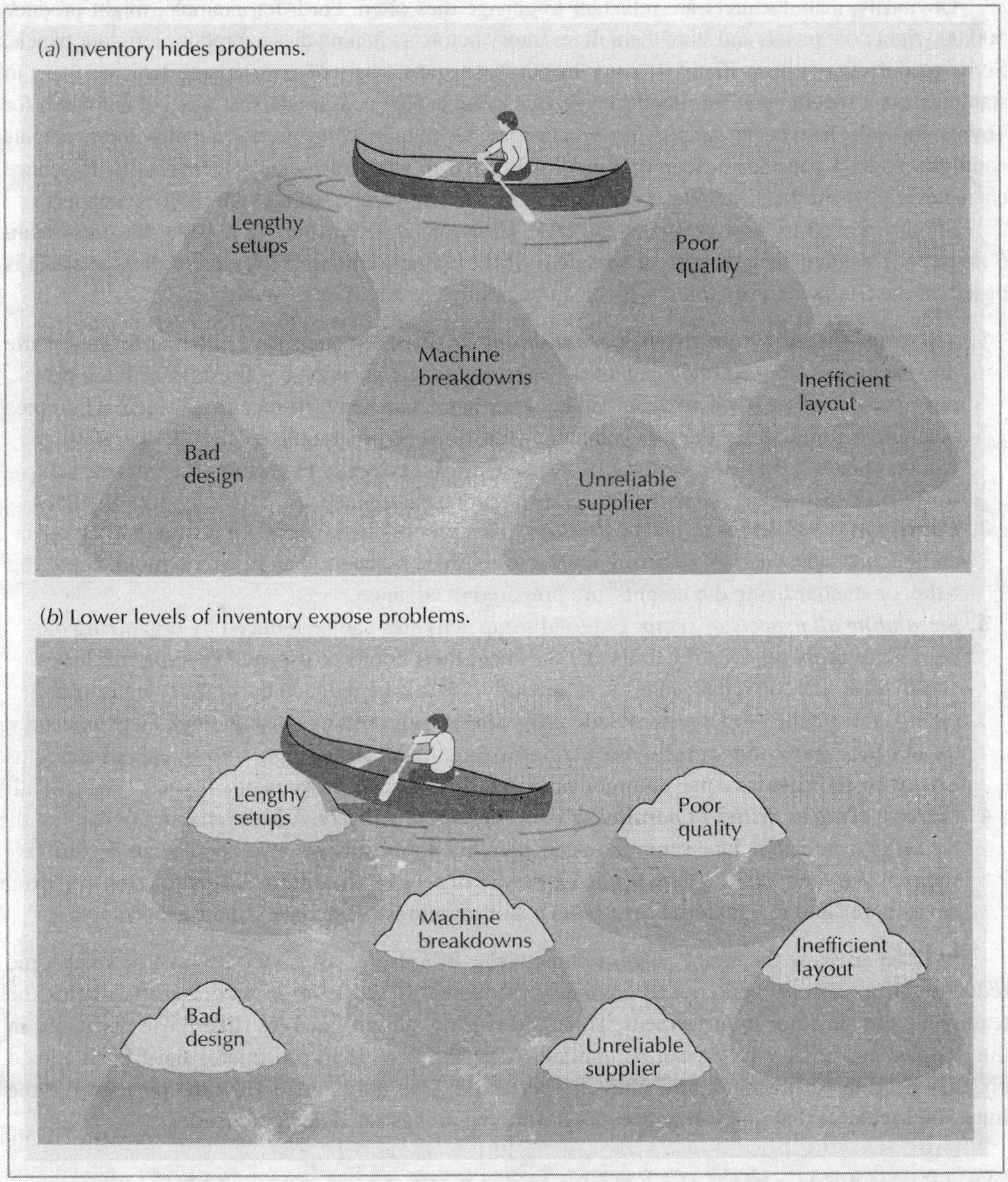

Figure 16.9

Reduced Inventory Makes Problems Visible

together, the method of movement is simplified, routings are standardized, or the need for movement is eliminated. *Waiting time* can be reduced through better scheduling of materials, workers and machines, and sufficient capacity. In many companies, however, lengthy *setup times* are the biggest bottleneck. Reduction of setup time is an important part of lean production.

QUICK SETUPS

Several processes in automobile manufacturing defy production in small lots because of the enormous amount of time required to set up the machines. Stamping is a good example. First, a large roll of sheet steel is run through a blanking press to produce stacks of flat blanks slightly larger than the size of the desired parts. Then, the blanks are inserted into huge stamping presses that contain a matched set of upper and lower dies. When the dies are held together under thousands of pounds of pressure, a three-dimensional shape emerges, such as a car door or fender. Because the dies weigh several tons each and have to be aligned with exact precision, die changes typically take an entire day to complete.

Obviously, manufacturers are reluctant to change dies often. Ford, for example, might produce 500,000 right door panels and store them in inventory before switching dies to produce left door panels. Some manufacturers have found it easier to purchase several sets of presses and dedicate them to stamping out a specific part for months or years. Due to capital constraints, that was not an option for Toyota. Instead, Ohno began simplifying die-changing techniques. Convinced that major improvements could be made, a consultant, Shigeo Shingo, was hired to study die setup systematically, to reduce changeover times further, and to teach these techniques to production workers and Toyota suppliers.

Shingo proved to be a genius at the task. He reduced setup time on a 1000-ton press from 6 hours to 3 minutes using a system he called SMED (single-minute exchange of dies). SMED is based on the following principles, which can be applied to any type of setup:

1. ***Separate internal setups from external setups***. **Internal setups** have to be performed while the machine is stopped; they cannot take place until the machine has finished with the previous operation. **External setups**, on the other hand, can be performed in advance, while the machine is running. By the time a machine has finished processing its current operation, the worker should have completed the external setup and be ready to perform the internal setup for the next operation. Applying this concept alone can reduce setup time by 30% to 50%.
2. ***Convert internal setups to external setups***. This process involves making sure that the operating conditions, such as gathering tools and fixtures, preheating an injection mold, centering a die, or standardizing die heights, are prepared in advance.
3. ***Streamline all aspects of setup***. External setup activities can be reduced by organizing the workplace properly, locating tools and dies near their points of use, and keeping machines and fixtures in good repair. Internal setup activities can be reduced by simplifying or eliminating adjustments. Examples include precoding desired settings, using quick fasteners and locator pins, preventing misalignment, eliminating tools, and making movements easier. Figure 16.10 provides some common analogies for these improvements.
4. ***Perform setup activities in parallel or eliminate them entirely***. Adding an extra person to the setup team can reduce setup time considerably. In most cases, two people can perform a setup in less than half the time needed by a single person. In addition, standardizing components, parts, and raw materials can reduce and sometimes eliminate setup requirements.

In order to view the setup process objectively, it is useful to assign the task of setup-time reduction to a team of workers and engineers. Videotaping the setup in progress often helps the team generate ideas for improvement. Time and motion study principles (like those discussed in the Supplement to Chapter 8) can be applied. After the new setup procedures have been agreed on, they need to be practiced until they are perfected. One only has to view the pit crews at the Indy 500 to realize that quick changeovers have to be orchestrated and practiced.

UNIFORM PRODUCTION LEVELS

The flow of production created by the pull system, kanbans, small lots, and quick setups can only be maintained if production is relatively steady. Lean production systems attempt to maintain **uniform production levels** by smoothing the production requirements on the final assembly line. Changes in final assembly often have dramatic effects on component production upstream. When this happens in a kanban system, kanbans for certain parts will circulate very quickly at some times and very slowly at others. Adjustments of plus or minus 10% in monthly demand can be absorbed by the kanban system, but wider demand fluctuations cannot be handled without substantially increasing inventory levels or scheduling large amounts of overtime.[4]

One way to reduce variability in production is to guard against unexpected demand through more accurate forecasts. To accomplish this, the sales division of Toyota takes the lead in production planning. Toyota Motor Sales conducts surveys of tens of thousands of people twice a year to estimate

[4]P. Y. Huang, L. P. Rees, and B. W. Taylor, "A Simulation Analysis of the Just-in-Time Technique (with Kanbans) for a Multiline, Multistage Production System," *Decision Sciences* (July 1983), pp. 326–345.

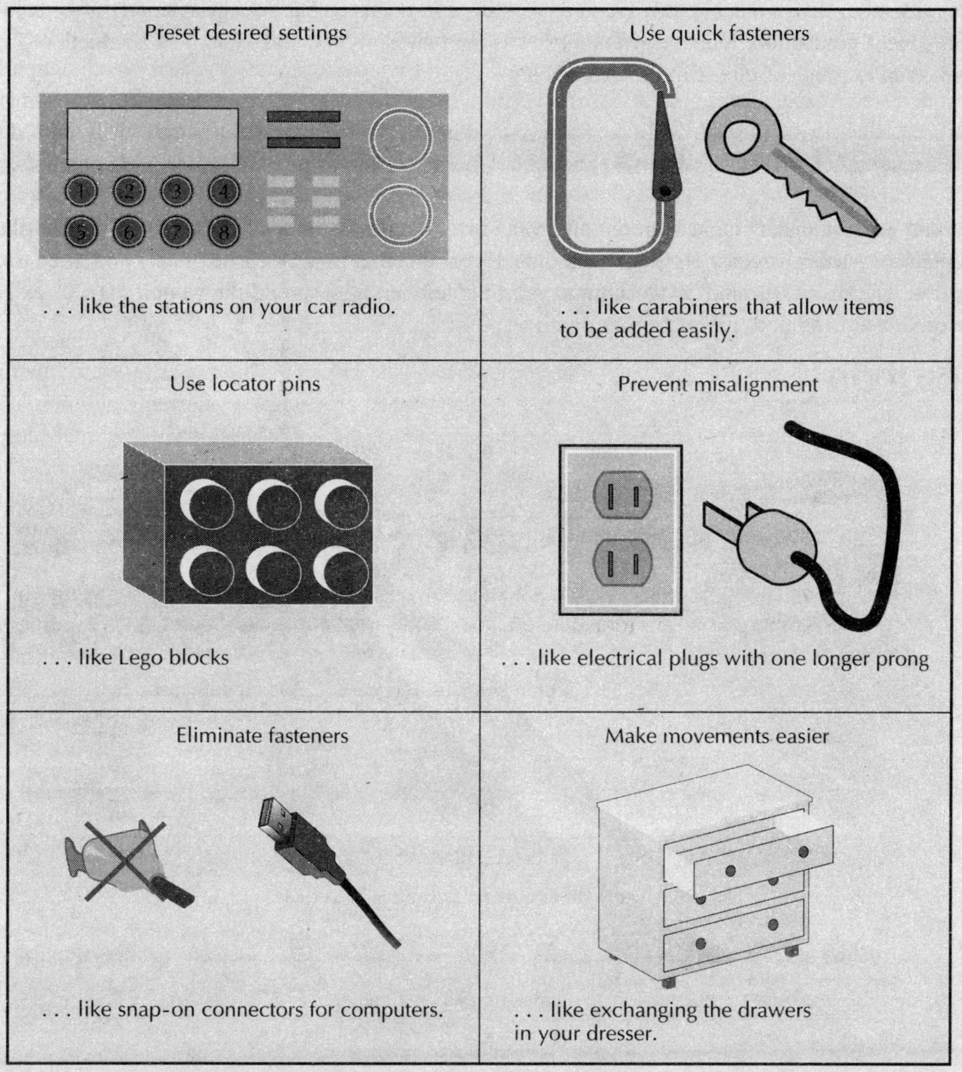

Figure 16.10

Some Common Techniques for Reducing Setup Time

demand for Toyota cars and trucks. Monthly production schedules are drawn up from the forecasts two months in advance. The plans are reviewed one month in advance and then again 10 days in advance. Daily production schedules, which by then include firm orders from dealers, are finalized four days from the start of production. Model mix changes can still be made the evening before or the morning of production. This flexibility is possible because schedule changes are communicated only to the final assembly line. Kanbans take care of dispatching revised orders to the rest of the system.

Another approach to achieving uniform production is to *level* or smooth demand across the planning horizon, a process known as **heijunka**. Demand is divided into small increments of time and spread out as evenly as possible so that the same amount of each item is produced each day, and item production is *mixed* throughout the day in very small quantities. The mix is controlled by the sequence of models on the final assembly line.

Toyota assembles several different vehicle models on each final assembly line. The assembly lines were initially designed this way because of limited space and resources and lack of sufficient volume to dedicate an entire line to a specific model. However, the mixed-model concept has since become an integral part of lean production systems. Daily production is arranged in the same ratio as monthly demand, and jobs are distributed as evenly as possible across the day's schedule. This means that at least some quantity of every item is produced daily, and the company will always have some quantity of an item available to respond to variations in demand. The mix of assembly also steadies component production, reduces inventory levels, and supports the pull system of production. Let's look at an example of mixed-model sequencing.

EXAMPLE 16.2

MIXED-MODEL SEQUENCING

Tyrone Motors makes cars, hybrids, and vans on a single assembly line at its Cleveland plant. September's sales forecast is for 220 vehicles. Hybrids sell at twice the rate of cars and three times the rate of vans. Assuming 20 working days in September, how should the vehicles (H, C, and V) be produced to smooth production as much as possible?

SOLUTION

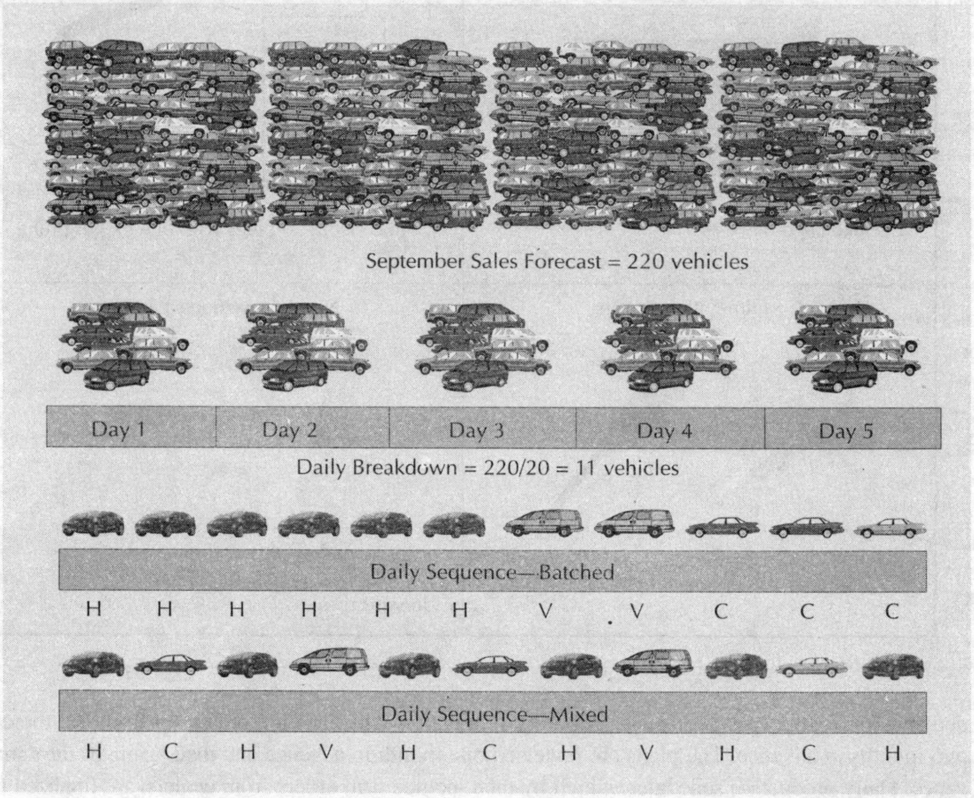

If the preceding example sounds extreme, it is not. Toyota assembles three models in 100 variations on a single assembly line at its Tahara plant, and the mix is juggled daily with almost no warning. The plant is highly automated, and each model carries with it a small yellow disc that transmits instructions to the next workstation. Cars roll off the final assembly line in what looks like unit production—a black Lexus sedan, a blue Camry, a red Lexus sports coupe, a white Corolla, and so on.

This is in sharp contrast to the large lots of similar items produced by mass production factories, in which luxury cars might be produced the first week and a half of the month, midsize cars the second week and a half, and small cars the final week. Under mass production, it's difficult to change product mix midway through the month, and small-car customers would have to wait three to four weeks before their orders would be available.

QUALITY AT THE SOURCE

For lean systems to work well, quality has to be extremely high. There is no extra inventory to buffer against defective units. Producing poor-quality items and then having to rework or reject them is a waste that should be eliminated. Producing in smaller lots encourages better quality. Workers can observe quality problems more easily; when problems are detected, they can be traced to their source and remedied without reworking too many units. Also, by inspecting the first and the last unit in a small batch or by having a worker make a part and then use the part, virtually 100% inspection can be achieved.

Visual Control

Quality improves when problems are made visible and workers have clear expectations of performance. Production systems designed with quality in mind include visible instructions for worker or machine action, and direct feedback on the results of that action. This is known as **visual control**. Examples include kanbans, standard operation sheets, andons, process control charts, and tool boards. A factory with visual control will look different from other factories. You may find machines or stockpoints in each section painted different colors, material-handling routes marked clearly on the floor, demonstration stands and instructional photographs placed near machines, graphs of quality or performance data displayed at each workstation, and explanations and pictures of recent improvement efforts posted by work teams. Figure 16.11 shows several examples of visual control.

Visual control of quality often leads to what the Japanese call a **poka-yoke**. A poka-yoke is any foolproof device or mechanism that prevents defects from occurring. For example, a dial on which desired ranges are marked in different colors is an example of visual control. A dial that shuts off a machine whenever the instrument needle falls above or below the desired range is a poka-yoke. Machines set to stop after a certain amount of production are poka-yokes, as are sensors that prevent the addition of too many items into a package or the misalignment of components for an assembly.

Kaizen

Quality in lean systems is based on **kaizen**, the Japanese term for "change for the good of all" or *continuous improvement*. Recall, we discussed kaizen earlier in Chapter 2. As a practical management system based on trial-and-error experiences in eliminating waste and simplifying operations, lean was created and is sustained through kaizen. Continuous improvement is not something that can be delegated to a department or a staff of experts. It is a monumental undertaking that requires the participation of every employee at every level. The essence of lean success is the willingness of workers to spot quality problems, halt operations when necessary, generate ideas for improvement, analyze processes, perform different functions, and adjust their working routines. In one year alone, workers at Toyota's Georgetown, Kentucky, plant suggested 500 kaizens, 99.8% of which were implemented. Team member ideas helped the plant install the first assembly line shared by a sedan and a minivan.

One of the keys to an effective kaizen is finding the *root cause* of a problem and eliminating it so that the problem does not reoccur. A simple, yet powerful, technique for finding the root cause is the **5 Why's**, a practice of asking "why?" repeatedly until the underlying cause is identified (usually requiring five questions). An often-cited example follows.[5]

5 Why's Example

Problem: The Washington Monument is deteriorating.

1. Why is the monument deteriorating? Because harsh chemicals are used to clean the monument.
2. Why are harsh chemicals used to clean the monument? Because there are a lot of birds in the area that deposit their droppings on the monument.

[5]This example appears in the iSixSigma dictionary, www.isixsigma.com, accessed May 5, 2007.

Figure 16.11

Examples of Visual Control

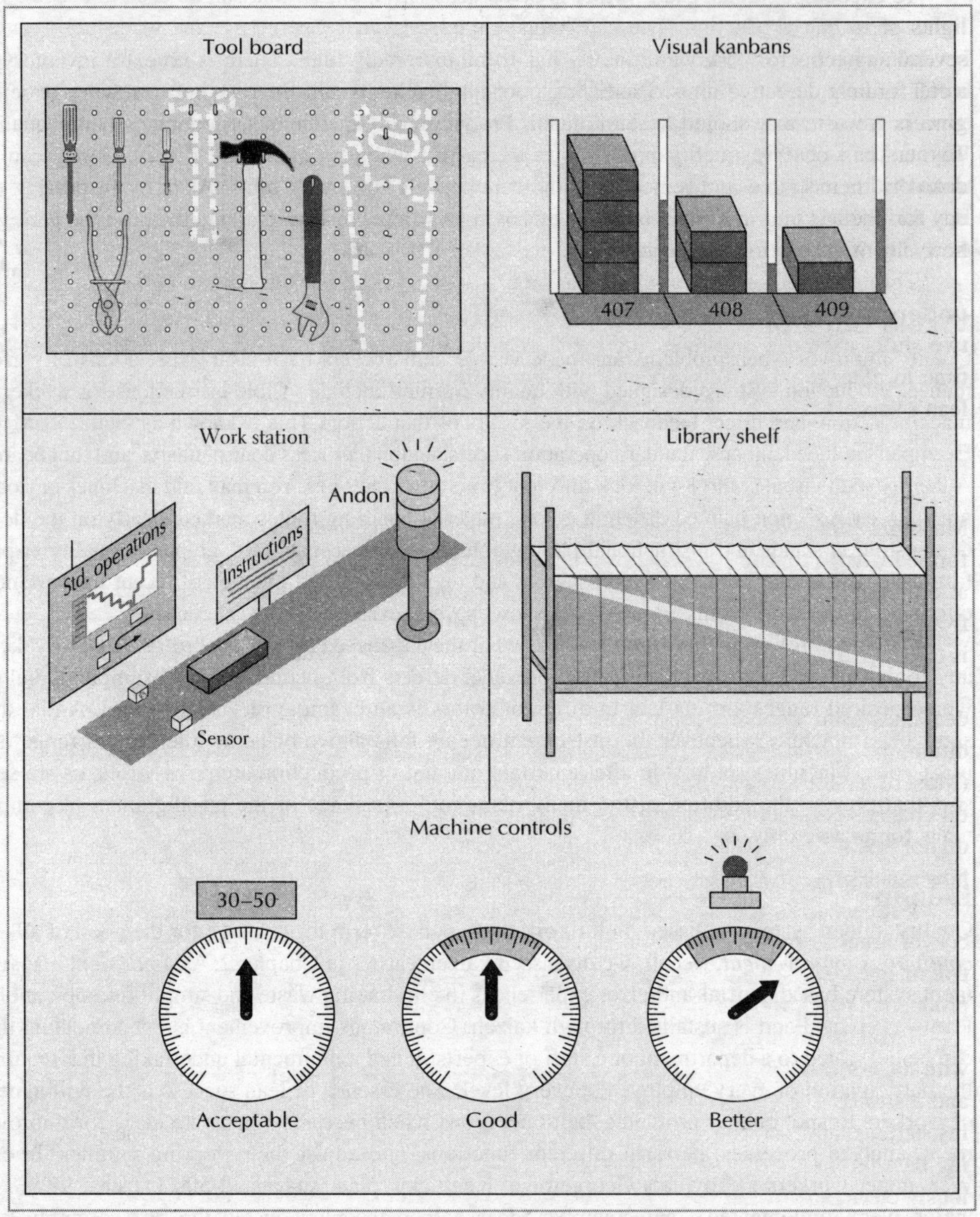

3. Why are there a lot of birds in the area? Because birds eat spiders, and there are a lot of spiders.
4. Why are there a lot of spiders? Because spiders eat gnats, and there are a lot of gnats.
5. Why are there a lot of gnats? Because they are attracted to bright lights at dusk.

Solution: Turn on the monument lights a half hour later.

Jidoka

It was the idea that workers could identify quality problems at their source, solve them, and never pass on a defective item that led Ohno to believe in zero defects. To that end, Ohno was determined that the workers, not inspectors, should be responsible for product quality. To go along with this responsibility, he also gave workers the unprecedented authority of **jidoka**—the authority to stop the production line if quality problems were encountered.

To encourage jidoka, each worker is given access to a switch that can be used to activate call lights or to halt production. The call lights, called **andons**, flash above the workstation and at several andon boards throughout the plant. Green lights indicate normal operation, yellow lights are a call for help, and red lights indicate a line stoppage. Supervisors, maintenance personnel, and engineers are summoned to troubled workstations quickly by flashing lights on the andon board. At Toyota, the assembly line is stopped for an average of 20 minutes a day because of jidoka. Each jidoka drill is recorded on easels kept at the work area. A block of time is reserved at the end of the day for workers to go over the list and work on solving the problems raised. For example, an eight-hour day might consist of seven hours of production and one hour of problem solving.

This concept of allocating extra time to a schedule for nonproductive tasks is called **undercapacity scheduling**. Another example of undercapacity scheduling is producing for two shifts each day and reserving the third shift for preventive maintenance activities. Making time to plan, train, solve problems, and maintain the work environment is an important part of lean's success.

TOTAL PRODUCTIVE MAINTENANCE

Machines cannot operate continuously without some attention. Maintenance activities can be performed when a machine breaks down to restore the machine to its original operating condition, or at different times during regular operation of the machine in an attempt to prevent a breakdown from occurring. The first type of activity is referred to as **breakdown maintenance**; the second is called **preventive maintenance**.

Breakdowns seldom occur at convenient times. Lost production, poor quality, and missed deadlines from an inefficient or broken-down machine can represent a significant expense. In addition, the cost of breakdown maintenance is usually much greater than preventive maintenance. (Most of us know that to be true from our own experience at maintaining an automobile. Regular oil changes cost pennies compared to replacing a car engine.) For these reasons, most companies do not find it cost-effective to rely solely on breakdown maintenance. The question then becomes, how much preventive maintenance is necessary and when should it be performed?

With accurate records on the time between breakdowns, the frequency of breakdowns, and the cost of breakdown and preventive maintenance, we can mathematically determine the best preventive maintenance schedule. But even with this degree of precision, breakdowns can still occur. Lean production requires more than preventive maintenance—it requires *total productive maintenance*.

Total productive maintenance (TPM) combines the practice of preventive maintenance with the concepts of total quality—employee involvement, decisions based on data, zero defects, and a strategic focus. Machine operators maintain their own machines with daily care, periodic inspections, and preventive repair activities. They compile and interpret maintenance and operating data on their machines, identifying signs of deterioration prior to failure.[6] They also scrupulously clean equipment, tools, and workspaces to make unusual occurrences more noticeable. Oil spots on a clean floor may indicate a machine problem, whereas oil spots on a dirty floor would go unnoticed. In Japan this is known as the 5 S's—*seiri, seiton, seiso, seiketsu,* and *shitsuke*—roughly translated as sort, set, shine, standardize, and sustain. Table 16.1 explains the 5 S's in more detail.

In addition to operator involvement and attention to detail, TPM requires management to take a broader, strategic view of maintenance. That means:

- Designing products that can easily be produced on existing machines;
- Designing machines for easier operation, changeover, and maintenance;
- Training and retraining workers to operate and maintain machines properly;
- Purchasing machines that maximize productive potential; and
- Designing a preventive maintenance plan that spans the entire life of each machine.

[6]Maintaining and repairing your own machine is called *autonomous maintenance*. Collecting data and designing maintenance remedies based on the data collected is referred to as *predictive maintenance*.

TABLE 16.1 5S Workplace Scan

5S's	Goal	Eliminate or Correct
1. Seiri (*sort*)	Keep only what you need	Unneeded equipment, tools, furniture; unneeded items on walls or bulletin boards, items blocking aisles or stacked in corners; unneeded inventory, supplies or parts; safety hazards
2. Seiton (*set in order*)	A place for everything and everything in its place	Items not in their correct places; correct places not obvious; aisles, workstations, and equipment locations not indicated; items not put away immediately after use
3. Seiso (*shine*)	Cleaning, and looking for ways to keep clean and organized	Floors, walls, stairs, equipment, and surfaces not clean; cleaning materials not easily accessible; lines, labels, or signs broken or unclean; other cleaning problems
4. Seiketsu (*standardize*)	Maintaining and monitoring the first three categories	Necessary information not visible; standards not known; checklists missing; quantities and limits not easily recognizable; items can't be located within 30 seconds
5. Shitsuke (*sustain*)	Sticking to the rules	Number of workers without 5S training; number of daily 5S inspections not performed; number of personal items not stored; number of times job instructions not available or up-to-date

SUPPLIER NETWORKS

Supplier support is essential to the success of lean production. Not only do suppliers need to be reliable, their production needs to be synchronized to the needs of the customer they are supplying. Toyota understood this and developed strong long-term working relationships with a select group of suppliers. Supplier plants encircled the 50-mile radius around Toyota City, making deliveries several times a day. Bulky parts such as engines and transmissions were delivered every 15 to 30 minutes. Suppliers who met stringent quality standards could forgo inspection of incoming goods. That meant goods could be brought right to the assembly line or area of use without being counted, inspected, tagged, or stocked.

Suppliers who try to meet the increasing demands of a lean customer without being lean themselves are overrun with inventory and exorbitantly high production and distribution costs. Lean supply involves:

1. ***Long-term supplier contracts.*** Suppliers are chosen on the basis of their ability to meet delivery schedules with high quality at a reasonable cost, and their willingness to adapt their production system to meet increasingly stringent customer requirements. Typical contracts are for three to five years, although some companies will choose a supplier for the life of the product.
2. ***Synchronized production.*** With longer-term contracts, suppliers are able to concentrate on fewer customers. Guaranteed, steady demand with advanced notice of volume changes allows the supplier to synchronize their production with that of the customer. Engineering and quality management assistance may also be provided to the supplier.
3. ***Supplier certification.*** Suppliers go through several stages before certification. Typically, their products undergo quality tests, their production facilities and quality systems are examined, and statistical measures of quality are sent with each shipment. After six months or so with no complications, a certification is issued that exempts the supplier from incoming quality and quantity inspections. In spite of certification, many companies bill their suppliers for the damage incurred by a defective part, such as the cost of a line shutdown or product recall.

4. ***Mixed loads and frequent deliveries.*** A lean supplier is an extension of the customer's assembly line. Small quantities may be delivered several times a day (or even hourly) directly to their point of use in the customer's factory. This usually involves smaller trucks containing a mixed load of goods. Different suppliers often join together to consolidate deliveries or share local warehouses.
5. ***Precise delivery schedules.*** Delivery windows to specific locations (docks, bays, or areas along an assembly line) can be as short as 15 minutes. Penalties for missing delivery times are high. One automobile company penalizes its suppliers $32,000 for each hour a delivery is late. With such tight schedules, signing for and paying for a shipment at the time of delivery is too time-consuming. Paying at regular intervals for shipments documented with bar codes or RFID[7] tags is more in tune with lean.
6. ***Standardized, sequenced delivery.*** Using standardized containers and exchanging full containers for empty ones upon delivery also speeds the delivery and replenishment process. In some cases, deliveries made directly to the manufacturer are sequenced in the order of assembly. Nissan, for example, receives deliveries of vehicle seats four times an hour and notifies the supplier two hours in advance with the exact sequence (size and color) in which seats are to be unloaded.
7. ***Locating in close proximity to the customer.*** With the increased number of deliveries in lean production, it is imperative that the source of supply be located close to the customer. When geographic distances between supplier and customer prohibit daily deliveries, suppliers may need to establish small warehouses near to the customer or consolidate warehouses with other suppliers. Trucking firms increasingly use consolidation warehouses as load-switching points for JIT delivery to various customers. Maintaining close proximity can mean relocating around the world, as shown by the number of suppliers who have moved to China and other Asian countries in support of their customers.

Implementing Lean Systems

Firms that have tried to implement lean by slashing inventory and demanding that their suppliers make frequent deliveries have missed the power of the system. Supplier deliveries and kanbans are some of the last elements of lean production to implement. Today, globalization and tough times have brought a new generation of manufacturers and suppliers into the lean fold.

The firms that are most successful in implementing lean production understand the breadth and interrelatedness of the concepts and have adapted them to their own particular environment. This makes sense when you consider the essence of lean—eliminate waste, speed up changeovers, work closely with suppliers, streamline the flow of work, use flexible resources, pay attention to quality, expose problems, and use worker teams to solve problems. None of these concepts or techniques are new or particularly revolutionary. How they are applied can differ considerably from company to company. What is unique and remarkable is how the pieces are tied together into a finely tuned operating system and how synchronized that system can be with both the external and internal business environments.

Lean applications on U.S. soil, whether in Japanese or U.S. run plants, differ somewhat from the original Japanese versions. Lean U.S. plants are typically larger, deliveries from suppliers are less frequent, more buffer inventory is held (because of the longer delivery lead times), and kanbans are very simple compared to lean plants in Japan. Worker-designed feedback systems are different, too. At the Nissan plant in Tennessee, workers are reminded to change workstations along an S-shaped assembly line by the changing tempo of piped-in music (from country to rock). Morning calisthenics are out for most U.S. plants, but the placement of ping-pong tables and basketball hoops alongside the assembly line for exercise during worker-designated breaks is popular. The slow pace of continuous improvement is hard to maintain for American workers. Thus, *kaizen blitzes*, intense process improvement over a week's time with immediate results, are easier and more energizing to conduct.

[7]RFID tags are radio frequency IDs that can store updated information on an item.

ALONG THE SUPPLY CHAIN

The Path to Lean at Nike's Supplier in Vietnam

Chang Shin, Inc. is one of Nike's main footwear manufacturers, producing 20 million pairs of shoes each year. Shin embarked on its lean journey 10 years ago, initially with little success. The company had several factories in Vietnam and China; quality was poor and deliveries late. The CEO attended a seminar on lean and traveled to Toyota to see lean in action. Although the tools of lean were impressive (such as 5S, kanbans, process standardization, cellular layouts, and quick changeovers), it was difficult to change the culture on the factory floor. Few saw the connection between footwear production and electronics or car production. Cost reduction was the main goal.

A lean consultant recommended that Chang Shin begin again very slowly. The company began with 5S. After two or three months, the factory was clean and orderly. Its appearance brought in more orders. The workers were proud of their accomplishments and were ready to move forward. Slowly, attitudes began to change. More employees were trained in lean concepts. Layout and machinery were changed. Inventory went down. Smaller machines were brought it. Workers were cross-trained and production lines became more flexible. Nike was instrumental in providing lean training, most recently at its NOS Innovation and Training Center for contract manufacturers in nearby Ho Chi Minh City.

After 10 years, Shin reports an increase in orders of 154% and an increase in productivity of 23%. Defective returns from customers are down 67%. Labor turnover is half the industry average. Each year the company gets 500,000 employee suggestions for process improvement. Last year, the company saved $2 million at one factory alone. Employees get a percentage of the money saved as an incentive. After a slow start and lots of hard work, Chang Shin has become a model lean factory for Nike.

1. What kind of supplier cooperation does this story illustrate?
2. Do you think lean can be applied in any industry? Explain.
3. Is lean necessarily a slow process? Why or why not?

Source: Based on "Interview with Whanil Jeong," Nike website, http://www.nikebiz.com/crreport/content/workers-and-factories/3-15-0-case-study-interview-with-whanil-jeong.php, accessed January 4, 2013.

THE BENEFITS OF LEAN PRODUCTION

A study of the average benefits accrued to U.S. manufacturers over a five-year period from implementing lean production are impressive: 90% reductions in manufacturing cycle time, 70% reductions in inventory, 50% reductions in labor costs, and 80% reductions in space requirements.

While not every company can achieve results at this level, lean production does provide a wide range of benefits, including:

1. Reduced inventory
2. Improved quality
3. Lower costs
4. Reduced space requirements
5. Shorter lead time
6. Increased productivity
7. Greater flexibility
8. Better relations with suppliers
9. Simplified scheduling and control activities
10. Increased capacity
11. Better use of human resources
12. More product variety

THE DRAWBACKS OF LEAN PRODUCTION

Lean production is not appropriate for every type of organization. Professor Rajan Suri, author of *Quick Response Manufacturing*, notes that the key to lean production is creating flow. To do this, lean manufacturers determine takt times, create a level schedule, and use kanbans to control production. This approach starts to have serious deficiencies when applied to companies that have high variability in demand (takt time breaks down), or large variety of low-volume products (too many kanbans in the system), or custom-engineered products (there are no kanbans for something that is yet to be designed).

Nor is lean production the best choice for high-volume repetitive items where mass production is more common. Even Toyota produces high-demand components (typically, small items that require stamping and forging) in lots as large as 10,000 units, sending them to subsequent processes in small batches only when requested.

Lean production can also present problems when unexpected changes in demand or supply occur. For example, a fire at one supplier's brake factory shut down three Toyota plants one year, and the Japanese tsunami delayed production of GM cars and Apple iPads for months. Add to that possible epidemics, natural disasters, financial meltdowns, terrorist attacks, and armed conflicts, and being completely lean is risky.

Thus, lean production must be compatible with a company's products, processes, and customers. Companies must also assess risk and uncertainty in their business environment, and adapt lean practices accordingly. Even with these drawbacks, however, we have found that most types of businesses can find some parts or processes that can benefit from lean concepts.

Lean Six Sigma

Lean and **Six Sigma** are natural partners for process improvement. The predominance of both techniques in today's corporate environment reinforces the value of both continuous and breakthrough improvements. Lean concentrates on eliminating waste and creating flow while Six Sigma reduces variability and enhances process capabilities. Lean is associated more with continuous improvement, whereas Six Sigma quality often requires breakthrough improvements.

Lean's kaizen initiatives enable Six Sigma by streamlining processes and empowering workers with teamwork and problem-solving skills. Six Sigma provides sophisticated statistical techniques to solve the more complex problems uncovered by lean systems. Together they accelerate the rate of process improvement and help sustain the results.

An important tool in Lean Six Sigma projects is value stream mapping, discussed in the next section.

Value Stream Mapping (VSM)

Value stream mapping (VSM) is a tool for analyzing process flow and eliminating waste. Maps of the current state and the future state of a system are created. VSM has several special icons, as shown in Exhibit 16.1, that differ from traditional flowcharts. These are related to lean production methods and include different types of kanbans, as well as material and information flows for both pull and push systems, and "aha" kaizen bursts. At the heart of the map are process icons with accompanying data boxes denoting the number of workers, cycle time (C/T), changeover time (C/O), and other relevant information about the process. Process steps are connected with arrows and typically include inventory or waiting time icons in-between the steps. A stepped timeline of metrics placed under the process flow separates value-added from non–value-added time or resources. This provides a basis for the improvement initiative, that is, redesigning the process with a new value stream map that reduces or eliminates the waste and inefficiencies that have been identified.

EXHIBIT 16.1 Value Stream Mapping Symbols in Microsoft Visio

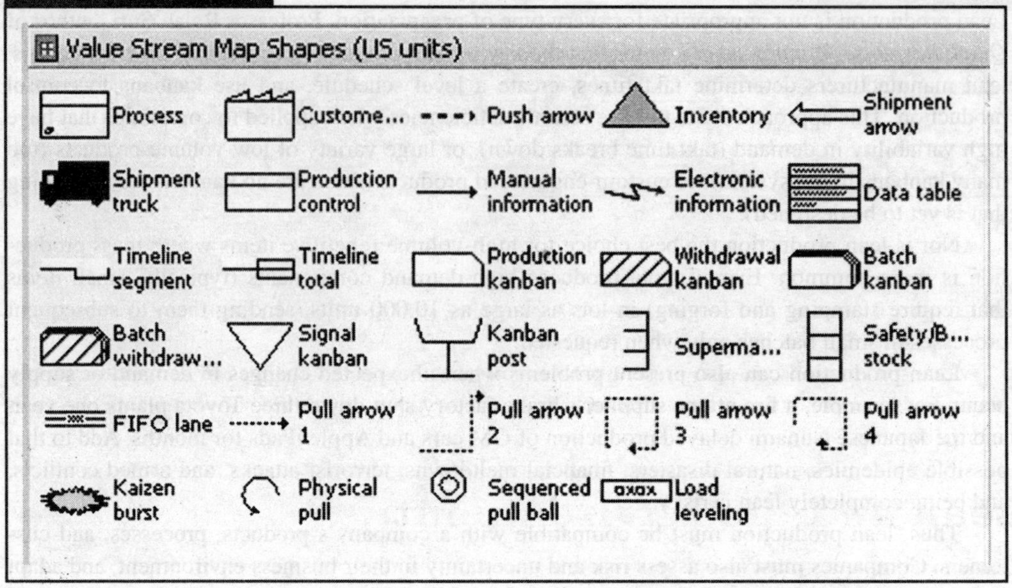

Exhibit 16.2 shows two steps of a process with both time and environmental metrics, and Exhibit 16.3 shows a value stream map for an emergency room. While initially used primarily in manufacturing, value stream maps have become an essential tool for improvements in the service sector. Creating the maps with a group of stakeholders helps create buy-in when process changes are proposed. The maps are created by "going to see" the process in action, rather than from memory.

EXHIBIT 16.2 A Simple Value Stream Map

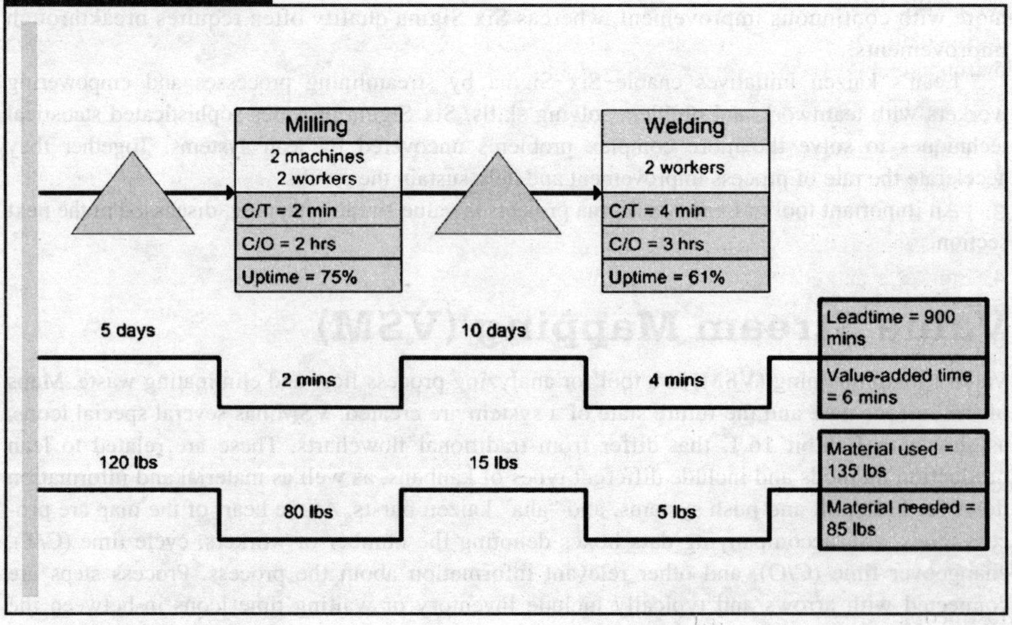

Key: C/T = cycle time
C/O = change over time

Source: Adapted from Environment Protection Agency, "Value Stream Mapping," *Lean and the Environment Toolkit*, retrieved from http://www.epa.gov/lean/toolkit/ch3.htm.

EXHIBIT 16.3 Emergency Room Value Stream Map

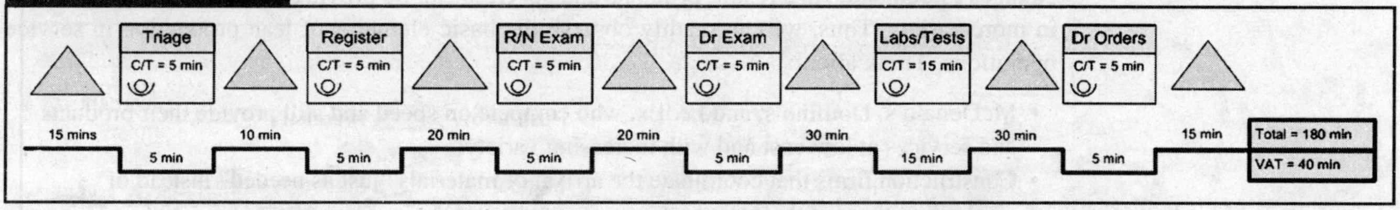

Key: C/T = cycle time
VAT = value added time

Source: Adapted from E. Dickson, S. Singh, D. Cheung, C. Wyatt, and A. Nugent, "Application of Lean Manufacturing Techniques in the Emergency Department," *The Journal of Emergency Medicine* 37, issue 2 (August 2009): pp. 177–182.

Value stream maps are also important tools for reducing energy and material consumption in a company's sustainability efforts. The next section describes the partnership between lean and the environment.

Lean and the Environment

Lean's mandate to eliminate waste and operate only with those resources that are absolutely necessary aligns well with environmental initiatives. Managers and workers can be trained to identify environmental wastes and improvement opportunities alongside the many other wastes and improvement opportunities uncovered by lean. This provides several benefits to business, industry, and consumers.

Environmental waste is often an indicator of poor process design and inefficient production. Applying lean concepts can significantly reduce material costs, energy costs, and regulatory compliance costs, as well as unnecessary risks to worker health and safety. Learning to see environmental wastes during process improvement efforts can open significant business improvement opportunities and further strengthen lean results. In addition, as consumer and societal concerns about the environment increase, companies that provide products or services with fewer environmental impacts can gain market share and create a sustainable competitive advantage.

Recognizing the potential gains from integrating lean and environmental initiatives, the U.S. Environmental Protection Agency (EPA) recommends that companies:

1. Commit to eliminate environmental waste through lean implementation. Add environmental waste to the seven wastes of lean.
2. Involve staff with environmental expertise in planning for and implementing lean events.
3. Find and drive out environmental wastes in specific processes by using lean process-improvement tools, such as the 5 Whys, visual control, and poka-yokes.
4. Empower and enable workers to eliminate environmental wastes in their work areas through 6S (e.g., 5S + safety) workplace evaluations.
5. Recognize new improvement opportunities by incorporating environmental, health, and safety icons and data into value stream maps. Include environmental metrics in the lean metrics of a process.[8]

As you can see, lean has many applications in the environment. We discuss lean in the service section next.

Lean Services

Most people who think of lean production as a system for reducing inventory do not consider the system to be applicable to services. However, you know from reading this chapter that lean production consists of more than low inventory levels. It eliminates waste, streamlines

[8]U.S. Environmental Protection Agency, *Lean and the Environment Toolkit*, retrieved from http://www.epa.gov/lean.

operations, promotes fast changeovers and close supplier relations, and adjusts quickly to changes in demand. As a result, products and services can be provided quickly, at less cost, and in more variety. Thus, we can readily observe the basic elements of lean production in service operations. Think about:

- McDonald's, Domino's, and FedEx, who compete on speed and still provide their products and services at low cost and with increasing variety;
- Construction firms that coordinate the arrival of materials "just as needed" instead of stockpiling them at the site;
- Multifunctional workers in department stores who work the cash register, stock goods, arrange displays, and make sales;
- Level selling with "everyday low prices" at Walmart and Food Lion;
- Work cells at fast-food restaurants that allow workers to be added during peak times and reduced during slow times;
- "Dollar" stores that price everything the same and simply count the number of items purchased as the customer leaves;
- Process mapping that has streamlined operations and eliminated waste in many services (especially in processing information);
- Medical facilities that have the flexibility to fill prescriptions, perform tests, and treat patients without routing them from one end of the building to another;
- JIT publishing that allows professors to choose material from a variety of sources and construct a custom-made book in the same amount of time off-the-shelf books can be ordered and at competitive prices;
- Lens providers, cleaners, and car-repair services that can turn around customer orders in an hour;
- Cleaning teams that follow standard operating routines in quickly performing their tasks;
- Supermarkets that replenish their shelves according to what the customer withdraws; and
- Retailers who introduce dozens of new clothing lines each year in smaller quantities.

In addition to these incidences of lean, entire service systems have been redesigned around lean principles. The most prevalent applications are lean retailing, lean banking, and lean healthcare. We also discuss leaning the supply chain.

LEAN RETAILING

Retail stores provide customers with more choices faster than ever before. *Lean retailing*, like lean production, involves smaller, more frequent orders and rapid replenishment of stock. For example, Zara, a Spanish fashion chain, ships new products to its stores around the world every few days, not once a season. The company produces over 11,000 different stock items per year, instead of several hundred. Time-to-market (from design to store) is less than 10 days. That means Zara can keep up with fashion trends and adjust its merchandise accordingly.[9]

LEAN BANKING

Lean banking is practiced by Bank of America, Citibank, Capital One, Jefferson Pilot, and Progressive Insurance, among others. The banking and insurance industries are particularly well suited to lean techniques because of their repetitive processes. Significant savings in both time and money can be achieved through differentiating processes, rationalizing decision approvals, simplifying service offerings, designing services in modules, and standardizing processes.

[9] John Tagliabue, "Spanish Clothing Chain Zara Grows by Being Fast and Flexible," *The New York Times* (May 30, 2003).

LEAN HEALTHCARE

Lean concepts are popular in the healthcare industry. One reason is the interest of corporations in keeping the cost of healthcare down. Pella Corporation loans its employees to a regional health center for "hot teams" to scrutinize medical operations. It was Boeing who convinced 30 executives from Seattle's Virginia Mason Medical Center to spend two weeks in Japan studying Toyota's methods.[10]

In Iowa, a group of manufacturers, including Maytag, formed a task force to facilitate lean best practices in their local healthcare systems. People from hospitals, healthcare providers, third-party insurance providers, and manufacturing executives met together to identify waste and map out the way money and information flows through the healthcare system. The group discovered that every insurance company and employer had specific plans and rules for processing employee healthcare claims, requiring different information on a multitude of forms. The forms were so confusing that much of the processor's time was spent calling the provider for clarifications and reworking returned claims.

At ThedaCare in Wisconsin, a dozen doctors, nurses, and staffers brainstormed ways of cutting a typical hour-long office visit to 30 minutes or less. They constructed a 25-foot process map of a pneumonia patient's office visit, concluding that 17 steps were useful and 51 were not. At the end of the session, the team concluded that doctor's assistants should be assigned to a pool rather than individual doctors and that lab tests should be performed in examining rooms rather than at a central location.

Flowcharts, mistake-proofing, flow management, quick setups, and kaizen are just a few of the lean healthcare tools.

LEANING THE SUPPLY CHAIN

One of the first elements of lean production to receive widespread acclaim among manufacturers was just-in-time inventory. Too often, companies pushed back inventory onto their suppliers in the name of just-in-time. While dominant companies in an industry sought lean objectives within their four walls, outside suppliers suffered. A number of suppliers in the U.S. auto industry were bankrupted by this approach. In the end, the need to hold excess inventory to fulfill a customer's just-in-time mandate resulted in a higher *total* supply chain cost.

Leaning a supply chain means "pulling" a smooth flow of material through a series of suppliers to support frequent replenishment orders and changes in customer demand. To accomplish this, firms need to share information and coordinate demand forecasts, production planning, and inventory replenishment with suppliers and their supplier's suppliers throughout the supply chain.

Developing and maintaining a lean production system within a firm is difficult enough; coordinating a lean supply chain across hundreds of different companies with different goals and cost structures is extremely challenging. The first step is to build a highly collaborative business environment that ensures all of the participants in the supply chain reap the rewards of a leaner system. Adopting the technology to support such a system is purely secondary.

Time, as well as cost, is reduced in a lean supply chain; however, recent trends toward outsourcing great distances lengthen supply chain time and make it more difficult not only to coordinate suppliers but also to ensure their commitment to lean goals. In response, some companies are *nearshoring* products that have volatile demand. Nike, for example, outsources the production of shoes to Asia, but locally produces personalized items such as bags.

[10]The material in this section comes from Patricia Panchak, "Lean Health Care? It Works!" *Industry Week* (November 1, 2003), and Bernard Wysocki, "Industrial Strength: To Fix Health Care, Hospitals Take Tips from Factory Floor," *Wall Street Journal* (April 9, 2004), p. A1.

SUMMARY

Lean production has truly changed the face of manufacturing and transformed the global economy. Originally known as just-in-time (JIT), it began at Toyota Motor Company as an effort to eliminate waste (particularly inventories), but evolved into a system for the continuous improvement of all aspects of manufacturing operations. *Lean production* is both a philosophy and a collection of management methods and techniques. The main advantage of the system is derived from the integration of the techniques into a focused, smooth-running management system.

In lean systems, workers are multifunctional and are required to perform different tasks, as well as aid in the improvement process. Machines are also multifunctional and are arranged in small, U-shaped work cells that enable parts to be processed in a continuous flow through the cell. Workers produce parts one at a time within the cells and transport parts between cells in small lots as called for by subassembly lines, assembly lines, or other work cells. The environment is kept clean, orderly, and free of waste so that unusual occurrences are visible.

Schedules are prepared only for the final assembly line, in which several different models are assembled on the same line. Requirements for component parts and subassemblies are then pulled through the system with kanbans. The principle of the pull system is not to make anything until requested to do so by the next station. The "pull" system will not work unless production is uniform, setups are quick, and lot sizes are low.

The pull system and kanbans are also used to order materials from outside suppliers. Suppliers are fewer in number and must be very reliable. They may be requested to make multiple deliveries of the same item in the same day, so their manufacturing system must be flexible, too. Deliveries are made directly to the factory floor, eliminating stockrooms and the waste of counting, inspecting, recording, storing, and transporting.

Lean production does not produce in anticipation of need. It produces only necessary items in necessary quantities at necessary times. Inventory is viewed as a waste of resources and an obstacle to improvement. Because there is little buffer inventory between workstations, quality must be extremely high, and every effort is made to prevent machine breakdowns.

When all these elements are in place, lean systems produce high-quality goods, quickly and at low cost. These systems also are able to respond to changes in customer demand. Lean production systems are most effective in repetitive environments, but elements of lean can be applied to almost any operation, including service operations. Lean retailing, lean banking, and lean healthcare are good examples.

KEY FORMULAS

Determining the number of kanbans

$$N = \frac{\bar{d}L + S}{C}$$

QUESTIONS

16-1. What is the purpose of lean production?

16-2. How did lean production evolve into a system of continuous improvement?

16-3. Why are flexible resources essential to lean production?

16-4. What does a cellular layout contribute to lean production?

16-5. Differentiate between a push and a pull production system.

16-6. How was the concept of kanban developed from the two-bin inventory system?

16-7. How are the kanban system and the reorder point system similar? How are they different?

16-8. Describe how the following kanbans operate:

a. Production and withdrawal kanbans
b. Kanban squares
c. Signal kanbans
d. Material kanbans
e. Supplier kanbans

16-9. What are the advantages of small-lot sizes?

16-10. Why do large-lot sizes not work well with pull systems?

16-11. Why are small-lot sizes not as effective in a push system?

16-12. Explain the principles of SMED. What does SMED try to achieve?

16-13. Why is uniform production important to lean? How is it achieved?

16-14. What are the advantages of mixed-model sequencing?

16-15. How are lean production and quality related? What is Lean Six Sigma?

16-16. How can a balance be struck between the cost of breakdown maintenance and the cost of preventive maintenance?

16-17. Explain the concept of total productive maintenance (TPM).

16-18. What role does the equipment operator play in TPM?

16-19. Preventive maintenance can be viewed as the process of maintaining the "health" of a machine. Using healthcare as an analogy, explain the differences and tradeoffs between breakdown maintenance, preventive maintenance, and total productive maintenance.

16-20. How are suppliers affected by lean production?

16-21. Suggest several ways that lean requirements can be made easier for suppliers.

16-22. Give examples of visual control. How does visual control affect quality?

16-23. What is a poka-yoke? Give an example.

16-24. Why is worker involvement important to kaizen? Find the Kaizen Institute on the Web and walk through the site. Summarize what you learned.

16-25. What are some typical benefits from implementing lean?

16-26. Which elements of lean are the most difficult to implement? Why?

16-27. In what type of environment is lean production most successful?

16-28. Give examples of lean services.

16-29. Lean has been applied extensively in the automobile industry. Report on other industries which use lean production.

16-30. Explain how lean and concern for the environment are related.

16-31. Discuss the problems of implementing lean production a) in an extended global supply chain, b) during periods of uncertainty or disruption, c) when managers make decisions solely based on cost.

PROBLEMS

16-1. As local developers prepare for an increase in housing starts, they must anticipate their demand for various materials. One such material is tile. Used in bathrooms, kitchens, and for decoration, tiles come in many shapes, colors, and sizes. In order to accommodate the varying needs, the tile manufacturer must schedule its production efficiently. Each month, developers order 30,000 boxes of quarry tile, 15,000 boxes of Italian mosaic tile, and 45,000 boxes of 4-inch bathroom tile. Determine a mixed-model sequence that will efficiently meet these needs. Assume 30 days per month.

16-2. An assembly station is asked to process 100 circuit boards per hour. It takes 20 minutes to receive the necessary components from the previous workstation. Completed circuit boards are placed in a rack that will hold 10 boards. The rack must be full before it is sent on to the next workstation. If the factory uses a safety factor of 10%, how many kanbans are needed for the circuit board assembly process?

16-3. It takes Aaron 15 minutes to produce 10 widgets to fill a container and 5 minutes to transport the container to the next station, where Maria works. Maria's process takes about 30 minutes. The factory uses a safety factor of 20%. Currently, five kanbans rotate between Aaron and Maria's stations. What is the approximate demand for widgets?

16-4. Stan Weakly can sort a bin of 100 letters in 10 minutes. He typically receives 600 letters an hour. A truck arrives with more bins every 30 minutes. The office uses a safety factor of 10%. How many kanbans are needed for the letter-sorting process?

16-5. The office administrator wishes to decrease the number of kanbans in the letter-sorting process described in Problem 16-4. Which of the following alternatives has the greatest effect on reducing the number of kanbans?

a. Eliminating the safety factor.
b. Receiving truck deliveries every 15 minutes
c. Increasing the bin capacity to 300 letters

What is the effect on inventory levels of decreasing the number of kanbans?

16-6. In a large microelectronics plant, the assembly cell for circuit boards has a demand for 200 units an hour. Two feeder cells supply parts A and B to the assembly cell (one A and one B for each board). Standard containers that look like divided trays are used. A container will hold 20 As or 10 Bs. It takes 10 minutes to fill up a container with As and 20 minutes to fill up a container with Bs. Transit time to the assembly cell is 5 minutes for both A and B. No safety factor is used. Set up a kanban control system for the assembly process.

16-7. Universal Motors installed a mixed model assembly line at its Huntsville plant last year when demand for SUVs was still strong. With the rising gas prices, however, SUV and van sales have plummeted, and demand for smaller, more fuel-efficient cars has surged. The plant has the capacity to produce 200 vehicles per day. Monthly demand for cars is estimated at 2,000 per month, vans at 1,000 per month and SUVs at 500 per month. The plant is operating at a slow-down schedule of 20 days per month.

a. Design a production sequence that will meet demand and level production of the various models.
b. How many times will that sequence be repeated per day?
c. Explain how the sequence you propose allows quicker adjustments to demand changes. What impact does it have on component demand?

16-8. Solvo produces three types of trucks on one assembly line: the long-haul (L), the short-haul (S) and the vocational truck (V). Next month the company has orders for 500 long-haul trucks, 750 short-haul trucks, and 250 vocational trucks. Chris Riggs, the production manager for Solvo, wants to try uniform production and mixed-model sequencing. Assuming 25 working days per month, what assembly sequence would you recommend and how many times per day should the sequence be repeated?

16-9. Backyard Equipment manufactures garden tillers, leaf blowers, and lawn mowers for home use in a mixed model assembly line. Annual demand is estimated as 4,500 for garden tillers, 3,000 for leaf blowers, and 9,000 for lawn mowers. The plant is currently operating one shift at an overtime schedule of 25 days per month. Backyard is pursuing the lean principles of uniform production and mixed model assembly.

a. Determine a mixed model production sequence that satisfies the goals of smoothing component production and assembling a variety of products each sequence.
b. How many times would the designed sequence be repeated per day to meet demand?

CASE STUDY

Making Cosmetics Bags Faster

Zibo Cosmetics Bag Ltd. is a major supplier of cosmetic bags throughout Asia. Since its owners started the company in a small fabrication facility, they have continued to expand and increase annual sales. A major component of their marketing and promotional plan is offering a range of cosmetic bags that will apply to a full range of uses in various situations. The bags come in a uniform size and shape as well as identical colors across all product lines.

This range of cosmetic bags includes a very utilitarian vinyl bag. This bag is the lowest cost bag but unless you look closely or handle it, you would have a difficult time differentiating it from the leather product line.

The leather product line is Zibo's top-of-the-line model. This bag is 100% top-grain leather that, with the exception of the handle, is carefully sewed by individuals.

The third product line is a cloth variety. This product line was recently introduced in response to customers' requests for something that was more durable than vinyl but not as expensive as leather. Keeping with the marketing strategy, Zibo is offering the new cloth cosmetic bag in the same size and colors as the other lines.

One common feature of the cosmetic bags is the handles. Regardless of product lines, all bags receive the same handle. This is the final component to be added to the bag. At the present time, each product line receives large lot size handle orders which are kept in inventory and used as required. The current practice is for a fixed interval inventory renewal process, where each product line receives a full week's handle production every third week. The delivered handle lot size is set to fulfill the next three weeks' fabrication schedule.

During the company expansions and moves, the fabrication lines were designed, constructed and operated as a product or assembly line process. While meeting the company's needs, this does not appear to be the lowest cost process.

In an attempt to better control manufacturing costs, Zibo's management team visited a Toyota manufacturing facility to see how they utilized the kanban system and cellular layout fabrication. Based on this visit, various studies, and reviews, Zibo's team believes that utilizing a kanban system and a cellular layout can reduce costs. They want to try the new system out for the handle assembling process.

The following diagram identifies the current fabrication facility layout.

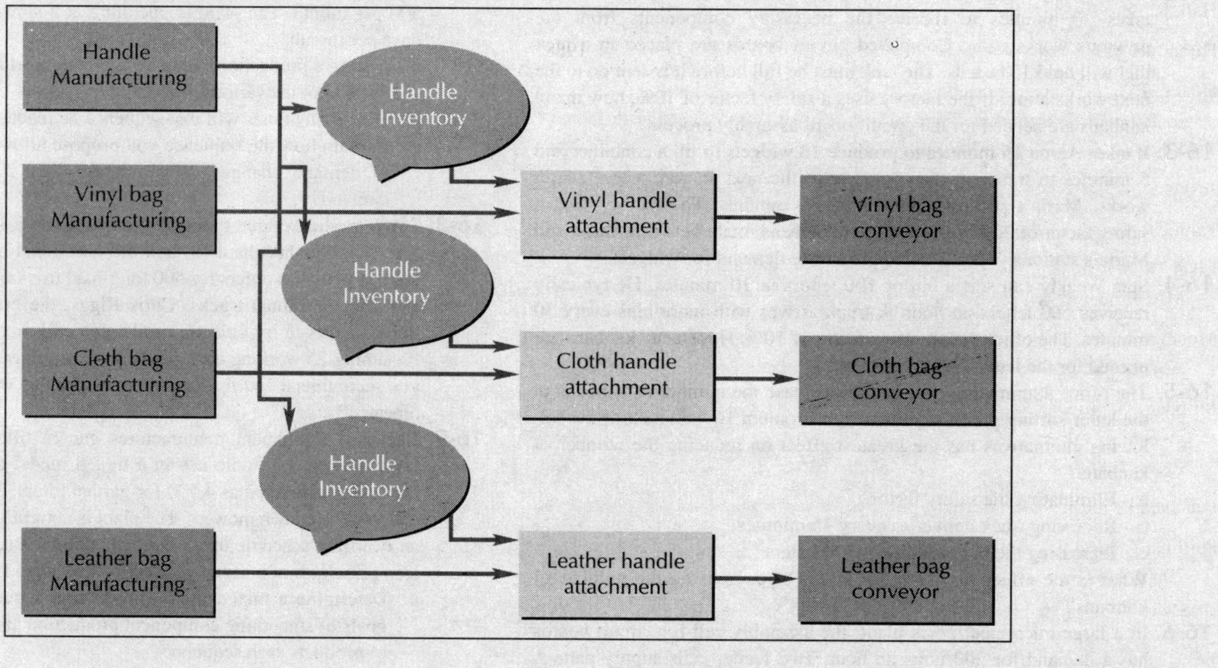

To finish fabricating the vinyl bag, a worker takes a handle from the handle inventory and a bag from the manufacturing inventory. The components are placed in an automated attachment machine which completes the fabrication. Once completed, the worker removes the bag and places it on the conveyor where it goes to packaging.

All bags follow the same process. The handle attachment machine is the same for each bag, but the length of time required varies according to the type of bag. The vinyl bag is the fastest in that it takes about a minute to complete. The leather bag is next and it takes about four minutes to complete the attachment. The cloth bag, being a new product, is taking about six minutes to make the final attachment.

Production demands have remained fairly constant with 96 vinyl, 48 leather, and 48 cloth bags every day. Time studies indicate that one employee can handle the three machines and meet the demand once every 10 minutes.

a. Determine a cellular layout which allows one employee to operate all three machines and meet the daily mix of bags required. Identify the sequence to be followed.

b. Determine the kanban container size required to meet a 15% safety factor, lead time of three days, average demand time of 10 minutes, and the number of containers close to three.

c. What do you see as a potential next step in improving the process?

REFERENCES

Abernathy, F., J. Dunlap, J. Hammond, and D. Weil. *A Stitch in Time: Lean Retailing and the Transformation of Manufacturing—Lessons from the Apparel and Textile Industries*. Oxford, UK: Oxford University Press, 1999.

Black, J. T. *The Design of the Factory with a Future*. New York: McGraw-Hill, 1991.

Bremner, B., and C. Dawson. "Can Anything Stop Toyota?" *BusinessWeek* (November 17, 2003), pp. 114–118.

Brown, S. "Toyota's Global Body Shop." *Fortune* (February 9, 2004), Industrial Edition, http://www.fortune.com/fortune/subs/columnist/0,15704,581557,00.html.

Bylinsky, G. "Heroes of Manufacturing." *Fortune* (March 20, 2000), pp. 192A–205A.

Cusomano, M. *The Japanese Automobile Industry*. Cambridge, MA: Harvard University Press, 1985.

Hall, R. *Zero Inventories*. Homewood, IL: Dow Jones-Irwin, 1983.

Hirano, H. *JIT Factory Revolution*. Cambridge, MA: Productivity Press, 1988.

Huang, P. Y., L. P. Rees, and B. W. Taylor. "A Simulation Analysis of the Just-in-Time Technique (with Kanbans) for a Multiline, Multistage Production System." *Decision Sciences* (July 1983), pp. 326–345.

Jusko, J. "A Look at Lean." *Industry Week* (December 6, 1999), pp. 88–91.

Kinni, T. *America's Best*. New York: Wiley, 1996.

Liker, J. *Becoming Lean: Inside Stories of U.S. Manufacturers*. Cambridge, MA: Productivity Press, 1998.

Monden, Y., ed. *Applying Just-In-Time: The American/Japanese Experience*. Atlanta: Industrial Engineering and Management Press, 1986.

Monden, Y. *Toyota Production System: An Integrated Approach to Just-in-Time*, 3rd ed. Atlanta: Industrial Engineering and Management Press, 1986.

Panchak, P. "Lean Health Care? It Works!" *Industry Week* (November 1, 2003).

Phillips, T. "Building the Lean Machine." *Advanced Manufacturing* (January 1, 2000). http://www.advancedmanufacturing.com.

Sepehri, M. *Just-in-Time, Not Just in Japan*. Falls Church, VA: American Production and Inventory Control Society, 1986.

Shingo, S. *Modern Approaches to Manufacturing Improvement*. Cambridge, MA: Productivity Press, 1990.

Sobek, D., J. Liker, and A. Ward. "Another Look at How Toyota Integrates Product Development." *Harvard Business Review* (July–August 1998), pp. 36–49.

Spear, S. "Comments on the Second Toyota Paradox." Teaching Note 9-602-035, Harvard Business School (March 2003).

Spear, S., and K. Bowen. "Decoding the DNA of the Toyota Production System." *Harvard Business Review* (September–October 1999), pp. 96–106.

Suzaki, K. *The New Manufacturing Challenge*. New York: Free Press, 1985.

Swank, C. "The Lean Service Machine." *Harvard Business Review* (October 2003), pp. 123–131.

Tagliabue, J. "Spanish Clothing Chain Zara Grows by Being Fast and Flexible." *The New York Times* (May 30, 2003).

Tierney, C. "Big Three Play Catch-Up to Toyota Plant Prowess." *Detroit News* (February 22, 2004).

The Toyota Production System. Company brochure. Japan: Toyota Motor Corporation, 1998.

Vasilash, G. "Lean Lessons." *Automotive Manufacturing and Production* (March 2001).

Vasilash, G. "Standardized Lean." *Automotive Manufacturing and Production* (February 2000). http://www.automfg.com.

Ward, A., J. Liker, J. Cristiano, and Durward Sobek II. "The Second Toyota Paradox: How Delaying Decisions Can Make Better Cars Faster." *Sloan Management Review* (Spring 1995), pp. 43–62.

Womack, J., D. Jones, and D. Roos. *The Machine That Changed the World*. New York: Macmillan, 1990.

Womack, J., and D. Jones. *Lean Thinking*. New York: Simon & Schuster, 1996.

Wysocki, B. "Industrial Strength: To Fix Health Care, Hospitals Take Tips from Factory Floor," *The Wall Street Journal* (April 9, 2004), p. A1.

CHAPTER 17

Scheduling

LEARNING OBJECTIVES

AFTER READING THIS CHAPTER, YOU WILL BE ABLE TO:

- Explain the multiple dimensions of a good schedule, and determine which type of schedule is appropriate for different types of productive systems.
- Use several different quantitative techniques for loading, sequencing, and monitoring work.
- Discuss advanced planning and scheduling systems, and contrast finite and infinite scheduling.
- Use the theory of constraints to identify the bottleneck and pace a system to the bottleneck operation.
- Create efficient and equitable employee schedules.

SCHEDULING APPAREL PRODUCTION

There are many types of production processes involved in the jeans supply chain, and thus many different scheduling problems. The production of denim fabric from cotton to fibers to yarn, through weaving, dyeing, and finishing, is highly automated, and has continuous production characteristics. Scheduling of textile equipment involves assigning production to different looms (the assignment method discussed in this chapter), determining the length of the production run or batch size (the economic production quantity from Chapter 13), and monitoring the equipment for performance (speed and feed of fabric, optimal weave patterns, mixtures of dye, heat treatment, multi-pass dyeing and finishing, quality control, maintenance scheduling, etc.). Fabric production is very different from garment construction and normally occurs in separate factories.

Jeans are a consumer product, which indicates that production is usually make-to-stock for a mass market. Customer orders (from retailers) are large but consist of a mix of considerably smaller lots of various styles, sizes, and measurements. Thus, the production process has some characteristics of batch production and some characteristics of mass production. One of the first steps in apparel production is cutting the fabric. Scheduling for this activity involves determining how different patterns can be cut from a swath of cloth so that waste is minimized. This is actually a classic linear programming problem (from Chapter 14S) known as the cutting stock problem. Genetic algorithms (discussed later in the chapter) can also be used to solve this problem. The fabric-cutting department usually feeds several downstream sewing departments and final assembly lines. The sewing process is the most labor intensive of the activities along the jeans supply chain, and scheduling here consists of assigning work to various sewers (called *loading*), and prioritizing the flow of work (called *sequencing*).

In this chapter, we explore different methods for day-to-day scheduling of operations, including employee scheduling and bottleneck scheduling.

Sources: Based on N. I. Karacapilidis, and C. P. Pappis, "Production Planning and Control in Textile Industry: A Case Study," *Computers in Industry* 30, no. 2 (2002); W. K. Wong, C. K. Kwong, P. Y. Mok, and W. H. Ip, "Genetic Optimization of JIT Operation Schedules for Fabric-Cutting Process in Apparel Manufacture," *Journal of Intelligent Manufacturing* 17 (2006): 342–354; "Real Time Monitoring and Planning for the Weaving Mill," *Weavemaster*, www.visionbms.com.

Scheduling specifies *when* labor, equipment, and facilities are needed to produce a product or provide a service. It is the last stage of planning before production takes place. The scheduling function differs considerably based on the type of operation:

- In *process industries,* such as chemicals and pharmaceuticals, scheduling might consist of determining the mix of ingredients that goes into a vat or when the system should stop producing one type of mixture, clean out the vat, and start producing another. Linear programming can find the lowest-cost mix of ingredients, and the production order quantity can determine the optimal length of a production run. These techniques are described in detail in Chapter 14 Supplement and Chapter 13, respectively.
- For *mass production,* the schedule of production is pretty much determined when the assembly line is laid out. Products simply flow down the assembly line from one station to the next in the same prescribed, nondeviating order every time. Day-to-day scheduling decisions consist of determining how fast to feed items into the line and how many hours per day to run the line. On a mixed-model assembly line, the *order* of products assembled also has to be determined. We discuss these issues in Chapters 7 and 16.
- For *projects,* the scheduling decisions are so numerous and interrelated that specialized project-scheduling techniques such as PERT and CPM have been devised. Chapter 9 is devoted to these planning and control tools for project management.
- For *batch* or *job shop production*, scheduling decisions can be quite complex. In previous chapters, we discussed *sales and operations planning*, which plans for the production of product lines or families*; master scheduling*, which plans for the production of individual end items or finished goods; and *material requirements planning* (MRP) and *capacity requirements planning* (CRP), which plan for the production of components and assemblies. Scheduling determines to which machine a part will be routed for processing, which worker will operate a machine that produces a part, and the order in which the parts are to be processed. Scheduling also determines which patient to assign to an operating room, which doctors and nurses are to care for a patient during certain hours of the day, the order in which a doctor is to see patients, and when meals should be delivered or medications dispensed.

What makes scheduling so difficult in a job shop is the variety of jobs (or patients) that are processed, each with distinctive routing and processing requirements. In addition, although the volume of each customer order may be small, there are probably a great number of different orders in the shop at any one time. This necessitates planning for the production of each job as it arrives, scheduling its use of limited resources, and monitoring its progress through the system.

This chapter concentrates on scheduling issues for job shop production. We also examine one of the most difficult scheduling problems for services—employee scheduling.

Objectives in Scheduling

There are many possible objectives in constructing a schedule, including

- Meeting customer due dates;
- Minimizing job lateness;
- Minimizing response time;
- Minimizing completion time;
- Minimizing time in the system;
- Minimizing overtime;
- Maximizing machine or labor utilization;
- Minimizing idle time; and
- Minimizing work-in-process inventory.

Job shop scheduling is also known as **production control**, *shop floor control* (SFC), and *production activity control* (PAC). Regardless of their primary scheduling objective, manufacturers typically have a *production control department* whose responsibilities consist of three activities:

1. ***Loading****—checking the availability of material, machines, and labor.* The MRP system plans for material availability. CRP converts the material plan into machine and labor requirements, and projects resource overloads and underloads. Production control assigns work to individual workers or machines, and then attempts to smooth out the load to make the MRP schedule "doable." Smoothing the load is called **load leveling.**
2. ***Sequencing****—releasing work orders to the shop and issuing dispatch lists for individual machines.* MRP recommends when orders should be released (hence the name *planned* order releases). After verifying their feasibility, production control actually releases the orders. When several orders are released to one machine center, they must be prioritized so that the worker will know which ones to do first. The **dispatch list** contains the sequence in which jobs should be processed. This sequence is often based on certain *sequencing rules*.
3. ***Monitoring****—maintaining progress reports on each job until it is completed.* This is important because items may need to be rescheduled as changes occur in the system. In addition to timely data collection, it involves the use of Gantt charts and input/output control charts.

Loading

Loading is the process of assigning work to limited resources. Many times an operation can be performed by various persons, machines, or work centers but with varying efficiencies. If there is enough capacity, each worker should be assigned to the task that he or she performs best, and each job to the machine that can process it most efficiently. In effect, that is what happens when CRP generates a load profile for each machine center. The routing file used by CRP lists the machine that can perform the job most efficiently first. If no overloads appear in the load profile, then production control can proceed to the next task of sequencing the work at each center. However, when resource constraints produce overloads in the load profile, production control must examine the list of jobs initially assigned and decide which jobs to reassign elsewhere. The problem of determining how best to allocate jobs to machines or workers to tasks can be solved with the *assignment method* of linear programming.

THE ASSIGNMENT METHOD

The *assignment method* is a specialized linear programming solution procedure for deciding which worker to assign to a task, or which job to assign to a machine. (See Supplement 14 for linear programming.) Given a table of tasks and resources, the procedure creates an *opportunity cost matrix* and selects the best assignment in consideration of tradeoffs among alternatives. With this technique, only one job may be assigned to each worker or machine. The procedure for a minimization problem is outlined as follows:

1. Perform *row reductions* by subtracting the minimum value in each row from all other row values.
2. Perform *column reductions* by subtracting the minimum value in each column from all other column values.
3. The resulting table is an *opportunity cost matrix*. Cross out all zeros in the matrix using the minimum number of horizontal or vertical lines.
4. If the number of lines equals the number of rows in the matrix, an optimal solution has been reached and assignments can be made where the zeros appear. Otherwise, *modify the matrix* by subtracting the minimum uncrossed value from all other uncrossed values and adding this same amount to all cells where two lines intersect. All other values in the matrix remain unchanged.
5. Repeat steps 3 and 4 until an optimal solution is reached.

EXAMPLE 17.1

ASSIGNING WORK AT WEBSTAR

WebStar, Inc. has four web projects to complete and four workers with varying degrees of expertise in web development for particular industries. Estimates of processing times (in hours) for each project by each worker are shown below. Development time costs an average of $100 an hour. Assign each worker to a project so that cost is minimized.

Initial Matrix	Project 1	Project 2	Project 3	Project 4
Bryan	10	5	6	10
Kari	6	2	4	6
Noah	7	6	5	6
Chris	9	5	4	10

SOLUTION

1. ***Row reduction**—Find the best assignment in each row. Subtract the smallest value in each row from all other row values.* The resulting number is the opportunity cost of assigning a worker to that project. For example, the best assignment for Bryan would be project 2. Thus, its value in the following matrix is zero. However, if Bryan were assigned to project 1 or 4, it would take (10 − 5) = 5 hours longer to complete, and if assigned to project 3, one hour longer.

Row Reduction	Project 1	Project 2	Project 3	Project 4
Bryan	5	0	1	5
Kari	4	0	2	4
Noah	2	1	0	1
Chris	5	1	0	6

2. ***Column reduction**—Find the best assignment in each column. Subtract the smallest value in each column from all other values in the column.* For example, project 1 can be completed the fastest with Noah as project leader, so it has an opportunity cost of zero. Assigning Bryan to project 1 would require 3 more hours of processing; thus, its opportunity cost is 3.

Column Reduction	Project 1	Project 2	Project 3	Project 4
Bryan	3	0	1	4
Kari	2	0	2	3
Noah	0	1	0	0
Chris	3	1	0	5

3. ***Look for unique assignments**—Examine the matrix and cover all zeros.* Remember that each person can only be assigned to one project and each project can only have one leader. A problem occurs when project 2 is the best for both Bryan and Kari, and project 3 is best for both Noah and Chris. In the following matrix, rows or columns containing optimal assignments are highlighted. This is called "covering all zeros." If the number of lines (or highlighting) is less than the number of rows, the matrix needs to be modified.

Initial Assignment	Project 1	Project 2	Project 3	Project 4
Bryan	3	0	1	4
Kari	2	0	2	3
Noah	0	1	0	0
Chris	3	1	0	5

4. ***Modify the matrix**—Find the smallest value of the entries that are not highlighted. Subtract that value from all other non-highlighted entries, and add it to the entries where the lines intersect.* Below we have subtracted 2 from the noncovered entries and added it to the intersection points (i.e., Noah's project 2 and project 3 values).

Modified Matrix	Project 1	Project 2	Project 3	Project 4
Bryan	1	0	1	2
Kari	0	0	2	1
Noah	0	3	2	0
Chris	1	1	0	3

5. ***Look for unique assignments****—Assign each worker to the best project available*. Bryan is assigned to project 2. With project 2 eliminated, Kari is assigned to project 1. Since project 1 has been eliminated, Noah is assigned to project 4. That leaves Chris for project 3.

Final Assignment	Project 1	Project 2	Project 3	Project 4
Bryan	1	0	1	2
Kari	0	0	2	1
Noah	0	3	2	0
Chris	1	1	0	3

6. ***Calculate performance***—Refer back to the original assignment matrix to find the times required to finish each project by the assigned worker. At a cost of $100 hour, the projects will cost $(5 + 6 + 4 + 6) \times \$100 = \$2{,}100$ to complete.

Final Matrix	Project 1	Project 2	Project 3	Project 4
Bryan	10	5	6	10
Kari	6	2	4	6
Noah	7	6	5	6
Chris	9	5	4	10

Smaller assignment problems, such as our example, are usually solved by hand. Larger ones can be solved in Excel with Solver, as shown in Exhibit 17.1. Assignment problems may also involve maximizing profit or customer satisfaction. When solving maximization problems by hand, each entry in the initial matrix should be subtracted from the largest matrix value before proceeding as a minimization problem. When solving with Excel, simply change the Solver objective function from min to max.

Sequencing

When more than one job is assigned to a machine or activity, the operator needs to know the order in which to process the jobs. The process of prioritizing jobs is called **sequencing**. If no particular order is specified, the operator would probably process the job that arrived first. This default sequence is called *first-come, first-served* (FCFS). If jobs are stacked on arrival to a machine, it might be easier to process the job first that arrived last and is now on top of the stack. This is called *last-come, first-served* (LCFS) sequencing.

Another common approach is to process the job first that is due the soonest or the job that has the highest customer priority. These are known as *earliest due date* (DDATE) and *highest customer priority* (CUSTPR) sequencing. Operators may also look through a stack of jobs to find one with a *similar setup* to the job that is currently being processed (SETUP). That would minimize the downtime of the machine and make the operator's job easier.

Variations on the DDATE rule include *minimum slack* (SLACK) and *smallest critical ratio* (CR). SLACK considers the work remaining to be performed on a job as well as the time remaining

EXHIBIT 17.1 The Assignment Method

EXCEL FILE

(a) Setup

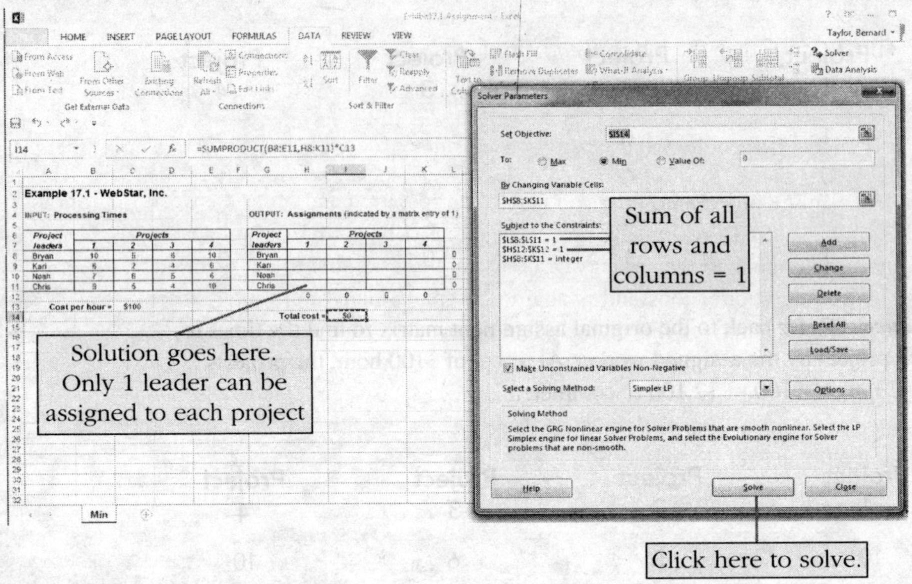

(b) Solution

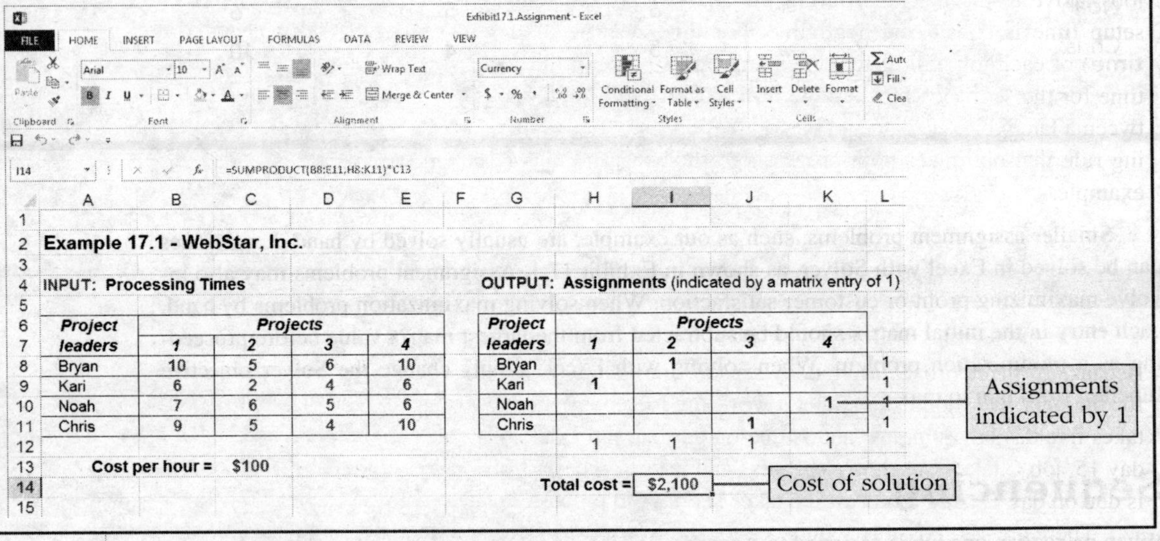

(until the due date) to perform that work. Jobs are processed first that have the least difference (or slack) between the two, as follows:

$$\text{SLACK} = (\text{due date} \quad \text{today's date}) - (\text{processing time})$$

The critical ratio uses the same information as SLACK, but recalculates the sequence as processing continues and arranges the information in ratio form. Mathematically, the CR is calculated as follows:

$$\text{CR} = \frac{\text{time remaining}}{\text{work remaining}} = \frac{\text{due date} - \text{today's date}}{\text{remaining processing time}}$$

If the work remaining is greater than the time remaining, the critical ratio will be less than 1. If the time remaining is greater than the work remaining, the critical ratio will be greater than 1. If the time remaining equals work remaining, the critical ratio exactly equals 1. The critical ratio allows us to make the following statements about our schedule:

If CR $>$ 1, then the job is *ahead of schedule*

If CR $<$ 1, then the job is *behind schedule*

If CR $=$ 1, then the job is exactly *on schedule*

Other sequencing rules examine processing time at a particular operation and order the work either by shortest processing time (SPT) or longest processing time (LPT). LPT assumes long jobs are important jobs and is analogous to the strategy of doing larger tasks first to get them out of the way. SPT focuses instead on shorter jobs and is able to complete many more jobs earlier than LPT. With either rule, some jobs may be inordinately late because they are always put at the back of a queue.

All these "rules" for arranging jobs in a certain order for processing seem reasonable. We might wonder which methods are best or if it really matters which jobs are processed first anyway. Perhaps a few examples will help answer those questions.

SEQUENCING JOBS THROUGH ONE PROCESS

The simplest sequencing problem consists of a queue of jobs at one machine or process. No new jobs arrive to the machine during the analysis, processing times and due dates are fixed, and setup time is considered negligible. For this scenario, the *completion time* (also called **flow time**) of each job will differ depending on its place in the sequence, but the overall completion time for the set of jobs (called the **makespan**) will not change. **Tardiness** is the difference between a late job's due date and its completion time. Even in this simple case, there is no sequencing rule that optimizes both processing efficiency and due date performance. Let's consider an example.

EXAMPLE 17.2

SIMPLE SEQUENCING RULES

Because of the approaching holiday season, Joe Palotty is scheduled to work seven days a week for the next two months. October's work for Joe consists of five jobs, A, B, C, D, and E. Job A takes five days to complete and is due on day 10, job B takes 10 days to complete and is due on day 15, job C takes two days to process and is due on day 5, job D takes eight days to process and is due on day 12, and job E, which takes six days to process, is due on day 8.

There are 120 possible sequences for the five jobs. Clearly, enumeration is impossible. Let's try some simple sequencing rules. Sequence the jobs by (a) first-come, first-served (FCFS), (b) earliest due date (DDATE), (c) minimum slack (SLACK), and (d) shortest processing time (SPT). Determine the completion time and tardiness of each job under each sequencing rule. Should Joe process his work as is—first-come, first-served? If not, what sequencing rule would you recommend to Joe?

SOLUTION

Prepare a table for each sequencing rule. Start the first job at time 0. (When today's date is not given, assume it is day 0.) Completion time is the sum of the start time and the processing time. The start time of the next job is the completion time of the previous job.

(Continued)

a. FCFS: Process the jobs in order of their arrival, A, B, C, D, E.

FCFS Sequence	Start Time	Processing Time	Completion Time	Due Date	Tardiness
A	0	5	5	10	0
B	5	10	15	15	0
C	15	2	17	5	12
D	17	8	25	12	13
E	25	6	31	8	23
Total			93		48
Average			93/5 = 18.60		48/5 = 9.6

b. DDATE: Sequence the jobs by earliest due date.

DDATE Sequence	Start Time	Processing Time	Completion Time	Due Date	Tardiness
C	0	2	2	5	0
E	2	6	8	8	0
A	8	5	13	10	3
D	13	8	21	12	9
B	21	10	31	15	16
Total			75		28
Average			75/5 = 15.00		28/5 = 5.6

c. SLACK: Sequence the jobs by minimum slack. The slack for each job is calculated as: (due date − today's date) − remaining processing time.

Job A $(10 - 0) - 5 = 5^*$

B $(15 - 0) - 10 = 5^*$

C $(5 - 0) - 2 = 3$

D $(12 - 0) - 8 = 4$

E $(8 - 0) - 6 = 2$

*break the tie arbitrarily with FCFS

Slack Sequence	Start Time	Processing Time	Completion Time	Due Date	Tardiness
E	0	6	6	8	0
C	6	2	8	5	3
D	8	8	16	12	4
A	16	5	21	10	11
B	21	10	31	15	16
Total			82		34
Average			82/5 = 16.40		34/5 = 6.8

d. SPT: Sequence the jobs by smallest processing time.

SPT Sequence	Start Time	Processing Time	Completion Time	Due Date	Tardiness
C	0	2	2	5	0
A	2	5	7	10	0
E	7	6	13	8	5
D	13	8	21	12	9
B	21	10	31	15	16
Total			74		30
Average			74/5 = 14.80		30/5 = 6

Summary

Rule	Average Completion Time	Average Tardiness	No. of Jobs Tardy	Maximum Tardiness
FCFS	18.60	9.6	3*	23
DDATE	15.00	5.6*	3*	16*
SLACK	16.40	6.8	4	16*
SPT	14.80*	6.0	3*	16*

*Best Value

All the sequencing rules complete the month's work by day 31, as planned. However, no sequencing rule is able to complete *all* jobs on time. The performance of FCFS is either met or exceeded by DDATE and SPT. Thus, Joe should take the time to sequence this month's work.

Whether Joe sequences his work by DDATE or SPT depends on the objectives of the company for whom he works. The particular jobs that are tardy may also make a difference.

The Excel solution to this problem is shown in Exhibit 17.2.

Are the preceding results a function of this particular example, or are they indicative of the types of results we will get whenever these rules are applied? Analytically, we can prove that for a set number of jobs to be processed on *one* machine, the SPT sequencing rule will minimize mean job completion time (also known as *flowtime*) and minimize mean number of jobs in the system. On the other hand, the DDATE sequencing rule will minimize mean tardiness. No definitive statements can be made concerning the performance of the other sequencing rules.

SEQUENCING JOBS THROUGH TWO SERIAL PROCESSES

Since few factories consist of just one process, we might wonder if techniques exist that will produce an optimal sequence for any number of jobs processed through more than one machine or process. **Johnson's rule** finds the fastest way to process a series of jobs through a two-step system in which every job follows the same sequence through two processes. Based on a variation

EXHIBIT 17.2 Using Excel for Sequencing Rules

EXCEL FILE

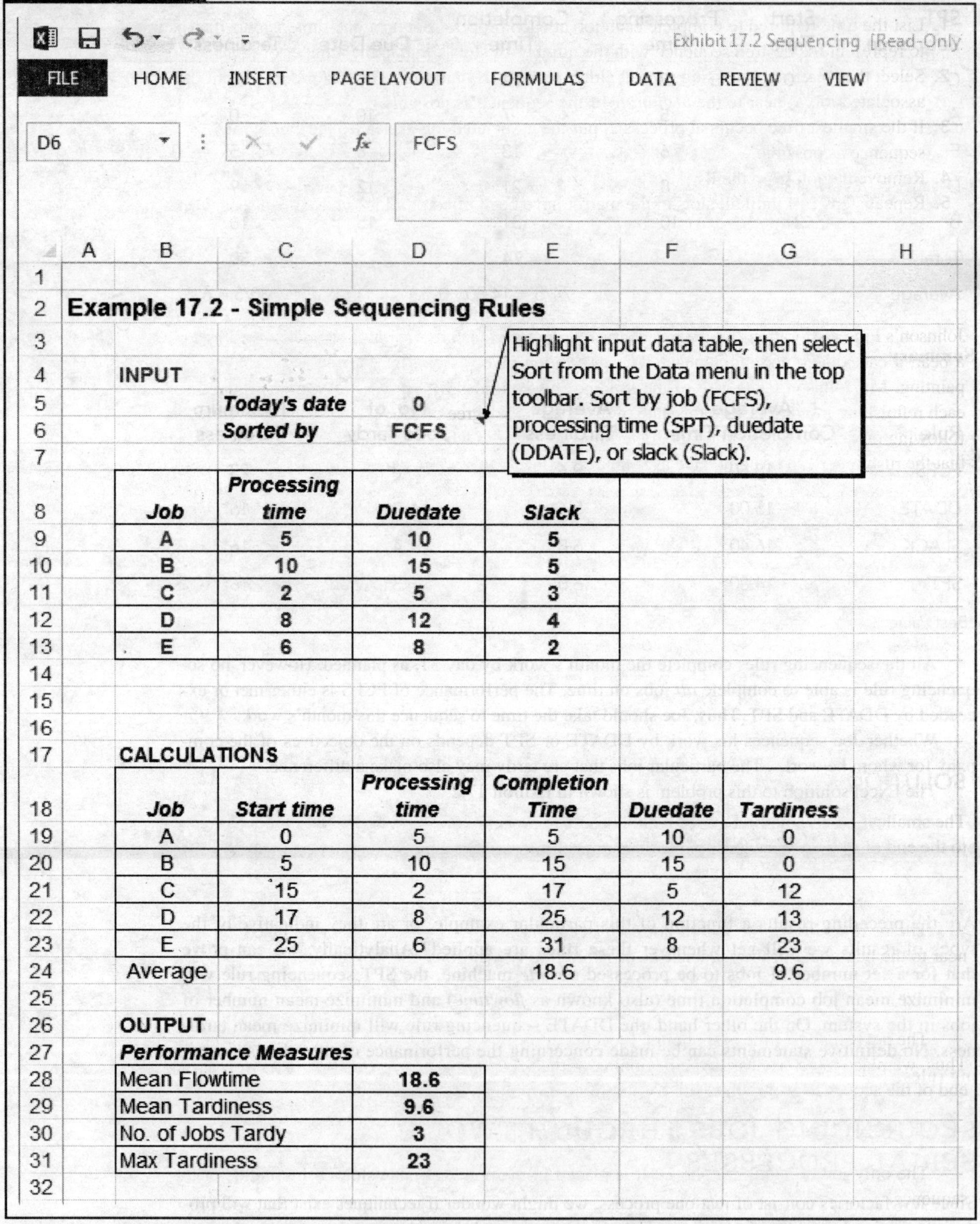

Example 17.2 - Simple Sequencing Rules

Highlight input data table, then select Sort from the Data menu in the top toolbar. Sort by job (FCFS), processing time (SPT), duedate (DDATE), or slack (Slack).

INPUT

Today's date **0**

Sorted by **FCFS**

Job	***Processing time***	***Duedate***	***Slack***
A	**5**	**10**	**5**
B	**10**	**15**	**5**
C	**2**	**5**	**3**
D	**8**	**12**	**4**
E	**6**	**8**	**2**

CALCULATIONS

Job	***Start time***	***Processing time***	***Completion Time***	***Duedate***	***Tardiness***
A	0	5	5	10	0
B	5	10	15	15	0
C	15	2	17	5	12
D	17	8	25	12	13
E	25	6	31	8	23
Average			18.6		9.6

OUTPUT

Performance Measures

Mean Flowtime	**18.6**
Mean Tardiness	**9.6**
No. of Jobs Tardy	**3**
Max Tardiness	**23**

of the SPT rule, it requires that the sequence be "mapped out" to determine the final completion time, or *makespan*, for the set of jobs. The procedure is as follows:

1. List the time required to complete each job at each process. Set up a one-dimensional matrix to represent the desired sequence with the number of slots equal to the number of jobs.
2. Select the smallest processing time at either process. If that time occurs at process 1, put the associated job as near to the *beginning* of the sequence as possible.
3. If the smallest time occurs at process 2, put the associated job as near to the *end* of the sequence as possible.
4. Remove the job from the list.
5. Repeat steps 2–4 until all slots in the matrix have been filled or all jobs have been sequenced.

EXAMPLE 17.3

JOHNSON'S RULE

Johnson's Fine Restorations has received a rush order to refinish five carousel animals—an alligator, a bear, a cat, a deer, and an elephant. The restoration involves two major processes: sanding and painting. Mr. Johnson takes care of the sanding; his son does the painting. The time required for each refinishing job differs with the state of disrepair and degree of detail of each animal. Given the following processing times (in hours), determine the order in which the jobs should be processed so that the rush order can be completed as soon as possible.

Job	Process 1	Process 2
A	6	8
B	11	6
C	7	3
D	9	7
E	5	10

SOLUTION

The smallest processing time, three hours, occurs at process 2 for job C, so we place job C as near to the end of the sequence as possible. C is now eliminated from the job list.

				C

The next smallest time is five hours. It occurs at process 1 for job E, so we place job E as near to the beginning of the sequence as possible. Job E is eliminated from the job list.

E				C

The next smallest time is six hours. It occurs at process 1 for job A and at process 2 for job B. Thus, we place job A as near to the beginning of the sequence as possible and job B as near to the end of the sequence as possible. Jobs A and B are eliminated from the job list.

E	A		B	C

The only job remaining is job D. It is placed in the only available slot, in the middle of the sequence.

E	A	D	B	C

(Continued)

This sequence will complete these jobs faster than any other sequence. The following bar charts (called *Gantt charts*) are used to determine the makespan or final completion time for the set of five jobs. Notice that the sequence of jobs (E, A, D, B, C) is the same for both processes and that a job cannot begin at process 2 until it has been completed at process 1. Also, a job cannot begin at process 2 if another job is currently in process. Time periods during which a job is being processed are labeled with the job's letter. The gray shaded areas represent idle time.

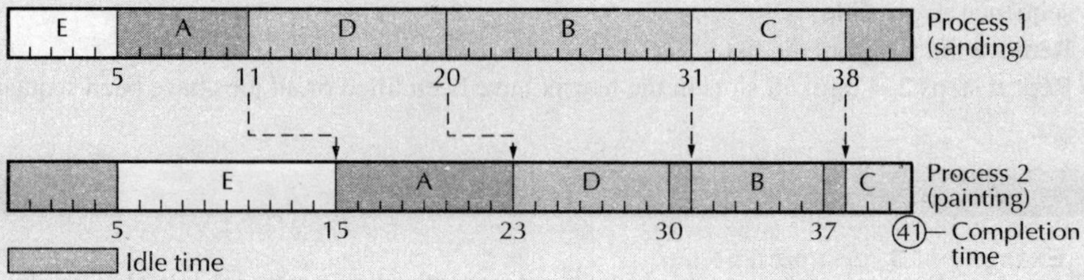

The completion time for the set of five jobs is 41 hours. Note that although Johnson's rule minimizes makespan and idle time, it does not consider job due dates in constructing a sequence, so there is no attempt to minimize job tardiness.

The Excel solution to this problem is shown in Exhibit 17.3.

GUIDELINES FOR SELECTING A SEQUENCING RULE

In a real-world job shop, jobs follow different routes through a facility that consists of many different machine centers or departments. A small job shop may have three or four departments; a large job shop may have 50 or more. From several to several hundred jobs may be circulating the shop at any given time. New jobs are released into the shop daily and placed in competition with existing jobs for priority in processing. Queues form and dissipate as jobs move through the system. A dispatch list that shows the sequence in which jobs are to be processed at a particular machine may be valid at the beginning of a day or week but become outdated as new jobs arrive in the system. Some jobs may have to wait to be assembled with others before continuing to be processed. Delays in completing operations can cause due dates to be revised and schedules changed.

The complexity and dynamic nature of most scheduling environments precludes the use of analytical solution techniques. The most popular form of analysis for these systems is *simulation*. Academia has especially enjoyed creating and testing sequencing rules in simulations of hypothetical job shops. One early simulation study alone examined 92 different sequencing rules. Although no optimal solutions have been identified in these simulation studies, they have produced some general guidelines for *when* certain sequencing rules may be appropriate. Here are a few of their suggestions:

1. ***SPT is most useful when the shop is highly congested.*** SPT tends to minimize mean flow time, mean number of jobs in the system (and thus work-in-process inventory), and percent of jobs tardy. By completing more jobs quickly, it theoretically satisfies a greater number of customers than the other rules. However, with SPT, some long jobs may be completed *very* late, resulting in a small number of very unsatisfied customers.

   For this reason, when SPT is used in practice, it is usually truncated (or stopped), depending on the amount of time a job has been waiting or the nearness of its due date. For example, many shared computer services process jobs by SPT. Jobs that are submitted are placed in several categories (A, B, or C) based on expected CPU time. The shorter jobs, or A jobs, are processed first, but every couple of hours the system stops processing A jobs and picks the first job from the B stack to run. After the B job is finished, the system returns to

EXHIBIT 17.3 Using Excel for Johnson's Rule **EXCEL FILE**

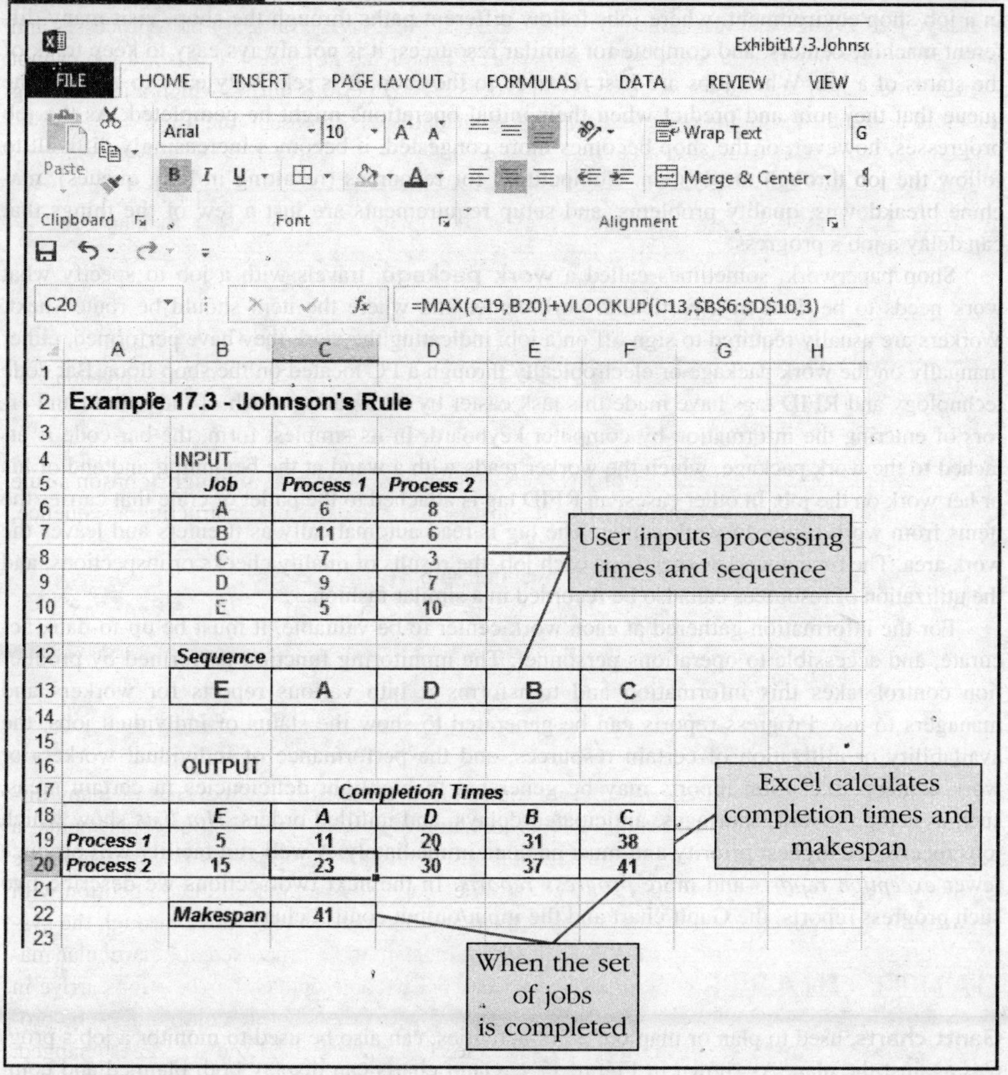

the A stack and continues processing. C jobs may be processed only once a day. Other systems that have access to due date information will keep a long job waiting until its SLACK is zero or its due date is within a certain range.

2. ***Use SLACK for periods of normal activity***. When capacity is not severely restrained, a SLACK-oriented rule that takes into account both due date and processing time will produce good results.
3. ***Use DDATE when only small tardiness values can be tolerated***. DDATE tends to minimize mean tardiness and maximum tardiness. Although more jobs will be tardy under DDATE than SPT, the degree of tardiness will be much less.
4. ***Use LPT if subcontracting is anticipated*** so that larger jobs are completed in-house, and smaller jobs are sent out as their due date draws near.
5. ***Use FCFS when operating at low-capacity levels.*** FCFS allows the shop to operate essentially without sequencing jobs. When the workload at a facility is light, any sequencing rule will do, and FCFS is certainly the easiest to apply.
6. ***Do not use SPT to sequence jobs that have to be assembled with other jobs at a later date***. For assembly jobs, a sequencing rule that gives a common priority to the processing of different components in an assembly, such as *assembly DDATE*, produces a more effective schedule.

Monitoring

In a job shop environment, where jobs follow different paths through the shop, visit many different machine centers, and compete for similar resources, it is not always easy to keep track of the status of a job. When jobs are first released to the shop, it is relatively easy to observe the queue that they join and predict when their initial operations might be completed. As the job progresses, however, or the shop becomes more congested, it becomes increasingly difficult to follow the job through the system. Competition for resources (resulting in long queues), machine breakdowns, quality problems, and setup requirements are just a few of the things that can delay a job's progress.

Shop paperwork, sometimes called a **work package**, travels with a job to specify what work needs to be done at a particular work center and where the item should be routed next. Workers are usually required to sign off on a job, indicating the work they have performed, either manually on the work package or electronically through a PC located on the shop floor. Bar code technology and RFID tags have made this task easier by eliminating much of the tedium and errors of entering the information by computer keyboard. In its simplest form, the bar code is attached to the work package, which the worker reads with a wand at the beginning and end of his or her work on the job. In other cases, an RFID tag is attached to the pallet or crate that carries the items from work center to work center. The tag is read automatically as it enters and leaves the work area. The time a worker spends on each job, the results of quality checks or inspections, and the utilization of resources can also be recorded in a similar fashion.

For the information gathered at each work center to be valuable, it must be up-to-date, accurate, and accessible to operations personnel. The monitoring function performed by production control takes this information and transforms it into various reports for workers and managers to use. Progress reports can be generated to show the status of individual jobs, the availability or utilization of certain resources, and the performance of individual workers or work centers. Exception reports may be generated to highlight deficiencies in certain areas, such as scrap, rework, shortages, anticipated delays, and unfilled orders. *Hot lists* show which jobs receive the highest priority and must be done immediately. A well-run facility will produce fewer *exception reports* and more *progress reports*. In the next two sections we describe two such progress reports, the Gantt chart and the input/output control chart.

GANTT CHARTS

Gantt charts, used to plan or map out work activities, can also be used to monitor a job's progress against the plan. As shown in Figure 17.1, Gantt charts can display both planned and completed activities against a time scale. In this figure, the dashed line indicating today's date crosses over the schedules for job 12A, job 23C, and job 32B.

From the chart we can quickly see that job 12A is exactly on schedule because the bar monitoring its completion exactly meets the line for the current date. Job 23C is ahead of schedule and job 32B is behind schedule.

Gantt charts have been used since the early 1900s and are still popular today. They may be created and maintained digitally or by hand. In some facilities, Gantt charts consist of large scheduling boards (the size of several bulletin boards) with magnetic strips, pegs, or string of different colors that mark job schedules and job progress for everyone to see. Gantt charts are a common feature of project management software, such as Microsoft Project.

INPUT/OUTPUT CONTROL

Input/output (I/O) control monitors the input to and output from each work center. Prior to such analysis, it was common to examine only the output from a work center and to compare the actual output with the output planned in the shop schedule. Using that approach in a job shop environment in which the performance of different work centers is interrelated may result in erroneous

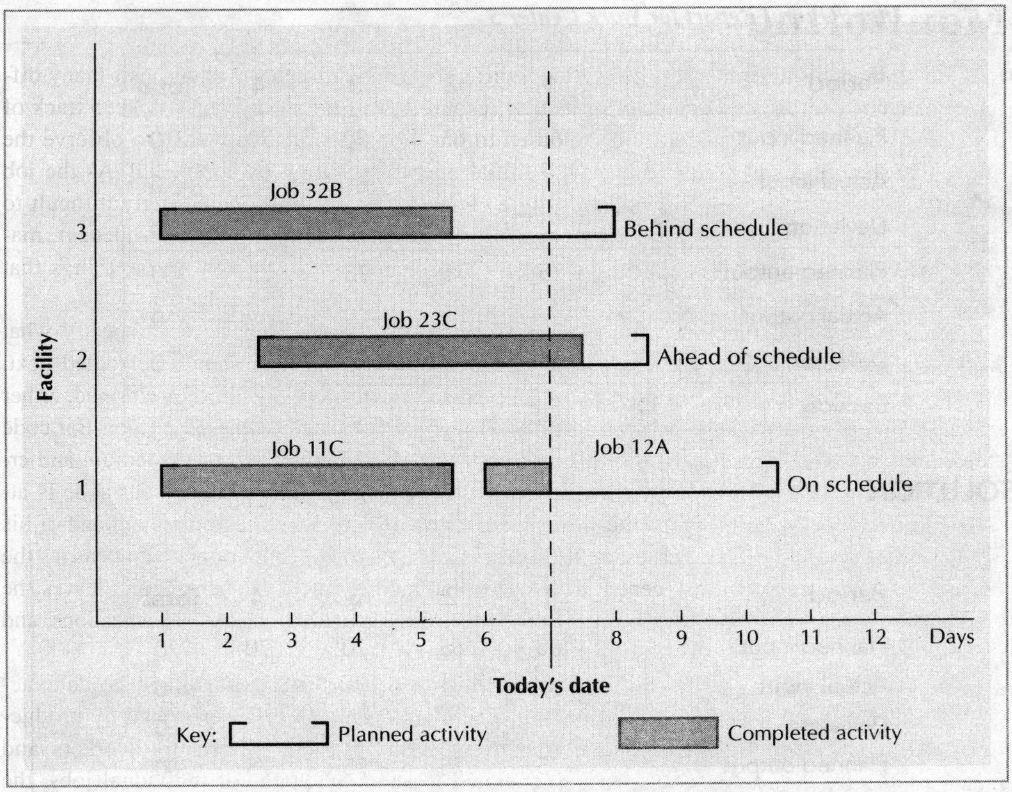

Figure 17.1
A Gantt Chart

conclusions about the source of a problem. Reduced output at one point in the production process may be caused by problems at the current work center, but it may also be caused by problems at previous work centers that *feed* the current work center. Thus, to identify more clearly the source of a problem, the *input* to a work center must be compared with the *planned input*, and the *output* must be compared with the *planned output*. Deviations between planned and actual values are calculated, and their cumulative effects are observed. The resulting backlog or waiting line of work to be completed is monitored to ensure that it stays within a manageable range.

The input rate to a work center can be controlled only for the initial operations of a job. These first work centers are often called *gateway* work centers, because the majority of jobs must pass through them before subsequent operations are performed. Input to later operations, performed at *downstream* work centers, is difficult to control because it is a function of how well the rest of the shop is operating—that is, where queues are forming and how smoothly jobs are progressing through the system. The deviation of planned to actual input for downstream work centers can be minimized by controlling the output rates of feeding work centers. The use of input/output reports can best be illustrated with an example.

EXAMPLE 17.4

INPUT/OUTPUT CONTROL

Hall Industries has begun input/output planning for its work centers. Below are the planned inputs and outputs for Work Center 5.

a. If production proceeds as planned, what will be the backlog at the end of period 4?
b. If actual input values are 60, 60, 65, 65 for periods 1 through 4, respectively, and output values cannot exceed 75, how much output can be expected from Work Center 5?
c. Is there a problem with production at Work Center 5?

(Continued)

Input/Output Report for Work Center 5

Period		1	2	3	4	Total
Planned input		65	65	70	70	270
Actual input						0
Deviation						0
Planned output		75	75	75	75	300
Actual output						0
Deviation						0
Backlog	30					

SOLUTION

a.

Period		1	2	3	4	Total
Planned input		65	65	70	70	270
Actual input						0
Deviation						0
Planned output		75	75	75	75	300
Actual output						0
Deviation						0
Backlog	30	20	10	5	0	

If everything goes as planned, the backlog will be zero by period 4.

b.

Period		1	2	3	4	Total
Planned input		65	65	70	70	270
Actual input		60	60	65	65	250
Deviation		–5	–5	–5	–5	–20
Planned output		75	75	75	75	300
Actual output		75	75	65	65	280
Deviation		0	0	–10	–10	–20
Backlog	30	15	0	0	0	

With the reduced input, the backlog is worked off sooner, but the total production cannot keep pace with what was planned.

c. Although Work Center 5 has produced only 280 units instead of the planned 300, the problem appears to be with the process that feeds Work Center 5. Notice the deviations from planned are the same for both the input and output values. An Excel solution to this example is shown in Exhibit 17.4.

EXHIBIT 17.4 A Grantt Chart for Textbook publishing

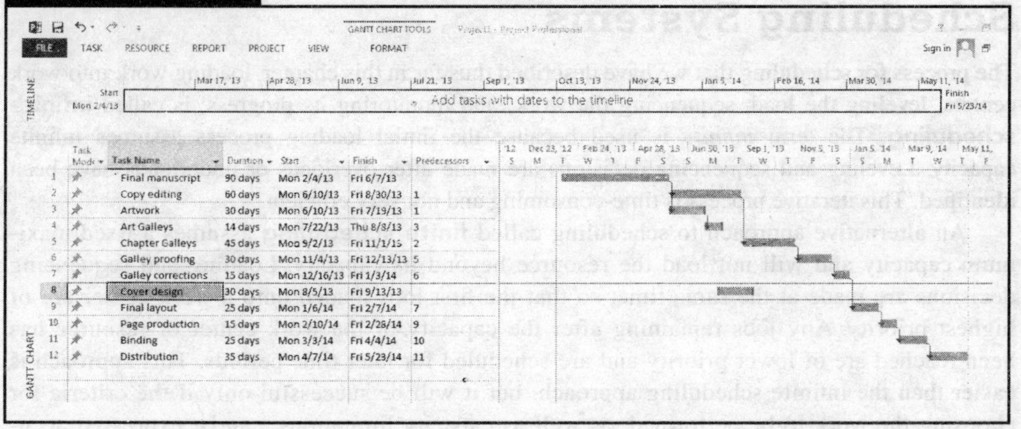

Gantt charts have been used for more than 75 years to plan and monitor schedules. Today, Gantt charts are more widely used than ever, often as part of the action plan from a quality-improvement team. This Gantt chart, created in Microsoft Project, is for publishing a textbook.

Input/output control provides the information necessary to regulate the flow of work to and from a network of work centers. Increasing the capacity of a work center that is processing all the work available to it will not increase output. The source of the problem needs to be identified. Excessive queues, or *backlogs*, are one indication that *bottlenecks* exist. To alleviate bottleneck work centers, the problem causing the backlog can be worked on, the capacity of the work center can be adjusted, or input to the work center can be reduced. Increasing the input to a bottleneck work center will not increase the center's output. It will merely clog the system further and create longer queues of work-in-process.

EXHIBIT 17.5 Using Excel for Input/Output Control

EXCEL FILE

Example 17.4 - Input / Output Control

Period		1	2	3	4	Total
Planned input		65	65	70	70	270
Actual input		60	60	65	65	250
Deviation		-5	-5	-5	-5	-20
Planned output		75	75	75	75	300
Actual output		75	75	65	65	280
Deviation		0	0	-10	-10	-20
Backlog	30	15	0	0	0	

User inputs planned and actual values

Excel calculates deviations and backlog

Advanced Planning and Scheduling Systems

The process for scheduling that we have described thus far in this chapter, loading work into work centers, leveling the load, sequencing the work, and monitoring its progress, is called **infinite scheduling**. The term *infinite* is used because the initial loading process assumes infinite capacity. Leveling and sequencing decisions are made after overloads or underloads have been identified. This iterative process is time-consuming and not very efficient.

An alternative approach to scheduling called **finite scheduling** assumes a fixed maximum capacity and will not load the resource beyond its capacity. Loading and sequencing decisions are made at the same time, so that the first jobs loaded onto a work center are of highest priority. Any jobs remaining after the capacity of the work center or resource has been reached are of lower priority and are scheduled for later time periods. This approach is easier than the infinite scheduling approach, but it will be successful only if the criteria for choosing the work to be performed, as well as capacity limitations, can be expressed accurately and concisely.

Finite scheduling systems use a variety of methods to develop their schedules, including mathematical programming, network analysis, simulation, constraint-based programming, genetic algorithms, neural networks, and expert systems. Because the scheduling system, not the human scheduler, makes most of the decisions, considerable time is spent incorporating the special characteristics and requirements of the production system into the database and knowledge base of the scheduling software. While some companies will develop their own finite scheduling software, most will purchase generic or industry-specific scheduling software as an add-on to their ERP system. This class of scheduling software, with libraries of algorithms and heuristics from which to choose, has become known as **advanced planning and scheduling (APS)**. SAP's APS system is called the Advanced Planner and Optimizer (APO), and JDA's is called Factory Planner. These systems also support collaborative planning and scheduling with trading partners. Both APO and Factory Planner use constraint-based programming and genetic algorithms to develop schedules. Figure 17.2 applies these techniques to sequence a set of jobs so that setup time is minimized.

Constraint-based programming (CBP) identifies a solution space and then systematically evaluates possible solutions subject to constraints on the system. In scheduling, when one job or person is assigned, the options for additional job assignments are reduced or further constrained. This cascading effect on the remaining jobs to be scheduled is called *constraint propagation*. In part (a) of Figure 17.2, all possible sequences are evaluated, with A-C-B and C-A-B yielding the best solutions.

Genetic algorithms are based on the natural selection properties of genetics. Starting from a feasible solution, alternative solutions or "offspring" are generated with slightly different characteristics. These are evaluated against an objective function and compared to subsequent solutions. The number of generations and number of offspring per generation are specified by the user. In this example, two generations are produced with two offspring per generation. That's more than enough offspring to try all possible combinations. Again, A-C-B and C-A-B are identified as optimal sequences.

As schedules are executed, another type of software, aptly named a **manufacturing execution system (MES)**, monitors work status, machine status, material usage and availability, and quality data. Alerts are sent to the APS system that shop conditions have changed and a scheduling revision is required.

Scheduling problems can be enormous in size, especially as the number of product options proliferate and linked schedules along a supply chain are considered. Some relief has come from the availability of more powerful computers and the use of artificial intelligence techniques. But the biggest impact has come from altered views of the production system. By grouping parts or products into families and scheduling bottleneck resources first, the scheduling problem is

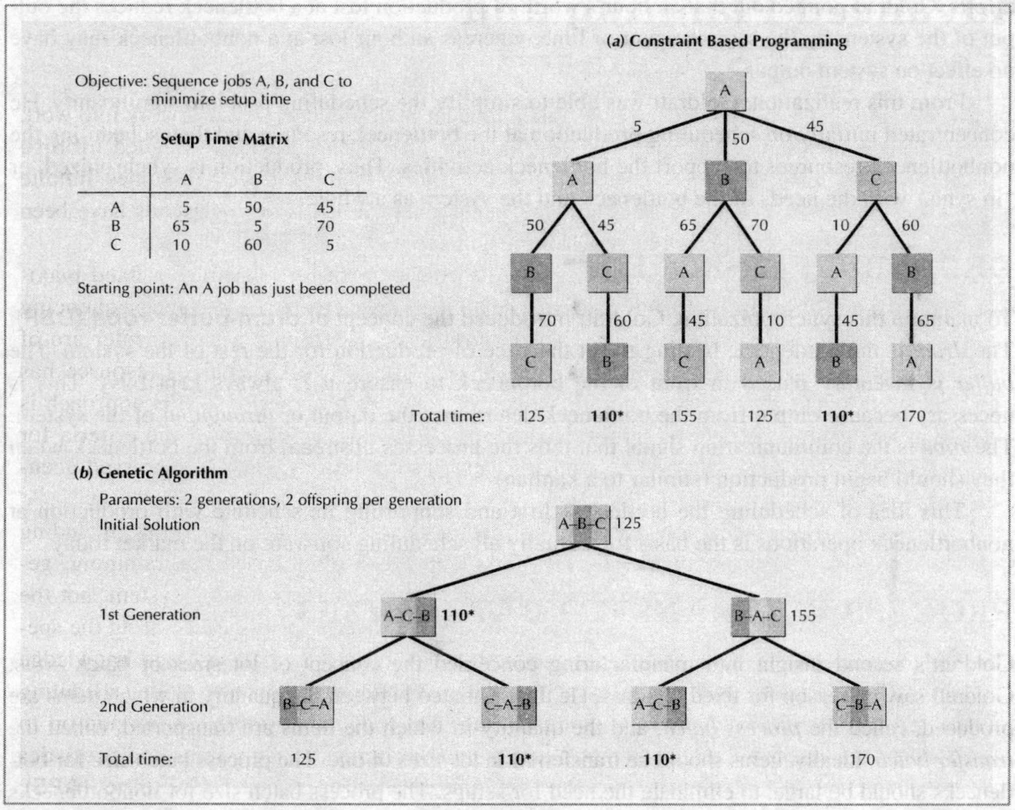

Figure 17.2

Advanced Planning and Scheduling Techniques

SOURCE: SAP AG, *Advanced Planner and Optimizer*, company brochure, 1999.

sufficiently reduced so that sophisticated solutions are feasible. In the next section, we present a common precept of today's scheduling systems, the *theory of constraints.*

Theory of Constraints

In the 1970s, an Israeli physicist named Eliyahu Goldratt responded to a friend's request for help in scheduling his chicken coop business. Lacking a background in manufacturing or production theory, Dr. Goldratt took a commonsense, intuitive approach to the scheduling problem. He developed a software system that used mathematical programming and simulation to create a schedule that realistically considered the constraints of the manufacturing system. The software produced good schedules quickly and was marketed in the early 1980s in the United States. After more than 100 firms had successfully used the scheduling system (called OPT), the creator sold the rights to the software and began marketing the theory behind the software instead. He called his approach to scheduling the **theory of constraints (TOC)**. General Motors and other manufacturers call its application *synchronous manufacturing.*

Decision making in manufacturing is often difficult because of the size and complexity of the problems faced. Dr. Goldratt's first insight into the scheduling problem led him to simplify the number of variables considered. He learned early that manufacturing resources typically are not used evenly. Instead of trying to balance the capacity of the manufacturing system, he decided that most systems are inherently unbalanced and that he would try to balance the *flow* of work through the system instead. He identified resources as bottleneck or nonbottleneck and observed that the flow through the system is controlled by the bottleneck resource. This resource should always have material to work on, should spend as little time as possible on nonproductive activities (e.g., setups, waiting for work), should be fully staffed, and should be the focus of improvement or automation efforts. Goldratt pointed out that an hour's worth of production lost at a bottleneck reduces the output of the system by the same amount of time, whereas an hour lost at a nonbottleneck may have no effect on system output.

From this realization, Goldratt was able to simplify the scheduling problem significantly. He concentrated initially on scheduling production at the bottleneck resource and then scheduling the nonbottleneck resources to support the bottleneck activities. Thus, production is synchronized, or "in sync," with the needs of the bottleneck and the system as a whole.

DRUM-BUFFER-ROPE

To maintain this synchronization, Goldratt introduced the concept of **drum-buffer-rope (DBR)**. The *drum* is the bottleneck, beating to set the pace of production for the rest of the system. The *buffer* is inventory placed in front of the bottleneck to ensure it is always kept busy. This is necessary because output from the bottleneck determines the output or *throughput* of the system. The *rope* is the communication signal that tells the processes upstream from the bottleneck when they should begin production (similar to a kanban).

This idea of scheduling the bottleneck first and supporting its schedule with production at nonbottleneck operations is the basis for virtually all scheduling software on the market today.

PROCESS VS. TRANSFER BATCH SIZES

Goldratt's second insight into manufacturing concerned the concept of lot sizes or batch sizes. Goldratt saw no reason for fixed lot sizes. He differentiated between the quantity in which items are produced, called the *process batch*, and the quantity in which the items are transported, called the *transfer batch*. Ideally, items should be transferred in lot sizes of one. The process batch size for bottlenecks should be large, to eliminate the need for setups. The process batch size for nonbottlenecks can be small because time spent in setups for nonbottlenecks does not affect the rest of the system.

The TOC scheduling procedure, illustrated in Example 17.5, follows these steps:

1. Identify the bottleneck.
2. Schedule the job first whose lead time to the bottleneck is less than or equal to the bottleneck processing time.
3. Forward schedule the bottleneck machine.
4. Backward schedule the other machines to sustain the bottleneck schedule.
5. Transfer in batch sizes smaller than the process batch size.

EXAMPLE 17.5

SYNCHRONOUS MANUFACTURING

The following diagram contains the product structure, routing, and processing time information for product A. The process flows from the bottom of the diagram upward. Assume one unit of items B, C, and D are needed to make each A. The manufacture of each item requires three operations at machine centers 1, 2, or 3. Each machine center contains only one machine. A machine setup time of 60 minutes occurs whenever a machine is switched from one operation to another (within the same item or between items).

Design a schedule of production for each machine center that will produce 100 A's as quickly as possible. Show the schedule on a Gantt chart of each machine center.

SOLUTION

The bottleneck machine is identified by summing the processing times of all operations to be performed at a machine.

Machine 1		Machine 2		Machine 3	
B1	5	B2	3	C1	2
B3	7	C3	15	D3	5
C2	10	D2	8	D1	10
Sum	22		26*		17

*Bottleneck

- Machine 2 is identified as the bottleneck, so we schedule machine 2 first. From the product structure diagram, we see that three operations are performed at machine 2—B2, C3, and D2. If we schedule item B first, B will reach machine 2 every five minutes (since B has to be processed through machine 1 first), but each B takes only three minutes to process at machine 2, so the bottleneck will be idle for two minutes of every five minutes. A similar result occurs if we schedule item D first on machine 2. The bottleneck will be idle for two minutes of every ten until D has finished processing. The best alternative is to schedule item C first. The first C will not reach machine 2 until time 12, but after that the bottleneck machine will remain busy.

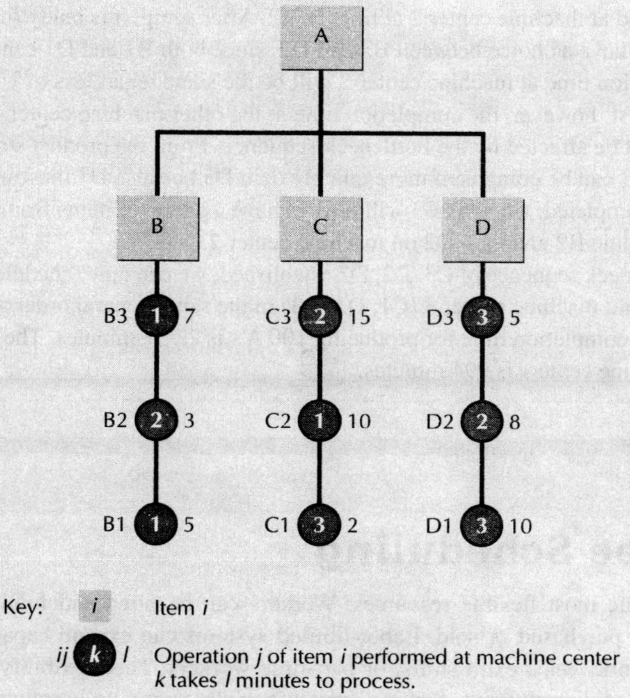

- We begin our Gantt charts by processing item C through the three machine centers. As shown in Figure 17.3, the Gantt charts look different from our earlier examples because we allow each item to be transferred to the next operation immediately after it is completed at the current operation (i.e., the transfer batch size is 1). We will still process the items in batches of 100 to match our demand requirements. The gray shaded areas represent idle time between operations due to setup time requirements or because a feeding operation has not yet been completed.

(Continued)

Figure 17.3

Gantt Chart Solution to Example 17.5

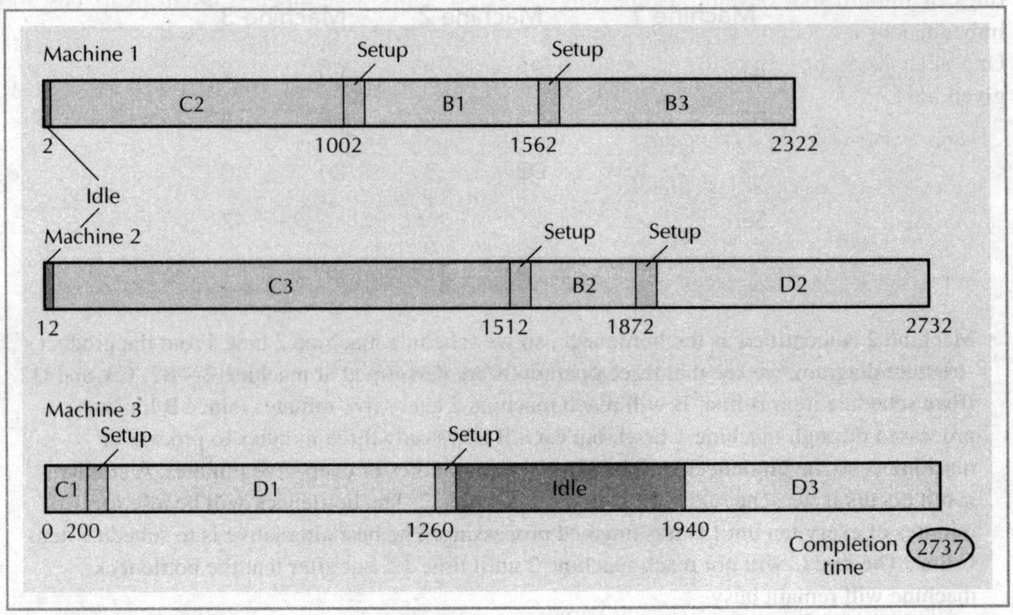

- C3 is completed at machine center 2 at time 1,512. After setup, it is ready for a new item at time 1572. We have a choice between B2 and D2, since both B1 and D1 can be completed by 1572. Completion time at machine center 2 will be the same regardless of whether B2 or D2 is processed first; however, the completion time at the other machine centers (and thus for product A) will be affected by the bottleneck sequence. From the product structure diagram, we note that B3 can be completed more quickly than D3 because D3 must wait three minutes for D2 to be completed, whereas B3 will always have a queue of items from B2 to work on. Thus, we schedule B2 and then D2 on machine center 2.
- With the bottleneck sequence of C3, B2, D2 established, we can now schedule machine center 1 (C2, B1, B3) and machine center 3 (C1, D1, D3) in the same general order as the bottleneck sequence. The completion time for producing 100 A's is 2,737 minutes. The total idle time at the three machine centers is 994 minutes.

Employee Scheduling

Labor is one of the most flexible resources. Workers can be hired and fired more easily than equipment can be purchased or sold. Labor-limited systems can expand capacity through overtime, expanded workweeks, extra shifts, or part-time workers. This flexibility is valuable but it tends to make scheduling difficult. Service firms especially spend an inordinate amount of time developing employee schedules. A supervisor might spend an entire week making up the next month's employee schedule. The task becomes even more daunting for facilities that operate on a 24-hour basis with multiple shifts.

The assignment method of linear programming discussed earlier in this chapter can be used to assign workers with different performance ratings to available jobs. Large-scale linear programming is currently used by McDonald's to schedule its large part-time workforce. American Airlines uses a combination of integer linear programming and expert systems for scheduling ticket agents to coincide with peak and slack demand periods and for the complicated scheduling of flight crews. Although mathematical programming certainly has found application in employee scheduling, most scheduling problems are solved by heuristics (i.e., rules of thumb) that develop a repeating pattern of work assignments. Often heuristics are imbedded in a decision support system to facilitate their use and increase their flexibility. One such heuristic[1] used for scheduling full-time workers with two days off per week, is given next.

Employee Scheduling Heuristic:

1. Let N = no. of workers available

   D_i = demand for workers on day i

   X = day working

   O = day off

2. Assign the first $N - D_1$ workers day 1 off. Assign the next $N - D_2$ workers day 2 off. Continue in a similar manner until all days have been scheduled.
3. If the number of workdays for a full-time employee is less than 5, assign the remaining workdays so that consecutive days off are possible or where unmet demand is highest.
4. Assign any remaining work to part-time employees, subject to maximum hour restrictions.
5. If consecutive days off are desired, consider switching schedules among days with the same demand requirements.

The heuristic just illustrated can be adapted to ensure that the two days off per week are consecutive. Other heuristics schedule workers two weeks at a time, with every other weekend off.

EXAMPLE 17.6

EMPLOYEE SCHEDULING

Diet-Tech employs five workers to operate its weight-reduction facility. Demand for service each week (in terms of minimum number of workers required) is given in the following table. Create an employee schedule that will meet the demand requirements and guarantee each worker two days off per week. Use O for day off and X for working.

Day of Week	M	T	W	Th	F	Sa	Su
No. of Workers	3	3	4	3	4	5	3
Taylor							
Smith							
Simpson							
Allen							
Dickerson							

SOLUTION

The completed employee schedule matrix is shown next.

(Continued)

[1]Kenneth R. Baker, and Michael J. Magazine, "Workforce Scheduling with Cyclic Demands and Days-off Constraints." *Management Science* 24, issue 2 (October 1977): pp.161–167.

V

Day of Week	M	T	W	Th	F	Sa	Su
No. of Workers	3	3	4	3	4	5	3
Taylor	O	X	X	O	X	X	X
Smith	O	X	X	O	X	X	X
Simpson	X	O	X	X	O	X	X
Allen	X	O	X	X	X	X	O
Dickerson	X	X	O	X	X	X	O

Following the heuristic, the first (5 − 3) = 2 workers, Taylor and Smith, are assigned Monday off. The next (5 − 3) = 2 workers, Simpson and Allen, are assigned Tuesday off. The next (5 − 4) = 1 worker, Dickerson, is assigned Wednesday off. Returning to the top of the roster, the next (5 − 3) = 2 workers, Taylor and Smith, are assigned Thursday off. The next (5 − 4) = 1 worker, Simpson, is assigned Friday off. Everyone works on Saturday, and the next (5 − 3) = 2 workers, Allen and Dickerson, get Sunday off.

The resulting schedule meets demand and has every employee working 5 days a week with 2 days off. Unfortunately, none of the days off are consecutive. By switching the initial schedules for Tuesday and Thursday (both with a demand of 3) and the schedules for Wednesday and Friday (both with a demand of 4), the following schedule results:

Day of Week	M	T	W	Th	F	Sa	Su
No. of Workers	3	3	4	3	4	5	3
Taylor	O	O	X	X	X	X	X
Smith	O	O	X	X	X	X	X
Simpson	X	X	O	O	X	X	X
Allen	X	X	X	O	X	X	O
Dickerson	X	X	X	X	O	X	O

In this revised schedule, the first three workers have consecutive days off. The last two workers have one weekend day off and one day off during the week.

AUTOMATED SCHEDULING SYSTEMS

Scheduling large numbers of workers at numerous locations requires a computerized scheduling system. Sophisticated employee scheduling software is available as a stand-alone system or as part of an ERP package. For example, Infor's Workforce Labor Scheduler system provides:

- **Staff scheduling** assigns qualified workers to standardized shift patterns, taking into account leave requests and scheduling conflicts. The solutions consider legal and social constraints such as labor laws for minors, overtime payment regulations, and legal or religious holidays that may differ by global location.

- **Schedule bidding** puts certain shift positions or schedule assignments up for bid and allows workers to post and trade schedules with others as long as coverage and skill criteria are met.
- **Schedule optimization** creates demand-driven forecasts of labor requirements and assigns workers to variable schedules (in some cases, as small as 15-minute blocks of time) that change dynamically with demand. The optimization is based on mathematical programming and artificial intelligence techniques.

SUMMARY

Scheduling techniques vary by type of production process. Scheduling in a job shop environment is difficult because jobs arrive at varying time intervals, require different resources and sequences of operations, and are due at different times. This lowest level of scheduling is referred to as shop floor control or production control. It involves assigning jobs to machines or workers (called loading), specifying the order in which operations are to be performed, and monitoring the work as it progresses. Techniques such as the assignment method are used for *loading*, various rules whose performance varies according to the scheduling objective are used for *sequencing*, and Gantt charts and input/output control charts are used for *monitoring*.

Realistic schedules must reflect capacity limitations. *Infinite scheduling* initially assumes infinite capacity and then manually "levels the load" of resources that have exceeded capacity. *Finite scheduling* loads jobs in priority order and delays those jobs for which current capacity is exceeded. The *theory of constraints* is a finite scheduling approach that schedules bottleneck resources first and then schedules other resources to support the bottleneck schedule. It also allows items to be transferred between resources in lot sizes that differ from the lot size in which the item is produced. Other advanced planning and scheduling techniques include mathematical programming, genetic algorithms, and simulation.

Employee scheduling is often difficult because of the variety of options available and the special requirements for individual workers. Scheduling heuristics are typically used to develop patterns of worker assignment. Automated workforce scheduling systems are becoming more commonplace.

KEY FORMULAS

Minimum Slack

$$\text{SLACK} = (\text{due date} - \text{today's date}) - (\text{processing time})$$

Critical Ratio

$$\text{CR} = \frac{\text{time remaining}}{\text{work remaining}} = \frac{\text{due date} - \text{today's date}}{\text{remaining processing time}}$$

SOLVED PROBLEMS

1. ASSIGNMENT PROBLEM

Wilkerson Printing has four jobs waiting to be run this morning. Fortunately, four printing presses are available. However, the presses are of different vintage and operate at different speeds. The approximate times (in minutes) required to process each job on each press are given next. Assign jobs to presses to minimize the press running times.

	PRESS			
JOB	*1*	*2*	*3*	*4*
A	20	90	40	10
B	40	45	50	35
C	30	70	35	25
D	60	45	70	40

SOLUTION

Row reduction:

10	80	30	0
5	10	15	0
5	45	10	0
20	5	30	0

Column reduction:

5	75	20	0
0	5	5	0
0	40	0	0
15	0	20	0

Cover all zeros:

5	75	20	0
0	5	5	0
0	40	0	0
15	0	20	0

The number of lines equals the number of rows, so this is the final solution. Make assignments:

5	75	20	0
0	5	5	0
0	40	0	0
15	0	20	0

Assign job A to press 4, job B to press 1, job C to press 3, and job D to press 2. Refer to the original matrix for actual processing times. The total machining time required is (10 + 40 + 35 + 45) = 130 minutes.

2. JOHNSON'S RULE

Clean and Shine Car Service has five cars waiting to be washed and waxed. The time required (in minutes) for each activity is given next. In what order should the cars be processed through the facility? When will the batch of cars be completed?

CAR	WASH	WAX
1	5	0
2	7	2
3	10	5
4	8	6
5	3	5

SOLUTION

Use Johnson's rule to sequence the cars. The lowest processing time is two minutes for waxing car 2. Since waxing is the second operation, we place car 2 as near to the end of the sequence as possible, in last place. The next-lowest time is three minutes for washing car 5. Since washing is the first operation, we place car 5 as near to the front of the sequence as possible, in first place. The next-lowest time is five minutes for washing car 1 and waxing car 3. Car 1 is scheduled in second place, and car 3 is put in next-to-last place (i.e., fourth). That leaves car 4 for third place.

The completion time for washing and waxing the five cars is 35 minutes. The washing facility is idle for two minutes at the end of the cycle. The waxing facility is idle for three minutes at the beginning of the cycle and four minutes during the cycle.

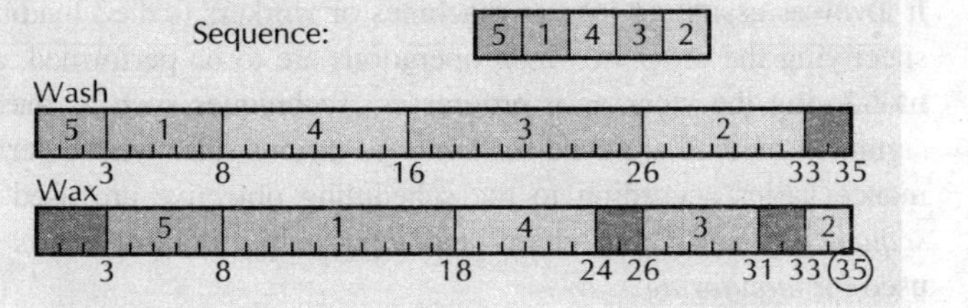

QUESTIONS

17-1. How do scheduling activities differ for projects, mass production, and process industries?

17-2. Why is scheduling a job shop so difficult?

17-3. What three functions are typically performed by a production control department?

17-4. Give examples of four types of operations (manufacturing or service) and suggest which scheduling objectives might be appropriate for each.

17-5. How can the success of a scheduling system be measured?

17-6. Describe the process of loading and load leveling. What quantitative techniques are available to help in this process?

17-7. What is the purpose of dispatch lists? How are they usually constructed?

17-8. When should the following sequencing rules be used? (a) SPT; (b) Johnson's rule; (c) DDATE; (d) FCFS.

17-9. Give examples of sequencing rules you use to prioritize work.

17-10. What information is provided by the critical ratio sequencing rule? How does it differ from SLACK?

17-11. How are work packages, hot lists, and exception reports used in a job shop?

17-12. What are Gantt charts, and why are they used so often?

17-13. Explain the concept behind input/output control. Describe how gateway work centers, downstream work centers, and backlogs affect shop performance.

17-14. Explain the difference between infinite and finite scheduling.

17-15. How does theory of constraints differ from traditional scheduling? How should bottleneck resources and nonbottleneck resources be scheduled? Why should transfer batches and process batches be treated differently?

17-16. Explain the drum-buffer-rope concept.

17-17. Discuss the similarities and differences between theory of constraints and lean production.

17-18. What are some typical issues involved in employee scheduling?

17-19. What quantitative techniques are available to help develop employee schedules? What quantitative techniques are available for advanced planning and scheduling systems?

17-20. Look for advanced planning and scheduling software on the Internet. Write a summary of the techniques presented.

PROBLEMS

17-1. At Valley Hospital, nurses beginning a new shift report to a central area to receive their primary patient assignments. Not every nurse is as efficient as another with particular kinds of patients. Given the following patient roster, care levels, and time estimates, assign nurses to patients to optimize efficiency. Also, determine how long it will take for the nurses to complete their routine tasks on this shift.

		Time Required (Hours) to Complete Routine Tasks			
Patient	**Care Level**	***Nurse 1***	***Nurse 2***	***Nurse 3***	***Nurse 4***
A. Jones	A2	3	5	4	3
B. Hathaway	B2	2	1	3	2
C. Bryant	B1	3	4	2	2
D. Sweeney	A1	4	3	3	4

17-2. Valley Hospital (from Problem 17-1) wants to focus on customer perceptions of quality, so it has asked its patients to evaluate the nursing staff and indicate preferences for assignment.

a. Reassign the nursing staff to obtain the highest customer approval rating possible (a perfect score is 100). What is the average rating of the assignment?

b. Compare the results with those from Problem 17-1. What other criteria could be used to assign nurses?

	Rating			
Patient	***Nurse 1***	***Nurse 2***	***Nurse 3***	***Nurse 4***
A. Jones	89	95	83	84
B. Hathaway	88	80	96	85
C. Bryant	87	92	82	84
D. Sweeney	93	82	36	94

17-3. Fibrous Incorporated makes products from rough tree fibers. Its product line consists of five items processed through one of five machines. The machines are not identical, and some products are better suited to some machines. Given the following production time in minutes per unit, determine an optimal assignment of product to machine:

	Machine				
Product	***A***	***B***	***C***	***D***	***E***
1	17	10	15	16	20
2	12	9	16	9	14
3	11	16	14	15	12
4	14	10	10	18	17
5	13	12	9	15	11

17-4. Karina Nieto works for New Products Inc., and one of her many tasks is assigning new workers to departments. The company recently hired six new employees and would like each one to be assigned to a different department. The employees have completed a two-month training session in each of the six departments from which they received the evaluations shown below (higher numbers are better). Determine how the new employees should be assigned to departments so that overall performance is maximized.

	Departments					
Employees	**Sales**	**Finance**	**Logistics**	**Marketing Research**	**Production**	**Customer Service**
Albertson	18	17	14	19	19	18
Bunch	17	15	12	14	20	17
Carson	15	15	13	17	20	18
Denali	19	16	18	18	18	20
Ebersole	18	15	12	17	19	17
Finch	16	16	16	18	20	17

17-5. Decenture has four new IT hires available for assignment to ERP implementation projects. Their expertise varies across platforms and technologies, resulting in different time estimates for completing project tasks. Given the expected time to completion (in weeks) for the list of project tasks below, determine the project assignment that will ensure the tasks are completed in the shortest amount of time.

Hires	**Project 1**	**Project 2**	**Project 3**	**Project 4**
Alex	8	10	17	9
Bhavna	3	8	5	6
Chen	10	12	11	9
Denise	6	13	9	7

17-6. Blue Jeans Modeling Agency specializes in providing wholesome youthful models for top women's magazines. Blue Jeans assigns models to clients with an understanding of client philosophies, target markets and product characteristics. The company rates its models on a scale of 1 to 5 (with 5 being best) as to how close they are to the client's ideal model. For a given month's issue, only one model can be assigned to each client, and models cannot appear in more than one magazine. Given the ratings below, assign models to clients so that total client satisfaction is maximized. What is the total client satisfaction score?

	Client				
Model	***Mon Ami***	***Sixteen***	***Title Nine***	***Eloquence***	***Claire***
Anita	1	2	1	4	5
Bella	5	4	3	2	1
Christy	4	1	2	3	5
Danielle	4	2	2	1	3
Elise	2	4	4	4	1

17-7. Evan Schwartz has six jobs waiting to be processed through his machine. Processing time (in days) and due date information for each job are as follows:

Job	Processing Time	Due Date
A	2	3
B	1	2
C	4	12
D	3	4
E	4	8
F	5	10

Sequence the jobs by FCFS, SPT, SLACK, and DDATE. Calculate the mean flow time and mean tardiness of the six jobs under each sequencing rule. Which rule would you recommend?

17-8. Today is day 4 of the planning cycle. Sequence the following jobs by FCFS, SPT, SLACK, and DDATE. Calculate the mean flow time and mean tardiness for each sequencing rule. Which rule would you recommend?

Job	Processing Time (in days)	Due Date
A	3	10
B	10	12
C	2	25
D	4	8
E	5	15
F	8	18
G	7	20

17-9. Jobs A, B, C, and D must be processed through the same machine center. Sequence the following jobs by (a) SPT and (b) SLACK. Calculate mean flow time, mean tardiness, and maximum tardiness. Which sequencing rule would you recommend? Why?

Job	Processing Time	Due Date
A	20	20
B	10	15
C	30	50
D	15	30

17-10. Jobs processed through Percy's machine shop pass through milling first, and then turning. The current backlog of jobs and hours required at each machine follow:

Job	Milling	Turning
A	5	4
B	2	5
C	3	1
D	1	0
E	4	2

Sequence the jobs so that the entire set of jobs is completed as soon as possible. Make a Gantt chart to map out the schedule on each machine and determine the makespan for the set of jobs.

17-11. Sassy U makes fashion jeans out of a variety of denim materials that differ in thickness, stiffness, drape and weave. Customers receive a sampling of product in each type of material before final orders are placed. Each day, bolts of denim cloth received from suppliers wait their turn in the cutting department. The cutting sequence is developed from an algorithm called *Johnson's Rule* which examines the time required for *spreading* the cloth on a cutting table (plus marking the pattern) and the time required for *cutting* it into pattern pieces that will later be sewn together. These times can vary considerably due to number of pattern pieces, pattern placement (matching stripes, for example), cloth thickness, and whether the cutting is to be performed by hand (with an electric knife) or by a CNC textile-cutting machine.

a. Given the time data below, determine the optimal sequence of denim cloth through the cutting room so that makespan is minimized.
b. Map out the spreading and cutting processes on a Gantt chart and calculate the makespan.
c. Using the sequence determined above, when will the stretch denim material leave the cutting room?

Cloth	Code	Spreading (hrs)	Cutting (hrs)
Organic Denim	O	2	6
Poly Denim	P	4	2
Quilted Denim	Q	6	3
Ramie Denim	R	2	1
Stretch Denim	S	3	5
Twill Denim	T	1	4

17-12. Restore is a small repair shop that makes customized parts for old equipment. All customer orders must be machined first, then polished. Determine a sequence that will minimize the time required to process all six jobs. Chart the schedule on a Gantt chart and indicate the makespan.

Jobs	Machining	Polishing
A	5.0	4.0
B	7.0	3.0
C	3.0	2.0
D	4.0	1.0
E	1.0	2.0
F	3.0	4.0

17-13. Precision Painters, Inc., has five house painting jobs in one neighborhood. The houses differ in size, state of repair, and painting requirements, but each house must be prepped (cleaned, old paint chipped off, primed) first, then painted. In what sequence should the houses be worked on in order to finish all five houses as soon as possible? Chart out your sequences on Gantt charts and calculate the makespan.

	Days	
Houses	*Prep*	*Paint*
Addison	4	2
Brown	3	6

	Days	
Houses	***Prep***	***Paint***
Clayton	6	4
Daniels	5	6
Ebersole	1	4

17-14. Sequence the houses in Problem 17-13 by SPT and LPT. How much time is saved with Johnson's rule?

17-15. Tracy has six chapters on her desk that must be typed and proofed as soon as possible. Tracy does the typing; the author does the proofing. Some chapters are easy to type but more difficult to proof. The estimated time (in minutes) for each activity is given here. In what order should Tracy type the chapters so that the entire batch can be finished as soon as possible? When will the chapters be completed?

Chapter	Typing	Proofing
1	30	20
2	90	25
3	60	15
4	45	30
5	75	60
6	20	30

17-16. The following data have been compiled for an input/output report at Work Center 7. Complete the report and analyze the results.

Period	1	2	3	4	5	Total
Planned input	50	55	60	65	65	
Actual input	50	50	55	60	65	
Deviation						
Planned output	65	65	65	65	65	
Actual output	60	60	60	60	60	
Deviation						
Backlog 30						

17-17. The input/output report for Work Center 6 is as follows. Complete the report and comment on the results.

Period	1	2	3	4	5	Total
Planned input	50	55	60	65	65	
Actual input	40	50	55	60	65	
Deviation						
Planned output	50	55	60	65	65	
Actual output	50	50	55	60	65	
Deviation						
Backlog 10						

17-18. Schedule the wait staff at Vincent's Restaurant based on the following estimates of demand. Each employee should have two or more days off per week.

Days of the Week	M	T	W	Th	F	Sa	Su
Employees Needed	2	3	4	4	5	5	4
Amy Russell							
Shannon Hiller							
Jessica Jones							
Tom Turner							
Evalin Trice							
Pierre Dubois							

17-19. Mr. Baskins, manager of Tom and Jerry's Ice Cream Shoppe, needs help scheduling servers for next week. Create a schedule that will meet the demand requirements given below and guarantee each server two days off per week.

	M	T	W	Th	F	Sa	Su
Daily Requirements	1	3	3	5	4	5	4
Anna							
Brent							
Caleb							
David							
Edhas							

17-20. Casey Belzer runs a machine shop that fabricates parts for sprayers used in foam insulation equipment. Due to increasing interest in green building practices and high energy costs, demand for his products has increased dramatically. The shop has three CNC machines that can serve a variety of purposes. As customer orders come in, a routing sheet is developed and the order is diagrammed as shown below. When demand was low, it didn't really matter how the jobs were scheduled. Now, Casey wants to finish each job as quickly as possible so he can move on to the next one. Help Casey develop a schedule that would finish a customer order for 200 units of part A as soon as possible. Assume one B, C, and D are needed for each A.

a. Find the bottleneck process.

b. According to the theory of constraints, which component (i.e., B, C, or D) should be scheduled first on the bottleneck process?

c. Which component should be scheduled last?

d. Map out the optimum schedule on a Gantt chart and calculate the completion time. Assume that the process batch size is 200 and the transfer batch size is one.

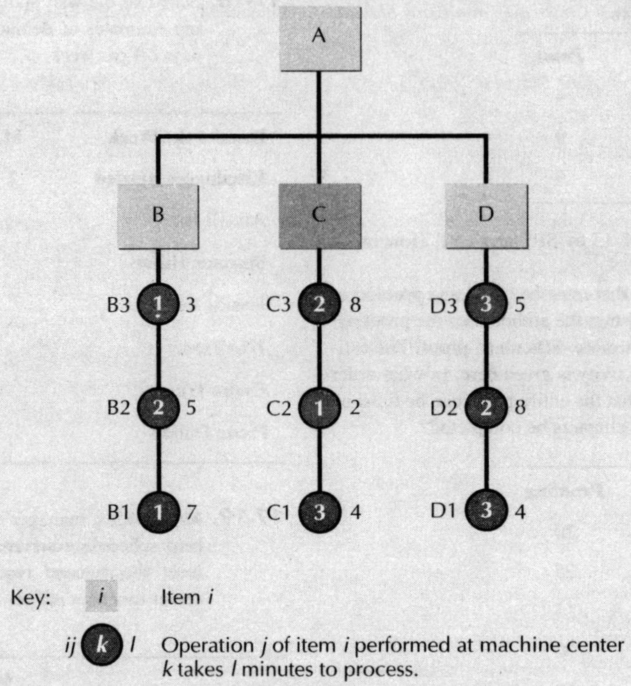

CASE STUDY

Developing the Best Manufacturing Schedule

Jiro's machine-shop has been asked to bid on the fabrication of six different versions of specialty door handles. The order will be for 100 handles each. The fabrication of each handle follows a two-step fabrication process:

Step 1 is where the actual handle piece is milled from a metal bank.

Step 2 involves attaching the handle to standard handle extension pieces. Depending on handle type, it takes different times to complete each of these steps.

Historically the machine shop has completed the work in batches. The first batch involves milling all the handles. Once all handles are ready, the company assembles all handles. Each process is based on a shortest process time rule.

Using the data below,

a. Determine the shortest time that the firm can manufacture one each of these handles.

b. Based on the time to build a single set of handles, determine how long it will take to fabricate all of the order.

c. Compare the total time to fabricate these handles with the time it historically takes for the machine shop to complete the job, based on a SPT batch process.

Handle	Mill	Assemble
1	23	14
2	12	6
3	24	11
4	7	6
5	15	13
6	11	22

REFERENCES

Baker, K., and M. Magazine. "Workforce Scheduling with Cyclic Demands and Days-Off Constraints." *Management Science* 24, issue 2 (October 1977): 161–167.

Conway, R., W. Maxwell, and L. Miller. *Theory of Scheduling*. Reading, MA: Addison-Wesley, 1967.

Goldratt, E. *What Is This Thing Called Theory of Constraints and How Should It Be Implemented?* Croton-on-Hudson, NY: North River Press, 1990.

Goldratt, E., and J. Cox. *The Goal: Excellence in Manufacturing*. Croton-on-Hudson, NY: North River Press, 1984.

Gupta, J. N. D. "An Excursion in Scheduling Theory." *Production Planning and Control* 13, issue 2 (2002): pp. 105–116.

Huang, P., L. Moore, and R. Russell. "Workload versus Scheduling Policies in a Dual-Resource Constrained Job Shop." *Computers and Operations Research* 11, issue 1 (1984): pp. 37–47.

Jacobs, R, W. Berry, D. C. Whybark, and T. Vollman. *Manufacturing Planning and Control for Supply Chain Management*. New York: McGraw-Hill, 2011.

Langevin, A., D. Riopel, and K. Stecke, "Transfer Batch Sizes in Flexible Manufacturing Systems." *Journal of Manufacturing Systems* (March–April 1999), pp. 140–151.

Pinedo, M. *Scheduling: Theory, Algorithms and Systems*. New York: Springer, 2008.

Russell, R., and B. W. Taylor. "An Evaluation of Sequencing Rules for an Assembly Shop." *Decision Sciences* 16, issue 2 (1985): pp. 196–212.

SAP AG. "Production Planning and Detailed Scheduling." Company brochure (December 1999).

Smith, K. A., and J. N. D. Gupta. "Neural Networks in Business." *Computers and Operations Research* 27, issue 1 (2000): pp. 1023–1044.

Umble, M., and M. L. Srikanth. *Synchronous Manufacturing: Principles for World Class Excellence*. Cincinnati: South-Western, 1990.

Xudong, H., R. Russell, and J. Dickey. "Workload Analysis Expert System and Optimizer." *Proceedings of the Seventh International Congress of Cybernetics and Systems,* Vol. 1, London (September 1987), pp. 68–72.

SUPPLEMENT A: GLOSSARY

5 Why's repeatedly ask "Why?" until a root cause is identified.

ABC system a method for classifying inventory items according to their dollar value to the firm based on the principle that only a few items account for the greatest dollar value of total inventory.

activity-on-arrow (AOA) a convention for constructing a CPM/PERT network in which the branches between nodes represent project activities.

activity-on-node (AON) a convention for constructing a CPM/PERT network in which the nodes represent project activities.

activity performance of an individual job or work effort that requires labor, resources, and time and is subject to management control.

adjusted exponential smoothing an exponential smoothing forecast adjusted for trend.

advanced planning and scheduling (APS) a software system that uses intelligent analytical tools and techniques to develop realistic schedules.

aggregate planning the process of determining the quantity and timing of production over an intermediate time frame.

agile project management an approach to project management that focuses on adaptability to rapid and unexpected change.

alternative workplace a combination of nontraditional work locations, settings, and practices that supplements or replaces the traditional office.

andons call lights installed at workstations to notify management and other workers of a quality problem in production.

appraisal costs costs of measuring, testing, and analyzing materials, parts, products, and the productive process to make sure they conform to design specifications.

arrival rate the rate (λ) at which customers arrive at a service facility during a specified period.

assemble-to-order a manufacturing environment in which major subassemblies are produced in advance of a customer's order and are then *configured to order*.

assembly chart a schematic diagram of a product that shows the relationship of component parts to parent assemblies, the groupings of parts that make up a subassembly, and the overall sequence of assembly.

attribute a product characteristic that can be evaluated with a discrete response such as yes or no, good or bad.

available-to-promise the quantity of items that can be promised to the customer; the difference between planned production and customer orders already received.

average error the cumulative error averaged over the number of time periods.

backlog accumulated customer orders to be completed at a later date.

backordering ordering an item that is temporarily out of stock.

backward pass starting at the end of a CPM/PERT network, a procedure for determining latest activity times.

backward scheduling scheduling backward from a due date to determine when to begin a job.

balance delay the total idle time of an assembly line.

balanced scorecard a performance assessment that includes metrics related to customers, processes, and learning and growing, as well as financials.

batch production the low-volume production of customized products.

benchmark a level of quality achievement established by one company that other companies seek to achieve (i.e., a goal).

benchmarking finding the best-in-class product or process, measuring one's performance against it, and making recommendations for improvements based on the results.

best-of-breed the selection of ERP modules from different vendors.

best operating level the percent of capacity utilization at which unit costs are lowest.

beta distribution a probability distribution traditionally used in CPM/PERT for estimating the mean and variance of project activity times.

big data very large volumes of both structured and unstructured data.

bill of material (BOM) a list of all the materials, parts, and assemblies that make up a product, including quantities, parent–component relationships, and order of assembly.

black belt in a Six Sigma program, the leader of a quality improvement project; a full-time position.

block diagram a schematic layout diagram that includes the size of each work area.

breakdown maintenance a maintenance activity that involves repairs needed to make a failed machine operational.

breakeven analysis a technique that determines the volume of demand needed to be profitable; it takes into account the trade-off between fixed and variable costs.

breakthrough strategy in Six Sigma, a five-step process for improvement projects: define, measure, analyze, improve, and control.

bullwhip effect occurs when demand variability is magnified at various upstream points in the supply chain.

calling population the source of customers to a waiting line.

capable-to-promise the quantity of items that can be produced and made available at a later date.

capacity cushion a percent of capacity held in reserve for unexpected occurrences.

capacity planning a long-term strategic decision that establishes the overall level of productive resources for a firm.

capacity requirements planning (CRP) a computerized system that projects the load from a given material plan onto the capacity of a system and identifies underloads and overloads.

capacity the maximum capability to produce.

carbon footprint a measure of the greenhouse gases produced by an activity, product or company.

carrying costs the cost of holding an item in inventory, including lost opportunity costs, storage, rent, cooling, lighting, interest on loans, and so on.

cause-and-effect diagram a graphical description of the elements of a specific quality problem; fishbone diagram.

cause-and-effect matrix a grid used to prioritize causes of quality problems.

c-chart a control chart based on the number of defects in a sample.

cellular layout a layout that creates individual cells to process parts or customers with similar requirements.

center-of-gravity technique a quantitative method for locating a facility at the center of movement in a geographic area based on weight and distance.

champion a member of top management who is responsible for project success in a Six Sigma program.

channels the number of parallel servers.

chase demand an aggregate planning strategy that schedules production to match demand and absorbs variations in demand by adjusting the size of the workforce.

cloud computing on-demand IT services usually delivered over the Internet; includes data storage as well as SaaS.

coefficient of determination the correlation coefficient squared; it measures the portion of the variation in the dependent variable that can be attributed to the independent variable.

coefficient of optimism (α) a measure of a decision maker's optimism, from 0 (completely pessimistic) to 1 (completely optimistic), used in the Hurwicz decision criterion.

collaborative planning, forecasting, and replenishment (CPFR) a process for two or more companies in a supply chain to synchronize their demand forecasts into a single plan to meet customer demand.

collaborative planning sharing information and synchronizing production plans across the supply chain.

collaborative product design (CPD) software system for collaborative design and development among trading partners.

competitiveness the degree to which a nation can produce goods and services that meet the test of international markets.

computer-aided design (CAD) a software system that uses computer graphics to assist in the creation, modification, and analysis of a design.

computer-aided design/computer-aided manufacturing (CAD/CAM) the ultimate design-to-manufacture connection.

computer-aided engineering (CAE) engineering analysis performed at a computer terminal with information from a CAD database.

computer-integrated manufacturing (CIM) automated manufacturing systems integrated through advanced information and communications technologies.

concurrent design a new approach to design that involves the simultaneous design of products and processes by design teams.

constraints linear relationships of decision variables representing the restrictions placed on the decision situation by the operating environment.

continuous inventory system a system in which the inventory level is continually monitored; when it decreases to a certain level, the reorder point, a fixed amount is ordered.

continuous production the production of a very-high-volume commodity product with highly automated equipment.

continuous replenishment supplying orders in a short period of time according to a predetermined schedule.

control chart a graph that visually shows if a sample is within statistical limits for defective items.

control limits the upper and lower bands of a control chart.

core competencies the activities that a company does best; the essential capabilities that create a firm's sustainable competitive advantage.

correlation a measure of the strength of the causal relationship between the independent and dependent variables in a linear regression equation.

cost index the ratio of quality cost to manufacturing cost.

craft production the process of handcrafting products or services for individual customers.

crash cost the cost of reducing the normal activity time.

crashing a method for shortening the project duration by reducing the time of one or more critical activities at a cost.

crash time the amount of time an activity is reduced.

critical path the longest path through a CPM/PERT network, indicating the minimum time in which a project can be completed.

cross-docking crossing of goods from one loading dock to another without being placed in storage.

cross training an employee learns more than one job in the organization.

cumulative error a sum of the forecast errors; also known as bias.

cumulative lead time the total length of time required to manufacture a product; also, the longest path through a product structure.

customer relationship management (CRM) software that plans and executes business processes that involve customer interaction, such as sales, marketing, fulfillment, and customer service.

cycle an up-and-down movement in demand over time.

cycle counting a method for auditing inventory accuracy that counts inventory and reconciles errors on a cyclical schedule rather than once a year.

cycle time the maximum amount of time an item is allowed to spend at each workstation if the targeted production rate is to be achieved; also, the time between successive product completions.

data mining is a process for analyzing large amounts of data to identify patterns, trends and relationships in groups.

decision analysis a set of quantitative decision-making techniques to aid the decision maker in dealing with decision situations in which uncertainty exists.

decision variables mathematical symbols that represent levels of activity of an operation.

delivery specification specify schedules, deliverables, and location.

delphi method a procedure for acquiring informed judgments and opinions from knowledgeable individuals to use as a subjective forecast.

dependent demand typically, component parts or materials used in the process to produce a final product.

design for environment (DFE) designing a product from material that can be recycled or easily repaired rather than discarded.

design for manufacture (DFM) designing a product so that it can be produced easily and economically.

design for Six Sigma (DFSS) a systematic methodology to design products and processes that meet customer expectations and can be produced at Six Sigma quality levels.

design for supply chain (DFSC) considering supply chain capabilities during product design.

design specification describe the service in enough detail to be replicated.

disaggregation the process of breaking down the aggregate plan into more detailed plans.

diseconomies of scale when higher levels of output cost more per unit to produce.

dispatch list a shop paper that specifies the sequence in which jobs should be processed; it is often derived from specific sequencing rules.

division of labor dividing a job into a series of small tasks each performed by a different worker.

DMADV define, measure, analyze, design and verify.

drum-buffer-rope a concept in the theory of constraints where the *drum* sets the pace of production, the *buffer* is placed in front of the bottleneck, and the *rope* communicates changes.

dummy an activity in a network that shows a precedence relationship but represents no passage of time.

earliest finish time (EF) the earliest time an activity can be completed.

earliest start time (ES) the earliest time an activity can begin subject to preceding activities.

earned value analysis (EVA) a standard procedure for measuring a project's progress, forecasting its completion time and cost, and measuring schedule and budget variation.

e-business the replacement of physical business processes with electronic ones.

eco-labeling a seal of approval for environmentally safe products.

economic order quantity (EOQ) a fixed-order quantity that minimizes total inventory costs.

economies of scale when it costs less per unit to produce higher levels of output.

efficiency how well a machine or worker performs compared to a standard output level.

electronic data interchange (EDI) a computer-to-computer exchange of business documents.

e-marketplaces websites where companies and suppliers conduct business-to-business activities.

empowerment the authority and responsibility of the workers to alert management about job-related problems.

enterprise resource planning (ERP) software that organizes and manages a company's business processes by sharing information across functional areas.

e-procurement business-to-business commerce in which purchases are made directly through a supplier's website.

equal likelihood (Laplace) criterion a decision criterion in which each state of nature is weighted equally.

ergonomics the application of human sciences like anatomy, physiology, and psychology to the design of the work environment and jobs, and objects and equipment used in work; fitting the task to the person.

event the completion or beginning of an activity in a project.

expected value a weighted average of decision outcomes in which each future state of nature is assigned a probability of occurrence.

expected value of perfect information (EVP) the maximum value that a decision maker would be willing to pay for perfect information about future states of nature.

expedite to speed up orders so that they are completed in less than their normal lead time.

explosion the process of determining requirements for lower-level items by multiplying the planned orders of parent items by the quantity per assembly of component items.

exponential smoothing an averaging method that weights the most recent data more strongly than more distant data.

extended producer responsibility (EPR) holding a company responsible for its product even after its useful life.

external failure costs costs of poor quality incurred after the product gets to the customer; that is, customer service, lost sales, and so on.

external setup setup activities that can be performed in advance while the machine is operating.

extreme points corner points, or protrusions, on the boundary of the feasible solution space in a linear programming model.

facility layout the arrangement of machines, departments, workstations, and other areas within a facility.

failure mode and effects analysis (FMEA) a systematic approach to analyzing the causes and effects of product failures.

fault tree analysis (FTA) a visual method for analyzing the interrelationships among failures.

feasible solution space an area that satisfies all constraints in a linear programming model simultaneously.

fill rate the fraction of orders placed by a customer with a supplier distribution center or warehouse that are filled within 24 hours.

finite scheduling an approach to scheduling that loads jobs in priority order and delays those jobs for which current capacity is exceeded.

fishbone diagram a graphical description of the elements of a specific quality problem; cause-and-effect diagram.

fitness for use a measure of how well a product or service does what the consumer thinks it is supposed to do and wants it to do.

fixed-position layout a layout in which the product remains at a stationary site for the entire manufacturing cycle.

fixed-time-period system also known as a periodic system; an inventory system in which a variable amount is ordered after a predetermined, constant passage of time.

flexibility in operations, the ability to adjust to changes in product mix, production volume, or product and process design.

flexible manufacturing system (FMS) programmable equipment connected by an automated material-handling system and controlled by a central computer.

flextime a work schedule in which fixed times of arrival and departure are replaced by a combination of fixed and variable times.

flow time the time that it takes for a job to "flow" through the system; that is, its completion time.

forecast error the difference between actual and forecasted demand.

form design the phase of product design concerned with how the product looks.

forward pass starting at the beginning of a CPM/PERT network, a procedure for determining earliest activity times.

forward scheduling scheduling forward from today's date to determine the earliest time a job can be completed.

functional design the phase of a product design concerned with how the product performs.

gainsharing an incentive plan that includes employees in a common effort to achieve a company's objectives in which they share in the gains.

Gantt chart a bar chart that shows a job's progress graphically or compares actual against planned performance; a graphical display using bars (or time lines) to show the duration of project activities and precedence relationships.

general-purpose machines perform several basic functions.

genetic algorithm a method that generates possible solutions based on genetic combinations of previous solutions.

goods tangible objects that can be created and sold at a later date.

graphical solution method a method for determining the solution of a linear programming problem using a two-dimensional graph of the model.

green belt in a Six Sigma program, a project team member, a part-time position.

heijunka the process of smoothing demand across a planning horizon.

horizontal job enlargement the scope of a job that includes all tasks necessary to complete a product or process.

hoshins the action plans generated from a policy deployment process.

Hurwicz criterion a decision criterion in which the decision payoffs are weighted by a coefficient of optimism, α.

independent demand final or finished products whose demand is not a function of, or dependent on, internal production activity.

index numbers ratios that measure quality costs relative to some base accounting values such as sales or product units.

infinite queue a waiting line that grows to any length.

infinite scheduling an approach to scheduling that initially assumes infinite capacity and then manually "levels the load" of resources that have exceeded capacity.

infrastructure the physical support structures in a community, including roads, water and sewage systems, and utilities.

innovation create a culture of change.

input/output (I/O) control a procedure for monitoring the input to and output from a work center to regulate the flow of work through a system.

interchangeable parts the standardization of parts initially as replacement parts; enabled mass production.

intermodal transportation combines several modes of transportation.

internal failure costs costs of poor-quality products discovered during the production process—that is, scrap, rework, and the like.

internal setup setup activities that can be performed only when the machine is stopped.

inventory a stock of items kept by an organization to meet internal or external customer demand; insurance against supply chain uncertainty held between supply chain stages.

inventory turns a supply chain performance metric computed by dividing the cost of goods sold by the average aggregate value of inventory.

item master file a file that contains inventory status and descriptive information on every item in inventory.

jidoka authority given to the workers to stop the assembly line when quality problems are encountered.

job a defined set of tasks that compose the work performed by employees that contributes to the production of a product or delivery of a service.

job rotation the horizontal movement between two or more jobs according to a plan or schedule.

Johnson's rule an algorithm for sequencing any number of jobs through two serial operations to minimize makespan.

just-in-time (JIT) smoothing the flow of material to arrive just as it is needed; evolved into a system for eliminating waste.

kaizen a Japanese term for a system of continuous improvement; involving everyone in the workplace in a process of gradual, organized, and continuous improvement.

kanban a card corresponding to a standard quantity of production (or size container) used in the pull system to authorize the production or withdrawal of goods.

kanban square a marked area designated to hold a certain amount of items; an empty square is the signal to produce more items.

key performance indicator (KPI) a metric used to measure supply chain performance; a set of measures that help managers evaluate performance in critical areas.

labor index the ratio of quality cost to direct labor hours.

landed cost total cost of producing, storing, and transporting a product to the site of consumption.

latest finish time (LF) the latest time an activity can be completed and still maintain the project critical path time.

latest start time (LS) the latest time an activity can begin and not delay subsequent activities.

lean production an adaptation of mass production that prizes quality and flexibility; both a philosophy and an integrated system of management that emphasizes the elimination of waste and the continuous improvement of operations.

lean Six Sigma a combination of lean's principles for eliminating waste with Six Sigma's reduction of variability; integrating Six Sigma and lean systems.

learning curve a graph that reflects the improvement rate of workers as a job is repeated and more units are produced.

level production an aggregate planning strategy that produces units at a constant rate and uses inventory to absorb variations in demand.

linear decision rule (LDR) a mathematical technique for aggregate planning.

linear programming a technique for general decision situations in which the decision is to determine a level of operational activity in order to achieve an objective, subject to restrictions.

linear regression a mathematical technique that relates a dependent variable to an independent variable in the form of a linear equation.

linear trend line a forecast using the linear regression equation to relate demand to time.

line balancing a layout technique that attempts to equalize the amount of work assigned to each workstation on an assembly line.

line of influence signs or activities that influence a customer to seek a service.

line of interaction point where a customer and service provider interact.

line of support point where a service provider interacts with support personnel.

line of visibility point that separates front-office and back-office activities.

load the standard hours of work assigned to a facility.

load-distance technique a quantitative method for evaluating various facility locations using a value that is a measure of weight and distance.

loading the process of assigning work to individual workers or machines.

load leveling the process of balancing underloads and overloads; the process of smoothing out the work assigned across time and the available resources.

load percent the ratio of load to capacity.

load profile a chart that compares released orders and planned orders with the capacity of a facility.

location factor rating a system for weighting the importance of different factors in the location decision, scoring the individual factors, and then developing an overall location score that enables a comparison of different location sites.

logistics the transportation and distribution of goods and services.

long-range forecast a forecast encompassing a period longer than two years into the future.

lost sales forfeited sales for out-of-stock items.

lot sizing determining the quantities in which items are usually made or purchased.

maintainability the ease with which a product is maintained or repaired.

makespan the time that it takes for a group of jobs to be completed—that is, the completion time of the last job in a group.

management coefficients model A regression technique for aggregate planning.

managing diversity includes education, awareness, communication, fairness, and commitment.

manufacturing cell a group of dissimilar machines brought together to manufacture a family of parts with similar shapes or processing requirements.

manufacturing execution systems (MES) manufacturing software that monitors operations, collects data, and controls processes on the shop floor.

mass customization the mass production of customized products.

mass production the high-volume production of a standardized product for a mass market.

master black belt in a Six Sigma program, a teacher and mentor for Black Belts; a full-time position.

master production schedule (MPS) a schedule for the production of end items (usually final products). It drives the MRP process that schedules the production of component parts.

material kanban a rectangular-shaped kanban used to order material in advance of a process.

material requirements planning (MRP) a computerized inventory control and production planning system for generating purchase orders and work orders of materials, components, and assemblies.

matrix organization an organizational structure of project teams that includes members from various functional areas in the company.

maximax criterion a decision criterion that results in the maximum of the maximum payoffs.

maximin criterion a decision criterion that results in the maximum of the minimum payoffs.

mean absolute deviation (MAD) the per-period average of the absolute difference between actual and forecasted demand.

mean absolute percent deviation (MAPD) the absolute forecast error measured as a percentage of demand.

mean squared error (MSE) the average of the squared forecast errors.

mean ($\bar{x}$-) chart a control chart based on the means of the samples taken.

minimax regret criterion a decision criterion that results in the minimum of the maximum regrets for each alternative.

mixed-model assembly line an assembly line that processes more than one product model.

mixed strategy varying two or more capacity factors to determine a feasible production plan.

modular bill of material a special bill of material used to plan the production of products with many optional features.

modular design combining standardized building blocks, or modules, in a variety of ways to create unique finished products.

most likely time the subjective estimate of the time that would occur most frequently if the activity were repeated many times.

motion study the study of the individual human motions used in a task.

motivation a willingness to work hard because that effort satisfies an employee need.

moving average average demand for a fixed sequence of periods including the most recent period.

muda anything other than the minimum amount of equipment, materials, parts, space, and time that are absolutely essential to add value to the product.

multifunctional workers workers who have been trained to perform more than one job or function.

multiple regression a mathematical relationship that relates a dependent variable to two or more independent variables.

Muther's grid a format for displaying manager preferences for department locations.

nation groups nations joined together into trading groups.

netting the process of subtracting on-hand quantities and scheduled receipts from gross requirements to produce net requirements.

objective function a linear mathematical relationship that describes the objective of an operation in terms of decision variables.

on-demand (direct-response) delivery requires the supplier to deliver goods when demanded by the customer.

operating characteristics measures of waiting line performance expressed as averages.

operations a function or system that transforms inputs into outputs of greater value.

operations management the design and operation of productive systems.

optimal solution the single best solution to a problem.

optimistic time the shortest possible time to complete the activity if everything went right.

order cycle the time between the receipt of orders in an inventory system.

order fulfillment the process of ensuring on-time delivery of a customer's order.

ordering costs the cost of replenishing the stock of inventory including requisition cost, transportation and shipping, receiving, inspection, handling, and so forth.

order qualifiers the characteristics of a product or service that qualify it to be considered for purchase.

order winner the characteristic of a product or service that wins orders in the marketplace.

organizational breakdown structure (OBS) a chart that shows which organizational units are responsible for work items.

outsourcing purchasing goods and services that were originally produced in-house from an outside supplier.

pareto analysis a method for identifying the causes of poor quality, which usually shows that most quality problems result from only a few causes.

participative problem solving involving employees directly in the quality-management process to identify and solve problems.

partnering a relationship between a company and its supplier based on mutual quality standards.

pattern test a statistical test to determine if the observations within the limits of a control chart display a nonrandom pattern.

payoff the outcome of a decision.

payoff table a means of organizing and illustrating the payoffs from different decisions given various states of nature.

***p*-chart** a control chart based on the proportion defective of the samples taken.

peak demand staffing for high levels of customer service.

perceptual map visual method for comparing customer perceptions of different products or services.

performance specification outline expectations and requirements.

periodic inventory system a system in which the inventory level is checked after a specific time period and a variable amount is ordered, depending on the inventory in stock.

periodic order quantity a lot sizing technique that orders at set time intervals.

pessimistic time (b) the longest possible time to complete the activity given that everything went wrong.

phases the number of sequential servers a customer must go through to receive service.

point-of-sale data computer records of sales at retail sites.

poka-yoke any foolproof device or mechanism that prevents defects from occurring.

policy deployment a planning system for converting strategy to measurable objectives throughout all levels of an organization.

positioning determining how a firm will compete in the marketplace.

postponement moving some final manufacturing steps like final assembly or product customization into the warehouse or distribution center.

precedence relationship the sequential relationship of project activities to each other.

precedence requirements physical restrictions on the order in which operations are performed.

prevention costs costs incurred during product design and manufacturing that prevent nonconformance to specifications.

preventive maintenance a system of daily maintenance, periodic inspection, and preventive repairs designed to reduce the probability of machine breakdown.

primary task the task that is most central to the operation of a firm; it defines the business that a firm is in and is often expressed in a mission statement.

process a group of related tasks with specific inputs and outputs.

process capability the range of natural variability in a process; the capability of a process to accommodate design specifications of a product.

process flowchart a diagram of the steps in a job, operation, or process; a document that uses standardized symbols to chart the productive and nonproductive flow of activities involved in a process; it may be used to document current processes or as a vehicle for process improvement.

process innovation the total redesign of a process.

process layout a layout that groups similar activities together into work centers according to the process or function they perform.

process planning the conversion of designs into workable instructions for manufacture, along with associated decisions on component purchase or fabrication, and process and equipment selection.

process plans a set of documents that detail manufacturing or service delivery specifications.

process strategy an organization's overall approach for physically producing goods and services.

procurement purchasing goods and services from suppliers.

production control scheduling and monitoring day-to-day production in a job shop.

production design the phase of product design concerned with how the product will be produced.

production flow analysis (PFA) a group technology technique that reorders part routing matrices to identify families of parts with similar processing requirements.

production index the ratio of quality cost to final product units.

production kanban a card authorizing the production of a container of goods.

production quantity model also known as the production lot-size model; an inventory system in which an order is received gradually and the inventory level is depleted at the same time it is being replenished.

productivity a measure of effectiveness in converting resources into products, generally computed as output divided by input; the ratio of output to input.

product layout a layout that arranges activities in a line according to the sequence of operations that are needed to assemble a particular product.

product lifecycle management (PLM) software that manages the product development process, product lifecycles, and design collaboration with suppliers and customers.

product structure file a file that contains computerized bills of material for all products.

profit sharing the company sets aside a portion of profits and distributes it among employees, usually at the end of the fiscal year.

prohibited route a transportation route over which items cannot be transported.

project the one-of-a-kind production of a product to customer order that requires a long time to complete and a large investment of funds and resources.

pull system a production system in which items are manufactured only when called for by the users of those items.

pure strategy varying only one capacity factor in aggregate planning.

push system a production system in which items are manufactured according to a schedule prepared in advance.

qualitative forecast methods nonquantitative, subjective forecasts based on judgment, opinion, experience, and expert opinion.

quality circles a small, voluntary group (team) of workers and supervisors formed to address quality problems in their area.

quality functional deployment (QFD) a structured process that translates the customer's voice into technical design.

quality impact on productivity fewer defects increase output and quality improvement reduces inputs.

quality management system (QMS) a system to achieve customer satisfaction that complements other company systems.

quality of conformance the degree to which the product or service meets the specifications required by design during the production process.

quality of design the degree to which quality characteristics are designed into a product or service.

quality–productivity ratio (QPR) a productivity index that includes productivity and quality costs.

quality revolution an emphasis on quality and the strategic role of operations.

quantitative forecast methods forecasts derived from a mathematical formula.

quantity discount a pricing schedule in which lower prices are provided for specific (higher) order quantities.

queue a single waiting line that forms in front of a service facility.

queue discipline the order in which customers are served.

radio frequency identification (RFID) radio waves used to transfer data, like an electronic product code, between an item with an embedded microchip and a reader.

random variations movements in demand that are not predictable and follow no pattern.

range (*R*-) chart a control chart based on the range (from the highest to the lowest values) of the samples taken.

range the difference between the smallest and largest values in a sample.

rapid prototyping quickly testing and revising a preliminary design model.

regression forecasting methods a class of mathematical techniques that relate demand to factors that cause demand behavior.

relationship diagram a schematic diagram that denotes location preference with different line thicknesses.

reliability the probability that a given part or product will perform its intended function for a specified period of time under normal conditions of use.

remanufacturing making new products from recycled parts.

reorder point a level of inventory in stock at which a new order is placed.

resilience the ability to bounce back, change, or adapt in response to a disaster, failure, or disruption.

responsibility assignment matrix (RAM) shows who in the organization is responsible for doing the work in the project.

revenue management the process of determining the percentage of seats or rooms to be allocated to different fare classes.

reverse auction a company posts items it wants to purchase on an Internet e-marketplace for suppliers to bid on.

reverse engineering carefully dismantling and inspecting a competitor's product to look for design features that can be incorporated into your own product.

risk pooling an approach to risk management that aggregates risk to reduce its impact.

robust design the design of a product or a service that can withstand variations in environmental and operating conditions.

run a sequence of sample values that display the same tendency in a control chart.

SaaS software as a service; on-demand access of software from a provider's site.

safety stock an amount added to the expected amount demanded during the lead time (the reorder point level) as a hedge against a stockout.

sales index the ratio of quality cost to sales.

sales & operations planning (S&OP) a process for coordinating supply and demand.

sample a portion of the items produced to use for inspection.

scheduling the determination of *when* labor, equipment, and facilities are needed to produce a product or provide a service.

scientific management the systematic analysis of work methods proposed by Frederick Taylor in the early 1900s.

scope statement a document that provides an understanding, justification, and expected result for the project.

SCOR the supply chain operations reference model; a diagnostic tool that provides a cross-industry standard for supply chain management.

search decision rule (SDR) a pattern search technique for aggregate planning.

seasonal factor a numerical value that is multiplied by the normal forecast to get a seasonally adjusted forecast.

seasonal pattern an oscillating movement in demand that occurs periodically in the short run and is repetitive.

sequencing the process of assigning priorities to jobs so that they are processed in a particular order.

sequential decision tree a graphical method for analyzing decision situations that require a sequence of decisions over time.

service blueprinting a specialized flow chart used for service processes.

service concept the purpose of a service; it defines the target market and the customer experience.

service level the probability that the amount of inventory on hand during the lead time is sufficient to meet expected demand.

service package the mixture of physical items, sensual benefits, and psychological benefits provided to the customer.

services acts, deeds or performances that provide value to the customer.

servicescapes the design of the physical environment (including signs, symbols, and artifacts) in which a service takes place.

service time the time required to serve a customer; the time period divided by service time yields the service rate (μ).

shortage costs temporary or permanent loss of sales that will result when customer demand cannot be met.

short- to mid-range forecast a forecast encompassing the immediate future, usually days or weeks, but up to two years.

signal kanban a triangular kanban used as a reorder point to signal production at the previous workstation.

simplex method a series of mathematical steps conducted within a tabular structure for solving a linear programming model.

simplification reducing the number of parts, subassemblies, or options in a product.

Six Sigma a measure of how much a given product or process deviates from perfection, or zero defects; the basis of a quality-improvement program.

slack the amount by which an activity can be delayed without delaying any of the activities that follow it or the project as a whole.

slack variable a variable added to a linear programming $\leq$ constraint to make it an equality.

smoothing constant the weighting factor given to the most recent data in exponential smoothing forecasts.

SOA service-oriented architecture; a software architecture that bundles together stand-alone services.

sourcing the selection of suppliers.

spend analysis a formal process for analyzing procurement data to lower costs.

standardization using commonly available parts that are interchangeable among products.

statement of work a written description of the objectives of a project.

statistical process control (SPC) a statistical procedure for monitoring the quality of the production process using control charts.

stockout an inventory shortage occurring when demand exceeds the inventory in stock.

strategy a common vision that unites an organization, provides consistency in decisions, and keeps the organization moving in the right direction.

supplier kanban a kanban that rotates between a factory and its supplier.

supply chain the facilities, functions, and activities involved in producing and delivering a product or service from suppliers (and their suppliers) to customers (and their customers).

supply chain management managing the flow of information, products, and services across a network of customers, enterprises, and supply chain partners in order to attain the level of synchronization that will make it more responsive to customer needs while lowering costs; software that plans and executes business processes related to supply chains.

surplus variable a variable subtracted from a ≥ linear programming constraint to make it an equality.

sustainability meeting present needs without compromising the ability of future generations to meet their needs.

takt time the cycle time of an operation paced to the rate of customer demand.

tardiness the difference between a job's due date and its completion time for jobs completed after their due date.

tariffs (duties) taxes on imported goods.

tasks individual, defined job activities that consist of one or more elements.

telecommuting employees work electronically from whatever location they choose, either exclusively or some of the time.

theory of constraints a finite scheduling approach that differentiates between bottleneck and nonbottleneck resources and between transfer batches and process batches.

time fence a date specified by management beyond which no changes in the master schedule are allowed.

time frame how far into the future something is forecasted.

time-phased bill of material an assembly chart shown against a time scale.

time phasing the process of subtracting an item's lead time from its due date to determine when an order should be released.

time series methods a class of statistical methods that uses historical demand data over a period of time to predict future demand.

tolerances allowable ranges of variation; product design specifications required by the customer.

total productive maintenance (TPM) an approach to machine maintenance that combines the practice of preventive maintenance with the concepts of total quality and employer involvement.

total quality management (TQM) the management of quality throughout the organization at all management levels and across all areas.

tracking signal a measure computed by dividing the cumulative error by MAD; used for monitoring bias in a forecast.

trade specialists specialists who help manage transportation and distribution operations in foreign countries.

transportation model transporting items from sources with fixed supplies to destinations with fixed demands at the minimum cost, time, etc.

transshipment model a special case of the transportation problem in which intermediate shipping points exist between the sources and final destinations.

trend a gradual, long-term up or down movement of demand.

undercapacity scheduling the allocation of extra time in a schedule for nonproductive tasks such as problem solving or maintenance.

uniform production levels the result of smoothing production requirements on the final assembly line.

unit load the quantity in which material is normally moved, such as a unit at a time, a pallet, or a bin of material.

usability ease of use of a product or service.

utilization factor (ρ) the probability the server is busy and the customer must wait.

utilization the percentage of available working time that a worker spends working or a machine operating.

value the creation of value for the customer is an important aspect of supply chain management.

value added tax (VAT) an indirect tax on the increase in value of a good at any stage in the supply chain from raw material to final product.

value analysis (VA) an analytical approach for eliminating unnecessary design features and functions.

value chain a series of activities from supplier to customer that add value to a product or service; a more contemporary name for a supply chain.

variable measure a product characteristic that can be measured, such as weight or length.

vendor-managed inventory (VMI) a system in which manufacturers instead of distributors generate orders.

vertical integration the degree to which a firm produces the parts that go into its products.

vertical job enlargement the degree of self-determination and control allowed to workers over their own work; also referred to as job enrichment.

visual control procedures and mechanisms for making problems visible.

warehouse management system (WMS) an automated system that runs the day-to-day operations of a warehouse or distribution center and keeps track of inventory.

weighted moving average a moving average with more recent demand values adjusted with weights.

withdrawal kanban a card authorizing the withdrawal and movement of a container of goods.

work breakdown structure (WBS) a method for subdividing a project into different hierarchical levels of components.

worker-machine chart a chart that illustrates on a time scale the amount of time an operator and a machine are working or are idle in a job.

work package shop paperwork that travels with a job to specify what work needs to be done at a particular machine center and where the item should be routed next.

XML extensible markup language; used to help different ERP systems communicate over the Internet.

yield a measure of productivity; the sum of good-quality and reworked units.

SUPPLEMENT B: INDEX

F

G

Q

R

S

SUPPLEMENT C: NORMAL CURVE TABLE

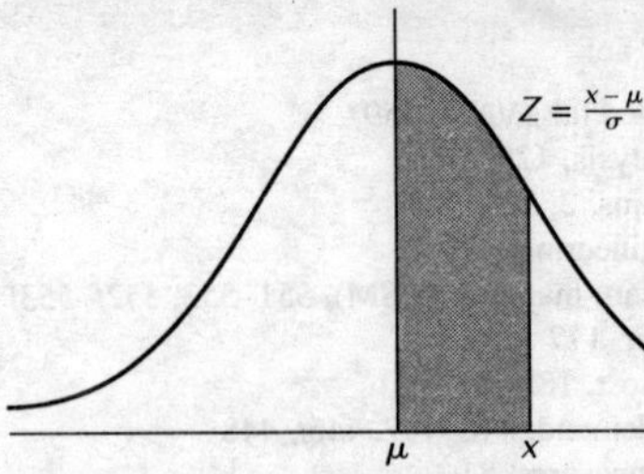

TABLE SC.1

Z	0.00	0.01	0.02	0.03	0.04	0.05	0.06	0.07	0.08	0.09
0.0	0.0000	0.0040	0.0080	0.0120	0.0160	0.0199	0.0239	0.0279	0.0319	0.0359
0.1	0.0398	0.0438	0.0478	0.0517	0.0557	0.0596	0.0636	0.0675	0.0714	0.0753
0.2	0.0793	0.0832	0.0871	0.0910	0.0948	0.0987	0.1026	0.1064	0.1103	0.1141
0.3	0.1179	0.1217	0.1255	0.1293	0.1331	0.1368	0.1406	0.1443	0.1480	0.1517
0.4	0.1554	0.1591	0.1628	0.1664	0.1700	0.1736	0.1772	0.1808	0.1844	0.1879
0.5	0.1915	0.1950	0.1985	0.2019	0.2054	0.2088	0.2123	0.2157	0.2190	0.2224
0.6	0.2257	0.2291	0.2324	0.2357	0.2389	0.2422	0.2454	0.2486	0.2517	0.2549
0.7	0.2580	0.2611	0.2642	0.2673	0.2704	0.2734	0.2764	0.2794	0.2823	0.2852
0.8	0.2881	0.2910	0.2939	0.2967	0.2995	0.3023	0.3051	0.3078	0.3106	0.3133
0.9	0.3159	0.3186	0.3212	0.3238	0.3264	0.3289	0.3315	0.3340	0.3365	0.3389
1.0	0.3413	0.3438	0.3461	0.3485	0.3508	0.3531	0.3554	0.3577	0.3599	0.3621
1.1	0.3643	0.3665	0.3686	0.3708	0.3729	0.3749	0.3770	0.3790	0.3810	0.3830
1.2	0.3849	0.3869	0.3888	0.3907	0.3925	0.3944	0.3962	0.3980	0.3997	0.4015
1.3	0.4032	0.4049	0.4066	0.4082	0.4099	0.4115	0.4131	0.4147	0.4162	0.4177
1.4	0.4192	0.4207	0.4222	0.4236	0.4251	0.4265	0.4279	0.4292	0.4306	0.4319
1.5	0.4332	0.4345	0.4357	0.4370	0.4382	0.4394	0.4406	0.4418	0.4429	0.4441
1.6	0.4452	0.4463	0.4474	0.4484	0.4495	0.4505	0.4515	0.4525	0.4535	0.4545
1.7	0.4554	0.4564	0.4573	0.4582	0.4591	0.4599	0.4608	0.4616	0.4625	0.4633
1.8	0.4641	0.4649	0.4656	0.4664	0.4671	0.4678	0.4686	0.4693	0.4699	0.4706
1.9	0.4713	0.4719	0.4726	0.4732	0.4738	0.4744	0.4750	0.4756	0.4761	0.4767
2.0	0.4772	0.4778	0.4783	0.4788	0.4793	0.4798	0.4803	0.4808	0.4812	0.4817
2.1	0.4821	0.4826	0.4830	0.4834	0.4838	0.4842	0.4846	0.4850	0.4854	0.4857
2.2	0.4861	0.4864	0.4868	0.4871	0.4875	0.4878	0.4881	0.4884	0.4887	0.4890
2.3	0.4893	0.4896	0.4898	0.4901	0.4904	0.4906	0.4909	0.4911	0.4913	0.4916
2.4	0.4918	0.4920	0.4922	0.4925	0.4927	0.4929	0.4931	0.4932	0.4934	0.4936
2.5	0.4938	0.4940	0.4941	0.4943	0.4945	0.4946	0.4948	0.4949	0.4951	0.4952
2.6	0.4953	0.4955	0.4956	0.4957	0.4959	0.4960	0.4961	0.4962	0.4963	0.4964
2.7	0.4965	0.4966	0.4967	0.4968	0.4969	0.4970	0.4971	0.4972	0.4973	0.4974
2.8	0.4974	0.4975	0.4976	0.4977	0.4977	0.4978	0.4979	0.4979	0.4980	0.4981
2.9	0.4981	0.4982	0.4982	0.4983	0.4984	0.4984	0.4985	0.4985	0.4986	0.4986
3.0	0.4987	0.4987	0.4987	0.4988	0.4988	0.4989	0.4989	0.4989	0.4990	0.4990

SUPPLEMENT D: ALONG THE SUPPLY CHAIN TOPICS

Chapter 1

- Human Rights and the Extended Supply Chain
- Two Different Strategies—ZARA and Uniqlo

Chapter 2

- Achieving Quality in Target's Supply Chain
- Two-Time Baldrige National Quality Award Winner, Ritz-Carlton Hotels
- Motorola's Six Sigma Quality
- Six Sigma Highlights
- North Shore University Hospital: A Six Sigma Project Example
- Six Sigma Success at Telefonica Group
- ISO 9001 Certification at Monarcas Morelia
- Orkin Uses ISO Certification to Improve Service Quality

Chapter 3

- Using Sampling and Statistics to Analyze MillerCoors Distribution Network Performance
- Using Control Charts for Improving Healthcare Quality
- Determining Quality Process Parameters for Starbucks Coffee Bags

Chapter 4

- Jugaad, Design for the Times
- Consider Nike's Flyknit Design

Chapter 5

- Dell's Service Now Includes Disaster Recovery
- Creating WOW Service at Zappos

Chapter 6

- 3D Printing and Other Advances in Additive Manufacturing

Chapter 7

- IKEA's Layout Design

Chapter 8

- Creating Sustainable Workplaces
- Telecommuting at Capital One, Bank of America, and Cisco
- English in the Workplace
- A Commitment to Diversity at UPS and Hershey's
- Target's Workplace Sustainability Standards for Its Global Suppliers' Employees

Chapter 9

- A Project to Fight AIDS in Swaziland
- Sustainability Projects Around the World
- Cross-Cultural Project Teams
- Innovative "Cloud" Projects at Facebook, Google, and Apple
- The Terminal 5 Project at Heathrow Airport
- Construction Mega-Projects Around the World

Chapter 10

- Supply Chain Resiliency at Cisco Systems
- Walmart's Commitment to Sustainability
- Achieving Sustainability While Reducing Costs and Increasing Profits
- Managing Ford's Supply Chain Risks and Helping the Automaker's Recovery

Chapter 11

- Achieving Warehouse Efficiency and Sustainability at Genzyme Corporation
- Adding a New Distribution Center to the Sephora Supply Chain
- Achieving Global Sustainability at HP in China
- Brazil as a Potential Near-Shore Supplier for the United States
- Reverse Globalization at K'NEX

Chapter 12

- Supply Chain Forecasting at Heineken USA
- Global Supply Chain Forecasting at Hershey's
- Demand Forecasting for Global Distribution at Zara
- Forecasting Airport Security Gate Arrivals at the Transportation Security Administration

Chapter 13

- Determining Supply Chain Strategy by Evaluating Inventory Costs at Hewlett-Packard

Chapter 14

- How LEGO Rebuilt Its Supply Chain and Found S&OP

Chapter 15

- Under Armour at the Top of Its Game with ERP

Chapter 16

- The Path to Lean at Nike's Supplier in Vietnam